VOLUME TWO

HANDBOOK OF SOCIAL CHOICE AND WELFARE

VOLUME TWO

HANDBOOK OF SOCIAL CHOICE AND WELFARE

Edited by

KENNETH J. ARROW

AMARTYA SEN

KOTARO SUZUMURA

ELSEVIER

AMSTERDAM • BOSTON • HEIDELBERG • LONDON
NEW YORK • OXFORD • PARIS • SAN DIEGO
SAN FRANCISCO • SINGAPORE • SYDNEY • TOKYO

North-Holland is an imprint of Elsevier

N·H

North-Holland is an imprint of Elsevier
The Boulevard, Langford Lane, Kidlington, Oxford OX5 1GB, UK
Radarweg 29, PO Box 211, 1000 AE Amsterdam, The Netherlands

British Library Cataloguing in Publication Data
A catalogue record for this book is available from the British Library

Library of Congress Cataloging-in-Publication Data
A catalog record for this book is available from the Library of Congress

ISBN–13: 978-0-444-50894-2

Printed and bound in the United States of America
11 12 13 14 15 10 9 8 7 6 5 4 3 2 1

CONTENTS

PREFACE

The *Handbook of Social Choice and Welfare* presents, in two volumes, essays on past and ongoing work in social choice theory and welfare economics. The first volume, which consists of twelve chapters in four parts—Part I (*Arrovian Impossibility Theorems*), Part II (*Voting Schemes and Mechanisms*), Part III (*Structure of Social Choice Rules*), and Part IV (*Welfare, Justice, and Poverty*)—, was published in 2002. This is the long overdue second volume of the *Handbook*, which also consists of four parts.

In Part V (*Foundations*), some very basic issues in welfare economics and social choice theory are discussed. The topics covered include the initial insights behind and the basic functions of social choice theory, the informational basis of normative and positive social choice theory, the status of competitive market mechanisms as social choice procedures, and the main ingredients of nonwelfaristic approaches in welfare economics and social choice theory along the line of the theory of functionings and capabilities.

Part VI (*Developments of the Basic Arrovian Schemes*) consists of four chapters that are lineal descendants of Part I in the first volume. Recollect that three chapters in Part I discussed the basic Arrovian schemes in an abstract space of social alternatives. Here, Part VI addresses itself to the important variations of the basic schemes, such as impossibility theorems on economic domains, topological theories of social choice, nonbinary social choice theory, and social choice theory with fuzzy preferences.

In Part VII (*Fairness and Rights*), several new dimensions in welfare economics and social choice theory are introduced through the well-known conflicts of values such as equity-efficiency tradeoffs, compensation and responsibility, the tension between the requirement of social efficiency and the claim of individual liberties and rights, and the social choice theoretical analysis of freedom, opportunity, and well-being.

Finally, Part VIII (*Voting and Manipulation*) goes back to the issues discussed in Part II of the first volume. Here the basic issues of strategy-proof social choice rules are covered as well as probabilistic and spatial models of voting, and the geometry of voting.

The literature on social choice theory is now quite vast, and we hope this collection of critical surveys in two volumes will be of interest to readers who would like to be introduced to the writings on human well-being and collective decision-making that have been pursued within this literature.

The initial plan of this *Handbook* was conceived soon after the publication of the Proceedings of the International Economic Association Roundtable Meeting on Social Choice Theory by us in 1996/1997. We are most grateful to the authors of the two volumes of the *Handbook* for their contributions. The editors apologize for the fact that some of the authors had to wait long for publication and had to update their chapters as the

other essays were coming in. We should also express our sincere gratitude to those readers of the first volume who provided important suggestions for the second volume, aside from encouraging us to complete what proved to be a remarkably ambitious project. We very much hope that the completed *Handbook* will live up to the expectations of our colleagues and readers.

We conclude this "extra" preface by reiterating the last paragraph of the Preface to the *Handbook* as a whole, which was printed in the first volume: "The primary purpose of this Handbook is to provide an accessible introduction to the current state of the art in social choice theory and welfare economics. But we also believe that the expounded theory has a strong and constructive message for pursuing human well-being and facilitating collective decision-making."

Kenneth Arrow
Amartya Sen
Kotaro Suzumura

A Statement from Kenneth Arrow and Amartya Sen

We would like to acknowledge our debt to Kotaro Suzumura for doing the lion's share of the editorial work, and for doing this ungrudgingly in a way that can be done only by a person of the remarkable generosity that Kotaro has. We are immensely grateful to him.

LIST OF CONTRIBUTORS

Chapter 13
Kenneth Arrow
Stanford University, Stanford, CA

Amartya Sen
Harvard University, Cambridge, MA

Kotaro Suzumura
Waseda University, Tokyo, Japan

Chapter 14
Amartya Sen
Harvard University, Cambridge, MA

Chapter 15
Peter J. Hammond
University of Warwick, Coventry, UK

Chapter 16
Kaushik Basu
Cornell University, Ithaca, NY

Luis F. López-Calva
United Nations Development Programme, New York, NY

Chapter 17
Michel Le Breton
Université de Toulouse, Toulouse, France

John A. Weymark
Vanderbilt University, Nashville, TN

Chapter 18
Nicholas Baigent
London School of Economics and Political Science, London, UK

Chapter 19
Rajat Deb
Southern Methodist University, Dallas, TX

Chapter 20
Richard Barrett
University of Birmingham, Birmingham, UK

Maurice Salles
l'Université de Caen, Caen, France

Chapter 21
William Thomson
University of Rochester, Rochester, NY

Chapter 22
Marc Fleurbaey
CNRS, University Paris-Descartes, Paris, France

François Maniquet
Université Catholique de Louvain, Louvain-La-Neuve, Belgium

Chapter 23
Kotaro Suzumura
Waseda University, Tokyo, Japan

Chapter 24
James E. Foster
Oxford Poverty and Human Development Initiative, Oxford, UK

Chapter 25
Salvador Barberà
Universitat Autònoma de Barcelona, Bellaterra, Spain

Chapter 26
Peter Coughlin
University of Maryland, College Park, MD

Chapter 27
Donald G. Saari
University of California, Irvine, CA

PART FIVE

Foundations

CHAPTER THIRTEEN

Kenneth Arrow on Social Choice Theory

Kenneth Arrow*, Amartya Sen, and Kotaro Suzumura*****
*Professor Emeritus, Stanford University, Stanford, CA
**Thomas W. Lamont University Professor, and Professor of Economics and Philosophy, Harvard University, Cambridge, MA
***Professor of Economics, Waseda University, Shinjuku-ku, Tokyo, Japan

Contents

Part I: An Editorial Note

Amartya Sen and Kotaro Suzumura

Kenneth Arrow founded the modern form of social choice theory in a path-breaking contribution at the middle of the twentieth century. We—the editors of the *Handbook of Social Choice and Welfare* other than Arrow—want to begin this final volume by noting the continuing need to read Arrow's decisive contribution in his epoch-making book, *Social Choice and Individual Values*, which started off the contemporary round of research on social choice theory. (Kenneth J. Arrow, *Social Choice and Individual Values*, New York: John Wiley & Sons, 1st edition, 1951, 2nd edition, 1963.)

We are also including in this chapter an interview that Kenneth Arrow gave to Professor Jerry Kelly some years ago, which was published in *Social Choice and Welfare* in 1987. This presents Arrow's thinking on the subject as it developed since his own pioneering contribution.

Finally, this chapter also includes some new observations by Arrow, "The Classification of Social Choice Propositions," dealing particularly with the distinction between normative and descriptive statements in social choice theory. These notes, which Arrow has written for this volume at a very difficult time for him, reflect, inevitably in a highly compressed form, some recent thoughts of the founder of the discipline on an important methodological issue in social choice theory.

Handbook of Social Choice and Welfare, Volume II
ISSN: 0169-7218, DOI: 10.1016/S0169-7218(10)00013-4

This is also an occasion for us—the editors other than Arrow—to acknowledge the huge benefit that the subject of social choice theory has received through the active contributions of the founder of this modern discipline over the last sixty years. We also would like to say how privileged we have been to work with Arrow in editing this two-volume *Handbook of Social Choice and Welfare.*

April 2010

Part II: An Interview with Kenneth J. Arrow

Kenneth Arrow and J. S. Kelly

The following is an edited transcript of an interview conducted on March 4, 1986, with Professor Arrow while he was visiting Syracuse University to deliver the Frank W. Abrams Lecture Series to be published as *The Uncertain Future and Present Action* by Syracuse University Press.[1] This interview was to elaborate on his description, presented in Volume 1 of his *Collected Papers* (Harvard University Press, 1983) of the origins of his work in collective choice theory.

JK. You started off the story in the collected papers with remarks about studying relational logic while you were in Townsend-Harris High School in New York City.

KA. Not in high school in the sense of [being] in my high school courses, but during this period I was an omnivorous reader and got into all sorts of things. One of them was Bertrand Russell's *Introduction to Mathematical Philosophy,* and it made a tremendous impression on me. It was the idea of logic that was in there. I don't really recall, for example, if there was a formal definition of a relation as a set of ordered pairs, but I learned the ideas of mathematical logic and its applications to mathematics in Russell's book. It seems to me that I also read one or two other logic books around that time.

JK. Later, when you went to City College of New York as a mathematics major, you encountered more mathematical logic.

KA. Yes, but again the logic study was on my own, there were no courses in it. I don't really remember exactly what I read. I remember once taking out the *Principia Mathematica,* but of course it's not the sort of thing one really reads from. I was looking up some theorems in it and things like that. I really am not prepared to tell you what I read, but at some point things like the idea of defining rational numbers by ordered pairs and equivalence classes by ordered pairs was something I got to know. I was fascinated

[1] According to Jerry Kelly, this lecture was never written up for publication.

by this and used to aggravate my professors by writing out proofs in very strictly logical form, avoiding words as much as possible and things of that kind.

JK. You did take a formal course with Tarski in the Philosophy Department; how did you happen to take that course?

KA. Yes. Well, I *knew* that Alfred Tarski was a great and famous logician, and there he was in my last term in school, and obviously I was going to take a course with Alfred Tarski. It turned out he had two courses. One was a kind of introductory course and I felt I knew more than *that*. The other course he gave was in the calculus of relations. To say it was in the *calculus* of relations meant that he gave an axiomatic treatment of relations, although he motivated it of course by motivating the axioms. You never had xRy; you only had R and S and T. You see, he never mentioned *individuals* in the formal theory. He had an axiomatic theory like an axiomatic treatment of set theory. Relations have some special aspects, in particular the idea of relative product, RS. If there is a z such that xRz and zSy, then $xRSy$. The relative square, $R^2 = RR$, is especially interesting; if the relative square is included in R you have transitivity.

So it was a fascinating thing, although it was really very elementary, really very easy. The concepts were not very subtle compared with the deep things he was working on like the truth principle.

JK. At this point you were involved in translating some of Tarski's work.

KA. He wrote a textbook called *Introduction to Logic* (Tarski 1941), which is one of the modern treatments, modern as of 1940. It had been published in German, may even have been orginally published in Polish. I didn't translate it. What happened was he had a translator and I read the proofs. I was just finishing college and he asked me to read the proofs for him. He didn't know any English, you see. This was the interesting thing. He came to this country in September 1939, for some kind of congress or conference and was trapped here by the outbreak of the war. He knew Polish, he knew German, but he didn't know any English, so he spent the Fall term learning some English so he could teach us in the Spring. At first we couldn't understand a word he was saying, but after about a week or so we began to catch on and we realized it wasn't *his* rate of progress it was *our* rate of progress that was relevant. His stresses were all wrong. He was aware of this and therefore felt he couldn't proofread in English. It's rather interesting as a coincidence that the translator was a German philosopher named Olaf Helmer, and Helmer comes back into my story eight years later.

It's interesting...Tarski, although his English was weak, had a very good sense of language, and he kept on asking me, "Is that really good English?" Not in the sense of being grammatically correct, but, well for example, Helmer was very fond of using the word "tantamount," and Tarski got the feeling that somehow it's not a word used very often. Actually his instincts for language were extremely good. I suppose that was connected with his general work on formalizations and metalanguages. Anyway, I was just a proofreader.

JK. You write that as a graduate student at Columbia you spent time, as an exercise, translating consumer theory in the logic of relations and orderings. What got you started on that and what did you get out of it?

KA. I went to Columbia because...well there were several problems. One was that we were extremely poor and the question of going anywhere depended on resources. Columbia had the great advantage, of course, that I could live at home, which wasn't true anywhere else. I didn't get any financial support for my first year, none at all.

But another of the things I had learned on my own at college was mathematical statistics, and I really had become fascinated with it. There was a course in statistics [at City College New York]; the teacher, a man by the name of Robinson, had no *real* knowledge of it I would say, basically—I won't even say he had a good reading list—but he did list one book, J. F. Kenney (1939), if I remember correctly, which happened to have an excellent bibliography. It was not one of those cookbooks in statistics but actually did have some attempts at mathematics. Kenney had references to R. A. Fisher and gave you enough to get you interested. So I started reading Fisher, and one of the first things was trying to work out his derivation of the distribution of the correlation coefficient under the null hypothesis, which was an integration in *n*-dimensional space. In Fisher it was done by intuition. I mean it's rigorous if you're sufficiently sophisticated; to me it was gibberish. But I knew enough multivariate calculus to be able to translate it into rigorous form, at least a form that I understood, and then I could see that he really was right. But I couldn't see it the way he wrote it. Then I suppose because of my logical background what was really important was reading the Neyman–Pearson papers, which were then new and written in rather obscure places, but they were available in the [CCNY] library. From Fisher alone, I think I would have been hopelessly confused about the logic of statistical tests, although Fisher was great on deriving distributions.

So, I knew I wanted to study mathematical statistics, which however was not a field, not a Department at Columbia. It was spread out in other Departments. I knew that Hotelling was one of the major figures, but he was in the Economics Department. I rather naively thought I would study mathematics and then would take the statistics from Hotelling. I had no interest in Economics.

I was in the Mathematics Department, taking courses like Functions of a Real Variable, but I was going to take courses from Hotelling. In the first term he happened to give a course in Mathematical Economics. So out of curiosity I took this and got completely transformed.

The course to an extent revolved around Hotelling's own papers. But, as it happens, they were kind of central. He gave a rigorous derivation of supply and demand. There was one paper on the theory of the firm, one on the theory of the consumer (Hotelling

1932, 1935). And he gave a rigorous derivation of demand functions in the consumer theory paper and derived the Slutsky equations. I think he knew about Slutsky's work, though I'm not sure he actually referred to Slutsky. So, anyway, this was one of the best papers around at the time. It's now a staple of our literature but then really was novel. One of the things, he was a very, *very* strong ordinalist, emphasized that all these results were invariant under monotone transformations, which was not a normal practice in economics at that time. Of course, all those who were coming of age, like Paul Samuelson, would jump to that position; it was the normal position of the avant garde.

Well, the idea was that it was an *ordering*. It was clear that what they were saying was "x is better than y" and that this is a transitive relationship. And I recognized that there were certain continuity axioms that had to be added to that. I was already familiar with that because there were certain similar things in the foundations of probability theory. In fact I think I worked that out for myself. I was playing around once in college trying to work out an axiom system for probability theory, that was work on an Honors paper or something, and I ran across a set of axioms by Karl Popper. Research methods were pretty primitive; I looked through the Union catalog and there was a reference to an article in *Mind* by Popper (1938). I realized that his axiom system really couldn't explain certain things that we take for granted, like the fact that cumulative distributions have a one-sided continuity property. So I realized that you need some kind of extra continuity axiom, and I sort of invented countable additivity all by myself. Later, of course, I found that Kolmogoroff and others had done this, but I could see there had to be an axiom.

So I was kind of familiar from having worked it out there that you needed these continuity axioms in order to close your preference theory system. It was easy to provide, and I suppose others were doing the same. I could also see that while it was clarifying for me, it was hardly a contribution to knowledge, because all I was doing was translating to a language that I knew. At least it got me thinking; whenever I saw a U for a utility function I translated to a preference ordering.

In fact one thing that struck me as an interesting problem—this is digressing a bit, but not entirely—why should there be a utility function representing an ordering? Hotelling had never really asked that question. Although he emphasized that the indifference map was the primitive, and the utility function only represented it, he didn't really ask, "Why should you have a representation in terms of numbers?" I was really thinking about this problem when I happened to run across some papers by Herman Wold (1943, 1944) who gave what he called a "Synthesis" in some papers in *Skandinavisk Aktuarietidskrift*, which gave a long treatment of demand analysis that did have essentially an axiomatic point of view. There he said you've got to prove there is a utility function representation. He was the first person I know to realize, in print, that this was a problem. He gave an answer, extremely weak because he needed strong assumptions.

Anyway, then I switched to Economics from Mathematics. I had gone to Hotelling asking for a letter of recommendation for a fellowship in the Mathematics Department and he said, "Well, I'm sure I don't have any influence in the Mathematics Department, but if you should enroll in Economics, I've found in the past they are willing to give one of my students a fellowship." I was bought.

Incidentically, I impressed him on about the second day of the class because he was fascinated by Edgeworth's taxation paradox; in fact his paper on the theory of the firm was called "Edgeworth's Taxation Paradox and the Nature of Supply and Demand Theory" (Hotelling 1932). Consider a case where there are first-class and third-class railroad tickets as in the English system. It turns out that if you impose a tax on one ticket then, with suitable demand functions, you could lower the price of both commodities. At the time there was a lot of excitement about that; the public finance people were pooh-poohing it, saying, "How can this be?" It had to do with the nature of interrelated demand curves and that was the big thing Hotelling stressed, that demand functions depended on *n* variables, not one variable. But he said he was puzzled by the fact that he had never been able to produce an example of Edgeworth's paradox with linear demand functions. So I sat down and wrote out the conditions for linear demand functions to yield the paradox; these conditions were certain inequalities on the coefficients and the inequalities were inconsistent. So I came in the next day and showed it to him. Really it was just a few lines, but from that point on he was really impressed with me. It was an extremely easy calculation, but thinking in inequality terms was not common. Little pieces were quite easy to prove, but you couldn't do it in the mechanical fashion that you were doing with, say, solving simultaneous equations or maximizations.

Anyway, I enrolled in Economics, and one of the things I read was a brand-new book, Hicks's *Value and Capital* (1939). You know, after reading through the mish-mash like Marshall and things like that, suddenly there was this clear, well-organized view, you knew exactly what was happening. Just the sort of thing to appeal to me. There was a whole, messy, confused literature on capital theory; all those great debates between Knight and von Hayek and all that. And now here was just the idea of dated commodities and suddenly scales fell from your eyes. A simple idea like dated commodities made whole issues transparent.

But as I read Hicks, I could see there were things left out. I turned to this again when I returned from the War, which was really pretty much of a hiatus in any work I was doing—I was gone and very busy for about three and a half years. I had done all my examinations before I had left. So now it was just a question of my thesis. I decided to take *Value and Capital* and redo it properly. I could see all kinds of specific points that were of concern. I wanted to combine it with Samuelson's (1941, 1942) stability theory, which he had developed in the meanwhile, the papers on dynamic stability in 1941 and 1942. Maybe I would add some stochastic elements to the story, because as a student of probability and statistics theory I could see noise in the system. Well, it was a lifetime of work, really; it was a very unrealistic thesis.

Hotelling was primarily interested in statistics at this time, and then he left for the University of North Carolina. And Abraham Wald wasn't interested in Economics anymore, either. The one I was closest to was Albert Hart, who was regarded then as a very promising theorist, but somehow wasn't able to do what he was capable of. Now people haven't even heard of Albert Gailord Hart. He had a good analysis of flexibility in a Festschrift for Henry Schultz (Lange, McIntyre, Yntema 1942), another figure who has faded, but I was never impressed by Henry Schultz. Hart considered a problem where you're thinking of buying a durable machine and you're uncertain as to the second period output; the trade-off is between a first machine that would be beautifully optimizing if you knew exactly the output but is not very good at slightly different outputs, and a second machine that has costs that are fairly uniform along a wide range. The second machine might sometimes be preferred, He gave a sequential analysis; the idea that your choice today can be dependent on your uncertainty about tomorrow. Elementary as that point may seem, it just hadn't been expressed anywhere; it was very revelatory and came out in this Festschrift for Henry Schultz (Hart 1942), published in 1942, 1943, or 1944.

Hart was friendly and respectful but not very mathematical. One of the things he brought to my attention was that firms are, after all, multiowner objects. It is true that all the owners are interested in the same thing, maximizing profit; however, from a Hicksian point of view, the owners might have different expectations. Then their recommended investment policies today would be different. Each one, trying to maximize the same thing, expected profit, would nevertheless have a different choice. Now, from a modern point of view, we would probably take a different position. In fact the whole idea on my part was wrong; I didn't take account of the very simple point that owners could sell their stock. I didn't think about that until I read Modigliani–Miller (1958) years later and realized that my whole attack had been wrong. Those who were most optimistic about the firm would, in effect, buy it out from everybody else, who would do something else with their money. So, in fact, in that context, the voting paradox is irrelevant. But I did not think of it that way, I thought of owners as glued to the firm, and just did not think about the stock market. Within that context I thought, well, how would they decide between two actions. A reasonable thing is to assume it goes by majority vote, a majority of shares, of course. I started writing this down and it occurred to me that I have a preference of the firm defined by the statement that a majority prefers investment A to investment B. Then, from my background, a natural question is, is this relation transitive? Well, it didn't take more than a couple of tries to see that this is not true.

The minute I saw it, I thought: This must be well known. In fact, I thought I might have seen it before. I have no idea from that day to this what I could have seen. However, it is the sort of thing that would appear maybe even in a puzzle page of a newspaper. It could have appeared in some quite trifling way. Anyway, I thought I'd seen it before, and I didn't think it was major; all I thought was it was a nuisance because it was spoiling my theory. I ended up trying to develop a theory on the basis of maximizing profits weighted by share numbers, using that as a maximand. Later I gave up the whole thing because it seemed very unwieldly and didn't cohere.

JK. Gave up that section or the whole dissertation?

KA. The whole dissertation. Large parts were in no way novel. At best, I learned some ideas about myopia in investment, things that in later years I pursued. At one point I had about thirty pages of outline of ideas and results, but somehow it didn't send me. I felt somehow it was supposed to lead ultimately to empirical work. I was rather discouraged because I was spending quite a bit of time at this. It was a couple of years.

JK. Now comes the Hicks lecture...

KA. Intransitivity was something I had discovered, but it was not on my mind; it was something I had dismissed. Hicks gave a lecture during the winter of 1946–1947. He had a very interesting idea. He was trying to find a definition of welfare inequality that was nevertheless consistent with ordinalism. What was meant by saying "individual A is better off than individual B"? Hicks' statement was the following: Suppose individual A prefers his own bundle to B's, and individual B also prefers A's bundle to his own. Then Hicks would say A is better off than B. Of course, this definition surfaced again about twenty years later in the work of Duncan Foley (1967), but I'd never heard of it before. I think I once found some indication that Trygve Haavelmo had had that idea, and I've tried to find the reference again but I've never succeeded in tracking it down. Hicks presented this lecture and went through a lot of variations of this point, but he said Joan Robinson had criticized it and he was a little worried about it. He said, of course, that people might be noncomparable. A could prefer his bundle to B's, and B could prefer his own to A's—he recognized that. I thought about it sitting there and finally said, "Would you want this property of 'being better off than' to be transitive?" I defined what I meant by transitive. "Well, in the case, your definition won't satisfy that, because the comparison between A and B is based on A and B's orderings, the comparison between B and C is based on B and C's orderings, and the comparison between A and C is based on A and C's orderings. And it's possible to have A better off than B, B better off than C, and C better off than A by this." So I guess somehow this idea of intransitivity fascinated me. Hicks said, "What? What? What?" I don't think he quite got the point. Hart was very quick; he was chairing the meeting, got the point, and tried explaining it. Interestingly, Hicks never published this. Now all this may be beside the point, because you may not want transitivity even though it seems natural. In Foley's work, for example, this issue doesn't arise. Foley just said a point is fair if nobody is better off than anybody else. But this story does show intransitivity was bubbling around inside me even though I wasn't conciously aware of pursuing this line as a subject of research.

At this time, I received an invitation to the Cowles Commission. At first I postponed a move because I was trying to finish my Hicksian dissertation before I went there, but I finally settled on finishing it there.

JK. Wasn't it unusual then to leave graduate school before finishing your dissertation?

KA. You know, my knowledge of what was typical wasn't very good. The people I knew were at Columbia. I didn't know what was going on at Harvard or Chicago. It was really very provincial. In fact from what I now know, the Columbia situation was unusually chaotic. One problem at Columbia, and I think it's true to this day, is that the sense of community among students and faculty is very weak; they're all dispersed. In particular the National Bureau of Economic Research was a very strong organization, and some of the leading Department members went off there, especially the great Wesley Clair Mitchell. So they weren't available. The Bureau was not near the University, and so they were just simply physically somewhere else. One had the feeling, in fact, that they never talked to each other.

JK. What led to your invitation to Cowles?

KA. They came around and asked Wald and he recommended me. While he was primarily trained as a statistician, nevertheless he was interested in economics. There weren't many in that category and so they asked him.

Cowles was a funny kind of place because they were kind of a persecuted sect; the mathematical and quantitative emphasis was exceptional and distrusted. My salary was $3200 per calendar year—it was a calendar-year appointment. Even by the standards of 1947, that wasn't very much.

JK. What were you hired to do?

KA. What they really wanted me to do was work on statistical problems but it was a freewheeling place. At the moment the emphasis was on the development of the econometrics of large-scale models. So-called "large": three equations, five equations. Larry Klein ended up with a 20-equation model. Now Tinbergen had even bigger models in his League of Nations study, but this was simultaneous equations estimation, which made the computational burden very much greater. I had some idea of using higher-order approximations. Others had gotten the asymptotic distributions, which were normal, and I had been taking a course in Edgeworth–Cramér expansions, which you get from higher-order approximations. These ideas were originated by Edgeworth and quite ignored; interestingly, Edgeworth authored quite a few new ideas in statistics, most of which were ignored and then rediscovered. Edgeworth had this method, and

Cramér rediscovered it. Actually, it was pretty high-powered mathematics, and it really was probably beyond me. I knew how to do it, but mathematical estimates of the error term in the approximation were a very subtle and complex matter.

But I was there to do anything I pleased, and I was very obviously interested in theory. There was a feeling that theoretical foundations were also an essential part. Finishing my thesis could fit into this.

JK. While you were at Cowles you worked on the single-peakedness result.

KA. I really spent a year there not doing much of anything, to tell you the truth. I wrote a few tiny papers, none of which amounted to anything. I was a great contributor to discussions: argumentative, finding exceptions, errors, and counterexamples. But I really felt very discouraged. Once, at lunch, we were talking about politics, left parties and right parties, and I remember drawing on a piece of paper the idea that a voter might have preferences over the parties. It wasn't so much that I saw the ideas—it was the only way I could think about it. It was not that I thought why don't we represent voters as having preferences—as soon as I thought about the question, it couldn't occur to me there was any other way of doing it. So I wrote this thing down and started looking at the question of majorities. It's really hard to describe it. All I can say is, once you've seen it, it's obvious; it takes an hour or two. If you ask the question, the answer is fairly obvious. I spent a day or two working it up as a formal proof. And in my usual way, I sort of stalled about a month on writing it up for publication. No, but that doesn't make any difference. I can't say I lost anything. It would just establish that I had the idea independently. But in a sense it didn't matter, because within about a month I picked up the *JPE,* and there's the paper by Duncan Black (1948) that had exactly that idea.

The coincidence I regard as an extremely interesting point in the history of thought. It's an idea which could easily have occurred to Condorcet. It doesn't depend in any way on the development of mathematics in the last 150 years.

JK. Except to a sensitivity to the logic of relations?

KA. I suppose so. Well, let me put it this way. The logic of relations was worked out at great length in the latter part of the nineteenth century. Let's say it depends on Boole and the idea of relations as ordered pairs—even that goes back to 1910 or 1911. But while the idea of relations as ordered pairs is a comforting idea, in the sense that you have a logical foundation, it isn't necessary. The fellow who developed a lot of the ideas about logical relations, rather sophisticatedly, was Charles Peirce, the philosopher and logician, founder of pragmatism around 1880 to 1910. It was picked up by a German named Schroder (1890–1905) who in good Germanic fashion wrote three large volumes around 1890. All the apparatus, all the sensitivity was there. If you needed more, the

Principia surely supplied all that was needed. Nobody asked that question; that's all I can say. Black, of course, had been building up to it; he really did have the idea of voting as a mechanism.

JK. Had you read anything of Black's before this paper?

KA. I honestly can't tell you. The stuff before was awfully formal and obvious. This was the only paper of his I seriously regard as having some excitement in it. So, anyway, there was my third encounter with orderings. But that really developed out of amusement.

Then that summer I went to Rand Corporation—again through sheer accident. My wife, whom I met as a graduate student in Chicago, had previously worked in the Agriculture Department. She'd arrived there as a clerk and became a professional, a statistician. Her boss was a very distinguished mathematical statistician named M. A. Girshick. So I was friendly with Girshick, who had gone to the Rand Corporation when it was started. The Air Force needed someone to tell them what was going on in the world, so they took all these wild characters and unleashed them. Girshick was one of those invited to go out there and he commenced to spend a couple of years. He often visited Chicago. He had been in contact with the Cowles Commission anyway, because some of his work in multivariate analysis really was very close mathematically—more than mathematically, close conceptually—to simultaneous equation estimation. He was giving advice to them; in fact, he had some ingenious ideas. He contributed a good deal to the development of the limited information method and was never really given full credit for that. Anyway, Girshick had this connection with Cowles independent of us, but when he came to Chicago he visited us.

One of the things Rand was doing was inviting large numbers of visitors for the summer so Girshick urged me to come. Summer in Santa Monica didn't seem like a bad idea to me, and it turned out to be far more intellectually exciting than anything I had planned because the halls were filled with people working on game theory. Everybody was fooling with zero-sum games, how to calculate them, the fundamental definition of the concepts; it was work at the conceptual level and at the technical level.

JK. Was game theory something you'd studied before you went to Rand?

KA. Not really. I mean I knew about the book and had been vaguely pecking away at it, but I hadn't really studied it at all carefully. It was not a big topic at the Cowles Commission, although Marschak had written a review of it.

Anyway, Olaf Helmer was among those who had been brought to Rand; a philosopher. There were several people there, as a matter of fact, who were basically philosophers; Abraham Kaplan was another. Helmer said to me one day: "There's one thing that disturbs me." They were taking game theory and applying it especially to

Soviet–U.S. relations: diplomatic conflict, potential tactical situations, war. However, the payoff functions were defined in terms of utility functions, as von Neumann and Morgenstern argued in their appendix, and these were derived on the basis of the individual. The trouble was, the Soviet Union and the United States were not individuals. What is the meaning of this? You've got to give him credit for proposing the problem.

Now I hadn't spent a lot of time or attention on welfare economics. I had really been trying to work on descriptive theory and general equilibrium theory considered as descriptive rather than as normative theory. But I did read. One of the things I did when I was supposed to be working on my thesis was read and read and read. It was the typical thing I was doing. I still do it to this day. I'm supposed to be doing something and I find myself picking up something allegedly relevant and reading it. You pick up a lot of information that way at times. I had read Oscar Lange's expository article (1942) on the foundations of welfare economics. Lange was extremely clear. It was only afterwards I began to feel his clarity was purchased at the price of depth. He set forth very clearly the conditions for a Pareto Optimum. But then he referred to the fact that one could consider maximizing a welfare function. You started off with $U_1, \ldots, U_n$, utility functions of individuals, and you want to maximize $W(U_1, \ldots, U_n)$ but then there are a whole subset of the maximizing conditions that don't involve W—those are essentially the conditions that define Pareto Optimality. If I recall correctly, he was quite clear on distinguishing these concepts, but he did have this W function and he gave a rather casual reference to Bergson. By this time, Samuelson's *Foundations of Economic Analysis* (Samuelson 1947) had been published, and he gives a very full account of welfare economics in Chapter 8, which he bases on Bergson's paper.

So I gave a quick reply to Helmer: "Economists have thought about that, and it's really explained by Bergson's social welfare function." "Oh, is that so," he said; "Why don't you write it up? I think it would be nice for us all to have an exposition of how the Bergson social welfare function settles this."

JK. So you just started to write this up.

KA. Well, of course, I dropped the U's which I never liked because I knew the U's were just disguises for R's for preference relations. I thought, while I was at it, I'd do an exposition starting from just the orderings. Then I started musing about what information is conveyed. Welfare comparisons could be regarded as a series of pairwise votes, and I was obviously interested in elections so that just seemed like the natural language to use. One natural method of taking a bunch of R's and putting them together would be by pairwise comparisons by majority voting. And I already knew *that* was going to lead to trouble! So I figured, well, majority voting was just one of a very large number of possibilities, you just have to be more ingenious. I started to write various possibilities down.

JK. For example…

KA. I'm pretty sure the Borda method came to my mind, because that was a very well-known method. I didn't know it was Borda, you understand.

JK. It was something you'd encountered before?

KA. That was very well known; it was a widely used custom. A club might do that. It was something that was done in practice.

JK. Did you ask any political scientists at Rand about voting procedures?

KA. I don't think at first they did have any political scientists. I don't know anybody I would have regarded as a political scientist. I don't think Rand was interested in traditional political science. Later I think they had more traditional political scientists, but even when they did they had people interested in area studies, Soviet experts. I don't think they ever had theoretical political scientists.

JK. So this experimentation was totally isolated. You didn't ask anybody about rules.

KA. Right, but that also reflected me. It seems to me I was trying at some point to systematically go through all possible rules. I took some examples and then considered related examples. Beyond that, I can't tell you which rules I explored. I did grasp that, at some point in this procedure, part of the point was I was only using information on the alternatives under consideration. But then that struck me as a very natural thing to do.

JK. Very crucial.

KA. That turned out to be *very* crucial. In fact, if I had realized how crucial it was, I might have been more disturbed. It seemed very natural. Afterwards, when I formalized it, I saw the importance of it. Now it was obvious enough that if you let *one* person make the decision, there isn't any particular problem. So I was assuming nondictatorship. But, I think it was a lucky thing, I assumed nondictatorship in a very strong form. You know at the start I was only looking at triples, because that had the essential problem. I was assuming there wasn't any dictator or any pairwise choice. And then you see, you need two or more individuals to be decisive. A little calculation shows that you can always produce orderings that violate this. It really is the Condorcet paradox restated. And then when I tried to extend it to more than triples, I retained this postulate.

So, in this first version, which I did show about a week later to Abraham Kaplan, there was this idea of showing that these conditions were incompatible. But I thought

I had really put a lot of emphasis on the assumption that there was no dictator on any pair; so, I thought, well there must *be* a solution if you allow different dictators on different pairs. This seemed to be absolutely crucial to the argument, and I thought about this for awhile. I thought it would be easy to produce an example where you have a different dictator on every pair. Now I didn't think that was a suitable solution anyway—I thought an assumption of nondictatorship was a correct assumption, even on one pair, so I wasn't too disturbed. But I thought, to clean out the exposition, to show exactly what was meant, I ought to produce an example where you have different dictators on different pairs. But no, if there's transitivity that means dictatorship sort of propagates itself. And finally one night when I wasn't sleeping too well, I could see the whole proof, you know after playing around with it for awhile. And that was a couple of weeks later, that I had the idea that the nondictatorship condition could be stated in this much weaker way, that the whole ordering can't be determined by one dictator.

JK. What did you feel at this point?

KA. I felt this was very exciting. I thought, "*This* is a dissertation." You know, it's a funny thing. One of my problems had been feeling that one has to be serious, and every time I'd thought about these voting questions they seemed like amusing diversions from the real gritty problem of developing a good descriptive theory. And in some sense I still have a little bit of that feeling. But when I got the result, I felt it was significant. I really did. It clearly didn't conform to my preordained ideas about what was significant. I would have said a priori if somebody told me about this, my temptation would be to say, "Well, that's very nice, but what importance is it?" But when I did it, I felt, yes, this is something. This was at least asking some very fundamental questions about the whole nature of social intercourse and particularly about legitimation of collective action.

This wasn't just a technical issue in game theory. The technical and the philosophical were intimately merged. My whole work in general, not only in this field but in others, has tended to deny the idea we can take off the technique and put it here and put the deep issues there. Some of the so-called technical issues are really of the essence of the so-called deep issues, and you really can't separate them at all. Each one illuminates the other. In fact they fuse together and in some cases they're identical. And nothing can better exemplify this than social choice theory, where the central issues and the technical issues were identical.

JK. Let's go down the list of some of the names you've acknowledged and tell us what they contributed. First the people at Rand: Abraham Kaplan.

KA. Well, he was one of the first persons to whom I showed the results. He was the only one who combined the philosophical side and at least some of the technical capacity to appreciate this. I don't recall getting anything specific from him, just an appreciation that it really was important.

JK. Youngs.

KA. I don't know why I thanked Youngs. Youngs was a mathematician with whom I discussed some issues of preference orderings and the like. I had been in close contact with him and I discussed some other aspects about preference orderings, really about individual preference orderings. I felt a kind of general intellectual debt.

JK. David Blackwell.

KA. Again, well, Blackwell was a genius. He and I worked very closely on other matters. He, Girshick, and I wrote a paper in 1949 on sequential analysis. He did contribute one other thing. There was this chapter [in *Social Choice and Individual Values*] which has never been followed up. I was raising the question about if the orderings were restricted in some ways, when does the paradox exist. If you go to the extreme of single-peakedness we know the answer. So the question is, supposing you have *some* restrictions on orderings but there is a lot of freedom left. I had a result, where the technical point was when could you extend a quasi-ordering to a full ordering, and it was Blackwell who told me about Szpilrajn's Theorem. However, unfortunately, my proof is not correct, because it suffers from the problem that Blau pointed out in 1957. I suspect the theorem is correct or some theorem like it is correct, but nobody's ever stated it and I've never gone back to it.

JK. J. C. C. McKinsey.

KA. McKinsey was a very interesting fellow. He was the one who educated all of us to what game theory was all about. So the influence was indirect, but in a way it was there. He was a beautiful expositor. He was a logician of considerable power and had done some work earlier on the formalization of logic; he was a disciple of Tarski's. The whole game theory ambience, and therefore in particular McKinsey—and Blackwell, for that matter, on the technical side—were influential in setting the whole tone to this.

JK. The next names are from Chicago: Tjalling Koopmans, Herbert Simon, Franco Modigliani, T. W. Anderson, Milton Friedman, David Easton.

KA. The exposition of the book was developed in the next year back in Chicago. I presented the material over a number of seminars. I was grateful to these people because they thought it was a good idea, encouraged me, and asked good questions; parts of the book are making clear points they found obscure.

Easton was a little different. He was the first political scientist I talked to about this. He gave me the references to the idealist position, which was sort of the opposite idea. In a way the idealist position was the only coherent defense that I could see in political philosophy. It wasn't a very acceptable position, but it was the only one that had at least a coherent view of why there ought to be a social ordering.

JK. Why did you call it a "Possibility" Theorem?

KA. That was Tjalling's idea. Originally I called it an impossibility theorem, but he thought that was too pessimistic! He was my boss and a very sweet man, so I changed it for him.

JK. There was a meeting of the Econometric Society where you presented these results.

KA. I guess I must have presented it at the December 1948 meeting.

JK. Who was there and what was the reaction?

KA. I remember Larry Klein was in the chair and Melvin Reder was reading another paper at the same session. My recollection is that there were 30 or 40 people in the room. I distinctly remember that in the audience was this contentious Canadian, David McCord Wright, who objected because among the objectives, I hadn't mentioned freedom as one of the essential values in social choice, and apparently he went out of the room saying that Klein and Arrow were communists—this was quoted to me at least by Kenneth May, who was also present.

I thought under the circumstances, I got a pretty good reception. I don't think anybody said, "We've seen a revolution before our eyes," but it *was* taken as a serious contribution. I wonder why it was accepted so well. There really was no resistance. It made my reputation.

There had been, of course, a fair amount of controversy about the foundations of welfare economics, beginning with papers by Roy Harrod (1938), John Hicks (1940), then Nicholas Kaldor (1939), then the long chapter in Samuelson's *Foundations,* then Tibor Scitovsky (1941) with intersecting community indifference curves. So unease about the foundations of economic policy was there. So the debate was serious—people were already concerned about these things.

Right after the summer I developed this, on the way back to Chicago, I stopped at Stanford to be interviewed for a job. Girshick had meanwhile moved to Stanford to contribute to starting a Statistics Department there. He was their star and he wanted me to join him. The Economics Department there had already in fact made me an offer a year earlier.

JK. Based on?

KA. What happened was due to Allen Wallis, who was Chancellor of the University of Rochester and is now, at the age of 75, Undersecretary of State for Economic Affairs. Wallis had been a Professor at Stanford before the war, he was the first really major appointment they ever made. He didn't return after the war, but he was highly regarded and apparently they asked him for recommendations. He had worked with Wald during the war, and Wald had spoken about me based on my work as a student at Columbia. It was very common at Stanford to appoint Assistant Professors who didn't have a PhD; they assumed we would finish. I was appointed without a PhD. In fact, I got tenure without a PhD.

JK. Really?

KA. Well, I'm being a little technical, but my statement is technically correct. In those days you couldn't get your degree until your dissertation was printed. So I had these theorems and then sent my changed proposal into Albert Hart, who got kind of excited about it. I defended the thesis in January of 1949. Stigler was on the examining committee, Bergson had come to Columbia in the meantime and they put him on the commitee. Of course, Bergson was asking some searching questions but was very fair and did have a high opinion of me. But I had no real interaction—I sent in my dissertation and got it approved.

Hart was immediately enthusiastic. He said, "I don't really understand it fully, but it sounds like you're dealing with very important issues," and I've heard later that around Columbia it was held to be an exciting event. Of course I had been regarded as a kind of a star student. In fact, one of the things that had worried me was whether I was just an eternal student.

Stanford had a custom where all initial appointments were for one year. They kept this idea since they frequently hired people without even interviewing them—because of the geography. Even Moses Abramovitz, who transformed the Department, was hired as a full Professor for just one year just before I came. The jet has ended all this. So I came as an Assistant Professor on a one-year appointment. My thesis had been approved, but I couldn't get a degree until it was printed. This was just about the end of that era. I must have been one of the last people to come under that rule. In fact, while the thing was in the process of being printed, I received a notice that if I submitted a typed manuscript, I could get my degree immediately. But that was kind of expensive, to have somebody retype that all up. I really lost about a year on my degree by deciding to go ahead on the printing. But then they gave me tenure on the basis of this unpublished dissertation. You couldn't do it today. It would never be approved today.

Then it is interesting—the reception question. Hart, who didn't work in this line, was very enthusiastic; he had spoken, I gather very well, around the Columbia faculty. The people at Stanford were very impressed; essentially all I had for them to see was this work—I hadn't done anything else except trivial stuff. They were so impressed that by the end of the interview day—within a day they were ready to make me an offer. So it's interesting to get this reception from all sorts of people not logically trained, not mathematically trained. And when the book came out, it made a great success. It is a little puzzling—at the time I took it as that's what happened. But in retrospect I sort of wonder why.

JK. Let's go to Blau's (1957) discovery of a mistake in your proof. That was eight years later; was that a great surprise?

KA. Yes, it certainly was. Blau was working that year at Stanford and showed it to me. I was surprised, but I knew right away that a universality assumption would correct things. It had seemed obvious to me that the nondictatorship property was hereditary, but it wasn't. I still think there is a better correction than that one, but I've never really gone back to work on it.

Blau's was a very, very nice result. It didn't obviously change the basic impact, but it did show my little attempts at generalization didn't work. It's interesting to see how easy it is to make a mistake on things that seem so airtight.

JK. Let's leave the origins now. Over the succeeding 40 years, what were the most important developments in social choice theory?

KA. Some of the work that has cohered around the original question is mathematically interesting but not very relevant to the original field. The literature that depends on small numbers of alternatives is in this category. I think the alternative space must be taken to be very large.

I also have qualms about results like those of Kirman and Sondermann (1972). What do we learn from Kirman–Sondermann exactly? When you have an infinity of voters, then the axioms as I wrote them become consistent and you can produce voting systems. But they are consistent because in some sense the dictator has a different meaning; banning a dictator is no longer enough. As it turns out, if you have a sequence of decisive sets, each of which is properly contained in its predecessor, the intersection of the whole sequence is empty, but everyone in that sequence is then less decisive. In some sense, the spirit of nondictatorship ought to rule that out.

Incidentally, there's a recent result I haven't had a chance to study by a former student of mine, Alain Lewis, who says if you confine yourself to recursive functions then the voting paradox occurs even with an infinite number of voters; in the strict sense, even with just the ordinary axioms. The examples Kirman and Sondermann use are nonconstructive; something with cofinite sets is not something you can actually construct—you just show it exists. But since they are only examples, that's not a proof that there isn't a constructive procedure. But Lewis says he's given a proof and I have to study it. If I can understand it.

JK. What about the Gibbard–Satterthwaite results?

KA. Gibbard's (1973) work was a bombshell. That was very exciting. I didn't know about Satterthwaite's (1975) work for a couple of years, but it was very much the same thing. I had taken the liberty of abstracting from manipulability in my thesis and I never went back to that issue. What's surprising is not really that there is an impossibility of nonmanipulability, but that the issues should be essentially the same. That strikes one as a remarkable coincidence.

I still find it surprising and feel that we might not have the right proof. Somehow you feel that if you had the right proof it would be obvious. But then I thought that about my work, too. My impossibility theorem ought to be totally obvious when looked at the right way. Yet every proof involves a trick. Maybe not a big trick; I don't think it's a mathematically hard theorem. But somehow if you had the right way of approaching it, it should be trivial. Yet, no matter how you present the proof, and they're all pretty close to equivalent, it's not yet trivial. For example, when ultrafilters came in, I thought, Aha! This is a beautiful way of showing it. But it turns out that to prove the decisive sets form an ultrafilter involves essentially all the original calculations.

JK. Still, it's a nice approach conceptually.

KA. I don't know. I'm less convinced than when I first saw it. It has the advantage of referring to a known body of knowledge. But this is a body of knowledge that is somewhat technical. You're bringing in a fair amount of technical apparatus, and it ought to pay for itself somewhere, if I may use an economic approach. It ought to pay for itself in making the proof trivial. But in fact you need just about every step in the original proof to show that the issue *is* one of a fixed ultrafilter. So therefore, why bring in all this apparatus? I was a little surprised by how little you get from all that apparatus. I can't help feeling there's some way out of it. In the same way, I always feel the Gibbard–Satterthwaite result should be more transparent than it is. But maybe it can't be done.

JK. What about Sen's (1970) Paretian liberal approach; does that interest you?

KA. I thought that was stunning and penetrating to a very important issue. But ... why do we have rights? What I am after all is a kind of utilitarian manqué. That is to say, I'd like to be utilitarian but the only problem is I have nowhere those utilities come from. The problem I have with utilitarianism is not that it is excessively rational, but that the epistemological foundations are weak. My problem is: What are those objects we are adding up? I have no objection to adding them up if there's something to add. But the one thing I retain from utilitarianism is that, basically, judgments are based on consequences. Certainly that's the sort of thing we do in the theory of the single individual under uncertainty; you make sure utility is defined only over the consequences. I view rights as arrangements that may help you in achieving a higher utility level. For example, if you are much better informed about a certain choice, because it's personal to you and not to me, I don't really know anything about it, I should delegate the choice to you.

JK. You don't want to allow preferences over processes?

KA. Well, one of the things I fear is emptiness. You put preferences over enough things, then anything that happens can be defended. It destroys the idea of discourse. Of course, it is a delicate issue, you can always say, of any particular process that it is specially privileged. You could take Nozick's point of view; you can have an absolute preference about certain processes. For example, we have a property system; if you and I make an agreement about anything within our property rights, that just fixes it, period. Now I've got to admit Nozick's courage is good. Suppose somebody invented a cure for cancer and allowed it to be used only at an extremely high price. Nozick says: No problem. Most everybody else would regard that as a fatal counterexample, but Nozick has the courage of his convictions. But that's a strong example of preference over processes. Most of the people who are advocating rights are very different, like Dworkin. They tend to support so to speak left-wing rights rather than right-wing rights, but once you grant that, who settles what rights are legitimate? The consequentialist view—I won't say that fully settles it either, but at least you have something to argue about. So this is why I'm a little unsympathetic to the rights issue—everybody just multiplies the rights all over the place and you get total paralysis.

Consider the consenting adult example—say homosexuality—and think about the concept of externality. Now why do we say intercourse among consenting adults should be allowed? One argues because there's no externality. But if I care, there *is* an externality. I actually allude to this even in the first edition of my book. It's just a rhetorical passage and doesn't enter the logic, but I mention that the concept of preference is just what everybody thinks their preferences are. Different people might have different ideas of externalities. I took the view that all preferences count. From the logical point of view, it doesn't matter; if you purify the preferences by rejecting the nosy preferences, the theorem applies to whatever is left. There is, of course, a technical problem in systematically combing out inadmissible preferences. Transitivity says you can't just look at separate preference pairs, you have to look at the whole system. That's what Gibbard's paper is really devoted to. Gibbard is not totally convincing, because there are some arbitrary choices in his elimination procedure; he doesn't make it compelling that his is the only way of doing it. It's just *a* way. It looked pretty devastating but it eliminated more than was really necessary.

I'm quite puzzled. People really care about consequences as they see them. If I'm really offended because people are seeing obscene material, well, I'm hurt. I really am hurt. I'm hurt just as much as if somebody blew smoke in my eyes—or whatever your favorite form of pollution is. Indeed a lot of people probably care much more. I really find it difficult to decide.

Unless somebody produces a logic of rights in terms of which we can *argue,* I really find the whole issue is unfocused. The reason why it is compelling is that there are at least some cases where we do feel strongly about the rights. It's not clear you can always reduce those to utilitarian considerations like information.

JK. One last question. What outstanding problem in social choice theory would you most like to see solved?

KA. Well, if I had to pick just one, it would be reformulating a weakened form of the independence of irrelevant alternatives which stops short of just dropping it completely. There are a lot of arguments used today, extended sympathy, for example, or the relevance of risk-bearing to social choice as in Harsanyi (1955) or Vickrey (1945), that do involve, if you look at them closely, use of irrelevant alternatives. Suppose I'm making a choice in Harsanyi's story among totally certain alternatives. I somehow use preferences among risky alternatives as part of the process of social decision-making. We use a chain of reasoning that goes through irrelevant alternatives. It seems quite open to acceptance, not at all unreasonable, that these are useful. I would not want to rule out in an argument, a line of reasoning that goes through a chain of transitivity via an irrelevant alternative. And yet I don't want to be in the position of saying, well the whole thing depends on the whole preference ordering. My current feeling is that that is the most central issue—the most likely way of really understanding issues.

JK. Are you anticipating that if you allow chains of transitivity over irrelevant alternatives you will obtain a "good" social choice procedure, or are you expecting a deeper impossibility theorem?

KA. I'm expecting—no, let me put it more cautiously—I'm *hoping* for a possibility result.

REFERENCES

Arrow, K. J. (1951). *Social choice and individual values*. New York: Wiley.

Arrow, K. J., Girshick, M. A. & Blackwell, D. (1949). Bayes and minimax solutions of sequential decision problems. *Econometrica, 17*, 213–244.

Black, D. (1948). On the rationale of group decision making. *Journal of Political Economics, 56*, 23–34.

Blau, J. (1957). The existence of social welfare functions. *Econometrica, 25*, 302–313.

Foley, D. (1967). Resource allocation and the public sector. *Yale Economic Essays*, 7, 45–98.

Gibbard, A. (1973). Manipulation of voting schemes: a general result. *Econometrica, 41*, 587–601.
Harrod, R. F. (1938). Scope and method of economics, *Economic Journal, 48*, 383-412.
Harsanyi, J. C. (1955). Cardinal welfare, individualistic ethics, and interpersonal comparisons of utility. *Journal of Political Economics, 63*, 309–321.
Hart, A. G. (1942). Risk, uncertainty and the unprofitability of compounding probabilities. In O. Lange, F. McIntyre & T. O. Yntema (Eds.), *Mathematical economics and econometrics: In memory of Henry Schultz* (pp. 110–118). University of Chicago Press.
Hicks, J. (1939). *Value and capital.* Oxford: Clarendon Press.
Hicks, J. R. (1940). The valuation of the social income, *Economica, 7*, 105-124.
Hotelling, H. (1932). Edgeworth's taxation paradox and the nature of demand and supply functions. *Journal of Political Economics, 40*, 571–616.
Hotelling, H. (1935). Demand functions with limited budgets. *Econometrica, 3*, 66–78.
Kaldor, N. (1939). Welfare propositions in economics and interpersonal comparisons of utility, *Economic Journal, 49*, 549-552.
Kenney, J. F. (1939). *Mathematics of statistics* (Vol. 2). Wokingham: Van Nostrand.
Kirman, A. & Sondermann, D. (1972). Arrow's theorem, many agents and invisible dictators. *Journal of Economic Theory, 5*, 267–277.
Lange, O. (1942). The foundations of welfare economics. *Econometrica, 10*, 215–228.
Lange, O., McIntyre, F. & Yntema, T. O. (Eds.) (1942). *Mathematical economics and econometrics: In memory of Henry Schultz*. University of Chicago Press.
Modigliani, F. & Miller, M. H. (1958). The cost of capital, corporation finance, and the theory of investment. *American Economic Review, 48*, 261–297.
Popper, K. (1938). A set of independent axioms for probability. *Mind, 47*, 275–277.
Samuelson, P. A. (1941, 1942). The stability of equilibrium. *Econometrica, 9*, 97–120; *10*, 1–25.
Samuelson, P. A. (1947). *Foundations of economic analysis*, Cambridge, Massachusetts, Harvard University Press.
Satterthwaite, M. A. (1975). Strategy-proofness and Arrow's conditions. *Journal of Economic Theory, 10*, 187–217.
Schroder, E. (1890–1905). *Vorlesungen über die Algebra der Logik* (Vol. 3). Leipzig: B. G. Teubner.
Scitovsky, T. (1942). A reconsideration of the theory of tarifs. *Review of Economic Study, 9*, 89–110.
Sen, A. (1970). The impossibility of a Paretian liberal. *Journal of Political Economics, 78*, 152–157.
Tarski, A. (1941). *Introduction to logic and the methodology of the deductive sciences.* New York: Oxford University Press (Appeared originally in Polish, 1936, and was translated into German, 1937).
Vickrey, W. S. (1945). Measuring marginal utility by reactions to risk. *Econometrica, 13*, 319–333.
Wold, H.O.A. (1943, 1944). A synthesis of pure demand analysis, I–III. *Skandinavisk Aktuarietidskrift, 26*, 85–118, 220–263; *27*, 69–120.

Part III : The Classification of Social Choice Propositions

Kenneth Arrow

Our modern concern with social choice and, indeed, with rational choice in general, is a project of the Enlightenment period of Western thought in the eighteenth century. Daniel Bernoulli's famous paper on rational choice under uncertainty certainly pioneers [this inquiry]. More relevant still are the works of Marquis de Condorcet, Jeremy Bentham, and David Hume.

The process of social choice is clearly a system with many elements, including the members of the society, and their interactions. To an important extent, the aims of these members affect the outcome, which in some sense "should assist" in achieving these ends. A few of the same considerations are seen in the emerging study of what are called "complex adaptive systems," a concept at least partly inspired by the theory of evolution. There is a concept of "fitness," which individual components of the system are increasing; the question is the outcome of the system as a whole, and the answer sought by ecologists is frequently in terms of some overall measure that might be called an aggregate fitness, for example, biomass.

Hume famously distinguished between normative and descriptive propositions, "is" and "ought" statements; one can never deduce a proposition that imposes an obligation (an "ought") from a series of statements that describe the world (statements of what "is"). Obviously, in some sense, this must be right, but the examination of social choice theory suggests that the dichotomy is more blurred than it seems.

I have written of my first encounter with the social choice paradox. I was in fact concerned with a purely descriptive issue, viz., investment choices by firms with many owners (corporations). In an economy extended in time, John Hicks held in *Value and Capital* (1939) that a firm's investment behavior could be described as maximizing its anticipated discounted profits. The different shareholders may well have different anticipations of the future. How then are investments determined? Each owner will have his or her own optimal investment policy, as determined by his or her anticipations of future prices. My natural hypothesis was that the choice between two investment plans is determined (in principle) by majority voting (share-weighted, of course). This choice defines a preference relation. Since, as I understood it, rationality required transitivity, I immediately checked whether majority voting satisfied this condition, and it took no more than a few minutes to find a counterexample. It was another five years before I learned that I had been "anticipated" by Condorcet more than 160 years earlier, but I did guess that someone must have already found this out.[2,3]

I tell this story to show how the same issue can be thought of as normative or descriptive from different points of view. The situation is somewhat similar to well-known optical illusions. The empirical, descriptive implications of the social choice paradox for political activity have been argued for by many political scientists, as I note below.

[2] Let me put on the record a small historical incident. I had in fact noted a similar paradox a few months earlier. Hicks gave a lecture at Columbia on an ordinalist definition of being better off without requiring interpersonal comparability [of utility], in fact, the same one developed later and independently by Duncan Foley under the name of "envy." He defined A to be "better off" than B if A's bundle is preferred to B's in both A's and B's preference orderings. Hicks understood clearly that this relation was incomplete. But, as I noted in a question to Hicks at the lecture, Hicks' relation could easily be intransitive, which would contradict the usual associations of the term "better off."

[3] As a descriptive problem, the issue is still with us. My formulation was in any case inadequate, because I did not allow for the possibility of selling the stock, i.e., a stockholder might opt for an investment project that will maximize the appeal of the firm's stock to the market in general, as measured by the market price even if the individual stockholder does not think that investment project will be optimal for the firm.

To return to the consideration of social choice as an adaptive system, the interactions within the system may be summarized as communications, expressions by the members of their specific properties. The process can again be analogized to an ecosystem, in which individual species or even individual phenotypes act in ways that reflect their properties and capabilities. There is no central agency with the relevant information. Social choice theory strips down the properties of the members to their preference scales. There is then a *communication system,* which must ultimately (given other knowledge, mainly the set of opportunities) determine the system's outcome.

Social choice theory starts with some hopefully reasonable conditions that relate the outcomes to the communications (or interactions). The conditions include those relating to the feasibility of communication itself. I am here going to assume that social choice depends on individual welfares ("welfarism"), without trying to argue the proposition. Hence, communications are of individual preferences, as stated, and the collective outcome has to be a function of the communications.

Let us look briefly at the stated conditions in *Social Choice and Individual Values,* Chapter 3. The key conditions are, of course, *Collective Rationality* (embodied in the definition of a social welfare function), the *Pareto Principle* (or, in a form that I like but has not caught on, the *Positive Association of Individual and Social Values*),[4] and the *Independence of Irrelevant Alternatives.*

Only the second condition is normative in the usual sense, and it is a weak one, at least from a welfarist viewpoint. This is one reason why the distinction between normative and descriptive propositions in social action is so blurred. If every goose wants to go in the same direction, the statement that the flock goes in that direction can be thought of indifferently as an "ought" or as an "is."

The condition of *Independence of Irrelevant Alternatives* seems to be primarily a question of feasibility, but it seems also to have a normative element. Consider the market as a system of social choice. We only expect consumers and producers to make choices constrained by the realities as they see them, constrained by budget sets and production possibility sets, and the market equilibrium is, in turn, constrained by feasibility, that is, the absence of excess supply.[5] Of course, elections and legislation clearly satisfy the conditions.

We can indeed imagine a social choice system that violates *Independence of Irrelevant Alternatives.* Consider all *conceivable* alternatives (not just those that are feasible), and require each individual to rank them. Calculate the Borda count for each individual, and choose the alternative with the highest Borda count among the feasible alternatives. This method will clearly satisfy both *Collective Rationality* and *Positive Association of Individual and Social Values* (or the *Pareto Principle*). The infeasible alternatives might be said to help

[4] This states that, if preferences change so that only one alternative rises in one or more individuals' preference scales and no other change takes place, then a social preference for that alternative over some other still holds.

[5] In writing this, it occurs to me that if one added to the description of the market some process of getting into equilibrium, then we would be using information about irrelevant alternatives. But it remains true that the equilibrium outcome depends only on preferences among relevant (i.e., feasible) alternatives.

measure the intensity of preferences. (If I put many infeasible alternatives between A and B, while you rank B just above A, the Borda count would in effect say that my preference for A over B is stronger than your preference for B over A.) Still, there is some sense, which I cannot further identify, that such a procedure is not satisfactory, so there does seem to be a normative element to *Independence of Irrelevant Alternatives*.

I conclude with some references to work on social choice as a descriptive theory. I have already noted one then-current example of intransitivity in actual legislation (*Social Choice and Individual Values*, Chapter 1, footnote 3).

With regard to elections, refutation can be only hypothetical, for instance, that an election outcome would have been different if an "irrelevant" change in preference or in the list of candidates (e.g., deletion of a loser) had occurred. It is obviously true that the outcome can depend on the election method, as Jean-Charles de Borda had already noted. Whenever full rankings are available, Condorcet intransitivities can often be found. Donald Saari has claimed that in the United States presidential election of 1860, a centrist candidate other than Lincoln would have been a Condorcet winner.

In legislation, the outcome can clearly depend on the order in which alternative proposals are voted on, a point on which there is a large literature. A conclusion drawn by many political scientists, such as William Riker, is that politics is inherently chaotic. Richard McKelvey has stated a famous theorem: Suppose the alternatives lie in an n-dimensional space ($n > 1$), we choose between alternatives by majority voting (as is standard in legislation), and there is no Condorcet winner. Given *any* two proposals, a and b, there exists a sequence of proposals, $\{a_i'\}(i = 0, \ldots, n)$ such that $a_0' = a, a_n' = b$, and a_i' defeats a_{i+1}' for all $i = 0, \ldots, n-1$. That is, by a suitably chosen agenda, any proposal can defeat any other if there is no Condorcet winner. Riker has clearly been influenced by results like this and by those of Norman Schofield. As Riker has said,

> *Disequilibrium, or the potential that the status quo can be upset, is the characteristic feature of politics. The sum of our new sophistication is, therefore, that political outcomes truly are unpredictable in the long run.... Politics is the dismal science because we learned from it that there are no fundamental equilibria to predict.*

Even the actions of the third branch of the government, the judicial, have been scrutinized for intransitivity, as in the studies of the United States Supreme Court by Frank Easterbrook and Maxwell Stearns. Courts deal with specific cases, so that contradictions cannot literally occur. But since principles are enunciated and binding, intransitivity appears as the creation of inconsistent precedents or at least inconsistent principles on which to base future decisions.

These fragmentary remarks serve in general to illustrate two propositions about social choice theory: (1) that the boundary between normative and descriptive statements is vague; and (2) that the implications of social choice paradoxes for descriptive political theory are to make empirical propositions harder to come by and to stress the unpredictability of political outcomes.

CHAPTER FOURTEEN

The Informational Basis of Social Choice[1]

Amartya Sen
Thomas W. Lamont University Professor, and Professor of Economics and Philosophy, Harvard University, Cambridge, MA.

Contents

Abstract

Any procedure of social choice makes use of some types of information and ignores others. For example, the method of majority decision concentrates on people's votes, but pays no direct attention to, say, their social standings, or their prosperity or penury, or even the intensities of their preferences. The differences between distinct procedures lie, to a substantial extent, on the kind of information that each procedure uses and what it has to ignore. The informational bases of the different social choice procedures tell us a great deal about how they respectively work and what they can or cannot achieve.

Keywords: information, welfarism, voting, social welfare, impossibility theorems.

1. INTRODUCTION

Social choice theory addresses a wide range of decisional and judgmental problems, dealing with a variety of procedures—from voting to making normative social assessments. It encompasses theories of elections and balloting on one side, to welfare economics on the other, as well as theories of normative measurement, such as the

[1] For helpful discussions I am grateful to Kenneth Arrow and Kotaro Suzumura.

Handbook of Social Choice and Welfare, Volume II
ISSN: 0169-7218, DOI: 10.1016/S0169-7218(10)00014-6

evaluation of national incomes, measurement of inequality and poverty, and appraisal of social welfare. These distinct problems often demand quite dissimilar approaches, and there is little hope of getting some uniform approach that would work equally satisfactorily for all the different exercises.[2] Nevertheless, all the social choice problems have the shared feature of relating "social"—or group—assessment to the values, preferences, choices, or some other characteristics of the respective individuals who form the collectivity of that society or group. It is with the informational basis of that generic approach that this chapter is concerned.

Any procedure of social choice makes use of some types of information and ignores others. For example, the method of majority decision concentrates on people's votes and, by implication, (given suitable assumptions) on their preferences. But it pays no direct attention to a variety of other kinds of information, such as their personal characters, their social standing, their prosperity or penury, or even the intensities of their preferences. But each of these ignored features can be very influential for other procedures of social choice. The differences between distinct procedures lie, to a substantial extent, on the kind of information that they respectively use and what they ignore. The informational bases of the respective social choice procedures tell us a great deal about their nature and underlying motivations, and about the differences that distinguish them from each other.

Much the same thing can be said about *principles* of social judgment or of normative social decisions. Their respective informational bases qualify the nature of the judgments that can—or cannot—be made. The informational bases can be explicitly stated, or implicitly characterized, by the axiomatic requirements imposed on each respective approach. Indeed, many of the "conditions" of social decisions that have received intense attention in recent decades, especially since Arrow's (1950, 1951) pioneering departure in axiomatic social choice theory, can be helpfully analyzed in terms of their informational demands, including informational prohibitions.

We can, in fact, go a long way in characterizing any normative principle, or any well-defined procedure of social choice, by identifying the information that it uses and, no less importantly, the information it ignores, as is discussed in Sen (1977b, 1979). It is tempting to ask whether a procedure, or a principle, of social choice can be fully delineated by its informational basis *alone?* The answer is very definitely in the negative, for reasons that are not far to seek. No matter how tight the informational conditions are that help us to move closely towards a certain principle p, there are at least three other principles that are not excluded by the very same informational requirements. First, a principle, let us call it anti-p, can demand the exact opposite of what principle p concludes (e.g., minimizing the utility sum-total does not demand any more information than the utilitarian maximization of that sum). Second, to resolve that all alternatives be

[2] I have discussed elsewhere, in Sen (1977a), why the distinctions involved are very important to acknowledge and accommodate. See also Suzumura (1982, 1983).

accepted as being equally good (what can be called *universal indifference*) does not demand any information at all (beyond the knowledge of that *blanket rule*). Third, resolving that no alternative can be ranked against any other (call it *universal unconnectedness*) also has little informational requirement.

However, the informational perspective can be used not only to make sure that there is enough information for the decisions involved, but also to demand that the processes or principles must actually respond to—or be sensitive to—particular types of information that characterize each specific principle or procedure. If we go beyond checking the sufficiency of available information to the necessity of taking discriminating note of particular information (a requirement of informational *responsiveness*), the last two of the three alternatives may turn out to be unacceptable. To illustrate with a simple example, an insistence on the necessity to be sensitive to the unanimous strict preferences of all individuals over a pair of social states $\{x, y\}$ may eliminate the possibility of being indifferent between them, or keeping them unranked, when everyone does in fact prefer x to y. But informational sensitivity alone, without a directional mandate, cannot yield the conclusion that x must, in this case, be socially preferred to y (or that x must be chosen over y, given that choice). Indeed, the exact opposite (that is, socially ranking y over x in response to every member of the society preferring x to y), while patently perverse, is also sensitive to the same information. Pareto and anti-Pareto do not, in fact, differ in informational requirement or in informational responsiveness—only in the *direction* of the response.

Substantive social choice theory cannot, therefore, be understood merely in terms of informational bases. There is no way of getting rid of the different ways in which the same information can be used in different procedures or principles. And yet the differences between distinct social choice principles or processes often rest primarily on their contrasting informational bases.

Indeed, many of the decisive steps in the history of social choice theory have turned on invoking some types of information and disavowing others. This chapter is concerned with tracing some of these historical steps, beginning with the early origins of the subject in the hands of eighteenth-century French mathematicians (such as Condorcet and Borda), then proceeding to the founding of modern social choice theory in the middle of the twentieth century (with the pioneering work of Kenneth Arrow in 1950 and 1951), and finally looking briefly at some of the more recent trends in the subject, particularly in normative social choice theory.[3]

[3] The balance of attention in this chapter is somewhat tilted in the direction of relatively broader results rather than more particularized findings. I have had the occasion to discuss and illustrate in another essay on social choice theory (Sen, 1986) how the classical debates on the principles and procedures of social choice have continuing relevance to the formal analyses and technical results in the more recent works that often deal with very specialized issues. The "older" contentious issues, related to informational bases, have similar resilience and durability.

2. DEMOCRATIC PRIORITIES AND INFORMATIONAL INCLUSIVENESS

The informational foundation of modern social choice theory relates closely to the basic democratic conviction that social judgments and public decisions must depend, in some transparent way, on individual preferences, broadly understood. The emergence of this democratic instinct relates closely to the ideas and events that surrounded the European Enlightenment. While it drew on various antecedent sources and inspirations, the democratic perspective received adequate delineation and wide public acknowledgement only during the Enlightenment, particularly in the late-eighteenth century, which also saw the French Revolution and American independence. The works of Borda (1781) and Condorcet (1785) on the properties of voting systems and of Bentham (1789) on the demands of utilitarian social aggregation were clearly influenced by this general intellectual climate.

Individual preferences can, of course, be variously interpreted in different democratic exercises, and this is well illustrated by the contrast between focusing on votes—and through them on people's voices (explored in the classic works of Borda or Condorcet)—on the one hand, and concentrating on the interests or judgments (explored in the pioneering writings of Adam Smith, Jeremy Bentham, or John Stuart Mill), on the other. These contrasts—between alternative interpretations of preferences—can be very important for some purposes, but in the present context, that of noting the democratic foundations of social choice theory, their differences are less important than what they have in common. For the moment I shall use the generic term *preference* to cover all these different interpretations of individual concerns that could be invoked, in one way or another, to serve as the informational bases of public decisions or social judgments.

In this elementary democratic foundation, there is also a strong understanding that at least in principle the preferences of everyone could count, without any a priori exclusions (even if it were to turn out, on the basis of further analyses, that some preferences would be more effective than others, sometimes radically so). No member of the collectivity could be eliminated as being foundationally irrelevant. That informational underpinning, which was established in the first generation of formal social choice theory that emerged in the eighteenth century, has been powerfully reinforced in modern social choice theory pioneered by Arrow (1951). While this rudimentary democratic feature may seem today to be rather straightforward, perhaps even mundane, it was a radical enough step at the time of its first consolidation. It firmly established a democratic inclusiveness in the informational basis of social choice.

The force of this departure can be brought out by examining the contrast between these new presumptions and the earlier interpretations of social choice in pre-Enlightenment politics or political economy. For example, Aristotle in ancient Greece and Kautilya in ancient India, both of whom lived in the fourth century before Christ, had explored various procedures for making appropriate social decisions, in their books respectively called *Politics* and *Economics*.[4] Aristotle had no great difficulty in excluding women and slaves from the process of social decision making, and Kautilya had little problem in confining critical decisions in the hands of those blessed by high social status (related to caste or political authority). Enormous informational exclusions were, in effect, authorized *before* the substantive investigation of social procedures properly began. The world of late-eighteenth century Europe broadened the needed informational foundation by overturning that exclusionary authorization. The pioneers of modern social choice theory were guided by their firm conviction that every member of a collectivity must, in principle, count in the decisions of that collectivity.[5]

This is meant to apply to choices for the society as a whole, as well as to those for a committee, or an academy, or a set of juries, or some other organizational panel or board. There is an insistence on no antecedent exclusion of the concerns of any individual member of the respective collectivity. The different decisional structures that were explored, such as majority rule, or utilitarian aggregation, or rank-order voting (the so-called "Borda rule") differed in the significance that can be attached to particular aspects of individual preferences: for example, whether to take note only of the ranking of each pair considered separately (ignoring other "irrelevant" alternatives), or to attach significance to the rank of a particular alternative in an overall ranking (as in Borda's well-known formula).[6] But in not excluding anyone's preference ordering from counting, they shared a basic belief in democratic inclusiveness in an elementary but powerful form.

Since contemporary social choice theory, pioneered by Arrow, emphatically shares this foundational democratic value, the discipline has continued to be loyal to this basic informational presumption. For example, when an axiomatic structure yields the existence of a dictator (Arrow 1951), as a joint implication of chosen axioms that seemed plausible enough (seen on their own), this is immediately understood as something of a major embarrassment for that set of axioms, rather than being taken to be just fine on the ground that it is a logical corollary of axioms that have been already accepted and endorsed. We cannot begin to understand the intellectual challenge involved in Arrow's impossibility theorem without coming to grips with the focus on inclusiveness that goes with a democratic commitment, which is deeply offended by a dictatorial procedure, even when it is entailed by axiomatic requirements that seem eminently acceptable.

4 For English translations of Aristotle's *Politics* and of Kautilya's *Arthashastra*, see, respectively, Barker (1958) and Shama Sastry (1967). *Arthashastra*, the Sanskrit title of Kautilya's book, which literally means "treatise on material wealth," is perhaps best translated as "economics," even though much of the book is devoted to studying systematic statecraft.

5 On the intellectual debates that engaged Enlightenment authors, including Condorcet, see Rothschild (2001).

6 The so-called "Borda rule" belongs to a general class of "positional rules," the properties of which have been extensively investigated by Gardenfors (1973), Fine and Fine (1974), and others; see Pattanaik's (2002) superb critical survey of this literature, in Vol. I of this *Handbook*. Condorcet's voting principles have been well discussed by Arrow (1963), Fishburn (1973), Suzumura (1983), Young (1988), among others.

The same applies, in one way or another, to the various subsequent results that followed Arrow's impossibility theorem. Arrow's specific impossibility result—with dictatorship's being implied by his other conditions—is not extendable to the case in which the transitivity of social preference is weakened, even rather slightly, to just "quasi-transitivity" (or the transitivity of strict preference only), unless the other conditions are redefined.[7] But as the requirement of "collective rationality" in the form of social transitivity or binariness is gradually relaxed, new results emerge that show that there must now be an oligarchy, or the existence of someone with veto power, or some other violation of what democracy demands.[8] Again, the tension that is generated by these results relates to the violation of informational inclusion that a democratic commitment entails.

It is important to recognize how radically the nature of the social choice search for a minimally acceptable social decision procedure has been shaped by the informational implications of a basic democratic conviction that was getting firmly established in the second half of the eighteenth century, just as social choice theory, in its early form, was being founded. Given the centrality of Arrow's result, which has profoundly shaped the direction that the development of social choice theory took over the second half of the twentieth century, it is perhaps useful to examine sequentially how the tension with democratic inclusiveness emerges from what looks merely like minimal demands of systematic and sensitive social choice. After some clarificatory discussion of the informational aspects of Arrow's social choice framework in the next section, a simple way of understanding and establishing Arrow's theorem (seen specifically in an informational perspective) is presented in Section 4.

3. INFORMATIONAL EXCLUSIONS AND SOCIAL CHOICE FRAMEWORK

In the general Arrovian framework, the social ranking R of the alternative social states is taken to be a function of the n-tuple of individual rankings $\{R_i\}$ of those states:

$$R = f(\{R_i\}) \tag{1}$$

[7] This nonextendability is shown in Sen (1969, 1970a). However, it can also be shown that in a choice-functional framework, Arrow's conditions can be suitably recharacterized, without changing their motivational justifications, to precipitate the dictatorship result without any condition of internal consistency of social choice whatsoever (as shown in Sen 1993). Thus reinterpreted, Arrow's conditions of independence, unrestricted domain, and the weak Pareto principle, together, continue to contradict democratic inclusiveness, even without any demand for *internal* consistency of social choice.

[8] Different types of results in this general line of investigation have been presented—or scrutinized—in Gibbard (1969, 1973), Sen (1970a, 1977a, 1993), Mas-Colell and Sonnenschein (1972), Fishburn (1973, 1974), Brown (1974, 1975), Binmore (1975, 1994), Campbell (1976), Deb (1976, 1977), Suzumura (1976a,b, 1983), Blau and Deb (1977), Kelly (1978), Blair and Pollak (1979, 1982), Grether and Plott (1982), Chichilnisky (1982), Chichilnisky and Heal (1983), Moulin (1983), Pattanaik and Salles (1983), Peleg (1984), Hammond (1985), Kelsey (1985), and Campbell and Kelly (1997).

The functional relation f, which we can call a "collective choice rule," is an Arrovian "social welfare function" when there is the further requirement that R as well as each R_i be a complete ordering of feasible social states.[9] In the discussion that follows, the immediate reference will be specifically to social welfare functions (SWF), but much of the discussion applies to collective choice rules in general.

Since conflict with informational inclusiveness is such a central feature of the Arrow impossibility theorem, it is important to be sure that the impossibility result is not being achieved simply by beginning with patently informational restrictions (in the formulation of social welfare functions). We have to ask: How inclusive is this general Arrovian formulation regarding the information that can be accommodated in the process of social choice? In answering this question, it is convenient to distinguish between "utility information" in the general sense (including information about preference rankings) and "nonutility information" regarding other features of states of affairs. It is easily checked that while the utility information that is allowed to be accommodated in an SWF is rather restricted, there is nothing in the form of an SWF itself that limits the admissibility of nonutility information.

Consider first the nature of allowable utility information. In (1), the form of $f(\{R_i\})$ does not allow the use of interpersonal comparison of utilities.[10] This is certainly a start-off restriction. In his initial formulation of the problem of social choice, Kenneth Arrow was moved by the view, common in positivist philosophy that was then influential in welfare economics, that "interpersonal comparison of utilities has no meaning" (Arrow 1951, p. 9). The utility information that is usable in this structure of social choice consists of n-tuples of individual preferences (or utility orderings) of the respective individuals—considered separately. This is a momentous informational exclusion, the removal of which can open up many constructive possibilities (as was discussed in Sen 1970a).

However, as far as nonutility information is concerned, the format of social welfare functions is remarkably permissive. Unless eliminated by specific axioms to be imposed on social welfare functions (on which more will be discussed presently), the framework can accommodate sensitivity to any part of the informational content of social states. There is a real comprehensiveness here, which is worth emphasizing, since it can be easily missed because of the apparent insistence, in the formulation of (1), that the n-tuple of individual preferences $\{R_i\}$ be the sole input into the choice process. The implications of this formulation require some elucidation, particularly since they are, in fact, critically important for later social choice theory, involving the use of nonutility

9 Different types of collective choice rules can be distinguished and individually investigated, as discussed in Sen (1970a). See also Fishburn (1973), Kelly (1978), and Suzumura (1983), among other treatises, for different classificatory systems.

10 Nor are cardinal utilities (whether or not comparable) admissible in this framework. This is not, however, a critical constraint for Arrow's impossibility theorem, since that result can be extended to the case of noncomparable cardinal utilities (see Theorem 8.2 in Sen 1970a), even though it does severely restrict the class of permissible social choice procedures (on which see Gevers 1979 and Roberts 1980a).

information related to liberties, rights, and nonwelfarist interpretations of justice, equity, and poverty.

The informational content of social states is not arbitrarily restricted in any way, and the social welfare function can take note of any information that can be accommodated within the specification of social states. There is need for some clarification here. Given the form of (1), with $R = f(\{R_i\})$, it may appear that no feature of social states can be influential in the choice over these states unless the individual preferences $\{R_i\}$ respond to that feature. In this interpretation, if a specific feature of a state of affairs (say, the level of income inequality, or the violation of some liberties, or the infringement of civil rights) is going to be directly influential in social choice, it must be *through* the impact of that feature on individual preferences over states of affairs. Indeed, in this interpretation, no feature of the states can have an influence on social choice through any channel *other than* individual preferences.

This interpretation, however, is not correct. Even though a social welfare function insists on a tight functional relation f between R and $\{R_i\}$, there is nothing in the mathematics of this requirement that would prevent the nature of the functional relation f to be itself responsive to any information that is included in the content of the respective social states that R and R_i order. The individual preference orderings are rankings of substantive social states, and the information about the social states can be taken into account in deciding on the mapping between the set of n-tuples of individual preferences and the set of social rankings to be determined by f.

However, this permissive format can be made informationally more restrictive through the effects of axioms that may be imposed on a social welfare function. Indeed, through this route it is possible to end up eliminating the direct usability of *all* nonutility information, so that the characteristics of social states are made totally inconsequential: social choice over them will then be determined only by their placing in the individual preference rankings. This condition is sometimes called "neutrality." This is perhaps an oddly reverent name for what is after all only an informational restriction, but the requirement can be seen as "neutralizing"—indeed eliminating—the influence of all nonutility (or nonpreference) information regarding social states. In effect, it yields an insistence that social decisions be taken only on the basis of individual preferences over the states, without paying any attention to the nature of these states (and the nonutility or nonpreference information about these states).

In the literature of moral philosophy, this "neutrality" condition and similar requirements are sometimes called "welfarism" (see Sen and Williams 1982), and that term has been in increasing use in social choice theory as well. Welfarism, narrowly defined, is the demand that social welfare (or whatever is taken as the social maximand) depends only on individual utilities: other features of states of affairs have no direct influence on social welfare (or the social maximand). In somewhat broader formulations, welfarism, corresponding to "neutrality," can be seen as a more permissive insistence that the social maximand depends only on individual utilities, or individual welfares, or individual evaluations of the worth of states of affairs (more on this presently).

It is possible to combine welfarism with very rich utility information (such as interpersonal comparability and cardinality), and indeed such enrichment of information would be particularly important for normative social judgments, including welfare economic assessments.[11] But when it is applied to social welfare functions that use individual utility information only in the form—as in (1)—of n-tuples of individual preferences (corresponding to noncomparable ordinal individual utilities), we get a combination that attempts to make do with very little information indeed. It must, however, be noted that Arrow does not invoke neutrality or welfarism in any form as a prior requirement. In a limited form that restriction emerges as an implication of other conditions, and a substantial part of the unexpected nature of Arrow's impossibility result (or the "General Possibility Theorem" as Arrow called it) relates, in fact, to this analytical demonstration.[12]

4. AXIOMATIC EXCLUSIONS AND ARROW'S IMPOSSIBILITY THEOREM

4.1. Arrow's Theorem

It is useful, in this perspective, to go through a simple proof of Arrow's impossibility theorem not merely because the result is so central to social choice theory, but also because of the light it throws on the way apparently mild axioms can, acting in combination, end up as very severe informational constraints. Arrow considered a set of very plausible-looking conditions relating social choice to the n-tuple of individual preferences, and showed that it is impossible to satisfy those conditions simultaneously.

The axioms used by Arrow (in the later, and neater, version in Arrow 1963) include *unrestricted domain, weak Pareto principle, nondictatorship,* and *the independence of irrelevant alternatives* (in addition to the structural conditions requiring that the set of individuals is finite and that the set of social states includes at least three distinct states). We define xR_iy as the statement that person i weakly prefers x to y (that is, either strictly prefers

11 This general issue is discussed more fully in Sen (1970a, 1977a, 1999).

12 Since it is often said that Arrow's impossibility theorem is a generalization of the old "paradox of voting," it is worth noting that this is only partly true. It is important, in particular, to recognize that while voting rules must satisfy neutrality, neither the form of Arrow's social welfare function, nor any of the individual axioms imposed by Arrow on that function, make any demand of neutrality. We are moved in the direction of neutrality by the *combination* of the axioms, and indeed the main work in proving Arrow's impossibility theorem consists, it can be argued, in deriving a property of neutrality from the combination of different axioms, through the use of axiomatic reasoning. In what follows, see Lemma L.1.

x to y, or is indifferent between them), and xP_iy as person i strictly prefers x to y. The weak and strict social preferences are denoted R and P, respectively.

Unrestricted domain (U) demands that the domain of the social welfare function, that is f in (1), includes all possible n-tuples of individual preferences $\{R_i\}$. The *weak Pareto principle* (P) says that if all persons prefer any x to any y, then x is socially preferred to y. *Nondictatorship* (D) excludes the possibility that any individual j could be so powerful that whenever, over the domain of f, he or she prefers any x to any y, society too strictly prefers x to y. And *independence of irrelevant alternatives* (I) can be seen as demanding that the social ranking of any pair $\{x, y\}$ must depend only on individual preferences over $\{x, y\}$. The Arrow impossibility theorem states that there does not exist any social welfare function f that can simultaneously fulfill U, P, D, and I.

We can define a set G of individuals as being "decisive" over the ordered pair $\{x, y\}$, denoted $D_G(x, y)$, if and only if whenever everyone in G prefers x to y, we must have xPy no matter what others prefer. Further, if G is decisive over every ordered pair, then G is simply called "decisive," denoted D_G. It is readily seen that nondictatorship is the requirement that no individual is decisive, whereas the weak Pareto principle is the requirement that the set of all individuals is decisive. The proof used here goes via two lemmas, which establish the implied informational exclusions, to obtain dictatorship from the weak Pareto principle.[13]

4.2. Proof of Arrow's Theorem

Lemma L.1 *If* $D_G(x, y)$ *for any ordered pair* $\{x, y\}$*, then* D_G.

To establish this, we have to show that $D_G(x, y) \rightarrow D_G(a, b)$, for all a and b. The demonstration proceeds by repetitions of essentially the same strategy in different possible cases depending on whether or not x or y is identical with either b or a. Consider the case in which the four states x, y, a, b are all distinct. Assume the following pattern of individual preferences: for all persons j in G: aP_jx, xP_jy, and yP_jb, and for all persons i not in G: aP_ix and yP_ib (with nothing being presumed about the ranking of the other pairs). By $D_G(x, y)$, we have xPy, and by the weak Pareto principle, we obtain aPx and yPb. Hence, through the transitivity of strict preference, we get: aPb. By the independence of irrelevant alternatives, aPb must depend on individual preferences only over $\{a, b\}$, and since only the preferences of people in G have been specified, clearly $D_G(a, b)$.

Lemma L.2 *For any G, if* D_G*, and if G has more than one person in it and can be, thus, partitioned into two nonempty parts* G_1 *and* G_2*, then either* D_{G1} *or* D_{G2}.

[13] The brief proof used here corresponds to the one outlined in Sen (1995, fns. 9 and 10, p. 4). Note that this proof drops the need to introduce the intermediate concept of "almost decisiveness" (used in Arrow 1951, 1963, and Sen 1970a), since it is redundant.

Assume that for all i in G_1: xP_iy, and xP_iz, with any possible ranking of y, z, and that for all j in G_2: xP_jy, and zP_jy, with any possible ranking of x, z. Nothing is required from the preferences of those not in G. Clearly, xPy by the decisiveness of G. If, now, xPz, then group G_1 would be decisive over this pair, since they alone definitely prefer x and z (the others can rank this pair in any way). If G_1 is not to be decisive (and thus by Lemma L.1 not to be decisive over any pair), we must have zRx for *some* set of individual preferences over x, z of nonmembers of G_1. Take that case. So we have zRx, and also xPy. We thus have, by transitivity of preferences, zPy. Since only G_2 members definitely prefer z to y, this entails that G_2 is decisive over this pair $\{z, y\}$. But, then, by L.1, G_2 is generally decisive. So either G_1 or G_2 must be decisive.

Completing the proof of Arrow's theorem can now proceed very rapidly. By the weak Pareto principle, the group of all individuals is decisive. It is, by assumption, finite. By successive twofold partitionings, and each time picking the decisive part (which exists, guaranteed by L.2), we arrive at a decisive individual, who must, thus, be a dictator.

4.3. Interpretation of the Proof

The proof just presented works through a sequential compounding of informational exclusions, beginning in a small way and ending with such a massive prohibition that the weak Pareto principle cannot be effectively distinguished from the existence of a dictator. In socially ranking x and y, the condition of independence of irrelevant alternatives excludes the use of information—both preferences related and any other—except what relates directly to the "relevant" alternatives, that is, x and y only. Starting with that small beginning and afforced by the unrestricted domain and the weak Pareto principle, we get to the result in Lemma L.1 that any group that is socially decisive over any pair of social states must be socially decisive over every pair of social states—no matter what these states are. So the specific information about the respective states, which we may have plentifully, will not be allowed to make any difference as far as decisiveness (based on individual preferences) is concerned.

Armed with this informational exclusion established in Lemma L.1, the proof proceeds in Lemma L.2 to economize also on preference information itself. If the information about the unanimous preference of a set G of individuals is adequate to rank social states (no matter what others want), then the information about the unanimous preference of some proper subset G^* of individuals, excluding some others in G, will be adequate as well. This opens the door, through sequential use, to go from the decisiveness of unanimous strict preference of all (thanks to the weak Pareto principle) to the decisiveness of strict preference of some one individual (that is, a dictator). The informational inclusiveness of a foundational democratic commitment is, thus, caught in a fierce internal contradiction: to empower *all* without discrimination (as incorporated in the weak Pareto principle) is to empower *one* irrespective of what others want (that is, a dictatorship).

5. ENRICHING INFORMATION FOR THE POSSIBILITY OF SOCIAL CHOICE

As was mentioned earlier, the *entailed* exclusion of nonutility information through Arrow's axioms adds to the *antecedent* exclusions directly incorporated in the formulation of a social welfare function through the nonadmissibility of interpersonal comparability and cardinality. Informational enrichment can be sought *either* through the route of enriching utility information, *or* through that of admitting nonutility information.

The former route has been particularly explored in social choice theory since the 1970s.[14] The formal structure is that of a "social welfare functional," which functionally relates social ranking R to n-tuples of individual utility functions $\{U_i\}$. The extent of measurability and cardinality of utilities is specified by "invariance conditions" imposed on social welfare functionals.[15] It can be shown that all the Arrow axioms, if translated into a broadened framework of "social welfare functionals" that allows richer utility information, can be simultaneously satisfied, even with just ordinal comparability of individual utilities, even without any cardinality. Furthermore, many other constructive possibilities are opened up once cardinal comparability is also allowed.[16] These extensions are hugely important for welfare economics and for normative social judgments in general.

This route (that is, enriching utility information while still keeping out nonutility information) does not immediately raise issues of inconsistency. But while the Arrow impossibility may be circumvented this way, this path does not still accommodate the use of nonutility information needed for specification of rights or liberties or nonwelfarist assessment of inequality or fairness. This is unfortunate since these norms have considerable appeal, and many "non-neutral" concerns have figured in the informal literature on social decisions and choices for a very long time. Even as formal social choice theory was getting founded through the pioneering works of Borda (1781), Condorcet (1785), and other mathematical analysts of voting and electoral processes, and also through the parallel line of investigation pursued by utilitarians such as Bentham (1789), other innovative departures were being made in the understanding of justice in a way that could not be fully translated into axioms defined in the neutral space of preferences. For example, the

[14] Vickrey (1945) and Harsanyi (1955) had earlier identified representation results that make use of information based on expected utility, interpreted as interpersonally comparable cardinal utilities, to obtain the value of social welfare in a summational form.

[15] The operation and use of invariance conditions is investigated in Sen (1970a,b), d'Aspremont and Gevers (1977), Gevers (1979), Maskin (1979), and Roberts (1980a), among other contributions.

[16] See, among other contributions, Sen (1970a, 1977b), Hammond (1976, 1985), d'Aspremont and Gevers (1977, 2002), Arrow (1977), Maskin (1978, 1979), Gevers (1979), Roberts (1980a,b), Suzumura (1983, 1996), Blackorby, Donaldson, and Weymark (1984), d'Aspremont (1985), Blackorby, Bossert, and Donaldson (2002), and d'Aspremont and Mongin (2008).

relevance and reach of the idea of rights were extensively explored by such pioneering authors as Mary Wollstonecraft (1790, 1792) and Thomas Paine (1791).[17] These concentrations were well reflected in the practical politics related to the French Revolution as well as American Independence, both of which made extensive use of the idea of fundamental rights.

Some of these rights involve conditions that relate to individual preferences of the people involved (for example, what one prefers in one's "personal domain" of liberty), but even here nonutility characteristics of the states of affairs have to be taken into account to give more effectiveness to each person over his or her own personal domain. These concerns were not explicitly accommodated in formal social choice theory in its classic formulations, but they have figured prominently in more recent developments in the social choice literature.[18]

6. ON COMBINING UTILITY AND NONUTILITY INFORMATION

There are, however, important problems in combining utility and nonutility information, since their disparate roles can yield possible inconsistencies. Indeed, this is one way of interpreting the so-called "liberal paradox," which involves a consistency problem in simultaneously accommodating, along with unrestricted domain, a minimal condition of liberty (involving the use of some nonutility information regarding personal features in social states) and the weak Pareto principle (involving very modest use of utility information).[19] Indeed, the "impossibility of the Paretian liberal" brings out this tension in a very simple case, and the conflicts can be much more complex when it is attempted to use richer utility information *along with* substantive use of nonutility descriptions of states of affairs.

These "hybrid" frameworks have not been extensively investigated yet, and there has in fact been some reluctance to leave the simplicity of welfarism even when trying to accommodate principles or procedures of social choice that are quintessentially nonwelfarist. Consider, for example, John Rawl's (1971) well-known theory of justice, which involves "the priority of liberty" as the first principle (a substantively nonwelfarist requirement), and also the Difference Principle, which uses lexicographic maximin in the space of primary goods, not utilities. While Rawls has been much invoked in social choice theory, nevertheless the axiomatizations of Rawls in welfare economics (and in social choice theory related to welfare economics) have tended to ignore his first principle

[17] The far-reaching relevance of these perspectives is discussed in Sen (2009).

[18] See Arrow, Sen, and Suzumura (1996/1997) and other chapters of this *Handbook of Social Choice Theory*, Vol. II, especially Part VII, including the chapters by William Thomson, Marc Fleurbaey and Francois Maniquet, and Kotaro Suzumura.

[19] The literature on the liberal paradox is by now quite vast. The special number of *Analyse & Kritik*, September 1996, includes a fine collection of papers on this subject, as well as extensive bibliographies of publications in this field.

altogether (except indirectly in the context of the so-called "liberal paradox") and have also redefined the Difference Principle in terms of utilities, in contrast with Rawls's own focus on primary goods.[20]

These recharacterizations of nonwelfarist principles (like Rawls's) in "welfarist" terms, while strictly speaking inaccurate, do have significant usefulness, for several distinct reasons. First, welfarism does appeal to the intuition of many social analysts.[21] In fact, many seem to find the welfarist version of Rawls's lexicographic maximin more acceptable than Rawls's own insistence on operating in the space of primary goods.[22]

Second, the utility-based formulation is open to alternative interpretations and can be relatively easily integrated with decision-theoretic normative reasoning. Indeed, as d'Aspremont and Gevers (2002) point out in their masterly critical survey of the literature on "social welfare functionals" in Volume I of this *Handbook*, this literature "can be reinterpreted as an application of multi-objective decision theory to the ethical observer's problem" (p. 464).

Third, the restricting of the entire informational basis of all the normative principles to one basic class of evaluative data (such as individual utilities or individual overall evaluations) can be a simple way of keeping the possibility of inconsistency (under discussion here) at bay, and this can be seen to be a considerable merit in itself. Indeed, even within such restrictions, a variety of different concerns can be accommodated, without internal tension. As d'Aspremont and Gevers (2002) point out, even the alternative approach of capabilities (on which see Chapter 16 by Kaushik Basu and Luis Felipe Lopez-Calva in this volume) can do this with its exploration of the possibility of accommodating "doings and beings" *within* the approach of "social welfare functionals." The problems that may have to be faced would arise not from the *objects* that influence individual utility or individual welfare or individual evaluation, but from any proposed use of other information to determine the relevance of—and the weights to be placed on—utility or welfare, or on evaluative conclusions of individuals.

Possible tensions arise when *other* data from the states of affairs are invoked in making social judgments or social choices: for example, in giving priority to a person's evaluation over her own "personal domain" (as in Rawlsian "priority of liberty" or in various conditions of "minimal liberty" used in social choice theory), or in attaching

20 See Phelps (1973, 1977), Hammond (1976), Maskin (1978, 1979), Meade (1976), Strasnick (1976), Arrow (1977), d'Aspremont and Gevers (1977), Sen (1977b), Gevers (1979), Roberts (1980a, 1980b), Atkinson (1983), Suzumura (1983, 1996), Blackorby, Donaldson, and Weymark (1984), d'Aspremont (1985). However, social choice theoretic reasoning has been used to question or defend the possibility of having a consistent index of bundles of diverse primary goods, on which see Plott (1978), Gibbard (1979), Blair (1988), and Sen (1991).

21 On this see Hammond (1976, 1982), d'Aspremont and Gevers (1977, 2002), Gevers (1979), Suzumura (1983, 1996), Broome (1991, 2004), Pattanaik and Suzumura (1994), d'Aspremont and Mongin (2008), Blackorby, Bossert, and Donaldson (2002), among other contributions.

22 I should explain that this is definitely not the judgment of this author, but he is able to distinguish between his own assessment and that of many analysts whose judgments he respects.

special importance to the centrality of certain capabilities (as in the philosophical or developmental approaches that give a special role to the fulfilment of certain basic capabilities).[23] The critical issue, as was discussed earlier, is so-called "neutrality"—a condition that can be directly imposed or indirectly precipitated through the use of other axioms, which restricts the class of permissible social welfare functions and social welfare functionals to reliance on utility information.[24] This requirement runs counter to the invocation of various foundational norms, reflected in, say, the Rawlsian principles of justice, or the Aristotelian focus on capabilities, or the Wollstonecraft–Paine concentration on the "vindication of rights."

The possibility of combining these different classes of foundational information reflected in different types of principles of social justice and equity—involving both utility and nonutility information—has not yet been investigated adequately. While celebrating what has already been achieved, it is important to identify this as an area in which more investigation will be needed in the future.[25] That would be of particular importance in making further use of social choice theory in analyzing and exploring theories of justice.

REFERENCES

Arrow, K. J. (1950). A difficulty in the concept of social welfare. *Journal of Political Economy, 58.*

Arrow, K. J. (1951). *Social choice and individual values.* New York: Wiley.

Arrow, K. J. (1963). *Social choice and individual values,* (enlarged 2nd ed.). New York: Wiley.

Arrow, K. J. (1977). Extended sympathy and the possibility of social choice. *American Economic Review, 67.*

Arrow, K. J., & Intriligator, M. (Eds.). (1986). *Handbook of mathematical economics.* Amsterdam: North-Holland.

Arrow, K. J., Sen, A. K., & Suzumura, K. (1996/1997). *Social choice re-examined.* London: McMillan, and New York: St. Martin's Press.

Atkinson, A. B. (1983). *Social justice and public policy.* Brighton: Wheatsheaf, and Cambridge, MA: MIT Press.

Barker, E. (1958). *The politics of Aristotle.* London: Oxford University Press.

Bentham, J. (1789). *An introduction to the principles of morals and legislation.* London: Payne; republished, Oxford: Clarendon Press, 1907.

Binmore, K. (1975). An example in group preference. *Journal of Economic Theory, 10.*

Binmore, K. (1994). *Playing fair: Game theory and the social contract* (Vol. I). Cambridge, MA: MIT Press.

Blackorby, C., Donaldson, D., & Weymark, J. (1984). Social choice with interpersonal utility comparisons: a diagrammatic introduction. *International Economic Review, 25.*

[23] See Sen (1982), Atkinson (1983), Suzumura (1983), Nussbaum and Sen (1993), Dutta (2002), among other contributions.

[24] In the format of social welfare functionals, strong neutrality follows from unrestricted domain, Pareto indifference, and independence in a binary form, as was established by d'Aspremont and Gevers (1977); see Theorem 3.7 in d'Aspremont and Gevers (2002, pp. 493–494). The conditions that yield something quite close to neutrality for social welfare functions, as shown in Lemma L.1 above, draw on similar informational demands imposed on that framework.

[25] This has been discussed in the exploration of social choice-based ideas of justice in Sen (2009).

Blackorby, C., Bossert, W., & Donaldson, D. (2002). Utilitarianism and the theory of justice. In K. J. Arrow, A. K. Sen & K. Suzumura (Eds.), *Handbook of social choice and welfare* (Vol. I). Amsterdam: North-Holland.

Blair, D. H. (1988). The primary-goods indexation problem in Rawls's theory of justice. *Theory and Decision, 24.*

Blair, D. H., & Pollak, R. A. (1979). Collective rationality and dictatorship: the scope of the Arrow theorem. *Journal of Economic Theory, 21.*

Blair, D. H., & Pollak, R. A. (1982). Acyclic collective choice rules. *Econometrica, 50.*

Blau, J. H., & Deb, R. (1977). Social decision functions and veto. *Econometrica, 45.*

Borda, J. C. (1781). Memoire sur les elections au Scrutin, *Histoire de l'Academie Royale des Sciences* (Paris); translated by Alfred de Grazia, Mathematical Derivation of an Election System, *Isis, 44.*

Broome, J. (1991). *Weighing goods: Equality, uncertainty and time.* Oxford: Blackwell Press.

Broome, J. (2004). *Weighing lives.* Oxford: Oxford University Press.

Brown, D. J. (1974). An approximate solution to Arrow's problem. *Journal of Economic Theory, 9.*

Brown, D. J. (1975). Acyclic aggregation over a finite set of alternatives, Cowles Foundation Discussion Paper No. 391, Yale University.

Campbell, D. E. (1976). Democratic preference functions. *Journal of Economic Theory, 12.*

Campbell, D. E., & Kelly, J. S. (1997). The possibility-impossibility boundary in social choice. In K. J. Arrow, A. K. Sen & K. Suzumura (Eds.), *Social choice re-examined* (Vol. I). New York: St. Martin's Press.

Chichilnisky, G. (1982). Topological equivalence of the Pareto condition and the existence of a dictator. *Journal of Mathematical Economics, 9.*

Chichilnisky, G., & Heal, G. (1983). Necessary and sufficient conditions for resolution of the social choice paradox. *Journal of Economic Theory, 31.*

de Condorcet, M. (1785). *Essai sur l'application de l'analyse à la probabilité des décisions rendues à la pluralite des voix.* Paris: L'Imprimerie Royale.

d'Aspremont, C. (1985). Axioms for social welfare ordering. In L. Hurwicz, D. Schmeidler & H. Sonnenschein (Eds.), *Social goods and social organization.* Cambridge: Cambridge University Press.

d'Aspremont, C., & Gevers, L. (1977). Equity and the informational basis of collective choice. *Review of Economic Studies, 44.*

d'Aspremont, C., & Gevers, L. (2002). Social welfare functionals and interpersonal comparability. In K. J. Arrow, A. K. Sen & K. Suzumura (Eds.), *Handbook of social choice and welfare* (Vol. 1). Amsterdam: North-Holland.

d'Aspremont, C., & Mongin, P. (2008). A welfarist version of Harsanyi's aggregation theorem. In M. Fleurbaey, M. Salles & J. A. Weymark (Eds.), *Justice, political liberalism and utilitarianism: Themes from Harsanyi and Rawls.* Cambridge: Cambridge University Press.

Deb, R. (1976). On constructing generalized voting paradoxes. *Review of Economic Studies, 43.*

Deb, R. (1977). On Schwartz's rule. *Journal of Economic Theory, 16.*

Dutta, B. (2002). Inequality, poverty and welfare. In K. J. Arrow, A. K. Sen & K. Suzumura (Eds.), *The handbook of social choice and welfare* (Vol. I). Amsterdam: North-Holland.

Fine, B. J., & Fine, K. (1974). Social choice and individual ranking. *Review of Economic Studies, 41.*

Fishburn, P. C. (1973). *The theory of social choice.* Princeton, NJ: Princeton University Press.

Fishburn, P. C. (1974). On collective rationality and a generalized impossibility theorem. *Review of Economic Studies, 41.*

Gardenfors, P. (1973). Positional voting functions. *Theory and Decision, 4.*

Gevers, L. (1979). On interpersonal comparability and social welfare orderings. *Econometrica, 47.*

Gibbard, A. F. (1969). Unpublished term paper at the Philosophy Department of Harvard University, discussed in Sen (1970a).

Gibbard, A. F. (1973). Manipulation of voting schemes: a general result. *Econometrica, 41.*

Gibbard, A. F. (1979). Disparate goods and Rawls' difference principle: a social choice theoretic treatment. *Theory and Decision, 11.*

Grether, D. M., & Plott, C. R. (1982). Nonbinary social choice: an impossibility theorem. *Review of Economic Studies, 49.*

Hammond, P. J. (1976). Equity, Arrow's conditions and Rawls' difference principle. *Econometrica, 44.*

Hammond, P. J. (1982). Liberalism, independent rights, and the Pareto principle. In L. J. Cohen, J. Los, H. Pfeiffer & K.-P. Podewski (Eds.), *Logic, methodology, and the philosophy of science* (Vol. 6). Amsterdam: North-Holland.

Hammond, P. J. (1985). Welfare economics. In G. Feiwel (Ed.), *Issues in contemporary microeconomics and welfare.* Albany: SUNY Press.

Harsanyi, J. C. (1955). Cardinal welfare, individualistic ethics and interpersonal comparisons of utility. *Journal of Political Economy, 63.*

Kelly, J. S. (1978). *Arrow impossibility theorems.* New York: Academic Press.

Kelsey, D. (1985). Acyclic choice without the Pareto principle. *Review of Economic Studies, 51.*

Mas-Colell, A., & Sonnenschein, H. (1972). General possibility theorems for group decisions. *Review of Economic Studies, 39.*

Maskin, E. (1978). A theorem on utilitarianism. *Review of Economic Studies, 45.*

Maskin, E. (1979). Decision-making under ignorance with implications for social choice. *Theory and Decision*, 11.

Meade, J. (1976). *The just economy.* London: Macmillan, and Albany, NY: State University of New York Press.

Moulin, H. (1983). *The strategy of social choice.* Amsterdam: North-Holland.

Nussbaum, M., & Sen, A. (Eds.), (1993). *The quality of life.* Oxford: Oxford University Press.

Paine, T. (1791). *The rights of man: Being an answer to Mr. Burke's attack on the French Revolution*, 1791; republished *The rights of man.* London: Dent, and New York: Dutton, 1906.

Pattanaik, P. K. (2002). Positional rules of collective decision-making. In K. J. Arrow, A. K. Sen & K. Suzumura (Eds.), *The handbook of social choice and welfare.* Amsterdam: North-Holland.

Pattanaik, P. K., & Salles, M. (Eds.). (1983). *Social choice and welfare.* Amsterdam: North-Holland.

Pattanaik, P. K., & Suzumura, K. (1994). Rights, welfarism, and social choice. *American Economic Review, 84.*

Peleg, B. (1984). *Game theoretic analysis of voting in committees.* Cambridge: Cambridge University Press.

Phelps, E. S. (Ed.). (1973). *Economic justice.* Harmondsworth: Penguin.

Phelps, E. S. (1977). Recent developments in welfare economics: Justice et équité. In M. D. Intriligator (Eds.), *Frontiers of quantitative economics* (Vol. 3). Amsterdam: North-Holland.

Plott, C. (1978). Rawls' theory of justice: An impossibility result. In H. W. Gottinger & W. Leinfellner (Ed.), *Decision theory and social ethics: Issues in social choice.* Dordrecht: Reidel.

Rawls, J. (1971). *A theory of justice.* Cambridge, MA: Harvard University Press.

Roberts, K. W. S. (1980a). Interpersonal comparability and social choice theory. *Review of Economic Studies, 47.*

Roberts, K. W. S. (1980b). Price independent welfare prescriptions. *Journal of Public Economics, 13.*

Rothschild, E. (2001). *Economic sentiments: Adam Smith, Condorcet and the Enlightenment.* Cambridge, MA: Harvard University Press.

Sen, A. K. (1969). Quasi-transitivity, rational choice and collective decisions. *Review of Economic Studies, 36.*

Sen, A. K. (1970a). *Collective choice and social welfare.* San Francisco: Holden Day, republished Amsterdam: North-Holland, 1979.

Sen, A. K. (1970b). The impossibility of a Paretian liberal. *Journal of Political Economy, 78.*

Sen, A. K. (1977a). Social choice theory: A re-examination. *Econometrica, 45,* reprinted in Sen (1982).

Sen, A. K. (1977b). On weights and measures: informational constraints in social welfare analysis. *Econometrica, 45*, reprinted in Sen (1982).
Sen, A. K. (1979). Informational analysis of moral principles. In R. Harrison (Ed.), *Rational action*. Cambridge: Cambridge University Press.
Sen, A. K. (1982). *Choice, welfare and measurement*. Oxford: Basil Blackwell, and Cambridge, MA: MIT Press.
Sen, A. K. (1986). Social choice theory. In K. J. Arrow & M. Intriligator (Eds.), *Handbook of mathematical economics*. Amsterdam: North-Holland.
Sen, A. K. (1991). *On indexing primary goods and capabilities*. mimeographed, Harvard University, July 1991.
Sen, A. K. (1993). Internal consistency of choice. *Econometrica, 61*.
Sen, A. K. (1995). Rationality and social choice. *American Economic Review, 85*.
Sen, A. K. (1999). The possibility of social choice. *American Economic Review, 109*.
Sen, A. K. (2009). *The idea of justice*. Cambridge, MA: The Belknap Press of Harvard University Press.
Sen, A., & Williams, B. (Eds.). (1982). *Utilitarianism and beyond*. Cambridge: Cambridge University Press.
Shama, S. R. (1967). *Kautilya's Arthashastra* (8th ed.). Mysore: Mysore Printing and Publishing House.
Smith, A. (1759). *The theory of moral sentiments*. (revised edition, 1790; republished, New York: Penguin, 2009).
Strasnick, S. (1976). Social choice and the derivation of Rawls's difference Principle. *Journal of Philosophy, 73*.
Suzumura, K. (1976a). Rational choice and revealed preference. *Review of Economic Studies, 43*.
Suzumura, K. (1976b). Remarks on the theory of collective choice. *Economica, 43*.
Suzumura, K. (1982), Equity, efficiency and rights in social choice. *Mathematical Social Sciences, 3*.
Suzumura, K. (1983). *Rational choice, collective decisions and social welfare*. Cambridge: Cambridge University Press.
Suzumura, K. (1996). Welfare, rights, and social choice procedure: a perspective. *Analyse & Kritik, 18*.
Vickrey, W. (1945). Measuring marginal utility by reactions to risk. *Econometrica, 13*.
Wollstonecraft, M. (1790, 1792). *A vindication of the rights of men, in a letter to the right Honourable Edmund Burke; occasions by his reflections on the revolution in France*, 1790, and, *A vindication of the rights of woman: With strictures on political and moral subjects*, 1792; both included in Mary Wollstonecraft, *A vindication of the rights of man and a vindication of the rights of women*, S. Tomaselli (Ed.), Cambridge: Cambridge University Press, 1995.
Young, H. P. (1988). Condorcet's theory of voting. *American Political Science Review, 82*.

CHAPTER FIFTEEN

Competitive Market Mechanisms as Social Choice Procedures

Peter J. Hammond
Department of Economics, University of Warwick, Coventry, U.K.

Contents

Handbook of Social Choice and Welfare, Volume II
ISSN: 0169-7218, DOI: 10.1016/S0169-7218(10)00015-8

Abstract

A competitive market mechanism is a prominent example of a nonbinary social choice rule, typically defined for a special class of economic environments in which each social state is an economic allocation of private goods, and individuals' preferences concern only their own personal consumption. This chapter begins by discussing which Pareto efficient allocations can be characterized as competitive equilibria with lump-sum transfers. It also discusses existence and characterization of such equilibria without lump-sum transfers. The second half of the chapter focuses on continuum economies, for which such characterization results are much more natural, given that agents have negligible influence over equilibrium prices.

Keywords: welfare theorems, general equilibrium, core equivalence, incentive compatibility.

JEL codes: D50, D61, D71, C71.

1. INTRODUCTION AND OUTLINE

1.1. Markets and Social Choice

Social choice theory concerns itself with the proper choice of a social state from a given feasible set of social states. The main question the theory addresses is how that social choice should depend on the profile of individual preferences. Early work by Arrow and various predecessors, including Condorcet, Borda, Dodgson, and Black, was about the construction of a social preference ordering—that is, a binary relation of weak preference that is complete and transitive. Later, Sen (1971, 1982, 1986) in particular initiated an investigation of more general social choice rules (SCRs) that may not maximize any binary relation, even one that may not be complete or transitive.

A "competitive" or *Walrasian* market mechanism, as defined in Section 3, is a prominent example of such a nonbinary social choice rule, although it has rarely been regarded as such either by social choice theorists or by economists studying general equilibrium.[1] Generally, this rule will be called the *Walrasian* SCR. It is typically defined for a special class of economic environments in which each social state is an economic allocation of private goods, and individuals' preferences concern only their own personal consumption. Moreover, the economic environments in the domain are also typically required to satisfy continuity and convexity assumptions guaranteeing the existence of a Walrasian equilibrium in the market economy.

Another major concern of social choice theory has been with various characterizations of a particular social choice rule. Accordingly, this chapter explores what sets of axioms are uniquely satisfied by the Walrasian mechanism, with or without various forms of lump-sum redistribution.

1.2. Finite Economies

The most obvious social choice property satisfied by a Walrasian mechanism is Pareto efficiency. Indeed, as discussed in Section 4.3, for economies with just one "representative" agent, or alternatively with several identical agents who all receive the same consumption vector, Pareto efficiency offers a complete characterization of the Walrasian mechanism under standard continuity, convexity, and aggregate interiority assumptions. Beyond this special case, however, standard textbook examples with two consumers and two goods demonstrate that Pareto efficiency alone is insufficient to characterize the Walrasian mechanism. Nevertheless, once one allows lump-sum redistribution,

[1] Sakai (2009) considers a "Walrasian social ordering" over allocations in economies with fixed individual endowments, constructed so that all optimal allocations are Walrasian, and all non-Walrasian allocations where each individual gains weakly from trade are indifferent. Such an ordering is of limited usefulness because it cannot meaningfully compare allocations of different endowments.

then most Pareto efficient allocations can be characterized as Walrasian equilibria. The main exceptions are extreme or "oligarchic" allocations in which some agents are so well off that they cannot benefit even from free gifts of goods that would otherwise be consumed by agents outside the oligarchy. Also, even such oligarchic allocations are compensated Walrasian equilibria with lump-sum transfers. These and some related results are presented in Section 4.

Characterizations of Walrasian equilibria without lump-sum transfers remain much more elusive, however, especially for economic environments with a fixed finite number of agents. First Section 5 presents conditions sufficient to ensure the existence of Walrasian equilibrium. Then Section 6 considers characterizations that apply to one economic environment with a fixed set of agents having a fixed type profile. Next, Section 7 considers characterizations with a fixed set of agents but a variable type profile. To conclude the results for "finite economies" with a finite set of individual agents, Section 8 allows the number of agents to vary as well as their type profile. Included are asymptotic characterizations such as the Debreu–Scarf Theorem, which hold when the number of agents tends to infinity.

1.3. Continuum Economies

In finite economies, each individual agent nearly always has influence over market prices. This calls into question the standard Walrasian hypothesis that agents take equilibrium prices as given. For this reason, attempts to provide social choice characterizations of Walrasian equilibria without lump-sum transfers become somewhat less problematic when this influence disappears because the economy has a continuum of agents.

Before considering how to characterize the Walrasian mechanism in a continuum economy, however, Section 9 suggests reasons for generalizing Aumann's (1964) standard concept to "statistical" continuum economies described by a joint distribution over "potential" agents' labels and their types. Efficiency and existence theorems for such economies are presented in Sections 10 and 11; these results are largely adaptations of the counterparts for finite economies in Sections 4 and 5. In continuum economies, however, most of the theorems hold even when agents have nonconvex preferences. To allow indivisible goods and other nonconvexities in agents' feasible sets, there are also extensions to the case when these sets are "piecewise convex" rather than convex. These extensions typically require an additional "dispersion" assumption.

Following these preliminary results, the next four sections offer several different characacterizations of Walrasian equilibrium allocations that are specific to continuum economies. First, Section 12 presents equivalence theorems for the core and some related solution concepts in a continuum economy. Next, given a continuum of agents whose possible types lie in a suitable smooth domain, Section 13 characterizes "full" Walrasian equilibrium allocations as those that satisfy "full" forms of both Pareto efficiency and absence of envy.[2] Next, Section 14 characterizes Walrasian mechanisms with strategyproofness replacing the absence of envy condition used in Section 13. Then Section 15 shows how, when anonymity is assumed, a "multilateral" version of strategyproofness on its own characterizes a Walrasian mechanism, without the need to assume any form of Pareto efficiency, or a smooth type domain.

Results based on the characterizations by Aumann and Shapley (1974) and by Aumann (1975) of Walrasian equilibria as value allocations will not be discussed here. Hart (2002) in particular offers an authoritative survey.

1.4. Public Goods and Externalities

The last section, Section 16, briefly discusses some possible extensions to accommodate public goods and externalities.

2. AGENT TYPES

This section contains essential preliminaries, including various assumptions concerning economic agents and their types. Thereafter, Section 3 provides key definitions for economics with a finite set of agents. Corresponding definitions for continuum economies are provided in Sections 9 and 11.

2.1. Commodity Space

For simplicity, and to help focus on the main issues in the existing literature, this chapter assumes throughout that there is a fixed finite set G of *goods* or *commodities*. The associated commodity space is the finite-dimensional Euclidean space $\mathbb{R}^G$.[3] The typical member of $\mathbb{R}^G$ is the vector $x = (x_g)_{g \in G}$. Let $\#G$ denote the number of goods $g \in G$, which is also the dimension of the commodity space $\mathbb{R}^G$.

2.2. Notation

The *Euclidean norm* of each $x \in \mathbb{R}^G$ will be denoted by $\|x\| := \sqrt{\sum_{g \in G} x_g^2}$.

[2] Here "full" means, somewhat loosely, that *all* agents are included, rather than merely almost all. Precise definitions appear in Section 13.

[3] This assumption excludes the overlapping generations models pioneered by Allais (1947) and Samuelson (1958), with both an infinite time horizon and an infinite set of agents. In particular, this is the main interesting class of economies in which, even though markets are ostensibly complete, nevertheless a Walrasian equilibrium allocation may well be Pareto inefficient. For further discussion, see the survey by Geanakoplos and Polemarchakis (1991) in particular.

Define the three inequalities $\geqq$, $>$, and $\gg$ on $\mathbb{R}^G$ so that, for each $a = (a_g)_{g \in G}$ and $b = (b_g)_{g \in G}$ in $\mathbb{R}^G$, one has:

(1) $a \geqq b$ iff $a_g \geq b_g$ for all $g \in G$;
(2) $a > b$ iff $a \geqq b$ and $a \neq b$;
(3) $a \gg b$ iff $a_g > b_g$ for all $g \in G$.

Given any set $S \subseteq \mathbb{R}^G$, let cl S denotes its closure, and **int** S its interior. Also, let:

(1) $pS := \{px \mid x \in S\}$ for any $p \in \mathbb{R}^G$;
(2) $\lambda S := \{\lambda x \mid x \in S\}$ for any $\lambda \in \mathbb{R}$.

Finally, given any two sets $A, B \subseteq \mathbb{R}^G$, define the *vector sum*

$$A + B := \{c \in \mathbb{R}^G \mid \exists a \in A, b \in B : c = a + b\}$$

and the *vector difference* $A - B := A + (-1)B$.

2.3. Consumption and Production Sets

As usual in classical "Arrow–Debreu" general equilibrium theory, assume any individual agent has a *consumption set* $X \subseteq \mathbb{R}^G$. Following Rader (1964, 1972, 1976, 1978), however, assume each agent is also endowed with a private *production set* $Y \subseteq \mathbb{R}^G$. One can also interpret Y as the agent's "opportunity set." The special case usually treated in general equilibrium theory is of a *pure exchange economy* in which an agent's set Y takes the form $\{e\}$ for a fixed initial *endowment vector* e. Often it is assumed that e is an interior point of X. Another common assumption is that X is the non-negative orthant $\mathbb{R}^G_+$.

Occasionally it will be assumed that either X or Y satisfies *free disposal*. In the case of the consumption set X, this means that, whenever $x \in X$ and $\tilde{x} \geqq x$, then $\tilde{x} \in X$. In the case of the production set Y, this means that, whenever $y \in Y$ and $\tilde{y} \leqq y$, then $\tilde{y} \in Y$.

Given the (net) consumption vector x and net production vector y, the agent must make up the difference between x and y by arranging to obtain the *net trade vector* $t := x - y$ from market purchases and sales, or from some more general kind of interaction with other agents.

Given the two sets X and Y, the agent has a *feasible set* of net trades given by the vector difference $T := X - Y$ of the consumption and production sets.[4]

2.4. Preferences for Consumption

Assume that each agent $i \in N$ has a (complete and transitive) *preference ordering* R on X. Let P and I denote the associated strict preference and indifference relations, respectively.

[4] One can define a corresponding feasible set T more generally, even when transactions costs further limit net trades—as they do, for example, in Diamantaras and Gilles (2004) or Sun, Yang, and Zhou (2004).

Given any fixed $\bar{x} \in X$, let

$$R(\bar{x}) := \{x \in X \mid x\, R\, \bar{x}\} \quad \text{and} \quad P(\bar{x}) := \{x \in X \mid x\, P\, \bar{x}\}$$

denote the *preference set* and *strict preference set*, respectively.

Preferences are said to be:

(i) (globally) *nonsatiated* if $P(\bar{x})$ is nonempty for every $\bar{x} \in X$;

(ii) *locally nonsatiated* (LNS) if, given any $\bar{x} \in X$ and any topogical neighborhood V of $\bar{x}$ in $\mathbb{R}^G$, there exists $x \in P(\bar{x}) \cap V$ (implying that the preference ordering has no local maximum);

(iii) *convex* if X and Y are both convex sets, and if for all $\bar{x} \in X$, the preference set $R(\bar{x})$ is convex;

(iv) *strictly convex* if they are convex and moreover, for all $x, \bar{x} \in X$ with $x \in R(\bar{x})$ and $x \neq \bar{x}$, every *strictly convex* combination $\tilde{x} := \alpha x + (1-\alpha)\bar{x}$ with $0 < \alpha < 1$ satisfies $\tilde{x}\, P\, \bar{x}$;

(v) *continuous* if X and Y are both closed sets, as are $R(\bar{x})$ and also the "dispreference" set $R^{i-}(\bar{x}) := \{x \in X \mid \bar{x}\, R\, x\}$ for each $\bar{x} \in X$;

(vi) *weakly monotone* if $x \in R(\bar{x})$ whenever $\bar{x} \in X$ and $x \geqq \bar{x}$;

(vii) *monotone* if preferences are weakly monotone and $x \in P(\bar{x})$ whenever $x \gg \bar{x}$;

(viii) *strictly monotone* if $x \in P(\bar{x})$ whenever $\bar{x} \in X$ and $x > \bar{x}$.

The first two of these properties each have important implications.

Lemma 1 *Suppose preferences are LNS. Then $\bar{x} \in \operatorname{cl} P(\bar{x})$ for all $\bar{x} \in X$.*

Proof. Given any $\bar{x} \in X$ and any $n = 1, 2, \ldots$, the LNS property implies that there exists $x_n \in P(\bar{x})$ with $\|x_n - \bar{x}\| < 2^{-n}$. Then the sequence x_n $(n = 1, 2, \ldots)$ converges to $\bar{x}$. So $\bar{x} \in \operatorname{cl} P(\bar{x})$. □

The following implication of convex preferences is used in many later proofs.

Lemma 2 *Suppose an agent's preferences are convex. Then $P(\bar{x})$ is convex for all $\bar{x} \in X$.*

Proof. Suppose that $x, \tilde{x} \in P(\bar{x})$. Because preferences are complete, it loses no generality to suppose that $x, \tilde{x}$ have been chosen so that $x\, R\, \tilde{x}$. Let $\hat{x} := \alpha\, x + (1-\alpha)\, \tilde{x}$ where $0 \leq \alpha \leq 1$. Because preferences are convex, $\hat{x} \in R(\tilde{x})$. But $\tilde{x}\, P\, \bar{x}$ and so, because preferences are transitive, $\hat{x}\, P\, \bar{x}$. □

Later, Section 4.6 uses a somewhat stronger convexity condition that appeared in Arrow and Debreu (1954), as well as Debreu (1959) and McKenzie (1959, 1961). Following Arrow and Hahn (1971, p. 78), say that preferences are *semi-strictly convex* if the feasible set X is convex and, in addition, whenever $x, \bar{x} \in X$ with $x\, P\, \bar{x}$ and $0 < \alpha \leq 1$, then $\alpha\, x + (1-\alpha)\, \bar{x}\, P\, \bar{x}$.

A sufficient condition for preferences to be semi-strictly convex is that there exists a *concave* (not merely quasi-concave) utility function $u : X \to \mathbb{R}$, which *represents* R in the sense that $u(x) \geq u(\bar{x})$ if and only if $x \; R \; \bar{x}$.[5]

It is easy to construct examples of preferences that are convex and nonsatiated, but are locally satiated. However, the same will not be true of semi-strictly convex preferences, as the following simple result shows.

Lemma 3 *Suppose that preferences are nonsatiated and semi-strictly convex. Then preferences are LNS.*

Proof. Suppose $\bar{x} \in X$ and let V denote any neighborhood of $\bar{x}$. Because preferences are nonsatiated, there exists $x \in P(\bar{x})$. Because preferences are semi-strictly convex, the convex combination $\tilde{x} := \alpha x + (1-\alpha)\bar{x}$ (with $0 < \alpha \leq 1$) belongs to $P(\bar{x})$. But $\tilde{x} \in V$ for all sufficiently small $\alpha > 0$. □

Lemma 4 *Suppose that preferences are nonsatiated, continuous, and semi-strictly convex. Then preferences are convex.*

Proof. Suppose that $\hat{x}, \tilde{x} \in R(\bar{x})$ with $\hat{x} \; R \; \tilde{x}$. By Lemma 3, preferences are LNS. So by Lemma 1 there exists a sequence $x_n \in P(\hat{x})$ that converges to $\hat{x}$ as $n \to \infty$. Because preferences are transitive, each $x_n \in P(\tilde{x})$. But preferences are also semi-strictly convex, so for each $\alpha \in (0,1)$ one has $\alpha x_n + (1-\alpha)\tilde{x} \in P(\tilde{x}) \subset R(\bar{x})$ for $n = 1, 2, \ldots$. Because preferences are continuous, so $\alpha x + (1-\alpha)\tilde{x} \in R(\bar{x})$ in the limit as $n \to \infty$, for each $\alpha \in (0,1)$. □

2.5. Regular Smooth Preferences

Some results presented later depend on particular smoothness assumptions that are frequently used in general equilibrium theory. Specifically, say that the agent has *regular smooth preferences* when:

(a) $X = \mathbb{R}^G_+$;

(b) $Y = \{e\}$ where $e \gg 0$;

(c) R is continuous, convex, and strictly monotone on X;

(d) R satisfies the *boundary condition* that, for any $\bar{x} \gg 0$, one has $x \in P(\bar{x})$ only if $x \gg 0$;

(e) R can be represented on X by a continuous utility function $u : \mathbb{R}^G_+ \to \mathbb{R}$ that is C^1 on $\mathbb{R}^G_{++}$.

Condition (d) receives its name because it allows an indifference curve to intersect the boundary of $\mathbb{R}^G_+$ only if it is a subset of that boundary.

[5] See Kannai (1977) for a comprehensive discussion of conditions guaranteeing that a convex preference relation can be represented by a concave utility function.

2.6. Preferences for Net Trades

The first part of this chapter, involving economies with finitely many agents, largely considers both agents' consumption and production vectors explicitly. Later, especially in the work involving a continuum of agents, notation will be reduced somewhat by considering only net trade vectors. Then it is convenient to ignore the distinction between an agent's consumption set X and production set Y. Instead, we focus on the *feasible net trade set* $T := X - Y$.

This reduction is facilitated by Rader's (1978) discussion of sufficient conditions for various important properties of an agent's preference relation R on X to carry over to the *derived preference relation for net trades*. This relation, denoted by $\succsim$, is defined on the feasible set $T = X - Y$ so that, for all $t, t' \in T$, one has $t \succsim t'$ if and only if, whenever $x' \in X$ and $y' \in Y$ with $t' = x' - y'$, there exist $x \in R(x')$ and $y \in Y$ such that $t = x - y$. Thus, $t \succsim t'$ if and only if, given any consumption vector $x' = y' + t' \in X$ that the agent can attain by combining a feasible production vector y' with t', there exists a weakly preferred consumption vector $x = y + t \in X$ that the agent can attain by combining an alternative feasible production vector y with t.

Suppose preferences are continuous and the set $\{(x, y) \in X \times Y \mid x - y = t\}$ is bounded for each t—so compact because it must also be closed. Then it is not hard to show that $\succsim$ is a (complete and transitive) preference ordering over T. Let $\succ$ and $\sim$ denote the associated strict preference and indifference relations, respectively.

Thus, when concentrating on net trades, little is lost by regarding the agent as having a fixed consumption set T and a fixed endowment vector 0, though then the requirement that $T \subseteq \mathbb{R}^G_+$ has to be relaxed.[6]

In a continuum economy, virtually none of the standard results require preferences to be convex. On the other hand, the assumption that T is a convex set will eventually play an important role. This is because the key "cheaper point" lemma of Section 3.7 may not hold when nonconvex feasible sets are allowed, so results concerning "compensated" equilibria may not extend to Walrasian equilibria.

Section 11 uses several assumptions on preferences for net trades to prove that equilibrium exists in a continuum economy. Of these, the simplest is that T *allows autarky* in the sense that $0 \in T$—i.e., feasibility does not require any net trade. Next, say that T is *bounded below* if there exists $\underline{t} \in \mathbb{R}^G$ such that $t \geqq \underline{t}$ for all $t \in T$. Finally, say that preferences for net trades are *weakly monotone* if $t \in T$ and $t \succsim_\theta t'$ whenever $t \geqq t'$ and $t' \in T$.

[6] A similar reduction based on net trade vectors works in more general models with individual transactions costs, like those of Foley (1970b), Diamantaras and Gilles (2004), or Sun, Yang, and Zhou (2004). Indeed, even when profitable arbitrage between different markets is possible, it is still enough to consider each agent's total net trade vector, after summing all transactions in every market.

2.7. A Compact Polish Space of Agents' Types

When the preference ordering $\succsim$ on T is complete, note that $t \in T$ iff $t \succsim t$. Accordingly, each pair $(T, \succsim)$ for which $\succsim$ is complete is entirely characterized by the *graph* of $\succsim$, defined as the set

$$G_{\succsim} := \{ (t,t') \in \mathbb{R}^G \times \mathbb{R}^G \mid t \succsim t' \}.$$

We typically assume that each possible $\succsim$ is continuous, which is true if and only if $G_{\succsim}$ is a closed set. Let Θ denote the domain of all possible continuous agent types—that is, all possible closed subsets of $\mathbb{R}^G \times \mathbb{R}^G$ that correspond to complete and continuous preference orderings.

As discussed in Debreu (1969), Hildenbrand (1974, pp. 15–19), and Mas-Colell (1985, Section A.5), the family of closed subsets of $\mathbb{R}^G \times \mathbb{R}^G$ can be given the topology of *closed convergence*. The results of Aliprantis and Border (1999, pp. 116–118) imply that the resulting topological space is compact and Polish.[7]

Let Θ denote the subfamily of graphs of preference orderings, which we regard as the space of possible agent types. It is easy to show that Θ is closed in the topology of closed convergence, so it is also compact and Polish.

Given any agent type $\theta \in \Theta$, let T_θ and $\succsim_\theta$ denote the corresponding feasible set of net trades and preference ordering, respectively. The topology of closed convergence on Θ is useful precisely because it gives the two correspondences $\theta \mapsto\!\!\!\to T_\theta$ and $\theta \mapsto\!\!\!\to G_{\succsim_\theta}$ closed graphs, and also makes them both lower hemi-continuous. Specifically:

Lemma 5

(1) *Suppose that (θ, t, t') is the limit as $n \to \infty$ of a convergent sequence $(\theta_n, t_n, t'_n)_{n=1}^{\infty}$ in $\Theta \times \mathbb{R}^G \times \mathbb{R}^G$ satisfying $t_n, t'_n \in T_{\theta_n}$ as well as $t_n \succsim_{\theta_n} t'_n$ for all $n = 1, 2, \ldots$. Then $t, t' \in T_\theta$ and $t \succsim_\theta t'$.*

(2) *Suppose that θ is the limit as $n \to \infty$ of a convergent sequence $(\theta_n)_{n=1}^{\infty}$ of agent types. Then any $t \in T_\theta$ is the limit of a convergent sequence $(t_n)_{n=1}^{\infty}$ of net trade vectors that satisfies $t_n \in T_{\theta_n}$ for each $n = 1, 2, \ldots$.*

(3) *Given any triple $(\theta, t, t') \in \Theta \times \mathbb{R}^G \times \mathbb{R}^G$ satisfying $t, t' \in T_\theta$ and $t \succ_\theta t'$, there exist neighborhoods U of θ, V of t and V' of t' such that $\tilde{t} \succ_{\tilde{\theta}} \tilde{t}'$ for all $\tilde{\theta} \in U$, all $\tilde{t} \in V \cap T_{\tilde{\theta}}$, and all $\tilde{t}' \in V' \cap T_{\tilde{\theta}}$.*

Proof. See, for example, Hildenbrand (1974, p. 98, Corollaries 1 and 3). □

[7] Recall that a topological space is *Polish* if it is separable (has a countable dense set) and has a metric that makes it complete (Cauchy sequences converge).

Say that *autarky is possible* for a type θ agent if $0 \in T_\theta$. Say that a type θ agent's feasible set T_θ has a *lower bound* $\underline{t}_\theta$ if $t \in T_\theta$ implies $t \geqq \underline{t}_\theta$.

From now on, given any $\theta \in \Theta$ and any $\bar{t} \in T_\theta$, let

$$R_\theta(\bar{t}) := \{t \in T_\theta \mid t \succsim_\theta \bar{t}\} \quad \text{and} \quad P_\theta(\bar{t}) := \{t \in T_\theta \mid t \succ_\theta \bar{t}\}$$

denote the associated weak and strict preference sets, respectively.

Given any type $\theta \in \Theta$ and any price vector $p \in \mathbb{R}^G \setminus \{0\}$, the net trade *Walrasian budget set* of a θ agent is $B_\theta(p) := \{t \in T_\theta \mid pt \leq 0\}$.

Lemma 6 *Suppose each T_θ has a lower bound $\underline{t}_\theta$, and $0 \in T_\theta$. Then for each $\theta \in \Theta$ and $p \gg 0$:*

(1) *$0 \in B_\theta(p)$, which is a compact set;*
(2) *the mapping $\theta \mapsto \underline{w}_\theta(p) := \inf pT_\theta$ is continuous.*

Proof.

(1) Obviously $0 \in B_\theta(p)$ for each p and θ. Because $\underline{t}_\theta$ is a lower bound and $p \gg 0$, each component t_g of any vector $t \in B_\theta(p)$ satisfies

$$p_g \underline{t}_g \leq p_g t_g \leq - \sum_{h \in G \setminus \{g\}} p_h t_h \leq - \sum_{h \in G \setminus \{g\}} p_h \underline{t}_{\theta h},$$

so $B_\theta(p)$ is bounded. Because $B_\theta(p)$ is evidently closed, it must be compact.

(2) By Lemma 5, the correspondence

$$\theta \mapsto\!\!\!\rightarrow T_\theta = \{t \in \mathbb{R}^G \mid (t,t) \in G_{\succsim_\theta}\}$$

has a closed graph and is lower hemi-continuous. Because each T_θ has a lower bound, continuity of the mapping $\theta \mapsto \underline{w}_\theta(p)$ follows from applying the maximum theorem to the problem of maximizing $-pt$ over the nonempty compact set $B_\theta(p)$. See, for example, Hildenbrand (1974, p. 30, corollary). □

2.8. Smooth Type Domains

The domain Θ of types is said to be *smooth* provided that it is a piecewise C^1-arc connected[8] subset of a normed linear space satisfying:

(a) for each $\theta \in \Theta$, the feasible set T_θ is closed, convex, satisfies free disposal, has 0 as an interior point, and has $\underline{t}_\theta$ as a lower bound;

[8] This means that, given any pair of types $\theta', \theta'' \in \Theta$, one can connect θ' to θ'' by an arc $s \mapsto \theta(s)$ mapping $[0,1]$ to Θ such that $\theta(0) = \theta'$, $\theta(1) = \theta''$, where the function $\theta(\cdot)$ is continuous and piecewise continuously differentiable w.r.t. s. For a more general discussion of smooth preferences, see especially Mas-Colell (1985).

(b) for each fixed $\theta \in \Theta$, the preference ordering $\precsim_\theta$ on T_θ can be represented by a C^1 *utility function* $u_\theta(t)$ of (t,θ) which is strictly increasing and strictly quasi-concave as a function of t;

(c) on the domain D of triples $(p,w,\theta) \in \mathbb{R}^G_{++} \times \mathbb{R} \times \Theta$ such that $w > \underline{w}_\theta(p)$, maximizing $u_\theta(t)$ w.r.t. t over the *Walrasian budget set* $\{t \in T_\theta \mid pt \leq w\}$ gives rise to a unique *Walrasian demand* vector $h_\theta(p,w)$ in the interior of T_θ that is a C^1 function of (p,w,θ);

(d) the *indirect utility function* defined on the domain D by $v_\theta(p,w) := u_\theta(h_\theta(p,w))$ is continuous, and has a positive partial derivative $(v_\theta)'_w = \partial v_\theta/\partial w$ w.r.t. w that is a continuous function of (w,θ);

(e) for each fixed $p \gg 0$, if the sequences θ_n and w_n in Θ and $\mathbb{R}$ respectively tend to θ and $+\infty$, then for any $t \in T_\theta$ one has $u_\theta(h_{\theta_n}(p,w_n)) > u_\theta(t)$ for all sufficiently large n.

Condition (e) is not standard, nor is it implied by the other conditions. It is used in Sections 13 and 14 to ensure that self-selection or incentive constraints prevent lump-sum transfers from diverging to $+\infty$.[9] When conditions (a) to (d) all hold, a sufficient condition for (e) to hold as well is that, given any fixed $t \in \mathbb{R}^G$, $p \gg 0$, and $\theta \in \Theta$, one has $h_\theta(p,w) \gg t$ for all large w. This condition clearly holds, for example, in the special *homothetic* case when $T_\theta = \{t \in \mathbb{R}^G \mid t + e_\theta \geqq 0\}$ for some fixed endowment vector $e_\theta \gg 0$, and the preference ordering $\precsim_\theta$ on T_θ gives rise to a Walrasian demand function satisfying $h_\theta(p,w) \equiv (w + p\,e_\theta)b_\theta(p) - e_\theta$ where $b_\theta(p) \in \mathbb{R}^G_{++}$ and $p\,b_\theta(p) = 1$ for all $p \gg 0$. More generally, condition (e) holds whenever the C^1 demand functions $h_{\theta g}(p,w)$ for each commodity $g \in G$ have income responses $\partial h_{\theta g}/\partial w$ that are all positive and bounded away from 0—that is, there exist functions $a_{\theta g}(p) > 0$ such that $\partial h_{\theta g}(p,w)/\partial w \geq a_{\theta g}(p)$ for all $w > \underline{w}_\theta(p)$.

3. WALRASIAN EQUILIBRIUM AND PARETO EFFICIENCY

3.1. Finite Set of Agents

As usual in social choice theory, let N denote the finite set of individuals. In the tradition of general equilibrium theory, these individuals may also be described as *agents* or *consumers*. Let $\#N$ denote the number of agents $i \in N$.[10]

Superscripts will indicate particular agents $i \in N$. Thus, X^i, Y^i, T^i, R^i, and $\precsim^i$ respectively denote agent i's consumption set, production set, set of feasible net trades,

[9] Luis Corchón has suggested to me that there may be a relationship between preferences violating condition (e) and the phenomenon of "immiserizing growth" that Bhagwati (1958, 1987) in particular has explored thoroughly. This deserves later investigation.

[10] Standard "Arrow–Debreu" theory also admits a finite set J of private producers that are owned jointly by one or more consumers and have production sets $Y^j \subseteq \mathbb{R}^G$ (all $j \in J$). This survey will not consider such jointly-owned producers.

preference ordering over X^i, and preference ordering over T^i. Similarly, x^i, y^i, and $t^i = x^i - y^i$ respectively denote agent i's consumption, production, and net trade vectors.

3.2. Feasible and Pareto Efficient Allocations

Let X^N and Y^N denote the Cartesian products $\prod_{i\in N} X^i$ and $\prod_{i\in N} Y^i$, respectively. Then $X^N \times Y^N$ is the set of *individually feasible* collections (x^N, y^N) satisfying $x^i \in X^i$ and $y^i \in Y^i$ for all $i \in N$. An *allocation* is a collection $(x^N, y^N) \in X^N \times Y^N$ that also satisfies the *resource balance constraint* $\sum_{i\in N}(x^i - y^i) = 0$. Note that an allocation is automatically feasible, by definition, although even so we shall often write of a "feasible allocation." Also note that free disposal is not assumed, although it will be satisfied if at least one individual agent's production set has this property.

A particular feasible allocation $(\hat{x}^N, \hat{y}^N)$ is said to be:

- *weakly Pareto efficient* (WPE) if no alternative feasible allocation (x^N, y^N) satisfies $x^i \; P^i \; \hat{x}^i$ for all $i \in N$;
- *Pareto efficient* (PE) if no alternative feasible allocation (x^N, y^N) satisfies $x^i \; R^i \; \hat{x}^i$ for all $i \in N$, with $x^h \; P^h \; \hat{x}^h$ for some $h \in N$.

In an example with two agents labeled 1 and 2 and only one good, an allocation can be weakly Pareto efficient but not Pareto efficient, provided that one agent has locally satiated preferences at that allocation. Indeed, suppose that agent 1 is made no worse off by giving up a small enough amount of the good, whereas agent 2 always prefers more of the good. Then transferring that small enough amount of the good from agent 1 to agent 2 makes the latter better off, but leaves agent 1 indifferent.

Another example shows that weak Pareto efficiency does not imply Pareto efficiency even when all agents have LNS preferences. Indeed, suppose there are three goods and three agents. Suppose agent 1 has preferences represented by the utility function $u^1(x^1) = x_1^1$, whereas agents 2 and 3 both have utility functions $u^i(x^i)$ that are strictly increasing in (x_2^i, x_3^i) $(i = 2, 3)$, but independent of x_1^i. Suppose each agent $i \in N$ has a fixed endowment vector $e^i \in \mathbb{R}^3$ of the three different goods. Then any allocation that allocates the total endowment of good 1 to agent 1 must be weakly Pareto efficient. Yet Pareto efficiency requires in addition that the total endowments of goods 2 and 3 must be efficiently distributed between agents 2 and 3.

3.3. Wealth Distribution and Walrasian Equilibrium

Let $p \in \mathbb{R}^G \setminus \{0\}$ denote the typical price vector. Note that the signs of the prices $p_g (g \in G)$ are not specified, as is appropriate without any assumption of either free disposal or monotone preferences.

Given any $p \in \mathbb{R}^G \setminus \{0\}$, the *Walrasian budget constraint* of any agent $i \in N$ is $px^i \leq py^i$. This requires the value of consumption at prices p not to exceed the value of production at those same prices.

A *Walrasian equilibrium* (or WE) is an allocation $(\hat{x}^N, \hat{y}^N)$ and a price vector $\hat{p} \in \mathbb{R}^G \setminus \{0\}$ such that, for each $i \in N$, both $\hat{p}\hat{x}^i \leq \hat{p}\hat{y}^i$ and also

$$x^i \in P^i(\hat{x}^i),\ y^i \in Y^i \Longrightarrow \hat{p}x^i > \hat{p}y^i.$$

Equivalently, each agent i's choices $(\hat{x}^i, \hat{y}^i)$ together maximize R^i w.r.t. (x^i, y^i), subject to the feasibility constraints $x^i \in X^i$, $y^i \in Y^i$, as well as the budget constraint $\hat{p}x^i \leq \hat{p}y^i$. Feasibility of the allocation guarantees that, at the equilibrium price vector $\hat{p}$, demand matches supply for each commodity.

As remarked in the introduction in Section 1, even though a WE allocation is always at least weakly Pareto efficient in the framework considered here, the converse is not true. At best, most weakly Pareto efficient allocations will be Walrasian equilibria only if agents' budget constraints are modified by specifying a more general *wealth distribution rule* (or by imposing a *lump-sum transfer system*).[11] This is defined as a collection $w^N(p)$ of functions $w^i(p)$ $(i \in N)$ which are homogeneous of degree one in p and satisfy $\sum_{i\in N} w^i(p) \equiv 0$. Here $w^i(p)$ represents agent i's net unearned wealth, which supplements the net profit py^i that i earns by producing and selling the net output vector y^i when the price vector is p. Often it is enough to consider a wealth distribution rule having the special form $w^i(p) \equiv p(\bar{x}^i - \bar{y}^i)$ for some fixed feasible allocation $(\bar{x}^N, \bar{y}^N)$.

Relative to the specified wealth distribution rule $w^N(p)$, a *Walrasian equilibrium with lump-sum transfers* (or WELT) consists of a (feasible) allocation $(\hat{x}^N, \hat{y}^N)$ together with a price vector $\hat{p} \in \mathbb{R}^G \setminus \{0\}$, such that, for each $i \in N$, both $\hat{p}(\hat{x}^i - \hat{y}^i) \leq w^i(\hat{p})$ and also

$$x^i \in P^i(\hat{x}^i),\ y^i \in Y^i \Longrightarrow \hat{p}(x^i - y^i) > w^i(\hat{p}). \tag{1}$$

Equivalently, for each $i \in N$, the pair $(\hat{x}^i, \hat{y}^i)$ must maximize R^i subject to $(x^i, y^i) \in X^i \times Y^i$ and the budget constraint $\hat{p}(x^i - y^i) \leq w^i(\hat{p})$.

Obviously, this definition implies that a WE is a WELT relative to the trivial wealth distribution rule given by $w^i(p) = 0$ for all $i \in N$ and all $p \in \mathbb{R}^G \setminus \{0\}$.

3.4. Compensated Walrasian Equilibrium

In order to demonstrate that most weakly Pareto efficient allocations can be achieved as WELTs, for a suitable wealth distribution rule and equilibrium price vector, it is useful to introduce the following routine extension of a concept due to McKenzie (1957).[12]

[11] The concept appears to originate in Gale and Mas-Colell (1975), although they use the term "income functions."

[12] See also Koopmans (1957, pp. 32–33). Debreu (1951, p. 281) mentions a similar concept, but in that paper fails to distinguish it from a WELT.

3.4.1. Definition

Given the wealth distribution rule $w^N(p)$, the particular allocation $(\hat{x}^N, \hat{y}^N)$ and price vector $\hat{p} \in \mathbb{R}^G \setminus \{0\}$ form a *compensated equilibrium with lump-sum transfers* (or CELT) if, for each $i \in N$, both $\hat{p}(\hat{x}^i - \hat{y}^i) \leq w^i(\hat{p})$ and also

$$x^i \in R^i(\hat{x}^i),\ y^i \in Y^i \Longrightarrow \hat{p}(x^i - y^i) \geq w^i(\hat{p}). \tag{2}$$

The only differences between a CELT satisfying (2) and a WELT satisfying (1) are that $P^i(\hat{x}^i)$ has been replaced by $R^i(\hat{x}^i)$, and the strict inequality has become weak.

A *compensated equilibrium* (or CE), without lump-sum transfers, occurs when $w^i(\hat{p}) = 0$ for all $i \in N$.

3.4.2. Arrow's Exceptional Case

The difference between compensated and (uncompensated) Walrasian equilibrium is illustrated by the following example, often referred to as *Arrow's exceptional case.*[13] The agent's feasible set is taken to be the non-negative quadrant $X = \mathbb{R}^2_+ = \{(x_1, x_2) \mid x_1, x_2 \geq 0\}$ in $\mathbb{R}^2$. Preferences are assumed to be represented by the utility function $u(x_1, x_2) = x_1 + \sqrt{x_2}$ restricted to the domain $X = \mathbb{R}^2_+$. So all the indifference curves are given by the equation $x_2 = (u - x_1)^2$ for $0 \leq x_1 \leq u$, and must therefore be parts of parabolae that touch the x_1-axis, as indicated by the dotted curves in Figure 15.1.

This agent has continuous, convex, and strictly monotone preferences, as is easily checked. In fact, preferences are "quasi-linear," with the special feature that the marginal willingness to pay for the second good becomes infinite as $x_2 \to 0$.

In this example, trouble arises at any consumption vector of the form $(x_1, 0)$ with x_1 positive, such as the point A in Figure 15.1. Any such consumption vector is clearly a compensated equilibrium for the agent at any price vector of the form $(0, p_2)$ where $p_2 > 0$. To make point A a Walrasian equilibrium at any price vector is impossible, however. The reason is that any Walrasian equilibrium price vector would have to be

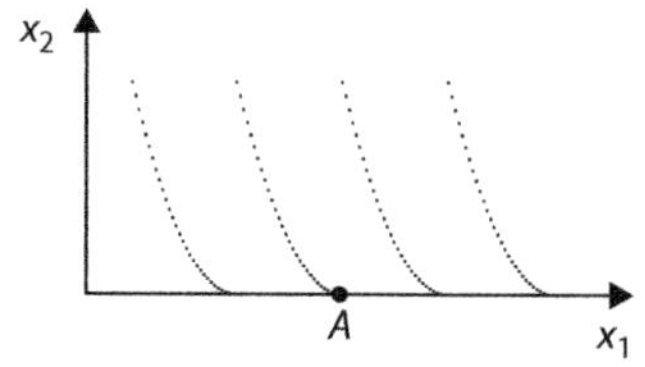

Figure 15.1. Arrow's Exceptional Case.

[13] The original example in Arrow (1951a) involved an Edgeworth box economy in which one of the two agents has non-monotone preferences. Koopmans (1957, p. 34) appears to have been the first to present a version of the example in which preferences are monotone.

a compensated equilibrium price vector, and so take the form $(0, p_2)$. Hence, the budget constraint would have to be $p_2 x_2 \leq 0$, which is equivalent to $x_2 \leq 0$. But then the agent could always move to preferred points by increasing x_1 indefinitely while keeping $x_2 = 0$.

3.5. Properties of Compensated and Walrasian Equilibria

Lemma 7 *In any CELT one has* $\hat{p}(\hat{x}^i - \hat{y}^i) = w^i(\hat{p})$ *for all* $i \in N$.

Proof. By definition, $\hat{p}(\hat{x}^i - \hat{y}^i) \leq w^i(\hat{p})$ for all $i \in N$. On the other hand, because $\hat{x}^i \in R^i(\hat{x}^i)$ and $\hat{y}^i \in Y^i$, the definition also implies that $\hat{p}(\hat{x}^i - \hat{y}^i) \geq w^i(\hat{p})$ for all $i \in N$. □

From now on, let $\pi^i(p)$ denote $\sup p\, Y^i$, agent i's supremum profit at the price vector $p \neq 0$.

Lemma 8 *For any agent* $i \in N$ *who has LNS preferences, in any CELT (or CE) one must have* $\hat{p}\hat{y}^i = \pi^i(\hat{p}) = \max p\, Y^i$.

Proof. Define $w := w^i(\hat{p}) + \pi^i(\hat{p})$. Suppose that $\bar{x}^i \in X^i$ satisfies $\hat{p}\bar{x}^i < w$. Then there exists a neighborhood V of $\bar{x}^i$ such that $\hat{p}x^i < w$ for all $x^i \in V$. Because preferences are LNS, there exists $\tilde{x}^i \in P^i(\bar{x}^i) \cap V$. By the definitions of w and $\pi^i(\hat{p})$, then there also exists $y^i \in Y^i$ such that $\hat{p}\tilde{x}^i < w^i(\hat{p}) + \hat{p}y^i$. So $\bar{x}^i$ cannot be part of a CELT at the price vector $\hat{p}$.

Conversely, if $(\hat{x}^i, \hat{y}^i)$ is part of a CELT at the price vector $\hat{p}$ and given the wealth level $w^i(\hat{p})$, then $\hat{p}\hat{x}^i \geq w$. By Lemma 7 and the definition of w, it follows that

$$\hat{p}\hat{y}^i = \hat{p}\hat{x}^i - w^i(\hat{p}) \geq w - w^i(\hat{p}) = \pi^i(\hat{p}).$$

The result follows from the definition of $\pi^i(\hat{p})$. □

Thus, in any CELT, each agent $i \in N$ with LNS preferences must have a net output vector $\hat{y}^i$ that maximizes net profit at the equilibrium price vector $\hat{p}$ over i's production set Y^i.

Lemma 9 *If all agents have LNS preferences, then any WELT is a CELT.*

Proof. Suppose that $(\hat{x}^N, \hat{y}^N, \hat{p})$ is a WELT relative to the wealth distribution rule $w^N(p)$. Consider any $i \in N$ and any $(x^i, y^i) \in R^i(\hat{x}^i) \times Y^i$. Because preferences are LNS, Lemma 1 implies that there exists a sequence $x^i_n \in P^i(\hat{x}^i)$ $(n = 1, 2, \ldots)$ which converges to x^i. The fact that $(\hat{x}^N, \hat{y}^N, \hat{p})$ is a WELT implies that $\hat{p}(x^i_n - y^i) > w^i(\hat{p})$ for all n. Taking the limit as $n \to \infty$ yields $\hat{p}(x^i - y^i) \geq w^i(\hat{p})$. This is enough to show that $(\hat{x}^N, \hat{y}^N, \hat{p})$ is a CELT as well as a WELT relative to the wealth distribution rule $w^N(p)$. □

Obviously Lemma 9 implies that if preferences are LNS, then Lemmas 7 and 8 are also true for any WELT. The following summarizes the results of Lemmas 7–9 in this case:

Theorem 10 *Suppose all agents have LNS preferences. Then the feasible allocation* $(\hat{x}^N, \hat{y}^N)$ *is a WELT at the price vector* $\hat{p} \neq 0$ *relative to the wealth distribution rule* $w^N(p)$ *if and only if, for all* $i \in N$*, one has:*

(1) $\hat{p}(\hat{x}^i - \hat{y}^i) = w^i(\hat{p})$*;*
(2) $\hat{p}\hat{y}^i = \pi^i(\hat{p})$*;*
(3) $x^i \in P^i(\hat{x}^i)$ *implies that* $\hat{p}x^i > \hat{p}\hat{x}^i$*.*

The same allocation is a CELT at the price vector $\hat{p}$ *if and only if, for all* $i \in N$*, properties (1) and (2) are satisfied, but (3) is replaced by:*

(3′) $x^i \in R^i(\hat{x}^i)$ *implies that* $\hat{p}x^i \geq \hat{p}\hat{x}^i$*.*

Proof. Properties (1), (2), and (3) together imply that

$$\hat{p}(x^i - y^i) > \hat{p}\hat{x}^i - \pi^i(\hat{p}) = \hat{p}(\hat{x}^i - \hat{y}^i) = w^i(\hat{p})$$

whenever $x^i \in P^i(\hat{x}^i)$ and $y^i \in Y^i$, as required for a WELT. When (3) is replaced by (3′), there is a CELT instead of a WELT. So the listed properties are sufficient.

Conversely, Lemmas 7–9 show the necessity of properties (1) and (2). In addition, if $(\hat{x}^N, \hat{y}^N, \hat{p})$ is indeed a WELT, then for any $i \in N$, putting $y^i = \hat{y}^i$ in the definition and using Lemma 8 implies that, whenever $x^i \in P^i(\hat{x}^i)$, then

$$\hat{p}(x^i - \hat{y}^i) > w^i(\hat{p}) = \hat{p}(\hat{x}^i - \hat{y}^i).$$

In particular, $\hat{p}x^i > \hat{p}\hat{x}^i$, thus verifying property (3). The proof that a CELT must satisfy property (3′) is similar. □

3.6. Walrasian Equilibrium with Equal Budgets

A *Walrasian equilibrium with equal budgets* (or WEEB) is a WELT $(\hat{x}^N, \hat{y}^N, \hat{p})$ relative to some wealth distribution rule satisfying the restriction that, in equilibrium, one has

$$\hat{p}\hat{x}^i = \frac{1}{\#N} \sum_{h \in N} \hat{p}\hat{y}^h \tag{3}$$

for all $i \in N$. In other words, all agents $i \in N$ have the same amount to spend on their respective (net) consumption vectors x^i. Such a WELT will be an equilibrium relative to the specific "egalitarian" wealth distribution rule defined by $w^i(p) := -\pi^i(p) + (1/\#N)\sum_{h \in N} \pi^h(p)$ for all price vectors $p \neq 0$. This rule collects each agent's supremum profit, and then distributes the total profit equally among all agents.

In the case of a standard exchange economy where $Y^i = \{e^i\}$ with $e^i \in \mathbb{R}^G_+$ for each $i \in N$, a WEEB is equivalent to a WE in the "equal split" exchange economy where each agent is endowed with an equal share $(1/\#N)\sum_{h\in N} e^h$ of the aggregate endowment, as discussed by Thomson (1983) and many others. More generally, let $\tilde{Y}$ denote the *mean production set* $(1/\#N)\sum_{h\in N} Y^h$. The *equivalent equal opportunity economy* is defined as one where each agent $i \in N$ is endowed with the production set $\tilde{Y}$ (instead of with Y^i). Say that the feasible allocation (x^N, y^N) in this equivalent economy has *symmetric production* if $y^h = y^i$ for all $h, i \in N$.

Theorem 11 *Corresponding to each WEEB* $(\hat{x}^N, \hat{y}^N, \hat{p})$ *in the original economy is a WE* $(\hat{x}^N, \tilde{y}^N, \hat{p})$ *with symmetric production in the equivalent equal opportunity economy.*

Proof. Suppose $(\hat{x}^N, \hat{y}^N, \hat{p})$ is a WEEB. Let $\tilde{y} := (1/\#N)\sum_{h\in N} \hat{y}^h \in \tilde{Y}$ and let $\tilde{y}^i := \tilde{y}$ (all $i \in N$), so that $\tilde{y}^N$ has symmetric production. Then $\sum_{i\in N} \hat{x}^i = \sum_{i\in N} \hat{y}^i = \sum_{i\in N} \tilde{y}^i$, and (3) implies that

$$\hat{p}\hat{x}^i = \frac{1}{\#N}\sum_{h\in N} \hat{p}\hat{y}^h = \hat{p}\tilde{y} = \hat{p}\tilde{y}^i \quad (\text{all } i \in N).$$

Also, given any $(x^i, y) \in P^i(\hat{x}^i) \times \tilde{Y}$, Theorem 10 implies that $\hat{p}x^i > \hat{p}\hat{x}^i$ and

$$\begin{aligned}\hat{p}y \leq \sup \hat{p}\tilde{Y} &= \sup \hat{p}\frac{1}{\#N}\sum_{i\in N} Y^i = \frac{1}{\#N}\sum_{i\in N} \sup \hat{p}Y^i \\ &= \frac{1}{\#N}\sum_{i\in N} \pi^i(\hat{p}) = \frac{1}{\#N}\sum_{i\in N} \hat{p}\hat{y}^i = \hat{p}\tilde{y}.\end{aligned}$$

Applying Theorem 10 once again shows that $(\hat{x}^N, \tilde{y}^N, \hat{p})$ is a WE in the equivalent equal opportunity economy.

Conversely, suppose that $(\hat{x}^N, \tilde{y}^N, \hat{p})$ is a WE with symmetric production in the equivalent equal opportunity economy. Let $\tilde{y}$ denote the common value of $\tilde{y}^i$ (all $i \in N$). Then $\hat{p}\hat{x}^i = \hat{p}\tilde{y}$ for all $i \in N$.

Furthermore, Theorem 10 implies that $\tilde{y} \in \arg\max \hat{p}\tilde{Y}$. By definition of $\tilde{Y}$, it follows that $\tilde{y} = (1/\#N)\sum_{i\in N} \hat{y}^i$ for some collection $\hat{y}^N \in Y^N$ satisfying $\hat{y}^i \in \arg\max \hat{p}Y^i$ for each $i \in N$. Then $\sum_{i\in N} \hat{x}^i = \#N\tilde{y} = \sum_{i\in N} \hat{y}^i$. Finally, because $(\hat{x}^N, \tilde{y}^N, \hat{p})$ is a WE, Theorem 10 also implies that $\hat{p}x^i > \hat{p}\hat{x}^i$ whenever $x^i \in P^i(\hat{x}^i)$. This completes the proof that $(\hat{x}^N, \hat{y}^N, \hat{p})$ is a WEEB. □

When $\tilde{Y}$ is convex, it loses no generality to assume that any WE in the equivalent equal opportunity economy has symmetric production. This need not be true when $\tilde{Y}$ is nonconvex, however.

3.7. The Cheaper Point Lemma

Given the wealth distribution rule $w^i(p)$ $(i \in N)$, say that agent i has *a cheaper point* at the price vector $\hat{p}$ if there exists $(\bar{x}^i, \bar{y}^i) \in X^i \times Y^i$ such that $\hat{p}(\bar{x}^i - \bar{y}^i) < w^i(\hat{p})$.

The usual way to prove that a CELT is a WELT involves the following fundamental result:[14]

Lemma 12 (The Cheaper Point Lemma) *Given any $i \in N$, suppose the feasible sets X^i and Y^i are convex, while i's preferences are continuous. Suppose that agent i has a cheaper point $(\bar{x}^i, \bar{y}^i)$ at the price vector $\hat{p}$. Then, if $(\hat{x}^i, \hat{y}^i)$ is any compensated equilibrium for i satisfying (2), it follows that $(\hat{x}^i, \hat{y}^i)$ is a Walrasian equilibrium for i satisfying (1).*

Proof. Suppose that $(\hat{x}^i, \hat{y}^i)$ is a compensated equilibrium for i. Consider any $(x^i, y^i) \in P^i(\hat{x}^i) \times Y^i$. Because X^i and Y^i are convex, while R^i is continuous, there exists λ with $0 < \lambda < 1$ small enough to ensure that $(1-\lambda)x^i + \lambda\bar{x}^i \in R^i(\hat{x}^i)$. Then $(1-\lambda)y^i + \lambda\bar{y}^i \in Y^i$. The hypothesis that $(\hat{x}^i, \hat{y}^i)$ is a compensated equilibrium for i implies that

$$\hat{p}[(1-\lambda)x^i + \lambda\bar{x}^i - (1-\lambda)y^i - \lambda\bar{y}^i] \geq w^i(\hat{p})$$

or equivalently,

$$(1-\lambda)\hat{p}(x^i - y^i) \geq w^i(\hat{p}) - \lambda\hat{p}(\bar{x}^i - \bar{y}^i). \tag{4}$$

But $(\bar{x}^i, \bar{y}^i)$ is a cheaper point for agent i, so $\hat{p}(\bar{x}^i - \bar{y}^i) < w^i(\hat{p})$. Because $\lambda > 0$, it follows that $w^i(\hat{p}) - \lambda\hat{p}(\bar{x}^i - \bar{y}^i) > (1-\lambda)w^i(\hat{p})$. Thus, (4) implies that

$$(1-\lambda)\hat{p}(x^i - y^i) > (1-\lambda)w^i(\hat{p}). \tag{5}$$

Dividing each side of (5) by $1-\lambda$, which is positive, yields $\hat{p}(x^i - y^i) > w^i(\hat{p})$, as required. □

This result motivates the following obvious adaptation of a definition suggested by Debreu (1962). Given the wealth distribution rule $w^N(p)$, a feasible allocation $(\hat{x}^N, \hat{y}^N)$ and price vector $\hat{p} \neq 0$ are said to be a *quasi-equilibrium with lump-sum transfers* (or QELT) provided that:

(1) for all $i \in N$, one has $\hat{p}(\hat{x}^i - \hat{y}^i) \leq w^i(\hat{p})$;
(2) for every agent $i \in N$ who has a cheaper point at prices $\hat{p}$, whenever $x^i \in P^i(\hat{x}^i)$ and $y^i \in Y^i$, then $\hat{p}(x^i - y^i) > w^i(\hat{p})$.

When preferences are LNS, it is easy to see that any QELT is a CELT. When the feasible set is convex and preferences are continuous, Lemma 12 clearly implies that any CELT allocation must be a QELT.

[14] Koopmans (1957, p. 34) ascribes this to the Remark in Section 5 of Debreu (1954), for whose "essence" Debreu gives credit to Arrow (1951a, Lemma 5).

3.8. The Unique Cheapest Point Case

Arrow's exceptional case as presented in Section 3.4.2 has the key feature that there is a whole line segment of cheapest points $(x_1, 0)$ at any relevant price vector of the form $(0, p_2)$ (with $p_2 > 0$). The next property explicitly rules this out.

Say that agent $i \in N$ has a *unique cheapest point* at the price vector $p \neq 0$, provided there is a unique $\underline{x}^i \in X^i$ such that $px^i > p\underline{x}^i$ for all $x^i \in X^i \setminus \{\underline{x}^i\}$.

Provided that $p \gg 0$, it is easy to check that a unique cheapest point exists in each of the following cases:

(1) X^i is closed, bounded below, and strictly convex;[15]
(2) $X^i = \mathbb{R}^G_+$;
(3) there is only one good, and X^i is a closed half-line that is bounded below.

Lemma 13 *Suppose agent $i \in N$ has convex feasible sets X^i and Y^i, as well as preferences that are LNS and continuous. Suppose that $(\hat{x}^i, \hat{y}^i) \in X^i \times Y^i$ is a CELT for agent i at the price vector $\hat{p} \neq 0$, and that agent i has a unique cheapest point at $\hat{p}$. Then $(\hat{x}^i, \hat{y}^i)$ is a WELT for agent i at the price vector $\hat{p}$.*

Proof. Because of Lemma 12, it is enough to consider the case when agent i has no cheaper point—that is, when $\hat{p}(x^i - y^i) \geq w^i(\hat{p})$ for all $(x^i, y^i) \in X^i \times Y^i$. In particular, putting $y^i = \hat{y}^i$ and using Lemma 7 yields

$$\hat{p}x^i \geq \hat{p}\hat{y}^i + w^i(\hat{p}) = \hat{p}\hat{x}^i$$

for all $x^i \in X^i$, so that $\hat{x}^i$ is a cheapest point of X^i.

Now consider any $x^i \in P^i(\hat{x}^i)$. Then $x^i \neq \hat{x}^i$ and so $\hat{p}x^i > \hat{p}\hat{x}^i$ because of the hypothesis that agent i has a unique cheapest point at $\hat{p}$. Theorem 10 implies that the CELT $(\hat{x}^i, \hat{y}^i)$ for agent i at the price vector $\hat{p}$ must be a WELT. □

3.9. Aggregate Interiority

The rest of this chapter makes frequent use of the *aggregate interiority* assumption. This requires 0 to be an interior point of the set $\sum_{i \in N}(X^i - Y^i)$ of *feasible aggregate net trade vectors* $\sum_{i \in N}(x^i - y^i)$ satisfying $x^i \in X^i$ and $y^i \in Y^i$ for all $i \in N$. This interiority assumption by itself ensures that there always exists at least one agent with a cheaper point:

Lemma 14 *Suppose aggregate interiority is satisfied. Then, given any wealth distribution rule $w^N(p)$ and any price vector $\hat{p} \in \mathbb{R}^G \setminus \{0\}$, at least one agent $h \in N$ has a feasible pair $(\bar{x}^h, \bar{y}^h) \in X^h \times Y^h$ satisfying $\hat{p}(\bar{x}^h - \bar{y}^h) < w^h(\hat{p})$.*

[15] This case is mentioned by Koopmans (1957, p. 32).

Proof. Because $0 \in \text{int} \sum_{i \in N} (X^i - Y^i)$, there exist $(\bar{x}^i, \bar{y}^i) \in X^i \times Y^i$ for all $i \in N$ such that $\hat{p} \sum_{i \in N} (\bar{x}^i - \bar{y}^i) < 0 = \sum_{i \in N} w^i(\hat{p})$. The result follows immediately. □

4. CHARACTERIZING PARETO EFFICIENT ALLOCATIONS

4.1. First Efficiency Theorem

The first result, based on Arrow (1951a), is very simple.

Theorem 15 *Any WELT is weakly Pareto efficient, and is Pareto efficient if all agents have LNS preferences.*

Proof. Let $(\hat{x}^N, \hat{y}^N, \hat{p})$ be any WELT. We show that $\sum_{i \in N} (x^i - y^i) \neq 0$ for any $(x^N, y^N) \in \prod_{i \in N} [P^i(\hat{x}^i) \times Y^i]$, so no such (x^N, y^N) is feasible.

Indeed, if $(x^i, y^i) \in P^i(\hat{x}^i) \times Y^i$ for all $i \in N$, the definition of WELT implies that $\hat{p}(x^i - y^i) > w^i(\hat{p})$. Summing over i gives

$$\hat{p} \sum_{i \in N} (x^i - y^i) > \sum_{i \in N} w^i(\hat{p}) = 0, \tag{6}$$

and so $\sum_{i \in N} (x^i - y^i) \neq 0$.

When all agents have LNS preferences, Lemma 7 implies that the WELT is a CELT. So if $(x^N, y^N) \in \prod_{i \in N} [R^i(\hat{x}^i) \times Y^i]$, then $\hat{p}(x^i - y^i) \geq w^i(\hat{p})$ for each i. If in addition $x^h \; P^h \; \hat{x}^h$ for any $h \in N$, then $\hat{p}(x^h - y^h) > w^h(\hat{p})$. Once again, summing over i gives (6). □

4.2. Second Efficiency Theorem

The second result, also based on Arrow (1951a), is much more involved than the first. Indeed, Arrow's exceptional case described in Section 3.4.2 is just one example showing the need for extra assumptions. We therefore begin with a simpler result:

Theorem 16 *Suppose agents' preferences are LNS and convex. Then any weakly Pareto efficient allocation $(\hat{x}^N, \hat{y}^N)$ is a CELT.*

Proof. For each $i \in N$, define the set $Z^i := P^i(\hat{x}^i) - Y^i$ of net trade vectors $x^i - y^i$ allowing i to achieve a consumption vector $x^i \in P^i(\hat{x}^i)$. By Lemma 2, the set $P^i(\hat{x}^i)$ is convex, and so therefore is Z^i, as the vector difference of two convex sets. Then weak Pareto efficiency implies that $0 \notin Z := \sum_{i \in N} Z^i$. Moreover, Z must be convex as the sum of convex sets. So there exists a price vector $\hat{p} \neq 0$ that defines a hyperplane $\hat{p} z = 0$ through the origin with the property that $\hat{p}z \geq 0$ for all $z \in Z$. Because $Z = \sum_{i \in N} Z^i$, it follows that

$$0 \leq \inf \hat{p} \sum_{i \in N} Z^i = \sum_{i \in N} \inf \hat{p} Z^i. \tag{7}$$

By Lemma 1, LNS preferences imply that $\hat{x}^i \in \mathrm{cl}\, P^i(\hat{x}^i)$, and so $\hat{x}^i - \hat{y}^i \in \mathrm{cl}\, Z^i$. It follows that

$$\inf \hat{p} Z^i \leq \hat{w}^i := \hat{p}(\hat{x}^i - \hat{y}^i) \tag{8}$$

for all $i \in N$. Now (7) and (8) together imply that

$$0 \leq \inf \hat{p} \sum_{i \in N} Z^i = \sum_{i \in N} \inf \hat{p} Z^i \leq \sum_{i \in N} \hat{w}^i = 0 \tag{9}$$

because $\sum_{i \in N} (\hat{x}^i - \hat{y}^i) = 0$ and so $\sum_{i \in N} \hat{w}^i = \hat{p} \sum_{i \in N} (\hat{x}^i - \hat{y}^i) = 0$. Hence, both inequalities in (9) must be equalities, which is consistent with (8) only if

$$\inf\{\hat{p}z^i \mid z^i \in Z^i\} = \hat{w}^i \quad \text{for all } i \in N. \tag{10}$$

Now suppose that $(x^i, y^i) \in R^i(\hat{x}^i) \times Y^i$. Because preferences are transitive, $P^i(x^i) \subset P^i(\hat{x}^i)$. Because preferences are LNS, Lemma 1 implies that there is a sequence of points $(x^i_n)_{n=1}^\infty$ in $P^i(x^i)$ that converges to x^i. But then $x^i_n - y^i \in P^i(\hat{x}^i) - Y^i = Z^i$ for all n. By (10), it follows that $\hat{p}(x^i_n - y^i) \geq \hat{w}^i$. So $\hat{p}(x^i - y^i) \geq \hat{w}^i = \hat{p}(\hat{x}^i - \hat{y}^i)$ in the limit as $n \to \infty$.

These properties imply that $(\hat{x}^N, \hat{y}^N, \hat{p})$ is a CELT. □

4.3. Identical Agents

Obviously, we say that *all agents are identical* in case the feasible sets X^i, Y^i and preference orderings R^i are all independent of i. Suppose, too, that the identical agents have LNS, continuous, and convex preferences. Following Lucas (1978) and Stokey, Lucas, and Prescott (1989, ch. 1), it has been common in macroeconomics to consider symmetric allocations in an economy with many identical agents. There is a particularly simple relationship between Walrasian equilibrium and Pareto efficiency in such a framework.

Consider any WE $(\hat{x}^N, \hat{y}^N, \hat{p})$. By Theorem 10, this must satisfy the budget equation $\hat{p}\hat{x}^i = \hat{p}\hat{y}^i$ for all $i \in N$ because preferences are LNS. Consider also the symmetric allocation $(\bar{x}^N, \bar{y}^N)$ defined for all $i \in N$ by

$$\bar{x}^i := \bar{x} := \frac{1}{\#N} \sum_{i \in N} \hat{x}^i \quad \text{and} \quad \bar{y}^i := \bar{y} := \frac{1}{\#N} \sum_{i \in N} \hat{y}^i$$

Because preferences are convex, it is easy to see that this is also a WE at the same price vector $\hat{p}$. It must therefore satisfy $\hat{x}^i \; I^i \; \bar{x}$ for all $i \in N$. Hence the original WE is equivalent to a symmetric WE that is also Pareto efficient.

More interesting is the converse. Suppose $(\hat{x}^N, \hat{y}^N)$ is a symmetric Pareto efficient allocation, with $\hat{x}^i = \hat{x}$ and $\hat{y}^i := \hat{y}$ for all $i \in N$. Of course, feasibility requires that $\hat{x} = \hat{y}$. Theorem 16 states that this allocation must be a CELT, for some price vector $\hat{p} \neq 0$, and given a wealth distribution rule $w^N(p)$ satisfying $w^i(\hat{p}) = \hat{p}\,(\hat{x}^i - \hat{y}^i)$ for all $i \in N$. But then $w^i(\hat{p}) = \hat{p}\,(\hat{x} - \hat{y}) = 0$ for all $i \in N$. So this CELT is actually a CE, without lump-sum transfers.

Finally, as mentioned in Section 3.9, we impose the standard aggregate interiority assumption requiring that $0 \in \operatorname{int} \sum_{i \in N} (X^i - Y^i)$. By Lemma 14, at least one agent $h \in N$ has a cheaper point $(\bar{x}^h, \bar{y}^h) \in X^h \times Y^h$ satisfying $\hat{p}\,(\bar{x}^h - \bar{y}^h) < 0$. Since all agents are identical, all must have cheaper points. By Lemma 12, it follows that $(\hat{x}, \hat{y}, \hat{p})$ is a Walrasian equilibrium. This proves that a symmetric Pareto efficient allocation is a WE under the assumptions stated above—namely, that agents have identical LNS, continuous and convex preferences, while $0 \in \operatorname{int} \sum_{i \in N} (X^i - Y^i)$.

4.4. Nonoligarchic Allocations

The following general conditions for a CELT to be a WELT, and so for a Pareto efficient allocation to be a WELT, originated in Hammond (1993), following ideas pioneered by McKenzie (1959, 1961).

For the weakly Pareto efficient allocation $(\hat{x}^N, \hat{y}^N)$, the proper subset $K \subset N$ (with both K and $N \setminus K$ nonempty) is said to be an *oligarchy* if there is no alternative feasible allocation satisfying $x^i \; P^i \; \hat{x}^i$ for all $i \in K$. In the case when $K = \{d\}$ for some $d \in N$, we may speak of d being a *dictator* who is unable to find any preferred alternative. On the other hand, a *nonoligarchic* weakly Pareto efficient (or NOWPE) allocation occurs if there is no oligarchy.

One way to interpret this definition is that the members of any oligarchy K are already so well off at the relevant allocation $(\hat{x}^N, \hat{y}^N)$ that they cannot benefit from any gift that an outside individual might make. Indeed, the members of K would not even wish to steal whatever little consumption is left to those agents who are excluded from the set K.

It may be instructive to consider these definitions in the context of an economy with three agents and just one good. As usual, agents are assumed always to prefer more of the good for their own consumption. Each agent is assumed to have a fixed positive endowment of the only good. Then the set of feasible non-negative consumption allocations is a triangle in three-dimensional space. The corners correspond to the dictatorial allocations that give all the total endowment to one of the three agents. On the other hand, those oligarchic allocations that are not also dictatorial occur on the relative interior of each edge of the feasible triangle.

Theorem 17 *Suppose agents' preferences are LNS, convex, and continuous. Suppose, too, that* $0 \in \operatorname{int} \sum_{i \in N} (X^i - Y^i)$. *Then any nonoligarchic weakly Pareto efficient (NOWPE) allocation* $(\hat{x}^N, \hat{y}^N)$ *is a WELT.*

Proof. By Theorem 16, the hypotheses here guarantee that $(\hat{x}^N, \hat{y}^N)$ is a CELT at some price vector $\hat{p} \neq 0$. It follows that some wealth distribution rule $w^N(p)$ that satisfies $w^i(\hat{p}) = \hat{p}(\hat{x}^i - \hat{y}^i)$ for all $i \in N$, and so $\sum_{i \in N} w^i(\hat{p}) = 0$. Let K be the set of all agents having cheaper points. By Lemma 14, K is nonempty.

Consider any collection $(x^N, y^N) \in X^N \times Y^N$ with $x^i \, P^i \, \hat{x}^i$ for all $i \in K$. Because each agent $i \in K$ has a cheaper point, Lemma 12 implies that

$$\hat{p}(x^i - y^i) > w^i(\hat{p}) \quad \text{for all } i \in K. \tag{11}$$

But no agent outside K has a cheaper point, so

$$\hat{p}(x^i - y^i) \geq w^i(\hat{p}) \quad \text{for all } i \in N \setminus K. \tag{12}$$

Because K must be nonempty, adding the sum of (11) over all $i \in K$ to the sum of (12) over all $i \in N \setminus K$ yields $\hat{p} \sum_{i \in N} (x^i - y^i) > \sum_{i \in N} w^i(\hat{p}) = 0$. Hence, (x^N, y^N) cannot be a feasible allocation. Unless $K = N$, it follows that K is an oligarchy.

Conversely, if $(\hat{x}^N, \hat{y}^N)$ is nonoligarchic, then $K = N$, so all agents have cheaper points. By Lemma 12, the CELT is actually a WELT. □

Corollary 18 *Under the hypotheses of Theorem 17, one has*

$$NOWPE \subseteq WELT \subseteq PE \subseteq WPE \subseteq CELT = QELT.$$

Proof. It has just been proved that NOWPE ⊆ WELT. Theorem 15 implies that WELT ⊆ PE. Obviously PE ⊆ WPE from the definitions in Section 3.2. Theorem 16 implies that WPE ⊆ CELT. Finally, CELT = QELT, as discussed at the end of Section 3.7. □

The next result is prompted by an idea due to Spivak (1978).

Theorem 19 *Suppose agents' preferences are LNS, convex and continuous. Let* $(\hat{x}^N, \hat{y}^N)$ *be a weakly Pareto efficient allocation in which* K *is an oligarchy. Then there is a price vector* $\hat{p} \neq 0$ *such that* $(\hat{x}^N, \hat{y}^N, \hat{p})$ *is a CELT in which each agent* $i \in N \setminus K$ *is at a cheapest point.*

Proof. The proof is similar to that of Theorem 16. For each $i \in K$, define $Z^i := P^i(\hat{x}^i) - Y^i$; for each $i \in N \setminus K$, however, define $Z^i := X^i - Y^i$. Then let $Z := \sum_{i \in K} Z^i$, which is obviously nonempty and convex. The definition of oligarchy implies that $0 \notin Z$. Hence there exists $\hat{p} \neq 0$ such that $\hat{p} z \geq 0$ for all $z \in Z$.

As in the proof of Theorem 16, for all $i \in N$ the net trade vector $\hat{x}^i - \hat{y}^i \in \mathrm{cl}\, Z^i$. Repeating the derivation of (10), one has

$$\inf \hat{p}\, Z^i = \hat{w}^i := \hat{p}\,(\hat{x}^i - \hat{y}^i) \quad \text{for all } i \in N. \tag{13}$$

For all $i \in K$, (13) implies that $\hat{p}\,(x^i - y^i) \geq \hat{w}^i$ whenever $(x^i, y^i) \in P^i(\hat{x}^i) \times Y^i$, and so, because preferences are LNS, whenever $(x^i, y^i) \in R^i(\hat{x}^i) \times Y^i$. For all $i \in N \setminus K$, (13) implies that $\hat{p}\,(x^i - y^i) \geq \hat{w}^i$ whenever $(x^i, y^i) \in X^i \times Y^i$, so $(\hat{x}^i, \hat{y}^i)$ is a cheapest point of $X^i \times Y^i$. Hence, relative to the specific wealth distribution rule $w^N(p)$ defined by $w^i(p) := p\,(\hat{x}^i - \hat{y}^i)$ (all $i \in N$, $p \in \mathbb{R}^G$), the triple $(\hat{x}^N, \hat{y}^N, \hat{p})$ is a CELT with each $i \in N \setminus K$ at a cheapest point. □

4.5. Exact Characterization of Nonoligarchic Allocations

Let CELT* indicate the subset of CELT allocations with the special property that *every* equilibrium price vector allows *every* agent a cheaper point. Let WELT* and QELT* be the corresponding subsets of WELT and QELT.

Theorem 20 *Suppose that agents' preferences are LNS, convex, and continuous, and that* $0 \in \mathrm{int} \sum_{i \in N} (X^i - Y^i)$. *Then one has the exact characterization NOWPE = WELT* = CELT* = QELT*, and also every NOWPE allocation is (fully) Pareto efficient.*

Proof. The cheaper point Lemma 12 makes the equality QELT* = CELT* = WELT* obvious. Also, the proof of Theorem 17 actually demonstrates the stronger result that NOWPE ⊆ CELT* = WELT* ⊆ WELT. And, of course, any WELT* allocation must be Pareto efficient, by Theorem 15. Finally, the contrapositive of Theorem 19 obviously implies that CELT* ⊆ NOWPE. □

4.6. Oligarchic Allocations and Hierarchical Prices

Theorem 20 characterizes only the nonoligarchic part of the Pareto frontier, avoiding the oligarchic extremes. A result due to Florig (2001a, 2003) goes far toward characterizing the oligarchic extremes that are not WELT allocations—see also Konovalov and Marakulin (2006).

As in Shafer and Sonnenschein's (1976) very general framework, Florig considers incomplete preferences over personal consumption that depends on other agents' consumption and production activities. These preferences may even be intransitive. By contrast, this section remains within the standard framework of this chapter, in which each agent has complete and transitive preferences that are independent of all other agents' consumption and production activities. The only difference will be the use of the stronger semi-strict convexity condition that was briefly discussed in Section 2.4.

Florig's (2001a) characterization relies on extended "hierarchical" price systems. It also uses (p. 532) a notion of weak Pareto efficiency that departs from the standard definition. To avoid confusion, here we use a different term and say that the feasible allocation $(\hat{x}^N, \hat{y}^N)$ is *incompletely Pareto efficient* if any Pareto superior allocation (x^N, y^N) satisfies both $x^h \; I^h \; \hat{x}^h$ and $x^h - y^h \neq \hat{x}^h - \hat{y}^h$ for at least one $h \in N$. Equivalently, no feasible allocation (x^N, y^N) in $\prod_{i \in N}[R^i(\hat{x}^i) \times Y^i]$ satisfies $\emptyset \neq N^{\neq} \subset N^{\succ}$, where

$$N^{\neq} := \{i \in N \mid x^i - y^i \neq \hat{x}^i - \hat{y}^i\} \quad \text{and} \quad N^{\succ} := \{i \in N \mid x^i \in P^i(\hat{x}^i)\}. \tag{14}$$

Obviously, any Pareto efficient allocation is incompletely Pareto efficient, and any incompletely Pareto efficient is weakly Pareto efficient. But in neither case does the converse hold, in general.

A *kth-order price system* is a $k \times \#G$ matrix $\mathbf{P}^k$ whose rows $p^r \in \mathbb{R}^G$ $(r = 1, 2, \ldots, k)$ are price vectors satisfying the *orthogonality condition* $p^r \cdot p^s := \sum_{g \in G} p^r_g p^s_g = 0$ whenever $r \neq s$. Obviously, this implies that $\mathbf{P}^k$ has rank k, where $k \leq \#G$. Then any commodity vector $z \in \mathbb{R}^G$ has a k-dimensional value given by the matrix product $\mathbf{P}^k z \in \mathbb{R}^k$.

Define the *lexicographic strict ordering* $>^k_L$ on $\mathbb{R}^k$ so that $a >^k_L b$ iff there exists $r \in \{1, 2, \ldots, k\}$ such that $a_s = b_s$ for $s = 1, \ldots, r-1$, but $a_r > b_r$. Let $\geq^k_L$ be the corresponding weak ordering. Of course, $>^k_L$ is a *total ordering* in the sense that $a \neq b$ implies either $a >^k_L b$ or $b >^k_L a$.

The feasible allocation $(\hat{x}^N, \hat{y}^N)$ is said to be a *hierarchical* WELT at the kth-order price system $\mathbf{P}^k$ if, for all $i \in N$, whenever $(x^i, y^i) \in P^i(\hat{x}^i) \times Y^i$, then $\mathbf{P}^k(x^i - y^i) >^k_L \mathbf{P}^k(\hat{x}^i - \hat{y}^i)$. Equivalently, because $\leq^k_L$ is a total ordering, for each $i \in N$ the pair $(\hat{x}^i, \hat{y}^i)$ must maximize R^i subject to individual feasibility and the *hierarchical Walrasian budget constraint* $\mathbf{P}^k(x^i - y^i) \leq^k_L \mathbf{P}^k(\hat{x}^i - \hat{y}^i)$.

Theorem 21 *Any hierarchical WELT allocation is incompletely Pareto efficient.*

Proof. Suppose the allocation $(\hat{x}^N, \hat{y}^N)$ is a hierarchical WELT at the kth-order price system $\mathbf{P}^k$. Suppose, too, the collection $(x^N, y^N) \in \prod_{i \in N}[R^i(\hat{x}^i) \times Y^i]$ satisfies $\emptyset \neq N^{\neq} \subset N^{\succ}$, where $N^{\neq}$ and $N^{\succ}$ are defined by (14). By definition of a hierarchical WELT, one has

$$\mathbf{P}^k(x^i - y^i) >^k_L \mathbf{P}^k(\hat{x}^i - \hat{y}^i) \quad \text{for all } i \in N^{\succ}. \tag{15}$$

Of course

$$\mathbf{P}^k(x^i - y^i) = \mathbf{P}^k(\hat{x}^i - \hat{y}^i) \quad \text{for all } i \in N \setminus N^{\neq}. \tag{16}$$

For (15) and (16) to be consistent, one must have $N^{\succ} \subset N^{\neq}$ and so, by hypothesis, $N^{\succ} = N^{\neq} \neq \emptyset$. Now one can sum (15) and (16) over all $i \in N$ in order to obtain $\mathbf{P}^k \sum_{i \in N}(x^i - y^i) >_L^k \mathbf{P}^k \sum_{i \in N}(\hat{x}^i - \hat{y}^i) = 0$, as is easy to check. Hence, (x^N, y^N) cannot be a feasible allocation when $\emptyset \neq N^{\neq} \subset N^{\succ}$. So $(\hat{x}^N, \hat{y}^N)$ is incompletely Pareto efficient. □

Theorem 22 *Suppose all agents' preferences are LNS, semi-strictly convex, and continuous. Then any incompletely Pareto efficient allocation $(\hat{x}^N, \hat{y}^N)$ is a hierarchical WELT.*

Proof. The proof is by recursive construction of successive orthogonal price vectors $p^r \in \mathbb{R}^G \setminus \{0\}$ $(r = 1, 2, \ldots)$. Let $\mathbf{P}^k := (p^1, \ldots, p^k)$ denote the resulting kth-order price system, and N^k the set of all agents $i \in N$ for whom $(\hat{x}^i, \hat{y}^i)$ is a hierarchical WELT at $\mathbf{P}^k$. Obviously $N^k \subseteq N^{k+1}$ $(k = 1, 2, \ldots)$. By Theorem 16, there exists a non-zero price vector $p^1 \in \mathbb{R}^G$, at which the allocation $(\hat{x}^N, \hat{y}^N)$ is a CELT. This is the first step.

It will be proved by induction on k that, for all $i \in N \setminus N^k$, whenever $(x^i, y^i) \in R^i(\hat{x}^i) \times Y^i$ and $p^r(x^i - y^i) = p^r(\hat{x}^i - \hat{y}^i)$ for $r = 1, \ldots, k-1$, then $p^k(x^i - y^i) \geq p^k(\hat{x}^i - \hat{y}^i)$. This is true when $k = 1$ because $(\hat{x}^N, \hat{y}^N, p^1)$ is a CELT.

If $N^k = N$, the proof is already complete. Otherwise, define the $(\#G - k)$-dimensional linear subspace $L^k := \{z \in \mathbb{R}^G \mid \mathbf{P}^k z = 0\}$ of vectors that are orthogonal to all the k mutually orthogonal price vectors $p^1, p^2, \ldots, p^k$. Consider the set $Z^k := \sum_{i \in N \setminus N^k} [P^i(\hat{x}^i) - Y^i]$ and the vector $\hat{z}^k := \sum_{i \in N \setminus N^k} (\hat{x}^i - \hat{y}^i) = -\sum_{i \in N^k} (\hat{x}^i - \hat{y}^i)$. Incomplete Pareto efficiency implies that $\hat{z}^k \notin Z^k$, so 0 is not a member of the convex set $(Z^k - \{\hat{z}^k\}) \cap L^k$. Also, for each $i \in N \setminus N^k$, nonsatiation and semi-strictly convex preferences together imply that $\hat{x}^i - \hat{y}^i$ is a boundary point of $[P^i(\hat{x}^i) - Y^i] \cap L^k$, so 0 is a boundary point of $(Z^k - \{\hat{z}^k\}) \cap L^k$. It follows that there exists a hyperplane $p^{k+1} z = 0$ in L^k that separates $(Z^k - \{\hat{z}^k\}) \cap L^k$ from 0, with $p^{k+1} z \geq 0$ for all $z \in (Z^k - \{\hat{z}^k\}) \cap L^k$. Arguing as in the proof of Theorem 16, for each $i \in N \setminus N^k$, this implies that $p^{k+1}(x^i - y^i) \geq p^{k+1}(\hat{x}^i - \hat{y}^i)$ whenever $(x^i, y^i) \in R^i(\hat{x}^i) \times Y^i$ satisfies $(x^i - y^i) - (\hat{x}^i - \hat{y}^i) \in L^k$. This completes the induction step.

Continue the construction, if necessary, until $k = \#G$. Arguing as in the proof of Lemmas 12 and 13, for each $i \in N \setminus N^{\#G-1}$, because $L^{\#G-1}$ has dimension one, one has $p^{\#G}(x^i - y^i) > p^{\#G}(\hat{x}^i - \hat{y}^i)$ whenever $(x^i, y^i) \in P^i(\hat{x}^i) \times Y^i$ satisfies $(x^i - y^i) - (\hat{x}^i - \hat{y}^i) \in L^{\#G-1}$. This implies that the feasible allocation $(\hat{x}^N, \hat{y}^N)$ is a hierarchical WELT given the price system $P = (p^1, \ldots, p^{\#G})$. □

5. WALRASIAN EQUILIBRIUM IN FINITE ECONOMIES

This section provides sufficient conditions for the Walrasian SCR to give a nonempty choice set. It will also be shown that, when WE allocations do exist, they must satisfy the "individual rationality" or weak gains from trade constraints requiring each agent to be no worse off than under autarky. Indeed, unless autarky happens to be at least weakly Pareto efficient, any WE allocation must make at least one agent strictly better off than under autarky.

5.1. Autarky

Autarky means that agents rely only on their own resources, including their own production possibilities, and do not trade with other agents at all. Accordingly, for each $i \in N$, say that $X^i \cap Y^i$ is agent i's *autarky consumption set*. We assume throughout this section that each $X^i \cap Y^i$ is nonempty and bounded, and also that agents' preferences are continuous. These assumptions imply that the sets X^i and Y^i are both closed, so $X^i \cap Y^i$ is obviously compact. It follows that there is a nonempty set

$$A^i := \{a^i \in X^i \cap Y^i \mid x^i \in X^i \cap Y^i \Longrightarrow a^i \; R^i \; x^i\}$$

of *optimal autarky consumption vectors*, all of which must be indifferent to each other. It follows that the set $R^i(a^i)$ is the same for all $a^i \in A^i$. From now on, we denote this set by $\hat{R}^i$.

5.2. Gains from Trade

Following both cooperative game theory and also social choice theory, the *individual rationality* or *participation* constraint of each agent $i \in N$ requires the consumption vector x^i to satisfy $x^i \in \hat{R}^i$. Thus, agent i is no worse off than under autarky. Using terminology closer to what is standard in general equilibrium theory, agent i experiences *weak gains from trade*.

Let $\hat{R}^N := \prod_{i \in N} \hat{R}^i$, and then define the *collective gains from trade set*

$$W := \{(x^N, y^N) \in \hat{R}^N \times Y^N \mid \sum_{i \in N} (x^i - y^i) = 0\}$$

of feasible allocations allowing each agent weak gains from trade. We assume that, like each agent's autarky set $X^i \cap Y^i$, the set W is also bounded. When preferences are continuous, it follows that W is also closed, so compact.

The following result ensures that any WE allocation $(\hat{x}^N, \hat{y}^N)$ confers collective gains from trade. In fact, a slightly stronger result is proved: except in trivial cases, at least one agent must experience strict gains from trade.

Theorem 23 (Gains from Trade Lemma) *Any WE $(\hat{x}^N, \hat{y}^N, \hat{p})$ satisfies $(\hat{x}^N, \hat{y}^N) \in W$. Furthermore, unless there happens to be an autarky allocation (x^N, y^N) with $x^i = y^i = a^i \in A^i$ (all $i \in N$) that is weakly Pareto efficient (or Pareto efficient if preferences are LNS), there must exist $h \in N$ such that $\hat{x}^h \; P^h \; a^h$ for all $a^h \in A^h$.*

Proof. For each $i \in N$, let a^i be any member of A^i. Because $(x^i, y^i) = (a^i, a^i)$ satisfies the Walrasian budget constraint $\hat{p}(x^i - y^i) \leq 0$, revealed preference implies that $\hat{x}^i \; R^i \; a^i$ in the Walrasian equilibrium. So $(\hat{x}^N, \hat{y}^N) \in W$.

Next, suppose that $\hat{x}^i \; I^i \; a^i$ for all $i \in N$. By the first efficiency theorem (Theorem 15), the WE allocation $(\hat{x}^N, \hat{y}^N)$ is weakly Pareto efficient (and Pareto efficient if preferences are LNS). So, therefore, is the autarky allocation $(\bar{x}^N, \bar{y}^N)$ with $\bar{x}^i = \bar{y}^i = a^i$ for all $i \in N$, because preferences are transitive. □

5.3. Existence of Compensated Walrasian Equilibrium

Theorem 24 (Compensated Equilibrium Existence) *Suppose that each agent $i \in N$ has LNS, convex, and continuous preferences, as well as a nonempty and bounded autarky consumption set $X^i \cap Y^i$. Suppose too that the collective gains from trade set W is bounded. Then there exists a compensated equilibrium $(\hat{x}^N, \hat{y}^N, \hat{p})$ with $(\hat{x}^N, \hat{y}^N) \in W$.*

Proof.

Step 1. The first step involves an ingenious construction that has become standard in general equilibrium existence proofs ever since Arrow and Debreu (1954). For each $i \in N$, let $\tilde{X}^i$ and $\tilde{Y}^i$ be compact convex subsets of $\mathbb{R}^G$ so large that W is contained within the interior of the Cartesian product set $\prod_{i \in N} (\tilde{X}^i \times \tilde{Y}^i)$. Then, for each $i \in N$, define the two constrained sets

$$\bar{X}^i := \tilde{X}^i \cap \hat{R}^i \quad \text{and} \quad \bar{Y}^i := \tilde{Y}^i \cap Y^i. \tag{17}$$

These are both convex, as intersections of two convex sets. Because $\tilde{X}^i$ and $\tilde{Y}^i$ are compact while $\hat{R}^i$ and Y^i are closed, the sets $\bar{X}^i$ and $\bar{Y}^i$ must be compact.

Step 2. Let D denote the domain of all price vectors $p \in \mathbb{R}^G$ (including 0) such that $\|p\| \leq 1$—that is, D is the unit ball in $\mathbb{R}^G$. Then, for each $i \in N$ and each $p \in D$, define the modified budget set

$$\bar{B}^i(p) := \{(x^i, y^i) \in \bar{X}^i \times \bar{Y}^i \mid p(x^i - y^i) \leq w(p)\}$$

where $w(p) := (\#N)^{-1}(1 - \|p\|)$.[16] This set is evidently compact and convex. It is also nonempty because it includes (a^i, a^i) for each $a^i \in A^i$.

Step 3. Next, we define the modified compensated demand set

$$\bar{\alpha}^i_C(p) := \{(x^i, y^i) \in \bar{B}^i(p) \mid (\tilde{x}^i, \tilde{y}^i) \in \bar{X}^i \times \bar{Y}^i, \; \tilde{x}^i \; P^i \; x^i \Longrightarrow p(\tilde{x}^i - \tilde{y}^i) \geq w(p)\}$$

[16] This modified wealth distribution rule adapts an approach that Bergstrom (1976) also uses in order to prove existence without assuming free disposal, while allowing prices to be negative as well as positive.

and verify that it is nonempty and convex. Indeed, $\bar{\alpha}^i_C(p)$ includes the nonempty modified uncompensated demand set

$$\bar{\alpha}^i_U(p) := \{(x^i, y^i) \in \bar{B}^i(p) \mid (\tilde{x}^i, \tilde{y}^i) \in \bar{B}^i(p) \Longrightarrow x^i \; R^i \; \tilde{x}^i\}$$

of pairs (x^i, y^i) that maximize agent i's continuous preference relation R^i over the compact set $\bar{B}^i(p)$.

To confirm that $\bar{\alpha}^i_C(p)$ is a convex set, suppose that $(x^i, y^i), (\hat{x}^i, \hat{y}^i)$ are any two points in $\bar{\alpha}^i_C(p)$ with $x^i \; R^i \; \hat{x}^i$, and let $(\bar{x}^i, \bar{y}^i) = \alpha(x^i, y^i) + (1 - \alpha)(\hat{x}^i, \hat{y}^i)$ with $0 \leq \alpha \leq 1$ be any convex combination. Because $\bar{B}^i(p)$ is a convex set, it includes $(\bar{x}^i, \bar{y}^i)$. The definition of $\bar{X}^i$ in (17) implies that $\bar{x}^i \; R^i \; \hat{x}^i$, because preferences are convex. Hence, whenever $(\tilde{x}^i, \tilde{y}^i) \in \bar{X}^i \times \bar{Y}^i$ with $\tilde{x}^i \; P^i \; \bar{x}^i$, then $\tilde{x}^i \; P^i \; \hat{x}^i$. By definition of $\bar{\alpha}^i_C(p)$, it follows that $p(\tilde{x}^i - \tilde{y}^i) \geq w(p)$. This shows that $(\bar{x}^i, \bar{y}^i) \in \bar{\alpha}^i_C(p)$, which must therefore be convex.

Also, for each $i \in N$ and each price vector $p \in D$, define the modified compensated net trade set

$$\bar{\zeta}^i_C(p) := \{z^i \in \mathbb{R}^G \mid \exists (x^i, y^i) \in \bar{\alpha}^i_C(p) : z^i = x^i - y^i\}.$$

This is also nonempty and convex for each p. So is the aggregate modified compensated net trade set defined by $\zeta(p) := \sum_{i \in N} \bar{\zeta}^i_C(p)$ for each $p \in D$.

Step 4. The next step is to show that the correspondence $p \mapsto\!\!\!\to \zeta(p)$ has a closed graph in $D \times \mathbb{R}^G$. To do so, suppose that the sequence of pairs $(p_n, z_n) \in D \times \mathbb{R}^G$ satisfies $z_n \in \zeta(p_n)$ for $n = 1, 2, \ldots$ and converges to a limit (p, z) as $n \to \infty$. Then for each $i \in N$ there exists, by definition, a corresponding sequence $(x^i_n, y^i_n) \in \bar{\alpha}^i_C(p_n)$ such that $z_n = \sum_{i \in N}(x^i_n - y^i_n)$ for $n = 1, 2, \ldots$. By construction, each profile (x^N_n, y^N_n) of consumption and production vectors is restricted to the compact set $\bar{X}^N \times \bar{Y}^N := \prod_{i \in N}(\bar{X}^i \times \bar{Y}^i)$. So there is a convergent subsequence with limit point $(x^N, y^N) \in \bar{X}^N \times \bar{Y}^N$. Because $z_n = \sum_{i \in N}(x^i_n - y^i_n)$ converges to z, it follows that $z = \sum_{i \in N}(x^i - y^i)$.

The rest of the argument loses no generality if one retains only the terms of this convergent subsequence, implying that $(x^N_n, y^N_n) \to (x^N, y^N)$ as $n \to \infty$. Then, because $(x^i_n, y^i_n) \in \bar{\alpha}^i_C(p_n) \subseteq \bar{B}^i(p_n)$ for each n, the budget constraint $p_n(x^i_n - y^i_n) \leq w(p_n)$ is satisfied. But $p_n \to p$ implies that $\|p_n\| \to \|p\|$ and so $w(p_n) \to w(p)$. Then, taking the limit as $n \to \infty$ shows that $p(x^i - y^i) \leq w(p)$. Hence, $(x^i, y^i) \in \bar{B}^i(p)$ for each $i \in N$.

Furthermore, whenever $(\tilde{x}^i, \tilde{y}^i) \in \bar{X}^i \times \bar{Y}^i$ satisfies $\tilde{x}^i \; P^i \; x^i$, then continuity of preferences implies that $\tilde{x}^i \; P^i \; x^i_n$ for each large n. Because $(x^i_n, y^i_n) \in \bar{\alpha}^i_C(p_n)$, it follows that $p_n(\tilde{x}^i - \tilde{y}^i) \geq w(p_n)$, so taking the limit as $n \to \infty$ shows that $p(\tilde{x}^i - \tilde{y}^i) \geq w(p)$. This confirms that $(x^i, y^i) \in \bar{\alpha}^i_C(p)$ for each $i \in N$.

But then $x^i - y^i \in \bar{\zeta}^i_C(p)$ for each $i \in N$, and so $z = \sum_{i \in N}(x^i - y^i) \in \zeta(p) = \sum_{i \in N} \bar{\zeta}^i_C(p)$. This confirms that the correspondence ζ has a closed graph.

Step 5. Next, let $\bar{Z} := \sum_{i \in N}(\bar{X}^i - \bar{Y}^i)$. Because all the sets $\bar{X}^i$ and $\bar{Y}^i$ are compact and convex, so are $\bar{Z}$ and $D \times \bar{Z}$.

The successive definitions of $\bar{B}^i(p)$, $\bar{\alpha}^i_C(p)$, $\bar{\zeta}^i_C(p)$, and $\zeta(p)$ together imply that $\zeta(p) \subseteq \bar{Z}$ for all $p \in D$. Define the correspondence $\phi : \bar{Z} \twoheadrightarrow D$ by

$$\phi(z) := \arg\max_p \{pz \mid p \in D\} = \begin{cases} \{z/\|z\|\} & \text{if } z \neq 0 \\ D & \text{if } z = 0 \end{cases}$$

because D is the unit ball in $\mathbb{R}^G$. Obviously $\phi(z)$ is nonempty and convex for all $z \in \bar{Z}$. Furthermore, because the mapping $z \mapsto z/\|z\|$ is continuous for all $z \neq 0$, and because $\bar{Z}$ and D are closed sets, it is easy to see that ϕ has a closed graph in $\bar{Z} \times D$.

Step 6. Consider, finally, the product correspondence $\psi : D \times \bar{Z} \twoheadrightarrow D \times \bar{Z}$ defined by $\psi(p, z) := \phi(z) \times \zeta(p)$. Because any Cartesian product of two convex sets is convex, while ϕ and ζ both have nonempty convex values throughout their respective domains $\bar{Z}$ and D, so does ψ throughout its domain $D \times \bar{Z}$. Also, the graph of the correspondence ψ is

$$\{(p, z, p', z') \in (D \times \bar{Z}) \times (D \times \bar{Z}) \mid p' \in \phi(z), z' \in \zeta(p)\}.$$

This is homeomorphic to the Cartesian product

$$\{(p, z') \in D \times \bar{Z} \mid z' \in \zeta(p)\} \times \{(z, p') \in \bar{Z} \times D \mid p' \in \phi(z)\}$$

of the graphs of ϕ and ζ, which are closed subsets of the respective compact sets $D \times \bar{Z}$ and $\bar{Z} \times D$. So the graph of ψ is a closed subset of the compact set $(D \times \bar{Z}) \times (D \times \bar{Z})$. Hence ψ actually has a compact graph.

To summarize, we have shown that $\psi : D \times \bar{Z} \twoheadrightarrow D \times \bar{Z}$ has a convex domain, nonempty convex values, and a compact graph. These properties allow Kakutani's fixed-point theorem to be applied. So there must exist $(\hat{p}, \hat{z}) \in D \times \bar{Z}$ with $(\hat{p}, \hat{z}) \in \psi(\hat{p}, \hat{z})$. This implies that $\hat{p} \in \phi(\hat{z})$ and $\hat{z} \in \zeta(\hat{p})$.

Step 7. The next step is to show that any fixed point $(\hat{p}, \hat{z})$ satisfies $\hat{z} = 0$. Indeed, the definition of ϕ implies that $\|p\| < 1$ for some $p \in \phi(z)$ only if $z = 0$. Hence either $\hat{z} = 0$, or $\|\hat{p}\| = 1$, or both.

Suppose $p \in D$ is any price vector satisfying $\|p\| = 1$. Then $z \in \zeta(p)$ only if $z = \sum_{i \in N}(x^i - y^i)$ for some collection $(x^N, y^N) \in \prod_{i \in N} \bar{\alpha}^i_C(p)$. But then

$p(x^i - y^i) \leq w(p)$ for all $i \in N$, implying that

$$pz = \sum_{i \in N} p(x^i - y^i) \leq \#Nw(p) = 1 - \|p\| = 0.$$

Yet $pz \leq 0$ for some $p \in \phi(z)$ only if $z = 0$. Because $\hat{p} \in \phi(\hat{z})$ and $\hat{z} \in \zeta(\hat{p})$, it follows that $\|\hat{p}\| = 1$ implies $\hat{z} = 0$. So $\hat{z} = 0$ whether or not $\|\hat{p}\| = 1$.

Step 8. It follows that $0 = \hat{z} = \sum_{i \in N}(\hat{x}^i - \hat{y}^i)$ for some collection $(\hat{x}^N, \hat{y}^N) \in \prod_{i \in N} \bar{\alpha}^i_C(\hat{p})$. In particular, $\hat{x}^i \in \bar{X}^i \subseteq \hat{R}^i$ for all $i \in N$. It follows that $(\hat{x}^N, \hat{y}^N)$ is a feasible allocation in the set W, a subset of the interior of $\prod_{i \in N}(\tilde{X}^i \times \tilde{Y}^i)$.

Step 9. Because each agent $i \in N$ has LNS preferences, by Lemma 1 there exists a sequence $x^i_n \in P^i(\hat{x}^i)$ that converges to $\hat{x}^i$. Because preferences are also transitive, one has $x^i_n \in \hat{R}^i$ for all $i \in N$ and for $n = 1, 2, \ldots$. Furthermore, $\hat{x}^i$ belongs to the interior of $\tilde{X}^i$, so $x^i_n \in \tilde{X}^i$ for large n, implying that $(x^i_n, \hat{y}^i) \in \bar{X}^i \times Y^i$. Because $(\hat{x}^i, \hat{y}^i) \in \bar{\alpha}^i_C(\hat{p})$, it follows that $\hat{p}(x^i_n - \hat{y}^i) \geq w(\hat{p})$ for large n. Taking the limit as $n \to \infty$ yields $\hat{p}(\hat{x}^i - \hat{y}^i) \geq w(\hat{p})$. But $(\hat{x}^i, \hat{y}^i) \in \bar{B}^i(\hat{p})$, so $\hat{p}(\hat{x}^i - \hat{y}^i) \leq w(\hat{p})$. This shows that $\hat{p}(\hat{x}^i - \hat{y}^i) = w(\hat{p})$ for all $i \in N$.

Then, because $0 = \sum_{i \in N}(\hat{x}^i - \hat{y}^i)$, summing over all $i \in N$ implies $w(\hat{p}) = 0$. By definition of $w(\hat{p})$, it follows that $\|\hat{p}\| = 1$, and also that $\hat{p}(\hat{x}^i - \hat{y}^i) = 0$ for all $i \in N$.

Step 10. Finally we verify that, for each agent $i \in N$, the pair $(\hat{x}^i, \hat{y}^i)$ is a compensated demand subject to the budget constraint $\hat{p}(x^i - y^i) \leq 0$. Because $(\hat{x}^N, \hat{y}^N) \in W$, a subset of the interior of $\prod_{i \in N}(\tilde{X}^i \times \tilde{Y}^i)$, it follows from the construction in Step 1 that $(\hat{x}^i, \hat{y}^i)$ is an interior point of the convex set $\tilde{X}^i \times \tilde{Y}^i$.

Now suppose that $(x^i, y^i) \in R^i(\hat{x}^i) \times Y^i$. For small enough $\lambda > 0$, the convex combination $(1 - \lambda)(\hat{x}^i, \hat{y}^i) + \lambda(x^i, y^i)$ belongs to $\tilde{X}^i \times \tilde{Y}^i$, as well as to $X^i \times Y^i$. In fact, because preferences are convex and transitive, this convex combination also belongs to $R^i(\hat{x}^i) \times Y^i \subseteq \hat{R}^i \times Y^i$, and so to $\bar{X}^i \times \bar{Y}^i$. But $(\hat{x}^i, \hat{y}^i) \in \bar{\alpha}^i_C(\hat{p})$ and $\|\hat{p}\| = 1$, so

$$\hat{p}[(1 - \lambda)(\hat{x}^i - \hat{y}^i) + \lambda(x^i - y^i)] \geq w(\hat{p}) = 0.$$

Because $\hat{p}(\hat{x}^i - \hat{y}^i) = 0$ and $\lambda > 0$, this implies that $\hat{p}(x^i - y^i) \geq 0$.

This last step completes the proof that $(\hat{x}^N, \hat{y}^N, \hat{p})$ is a compensated equilibrium satisfying $\hat{x}^i \in \hat{R}^i$ for all $i \in N$. □

5.4. Directional Irreducibility and Existence of Walrasian Equilibrium

To show that the CE of Theorem 24 is a WE, the obvious procedure is to apply the cheaper point Lemma 12. A sufficient condition for this to be valid is that each agent's autarky set $X^i \cap Y^i$ should have an interior point. Yet this seems unduly restrictive because, for example, it requires each agent to have the capacity to supply a positive net quantity of all goods simultaneously.

Instead, we start with the standard aggregate interiority assumption of Section 3.9 requiring that $0 \in \text{int} \sum_{i \in N} (X^i - Y^i)$. This ensures that at least one agent has a cheaper point. Some additional condition is still required, however, in order to ensure that *every* individual agent has a cheaper point. Any such additional condition will differ somewhat from the nonoligarchy assumption used in the latter part of Section 4. For one thing, we cannot simply assume that all feasible allocations are nonoligarchic because our continuity and boundedness assumptions actually guarantee the existence of oligarchic allocations. Assume instead that, given any feasible allocation and any proper subset of agents $K \subset N$, the agents in $N \setminus K$ start with resources allowing them to offer an aggregate net supply vector that is desired by the agents in K. In case the agents in K all have cheaper points in some compensated equilibrium, this condition ensures that this aggregate net supply vector of the other agents has positive value at the equilibrium price vector.

Arrow and Debreu (1954) were the first to introduce a condition of this kind. Adapted to the framework used here, their condition requires the existence of two nonempy sets $G_D, G_P \subset G$—of *desirable commodities* and *productive inputs*, respectively—with the properties:

(1) given any $i \in N$, any $x^i \in X^i$, and any $g \in G_D$, there exists $\tilde{x}^i \in P^i(x^i)$ such that $\tilde{x}^i_h = x^i_h$ for all $h \in G \setminus \{g\}$, while $\tilde{x}^i_g > x^i_g$;

(2) given any $g \in G_P$ and any $y \in \sum_{i \in N} Y^i$, there exists $\tilde{y} \in \sum_{i \in N} Y^i$ such that $\tilde{y}_h \geq y_h$ for all $h \in G \setminus \{g\}$, with $\tilde{y}_h > y_h$ for at least one $h \in G_D$;

(3) given any $i \in N$, there exist $g \in G_P$ and $(\bar{x}^i, \bar{y}^i) \in X^i \times Y^i$ such that $\bar{x}^i \leqq \bar{y}^i$ with $\bar{x}^i_g < \bar{y}^i_g$.

McKenzie (1959, 1961) introduced a more general sufficient condition. He defined an economy as *irreducible* provided that, for any proper subset $K \subset N$ and any feasible allocation $(\hat{x}^N, \hat{y}^N)$, there exist $(x^N, y^N) \in X^N \times Y^N$ such that $x^i \; P^i \; \hat{x}^i$ for all $i \in K$ and $\sum_{i \in K} [(x^i - y^i) - (\hat{x}^i - \hat{y}^i)] = -\sum_{i \in N \setminus K} (x^i - y^i)$—or, equivalently, $\sum_{i \in N} (x^i - y^i) + \sum_{i \in N \setminus K} (\hat{x}^i - \hat{y}^i) = 0$.[17] This condition can be interpreted as requiring the existence of appropriate consumption and production vectors $(x^i, y^i) \in X^i \times Y^i$ for all $i \in N \setminus K$ such that, if the feasible aggregate net supply vector $-\sum_{i \in N \setminus K}(x^i - y^i)$ became available from outside the economy, these additional exogenous resources could be distributed as incremental net trade vectors $(x^i - y^i) - (\hat{x}^i - \hat{y}^i)$ to the agents $i \in K$ in a way that benefits them all simultaneously, without affecting the other agents $i \in N \setminus K$ at all. It is easy to check that an economy satisfying the Arrow–Debreu condition just described earlier must be irreducible.

[17] This follows an earlier idea due to Gale (1957)—see also Gale (1976), Eaves (1976), and Hammond (1993).

In order to ensure that a CE is a WE, a number of variations of McKenzie's original definitions have been propounded, including Arrow and Hahn's (1971) concept of "resource relatedness"—direct or indirect. Some systematic exploration of these concepts was attempted in Spivak (1978) and Hammond (1993). The discussion has since been advanced by Florig (2001b) and by McKenzie (2002) himself.[18] Rather than pursue this further, the discussion here concentrates on a version of irreducibility that seems weaker than all other versions, yet remains sufficient for any CE to be a WE. Following the recent suggestion of Florig (2001b, p. 189), this weakened definition has the property that "only directions matter and not magnitudes."

First, given the particular feasible allocation $(\hat{x}^N, \hat{y}^N)$, define $U^i(\hat{x}^i, \hat{y}^i)$ as the convex cone of vectors $\lambda[(x^i - y^i) - (\hat{x}^i - \hat{y}^i)]$ with $\lambda > 0$, $x^i \in P^i(\hat{x}^i)$, and $y^i \in Y^i$. Thus, $U^i(\hat{x}^i, \hat{y}^i)$ consists of directions that allow agent i's net trade vector to be improved by moving an appropriate distance away from $\hat{x}^i - \hat{y}^i$.

Second, define $V^i(\hat{x}^i, \hat{y}^i)$ as the closed convex cone of vectors $\lambda[(x^i - y^i) - (\hat{x}^i - \hat{y}^i)]$ with $\lambda \geq 0$ and $(x^i, y^i) \in X^i \times Y^i$. Thus, $V^i(\hat{x}^i, \hat{y}^i)$ consists of directions in which it is feasible to change agent i's net trade vector by moving an appropriate distance away from $\hat{x}^i - \hat{y}^i$.

Third, define W^i as the convex cone of vectors $-\mu(x^i - y^i)$ with $\mu \geq 0$, $x^i \in X^i$, and $y^i \in Y^i$. Thus, W^i consists of directions in which resources can be removed from agent i without violating individual feasibility.

Finally, define Z^i as the convex cone of vectors $-\nu(\hat{x}^i - \hat{y}^i)$ with $\nu \geq 0$. Thus, Z^i is the half-line of nonpositive multiples of $\hat{x}^i - \hat{y}^i$ when $\hat{x}^i \neq \hat{y}^i$; but $Z^i = \{0\}$ when $\hat{x}^i = \hat{y}^i$.

With these definitions, the economy is said to be *directionally irreducible* provided that, for any proper subset $K \subset N$ (with both K and $N \setminus K$ nonempty) and any feasible allocation $(\hat{x}^N, \hat{y}^N)$, the two sets

$$\sum_{i \in K} U^i(\hat{x}^i, \hat{y}^i) + \sum_{i \in N \setminus K} V^i(\hat{x}^i, \hat{y}^i) \quad \text{and} \quad \sum_{i \in N \setminus K} W^i + \sum_{i \in N} Z^i$$

intersect. This is obviously a weaker condition than McKenzie's (1959, 1961) original version of the irreducibility assumption.

Theorem 25 *Suppose agents have convex consumption and production sets, as well as LNS and continuous preferences. Suppose too* $0 \in \operatorname{int} \sum_{i \in N} (X^i - Y^i)$, *and the economy is directionally irreducible. Then any CE is a WE.*

[18] Translated to the present context, McKenzie (2002, p. 172) defines an economy as irreducible when, for any proper subset $K \subset N$ and any feasible allocation $(\hat{x}^N, \hat{y}^N)$, there exist $(x^i, y^i) \in X^i \times Y^i$ for all $i \in K$ and a scalar $\lambda > 0$ such that $x^i \, P^i \, \hat{x}^i$ for all $i \in K$ and

$$\sum_{i \in K} [(x^i - y^i) - (\hat{x}^i - \hat{y}^i)] + \lambda \sum_{i \in N \setminus K} (x^i - y^i) = 0.$$

Proof. Let $(\hat{x}^N, \hat{y}^N, \hat{p})$ be a CE. Because $0 \in \textbf{int} \sum_{i \in N} (X^i - Y^i)$, Lemma 14 implies that there exist $h \in N$ and $(\underline{x}^h, \underline{y}^h) \in X^h \times Y^h$ such that $\hat{p}(\underline{x}^h - \underline{y}^h) < 0$.

Let K be any proper subset of N whose members all have such cheaper points. By directional irreducibility, there exist:

(1) $(x^N, y^N) \in X^N \times Y^N$ and $\lambda^i \geq 0$ (all $i \in N$) with $x^i \; P^i \; \hat{x}^i$ and $\lambda^i > 0$ for all $i \in K$;
(2) $(\bar{x}^i, \bar{y}^i) \in X^i \times Y^i$ and $\mu^i \geq 0$ for all $i \in N \setminus K$;
(3) $\nu^i \geq 0$ for all $i \in N$;

such that

$$\sum_{i \in N} \lambda^i [(x^i - y^i) - (\hat{x}^i - \hat{y}^i)] + \sum_{i \in N \setminus K} \mu^i (\bar{x}^i - \bar{y}^i) + \sum_{i \in N} \nu^i (\hat{x}^i - \hat{y}^i) = 0. \tag{18}$$

Because $(\hat{x}^N, \hat{y}^N, \hat{p})$ is a CE, Lemma 12 implies that $\hat{p}(x^i - y^i) > 0$ for all $i \in K$. Also, because preferences are LNS, Theorem 10 implies that $\hat{p}(\hat{x}^i - \hat{y}^i) = 0$ for all $i \in N$. From (18) it follows that

$$\hat{p} \sum_{i \in N \setminus K} [\lambda^i (x^i - y^i) + \mu^i (\bar{x}^i - \bar{y}^i)] = -\hat{p} \sum_{i \in K} \lambda^i (x^i - y^i) < 0.$$

So at least one $i \in N \setminus K$ has either $\lambda^i \hat{p}(x^i - y^i) < 0$ or $\mu^i \hat{p}(\bar{x}^i - \bar{y}^i) < 0$. Because $\lambda^i \geq 0$ and $\mu^i \geq 0$ for all $i \in N \setminus K$, at least one $i \in N \setminus K$ has either (x^i, y^i) or $(\bar{x}^i, \bar{y}^i)$ as a cheaper point. Hence, K cannot include all agents with cheaper points. The only remaining possibility is that all agents have cheaper points. By Lemma 12, this implies that the CE is actually a WE. □

5.5. Extended Irreducibility

Developing a suggestion of Spivak (1978) along the lines of Hammond (1993), it will be shown that a slight weakening of irreducibility is a necessary condition for being able to apply the line of reasoning used to prove Theorem 25.

The economy is said to be *extended irreducible* provided that, for any proper subset $K \subset N$ and any feasible allocation $(\hat{x}^N, \hat{y}^N)$, there exist $(x^N, y^N) \in X^N \times Y^N$ and $\nu^i \in [0, 1]$ (all $i \in N$) such that $x^i \; P^i \; \hat{x}^i$ for all $i \in K$ and $\sum_{i \in N} (x^i - y^i) + \sum_{i \in N \setminus K} (\hat{x}^i - \hat{y}^i) = \sum_{i \in N} \nu^i (\hat{x}^i - \hat{y}^i)$.

Theorem 26 *Suppose autarky is feasible for each agent, while preferences are LNS, convex, and continuous. Unless the economy is extended irreducible, there exists a CE with a nonempty set of agents at their cheapest points.*

Proof. Unless the economy is extended irreducible, there exist a proper subset $K \subset N$ and a feasible allocation $(\hat{x}^N, \hat{y}^N)$ such that

$$0 \notin Z := \sum_{i \in K} [P^i(\hat{x}^i) - Y^i] + \sum_{i \in N \setminus K} (\{\hat{x}^i - \hat{y}^i\} + X^i - Y^i)$$
$$- \sum_{i \in N} \{\nu^i(\hat{x}^i - \hat{y}^i) \mid \nu^i \in [0,1]\}. \tag{19}$$

Because Z is the sum of convex sets, it is convex. So it can be separated from the origin. Hence, there exists a price vector $p \neq 0$ such that

$$0 \leq \inf p\, Z. \tag{20}$$

For all $i \in K$, let

$$\alpha^i := \inf p\,[P^i(\hat{x}^i) - Y^i] \leq w^i := p\,(\hat{x}^i - \hat{y}^i), \tag{21}$$

where the inequality holds because preferences are LNS and so $(\hat{x}^i, \hat{y}^i) \in \operatorname{cl} P^i(\hat{x}^i) \times Y^i$. Next, for all $i \in N \setminus K$, let

$$\beta^i := \inf p\,(X^i - Y^i) \leq 0, \tag{22}$$

where the inequality holds because autarky is feasible. From (19) to (22),

$$0 \leq \sum_{i \in K} \alpha^i + \sum_{i \in N \setminus K} (w^i + \beta^i) + \sum_{i \in N} \inf\{-\nu^i w^i \mid \nu^i \in [0,1]\}$$
$$\leq \sum_{i \in N} (w^i + \min\{0, -w^i\}) = \sum_{i \in N} \min\{0, w^i\} \leq 0. \tag{23}$$

Hence $0 = \sum_{i \in N} \min\{0, w^i\}$, which is only possible when $w^i \geq 0$ for all $i \in N$. But (21) and feasibility of the allocation $(\hat{x}^N, \hat{y}^N)$ together imply that $\sum_{i \in N} w^i = \sum_{i \in N} p\,(\hat{x}^i - \hat{y}^i) = 0$, so $w^i = 0$ for all $i \in N$. Then (23) reduces to

$$0 = \sum_{i \in K} \alpha^i + \sum_{i \in N \setminus K} \beta^i. \tag{24}$$

But (21) implies that $\alpha^i \leq w^i = 0$ for all $i \in K$, whereas (22) implies that $\beta^i \leq 0$ for all $i \in N \setminus K$. From (24), these inequalities imply that $\alpha^i = 0$ for all $i \in K$ and $\beta^i = 0$

for all $i \in N \setminus K$. Substituting these into the definitions (21) and (22), one obtains

$$\inf p\,[P^i(\hat{x}^i) - Y^i] = 0 \quad \text{for all } i \in K$$

$$\text{and} \quad \inf p\,(X^i - Y^i) = 0 \quad \text{for all } i \in N \setminus K.$$

Because preferences are LNS, these properties together imply that $(\hat{x}^N, \hat{y}^N, p)$ is a CE in which each agent $i \in N \setminus K$ is at a cheapest point. □

6. CHARACTERIZATIONS OF WE WITH A FIXED PROFILE OF AGENTS' TYPES

6.1. Walrasian Acceptability

Thomson (1983) offers a characterization of Walrasian equilibrium with equal budgets (actually, from equal division) based on a notion of equity related to a criterion he calls "acceptability." The following adaptation and simplification treats Walrasian equilibrium more generally, based on net trade vectors.

Let Π^N denote the set of permutations $\sigma : N \to N$. Say that the feasible allocation $(\hat{x}^N, \hat{y}^N)$ is *Walrasian acceptable* if it is a WELT and, for each $\sigma \in \Pi^N$, relative to the *permuted wealth distribution rule* $\tilde{w}^N(p)$ defined by

$$\tilde{w}^i(p) := p\,(\hat{x}^{\sigma(i)} - \hat{y}^{\sigma(i)}) \tag{25}$$

for all $p \in \mathbb{R}^G \setminus \{0\}$, there exists a WELT $(\tilde{x}^N, \tilde{y}^N, \tilde{p})$ such that $\hat{x}^i \; R^i \; \tilde{x}^i$ for all $i \in N$. Thus, no matter how the equilibrium net trade vectors $\hat{x}^i - \hat{y}^i$ are permuted in order to determine an alternative wealth distribution rule, there always exists a new WELT relative to this alternative rule that no agent prefers to the original WELT.

Theorem 27 *Provided that preferences are LNS, any WE allocation is Walrasian acceptable.*

Proof. If $(\hat{x}^N, \hat{y}^N, \hat{p})$ is a WE and preferences are LNS, Theorem 10 implies that $\hat{p}\,(\hat{x}^i - \hat{y}^i) = 0$ for all $i \in N$. It follows that the same WE is a WELT relative to each permuted wealth distribution rule defined by (25). □

Theorem 28 *If $(\hat{x}^N, \hat{y}^N)$ is Walrasian acceptable, then there exists a price vector $\tilde{p} \neq 0$ such that $(\hat{x}^N, \hat{y}^N, \tilde{p})$ is a WE.*

Proof. Label the set N of individuals as i_k $(k = 1, 2, \ldots, \#N)$. Then let $\sigma \in \Pi^N$ be the particular permutation defined by $\sigma(i_k) := i_{k+1}$ for all $k = 1, 2, \ldots, \#N - 1$ and

$\sigma(i_{\#N}) := i_1$. By hypothesis, there must exist a WELT $(\tilde{x}^N, \tilde{y}^N, \tilde{p})$ relative to the permuted rule (25) such that $\hat{x}^i \; R^i \; \tilde{x}^i$ for all $i \in N$. Because preferences are LNS, Lemma 9 and Theorem 10 imply that

$$\tilde{p}(\hat{x}^i - \hat{y}^i) \geq w^i(\tilde{p}) = \tilde{p}(\hat{x}^{\sigma(i)} - \hat{y}^{\sigma(i)})$$

for all $i \in N$. By definition of σ, it follows that $\tilde{p}(\hat{x}^i - \hat{y}^i)$ is independent of i. But $\sum_{i \in N}(\hat{x}^i - \hat{y}^i) = 0$, so $\tilde{p}(\hat{x}^i - \hat{y}^i) = 0$ for all $i \in N$.

Finally, suppose $(x^i, y^i) \in P^i(\hat{x}^i) \times Y^i$. Then $x^i \in P^i(\tilde{x}^i)$ because $\hat{x}^i \; R^i \; \tilde{x}^i$ and preferences are transitive. But $(\tilde{x}^N, \tilde{y}^N, \tilde{p})$ is a WELT, so

$$\tilde{p}(x^i - y^i) > w^i(\tilde{p}) = \tilde{p}(\hat{x}^{\sigma(i)} - \hat{y}^{\sigma(i)}) = 0.$$

This proves that $(\hat{x}^N, \hat{y}^N, \tilde{p})$ is a WE. □

6.2. Equal Rights to Multiple Proportional Trade

The following discussion of "equal rights to trade" develops some of the ideas in Schmeidler and Vind (1972). It offers a different "fairness" characterization of Walrasian equilibrium without lump-sum transfers.

6.2.1. Definitions

In this section we assume that each agent $i \in N$ has a feasible set of net trades T^i and an associated preference ordering $\succsim^i$ on T^i, as described in Section 2.6. Let $F := \{t^N \in T^N \mid \sum_{i \in N} t^i = 0\}$ denote the feasible set of *balanced allocations* of net trade vectors to the different agents in the economy.

Given the allocation $\bar{t}^N \in F$, agent i is said to *envy* agent h if $\bar{t}^h \in T^i$ with $\bar{t}^h \succ^i \bar{t}^i$. On the other hand, the allocation $\bar{t}^N \in F$ is *envy-free* if $\bar{t}^i \succsim^i \bar{t}^h$ for all $h, i \in N$ such that $\bar{t}^h \in T^i$. Say that the allocation $\bar{t}^N \in F$ is *strongly envy-free* if $\bar{t}^i \succsim^i \sum_{h \in N} n^h \bar{t}^h$ for all $i \in N$ and all collections of non-negative integers $n^h \in \mathbb{Z}_+$ $(h \in N)$ such that $\sum_{h \in N} n^h \bar{t}^h \in T^i$.[19]

Next, say that the feasible allocation $\bar{t}^N \in F$ offers *equal rights to trade* if there exists a common *trading set* $B \subseteq \mathbb{R}^G$ such that, for all $i \in N$, both $\bar{t}^i \in B$ and also $t^i \in B \cap T^i \Longrightarrow \bar{t}^i \succsim^i t^i$.

Because $\bar{t}^h \in B$ for all $h \in N \setminus \{i\}$, offering the common trading set B gives all agents $i \in N$ the right to choose, in particular, any other agent's net trade vector $\bar{t}^h$ instead

[19] Schmeidler and Vind (1972) call such allocations "strongly fair." Note too that what they describe as a "Walras net trade" has only to satisfy the budget constraint $pt = 0$ at the specified price vector $p \neq 0$; if preference maximization also holds, even in a restricted set, they call the net trade vector "competitive."

of their own, provided that $\bar{t}^h \in T^i$. Accordingly, equal rights to trade imply that the allocation $\bar{t}^N$ is envy-free.

Say that there are *equal rights to multiple trade* if the set B is closed under addition—that is, $B + B \subseteq B$. Thus, an agent $i \in N$ who has the right to trade either of the net trade vectors $t^i, \tilde{t}^i$ in B also has the right to the combined net trade vector $t^i + \tilde{t}^i$. As Schmeidler and Vind (1972, Theorem 1) demonstrate, if $\bar{t}^N \in F$ offers equal rights to multiple trade within a set B satisfying $0 \in B$, then $\bar{t}^N$ is strongly envy-free.

Also, say that there are *equal rights to proportional trade* if the set B is closed under multiplication by any non-negative scalar—that is, $\lambda B \subseteq B$ for all $\lambda \geq 0$, implying that B is a cone. Thus, each agent enjoys the right to any multiple of an allowable net trade vector, with both supplies and demands re-scaled in the same proportion. This extension is related to, but somewhat different from, Schmeidler and Vind's (1972) divisibility condition. Finally, say that there are *equal rights to multiple proportional trade* if both of the last two properties are satisfied, implying that $\lambda B + \mu B \subseteq B$ whenever $\lambda, \mu \geq 0$, so B must be a convex cone.

Obviously, if $(\bar{t}^N, p)$ is a WE, then there are equal rights to multiple proportional trade within the *Walrasian budget set* $B_p := \{t \in \mathbb{R}^G \mid pt = 0\}$, a linear subspace of $\mathbb{R}^G$.

6.2.2. Two Preliminary Lemmas

Given any allocation $\bar{t}^N \in F \subseteq (\mathbb{R}^G)^N$, let $L(\bar{t}^N)$ denote the linear subspace of $\mathbb{R}^G$ spanned by the associated set $\{\bar{t}^i \mid i \in N\}$ of net trade vectors. The following simple result will be used later:

Lemma 29 *Suppose preferences are nonsatiated, and the feasible allocation $\bar{t}^N \in F$ offers equal rights to multiple proportional trade within the convex cone B. Then $L(\bar{t}^N) \subseteq B$, and $L(\bar{t}^N)$ is of dimension $\#G - 1$ at most.*

Proof. First, because $\bar{t}^N \in F$ and so $\sum_{i \in N} \bar{t}^i = 0$, note that $-\bar{t}^i = \sum_{h \in N \setminus \{i\}} \bar{t}^h$. Second, by definition of equal rights to trade within B, one has $\bar{t}^h \in B$ for all $h \in N$. Because B is a convex cone, this implies that $-\bar{t}^i \in B$ for all $i \in N$. It follows that B must contain every linear combination $\sum_{i \in N} \lambda^i \bar{t}^i$ of the set $\{\bar{t}^i \mid i \in N\}$ of net trade vectors, no matter what the sign of each scalar $\lambda^i \in \mathbb{R}$ may be. This proves that $L(\bar{t}^N) \subseteq B$.

Next, because $\succsim^i$ is nonsatiated, there exists $\hat{t}^i \in T^i$ with $\hat{t}^i \succ^i \bar{t}^i$. Because there are equal rights to trade within the set B, one has $t^i \in B \cap T^i \Longrightarrow \bar{t}^i \succsim^i t^i$, so B cannot include $\hat{t}^i$. Nor therefore can the subset $L(\bar{t}^N)$ of B. This proves that $L(\bar{t}^N)$ must be of dimension less than $\#G$. □

The next result is in the spirit of Schmeidler and Vind (1972, Theorem 4).

Lemma 30 *Suppose that the feasible allocation $\bar{t}^N \in F$ offers equal rights to multiple proportional trade within some common convex cone B that contains a linear subspace $L \subseteq \mathbb{R}^G$ of dimension $\#G - 1$. Then $\bar{t}^N$ is a WE at some price vector $p \neq 0$.*

Proof. If L is a subspace of dimension $\#G-1$, it is a hyperplane through the origin, so $L = B_p := \{t \in \mathbb{R}^G \mid pt = 0\}$ for some $p \neq 0$. But each agent $i \in N$ has the right to trade within B_p, so $\bar{t}^i \in B_p$ and also $t^i \in B_p \cap T^i \Longrightarrow \bar{t}^i \succsim^i t^i$. Because $\bar{t}^N \in F$, it follows that $(\bar{t}^N, p)$ is a WE. □

6.2.3. Pareto Efficiency

So far, equal rights to multiple proportional trade are consistent with the common budget set B being a linear subspace of low dimension—in fact, even $B = \{0\}$ is possible, with enforced autarky. Supplementing equal rights to trade with Pareto efficiency avoids this trivial case, unless autarky happens to be Pareto efficient anyway. This leads to the following characterization:[20]

Theorem 31 *Suppose agents' preferences for net trades are LNS and convex. Let $\bar{t}^N \in F$ be any weakly Pareto efficient allocation offering equal rights to multiple proportional trade. Assume that at least one agent $h \in N$ has preferences represented by a utility function $u^h(t^h)$ that is differentiable at $\bar{t}^h$. Then $\bar{t}^N$ is a CE at some price vector $p \neq 0$.*

Proof. Let p denote the gradient vector of u^h at $\bar{t}^h$. Given any $v \in L(\bar{t}^N)$, one has $\bar{t}^h + \lambda v \in L(\bar{t}^N)$ for all $\lambda > 0$ because $\bar{t}^h \in L(\bar{t}^N)$ and $L(\bar{t}^N)$ is a linear subspace. By Lemma 29, equal rights to multiple proportional trade within the convex cone B imply that $L(\bar{t}^N) \subseteq B$. So $\bar{t}^h + \lambda v \in B$ for all $\lambda > 0$, from which it follows that $\bar{t}^h \succsim^h \bar{t}^h + \lambda v$. By definition of p, it follows that $pv \leq 0$. But this is true for all v in the linear subspace $L(\bar{t}^N)$, so $pv = 0$ for all $v \in L(\bar{t}^N)$. In particular, $p\bar{t}^i = 0$ for all $i \in N$.

By Theorem 16, the Pareto efficient allocation $\bar{t}^N$ must be a CELT at some common supporting price vector $\bar{p} \neq 0$. Because p is the gradient vector of u^h at $\bar{t}^h$, the common supporting price vector $\bar{p}$ must be a positive multiple of p, so can be replaced by p. But $p\bar{t}^i = 0$ for all $i \in N$, so $\bar{t}^N$ is a CE at the price vector $p \neq 0$. □

6.3. Interactive Opportunity Sets

One of the oldest ideas in economics is that agents who exploit arbitrage or other trading opportunities will be driven toward a Walrasian equilibrium. Some relatively recent attempts to formalize this idea have appeared in Fisher (1981, 1983)—see also Fisher and Saldanha (1982), as well as Stahl and Fisher (1988). That work, however, typically assumes that all agents trade at a common price vector, and asks when awareness of disequilibrium will lead that price vector to change.[21] Instead, this section summarizes some striking results due to Serrano and Volij (2000) that derive rather than presume the existence of (uniform) market price vectors.

[20] More general results of this kind appear in Hammond (2003).

[21] For a different approach to arbitrage opportunities, see Makowski and Ostroy (1995, 1998, 2001), as well as the discussion in Section 15.2.

Consider the general framework of Section 3.1 in which agents $i \in N$ have types described by consumption sets X^i, production sets Y^i, and preference orderings R^i. Serrano and Volij suggest constructing recursively a sequence $Z^{i,m}(x^N)$ $(m = 0, 1, 2, \ldots)$ of *multilateral interactive opportunity sets* defined for each agent $i \in N$ and each profile of consumption vectors $x^N \in X^N$.[22] The construction starts when $m = 0$ with the obvious sets $Z^{i,0}(x^N) := Y^i$ of consumption vectors that each agent $i \in N$ can achieve without any trade at all. Given any fixed m and $x^N \in X^N$, as well as the previously constructed sets $Z^{i,m}(x^N)$ $(i \in N)$, the next step is to construct the set

$$Z^{i,m+1}(x^N) := Z^{i,m}(x^N) - \sum_{h \in N \setminus \{i\}} \left([R^h(x^h) - Z^{h,m}(x^N)] \cup \{0\} \right) \tag{26}$$

for each agent $i \in N$. Thus $\hat{x}^i \in Z^{i,m+1}(x^N)$ iff $\hat{x}^i = \tilde{x}^i - \sum_{h \in K} t^h$ for some combination of a consumption vector $\tilde{x}^i \in Z^{i,m}(x^N)$, a set of trading partners $K \subseteq N \setminus \{i\}$, and a collection of incremental net trade vectors $t^h \in R^h(x^h) - Z^{h,m}(x^N)$ that leave all the agents $h \in K$ no worse off than they are at x^N, provided they also make appropriate use of their mth-order opportunity sets $Z^{h,m}(x^N)$. This construction evidently implies that $Z^{i,m}(x^N) \subseteq Z^{i,m+1}(x^N)$ for all $i \in N$ and for $m = 0, 1, 2, \ldots$. So the limit sets $Z^i(x^N) := \cup_{m=0}^{\infty} Z^{i,m}(x^N)$ are well defined, for each $i \in N$ and $x^N \in X^N$.

An alternative construction leads to a sequence $\tilde{Z}^{i,m}(x^N)$ $(m = 0, 1, 2, \ldots)$ of *bilateral interactive opportunity sets*, with $\tilde{Z}^{i,0}(x^N) := Y^i$ as before, but with (26) replaced by

$$\tilde{Z}^{i,m+1}(x^N) := \tilde{Z}^{i,m}(x^N) - \left(\cup_{h \in N \setminus \{i\}} [R^h(x^h) - Z^{h,m}(x^N)] \cup \{0\} \right). \tag{27}$$

This is equivalent to letting i trade with at most one other agent $h \in N \setminus \{i\}$ when adding an incremental net trade vector to the elements of $\tilde{Z}^{i,m}(x^N)$. As before, $\tilde{Z}^{i,m}(x^N) \subseteq \tilde{Z}^{i,m+1}(x^N)$ for $m = 0, 1, 2, \ldots$, so one can define each limit set $\tilde{Z}^i(x^N) := \cup_{m=0}^{\infty} \tilde{Z}^{i,m}(x^N)$ (for all $i \in N$ and $x^N \in X^N$). Given any $i \in N$ and $x^N \in X^N$, an obvious argument by induction on m shows that $\tilde{Z}^{i,m}(x^N) \subseteq Z^{i,m}(x^N)$ for $m = 0, 1, 2, \ldots$, so $\tilde{Z}^i(x^N) \subseteq Z^i(x^N)$.

Serrano and Volij (2000) derive their results under the assumption that there is a pure exchange economy with $X^i = \mathbb{R}^G_+$ and $Y^i = \{e^i\} \subset \mathbb{R}^G_{++}$ for all $i \in N$, and with continuous monotone preference orderings R^i on $\mathbb{R}^G_+$. Their Proposition 1 then states that the multilateral and bilateral interactive opportunity sets $Z^i(x^N)$ and $\tilde{Z}^i(x^N)$ are always identical. The following summarizes their Theorem 1′:

[22] Serrano and Volij (2000) use the term "interactive choice set." In social choice theory, however, it is common to reserve the term "choice set" for the set of *chosen* options rather than the feasible set of available options.

Theorem 32 *In a pure exchange economy with strictly positive endowments and continuous monotone preference orderings, the allocation $\hat{x}^N$ is a WE if and only if the consumption vector $\hat{x}^i$ of each agent $i \in N$ maximizes R^i over either of the (identical) opportunity sets $Z^i(\hat{x}^N)$ and $\tilde{Z}^i(\hat{x}^N)$.*

The key idea of the proof they provide is expressed in their Theorem 4. This states that if the consumption profile x^N admits the existence of any $\tilde{x}^i \in P^i(x^i) \cap Z^i(x^N)$, then in a large enough replica economy of the kind described in Section 8.1, agent i can gain by joining a coalition that blocks x^N. So the result follows from the well-known Debreu–Scarf limit theorem for the core of an infinitely replicated economy of that kind.

Note that if preferences are not convex, Theorem 32 still holds formally, though there may be no WE.

7. CHARACTERIZATIONS OF WE WITH A VARIABLE PROFILE OF AGENTS' TYPES

7.1. Minimal Message Spaces

Consider pure exchange economies in which the type of each agent $i \in N$ can be expressed as $\theta^i = (X^i, e^i, R^i)$, where $X^i \subseteq \mathbb{R}^G$ is a consumption set, the production set Y^i is $\{e^i\}$ for some fixed endowment vector in $e^i \in \mathbb{R}^G_{++}$, and the preference ordering R^i on X^i can be represented by a continuous, strictly increasing, and quasi-concave utility function $u^i : X^i \to \mathbb{R}$. Following Jordan (1982), assume also that the consumption set X^i is $\mathbb{R}^G_{++}$ if the closure of the weak preference set $R^i(\bar{x}^i)$ is contained in $\mathbb{R}^G_{++}$ for each $\bar{x}^i \in \mathbb{R}^G_{++}$; otherwise, $X^i = \mathbb{R}^G_+$. Finally, assume that each utility function u^i is either concave or strictly quasi-concave. Let Θ^i denote the domain of such types.

Let $\theta^N := (\theta^i)_{i \in N}$ denote the typical type profile, and $\Theta^N := \prod_{i \in N} \Theta^i$ the associated domain of all such profiles. Because the relevant conditions of Section 5 are satisfied, a Walrasian equilibrium exists for each profile $\theta^N \in \Theta^N$.

A *message process* is a pair (μ, M), where M is an abstract topological *message space*, and $\mu : \Theta^N \twoheadrightarrow M$ is a nonempty valued correspondence on the domain Θ^N of type profiles. As in Section 6.2, let $F := \{t^N \in (\mathbb{R}^G)^N \mid \sum_{i \in N} t^i = 0\}$ denote the feasible set of balanced allocations of net trade vectors to the different agents in the economy. Given the message space M, an *outcome function* is a mapping $g : M \to F$. Then say that the triple (μ, M, g) is an *allocation mechanism* if (μ, M) is a message process and g is an outcome function. Finally, say that two mechanisms (μ, M, g) and (μ', M', g') are *equivalent* if there exists a homeomorphism $h : M \to M'$ between the two message spaces such that $g'(h(m)) = g(m)$ for all $m \in M$, and

$$\mu'(\theta^N) = h(\mu(\theta^N)) = \{m' \in M' \mid \exists m \in \mu(\theta^N) : m' = h(m)\}$$

for all $\theta^N \in \Theta^N$. In particular, equivalence implies that

$$g'(\mu'(\theta^N)) = g'(h(\mu(\theta^N))) = g(\mu(\theta^N))$$

for all $\theta^N \in \Theta^N$, so the two equivalent mechanisms must have an identical range of possible outcomes.

Let $\Delta^0 := \{p \in \mathbb{R}^G_{++} \mid \sum_{g \in G} p_g = 1\}$ denote the relative interior of the unit simplex in $\mathbb{R}^G$, whose members are normalized strictly positive price vectors. Given any price vector $p \in \Delta^0$, agent $i \in N$, and type $\theta^i = (X^i, e^i, R^i)$, define

$$\begin{aligned} &\beta(p;\theta^i) := \{t \in \mathbb{R}^G \mid pt \leq 0,\ t + e^i \in X^i\} \\ \text{and} \quad &\tau(p;\theta^i) := \{t \in \beta(p;\theta^i) \mid \tilde{t} \in \beta(p;\theta^i) \Longrightarrow t + e^i\ R^i\ \tilde{t} + e^i\} \end{aligned}$$

as the Walrasian budget and demand sets, respectively. The *Walrasian* allocation mechanism is the triple (μ_W, M_W, g_W), where:

$$\begin{aligned} M_W &:= \{(p, t^N) \in \Delta^0 \times F \mid pt^i = 0 \text{ (all } i \in N)\}; \\ \mu_W(\theta^N) &:= \cap_{i \in N} \{(p, t^N) \in M_W \mid t^i \in \tau(p;\theta^i)\}; \\ g_W(p, t^N) &:= t^N. \end{aligned}$$

Note that the space M_W is a connected manifold in $\mathbb{R}^G \times (\mathbb{R}^G)^N$ of dimension $d := \#N(\#G - 1)$. Also, because $t^N \in F$ implies $\sum_{i \in N} t^i = 0$ and $t^i \in \tau(p;\theta^i)$ for all $i \in N$, it follows that $\mu_W(\theta^N)$ is the set of all Walrasian equilibria.

Following Hurwicz's (1960, 1972) original ideas, Mount and Reiter (1974) and Hurwicz (1977) pioneered the formal study of such allocation mechanisms. They required that all possible outcomes $t^N \in g(\mu(\theta^N))$ of the mechanism should be Pareto efficient allocations satisfying weak gains from trade or "individual rationality"—that is, $t^i + e^i\ R^i\ e^i$ for all $i \in N$. They also required the mechanism to be *informationally decentralized* in the sense that $\mu(\theta^N) = \cap_{i \in N} \mu^i(\theta^i)$ for a profile of correspondences $\mu^i : \Theta^i \twoheadrightarrow M$ defined on Θ^i, the domain of possible types θ^i for agent i. Obviously the Walrasian mechanism satisfies all these conditions. They showed that any other mechanism with all these properties requires a message space of dimension at least d, the dimension of the Walrasian message space M_W.[23]

These results do not characterize the Walrasian allocation mechanism uniquely because they fail to exclude other mechanisms that might use a message space of dimension d to generate as outcomes general WELT allocations satisfying weak gains from trade, rather than WE allocations specifically. Jordan (1982), however, provides

[23] Various corrections, elaborations, and extensions appear in Reiter (1977), Walker (1977), Osana (1978, 2005), Sato (1981), and Chander (1983).

conditions guaranteeing that *only* mechanisms equivalent to the Walrasian allocation mechanism are informationally decentralized and use a message space of dimension not exceeding d in order to generate Pareto efficient allocations satisfying weak gains from trade. In this sense, his results characterize the Walrasian mechanism uniquely.[24]

To derive their results, Mount and Reiter in particular imposed a "local threadedness" condition on the correspondence $\mu : \Theta^N \twoheadrightarrow M$ requiring that, for each $\bar{\theta}^N \in \Theta^N$, there should exist a neighborhood U of $\bar{\theta}^N$ and a continuous selection $f : U \to M$ satisfying $f(\theta^N) \in \mu(\theta^N)$ for all $\theta^N \in U$.[25] Jordan imposes a different "regularity" assumption requiring μ to be a continuous single-valued function on the restricted domain Θ^N_{CD} of "Cobb–Douglas" environments in which each $X^i = \mathbb{R}^G_+$ and each utility function takes the form $u^i(x^i) \equiv \prod_{g \in G} (x^i_g)^{\alpha^i_g}$ for some parameter vector $\alpha^i \in \mathbb{R}^G_{++}$.[26] This regularity assumption ensures that the characterization result holds for the domain Θ^N_{CD}; it is extended to the whole of Θ^N by requiring the range set $\mu(\Theta^N_{\mathrm{CD}})$ to be a relatively closed subset of the message space M. Jordan provides examples showing that these two extra assumptions are indispensable for his result.[27]

Work by Hurwicz and Marschak (2003) demonstrates an analogous form of informational superiority for the Walrasian mechanism when it is approximated by a mechanism using a finite message space, and the size rather than the dimension of that space is used to measure the cost of the mechanism.

7.2. Gevers' Theorem

7.2.1. Maskin Monotonicity

Consider a pure exchange economy where each agent $i \in N$ has $X^i = \mathbb{R}^G_+$ and $Y^i = \{e^i\}$ for a fixed endowment vector $e^i \in \mathbb{R}^G_{++}$. Let $\mathcal{D}^i$ denote the domain of preference orderings R^i on $\mathbb{R}^G_+$ satisfying regularity conditions (a)–(d) of Section 2.5. In particular, each R^i must be convex, continuous, strictly monotone, and have indifference curves staying away from the boundary of $\mathbb{R}^G_+$. Let $\mathcal{D}^N := \prod_{i \in N} \mathcal{D}^i$ be the domain of *preference profiles* R^N with these properties.

Given the fixed *endowment profile* $e^N := (e^i)_{i \in N}$, define the set

$$F_{e^N} := \{x^N \in X^N = (\mathbb{R}^G)^N \mid \sum_{i \in N} (x^i - e^i) = 0\}$$

24 More results of this kind appear in Calsamiglia and Kirman (1993) and in Tian (2004, 2006).

25 Mount and Reiter (1974, Definition 6, p. 173) originally described this property as being "locally sliced," and the continuous selection f as a "local slice." Reiter (1977, p. 230) introduces the new term. Later, Jordan (1982) demonstrates a version of Mount and Reiter's main result using the weaker condition that a continuous selection $f : U \to M$ exists for just one open set $U \subset \Theta^N$.

26 It is easy to show that the gross substitutability condition $\partial x^i_g / \partial p_h \geq 0$ (all $h \neq g$) is satisfied in every environment $\theta^N \in \Theta^N_{\mathrm{CD}}$, so $\mu_W(\theta^N)$ must be singleton-valued—see Arrow and Hahn (1971).

27 Segal (2007, Section 7.1) has since derived an analogous characterization without such extra assumptions. Moreover, other parts of the paper derive similar results for particular nonconvex environments and for social goals other than Pareto efficiency.

of all feasible consumption profiles. Then let $\Phi_{e^N} : \mathcal{D}^N \twoheadrightarrow X^N$ denote a *social choice rule* (or SCR) which, for each $R^N \in \mathcal{D}^N$, specifies a nonempty choice set $\Phi_{e^N}(R^N) \subseteq F_{e^N}$. Say that Φ_{e^N} is *singleton valued* if there exists a mapping $\phi_{e^N} : \mathcal{D}^N \to X^N$ such that $\Phi_{e^N}(R^N) \equiv \{\phi_{e^N}(R^N)\}$.

The following definition is due to Maskin (1999).[28] Say that the SCR is *Maskin monotonic* provided that any $x^N \in \Phi_{e^N}(R^N)$ also belongs to $\Phi_{e^N}(\tilde{R}^N)$ whenever the two preference profiles R^N and $\tilde{R}^N$ satisfy $x^i \; R^i \; \bar{x}^i \Longrightarrow x^i \; \tilde{R}^i \; \bar{x}^i$ for all $i \in N$ and all $\bar{x}^i \in X^i$. One reason for being interested in this property is that it is necessary and sufficient for Nash implementability of Walrasian equilibrium when $\#N \geq 3$.[29] The following result is suggested by Hurwicz (1979) and (1986, p. 1473)—see also Thomson (1979).

Theorem 33 *In a pure exchange economy with fixed endowment profile e^N, let $\mathcal{D}^N$ be the domain of preference profiles that satisfy the smoothness conditions (a)–(d) of Section 2.5. Suppose $\phi_{e^N}(R^N)$ is a singleton-valued social choice rule on $\mathcal{D}^N$ that is continuous, Maskin monotonic, and generates Pareto efficient allocations satisfying weak gains from trade. Then $\phi_{e^N}(R^N)$ must be a Walrasian equilibrium for all $R^N \in \mathcal{D}^N$.*

7.2.2. Constrained Walrasian Equilibrium

Theorem 33 requires the boundary condition (d) of Section 2.5. Without it, there is a counterexample announced by Hurwicz (1986) that eventually appeared in Hurwicz, Maskin, and Postlewaite (1995)—see also Thomson (1999).

Alternatively one could omit the boundary condition, but allow a somewhat modified SCR $\phi_{e^N}(R^N)$ instead. Recall our assumption here that each agent $i \in N$ has $X^i = \mathbb{R}^G_+$ and $Y^i = \{e^i\}$ for a fixed endowment vector $e^i \in \mathbb{R}^G_{++}$. In this case, a *constrained Walrasian equilibrium* is defined as a pair $(\hat{x}^N, \hat{p})$ consisting of a feasible allocation and a price vector with the properties that, for all $i \in N$, one has $\hat{p}\hat{x}^i \leq \hat{p}\hat{e}^i$, and also $\hat{p}x^i > \hat{p}\hat{e}^i$ whenever both $x^i \in P^i(\hat{x}^i)$ and $x^i \leqq \sum_{h \in N} e^h_g$. In an economy with two agents and two goods, the latter is an additional constraint preventing any one agent's demand vector from going outside the Edgeworth box.

With this new definition, a modified form of Theorem 33 drops the boundary condition (d) of Section 2.5, but concludes only that $\phi_{e^N}(R^N)$ must be a constrained Walrasian equilibrium for all $R^N \in \mathcal{D}^N$. For details, see Hurwicz (1986, p. 1473) and also Tian (1992), Nagahisa (1994), and Bochet (2007).

When preferences do satisfy the boundary condition, any such additional constraint is irrelevant, and the constrained and unconstrained Walrasian equilibria coincide.

[28] An early version of Maskin's paper was widely circulated in 1977. See also Dasgupta, Hammond, and Maskin (1979).
[29] Maskin's (1999) demonstration of sufficiency relies on a condition he calls "no veto power." This is vacuously satisfied in an exchange economy with $\#N \geq 3$ when agents have strictly monotone preferences.

7.2.3. Welfarist Social Choice Rules

Except for domains of preference profiles that are much more restrictive than those satisfying regularity conditions (a)–(d) of Section 2.5, there are typically multiple Walrasian equilibria for some preference profiles.[30] So it is natural to consider an SCR Φ_{e^N} that need not be singleton-valued on all of $\mathcal{D}^N$.

A condition that Thomson (1983, p. 223) called "property P" was later used by Gevers (1986, p. 102) under the name "nondiscrimination between Pareto indifferent allocations." Later writers often call it simply "Pareto indifference." However, it is really a choice-theoretic version of the "welfarism" condition that Sen (1979, p. 538) described for social rankings—namely: "Social welfare is a function of personal utility levels, so that any two social states must be ranked entirely on the basis of personal utilities in the respective states (irrespective of the nonutility features of the states)."[31]

Accordingly, here we say, somewhat more concisely, that the SCR Φ is *welfarist* if, whenever the preference profile $R^N \in \mathcal{D}^N$ and the two allocations $\tilde{x}^N, \hat{x}^N \in F_{e^N}$ satisfy $\tilde{x}^i \; I^i \; \hat{x}^i$ for all $i \in N$, then $\tilde{x}^N \in \Phi_{e^N}(R^N) \Longleftrightarrow \hat{x}^N \in \Phi_{e^N}(R^N)$.

Let $\Phi^W_{e^N}$ denote the *Walrasian* SCR defined so that, for each $R^N \in \mathcal{D}^N$, the value $\Phi^W_{e^N}(R^N)$ is the set of all Walrasian allocations in the pure exchange economy $\mathcal{E}$ defined by e^N and R^N. The following result confirms that this Walrasian SCR is welfarist, as is the WELT SCR for a given wealth distribution.

Lemma 34 *Assume preferences are LNS. Suppose that $(\hat{x}^N, \hat{p})$ is a WELT in the economy $\mathbf{E} = (e^N, R^N)$, and that $\tilde{x}^N \in F_{e^N}$ satisfies $\tilde{x}^i \; I^i \; \hat{x}^i$ for all $i \in N$. Then $(\tilde{x}^N, \hat{p})$ is also a WELT in $\mathcal{E}$, with $\hat{p}\tilde{x}^i = \hat{p}\hat{x}^i$ for all $i \in N$.*

Proof. Because preferences are LNS, Lemma 9 implies that $(\hat{x}^N, \hat{p})$ is a CELT. But $\tilde{x}^i \; I^i \; \hat{x}^i$ for all $i \in N$, so $\hat{p}\tilde{x}^i \geq \hat{p}\hat{x}^i$ for all $i \in N$. Also, feasibility implies that $\sum_{i \in N} \tilde{x}^i = \sum_{i \in N} \hat{x}^i = \sum_{i \in N} e^i$, so $\hat{p}\tilde{x}^i = \hat{p}\hat{x}^i$ for all $i \in N$. Now, for any $i \in N$, whenever $x^i \in P^i(\tilde{x}^i)$, one has $x^i \in P^i(\hat{x}^i)$ because preferences are transitive, so $\hat{p}x^i > \hat{p}\hat{x}^i = \hat{p}\tilde{x}^i$ because $(\hat{x}^N, \hat{p})$ is a WELT. This confirms that $(\tilde{x}^N, \hat{p})$ is a WELT. □

7.3. A Maximally Selective Social Choice Rule

Consider a fixed endowment profile e^N and a family $\mathcal{S}$ of social choice rules $\Phi_{e^N} : \mathcal{D}^N \to F_{e^N}$ that satisfy:

(1) $\Phi^W_{e^N} \in \mathcal{S}$;

(2) for all $\Phi_{e^N} \in \mathcal{S}$, one has $\Phi^W_{e^N}(R^N) \subseteq \Phi_{e^N}(R^N)$ throughout the domain of exchange economies.

[30] See Arrow and Hahn (1971) for discussions of when Walrasian equilibria are unique.

[31] This welfarism condition, of course, was a prime target of Sen's critique of welfare economics both then and often since.

Then the class $\mathcal{S}$ includes a unique *maximally selective* SCR $\Phi^{\mathcal{S}}_{e^N} : \mathcal{D}^N \to F_{e^N}$ defined by $\Phi^{\mathcal{S}}_{e^N}(R^N) := \bigcap_{\Phi \in \mathcal{S}} \Phi_{e^N}(R^N)$. Obviously, the hypotheses (1) and (2) above imply that $\Phi^W_{e^N}(R^N) \equiv \Phi^{\mathcal{S}}_{e^N}(R^N)$. So the Walrasian SCR is characterized uniquely and completely as the maximally selective or most refined member of $\mathcal{S}$, but only in a way that treats refinement as a desirable end in itself.

The following main result of Gevers (1986) is a modification of Theorem 33 to allow social choice rules that may not have singleton values.

Theorem 35 *In a pure exchange economy with fixed endowment profile e^N, let $\mathcal{D}^N$ be the domain of preference profiles that satisfy the smoothness conditions (a)–(d) of Section 2.5. Then the Walrasian SCR $\Phi^W_{e^N}$ on $\mathcal{D}^N$ is maximally selective amongst those SCRs that are Maskin monotonic, and generate Pareto efficient allocations satisfying weak gains from trade.*

Related results have been discussed by, amongst others, Nagahisa (1991), Thomson (1987, pp. 387–389), Tadenuma and Thomson (1995), Maniquet (1996), and most recently by Hayashi and Sakai (2009).

7.4. Local Independence in Smooth Economies

Nagahisa and Suh (1995) refine an earlier characterization of the Walras rule proposed by Nagahisa (1991). They also characterize Walras equilibrium with equal budgets.

Let $\mathcal{D}^i$ now denote the domain of regular smooth preferences satisfying all the smoothness conditions of Section 2.5. Let $\mathcal{D}^N := \prod_{i \in N} \mathcal{D}^i$. Let $\Phi_{e^N} : \mathcal{D}^N \twoheadrightarrow X^N$ be the SCR.

Say that the SCR Φ_{e^N} gives *envy-free* allocations if, for each R^N and each $x^N \in \Phi_{e^N}(R^N)$, one has $x^i \; R^i \; x^h$ for all $h, i \in N$.

For each agent $i \in N$, for each smooth preference ordering $R^i \in \mathcal{D}^i$ represented by a utility function u^i that is C^1 on $\mathbb{R}^G_{++}$, for each net consumption vector $x^i \in \mathbb{R}^G_{++}$, and for each pair of goods $f, g \in G$, let

$$s^i_{fg}(R^i, x^i) := \frac{\partial u^i}{\partial x^i_f}(x^i) \Big/ \frac{\partial u^i}{\partial x^i_g}(x^i)$$

denote agent i's *marginal rate of substitution* between f and g at x^i. Note that this depends only on agent i's preference ordering R^i, not on the utility function used to represent it.

Say that the SCR satisfies *local independence* provided that, for each pair of preference profiles $R^N, \tilde{R}^N \in \mathcal{D}^N$ and each allocation $x^N \in X^N$, satisfying $s^i_{fg}(R^i, x^i) = s^i_{fg}(\tilde{R}^i, x^i)$ for all $i \in N$ and all $f, g \in G$, then $x^N \in \Phi_{e^N}(R^N)$ if and only if $x^N \in \Phi_{e^N}(\tilde{R}^N)$. This is clearly a local version of the familiar "independence of irrevelant alternatives" axiom in social choice theory. Also, if individuals do have smooth preferences, and if $x^i \; R^i \; \bar{x}^i$ implies $x^i \; \tilde{R}^i \; \bar{x}^i$ for all $\bar{x}^i \in X^i$, then $s^i_{fg}(R^i, x^i) = s^i_{fg}(\tilde{R}^i, x^i)$ for all $f, g \in G$.

When preferences are smooth, it follows that local independence implies the Maskin monotonicity condition described in Section 7.2.1.

With these definitions, Nagahisa and Suh's main characterization results for Walrasian equilibria with and without equal budgets can be stated as follows:

Theorem 36 *The SCR* $R^N \mapsto \Phi_{e^N}(R^N)$ *is Walrasian if and only if it is locally independent, Pareto efficient, and satisfies weak gains from trade.*

Theorem 37 *The SCR* $R^N \mapsto \Phi_{e^N}(R^N)$ *is WEEB if and only if it is locally independent, and also generates allocations that are both Pareto efficient and envy-free.*

In each case it is easy to check that the relevant SCR has the claimed properties. Proofs that these properties are complete characterizations can be found in Nagahisa and Suh (1995). They also provide examples that go most of the way toward showing how the smoothness and other conditions are required for these results to be valid.

7.5. Strategyproofness with Exogenous Prices

7.5.1. Strategyproof Mechanisms in a Finite Economy

A *net trade allocation mechanism* $t^N(\theta^N)$ specifies the profile of agents' net trade vectors $t^N \in T^N$ satisfying $\sum_{i \in N} t^i = 0$ as a function of their type profile θ^N. The mechanism is said to be (individually) *strategyproof* if the *incentive constraint* $t^i(\theta^N) \succsim_{\theta^i} t^i(\tilde{\theta}^i, \theta^{-i})$ is satisfied whenever $t^i(\tilde{\theta}^i, \theta^{-i}) \in T_{\theta^i}$, where θ^{-i} denotes $\langle \theta^h \rangle_{h \in N \setminus \{i\}}$, with i's type omitted. This definition implies that no individual $i \in N$ whose true type is $\theta^i \in \Theta$ has the incentive to manipulate the mechanism by acting as a type $\tilde{\theta}^i$ agent would.

In finite economies, a mechanism that produces a Walrasian equilibrium allocation for every type profile will rarely be strategyproof. This is because agents can typically manipulate prices to their own advantage by acting in the market as if they were a different type of agent who is willing to undertake only a smaller volume of trade. Moreover, strategyproofness is inconsistent with Pareto efficiency unless the mechanism allows allocations that either violate individual rationality, as in Serizawa (2002), or else are arbitrarily close to the extremes of the feasible set, as in Serizawa and Weymark (2003). For similar negative results, see Kato and Ohseto (2002, 2004) and Ju (2004).

Makowski, Ostroy, and Segal (1999) present some more positive results concerning WE allocations on a restricted domain. These involve cases where at least one agent has a flat indifference surface in some neighborhood of a Walrasian equilibrium allocation. If this neighborhood is sufficiently large, then individual agents cannot manipulate prices except by distorting their desired net trades so much that they become worse off.

7.5.2. A Linear Technology

Similar positive results might be expected in economies with production where equilibrium prices happen to be determined entirely by exogenous supply conditions, independent of demand. The "nonsubstitution theorem" due to Samuelson (1951), Koopmans (1951), Arrow (1951b), and Georgescu-Roegen (1951) describes an important case when this is true—see also Mirrlees (1969) for a "dynamic" extension to steady growth paths. For recent work on sufficient conditions for a technology to be linear, at least in some neighborhood of a given aggregate demand vector, see Bergstrom (1996) and Villar (2003). One line of work not cited there explores relevant links between factor price equalization and price invariance (or what Bhagwati and Wan (1979) call "stationarity") in the theory of international trade for small open economies—see, for example, Diewert (1983) and Hammond (1986).

Formally, suppose that there is a linear technology described by an aggregate production possibility set which is the half-space $Y := \{y \in \mathbb{R}^G \mid \bar{p}y \leq \bar{p}e\}$ for some fixed price vector $\bar{p} \gg 0$ and some exogenous aggregate endowment vector $e \in \mathbb{R}^G_{++}$. Suppose too that each type $\theta \in \Theta$ of agent has the same consumption set $\mathbb{R}^G_+$, and a variable preference ordering R_θ that is continuous and strictly monotone on $\mathbb{R}^G_+$.

For this important special case, given the fixed price vector $\bar{p} \gg 0$, let

$$\gamma_\theta(w) := \{x \in \mathbb{R}^G_+ \mid \bar{p}x \leq w;\ x' \in P_\theta(x) \Longrightarrow \bar{p}x' > w\}$$

denote the Walrasian demand set of a type θ agent when confronted with the budget constraint $\bar{p}x \leq w$, where $w \in \mathbb{R}_+$. Now suppose that $\theta^N \mapsto x^N(\theta^N) \in (\mathbb{R}^G_+)^N$ is a consumption mechanism that generates a WELT allocation for each type profile $\theta^N \in \Theta^N$. That is, there exist wealth transfer functions $\theta^N \mapsto w^N(\theta^N) \in \mathbb{R}^N_+$ satisfying $\sum_{i \in N} w^i(\theta^N) = \bar{p}e$ with the property that $x^i(\theta^N) \in \gamma_{\theta^i}(w^i(\theta^N))$ for all $i \in N$ and all type profiles $\theta^N \in \Theta^N$.

Suppose that $w^i(\theta^N) \equiv w^i$, independent of θ^N, for all $i \in N$. In this case, each consumer $i \in N$ faces the same budget constraint $\bar{p}x \leq w^i$ and feasibility constraint $x \in \mathbb{R}^G_+$ for all θ^N, so evidently the incentive constraint $x^i(\theta^N) \succsim_{\theta^i} x^i(\tilde{\theta}^i, \theta^{-i})$ is always satisfied. Hence the mechanism is individually strategyproof; indeed, it is even coalitionally strategyproof in the strong sense that $x^i(\theta^N) \succsim_{\theta^i} x^i(\tilde{\theta}^N)$ for all $i \in N$ and all pairs of type profiles $\theta^N, \tilde{\theta}^N$.

A converse result would give sufficient conditions for Pareto efficient allocations generated by a strategyproof mechanism to be WELT allocations with $w^i(\theta^N)$ independent of θ^N, for all $i \in N$. Under the smooth type domain hypothesis of Section 2.8, a variant of the arguments used in Section 13.2 could be applied. Alternatively, under extra assumptions discussed below, Maniquet and Sprumont (1999) provide the following two different characterizations of consumption mechanisms $\theta^N \mapsto x^N(\theta^N)$ that generate WELT allocations with transfers satisfying $w^i(\theta^N) = \frac{1}{n}\bar{p}e$ for all $i \in N$ and all $\theta^N \in \Theta^N$:

(1) they are strategyproof, Pareto efficient, and give identical agents equally good consumption vectors (see their Theorem 2);

(2) they are coalitionally strategyproof, Pareto efficient, and give all agents equally good consumption allocations whenever all agents have identical preferences (see their Theorem 4).

The first extra assumption requires the range of different correspondences $\gamma_\theta : \mathbb{R}_+ \twoheadrightarrow \mathbb{R}^G_+$ to have the property that, given any continuous and increasing *wealth consumption curve* $c : \mathbb{R}_+ \to \mathbb{R}^G_+$ satisfying $\bar{p}\, c(w) = w$ for all $w \in \mathbb{R}_+$, there exist a $\theta \in \Theta$ and a differentiable utility function $x \mapsto u_\theta(x)$ representing $\succsim_\theta$ on $\mathbb{R}^G_+$ such that $\gamma_\theta(w) = \{c(w)\}$. Finally, result (2) relies on a second extra assumption requiring that for all $\theta, \theta' \in \Theta$ and all $w \in \mathbb{R}_+$, there exists $\theta'' \in \Theta$ such that $\gamma_\theta(w) \cup \gamma_{\theta'}(w) \subseteq \gamma_{\theta''}(w)$. Of course, this last assumption rules out single-valued demand functions except in the trivial case where every type of agent has exactly the same Walrasian demand correspondence $w \mapsto\!\!\!\twoheadrightarrow \gamma_\theta(w)$.

8. CHARACTERIZATIONS OF WE WITH A VARYING NUMBER OF AGENTS

8.1. The Core and Edgeworth Equilibrium

Let $\mathcal{E}$ denote the economy described in Section 3.1, with a finite set of agents N whose consumption and production sets are X^i and Y^i, respectively, and whose preference orderings are R^i, for all $i \in N$. Consider any feasible allocation $(\bar{x}^N, \bar{y}^N)$ in $\mathcal{E}$. Given a coalition $K \subseteq N$, say that K *blocks* $(\bar{x}^N, \bar{y}^N)$, and that K is a *blocking coalition*, if there is a *blocking allocation* $(x^K, y^K) \in \prod_{i \in K}[P^i(\bar{x}^i) \times Y^i]$ satisfying $\sum_{i \in K}(x^i - y^i) = 0$.[32] On the other hand, the feasible allocation $(\hat{x}^N, \hat{y}^N)$ is in the *core* if there is no blocking coalition. Obviously, any core allocation is weakly Pareto efficient because otherwise the "grand coalition" N would block it.

Theorem 38 *Suppose agents' preferences are LNS and $(\hat{x}^N, \hat{y}^N, \hat{p})$ is a WE. Then the equilibrium allocation $(\hat{x}^N, \hat{y}^N)$ is in the core.*

Proof. Let $K \subseteq N$ be any coalition. Suppose $(x^K, y^K) \in \prod_{i \in K}[P^i(\hat{x}^i) \times Y^i]$. Because $(\hat{x}^N, \hat{y}^N, \hat{p})$ is a WE, it follows that $\hat{p}\,(x^i - y^i) > 0$ for all $i \in K$. This contradicts $\sum_{i \in K}(x^i - y^i) = 0$, so there can be no blocking coalition. □

Given the economy $\mathcal{E}$ and any natural number $r \in \mathbb{N}$, let $\mathcal{E}^r$ denote the rth *replica economy* in which each agent $i \in N$ is replicated r times. These replicated agents have labels ik $(k = 1, 2, \ldots, r)$. Their respective consumption and production sets and preference orderings satisfy $X^{ik} = X^i$, $Y^{ik} = Y^i$, and $R^{ik} = R^i$ for all $k = 1, 2, \ldots, r$.

[32] Alternatively, a *weak blocking allocation* satisfies $(x^K, y^K) \in \prod_{i \in K}[R^i(\bar{x}^i) \times Y^i]$, as well as $\sum_{i \in K}(x^i - y^i) = 0$ and $x^h\ P^h\ \bar{x}^h$ for some $h \in K$. This weakening would make little difference to the results presented here.

Following Aliprantis, Brown, and Burkinshaw (1987a, 1987b), define an *Edgeworth equilibrium* in the economy $\mathcal{E}$ as a feasible allocation $(\hat{x}^N, \hat{y}^N)$, such that the core of each replica economy $\mathcal{E}^r$ $(r = 1,2,\ldots)$ includes the *replica allocation* $(x^{N\times\{1,2,\ldots,r\}}, y^{N\times\{1,2,\ldots,r\}})$ satisfying $x^{ik} = \hat{x}^i$ and $y^{ik} = \hat{y}^i$ for all $i \in N$ and all $k = 1,2,\ldots,r$.[33] We denote this rth replica allocation by $(\hat{x}^N, \hat{y}^N)^r$.

Theorem 39 *Suppose agents' preferences are LNS and $(\hat{x}^N, \hat{y}^N, \hat{p})$ is a WE. Then the equilibrium allocation $(\hat{x}^N, \hat{y}^N)$ is an Edgeworth equilibrium.*

Proof. Because $(\hat{x}^N, \hat{y}^N, \hat{p})$ is a WE in the economy $\mathcal{E}$, so is $((\hat{x}^N, \hat{y}^N)^r, \hat{p})$ in the replica economy $\mathcal{E}^r$. Theorem 38 implies that $(\hat{x}^N, \hat{y}^N)^r$ belongs to the core of $\mathcal{E}^r$ for each $r = 1,2,\ldots$. So $(\hat{x}^N, \hat{y}^N)$ is an Edgeworth equilibrium. □

The following converse result is based on Debreu and Scarf's (1963) limit theorem for the core. Agents are assumed to have convex consumption and production sets. Preferences need not be convex, however, though if they are not, there may be neither a CE nor an Edgeworth equilibrium.

Theorem 40 *Suppose agents have convex consumption and production sets for which autarky is feasible, as well as preferences that are LNS and continuous. Then a feasible allocation $(\hat{x}^N, \hat{y}^N)$ is an Edgeworth equilibrium only if there exists a price vector $\hat{p} \neq 0$ such that $(\hat{x}^N, \hat{y}^N, \hat{p})$ is a CE.*

Proof. Given the feasible allocation $(\hat{x}^N, \hat{y}^N)$, define Z as the convex hull of $\cup_{i\in N}[P^i(\hat{x}^i) - Y^i]$.

Suppose $0 \in Z$. Then there must exist a natural number m and, for each $q = 1,2,\ldots,m$, corresponding convex weights $\alpha_q \in (0,1]$, agents $i_q \in N$, consumption vectors $x_q \in P^{i_q}(\hat{x}^{i_q})$, and production vectors $y_q \in Y^{i_q}$, such that $\sum_{q=1}^m \alpha_q = 1$ and $0 = \sum_{q=1}^m \alpha_q (x_q - y_q)$. For each $q \in \{1,2,\ldots,m\}$ and $r = 1,2,\ldots$, let n_{qr} be the smallest integer that is greater or equal to $r\alpha_q$. Then define

$$(\tilde{x}_{qr}, \tilde{y}_{qr}) := \frac{r\alpha_q}{n_{qr}}(x_q, y_q) + \left(1 - \frac{r\alpha_q}{n_{qr}}\right)(a^{i_q}, a^{i_q})$$

where each $a^{i_q} \in X^{i_q} \cap Y^{i_q}$ is any feasible autarky consumption vector for agent i_q. Because $r\alpha_q \leq n_{qr}$ and the sets X^i and Y^i are assumed to be convex for all $i \in N$, the convex combination $(\tilde{x}_{qr}, \tilde{y}_{qr}) \in X^{i_q} \times Y^{i_q}$ for $q = 1,2,\ldots,m$ and for $r = 1,2,\ldots$. Moreover,

$$\sum_{q=1}^m n_{qr}(\tilde{x}_{qr} - \tilde{y}_{qr}) = \sum_{q=1}^m r\alpha_q (x_q - y_q) = 0.$$

[33] Vind (1995) carefully discusses the (rather tenuous) relationship between perfect competition, the core, and Edgeworth's (1881) concept of "final equilibrium."

Finally, $0 \leq n_{qr} - r\alpha_q < 1$ so $r\alpha_q / n_{qr} \to 1$ as $r \to \infty$, implying $\tilde{x}_{qr} \to x_q$. Because preferences are continuous, for all sufficiently large r one has $\tilde{x}_{qr} \in P^{i_q}(\hat{x}^{i_q})$ for all $q = 1, 2, \ldots, m$. Now define $Q^i := \{q \in \{1, 2, \ldots, m\} \mid i_q = i\}$ for each $i \in N$, as well as $s := \sum_{q=1}^{m} n_{qr}$. Then a coalition that consists of $\sum_{q \in Q^i} n_{qr}$ replicas of each agent $i \in N$ can block the replicated allocation $(\hat{x}^N, \hat{y}^N)^s$ in the replica economy $\mathcal{E}^s$ by allocating $(\tilde{x}_{qr}, \tilde{y}_{qr})$ to n_{qr} replicas of agent i_q, for $q = 1, 2, \ldots, m$. Thus, $(\hat{x}^N, \hat{y}^N)$ is not an Edgeworth equilibrium.

Conversely, if $(\hat{x}^N, \hat{y}^N)$ is an Edgeworth equilibrium, then $0 \notin Z$. Because Z is convex by construction, there exists a price vector $\hat{p} \neq 0$ such that $\hat{p}z \geq 0$ for all $z \in Z$, and so for all $z \in \cup_{i \in N}[P^i(\hat{x}^i) - Y^i]$. But preferences are LNS, so $\hat{x}^i \in \text{cl}\, P^i(\hat{x}^i)$. It follows that $\hat{x}^i - \hat{y}^i \in \text{cl}\, P^i(\hat{x}^i) - Y^i$, so $\hat{p}(\hat{x}^i - \hat{y}^i) \geq 0$ for all $i \in N$. But $\sum_{i \in N}(\hat{x}^i - \hat{y}^i) = 0$ because $(\hat{x}^N, \hat{y}^N)$ is feasible, so $\hat{p}(\hat{x}^i - \hat{y}^i) = 0$ for all $i \in N$. Finally, whenever $(x^i, y^i) \in R^i(\hat{x}^i) \times Y^i$, then $x^i \in \text{cl}\, P^i(\hat{x}^i)$, so $x^i - y^i \in \text{cl}\, P^i(\hat{x}^i) - Y^i$. Hence, $\hat{p}(x^i - y^i) \geq 0$. These results imply that $(\hat{x}^N, \hat{y}^N, \hat{p})$ is a CE. □

Theorem 41 *Suppose agents have convex consumption and production sets for which autarky is feasible, and* $0 \in \text{int} \sum_{i \in N}(X^i - Y^i)$. *Suppose preferences are LNS and continuous, and the economy is directionally irreducible, as defined in Section 5.4. Then a feasible allocation* $(\hat{x}^N, \hat{y}^N)$ *is an Edgeworth equilibrium if and only if there exists a price vector* $\hat{p} \neq 0$ *such that* $(\hat{x}^N, \hat{y}^N, \hat{p})$ *is a WE.*

Proof. By Theorem 39, any WE allocation is an Edgeworth equilibrium. Conversely, any Edgeworth equilibrium is a CE allocation, by Theorem 40. Under the stated hypotheses, Theorem 25 guarantees that any CE is a WE. □

8.2. Another Limit Theorem

Edgeworth equilibria refine the core by requiring that the same allocation, when replicated, belongs to the core of the corresponding replica economy. Nagahisa (1994, Theorem 5) has used alternative refinements of the core in replica economies of different size in order to characterize Walrasian equilibrium. These results, however, rest on rather strong assumptions, including the Maskin monotonicity condition considered in Section 7.2.1, as well as the welfarism axiom used in 7.2.3.

8.3. Stability

8.3.1. A Walrasian Social Choice Rule

Let $\mathcal{E} := \langle N, \theta^N \rangle$ denote a typical *economic environment* of pure exchange, with N as the variable finite set of agents, each of whom has a type $\theta^i = (X^i, e^i, R^i)$ described by a consumption set $X^i \subseteq \mathbb{R}^G_+$, a fixed endowment vector $e^i \in \mathbb{R}^G_{++}$, and a preference ordering R^i. In this section we assume that preferences are strictly monotone and convex.

Given any environment $\mathcal{E}$, let

$$F(\mathcal{E}) := \{x^N \in X^N \mid \sum_{i\in N}(x^i - e^i) = 0\} \subset (\mathbb{R}^G)^N$$

denote the set of all feasible consumption allocations in $\mathcal{E}$. Let WE($\mathcal{E}$) and WELT($\mathcal{E}$) denote the (possibly empty) sets of feasible allocations $\hat{x}^N \in F(\mathcal{E})$ for which there exists an equilibrium price vector $\hat{p} \neq 0$ such that $(\hat{x}^N, \hat{p})$ is, respectively, a WE and a WELT in the environment $\mathcal{E}$. Because preferences are assumed to be strictly monotone, any WE or WELT equilibrium price vector must satisfy $\hat{p} \gg 0$.

Define the respective domains $\mathbf{E}_1$ and $\mathbf{E}_2$ of environments $\mathcal{E}$ so that WE($\mathcal{E}$) $\neq \emptyset$ iff $\mathcal{E} \in \mathbf{E}_1$ and WELT($\mathcal{E}$) $\neq \emptyset$ iff $\mathcal{E} \in \mathbf{E}_2$. Because WE($\mathcal{E}$) $\subseteq$ WELT($\mathcal{E}$) for all $\mathcal{E}$, obviously $\mathbf{E}_1 \subseteq \mathbf{E}_2$.

Next, define a *social choice rule* (or SCR) as a mapping $\Phi : \mathbf{E} \twoheadrightarrow (\mathbb{R}^G)^N$ that satisfies $\emptyset \neq \Phi(\mathcal{E}) \subseteq F(\mathcal{E})$ for all environments $\mathcal{E}$ in a specified domain $\mathbf{E}$. Obviously, the *Walrasian social choice rule* WE($\cdot$) and the more general WELT($\cdot$) are two such rules, which are defined on the domains $\mathbf{E}_1$ and $\mathbf{E}_2$, respectively, and satisfy $\emptyset \neq$ WE($\mathcal{E}$) $\subset$ WELT($\mathcal{E}$) for all environments $\mathcal{E} \in \mathbf{E}_1$. Of course, when seeking a characterization of Walrasian equilibrium, it is natural to limit attention to environments in which a Walrasian equilibrium—or at least a WELT—exists. We assume therefore that the domain $\mathbf{E}$ satisfies $\mathbf{E}_1 \subseteq \mathbf{E} \subseteq \mathbf{E}_2$.

8.3.2. Stability under Nonessential Addition

Thomson (1988) in particular introduced axioms relating values $\Phi(\mathcal{E})$ of the SCR for economic environments where the set of agents N can vary. He discussed several different SCRs, including Walrasian equilibrium with equal budgets. Here, two of his axioms will be adapted to our more general setting in order to characterize the Walrasian SCR WE($\cdot$) as a particular restriction of WELT($\cdot$).[34]

First, say that $\mathcal{E} = \langle N, \theta^N \rangle$ is a *subeconomy* of $\tilde{\mathcal{E}} = \langle \tilde{N}, \tilde{\theta}^{\tilde{N}} \rangle$, and write $\mathcal{E} \subseteq \tilde{\mathcal{E}}$, whenever $N \subset \tilde{N}$ and also $\tilde{\theta}^N = \theta^N$.

Next, say that the SCR Φ is *stable under nonessential addition* if, whenever $\mathcal{E} \in \mathbf{E}$, $\mathcal{E} \subset \tilde{\mathcal{E}}$, and a chosen allocation $\hat{x}^N \in \Phi(\mathcal{E})$ has an extension $\hat{x}^{\tilde{N}} \in F(\tilde{\mathcal{E}})$ that is Pareto efficient in $\tilde{\mathcal{E}}$ and satisfies $\tilde{x}^i = \tilde{e}^i$ for all $i \in \tilde{N} \setminus N$, then $\tilde{\mathcal{E}} \in \mathbf{E}$ and the extended allocation

[34] In order to avoid unnecessary complications because a Pareto efficient allocation may not be a WELT, or even a CELT, we will assume directly that $\Phi(\mathcal{E}) \subseteq$ WELT($\mathcal{E}$) for all $\mathcal{E} \in \mathbf{E}$, rather than that each allocation in $\Phi(\mathcal{E})$ is Pareto efficient. In particular, there is no need to assume that preferences are continuous. A related reason for departing from Thomson's original framework is that the proof of Theorem 5 he offers appears to need modifications and additional assumptions that guarantee that if there is a unique normalized equilibrium price vector, then every Walrasian equilibrium allocation is included in the social choice set.

$\hat{x}^{\tilde{N}} \in \Phi(\tilde{\mathcal{E}})$. Thus, if an economy is enlarged by adding new agents to whom allocating a zero net trade vector extends Pareto efficiently a chosen allocation in the original economy $\mathcal{E}$, then that extended allocation should be a possible choice in the enlarged economy $\tilde{\mathcal{E}}$.

Lemma 42 *Suppose* $\mathbf{E} \subseteq \mathbf{E}_2$, *and the SCR* Φ *is stable under nonessential addition while satisfying* $\Phi(\mathcal{E}) \subseteq \text{WELT}(\mathcal{E})$ *for each* $\mathcal{E} \in \mathbf{E}$. *Suppose too that* $\hat{x}^N \in \Phi(\mathcal{E}^*) \setminus \text{WE}(\mathcal{E}^*)$ *where* $\mathcal{E}^* \in \mathbf{E}$. *Then there exist* $\tilde{\mathcal{E}} \in \mathbf{E}$ *and* $\tilde{x}^{\tilde{N}} \in \Phi(\tilde{\mathcal{E}})$ *with at least one agent envying another's net trade vector.*

Proof. By hypothesis, there exists $\hat{p} \gg 0$ at which $\hat{x}^N$ is a WELT in the environment $\mathcal{E}^*$. Construct a new environment $\tilde{\mathcal{E}}$ with $\tilde{N} := N \cup \{0\}$ and $\mathcal{E}^* \subset \tilde{\mathcal{E}}$ by adding to N one extra agent labeled $0 \notin N$ with consumption set $X^0 = \mathbb{R}^G_+$, endowment vector $e^0 \in \mathbb{R}^G_{++}$, and with R^0 represented by the linear utility function defined by $u^0(x) := \hat{p}x$ for all $x \in \mathbb{R}^G_+$. Consider too the extended allocation $\tilde{x}^{\tilde{N}} \in F(\tilde{\mathcal{E}})$ with $\tilde{x}^i = \hat{x}^i$ for all $i \in N$ and $\tilde{x}^0 = e^0$. Then $(\tilde{x}^{\tilde{N}}, \hat{p})$ is a WELT in $\tilde{\mathcal{E}}$. Because preferences are strictly monotone and so LNS, Theorem 15 implies that this allocation is Pareto efficient. Because Φ is stable under nonessential addition, it follows that $\tilde{\mathcal{E}} \in \mathbf{E}$ and $\tilde{x}^{\tilde{N}} \in \Phi(\tilde{\mathcal{E}})$.

By hypothesis, $\hat{x}^N$ is not a WE allocation, so $\hat{p}(\hat{x}^i - e^i) \neq 0$ for some $i \in N$. Because $\sum_{i \in N}(\hat{x}^i - e^i) = 0$, there must exist $h \in N$ such that $\hat{p}(\hat{x}^h - e^h) > 0$. So agent 0's utility function satisfies

$$u^0(e^0 + \tilde{x}^h - e^h) - u^0(e^0 + 0) = \hat{p}(\tilde{x}^h - e^h) > 0.$$

This proves that agent 0 with net trade vector 0 envies agent h with net trade vector $\tilde{x}^h - e^h$. □

8.3.3. Stability under Nonessential Deletion

Next, say that the SCR Φ is *stable under nonessential deletion* if, whenever $\tilde{\mathcal{E}} \in \mathbf{E}$, $\mathcal{E} \subset \tilde{\mathcal{E}}$, and a chosen allocation $\tilde{x}^{\tilde{N}} \in \Phi(\tilde{\mathcal{E}})$ satisfies $\tilde{x}^i = e^i$ for all $i \in \tilde{N} \setminus N$, then $\mathcal{E} \in \mathbf{E}$ and the restricted allocation $\tilde{x}^N \in \Phi(\mathcal{E})$. In other words, ignoring agents whose chosen net trade vectors in $\tilde{\mathcal{E}}$ happen to be zero leaves an allocation to the other agents that is chosen in the subeconomy $\mathcal{E}$.

Lemma 43 *Suppose* Φ *is welfarist and also stable under nonessential deletion on the domain* $\mathbf{E}$, *where* $\mathbf{E}_1 \subset \mathbf{E}$. *Suppose too that* $\Phi(\mathcal{E}) \subseteq \text{WE}(\mathcal{E})$ *for each* $\mathcal{E} \in \mathbf{E}$. *Then* $\mathbf{E} = \mathbf{E}_1$ *and* $\Phi(\mathcal{E}) = \text{WE}(\mathcal{E})$ *for all* $\mathcal{E} \in \mathbf{E}$.

Proof. Let $(\hat{x}^N, \hat{p})$ be any WE in the environment $\mathcal{E}$. Construct a new environment $\tilde{\mathcal{E}}$ with $\tilde{N} := N \cup \{0\}$ and $\mathcal{E} \subset \tilde{\mathcal{E}}$ by adding to N one extra agent $0 \notin N$ with consumption set $X^0 = \mathbb{R}^G_+$, preference ordering R^0 represented by the linear utility function

$u^0(x) \equiv \hat{p}x$, and endowment vector $e^0 \in \mathbb{R}^G_{++}$ whose respective components are

$$e^0_g := \frac{1}{\hat{p}_g} \sum_{h \in G} \sum_{i \in N} \hat{p}_h e^i_h \text{ (all } g \in G). \tag{28}$$

Consider too the allocation $\tilde{x}^{\tilde{N}} \in F(\tilde{\mathcal{E}})$ with $\tilde{x}^i = \hat{x}^i$ for all $i \in N$ and with $\tilde{x}^0 = e^0$. Evidently $(\tilde{x}^{\tilde{N}}, \hat{p})$ is a WE in the environment $\tilde{\mathcal{E}}$. In particular $\tilde{\mathcal{E}} \in \mathbf{E}_1$, so $\tilde{\mathcal{E}} \in \mathbf{E}$, which implies that $\Phi(\tilde{\mathcal{E}}) \neq \emptyset$.

Given any alternative price vector $p \gg 0$, define

$$\alpha(p) := \min\{p_g/\hat{p}_g \mid g \in G\} \quad \text{and} \quad G(p) := \arg\min\{p_g/\hat{p}_g \mid g \in G\}. \tag{29}$$

Then the Walrasian consumption vector $x^0(p)$ demanded by agent 0 obviously satisfies $x^0_g(p) = 0$ for all $G \setminus G(p)$, so (29) implies that

$$\sum_{g \in G(p)} \hat{p}_g x^0_g(p) = \frac{1}{\alpha(p)} \sum_{g \in G(p)} p_g x^0_g(p) = \frac{1}{\alpha(p)} \sum_{g \in G} p_g e^0_g \geq \sum_{g \in G} \hat{p}_g e^0_g. \tag{30}$$

From (30) and (28) it follows that

$$\sum_{g \in G(p)} \hat{p}_g [x^0_g(p) - e^0_g] \geq \sum_{g \in G \setminus G(p)} \hat{p}_g e^0_g = \sum_{g \in G \setminus G(p)} \sum_{h \in G} \sum_{i \in N} \hat{p}_h e^i_h. \tag{31}$$

Whenever p is not proportional to $\hat{p}$ and so $G \setminus G(p) \neq \emptyset$, (31) implies that

$$\sum_{g \in G(p)} \hat{p}_g [x^0_g(p) - e^0_g] > \sum_{g \in G(p)} \hat{p}_g \sum_{i \in N} e^i_g$$

and so $x^0_h(p) - e^0_h > \sum_{i \in N} e^i_h$ for at least one $h \in G(p)$. But $x^i_h(p) \geq 0$ for all $i \in N$, so $\sum_{i \in \tilde{N}} [x^i_h(p) - e^i_h] \geq x^0_h(p) - e^0_h - \sum_{i \in N} e^i_h > 0$ for this $h \in G(p)$. We conclude that the only possible Walrasian equilibrium price vectors in the environment $\tilde{\mathcal{E}}$ must be proportional to $\hat{p}$. Because $(\tilde{x}^{\tilde{N}}, \hat{p})$ is a WE, it is easy to see that any other WE allocation $x^{\tilde{N}}$ must satisfy $x^i \, I^i \, \tilde{x}^i$ for all $i \in N$. But $\emptyset \neq \Phi(\tilde{\mathcal{E}}) \subseteq \text{WE}(\tilde{\mathcal{E}})$ and the SCR is assumed to satisfy welfarism, so $\tilde{x}^{\tilde{N}} \in \Phi(\tilde{\mathcal{E}})$. Because $\tilde{x}^0 = e^0$, stability under nonessential deletion implies that $\mathcal{E} \in \mathbf{E}$ and that $\hat{x}^N = \tilde{x}^N \in \Phi(\mathcal{E})$. Since this is true for any WE $(\hat{x}^N, \hat{p})$, it follows that $\text{WE}(\mathcal{E}) \subseteq \Phi(\mathcal{E})$ and so, by the hypotheses of the Lemma, that $\text{WE}(\mathcal{E}) = \Phi(\mathcal{E})$. □

Theorem 44 *Suppose that the SCR Φ is defined on a domain $\mathbf{E}$ with $\mathbf{E}_1 \subseteq \mathbf{E} \subseteq \mathbf{E}_2$ and $\Phi(\mathcal{E}) \subseteq \text{WELT}(\mathcal{E})$ for all $\mathcal{E} \in \mathbf{E}$. Suppose too that Φ is welfarist, generates envy-free net trades,* *and is stable under both nonessential deletion and nonessential addition. Then Φ is the Walrasian social choice rule—that is, $\Phi(\mathcal{E}) = \mathrm{WE}(\mathcal{E}) \neq \emptyset$ for all $\mathcal{E} \in \mathbf{E}$, where $\mathbf{E} = \mathbf{E}_1$.*

Proof. Because Φ generates envy-free net trades and is stable under nonessential addition, Lemma 42 implies that $\Phi(\mathcal{E}) \subseteq \mathrm{WE}(\mathcal{E})$ for all $\mathcal{E} \in \mathbf{E}$. The result then follows from Lemma 43. □

It is worth noting that the above proofs require only that the two stability properties hold when $\#(\tilde{N} \setminus N) = 1$—that is, when only one agent at a time is added or deleted from the economic environment.

8.4. Consistency and Converse Consistency

An alternative approach to characterizing Walrasian allocations through properties of social choice rules with a variable set of agents uses some key ideas pioneered by Thomson (1988) for fair division problems. Van den Nouweland, Peleg, and Tijs (1996) have adapted these ideas to Walrasian allocations—see also Dagan (1995, 1996). Their main results apply to pure exchange economic environments in which agents all have regular smooth preferences as defined in Section 2.5.[35] In particular, each agent's type $\theta^i = (X^i, e^i, R^i)$ is described by a consumption set $X^i = \mathbb{R}^G_+$, an endowment vector $e^i \in \mathbb{R}^G_{++}$, and a smooth preference ordering R^i that is strictly monotone, convex, and continuous. But each environment $\mathcal{E} := \langle N, \theta^N, z\rangle$ is a *generalized economy*, with z as an exogenously given aggregate net supply vector. The associated *feasible set* is defined by

$$F(N, \theta^N, z) := \{x^N \in (\mathbb{R}^G_+)^N \mid \sum_{i \in N} (x^i - e^i) = z\}.$$

Say that $(\hat{x}^N, \hat{p})$ is a WE in the environment $\mathcal{E} = \langle N, \theta^N, z\rangle$ provided that $\hat{x}^N \in F(\mathcal{E})$, and $\hat{x}^i$ is a Walrasian demand at the price vector $\hat{p}$, for each $i \in N$. When preferences are LNS, this implies that $\hat{p}z = \sum_{i \in N} \hat{p}(\hat{x}^i - \hat{e}^i) = 0$.

A *solution* or *social choice rule* (SCR) on a *domain* $\mathbf{E}$ of environments $\mathcal{E}$ is a correspondence $\Phi : \mathbf{E} \twoheadrightarrow (\mathbb{R}^G_+)^N$ satisfying $\emptyset \neq \Phi(\mathcal{E}) \subseteq F(\mathcal{E})$ for all $\mathcal{E} \in \mathbf{E}$.[36]

Given any environment $\mathcal{E} = \langle N, \theta^N, z\rangle$ with $\#N \geq 2$, any proper subset K of N, and any consumption allocation $x^N \in F(N, \theta^N, z)$, define the *reduced environment*

$$\mathcal{E}^K(x^N) := \langle K, \theta^K, z - \sum_{i \in N \setminus K} (x^i - e^i)\rangle.$$

[35] This is somewhat imprecise. More exactly, instead of assuming that there is a C^1 utility function, they require only the existence of a unique normalized supporting price vector at each $x \in \mathbb{R}^G_{++}$.

[36] Van den Nouweland, Peleg, and Tijs (1996) allow $\Phi(\mathcal{E})$ to be empty in some generalized economies. It seems preferable to exclude this possibility, though the full implications for the domain $\mathbf{E}$ where Φ can be defined have yet to be explored.

The SCR Φ on the domain $\mathbf{E}$ is said to be *consistent* if, given any $\mathcal{E} = \langle N, \theta^N, z \rangle \in \mathbf{E}$, any proper subset K of N, and any consumption allocation $x^N \in \Phi(\mathcal{E})$, one has $\mathcal{E}^K(x^N) \in \mathbf{E}$ and $x^K \in \Phi(\mathcal{E}^K(x^N))$.

On the other hand, the SCR Φ on the domain $\mathbf{E}$ is said to be *converse consistent* if, given any $\mathcal{E} = \langle N, \theta^N, z \rangle \in \mathbf{E}$, and any consumption allocation x^N that is Pareto efficient in the environment $\mathcal{E}$, then $x^N \in \Phi(\mathcal{E})$ provided that $\mathcal{E}^K(x^N) \in \mathbf{E}$ and $x^K \in \Phi(\mathcal{E}^K(x^N))$ for every proper subset K of N.

Consistency and converse consistency are essentially strengthenings of Thomson's (1988) conditions of stability under nonessential deletion and addition, respectively, as described in Section 8.3. The strengthenings allow the no-envy condition of Theorem 44 to be dropped. However, one other condition of "Pareto efficiency in two-agent environments" is still needed in the following characterization result.

Theorem 45 *Suppose that the SCR Φ is defined on the restricted domain $\mathbf{E}$ of all regular smooth generalized economic environments in which a Walrasian equilibrium exists. Then Φ is the Walrasian rule if and only if it satisfies both consistency and converse consistency, and in addition, whenever $\#N = 2$, then every $x^N \in \Phi(\mathcal{E})$ is Pareto efficient relative to the feasible set $F(\mathcal{E})$.*

8.5. Consistency and Converse Consistency with Interactive Opportunity Sets

Serrano and Volij (1998) provide an alternative characterization using a different notion of reduced environment. Also, instead of considering generalized environments that each include an exogenous net supply vector z, they use the more standard framework of Section 3.1 in which each agent $i \in N$ has a consumption set X^i, a production set Y^i, and a preference ordering R^i.

Another important difference is that the concept of a reduced environment involves a modified version of Serrano and Volij's (2000) multilateral interactive opportunity sets whose construction was discussed in Section 6.3. Specifically, the sequences $Z_S^{i,m}(x^N)$ $(m = 0, 1, 2, \ldots)$ are defined for each (nonempty) coalition $S \subseteq N$, each agent $i \in S$, and each consumption allocation $x^N \in X^N$. The construction starts as before with $Z_S^{i,0}(x^N) := Y^i$ when $m = 0$. Thereafter, given any fixed m and the sets $Z_S^{i,m}(x^N)$ (all $i \in S$), the next set for agent i is

$$Z_S^{i,m+1}(x^N) := Z_S^{i,m}(x^N) - \sum_{h \in S \setminus \{i\}} \Big([R^h(x^h) - Z_S^{h,m}(x^N)] \cup \{0\} \Big).$$

This is an obvious modification of (26). As before, $Z_S^{i,m}(x^N) \subseteq Z_S^{i,m+1}(x^N)$ for $m = 0, 1, 2, \ldots$, so the limit set $Z_S^i(x^N) := \cup_{m=0}^{\infty} Z_S^{i,m}(x^N)$ is well defined.

Next, given the environment $\mathcal{E} = \langle N, \theta^N \rangle$, the coalition $K \subseteq N$, and the consumption allocation $x^N \in X^N$, define the *reduced environment* $\mathcal{E}^K(x^N) := \langle K, \theta^K(x^N) \rangle$ where

$\theta^i(x^N) := \langle X^i, Y^i_K(x^N), R^i\rangle$ for all $i \in K$, with $Y^i_K(x^N) := \cup_{S\subseteq N\setminus K} Z^i_{\{i\}\cup S}(x^N)$. Thus agent i's opportunity set $Y^i_K(x^N)$ when interacting with coalition K in the reduced environment $\mathcal{E}^K(x^N)$ reflects the possibilities for trade outside this coalition, as represented by the sets $Z^i_{\{i\}\cup S}(x^N)$ for $S \subseteq N \setminus K$. The corresponding definitions of *consistency* and of *converse consistency with interactive opportunity sets* are exactly the same as the definitions in Section 8.4, though they apply to different sets $\mathcal{E}$ and $\mathcal{E}^K(x^N)$.

The following characterization result uses the set A^i of optimal autarky allocations for each agent $i \in N$, as defined in Section 5.1:

Theorem 46 *The SCR Φ is the Walrasian rule if and only if it satisfies both consistency and converse consistency with interactive opportunity sets, and in addition $\Phi(\mathcal{E}) \subseteq A^i$ whenever $\#N = \{i\}$.*

8.6. Minimal Message Spaces

Minimal message spaces were briefly mentioned at the end of Section 7.1 for economies with a fixed set of agents but a variable type profile. Sonnenschein (1974) used a similar idea, requiring that there should be no redundant messages, in order to characterize the Walrasian mechanism as a rule that selects core allocations while satisfying other axioms. Amongst these the most prominent is the "swamping" axiom S: Given any allowable message and any finite economy, that message is in the equilibrium message set for some larger finite economy that extends the original finite economy. Thus, given any message, the presence of any fixed set of agents in the economy does not preclude that message occurring in equilibrium when a large enough number of other agents are added to the economy.

9. STATISTICAL CONTINUUM ECONOMIES

9.1. Continuum Economies

Let Θ denote the (metric) space of agent types, as defined in Section 2.7. In Section 3.1 a *finite economy* was defined implicitly in the obvious way as a mapping $i \mapsto \theta^i$ from the finite set N to Θ. Following Aumann (1964), the standard model of a *continuum economy* involves the set of agents $N = [0,1]$, and a mapping $i \mapsto \theta^i$ from N to Θ. Not every mapping makes economic sense, however. Instead, it is usual to assume that N is given its *Borel σ-field*, defined as the smallest family $\mathcal{B}$ of subsets of N that includes:

(1) all relatively open sets;
(2) the complement $N \setminus B$ of any set $B \in \mathcal{B}$;
(3) the union $\cup_{n=1}^{\infty} B_n$ of any countable family of sets $B_n \in \mathcal{B}$ $(n = 1,2,\ldots)$.

The members of $\mathcal{B}$ are called *Borel sets*. We also define *Lebesgue measure* λ on the Borel σ-field $\mathcal{B}$. It is the unique mapping $\lambda : \mathcal{B} \to [0,1]$ such that $\lambda([a,b]) = b - a$ whenever

$[a,b]$ is an interval with $0 \leq a \leq b \leq 1$, and which is *countably additive* in the sense that $\lambda(B) = \sum_{n=1}^{\infty} \lambda(B_n)$ whenever B is the union $\cup_{n=1}^{\infty} B_n$ of the countable family of pairwise disjoint sets $B_n \in \mathcal{B}$ $(n = 1, 2, \ldots)$.

As a metric space, Θ also has a Borel σ-field, which we denote by $\mathcal{F}$. It has then been usual to assume, following Hildenbrand (1974), that the mapping $i \mapsto \theta^i$ from N to Θ is *measurable*—that is, for each Borel set $K \in \mathcal{F}$, the set $\theta^{-1}(k) := \{i \in N \mid \theta^i \in K\}$ should belong to $\mathcal{B}$.

Such measurability is highly restrictive, however. To see why, suppose Θ is an *n-parameter domain* of agent types for which there is a homeomorphism between Θ and a subset of $\mathbb{R}^n$. Then any measurable mapping $i \mapsto \theta^i$ from N to Θ must be "nearly continuous"—specifically, given any $\epsilon > 0$, there exists a compact set $K_\epsilon \subseteq N$ with $\lambda(K_\epsilon) > 1 - \epsilon$ such that the mapping $i \mapsto \theta^i$ restricted to K_ϵ is continuous. Indeed, this is a direct application of Lusin's Theorem, a well-known result in measure theory.[37]

9.2. Statistical Economies

Usually all that matters about agents' types θ^i $(i \in N)$ is their *distribution*. This is represented by a (probability) measure μ on Θ, with $\mu(K) \geq 0$ as the proportion of agents having $\theta \in K$, for each Borel set K. This measure must satisfy the standard conditions that $\mu(\Theta) = 1$, and also $\mu(\cup_{n=1}^{\infty} K_n) = \sum_{n=1}^{\infty} \mu(K_n)$ whenever the sets K_n $(n = 1, 2, \ldots)$ are pairwise disjoint.

9.3. Statistical Continuum Economies

Although the distribution μ on Θ captures most important features of agents' types, it need not represent the fact that there are many agents. For example, if there happen to be two types θ' and θ'' such that the distribution satisfies $\mu(\{\theta'\}) = \mu(\{\theta'\}) = \frac{1}{2}$, this could be because there are only two agents, or because there is a continuum of agents of whom exactly half have each of these two types.

Also, in some contexts it is important to allow asymmetric allocations in which some agents of the same type receive different net trade vectors. Indeed, in nonconvex environments, this may be essential in any Walrasian equilibrium. Obviously, this requires a mathematical framework rich enough to allow the net trade vector t^i of each agent $i \in N$ to depend not only on i's type θ^i, but possibly also directly on i.

For these reasons, the formulation used here involves the entire Cartesian product $N \times \Theta$ of label–type pairs or "potential" agents (i, θ). Then N is the set of actual agents i who each have a type θ^i that may vary. We do not assume that the mapping $i \mapsto \theta^i$ is measurable. Instead, we assume that the economy is described by the joint distribution

[37] See Aliprantis and Border (1999), as well as Loeb and Talvila (2004), who show that the same property would hold whenever the metric space Θ is second countable—or *a fortiori*, separable.

of pairs (i,θ). This involves considering the *product* σ*-field* $\mathcal{B}\otimes\mathcal{F}$, defined as the smallest σ-field that contains all *measurable rectangles* of the form $B\times F$ with $B\in\mathcal{B}$ and $F\in\mathcal{F}$. Then the *joint distribution* of (i,θ) is a probability measure ν defined on the measurable sets in $\mathcal{B}\otimes\mathcal{F}$.

An important restriction on the probability measure ν that describes the statistical continuum economy is that it should *conform* with λ on $\mathcal{B}$, meaning that $\nu([a,b]\times\Theta)=\lambda([a,b])=b-a$ whenever $0\leq a\leq b\leq 1$. More generally, the marginal measure $\text{marg}_N\,\nu$ of ν on N should be the Lebesgue measure λ—that is,

$$\nu(B\times\Theta)=\lambda(B)\text{ whenever }B\in\mathcal{B}. \tag{32}$$

Let $\mathcal{M}_\lambda(N\times\Theta)$ denote the set of probability measures on the product σ-field $\mathcal{B}\otimes\mathcal{F}$ of $N\times\Theta$ that satisfy (32).

It is worth noting that each continuum economy, described by a measurable mapping $i\mapsto\theta^i$, is included as a special case. Indeed, such a continuum economy is fully described by the measure ν restricted to the graph

$$\Gamma:=\{(i,\theta)\in N\times\Theta\mid\theta=\theta^i\}$$

of the measurable mapping $i\mapsto\theta^i$, with $\nu((B\times\Theta)\cap\Gamma)=\lambda(B)$ for all $B\in\mathcal{B}$.

Following an extension of an idea due to Hildenbrand (1974, p. 138), consider a randomly drawn infinite sequence of pairs $(i,\theta)\in N\times\Theta$. Then we can interpret the joint measure ν as the theoretical limit of the sequence of empirical distributions that result when:

- the identifiers i are i.i.d. random draws from the uniform distribution described by the Lebesgue measure λ on $N=[0,1]$;
- the type θ of each agent $i\in N$ is drawn from that agent's conditional distribution $\nu(\cdot|i)$ on Θ.

In fact the pairs (i,θ) in the random sequence are mutually independent random variables with identical distribution $\nu\in\mathcal{M}_\lambda(N\times\Theta)$. Because both N and Θ are Polish spaces, so is their product. Now apply Varadarajan's (1958) version of the well-known Glivenko–Cantelli theorem in probability theory.[38] It implies that the two empirical distributions of i and of (i,θ) that result from the first n pairs of the sequence almost surely have weak limits (as probability measures) as $n\to\infty$ equal to λ and to ν, respectively.

9.4. Allocation Mechanisms

A (net trade) *allocation mechanism* given ν is a mapping $(i,\theta)\mapsto t^i_\theta$ from $N\times\Theta$ to $\mathbb{R}^G$ that is *measurable* in the sense that the set $\{(i,\theta)\in N\times\Theta\mid t^i_\theta\in S\}$ belongs to $\mathcal{B}\otimes\mathcal{F}$ for

[38] See Dudley (1989, Theorem 11.4.1).

every Borel set S of the Euclidean space $\mathbb{R}^G$, and also *feasible* in the sense that $t^i_\theta \in T_\theta$ for ν-a.e. $(i,\theta) \in N \times \Theta$, while the *mean net trade vector* defined by the integral $\int_{N\times\Theta} t^i_\theta \, d\nu$ is equal to 0. Such an allocation mechanism will typically be denoted by $t^{N\times\Theta}$.

It is obviously natural to consider such allocation mechanisms in a statistical economy described by a distribution ν over $N \times \Theta$. But even when the economy is described by a measurable mapping $i \mapsto \theta^i$ from $N = [0,1]$ to Θ, some characterizations of Walrasian equilibrium require specifying what net trade vector t^i_θ agent i would receive in the counterfactual event that i's type were to change to some arbitrary type $\theta \neq \theta^i$. In particular, this is important when considering strategyproofness.

9.5. Pareto Efficiency

Say that the particular allocation mechanism $\hat{t}^{N\times\Theta}$ is *weakly Pareto efficient* if there is no alternative allocation mechanism $t^{N\times\Theta}$ with

$$\nu\left(\{(i,\theta) \in N \times \Theta \mid t^i_\theta \in P_\theta(\hat{t}^i_\theta)\}\right) = 1.$$

Say that the allocation mechanism $\hat{t}^{N\times\Theta}$ is *Pareto efficient* if there is no alternative allocation mechanism $t^{N\times\Theta}$ with

$$\nu\left(\{(i,\theta) \in N \times \Theta \mid t^i_\theta \in R_\theta(\hat{t}^i_\theta)\}\right) = 1,$$
$$\text{while} \quad \nu\left(\{(i,\theta) \in N \times \Theta \mid t^i_\theta \in P_\theta(\hat{t}^i_\theta)\}\right) > 0.$$

9.6. Walrasian and Compensated Equilibria

Without any lump-sum wealth redistribution, an agent with type θ has a corresponding *Walrasian budget set* at a given price vector $p \in \mathbb{R}^G \setminus \{0\}$ defined by

$$B_\theta(p) := \{t \in T_\theta \mid p\,t \leq 0\},$$

as well as a *Walrasian demand set* defined by

$$\xi_\theta(p) := \{t \in B_\theta(p) \mid t' \in P_\theta(t) \Longrightarrow p\,t' > 0\}.$$

The corresponding *compensated demand set*, on the other hand, is defined by

$$\xi^C_\theta(p) := \{t \in B_\theta(p) \mid t' \in R_\theta(t) \Longrightarrow p\,t' \geq 0\}.$$

Suppose that $\hat{t}^{N\times\Theta}$ is a feasible allocation mechanism, and $\hat{p} \neq 0$ a price vector. Then the pair $(\hat{t}^{N\times\Theta}, \hat{p})$ is a Walrasian equilibrium (or WE) if $\hat{t}^i_\theta \in \xi_\theta(\hat{p})$ for ν-a.e. pair $(i,\theta) \in N \times \Theta$. The same pair is a compensated equilibrium (or CE) if $\hat{t}^i_\theta \in \xi^C_\theta(\hat{p})$ for ν-a.e. pair $(i,\theta) \in N \times \Theta$.

9.7. Lump-Sum Wealth Redistribution

Wealth distribution rules for finite economies, along with associated Walrasian equilibria, were defined in Section 3.3. In the statistical continuum economy described by the distribution ν on $N \times \Theta$, a *wealth distribution rule* $w^{N\times\Theta}(p)$ is a real-valued function $(i,\theta,p) \mapsto w^i_\theta(p)$ defined on $N \times \Theta \times (\mathbb{R}^G \setminus \{0\})$ that is measurable w.r.t. (i,θ), continuous and homogeneous of degree one w.r.t. p, while satisfying $\int_{N\times\Theta} w^i_\theta(p)\,d\nu = 0$ for each $p \neq 0$. With this as the wealth distribution rule, the definitions in Section 9.6 of Walrasian budget set, Walrasian demand set, and compensated demand set change in the obvious way to become

$$B^i_\theta(p) := \{t \in T_\theta \mid pt \leq w^i_\theta(p)\},$$
$$\xi^i_\theta(p) := \{t \in B^i_\theta(p) \mid t' \in P_\theta(t) \implies pt' > w^i_\theta(p)\},$$
$$\xi^{iC}_\theta(p) := \{t \in B^i_\theta(p) \mid t' \in R_\theta(t) \implies pt' \geq w^i_\theta(p)\},$$

respectively. These three sets depend on i as well as θ only because $w^i_\theta(p)$ is allowed to depend on i.

Relative to the wealth distribution rule $w^{N\times\Theta}(p)$, the pair $(\hat{t}^{N\times\Theta},\hat{p})$ consisting of the feasible allocation mechanism $\hat{t}^{N\times\Theta}$ and the price vector $\hat{p} \neq 0$ is a WELT (respectively, CELT) if $\hat{t}^i_\theta \in \xi^i_\theta(\hat{p})$ (respectively, $\hat{t}^i_\theta \in \xi^{iC}_\theta(\hat{p})$) for ν-a.e. pair $(i,\theta) \in N \times \Theta$.

9.8. Walrasian Equilibrium with Equal Budgets

The analysis of Section 3.6 is easily extended to the present continuum economy setting. Thus, results that characterize WE can be used to characterize WEEB instead by applying them to equivalent equal opportunity economies in which $T_\theta = X_\theta - Y$ for each type $\theta \in \Theta$, where X_θ is the consumption set, and Y is the common opportunity set.

10. EFFICIENCY THEOREMS IN CONTINUUM ECONOMIES

10.1. First Efficiency Theorem

The first efficiency theorem is a routine extension of Theorem 15.

Theorem 47 *Any WELT is weakly Pareto efficient; it is Pareto efficient if all agents have LNS preferences.*

Proof. Let $(\hat{t}^{N\times\Theta},\hat{p})$ be any WELT. Suppose that the mapping $(i,\theta) \mapsto t^i_\theta$ is measurable w.r.t. the product σ-field on $N \times \Theta$, while satisfying $t^i_\theta \in P_\theta(\hat{t}^i_\theta)$ for ν-a.e. $(i,\theta) \in N \times \Theta$. Because $\hat{t}^i_\theta \in \xi^i_\theta(\hat{p})$ for ν-a.e. (i,θ), it follows that $\hat{p}t^i_\theta > w^i_\theta(\hat{p})$ for ν-a.e. (i,θ).

Integrating this inequality over $N \times \Theta$ gives

$$\int_{N\times\Theta} \hat{p}\, t^i_\theta \, \mathrm{d}\nu > \int_{N\times\Theta} w^i_\theta(p)\, \mathrm{d}\nu = 0. \tag{33}$$

This implies that $\int_{N\times\Theta} t^i_\theta \, \mathrm{d}\nu \neq 0$, so the mapping $(i,\theta) \mapsto t^i_\theta$ does not give a feasible allocation. Conversely, no feasible allocation $t^{N\times\Theta}$ can satisfy $t^i_\theta \in P_\theta(\hat{t}^i_\theta)$ for ν-a.e. $(i,\theta) \in N \times \Theta$.

In the case when $\succsim_\theta$ is LNS for ν-a.e. (i,θ), Lemma 9 implies that the WELT is a CELT. So if the mapping $(i,\theta) \mapsto t^i_\theta$ is measurable w.r.t. the product σ-field on $N \times \Theta$, while satisfying $t^i_\theta \in R_\theta(\hat{t}^i_\theta)$ for ν-a.e. $(i,\theta) \in N \times \Theta$, then $\hat{p}\, t^i_\theta \geq w^i_\theta(\hat{p})$ for ν-a.e. (i,θ). And if $t^i_\theta \in P_\theta(\hat{t}^i_\theta)$ for a non-null set of pairs (i,θ), then $\hat{p}\, t^i_\theta > w^i_\theta(\hat{p})$ in that set, implying that (33) holds as before. □

10.2. Second Efficiency Theorem

The following result is the obvious counterpart of Theorem 16, bearing in mind that a continuum of (potential) agents allows one to relax the assumption that preferences are convex. On the other hand, we assume preferences are continuous in order to allow the measure ν to be constructed on $N \times \Theta$. The proof is an obvious adaptation of that found in Hildenbrand (1974, p. 232).

Theorem 48 *Suppose that agents' preferences are LNS and continuous. Then any weakly Pareto efficient allocation is a CELT.*

Proof. Suppose that the feasible allocation $\hat{t}^{N\times\Theta}$ is weakly Pareto efficient. Recall from Section 2.7 that each agent's type θ is identified with the closed graph of the preference ordering $\succsim_\theta$. Together with the measurability of the mapping $(i,\theta) \mapsto \hat{t}^i_\theta$, this ensures that the correspondence $(i,\theta) \twoheadrightarrow P_\theta(\hat{t}^i_\theta)$ has a measurable graph. Define the set

$$Z := \int_{N\times\Theta} P_\theta(\hat{t}^i_\theta)\, \mathrm{d}\nu \tag{34}$$

of all possible integrals of measurable selections $(i,\theta) \mapsto t^i_\theta \in P_\theta(\hat{t}^i_\theta)$. Because preferences are LNS, one has $\hat{t}^i_\theta \in \operatorname{cl} P_\theta(\hat{t}^i_\theta)$ for all $(i,\theta) \in N \times \Theta$. But the correspondence $(i,\theta) \twoheadrightarrow P_\theta(\hat{t}^i_\theta)$ has a measurable graph and preferences are continuous, so there exists a measurable function $(i,\theta) \mapsto t^i_\theta \in P_\theta(\hat{t}^i_\theta)$ such that $t^i_\theta - \hat{t}^i_\theta$ is bounded. Then, because $\int_{N\times\Theta} \hat{t}^i_\theta \mathrm{d}\nu = 0$, the function $(i,\theta) \mapsto t^i_\theta$ is an integrable selection from the correspondence $(i,\theta) \twoheadrightarrow P_\theta(\hat{t}^i_\theta)$. This implies that Z is nonempty. Because the measure ν is nonatomic, it is well known that Z must be convex—see, for example, Hildenbrand (1974, p. 62, Theorem 3).

Weak Pareto efficiency of $\hat{t}^{N\times\Theta}$ implies that $0 \notin Z$. By the separating hyperplane theorem, there exists $\hat{p} \neq 0$ such that

$$0 \leq \inf \hat{p} Z = \int_{N\times\Theta} \inf \hat{p} P_\theta(\hat{t}^i_\theta)\, d\nu, \tag{35}$$

where the equality is implied by (34) and Hildenbrand (1974, p. 63, Prop. 6). But $\hat{t}^i_\theta \in \text{cl}\, P_\theta(\hat{t}^i_\theta)$ because preferences are LNS, so

$$\inf \hat{p} P_\theta(\hat{t}^i_\theta) \leq \hat{p}\, \hat{t}^i_\theta \text{ for all } (i,\theta) \in N \times \Theta. \tag{36}$$

Because $0 = \int_{N\times\Theta} \hat{t}^i_\theta\, d\nu$, it follows from (35) and (36) that

$$0 \leq \int_{N\times\Theta} \inf \hat{p} P_\theta(\hat{t}^i_\theta)\, d\nu \leq \int_{N\times\Theta} \hat{p}\, \hat{t}^i_\theta\, d\nu = 0. \tag{37}$$

Together (36) and (37) imply that $\inf \hat{p} P_\theta(\hat{t}^i_\theta) = \hat{p}\, \hat{t}^i_\theta$ for ν-a.e. $(i,\theta) \in N \times \Theta$. In particular, because preferences are LNS, for ν-a.e. (i,θ) one has $\hat{p}\, t \geq \hat{p}\, \hat{t}^i_\theta$ whenever $t \in R_\theta(\hat{t}^i_\theta)$. This implies that $(\hat{t}^{N\times\Theta}, \hat{p})$ is a CELT relative to the specific wealth distribution rule $w^{N\times\Theta}(p)$ defined by $w^i_\theta(p) := p\, \hat{t}^i_\theta$ for all $i \in N$, $\theta \in \Theta$ and $p \in \mathbb{R}^G \setminus \{0\}$. □

10.3. Nonoligarchic Allocations

Convex preferences were not needed to prove Theorem 48. Convex feasible sets, however, are assumed in the following argument concerning sufficient conditions for a CELT to be a WELT. When each T_θ is convex, the definition and results of Section 4.4 are fairly easily extended to continuum economies. Specifically, given the weakly Pareto efficient allocation $\hat{t}^{N\times\Theta}$, the set $K \subset N \times \Theta$ with $0 < \nu(K) < 1$ is said to be an *oligarchy* if there is no alternative feasible allocation $t^{N\times\Theta}$ satisfying $t^i_\theta \succ_\theta \hat{t}^i_\theta$ for ν-a.e. $(i,\theta) \in K$.

Theorem 49 *Assume agents' preferences are LNS and continuous, and each feasible set T_θ is convex. Assume too that $0 \in \text{int} \int_{N\times\Theta} T_\theta\, d\nu$. Then any nonoligarchic weakly Pareto efficient (NOWPE) allocation is a WELT.*

Proof. Let $\hat{t}^{N\times\Theta}$ be any weakly Pareto efficient allocation. By Theorem 48, this allocation is a CELT at some price vector $\hat{p} \neq 0$. Let K be the set of all potential agents $(i,\theta) \in N \times \Theta$ with cheaper points $\underline{t}^i_\theta \in T_\theta$ satisfying $\hat{p}\, \underline{t}^i_\theta < \hat{p}\, \hat{t}^i_\theta$. By the definitions of a statistical continuum economy and of an allocation mechanism, the set K is measurable. Because $0 \in \text{int} \int_{N\times\Theta} T_\theta\, d\nu$, there exists an integrable mapping $(i,\theta) \mapsto \bar{t}^i_\theta \in T_\theta$ on $N \times \Theta$ such that $\hat{p} \int_{N\times\Theta} \bar{t}^i_\theta\, d\nu < 0$. Because $\hat{p} \int_{N\times\Theta} \hat{t}^i_\theta\, d\nu = 0$, there must exist a non-null measurable set $H \subset N \times \Theta$ such that $\hat{p}\bar{t}^i_\theta < \hat{p}\hat{t}^i_\theta$ for all $(i,\theta) \in H$. So $H \subset K$, implying that K is non-null.

Consider any measurable mapping $(i,\theta) \mapsto t^i_\theta$ satisfying both $t^i_\theta \in T_\theta$ for ν-a.e. $(i,\theta) \in N \times \Theta$ and $t^i_\theta \succ_\theta \hat{t}^i_\theta$ for ν-a.e. $(i,\theta) \in K$. Because each agent $i \in K$ has a cheaper point, Lemma 12 implies that $\hat{p}t^i_\theta > \hat{p}\hat{t}^i_\theta$ for ν-a.e. $(i,\theta) \in K$. But no agent outside K has a cheaper point, so $\hat{p}t^i_\theta \geq \hat{p}\hat{t}^i_\theta$ for ν-a.e. $(i,\theta) \in (N \times \Theta) \setminus K$. Because K must be non-null, it follows that

$$\hat{p} \int_{N\times\Theta} t^i_\theta \, d\nu > \hat{p} \int_{N\times\Theta} \hat{t}^i_\theta \, d\nu = 0.$$

Hence $\int_{N\times\Theta} t^i_\theta \, d\nu \neq 0$, so $t^{N\times\Theta}$ cannot be a feasible allocation. Except when $\nu(K) = 1$, it follows that $\hat{t}^{N\times\Theta}$ is oligarchic, with K as an oligarchy.

Conversely, if $\hat{t}^{N\times\Theta}$ is a NOWPE allocation, then $\nu(K) = 1$, so almost all agents have cheaper points. So the CELT $(\hat{t}^{N\times\Theta}, \hat{p})$ is actually a WELT. □

10.4. Individual Nonconvexities

When the individual feasible sets T_θ are nonconvex for a non-null set of potential agents (i,θ), the cheaper point Lemma 12 cannot be applied, and the conclusion of Theorem 49 may not hold. Examples illustrating this possibility can be found in Dasgupta and Ray (1986) as well as Coles and Hammond (1995) and also Hammond and Sempere (2006, 2009). Additional assumptions will be presented here that do guarantee that a weakly Pareto efficient allocation is a WELT.

Any individual feasible set T_θ is said to be *piecewise convex* if there exists a countable (i.e., finite or countably infinite) collection T^m_θ $(m \in M_\theta \subseteq \mathbb{N})$ of closed convex sets such that $T_\theta = \cup_{m\in M_\theta} T^m_\theta$. That is, even if T_θ is not convex, it must be the union of a countable collection of *convex components* or "pieces." These components may be disjoint, but they may also intersect.

Piecewise convexity excludes some nonconvex feasible sets such as

$$\{t \in \mathbb{R}^2 \mid t \geqq (-1,-1),\ (t_1+1)^2 + (t_2+1)^2 \geq 1\}.$$

But it allows many forms of setup cost. It also allows indivisible goods, which are consistent with a feasible set such as $\{t \in \mathbb{R}^D \times \mathbb{Z}^H \mid t \geqq \underline{t}\}$ for some fixed lower bound $\underline{t} \in \mathbb{R}^D \times \mathbb{Z}^H$, where D is the set of divisible goods, and $H := G \setminus D$ is the set of indivisible goods, with $\mathbb{Z}$ denoting the set of integers.

Given any agent type $\theta \in \Theta$ and any net trade vector $t \in T_\theta$, define the set

$$M_\theta(t) := \{m \in M_\theta \mid P_\theta(t) \cap T^m_\theta \neq \emptyset\} \tag{38}$$

of natural numbers $m \in \mathbb{N}$ that index those convex components T_θ^m that intersect the strict preference set $P_\theta(t)$. Given a price vector $p \neq 0$, let

$$W_\theta(p,t) := \{\inf p\, T_\theta^m \mid m \in M_\theta(t)\} \tag{39}$$

be the associated countable set of *critical* wealth levels at which a type θ agent can just afford to reach one of the convex components $T_\theta^m (m \in M_\theta(t))$. Extending the second efficiency theorem to allow individual nonconvexities will rely on the following generalization of the cheaper point Lemma 12.

Lemma 50 *Let $(i,\theta) \in N \times \Theta$ be any potential agent with a piecewise convex feasible set T_θ and continuous preferences. Suppose that the net trade vector $\hat{t}_\theta^i$ is any CELT for (i,θ) at the price vector $p \neq 0$—that is, suppose*

$$t \in R_\theta(\hat{t}_\theta^i) \Longrightarrow p\,t \geq p\,\hat{t}_\theta^i. \tag{40}$$

Suppose too that $p\,\hat{t}_\theta^i \notin W_\theta(p,\hat{t}_\theta^i)$. Then $\hat{t}_\theta^i$ is a WELT for (i,θ)—that is,

$$t \in P_\theta(\hat{t}_\theta^i) \Longrightarrow p\,t > p\,\hat{t}_\theta^i.$$

Proof. Consider any $t \in P_\theta(\hat{t}_\theta^i)$. Piecewise convexity of T_θ implies that $t \in T_\theta^m$ for some $m \in M_\theta(\hat{t}_\theta^i)$. The hypothesis $p\,\hat{t}_\theta^i \notin W_\theta(p,\hat{t}_\theta^i)$ implies that $p\,\hat{t}_\theta^i \neq \inf p\, T_\theta^m$. One possibility is that $p\,\hat{t}_\theta^i < \inf p\, T_\theta^m$, in which case $p\,t > p\,\hat{t}_\theta^i$, as required.

Alternatively $p\,\hat{t}_\theta^i > \inf p\, T_\theta^m$, and so there exists $\underline{t} \in T_\theta^m$ such that $p\,\underline{t} < p\,\hat{t}_\theta^i$. In this case, define $\tilde{t} := (1-\alpha)t + \alpha\,\underline{t}$ where $0 < \alpha < 1$. But T_θ^m is convex, $t \in P_\theta(\hat{t}_\theta^i)$, and preferences are continuous. Hence one has $\tilde{t} \in R_\theta(\hat{t}_\theta^i)$ for a suitably small α. So (40) implies that $p\,\tilde{t} \geq p\,\hat{t}_\theta^i$. But $p\,\underline{t} < p\,\hat{t}_\theta^i$ and $0 < \alpha < 1$, so

$$p\,t = \frac{1}{1-\alpha}(p\,\tilde{t} - \alpha\, p\,\underline{t}) > \frac{1}{1-\alpha}(p\,\hat{t}_\theta^i - \alpha\, p\,\hat{t}_\theta^i) = p\,\hat{t}_\theta^i.$$

Because this argument works for all $t \in P_\theta(\hat{t}_\theta^i)$, the result follows. □

To reduce notation, let $W_\theta^*(p,\hat{t}_\theta^i)$ denote the set $W_\theta(p,\hat{t}_\theta^i) \setminus \{\inf p\, T_\theta\}$. Then, to elaborate the basic idea used by Mas-Colell (1977), Yamazaki (1978, 1981) and Coles and Hammond (1995), say that the CELT $(\hat{t}^{N\times\Theta},p)$ is *dispersed* if

$$\nu(\{(i,\theta) \in N \times \Theta \mid p\,\hat{t}_\theta^i \in W_\theta^*(p,\hat{t}_\theta^i)\}) = 0. \tag{41}$$

In other words, the set of potential agents who have both cheaper points and critical wealth levels should be of measure zero.

Theorem 51 *Suppose each agent's feasible set T_θ is piecewise convex, with $0 \in \operatorname{int} \int_{N\times\Theta} T_\theta \, d\nu$. Suppose too that preferences are LNS and continuous. Then any CELT that is nonoligarchic and dispersed must be a WELT.*

Proof. Let $(\hat{t}^{N\times\Theta}, p)$ be a CELT. As in the proof of Theorem 49, let K be the set of all $(i,\theta) \in N \times \Theta$ for which there is a cheaper point $\underline{t}^i_\theta \in T_\theta$ satisfying $p\underline{t}^i_\theta < p\hat{t}^i_\theta$. Because $0 \in \operatorname{int} \int_{N\times\Theta} T_\theta \, d\nu$, the set K must be non-null.

Consider any measurable mapping $(i,\theta) \mapsto t^i_\theta$ satisfying both $t^i_\theta \in T_\theta$ for ν-a.e. $(i,\theta) \in N \times \Theta$ and $t^i_\theta \succ_\theta \hat{t}^i_\theta$ for ν-a.e. $(i,\theta) \in K$. Because the CELT is assumed to be dispersed and each agent $(i,\theta) \in K$ has a cheaper point, for ν-a.e. $(i,\theta) \in K$ one has $p\hat{t}^i_\theta \notin W_\theta(p, \hat{t}^i_\theta)$ and so, by Lemma 50, $\hat{p}t^i_\theta > \hat{p}\hat{t}^i_\theta$. But no agent outside K has a cheaper point, so $\hat{p}t^i_\theta \geq \hat{p}\hat{t}^i_\theta$ for ν-a.e. $(i,\theta) \in (N \times \Theta) \setminus K$. Because K must be non-null, it follows that

$$\hat{p} \int_{N\times\Theta} t^i_\theta \, d\nu > \hat{p} \int_{N\times\Theta} \hat{t}^i_\theta \, d\nu = 0.$$

Hence, $t^{N\times\Theta}$ cannot be a feasible allocation. Unless $\nu(K) = 1$, it follows that K is an oligarchy.

Conversely, if $\hat{t}^{N\times\Theta}$ is nonoligarchic, then $\nu(K) = 1$, implying that almost all agents have cheaper points. Then dispersion implies $p\hat{t}^i_\theta \notin W_\theta(p, \hat{t}^i_\theta)$ for ν-a.e. $(i,\theta) \in N \times \Theta$. By Lemma 50, the CELT is actually a WELT. □

A sufficient condition for (41) to hold is that $p, \hat{t}^i_\theta \notin W^*_\theta := \cup_{m\in M_\theta} \{\inf p\, T^m_\theta\} \setminus \{\inf p\, T_\theta\}$ for ν-a.e. $(i,\theta) \in N \times \Theta$. Because W^*_θ is a countable subset of $\mathbb{R}$, this may not be very restrictive. It is not restrictive at all when each T_θ is convex, in which case we can regard each T_θ as consisting of a single convex component, implying that W^*_θ is empty.

11. STATISTICAL CONTINUUM ECONOMIES: EXISTENCE THEOREMS

11.1. Integrably Bounded Gains from Trade Sets

The compensated equilibrium existence theorem for finite economies presented in Section 5.3 does not extend immediately to a continuum economy. With infinitely many agents, the set of feasible allocations and the gains from the trade set are both subsets of an infinite-dimensional space, which creates technical difficulties. In particular, the collective gains from the trade set defined in Section 5.3 is unlikely to be bounded because, as the number of agents tends to infinity, one or more of those agents may be able to extract unbounded quantities of some goods from other agents even if all of them remain no worse off than under autarky. Even if one imposes "equal treatment," requiring all agents of the same type to receive an identical allocation, the collective gains from trade set becomes unbounded as the number of different agent types tends to infinity.

To overcome these obstacles to existence, we restrict attention to agent types $\theta \in \Theta$ for which the feasible sets of net trade vectors T_θ allow autarky. We also assume that the weak gains from trade sets $R_\theta(0)$ are collectively *integrably bounded below*—that is, there exist lower bounds $\underline{t}_\theta$ (all $\theta \in \Theta$) such that $t \geqq \underline{t}_\theta$ for all $t \in R_\theta(0)$; moreover each lower bound $\underline{t}_\theta \leqq 0$ can be selected so that the mapping $\theta \mapsto \underline{t}_\theta$ is ν-integrable (meaning that $\int_{N\times\Theta} |\underline{t}_{\theta g}|\, d\nu < \infty$ for each $g \in G$), with $\int_{N\times\Theta} \underline{t}_\theta\, d\nu \ll 0$. In Section 11.5 it is also assumed that preferences are weakly monotone, and in Section 11.6, that individual agents' feasible sets are convex. Convexity of preferences, however, is not required.

Eventually, Sections 11.7 and 11.8 even relax convexity of the feasible sets of net trades in order to allow indivisible goods. The appropriately modified existence proof uses dispersion ideas similar to those of Section 10.4.

11.2. Continuity of the Budget and Demand Correspondences

The existence proofs in this section will rely on important continuity properties of the compensated demand correspondence when the space of agents' continuous types Θ is given the topology described in Section 2.7.

The first result concerns variations in θ when p is fixed.

Lemma 52 *For each fixed $p \neq 0$, the correspondence $\theta \mapsto\!\!\!\rightarrow \xi^C_\theta(p)$ has a closed graph in $\Theta \times \mathbb{R}^G$.*

Proof. Let $(\theta_n, t_n)_{n=1}^\infty$ be any sequence of points that belong to the graph of $\theta \mapsto\!\!\!\rightarrow \xi^C_\theta(p)$ because $t_n \in \xi^C_{\theta_n}(p)$ for $n = 1, 2, \ldots$. Suppose too that the sequence converges to $(\bar\theta, \bar t)$ as $n \to \infty$. Because $t_n \in T_{\theta_n}$ for each n, it follows from part (1) of Lemma 5 that $\bar t \in T_{\bar\theta}$. Also $p\,t_n \leq 0$ for each n. Taking the limit as $n \to \infty$ gives $p\bar t \leq 0$, so $\bar t \in B_{\bar\theta}(p)$.

Suppose $\tilde t \in P_{\bar\theta}(\bar t)$. Parts (2) and (3) of Lemma 5 imply that there exists a sequence $(\tilde t_n)_{n=1}^\infty$ converging to $\tilde t$ whose terms satisfy $\tilde t_n \in P_{\theta_n}(t_n)$ for all large n. Because $t_n \in \xi^C_{\theta_n}(p)$ for each n, it follows that $p\tilde t_n \geq 0$ for all large n, and so $p\tilde t \geq 0$ in the limit as $n \to \infty$.

Finally, because agents' preferences are LNS and transitive, any $t' \in R_{\bar\theta}(\bar t)$ is the limit of a sequence $(t'_n)_{n=1}^\infty$ in $P_{\bar\theta}(\bar t)$ that converges to t'. The previous paragraph showed that $p\,t'_n \geq 0$ for $n = 1, 2, \ldots$, so $p\,t' \geq 0$ in the limit. Hence $\bar t \in \xi^C_{\bar\theta}(p)$, thus confirming that the graph of $\theta \mapsto\!\!\!\rightarrow \xi^C_\theta(p)$ is closed. □

The second result concerns variations in p when θ is fixed.

Lemma 53 *For each fixed θ, the correspondence $p \mapsto\!\!\!\rightarrow \xi^C_\theta(p)$ has a relatively closed graph in $(\mathbb{R}^G \setminus \{0\}) \times \mathbb{R}^G$.*

Proof. Suppose that $(p_n, t_n)_{n=1}^{\infty}$ is any sequence of points that are in the graph of $p \mapsto\!\!\!\to B_\theta(p)$ because $p_n \neq 0$ and $t_n \in B_\theta(p_n)$ for $n = 1, 2, \ldots$. Suppose too that the sequence converges to $(\bar{p}, \bar{t})$ as $n \to \infty$, where $\bar{p} \neq 0$. Then $\bar{t} \in T_\theta$ because T_θ is closed. Also $p_n\, t_n \leq 0$ for each n, so taking the limit as $n \to \infty$ implies that $\bar{p}\bar{t} \leq 0$. This confirms that $\bar{t} \in B_\theta(\bar{p})$.

Suppose in addition that each point of the convergent sequence $(p_n, t_n)_{n=1}^{\infty}$ is in the graph of $p \mapsto\!\!\!\to \xi_\theta^C(p)$. Consider any $t' \in P_\theta(\bar{t})$. Because preferences are continuous and $t_n \to \bar{t}$ as $n \to \infty$, it follows that $t' \succ_\theta t_n$ for large enough n. But each $t_n \in \xi_\theta^C(p_n)$, so $p_n t' \geq 0$ for all large n. Taking the limit as $n \to \infty$ implies that $\bar{p}t' \geq 0$. Because preferences are LNS, the same must be true whenever $t' \in R_\theta(\bar{t})$. This proves that $\bar{t} \in \xi_\theta^C(\bar{p})$, thus confirming that the graph of $p \mapsto\!\!\!\to \xi_\theta^C(p)$ is closed. □

One reason for using the compensated demand correspondence $\xi_\theta^C(\cdot)$ is precisely that the usual Walrasian demand correspondence $\xi_\theta(\cdot)$ may not have a closed graph near any price vector p at which there is no cheaper point $t \in T_\theta$ satisfying $pt < 0$.

11.3. Integrably Bounded Restricted Budget and Demand Correspondences

Any Walrasian net trade vector $\hat{t}_\theta^i \in \xi_\theta(p)$ satisfies $0 \notin P_\theta(\hat{t}_\theta^i)$ and so, because preferences are complete, $\hat{t}_\theta^i \in R_\theta(0)$. Consequently, any WE $(\hat{t}^{N\times\Theta}, \hat{p})$ satisfies weak gains from trade. A CE need not, however, unless each $\xi_\theta^C(p)$ is replaced by the *restricted compensated demand set*

$$\bar{\xi}_\theta^C(p) := \xi_\theta^C(p) \cap R_\theta(0) = \{ t \in \bar{B}_\theta(p) \mid t' \in R_\theta(t) \Longrightarrow pt' \geq 0 \},$$

where $\bar{B}_\theta(p) := B_\theta(p) \cap R_\theta(0) = \{ t \in R_\theta(0) \mid pt \leq 0 \}$ is the *restricted budget set*. The following proofs demonstrate existence of a *restricted* CE $(\hat{t}^{N\times\Theta}, \hat{p})$ satisfying weak gains from trade because $\hat{t}_\theta^i \in \bar{\xi}_\theta^C(\hat{p})$ for ν-a.e. $(i, \theta) \in N \times \Theta$.

Say that a correspondence $F : N \times \Theta \twoheadrightarrow \mathbb{R}^G$ is *integrably bounded* if there exist integrable functions $(i,\theta) \mapsto a_\theta^i$ and $(i,\theta) \mapsto b_\theta^i$ such that, for ν-a.e. $(i,\theta) \in N \times \Theta$, one has $a_\theta^i \leqq t_\theta^i \leqq b_\theta^i$ whenever $t_\theta^i \in F_\theta^i$.

Lemma 54 *Suppose the feasible sets T_θ allow autarky, and the weak gains from trade sets $R_\theta(0)$ are bounded below by the ν-integrable function $\theta \mapsto \underline{t}_\theta$. Suppose preferences are LNS and continuous. Then for each fixed $p \gg 0$ the restricted compensated demand correspondence $(i,\theta) \mapsto\!\!\!\to \bar{\xi}_\theta^C(p)$ has nonempty compact values that are integrably bounded, as well as a closed graph.*

Proof. By definition, each $t \in \bar{B}_\theta(p)$ satisfies $t \in R_\theta(0)$ and so $t \geqq \underline{t}_\theta$. Because $p \gg 0$, the argument used to prove Lemma 6 shows that any $t \in \bar{B}_\theta(p)$ also satisfies $t \leqq \bar{t}_\theta(p)$, where

$\bar{t}_\theta(p)$ is the vector with components defined by

$$\bar{t}_{\theta g}(p) := -\sum_{h \in G \setminus \{g\}} p_h \underline{t}_{\theta h} / p_g \quad (\text{all } g \in G). \tag{42}$$

Hence $\bar{B}_\theta(p)$ is bounded. Also, because $\underline{t}_\theta$ is ν-integrable, (42) implies that so is $\bar{t}_\theta(p)$. Because $\bar{B}_\theta(p)$ is evidently a closed set, it must be compact. Obviously $0 \in \bar{B}_\theta(p)$ for each p and θ, so it is nonempty.

As discussed at the start of this section, $\xi_\theta(p) \subset R_\theta(0)$. So $\xi_\theta(p)$ consists of net trade vectors t that maximize $\succsim_\theta$ subject to $t \in \bar{B}_\theta(p)$. But the restricted budget set $\bar{B}_\theta(p)$ is compact. Because preferences are continuous, it follows that the Walrasian demand set $\xi_\theta(p)$ is nonempty. Also, because preferences are LNS, the proof of Lemma 9 shows that $\xi_\theta(p) \subseteq \xi_\theta^C(p)$. Hence $\xi_\theta(p) \subseteq R_\theta(0) \cap \xi_\theta^C(p) = \bar{\xi}_\theta^C(p)$, which implies that $\bar{\xi}_\theta^C(p)$ is nonempty.

Finally, let G_R and $G_C(p)$ denote the graphs of $\theta \mapsto\!\!\!\to R_\theta(0)$ and $\theta \mapsto\!\!\!\to \xi_\theta^C(p)$, respectively. Then G_R and $G_C(p)$ are both closed, by part (1) of Lemma 5 and Lemma 52, respectively. So therefore is $N \times [G_R \cap G_C(p)]$, which is the graph of $(i,\theta) \mapsto\!\!\!\to \bar{\xi}_\theta^C(p)$. In particular $\bar{\xi}_\theta^C(p)$ must be a closed set, for each fixed θ and p. As a closed subset of the compact set $\bar{B}_\theta(p)$, it must be compact. □

11.4. Existence of Compensated Equilibrium with Free Disposal

We begin by using arguments due to Khan and Yamazaki (1981) and Yamazaki (1981) to prove existence of a CE *with free disposal* $(\hat{t}^{N\times\Theta}, \hat{p})$. This is defined as a pair satisfying $\hat{t}_\theta^i \in \xi_\theta^C(\hat{p})$ for ν-a.e. $(i,\theta) \in N \times \Theta$, as well as $\hat{z} := \int_{N\times\Theta} \hat{t}_\theta^i \, d\nu \leqq 0$, $\hat{p} > 0$, and $\hat{p}\hat{z} = 0$. Because $\hat{p} > 0$ whereas $\hat{z} \leqq 0$, it follows that $\hat{p}_g \hat{z}_g = 0$ for all $g \in G$, implying the *rule of free goods*—if $\hat{z}_g < 0$ then $\hat{p}_g = 0$, whereas $\hat{z}_g = 0$ if $\hat{p}_g > 0$. Furthermore, because $\hat{p}\hat{z} = 0$ while $\hat{p}_g \hat{t}_\theta^i \leq 0$ for ν-a.e. $(i,\theta) \in N \times \Theta$, one has $\hat{p}_g \hat{t}_\theta^i = 0$ for ν-a.e. $(i,\theta) \in N \times \Theta$.

Lemma 55 *Suppose agents' feasible sets T_θ allow autarky, and the weak gains from trade sets $R_\theta(0)$ are bounded below by the integrable function $\theta \mapsto \underline{t}_\theta$. Suppose too that preferences are LNS and continuous. Then there exists a compensated equilibrium with free disposal satisfying weak gains from trade.*

Proof. Let $\Delta := \{p \in \mathbb{R}_+^G \mid \sum_{g\in G} p_g = 1\}$ denote the unit simplex of normalized nonnegative price vectors, with interior Δ^0 of normalized strictly positive price vectors. For each $n = 1, 2, \ldots,$ define the nonempty domain

$$D_n := \left\{p \in \Delta \mid p_g \geq 1/(\#G + n) \ (\text{all } g \in G)\right\}.$$

Note that, for each fixed $\theta \in \Theta$, whenever $t_\theta \in \bar{B}_\theta(p)$ and $p \in \Delta$, then

$$p_g\, t_{\theta g} = -\sum_{h \in G \setminus \{g\}} p_h\, t_{\theta h} \leq -\sum_{h \in G \setminus \{g\}} p_h\, \underline{t}_{\theta h} \leq \max\{-\underline{t}_{\theta h} \mid h \in G\}.$$

Hence, whenever $p \in D_n$ and $t_\theta \in \bar{B}_\theta(p)$, then $\underline{t}_\theta \leqq t_\theta \leqq \bar{t}_\theta$ where $\underline{t}_\theta \leqq 0$ and the respective components of $\bar{t}_\theta$ are given by

$$\bar{t}_{\theta g} := (\#G + n) \max\{-\underline{t}_{\theta h} \mid h \in G\} \quad (\text{all } g \in G). \tag{43}$$

That is, every $t_\theta \in \bar{B}_\theta(p)$ satisfies $\underline{t}_\theta \leqq t_\theta \leqq \bar{t}_\theta$ uniformly for all $p \in D_n$.

Next, for each $n = 1, 2, \ldots,$ define the aggregate excess compensated demand correspondence $\zeta_n : D_n \twoheadrightarrow \mathbb{R}^G$ by

$$p \mapsto\!\!\!\rightarrow \zeta_n(p) := \int_{N \times \Theta} \bar{\xi}_\theta^C(p)\, d\nu.$$

By Lemma 54, the correspondence $(i, \theta) \mapsto\!\!\!\rightarrow \bar{\xi}_\theta^C(p)$ has nonempty values and is integrably bounded, while its graph is closed and so measurable. So for each fixed $p \in D_n$, there exists an integrable selection from $(i, \theta) \mapsto\!\!\!\rightarrow \bar{\xi}_\theta^C(p)$, implying that $\zeta_n(p)$ is nonempty. Also, $\zeta_n(p)$ is convex because ν is nonatomic. But preferences are LNS, so for all $\theta \in \Theta$ one has $pt = 0$ whenever $t \in \xi_\theta^C(p)$ and so whenever $t \in \bar{\xi}_\theta^C(p) = \xi_\theta^C(p) \cap R_\theta(0)$. It follows that $pz = 0$ whenever $z \in \zeta_n(p)$. Moreover, because $\underline{t}_\theta \leqq t_\theta \leqq \bar{t}_\theta$ for all $t_\theta \in \bar{\xi}_\theta^C(p)$ where $\theta \mapsto \underline{t}_\theta$ is ν-integrable, it follows from (43) that $\theta \mapsto \bar{t}_\theta$ is also ν-integrable, and that

$$\int_{N \times \Theta} \underline{t}_\theta\, d\nu \leqq z \leqq \int_{N \times \Theta} \bar{t}_\theta\, d\nu \tag{44}$$

for all $z \in \zeta_n(p)$ and all $p \in D_n$. Hence, the arguments in Hildenbrand (1974, p. 73, Props. 7 and 8) establish: (1) because each set $\bar{\xi}_\theta^C(p)$ is closed and (44) holds, the correspondence ζ_n is compact-valued; (2) the graph of $\zeta_n : D_n \twoheadrightarrow \mathbb{R}^G$ is closed. Using (44) once again, it follows that the graph of ζ_n is compact.

For $n = 1, 2, \ldots,$ one can find a compact convex set $Z_n \subset \mathbb{R}^G$ large enough so that the graph of ζ_n is a subset of $D_n \times Z_n$. Then define $\phi_n(z) := \arg\max\{pz \mid p \in D_n\}$ for each $z \in Z_n$. Obviously $\phi_n(z)$ is nonempty and convex.

As in the proof of Theorem 24, one can show that the graph of the correspondence ϕ_n is closed, and so compact as a closed subset of the compact set $Z_n \times D_n$. Consider next the correspondence $\psi_n : D_n \times Z_n \twoheadrightarrow D_n \times Z_n$, which is defined for each

$n = 1, 2, \ldots$ by $\psi_n(p, z) := \phi_n(z) \times \zeta_n(p)$. This correspondence has a convex domain and nonempty convex values. Its graph is easily seen to be the Cartesian product of the graph of ϕ_n with the graph of ζ_n, and so compact as the Cartesian product of two compact sets. Hence, Kakutani's theorem can be applied to demonstrate the existence of a fixed point $(p_n, z_n) \in D_n \times Z_n$ for each $n = 1, 2, \ldots$. This fixed point satisfies $(p_n, z_n) \in \psi_n(p_n, z_n)$ and so $p_n \in \phi_n(z_n)$, $z_n \in \zeta_n(p_n)$. In particular, for all $p \in D_n$ one has $p z_n \leq p_n z_n = 0$.

Because the vector $(\#G)^{-1}(1, 1, \ldots, 1) \in D_n$, this result and (44) imply that

$$z_n \in Z^* := \{z \in \mathbb{R}^G \mid z \geqq \int_{N\times\Theta} \underline{t}_\theta \, d\nu; \ \frac{1}{\#G} \sum_{g\in G} z_{ng} \leq 0\}.$$

So the sequence $(p_n, z_n)_{n=1}^\infty$ lies in the compact subset $\Delta \times Z^*$ of $\mathbb{R}^G \times \mathbb{R}^G$, and must have a convergent subsequence. Retaining only the terms of this subsequence, we can assume that (p_n, z_n) converges to some pair $(\hat{p}, z^*) \in \Delta \times \mathbb{R}^G$.

Next, any $p \in \Delta^0$ satisfies $p \in D_n$ for all large n, so $p z_n \leq p_n z_n = 0$. Taking limits yields $p z^* \leq 0$ for all $p \in \Delta^0$, so $z^* \leqq 0$.

By definition of ζ_n, for $n = 1, 2, \ldots$ one has $z_n = \int_{N\times\Theta} t^i_{\theta n} \, d\nu \geqq \int_{N\times\Theta} \underline{t}_\theta \, d\nu$ where $t^i_{\theta n} \in \xi^C_\theta(p_n)$ for ν-a.e. $(i, \theta) \in N \times \Theta$. Now we apply "Fatou's lemma in several dimensions" due to Schmeidler (1970)—see also Hildenbrand (1974, p. 69, Lemma 3). Because $(i, \theta) \mapsto v^i_{\theta n} := t^i_{\theta n} - \underline{t}_\theta$ $(n = 1, 2, \ldots)$ is a sequence of ν-integrable functions from $N \times \Theta$ into $\mathbb{R}^G_+$, and because

$$\int_{N\times\Theta} v^i_{\theta n} \, d\nu = z_n - \int_{N\times\Theta} \underline{t}_\theta \, d\nu \to \hat{v} := z^* - \int_{N\times\Theta} \underline{t}_\theta \, d\nu,$$

as $n \to \infty$, there exists an integrable function $(i, \theta) \mapsto v^i_\theta \in \mathbb{R}^G_+$ such that v^i_θ is an accumulation point of the sequence $v^i_{\theta n}$ for ν-a.e. $(i, \theta) \in N \times \Theta$, and also $\int_{N\times\Theta} v^i_\theta \, d\nu \leqq \hat{v}$. Next, define $\hat{t}^i_\theta := v^i_\theta + \underline{t}_\theta$ for all $(i, \theta) \in N \times \Theta$. For ν-a.e. $(i, \theta) \in N \times \Theta$, this implies that $\hat{t}^i_\theta$ is an accumulation point of the sequence $t^i_{\theta n}$. Because $t^i_{\theta n} \in \xi^C_\theta(p_n)$, while $p_n \to \hat{p}$ and ξ^C_θ has a closed graph, it follows that $\hat{t}^i_\theta \in \xi^C_\theta(\hat{p})$. Furthermore

$$\hat{z} := \int_{N\times\Theta} \hat{t}^i_\theta \, d\nu = \int_{N\times\Theta} (v^i_\theta + \underline{t}_\theta) \, d\nu \leqq \hat{v} + \int_{N\times\Theta} \underline{t}_\theta \, d\nu = z^* \leqq 0.$$

Finally, because preferences are LNS, one has $\hat{p}\,\hat{t}^i_\theta = 0$ for ν-a.e. $(i, \theta) \in N \times \Theta$, so $\hat{p}\,\hat{z} = \int_{N\times\Theta} \hat{p}\,\hat{t}^i_\theta \, d\nu = 0$. This completes the proof that $(\hat{t}^{N\times\Theta}, \hat{p})$ is a CE with free disposal that satisfies weak gains from trade. □

11.5. Monotone Preferences and Existence of Compensated Equilibrium

When preferences are weakly monotone, a CE without free disposal exists:

Lemma 56 *Suppose agents' preferences are weakly monotone, and* $(\hat{t}^{N\times\Theta}, \hat{p})$ *is a CE with free disposal. Then there exists a CE* $(\tilde{t}^{N\times\Theta}, \hat{p})$ *with the same equilibrium price vector and with* $\tilde{t}^i_\theta \geqq \hat{t}^i_\theta$ *for* ν*-a.e.* $(i,\theta) \in N \times \Theta$.

Proof. First, let $\hat{z} := \int_{N\times\Theta} \hat{t}^i_\theta \, d\nu$. Then $\hat{z} \leqq 0$ and $\hat{p}\hat{z} = 0$ by definition of CE with free disposal. Second, define $\tilde{t}^i_\theta := \hat{t}^i_\theta - \hat{z}$ for all (i,θ). This definition implies that $\int_{N\times\Theta} \tilde{t}^i_\theta \, d\nu = \int_{N\times\Theta} \hat{t}^i_\theta \, d\nu - \hat{z} = 0$, and also that $\hat{p}\tilde{t}^i_\theta = \hat{p}(\hat{t}^i_\theta - \hat{z}) = \hat{p}\hat{t}^i_\theta \leq 0$ for ν-a.e. $(i,\theta) \in N \times \Theta$. Weak monotonicity of preferences then implies that $\tilde{t}^i_\theta \in R_\theta(\hat{t}^i_\theta)$ for ν-a.e. $(i,\theta) \in N \times \Theta$. Since preferences are transitive, one must have $\hat{p}t \geq 0$ whenever $t \succsim_\theta \tilde{t}^i_\theta$, because the same is true whenever $t \succsim_\theta \hat{t}^i_\theta$. Hence $\tilde{t}^i_\theta \in \xi^C_\theta(\hat{p})$ for ν-a.e. $(i,\theta) \in N \times \Theta$. This confirms that $(\tilde{t}^{N\times\Theta}, \hat{p})$ is a CE satisfying $\tilde{t}^i_\theta \geqq \hat{t}^i_\theta$ for ν-a.e. $(i,\theta) \in N \times \Theta$. □

Obviously, when the equilibrium allocation $\hat{t}^{N\times\Theta}$ satisfies weak gains from trade, so does $\tilde{t}^{N\times\Theta}$, because preferences are transitive and weakly monotone.

11.6. Existence of Walrasian Equilibrium

Convexity of preferences was not required to prove Lemma 55. Convexity of each feasible set T_θ, however, *is* needed for the following argument showing that a CE is a WE provided that $0 \in \operatorname{int} \int_{N\times\Theta} T_\theta \, d\nu$ and the economy satisfies a suitable irreducibility assumption. This assumption will adapt the condition used in Section 5.4 for a continuum economy in much the same way as Hildenbrand (1972, p. 85) adapted McKenzie's (1959, 1961) original assumption.

Given the particular feasible allocation $\hat{t}^{N\times\Theta}$ and any $(i,\theta) \in N \times \Theta$, define $U^i_\theta(\hat{t}^i_\theta)$ as the cone of vectors $\alpha(t - \hat{t}^i_\theta)$ with $\alpha > 0$ and $t \in P_\theta(\hat{t}^i_\theta)$. Similarly, define $V^i_\theta(\hat{t}^i_\theta)$ as the closed cone of vectors $\alpha(t - \hat{t}^i_\theta)$ with $\alpha \geq 0$ and $t \in T_\theta$. Next, define W_θ as the cone of vectors $-\beta t$ with $\beta \geq 0$ and $t \in T_\theta$. Finally, define Z^i_θ as the cone of vectors $-\gamma \hat{t}^i_\theta$ with $\gamma \geq 0$. Then the economy is said to be *directionally irreducible* provided that, for any subset $K \subset N \times \Theta$ with $0 < \nu(K) < 1$ and any feasible allocation $\hat{t}^{N\times\Theta}$, the two sets

$$\int_K U^i_\theta(\hat{t}^i_\theta) \, d\nu + \int_{(N\times\Theta)\setminus K} V^i_\theta(\hat{t}^i_\theta) \, d\nu \quad \text{and} \quad \int_{(N\times\Theta)\setminus K} W_\theta \, d\nu + \int_{N\times\Theta} Z^i_\theta \, d\nu$$

intersect.

Theorem 57 *Suppose that agents' feasible sets* T_θ *are convex, and that* $0 \in \operatorname{int} \int_{N\times\Theta} T_\theta \, d\nu$. *Suppose too that agents' preferences are LNS and continuous, and the economy is directionally irreducible. Then any CE is a WE.*

Proof. Let $(\hat{t}^{N\times\Theta},\hat{p})$ be a CE. Because $0 \in \text{int} \int_{N\times\Theta} T_\theta \, d\nu$, a non-null set of agents $(i,\theta) \in N \times \Theta$ have "cheaper points" $\underline{t}^i_\theta \in T_\theta$ satisfying $\hat{p}\underline{t}^i_\theta < 0$.

Let K be any measurable subset of $N \times \Theta$ satisfying $0 < \nu(K) < 1$ whose members all have such cheaper points. By directional irreducibility, there exist measurable selections:

(1) $(i,\theta) \mapsto t^i_\theta \in T_\theta$ and $(i,\theta) \mapsto \alpha^i_\theta \geq 0$ (for ν-a.e. $(i,\theta) \in N \times \Theta$) with $t^i_\theta \succ_\theta \hat{t}^i_\theta$ and $\alpha^i_\theta > 0$ for ν-a.e. $(i,\theta) \in K$;
(2) $(i,\theta) \mapsto \bar{t}^i_\theta \in T_\theta$ and $(i,\theta) \mapsto \beta^i_\theta \geq 0$ (for ν-a.e. $(i,\theta) \in (N \times \Theta) \setminus K$);
(3) $(i,\theta) \mapsto \gamma^i_\theta \geq 0$ (for ν-a.e. $(i,\theta) \in N \times \Theta$);

such that

$$\int_K \alpha^i_\theta (t^i_\theta - \hat{t}^i_\theta) \, d\nu + \int_{(N\times\Theta)\setminus K} [\alpha^i_\theta (t^i_\theta - \hat{t}^i_\theta) + \beta^i_\theta \bar{t}^i_\theta] \, d\nu + \int_{N\times\Theta} \gamma^i_\theta \hat{t}^i_\theta \, d\nu = 0$$

and so

$$\int_{N\times\Theta} \alpha^i_\theta t^i_\theta \, d\nu + \int_{(N\times\Theta)\setminus K} \beta^i_\theta \bar{t}^i_\theta \, d\nu = \int_{N\times\Theta} (\alpha^i_\theta - \gamma^i_\theta) \hat{t}^i_\theta \, d\nu. \tag{45}$$

Because $(\hat{t}^{N\times\Theta},\hat{p})$ is a CE and preferences are LNS, one has $\hat{p}\hat{t}^i_\theta = 0$ for ν-a.e. $(i,\theta) \in N \times \Theta$. Also, Lemma 12 and the definition of K imply that $\hat{p}\, t^i_\theta > 0$ for ν-a.e. $(i,\theta) \in K$. From (45), it follows that

$$\int_{(N\times\Theta)\setminus K} \hat{p}\,(\alpha^i_\theta t^i_\theta + \beta^i_\theta \bar{t}^i_\theta) \, d\nu = -\int_K \alpha^i_\theta \hat{p}\, t^i_\theta \, d\nu - \int_{N\times\Theta} \gamma^i_\theta \hat{p}\hat{t}^i_\theta < 0.$$

So there is a non-null subset $K' \subseteq (N \times \Theta) \setminus K$ such that either $\alpha^i_\theta \hat{p}\, t^i_\theta < 0$ or $\beta^i_\theta \hat{p}\bar{t}^i_\theta < 0$ for all $(i,\theta) \in K'$. Because $\alpha^i \geq 0$ for ν-a.e. $(i,\theta) \in N \times \Theta$ and $\beta^i \geq 0$ for ν-a.e. $(i,\theta) \in (N \times \Theta) \setminus K$, there is a non-null set of $(i,\theta) \in (N \times \Theta) \setminus K$ for whom either $\hat{p}\, t^i_\theta < 0$ or $\hat{p}\bar{t}^i_\theta < 0$, so (i,θ) has a cheaper point. Hence, no subset K of $N \times \Theta$ with $\nu(K) < 1$ can include almost all pairs (i,θ) with cheaper points. The only other possibility is that almost all (i,θ) must have cheaper points. By Lemma 12, this implies that the CE is actually a WE. □

11.7. Indivisible Goods and Constrained Monotone Preferences

Because monotone preferences require each feasible set T_θ to allow free disposal, they obviously rule out indivisible goods. So does the assumption in Section 11.6 that each T_θ is a convex set. Nevertheless, many results for continuum economies discussed here can be extended to indivisible goods, using methods such as those discussed in Mas-Colell (1977) and Yamazaki (1978, 1981). One has to weaken the monotone preferences assumption, and also assume sufficient dispersion in the marginal distribution of agents' feasible sets T_θ induced by distribution measure $\nu \in \mathcal{M}_\lambda(N \times \Theta)$.

Assume that G can be partitioned into the sets D of *divisible* and H of *indivisible* goods. Instead of $\mathbb{R}^G$, the natural commodity space becomes $\mathbb{R}^D \times \mathbb{Z}^H$, where $\mathbb{Z}^H$ is the Cartesian product of $\#H$ copies of $\mathbb{Z}$, the set of all integers. Obviously we assume that $T_\theta \subseteq \mathbb{R}^D \times \mathbb{Z}^H$ for all $\theta \in \Theta$. Note that preferences can be LNS only if D is nonempty.[39]

Within this restricted commodity space, say that preferences are *constrained weakly monotone* if $t' \in R_\theta(t)$ whenever $t \in T_\theta$ and $t' \geqq t$ with $t' \in \mathbb{R}^D \times \mathbb{Z}^H$.

Lemma 58 *Suppose agents' preferences are constrained weakly monotone, and* $(\hat{t}^{N\times\Theta}, \hat{p})$ *is a CE with free disposal. Then there exists a CE* $(\tilde{t}^{N\times\Theta}, \hat{p})$ *with the same equilibrium prices and with* $\tilde{t}^i_\theta \geqq \hat{t}^i_\theta$ *for* ν*-a.e.* $(i,\theta) \in N \times \Theta$.

Proof. As in the proof of Lemma 55, let $\hat{z} := \int_{N\times\Theta} \hat{t}^i_\theta \, d\nu$. Then $\hat{z} \leqq 0$ and $\hat{p}\hat{z} = 0$ by definition of CE with free disposal. For each indivisible good $g \in H$, define $z^*_g \in \mathbb{Z}_-$ as the largest integer that does not exceed $\hat{z}_g \leq 0$, and let $Z^*_g := \int_{N\times\Theta}\{z^*_g, 0\} d\nu$. Because the measure ν is nonatomic, the set Z^*_g is convex, so it contains the whole interval $[z^*_g, 0]$, including $\hat{z}_g$. Hence, for each $g \in H$ there is a measurable selection $(i,\theta) \mapsto z^i_{\theta g}$ from the correspondence $(i,\theta) \twoheadrightarrow \{z^*_g, 0\} \subset \mathbb{Z}_-$ such that $\hat{z}_g = \int_{N\times\Theta} z^i_{\theta g} d\nu$.

To include divisible goods as well, given any $(i,\theta) \in N \times \Theta$ simply define $z^i_{\theta g} := \hat{z}_g$ for all $g \in D$ and let z^i_θ be the vector $(z^i_{\theta g})_{g\in G} \in \mathbb{R}^G_-$. Then $\hat{z} = \int_{N\times\Theta} z^i_\theta d\nu$ for the measurable function $(i,\theta) \mapsto z^i_\theta \in \mathbb{R}^D_- \times \mathbb{Z}^H_-$. Now define $\tilde{t}^i_\theta := \hat{t}^i_\theta - z^i_\theta$ for all $(i,\theta) \in N \times \Theta$. Because both $\hat{t}^i_\theta$ and z^i_θ always belong to $\mathbb{R}^D \times \mathbb{Z}^H$, so does each $\tilde{t}^i_\theta$. Also $\tilde{t}^i_\theta \geqq \hat{t}^i_\theta$ for all $(i,\theta) \in N \times \Theta$ because $z^i_\theta \leqq 0$. Finally, the rule of free goods stated in Section 11.4 implies that $z^i_{\theta g} = 0$ unless $\hat{p}_g = 0$, so $\hat{p}\tilde{t}^i_\theta = \hat{p}\hat{t}^i_\theta \leq 0$ for ν-a.e. $(i,\theta) \in N \times \Theta$.

The rest of the proof closely follows that of Lemma 56, so will be omitted. □

11.8. Dispersion and Existence of Walrasian Equilibrium

As in Section 10.4, assume that each agent's feasible set T_θ is piecewise convex—that is, that $T_\theta = \cup_{m\in M_\theta} T^m_\theta$ where $M_\theta \subseteq \mathbb{N}$. Now adapt the definitions (38), (39), and (41) in Section 10.4. Given any $\theta \in \Theta$, first define

$$\hat{M}_\theta := \{m \in M_\theta \mid P_\theta(0) \cap T^m_\theta \neq \emptyset\}$$

where $P_\theta(0)$ is the set of net trade vectors that are strictly preferred to autarky. Second, given a price vector $p \neq 0$, let

$$\hat{W}_\theta(p) := \{\inf p\, T^m_\theta \mid m \in \hat{M}_\theta\}$$

[39] For weaker results when all goods are indivisible and so D is empty, see for example Inoue (2006, 2008).

be the associated countable set of critical wealth levels. Finally, say that agents have *dispersed feasible sets* if for all $p > 0$ one has

$$\nu(\{(i,\theta) \in N \times \Theta \mid 0 \in \hat{W}_\theta(p) \setminus \{\inf p\, T_\theta\}\}) = 0.$$

Lemma 59 *Suppose that agents' feasible sets T_θ are piecewise convex and dispersed, while $0 \in \operatorname{int} \int_{N\times\Theta} T_\theta \, d\nu$. Suppose too that agents' preferences are LNS and continuous, and that the economy is directionally irreducible. Then any CE satisfying weak gains from trade is a WE.*

Proof. Suppose $(\hat{t}^{N\times\Theta}, \hat{p})$ is a CE satisfying weak gains from trade. Consider any $(i,\theta) \in N \times \Theta$ who has a cheaper point because $\inf \hat{p}\, T_\theta < 0$. Any $t \in P_\theta(\hat{t}^i_\theta)$ satisfies $t \in P_\theta(0)$ because preferences are transitive, so $t \in T^m_\theta$ for some $m \in \hat{M}_\theta$. Because agents have LNS preferences and dispersed feasible sets, it follows that $\hat{p}\hat{t}^i_\theta \notin \hat{W}_\theta(\hat{p})$. So almost any potential agent $(i,\theta) \in N \times \Theta$ with a cheaper point meets the conditions required for Lemma 50 to show that any $t \in P_\theta(\hat{t}^i_\theta)$ satisfies $\hat{p}\, t > 0$. This observation implies that all the arguments used to prove Theorem 57 still apply, so the CE is a WE. □

Theorem 60 *Suppose agents' feasible sets T_θ allow autarky, are piecewise convex and dispersed, while satisfying $0 \in \operatorname{int} \int_{N\times\Theta} T_\theta \, d\nu$. Suppose their weak gains from trade sets are integrably bounded below. Suppose preferences are LNS, continuous, and constrained weakly monotone. Suppose finally that the economy is directionally irreducible. Then there exists a WE.*

Proof. This follows by combining the results of Lemmas 55, 58, and 59. □

12. EQUIVALENCE THEOREMS FOR THE CORE AND f-CORE

12.1. The Core and f-Core

The feasible allocation mechanism $\hat{t}^{N\times\Theta}$ is in the *core* if there is no *blocking coalition* $K \subseteq N \times \Theta$ satisfying $\nu(K) > 0$ with a *blocking mechanism* t^K in the form of a measurable mapping $(i,\theta) \mapsto t^i_\theta$ from K to $\mathbb{R}^G$ that satisfies $t^i_\theta \in P_\theta(\hat{t}^i_\theta)$ for ν-a.e. $(i,\theta) \in K$, as well as $\int_K t^i_\theta d\nu = 0$—that is, feasibility within K. This is an obvious extension of the earlier definition of the core for a finite economy in Section 8.1. It also generalizes Aumann's (1964) original definition for a continuum economy, as well as Hildenbrand (1974).

The feasible allocation mechanism $\hat{t}^{N\times\Theta}$ is in the *f-core* if there is no finite family of pairwise disjoint non-null sets $K_1, \ldots, K_m \subset N \times \Theta$ and corresponding natural numbers $n_1, \ldots, n_m \in \mathbb{N}$ such that, for some $r > 0$, there is a blocking coalition $K \subseteq \cup_{j=1}^m K_j$ with $\nu(K \cap K_j) = r\, n_j \;\; (j = 1, \ldots, m)$ and so $\nu(K) = r \sum_{j=1}^m n_j$, while the blocking mechanism t^K satisfies $t^i_\theta = \bar{t}_j$ for all $(i,\theta) \in K_j$ for some finite collection $\bar{t}_1,\dots,\bar{t}_m \in \mathbb{R}^G$ with $\sum_{j=1}^m n_j \bar{t}_j = 0$.[40]

Thus an allocation is not in the f-core only if some blocking coalition K can be decomposed into a continuum of finite subcoalitions, each consisting of $\sum_{j=1}^m n_j$ members, with each subcoalition choosing exactly the same pattern of net trade vectors for its members. In particular, blocking is possible even when trade is restricted to take place separately within finite subcoalitions. Obviously, therefore, any allocation in the core also belongs to the f-core.

12.2. Walrasian Equilibria Belong to the Core

This section provides sufficient conditions for both the core and the f-core to coincide with the set of WE allocations. The first part of this equivalence result is easy:

Theorem 61 *If $(\hat{t}^{N\times\Theta}, \hat{p})$ is any WE, then $\hat{t}^{N\times\Theta}$ belongs to the core.*

Proof. Let $K \subseteq N \times \Theta$ be any non-null set. Suppose the measurable mapping $t : K \to \mathbb{R}^G$ satisfies $t^i_\theta \in P_\theta(\hat{t}^i_\theta)$ for ν-a.e. $(i,\theta) \in K$. Because $\hat{t}^i_\theta \in \xi_\theta(\hat{p})$ for ν-a.e. $(i,\theta) \in N \times \Theta$, it follows that $\hat{p}\, t^i_\theta > 0$ for ν-a.e. $(i,\theta) \in K$. This implies that $\int_K \hat{p}\, t^i_\theta d\nu > 0$, so $\int_K t^i_\theta d\nu \neq 0$. Thus, t^K cannot be a blocking mechanism, so no blocking mechanism exists. □

12.3. f-Core Allocations Are Compensated Equilibria

First, we introduce a new assumption on agents' preferences. To do so, let $\mathbb{Q} \subset \mathbb{R}$ denote the set of *rational numbers*—that is, ratios of integers m/n where $m, n \in \mathbb{Z}$. Of course, $\mathbb{Q}$ is countable. Then let $\mathbb{Q}^G \subset \mathbb{R}^G$ denote the collection of vectors whose coordinates are all rational; it is also countable.

Next, say that the preferences described by the pair $(T_\theta, \succsim_\theta)$ are *locally nonsatiated in rational net trade vectors* (or LNS in $\mathbb{Q}^G$) if, for any $t \in T_\theta$ and any neighborhood V of t in $\mathbb{R}^G$, there exists $t' \in V \cap \mathbb{Q}^G$ such that $t' \in P_\theta(t)$. This obviously strengthens the LNS assumption that has been used so often in this chapter. Indeed, suppose that $G = \{1,2\}$ and that there exists a scalar $\xi > 0$ for which $T_\theta = \{t \in \mathbb{R}^G_+ \mid t_2 = \xi\, t_1\}$. Suppose too that, given any $t, t' \in T_\theta$, one has $t \succsim_\theta t' \iff t_1 \geq t'_1$. These preferences are obviously LNS for all $\xi > 0$. But $T_\theta \cap \mathbb{Q}^G = \{(0,0)\}$ when ξ is irrational, so preferences are LNS in $\mathbb{Q}^G$ if and only if ξ is rational.

Nevertheless, the assumption is still weak enough to be satisfied by any monotone preference relation.

[40] The above definition of the f-core is based on Kaneko and Wooders (1986) and Hammond, Kaneko, and Wooders (1989)—see also Hammond (1999a). The first two of these papers also show that any feasible allocation mechanism $\hat{t}^{N\times\Theta}$ can be achieved as the limit of a sequence of mechanisms in which finite coalitions form to trade amongst their members.

Lemma 62 *Monotone preferences are LNS in $\mathbb{Q}^G$.*

Proof. Suppose that the preferences described by the pair $(T_\theta, \precsim_\theta)$ are monotone. Given any $t \in T_\theta$ and any neighborhood V of t in $\mathbb{R}^G$, there exists $t' \gg t$ such that $t' \in V \cap \mathbb{Q}^G$, and then $t' \in P_\theta(t)$. □

The following result does not rely on convexity, continuity, or montonicity of preferences. The proof relies on a key idea introduced in Aumann (1964).

Theorem 63 *Suppose preferences are LNS in $\mathbb{Q}^G$. Then any allocation $t^{N\times\Theta}$ in the f-core is a CE at some price vector $p \neq 0$.*

Proof. By definition, the mapping $(i,\theta) \mapsto t^i_\theta$ associated with the allocation $t^{N\times\Theta}$ must be measurable w.r.t. the product σ-field on $N \times \Theta$. For each $t \in \mathbb{Q}^G$, define $\hat{K}(t) := \{(i,\theta) \in N \times \Theta \mid t \in P_\theta(t^i_\theta)\}$, which is also measurable when $N \times \Theta$ is given the product σ-field.

Let $K_0 := \cup\{\hat{K}(t) \mid t \in \mathbb{Q}^G,\ \nu(\hat{K}(t)) = 0\}$. As the union of a countable family of null sets, the set K_0 is measurable and $\nu(K_0) = 0$. Then let $K' := (N \times \Theta) \setminus K_0$ and define C as the convex hull of the set $\cup_{(i,\theta)\in K'}[\mathbb{Q}^G \cap P_\theta(t^i_\theta)]$.

Suppose $0 \in C$. Then there must exist a natural number m and a collection $(i_j, \theta_j, t_j, r_j)$ $(j = 1, \ldots, m)$ of points in $K' \times \mathbb{Q}^G \times [0,1]$ such that $t_j \in P_{\theta_j}(t^{i_j}_{\theta_j})$ (each j), whereas the non-negative real numbers r_j $(j = 1, \ldots, m)$ are convex weights satisfying

$$\sum_{j=1}^{m} r_j = 1 \quad \text{and also} \quad \sum_{j=1}^{m} r_j\, t_j = 0. \tag{46}$$

After excluding any $(i_j, \theta_j, t_j, r_j)$ for which $r_j = 0$, it loses no generality to assume that $r_j > 0$ for $j = 1, \ldots, m$.

Because each $t_j \in \mathbb{Q}^G$, every coefficient in the system (46) of simultaneous equations in the convex weights r_j $(j = 1, \ldots, m)$ must be rational. Moreover, the system can be solved by pivoting operations or Gaussian elimination. Since (46) has at least one solution, there must be a *rational* solution. Multiplying this solution by the least common denominator of the rational fractions r_j, the result is a collection of natural numbers $n_j \in \mathbb{N}$ $(j = 1, \ldots, m)$ such that $0 = \sum_{j=1}^{m} n_j t_j$.

Because each $(i_j, \theta_j) \notin K_0$, by definition there is no $t'_j \in \mathbb{Q}^G$ with $(i_j, \theta_j) \in \hat{K}(t'_j)$ and $\nu(\hat{K}(t'_j)) = 0$. It follows that $\nu(\hat{K}(t_j)) > 0$ $(j = 1, \ldots, m)$.

Define $r := \min_j \{\nu(\hat{K}(t_j))\}/\sum_{j=1}^{m} n_j$. Then $r > 0$. For each $j = 1, 2, \ldots, m$, let K_j be any subset of $\hat{K}(t_j)$ having measure $n_j\, r$, and suppose that the different sets K_j are pairwise disjoint. Even if all the sets $\hat{K}(t_j)$ are equal, this will still be possible. Let $K := \cup_{j=1}^{m} K_j$.

Then define t^K so that each potential agent $(i_j, \theta_j) \in K_j$ gets t_j instead of $t^{i_j}_{\theta_j}$. Because $\sum_{j=1}^{m} n_j t_j = 0$, this t^K is a blocking allocation. So $t^{N\times\Theta}$ does not belong to the f-core.

Conversely, if $t^{N\times\Theta}$ does belong to the f-core, it has just been proved that $0 \notin C$. By definition, C is convex, so there must exist $p \neq 0$ such that $pz \geq 0$ for all $z \in C$. In particular, whenever $(i,\theta) \in K'$ and $t \in \mathbb{Q}^G \cap P_\theta(t^i_\theta)$, then $t \in C$ and so $pt \geq 0$. Because $\mathbb{Q}^G$ is dense in $\mathbb{R}^G$, it follows that $pt \geq 0$ whenever there exists $(i,\theta) \in K'$ such that $t \in P_\theta(t^i_\theta)$, and so, by LNS, such that $t \in R_\theta(t^i_\theta)$. In particular, $pt^i_\theta \geq 0$ for all $(i,\theta) \in K'$. But $\nu(K') = 1$ and $\int_{N\times\Theta} t^i_\theta d\nu = 0$. So for ν-a.e. (i,θ) one has $pt^i_\theta = 0$, as well as $pt \geq 0$ whenever $t \in R_\theta(t^i_\theta)$. This proves that $(t^{N\times\Theta}, p)$ is a CE. □

Corollary 64 *Suppose agents' preferences are LNS in $\mathbb{Q}^G$. Then WE $\subseteq$ Core $\subseteq f$-Core $\subseteq$ CE.*

Proof. In Section 12.1 it was noted that Core $\subseteq f$-Core. The result follows immediately from Theorems 61 and 63. □

The following equivalence theorem provides two characterizations of WE:

Theorem 65 *Suppose that agents' feasible sets T_θ are piecewise convex and dispersed, while $0 \in \text{int} \int_{N\times\Theta} T_\theta \, d\nu$. Suppose agents' preferences are LNS in $\mathbb{Q}^G$ as well as continuous, and that the economy is directionally irreducible. Then WE = Core = f-Core.*

Proof. This is obvious from Lemma 59 and Corollary 64. □

Of course a special case of Theorem 65 is when each T_θ is convex instead of piecewise convex; then dispersion is automatically satisfied.

12.4. Coalitional Fairness

Varian (1974) defines a feasible allocation $\hat{t}^{N\times\Theta}$ as *c-fair* if, whenever $K, L \subseteq N \times \Theta$ with $0 < \nu(L) \leq \nu(K) \leq 1$, there is no measurable mapping $(i,\theta) \mapsto t^i_\theta \in T_\theta$ from L to $\mathbb{R}^G$ satisfying $\int_L t^i_\theta d\nu = \int_K \hat{t}^i_\theta d\nu$ with $t^i_\theta \in R_\theta(\hat{t}^i_\theta)$ for ν-a.e. $(i,\theta) \in L$, as well as $\nu(\{(i,\theta) \in L \mid t^i_\theta \in P_\theta(\hat{t}^i_\theta)\}) > 0$.[41] Thus, no smaller coalition can do better by sharing an equal aggregate net trade vector between its members. Varian also defines $\hat{t}^{N\times\Theta}$ as *c′-fair* if the condition $\int_L t^i_\theta d\nu = \int_K \hat{t}^i_\theta d\nu$ is replaced by $[1/\nu(L)] \int_L t^i_\theta d\nu = [1/\nu(K)] \int_K \hat{t}^i_\theta d\nu$. Thus, no smaller coalition can do better with an equal mean net trade vector.

Theorem 66 *Provided agents have LNS preferences, any WE allocation is both c-fair and c′-fair.*

Proof. Suppose that $(\hat{t}^{N\times\Theta}, \hat{p})$ is a WE. Suppose too that $K, L \subseteq N \times \Theta$ are measurable with $0 < \nu(L) \leq \nu(K) \leq 1$, and that the measurable mapping $(i,\theta) \mapsto t^i_\theta \in T_\theta$ from L to $\mathbb{R}^G$ satisfies $t^i_\theta \in R_\theta(\hat{t}^i_\theta)$ for ν-a.e. $(i,\theta) \in L$, as well as $\nu(\{(i,\theta) \in L \mid t^i_\theta \in P_\theta(\hat{t}^i_\theta)\}) > 0$.

[41] Varian (1974) acknowledges being inspired by Karl Vind's unpublished lecture notes.

Because preferences are LNS, $\hat{p}t^i_\theta \geq \hat{p}\hat{t}^i_\theta = 0$ for ν-a.e. $(i,\theta) \in L$, with strict inequality on a non-null subset of L. It follows that

$$\int_L \hat{p}t^i_\theta \, d\nu > 0 = \int_L \hat{p}\hat{t}^i_\theta \, d\nu = \int_K \hat{p}\hat{t}^i_\theta \, d\nu.$$

This contradicts both $\int_L t^i_\theta \, d\nu = \int_K \hat{t}^i_\theta \, d\nu$ and $\int_L t^i_\theta \, d\nu/\nu(L) = \int_K \hat{t}^i_\theta \, d\nu/\nu(K)$. Hence, the equilibrium allocation $\hat{t}^{N\times\Theta}$ is both c-fair and c'-fair. □

Conversely:

Theorem 67 *If the feasible allocation $\hat{t}^{N\times\Theta}$ is c-fair, or c'-fair, then it belongs to the core.*

Proof. Suppose, on the contrary, that the feasible allocation $\hat{t}^{N\times\Theta}$ is not in the core. Then there exists a blocking coalition $L \subseteq N \times \Theta$ with an allocation t^L to its members such that $\int_L t^i_\theta \, d\nu = 0$ and $t^i_\theta \in P_\theta(\hat{t}^i_\theta)$ for ν-a.e. $(i,\theta) \in L$. Because feasibility requires that $\int_{N\times\Theta} \hat{t}^i_\theta \, d\nu = 0$, taking $K = N \times \Theta$ in the above definitions implies that $\hat{t}^{N\times\Theta}$ is neither c-fair nor c'-fair. □

Again, under the hypotheses of Theorem 65, Theorems 66 and 67 show that Walrasian equilibria can be characterized as c-fair (or c'-fair) allocations.

12.5. A Bargaining Set

Mas-Colell (1989) has developed an interesting coarsening of the core, similar to the bargaining set in a cooperative game. It offers an alternative characterization of Walrasian equilibrium for continuum economies—at least for a standard pure exchange economy in which the feasible set of each agent type $\theta \in \Theta$ is $T_\theta = \{t \in \mathbb{R}^G \mid t + e_\theta \geqq 0\}$, where $\theta \mapsto e_\theta \in \mathbb{R}^G_{++}$ is measurable. It will also be assumed that preferences for net trades are strictly monotone.

Given any feasible allocation $\hat{t}^{N\times\Theta}$, say that (K, t^K) is an *objection* if:

(1) K is a non-null measurable subset of $N \times \Theta$;
(2) t^K is an integrable mapping $(i,\theta) \mapsto t^i_\theta$ from K to $\mathbb{R}^G$ satisfying:

  (a) $\int_K t^i_\theta \, d\nu = 0$;
  (b) $t^i_\theta \in R_\theta(\hat{t}^i_\theta)$ for ν-a.e. $(i,\theta) \in K$;
  (c) $\nu(\{(i,\theta) \in K \mid t^i_\theta \succ_\theta \hat{t}^i_\theta\}) > 0$.

This is similar to when K is a blocking coalition, except that a non-null subset of K may only weakly prefer the new allocation.

Given any feasible allocation $\hat{t}^{N\times\Theta}$ and any objection (K, t^K), say that the pair $(\tilde{K}, \tilde{t}^{\tilde{K}})$ is a *counter-objection* to the objection if:

(1) $\tilde{K}$ is a non-null measurable subset of $N \times \Theta$;
(2) $\tilde{t}^{\tilde{K}}$ is an integrable mapping $(i,\theta) \mapsto \tilde{t}^i_\theta$ from $\tilde{K}$ to $\mathbb{R}^G$ satisfying:

(a) $\int_{\tilde{K}} \tilde{t}_\theta^i \, d\nu = 0$;
(b) $\tilde{t}_\theta^i \in P_\theta(t_\theta^i)$ for ν-a.e. $(i,\theta) \in \tilde{K} \cap K$;
(c) $\tilde{t}_\theta^i \in P_\theta(\hat{t}_\theta^i)$ for ν-a.e. $(i,\theta) \in \tilde{K} \setminus K$.

Next, given any feasible allocation $\hat{t}^{N\times\Theta}$ and the objection (K, t^K), say that the objection is *justified* if there is no counter-objection. Finally, the *bargaining set* is defined as the set of all allocations for which there is no justified objection. That is, every objection is subject to a counter-objection.

This is Mas-Colell's (1989) equivalence theorem:

Theorem 68 *Suppose that for each $\theta \in \Theta$ one has $T_\theta = \{t \in \mathbb{R}^G \mid t + e_\theta \geqq 0\}$ where $\theta \mapsto e_\theta \in \mathbb{R}^G_{++}$ is measurable. Suppose too that each $\succsim_\theta$ is continuous and strictly monotone. Then feasible allocation $\hat{t}^{N\times\Theta}$ belongs to the bargaining set if and only if there exists $\hat{p} \gg 0$ such that $(\hat{t}^{N\times\Theta}, \hat{p})$ is a WE.*

No formal proof will be given here. However, it is easy to see that, given LNS preferences, any WE allocation allows no objection whatsoever, just as a WE allocation cannot be blocked and so belongs to the core. Conversely, to see that any allocation in the bargaining set is a WE, an important step is to realize that only *Walrasian objections* need be considered. These are defined as objections (K, t^K) to the feasible allocation $\hat{t}^{N\times\Theta}$ for which there exists a price vector $p > 0$ such that, for ν-a.e. $(i,\theta) \in N \times \Theta$, whenever $\tilde{t} \in T_\theta$:

(1) $(i,\theta) \in K$ and $\tilde{t} \in R_\theta(t_\theta^i)$ together imply $p\tilde{t} \geq 0$;
(2) $(i,\theta) \in (N \times \Theta) \setminus K$ and $\tilde{t} \in R_\theta(\hat{t}_\theta^i)$ together imply $p\tilde{t} \geq 0$.

No attempt has been made to weaken the hypotheses of Theorem 68 to those under which core equivalence has been proved, though one suspects some steps could be made in this direction—see, for example, Yamazaki (1995).

Extending this concept, as well as Ray's (1989) work on credible coalitions, Dutta et al. (1989) consider a "consistent" bargaining set for general cooperative games in characteristic function form. This set is based on chains of successive objections, each of which is an objection to the immediately preceding objection. A further objection to any such chain is *valid* if there is no valid counter-objection to this extended chain; the further objection is *invalid* if there is a valid counter-objection. This is a circular definition, but the circularity can be circumvented—see, for example, Greenberg (1990). Note that, in the case of an exchange economy, any allocation in this consistent bargaining set must be in the bargaining set, because consistency makes it harder to find a valid counter-objection to any given objection. On the other hand, any allocation in the core must be in the consistent bargaining set. This is because any allocation in the core is not blocked, so there can be no objection at all, let alone a valid objection. Of course, when the equivalence theorem holds, and both bargaining set and core consist of the set of Walrasian equilibrium allocations, then the same set is also the consistent bargaining set as well.

Other properties and notable variations of the core and of Mas-Colell's bargaining set for exchange economies have been discussed by Vind (1992), Hara (2002, 2005), Serrano and Vohra (2005).

13. ENVY-FREE MECHANISMS

13.1. Full f-Pareto Efficiency

The main result of this section is considerably simplified if one imposes a stronger form of Pareto efficiency. The weakly Pareto efficient allocation $\hat{t}^{N\times\Theta}$ is said to be *fully f-Pareto efficient* if no finite coalition $C \subset N \times \Theta$ of potential agents can find net trade vectors $t^i_\theta \in T_\theta$ (all $(i,\theta) \in C$) satisfying both $\sum_{(i,\theta)\in C} t^i_\theta = \sum_{(i,\theta)\in C} \hat{t}^i_\theta$ and $t^i_\theta \in P_\theta(\hat{t}^i_\theta)$ for all $(i,\theta) \in C$.

This definition is somewhat similar to that of Hammond (1999a) for the f-core of an economy in which each individual $(i,\theta) \in N \times \Theta$ has initial endowment $\hat{t}^i_\theta$ instead of 0. One key difference, however, is that the coalition C can be drawn from *all* of $N \times \Theta$, not just from agents outside some null set.

It is important to realize that fully f-Pareto efficient allocations do exist. Indeed, say that the WELT $(\hat{t}^{N\times\Theta}, \hat{p})$ is *full* if the allocation satisfies the extra condition that $\hat{t}^i_\theta \in \xi^i_\theta(\hat{p})$ for *all* $(i,\theta) \in N \times \Theta$—not merely for ν-a.e. $(i,\theta) \in N \times \Theta$. Then it is easy to show that any full WELT allocation is fully f-Pareto efficient, using an argument similar to the proof of the first efficiency Theorem 15 for a finite economy. Moreover, the Walrasian demand set $\xi^i_\theta(\hat{p})$ will be nonempty for all $(i,\theta) \in N \times \Theta$ when every preference ordering $\succsim_\theta$ is continuous and the Walrasian budget set $B^i_\theta(\hat{p}) = \{t \in T_\theta \mid \hat{p}\,t \leq w^i_\theta\}$ is compact for all $(i,\theta) \in N \times \Theta$—because, for example, $\hat{p} \gg 0$ and every set T_θ is closed and bounded below. Then any WELT can be converted into a full WELT by changing the allocations to at most a null set of potential agents (i,θ) so that they satisfy $\hat{t}^i_\theta \in \xi^i_\theta(\hat{p})$. Such changes, of course, have no effect on the mean net trade vector $\int_{N\times\Theta} \hat{t}^i_\theta \, d\nu = 0$ or on the equilibrium price vector $\hat{p}$.

On the other hand, with smooth preferences such as those satisfying conditions (a) and (b) in Section 2.8, any fully f-Pareto efficient and interior allocation $\hat{t}^{N\times\Theta}$ must equate all agents' (positive) marginal rates of substitution between any pair of goods. Hence, there must exist a common suitably normalized price vector $\hat{p} \gg 0$ such that $(\hat{t}^{N\times\Theta}, \hat{p})$ is a full WELT.

13.2. Self-Selective Allocations

The allocation $\hat{t}^{N\times\Theta}$ is said to be *self-selective* if $\hat{t}^i_\theta \succsim_\theta \hat{t}^i_\eta$ whenever $(i,\theta,\eta) \in N \times \Theta \times \Theta$ satisfies $\hat{t}^i_\eta \in T_\theta$. Thus, each potential agent $(i,\theta) \in N \times \Theta$ weakly prefers the allocated net trade vector $\hat{t}^i_\theta$ to any feasible $\hat{t}^i_\eta \in T_\theta$ allocated to an alternative type $\eta \in \Theta$.

The following lemma plays an important role in subsequent proofs.

Lemma 69 *Suppose there is a smooth type domain Θ, as defined in Section 2.8. Let $(\hat{t}^{N\times\Theta}, p)$ be any full WELT with $p \gg 0$ and with $\hat{t}^i_\theta = h_\theta(p, w^i_\theta)$ where $w^i_\theta = p\,\hat{t}^i_\theta > \underline{w}_\theta(p) = \inf p\,T_\theta$ for all $(i,\theta) \in N \times \Theta$. Then the allocation $\hat{t}^{N\times\Theta}$ is self-selective if and only if $w^i_\theta \equiv w^i$, independent of θ, for all $(i,\theta) \in N \times \Theta$.*

Proof. Suppose $w^i_\theta \equiv w^i$, independent of θ. Then given any $(i,\theta,\eta) \in N \times \Theta \times \Theta$, one has $p\,\hat{t}^i_\eta = w^i$. So the definition of a full WELT implies that $\hat{t}^i_\theta = h_\theta(p, w^i_\theta) \succsim_\theta \hat{t}^i_\eta$ whenever $\hat{t}^i_\eta \in T_\theta$. Hence, the allocation $\hat{t}^{N\times\Theta}$ is self-selective.

Conversely, suppose $(\hat{t}^{N\times\Theta}, \hat{p})$ is a full WELT in which the allocation $\hat{t}^{N\times\Theta}$ is self-selective. Consider any fixed $i \in N$. Let $(\theta_n)_{n=1}^\infty$ be any convergent sequence with limit θ. By smoothness condition (c) in Section 2.8, the WELT net trade vectors $h_{\theta_n}(p, w^i_{\theta_n})$ and $h_\theta(p, w^i_\theta)$ are interior points of T_{θ_n} and T_θ, respectively. By part (2) of Lemma 5, one has $h_{\theta_n}(p, w^i_{\theta_n}) \in T_\theta$ and $h_\theta(p, w^i_\theta) \in T_{\theta_n}$ for all large n, so self-selection implies that

$$v_{\theta_n}(p, w^i_{\theta_n}) = u_{\theta_n}(h_{\theta_n}(p, w^i_{\theta_n})) \geq u_{\theta_n}(h_\theta(p, w^i_\theta)) \tag{47}$$

$$\text{and} \quad v_\theta(p, w^i_\theta) = u_\theta(h_\theta(p, w^i_\theta)) \geq u_\theta(h_{\theta_n}(p, w^i_{\theta_n})). \tag{48}$$

Because $w^i_\theta > \underline{w}_\theta(p)$, part (2) of Lemma 6 implies $w^i_\theta > \underline{w}_{\theta_n}(p)$ for all large n. Also, by smoothness conditions (b) and (d) of Section 2.8, the functions u_θ and v_θ are continuous w.r.t. θ. So given any small enough $\epsilon > 0$ and any sufficiently large n, (47) implies that

$$\begin{aligned} v_\theta(p, w^i_{\theta_n}) + \epsilon > v_{\theta_n}(p, w^i_{\theta_n}) &\geq u_{\theta_n}(h_\theta(p, w^i_\theta)) \\ &> u_\theta(h_\theta(p, w^i_\theta)) - \epsilon = v_\theta(p, w^i_\theta) - \epsilon, \end{aligned} \tag{49}$$

and so $v_\theta(p, w^i_{\theta_n}) \geq v_\theta(p, w^i_\theta)$. But $v_\theta(p, w)$ is strictly increasing in w, and so $w^i_{\theta_n} \geq w^i_\theta$. Therefore $w_* := \liminf_{n\to\infty} w^i_{\theta_n}$ exists and is finite, with $w_* \geq w^i_\theta$.

Next, because of smoothness condition (e), the constraint (48) implies that no subsequence of $w^i_{\theta_n}$ can tend to $+\infty$, so the sequence is bounded above. Hence, $w^* := \limsup_{n\to\infty} w^i_{\theta_n}$ exists and is finite, with

$$w^* \geq w_* \geq w^i_\theta > \underline{w}_\theta(p). \tag{50}$$

But some subsequence of $(\theta_n, w^i_{\theta_n})$ must converge to (θ, w^*). By smoothness condition (c), the corresponding subsequence of $h_{\theta_n}(p, w^i_{\theta_n})$ converges to $h_\theta(p, w^*)$. Taking the limit of (48) for this subsequence implies that

$$v_\theta(p, w^i_\theta) \geq u_\theta(h_\theta(p, w^*)) = v_\theta(p, w^*).$$

Because $v_\theta(p, w)$ is strictly increasing w.r.t. w, it follows that $w^i_\theta \geq w^*$. In combination with (50), this shows that $w_* = w^i_\theta = w^*$. By definition of w_* and w^*, it follows that

$w^i_{\theta_n} \to w^i_\theta$. Because θ_n was an arbitrary convergent sequence, this proves that w^i_θ is a continuous function of θ.

Next, consider any piecewise C^1-arc $s \mapsto \theta(s)$ mapping $[0,1]$ to Θ. Suppose that $s \mapsto \theta(s)$ is C^1 in the open interval $(\underline{s}, \bar{s}) \subset [0,1]$. Consider any disjoint pair $s, s' \in (\underline{s}, \bar{s})$. Because $v_{\theta(s)}(p,w)$ and $v_{\theta(s')}(p,w)$ are both C^1 functions of w, the mean-value theorem implies that there must exist w, w' in the interval between $w^i_{\theta(s)}$ and $w^i_{\theta(s')}$ such that

$$v_{\theta(s)}(p, w^i_{\theta(s')}) - v_{\theta(s)}(p, w^i_{\theta(s)}) = (w^i_{\theta(s')} - w^i_{\theta(s)})\,(v_{\theta(s)})'_w(p,w) \tag{51}$$

$$\text{and} \quad v_{\theta(s')}(p, w^i_{\theta(s')}) - v_{\theta(s')}(p, w^i_{\theta(s)}) = (w^i_{\theta(s')} - w^i_{\theta(s)})\,(v_{\theta(s')})'_w(p,w'). \tag{52}$$

Because w^i_θ is continuous in θ, smoothness condition (d) implies that $v_\theta(p, w^i_\theta)$ is also continuous in θ. Then smoothness condition (c) and Lemma 5 together imply that $h_{\theta(s')}(p, w^i_{\theta(s')}) \in T_{\theta(s)}$ and $h_{\theta(s)}(p, w^i_{\theta(s)}) \in T_{\theta(s')}$ whenever s' is sufficiently close to s. Consequently the self-selection constraints and the definitions of $v_{\theta(s)}$, $v_{\theta(s')}$ imply that

$$v_{\theta(s)}(p, w^i_{\theta(s)}) = u_{\theta(s)}(h_{\theta(s)}(p, w^i_{\theta(s)})) \geq u_{\theta(s)}(h_{\theta(s')}(p, w^i_{\theta(s')})) \tag{53}$$

$$\text{and} \quad v_{\theta(s')}(p, w^i_{\theta(s')}) = u_{\theta(s')}(h_{\theta(s')}(p, w^i_{\theta(s')})) \geq u_{\theta(s')}(h_{\theta(s)}(p, w^i_{\theta(s)})). \tag{54}$$

Dividing (52) by the positive number $(v_{\theta(s)})'_w(p,w')$ and (51) by $(v_{\theta(s')})'_w(p,w)$, then using (54) and (53), respectively, one can derive

$$\frac{u_{\theta(s')}(h_{\theta(s)}(p, w^i_{\theta(s)})) - u_{\theta(s')}(h_{\theta(s')}(p, w^i_{\theta(s)}))}{(v_{\theta(s')})'_w(p,w')} \leq w^i_{\theta(s')} - w^i_{\theta(s)}$$
$$\leq \frac{u_{\theta(s)}(h_{\theta(s)}(p, w^i_{\theta(s')})) - u_{\theta(s)}(h_{\theta(s')}(p, w^i_{\theta(s')}))}{(v_{\theta(s)})'_w(p,w)}.$$

Next, divide each term of these inequalities by $s' - s$ (when $s' \neq s$) and then take the limit as $s' \to s$. Because then $\theta(s') \to \theta(s)$, the smoothness conditions of Section 2.8 imply that the derivative $\frac{d}{ds} w^i_{\theta(s)}$ exists and also that

$$\begin{aligned}(v_\theta)'_w(p,w^i)\frac{d}{ds} w^i_{\theta(s)} &= -\frac{d}{ds} u_\theta(h_{\theta(s)}(p,w^i)) \\ &= -\sum_{g \in G} (u_\theta)'_g(h_{\theta(s)}(p,w^i))\frac{d}{ds} h_{\theta(s)g}(p,w^i)\end{aligned} \tag{55}$$

where $\theta = \theta(s)$ and $w^i = w^i_{\theta(s)}$ with s fixed, and where $(u_\theta)'_g$ denotes $\partial u_\theta / \partial t_g$. But the usual first-order conditions for utility maximization subject to the constraint $pt \leq w^i$ are $(u_\theta)'_g = (v_\theta)'_w p_g$ for each $g \in G$. So (55) simplifies to

$$\frac{d}{ds} w^i_{\theta(s)} = -\sum_{g \in G} p_g \frac{d}{ds} h_{\theta(s)g}(p,w^i). \tag{56}$$

Differentiating the budget identity $w^i \equiv \sum_{g \in G} p_g \, h_{\theta(s)g}(p, w^i)$ w.r.t. s shows, however, that the right-hand side of (56) must equal zero. Hence, $\frac{\mathrm{d}}{\mathrm{d}s} w^i_{\theta(s)} = 0$ along any C^1 path $s \mapsto \theta(s)$ in Θ, implying that $w^i_{\theta(s)}$ is constant throughout the interval $(\underline{s}, \bar{s})$. By continuity, w^i_θ must also be constant along any piecewise C^1 arc in the type domain Θ. So the hypothesis in Section 2.8 that Θ is piecewise C^1-arc connected implies that w^i_θ is independent of θ everywhere. □

13.3. Counterexample

The following example in Figure 15.2 shows that Lemma 69 may not hold if the type domain Θ is not piecewise C^1-arc connected, as required by the smoothness assumption of Section 2.8.

Example 70 Suppose there are two goods—books (b) and a second good (c) that we will call "conspicuous consumption," following Veblen. There are two types of agent, the scholarly (S) and the prodigal (P). All agents of the same type receive the same allocation of books and of conspicuous consumption. The consumption vectors of the two types are t_S and t_P, respectively, as illustrated in Figure 15.2. In particular, the scholarly receive relatively more books and the prodigal receive relatively more conspicuous consumption. This allocation is self-selective and also a WELT, given that the agents of each type have their common allocations supported by parallel budget lines touching their appropriate convex indifference curves, as indicated in Figure 15.2. But the allocation is not a WE. In fact, there is redistribution of wealth from agents of type S to those of type P, with $w^i_P = w_P > w_S = w^i_S$ for all $i \in N$.

13.4. Fully Fair Allocations

It is easy to extend the ideas of Foley (1967) and Varian (1974) to a continuum economy. First, say that the allocation $\hat{t}^{N \times \Theta}$ is *envy-free* if

$$(\nu \times \nu)\big(\{\, (i, \theta, j, \eta) \in N \times \Theta \times N \times \Theta \mid \hat{t}^j_\eta \in P_\theta(\hat{t}^i_\theta) \,\}\big) = 0.$$

Departing slightly from Varian (1974), say that the allocation is ν-*fair* (rather than "fair") if it is both Pareto efficient and envy-free.

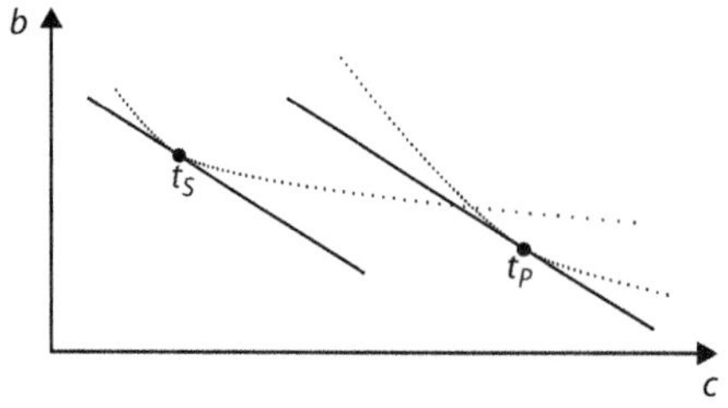

Figure 15.2. Self-Selective Allocation of Books and Conspicuous Consumption.

As with Lemma 69, it is easier to work with strengthened definitions. Thus, say that the allocation $\hat{t}^{N\times\Theta}$ is *fully envy-free* if $\hat{t}^i_\theta \succsim_\theta \hat{t}^j_\eta$ for all combinations (i,j,θ,η) such that $i \neq j$ and $\hat{t}^j_\eta \in T_\theta$. And that the allocation is *fully ν-fair* if it is fully f-Pareto efficient and fully envy-free.

The following simplifies the main result of Champsaur and Laroque (1981):

Theorem 71 *Suppose the type domain Θ is smooth. Any interior allocation $\hat{t}^{N\times\Theta}$ is fully ν-fair if and only if it is a full WE for a suitable price vector p.*

Proof. Following the discussion in Section 13.1, it is obvious that any full WE allocation is fully f-Pareto efficient and fully envy-free, so fully ν-fair.

To prove the converse, note that because Θ is smooth and the interior allocation $\hat{t}^{N\times\Theta}$ is fully f-Pareto efficient, the argument that concluded Section 13.1 implies that there must exist a price vector $p \gg 0$ such that $(\hat{t}^{N\times\Theta}, p)$ is a full WELT. There is an associated wealth distribution rule $w^{N\times\Theta}$ specified by the measurable function $(i,\theta) \mapsto w^i_\theta$ where $w^i_\theta := p\hat{t}^i_\theta > \underline{w}_\theta(p)$ for all $(i,\theta) \in N \times \Theta$, and also $\int_{N\times\Theta} w^i_\theta d\nu = 0$.

In addition, because the allocation is fully envy-free, for each fixed $\theta \in \Theta$ it must satisfy $\hat{t}^i_\theta \succsim_\theta \hat{t}^j_\theta$ for all pairs $i,j \in N$. Now consider the unit interval N as a type domain. Given the fixed $\theta \in \Theta$, the set N trivially satisfies the assumptions of Section 2.8 needed to make it a smooth type domain. So Lemma 69 can be applied with N instead of Θ as the type domain. It follows that $w^i_\theta \equiv w_\theta$ and so $\hat{t}^i_\theta = h_\theta(p, w_\theta) =: \bar{t}_\theta$, both independent of i.

Again, because the allocation is fully envy-free, it follows that $\bar{t}_\theta \succsim_\theta \bar{t}_\eta$ for all $(\theta,\eta) \in \Theta \times \Theta$ such that $\bar{t}_\eta \in T_\theta$. Now Lemma 69 can be applied once more to the self-selective allocation $(i,\theta) \mapsto \bar{t}_\theta$ with Θ as the smooth type domain. It implies that $w_\theta \equiv w$, independent of θ. But $\int_{N\times\Theta} w^i_\theta d\nu = 0$, so $w = 0$. It follows that $(\hat{t}^{N\times\Theta}, p)$ is a full WE. □

14. STRATEGYPROOF MECHANISMS IN A CONTINUUM ECONOMY

14.1. Individual Strategyproofness

Section 7.5.1 briefly considered strategyproof allocation mechanisms in finite economies, and cited the negative results of Serizawa and Weymark (2003) in particular. In continuum economies, statistical or not, the picture is much more rosy (Hammond 1979).

When characterizing WE allocations, it is natural to consider a restricted domain of statistical continuum economies for which a WE exists. Accordingly, let $\mathcal{D} \subseteq \mathcal{M}_\lambda(N \times \Theta)$ denote a domain of measures ν with $\text{marg}_N\, \nu = \lambda$. Given this domain, define an *allocation mechanism* as a mapping $f : \mathcal{D} \times N \times \Theta \to \mathbb{R}^G$ satisfying $f(\nu, i, \theta) \in T_\theta$ for ν-a.e.

(i,θ) in $N \times \Theta$ which, for each fixed $\nu \in \mathcal{D}$, also has the property that the mapping $(i,\theta) \mapsto f(\nu,i,\theta)$ is ν-integrable with $\int_{N\times\Theta} f(\nu,i,\theta)d\nu = 0$. Thus, for each $\nu \in \mathcal{D}$, the mapping $(i,\theta) \mapsto t^i_\theta(\nu) := f(\nu,i,\theta)$ determines a feasible allocation $t^{N\times\Theta}(\nu)$.

Such an allocation mechanism is said to be (individually) *strategyproof* if, for all $\nu \in \mathcal{D}$ and all $(i,\theta) \in N \times \Theta$, it satisfies the *incentive constraint*

$$f(\nu,i,\theta) \succsim_\theta f(\nu,i,\tilde{\theta}) \text{ for all } \tilde{\theta} \text{ such that } f(\nu,i,\tilde{\theta}) \in T_\theta. \tag{57}$$

This formulation reflects the negligible influence each individual in a continuum economy has on the joint distribution ν of labels $i \in N$ and apparent types $\theta \in \Theta$. In fact, the mechanism f is strategyproof if and only if, for each $\nu \in \mathcal{D}$, the allocation $t^{N\times\Theta}(\nu)$ it generates satisfies the self-selection constraints $t^i_\theta \succsim_\theta t^i_\eta$ whenever $(i,\theta,\eta) \in N \times \Theta \times \Theta$ satisfy $t^i_\eta \in T_\theta$. This convenient property is generally false in finite economies.

Note that the incentive constraint (57) is required to hold for *all* $(i,\theta) \in N \times \Theta$ without exception, not merely for ν-a.e. (i,θ). This strong definition simplifies later results. The strengthening is essentially harmless, because the decentralization theorem that follows gives weak sufficient conditions allowing a mechanism that satisfies (57) for ν-a.e. $(i,\theta) \in N \times \Theta$ to be adapted easily by choosing an appropriate value of $f(\nu,i,\theta)$ on the exceptional null set so that the new mechanism satisfies (57) for all (i,θ). In this connection, it is instructive to compare the contrasting approaches and results of Mas-Colell and Vives (1993) with those of Guesnerie (1995).

Several later results specifically concern *anonymous* mechanisms, defined as satisfying the symmetry requirement that f be independent of i.[42]

14.2. Decentralization Theorem

A *budget correspondence* is a mapping $B : \mathcal{D} \times N \twoheadrightarrow \mathbb{R}^G$ that specifies each individual's budget set $B^i(\nu)$ in $\mathbb{R}^G$ as a function of $i \in N$ and $\nu \in \mathcal{D}$, with the property that the set $\{(i,t) \in N \times \mathbb{R}^G \mid t \in B^i(\nu)\}$ should be measurable for every $\nu \in \mathcal{D}$. Note that the set $B^i(\nu)$ is required to be *independent* of $\theta \in \Theta$. It can depend on the identifier i, however, which is observable by definition. For example, $B^i(\nu)$ can depend on agent i's observable characteristics, such as date of birth or other officially recorded demographic events. Indeed, most social security systems and other pension schemes have exactly this feature.

The budget correspondence $(\nu,i) \mapsto\!\!\!\rightarrow B^i(\nu)$ is said to *decentralize* the mechanism $f(\nu,i,\theta)$, provided that for all $\nu \in \mathcal{D}$ and all $(i,\theta) \in N \times \Theta$, one has $f(\nu,i,\theta) \in B^i(\nu)$

[42] Formally, as Guesnerie (1995) in particular points out, this is a weak definition of anonymity requiring only *recipient anonymity*, with $f(\nu,i,\theta)$ independent of i. It does not require the *anonymity in influence*, with $f(\nu,i,\theta) \equiv \phi(\mu,i,\theta)$ where μ is the marginal distribution on Θ induced by the joint distribution ν on $N \times \Theta$. This distinction makes little difference to the following results, however.

and also

$$t \in B^i(\nu) \cap T_\theta \Longrightarrow f(\nu,i,\theta) \succsim_\theta t.$$

The following very simple characterization is taken from Hammond (1979).

Theorem 72 *The mechanism $f(\nu,i,\theta)$ is strategyproof if and only if it can be decentralized.*

Proof. First, suppose $B^i(\nu)$ decentralizes f. Because $f(\nu,i,\tilde{\theta}) \in B^i(\nu)$, obviously $f(\nu,i,\theta) \succsim_\theta f(\nu,i,\tilde{\theta})$ whenever $f(\nu,i,\tilde{\theta}) \in T_\theta$. So the incentive constraints (57) are satisfied.

Conversely, construct the set

$$B^i(\nu) := f(\nu,i,\Theta) := \{t \in \mathbb{R}^G \mid \exists\theta \in \Theta : t = f(\nu,i,\theta)\} \tag{58}$$

as the range of f as θ varies over Θ, with (ν,i) fixed. Strategyproofness implies that this must be a decentralization. □

Guesnerie (1995) has a very similar result, which he calls the "taxation principle" because it implies, for instance, that an allocation mechanism that is used to redistribute wealth or to finance the provision of public goods will be strategyproof if and only if it presents all indistinguishable agents with the same (generally nonlinear) budget constraint after the effects of all taxes and subsidies are taken into account.

Obviously many different budget correspondences are possible, giving rise to many different strategyproof mechanisms. Indeed, suppose preferences are continous and the budget correspondence has values that make $B^i(\nu) \cap T_\theta$ a nonempty compact subset of $\mathbb{R}^G$ throughout the domain $\mathcal{D} \times N \times \Theta$. Then Theorem 72 implies that there exists a strategyproof mechanism satisfying

$$f(\nu,i,\theta) \in \{t \in B^i(\nu) \cap T_\theta \mid t' \in B^i(\nu) \cap T_\theta \Longrightarrow t \succsim_\theta t'\}$$

for all $(\nu,i,\theta) \in \mathcal{D} \times N \times \Theta$. In particular, there is the *Walrasian* budget correspondence with lump-sum transfers. This is defined by

$$B^i(\nu) := \{t \in \mathbb{R}^G \mid p(\nu)\, t \leq w^i(p(\nu),\nu)\}$$

where $p(\nu)$ should be chosen to clear markets given the wealth distribution rule $(i,p,\nu) \mapsto w^i(p,\nu)$—which must be ν-integrable and satisfy $\int_N w^i(p,\nu)\, d\lambda = 0$ for all (p,ν). An obvious corollary of Theorem 72 is that the associated mechanism that generates WELT allocations must be strategyproof.

Suppose that agents' preferences are LNS, continuous, and convex, and that the allocation mechanism $f(\nu,i,\theta)$ is anonymous and strategyproof, while also generating

Pareto efficient interior allocations (which must therefore be WELT allocations). Then Theorem 72 implies the existence of a decentralization $B(\nu)$, independent of i and θ. Nevertheless, the mechanism need not generate WE allocations without lump-sum transfers, as Example 70 in Section 13.3 illustrates. Note that the decentralization in that example could be the two-point set $B(\nu) = \{t_S, t_P\}$, or some obvious variation including these points. It does not have to be, and actually cannot be, a Walrasian budget decentralization with one common budget line facing both types of agent. This example can be avoided, however, under the smooth type domain hypothesis set out in Section 2.8.

14.3. Limits to Redistribution

The following Lemma is based on extensions and corrections by Champsaur and Laroque (1981, 1982) of a result stated by Hammond (1979) and also partly corrected in the appendix to Hammond (1987).

Lemma 73 *Suppose that Θ is a smooth type domain. Then the mechanism $f : \mathcal{D} \times N \times \Theta$ is strategyproof and yields fully f-Pareto efficient interior allocations if and only if, for each $\nu \in \mathcal{D}$ it generates a fully WELT allocation relative to a wealth distribution rule $w^{N\times\Theta}(\nu)$ satisfying $w^i_\theta(\nu) \equiv w^i(\nu)$, independent of θ, where $w^i(\nu) > \underline{w}_\theta(p(\nu)) := \inf p(\nu)\, T_\theta$ for all $(\nu, i, \theta) \in \mathcal{D} \times N \times \Theta$.*

Proof. Sufficiency follows from Theorem 72, with $B^i(\nu)$ as the Walrasian budget set $\{t \in \mathbb{R}^G \mid p(\nu)\, t \leq w^i(p(\nu), \nu)\}$ for each $\nu \in \mathcal{D}$ and $i \in N$, where $w^N(p, \nu)$ is the wealth distribution rule, independent of θ, and where $p = p(\nu)$ denotes any WELT price vector that solves $\int_{N\times\Theta} h_\theta(p, w^i(p, \nu))\, d\nu = 0$. Then smoothness condition (c) in Section 2.8 ensures that the fully WELT allocation is interior.

Conversely, fix any $\nu \in \mathcal{D}$ and suppose the allocation $\hat{t}^{N\times\Theta}(\nu)$ defined by $\hat{t}^i_\theta(\nu) := f(\nu, i, \theta)$ is fully f-Pareto efficient and interior. By the argument that concludes Section 13.1, it must generate a fully WELT allocation that is decentralizable by budget constraints of the form $p(\nu)\, t \leq w^i_\theta(\nu)$ for all $(i, \theta) \in N \times \Theta$. Because of interiority, note that $w^i_\theta(\nu) > \underline{w}_\theta(p(\nu))$ for all $(i, \theta) \in N \times \Theta$. Also, strategyproofness implies that the allocation $\hat{t}^{N\times\Theta}(\nu)$ must be self-selective, as defined in Section 13.2. The result follows from Lemma 69. □

14.4. Anonymity

The limits to redistribution presented in Section 14.3 make it easy to derive our main characterization of WE allocation mechanisms on smooth type domains.

Theorem 74 *Suppose Θ is a smooth type domain, and the allocation mechanism $f(\nu, i, \theta)$ is anonymous and strategyproof. Suppose too that the resulting allocation $f(\nu, i, \theta)$ is interior and* *fully f-Pareto efficient for each $\nu \in \mathcal{D}$. Then the allocation defined by $f(\nu, i, \theta)$ must be a full WE for each $\nu \in \mathcal{D}$.*

Proof. Given the wealth distribution rule $w^i(\nu)$ of Lemma 73, one has $f(\nu, i, \theta) = h_\theta(p(\nu), w^i(\nu))$ for all (i, θ). For each pair $i, j \in N$, anonymity implies that $h_\theta(p(\nu), w^i(\nu)) = h_\theta(p(\nu), w^j(\nu))$, so

$$w^i(\nu) = p(\nu)\, h_\theta(p(\nu), w^i(\nu)) = p(\nu)\, h_\theta(p(\nu), w^j(\nu)) = w^j(\nu).$$

Hence $w^i(\nu) = w(\nu)$, independent of i, for all $i \in N$. But $\int_{N \times \Theta} w^i(\nu)\, d\nu = 0$, so $w(\nu) = 0$. The allocation must therefore be a full WE. □

There is an obvious converse of Theorem 74—with a smooth type domain, any mechanism generating a full WE allocation for each $\nu \in \mathcal{D}$ must be anonymous. Indeed, this is true whenever preferences are merely strictly convex.

14.5. Weak Gains from Trade with an Inclusive Type Domain

The second characterization of a WE allocation mechanism for a smooth type domain Θ relies on two additional conditions.

Say that the mechanism $f(\nu, i, \theta)$ satisfies *full weak gains from trade* provided that $f(\nu, i, \theta) \succsim_\theta 0$ for all $(\nu, i, \theta) \in \mathcal{D} \times N \times \Theta$.

Say that the smooth type domain Θ is *inclusive* if

$$\{ u'_\theta(0) / \| u'_\theta(0) \| \mid \theta \in \Theta \} = \Delta^0$$

—that is, if the domain of normalized utility gradient vectors at the autarky allocation is equal to the relative interior of the unit simplex Δ in $\mathbb{R}^G$. Equivalently, given any $p \gg 0$, there must exist $\theta \in \Theta$ such that $h_\theta(p, 0) = 0$.

Theorem 75 *Suppose there is an inclusive smooth type domain Θ. Suppose too that $f(\nu, i, \theta)$ is an interior, strategyproof, and fully f-Pareto efficient mechanism that satisfies full weak gains from trade. Then the allocation defined by $f(\nu, i, \theta)$ must be a WE for each $\nu \in \mathcal{D}$.*

Proof. By Lemma 73, given any fixed $\nu \in \mathcal{D}$, the allocation $t^{N \times \Theta}(\nu)$ defined by $t^i_\theta(\nu) := f(\nu, i, \theta)$ for all $(i, \theta) \in N \times \Theta$ must be a full WELT at some price vector $p(\nu) \gg 0$ relative to some wealth distribution rule $w^N(\nu)$ that does not depend on θ. Full weak gains from trade imply that $f(\nu, i, \theta) = h_\theta(p(\nu), w^i(\nu)) \succsim_\theta 0$ for all $(i, \theta) \in N \times \Theta$. Because the type domain is inclusive, there exists $\theta \in \Theta$ such that $h_\theta(p(\nu), 0) = 0 \precsim_\theta h_\theta(p(\nu), w^i(\nu))$ and so $w^i(\nu) \geq 0$ for all $i \in N$. But the wealth distribution rule must satisfy $\int_N w^i(\nu)\, d\lambda = 0$, so $w^i(\nu) = 0$ for λ-a.e. $i \in N$. Hence, each full WELT must be a WE, without lump-sum transfers. □

14.6. Strategyproof Mechanisms of Maximal Dimension

Say that the mechanism $f(\nu, i, \theta)$ has *dimension n* at ν if for ν-a.e. $(i, \theta) \in N \times \Theta$ there exists a set V_θ^i that is homeomorphic to an open ball in $\mathbb{R}^n$ such that $f(\nu, i, \theta) \in V_\theta^i \subseteq f(\nu, i, \Theta)$, where $f(\nu, i, \Theta)$ is the range set defined in (58). Because a Walrasian mechanism satisfies $p(\nu) f(\nu, i, \theta) = 0$ for ν-a.e. (i, θ), it has dimension $n \leq \#G - 1$ at each ν in its domain. The main result of Dubey, Mas-Colell, and Shubik (1980) suggests the following:[43]

Theorem 76 *Suppose that agents' preferences are both monotone and semi-strictly convex. Suppose too that f is an anonymous strategyproof mechanism whose dimension at ν is $n \geq \#G - 1$. Then the corresponding allocation $t^{N \times \Theta}(\nu)$ must be a symmetric WE.*

Proof. Fix the distribution ν and write $t^{N \times \Theta}$ instead of $t^{N \times \Theta}(\nu)$. Anonymity implies that $t_\theta^i \equiv f(\nu, \theta)$ for all $(i, \theta) \in N \times \Theta$. Let L denote the linear space spanned by the range set $f(\nu, \Theta)$. Evidently $t_\theta^i \in L$ for all $(i, \theta) \in N \times \Theta$.

Define K_1 and K_2 as the sets of potential agents $(i, \theta) \in N \times \Theta$ for whom there exist, respectively: (i) a vector $v \in L \cap P_\theta(t_\theta^i)$; (ii) a set V homeomorphic to an open ball in $\mathbb{R}^n$ such that $t_\theta^i \in V \subseteq f(\nu, \Theta)$. For any $(i, \theta) \in K_1 \cap K_2$ and any $\alpha \in (0, 1)$ sufficiently small, the convex combination $\tilde{t}_\theta^i := (1 - \alpha) t_\theta^i + \alpha v \in V$. Because preferences are semi-strictly convex, it follows that $\tilde{t}_\theta^i \in P_\theta(t_\theta^i) \cap f(\nu, \Theta)$. Strategyproofness implies, therefore, that $K_1 \cap K_2$ must be empty.

Consider any $(i, \theta) \in K_2$. Then $(i, \theta) \notin K_1$, implying that $t_\theta^i \succsim_\theta v$ whenever $v \in L \cap T_\theta$. But the mechanism has dimension n, so $\nu(K_2) = 1$. Because preferences are monotone and so nonsatiated, it follows that $L \neq \mathbb{R}^G$. Therefore $n = \#G - 1$. So there exists $p \neq 0$ such that L is the hyperplane $\{v \in \mathbb{R}^G \mid pv = 0\}$.

Now, for each $(i, \theta) \in K_2$, the two convex sets L and $P_\theta(t_\theta^i)$ must be disjoint, as well as nonempty, with $t_\theta^i \in L$. But preferences are monotone and so LNS, so t_θ^i is a boundary point of $P_\theta(t_\theta^i)$. It follows that the hyperplane L itself must separate L from $P_\theta(t_\theta^i)$. Also, after a suitable choice of the sign of p, one has $pt \geq 0$ for all $t \in \mathbb{R}_{++}^G$, so $p > 0$ and also $pt \geq 0$ for all $t \in P_\theta(t_\theta^i)$. Because L and $P_\theta(t_\theta^i)$ are disjoint, in fact $pt > 0$ for all $t \in P_\theta(t_\theta^i)$. But $\nu(K_2) = 1$, so $(t^{N \times \Theta}, p)$ is a WE. □

[43] Dubey, Mas-Colell, and Shubik consider a *strategic market game* in which each player faces a strategy space S, assumed to be a subset of some separable Banach space. Four axioms called anonymity, continuity, convexity, and aggregation together guarantee that S is convex, and that the outcome of the market game is a feasible allocation $t^{N \times \Theta}$ with the property that almost every potential agent's net trade vector t_θ^i can be expressed as a jointly continuous function $F_{\bar{s}}(s_\theta^i)$ of their own strategy choice s_θ^i and of the mean strategy choice $\bar{s} := \int_{N \times \Theta} s_\theta^i d\nu$. Theorem 76 relies on considerably weaker versions of these assumptions. In particular, the aggregation axiom is dispensed with entirely. Nor is it assumed that $F_{\bar{s}}(s_\theta^i)$ is continuous w.r.t. $\bar{s}$. The latter generalization is important because there may be no continuous selection from the Walrasian equilibrium correspondence. On the other hand, we limit attention to strategyproof direct revelation mechanisms instead of general strategic market games.

15. MANIPULATION BY FINITE COALITIONS

15.1. Multilateral Strategyproofness

In Example 70 of Section 13.3, though the allocation (t_S, t_P) is strategyproof, it could be manipulated by agents exchanging books for conspicuous consumption "on the side," after at least one scholar in a finite coalition has claimed to be prodigal. With this in mind, say that the allocation mechanism $f(\nu, i, \theta)$ is *multilaterally strategyproof* if, for each $\nu \in \mathcal{D}$, no finite coalition $C \subset N$ with (potential) types $\theta^i \in \Theta$ can find "manipulative" types $\tilde{\theta}^i \in \Theta$ and net trade vectors $t^i \in \mathbb{R}^G$ $(i \in C)$ satisfying $\sum_{i \in C} t^i = 0$ as well as $f(\nu, i, \tilde{\theta}^i) + t^i \in P_\theta(f(\nu, i, \theta^i))$ for all $i \in C$.[44]

Considering the case when $\#C = 1$ and so $t^i = 0$, it is obvious that multilateral strategyproofness entails (individual) strategyproofness.

Following Guesnerie (1981, 1995) in particular, a useful distinction can be made between:

(1) "nonexchangeable" goods for which nonlinear pricing is possible;

(2) "exchangeable" goods for which trade on the side cannot be prevented, so only linear pricing is multilaterally strategyproof.

In order to characterize Walrasian equilibrium, the following results concentrate on the case when all goods are exchangeable.

Theorem 77 *If $f(\nu, i, \theta)$ selects a full WE allocation for each $\nu \in \mathcal{D}$, then f is multilaterally strategyproof.*

Proof. For each $\nu \in \mathcal{D}$, there exists a WE price vector $p = p(\nu) \neq 0$ such that, for all $(i, \theta) \in N \times \Theta$, one has $pf(\nu, i, \theta) \leq 0$ and also $\hat{t} \succ_\theta f(\nu, i, \theta) \Longrightarrow p\hat{t} > 0$. Suppose $C \subset N$ and, for all $i \in C$, the actual types $\theta^i \in \Theta$, potential types $\tilde{\theta}^i \in \Theta$, and net trade vectors $\tilde{t}^i \in \mathbb{R}^G$ together satisfy $f(\nu, i, \tilde{\theta}^i) + \tilde{t}^i \in P_{\theta^i}(f(\nu, i, \theta^i))$. Then $p[f(\nu, i, \tilde{\theta}^i) + \tilde{t}^i] > 0 \geq pf(\nu, i, \tilde{\theta}^i)$ for all $i \in C$, implying that $\sum_{i \in C} p\tilde{t}^i > 0$. Thus $\sum_{i \in C} \tilde{t}^i = 0$ is impossible. □

Theorem 78 *Suppose preferences are LNS in $\mathbb{Q}^G$, as defined in Section 12.3. Suppose the mechanism $f(\nu, i, \theta)$ is multilaterally strategyproof for all $\nu \in \mathcal{D}$. Then each allocation $(i, \theta) \mapsto f(\nu, i, \theta)$ is a CELT w.r.t. a wealth distribution rule satisfying $w^i_\theta(\nu) = w^i(\nu)$, independent of θ, with $\int_N w^i(\nu) d\lambda = 0$.*

[44] Similar ideas have been applied in different contexts by Gale (1980, 1982), Guesnerie (1981, 1995), Jacklin (1987), Blackorby and Donaldson (1988), Haubrich (1988), Haubrich and King (1990), and Hammond (1987, 1999b).

Proof. Given any fixed $\nu \in \mathcal{D}$, we adapt the proof of Theorem 63 showing that any f-core allocation is a CE. To do so, first define the "manipulative set"

$$M := \{ (i,\theta,t) \in N \times \Theta \times \mathbb{R}^G \mid \exists \tilde{\theta} \in \Theta : f(\nu,i,\tilde{\theta}) + t \succ_\theta f(\nu,i,\theta) \}.$$

For each (i,θ,t), define the associated sections

$$M_\theta^i := \{ t' \in \mathbb{Q}^G \mid (i,\theta,t') \in M \}$$
$$\text{and} \quad M(t) := \{ (i',\theta') \in N \times \Theta \mid (i',\theta',t) \in M \}$$

of the set M. Next, define

$$K' := \cup\{ M(t) \mid t \in \mathbb{Q}^G,\ \nu(M(t)) > 0 \},$$

which must satisfy $\nu(K') = 1$. Then let C be the convex hull of $\cup_{(i,\theta)\in K'} M_\theta^i$.

Arguing as in the proof of Theorem 63, multilateral strategyproofness implies that $0 \notin C$. Hence, for each fixed $\nu \in \mathcal{D}$, there exists a separating price vector $p(\nu) \neq 0$ such that, for all $(i,\theta) \in K'$, one has $p(\nu)t \geq 0$ whenever $t \in M_\theta^i$ because $t \in \mathbb{Q}^G$ and there exists $\tilde{\theta} \in \Theta$ such that $f(\nu,i,\tilde{\theta}) + t \succsim_\theta f(\nu,i,\theta)$.

In particular, putting $t = f(\nu,i,\theta) - f(\nu,i,\tilde{\theta})$ implies that $p(\nu)t \geq 0$ and so $p(\nu)f(\nu,i,\theta) \geq p(\nu)f(\nu,i,\tilde{\theta})$ whenever $(i,\theta),(i,\tilde{\theta}) \in K'$. Because θ and $\tilde{\theta}$ can be interchanged, this makes it possible to define $w^i(\nu)$ for each $i \in N$ so that $p(\nu)f(\nu,i,\theta) = w^i(\nu)$, independent of θ, for all $(i,\theta) \in K'$. Also, when $\tilde{\theta} = \theta$, putting $\tilde{t} = f(\nu,i,\theta) + t$ implies that, for all $(i,\theta) \in K'$, whenever $\tilde{t} \succsim_\theta f(\nu,i,\theta)$, then $p(\nu)t \geq 0$ and so $p(\nu)\tilde{t} \geq p(\nu)f(\nu,i,\theta)$. Because $\nu(K') = 1$, this shows that $f(\nu,i,\theta)$ is a CELT at prices $p(\nu)$, as claimed. □

Corollary 79 *Suppose preferences are LNS in $\mathbb{Q}^G$. If the anonymous mechanism $f(\nu,\theta)$ is multilaterally strategyproof, then it produces CE allocations.*

Proof. By Theorem 78, for each fixed $\nu \in \mathcal{D}$ the allocation generated by $f(\nu,\theta)$ must be a CELT w.r.t. a wealth distribution rule satisfying $w_\theta^i(\nu) \equiv w(\nu)$, independent of both i and θ, for ν-a.e. $(i,\theta) \in N \times \Theta$. But then $\int_{N\times\Theta} w_\theta^i(\nu) d\nu = 0$, so $w(\nu) = 0$. □

The conditions discussed in Sections 11.6 and 11.8 can be used to ensure that the CE allocations are WE.

15.2. Arbitrage-Free Allocations

Manipulation by finite coalitions can be regarded as one form of arbitrage. For finite economies, a second form of arbitrage was considered in Section 6.3. Yet another form is the subject of Makowski and Ostroy (1998).

Consider a particular feasible allocation $\hat{t}^{N\times\Theta}$. Let $\mathcal{F}$ denote the family of all finite subsets of $N \times \Theta$, and define the "arbitrage opportunity set"

$$\hat{Z} := \bigcup_{K\in\mathcal{F}} \sum_{(i,\theta)\in K} -[R_\theta(\hat{t}^i_\theta) - \{\hat{t}^i_\theta\}]. \tag{59}$$

Thus $z \in \hat{Z}$ if and only if there is a finite coalition $K \subset N \times \Theta$ of potential agents, together with a collection $a^i_\theta \in \mathbb{R}^G$ ($(i,\theta) \in K$) of "potential arbitrage" net trade vectors satisfying $\hat{t}^i_\theta + a^i_\theta \in R_\theta(\hat{t}^i_\theta)$ for all $(i,\theta) \in K$, such that $z = -\sum_{(i,\theta)\in K} a^i_\theta$. Strengthening and also considerably simplifying Makowski and Ostroy's (1998) key definition, say that the allocation $\hat{t}^{N\times\Theta}$ is a *full arbitrage equilibrium* if $\hat{t}^i_\theta \succsim_\theta z$ for all $z \in \hat{Z} \cap T_\theta$ and all $(i,\theta) \in N \times \Theta$.[45] In such an equilibrium, no agent can benefit from potential arbitrage net trades.

Next, say that the allocation $\hat{t}^{N\times\Theta}$ is *fully perfectly competitive* if it is a full arbitrage equilibrium, and if there exists $p \neq 0$ such that the half-space

$$H^-(p) := \{z \in \mathbb{R}^G \mid pz \leq 0\} \tag{60}$$

is the closure of the set $\hat{Z}$. Makowski and Ostroy (1998) impose assumptions that imply in particular a *boundary assumption* requiring the strict preference set $P_\theta(t)$ to be open, for all $\theta \in \Theta$ and $t \in T_\theta$. Their major result is that, for generic continuum economies, the "flattening effect of large numbers" of agents ensures that the closure of the set $\hat{Z}$ is indeed such a half-space. So, if the allocation $\hat{t}^{N\times\Theta}$ is an arbitrage equilibrium, in generic economies it is also perfectly competitive. This leads to a characterization of full Walrasian equilibrium because of a result that, in the simplified framework considered here, takes the form:

Theorem 80

(1) *Provided that preferences are LNS, any full WE is a full arbitrage equilibrium.*

(2) *Suppose that preferences are LNS and continuous, and that they satisfy the boundary assumption. Then any fully perfectly competitive allocation is a WE.*

Proof.

(1) Suppose $(\hat{t}^{N\times\Theta}, p)$ is a full WE. Because preferences are LNS, it is a full CE also. So for any $(i,\theta) \in N \times \Theta$, one has $pt \geq 0 = p\hat{t}^i_\theta$ whenever $t \in R_\theta(\hat{t}^i_\theta)$. Hence $pz \leq 0$ whenever $z \in -[R_\theta(\hat{t}^i_\theta) - \{\hat{t}^i_\theta\}]$. So $z \in \hat{Z} \cap T_\theta$ implies that $pz \leq 0$ and so $\hat{t}^i_\theta \succsim_\theta z$. It follows that $\hat{t}^{N\times\Theta}$ is a full arbitrage equilibrium.

[45] Makowski and Ostroy's (1998) actual definition of an "arbitrage equilibrium" in effect requires this condition to hold for almost all $(i,\theta) \in N \times \Theta$. It also limits the finite coalitions K in a way that depends on the support of the distribution on $\mathbb{R}^G \times \Theta$ that is induced by the allocation $\hat{t}^{N\times\Theta}$.

(2) Suppose the allocation $\hat{t}^{N\times\Theta}$ is fully perfectly competitive. Let $p \neq 0$ be a price vector such that the half-space $H^-(p)$ defined in (60) is the closure of the set $\hat{Z}$ defined in (59).

Consider any $(i,\theta) \in N \times \Theta$ and any $t \in P_\theta(\hat{t}^i_\theta)$. By the boundary assumption, there exists an open set V in $\mathbb{R}^G$ such that $t \in V \subseteq P_\theta(\hat{t}^i_\theta)$. But $\hat{t}^{N\times\Theta}$ is fully perfectly competitive, so a full arbitrage equilibrium, implying that $P_\theta(\hat{t}^i_\theta) \subseteq T_\theta \setminus \hat{Z}$. Hence $\hat{Z} \subseteq T_\theta \setminus V$. But $H^-(p)$ is the closure of $\hat{Z}$ and $T_\theta \setminus V$ is closed, so $H^-(p) \subseteq T_\theta \setminus V$. Because $V \subseteq T_\theta$, this implies that $pt' > 0$ for each $t' \in V$, including t.

Because preferences are LNS, the previous paragraph shows that $p\hat{t}^i_\theta \geq 0$. This is true for all $(i,\theta) \in N \times \Theta$. But the allocation $\hat{t}^{N\times\Theta}$ is feasible, so $p \int_{N\times\Theta} \hat{t}^i_\theta d\nu = 0$, which is only possible when $p\hat{t}^i_\theta = 0$ for ν-a.e. $(i,\theta) \in N \times \Theta$. Hence, $(\hat{t}^{N\times\Theta}, p)$ must be a WE.[46] □

16. OTHER ENVIRONMENTS

16.1. Public Goods

Competitive market mechanisms are unlikely to perform well when there are public goods. Nevertheless, versions of the efficiency theorems in Section 4 do hold. Indeed, Foley (1970a) and Milleron (1972) suggest how an economy with public goods could be regarded as a special kind of economy with private goods that include "personalized" copies of each public good. Because these copies have to be produced in equal amounts for all consumers, the resulting private good economy cannot have even weakly monotone preferences. Yet most of the results in Sections 4 and 5 for Walrasian equilibria in finite economies with private goods do not rely on preferences being monotone. So these results extend immediately to corresponding results for Lindahl or ratio equilibria (Kaneko 1977) in economies with both public and private goods. So may some of the later results in Sections 6 and 7, though this remains to be investigated.

One complication that does arise is that, as the number of agents increases, so does the number of dimensions in the relevant commodity space, including the personalized copies of each public good. For this reason, results like those in Section 7 are not easy to extend to public goods. In particular, the core of a replica economy with public goods may not shrink fast enough to exclude lump-sum transfers, even in the limit. Nevertheless Van den Nouweland, Tijs, and Wooders (2002) do find a counterpart to the main result of Section 8.4.

[46] It may not be a full WE because one could have $p\hat{t}^i_\theta > 0$ on a null subset of $N \times \Theta$.

When there is a continuum of agents, there is also a continuum of personalized copies of each public good, so the commodity space becomes infinite-dimensional. More specifically, Muench (1972) in particular has shown how core equivalence is lost. Strategyproofness, however, can be satisfied, at least formally, as discussed in Hammond (1979). Indeed, a generalization of Theorem 74 could be used to characterize Lindahl equilibria. Though formally strategyproof, however, these mechanisms for continuum economies lack counterparts that are approximately strategyproof in large finite economies—the free-rider problem is hard to overcome.

Other extensions to public goods of the results presented in this chapter are likely to be even less straightforward. Some recent work on the topic includes Silvestre (2003), Buchholz and Peters (2007), and Florenzano (2009).

16.2. Externalities

In principle, externalities can be treated rather like public goods, by adding dimensions to the commodity space. Appropriate Pigou taxes or subsidies on private activities that create each externality can then be used to help steer the economy toward a Pareto efficient allocation. The definition of an appropriately modified Walrasian equilibrium, however, may not be so straightforward, because the "property rights" that determine agents' endowments need to be specified. Do polluters have the right to create as much pollution as suits them, or should they be required to pay for all the damage they create?

A special case is when each agent's feasible set is conditioned by one or more aggregate externalities that get created by all agents together, and preferences extend over such aggregate externalities. Each such externality is effectively a public good (or public bad) for which Lindahl prices are appropriate. The right (or duty) to create such an externality, however, should be allocated by prices that can be regarded as per unit Pigou taxes or subsidies, the same for all agents. A detailed analysis is presented in Hammond (1998). A major complication pointed out by Starrett (1972) is that negative externalities of this kind are incompatible with convex production possibilities, so the usual second efficiency theorem is inapplicable.

Similar extensions to a continuum economy are fairly straightforward, with the aggregate externalities becoming "widespread externalities" of the kind considered by Kaneko and Wooders (1986, 1989, 1994), Hammond, Kaneko, and Wooders (1989), and Hammond (1995, 1999a).

Though the allocations generated by competitive market mechanisms are unlikely to be Pareto efficient in the presence of externalities, they may nevertheless meet some weaker criterion of constrained Pareto efficiency. Grossman (1977) and Repullo (1988) considered forms of constrained Pareto efficiency that apply when markets are incomplete. Somewhat similar ideas are applied to economies with a continuum of agents and widespread externalities in Hammond (1995). Particularly appealing may be the main result of Hammond, Kaneko, and Wooders (1989)—as well as the corresponding result in Hammond (1999a)—that characterizes f-core allocations as "Nash–Walrasian equilibria" in which each agent treats the aggregate externalities as fixed. This is consistent with using Pigou pricing to allocate efficiently agents' rights to contribute to those externalities. Some particular widespread externalities that arise in sequential environments with policy feedback are considered in Hammond (1999c, 2007).

ACKNOWLEDGMENTS

Parts of this chapter were presented in 1998 during the course of three lectures at the Institute of Economic Research at Hitotsubashi University during a visit financed by the Japanese Ministry of Education. My thanks to Kotaro Suzumura as a host, and to him and his colleagues for their interest and comments. Thanks also to Kenneth Arrow, both for his numerous helpful suggestions in his capacity as editor, and for being a patient and understanding colleague. Finally, my thanks to William Thomson for detailed suggestions concerning Sections 7 and 8 in particular, not all of which I have been able to follow.

REFERENCES

Aliprantis, C. D., & Border, K. (1999). *Infinite dimensional analysis: a Hitchhiker's guide* (2nd ed.). Berlin: Springer.

Aliprantis, C. D., Brown, D. J., & Burkinshaw, O. (1987a). Edgeworth equilibria. *Econometrica, 55*, 1109–1137.

Aliprantis, C. D., Brown, D. J., & Burkinshaw, O. (1987b). Edgeworth equilibria in production economies. *Journal of Economic Theory, 43*, 252–291.

Allais, M. (1947). *Economie et intérêt*. Paris: Imprimerie Nationale.

Arrow, K. J. (1951a). An extension of the basic theorems of classical welfare economics. In J. Neyman (Ed.), *Proceedings of the second Berkeley symposium on mathematical statistics and probability* (pp. 507–532). Berkeley: University of California Press; reprinted in *Collected papers of Kenneth J. Arrow, Vol. 2: general equilibrium*. Cambridge, MA: Belknap Press of Harvard University Press, 1983.

Arrow, K. J. (1951b). Alternative proof of the substitution theorem for Leontief models in the general case. In T. C. Koopmans (Ed.) *Activity analysis of production and allocation* (ch. 9, pp. 155–164). New York: Wiley; reprinted in *Collected papers of Kenneth J. Arrow, Vol. 2: general equilibrium* Cambridge, MA: Belknap Press of Harvard University Press, 1983.

Arrow, K. J., & Debreu, G. (1954). Existence of equilibrium for a competitive economy. *Econometrica, 22*, 265–290.

Arrow, K. J., & Hahn, F. H. (1971). *General competitive analysis*. San Francisco: Holden-Day.

Aumann, R. J. (1964). Markets with a continuum of traders. *Econometrica, 32*, 39–50.

Aumann, R. J. (1975). Values of markets with a continuum of traders. *Econometrica, 43*, 611–646.

Aumann, R. J., & Shapley, L. (1974). *Values of non-atomic games*. Princeton: Princeton University Press.

Bergstrom, T. C. (1976). How to discard 'free disposability'—at no cost. *Journal of Mathematical Economics, 3*, 131–134.

Bergstrom, T. C. (1996). Nonsubstitution theorems for a small trading country. *Pacific Economic Review, 1*, 117–135.

Bhagwati, J. N. (1958). Immiserizing growth: a geometrical note. *Review of Economic Studies, 25,* 201–205.

Bhagwati, J. N. (1987). Immiserizing growth. In J. Eatwell, M. Milgate & P. Newman (Eds.), *The new Palgrave: a dictionary of economics.* London: Macmillan.

Bhagwati, J. N., & Wan, H. (1979). The "stationarity" of shadow prices of factors in project evaluation, with or without distortions. *American Economic Review, 69,* 261–273.

Blackorby, C., & Donaldson, D. (1988). Cash versus kind, self-selection, and efficient transfers. *American Economic Review, 78,* 691–700.

Bochet, O. (2007). Implementation of the Walrasian correspondence: the boundary problem. *International Journal of Game Theory, 36,* 301–316.

Buchholz, W., & Peters, W. (2007). Justifying the Lindahl solution as an outcome of fair cooperation. *Public Choice, 133,* 157–169.

Calsamiglia, X., & Kirman, A. (1993). A unique informationally efficient and decentralized mechanism with fair outcomes. *Econometrica, 61,* 1147–1172.

Champsaur, P., & Laroque, G. (1981). Fair allocations in large economies. *Journal of Economic Theory, 25,* 269–282.

Champsaur, P., & Laroque, G. (1982). A note on incentives in large economies. *Review of Economic Studies, 49,* 627–635.

Chander, P. (1983). On the informational size of message spaces for efficient resource allocation processes. *Econometrica, 51,* 919–938.

Coles, J. L., & Hammond, P. J. (1995). Walrasian equilibrium without survival: equilibrium, efficiency, and remedial policy. In K. Basu, P. K. Pattanaik & K. Suzumura (Eds.), *Choice, welfare, and development: a Festschrift in honor of Amartya K. Sen* (ch. 3, pp. 32–64). Oxford: Oxford University Press.

Dagan, N. (1995). Consistent solutions in exchange economies: a characterization of the price mechanism. Economics Working Paper 141, Universitat Pompeu Fabra, Barcelona. http://www.econ.upf.edu/docs/papers/downloads/141.pdf.

Dagan, N. (1996). Consistency and the Walrasian allocations correspondence. Economics Working Paper 151, Universitat Pompeu Fabra, Barcelona. http://www.econ.upf.edu/docs/papers/downloads/151.pdf.

Dasgupta, P. S., Hammond, P. J., & Maskin, E. S. (1979). The implementation of social choice rules: some general results on incentive compatibility. *Review of Economic Studies, 46,* 185–216.

Dasgupta, P., & Ray, D. (1986). Inequality as a determinant of malnutrition and unemployment: theory. *Economic Journal, 96,* 1011–1034.

Debreu, G. (1951). The coefficient of resource utilization. *Econometrica, 22,* 273–292.

Debreu, G. (1954). Valuation equilibrium and Pareto optimum. *Proceedings of the National Academy of Sciences, 40,* 588–592; reprinted in *Mathematical economics: twenty papers of Gerard Debreu.* Cambridge: Cambridge University Press, 1983.

Debreu, G. (1959). *Theory of value: an axiomatic analysis of economic equilibrium.* New York: John Wiley.

Debreu, G. (1962). New concepts and techniques for equilibrium analysis. *International Economic Review, 3,* 257–273.

Debreu, G. (1969). Neighboring economic agents. In *La Décision* (Colloques Internationaux du Centre de la Recherche Scientifique), *171,* 85–90; reprinted in *Mathematical economics: twenty papers of Gerard Debreu.* Cambridge: Cambridge University Press, 1983.

Debreu, G., & Scarf, H. (1963). A limit theorem on the core of an economy. *International Economic Review, 4,* 235–246.

Diamantaras, D., & Gilles, R. P. (2004). On the microeconomics of specialization. *Journal of Economic Behavior and Organization, 55,* 223–236.

Diewert, W. E. (1983). Cost–benefit analysis and project evaluation: a comparison of alternative approaches. *Journal of Public Economics, 22,* 265–302.

Dubey, P., Mas-Colell, A., & Shubik, M. (1980). Efficiency properties of strategic market games: an axiomatic approach. *Journal of Economic Theory, 22*, 339–362.

Dudley, R. M. (1989). *Real analysis and probability*. New York: Chapman & Hall.

Dutta, B., Ray, D., Sengupta, K., & Vohra, R. (1989). A consistent bargaining set. *Journal of Economic Theory, 49*, 93–112.

Eaves, B. C. (1976). A finite algorithm for the linear exchange model. *Journal of Mathematical Economics, 3*, 197–203.

Edgeworth, F. Y. (1881). *Mathematical psychics*. London: Kegan Paul.

Fisher, F. M. (1981). Stability, disequilibrium awareness, and the perception of new opportunities. *Econometrica, 49*, 279–317.

Fisher, F. M. (1983). *Disequilibrium foundations of equilibrium economics*. Cambridge: Cambridge University Press.

Fisher, F. M., & Saldanha, F. M. C. B. (1982). Stability, disequilibrium awareness, and the perception of new opportunities: some corrections. *Econometrica, 50*, 781–783.

Florenzano, M. (2009). Walras–Lindahl–Wicksell: what equilibrium concept for public goods provision? I—The convex case. Documents de Travail du Centre d'Economie de la Sorbonne. http://halshs.archives-ouvertes.fr/docs/00/36/78/67/PDF/09009.pdf.

Florig, M. (2001a). Hierarchic competitive equilibria. *Journal of Mathematical Economics, 35*, 515–546.

Florig, M. (2001b). On irreducible economies. *Annales d'Économie et de Statistique, 61*, 183–199.

Florig, M. (2003). Corrections to hierarchic competitive equilibria. Cahiers de la MSE, Série Bleue; available at ftp://mse.univ-paris1.fr/pub/mse/cahiers2003/B03065.pdf.

Foley, D. K. (1967). Resource allocation and the public sector. *Yale Economic Essays, 7*, 45–198.

Foley, D. K. (1970a). Lindahl's solution and the core of an economy with public goods. *Econometrica, 38*, 66–72.

Foley, D. K. (1970b). Economic equilibrium with costly marketing. *Journal of Economic Theory, 2*, 276–291.

Gale, D. (1957). Price equilibrium for linear models of exchange. Technical Report P-1156, RAND Corporation.

Gale, D. (1976). The linear exchange model. *Journal of Mathematical Economics, 3*, 204–209.

Gale, D. M. (1980). Money, information and equilibrium in large economies. *Journal of Economic Theory, 23*, 28–65.

Gale, D. M. (1982). *Money: in equilibrium*. Welwyn: James Nisbet.

Gale, D., & Mas-Colell, A. (1975). An equilibrium existence theorem for a general model without ordered preferences. *Journal of Mathematical Economics, 2*, 9–15.

Geanakoplos, J., & Polemarchakis, H. (1991). Overlapping generations. In W. Hildenbrand & H. Sonnenschein (Eds.), *Handbook of mathematical economics*, Vol. IV (ch. 35, pp. 1899–1960). Amsterdam: North-Holland.

Georgescu-Roegen, N. (1951). some properties of a generalized Leontief model. In T. C. Koopmans (Ed.), *Activity analysis of production and allocation* (ch. 10, pp. 165–176). New York: Wiley.

Gevers, L. (1986). Walrasian social choice: some axiomatic approaches. In W. P. Heller, R. M. Starr & D. A. Starrett (Eds.), *Social choice and public decision making: Essays in honor of Kenneth J. Arrow*, Vol. I (ch. 5, pp. 97–114). Cambridge: Cambridge University Press.

Greenberg, J. (1990). *The theory of social situations: an alternative game-theoretic approach*. Cambridge: Cambridge University Press.

Grossman, S. J. (1977). A characterization of the optimality of equilibrium in incomplete markets. *Journal of Economic Theory, 15*, 1–15.

Guesnerie, R. (1981). On taxation and incentives: Further reflections on the limits of redistribution. Discussion Paper No. 89, Sonderforschungsbereich 21, University of Bonn; revised as ch. 1 of Guesnerie (1995).

Guesnerie, R. (1995). *A contribution to the pure theory of taxation*. Cambridge: Cambridge University Press.

Hammond, P. J. (1979). Straightforward individual incentive compatibility in large economies. *Review of Economic Studies, 46,* 263–282.

Hammond, P. J. (1986). Project evaluation by potential tax reform. *Journal of Public Economics, 30,* 1–36.

Hammond, P. J. (1987). Markets as constraints: multilateral incentive compatibility in continuum economies. *Review of Economic Studies, 54,* 399–412.

Hammond, P. J. (1993). Irreducibility, resource relatedness, and survival in equilibrium with individual non-convexities. In R. Becker, M. Boldrin, R. Jones & W. Thomson (Eds.), *General equilibrium, growth, and trade II: the legacy of Lionel W. McKenzie* (ch. 4, pp. 73–115). San Diego: Academic Press.

Hammond, P. J. (1995). Four characterizations of constrained Pareto efficiency in continuum economies with widespread externalities. *Japanese Economic Review, 46,* 103–124.

Hammond, P. J. (1998). The efficiency theorems and market failure. In A. P. Kirman (Ed.), *Elements of general equilibrium analysis* (ch. 6, pp. 211–260). Oxford: Basil Blackwell.

Hammond, P. J. (1999a). On f-core equivalence in a continuum economy with general widespread externalities. *Journal of Mathematical Economics, 32,* 177–184.

Hammond, P. J. (1999b). Multilaterally strategy-proof mechanisms in random Aumann–Hildenbrand macroeconomies. In M. Wooders (Ed.), *Topics in game theory and mathematical economics: essays in honor of Robert J. Aumann* (pp. 171–187). Providence, RI: American Mathematical Society.

Hammond, P. J. (1999c). History as a widespread externality in some Arrow–Debreu market games. In G. Chichilnisky (Ed.), *Markets, information and uncertainty: essays in economic theory in honor of Kenneth J. Arrow* (ch. 16, pp. 328–361). Cambridge: Cambridge University Press.

Hammond, P. J. (2003). Equal rights to trade and mediate. *Social Choice and Welfare, 21,* 181–193.

Hammond, P. J. (2007). History: sunk cost or widespread externality? *Rivista Internazionale di Scienze Sociali, 115,* 161–185.

Hammond, P. J., Kaneko, M., & Wooders, M. H. (1989). Continuum economies with finite coalitions: core, equilibrium and widespread externalities. *Journal of Economic Theory, 49,* 113–134.

Hammond, P. J., & Sempere, J. (2006). Gains from trade versus gains from migration: what makes them so different? *Journal of Public Economic Theory, 8,* 145–170.

Hammond, P. J., & Sempere, J. (2009). Migration with local public goods and the gains from changing places. *Economic Theory, 41,* 359–377.

Hara, C. (2002). The anonymous core of an exchange economy. *Journal of Mathematical Economics, 38,* 545–556.

Hara, C. (2005). Bargaining set and anonymous core without the monotonicity assumption. *Journal of Mathematical Economics, 41,* 91–116.

Hart, S. (2002). Values of perfectly competitive economies. In R. Aumann & S. Hart (Eds.), *Handbook of game theory with economic applications,* Vol. III (ch. 57, pp. 2169–2184). Amsterdam: North-Holland.

Haubrich, J. G. (1988). Optimal financial structure in exchange economies. *International Economic Review, 29,* 217–235.

Haubrich, J. G., & King, R. G. (1990). Banking and insurance. *Journal of Monetary Economics, 26,* 361–386.

Hayashi, T., & Sakai, T. (2009). Nash implementation of competitive equilibria in the job-matching market. *International Journal of Game Theory, 38,* 453–467.

Hildenbrand, W. (1972). Metric measure spaces of economic agents. In L. Le Cam, J. Neyman & E. L. Scott (Eds.), *Proceeedings of the sixth Berkeley symposium on mathematical statistics and probability,* Vol. II (pp. 81–95). Berkeley: University of California Press.

Hildenbrand, W. (1974). *Core and equilibrium of a large economy.* Princeton: Princeton University Press.

Hurwicz, L. (1960). Optimality and informational efficiency in resource allocation processes. In K. J. Arrow, S. Karlin & P. Suppes (Eds.), *Mathematical methods in the social sciences 1959* (pp. 27–46). Stanford: Stanford University Press.

Hurwicz, L. (1972). On informationally decentralized systems. In C. B. McGuire & R. Radner (Eds.), *Decisions and organization* (ch. 14, pp. 297–336). Amsterdam: North-Holland.

Hurwicz, L. (1977). On the dimensional requirements of informationally decentralized Pareto-satisfactory processes. In K. J. Arrow & L. Hurwicz (Eds.), *Studies in resource allocation processes* (pp. 413–424). Cambridge: Cambridge University Press.

Hurwicz, L. (1979). On allocations attainable through Nash equilibria. *Journal of Economic Theory, 21*, 140–165.

Hurwicz, L. (1986). Incentive aspects of decentralization. In K. J. Arrow & M. D. Intriligator (Eds.), *Handbook of mathematical economics*, Vol. III (ch. 28, pp. 1441–1482). Amsterdam: North-Holland.

Hurwicz, L., & Marschak, T. (2003). Finite allocation mechanisms: approximate Walrasian versus approximate direct revelation. *Economic Theory, 21*, 545–572.

Hurwicz, L., Maskin, E., & Postlewaite, A. (1995). Feasible implementation of social choice correspondences by Nash equilibria. In J. O. Ledyard (Ed.), *The economics of informational decentralization: complexity, efficiency, and stability: essays in honor of Stanley Reiter* (pp. 367–433). Dordrecht: Kluwer Academic Publishers.

Inoue, T. (2006). Do pure indivisibilities prevent core equivalence? Core equivalence theorem in an atomless economy with purely indivisible commodities only. *Journal of Mathematical Economics, 42*, 228–254.

Inoue, T. (2008). Indivisible commodities and the nonemptiness of the weak core. *Journal of Mathematical Economics, 44*, 96–111.

Jacklin, C. J. (1987). Demand deposits, trading restrictions, and risk sharing. In E. C. Prescott & N. Wallace (Eds.), *Contractual arrangements for intertemporal trade* (pp. 26–47). Minneapolis: University of Minnesota Press.

Jordan, J. S. (1982). The competitive allocation process is informationally efficient uniquely. *Journal of Economic Theory, 28*, 1–18.

Ju, B.-G. (2004). Continuous selections from the Pareto correspondence and non-manipulability in exchange economies. *Journal of Mathematical Economics, 40*, 573–592.

Kaneko, M. (1977). The ratio equilibrium and a voting game in public goods economy. *Journal of Economic Theory, 16*, 123–136.

Kaneko, M., & Wooders, M. H. (1986). The core of a game with a continuum of players and finite coalitions: the model and some results. *Mathematical Social Sciences, 12*, 105–137.

Kaneko, M., & Wooders, M. H. (1989). The core of a continuum economy with widespread externalities and finite coalitions: from finite to continuum economies. *Journal of Economic Theory, 49*, 135–168.

Kaneko, M., & Wooders, M. H. (1994). Widespread externalities and perfectly competitive markets: examples. In R. P. Gilles & P. H. M. Ruys (Eds.), *Imperfections and behavior in economic organizations* (ch. 4, pp. 71–87). Boston: Kluwer Academic Publishers.

Kannai, Y. (1977). Concavifiability and construction of concave utility functions. *Journal of Mathematical Economics, 4*, 1–56.

Kato, M., & Ohseto, S. (2002). Toward general impossibility theorems in pure exchange economies. *Social Choice and Welfare, 19*, 659–664.

Kato, M., & Ohseto, S. (2004). Non-dummy agents in pure exchange economies. *Japanese Economic Review, 55*, 212–220.

Khan, M. A., & Yamazaki, A. (1981). On the cores of economies with indivisible commodities and a continuum of traders. *Journal of Economic Theory, 24*, 218–225.

Konovalov, A., & Marakulin, V. (2006). Equilibria without the survival assumption. *Journal of Mathematical Economics, 42*, 198–215.

Koopmans, T. C. (1951). Alternative proof of the substitution theorem for Leontief models in the case of three industries. In T. C. Koopmans (Ed.), *Activity analysis of production and allocation* (ch. 8, pp. 147–154). New York: Wiley.

Koopmans, T. C. (1957). *Three essays on the state of economic science*. New York: Wiley.

Loeb, P. A., & Talvila, E. (2004). Lusin's theorem and Bochner integration. *Scientiae Mathematicae Japonicae, 10*, 55–62.

Lucas, R. E. (1978). Asset prices in an exchange economy. *Econometrica, 46*, 1429–1446.

Makowski, L., & Ostroy, J. M. (1995). Appropriation and efficiency: a revision of the first theorem of welfare economics. *American Economic Review, 85*, 808–827.

Makowski, L., & Ostroy, J. M. (1998). Arbitrage and the flattening effect of large numbers. *Journal of Economic Theory, 78*, 1–31.

Makowski, L., & Ostroy, J. M. (2001). Perfect competition and the creativity of the market. *Journal of Economic Literature, 39*, 479–535.

Makowski, L., Ostroy, J., & Segal, U. (1999). Efficient incentive compatible mechanisms are perfectly competitive. *Journal of Economic Theory, 85*, 169–225.

Maniquet, F. (1996). Horizontal equity and stability when the number of agents is variable in the fair division problem. *Economics Letters, 50*, 85–90.

Maniquet, F., & Sprumont, Y. (1999). Efficient strategy-proof allocation functions in linear production economies. *Economic Theory, 14*, 583–595.

Mas-Colell, A. (1977). Indivisible commodities and general equilibrium theory. *Journal of Economic Theory, 16*, 443–456.

Mas-Colell, A. (1985). *The theory of general economic equilibrium: a differentiable approach*. Cambridge: Cambridge University Press.

Mas-Colell, A. (1989). An equivalence theorem for a bargaining set. *Journal of Mathemetical Economics, 18*, 129–139.

Mas-Colell, A., & Vives, X. (1993). Implementation in economies with a continuum of agents. *Review of Economic Studies, 60*, 613–629.

Maskin, E. (1999). Nash equilibrium and welfare optimality. *Review of Economic Studies, 66*, 23–38.

McKenzie, L. W. (1957). Demand theory without a utility index. *Review of Economic Studies, 24*, 185–189.

McKenzie, L. W. (1959, 1961). On the existence of general equilibrium for a competitive market; and ———: some corrections. *Econometrica, 27*, 54–71; and *29*, 247–248.

McKenzie, L. W. (2002). *Classical general equilibrium theory*. Cambridge, MA: MIT Press.

Milleron, J.-C. (1972). Theory of value with public goods: a survey article. *Journal of Economic Theory, 5*, 419–477.

Mirrlees, J. A. (1969). The dynamic nonsubstitution theorem. *Review of Economic Studies, 36*, 67–76.

Mount, K., & Reiter, S. (1974). The informational size of message spaces. *Journal of Economic Theory, 8*, 161–192.

Muench, T. J. (1972). The core and the Lindahl equilibrium of an economy with a public good: an example. *Journal of Economic Theory, 4*, 241–255.

Nagahisa, R.-I. (1991). A local independence condition for characterization of Walrasian allocations rule. *Journal of Economic Theory, 54*, 106–123.

Nagahisa, R.-I. (1994). A necessary and sufficient condition for Walrasian social choice. *Journal of Economic Theory, 62*, 186–208.

Nagahisa, R.-I., & Suh, S.-C. (1995). A characterization of the Walras rule. *Social Choice and Welfare, 12*, 335–352.

Osana, H. (1978). On the informational size of message spaces for resource allocation processes. *Journal of Economic Theory, 17*, 66–77.

Osana, H. (2005). Externalities do not necessarily require larger message spaces for realizing Pareto-efficient allocations. *Review of Economic Design, 9*, 227–269.

Rader, T. (1964). Edgeworth exchange and general economic equilibrium. *Yale Economic Essays, 4*, 133–180.

Rader, T. (1972). *Theory of microeconomics*. New York: Academic Press.

Rader, T. (1976). Pairwise optimality, multilateral efficiency, and optimality, with and without externalities. In S. A. Y. Lin (Ed.), *Theory and measurement of economic externalities*. New York: Academic Press.

Rader, T. (1978). Induced preferences on trades when preferences may be intransitive and incomplete. *Econometrica, 46*, 137–146.

Ray, D. (1989). Credible coalitions and the core. *International Journal of Game Theory, 18*, 185–187.

Reiter, S. (1977). Information and performance in the (new)^2 welfare economics. *American Economic Review (Papers and Proceedings), 67*, 226–234.

Repullo, R. (1988). A new characterization of the efficiency of equilibrium with incomplete markets. *Journal of Economic Theory, 44*, 217–230.

Sakai, T. (2009). Walrasian social orderings in exchange economies. *Journal of Mathematical Economics, 45*, 16–22.

Samuelson, P. A. (1951). Abstract of a theorem concerning substitability in open Leontief models in the general case. In T. C. Koopmans (Ed.), *Activity analysis of production and allocation* (ch. 7, pp. 142–146). New York: Wiley.

Samuelson, P. A. (1958). An exact consumption-loan model of interest with or without the social contrivance of money. *Journal of Political Economy, 66*, 467–482.

Sato, F. (1981). On the informational size of message spaces for resource allocation processes in economies with public goods. *Journal of Economic Theory, 24*, 48–69.

Schmeidler, D. (1970). Fatou's lemma in several dimensions. *Proceedings of the American Mathematical Society, 24*, 300–306.

Schmeidler, D., & Vind, K. (1972). Fair net trades. *Econometrica, 40*, 637–642.

Segal, I. (2007). The communication requirements of social choice rules and supporting budget sets. *Journal of Economic Theory, 136*, 341–378.

Sen, A. K. (1971). *Collective choice and social welfare*. San Francisco: Holden-Day.

Sen, A. K. (1979). Personal utilities and public judgements: Or what's wrong with welfare economics. *Economic Journal, 89*, 537–558.

Sen, A. K. (1982). *Choice, welfare, and measurement*. Oxford: Basil Blackwell.

Sen, A. K. (1986). Social choice theory. In K. J. Arrow & M. D. Intriligator (Eds.), *Handbook of mathematical economics*, Vol. III (ch. 22, pp. 1073–1181). Amsterdam: North-Holland.

Serizawa, S. (2002). Inefficiency of strategy-proof rules for pure exchange economies. *Journal of Economic Theory, 106*, 219–241.

Serizawa, S., & Weymark, J. A. (2003). Efficient strategy-proof exchange and minimum consumption guarantees. *Journal of Economic Theory, 109*, 246–263.

Serrano, R., & Volij, O. (1998). Axiomatizations of neoclassical concepts for economies. *Journal of Mathematical Economics, 30*, 87–108.

Serrano, R., & Volij, O. (2000). Walrasian allocations without price-taking behavior. *Journal of Economic Theory, 95*, 79–106.

Serrano, R., & Volij, O. (2002). Bargaining and bargaining sets. *Games and Economic Behavior, 39*, 292–308.

Shafer, W., & Sonnenschein, H. (1976). Equilibrium with externalities, commodity taxation, and lump sum transfers. *International Economic Review, 17*, 601–611.

Silvestre, J. (2003). Wicksell, Lindahl, and the theory of public goods. *Scandinavian Journal of Economics, 105*, 527–553.

Sonnenschein, H. (1974). An axiomatic characterization of the price mechanism. *Econometrica, 42*, 425–433.

Spivak, A. (1978). A note on Arrow–Hahn's resource relatedness (or McKenzie's irreducibility). *International Economic Review, 19*, 527–531.

Stahl, D. O., & Fisher, F. M. (1988). On stability analysis with disequilibrium awareness. *Journal of Economic Theory, 46*, 309–321.

Starrett, D. A. (1972). Fundamental nonconvexities in the theory of externalities. *Journal of Economic Theory, 4*, 180–199.

Stokey, N. L., Lucas, R. E., & Prescott, E. C. (1989). *Recursive methods in economic dynamics*. Cambridge, MA: Harvard University Press.

Sun, G.-Z., Yang, X., & Zhou, L. (2004). General equilibria in large economies with endogenous structure of division of labor. *Journal of Economic Behavior and Organization, 55*, 237–256.

Tadenuma, K., & Thomson, W. (1995). Games of fair division. *Games and Economic Behavior, 9*, 191–204.

Thomson, W. (1979). On allocations attainable through Nash equilibria: a comment. In J. -J. Laffont (Ed.), *Aggregation and revelation of preferences* (ch. 23, pp. 420–431). Amsterdam: North-Holland.

Thomson, W. (1983). Equity in exchange economies. *Journal of Economic Theory, 29*, 217–244.

Thomson, W. (1987). The vulnerability to manipulative behavior of economic mechanisms designed to select equitable and efficient outcomes. In T. Groves, R. Radner & S. Reiter (Eds.), *Information, incentives and economic mechanisms* (ch. 14, pp. 375–396). Minneapolis: University of Minnesota Press.

Thomson, W. (1988). A study of choice correspondences in economies with a variable number of agents. *Journal of Economic Theory, 46*, 237–254.

Thomson, W. (1999). Monotonic extensions on economic domains. *Review of Economic Design, 1*, 13–33.

Tian, G. (1992). Implementation of the Walrasian correspondence without continuous, convex, and ordered preferences. *Social Choice and Welfare, 9*, 117–130.

Tian, G. (2004). A unique informationally efficient allocation mechanism in economies with consumption externalities. *International Economic Review, 33*, 79–111.

Tian, G. (2006). The unique informational efficiency of the competitive mechanism in economies with production. *Social Choice and Welfare, 26*, 155–182.

van den Nouweland, A., Peleg, B., & Tijs, S. (1996). Axiomatic characterizations of the Walras correspondence for generalized economies. *Journal of Mathematical Economics, 25*, 355–372.

van den Nouweland, A., Tijs, S., & Wooders, M. H. (2002). Axiomatization of ratio equilibria in public good economies. *Social Choice and Welfare, 19*, 627–636.

Varadarajan, V. S. (1958). On the convergence of sample probability distributions. *Sankhyā, 19*, 23–26.

Varian, H. (1974). Equity, envy, and efficiency. *Journal of Economic Theory, 9*, 63–91.

Villar, A. (2003). The generalized linear production model: solvability, nonsubstitution, and productivity measurement. *Advances in Theoretical Economics, 3*(1), Article 1. http://www.bepress.com/bejte.

Vind, K. (1992). Two characterizations of bargaining sets. *Journal of Mathematical Economics, 21*, 89–97.

Vind, K. (1995). Perfect competition or the core. *European Economic Review, 39*, 1733–1745.

Walker, M. (1977). On the informational size of message spaces. *Journal of Economic Theory, 15*, 366–375.

Yamazaki, A. (1978). An equilibrium existence theorem without convexity assumptions. *Econometrica, 46*, 541–555.

Yamazaki, A. (1981). Diversified consumption characteristics and conditionally dispersed endowment distribution: regularizing effect and existence of equilibria. *Econometrica, 49*, 639–654.

Yamazaki, A. (1995). Bargaining sets in continuum economies. In T. Maruyama & W. Takahashi (Eds.), *Nonlinear and convex analysis in economic theory* (pp. 289–299). Berlin: Springer-Verlag.

CHAPTER SIXTEEN

Functionings and Capabilities

Kaushik Basu* **and Luis F. López-Calva****
*Department of Economics, Cornell University, Ithaca, NY
**United Nations Development Programme, Regional Bureau for Latin America and the Caribbean, New York, NY

Contents

Abstract

Traditional economics identifies a person's well-being with the goods and services the person consumes and the utility that the person gets from such consumption. This, in turn, has led to the widely used approach of welfarism that uses individual utilities as ingredients for evaluating a society's aggregate welfare. This approach has long been contested as being too restrictive in its view of what constitutes human well-being and for its commodity fetish. What has injected new life into this critique is the emergence of an alternative approach, which replaces the traditional concern for commodities and utility with functionings and capabilities. While the origins of this "capabilities approach" go back to the works of John Stuart Mill, Adam Smith, and, in spirit if not in form, to Aristotle, it was the seminal contribution of Amartya Sen in the form of his 1979 *Tanner Lectures* that gave it shape and structure. Subsequent works by Sen and an enormous outpouring of writing by various authors in economics, philosophy, and sociology have made this a major field of inquiry, which has also led to important practical applications. The present chapter is a survey of this new field of study. In Sen's terminology a "functioning" is what an individual chooses to do or to be, in contrast to a "commodity," which is an instrument which enables her to achieve different functionings. While functioning is central to the notion of human well-being, it is not merely the achieved functionings that matter but the freedom that a person has in choosing from the set of feasible functionings, which is referred to as the person's "capability." Beginning with a discussion of these ideas in history, the present chapter tries to present a comprehensive review of the recent literature, including formalizations and applications. It is important to recognize that a full formalization may not be feasible, since there are important dimensions of life that are germane to the capabilities approach that may be impossible to capture in a single

Handbook of Social Choice and Welfare, Volume II
ISSN: 0169-7218, DOI: 10.1016/S0169-7218(10)00016-X

formalization. Nevertheless, the capability approach itself has been immensely useful in the context of studying poverty, gender issues, political freedom, and the standard of living. It has also resulted in the creation of the Human Development Index (HDI), popularized by UNDP's Human Development Reports since 1990. This chapter critically examines the HDI and recent advances in the human development literature.

Keywords: capabilities; capability approach; freedom; functionings; well-being.
JEL codes: D60, D71, I3, I31.

1. THE CAPABILITIES APPROACH: AN INTRODUCTION

Traditional welfare economics tends to identify a person's well-being with the person's command over goods and services. This naturally leads to a focus on income, since a person's income determines how much he or she can consume. Going a step further, this approach often views each person as being endowed with a "utility or welfare function," and the person's income as an important variable that determines the level of utility that the person enjoys. *Social* welfare, according to this approach, is represented by aggregating the utility levels of all individuals in society.

An alternative route to this beaten track is the "capabilities approach," which replaces the traditional concern for commodities and utility with, respectively, functionings and capability. While the origins of the capabilities approach go back to John Stuart Mill, Adam Smith, and in fact Aristotle, it is only over the last one or two decades—after these early suggestions were resurrected, reinterpreted, and partially formalized by Sen (1980, 1985)—that the capabilities approach gained some currency within the economics profession, culminating in the heroic effort undertaken by the annual *Human Development Reports*, which try to make some of these ideas operational.

While the capabilities approach now has a substantial literature, discussing and debating the ideas, exploring variants, and applying them to evaluating the standard of living of different nations or regions, the crux of its discord with traditional welfare economics is to be found in the distinction between "goods" and "functionings" and also between achievement and freedom. A *functioning* is what a person manages to do or to be. A *good* can *enable* a functioning but is distinct from it. A bicycle is a good, whereas being able to transport oneself rapidly to work (or, more importantly to most people, away from work) is a functioning. Two persons, each owning a bicycle, may not be able to achieve the same functioning. If, for instance, one of them happens to be handicapped, she may not be able to use the bike to go as far as the other person can. This is one of the central operational distinctions between commodities and functionings. Whereas we need not know anything about the individual concerned in asserting that he owns a certain good (for instance, a bike), we may need to know a good deal about a person, over and above what commodities he owns, in order to know what functionings he can achieve.

Just as a functioning must not be confused with a commodity, which may well play an enabling role, a functioning must not be confused with utility. It is possible to develop the capabilities approach without reference to utility, but it is not incompatible with the idea of human beings striving to achieve a certain level of or even aiming to maximize utility. If we were to use the idea of utility in conjunction with functionings, then it is important to recognize that functionings are prior to utility. Just as commodities make it possible to achieve certain functionings, functionings may enable a person to reach certain levels of utility.

However, the functionings *achieved* by a person may not be sufficient in determining a person's overall quality of life or well-being. For the latter we need to know, minimally, the person's "capability," the functionings that the person *could* have achieved. Hence, capability is closely related to the idea of opportunity, freedom, and advantage. According to the capabilities approach, in determining the overall quality of life of a person, it is not enough to know what functionings he achieved, for instance that he did not go to Florida and instead remained in Poland. We need to know, if he *could* have gone to Florida and chose not to, or he did not have the money to go to Florida, or was denied a visa to get to the United States.

It should be clear that it is not just a comparison of capabilities that we need to undertake but also the choice that a person made. So, at a minimum what we need to know about each person is a set and a singleton—the set from which she was free and able to choose, and the singleton that she actually achieved (see Suzumura and Xu 1999). At times we may for simplicity's sake focus on the achieved functionings alone or the capabilities set alone without information on what functionings were achieved, but given free information, we would ideally want information on both in assessing a person's or a society's quality of life.

Another thing that must be evident is, as Sen (1994) has stressed, that the capabilities approach suffers from the embarrassment of riches because in life the functionings that we may or may not achieve are manifold. This approach recognizes that real society is peopled with characters whose entire quality of life cannot fully be captured by a unique real number, characters who have distinct notions of well-being, happiness, and desire-fulfillment. One consequence of this is that the idea of capability is not fully formalized and perhaps not even fully formalizable. How easily a concept yields to formalization is often treated by economists as an index of the concept's usefulness. To take such a view would, however, be erroneous. There are many important ideas or concepts, for example, utility, liberty, or happiness, which may be impossible to capture fully in a single formalization but are nevertheless useful. That is the view we take of capability here. One consequence of taking such a view is that, in trying to empirically compare the quality of life achieved by different societies using the capabilities approach, we may need to focus on a few salient functionings (risking the charge of idiosyncracy). Do people in society x have the option of a long and healthy life? Are people able to live lives free of political oppression? Are people able to read and write and therefore enjoy literature and communication with others? Do people have enough to eat and drink? Of course, empirically one has to face tricky questions like whether one should provide the information on achieved functionings as a vector or aggregate them into a single number (see Ray 1998, for discussion). But the dilemma should not be used as reason not to do either.

2. THE IDEAS IN HISTORY

The origin of the idea of functionings and capability can be traced back to Aristotle. The two fundamental observations related to this concept take place in his discussion on political distribution in *Politics* (Book VII, chapters 1–2) and the concept of the "good" and the "good man" in the *Nicomachean Ethics* (Book I, chapter 7). The Aristotelian foundation has been discussed at length by Nussbaum (1988, 1992) and Cohen (1993). In *Politics* (mainly VII.1–2), when discussing the idea of the "best political arrangement," Aristotle argues that the aim of political planning is the distribution of the conditions for a good life to the people in the city. These conditions are understood by him as producing capabilities, that is, the possibilities of having a "flourishing life." It is not the allotment of commodities that we should be concerned about, but the possibility to function in a certain human way, as explained in the interpretation by Nussbaum (1988).[1] When we ask concretely what he meant by the idea of "functioning in certain human ways," it is useful to look at his argument on "human functioning" in the *Nicomachean Ethics,* which we shall discuss presently. These two references are the core that establish the Aristotelian foundation of Sen's criticism of utilitarianism and of the Rawlsian ethics in his *Tanner Lectures* (Sen 1980; see also Robeyns 2009).

Aristotle has a famous argument on human functioning in his discussion of "the good human life."[2] While admitting that most human beings live their lives in the pursuit of happiness, he argues against a purely hedonistic view of life and proposes a different definition of the good human life. This definition emphasizes the rational nature of

[1] Nussbaum (1988) says that "Aristotle's statement of the [proposed] view is full of internal obscurity and inconsistency; and sorting our way through all of this will take us at times away from a straightforward investigation of the view" (p. 145). Discussion and criticisms of Nussbaum's interpretation of Aristotle can be found in Crocker (1995) and Des Gasper (1997b).

[2] The concept of the "good life," the one in which you reach the state of happiness as the final end, is related to the Greek words *eudaimonia* ("good state, sense of peace and happiness") and *makarios* ("being pure, free of sins, being happy"). Nussbaum argues in different writings that Aristotle used these two words interchangeably to refer to a "flourishing life" or a "good life." On the other hand, the Greek word *dunamin,* used by Aristotle in his discussion of the human good, can be translated as "capability of existing or acting," though it has been sometimes translated as "potentiality." See Sen (1993).

human beings as the specific difference that makes them distinct from animals. Aristotle tells us that "now the mass of mankind are evidently quite slavish of their tastes, preferring a life suitable to beasts."[3] In this way, he would argue later that a good human life would not only require adequate functioning in terms of "nutrition and growth," a purely animal feature, but the possibility of exercising choice and practical reason. A purely hedonistic life, as well as one devoted to contemplation or to the accumulation of wealth, are rejected as definitions of a "good human life."[4]

He establishes thus that a good life is one in which a person can function not only in the biological sense but also by exercising choice and reason. On the other hand, "it is evident that the best political arrangement is that according to which anyone whatsoever might do best and live a flourishing life (*zoie makarios*)" (*Politics,* VII.2). The fact that "anyone whatsoever might do best" gives us the egalitarian perspective, but egalitarian in the realm of capabilities, as possibilities to function as human beings. This involves biological functions, as well as possibilities to exercise reason and actively participate in the political life.[5] This perspective is called the "Distributive Conception" in Nussbaum (1988).

More than twenty centuries later, Marx (1973) and Marx and Engels (1947) proposed a view of human functioning and effective freedom that can be interpreted from an Aristotelian perspective. Marx described a commendable human life as not only one in which the person's material needs are satisfied (biological functioning), but also as one in which the human being is able to use reason. He makes a strong case for differentiating activities that are purely animal from those which distinguish men and women as human beings. When discussing the meaning of "alienation of labor," Marx says that "man (the worker) feels that he is acting freely only in his animal functions—eating, drinking, and procreating, or at most in his dwelling and adornment—while in his human functions, he is nothing more than animal" (Marx 1973). For Marx, the biological needs of eating, drinking, or procreation, are "genuinely human functions," but without freedom of choice and freedom from immediate want, these will be performed in a merely animal way.[6]

Not only was Marx using the concept of "human functions," but Marx and Engels (1947) also discussed the idea of effective freedom in a way that we can relate to the concept of functionings and capabilities. The real liberation of human beings is discussed

[3] *Nicomachean Ethics,* I.5. Also, in a different translation, "Choosing a life of dumb grazing animals" (Nussbaum 1988).

[4] The life of money-making is one undertaken under compulsion, and wealth is evidently not the good we are seeking; for it is merely useful and for the sake of something else. And so one might rather take the aforenamed objects to be ends; for they are loved for themselves. But it is evident that not even these are ends; yet many arguments have been wasted on the support of them" (*Nicomachean Ethics,* I.6).

[5] The idea of the ability to participate in the political life has been discussed in Bohman (1997) and Sen (1998).

[6] For this interpretation of Marx's writings see Nussbaum (1988). Des Saint Croix (1981) discusses the influence of Aristotle in Marx's writings.

as being related to economic progress and the strengthening of real capabilities. Thus they tell us:

That real liberation is not possible outside the real world and through real means, that it is not possible to abolish slavery without the steam machine, the mule jenny, that it is not possible to abolish a regime of serfdom without an improved agriculture, that, in general, it is not possible to free men if they cannot be assured access to food, drink, housing, and good quality-clothing. (p. 22)

But they also add that the liberated society would

make it possible for me to do one thing to-day and another tomorrow, to hunt in the morning, fish in the afternoon, rear cattle in the evening, criticize after dinner, just as I have in mind, without ever becoming hunter, fisherman, shepherd or critic. (p. 22)

These statements also show a view of freedom in the sense of what individuals, everything considered, are indeed able to do, as opposed to what they are formally prevented from doing. This introduces the discussion of what shall be called "actual freedom," as opposed to "formal freedom," the latter being consistent with the view of the classical liberals. T. H. Green, foreshadowing the famous later work of Isaiah Berlin, wrote on this topic, emphasizing the distinction between freedom in the sense of not being prevented from doing something and the actual ability to do something. Green (1900) tells us that:

We shall probably all agree that freedom, rightly understood, is the greatest of blessings; that its attainment is the true end of all our efforts as citizens. But when we thus speak of freedom, we should consider carefully what we mean by it. We do not mean merely freedom from restraint or compulsion.... When we speak of freedom as something to be so highly prized, we mean a positive power or capacity of doing or enjoying something worth doing or enjoying, and that, too, something that we do or enjoy in common with others. (p. 371)

Development of better living conditions seems to be related to that *positive* capacity of doing things, as in Aristotle's and Marx's writings. Green says that "in a sense no man is so well able to do as he likes as the wandering savage... He has no master... Yet, we do not count him really free, because the freedom of the savage is not strength, but weakness" (p. 371). One sees in this echoes of Berlin (1969) ideas of "positive freedom" and "negative freedom," the latter being as understood by the classical liberals. Berlin says:[7]

The first of these political senses of freedom or liberty...which (following much precedent) I shall call the "negative" sense, is involved in the answer to the question "what is the area within which the subject—a person or group of persons—is or should be left to do or be what he is able to do or be, without interference by other persons?" The second, which I shall call the "positive" sense, is involved in the answer to the question "what or who, is the source of control or interference that can determine someone to do, or be, this rather than that?" The two questions are clearly different, even though the answers to them may overlap. (p. 122)

[7] The original publication of the essay "Two Concepts of Liberty" took place in 1958. Sen discusses this perspective in, for example, Sen (1989).

The fact that the goods are required to satisfy the need to function biologically and socially, as well as to be able to exercise reason and choice, is at the core of the capability approach (see, for instance, Roemer 1996, and Herrero 1996). This idea is also related to Smith (1776). Smith discusses the notion that commodities give individuals not only consumption possibilities but the ability to interact socially as well. This is the way in which Smith (1776) defines "*necessaries*":

> *By necessaries I understand, not only the commodities which are indispensably necessary for the support of life, but whatever the custom of the country renders it indecent for creditable people, even of the lowest order, to be without. A linen shirt, for example, strictly speaking, is not a necessary of life. The Greeks and Romans lived, I supposed, very comfortably, though they had no linen. But in present times, through the greater part of Europe, a creditable day-labourer would be ashamed to appear in public without a linen shirt, the want of which would be supposed to denote that disgraceful degree of poverty.... (pp. 870–871)*

When Malinowski (1921), describing the primitive economy of the Trobriand Islanders off the coast of New Guinea, notes that "to the natives the possession and display of food are of immense value and importance *in themselves*" (p. 8, my italics), he is referring to the same idea of goods being used to give social dignity. "One of the greatest insults," writes Malinowski, "that can be uttered is to call someone 'man with no food,' and it would be bitterly resented and probably a quarrel would ensue. To be able to boast of having food, is one of their chief glories and ambitions" (p. 8).

This perspective is an example of the instrumental nature of commodities acquisition, as a means to achieve certain human functionings that include social interaction, dignity, and the participation in the life of the community. Sen (1983a) would discuss later, based on Smith's definition, the concept of poverty as being *relative* in the realm of commodities but *absolute* in the realm of capabilities.

The foundations of Sen's new perspective on well-being are thus Aristotle's concept of the "good life" and the "goodness" of a political arrangement, as well as Marx's view of a true human life and real liberation. Moreover, those ideas are enriched by Smith's definition of necessary goods and by T. H. Green's and Berlin's distinction between "positive" and "negative" freedom.

3. SEN'S CRITIQUE AND FORMULATION

Even though the concept of capabilities is related to the subject of human well-being in general, its contemporary treatment originated in Sen's *Tanner Lectures* (Sen 1980) at Stanford University in 1979, which were focused on alternative interpretations of egalitarianism. Starting with a critique of utilitarianism and Rawlsianism, Sen (1980) went on to develop the idea of "functioning" and proposed "capability" as a new answer to the question, "Equality of what?" In a series of subsequent papers (Sen 1985, 1987, 1990, 1992, 1993) he developed these ideas further and tried to establish capabilities as a general approach to evaluating human condition.

Chronological fidelity is not always desirable when surveying a field of study, but in this case it is useful to start with Sen's *Tanner Lectures* (Sen 1980). In these lectures Sen began with an evaluation of utilitarianism as a moral principle. Utilitarianism requires that given a choice from among several alternatives, we select the one that maximizes the sum total of utility among all human beings.[8] This, combined with the standard assumption that marginal utility from income for each person diminishes as a person has more income, implies that under utilitarianism when a fixed income is being distributed among a set of individuals, this will be done so that each person gets the same marginal utility. Hence, to the question "Equality of what?" the utilitarian answer is "marginal utility." Sen then goes on to remind us that this may be fine when the human beings in question happen to be similar but comes apart once we recognize the essential diversity of human beings.

Sen criticizes utilitarianism both by appealing to more general moral principles that conflict with it (the "prior-principle critique"), and constructing examples of special cases that check our "moral intuition" (the "case-implication critique").

To take first the case-implication critique, he considers the example of a person with a handicap who has great need for money and another person who has no handicaps but is a pleasure machine who derives a lot of satisfaction from every dollar that she is able to spend. Plainly, equalizing marginal utility requires giving more money to the latter. The needy person, in other words, gets less, which does not seem to square up with our moral intuition about equity.

Sen also considers Rawls's critique that people behind a "veil of ignorance" would not opt for a society that maximizes the sum total of utility, opting instead for a more equitable distribution of utility. In the spirit of prior-principle critique, Rawls (1971) also emphasized how utilitarianism does injustice to some of our basic notions of liberty and equality.

Rawls proposed a principle in which society is evaluated in terms of the level achieved by the worst-off person in society, measured over an index of primary goods—the so-called "maximin" principle.[9] Economists usually attribute to Rawls a different principle that follows the same criterion but measures the level on the dimension of utility. But as Sen points out, this and also the closely related "leximin" go to the other extreme of utilitarianism in ignoring claims arising from the intensity of one's needs.

[8] The classical reference on the utilitarian perspective is Bentham (1789). For the axiomatic foundations of utilitarianism, see d'Aspremont and Gevers (1977), Maskin (1978), Roberts (1980), and Basu (1983).

[9] For the axiomatic foundations of this principle see Hammond (1976), Strasnick (1976), and d'Aspremont and Gevers (1977).

Utilitarianism and Rawls's criterion as interpreted by economists belong to the more general category of "welfarism." Welfarism, which in turn is a special case of consequentialism, is the view that the goodness of a society can be judged entirely from information on the utility levels achieved by every human being in that society (see Scanlon 2001, Sen 1977). The most important prior-principle critique that Sen mounts against utilitarianism is to argue that, in evaluating a society or state of affairs fully, we must make room for nonutility information.

The critique does not apply to the moral criterion that Rawls had originally developed. Rawls (1971) moved away from welfarism by eliminating the emphasis on utilities and proposing a view based on what he called *primary goods*.[10] Rawls's criterion would be the first step towards a formal theory in which equality of opportunity becomes the concept of moral importance for distributive justice. The Rawlsian principle of justice can be summarized by the following mandate: *maximize the minimum, over all persons, of the bundle of primary goods*.[11] This mandate is called the "difference principle." The definition of primary goods is of essential importance for the understanding of Rawls's theory.

Following Rawls (1971, 1982), we can identify five groups of primary goods:

(a) basic liberties,
(b) freedom of movement and choice of occupation,
(c) powers and prerogatives of offices and positions of public responsibility,
(d) income and wealth, and
(e) the social bases of self-respect.

Rawls proposes that the first two sets are formally prior to the pursuit of the other three. The political setting must first provide the conditions stated in (a) and (b) in order for the economic system to provide the conditions for (c), (d), and (e).

From a prior-principle point of view, Sen argues that the difference principle can be criticized for being concerned with means (commodities), not ends (freedoms). Indeed, it has some tendency to be "primary good fetishist" in analogy with Marx's (1973) discussion of "commodity fetishism." Moreover, by applying the case-implication critique we would find that the difference principle could be unacceptably indifferent to heterogeneity.

Consider the case of a person with a handicap who has a marginal utility disadvantage: He is not very efficient at converting dollars into utils at the margin. In addition, suppose that he is no worse off than others in utility terms despite his handicap, perhaps because he has an innately jolly disposition, or because of a deep religiosity. It is now evident that neither utilitarianism nor the leximin criterion will do much for him. Indeed, he seems to be beyond the reach of virtually all reasonable welfarist principles. What about authentic

[10] He has elaborated on his original theory in Rawls (1975, 1982, 1985).

[11] There is of course some ambiguity in this, because it is not always obvious how one compares between bundles. This is addressed later through the work of Herrero (1996).

Rawlsianism, based on deprivation in terms of primary goods? Unfortunately that, too, is limited by its concern for goods, even though "goods" are defined in a fairly broad way.

Roemer (1996) has also criticized Rawls, though on different grounds. This criticism relates to the fact that the difference principle does not consider people's evaluation of their state. He shows that Rawls's notion of primary goods "must depend on the conceptions of the good that individuals have, though it cannot be recovered solely by knowing those conceptions" (Roemer 1996, p. 169). The conceptions of the good by individuals are related to their "life plans," in Rawls's terminology, so utility would be interpreted in that sense as "satisfaction" or "desire-fulfillment."[12] The relevance of responsibility—deciding on one's life plan—would become the feature analyzed in later discussions on inequality. This point relates to one of the most important features of Rawls's and Sen's theory, namely the emphasis that is put on *ex ante* opportunity, as opposed to *ex post* outcomes. The typical utilitarian solution is clearly based on the latter.

Another feature of Rawls's theory consists of using the "veil of ignorance" argument to claim that individuals behind that "veil" would choose the maximin principle over an index of primary goods as the accepted social contract.[13] By constructing a formalization of this statement, Roemer (1996, chapter 5) has tried to show that the argument is flawed. Using von Neumann–Morgenstern utility functions for the *souls* behind the "veil of ignorance" choosing a social contract—a tax scheme that redistributes resources according to the Maximin principle—it is shown that maximin would not be chosen by the agents, unless they are infinitely risk-averse.[14]

Summarizing, Rawls defends the difference principle from two perspectives: first, by claiming its "impartiality" (justice as fairness), and second, by appealing to "mutual advantage" (choosing social contract from behind the "veil of ignorance"). Both arguments are criticized by Sen (1980, 1993) and Roemer (1996). Those Rawlsian ideas, however, set the basic notion of justice as equality of *ex ante* opportunity, as opposed to the emphasis on outcomes embedded in the welfaristic theories of justice.[15]

[12] While for Sen utility is a sense of pleasure or happiness.

[13] The idea of the "veil of ignorance" comes originally from Adam Smith. See Harsanyi (1982).

[14] Instead of assuming infinite risk-aversion of the agents, Roemer (1996) suggests that we consider choice under ignorance, as in Maskin (1979), in which the choice of an alternative that maximizes the minimum possible utility is advocated, in a framework in which agents do not know the probability distributions over goods and states. Maskin (1978) actually refers to his work (published later as Maskin 1979) saying that, if the framework of decision making under ignorance is considered, the utilitarian rule is an "immediate consequence."

[15] Kolm (1972) independently developed an egalitarian theory similar to Rawls's, in fact, almost simultaneously. Kolm also emphasizes the existence of a basic set of goods as an index to evaluate equality. He claims that "Fundamentally, all individuals have the same needs, the same tastes, and the same desires" (Kolm 1972, p. 79). In that sense, he is consistent with Rawls in the sense that there exists a basic set of goods whose provision guarantees equality of opportunity across individuals. Individuals that seem to be different are so because of some specific feature that can be added to the commodity space, as long as it is needed for individuals to look the same. Once that reductionist process takes place, we arrive at the level of some "fundamental preferences," under which all individuals are the same.

What we need, so argues Sen (1980), is a moral system that is concerned not just with "good things," but

> *with what these good things do to human beings... I believe what is at issue is the interpretation of needs in the form of basic capabilities. The interpretation of needs and interests is often implicit in the demand for equality. This type of equality I shall call basic capability equality (p. 218).*

Thus, through this discussion of equality, the idea of capability and, implicitly, functioning was conceived.

The formalizations of this approach occurred later. One of the first efforts was by Sen (1985), who tried to give structure to the perspective of well-being based on the concepts of functionings and capabilities. Goods have an instrumental value in that they allow individuals to "function." A functioning is an achievement of a person: what he or she manages to do or to be. Formally, we start from the commodities vector. Let us use $\mathbf{x}_i$ to denote the vector of commodities possessed by person i.

Following Gorman (1968) and Lancaster (1966), Sen used the fact that commodities can be converted into characteristics. Thus if c is the function converting a commodity vector into a vector of characteristics, the vector of characteristics consumed by person i will be given by $c(\mathbf{x}_i)$.[16] Next, let f_i be person i's "personal utilization function," that is, a function that converts characteristics into functionings. Given that in this exercise c is exogenous to the person, we could actually think of f_i as a function, which directly converts commodity vectors into functionings. But let us for now continue with Sen's treatment. In Sen's model f_i is partly a matter of person i's choice. She chooses a utilization function from a feasible set, $\mathbf{F}_i$, of utilization functions.

A *functioning* is a function that tells us what person i has achieved (a *being*) given her choice of a utilization function $f_i \in \mathbf{F}_i$. We represent it as:

$$\mathrm{b}_i = f_i\left(c\left(\mathbf{x}_i\right)\right).$$

The vector b_i represents the *beings* that a person has managed to accomplish by using the commodities she possesses and choosing a utilization function from $\mathbf{F}_i$. Those functionings are, for example, being well-nourished, well-clothed, mobile, and participating actively in the life of the community. In the Aristotelian view, these would imply "functioning in a human way."

Next, define $\mathbf{P}_i(\mathbf{x}_i)$ as the set of functioning vectors *feasible* for person i as:

$$\mathbf{P}_i\left(\mathbf{x}_i\right) = \left[\mathrm{b}_i | \mathrm{b}_i = f_i\left(c\left(\mathbf{x}_i\right)\right), \quad \text{for some} \quad f_i \in \mathbf{F}_i\right].$$

Let us suppose the person i has access to any of the set of vectors of commodities in $\mathbf{X}_i$. Then $\mathbf{X}_i$ is her entitlements. Now, we can define the effective "freedom" that

[16] The function does not have to be necessarily linear.

a person has, given her command over commodities and her individual possibilities of converting the characteristics of goods into functionings. Such a set represents person *i*'s *capabilities.* Formally, person *i*'s *capability* is given by:

$$\mathbf{Q}_i = \left[\mathrm{b}_i | \mathrm{b}_i = f_i\left(c\left(\mathbf{x}_i\right)\right), \quad \text{for some} \quad f_i \in \mathbf{F}_i, \quad \text{and some} \quad x_i \in \mathbf{X}_i\right].$$

This sums up Sen's own formalization of one way of going from commodities, via functionings, to capability.

4. FURTHER FORMALIZATIONS

Roemer (1996) noted that the approach proposed by Sen has four similarities with that of Rawls: (a) both are nonwelfarist, (b) both are egalitarian, (c) both emphasize *ex-ante* opportunity as opposed to *ex-post* outcome evaluation, and (d) both take a concept of freedom from the perspective of actual possibility to achieve, as opposed to formal liberty that considers only legal barriers to individual action. Utilitarianism is nonegalitarian and emphasizes outcomes. On the other hand, from characteristics (c) and (d) we can see the relevance these theories assign to individual responsibility. A comprehensive review of the formalization of this approach and its empirical applications is found in Kuklys (2005).

Dworkin (1981) has suggested an approach that assigns a higher importance to individual responsibility, thus advocating "equality of resources." That would eliminate the "paternalistic" bias in the capabilities view and would force individuals to be responsible for their life plans. The importance of individual life plans and responsibility had already been discussed in Rawls (1971). "Agency achievement" is the term used by Foster and Sen (1997) when discussing the satisfaction of those individual plans. Roemer (1986) has shown that, under a specific interpretation of what resources are, equality of resources and equality of welfare cannot be distinguished, which would put Dworkin's idea within the realm of the welfaristic perspective.

The concept of a *functioning* represents the *state* of a person, a set of things that she manages to do or to be in her life. The *capabilities* reflect the alternative combination of functionings that a person can achieve, from which the individual will choose one collection. If, say, there are *n* relevant functionings, then that person's level of achievement will be represented by an *n*-tuple. Well-being will be defined as the *quality* of a person's being, based on those functionings the person can indeed choose from. How many and what specific functionings should be included in evaluating a person's well-being has been a subject of debate. However, as Sen (1992, p. 31) has claimed, "We may be able to go a fairly long distance with a relatively small number of centrally important functionings and the corresponding basic capabilities," especially when analyzing issues like poverty in developing countries. Those centrally important functionings would include the ability to be well-nourished and well-sheltered, as well as the capability of escaping avoidable morbidity and premature mortality, among some basic ones.

Suppose now that the problem of choosing the relevant functionings is somehow resolved. Given that functionings are vectors, there is a large problem of aggregation that is bound to occur as soon as we try to use this approach for normative purposes. Suppose we decide to follow Rawls and commend the society in which the capability of the least capable person is the highest. How shall we do so? This is exactly the question that Herrero (1996) investigates in an important paper based on Roemer (1988).

Herrero's (1996) and Roemer's (1996) exercises in interpreting Rawls's difference principle in terms of capability sets provides a nice example of one way in which we may proceed to formalize the capability approach. As noted previously in Section 3, economists using Rawls's principle have usually worked with utility as the indicator of individual well-being. Rawls himself had based much of his normative analysis on the primary goods consumed by individuals. Herrero moves away from both utility and primary goods to capabilities. Rawls's difference principle would then recommend that we maximize the capability of the person having the smallest capability. Since a person's capability is a set of functionings, it is not always obvious whether one person has a larger capability than another (consider the case where the capability set of neither is a subset of the other's). Hence, we are immediately confronted with the problem of comparison, which somehow needs to be formalized. Herrero proceeds to develop her argument axiomatically. In what follows we provide a sketch of her model, while cautioning the reader that there may be other ways to formalize the capabilities approach.

Let us suppose that there are h commodities and $\Re^h_+$ is the set of all possible commodity bundles. There are m functionings and $\Re^m$ is the set of all possible functionings. For each person i there exists a correspondence $C_i : \Re^h_+ \to \Re^m$ such that, for all $\mathbf{x} \in \Re^h_+$, $C_i(\mathbf{x})$ is the set of all functioning vectors available to person i. In Herrero's model, $C_i(\mathbf{x})$ is person i's *capability* or *capability set*. Note that, in keeping with the discussion in the previous sections a person's capability depends not just on the goods he consumes but also on who he happens to be. Hence, the subscript i. In what follows, we use $B(\mathbf{X})$ to denote the set of boundary points of the set $\mathbf{X} \subset \Re^m$. The following conditions are assumed throughout this exercise:

(1) $C_i(0) = \varnothing$
(2) If $\mathbf{x} > \mathbf{y}$, then $C_i(\mathbf{x}) \supseteq C_i(\mathbf{y}), \forall \mathbf{x}, \mathbf{y} \in \Re^h_+$
(3) $\forall \mathbf{x} \in \Re^h_+, C_i(\mathbf{x})$ is such that, $\forall g \in B(C_i(\mathbf{x})), [0, g) \subset C_i(\mathbf{x}) \backslash B(C_i(\mathbf{x}))$
(4) $\forall \mathbf{x} \in \Re^h_+, C_i(\mathbf{x})$ is compact
(5) If $\{\mathbf{x}_n\}$ is a sequence such that $\mathbf{x}_n \to x, f_n \in C_i(\mathbf{x}_n)$, and $f_n \to f$, then $f \in C_i(\mathbf{x})$
(6) $\exists \mathbf{x} \in \Re^h_+$ such that $f \in C_i(\mathbf{x})$ and $f \gg 0$

Conditions (1) through (6) are a combination of self-evident axioms and some technical conditions needed for the results to be proven in Herrero's (1996) setting.

A person's utility depends both on the goods he consumes and the functionings he achieves. Hence, person i's utility function, v_i, may be thought of as a function

$$v_i : \Re^h \times \Re^m \rightarrow \Re.$$

While Sen does not always assume utility maximizing behavior on the part of agents, we shall here go along with Herrero (1996) and assume that if person i consumes a commodity bundle $\mathbf{x}$, she will choose a functioning vector f^* such that

$$v_i\left(\mathbf{x}, f^*\right) \geq v_i\left(\mathbf{x}, f\right), \forall f \in C_i(\mathbf{x}).$$

Let us now define

$$v_i(\mathbf{x}) = \max_{f \in C_i(\mathbf{x})} v_i(\mathbf{x}, f).$$

It is interesting to note that this formulation is general enough to allow for the possibility that even if a person's capability increases, her utility falls. In other words, we can have

$$C_i(\mathbf{x}) \subset C_i(\mathbf{y}) \quad \text{but} \quad v_i(\mathbf{x}) > v_i(\mathbf{y}).$$

The normative problem in this model is posed in terms of a planner, who has a vector, $\mathbf{w}$, of commodities to be distributed among the n individuals in society. The planner's aim is the Rawlsian one of maximizing the capability of the individual with the least capability. So she has to confront head on the problem of comparing capability sets. Comparison of sets, when this has to be consistent with some underlying preference over the elements of the sets, is problematic (see, for example, Kannai and Peleg 1984, and Barberá and Pattanaik 1984). Herrero circumvents this by thinking of an index of capability sets, which is a primitive.

Individual i's *capability index* is a concave and continuous function, $c_i : \Re^h_+ \rightarrow \Re$, such that $c_i(0) = 0$, $C_i(\mathbf{x}) \subset C_i(\mathbf{y})$ implies $c_i(\mathbf{x}) \leq c_i(\mathbf{y})$, and $\lim_{t\rightarrow\infty}(1/t)c_i(tx) = 0, \forall \mathbf{x} \in \Re^h_+$. The interpretation of this is as follows. If $c_i(\mathbf{x}) = r$, then person i having a capability set $C_i(\mathbf{x})$ is described as having a capability index of r. An increasing capability index suggests greater capability.

A planner's problem may now be expressed as a quadruple $\sigma = < n, h, w, \mathbf{c} >$, where we are describing any distribution problem by the following pieces: number of agents in the economy, n; number of commodities, h; available resources for distribution, $w \in \Re^h_+$; and an n-tuple of capability indices, $\mathbf{c} = (c_1, \ldots, c_n)$, where $c : \Re^h_+ \rightarrow \Re$. Let Σ be the collection of all possible planner's problems. This formulation, mathematically, is the same as the one in Roemer (1988).

Given a planner's problem σ, the set of all feasible allocations, $Z(\sigma)$, is defined as follows:

$$Z(\sigma) = \left\{ (x_1, \ldots, x_n) \mid \sum_{i=1}^{n} x_i \leq w \quad \text{and} \quad x_i \geq 0, \forall i \right\}.$$

We are now in a position to formalize the Rawlsian Solution (with capabilities as fundamentals) of a planner's problem. Given $r \in \Re^n$, let $\alpha(r)$ be a permutation of r such that $\alpha_1(r) \leq \alpha_2(r) \leq \ldots \leq \alpha_n(r)$. Given that $r, k \in \Re^n$, we write $r\rangle^L k$ if $\exists\ i$ such that $r_i > k_i$ and, for all $j < i$, $r_j = k_j$.

The Rawlsian solution of a planner's problem σ is denoted by $L(\sigma)$ and defined as follows:

$$L(\sigma) = \{\mathbf{z} \in Z(\sigma) | [\alpha(c(\mathbf{y}))\rangle^L \alpha(c(\mathbf{z})) \Rightarrow \mathbf{y} \notin Z(\sigma)]\}.$$

$L(\sigma)$ is the collection of those feasible allocations that endow the n individuals with capabilities such that no n-tuple of capabilities exist that is feasible and lexicographically dominates this (that is, dominates in terms of the binary relation $\rangle^L$). Herrero also considers $L(\sigma)$ as the collection of fair allocations a la Sen, since "they provide equal capability indices up to the point at which it does not come into conflict with optimality in capability terms" (Herrero 1996, p. 79).

A logically interesting exercise that is undertaken in Herrero (1996) is to consider mechanisms and desirable axioms (in the spirit of Roemer 1988 and Nieto 1992), which turn out to be equivalent to the Rawlsian solution. To convey an idea of this, define an *allocation mechanism*, F, to be a mapping

$$F: \sum \rightarrow 2^{z(\sigma)}$$

such that $\forall \sigma \in \Sigma, F(\sigma)$ is nonempty.

The axioms that Herrero imposes on F are, stated informally, as follows:

(i) If two allocations are indistinguishable in terms of their capability implications, then if the allocation mechanism chooses one of them, it must pick the other.

(ii) The chosen allocations must be Pareto optimal in capabilities (instead of the usual utilities).

(iii) F must be anonymous over the agents.

(iv) Suppose a certain good, k, is "personal" for agent i in the sense that the capability set of other agents is independent of their consumption of k. Then F should have the property that a change in the planner's problem that simply eliminates the personal good should leave the allocation unchanged for everybody over the other goods.

(v) If the amount of personal good for agent j increases, j's capability index should not fall.

(vi) If some agents disappear with the goods allocated to them, the allocation made in the revised planner's problem should be such that all other agents get exactly what they got before the agent's disappearance.

Herrero proves that F satisfies axioms (i) to (vi) if and only if it is the Rawlsian solution, as defined earlier.

As always, the advantage of an axiomatization is that it allows us to evaluate a large moral principle by breaking it up into parts. To us it seems that axioms (iii) and (vi) are the ones that can be contested. Sen himself has challenged anonymity, though there is less scope for that criticism in this framework since individuals are allowed to have different C_i and c_i functions.

Nevertheless, there may be traits associated with who the person happens to be that anonymity, that is, axiom (iii), tends to ignore. Axiom (vi) suggests a kind of absence of externality, which may well be questioned.

This formal exercise may not fully capture the intuition behind the capabilities approach, but it sets up a useful agenda and also helps to potentially break up and evaluate the whole new approach.

Once the allocation is made in a way consistent with the leximin rule in the dimension of capabilities, it is worth investigating what is the result in the dimension of utilities, under the given assumptions. When defining and constructing the set of capability-Pareto optimal allocations, the information regarding utilities is irrelevant. No clear relation can be derived, in principle, between allocations that are capability-Pareto optimal and the set of Pareto optimal allocations in the utility sense.

This link can be established, however, as long as the utilities depend on functionings that are relevant for the capability index in a specific way.[17] The specific assumption that Herrero examines is one with the property that $c_i(\mathbf{x}_i) > c_i(\mathbf{y}_i)$ implies $u_i(\mathbf{x}_i) > u_i(\mathbf{y}_i)$, that is, a higher capability index implies higher utility.[18] This assumption can be added to the description of the allocation problem. That specific property of the utility functions is added to the information set. Thus, the problem is characterized by $\tau = \{\sigma, \mathbf{u}\} = \{< n, h, w, \mathbf{c} >, \mathbf{u}\}$, where σ describes the problem, as before, and $\mathbf{u} = (u_1, \ldots, u_n)$, $u_i : \Re^n \rightarrow \Re, \forall i = 1, \ldots, n$, and $c_i(\mathbf{x}_i) > c_i(\mathbf{y}_i) \Rightarrow u_i(\mathbf{x}_i) > u_i(\mathbf{x}_i)$.

Under this framework, two important results relating capabilities and utilities can be established. The first one states that when an allocation is chosen from the set of

[17] Commodities can be divided into a set that is relevant for the "basic" functionings and those that are only valued by specific individuals, called "personal" commodities, or "primary" and "secondary" resources, as in Roemer (1996).

[18] This is, of course, a rather straightforward assumption. But it is worth keeping in mind that this assumption is compatible with $c_i(\mathbf{x}_i) = c_i(\mathbf{y}_i)$ and $u_i(\mathbf{x}_i) > u_i(\mathbf{y}_i)$.

capabilities-Pareto optimal allocations, recontracting among agents aimed at improving well-being cannot result in a suboptimal outcome in capability terms. Moreover, if the positive relationship between comparable capability indices and utilities does exist, the intersection between the set of capabilities-Pareto optimal allocations and *u*-Pareto optimal allocations is not empty.

Finally, one more assumption allows us to establish the result that the set of capabilities-Pareto optimal allocation is contained in the set of utility-Pareto optimal allocations in problems of this class. The assumption is "local nonsatiation" of the capability indices. Though restrictive, within that setting it is possible to state that choosing an allocation that is optimal in capability terms would also imply that the allocation is optimal in utility terms. Herrero (1996) goes beyond these results to show under what conditions the mechanisms would necessarily result in allocations that are Pareto optimal in capability terms. As explained earlier, the most important assumption that drives the result of the interaction between capabilities and utilities is that capabilities and utilities move in the same direction.

Other formalizations have emerged from the idea that capability is a fuzzy concept.[19] The idea that deprivation is not an "all-or-nothing" condition lies behind that conception. Instead of assigning a 1 or 0 to elements depending on whether they belong or not to a specific set, it uses a function, called "membership function," which takes values in the closed interval [0,1], corresponding to the degree of membership. Chiappero-Martinetti (1994, 1996) shows the empirical obstacles and possible solutions to the implementation of "fuzzy" measurement of well-being from the capabilities perspective. Relevant examples include Chakravarty (2006) and Qizilbash and Clark (2005).

Once one enters the domain of the "partial," new avenues of inquiry open up. Basu and Foster (1998), for instance, consider the case of education, where the mere presence of a literate person in the household confers some partial benefits of literacy on the illiterate members of the household. The deprivation of illiteracy in their model is total if a person is an "isolated illiterate," that is, an illiterate who lives in a household with no literate member, and partial if the person is a "proximate illiterate." It may be possible in the future to exploit the algebraic affinity between such a model and Chiappero-Martinetti's (1996) fuzzy approach to gain new insights.

5. CAPABILITY, PREFERENCE, AND CHOICE

The subject of capability is closely related to that of freedom (see Arrow 1995, 2006, Pettit 2001, Alkire 2007).[20] Viewed as a concomitant of freedom capability gives

[19] On this, see Chiappero-Martinetti (1994, 1996) and Sen's (1994) comments on that work. For previous work on the application of fuzzy set theory to the measurement of inequality see Basu (1987b).

[20] Also see Sen (2004, 2006).

rise to some special problems, especially when we consider the choices of several individuals. To put this in a simple framework, it is best to start with the formulation of Foster and Sen (1997, pp. 199–203). They begin by assuming that there are n different kinds of functionings; a capability set, K, is a subset of $\Re^n$; and a person facing a capability set chooses some point, x, in the capability set. A focus on achievement would require us to focus exclusively on choices. Most traditional evaluations of well-being in economics do precisely that. Suzumura and Xu (1999) call this "pure consequentialism."

Before going to the case of several individuals let us examine one especially interesting argument put forward by Foster and Sen (1997), which makes the concern for capability almost a *logical* consequence of the concern for functioning. This stems from the realization that, at one level, the "ability to choose" is itself a kind of functioning. Hence, a functioning vector x chosen from the opportunity set S and the functioning vector x chosen from the set T may be thought of as denoting different achievements in functioning (see Foster and Sen 1997, p. 202). There is scope for some ambiguity here about what constitutes the functionings' space. Though Foster and Sen are imprecise in stating this, the essential idea is formalizable and important. The first step in formalizing this is to recognize that the functioning representing the ability to choose is a very different kind of functioning from the other functionings that they talk about. Let us call these other functionings the *basic* functionings and the functioning of choosing as a *supervenient* functioning. When Foster and Sen begin by assuming that there are n different kinds of functionings and they use $\Re^n$ to represent the functionings' space, clearly what they are talking about is basic functionings, because the interesting characteristic of the functioning of choosing (the supervenient functioning) is that it cannot be represented by real numbers because it is supervenient on the other functionings. Moreover, typically, one cannot choose between different levels of this functioning.[21]

The supervenient functioning level presented to a person is represented by a subset of the other functionings—the subset from which the person is allowed to choose. In other words, in this more generalized space, a capability set is:

$$\{(x, K) : x \varepsilon K\},$$

where $K \subset \Re^n$. When a person facing such a capability set chooses a point, for instance (x, K), the information about the capability that he faced is contained in his choice. Hence, an evaluation based on achieved (or chosen) functionings can be made sensitive

[21] The reason why this need not always be so is that individuals can at times choose the set from which they choose. Schelling (1985) and Akerlof (1991), in particular, have written about how individuals do at times take actions to restrict the set from which they choose. People often set rules for themselves that they then treat as constraints: I will not smoke more that 10 cigarettes a day or, if I drink more than one drink I will not drive. Alternatively, they often make choices that restrict their own future options, such as the person who does not carry his cigarette pack with him or the woman who throws away the painkiller before the labor pain begins. Basu (2000) shows that such behavior may be fully compatible with individual rationality.

to the capability set that the person faced. In this formulation, an evaluation based on capabilities alone is more restrictive than an evaluation based on the chosen functionings.

This formulation in terms of basic and supervenient functionings is a coherent one, as we tried to show above, and can be used for the actual evaluation of the quality of life of peoples; but we shall not pursue this line further. There are other problems to tackle concerning capabilities, even without going into this more sophisticated structure. So let us remain with the structure presented by Foster and Sen, where the functionings' space is given by $\Re^n$, a capability set is a subset of $\Re^n$, and a chosen functioning vector is an element of the capability set.

There is, first of all, the question of ranking *sets* of functionings, to capture the idea of "greater capability." That is, when can we say that one set represents a larger amount of capability or freedom than another set? This has been the subject of some inquiry (Kannai and Peleg 1984, Barberá and Pattanaik 1984, Pattanaik and Xu 1990) and it has had its share of impossibility theorems. But that takes us more into the domain of freedom. Staying closer to the concept of capability, we want to here draw attention to a very different kind of controversy—an ambiguity in the concept of opportunity as defined in economics. To understand this, the contents of the sets are unimportant. It does not matter whether they consist of commodities or functionings or something else. So let us introduce the problem, as in Basu (1987a), by using the standard Walrasian general equilibrium as the benchmark.

Keeping the framework abstract (and therefore widely applicable) let us use X to denote the universal set of alternatives. Assume X is finite and has at least three elements. We shall say that (x, A) is an extended alternative if $x 0 A \subset X$. An extended alternative, such as (x, A), denotes the action of choosing x when the set A of alternatives is available to choose from. The central idea that Suzumura and Xu (1999) introduce, formalizing the notion that human beings care not just about their final choice but also their freedoms, is to argue that human beings have preferences over extended alternatives. To formalize this, suppose Ω is the set of all possible extended alternatives. An individual's extended preference, R, is defined as an ordering (that is, a reflexive, complete, and transitive binary relation) on Ω. It will now be seen that imposing some mild-looking axioms on R can lock us into taking a very structured view of "how" capabilities enter human preferences.

We shall in particular consider three among the several axioms that Suzumura and Xu (1999) have discussed. Let us use P and I to denote the asymmetric and symmetric parts of R.

Axiom I (Independence) For all $(x, A), (y, B) 0 \Omega$ and $z \notin A \cup B$, $(x, A) R\ (y, B)$ if and only if $(x, A \cup \{z\}) R (y, B \cup \{z\})$.

Axiom S (Simple Independence) For all distinct alternatives $x, y, z\ 0\ X$, $(x, \{x, y\})$ $I(x, \{x, z\})$.

Axiom M (Monotonicity) For all $x \, 0 \, X$, there exists $(x, A) \, 0 \, \Omega$ such that $(x, X)P(x, A)$.

The interpretations of these axioms are straightforward. Axiom I says that if a person is indifferent between choosing x from A and choosing x from B, then if the capability set is expanded by adding another alternative (z), while keeping the choice the same, the person must continue to be indifferent over the new pair of extended alternatives. Axiom S says that when a person chooses from a pair of alternatives, as long as the chosen element is the same, the person must be indifferent. And finally, Axiom M asserts that for every alternative x, there exists a sufficiently small set $A \subset X$ such that a person prefers to choose x from X than x from A. A special instance of this is the assertion $(x, X)P(x, \{x\})$, for all $x \in X$.

These three axioms together, however, turn out to be very restrictive, as the following theorem, proved by Suzumura and Xu (1999), shows.

Theorem 1 *If R satisfies axioms* I, S, *and* M, *then for all* $(x, A), (x, B) \in \Omega$, $(x, A)R(x, B) \leftrightarrow \#A \geq \#B$.

In other words, a person whose preference satisfies these three axioms is concerned about capability, but his concern for capability takes a rather narrow "counting" approach. The more alternatives he is able to reject, the better off he is.

Apart from the analytical elegance of the theorem, it is valuable in showing how the concern for capability emerges easily from elementary notions regarding human preference. On the other hand, it demonstrates how quickly we can get locked into a rather mechanistic view of preferences for freedom. To break out of this we can try to relax these axioms—several variants of these are discussed by Suzumura and Xu (1999)—but, more interestingly, we can question the domain of this discourse. How reasonable is it to assume that the domain of human preference is Ω?

Consider the case where a person prefers z to x and x to y. Then the person is likely to view the feasible set $\{x, y\}$ very differently from $\{x, z\}$. And Axiom S begins to look less plausible than it did earlier. Moreover, it is no longer clear how we should interpret the extended alternative $(x, \{x, z\})$ since the person will not ever choose x when x and z are available. If by $(x, \{x, z\})$ we mean a situation where x is forced on this person from $\{x, z\}$, then it is not clear that "choosing" is the right word to describe this person's achieving x. In light of this, one way to modify the Suzumura–Xu framework is to restrict their domain, based on the agent's preference, R, on X.

Given R, let us define $\Omega(R)$ as the domain of all possible extended alternatives as follows: $(x, A) \in \Omega(R)$ if and only if $x \, 0 \, A \subset X$ and xRy, for all $y \, 0 \, A$. It will be interesting to explore the consequences of imposing reasonable axioms on the person's extended ordering on this more restricted domain. But such an exercise lies beyond the scope of this chapter.

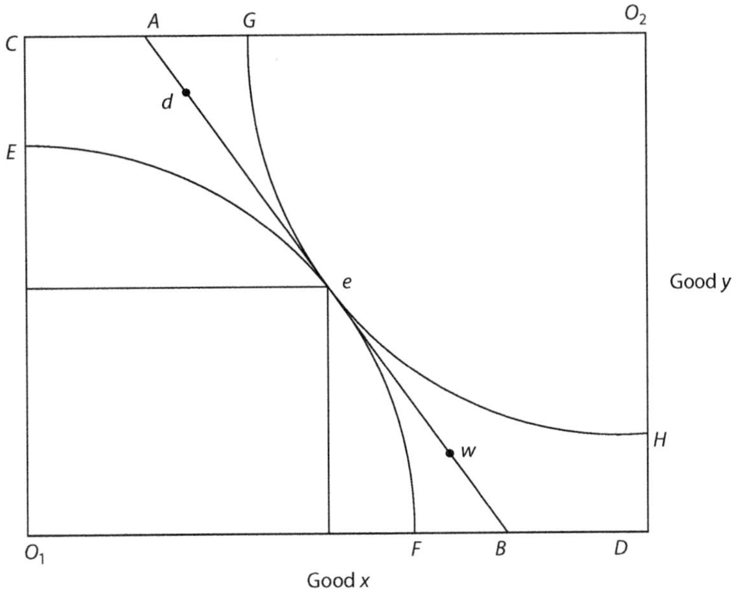

Figure 16.1. Edgeworth Box and Strategic Interaction.

Let us now turn to the problem of interpersonal freedoms. Let Figure 16.1 be a usual Edgeworth box of a two-person, two-good exchange economy. It depicts a general equilibrium. Let w be the point representing initial endowment. They face prices depicted by the line AB. Given the indifference curves as shown, equilibrium occurs at e. In this economy, person 1's *choice* or *achievement* is point e, but his *opportunity set* or *capability* (the concept here being restricted to the domain of commodities rather than functionings) is $CABO_1$. Likewise for person 2, whose opportunity set is $ABDO_2$.

The question that we want to raise now is whether these individuals are "really" free to choose any points within their opportunity sets. In an important sense the answer is no. This is because what is actually open to one person depends on what the other person chooses. For instance, in Figure 16.1 it is not possible for one person to choose point w and the other to choose d. Similarly, if person 2 chooses point e, person 1 cannot choose point d; person 1's belief (in the competitive model) that he can choose d is, in a sense, illusory. Once person 2 has chosen e, the only choices open to person1 are the points in the rectangle between e and O_1.

Given that opportunity sets have this element of illusion of choices, how much significance can we attach to opportunity sets as expressions of opportunity or capability or advantage? Also, once this problem is appreciated, it becomes clear that opportunities can be increased vastly without changing anything of significance. Consider the closed set bounded by $DFeECO_2$. From this remove all points on the curve FeE, except e.

Let us call the set that remains Z_2. If instead of restricting person 2's opportunity set to $ABDO_2$ we allow him to choose from the set Z_2, the equilibrium would remain unchanged. If we were evaluating this society in terms of opportunities open to individuals, this exercise of making person 2's opportunity set Z_2 would make this society appear better, but clearly our evaluation of this society should not hinge on such ploys.

To understand the problem further note that because agents 1 and 2 cannot simultaneously choose points d and e does not mean that they do not have the freedom to choose those points. The trouble stems from the fact that you cannot invariably say that they *have* the freedom to choose those points.

Consider a cocktail party for 100 persons. At the venue of the party there are 10 chairs, but most people show a preference for standing around, drinking and chatting; so that one chair remains vacant throughout. It seems reasonable to say that each person has the freedom to sit. This is so even though everybody cannot exercise this freedom. Next think of a train compartment with 10 seats for which 100 passengers have been sold tickets. These are polite people and so one seat remains vacant throughout the journey, no one wanting to appear impolite and grabbing the last seat. Here it would be wrong to say that everybody has the freedom to sit, even though at a purely behavioral level the situations (the party and the train) are the same. If there were no seats or chairs, we could unequivocally assert that people did not have the freedom or opportunity to sit; if there were 100 seats, we could say equally firmly that everybody had the opportunity to sit. What is interesting about the intermediate case, as illustrated by the above examples, is that freedom or capability has more to it than pure physical availability. One person's freedom can depend on another person's preference. At the party no one wanted to take that seat whereas in the train there were many who would have liked to have taken that last seat. That is what changes the fact that at the party each person has the freedom to sit, but in the train that is not the case.

It should be emphasized that this is not an argument that dismisses the importance of freedom nor one that claims that individuals in a Walrasian economy face no freedom. It simply shows that the extent of freedom faced by an individual in such an economy is a philosophically contested matter; that the traditional textbook view of equating this with the opportunity set may be too simplistic. Interestingly, this problem does not arise in a game-theoretic characterization of an economy or a game-form depiction of the choice problem faced by individuals (see, for example, Deb 1994, Fudenberg and Tirole 1993, Gaertner, Pattanaik, and Suzumura 1992), because in a game, as opposed to a market economy or a pseudo-game, an individual's set of opportunities or strategy set is independent of other people's choices.

This problem makes capabilities much harder to use in the actual evaluation of social states or societies, and so may mean that for the time being one is forced to use achieved functionings as the basis for evaluating societies. This is the line taken by Brandolini and D'Alessio (1998), the approach taken by the Swedish approach to social welfare

(Erikson 1993), and also the basis of the human development index of the UNDP, as in Section 8.[22]

6. APPLICATIONS OF THE CAPABILITIES APPROACH TO POVERTY MEASUREMENT AND GENDER ISSUES

Several applications of the capabilities approach to well-being have been used in the literature. One application is related to the concept of poverty, seen as "capability deprivation" (Sen 1983a, 1992, 1998). Poverty can be seen as being relative in the dimension of income, but absolute in the realm of capabilities (Sen 1983a).

The idea that poverty is not completely understood just by looking at income data is not new. In 1901 Rowntree wrote the book *Poverty: A Study of Town Life,* already calling for a distinction between "primary" and "secondary" poverty. Only the former was defined in terms of inadequacy of income, incorporating in the latter aspects such as influences that affect the family's consumption behavior. Rowntree's book also highlighted the need for defining several poverty lines because of variations in people's characteristics.[23]

In the late 1970s, new research tried to incorporate the "fact" that poverty has a multidimensional nature (Townsend 1979), though this was done without making use of the capabilities approach. One example of this is the so-called "Scandinavian Approach to Welfare Research" (Erikson 1993, Erikson and Uusiatlo 1987). This multidimensional approach to poverty measurement has been formalized by Bourguignon and Chakravarty (2003), and there are also papers that combine the capabilities approach to poverty with the multidimensional approach.[24] In the first decade of the twenty-first century the literature addressing multidimensionality has been related to methods based on axiomatic derivations of poverty indices. Examples in this field include the contributions of Bourguignon and Chakravarty (2003) and Alkire and Foster (2008).

The closest empirical approach to the idea of capabilities in poverty assessment, the "Scandinavian" approach, started with research centered around the Swedish Level of Living Surveys from 1968 to 1981. The Swedish multidimensional approach included nine groups of indicators of standard of living, namely health and access to health care,

[22] An idea that has gained ground in the recent literature refers to "adaptive preferences," where people might adapt to unfavorable circumstances, suppressing their wants and needs, rendering the evaluation of well-being complex. Several authors have posed interesting answers to this issue, for example Teschl and Comim (2005), and Qizilbash (2006).

[23] See Foster and Sen (1997), without A.7.4.

[24] An example of empirical evaluation of well-being explicitly from the functionings perspective is Brandolini and D'Alessio (1998). An attempt to construct poverty indices from the capabilities perspective taking into account implementation issues is Desai (1990). See also Balestrino (1992, 1994). A theoretical discussion of the applicability of the framework can be found in Alkire and Black (1997), and an extensive discussion of the foundations and the usefulness of the approach is in Alkire (2000).

employment and working conditions, economic resources, education and skills, family and social integration, housing, security of life and property, recreation and culture, and political resources. Each component included several indicators.[25] Though this approach is akin to the capabilities approach, criticisms have been made that in measuring certain indicators of well-being the approach is not clear as to what exactly is being measured. For example, "housing" is measured by people having access to a dwelling, whereas from a conceptual perspective the concept of "homelessness" is broader than the idea of not "having access to a shelter" (Brandolini and D'Alessio 1998, Foster and Sen 1997). The Scandinavian approach established, however, a broad framework for an empirical application of the capabilities approach, for a certain set of functionings.

Why is it necessary to introduce this new concept instead of the existing income-based poverty assessment? According to Sen (1998), there are three reasons for this: (i) income is only instrumentally important, whereas poverty can be sensibly characterized in terms of capability deprivation; (ii) there are influences on capability deprivation—on poverty—that are different from lowness of income; and, (iii) the instrumental relation between low income and low capability varies across communities and even across families and individuals.

The second point has to do with the capacity of individuals to convert income into functionings, introducing the aspects of disability, which were discussed in Sen's original formulation of the capabilities approach.[26] Establishing poverty lines in terms of income implicitly assumes equal capacity of conversion, which may not necessarily be true. The third point, that of the variability of the relation between income and functionings across communities, families, and individuals, allows us to deal with issues like gender discrimination in intra-household allocation of resources.[27] From the new perspective it is possible to identify instances of "functioning-poverty" even in relatively affluent societies and for levels of income that would not be regarded as being below an income-based poverty line.[28] Empirical work carried out by Ruggeri (1997, 1999) has shown that the identification of poverty may differ once the multidimensional approach is used instead of the common monetary poverty lines.[29] A similar conclusion is reached by Klasen (2000), using data for South Africa. Finally, another interesting application uses data for the unemployed population in Belgium to show that income is a poor indicator of capability deprivation for Belgian men (Schokkaert and Van Ooteghem 1990).

[25] For example, for "health and access to health care," the survey would typically include indicators such as ability to walk 100 meters, symptoms of illness, and contacts with doctors and nurses Erikson 1993.

[26] For more recent contributions in addressing the capability set of the disabled see Terzi (2005).

[27] See Sen (1998, Chapter 5) and Valdez (1995). For a criticism of the capabilities approach from the perspective of gender justice see Qizilbash (1997) and Robeyns (2008).

[28] An interesting case study is Balestrino (1996), based on a report requested by the Bishop of Pistoia, Italy, about poverty in that region.

[29] These applications use data for Chile (Ruggeri 1997) and Peru (Ruggeri 1999).

The Human Development Reports, published by the United Nations, have applied these principles to the measurement of human development from the perspective of gender equality. This resulted in the "gender-related development index," which corrects the Human Development Index for disparity of achievement between women and men (UNDP 1997). Razavi (1996) is another example in which the concept is used for the analysis of gender discrimination using village-level data from Iran.[30]

Besides the use of the capabilities approach in the analysis of well-being, inequality, poverty, the standard of living, and gender issues, there are other applications in the literature. These include political participation (Bohman 1997), freedom (Bavetta 1996, Carter 1996, Sen 1998), project evaluation, and environmental issues (Casini and Bernetti 1996), and health (Coast, Smith, and Lorgelly 2008).

7. CAPABILITY AND EXCLUSION

The link between capability and poverty, as discussed in Section 6, is an important one. Access to the market is a form of capability that can enable a person to escape abject poverty. Yet in poor countries many people do not have access to markets, which all of us seem to take for granted. This is more than a matter of possessing enough money. It has to do with the structure of markets and the nature of industrial organization. Atkinson (1995) has explored this link between capability and market exclusion. In his own words, what he was trying to explore was "the link between a specified capability and the distribution of income in the society, by introducing an aspect not typically considered: the conditions under which goods are supplied" (Atkinson 1995, p. 18). His model is based on Sen's (1983a, p. 161) view: "At the risk of oversimplification, I would like to say that poverty is an absolute notion in the space of capabilities, but very often it will take a relative form in the space of commodities or characteristics."

To understand the core idea behind Atkinson's model assume that we have an economy in which there are n workers and the productivity of the workers vary, uniformly, from $\underline{w}$ to $\underline{\underline{w}}$, where $\underline{\underline{w}} > w$. The "productivity" of a worker is defined in terms of what the worker can produce in this village. In other words, the least productive worker will produce $\underline{w}$ units of output when employed by a firm *in this village,* and the most productive worker will produce $\underline{\underline{w}}$ units when employed by a firm *in this village.* And the number of workers who have productivity in the interval $[\underline{m}, \underline{\underline{m}}]$, where $[\underline{m}, \underline{\underline{m}}] \subset [\underline{w}, \underline{\underline{w}}]$, is given by $(\underline{\underline{m}} - \underline{m})n/(\underline{\underline{w}} - \underline{w})$.

[30] For a discussion on the application of the capabilities approach to gender justice and women's capabilities, see Nussbaum (1995a, 1995b, and 1999, Chapter 1, "Women and Cultural Universals").

We shall now consider the market for bicycles. A bicycle is a commodity but one that can enable a person to achieve functionings otherwise not available, as in de Sica's classic film, *The Bicycle Thief.* The person can, for instance, enable him to ride to a neighboring village, where there is more capital and so one can earn more than in this village. Let us now, following Sen (1985), allow for the fact that what a bicycle can achieve for a person depends on who the person happens to be. Let us in particular assume that for a person with productivity $m \in [\underline{w}, \underline{\underline{w}}]$, the availability of a bicycle enhances what he can produce by himself. In other words, what he can earn with a bicycle is $(1 + h)m$ (by going to the neighboring village for work).

To see how some individuals may be excluded from the market, we have to now turn to the organization of the bicycle industry. Note that if the price of a bicycle is p, only those individuals will buy bicycles whose productivity, m, is such that $hm \geq p$.

Let c be the cost of manufacturing a bicycle. If $h\underline{w} < c$, then from the society's point of view it is inefficient to provide everybody with a bicycle. To rule this obvious kind of exclusion out, we shall henceforth assume that $h\underline{w} > c$. In other words, it is inefficient to exclude anybody from having a bicycle. We shall now show how, if the market is allowed to function without intervention, some individuals, in particular those with handicaps, will get excluded from the market.

The case of perfect competition in the bicycle market is easily dealt with, and is a useful benchmark. If by perfect competition we mean price-taking behavior and free entry of firms to the industry, then it is clear that the price of each bicycle will drop to c and all n individuals will get to own a bicycle.

The interesting cases arise when the industry is not fully competitive. For reasons of brevity, let us confine our attention to the case of pure monopoly, where the monopolist has to set one price for all buyers (that is, there is no price discrimination). If the monopolist sets price equal to p, his profit, π, will clearly be given as follows:

$$\pi = \{(\underline{\underline{w}} - (p/h))/(\underline{\underline{w}} - \underline{w})\}n(p - c).$$

From the first-order condition, it is evident that the monopolist will set the price at $p*$, such that:

$$p* = (h\underline{\underline{w}} + c)/2.$$

This means that all individuals with productivity below $p*/h$ are excluded from the bicycle market. It is not in the interest of the monopolist to sell to individuals who are relatively less productive and, therefore, relatively poor. The number of persons thus excluded is given by e^*, where

$$e^* = n[\{(h\underline{\underline{w}} + c)/2h\} - \underline{w}]/(\underline{\underline{w}} - \underline{w}).$$

It may be checked that, since $c > h\underline{\underline{w}}$, hence $e^* > 0$. Hence, a positive number of individuals will be excluded even though each person values a bicycle more than the cost of producing a bicycle.

From the definition of p^* above, it follows that all individuals with productivity less than w^* will be excluded from the cycle market, where w^* is given by:

$$w^* = (h\underline{\underline{w}} + c)/2h.$$

It is now easy to see that a person's capability can alter even without any change that is internal to her, purely by virtue of changes in other people's income, or by the income distribution or the arrival of immigrants, or by the out-migration of people. Just to take an example, suppose that the distribution of income worsens in this society, so that the richest person becomes richer, that is, $\underline{\underline{w}}$ becomes higher. This will cause w^* to rise, so that a longer tail of low productivity persons are now denied access to a bicycle. Likewise, if a group of wealthy migrants (productivity above $\underline{\underline{w}}$) come into this economy, then a larger number of poor persons will be excluded from the market. In the language of famines, the entitlements of poor individuals may diminish, without any change in the productive capacity of the economy or any innate change in the poor people. This also illustrates the possibility of an entitlement-based famine (Sen 1981), without any diminution, not just in production but in productive capacity.

Atkinson (1995) has taken this model further, and it is in fact possible to treat this as a base model to raise a variety of questions concerning poverty and famines caused by what appear to be unrelated factors, such as changes in the market structure and alterations in income distribution at the upper end of the income distribution, which seemingly leave the poor unaffected. But in the present context, the model is best viewed as one that brings "together the notion of poverty, in terms of an incapacity to function arising from the inability to purchase goods essential to that functioning, and the treatment of price and quality decisions in the industrial organization literature" (Atkinson 1995, p. 29).

8. THE HUMAN DEVELOPMENT INDEX

One important practical consequence of the capabilities approach is the emergence of the human development index (HDI), which is computed and made available annually since 1990 in the Human Development Reports of the UNDP. There is now a substantial literature using, criticizing, and advancing further these indices,[31] and the HDI has become part of the popular basis for criticizing or praising societies.

[31] Also see Anand and Ravallion (1993), Dasgupta and Weale (1992), Desai (1991), Ray (1998), Srinivasan (1994). Recent contributions are Foster, López-Calva and Szekely (2005) and Seth (2009).

The HDI is a method of ranking economies based on three summary measures of functioning. The three measures pertain to life expectancy or the basic functioning of living, literacy, or the ability to read, write, and communicate better, and finally, the economic standard of living, or the ability to buy goods and services that one desires.

To understand this more formally, let an average person's life expectancy at birth (in a certain nation) be given by l. Next let us turn to education. A nation's educational achievement is calculated by the *Human Development Report 1998* as follows. First the nation's adult literacy rate is measured, then the nation's school enrolment ratio is measured, and then a weighted average of these two is calculated with a weight of 2/3 on literacy and 1/3 on enrolment. Let us denote the nation's educational achievement level, thus calculated, by e. Finally, a nation's economic standard of living is measured by taking its "adjusted" per capita income. The adjustment is of the following kind. First the nation's per capita income with purchasing power parity correction is estimated. Then for incomes above a certain level the adjusted income is treated as one discounted by Atkinson's formula for the utility of income (see UNDP 1998, p. 107). Let a country's adjusted per capita income be given by y.

Now, for each of these three indices, l, e, and y, levels are chosen for the maximum and the minimum that a nation can have. Let us denote these by, respectively, L, E, and Y, and λ, ε, and ξ. These are of course somewhat arbitrary. Thus, for instance, the maximum possible life expectancy at birth is treated as 85 years and the minimum as 25 years. Once these estimations and choice of benchmarks have been made, the HDI is easy to derive. The country's HDI, denoted by H, is given as follows.

$$H = 1/3\{[l-\lambda]/[L-\lambda] + [e-\varepsilon]/[E-\varepsilon] + [y-\xi]/[Y-\xi]\}.$$

Table 16.1 below takes a sample of ten nations and gives their HDIs and GDP per capita. It is evident from column 3 that the ranks depend importantly on whether we use human development or GDP to evaluate a nation's well-being.

Australia has a lower per capita income than the United States but a higher HDI—in fact, Australia has the world's second highest HDI. Of all the countries reported in Table 16.1 Qatar has the highest per capita income, but it comes way down when it comes to human development. It is pulled down mainly by its lower life expectancy relative to its per capita income. In the case of countries like Qatar and Saudi Arabia, the GDP per capita is a poor indicator of the level of development, as evaluated from a broader perspective that is consistent with the capabilities approach. Qatar and Saudi Arabia go down 30 and 19 places in their ranking in the world, respectively, when the HDI criterion is used.

Other countries, however, rank better from the HDI perspective than they would if one were to consider only their GDP per capita. This is the case of Cuba and Costa Rica, which go up by 44 and 19 places, respectively, under the HDI perspective. In

Table 16.1 Human Development Index, GDP per Capita, and Rankings, 2007

Country	HDI	Real GDP per capita (US$, PPP)	HDI rank minus GDP rank[a]
Australia	0.970	34,923	20
USA	0.956	45,592	−4
Austria	0.955	37,370	1
Qatar	0.910	74,882	−30
Cuba	0.863	6,876[b]	44
Costa Rica	0.854	10,842	19
Mexico	0.854	14,104	5
Saudi Arabia	0.843	22,935	−19
China	0.772	5,383	10
Sri Lanka	0.759	4,243	14
India	0.612	2,753	−6
Nigeria	0.511	1,969	−17

[a] A positive number means that the HDI ranking is higher than the GDP ranking for that country.
[b] Data refers to year other than that specified.
Source: UNDP, *Human Development Report 2009,* Table H.

other cases, such as Austria and Mexico, the criterion does not seem to matter much for the comparison year. It is worth mentioning here that the GDP criterion is also less stable and can be affected by exchange rate disruptions and macroeconomic crisis, whereas the HDI rank is more robust to those short-run fluctuations.

One criticism of the HDI voiced often is that aggregating over literacy, life expectancy, and income is like adding apples and oranges. While such aggregation does hide information and is justifiably a source of concern, we must not go overboard in resisting aggregation. For one thing, there are contexts where we do add apples and oranges. We would do so, for instance, if someone asked us how many fruits there are in a basket that contains apples, oranges, and plums. Secondly, the concept of national income, used so ubiquitously, is itself highly aggregative. Whether a particular aggregation is right or wrong depends on the question that we are trying to answer. There is nothing fundamentally right or wrong in adding different entities together. Once people get to understand intuitively what a measure means, they are willing to accept it. A problem with the HDI is that its aggregation is not simple enough. Perhaps the best way to use the index is in conjunction with the disaggregated data on each country. Thus we could view a country's well-being as represented by a vector. What is interesting about the HDI is not the exact measure but its emphasis on a multidimensional, functionings-based view of development. That there was a need for this is evident from the rapidity with which it has caught on. The World Bank's move to adopt a "comprehensive development framework" is also a move in a similar direction.

9. CONCLUDING REMARKS

The capabilities approach opened an alternative route to welfare economics, traditionally focused on the analysis of well-being from the point of view of command over goods and services. In this new approach, commodities and utility are replaced by functionings and capability. Goods are only relevant in the sense that they allow people to achieve different "doings" or "beings," called functionings. The set of functionings available to a person represents her capability set.

The idea that goods allow people to "function" in a human way and to interact socially goes back to Aristotle, Adam Smith, John Stuart Mill, and Karl Marx. Moreover, the principle that real freedom does not depend on what people are "prevented from doing" by the law but what people are indeed able to do in a "positive sense" has been taken from Karl Marx, T. H. Green, and Isaiah Berlin. Amartya Sen proposed the new approach in his *Tanner Lectures* (Sen 1980) at Stanford University in 1979. After early attempts by Sen himself, several alternative formalizations have been proposed.

Applications of the functionings and capabilities approach have been attempted in the contexts of poverty measurement, gender issues, political freedom, and standard of living assessment. The most important attempt to make the approach operational was the creation of the *Human Development Reports* by the United Nations and the construction of the Human Development Index (HDI). The way countries rank in terms of development when measured by the HDI tends to differ, in some cases widely so, from those rankings based solely on income per capita.

Capability is closely related to the idea of opportunity or advantage. Ideally, in order to fully evaluate a person's well-being from this perspective, we would need to know the set of functionings from which he was indeed able to choose freely—the capability set—as well as a singleton: the functionings that were achieved. The problem of measuring "opportunity" can, however, be problematic from a philosophical perspective, especially when a person's opportunity depends on other people's choices. It is evident, therefore, that for some time to come, the attempts at applying the capabilities approach will run hand in hand with research to give greater rigor to its theoretical foundations.

It is, however, worth keeping in mind that the capabilities approach may well turn out to be (as with some other larger ideas in moral philosophy and social analysis, such as liberty or utility) not amenable to a single overarching formalization. We may have to contend with alternative specific formalizations and algorithms for dealing with different aspects of it. This may be viewed as a criticism of this approach. But it may also be its strength.

ACKNOWLEDGMENTS

We would like to thank Andrea Brandolini, Ingrid Robeyns, Amartya Sen, Kotaro Suzumura, and Eduardo Zambrano for many helpful comments and suggestions.

REFERENCES

Akerlof, G. (1991). Procastination and obedience. *The American Economic Review, 81.*

Alkire, S., & Black, R. (1997). A practical reasoning theory of development ethics: furthering the capabilities approach. *Journal of International Development, 9*, 263–279.

Alkire, S. (2000). *Sen's capability approach and poverty reduction.* Mimeo, University of Oxford.

Alkire, S. (2007). Instrumental freedoms and human capabilities. In Esquith (Ed.), Justice and Poverty. Ed. with Comim & Qizilbash. Cambridge: Cambridge University Press.

Alkire, S., & Foster, J. (2008). Counting and multidimensional poverty measurement. *OPHI Working Paper Series,* No. 07, OPHI.

Anand, S., & Ravallion, M. (1993). Human development in poor countries: on the role of private incomes and public services. *Journal of Economic Perspectives, 7.*

Aristotle. *The Nicomachean ethics.* Edition by Oxford University Press, 1980.

Aristotle. *Politics.* Edition by The University of Chicago Press, 1984.

Arrow, K. (1995). A note on freedom and flexibility, in Basu, Pattanaik & Suzumura (1995).

Arrow, K. (2006). Freedom and social choice: notes from the margins. *Utilitas, 18*(1), 52–60.

Atkinson, A. (1995). Capabilities, exclusion, and the supply of goods, in Basu, Pattanaik, & Suzumura (1995).

Baharad, E., & Nitzan, S. (2000). Extended preferences and freedom of choice. *Social Choice and Welfare, 17,* 629–637.

Balestrino, A. (1992). Poverta come 'non-funzionamiento': un approccio alla definizione di indici sintetici. *Economia Politica IX*(2), agosto.

Balestrino, A. (1994). Poverty and functionings: issues in measurement and public action. *Giornale Degli Economisti e Annali di Economia, LIII (N.S.)*(7–9), Luglio-Settembre.

Balestrino, A. (1996). A note on functioning-poverty in affluent societies. *Notizie di Politeia, 12*(43–44).

Barberá, S., & Pattanaik, P. K. (1984). Extending an order on a set to the power set: some remarks on Kannai and Peleg's approach. *Journal of Economic Theory, 32.*

Basu, K. (1983). Cardinal utility, utilitarianism, and a class of invariance axioms in welfare analysis. *Journal of Mathematical Economics, 12.*

Basu, K. (1987a). Achievements, capabilities, and the concept of well-being. *Social Choice and Welfare, 4,* 69–76.

Basu, K. (1987b). Axioms for fuzzy measures of inequality. *Mathematical Social Sciences, 14.*

Basu, K. (1996). Bargaining with set-valued disagreement. *Social Choice and Welfare, 13,* 61–74.

Basu, K. (2000). *Prelude to political economy: a study of the social and political foundations of economics.* Oxford University Press.

Basu, K., & Foster, J. (1998). On measuring literacy. *Economic Journal, 108,* 1733–1749.

Basu, K., Pattanaik, P. K., & Suzumura, K. (Eds.). (1995). *Choice, welfare and development.* Oxford University Press.

Bavetta, S. (1996). Individual liberty, control, and the 'freedom of choice' literature. *Notizie di Politeia, 12*(43–44).

Bentham, J. (1789). *An introduction to the principles of morals and legislation.* Edition by Oxford, Clarendon, 1907.

Berlin, I. (1969). Two concepts of liberty. In Berlin, I. (ed.) *Four essays on liberty,* pp. 118–172. Oxford: Oxford University Press.

Bohman, J. (1997). Deliberative democracy and effective social freedom: capabilities, resources, and opportunities, in Bohman & Rehg (1997).

Bohman, J., & Rehg, W. (1997). *Deliberative democracy—essays on reason and politics.* MIT Press.

Bohman, J., & Rehg, W. (2003). The measurement of multidimensional poverty. *Journal of Economic Inequality, 1*(1), 25–49.

Bourguignon, F., & Chakravarty, S. (2003). The measurement of multidimensional poverty. *Journal of Economic Inequality, 1*(1), 25–49.

Brandolini, A., & D'Alessio, G. (1998). *Measuring well-being in the functioning space.* Mimeo, Banca d'Italia, Research Department.

Carter, I. (1996). The concept of freedom in the work of Amartya Sen: an alternative analysis consistent with freedom's independent value. *Notizie di Politeia, 12*(43–44).

Casini, L., & Bernetti, I. (1996). Public project evaluation, environment, and Sen's theory. *Notizie di Politeia, 12*(43–44).

Chakraborty, A. (1996). On the possibility of a weighting system for functionings. *Indian Economic Review, XXXI*(2), 241–250.

Chakravarty, S. R. (2006). An axiomatic approach to multidimensional poverty measurement via fuzzy sets. In A. Lemmi & G. Betti (Eds.), *Fuzzy set approach to multidimensional poverty measurement.* New York: Springer.

Chiappero-Martinetti, E. (1994). A new approach to evaluation of well-being and poverty by fuzzy set theory. *Giornale Degli Economisti e Annali di Economia, LIII (N.S.)*(7–9), Luglio-Settembre.

Chiappero-Martinetti, E. (1996). Standard of living evaluation based on Sen's approach: some methodological suggestions. *Notizie di Politeia, 12*(43–44).

Coast, J., Smith, R. D., & Lorgelly, P. (2008). Welfarism, extra-welfarism and capability: the spread of ideas in health economics. *Social Science & Medicine, 67*(7), 1190–1198.

Cohen, G. A. (1993). Equality of what? On welfare, goods, and capabilities, in Nussbaum & Sen (1993).

Crocker, D. A. (1995). Functioning and capability: the foundations of Sen's and Nussbaum's development ethic, in Nussbaum & Glover (1995).

Dasgupta, P., & Weale, M. (1992). On measuring the quality of life. *World Development, 20*(1), 119–131.

d'Aspremont, C., & Gevers, L. (1977). Equity and the informational basis of collective choice. *The Review of Economic Studies, 46.*

Deb, R. (1994). Waiver, effectivity and rights as game forms. *Economica, 61.*

Desai, M. (1990). *Poverty and capability: towards an empirically implementable measure.* Mimeo, London School of Economics.

Desai, M. (1991). Human development: concept and measurement. *European Economic Review, 35,* 350–357.

Des Gasper. (1997a). Development ethics, capabilities, and the work of W.I.D.E.R. *Journal of International Development, 9*(2), 231–233.

Des Gasper. (1997b). Sen's capability approach and Nussbaum's capabilities ethic. *Journal of International Development, 9*(2), 281–302.

Des Saint Croix, G. E. M. (1981). *The class struggle in the ancient Greek world.* London.

Dworkin, R. (1981). What is equality? Part I: Equality of welfare. *Philosophy and Public Affairs, 10*(3).

Erikson, R. (1993). Description of inequality: the Swedish approach to welfare research, in Nussbaum & Sen (1993).

Erikson, R., & Uusiatlo, H. (1987). The Scandinavian approach to welfare research, in Erikson, Hansen, Ringen, & Uusitalo (1993).

Erikson, R., Hansen, E. J., Ringen, S., & Uusitalo, H. (Eds.). (1993). *The Scandinavian model, welfare states and welfare research.* Armonk, NY: Sharpe.

Foster, J., & Sen, A. (1997). *Annexe,* in Sen, A. *On economic inequality.* Expanded edition, Oxford: Oxford University Press.

Foster, J., López-Calva, L. F., & Szekely, M. (2005). Measuring the distribution of human development: methodology and an application to Mexico. *Journal of Human Development and Capabilities, 6*(1), 5–25.

Fudenberg, D., & Tirole, J. (1993). *Game theory.* MIT Press.

Gaertner, W., Pattanaik, P. K., & Suzumura, K. (1992). Individual rights revisited. *Economica, 59.*

Gorman, W. M. (1968). The structure of utility functions. *The Review of Economic Studies, 35.*

Goto, R., Suzumura, K., & Yoshihara, N. (1999). On the existence of procedurally fair allocation rules in economic environments. Discussion Paper Series A No. 379, Institute of Economic Research, Hitotsubashi University.

Grabel, N. (1994). Can a ranking of opportunity sets attach an intrinsic importance to freedom of choice? *American Economic Review, 84,* 454–458.

Green, T. H. (1900). Lecture on liberal legislation and freedom of contract, in Nettleship (1900).

Hammond, P. J. (1976). Equity, Arrow's conditions, and Rawls' difference principle. *Econometrica, 44.*

Harsanyi, J. (1982). Morality and the theory of rational behaviour, in Sen & Williams (1982).

Herrero, C. (1996). Capabilities and utilities. *Economic Design, 2*(1), 69–88.

Kannai, Y., & Peleg, B. (1984). A note on the extension of an order on a set to the power set. *Journal of Economic Theory, 32.*

Klasen, S. (2000). Measuring poverty and deprivation in South Africa. *The Review of Income and Wealth, 46,* 33–58.

Kolm, S. C. (1972). *Justice et Equité,* Paris, Editions du Centre National de la Recherche Scientifique.

Kuklys, W. (2005). *Amartya Sen's capability approach: theoretical insights and empirical applications.* Berlin: Springer Verlag.

Lancaster, K. J. (1966). A new approach to consumer theory. *Journal of Political Economy, 74.*

Malinowski, B. (1921). The primitive economics of the Trobriand Islanders. *Economic Journal, 31,* 1–16.

Marx, K. (1973). *The economic and philosophic manuscripts of 1944.* English translation, London: Lawrence and Wishart.

Marx, K., & Engels, F. (1947). *The German ideology.* English translation, New York: International Publishers, 1947.

Marx, K., & Engels, F. (1867). *Capital* (Vol. I). English translation, London: Allen and Unwin, 1938.

Maskin, E. (1978). A theorem of utilitarianism. *The Review of Economic Studies, 45.*

Maskin, E. (1979). Decision making under ignorance with implications for social choice. *Theory and Decision, 11.*

McMurrin, S. M. (Ed.). (1980). *Tanner lectures in human values* (Vol. 1). Cambridge University Press.

Mill, J. S. (1859). *On liberty.* (Reprinted as part of *Utilitarianism, Liberty and Representative Government.* London: Dent and Sons, 1971).

Nettleship, R. L. (1900). *Works of Thomas Hill Green, Vol. III, Miscelaneous and Memoir.* London: Fourth Impression, Longmans, Green, and Co.

von Neumann, J., & Morgenstern, O. (1944). *The theory of games and economic behavior.* Princeton: Princeton University Press.

Nieto, J. (1992). The lexicographic egalitarian solution on economic environments. *Social Choice and Welfare, 9.*

Nussbaum, M. C. (1988). Nature, function, and capability: Aristotle on political distribution. *Oxford Studies in Ancient Philosophy, 6*(Suppl. Vol.), 145–184.

Nussbaum, M. C. (1992). Human functioning and social justice: in defense of Aristotelian essentialism. *Political Theory, 20*(2), 202–246.

Nussbaum, M. C. (1995a). Human capabilities, female human beings, in Nussbaum & Glover (1995).

Nussbaum, M. C. (1995b). Emotions and women's capabilities, in Nussbaum & Glover (1995).

Nussbaum, M. C. (1999). *Sex and social justice.* New York: Oxford University Press.

Nussbaum, M. C., & Glover, J. (Eds.). (1995). *Women, culture, and development.* Oxford: Clarendon Press.

Nussbaum, M. C., & Sen, A. (Eds.). (1993). *The quality of life.* Oxford University Press.

Pattanaik, P. K., & Xu, Y. (1990). On ranking opportunity sets in terms of freedom of choice. *Reserches Économiques de Louvain, 56.*

Pettit, P. (2001). Capability and freedom: a defence of Sen. *Economics and Philosophy, 17.*

Qizilbash, M. (1997). A weakness of the capability approach with respect to gender justice. *Journal of International Development, 9*(2), 251–262.
Qizilbash, M. (1996). Capabilities, well-being, and human development: a survey. *Journal of Development Studies,* 33(2).
Qizilbash, M., & Clark, D. (2005). The capability approach and fuzzy poverty measures: an application to the South African context. *Social Indicators Research, 74,* 103–139.
Qizilbash, M. (2006). Well-being, adaptation and human limitations. *Royal Institute of Philosophy Supplement, 81,* 83–110.
Ray, D. (1998). *Development economics.* Princeton University Press.
Rawls, J. (1971). *A theory of justice.* Harvard University Press.
Rawls, J. (1975). Fairness to goodness. *Philosophical Review, 84.*
Rawls, J. (1982). Social unity and primary goods, in Sen & Williams (1982).
Rawls, J. (1985). Justice as fairness: political not metaphysical. *Philosophy and Public Affairs, 14.*
Razavi, S. (1996). Excess female mortality: an indicator of female subordination? A note drawing on village-level evidence from southeastern Iran. *Notizie di Politeia, 12*(43–44).
Roberts, K. (1980). Interpersonal comparability and social choice theory. *The Review of Economic Studies, 47.*
Robeyns, I. (2000). The capability approach: theory and empirical applications to welfare economics. Wolfson College, University of Cambridge.
Robeyns, I. (2008). Sen's capability approach and feminist concerns. In S. Alkire, F. Comim, & M. Qizilbash (Eds.), *The capability approach: concepts, measures and applications* (pp. 82–104). Cambridge University Press.
Robeyns, I. (2009). Justice as fairness and the capability approach. In K. Basu & R. Kanbur (Eds.), *Arguments for a better world. Essays for Amartya Sen's 75th Birthday,* Oxford University Press.
Roemer, J. E. (1986). Equality of resources implies equality of welfare. *The Quarterly Journal of Economics,* November.
Roemer, J. E. (1985). Equality of talent. *Economics and Philosophy, I,* 151–186.
Roemer, J. E. (1988). Axiomatic bargaining theory on economic environments. *Journal of Economic Theory, 45,* 1–21.
Roemer, J. E. (1996). *Theories of distributive justice.* Harvard University Press.
Rowntree, S. (1901). *Poverty: A study of town life.* London: Macmillan.
Ruggeri L. C. (1997). Poverty and its many dimensions: the role of income as an indicator. *Oxford Development Studies, 25,*(3).
Ruggeri L. C. (1999). The many dimensions of deprivation in Peru: theoretical devices and empirical evidence. Queen Elizabeth House Working Paper Series No. 29, Oxford University.
Scanlon, T. M. (2001). Sen and consequentialism. *Economics and Philosophy, 17.*
Schelling, T. (1985). Enforcing rules on oneself. *Journal of Law, Economics, and Organization, 1.*
Schokkaert, E., & Van Ooteghem, L. (1990). Sen's concept of the living standard applied to the Belgian unemployed. *Recherches Economiques de Louvain, 56,* 429–450.
Sen, A. (1977). On weights and measures: information constraints in social welfare. *Econometrica, 45.*
Sen, A. (1980). Equality of what?, in McMurrin, S. (ed.). *The Tanner Lectures on Human Values, Vol. 1.* Cambridge: Cambridge University Press.
Sen, A. (1981). *Poverty and famines: an essay on entitlement and deprivation.* Oxford: Clarendon Press.
Sen, A. (1983a). Poor, relatively speaking. *Oxford Economic Papers, 35,* 153–169.
Sen, A. (1983b). Development: which way now? *The Economic Journal, 93,* 745–762.
Sen, A. (1984a). Rights and capabilities, in Sen (1984b).
Sen, A. (1984b). *Resources, values, and development.* Harvard University Press.
Sen, A. (1985). *Commodities and capabilities.* North-Holland.
Sen, A. (1987). *The standard of living.* The Tanner Lectures, Cambridge University Press.
Sen, A. (1988). Freedom of choice: concept and content. *European Economic Review, 32,* 269–294.

Sen, A. (1989). Food and freedom. *World Development, 17*(6), 769–781.
Sen, A. (1990). Development as capability expansion, in Griffin & Knight (1990).
Sen, A. (1992). *Inequality reexamined.* Harvard University Press.
Sen, A. (1993). Capability and well-being, in Nussbaum & Sen (1993).
Sen, A. (1994). Well-being, capability, and public policy. *Giornale Degli Economisti e Annali di Economia, LIII (N.S.)*(7–9), Luglio-Settembre.
Sen, A. (1996). Freedom, capabilities, and public action: a response. *Notizie di Politeia, 12*(43–44).
Sen, A. (1997). *On economic inequality, expanded edition* (with an annexe by J. Foster & A. Sen), Oxford University Press.
Sen, A. (1998). *Development as freedom.* Oxford: Oxford University Press.
Sen, A., & Williams, B. (Eds.). (1982). *Utilitarianism and beyond.* Cambridge University Press.
Sen, A. (2004). *Rationality and freedom.* Harvard University Press.
Sen, A. (2006). Reason, freedom and well-being. *Utilitas, 18*(01), 80–96.
Seth, S. (2009). Inequality, interactions, and human development. *Journal of Human Development and Capabilities, 10*(3), 375–396.
Smith, A. (1776). *An inquiry into the nature and causes of the wealth of nations.* Edition by Oxford University Press, 1976.
Srinivasan, T. N. (1994). Human development: a new paradigm or the reinvention of the wheel. *The American Economic Review, Papers and Proceedings, 84.*
Strasnick, S. (1976). Social choice theory and the derivation of Rawls' difference principle. *Journal of Philosophy, 73.*
Suzumura, K. (1999). Consequences, opportunities, and procedures. *Social Choice and Welfare, 16,* 17–40.
Suzumura, K., & Xu, Y. (1999). *Characterizations of consequentialism and non-consequentialism.* Mimeo, Hitotsubashi University.
Suzumura, K., & Xu, Y. (1999a). *Welfarist-consequentialism, similarity of attitudes, and Arrow's general impossibility theorem.* Mimeo, Hitotsubashi University.
Terzi, L. (2005). A capability perspective on impairment, disability and special educational needs: towards social justice in education. *Theory and Research in Education, 3*(2), 197–223.
Teschl, M., & Comim, F. (2005). Adaptive preferences and capabilities: some preliminary conceptual explorations. *Review of Social Economy, 632,* 229–248.
Townsend, P. (1979). *Poverty in the United Kingdom.* London: Penguin.
Valdez, M. (1995). Inequality in capabilities between men and women in Mexico, in Nussbaum & Glover (1995).
Walsh, V. (1996). Amartya Sen on inequality, capabilities, and needs: review article. *Science and Society, 59*(4), 1995–1996.
Williams, B. (1987). The standard of living, in Sen (1987).
UNDP; *Human Development Report,* 1997, 1998, and 2009. New York: Oxford University Press.

PART SIX

Developments of the Basic Arrovian Schemes

CHAPTER SEVENTEEN

Arrovian Social Choice Theory on Economic Domains

Michel Le Breton* and John A. Weymark**
*GREMAQ and IDEI, Université de Toulouse 1, Toulouse, France
**Department of Economics, Vanderbilt University, Nashville, TN

Contents

Handbook of Social Choice and Welfare, Volume II
ISSN: 0169-7218, DOI: 10.1016/S0169-7218(10)00017-1

Abstract

This article surveys the literature that investigates the consistency of Arrow's social choice axioms when his unrestricted domain assumptions are replaced by domain conditions that incorporate the restrictions on agendas and preferences encountered in economic environments. Both social welfare functions and social choice correspondences are considered.

Keywords: social choice, Arrow's Theorem, restricted domains.
JEL code: D71.

1. INTRODUCTION

A social welfare function specifies a social ordering of a set of alternatives for each profile of individual preferences in some domain of preference profiles. Arrow's Theorem (see Arrow 1963) demonstrates that it is impossible for a social welfare function to satisfy Independence of Irrelevant Alternatives (the social ranking of a pair of alternatives only depends on the individual rankings of these alternatives), Weak Pareto (if everyone strictly prefers one alternative to a second, then so does society), and Nondictatorship (nobody's strict preferences are always respected) if the preference domain is unrestricted and there are at least three alternatives being ranked.

This theorem is not directly applicable to economic problems. In economic models, both the social alternatives and the individual preferences exhibit considerable structure. For example, (i) alternatives could be allocations of private goods with individuals restricted to having selfish, continuous, monotonic, and convex preferences; (ii) alternatives could be vectors of public goods with individual preferences required to be continuous, monotonic, and convex; or (iii) alternatives could be lotteries with preferences required to satisfy the axioms of expected utility theory. In each of these examples, the domain of admissible preference profiles is restricted, in contrast to Arrow's Theorem in which it is assumed that the preference domain is unrestricted.

Arrow's Theorem can also be formulated in terms of a social choice correspondence. In this case, the objective is to choose a set of socially optimal alternatives from a feasible subset of the alternatives called an agenda. A social choice correspondence specifies a nonempty subset of the agenda for each admissible preference profile and each admissible agenda. In its choice-theoretic formulation, Arrow's Theorem shows that Arrow's Choice Axiom (for a fixed preference profile, if agenda A is a subset of agenda B and some alternative from A is chosen when the agenda is B, then the set of alternatives chosen from A consists of the restriction to A of the set of alternatives chosen from B), Independence of Infeasible Alternatives (the social choice only depends on the preferences for feasible alternatives), and the choice correspondence versions of Weak Pareto (only weakly Pareto optimal alternatives are chosen), and Nondictatorship (the chosen alternatives are not always a subset of one individual's best feasible alternatives) are inconsistent if the preference domain is unrestricted and the agenda domain includes all the two- and three-element subsets of the universal set.[1]

The requirement that some of the agendas are finite is unnatural in many economic problems. For example, an agenda could be an Edgeworth box in an exchange economy or, alternatively, all of the allocations that are feasible for a production economy with given production technologies and resource endowment. By varying the technologies or the endowment, new agendas are obtained.

In this chapter, we survey the literature that investigates the consistency of Arrow's axioms when natural economic restrictions are placed on the universal set of alternatives, on preferences, and on agendas. We consider social welfare functions in Part I and social choice correspondences in Part II.

Prior to Arrow (1951), social choice theory focused on the properties of particular social decision procedures, such as majority rule. One of the innovative features of Arrow's work is that it shifted attention from the analysis of a given social decision rule to the question of whether *any* social decision procedure can satisfy a prespecified list of appealing properties. The answer to this question depends on the domain for which the social choice rule is meant to apply. Domains for which the Arrow axioms can be jointly satisfied are called *Arrow-consistent.*

The literature on the Arrow-consistency of the preference domain of a social welfare function has two main branches. In one branch of this literature, the objective is to find necessary and sufficient conditions for the domain to be Arrow-consistent when little or no a priori structure is placed on the set of alternatives. Not much is known about the implications of this line of research for economic domains, so it will not be considered in this survey.[2]

In the other branch of this literature, the objective is more modest. Instead of attempting to completely characterize the preference domains that are Arrow-consistent,

[1] For some agenda domains, Arrow's Choice Axiom is the choice-theoretic analogue of Arrow's assumption that social preferences are orderings.

[2] See Gaertner (2001, 2002) for discussions of this literature. Some of of the contributions to this literature assume that every individual exhibits a strict preference between any pair of alternatives or assume that the set of alternatives is finite, neither of which is a natural assumption in economic problems when the alternatives include divisible goods.

the objective is to determine whether the preference domain in a specific economic problem is Arrow-consistent and, if so, to identify social welfare functions that satisfy all of the Arrow axioms on this domain. This research program has been aided by the development of various sufficient conditions for a preference domain to be Arrow-inconsistent that can be applied in a wide range of economic applications.

While, in retrospect, the work of Black (1948) on single-peaked preferences when the set of alternatives is one-dimensional and of Arrow (1951, Chapter VI) and Blau (1957) on the allocation of multiple private goods can be seen as contributing to this research programme, it was the pathbreaking contribution of Kalai, Muller, and Satterthwaite (1979) that set the stage for most of the subsequent developments on the Arrow-consistency of domains of economic preferences.[3] They introduced the concept of a saturating domain and showed that it is a sufficient condition for the preference domain of a social welfare function to be Arrow-inconsistent when individuals are required to have the same set of admissible preferences. The method of proof used to establish this theorem is now known as the local approach. Some version of this methodology is used to prove most of the results we survey in Part I. As we shall see, except when alternatives are one-dimensional and preferences are single-peaked, it is typically the case that some version of Arrow's impossibility theorem holds for economic domains of interest.

The research on the consistency of Arrow's axioms on economic domains when the social choice correspondence framework is used originates with Bailey (1979), who questioned the relevance of Arrow's Theorem for exchange economies. Here, the results are more mixed. While the choice-theoretic versions of Arrow's axioms are inconsistent on many economic domains, a number of domains have been identified for which they are consistent. In contrast to the research on social welfare functions, the strategies used to determine whether various economic domains for social choice correspondences are Arrow-consistent or not have largely been domain-specific. As a consequence, the literature surveyed in Part II is less well developed than the literature surveyed in Part I.

We begin Part I with a review of Arrow's Theorem for social welfare functions. Single-peaked preferences on a one-dimensional set of alternatives are considered in Section 3. In Section 4, we discuss saturating domains and the local approach. We illustrate the application of the local approach in Section 5 by showing that a number of economic domains for public alternatives are saturating. In Section 6, we discuss a topological approach to identifying Arrow-consistent domains due to Redekop (1991). Private goods are considered in Sections 7, 8, and 9. In Section 10, we discuss problems

[3] Also influential is the earlier unpublished work of Maskin (1976). Maskin showed that when there are at least two private goods, Weak Pareto and Nondictatorship are inconsistent with a non-negative responsiveness condition (a strengthening of Independence of Irrelevant Alternatives) on the domain of selfish, continuous, monotonic, and convex preferences if each individual consumption set is a positive orthant.

in which the set of alternatives does not have a Cartesian structure. This situation arises when feasibility constraints place restrictions on the set of alternatives, as is the case, for example, in exchange economies. In Section 11, we consider some implications of requiring a social welfare function to generate socially-best alternatives on some subsets of alternatives.

Part II begins by describing a choice-theoretic version of Arrow's Theorem. This is followed in Section 13 by a discussion of a number of problems in which the agenda domain is restricted but the preference domain is not. This structure is exhibited by some voting models. In Section 14, we present a possibility theorem for a one-dimensional set of alternatives when preferences are single-peaked and agendas are compact intervals. In Section 15, we discuss some possibility theorems for multidimensional sets of alternatives when preferences are representable by analytic utility functions. Euclidean spatial preferences have this property. In Section 16, we consider some classical domains of spatial and economic preferences when agendas satisfy natural feasibility restrictions. In Section 17, the implications of a stronger independence condition are discussed for models similar to the ones considered in Section 16. Some concluding remarks are presented in Section 18.

Any survey of the literature on Arrovian social choice theory on economic domains would be incomplete without some discussion of the proof strategies that have been employed. Accordingly, for most of the results we discuss, we either present a proof or we provide heuristic arguments that convey the main intuition of a formal proof. By proceeding in this way, we hope that the reader will gain some appreciation for why significant progress has been made in understanding when the domain of a social welfare function is Arrow-inconsistent and why less progress has been made in understanding when Arrow's axioms for social choice correspondences are consistent.

Part I: Social Welfare Functions

2. ARROW'S THEOREM

Almost all of the research that we survey builds on Arrow's (1951, 1963) classic work. In this section, we provide a brief introduction to Arrow's impossibility theorem for social welfare functions. For more complete discussions, see, for example, Sen (1970) or Campbell and Kelly (2002).

We consider a finite set of individuals $N = \{1, \ldots, n\}$ with $n \geq 2$ and a universal set of alternatives X. $\mathcal{R}$ is the *set of all orderings* of X; that is, $\mathcal{R}$ is the set of all reflexive, complete, and transitive binary relations on X. For each ordering R in $\mathcal{R}$, strict preference P and indifference I are defined in the usual way: (a) xPy if and only if xRy and $\neg(yRx)$ and

(b) xIy if and only if xRy and yRx. Each person has a preference ordering $R_i \in \mathcal{R}$ on X. A *preference profile* $\mathbf{R} = (R_1, \ldots, R_n)$ is an n-tuple of individual preference orderings on X. Two preferences $R^1, R^2 \in \mathcal{R}$ coincide on $A \subseteq X$ if for all $x, y \in A$, $xR^1y \leftrightarrow xR^2y$.[4] Two profiles $\mathbf{R}^1, \mathbf{R}^2 \in \mathcal{R}^n$ coincide on $A \subseteq X$ if R_i^1 and R_i^2 coincide on A for all $i \in N$.

The collection of admissible profiles $\mathcal{D}$, a nonempty subset of $\mathcal{R}^n$, is called the *preference domain.* Collective decisions are only required for profiles in the preference domain. A *social welfare function* on $\mathcal{D}$ is a mapping $F\colon \mathcal{D} \rightarrow \mathcal{R}$ that assigns a social preference ordering $F(\mathbf{R})$ of X to each admissible profile $\mathbf{R}$. To simplify the notation, henceforth $F(\mathbf{R})$ is denoted as R.

Arrow (1951) supposed that the social welfare function must be determined before the individual preferences are known. If no structure is assumed about what form these preferences might take (other than that they are orderings), the social welfare function needs to be able to determine a social ordering of the alternatives for any conceivable preference profile.

Unrestricted Preference Domain

$\mathcal{D} = \mathcal{R}^n$.

In addition to his domain assumption, Arrow proposed three properties for a social welfare function to satisfy. The first of these axioms requires the social ranking of any pair of alternatives to depend only on the individual rankings of these alternatives.

Independence of Irrelevant Alternatives (IIA)

For all $x, y \in X$ and all $\mathbf{R}^1, \mathbf{R}^2 \in \mathcal{D}$, if $\mathbf{R}^1$ and $\mathbf{R}^2$ coincide on $\{x, y\}$, then R^1 and R^2 coincide on $\{x, y\}$.

Arrow's Weak Pareto axiom requires the social welfare function to respect unanimous strict rankings on pairs of alternatives.

Weak Pareto (WP)

For all $x, y \in X$ and all $\mathbf{R} \in \mathcal{D}$, if xP_iy for all $i \in N$, then xPy.

An individual $d \in N$ is a *dictator on the ordered pair* $(x, y) \in X^2$ if xPy for all $\mathbf{R} \in \mathcal{D}$ such that xP_dy. An individual $d \in N$ is a *dictator on the subset* $A \subseteq X$ if d is a dictator on the ordered pair (x, y) for all $x, y \in A$. An individual $d \in N$ is a *dictator* if d is a dictator on X. A social welfare function is *dictatorial* if there exists a dictator. Note that a dictatorial social welfare function only needs to respect the dictator's strict preferences. Arrow's final axiom requires the social welfare function to be nondictatorial.

[4] We distinguish between $\subseteq$ (weak set inclusion) and $\subset$ (strict set inclusion).

Nondictatorship (ND)
There is no dictator.

Detailed discussions of these axioms may be found in Sen (1970). As noted in Section 1, an *Arrow-consistent domain* for a social welfare function is a preference domain for which there exists a social welfare function satisfying IIA, WP, and ND.[5] If no social welfare function exists for which these three axioms are satisfied, then the preference domain is *Arrow-inconsistent*.

If a preference domain is Arrow-consistent, one may want to see if it is possible for a social welfare function to satisfy further desirable properties. For example, Weak Pareto could be strengthened to Strong Pareto, the requirement that if nobody prefers y to x and somebody prefers x to y, then x should be socially preferred to y.

Strong Pareto (SP)
For all $x, y \in X$ and all $\mathbf{R} \in \mathcal{D}$, if xR_iy for all $i \in N$ and xP_jy for some $j \in N$, then xPy.

Nondictatorship could be strengthened by requiring the social welfare function to treat individuals symmetrically in the sense that if we permute the individual preferences, then the social ordering is unchanged.

Anonymity (ANON)
For all $\mathbf{R}^1, \mathbf{R}^2 \in \mathcal{D}$, if $\mathbf{R}^1$ is a permutation of $\mathbf{R}^2$, then $F(\mathbf{R}^1) = F(\mathbf{R}^2)$.

Arrow's Theorem shows that it is impossible for a social welfare function to satisfy his three axioms when the preference domain is unrestricted. In other words, the domain $\mathcal{R}^n$ is Arrow-inconsistent.

Theorem 1 *If* $|X| \geq 3$*, there is no social welfare function with an unrestricted preference domain that satisfies* IIA, WP, *and* ND.[6]

Standard proofs of the social welfare function version of Arrow's Theorem, such as the one found in Sen (1970), show that a social welfare function must be dictatorial if it satisfies the other assumptions of Arrow's Theorem. Before describing the main steps in the proof of Arrow's Theorem, we need to introduce some further definitions. A nonempty group $G \subseteq N$ is *almost decisive* for the ordered pair $(x, y) \in X^2$ if x is socially strictly preferred to y when everyone in G strictly prefers x to y and everyone else has the

[5] This terminology is due to Redekop (1991). This definition does not explicitly mention the set of alternatives X being considered. However, X can always be inferred from knowledge of the preference domain.

[6] This version of Arrow's Theorem may be found in Chapter VIII of Arrow (1963). The original statement of the theorem in Arrow (1951) contains a minor error, a fact discovered by Blau (1957). Blau provided a correct statement of the impossibility theorem, but, as noted by Arrow (1963), Blau's version of the theorem contains a redundant axiom.

opposite strict ranking. G is *decisive* for the ordered pair $(x, y) \in X^2$ if x is socially strictly preferred to y when everyone in G strictly prefers x to y, regardless of the preferences of the other individuals. The proof of Arrow's Theorem proceeds by first showing that if a group G is almost decisive for some pair of distinct alternatives, then it is decisive for all pairs of alternatives, in which case G is said to be *decisive*. Next, it is shown that if any group of two or more individuals is decisive, then it contains a smaller decisive group. WP ensures that the set of all individuals is decisive. Hence, by the previous step in this argument, some individual is decisive; that is, there is a dictator. At various steps in this argument, it is necessary to construct profiles with particular configurations of preferences on pairs or triples of alternatives. On economic domains, these profiles may not exist.

A *linear ordering* on X is an ordering in which no distinct alternatives are indifferent to each other. The *set of linear orderings* of X is $\mathcal{L}$.

Unrestricted Linear Preference Domain
$\mathcal{D} = \mathcal{L}^n$.

Straightforward modifications to the standard proofs of Arrow's Theorem show that $\mathcal{L}^n$ is also an Arrow-inconsistent domain.

3. SINGLE-PEAKED PREFERENCES

In this section, we suppose that the set of alternatives is one-dimensional and that preferences are single-peaked. The analysis of social choice with single-peaked preferences was first considered by Black (1948) in his pioneering work on majority rule. Black's research predates that of Arrow and is nonaxiomatic. Subsequently, Moulin (1980) initiated the axiomatic study of strategyproof social choice for this preference domain. We show how Moulin's generalized median voting schemes can be used to establish the Arrow-consistency of the domain of single-peaked preference profiles. We also discuss the recent characterization by Ehlers and Storcken (2008) of all the social welfare functions that satisfy IIA and WP on this domain.

For concreteness, we assume that X is a nondegenerate interval of $\mathbb{R}$. X can be given a variety of interpretations. For example, if $X = \mathbb{R}_+$, an alternative can be interpreted as being the quantity of a public good. Alternatively, an alternative can be a political candidate's ideology, as measured on a left-right spectrum. In either case, it is natural to suppose that preferences are single-peaked. A preference $R \in \mathcal{R}$ is *single-peaked* on $X \subseteq \mathbb{R}$ if there exists a $\beta \in X$ such that xPy whenever $\beta \leq x < y$ or $\beta \geq x > y$. The alternative β is the *peak* of R. Let $\mathcal{S}_P$ denote the *set of all single-peaked preferences* and $\mathcal{S}_P^n$

denote the *set of all profiles of single-peaked preferences* on X.[7] In this section, we consider the preference domain $\mathcal{S}_P^n$.

Unrestricted Single-Peaked Preference Domain
$\mathcal{D} = \mathcal{S}_P^n$.

Let $\mathcal{B}$ denote the *set of all binary relations* on X. The *method of majority rule* on $\mathcal{D}$ is a mapping $M: \mathcal{D} \to \mathcal{B}$ that weakly ranks one alternative above another if and only if the former is weakly preferred to the latter by a majority of individuals. Formally, for all $x, y \in X$ and all $\mathbf{R} \in \mathcal{D}$,

$$xM(\mathbf{R})y \leftrightarrow |\{i \in N \mid xR_iy\}| \geq |\{i \in N \mid yR_ix\}|.$$

In general, the method of majority rule is not a social welfare function because it does not always result in a social ordering of the alternatives. However, Black (1948) has shown that if preferences are single-peaked and there are an odd number of individuals, then the majority-rule social preference relation is, in fact, an ordering.[8]

Theorem 2 *If X is a nondegenerate interval of $\mathbb{R}$ and $|N|$ is odd, then the method of majority rule is a social welfare function on an unrestricted single-peaked preference domain.*[9]

Theorem 2 can be used to help establish Black's median-voter theorem. Black's Theorem shows that, for any profile $\mathbf{R} \in \mathcal{S}_P^n$, the median of the individual preference peaks is equal to the alternative in X that is top-ranked according to the majority-rule preference relation $M(\mathbf{R})$ if n is odd.

The binary relation $\leq$ (resp. $\geq$) on X declares x to be weakly preferred to y if and only if $x \leq y$ (resp. $x \geq y$). If the infimum (resp. supremum) of X is not in X, $\leq$ (resp. $\geq$) is not single-peaked on X. However, the extensions of these relations to the closure $\bar{X}$ of X are single-peaked.[10] It is sometimes useful to augment the set of single-peaked preferences with these binary relations. Let $\mathcal{S}_P^* = \mathcal{S}_P \cup \{\leq, \geq\}$. Theorem 2 also holds for the preference domain $(\mathcal{S}_P^*)^n$.

Example 1 shows that it is possible to satisfy all of the Arrow axioms, with ND strengthened to ANON, on the domain of single-peaked preference profiles. Thus, this preference domain is Arrow-consistent.[11]

[7] In the absence of a natural order on the set of alternatives, single-peakedness is best thought of as a restriction on preference profiles. See Arrow (1951) and Austen-Smith and Banks (1999).

[8] See Gaertner (2001, 2002) for a discussion of other domain restrictions that ensure that majority rule yields transitive social preferences.

[9] See Arrow (1951) for a proof of this theorem. When the number of individuals is even, the social binary relation resulting from majority rule when preferences are single-peaked is reflexive and complete and the corresponding strict preference relation is transitive, but the social indifference relation may be intransitive.

[10] If $X = \mathbb{R}$, its closure is $\mathbb{R} \cup \{-\infty, \infty\}$.

[11] Arrow (1951) has used Theorem 2 to show that the method of majority rule satisfies all of the axioms used in the original version of his theorem on the domain of single-peaked preference profiles when the number of individuals is odd.

Example 1 Let X be a nondegenerate interval of $\mathbb{R}$. A social welfare function $F\colon \mathcal{S}_P^n \to \mathcal{R}$ is a generalized median social welfare function if there exists a profile $\mathbf{R}^P \in (\mathcal{S}_P^*)^{n-1}$ such that for all $\mathbf{R} \in \mathcal{S}_P^n$, $F(\mathbf{R}) = M(\mathbf{R}, \mathbf{R}^P)$. That is, we apply the method of majority rule to a profile consisting of the preferences of the n real individuals and the preferences of $n-1$ phantom voters.[12] The preferences of these phantom voters are fixed. Because there are an odd number of real and phantom individuals, Theorem 2 implies that F is a social welfare function. Generalized median social welfare functions are the social welfare function analogues of a class of social choice functions introduced by Moulin (1980).

The method of majority rule is based on pairwise comparisons, so F satisfies IIA. Because there are more real individuals than phantoms, if all of the real individuals strictly prefer x to y, then a majority of all the individuals, both real and phantom, prefer x to y. Hence, F satisfies WP. Permuting preferences has no effect on the number of individuals who rank x above y, so F also satisfies ANON.

In Example 1, if n is odd, there are an even number of phantom voters. By choosing $\mathbf{R}^P$ so that half of the phantoms have the preference $\leq$ and the other half have the preference $\geq$, the phantom voters just cancel each other out, and so have no influence on the social ranking. With this profile of phantom preferences, the corresponding generalized median social welfare function is simply the ordinary method of majority rule considered by Black (1948).

A nonempty group $G \subseteq N$ is *semidecisive* for the ordered pair $(x, y) \in X^2$ if x is socially weakly preferred to y when everyone in G strictly prefers x to y and everyone else has the opposite strict preference. Suppose that X is a nondegenerate interval of $\mathbb{R}$, $x, y, z \in X$ with $x < y < z$ or $z < y < x$, and $\emptyset \neq G \subseteq N$. Ehlers and Storcken (2008) have shown that the decisiveness properties described in our sketch of the proof of Arrow's Theorem only hold in a weaker form when preferences are single-peaked. Specifically, they have shown that if a social welfare function with an unrestricted single-peaked preference domain satisfies IIA and WP, then (i) if G is semidecisive for (x, y), then it is decisive for (x, z) and (ii) if G is semidecisive for (x, z), then it is decisive for (y, z). These decisiveness properties are compatible with nondictatorial rules.

As in Example 1, the social welfare functions in the Ehlers–Storcken characterization theorem use a set of fixed preferences to augment the actual profile of preferences. However, these supplementary preferences are drawn from a slightly more general class of preferences than the class of single-peaked preferences. A preference $R \in \mathcal{R}$ is *strictly quasiconcave* on an interval X of $\mathbb{R}$ if for any $x, y, z \in X$ with $x < y < z$, either yPx or yPz; that is, there is a single-peaked preference on X that coincides with R on $\{x, y, z\}$. With a strictly quasiconcave preference, there exists a *quasi-peak* $\beta \in \bar{X}$ such that (i) xPy

[12] This terminology is due to Border and Jordan (1983).

if either $y < x < \beta$ or $\beta > x > y$ and (ii) if $\beta \in X$, then either $\beta P x$ for all $x < \beta$ or $\beta P x$ for all $x > \beta$. Note that the quasi-peak can be worse than some of the alternatives on one, but not both, sides of it. If both of the conditions in (ii) hold, R is a single-peaked preference.

In the Ehlers–Storcken construction, there is a fixed strictly quasiconcave preference assigned to each possible subset of N, including the empty set. For all $S \subseteq N$, let R^S denote the preference assigned to the set S and β^S denote its quasi-peak. Let $\mathbf{R}^V$ denote the profile of these preferences. The profile $\mathbf{R}^V$ is *monotone* if for all $S, T \subseteq N$ for which $S \subseteq T$ and for all $w, x, y, z \in X$ for which $w < x < y < z$, (i) $xR^S y \to xP^T z$, (ii) $xR^S z \to yP^T z$, (iii) $yR^T x \to yP^S w$, and (iv) $yR^T w \to xP^S w$. The profile $\mathbf{R}^V$ is *strongly monotone* if for all $S, T \subseteq N$ for which $S \subseteq T$ and for all $x, y \in X$ for which $x < y$, (i) $xR^S y \to xR^T y$ and (ii) $xP^S y \to xP^T y$. It is readily verified that $\mathbf{R}^V$ is monotone if it is strongly monotone. The profile $\mathbf{R}^V$ is *symmetric* if $R^S = R^T$ when $|S| = |T|$.

For any pair of distinct alternatives $x, y \in X$, let $\tau_{\{x,y\}}$ be a social welfare function with an unrestricted preference domain for the set of alternatives $\{x, y\}$. A *pairwise assignment rule* τ is a family of such functions, one for each pair of distinct alternatives in X. The family τ is *symmetric* if $\tau_{\{x,y\}}$ is an anonymous social welfare function for all distinct $x, y \in X$. If each $\tau_{\{x,y\}}$ is the method of majority rule for $\{x, y\}$, then τ is the *majority-rule pairwise assignment rule*.

Ehlers–Storcken Social Welfare Functions

Given a monotone profile $\mathbf{R}^V$ of strictly quasiconcave preferences on X for which $R^\emptyset = \geq$ and $R^N = \leq$ and given a pairwise assignment rule τ, the Ehlers–Storcken social welfare function $F_\tau^{\mathbf{R}^V}: \mathcal{S}_p^n \to \mathcal{R}$ associated with $\mathbf{R}^V$ and τ is defined as follows. For all $\mathbf{R} \in \mathcal{S}_p^n$, $F_\tau^{\mathbf{R}^V}(\mathbf{R})$ is reflexive. Let $\mathbf{R} \in \mathcal{S}_p^n$ and consider $x, y \in X$ with $x < y$. Let $S = \{i \in N \mid xP_i y\}$ and $T = \{i \in N \mid xI_i y\}$.

- **(i)** If there exists a $z \in (x, y)$ such that $xR^S z$ or there exists a $z \in X$ with $z < x$ such that $zR^S y$, then $xF_\tau^{\mathbf{R}^V}(\mathbf{R})y$ and $\neg(yF_\tau^{\mathbf{R}^V}(\mathbf{R})x)$.
- **(ii)** If there exists a $z \in (x, y)$ such that $yR^{S \cup T} z$ or there exists a $z \in X$ with $z > y$ such that $zR^{S \cup T} x$, then $yF_\tau^{\mathbf{R}^V}(\mathbf{R})x$ and $\neg(xF_\tau^{\mathbf{R}^V}(\mathbf{R})y)$.
- **(iii)** Otherwise, $F_\tau^{\mathbf{R}^V}$ coincides with $\tau_{\{x,y\}}$ on $\{x, y\}$.[13]

The social preference assigned to any profile in $\mathcal{S}_p^n$ by $F_\tau^{\mathbf{R}^V}$ is constructed using the family of fixed preferences $\{R^S\}_{S \subseteq N}$ and the pairwise assignment rule τ. A striking feature of the social preference $F_\tau^{\mathbf{R}^V}(\mathbf{R})$ is that it is strictly quasiconcave. See Ehlers and Storcken (2008). It is fairly easy to show that if (i) holds, then $xP^S y$, and if (ii) holds,

[13] The monotonicity of $\mathbf{R}^V$ ensures that it is not possible to satisfy the hypotheses of both (i) and (ii) in the definition of $F_\tau^{\mathbf{R}^V}$ for a given profile and pair of alternatives.

then $yP^{SUT}x$. For example, if $x < z < y$ and xR^Sz, because R^S is strictly quasiconcave, $\beta^S \leq z$, which implies that zP^Sy. Hence, by transitivity, xP^Sy. As a consequence, $F_\tau^{\mathbf{R}^V}(\mathbf{R})$ coincides with R^S on $\{x,y\}$ in case (i) and it coincides with R^{SUT} on $\{x,y\}$ in case (ii). Ehlers and Storcken have shown that when case (iii) holds, (a) z is socially preferred to both x and y for all $z \in (x,y)$ and (b) x and y are both socially preferred to all of the other alternatives. If $F_\tau^{\mathbf{R}^V}(\mathbf{R})$ is continuous at both x and y, this would imply that x and y are socially indifferent. However, discontinuities are permitted, and it is in fact possible to arbitrarily rank x and y in case (iii) while preserving the strict quasiconcavity of $F_\tau^{\mathbf{R}^V}(\mathbf{R})$. This is why any pairwise assignment rule τ can be used to order x and y in this case. Note that in order to satisfy IIA, τ can only depend on the individual rankings of x and y.

Theorem 3 is the Ehlers–Storcken characterization theorem for the domain of single-peaked preferences.

Theorem 3 *If X is a nondegenerate interval of $\mathbb{R}$, then a social welfare function with an unrestricted single-peaked preference domain satisfies* IIA *and* WP *if and only if it is an Ehlers–Storcken social welfare function.*

By construction, $F_\tau^{\mathbf{R}^V}$ satisfies IIA. To see why WP is satisfied, suppose that $x < y$ and consider a profile in $\mathcal{S}_P^n$ in which everyone's peak is at x. Thus, the set S in the definition of $F_\tau^{\mathbf{R}^V}$ is N. For any $z \in (x,y)$, we have xP^Nz because $R^N = \leq$, so x is socially preferred to y by (i). By IIA, this is the social ranking whenever everyone prefers x to y. An analogous argument using (ii) applies when everyone prefers y to x. To complete the necessity part of the proof, it must be shown that $F_\tau^{\mathbf{R}^V}(\mathbf{R})$ is an ordering for all $\mathbf{R} \in \mathcal{S}_P^n$. The proof that $F_\tau^{\mathbf{R}^V}(\mathbf{R})$ is transitive is quite lengthy, as is the proof of the sufficiency part of this theorem. See Ehlers and Storcken (2008) for the details.

An Ehlers–Storcken social welfare function satisfies ANON if and only if the profile $\mathbf{R}^V$ and the pairwise assignment rule τ are both symmetric. This observation is used in Theorem 4 to provide sufficient conditions for an Ehlers–Storcken social welfare function to be a generalized median social welfare function.

Theorem 4 *If X is a nondegenerate interval of $\mathbb{R}$, $R^S \in \mathcal{S}_P^*$ for all $S \subseteq N$ with $R^\emptyset = \geq$ and $R^N = \leq$, $\mathbf{R}^V$ is symmetric and strongly monotone, and τ is the majority-rule pairwise assignment rule, then $F_\tau^{\mathbf{R}^V}: \mathcal{S}_P^n \to \mathcal{R}$ is a generalized median social welfare function.*[14]

Proof. The symmetry of $\mathbf{R}^V$ allows us to identify $\mathbf{R}^V$ with a profile of $n+1$ strictly quasiconcave preferences $(R_{n+1},\ldots,R_{2n+1})$, where $R_{n+t} = R^S$ if $|S| = t-1$. Consider any $\mathbf{R} \in \mathcal{S}_P^n$ and any $x,y \in X$ with $x < y$. Note that the majority relations $M(\mathbf{R},R_{n+1},\ldots,R_{2n+1})$ and $M(\mathbf{R},R_{n+2},\ldots,R_{2n})$ are equivalent because $R_{n+1} = \geq$ and $R_{2n+1} = \leq$, which cancel each other out. Thus, it is sufficient to show that

[14] Theorem 4 is a special case of a theorem in Ehlers and Storcken (2008).

$M(\mathbf{R}, R_{n+1}, \ldots, R_{2n+1})$ coincides with $F_\tau^{\mathbf{R}^V}(\mathbf{R})$ on $\{x, y\}$. As above, let $S = \{i \in N \mid xP_iy\}$ and $T = \{i \in N \mid xI_iy\}$.

First, suppose that x is strictly preferred to y according to $F_\tau^{\mathbf{R}^V}(\mathbf{R})$. This preference is only compatible with cases (i) and (iii) in the definition of $F_\tau^{\mathbf{R}^V}$. In the latter case, the conclusion follows directly from the assumption that τ is the majority-rule pairwise assignment rule. In the former case, we must have xP^Sy; that is, $xP_{n+|S|+1}y$. Strong monotonicity then implies that $xP_{n+|T|+1}y$ for all $T \supseteq S$. Thus, in the profile $(\mathbf{R}, R_{n+1}, \ldots, R_{2n+1})$, the individuals in S and the phantom individuals in $\{n + |S| + 1, \ldots, 2n + 1\}$ all strictly prefer x to y. Hence, x is strictly preferred to y by at least $n + 1$ individuals, which is a strict majority.

Second, suppose that y is strictly preferred to x according to $F_\tau^{\mathbf{R}^V}(\mathbf{R})$, which is only consistent with cases (ii) and (iii). As above, case (iii) is trivial, so suppose that (ii) applies, which implies that $yP_{n+|S \cup T|+1}x$. It then follows from strong monotonicity that $yP_{n+|U|+1}x$ for all $U \subseteq S \cup T$. Thus, in the profile $(\mathbf{R}, R_{n+1}, \ldots, R_{2n+1})$, the individuals in $N \backslash \{S \cup T\}$ and in $\{n + 1, \ldots, n + |S \cup T| + 1\}$ strictly prefer y to x, which is a strict majority.

If x is indifferent to y according to $F_\tau^{\mathbf{R}^V}(\mathbf{R})$, case (iii) must apply, and the conclusion is trivial. □

4. SATURATING PREFERENCE DOMAINS

Kalai, Muller, and Satterthwaite (1979) have identified a sufficient condition for a preference domain to be Arrow-inconsistent when everyone has the same set of admissible preferences. Domains satisfying their sufficient condition are called saturating. This structural property of a preference domain is satisfied in many economic and political applications. The methodology used to show that a saturating domain is Arrow-inconsistent is known as the local approach. In this section, we describe the local approach and present some general results about saturating preference domains.

4.1. Preliminaries

As a maintained assumption, we assume throughout this section that the set of admissible preference orderings for any one individual is independent of the preferences of the other individuals. Thus, the preference domain can be expressed as the product of *individual preference domains* $\mathcal{D}_i \subseteq \mathcal{R}$, $i \in N$.

Cartesian Preference Domain
$\mathcal{D} = \prod_{i=1}^n \mathcal{D}_i$, where $\mathcal{D}_i \subseteq \mathcal{R}$ for all $i \in N$.

If each person has the same set of admissible preferences, the preference domain is *common*.

Common Preference Domain
$\mathcal{D}$ is a Cartesian preference domain with $\mathcal{D}_i = \mathcal{D}_j$ for all $i, j \in N$.

When the preference domain is common, we let $\mathcal{D}_*$ denote the common individual preference domain. For a social welfare function F on a common preference domain, although each person's preferences are required to be in $\mathcal{D}_*$, the social preferences are merely required to be in $\mathcal{R}$.

Before considering further restrictions on the preference domain, we need to introduce some additional notation. For any subset A of X, $\mathcal{R}|_A$ denotes the restriction of $\mathcal{R}$ to A, $\mathcal{D}|_A$ denotes the restriction of $\mathcal{D}$ to A, and $F|_A$ denotes the restriction of F to A. More precisely, $F|_A$ is the social welfare function with domain $\mathcal{D}$ and range $\mathcal{R}|_A$ defined by $F|_A(\mathbf{R}) = F(\mathbf{R})|_A$.

In the theorems and examples we consider, it is necessary to determine how rich the preference domain is when restricted to certain subsets of X. The following kinds of sets of alternatives are used extensively.

Trivial Subset
A subset A of X is trivial with respect to $\mathcal{D}_i$ if $|\mathcal{D}_i|_A| = 1$. The set A is trivial with respect to $\mathcal{D}$ if there is some $i \in N$ such that A is trivial with respect to $\mathcal{D}_i$.

A subset is trivial (with respect to $\mathcal{D}$) if there is some individual who has only one admissible preference ordering over this set of alternatives. A *trivial pair* is a trivial subset containing only two alternatives. Sets that are not trivial are called *nontrivial.* Note that a nontrivial set with respect to $\mathcal{D}$ must be nontrivial for all individuals.

Free Subset
A subset A of X is free with respect to $\mathcal{D}_i$ if $\mathcal{D}_i|_A = \mathcal{R}|_A$. The set A is free with respect to $\mathcal{D}$ if it is free with respect to $\mathcal{D}_i$ for all $i \in N$.

A subset is free (with respect to $\mathcal{D}$) if everyone's preferences are unrestricted on this set of alternatives. A *free triple* is a free subset containing three alternatives. A free subset (containing more than one alternative) is obviously nontrivial. However, a nontrivial set need not be free.

Strong Connection
Two pairs A and B contained in X are strongly connected with respect to $\mathcal{D}_i$ (resp. $\mathcal{D}$) if $A \cup B$ is a free triple with respect to $\mathcal{D}_i$ (resp. $\mathcal{D}$).

Connection
Two pairs A and B contained in X are connected with respect to $\mathcal{D}_i$ (resp. $\mathcal{D}$) if there exists a finite sequence of pairs contained in X, $A_1, \ldots, A_r$, with $A_1 = A$ and $A_r = B$

such that A_j and A_{j+1} are strongly connected with respect to $\mathcal{D}_i$ (resp. $\mathcal{D}$) for all $j = 1, \ldots, r-1$.

In the subsequent discussion, when we refer to two pairs as being strongly connected or connected, we are implicitly assuming that this is relative to $\mathcal{D}$. Two pairs that are strongly connected have exactly one alternative in common and the preference domain is unrestricted on their union. If two pairs of alternatives are connected, the preference domain need not be unrestricted on their union; it is only necessary that there exist a way to link the pairs together so that each adjacent pair in the chain is strongly connected. In general, two pairs A and B may be connected with respect to $\mathcal{D}_i$ for all $i \in N$ without being connected because there is not a *single* sequence of pairs that connects the pairs A and B in all of the individual preference domains $\mathcal{D}_i$. That is, it may only be possible to connect A and B in i and j's preference domains using different intermediate pairs of alternatives. However, if there is a common preference domain, because the preference domain is Cartesian, any pairs that are connected (strongly connected) for any individual are obviously connected (strongly connected) for $\mathcal{D}$.

For any subset A of X, $F|_A$ is a function of $\mathcal{D}|_A$ if IIA is satisfied. This insight plays a central role in the results discussed in Part I. It implies that the structure of a social welfare function on A just depends on the restriction of the preference domain to A. In particular, if F satisfies IIA and WP and if $\mathcal{D}|_A = \mathcal{R}^n|_A$ and $|A| \geq 3$, then Theorem 1 (Arrow's Theorem) implies that $F|_A$ is dictatorial; that is, there exists a dictator on A. Naturally, (when IIA and WP are satisfied) we may use the same line of reasoning for any other set of alternatives B to conclude that there is a dictator on B if $\mathcal{D}|_B = \mathcal{R}^n|_B$ and $|B| \geq 3$. However, in general, the dictator on B need not be the same as the dictator on A. The following example, which appears in Fishburn (1976) and in Kalai, Muller, and Satterthwaite (1979), illustrates this point.

Example 2 Let $N = \{1,2\}$ and $X = \{x_1, x_2, x_3, x_4, x_5, x_6\}$. Let $\mathcal{D}$ be a common preference domain with $\mathcal{D}_* = \{R \in \mathcal{R} \mid x_i P x_j \text{ for all } i = 1,2,3 \text{ and all } j = 4,5,6\}$. In this example, $\{x_1, x_2, x_3\}$ and $\{x_4, x_5, x_6\}$ are free triples. Hence, if F is a social welfare function on $\mathcal{D}$ satisfying IIA and WP, there must exist a dictator on each of these free triples. Define the social welfare function F by setting, for all $\mathbf{R} \in \mathcal{D}$,

(i) $xRy \leftrightarrow xR_1y$ for $x, y \in \{x_1, x_2, x_3\}$,
(ii) $xRy \leftrightarrow xR_2y$ for $x, y \in \{x_4, x_5, x_6\}$,
(iii) xPy if $x \in \{x_1, x_2, x_3\}$ and $y \in \{x_4, x_5, x_6\}$.

This is a well-defined social welfare function because, for all profiles in the domain, the social preference is an ordering. For example, if $x \in \{x_1, x_2, x_3\}$ and $y, z \in \{x_4, x_5, x_6\}$, by (iii) we must have both xPy and xPz, which ensures that restricted to $\{x, y, z\}$, R is an ordering regardless of how y and z are ranked. F satisfies IIA and WP, but it is not dictatorial.

The following example demonstrates that an Arrow-consistent domain can be both a superset and subset of Arrow-inconsistent domains.

Example 3 Suppose that $|X| \geq 3$. Let R^* denote the ordering on X in which all alternatives are indifferent to each other. Bordes and Le Breton (1990b) have shown that the preference domain $(\mathcal{L} \cup \{R^*\})^n$ is Arrow-consistent. This domain contains no free triples. Note that $(\mathcal{L} \cup \{R^*\})^n$ contains $\mathcal{L}^n$ and is contained in $\mathcal{R}^n$, both of which are Arrow-inconsistent.[15]

An example of a social welfare function F that satisfies all of the Arrow axioms on this domain can be constructed as follows. For all $\mathbf{R} \in \mathcal{D}$ for which $R_i \neq R^*$ for all $i \in N$, let $F(\mathbf{R}) = R_1$. For any other $\mathbf{R} \in \mathcal{D}$, let $F(\mathbf{R}) = R_2$. F clearly satisfies WP and ND. If $\mathbf{R}^1$ and $\mathbf{R}^2$ coincide on $\{x, y\}$, then either both profiles are in $\mathcal{L}^n$ or someone has the preference R^* in both profiles. Hence, F satisfies IIA.

4.2. The Kalai–Muller–Satterthwaite Theorem

There is no dictator in Example 2 because no pair of alternatives from either of the free triples is connected to any of the pairs contained in the other free triple. Connectedness is a common feature of the preference domains found in a number of economic and political models. In this section, we present the Kalai–Muller–Satterthwaite Theorem, which shows that if all the nontrivial pairs are connected, then the preference domain is Arrow-inconsistent.

A preference domain is *saturating* when all nontrivial pairs are connected and there are at least two nontrivial pairs.

Saturating Preference Domain

An individual preference domain $\mathcal{D}_i$ (resp. a preference domain $\mathcal{D}$) is saturating if (a) there exist at least two nontrivial pairs with respect to $\mathcal{D}_i$ (resp. $\mathcal{D}$) and (b) any two nontrivial pairs are connected with respect to $\mathcal{D}_i$ (resp. $\mathcal{D}$).

For any saturating preference domain, any nontrivial pair must belong to a free triple. Hence, it is a free pair. The definition of a saturating preference domain introduced by Kalai, Muller, and Satterthwaite (1979) assumes that the preference domain is common. The more general definition presented here first appeared in Le Breton and Weymark (1996). In generalizing the Kalai–Muller–Satterthwaite definition to an arbitrary Cartesian preference domain, all nontrivial pairs are required to be connected, rather than merely requiring each individual preference domain to be saturating. In general, the Le Breton–Weymark definition of a saturating preference domain is not

[15] Kelly (1994) has characterized all the Arrow-inconsistent Cartesian preference domains $\mathcal{D}$ for which $\mathcal{L}^n \subseteq \mathcal{D} \subseteq \mathcal{R}^n$. A domain of linear preference profiles $\mathcal{D}$ is *super-Arrovian* if $\mathcal{D}$ is Arrow-inconsistent and every domain $\mathcal{D}'$ with $\mathcal{D} \subseteq \mathcal{D}' \subseteq \mathcal{L}^n$ is also Arrow-inconsistent. Fishburn and Kelly (1997) have provided a characterization of the Arrow-inconsistent domains that are also super-Arrovian.

equivalent to the requirement that each of the individual preference domains is saturating; as noted earlier, in the latter case, nontrivial pairs for different individuals may be connected using different sequences of pairs of alternatives. However, if there is a common preference domain, then the definition of a saturating preference domain given here is obviously equivalent to requiring the common individual preference domain $\mathcal{D}_*$ to be saturating.

A preference domain satisfies the *free triple property* if every triple of distinct alternatives is free. If every triple is free, then every pair is nontrivial. Further, any two pairs are connected. For example, $\{x,y\}$ and $\{u,v\}$ are connected by the pair $\{y,u\}$ if $u \notin \{x,y\}$. Hence, any preference domain that satisfies the free triple property is saturating. In particular, an unrestricted preference domain has the free triple property, and so must be saturating. However, a preference domain can be saturating without satisfying the free triple property, as Example 4 demonstrates.[16]

Example 4 Let $N=\{1,2\}$ and $X=\{x_1,x_2,x_3,x_4\}$. Let $\mathcal{D}$ be a common preference domain with $\mathcal{D}_*=\{R\in\mathcal{R} \mid x_iPx_4 \text{ for all } i=1,2,3\}$. In this example, $\{x_1,x_2,x_3\}$ is a free triple. Any pair containing x_4 is trivial.

Kalai, Muller, and Satterthwaite (1979) have established the following generalization of Arrow's Theorem.

Theorem 5 *If a social welfare function with a common saturating preference domain satisfies* IIA *and* WP, *then it is dictatorial.*

Proof. By the definition of a saturating preference domain, there are at least two nontrivial pairs. Let $\{x,y\}$ and $\{u,v\}$ be any two such pairs of alternatives. By the definition of a saturating preference domain, these pairs are connected; that is, there exists a finite sequence of pairs of alternatives, say $\{x_1,x_2\},\{x_2,x_3\},\ldots,\{x_{r-1},x_r\}$ such that $\{x,y,x_1\},\{y,x_1,x_2\}$, $\{x_1,x_2,x_3\},\ldots,\{x_{r-1},x_r,u\}$, and $\{x_r,u,v\}$ are free triples.

By Arrow's Theorem (Theorem 1), there is a dictator on each of these free triples. Consider the first two free triples in this sequence. They have the pair $\{y,x_1\}$ in common. As a consequence, the dictator must be the same for both of these two free triples. By a similar reasoning, we can conclude that each adjacent pair of free triples in the sequence has a common dictator. Thus, there is a dictator on the set $\{x,y,x_1,\ldots,x_r,u,v\}$. Any other pair of nontrivial alternatives must be connected to $\{x,y\}$ (and to $\{u,v\}$). It then follows from the preceding argument that there is a single dictator, say d, on the set of all nontrivial pairs. Because there is a common preference domain, everyone has the same preferences on any trivial pair. WP implies that d is a dictator on the trivial pairs. Thus, d dictates on all of X. □

[16] The statements in this paragraph are also valid for individual preference domains.

Variants of this proof have been used extensively to establish Arrovian impossibility theorems on economic and political domains. This method of proof originated with Kalai, Muller, and Satterthwaite (1979) and is now known as the *local approach*. The reason for this terminology is that the proof consists of first showing that there is a local dictator on a free triple of alternatives and then showing that this local dictator can be transformed into a global dictator (on the nontrivial pairs) by the connectedness implied by the assumptions on the preference domain.

An implication of the Kalai–Muller–Satterthwaite Theorem is that a common preference domain must not be saturating if it is Arrow-consistent. This is the case for the domain of single-peaked preference profiles $\mathcal{S}_P^n$ considered in Section 3. Consider any three points $x, y, z \in \mathbb{R}$ with $x < y < z$. With a single-peaked preference, it is not possible to rank x first, z second, and y third. Hence, there are no free triples and, therefore, $\mathcal{S}_P^n$ is not saturating.

4.3. Further Properties of Saturating Preference Domains

The Kalai–Muller–Satterthwaite Theorem shows that a sufficient condition for a preference domain to be Arrow-inconsistent is that it is common and saturating. In this section, we investigate the robustness of this result.

Example 5 demonstrates that a common preference domain need not be saturating in order for it to be Arrow-inconsistent.

Example 5 Let $N = \{1,2\}$ and $X = \{x_1, x_2, x_3, x_4\}$. Let $\mathcal{D}$ be a common preference domain with $\mathcal{D}_* = \{R \in \mathcal{R} \mid x_1 I x_4 \text{ or } x_1 P x_2 P x_4\}$. All of the pairs are nontrivial, but the pair $\{x_1, x_4\}$ is not connected to any other pair, so the preference domain is not saturating. Suppose that F is a social welfare function on $\mathcal{D}$ satisfying IIA and WP. It follows from the fact that $\{x_1, x_2, x_3\}$ and $\{x_2, x_3, x_4\}$ are free triples with the two elements $\{x_2, x_3\}$ in common that there is a dictator d on every pair with the possible exception of $\{x_1, x_4\}$. On this preference domain, for any profile $\mathbf{R}$ with $x_1 P_d x_4$, it is also the case that $x_1 P_d x_2$ and $x_2 P_d x_4$. We have already established that we must have $x_1 P x_2$ and $x_2 P x_4$ for such a profile. By the transitivity of social preference, it follows that $x_1 P x_4$; that is, d is a dictator. Hence, $\mathcal{D}$ is Arrow-inconsistent.

Both Arrow's Theorem (Theorem 1) and the Kalai–Muller–Satterthwaite Theorem (Theorem 5) assume that the preference domain is not only saturating, but also that it is common. Example 6 shows that the common preference domain assumption is essential for these results; that is, there exist saturating preference domains that are Arrow-consistent.

Example 6 Let $N = \{1,2\}$, $X = \{x_1, x_2, x_3, x_4\}$, $\mathcal{D}_1 = \{R_1 \in \mathcal{R} \mid x_4 P_1 x_i \text{ for } i = 1,2,3\}$, and $\mathcal{D}_2 = \{R_2 \in \mathcal{R} \mid x_i P_2 x_4 \text{ for } i = 1,2,3\}$. The social welfare function defined by setting xRy if and only if xR_1y when $x, y \in \{x_1, x_2, x_3\}$ and xPx_4 when $x \in \{x_1, x_2, x_3\}$ satisfies IIA, WP, and ND. The preference domain $\mathcal{D}$ is saturating, but it is not common.

In this example, preferences are unrestricted on the set $A = \{x_1, x_2, x_3\}$ and any pair of alternatives in this set is nontrivial. All other pairs, that is, pairs formed with x_4 as one of the alternatives, are trivial. On the trivial pairs, the two individuals have opposite strict preferences. The social welfare function makes person one a dictator on A and person two a dictator on all of the trivial pairs. For example, person two is a dictator on $B = \{x_3, x_4\}$. Although there are "local" dictators on A and B and these two sets overlap, because the intersection of these sets only contains a single alternative, there does not have to be a single dictator on their union. For the local approach to apply, the two sets must have at least two elements in common.[17]

Although the preference domain in Example 6 is Arrow-consistent, the social welfare function used to show the consistency is not very appealing because on every pair of alternatives, someone is a dictator. Furthermore, the same person is the dictator on every nontrivial pair. Theorem 6 demonstrates that the latter property is a general feature of saturating preference domains.

Theorem 6 *If a social welfare function with a saturating preference domain satisfies* IIA *and* WP, *then there is an individual $d \in N$ who is a dictator on every nontrivial pair.*

Proof. Inspection of the proof of Theorem 5 reveals that the part of that proof dealing with nontrivial pairs makes no use of the assumption that the preference domain is common.[18] □

As we shall see in the next section, many of the commonly used economic and political preference domains are saturating when alternatives are purely public. Unfortunately, Theorem 5 shows that all common saturating preference domains are Arrow-inconsistent. Furthermore, if the preference domain is both saturating and Arrow-consistent, Theorem 6 informs us that the social welfare function is dictatorial on every nontrivial pair of alternatives.

5. EXAMPLES OF SATURATING PREFERENCE DOMAINS

For a common preference domain, the Kalai–Muller–Satterthwaite Theorem (Theorem 5) tells us that the domain is Arrow-inconsistent if it is saturating. There are three main steps involved in showing that a preference domain is saturating. First,

[17] Example 6 is similar to the example used by Blau (1957) to show that the statement of Arrow's Theorem in Arrow (1951) is incorrect.

[18] Note that the assumption in Theorem 6 that the preference domain is saturating cannot be replaced with the assumption that each person's individual preference domain is saturating, as we need to have nontrivial pairs connected by a common sequence of intermediate alternatives for our proof to be valid.

the nontrivial pairs are identified. Second, the free triples are identified. Finally, it must be determined how to connect the nontrivial pairs with free triples.[19] In practice, this last step is often the hardest, but in many interesting applications it is still relatively simple. In this section, we illustrate this procedure with some examples of common saturating preference domains. In these examples, the universal set of alternatives X is a subset of the m-dimensional Euclidean space $\mathbb{R}^m$.[20]

Example 7 In this example, we consider the domain of continuous preferences on any connected subset X of $\mathbb{R}^m$. A preference ordering $R \in \mathcal{R}$ is continuous if for all $x \in X$, the sets $\{y \in X \mid yRx\}$ and $\{y \in X \mid xRy\}$ are both closed. The preference domain consisting of all profiles of continuous preference orderings has the free triple property and, hence, is saturating because continuity places no restriction on how a triple of alternatives can be ordered. For example, suppose that we want to find a continuous preference R for which $xPyPz$. We can find a neighborhood $N(x)$ of x in X such that $y, z \notin N(x)$. By Urysohn's Theorem (see Munkres 1975), there exists a continuous function $V^1\colon X \to \mathbb{R}$ for which (i) $V^1(x) = 2 \geq V^1(w)$ for all $w \in X$ and (ii) $V^1(w) = 0$ for all $w \notin N(x)$. Similarly, there exists a neighborhood $N(y)$ of y in X such that $x, z \notin N(y)$ and a continuous function $V^2\colon X \to \mathbb{R}$ for which (i) $V^2(y) = 1 \geq V^2(w)$ for all $w \in X$ and (ii) $V^2(w) = 0$ for all $w \notin N(y)$. The function $U = V^1 + V^2$ is a utility function representing a continuous preference R on X for which $xPyPz$.[21]

Example 8 We now consider the domain of classic economic preferences when there are two or more divisible public goods. Before presenting the details of this example, we need a few more definitions. Suppose X is a connected subset of $\mathbb{R}^m$. A preference ordering $R \in \mathcal{R}$ is monotone (resp. strictly monotone) if xPy for all $x, y \in X$ such that $x \gg y$ (resp. $x > y$).[22] A preference ordering $R \in \mathcal{R}$ is convex (resp. strictly convex) if for all distinct $x, y \in X$ and all $\lambda \in (0, 1)$, xRy implies that $[\lambda x + (1 - \lambda)y]Ry$ (resp. $[\lambda x + (1 - \lambda)y]Py$).

In our example, $X = \mathbb{R}^m_+$ with $m \geq 2$ and individuals can have any continuous, strictly monotonic, convex preference ordering on X.[23]

Classical Public Goods Preference Domain

$\mathcal{D}$ is the set of all profiles of continuous, strictly monotonic, convex preference orderings on X.

[19] This is the procedure used earlier to show that a preference domain is saturating if every triple is free.
[20] We let $\mathbb{R}^m_+$ denote the non-negative orthant, $\mathbb{R}^m_{++}$ denote the positive orthant, and 0_m denote the origin in $\mathbb{R}^m$.
[21] For a rigorous proof that this domain has the free triple property, see Campbell (1992b, Chapter 8).
[22] We use the following vector notation: (a) $x \geq y$ means $x_i \geq y_i$ for all $i = 1, \ldots, m$; (b) $x > y$ means $x_i \geq y_i$ for all $i = 1, \ldots, m$ with strict inequality for some i; and (c) $x \gg y$ means $x_i > y_i$ for all $i = 1, \ldots, m$.
[23] If $m = 1$, there is only one possible individual preference ordering. WP then makes everyone a dictator. ND is clearly not appropriate on such a degenerate preference domain.

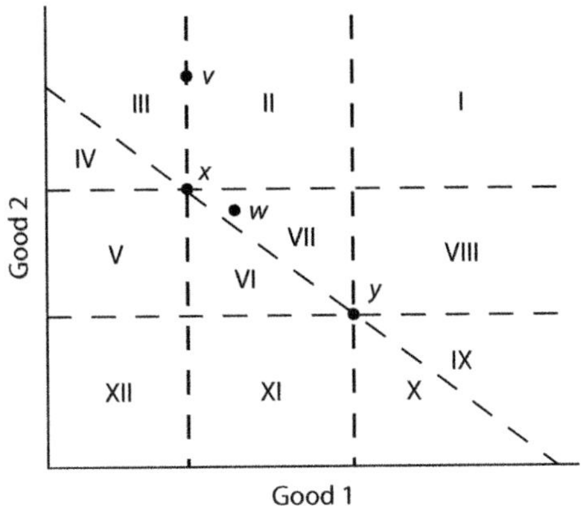

Figure 17.1. Free Pairs and Triples for Classical Public Goods Preferences.

For future reference, let $\mathcal{C}_{pu}$ denote the preference domain for this example. An alternative can be interpreted as being a vector of m public goods, with the individual preferences assumed to satisfy the usual regularity conditions found in microeconomic theory. Kalai, Muller, and Satterthwaite (1979) have shown that this preference domain is saturating. We sketch a proof for the case of $m = 2$.[24]

Step 1. We first identify the nontrivial pairs. Strict monotonicity of the preferences implies that any pair of alternatives $\{x, y\}$ with $x > y$ must be a trivial pair. It is easy to verify that if neither $x > y$ nor $y > x$ holds, then $\{x, y\}$ is nontrivial. Simple geometry can be used to confirm this fact. For example, the pair $\{x, y\}$ shown in Figure 17.1 is nontrivial.[25]

Step 2. We now identify the free triples. Consider the nontrivial pair $\{x, y\}$ shown in Figure 17.1. It is easy to check that $\{x, y, z\}$ is a free triple if and only if z is in one of the open regions marked III, VI, and IX. (If x is on the vertical axis, there is no region III. Analogously, if y is on the horizontal axis, there is no region IX.) For example, consider the free triple $A = \{x, y, z\}$ shown in Figure 17.2. There are thirteen (weak) orderings of A. Suppose, for concreteness, we want to confirm that there is an admissible preference ordering with xPy and yPz. In this case, using a preference ordering with indifference curves similar to those shown in Figure 17.2 will do. It is straightforward to check that for any of the other twelve orderings of A, there is an ordering R in the domain with

[24] The basic structure of the the proof when $m \geq 2$ is similar.

[25] Note that if the individual preference domains include all the continuous, monotone, and convex preference orderings (i.e., strict monotonicity is relaxed to monotonicity), a pair such as $\{v, x\}$ in Figure 17.1 is no longer trivial.

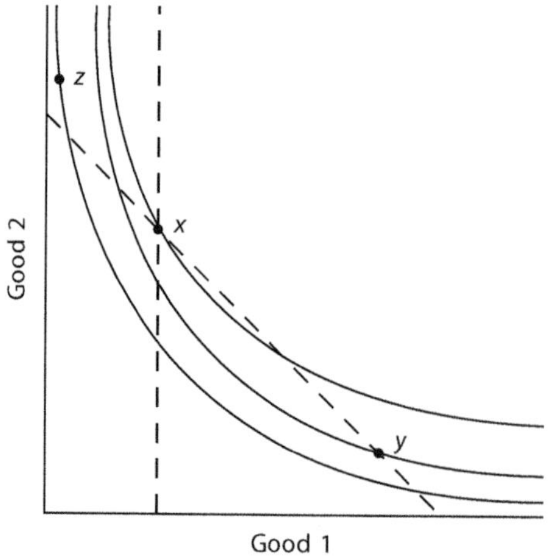

Figure 17.2. A Free Triple for Classical Public Goods Preferences.

$R|_A$ coinciding with the prespecified ordering of $\{x, y, z\}$. Strict monotonicity prevents any alternative in the regions marked I, II, V, VIII, XI, and XII in Figure 17.1 from being part of a free triple with x and y. Also requiring preferences to be convex precludes any alternative in the regions marked IV, VII, and X from being part of a free triple with x and y. For example, consider the alternative w shown in Figure 17.1 and suppose we want to have xIy and yPw. This is obviously impossible with strictly monotonic, convex preferences, so $\{w, x, y\}$ is not a free triple.

Step 3. We now show how to connect nontrivial pairs. Consider the two nontrivial pairs $\{x, y\}$ and $\{u, v\}$ shown in Figure 17.3. All four of these alternatives have been chosen to be in the positive orthant. We introduce two new alternatives w and z, with w lying on the vertical axis and z lying on the horizontal axis. By choosing these points to be sufficiently far from the origin, the preceding argument shows that $\{u, v, z\}$, $\{v, z, w\}$, $\{z, w, x\}$, and $\{w, x, y\}$ are free triples. Thus, by simply considering the two additional alternatives w and z, we are able to connect $\{u, v\}$ with $\{x, y\}$ using the sequence of nontrivial pairs $\{u, v\}$, $\{v, z\}$, $\{z, w\}$, $\{w, x\}$, and $\{x, y\}$. When either of the nontrivial pairs $\{x, y\}$ or $\{u, v\}$ has an element on one of the axes, the connection argument is not quite as easy. First, such a nontrivial pair must be connected to a nontrivial pair in the interior of X and then the argument proceeds as above.

In a series of articles summarized in Campbell (1992b, 1996), Campbell has developed an interesting variation of the local approach that can be used to show that economic domains like the one considered in Example 8 are Arrow-inconsistent. His approach may be illustrated using the preference domain of Example 8 with $m = 2$, but with $X = \mathbb{R}^2_{++}$.

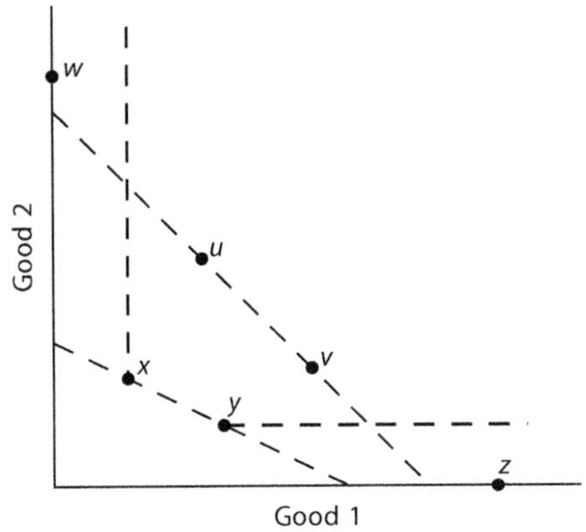

Figure 17.3. The Connection Argument for Classical Public Goods Preferences.

A *strictly convex downward-sloping curve* is the graph of a function $h: \mathbb{R}_{++} \to \mathbb{R}_{++}$ that is continuous, unbounded above, strictly convex, and decreasing. Let $\mathcal{I}$ be the set of all such curves. Each of the curves in $\mathcal{I}$ can be thought of as being a subset of the set of alternatives X. It is not difficult to see that for any $C \in \mathcal{I}$, any triple of distinct alternatives in C is a free triple. For example, if the curve C contains the alternatives x and y shown in Figure 17.1, then any third alternative z in C must lie either in region III, VI, or IX, which makes $\{x, y, z\}$ a free triple. If a social welfare function with this domain satisfies IIA and WP, Arrow's Theorem implies that there is a "local" dictator, say $i(C)$, on C. We claim that there exists an $i \in N$ such that $i(C) = i$ for all $C \in \mathcal{I}$. Consider two strictly convex downward-sloping curves C^1 and C^2 defined by the functions h^1 and h^2, respectively. If these curves intersect, then the curve C^3 defined by taking the supremum of $h^1(s)$ and $h^2(s)$ for all $s \in \mathbb{R}_{++}$ is also in $\mathcal{I}$. Because the curves C^1 and C^3 have more than one alternative in common (in fact, they have a continuum of alternatives in common), $i(C^1) = i(C^3)$. Similarly, $i(C^2) = i(C^3)$ and, hence, the dictators on C^1 and C^2 are the same. If C^1 and C^2 do not intersect, it is possible to find a third curve that intersects them both, and this curve can be used to connect the first two.[26]

Example 9 In this example, a preference ordering $R \in \mathcal{R}$ on a subset X of $\mathbb{R}^m$ is linear if there exists a $\pi \in \mathbb{R}^m$ such that for all $x, y \in X$, xRy if and only if $\pi x \geq \pi y$.[27] A linear preference ordering is continuous and has hyperplanes (linear surfaces) for indifference contours.

[26] If $X = \mathbb{R}^2_+$ instead of $\mathbb{R}^2_{++}$, the preceding argument does not show that the dictator on the interior of X is a dictator on all of X. To extend his argument to all of the non-negative orthant, Campbell assumed that social preferences are continuous.

[27] These linear preferences should not be confused with the linear preference orderings introduced earlier. Unfortunately, the same name is used for both kinds of preference. Except in this and the following example, a linear preference refers to an ordering for which no two distinct alternatives are indifferent.

The set of alternatives is $X = \mathbb{R}^m_+$ with $m \geq 3$ and the preference domain is the set of all profiles of continuous, strictly monotonic, and linear preference orderings on X. Kalai, Muller, and Satterthwaite (1979) have shown that this preference domain is saturating. We refer the reader to their article for the details. In fact, Kalai, Muller, and Satterthwaite used linear preferences to perform the connection operations in their proof that the preference domain in Example 8 is saturating when $m \geq 3$.

The assumption that $m \geq 3$ is essential for this domain of preferences to be saturating. Kalai, Muller, and Satterthwaite (1979) have shown that the preference domain considered in this example is Arrow-consistent when $m = 2$ and, hence, it is not saturating.[28] A social welfare function satisfying all of the Arrow axioms on this domain when $m = 2$ can be constructed as follows. For each profile of preferences in the domain, the social preference is set equal to the preference of the individual whose indifference curves have the median slope, with ties broken in favor of the smallest median slope if there are two medians.[29]

Example 10 In this example, X is the $(m-1)$-dimensional unit simplex $S^{m-1} = \{x \in \mathbb{R}^m_+ \mid \sum_{i=1}^m x_i = 1\}$. The preference domain is the set of all profiles of linear preference orderings on X, where a linear preference is as defined in Example 9. X can be interpreted as being the set of lotteries over m outcomes or prizes; that is, an alternative x is a probability vector with x_j being the probability of obtaining the jth prize. The common individual preference domain can then be interpreted as being the set of expected utility preferences axiomatized by von Neumann and Morgenstern (1947). The vector π that characterizes a linear preference ordering is the vector of von Neumann–Morgenstern utilities for the m prizes, where π_j is the von Neumann–Morgenstern utility of the jth prize. With this interpretation, x is weakly preferred to y if and only if the expected utility of the lottery x is at least as large as the expected utility of the lottery y.

For $m \geq 3$, Le Breton (1986) has shown that this preference domain is saturating. We outline the proof for the $m = 3$ case.[30]

Step 1. It is obvious that every pair is nontrivial.

Step 2. A triple $\{x, y, z\}$ is free if and only if its three elements are not colinear. For example, $\{x, y, z\}$ in Figure 17.4 is a free triple. If, for example, we want to find a linear preference ordering that has zPx and xIy, all of the indifference

[28] With a (strictly) monotone, linear preference ordering, the triple $\{x, y, z\}$ shown in Figure 17.2 is not free because it is not possible to have all three elements of the triple indifferent to each other.

[29] Kalai, Muller, and Satterthwaite (1979) do not include the tie-breaking rule, so their social welfare function is not well-defined if there are an even number of individuals. Tie-breaking rules other than the one considered here may not satisfy IIA. See Bossert and Weymark (1993) for a detailed discussion of this two-dimensional problem. Kalai, Muller, and Satterthwaite's analysis of this example is based, in part, on Nitzan (1976).

[30] Again, the argument is easily extended to higher dimensions. When $m = 2$, each person has only three possible preference orderings.

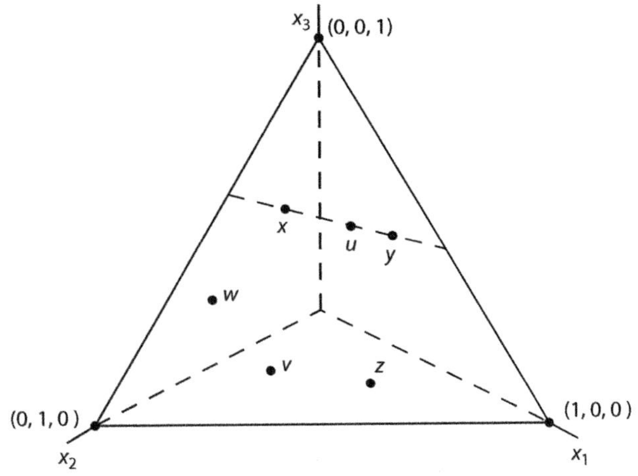

Figure 17.4. The Connection Argument for Expected Utility Preferences.

curves must be parallel to the dashed line through x and y with (0, 1, 0) being the most preferred alternative in X. It is easy to verify that each of the other possible configurations of preference on $\{x, y, z\}$ can be obtained with a linear preference.[31] A colinear triple such as $\{u, x, y\}$ in Figure 17.4 is not free; with linear preferences, if xIy, we must also have uIy.

Step 3. We now show how to connect nontrivial pairs. Consider the two pairs $\{x, y\}$ and $\{u, v\}$ shown in Figure 17.4. To make things interesting, we have chosen u so that it is colinear with x and y. It is clear that we can always choose two alternatives w and z in X so that each of the following triples consists of alternatives that are not colinear: $\{x, y, z\}$, $\{y, z, w\}$, $\{z, w, u\}$, and $\{w, u, v\}$. Figure 17.4 illustrates this construction. We connect $\{u, v\}$ with $\{x, y\}$ using the sequence of nontrivial pairs $\{x, y\}$, $\{y, z\}$, $\{z, w\}$, $\{w, u\}$, and $\{u, v\}$. Thus, we are able to connect the two nontrivial pairs $\{x, y\}$ and $\{u, v\}$ using only two additional alternatives, and this is the case even if any of the original alternatives lie on the boundary of X.[32]

Example 11 In this example, we further restrict the domain of classical public goods preferences considered in Example 8 by also assuming that preferences are analytic with

[31] If we want to have all three elements of the triple $\{x, y, z\}$ in Figure 17.4 indifferent to each other, then there must be universal indifference over all lotteries in X.

[32] Note that preferences are trivially strictly monotonic on a simplex. Thus, the preference domain in this example can be thought of as the restriction of the preference domain in the preceding example (where X is the non-negative orthant) to a simplex. On the non-negative orthant, strict monotonicity places considerable structure on the preferences, which helps account for the fact that the set of strictly monotone, linear preferences is saturating when the set of alternatives is the two-dimensional simplex, but it is not saturating when the set of alternatives is the two-dimensional non-negative orthant.

no critical points. Recall that $X = \mathbb{R}^m_+$ with $m \geq 2$ and $\mathcal{C}_{pu}$ is the common individual preference domain in Example 8. A preference R on a connected subset of $\mathbb{R}^m$ is analytic if it can be represented by an analytic utility function; that is, by a utility function that has the property that at any point x in the domain, there is a neighborhood of x on which the function can be expressed exactly as a Taylor series. A preference R on a connected subset of $\mathbb{R}^m$ has no critical point if it can be represented by a utility function whose gradient never vanishes. Let $\mathcal{M}_c$ denote the set of all strictly monotone, convex, analytic preferences with no critical points on $\mathbb{R}^m_+$. $\mathcal{M}_c$ is a subset of $\mathcal{C}_{pu}$. Many of the functional forms used for utility functions, such as Cobb–Douglas and CES, are analytic with no critical points, at least on the positive orthant.

Le Breton and Weymark (2002) have shown that the domain $\mathcal{M}_c^n$ is Arrow-inconsistent.[33] In fact, this domain is saturating, as we now show. Kannai (1974) has demonstrated that $\mathcal{M}_c$ is a dense subset of $\mathcal{C}_{pu}$.[34] It follows from this fact that the nontrivial pairs and free triples of $\mathcal{M}_c$ and $\mathcal{C}_{pu}$ are exactly the same. To see why, let $\{x, y, z\}$ be a free triple with respect to $\mathcal{C}_{pu}$. Let $R \in \mathcal{C}_{pu}$ be such that $xPyPz$. From Kannai's result, we then deduce that there exists a preference $R' \in \mathcal{M}_c$ such that $xP'yP'z$. This argument shows that any of six strict orderings on $\{x, y, z\}$ can be obtained with a preference in $\mathcal{M}_c$. To show that we can also obtain the other seven possible weak orderings, we use the preceding argument in conjunction with the fact that analyticity is preserved by convex combinations. For example, to obtain a preference $R \in \mathcal{M}_c$ with $xIyPz$, we first consider $R', R'' \in \mathcal{M}_c$ for which $xP'yP'z$ and $yP'xP'z$. Next, let U' and U'' be two analytic utility functions with no critical points representing R' and R'', respectively, and having values in $\mathbb{R}_+$. By choosing $\lambda \in [0, 1]$ appropriately, the utility function $\lambda U' + (1 - \lambda)U''$ represents a preference $R_\lambda \in \mathcal{M}_c$ for which $xI_\lambda yP_\lambda z$. Thus, the free triples of $\mathcal{M}_c$ and $\mathcal{C}_{pu}$ coincide. Similar arguments show that the nontrivial pairs coincide as well. Therefore, we can use the connection argument in Example 8 to show that $\mathcal{M}_c$ and, hence, $\mathcal{M}_c^n$ is saturating.

Example 12 In this example, we consider Euclidean spatial preferences. A preference $R \in \mathcal{R}$ on a subset X of $\mathbb{R}^m$ is a Euclidean spatial preference if there exists a point $\beta \in X$ such that for all $x, y \in X$, xRy if and only if $\|x - \beta\| \leq \|y - \beta\|$, where $\|\cdot\|$ denotes the Euclidean norm on $\mathbb{R}^m$.[35] With a Euclidean spatial preference, alternatives are ranked by their Euclidean distance from a point of global satiation β known as a bliss or an ideal point. A Euclidean spatial preference is analytic because it can be represented by a quadratic function with a critical point at the bliss point. When $m = 1$, a Euclidean

[33] Le Breton and Weymark assumed that all admissible preferences are strictly convex, not just convex, but this is not essential for their argument.

[34] A is a *dense* subset of B if B is contained in the closure of A.

[35] More generally, spatial preferences are convex preferences with a point of global satiation. We consider general spatial preferences in Section 16.3.

spatial preference is a continuous single-peaked preference that is symmetric with respect to the bliss point.

Spatial preferences are used extensively by political scientists in formal voting models. In these applications, X is referred to as an issue space. The coordinates of X might, for example, measure the budgets for different categories of public expenditure (police, garbage collection, etc.), with voters assumed to have spatial preferences. Spatial preferences are also found in some economic models of public good provision. In these applications, the presence of a satiation point arises because attention is restricted to allocations satisfying a budget constraint. For an introduction to spatial models, see Austen-Smith and Banks (1999).

For the case in which $X = \mathbb{R}^m$ with $m \geq 2$, Border (1984) has shown that Arrow's axioms are inconsistent on the domain of all profiles of Euclidean spatial preferences. Border's proof of this result is long and complicated.[36] An alternative way of establishing Border's theorem is to first show that this preference domain is saturating and then use Theorem 5 to conclude that the domain is Arrow-inconsistent. A proof along these lines, due to Le Breton, may be found in Le Breton and Weymark (1996). Both methods of proof take advantage of the fact that X has no boundary points. However, in spatial models, it is more natural to suppose that alternatives have non-negative components. Accordingly, here we suppose that $X = \mathbb{R}^m_+$.

Let $\mathcal{E}$ denote the set of all spatial preferences orderings on $\mathbb{R}^m_+$. Le Breton and Weymark (2002) have shown that the domain $\mathcal{E}^n$ is saturating when $m \geq 2$.[37] We provide an alternative proof that $\mathcal{E}^n$ is saturating for the case of $m = 2$.[38]

Step 1. It is obvious that every pair is nontrivial.

Step 2. Campbell (1993) has shown that if a triple $\{x, y, z\}$ is cocircular with a bliss point in the interior of X, then $\{x, y, z\}$ is a free triple. We illustrate the argument by showing that there exists an $R \in \mathcal{E}$ such that $xPyPz$. Consider the line segment $[x, y]$ joining x and y. Let H_{xy} be the line (hyperplane in higher dimensions) containing the midpoint of $[x, y]$ that is orthogonal to $[x, y]$. In spatial voting models, H_{xy} is referred to as the median line for the alternatives x and y. By assumption, x, y, and z are equidistant from a point β in the interior of X. Hence, by construction, β is in H_{xy}. Let A^1 and A^2 be, respectively, the short and the long arcs with extremities x and y on the circle with center β and radius $\|x - \beta\|$.[39] It is transparent from Figure 17.5 that if $z \in A^1$, then by moving β slightly farther from $\frac{(x+y)}{2}$, say to β', then we obtain a preference $R' \in \mathcal{E}$ for

[36] Redekop (1993c) has established a version of Border's Theorem that does not require the domain to include all profiles of Euclidean spatial preferences.

[37] Campbell (1993) has established a related result with the additional assumption that social preferences are continuous.

[38] This method of proof is easily generalized to higher dimensions.

[39] If the two arcs are the same length, they can be labeled arbitrarily.

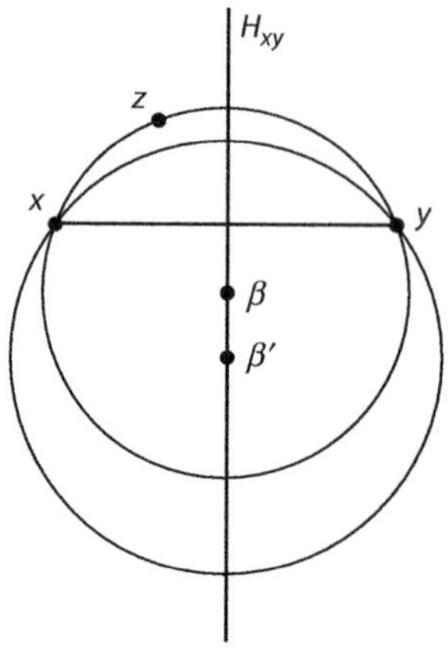

Figure 17.5. Free Triples for Euclidean Spatial Preferences.

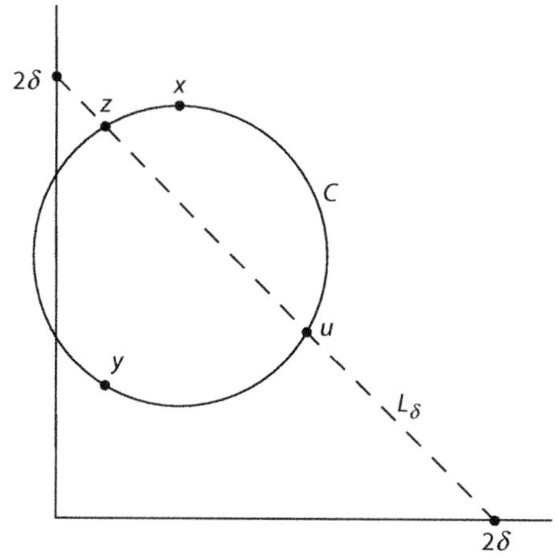

Figure 17.6. Step 3 of the Connection Argument for Euclidean Spatial Preferences.

which $xI'yP'z$. Note that this might not be possible if β is on the boundary of X. To obtain an $R \in \mathcal{E}$ for which $xPyPz$, one merely has to move β' slightly closer to x than to y. On the other hand, if $z \in A^2$, the preference R' in this argument is obtained by moving the bliss point β closer to $\frac{(x+y)}{2}$.

Step 3. We now show that any pair of alternatives is connected to a pair of alternatives whose corresponding median line is parallel to the 45° line. Let $\{x, y\}$ be an arbitrary pair in X and let C be a circle containing x and y whose bliss point β is in the interior of X. Let $\{L_\delta\}_{\delta \geq 0}$ be the family of lines that are orthogonal to the 45° line, parametrized by the point of intersection (δ, δ) with the 45° line. As illustrated in Figure 17.6, there exists a $\delta > 0$ and distinct $u, z \in \mathbb{R}^2_+ \setminus \{x, y\}$ such that $u, z \in C \cap L_\delta$. Because u, x, y, and z are cocircular and β is in the interior of X, it now follows from Step 2 that $\{x, y, z\}$ and $\{y, z, u\}$ are free

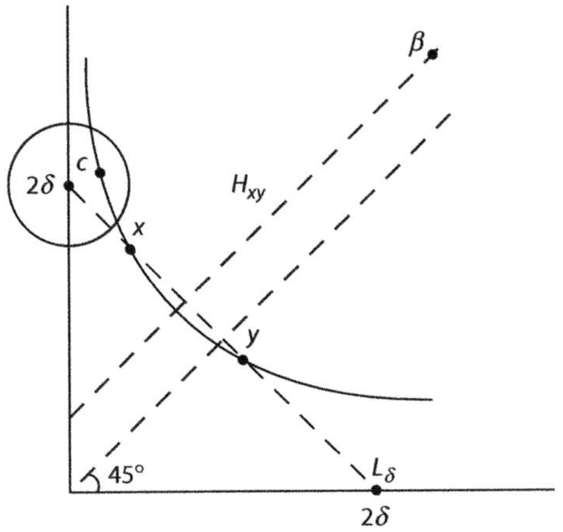

Figure 17.7. Step 4 of the Connection Argument for Euclidean Spatial Preferences.

triples. Hence, $\{x,y\}$ is connected to $\{z,u\}$. By construction the median line for $\{z,u\}$ is parallel to the 45° line.

Step 4. Next, we show that if u, x, y, and z are in $L_\delta \cap X$ for some $\delta > 0$, then $\{x,y\}$ and $\{z,u\}$ are connected. Let $\{x,y\}$ be a pair in $L_\delta \cap X$ with $\delta > 0$. Let $L_\delta^+ = \{c = (c_1,c_2) \in X \mid c_1 + c_2 > 2\delta\}$. We claim that there exists an $\varepsilon > 0$ such that $\{x,y,c\}$ is a free triple for all c in $[B((0,2\delta),\varepsilon) \cup B((2\delta,0),\varepsilon)] \cap L_\delta^+$, where $B(\bar{x},\varepsilon)$ is an open ball of radius ε centered at $\bar{x}$. The argument is illustrated in Figure 17.7. For concreteness, consider any $c \in B((0,2\delta),\varepsilon) \cap L_\delta^+$. By moving sufficiently far from the origin on H_{xy}, we can find a β such that x, y, and c are equidistant from β. It then follows from Step 2 that $\{x,y,c\}$ is a free triple.

To conclude the proof of this step, let ε be small enough for the claim to apply to each of the pairs $\{x,y\}$, $\{y,z\}$, and $\{z,u\}$. Again, for concreteness, consider any $c \in B((0,2\delta),\varepsilon) \cap L_\delta^+$. The pairs $\{x,y\}$ and $\{z,u\}$ are connected through the sequence of triples $\{x,y,c\}$, $\{y,c,z\}$, and $\{c,z,u\}$.

Step 5. Suppose that $0 < \delta < \delta'$. To complete the proof, we show that any pair in L_δ is connected to any pair in $L_{\delta'}$. Let β be the midpoint of the line segment $[(\delta,\delta),(\delta',\delta')]$, as illustrated in Figure 17.8. Choose $\varepsilon > 0$ sufficiently small that the circle centered at β with radius $\|\beta - (\delta,\delta)\| + \varepsilon$ intersects both $L_\delta \cap X$ and $L_{\delta'} \cap X$ twice. Let $\{x,y\}$ and $\{z,u\}$ be the points of intersection with L_δ and $L_{\delta'}$, respectively. By Step 2, $\{x,y,z\}$ and $\{y,z,u\}$ are free triples. Hence, $\{x,y\}$ is connected to $\{z,u\}$. It then follows from Step 4 that any pair in L_δ is connected to any pair in $L_{\delta'}$.[40]

[40] This proof makes use of the fact that the set of alternatives is unbounded from above. Ehlers and Storcken (2009) have shown that the domain of Euclidean spatial preferences is Arrow-inconsistent when X is contained in the closure of its interior and the interior of X is nonempty and connected. (As in Example 12, X is a subset of $\mathbb{R}^m$ with $m \geq 2$.) These assumptions are satisfied if X is a compact subset of $\mathbb{R}^m_+$ with a nonempty interior.

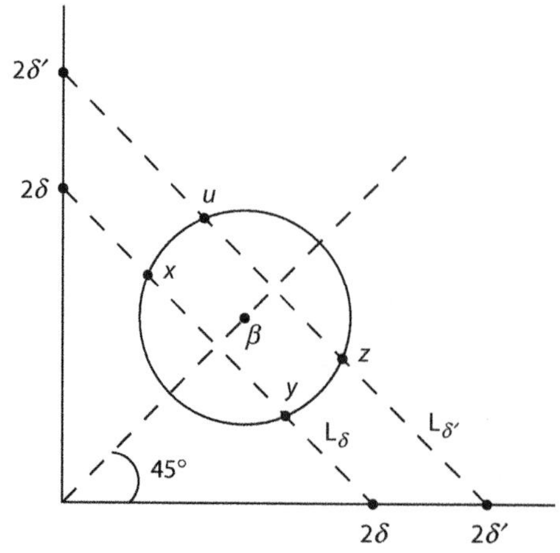

Figure 17.8. Step 5 of the Connection Argument for Euclidean Spatial Preferences.

Example 13 In this example, we consider continuous separable and continuous, additively separable preferences. Let $m \geq 2$ and suppose that X is a product set $X^1 \times X^2 \times \cdots \times X^m$, where each X^k is a subset of $\mathbb{R}$ with $|X^k| \geq 2$.[41] A preference ordering $R \in \mathcal{R}$ is separable if for all nonempty $\tilde{M} \subset M = \{1, \ldots, m\}$, all $z^{\tilde{M}}, u^{\tilde{M}} \in \Pi_{k \in \tilde{M}} X^k$, and all $x^{M \setminus \tilde{M}}, y^{M \setminus \tilde{M}} \in \Pi_{k \in M \setminus \tilde{M}} X^k$, $(x^{M \setminus \tilde{M}}, z^{\tilde{M}}) R (y^{M \setminus \tilde{M}}, z^{\tilde{M}})$ if and only if $(x^{M \setminus \tilde{M}}, u^{\tilde{M}}) R (y^{M \setminus \tilde{M}}, u^{\tilde{M}})$. With a separable preference, there are orderings on each of the components of X that are independent of the values of the other components. A preference ordering R is additively separable if for all $k \in M$, there exists a function $V^k \colon X^k \to \mathbb{R}$ such that for all $x, y \in X$, xRy if and only if $\sum_{k=1}^m V^k(x^k) \geq \sum_{k=1}^m V^k(y^k)$. In what follows, we denote by $\mathcal{R}_{CS}$ and $\mathcal{R}_{CAS}$, respectively, the set of continuous separable and continuous, additively separable preference orderings on X. Clearly, $\mathcal{R}_{CAS}$ is a subset of $\mathcal{R}_{CS}$.

The joint assumption that the set of alternatives is a product set and preferences are separable or additively separable has been considered by many authors from a strategic perspective. See, for example, Le Breton and Weymark (1999). Le Breton and Weymark have considered an example in which proportional taxes can be levied at different rates on the individual endowments of two private goods in order to finance the production of public goods. In their example, $X = [0, 1]^2$ is the set of possible pairs of tax rates and the individual preference domain is the subset of preferences in $\mathcal{R}_{CAS}$ that can be represented by continuously differentiable utility functions.

We show that $\mathcal{R}^n_{CAS}$ is saturating by demonstrating that $\mathcal{R}_{CAS}$ has the free triple property. A fortiori, $\mathcal{R}^n_{CS}$ is saturating as well.

[41] The following analysis can be easily generalized to the product of m metric spaces.

For any $x, y \in X$, let $M(x,y) = \{k \in M \mid x_k \neq y_k\}$ be the set of components on which x and y differ. Let $\{x,y,z\}$ be a triple of distinct alternatives in X. For concreteness, we show that there exists an R in $\mathcal{R}_{CAS}$ such that $xPyPz$. We consider three cases.

Case 1. $M(x,y) \cap M(x,z) \cap M(y,z) \neq \emptyset$. Consider $\bar{k} \in M(x,y) \cap M(x,z) \cap M(y,z)$. As in Example 7, we can construct a continuous function $V^{\bar{k}}\colon X^{\bar{k}} \to \mathbb{R}$ for which $V^{\bar{k}}(x_{\bar{k}}) = 2$, $V^{\bar{k}}(y_{\bar{k}}) = 1$, and $V^{\bar{k}}(z_{\bar{k}}) = 0$. For all other $k \in M$, let $V^k(w_k) = 0$ for all $w_k \in X^k$. The function $U = \sum_{k \in M} V^k$ is a utility function representing a preference $R \in \mathcal{R}_{CAS}$ for which $xPyPz$.

Case 2. $M(x,y) \cap M(x,z) = \emptyset$. Consider $\bar{k} \in M(x,z)$. By assumption, $x_{\bar{k}} = y_{\bar{k}}$. By Urysohn's Theorem, there exists a continuous function $V^{\bar{k}}\colon X^{\bar{k}} \to \mathbb{R}$ for which $V^{\bar{k}}(x_{\bar{k}}) = V^{\bar{k}}(y_{\bar{k}}) = 2$ and $V^{\bar{k}}(z_{\bar{k}}) = 0$. Next, consider $\tilde{k} \in M(x,y)$. By assumption, $x_{\tilde{k}} = z_{\tilde{k}}$. By Urysohn's Theorem, there exists a continuous function $V^{\tilde{k}}\colon X^{\tilde{k}} \to \mathbb{R}$ for which $V^{\tilde{k}}(x_{\tilde{k}}) = V^{\tilde{k}}(z_{\tilde{k}}) = 1$ and $V^{\tilde{k}}(y_{\tilde{k}}) = 0$. For all other $k \in M$, let $V^k(w_k) = 0$ for all $w_k \in X^k$. As in Case 1, the function $U = \sum_{k \in M} V^k$ is a utility function representing a preference $R \in \mathcal{R}_{CAS}$ for which $xPyPz$.

Case 3. $M(x,y) \cap M(x,z) \cap M(y,z) = \emptyset$ and $M(x,y) \cap M(x,z) \neq \emptyset$. For $\bar{k} \in M(x,y) \cap M(x,z)$, Urysohn's Theorem implies that there exists a continuous function $V^{\bar{k}}\colon X^{\bar{k}} \to \mathbb{R}$ for which $V^{\bar{k}}(x_{\bar{k}}) = 2$ and $V^{\bar{k}}(y_{\bar{k}}) = V^{\bar{k}}(z_{\bar{k}}) = 0$. For $\tilde{k} \in M(y,z)$, Urysohn's Theorem implies that there exists a continuous function $V^{\tilde{k}}\colon X^{\tilde{k}} \to \mathbb{R}$ for which $V^{\tilde{k}}(x_{\tilde{k}}) \in \{0,1\}$ (this value is 0 if $x_{\tilde{k}} = z_{\tilde{k}}$ and it is 1 if $x_{\tilde{k}} = y_{\tilde{k}}$), $V^{\tilde{k}}(y_{\tilde{k}}) = 1$, and $V^{\tilde{k}}(z_{\tilde{k}}) = 0$. For all other $k \in M$, let $V^k(w_k) = 0$ for all $w_k \in X^k$. As in the previous cases, the function $U = \sum_{k \in M} V^k$ is a utility function representing a preference $R \in \mathcal{R}_{CAS}$ for which $xPyPz$.

Similar constructions can be used to generate any of the other orderings of $\{x,y,z\}$.

Example 14 In this example, we consider a domain of preferences encountered in the study of income inequality. Let $X = S^{m-1}$ with $m \geq 3$ and suppose that the preference domain consists of all profiles of continuous and strictly Schur-convex orderings of X. An ordering R of S^{m-1} is strictly Schur-convex if for all $x, y \in X$, (a) xRy whenever $x = By$ for some bistochastic matrix B and (b) xPy whenever $x = By$ for some bistochastic matrix B that is not a permutation matrix.[42] The set X can be interpreted as being the set of all possible distributions of a unit of income, with the preference domain interpreted as being the set of all profiles of inequality orderings of X.[43] For symmetric orderings on

[42] A square matrix B is bistochastic if it is non-negative and all of its row and column sums are equal to one. A bistochastic matrix whose entries are all zeroes or ones is a permutation matrix.

[43] The details of this example are unchanged if there is any fixed amount of income $c > 0$ to distribute. Note that if $m = 2$, each person has only one possible preference ordering.

a simplex, strict Schur-convexity is equivalent to the Pigou–Dalton condition, which requires that an equalizing transfer from a richer to a poorer person results in a preferred distribution.[44]

Le Breton and Trannoy (1987) have shown that this preference domain is saturating. To show that all nontrivial pairs are connected involves introducing a rather large number of intermediate pairs, so we refer the reader to their article for the details of the argument.

In all the examples considered so far in this section, the preference domains are common and saturating. Hence, they are Arrow-inconsistent. We conclude this section with an example of a common preference domain that is Arrow-consistent and, therefore, not saturating. Nevertheless, in this example, there are subsets of alternatives on which the preference domain is saturating, so the local approach can be used to infer quite a bit about the structure of a social welfare function that satisfies the three Arrow axioms.

Example 15 In this example, individuals have probability relations on a finite set of events. We assume that there are $m \geq 4$ states of nature. Each state of nature corresponds to the possible realization of a random variable. An event is a subset of $M = \{1, \ldots, m\}$. The set of alternatives X is the set of all possible events. An ordinal probability is an ordering R on X that can be represented by a probability measure, that is, by a function p: $M \to [0,1]$ for which for all $x, y \in X$, xRy if and only if $\sum_{k \in x} p_k \geq \sum_{k \in y} p_k$, where $p_k = p(k)$. The preference domain is the set of all ordinal probabilities on X. This preference domain has been considered by Lainé, Le Breton, and Trannoy (1986) and Weymark (1997).

This example can be restated using the framework of Example 13. Let $X^* = \prod_{k \in M} X^{*k}$, where $X^{*k} = \{0,1\}$ for all $k \in M$. The event $x \in X$ can be reinterpreted as being the point $x^* \in X^*$ for which $x^*_k = 1$ if $k \in x$ and $x^*_k = 0$ if $k \notin x$. With this reinterpretation, the set of ordinal probabilities on X^* is a strict subset of $\mathcal{R}_{CAS}$, the set of continuous, additively separable preferences on X^*.[45] The set inclusion is strict because an ordinal probability satisfies monotonicity, among other properties.

In terms of our initial formulation of this example, any triple of events in which no event is a subset of any other event in the triple is free. To see why, let $\{x, y, z\}$ be such a triple of events. Let $w = x \cap y \cap z$. By assumption, $\bar{x} = x \backslash w$, $\bar{y} = y \backslash w$, and $\bar{z} = z \backslash w$ are all nonempty. By construction, $\bar{x} \cap \bar{y} \cap \bar{z} = \emptyset$. Suppose, for example, that we want to find an ordinal probability R for which $xPyPz$. We consider two cases.

Case 1. $\bar{x} \cap \bar{y} \neq \emptyset$. In this case, we choose a probability measure p on X such that $\sum_{k \in \bar{x} \cap \bar{y}} p_k = 1 - \varepsilon$ and $\sum_{k \in \bar{x} \backslash \bar{y}} p_k = \varepsilon$, where $\varepsilon > 0$. Note that $p_i = 0$ for all

[44] In this application, a preference order R on S^{m-1} is symmetric if for all $x, y \in X$, xIy whenever $x = By$ for some permutation matrix B.

[45] Continuity is vacuous in this finite setting.

$i \in w$. Because $\bar{x} \cap \bar{y} \cap \bar{z} = \emptyset$, for sufficiently small ε, this p represents an ordinal probability for which $xPyPz$.

Case 2. $\bar{x} \cap \bar{y} = \emptyset$. By construction, $\bar{x} \backslash \bar{z} \neq \emptyset$ and $\bar{y} \backslash \bar{z} \neq \emptyset$. In this case, we choose p such that $\sum_{k \in \bar{x} \backslash \bar{z}} p_k = 1 - \varepsilon$ and $\sum_{k \in \bar{y} \backslash \bar{z}} p_k = \varepsilon$, where $\varepsilon > 0$. As in Case 1, when ε is sufficiently small, p represents an ordinal probability for which $xPyPz$.

All of the other orderings of $\{x, y, z\}$ can be obtained in a similar fashion.

It follows from the preceding discussion that if neither $x \subseteq y$ nor $y \subseteq x$, then $\{x, y\}$ is a free pair. A pair of events $\{x, y\}$ for which $x \subset y$ is neither trivial nor free if $x \neq \emptyset$ or $y \neq M$. The reason is that an ordinal probability can rank these events in only one of two ways: xIy or yPx. Hence, this preference domain is not saturating. Because M is always more likely than $\emptyset$, $\{\emptyset, M\}$ is a trivial pair. In fact, this is the only trivial pair.

Let $X(k)$ denote the set of all events containing exactly k states. For $k \notin \{0, m\}$, because no two events in $X(k)$ can be ordered by set inclusion, the restriction of the preference domain to $X(k)$ has the free triple property. Thus, restricted to $X(k)$ for $k \notin \{0, m\}$, the preference domain is saturating. More generally, Lainé, Le Breton, and Trannoy (1986) have shown that any nontrivial pair of events can be connected to any other pair of nontrivial events provided that neither of the event pairs is a single-state event and its complement.[46] The problem with a pair such as $\{\{1\}, \{2, 3, \ldots, m\}\}$ is that any other event must be a subset or superset of one of these two events, so the pair cannot be embedded in a free triple.

Now consider a social welfare function defined on the domain of profiles of ordinal probabilities satisfying IIA and WP. Lainé, Le Breton, and Trannoy (1986) have shown that there is an individual d who is a dictator on any ordered pair of events (x, y) for which (i) $|x| > 1$ or (ii) $|x| = 1$ and y is not the complement of x.[47] We sketch the proof.

In view of the preceding discussion, the argument used to establish the Kalai–Muller–Satterthwaite Theorem shows that there is an individual d who is a dictator on any nontrivial pair except a single-set event and its complement. If $x \subseteq y$, no ordinal probability R can have xPy, so d is trivially a dictator on the ordered pair (x, y) when $x \subseteq y$. Because everyone ranks M above $\emptyset$, *WP* implies that d dictates on the ordered pair $(M, \emptyset)$.

To show that d dictates on the ordered pair $(\{1, 2\}, \{1\})$, consider a profile $\mathbf{R}$ in which $\{1, 2\} P_d \{1\}$. Because $\{\{1, 2\}, \{1, 3\}\}$ is a free pair, there exists a profile $\mathbf{R}'$ of ordinal probabilities with the properties that (i) $\{1, 2\} P'_d \{1, 3\}$, (ii) $\{1, 3\} P'_i \{1\}$ for all $i \in N$, and (iii) for all $i \in N$, $\{1, 2\} P'_i \{1\}$ if and only if $\{1, 2\} P_i \{1\}$. Because d is a dictator on $\{\{1, 2\}, \{1, 3\}\}$, we have $\{1, 2\} P' \{1, 3\}$. By WP, we have $\{1, 3\} P' \{1\}$. Transitivity of P' then implies that $\{1, 2\} P' \{1\}$. Hence, by IIA, $\{1, 2\} P \{1\}$ and, therefore, d is a dictator on $(\{1, 2\}, \{1\})$.

[46] This is not true if there are only three states. For example, it is not possible to connect $\{\{1\}, \{2\}\}$ with $\{\{1, 2\}, \{2, 3\}\}$ when $m = 3$ because there are no free triples containing two events with different cardinalities.

[47] The same conclusion holds when $m = 3$ if the social preference relation is also required to be an ordinal probability.

Similar arguments can be used to show that d is a dictator on any of the other ordered pairs not yet considered except a pair of the form $\{\{k\}, M\backslash\{k\}\}$. We cannot utilize a third event, as above, to show that d dictates on this pair because this third event, say x, must be a superset of $\{k\}$, and no ordinal probability can rank $\{k\}$ above x, as would be required to appeal to WP.[48]

6. TOPOLOGICAL DOMAIN RESTRICTIONS FOR PUBLIC GOODS

In the preceding two sections, we have shown that saturating preference domains are Arrow-inconsistent and that many domains of economic preferences are saturating. In a series of articles, Redekop (1991, 1993a, 1993c, 1996) has identified topological restrictions on the preference domain that imply that the domain is Arrow-inconsistent. Redekop begins by first restricting the set of admissible preference profiles to a domain of economic preferences that is Arrow-inconsistent. He then shows that in order for a subset of this domain to be Arrow-consistent, it must be topologically small. Redekop has considered two different ways of formalizing the idea that a preference domain is topologically small. They both capture the idea that topologically small preference domains do not exhibit much diversity in preference. Thus, Redekop's theorems demonstrate that if the domain exhibits much preference diversity, then it is Arrow-inconsistent. More precisely, if the basic structure of the preference domain is not altered by small perturbations in the preferences, then it is Arrow-inconsistent.

In this section, we provide an introduction to Redekop's work by considering one of his theorems and its proof in some detail. The strategy used in this proof has been adapted by Redekop to show the Arrow-inconsistency of a wide variety of economic preference domains. While we briefly describe some of these results in this section, it is not possible to consider them in any detail. More detail may be found in Redekop (1995), which is a relatively nontechnical survey of the theorems established in Redekop (1991, 1993a, 1993c, 1996). We also comment on how Redekop's domain restrictions and proof strategy are related to saturating domains and the local approach.

In the theorem we consider in this section, $X = \mathbb{R}^m_+$ with $m \geq 2$. An alternative in X is interpreted as being a vector of m public goods. Individual preferences are a priori restricted to be continuous and monotonic. Let $\mathcal{C}_{cm}$ denote the set of all such preference orderings on X. The universal domain of preference profiles is thus $\mathcal{C}^n_{cm}$.

A *topology* on a set S is a collection of subsets $\mathcal{T}$ of S that includes (i) both S and $\emptyset$, (ii) all finite intersections of sets in $\mathcal{T}$, and (iii) all unions of sets in $\mathcal{T}$. The sets in $\mathcal{T}$

48 For further discussion of Arrovian aggregation of ordinal probabilities, see Lainé, Le Breton, and Trannoy (1986) and Weymark (1997).

are the open subsets of S. A *basis* for $\mathcal{T}$ is a collection of sets contained in $\mathcal{T}$ with the property that any nonempty set in $\mathcal{T}$ is the union of sets in the basis. Thus, a topology is characterized by a basis. The sets in a basis are called *basic open sets*. For a topology on $\mathcal{C}_{cm}$, we use the questionnaire topology $\mathcal{T}_Q$ introduced in Redekop (1993b).[49] A basis for $\mathcal{T}_Q$ is the collection of sets of the form:

$$Q((x_1, y_1), \ldots, (x_r, y_r)) = \bigcap_{i=1}^{r} \{R \in \mathcal{C}_{cm} \mid x_i P y_i\},$$

where the x_i and y_i are alternatives in X. A basic open set is constructed by specifying strict rankings for a finite number of paired comparisons and then identifying all of the continuous monotonic preferences that exhibit these rankings. A subset of a topological space is *somewhere dense* if its closure contains an open set; otherwise, it is *nowhere dense*. It is natural to regard an individual preference domain as being topologically small if it is nowhere dense with respect to the questionnaire topology.

Suppose that the preference domain is common and that the individual preference domain $\mathcal{D}_*$ is a subset of $\mathcal{C}_{cm}$. Redekop (1991) has shown that a necessary condition for $\mathcal{D} = \mathcal{D}_*^n$ to be Arrow-consistent is that $\mathcal{D}_*$ be nowhere dense. Equivalently, a sufficient condition for $\mathcal{D}_*^n$ to be Arrow-inconsistent is that $\mathcal{D}_*$ be somewhere dense.

Theorem 7 *If $X = \mathbb{R}_+^m$ with $m \geq 2$ and $\mathcal{D}_* \subseteq \mathcal{C}_{cm}$ is somewhere dense, then there is no social welfare function $F\colon \mathcal{D}_*^n \rightarrow \mathcal{R}$ that satisfies* IIA, WP, *and* ND.

Thus, a preference domain $\mathcal{D}_*^n \subseteq \mathcal{C}_{cm}^n$ is Arrow-inconsistent if the closure of the individual preference domain contains at least one basic open set of preferences. A basic open set of preferences exhibits sufficient preference diversity for Arrow's axioms to be incompatible because, in addition to the restrictions imposed by continuity and monotonicity, the pairwise rankings are only restricted on a finite number of pairs of alternatives.

Theorem 7 is established by showing that there is a dictator if the individual preference domain is somewhere dense and the social welfare function F satisfies IIA and WP. The proof has three main parts. First, it is shown that for every $x \in X$, there is an open set $O(x) \subseteq X$ containing x and an individual $d(x) \in N$ such that $d(x)$ is a dictator on $O(x)$. Such an individual is called a *local dictator*. Second, it is shown that the same individual, say d, is a local dictator for all $x \in X$. These results only establish that d is a dictator on pairs of alternatives that are close together in the sense that they are in the same open set $O(x)$ for some $x \in X$. The final part of the proof shows that, in fact, d is a dictator on all of X.

[49] More familiar topologies for a space of preferences are the Kannai (1970) topology and the topology of closed convergence. Redekop (1993b) has shown that these two topologies coincide with the questionnaire topology on $\mathcal{C}_{cm}$.

To show that there is a local dictator for each $x \in X$, Redekop used an innovative version of the local approach. To describe it, we need to introduce some further definitions. A subset A of X is *strictly free* with respect to $\mathcal{D}_*$ if $\mathcal{L}|_A \subseteq \mathcal{D}_*|_A$; that is, every linear ordering of the alternatives in A is feasible. Two pairs $A, B \subseteq X$ are *strictly connected* with respect to $\mathcal{D}_*$ if there exists a sequence of pairs in X, $A_1, \ldots, A_r$, with $A_1 = A$ and $A_r = B$ such that $A_j \cup A_{j+1}$ is a strict free triple with respect to $\mathcal{D}_*$ for all $j = 1, \ldots, r-1$. An individual $d \in N$ is a *strict dictator* on $\{x, y\} \subseteq X$ if xPy for all $\mathbf{R} \in \mathcal{D}$ for which $xP_d y$ and $\neg(xI_i y)$ for all $i \neq d$. A set $A \subseteq X$ is *coordinatewise undominated* if $x \not\geq y$ and $y \not\geq x$ for all distinct $x, y \in A$.

Redekop's proof begins by identifying an open set $O'(x)$ containing x in which every triple that is coordinatewise undominated is a strict free triple. By the linear preference version of Arrow's theorem, there is a strict dictator on these triples. Next, it is shown that there is an open subset $O(x)$ of $O'(x)$ containing x in which coordinatewise undominated pairs are strictly connected, from which it follows that there is a strict dictator on all such pairs. To complete the first part of the proof, it remains to show that this implies that there is a dictator on $O(x)$. As Redekop (1991, p. 408) has noted, his approach is doubly local because he uses a version of the Kalai–Muller–Satterthwaite local approach on a small open set. We now turn to the details of this argument.

Lemma 1 *If $X = \mathbb{R}^m_+$ with $m \geq 2$, $\mathcal{D}_* \subseteq \mathcal{C}_{cm}$ is somewhere dense, and $F: \mathcal{D}^n_* \to \mathcal{R}$ is a social welfare function that satisfies* IIA *and* WP, *then, for all $x \in X$, there is a local dictator.*

Proof. The proof proceeds in a series of steps. The first five steps only assume that $\mathcal{D}_*$ is a somewhere dense subset of $\mathcal{C}_{cm}$.

Step 1. Let O be an open subset of $\mathcal{C}_{cm}$ and U_R be a continuous utility representation of $R \in O$. We first show that there exists an $\bar{\varepsilon} > 0$ such that whenever $0 < \varepsilon < \bar{\varepsilon}$ and $g: X \to [0,1]$ is a continuous nondecreasing function, then $R_\varepsilon \in O$, where R_ε is defined by

$$xR_\varepsilon y \leftrightarrow U_R(x) + \varepsilon g(x) \geq U_R(y) + \varepsilon g(y)$$

for all $x, y \in X$.[50] Because O is open, it contains a basic open set $B = Q((x_1, y_1), \ldots, (x_r, y_r))$, where $x_j P y_j$ for all $j = 1, \ldots, r$. Let

$$\bar{\varepsilon} = \frac{1}{2} \min_{1 \leq j \leq r} [U_R(x_j) - U_R(y_j)].$$

It is straightforward to verify that $U_R(x_j) + \varepsilon g(x_j) > U_R(y_j) + \varepsilon g(y_j)$ for all $j = 1, \ldots, r$ when $0 < \varepsilon < \bar{\varepsilon}$. Hence, $R_\varepsilon \in B \subseteq O$.

50 A function $g: \mathbb{R}^m_+ \to \mathbb{R}$ is *nondecreasing* if $g(x) \geq g(y)$ for all $x, y \in \mathbb{R}^m_+$ for which $x \gg y$. Note that because the inequality in this definition is weak, g may not represent a monotone preference. However, because R is monotone, so is R_ε when g is nondecreasing.

Step 2. Consider any coordinatewise undominated subset $\{a,b,c\}$ of X. For all $y \in \{a,b,c\}$, let $A_y = \{z \in X \mid z \geq y\}$. Define the function $\rho_y\colon X \to \mathbb{R}$ by setting

$$\rho_y(x) = \min_{z \in A_y} \|x - z\|$$

for all $x \in X$. Let

$$m = \min_{x \neq y} \rho_y(x),$$

where the minimum is taken over pairs $\{x,y\} \subseteq \{a,b,c\}$ for which $x \neq y$. Because $x \notin A_y$ for all such pairs and the A_y are closed, $m > 0$. Now define the functions $h_a\colon X \to [0,1]$ and $h_b\colon X \to [0,1]$ by setting, for all $x \in X$,

$$h_a(x) = 1 - \frac{\min(m, \rho_a(x))}{m}$$

and

$$h_b(x) = 1 - \frac{\min(m, \rho_b(x))}{m}.$$

The function h_α, $\alpha = a,b$, assigns a value of 1 to all $x \in A_\alpha$, a value of 0 to all x that are at least distance m from A_α, and a value of $1 - \|z - A_\alpha\|$ to all other x. Hence, h_a and h_b are both continuous and nondecreasing. Further, because of the way m has been chosen, $h_a(a) = h_b(b) = 1$ and $h_a(b) = h_a(c) = h_b(a) = h_b(c) = 0$.

Step 3. We now show that for all $x \in X$, there exists an open subset $O'(x)$ of X containing x such that any coordinatewise undominated triple in $O'(x)$ is a strict free triple with respect to the closure $\bar{\mathcal{D}}_*$ of $\mathcal{D}_*$.

Because $\mathcal{D}_*$ is somewhere dense in $\mathcal{C}_{cm}$, there exists a basic open set B contained in $\bar{\mathcal{D}}_*$. Consider any $R \in B$. Let U be a continuous utility representation of R. Define $\bar{\varepsilon}$ as in Step 1. For $0 < \varepsilon < \bar{\varepsilon}$, by the continuity of U at x, we can choose δ sufficiently small so that

$$\sup_{\|z-x\|<\delta} |U(x) - U(z)| < \frac{\varepsilon}{9}.$$

Let

$$O'(x) = \{z \in X \mid \|z - x\| < \delta\}.$$

To complete the proof of this step, we consider any coordinatewise undominated subset $\{a,b,c\}$ of $O'(x)$ and, without loss of generality, show that we can find an $R' \in B$ such that $aP'bP'c$.

For the set $\{a, b, c\}$, define the functions h_a and h_b as in Step 2. Let $g\colon X \to [0, 1]$ be the function defined by setting, for all $z \in X$,

$$g(z) = \frac{2}{3}h_a(z) + \frac{1}{3}h_b(z).$$

Because h_a and h_b are continuous and nondecreasing, so is g. Hence, using g to define R_ε as in Step 1, we conclude that $R_\varepsilon \in B$ when $0 < \varepsilon < \bar{\varepsilon}$.

By construction, $g(a) = \frac{2}{3}$, $g(b) = \frac{1}{3}$, and $g(c) = 0$. Therefore,

$$\begin{aligned}[U(a) + \varepsilon g(a)] - [U(b) + \varepsilon g(b)] &= \frac{1}{3}\varepsilon + [U(a) - U(b)] \\ &\geq \frac{1}{3}\varepsilon - |U(a) - U(b)| \\ &\geq \frac{1}{3}\varepsilon - |U(a) - U(x)| - |U(b) - U(x)] \\ &> \frac{\varepsilon}{9},\end{aligned}$$

where the last inequality follows from the choice of the δ used to construct $O'(x)$. Hence, $aP_\varepsilon b$. We can similarly show that $bP_\varepsilon c$. Setting $R' = R_\varepsilon$ for any $0 < \varepsilon < \bar{\varepsilon}$ completes the proof of this step.

Step 4. Suppose that $R \in \bar{\mathcal{D}}_*$ is such that $\bar{x}P\bar{y}P\bar{z}$. Because sets of the form $\{\bar{R} \in \mathcal{C}_{cm} \mid a\bar{P}b\}$ are open, there must exist an $R' \in \mathcal{D}_*$ such that $\bar{x}P'\bar{y}P'\bar{z}$. Hence, if $\{x, y, z\}$ is a strict free triple with respect to $\bar{\mathcal{D}}_*$, it is also a strict free triple with respect to $\mathcal{D}_*$. By Step 3, we therefore conclude that any coordinatewise undominated triple in $O'(x)$ is a strict free triple with respect to $\mathcal{D}_*$.

Step 5. Next, we show that there exists an open set $O(x) \subseteq O'(x)$ containing x with the property that if $\{v, w, y, z\} \subset O(x)$ and both $\{v, w\}$ and $\{y, z\}$ are coordinatewise undominated, then $\{v, w\}$ and $\{y, z\}$ are strictly connected with respect to $\mathcal{D}_*$.

We first consider the case in which x has at least two positive components. Without loss of generality, we assume that $x_1 > 0$ and $x_2 > 0$. The proof is similar to the one used to establish Step 3 in Example 8 (and illustrated in Figure 17.3). However, in order to use Step 4 to identify strict free triples, now the two alternatives, say s and t, that are used to form the intermediate pairs in the connection argument must be chosen from $O'(x)$. Further, in order for s and t to form a strict free triple with either $\{v, w\}$ or $\{y, z\}$, v, w, y, and z must be sufficiently close together. This will be the case if $\{v, w, y, z\} \subset O(x)$, where

$$O(x) = \{z \in X \mid \|z - x\| < \Delta\}$$

for $\Delta > 0$ sufficiently small that (i) $\|z - x\| < 3\Delta$ implies $z \in O'(x)$ and (ii) $\Delta < \min(x_1/3, x_2/3)$. If we now let $s = x + 2\Delta(1, -1, 0, \ldots, 0)$ and $t = x + 2\Delta(-1, 1, 0, \ldots, 0)$, we have $\{s, t\} \subset O'(x) \backslash O(x)$. In addition, s and t either singly or jointly form a coordinatewise undominated set when combined with any coordinatewise undominated subset of $O(x)$. Suppose that $\{v, w\}$ and $\{y, z\}$ are coordinatewise undominated subsets of $O(x)$. It then follows from Step 4 that $\{v, w, s\}$, $\{w, s, t\}$, $\{s, t, y\}$, and $\{t, y, z\}$ are strict free triples. Hence, $\{v, w\}$ and $\{y, z\}$ are strictly connected with respect to $\mathcal{D}_*$.

If x has at most one positive component, the connection argument is somewhat more complex. See Redekop (1991, pp. 416–417) for the details.

Step 6. Henceforth, we assume that $F\colon \mathcal{D}_*^n \to \mathcal{R}$ is a social welfare function that satisfies IIA and WP. We now show that some individual is a strict dictator for all distinct $\{y, z\} \subset O(x)$.

If $\{y, z\}$ is coordinatewise undominated, we can find a third alternative $w \in O(x)$ such that $\{w, y, z\}$ is coordinatewise undominated. By Step 4, this is a strict free triple. Hence, by the linear preference version of Arrow's Theorem, there is a strict dictator, say $d(x)$, on this triple. By Step 5, $\{y, z\}$ can be strictly connected to any other coordinatewise undominated pair in $O(x)$. Hence, by the argument used in the proof of Theorem 5, $d(x)$ is a strict dictator on all coordinatewise undominated pairs in $O(x)$.

Now consider the case in which $y > z$, $yP_{d(x)}z$, and $\neg(yI_jz)$ for all $j \neq d(x)$. Because preferences are monotone, this is only possible if yP_iz for all $i \in N$. Hence, by WP, we have yPz. Thus, $d(x)$ is a strict dictator for all distinct $\{y, z\} \subset O(x)$.

Step 7. Finally, we show that $d(x)$ is a dictator on $O(x)$. Consider any distinct $y, z \in O(x)$ and suppose that $yP_{d(x)}z$. Let $J_1 = \{j \in N \mid yP_jz\}$ and $J_2 = \{j \in N \mid zP_jy\}$. Because preferences are continuous, (i) for all $j \in J_1$, we can find an open set $O_j(z)$ containing z such that yP_jw for all $w \in O_j(z)$ and (ii) for all $j \in J_2$, we can find an open set $O_j(z)$ containing z such that wP_jz for all $w \in O_j(z)$. Because $\tilde{O} = O(x) \bigcap_{j \in (J_1 \cup J_2)} O_j(z)$ is an open set containing z, we can find a $v \in \tilde{O}$ with $v \gg z$. Everybody has a strict preference on $\{v, y\}$. In particular, $yP_{d(x)}v$. Hence, by Step 6, we have yPv. WP and the monotonicity of preferences imply that vPz. Transitivity of P then implies that yPz, so $d(x)$ is a dictator on $O(x)$. □

The use of the linear preference version of Arrow's Theorem in the proof of Lemma 1 is essential. To see why, suppose that $\mathcal{D}_* = \{R \in \mathcal{C}_{cm} \mid \neg(xIy)\}$ for some coordinatewise undominated pair of alternatives $\{x, y\}$. It is clear from the definition of the questionnaire topology that $\mathcal{D}_*$ is itself an open set, so $\mathcal{D}_*$ is somewhere dense. However, $\{x, y\}$ is not part of any free triple.

The next part of the proof of Theorem 7 establishes that the same person is the local dictator for all $x \in X$.

Lemma 2 *If $X = \mathbb{R}^m_+$ with $m \geq 2$, $\mathcal{D}_* \subseteq \mathcal{C}_{cm}$ is somewhere dense, and for all $x \in X$, there is a local dictator $d(x)$, then there is a $d \in N$ such that $d = d(x)$ for all $x \in X$.*

Proof. For all $x \in X$, let $O(x)$ be an open set containing x on which $d(x)$ is a local dictator. By Step 4 of the preceding proof, we can choose $O(x)$ sufficiently small so that every coordinatewise undominated pair in $O(x)$ is strictly free. For all $i \in N$, let $X_i = \{\cup_{x \in X} O(x) \mid i = d(x)\}$. These are open sets that cover X. If $X_i = \emptyset$ for all $i \neq d$, then d is a local dictator for all $x \in X$. Because X is connected, the only other possibility is that there exist distinct $i, j \in N$ such that $X_i \cap X_j$ contains a coordinatewise undominated pair $\{y, z\}$. But then there exists a profile $\mathbf{R} \in \mathcal{D}$ in which yP_iz and zP_jy. Because both i and j dictate on this pair, we have a contradiction. Hence, this case is not possible. □

The proof of Theorem 7 is completed by showing that the local dictator in Lemma 2 in fact dictates on all of X. The proof makes use of a property of preferences that Redekop (1991) calls the continuous climb property. A preference ordering R on X (i) satisfies the *continuous climb property for the ordered pair* (x, y) if xPy and there exists a continuous function $\gamma : [0,1] \to X$ such that $\gamma(0) = y$, $\gamma(1) = x$, and $\gamma(s)P\gamma(t)$ whenever $s > t$ and (ii) it satisfies the *continuous climb property* if it satisfies the continuous climb property for all ordered pairs (x, y) for which xPy. It is quite easy to show that if R is strictly monotonic, then R has the continuous climb property. Unfortunately, if a preference is monotonic, but not strictly monotonic, such a path may not exist if x or y is on the boundary of X. The following example, due to Redekop (1991), illustrates the problem.

Example 16 Let $X = \mathbb{R}^2_+$ and suppose that R is represented by a utility function U for which (i) $U(x) = x_1$ if $x_1 \leq 1$ and (ii) $U(x) = 1 + (x_1 - 1)x_2$ otherwise. Note that $R \in \mathcal{C}_{cm}$. Let $x = (2, 0)$ and $y = (0, 1)$. We have xPy, but there is no alternative near x that is worse than x according to R and, hence, no path with the continuous climb property connects x and y.

Proof of Theorem 7. Let d be the local dictator identified in Lemma 2. Consider a profile $\mathbf{R} \in \mathcal{D}$ and a pair of alternatives $x, y \in X$ for which xP_dy.

First, suppose that R_d satisfies the continuous climb property for (x, y) and let Γ be a continuous monotonic path (with respect to R_d) from y to x. For all $z \in \Gamma$, let $O(z)$ be the open set identified in Lemma 1. Because these sets cover Γ and Γ is compact, a finite subset of these sets also covers Γ. Let $\{O(z_1), \ldots, O(z_r)\}$ be such a finite cover, where $z_rP_dz_{r-1}P_d \cdots P_dz_1$. Let $\{x_1, \ldots, x_{r+1}\}$ be such that $\{x_k, x_{k+1}\} \subset O(z_k)$ for all $k = 1, \ldots, r$ with $x_1 = y$ and $x_r = x$. Because d dictates on each of the $O(z_k)$, we have $x_{k+1}Px_k$ for all $k = 1, \ldots, r$. Transitivity then implies that xPy.

Now, suppose that R_d does not satisfy the continuous climb property for (x, y). This can only occur if x is on the boundary of X with $x \neq 0_m$. If $y = \lambda x$ for some $\lambda \in [0, 1)$, then for any strictly monotonic preference $R'_d \in \mathcal{D}_*$, the profiles $\mathbf{R}$ and $\mathbf{R}' = (R_1, \ldots, R_{d-1}, R'_d, R_{d+1}, \ldots, R_n)$ coincide on $\{x, y\}$. Because R'_d satisfies the continuous climb property, by the first part of this proof, we have $xP'y$. Hence, by IIA, we also have xPy.

The argument when $y \neq \lambda x$ for some $\lambda \in [0, 1)$ is quite lengthy, so we only sketch the main idea. A complete proof may be found in Redekop (1991). In this case, it can be shown that there exist $\bar{\lambda} \in (0, 1)$, $z \in \mathbb{R}^m_{++}$, and $R_d \in \mathcal{C}_{cm}$ such that (i) d dictates on $(\bar{\lambda}x, z)$ and (ii) $xP_d(\bar{\lambda}x)P_d zP_d y$. We have already established that $xP(\bar{\lambda}x)$ and zPy. Because d dictates on $(\bar{\lambda}x, z)$, we therefore have xPy by the transitivity of R. □

The complications that arise in the last step of the proof would not occur if the domain only included strictly monotonic preferences or if $X = \mathbb{R}^m_{++}$. With either of these two assumptions, only minor modifications need to be made to the preceding proof to show that a somewhere dense set of profiles $\mathcal{D} \subseteq \mathcal{C}^n_{cm}$ is Arrow-inconsistent, even if $\mathcal{D}$ is not the Cartesian product of individual preference domains.[51]

The profiles that create problems in the proof of Theorem 7 have the property that individual d has a preference R_d that (i) is monotonic, but not strictly monotonic, and (ii) is not contained in the closure of any open set in $\mathcal{D}_*$. Redekop's alternative definition of a topologically small set rules out this possibility by requiring that when any profile $\mathbf{R}$ is feasible, so is some open set containing $\mathbf{R}$, as would be the case if the true profile cannot be identified with precision. Formally, a domain of preferences $\mathcal{D}_*$ (resp. preference profiles $\mathcal{D}$) is *near-open* if $\bar{\mathcal{D}}_* = \bar{O}$ for some open set O of preferences (resp. if $\bar{\mathcal{D}} = \bar{O}$ for some open set O of preference profiles). Clearly, if $\mathcal{D}_*$ is near-open, then $\mathcal{D}_*$ is somewhere dense in $\mathcal{C}_{cm}$. However, the reverse implication need not hold. For example, if $\mathcal{D}_* = \{R \in \mathcal{C}_{cm} \mid xPy\} \cup \bar{R}$, where $\{x, y\}$ is coordinatewise undominated, $\bar{R} \in \mathcal{C}_{cm}$, and $y\bar{P}x$, then $\mathcal{D}_*$ is somewhere dense, but not near-open. Without requiring that $\mathcal{D} \subseteq \mathcal{C}^n_{cm}$ be a Cartesian product, Redekop (1991) has shown that near-openness of $\mathcal{D}$ is sufficient for $\mathcal{D}$ to be Arrow-inconsistent when $X = \mathbb{R}^n_+$.

In view of Redekop's impossibility theorems for somewhere dense and near-open domains and the impossibility results for saturating domains presented in Sections 4 and 5, it is natural to enquire if there is any logical relationship between these domain restrictions. Using the definition of the questionnaire topology, it is easy to verify that the domain of continuous, strictly monotonic, convex preferences $\mathcal{C}_{pu}$ in Example 8 is nowhere dense, although we know that it is saturating. Suppose that $\{x, y\}$ is coordinatewise undominated and $\bar{R} \in \mathcal{C}_{cm}$ is such that $x\bar{I}y$. Let $\mathcal{D} = [\{R \in \mathcal{C}_{cm} \mid xPy \text{ or } yPx\} \cup \bar{R}]^n$.

[51] The product topology is used for the domain of preference profiles $\mathcal{C}^n_{cm}$. A basis for this topology is $\mathcal{T}^n_Q$, the n-fold Cartesian product of $\mathcal{T}_Q$.

Because $\{x, y\}$ is a free pair that is not part of any free triple, this domain is not saturating. However, $\bar{\mathcal{D}} = \mathcal{C}^n_{cm}$, so the domain is near-open and, hence, somewhere dense. Thus, the concept of a saturating domain and Redekop's domain restrictions are logically independent.[52]

Redekop (1991) has noted that there is a sense in which somewhere dense domains are unreasonably large. For the public goods problem considered in this section, we have seen that this domain condition ensures that there is sufficient preference diversity so that each alternative is contained in some open set whose coordinatewise undominated triples are strictly free. However, because a basic open set B is constructed by specifying strict rankings for only a finite number of paired comparisons and then identifying all of the continuous monotonic preferences that exhibit these rankings, no restrictions other than continuity and monotonicity are placed on preferences in B if we remove a neighborhood of the origin from X that is large enough to contain all the alternatives that are used to generate B. Hence, requiring a domain to be somewhere dense also implies that any basic open set of preferences coincides with $\mathcal{C}_{cm}$ on sets of alternatives that are sufficiently far from the origin. Thus, it could be argued, open sets of preferences permit too much preference diversity when comparing alternatives far from the origin. Redekop (1991) has identified a finer topology on the space of preferences that restricts the preference diversity on such sets without limiting the diversity that is present in the neighborhood of each alternative and has shown that his public goods impossibility theorems remain valid when this topology is used to define open sets of preferences.

In Theorem 7, preferences have been a priori restricted to be continuous and monotonic. As we have seen, the domain of continuous, strictly monotonic, convex preferences $\mathcal{C}_{pu}$ in Example 8 is nowhere dense relative to $\mathcal{C}_{cm}$, so Theorem 7 does not apply to the domain of classical public goods preferences. If we are confident that everyone's preferences lie in $\mathcal{C}_{pu}$, this is the "universal" set of preferences that should be used when identifying a domain of preferences as being topologically small. Similarly, if there are other restrictions on preferences that we are confident are satisfied, then the universal set of preferences should be restricted even further. Remarkably, Redekop has shown that his public goods impossibility theorems are quite robust to the specification of the underlying class of preferences. For example, Redekop (1993a) has shown that $\mathcal{D}^n_*$ is Arrow-inconsistent if $\mathcal{D}_*$ is a near-open subset of $\mathcal{C}_{pu}$ or if it is a near-open subset of the homothetic preferences in $\mathcal{C}_{pu}$.[53] Similarly, we may know that preferences lie in some parametric class, say the set of Cobb–Douglas preferences, the set of linear preferences considered in Example 9, or the set of Euclidean spatial preferences

[52] A domain is *strictly saturating* if there are at least two strictly free pairs and every pair of strictly free pairs is strictly connected. Redekop (1991) has shown that if $X = \mathbb{R}^m_{++}$, $\mathcal{D}$ is a common preference domain, and $\mathcal{D}$ is a near-open subset of $\mathcal{C}^n_{cm}$, then $\mathcal{D}$ is strictly saturating.

[53] It is an open question if these results can be extended to preference domains that are not common.

considered in Example 12. Provided that this parametric class is sufficiently rich, as in these three examples, Redekop (1993c) has shown that the incompatibility of Arrow's axioms can only be avoided on topologically small subsets of these domains when there are at least three goods.[54]

In addition to the public goods economies discussed here, Redekop (1993a, 1996) has considered private goods economies (see Section 9), economies with both public and private goods, economies with stochastic alternatives, deterministic intertemporal economies with an infinite number of time periods, and infinite-horizon economies with uncertain consumption streams. In each case, the basic message conveyed by Theorem 7 is unchanged—Arrow-consistent domains are topologically small.[55] These results are surveyed in Redekop (1995).

7. SUPERSATURATING PREFERENCE DOMAINS

So far, we have restricted attention to problems in which the social alternatives are purely public. As a consequence, the analysis is not immediately applicable to problems with private goods. As we shall see, the techniques used to study public alternatives in Sections 4 and 5 can be readily adapted to study private alternatives as well. However, to fully exploit the structure imposed on the problem by the private goods assumption, it is necessary to consider refinements of the concept of a saturating preference domain. In this section, we consider a restriction on the individual preference domains that ensures that the domain of preference profiles is saturating when individuals only care about their own private consumption.

For the private domains we consider in this and the following two sections, X is a Cartesian set of alternatives.

Cartesian Set of Alternatives

$X = \prod_{i=1}^{n} X_i$.

Thus, a social alternative is a vector $(x^1, \ldots, x^n)$, where $x^i \in X_i$ is the component of the social alternative relevant to person i. We refer to x^i as i's *consumption bundle* and to X_i as i's *consumption set*. In adopting this terminology, we are not requiring consumption bundles to be vectors in a Euclidean space, although that is in fact the case in the

[54] The restriction that $m \geq 3$ is essential in some cases, as we know from our discussion of the set of linear preferences in Example 9.

[55] When there are private goods, Redekop deletes the origin from each person's consumption set. As we shall see in the next two sections, standard domains of economic preferences for private goods are Arrow-consistent if this is not done.

applications we consider. We let $(y^i;x_{-i})$ denote $(x^1,\ldots,x^{i-1},y^i,x^{i+1},\ldots,x^n)$, where $x_{-i}=(x^1,\ldots,x^{i-1},x^{i+1},\ldots,x^n)$.[56]

As in the previous sections, we maintain the assumption that $\mathcal{D}$ is a Cartesian preference domain. When the alternatives are private, we assume that individuals are selfish; that is, in comparing two social alternatives, each individual is only concerned with his or her own consumption. Formally, for each $i \in N$, a preference ordering $R_i \in \mathcal{D}_i$ is *selfish* if there exists an ordering Q_i on X_i such that for all $x,y \in X$, xR_iy if and only if $x^iQ_iy^i$, where x^i and y^i are i's consumption bundles in the alternatives x and y, respectively. We refer to Q_i as i's *induced private preference.*

Selfish Preference Domain

For each $i \in N$, an individual preference domain $\mathcal{D}_i$ on a Cartesian set of alternatives X is selfish if R_i is selfish for all $R_i \in \mathcal{D}_i$. A preference domain $\mathcal{D}$ on a Cartesian set of alternatives X is selfish if the individual preference domain $\mathcal{D}_i$ on X is selfish for each $i \in N$.

For a selfish individual preference domain $\mathcal{D}_i$, the set of induced private orderings of X_i corresponding to $\mathcal{D}_i$ is denoted by $\mathcal{Q}_i$ and is called i's *induced private preference domain.* Note that a pair of social alternatives x and y is nontrivial for person i with respect to $\mathcal{D}_i$ if and only if the corresponding pair of private consumption bundles x^i and y^i is nontrivial with respect to $\mathcal{Q}_i$. Similarly, a triple of social alternatives $\{w,x,y\}$ is a free triple with respect to $\mathcal{D}_i$ if and only if the corresponding triple of private consumption bundles $\{w^i,x^i,y^i\}$ is free with respect to $\mathcal{Q}_i$.

A selfish preference domain (provided each person is not indifferent between all alternatives) is clearly not common. Consequently, Theorem 5, which establishes that a common saturating preference domain is Arrow-inconsistent, is not relevant when individuals have selfish preferences. However, Theorem 6, which shows that there is a dictator on every nontrivial pair when the social welfare function satisfies IIA and WP and the preference domain is saturating, does apply to selfish preference domains.

In order to help identify saturating preference domains when there are private alternatives, it is useful to consider the concept of a *supersaturating preference domain,* which is a domain restriction introduced by Bordes and Le Breton (1989).

Supersaturating Preference Domain

An individual preference domain $\mathcal{D}_i$ is supersaturating if (a) $\mathcal{D}_i$ is saturating and (b) for all nontrivial pairs $\{x,y\}$ with respect to $\mathcal{D}_i$ in X, there exist $u,v \in X$ such that $u,v \notin$

[56] The assumption that the set of alternatives has a Cartesian structure is not satisfied in all private goods problems. For example, if the set of social alternatives is the set of allocations in an Edgeworth box, the consumption bundles of the two individuals are restricted by an overall resource constraint. We consider non-Cartesian sets of alternatives in Section 10.

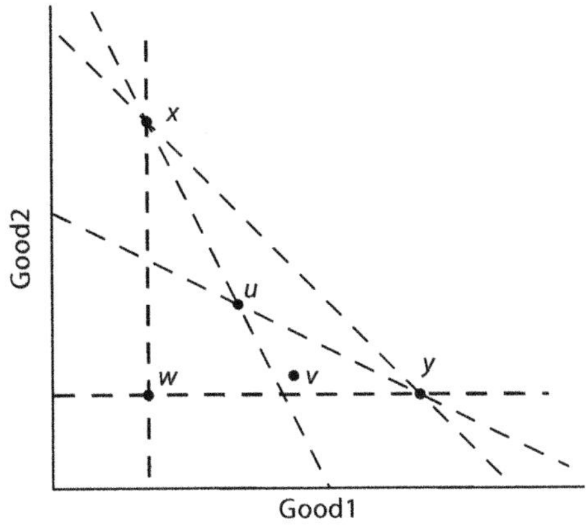

Figure 17.9. The Classical Public Goods Preference Domain is Supersaturating.

$\{x, y\}$ and $\{x, y, u\}$, $\{x, y, v\}$, $\{x, u, v\}$, and $\{y, u, v\}$ are free triples with respect to $\mathcal{D}_i$.[57] A preference domain $\mathcal{D}$ is supersaturating if $\mathcal{D}_i$ is supersaturating for all $i \in N$.

Although Bordes and Le Breton (1989) introduced the concept of a supersaturating preference domain to study selfish preferences for private alternatives, preference domains for public alternatives can be supersaturating as well. For example, the domain of classical economic preferences for public goods considered in Example 8 is a supersaturating preference domain. Recall that in this example, X is $\mathbb{R}^m_+$ with $m \geq 2$ and the common individual preference domain $\mathcal{D}_*$ is the set of continuous, strictly monotonic, and convex preferences $\mathcal{C}_{pu}$. We have already seen that this individual preference domain is saturating, so to establish that it is supersaturating it is sufficient to check that condition (b) is satisfied. We do this for the two-good case. Suppose that x and y are a nontrivial pair; that is, neither $x > y$ nor $y > x$. These alternatives are illustrated in Figure 17.9. We do not rule out the possibility that either x or y (or both) is on one of the axes. Let $w = (\min\{x_1, y_1\}, \min\{x_2, y_2\})$. Choose u so that it is in the interior of the triangle formed by the points w, x, and y, as shown in the diagram. Our discussion of Example 8 shows that $\{x, y, u\}$ is a free triple. Choose v so that it lies below the line through u and y, but above the lines through u and x and through w and y. By again appealing to our discussion of Example 8, we conclude that $\{x, y, v\}$, $\{x, u, v\}$, and $\{y, u, v\}$ are free triples with respect to $\mathcal{D}_*$, which completes the demonstration that $\mathcal{D}_*$ is supersaturating (when $m = 2$).

To help understand condition (b) in the definition of an individual supersaturating preference domain, we introduce the concept of a *self-cycle*.

[57] Bordes and Le Breton (1989) have shown that (a) and (b) are logically independent.

Self-Cycle

A sequence of pairs $A_1, \ldots, A_r$ in X is a self-cycle with respect to $\mathcal{D}_i$ (resp. $\mathcal{D}$) if $A_1 = A_r$ and A_j and A_{j+1} are strongly connected with respect to $\mathcal{D}_i$ (resp. $\mathcal{D}$) for all $j = 1, \ldots, r-1$.

A self-cycle is a sequence of pairs connecting a pair of alternatives to itself. If condition (b) in the definition of an individual supersaturating preference domain is satisfied, then for each nontrivial pair of alternatives $\{x, y\}$, we can construct a self-cycle containing three distinct pairs and we can construct a self-cycle containing four distinct pairs. The first of these self-cycles is given by the sequence $\{x, y\}$, $\{y, u\}$, $\{u, x\}$, and $\{x, y\}$. The second of these self-cycles is given by the sequence $\{x, y\}$, $\{y, u\}$, $\{u, v\}$, $\{v, x\}$, and $\{x, y\}$. In both of these sequences, any two adjacent pairs form a free triple. For the domain of economic preferences for public goods considered in Example 8, Figure 17.9 illustrates these self-cycles. By combining an appropriate number of these two self-cycles, $\{x, y\}$ can be connected to itself with a self-cycle containing r pairs for any positive integer r except 2, 3, and 6.

For private alternatives, because preferences are selfish, the induced private preference domain $\mathcal{Q}_i$ inherits many of the structural properties of the individual preference domain $\mathcal{D}_i$.

Lemma 3 *If X is a Cartesian set of alternatives and $\mathcal{D}$ is a selfish preference domain, then for each $i \in N$, the individual preference domain $\mathcal{D}_i$ is saturating (resp. supersaturating) on X if and only if the induced private preference domain $\mathcal{Q}_i$ is saturating (resp. supersaturating) on X_i.*

The intuition for Lemma 3 is quite simple. Because preferences are selfish, an individual's ranking of a pair of alternatives is completely determined by the individual's preference for the corresponding consumption bundles. Hence, all of the richness in the individual preference domain $\mathcal{D}_i$ is embodied in the induced individual preference domain $\mathcal{Q}_i$.[58]

Example 17 shows that the private goods counterpart to the public preference domain considered in Example 8 is supersaturating.

Example 17 In this example, we consider the classical domain of economic preferences for private goods. Before describing our example, we first need one more definition. Suppose that X is both a Cartesian set of alternatives and a subset of a Euclidean space. For each $i \in N$, a selfish preference ordering $R_i \in \mathcal{R}$ is strictly monotonic in own consumption if the corresponding induced private preference Q_i is strictly monotonic on X_i.

The set of alternatives is $X = \prod_{i=1}^{n} X_i$, where $X_i = \mathbb{R}_+^m$ for all $i \in N$, where $m \geq 2$. The preference domain is the domain of classical private goods preferences, which we denote by $\mathcal{C}_{pr}$.

[58] A formal proof of Lemma 3 may be found in Le Breton and Weymark (1996).

Classical Private Goods Preference Domain
For all $i \in N, \mathcal{D}_i$ is the set of all selfish, continuous, strictly monotonic in own consumption, convex preference orderings on X.

Because the set of alternatives is Cartesian and individual preferences are selfish, by Lemma 3, $\mathcal{D}_i$ is supersaturating on X if and only if the induced private preference domain $\mathcal{Q}_i$ is supersaturating on X_i. The induced private preference domain $\mathcal{Q}_i$ is formally the same as the public preference domain considered in Example 8. As we have already seen, this domain is supersaturating, from which it follows that $\mathcal{D}_i$ is supersaturating as well. Because $\mathcal{D}_i$ is supersaturating for all $i \in N$, the preference domain $\mathcal{D}$ is supersaturating.[59]

By definition, an individual preference domain $\mathcal{D}_i$ is saturating if it is supersaturating. In general, it does not follow that a preference domain $\mathcal{D}$ is saturating if it is supersaturating. However, if a preference domain $\mathcal{D}$ is both selfish and supersaturating, then it must also be saturating.

Theorem 8 *For a Cartesian set of alternatives X, if the preference domain $\mathcal{D}$ is both selfish and supersaturating, then it is also saturating.*[60]

Proof. Because the individual preference domains are saturating, for each $i \in N$, we can find alternatives $w(i)$, $x(i)$, $y(i)$, and $z(i)$ in X such that $\{x(i), y(i)\} \neq \{w(i), z(i)\}$ and such that both pairs of alternatives are nontrivial with respect to $\mathcal{D}_i$. Let $w = (w^1(1), \ldots, w^n(n))$, $x = (x^1(1), \ldots, x^n(n))$, $y = (y^1(1), \ldots, y^n(n))$, and $z = (z^1(1), \ldots, z^n(n))$. Because X is Cartesian, each of these four alternatives is in X. Because preferences are selfish, the pairs $\{x, y\}$ and $\{w, z\}$ are nontrivial with respect to $\mathcal{D}$. Thus, there exist at least two nontrivial pairs with respect to $\mathcal{D}$.

Now let $\{x, y\}$ and $\{w, z\}$ be any two nontrivial pairs with respect to $\mathcal{D}$. From Lemma 3, we know that for all $i \in N$, the induced private preference domains $\mathcal{Q}_i$ are supersaturating on X_i and the pairs of consumption bundles $\{x^i, y^i\}$ and $\{w^i, z^i\}$ are nontrivial with respect to $\mathcal{Q}_i$. Because $\mathcal{Q}_i$ is saturating, we can connect $\{x^i, y^i\}$ and $\{w^i, z^i\}$ using a sequence S_i of pairs of consumption bundles starting with $\{x^i, y^i\}$ and ending with $\{w^i, z^i\}$. Because $\mathcal{Q}_i$ is supersaturating, we can find consumption bundles u^i and v^i in X_i such that $\{x^i, y^i, u^i\}$, $\{x^i, y^i, v^i\}$, $\{x^i, u^i, v^i\}$, and $\{y^i, u^i, v^i\}$ are free triples with respect to $\mathcal{Q}_i$. Furthermore, $\{x^i, y^i\}$ is connected to itself using either the sequence of pairs (I): $\{x^i, y^i\}$, $\{y^i, u^i\}$, $\{u^i, x^i\}$, and $\{x^i, y^i\}$ or the sequence of pairs (II): $\{x^i, y^i\}$, $\{y^i, u^i\}$, $\{u^i, v^i\}$, $\{v^i, x^i\}$, and $\{x^i, y^i\}$.

Consider the sequences S_1 and S_2. Without loss of generality, we can suppose that S_1 is no longer than S_2. Suppose S_2 has k more pairs than S_1. If k is positive, we add self-cycles to the beginning of S_1 and S_2 until the two sequences are the same length.

[59] The assumption that each person consumes the same number of private goods is not essential in this example.
[60] This theorem is based on Lemma 2 in Bordes and Le Breton (1989).

If $k = 1$, this is accomplished by adding one type-II self-cycle to the beginning of S_1 and by adding one type-I self-cycle to the beginning of S_2. If $k = 2$, we add two type-I self-cycles to the beginning of S_1 and add one type-II self-cycle to the beginning of S_2. If $k = 3$, we simply add one type-I self-cycle to the beginning of S_1. If $k > 3$, by first adding an appropriate number of type-I self-cycles to the beginning of S_1, the difference in the lengths of the two sequences can be made not to exceed three, and one of the preceding procedures can be used to equate the length of the sequences.

Now that the sequences for the first two individuals are the same length, we use similar operations to equalize the length of the sequences connecting $\{x^i, y^i\}$ and $\{w^i, z^i\}$ for $i = 1, 2, 3$. Continuing in like fashion, we equalize the lengths of the connection paths joining $\{x^i, y^i\}$ and $\{w^i, z^i\}$ for all $i \in N$. For each individual, we now have a sequence of consumption bundles $(x^i, y^i, s^{i1}, \ldots, s^{it}, w^i, z^i)$ containing $t + 4$ elements, with each adjacent pair in the sequence forming the intermediate pairs used to connect $\{x^i, y^i\}$ and $\{w^i, z^i\}$ with respect to $\mathcal{Q}_i$. Next, we form a sequence of alternatives in X by combining these individual consumption bundles. That is, we construct the sequence $x = (x^1, \ldots, x^n)$, $y = (y^1, \ldots, y^n)$, $s^1 = (s^{11}, \ldots, s^{n1}), \ldots, s^t = (s^{1t}, \ldots, s^{nt})$, $w = (w^1, \ldots, w^n)$, $z = (z^1, \ldots, z^n)$. Each adjacent pair in this sequence is strongly connected, which establishes that the pairs $\{x, y\}$ and $\{w, z\}$ are connected in $\mathcal{D}$. Hence, $\mathcal{D}$ is saturating. □

An immediate implication of Theorems 6 and 8 is that if a private preference domain is supersaturating, then there must be a dictator on every nontrivial pair if the social welfare function satisfies IIA and WP.

Theorem 9 *For a Cartesian set of alternatives X, if a social welfare function on a preference domain that is both selfish and supersaturating satisfies* IIA *and* WP, *then there is an individual $d \in N$ who is a dictator on every nontrivial pair of social alternatives.*

The usefulness of Theorem 9 is limited by the fact that a pair of social alternatives is nontrivial if and only if the corresponding pairs of private consumption bundles are nontrivial for each individual. For example, with the classical economic preferences for private goods considered in Example 17, the social alternatives x and y are a nontrivial pair if and only if for all individuals neither $x^i > y^i$ nor $y^i > x^i$. Because this domain satisfies the assumptions of Theorem 9, there is a dictator on the nontrivial pairs. However, if we want to compare a pair of social alternatives in which even a single individual's consumption bundle is the same in both alternatives or in which some individual receives more of all goods in one of the two alternatives, then Theorem 9 tells us nothing about the social ranking.

Using the essential idea underlying an example in Blau (1957), Border (1983) has shown that the domain $\mathcal{C}_{pr}$ of classical economic preferences for private goods considered in Example 17 is Arrow-consistent. In Example 18, we present the social welfare function Border used to demonstrate this result.

Example 18 In this example, the set of alternatives X and the preference domain $\mathcal{D}$ are the same as in Example 17 but with $n = 2$.[61] By construction, the set of alternatives is Cartesian and the preference domain is selfish. We have already established that the preference domain is also supersaturating. Consider the following four subsets of X: $A_1 = \{x \in X \mid x^1 \neq 0_m \text{ and } x^2 \neq 0_m\}$, $A_2 = \{x \in X \mid x^1 \neq 0_m \text{ and } x^2 = 0_m\}$, $A_3 = \{x \in X \mid x^1 = 0_m \text{ and } x^2 \neq 0_m\}$, and $A_4 = \{(0_m, 0_m)\}$. These four sets form a partition of X. In A_1 both individuals consume some of at least one good. In each of the other sets, at least one person receives nothing. The social welfare function is defined by setting, for all $\mathbf{R} \in \mathcal{D}$,

(i) $\forall x, y \in A_1, xRy \leftrightarrow xR_2y$,
(ii) $\forall x, y \in A_2, xRy \leftrightarrow xR_1y$,
(iii) $\forall x, y \in A_3, xRy \leftrightarrow xR_2y$,
(iv) $\forall i < j, \forall x \in A_i, \forall y \in A_j, xPy$.

This social welfare function is nondictatorial. Person two dictates on alternatives in A_1. However, person two is not an overall dictator. If $x \in A_3$ and $y \in A_2$, then xP_2y because two's consumption is nonzero in A_3 and is zero in A_2. But, by (iv), the social preference is yPx.

This social welfare function satisfies WP because the social preference always agrees with the individual preference of at least one person. This fact is obvious if we compare two alternatives from the same cell in the partition. It is not difficult to verify this claim when the alternatives come from different cells. For example, if $x \in A_3$ and $y \in A_2$, the social preference coincides with person one's preference.

We leave it to the reader to confirm that IIA is satisfied and that the social preferences are orderings.[62]

8. HYPERSATURATING PREFERENCE DOMAINS

With public alternatives, the Kalai–Muller–Satterthwaite Theorem tells us that if the preference domain is common and saturating, then it is Arrow-inconsistent. In

[61] It is a straightforward matter to extend this example to larger populations.

[62] Donaldson and Roemer (1987) have considered private goods environments in which the number of goods is variable. They introduced an axiom that places restrictions on how the social rankings for different numbers of goods are related to each other. When combined with Pareto Indifference (the requirement that two alternatives are socially indifferent when everyone is indifferent between them), this consistency condition implies IIA. Donaldson and Roemer have noted that their consistency axiom is violated if, for each fixed number of goods, alternatives are socially ranked as in Example 18.

the preceding section, we learned that with a Cartesian set of private alternatives, the preference domain is saturating if the individual preference domains are selfish and supersaturating. With selfish preferences, it is not possible for individuals to have the same individual preference domains and, therefore, we cannot use the Kalai–Muller–Satterthwaite Theorem to establish that a private alternatives preference domain is Arrow-inconsistent when individuals only care about their own consumption. In this section, we consider a refinement of the concept of a supersaturating preference domain that implies that the domain is Arrow-inconsistent when the set of alternatives is Cartesian and preferences are selfish.

To help understand why a domain like the classical domain of private goods preferences considered in Examples 17 and 18 is Arrow-consistent, we introduce the concept of a trivial pair being *separable* for an individual.

Separable Trivial Pair

A pair of alternatives $\{x, y\}$ in X that is trivial for i is separable with respect to $\mathcal{D}_i$ if there exists a $z \in X$ such that the pairs $\{x, z\}$ and $\{y, z\}$ are nontrivial for i and either (a) xP_iy for all $R_i \in \mathcal{D}_i$ and there exists an $R'_i \in \mathcal{D}_i$ such that $xP'_izP'_iy$, or (b) yP_ix for all $R_i \in \mathcal{D}_i$ and there exists an $R'_i \in \mathcal{D}_i$ such that $yP'_izP'_ix$.

The concept of a separable trivial pair is implicit in Bordes and Le Breton (1989).[63] Informally, a trivial pair $\{x, y\}$ is separable for person i if i is not indifferent between x and y and there is an admissible preference ordering for i and an alternative z such that z is intermediate in preference between x and y and such that $\{x, z\}$ and $\{y, z\}$ are nontrivial pairs for i.

Bordes and Le Breton (1989) used the notion of a separable trivial pair to define a *hypersaturating preference domain.*

Hypersaturating Preference Domain

An individual preference domain $\mathcal{D}_i$ is hypersaturating if (a) $\mathcal{D}_i$ is supersaturating and (b) all trivial pairs $\{x, y\}$ with respect to $\mathcal{D}_i$ in X for which $\neg(xI_iy)$ for all $R_i \in \mathcal{D}_i$ are separable for i. A preference domain $\mathcal{D}$ is hypersaturating if $\mathcal{D}_i$ is hypersaturating for all $i \in N$.

With a hypersaturating preference domain, all non-indifferent trivial pairs are separable for each individual. The preference domain in Examples 17 and 18 is not hypersaturating because for each individual we can find trivial pairs consisting of two non-indifferent alternatives that are not separable. For example, if $x \gg y = (0_m, 0_m)$, $\{x, y\}$ is a trivial pair for both individuals for the preference domain considered in Example 18. Both individuals prefer x to y, but x and y cannot be separated.

[63] A closely related idea is used in Kalai and Ritz (1980).

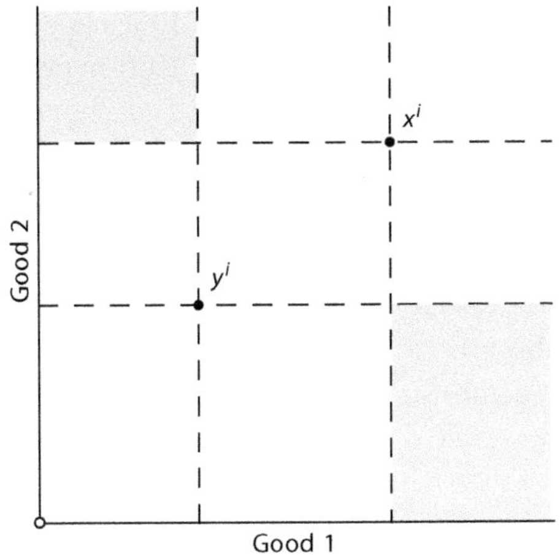

Figure 17.10. A Separable Trivial Pair for Classical Private Goods Preferences.

Lemma 4 provides the analogue to Lemma 3 for hypersaturating individual preference domains.

Lemma 4 *If X is a Cartesian set of alternatives and $\mathcal{D}$ is a selfish preference domain, then for each $i \in N$, the individual preference domain $\mathcal{D}_i$ is hypersaturating on X if and only if the induced private preference domain $\mathcal{Q}_i$ is hypersaturating on X_i.*

Although the preference domain of classical economic preferences for private goods is not hypersaturating when each consumption set is a non-negative orthant, it is hypersaturating if either the origin is removed from each person's consumption set or if all goods must be consumed in positive amounts.

Example 19 In this example, the preference domain is the domain of classical private goods preferences considered in Example 17, but now the origin is removed from each person's consumption set so that $X_i = \mathbb{R}^m_+ \backslash \{0_m\}$ for all $i \in N$, where $m \geq 2$.

By Lemma 4, to show that this preference domain is hypersaturating, it is sufficient to show that the induced private preference domain $\mathcal{Q}_i$ is hypersaturating on $\mathbb{R}^m_+ \backslash \{0_m\}$ for all $i \in N$. The discussion of Example 17 shows that $\mathcal{Q}_i$ is supersaturating. (Deleting the origin from the consumption set does not affect this argument.) We illustrate the rest of the proof that $\mathcal{Q}_i$ is hypersaturating for the case in which $m = 2$. On X_i, the pair $\{x^i, y^i\}$ is trivial for i with x^i preferred to y^i if and only if $x^i > y^i$, as illustrated in Figure 17.10. The pair $\{x^i, y^i\}$ can be separated by any consumption bundle z^i in the shaded regions of the diagram. Note that if y^i is on one of the axes, then there is only one such region (whether or not x^i is on this axis as well).

Example 20 This example is identical to Example 19 except that now $X_i = \mathbb{R}^m_{++}$ for all $i \in N$. The reasoning used to show that Example 19 is hypersaturating also shows that this preference domain is hypersaturating.[64]

Border (1983) has shown that the preference domain in Example 20 is Arrow-inconsistent. See also the related result in Maskin (1976).[65] When there are two individuals, the universal set of alternatives in Example 19 is equal to the set A_1 in Example 18. Recall that the social welfare function in Example 18 is dictatorial on A_1. Theorem 10 shows that this is no accident. For a Cartesian set of alternatives and selfish preferences, Theorem 10 demonstrates that a preference domain is Arrow-inconsistent if it is hypersaturating. This result, which is due to Bordes and Le Breton (1989), is a private good analogue to the Kalai–Muller–Satterthwaite Theorem (Theorem 5) for public alternatives.

Theorem 10 *For a Cartesian set of alternatives X, if a social welfare function on a preference domain that is both selfish and hypersaturating satisfies* IIA *and* WP, *then it is dictatorial.*

Proof. Because a hypersaturating preference domain is supersaturating, it follows from Theorem 9 that there is an individual d who is a dictator on the nontrivial pairs. We show that d is also a dictator on the trivial pairs.

Consider any trivial pair $\{x, y\}$ and let $\mathbf{R} = (R_1, \ldots, R_n)$ be any profile in $\mathcal{D}$ for which $xP_d y$. We now show that there is an alternative $z \in X$ such that for all $i \in N$, (i) $\{x^i, z^i\}$ and $\{y^i, z^i\}$ are nontrivial pairs of consumption bundles for the induced private preference domain $\mathcal{Q}_i$ and (ii) there exists an induced private preference $Q_i' \in \mathcal{Q}_i$ for which i weakly prefers x^i to z^i (resp. z^i to x^i) and weakly prefers z^i to y^i (resp. y^i to z^i) if and only if i weakly prefers x^i to y^i (resp. y^i to x^i) according to Q_i. Note that the pair of consumption bundles $\{x^i, y^i\}$ need not be trivial for all i. By Lemma 4, the induced private preference domain $\mathcal{Q}_i$ is hypersaturating for all $i \in N$. Because $\mathcal{Q}_i$ is saturating, if $\{x^i, y^i\}$ is nontrivial for i, there must be a free triple with respect to $\mathcal{Q}_i$ that includes $\{x^i, y^i\}$. In this case, z^i can be chosen to be the third member of this triple and the requisite preference clearly exists. If $\{x^i, y^i\}$ is trivial for i, it follows immediately from the fact that $\mathcal{Q}_i$ is hypersaturating that z^i and Q_i' exist when i is not indifferent between x^i and y^i according to Q_i. If i is indifferent, the argument is more involved. See Bordes and Le Breton (1989) or Le Breton and Weymark (1996) for the details. Because preferences are selfish, it follows that $\{x, z\}$ and $\{y, z\}$ are nontrivial pairs of social alternatives.

[64] See Bordes and Le Breton (1989) for other examples of hypersaturating preference domains with private alternatives.

[65] Arrow (1951, Chapter VI) showed that free triples exist when there are private goods and individuals have selfish preferences that are monotone in own consumption. The original (erroneous) version of Arrow's impossibility theorem did not utilize unrestricted domain, but instead simply assumed that there exists a free triple. This led Arrow to falsely conclude that a private goods version of his impossibility theorem follows immediately from his more general theorem.

For all $i \in N$, let R'_i be the selfish preference on X corresponding to Q'_i and let $\mathbf{R}' = (R'_1, \ldots, R'_n)$. By construction, $xP'_d z$ and $zP'_d y$. Because $\{x, z\}$ and $\{y, z\}$ are nontrivial pairs, d is a dictator on these two pairs. Thus, $xP'z$ and $zP'y$. By the transitivity of social preference, it follows that $xP'y$. IIA then implies that $xP_d y$. Hence, person d is a dictator.[66] □

The classical domain of economic preferences for private goods is Arrow-consistent if the origin is included in the individual consumption sets, as in Examples 17 and 18. On this domain, the preceding argument does not apply whenever the pair $\{x, y\}$ includes the origin, as such a pair cannot be separated. However, it follows from Theorem 10 and Example 19 that the only social welfare functions that satisfy all of the Arrow axioms on such domains are dictatorial on the subset of alternatives obtained by deleting the origin from each person's consumption set. In other words, only if at least one of the alternatives being compared has someone with zero consumption may the individual who is "almost dictatorial" have his or her strict preference overridden. The social welfare function in Example 18 has this property. It thus seems that with private alternatives, just like with public alternatives, restricting the preference domain does not provide a satisfactory way of avoiding Arrow's dilemma.

9. TOPOLOGICAL DOMAIN RESTRICTIONS FOR PRIVATE GOODS

Redekop (1993a) has established private goods counterparts to the topological public goods results discussed in Section 6. In this section, we describe a private good analogue to Theorem 7. We also consider a theorem of Redekop's that shows that a preference domain for private goods can be Arrow-consistent even if everyone has identical preferences for own consumption.

Throughout this section, the set of alternatives is $X = \prod_{i=1}^{n} X_i$, where $X_i = \mathbb{R}^m_+ \backslash \{0_m\}$ for all $i \in N$ with $m \geq 2$. We also assume that preferences are selfish. In Redekop's "identical preferences" theorem, the preference domain $\mathcal{D}$ is not Cartesian. When this is the case, $\mathcal{D}$ is selfish if for all $\mathbf{R} \in \mathcal{D}$ and all $i \in N$, R_i is selfish.

Let $\mathcal{C}_{csm}$ denote the set of continuous and strictly monotonic preference orderings on $\mathbb{R}^m_+ \backslash \{0_m\}$. Redekop (1993a) has shown that a selfish Cartesian preference domain is

[66] The argument we used to show that d is a dictator on the ordered pair $(\{1,2\}, \{1\})$ in our discussion of ordinal probabilities (Example 15) is similar. As in the proof of Theorem 10, we introduced a third pair of alternatives $\{1,3\}$ to separate $\{1,2\}$ from $\{1\}$. The pairs $\{\{1,2\}, \{1,3\}\}$ and $\{\{1,3\}, \{1\}\}$ are both nontrivial, but only the former is free. Because $\{\{1,3\}, \{1\}\}$ is not a free pair, we had to use IIA and WP before we could appeal to transitivity, and we could not use our finding that d is a dictator on $(\{1,2\}, \{1\})$ to also conclude that d is a dictator on $(\{1\}, \{1,2\})$.

Arrow-inconsistent if each person has an induced individual preference domain that is a near-open subset of $\mathcal{C}_{csm}$.

Theorem 11 *If* $X = (\mathbb{R}^m_+ \backslash \{0_m\})^n$ *with* $m \geq 2$, *the Cartesian preference domain* $\mathcal{D}$ *is selfish, and, for all* $i \in N$, *the induced individual preference domain* $\mathcal{Q}_i$ *is a near-open subset of* $\mathcal{C}_{csm}$, *then there is no social welfare function* $F\colon \mathcal{D} \to \mathcal{R}$ *that satisfies* IIA, WP, *and* ND.

Note that the individual preference domains for own consumption in this theorem can be person-specific. The strategy used to prove Theorem 11 is similar to the one used to prove Theorem 7, except for the way that the open sets are constructed on which an individual is a local dictator. See Redekop (1993a) for the details. By assuming that preferences for own consumption are strictly monotonic, not just monotonic, and by assuming that each $\mathcal{Q}_i$ is a near-open subset of $\mathcal{C}_{csm}$, rather than being simply a somewhere dense subset of $\mathcal{C}_{csm}$, the technical problems described in Section 6 can be avoided.

With public goods, if the preference domain is restricted so that everyone always has identical preferences, then no pair or triple of alternatives is strictly free. However, with private goods, even if everyone has identical preferences for own consumption, it is relatively easy to construct strict free triples, provided that the common induced individual preference domain exhibits sufficient preference diversity. The reason for this is that each individual's consumption bundle can be varied independently. For example, suppose that $\mathcal{Q}_i = \mathcal{C}_{csm}$ for all $i \in N$, but in any admissible preference profile, everyone has the same induced private preference. Consider three alternatives x, y, and z for which the $3n$ vectors of private consumptions $x^1, y^1, z^1, \ldots, x^n, y^n, z^n$ are coordinatewise undominated. It is easy to see that $\{x, y, z\}$ is a strict free triple, even though everyone has the same preferences for own consumption.

A selfish preference domain for private goods $\mathcal{D}$ has a *common private preference domain* if $\mathcal{Q}_i = \mathcal{Q}_j$ for all $i, j \in N$. Let $\mathcal{Q}$ denote this common set of preferences for own consumption. A selfish preference domain for private goods $\mathcal{D}$ exhibits *identity of preferences for own consumption* if for all $\mathbf{R} \in \mathcal{D}$, $Q_i = Q_j$ for all $i, j \in N$. Redekop (1993a) has shown that a preference domain is Arrow-inconsistent if the domain has both of these properties and $\mathcal{Q}$ is a near-open subset of $\mathcal{C}_{csm}$.

Theorem 12 *If* $X = (\mathbb{R}^m_+ \backslash \{0_m\})^n$ *with* $m \geq 2$, *the preference domain* $\mathcal{D}$ *is selfish with a common private preference domain* $\mathcal{Q}$, $\mathcal{D}$ *exhibits identity of preferences for own consumption, and* $\mathcal{Q}$ *is a near-open subset of* $\mathcal{C}_{csm}$, *then there is no social welfare function* $F\colon \mathcal{D} \to \mathcal{R}$ *that satisfies* IIA, WP, *and* ND.

The proof of Theorem 12 is similar to the proof of Theorem 11. See Redekop (1993a). An implication of this theorem is that the Cartesian structure of the alternatives and the selfishness of preferences play significant roles in generating the preference diversity needed to show that a domain is Arrow-inconsistent when there are private goods.

As in Section 6, the theorems presented in this section are quite robust to the specification of the "universal" set of preferences that is used to identify when a domain is topologically large. In particular, these theorems also hold when $\mathcal{C}_{csm}$ is replaced by the set of continuous, strictly monotonic, and convex preference orderings on $\mathbb{R}^m_+ \backslash \{0_m\}$. See Redekop (1993a, 1995). Thus, Redekop's topological approach can be used to provide an alternative proof that the domain of classical private goods preferences $\mathcal{C}_{pr}$ in Example 19 is Arrow-inconsistent.

10. NON-CARTESIAN SETS OF ALTERNATIVES

So far, our discussion of private alternatives has assumed that the set of alternatives is a Cartesian product set $\Pi_{i=1}^n X_i$. In this section, the set of alternatives is a proper subset of a product set. If an alternative is an allocation of goods, this setting arises naturally when the set of alternatives X incorporates feasibility constraints—allocation decisions for one individual limit what can be done for the remaining individuals. There are no general results when the set of alternatives is not Cartesian. However, Bordes and Le Breton (1990a) and Bordes, Campbell, and Le Breton (1995) have shown that a modification of the local approach permits one to establish Arrow-inconsistency in some important non-Cartesian examples. We consider their analyses of the assignment problem and of exchange economies.[67]

10.1. Assignments of Indivisible Objects

We assume that there is a set G of n indivisible goods. Without loss of generality, we can assume that $G = N = \{1, 2, \ldots, n\}$. For example, the elements of G could be seats in a theater, places to park a car, dorm rooms in a college, etc. In terms of our earlier notation, for all $i \in N$, i's consumption set X_i is G. However, each object can only be assigned to one individual, so the set of feasible alternatives X is a proper subset of G^n. Thus, an alternative is an assignment of the n goods to the n individuals, each individual receiving exactly one good. Formally, an *assignment* x is a bijection from N onto G. Because $G = N$, we can identify X with Σ_n, the *set of permutations* of N. In the subsequent discussion, we single out two kinds of permutations. A *transposition* transposes two elements of N. Let Θ_n denote the *set of transpositions* of N. For all $i \in N$, a *circular permutation* maps i into $i + t$ for some $t \in \{0, \ldots, n-1\}$, where addition is modulo n. Let

[67] Non-Cartesian sets of alternatives that arise because of feasibility constraints are also a feature of the overlapping generations economies considered by Campbell (1992b, 1992d).

C_n denote the *set of circular permutations* of N. For $\sigma \in \Sigma_n$, σC_n is the set obtained by applying the permutation σ to each of the elements in C_n.

It is assumed that an individual only cares about the good allocated to him or her. In other words, for all $i \in N$, all $R_i \in \mathcal{D}_i$, and all $x, y \in X$, if $x_i = y_i$, then xI_iy. We make no further restrictions on individual preferences other than that they lie in $\mathcal{R}$ (the set of orderings of X). Note that this implies that all of the objects in G must be different. Let $\mathcal{R}_{iA}$ denote i's set of admissible individual preferences.

Bordes and Le Breton (1990a) have shown that if $n \geq 4$, then the preference domain $\Pi_{i=1}^{n} \mathcal{R}_{iA}$ is Arrow-inconsistent. Before considering their theorem, we first show why the $n = 3$ case is not covered by their result.

Example 21 When $n = 3$, X contains six alternatives. We group them into the sets $A_1 = \{(1,2,3), (2,3,1), (3,1,2)\}$ and $A_2 = \{(1,3,2), (3,2,1), (2,1,3)\}$. In each of these alternatives, the ith component is the good assigned to person i. Note that A_1 is the set of circular permutations C_3, (1,3,2) is obtained by transposing the assignment of goods 2 and 3 in (1,2,3), and A_2 is the set of assignments obtained by applying circular permutations to (1,3,2). Both A_1 and A_2 are free triples, so any social welfare function with preference domain $\Pi_{i=1}^{n} \mathcal{R}_{iA}$ is dictatorial on each of these triples if IIA and WP are satisfied.

Define the social choice welfare function $F\colon \Pi_{i=1}^{n} \mathcal{R}_{iA} \to \mathcal{R}$ by setting, for all $\mathbf{R} \in \Pi_{i=1}^{n} \mathcal{R}_{iA}$,

(i) $xRy \leftrightarrow xR_1y$ for $x, y \in A_1$,
(ii) $xRy \leftrightarrow xR_2y$ for $x, y \in A_2$,
(iii) xPy if $x \in A_1$ and $y \in A_2$.

For the same reason as in Example 2, this is a well-defined social welfare function. F satisfies all the Arrow axioms.[68]

Theorem 13 is Bordes and Le Breton's impossibility theorem for the assignment problem.

Theorem 13 *If* $X = \Sigma_n$ *and* $n \geq 4$*, there is no social welfare function with preference domain* $\Pi_{i=1}^{n} \mathcal{R}_{iA}$ *that satisfies* IIA, WP, *and* ND.

Proof. We present the the proof for the case of $n \geq 5$.[69] Suppose that $F\colon \Pi_{i=1}^{n} \mathcal{R}_{iA} \to \mathcal{R}$ satisfies IIA and WP. The proof proceeds in a series of steps.

[68] Note that if $x \in A_1$ and $y \in A_2$, the weak Pareto principle is vacuous because these alternatives are not Pareto ranked (someone receives the same good in both assignments). We also have dictators on the two subsets of alternatives in Example 2, but the two sets are Pareto ranked in that example.

[69] The case $n = 4$ calls for a special treatment. See Bordes and Le Breton (1990a).

Step 1. We first show that for all $\sigma \in \Sigma_n$, there is a dictator $d(\sigma)$ on σC_n. Because each person receives a different object in each alternative in C_n, preferences are unrestricted on C_n. For the same reason, preferences are unrestricted on any common permutation of the alternatives in C_n. Hence, the existence of a dictator on σC_n follows from Arrow's Theorem.

Step 2. We next show that for all $\sigma \in \Sigma_n$, all $\theta \in \Theta_n$, and all $x \in C_n$, there exist $x', x'' \in C_n$ such that $\{\sigma x, \theta\sigma x', \theta\sigma x''\}$ is a free triple.[70] Suppose that θ transposes the assignment of goods i and j. We have already seen that each person receives a different object in each alternative in σC_n. If for all alternatives in σC_n except σx, we transpose the assignment of goods i and j, it will still be the case that everyone receives a different object in each alternative in $\theta\sigma C_n \backslash \{\theta\sigma x\}$. To complete the proof of this step, we need to show that there are at least two of these transposed alternatives, say $\theta\sigma x'$ and $\theta\sigma x''$, in which everyone receives different objects in $\{\sigma x, \theta\sigma x', \theta\sigma x''\}$.

Let $i^* = (\sigma x)^{-1}(i)$ and $j^* = (\sigma x)^{-1}(j)$ be the individuals who receive objects i and j, respectively, in σx. For any $k \neq i^*, j^*$, transposing the assignment of objects i and j in σx has no effect on what k receives, so $\sigma x(k) = \theta\sigma x(k)$. For any circular permutation y distinct from x, $x(k) \neq y(k)$ and, hence, $\sigma x(k) \neq \theta\sigma y(k)$ for $k \neq i^*, j^*$. For each individual and each object, there is exactly one assignment in C_n in which this individual receives this object. Hence, there exists exactly one $x_{i^*} \in C_n$ such that $i = \sigma x(i^*) = \theta\sigma x_{i^*}(i^*)$ and exactly one $x_{j^*} \in C_n$ such that $j = \sigma x(j^*) = \theta\sigma x_{j^*}(j^*)$.

Let $E = \theta\sigma C_n \backslash \{\theta\sigma x, \theta\sigma x_{i^*}, \theta\sigma x_{j^*}\}$. Because $n \geq 5$, $|E| \geq 2$. Let $\theta\sigma x'$ and $\theta\sigma x''$ be any two distinct elements of E. For each $k \neq i^*, j^*$, from the preceding discussion, we know that k receives distinct objects in σx, $\theta\sigma x'$, and $\theta\sigma x''$ because x, x', and x'' are distinct. Because these circular permutations are distinct, individuals i^* and j^* receive different objects in $\theta\sigma x$, $\theta\sigma x'$, and $\theta\sigma x''$. By the construction of E, neither i^* nor j^* receives objects i or j in either $\theta\sigma x'$ or $\theta\sigma x''$. Hence, i^* and j^* also receive distinct objects in σx, $\theta\sigma x'$, and $\theta\sigma x''$.

Step 3. We now show that for all $\sigma \in \Sigma_n$ and all $\theta \in \Theta_n$, $d(\sigma) = d(\theta\sigma)$. Let σ_1 be any element of σC_n. By Step 2, there exist $\sigma_2, \sigma_3 \in \theta\sigma C_n$ such that $\{\sigma_1, \sigma_2, \sigma_3\}$ is a free triple. As in Step 2, suppose that θ transposes the assignment of goods i and j. Let i^{**} and j^{**} be the individuals who receive objects i and j, respectively, in σ_2. Because $\theta\theta$ is the identity transform, $\theta\sigma_2 \in \sigma C_n$. We know that everyone receives a different object in every assignment in σC_n. Thus, for any $\sigma_4 \in \sigma C_n \backslash \{\sigma_1, \theta\sigma_2\}$, everyone except possibly i^{**} or j^{**} must receive different objects in σ_1, σ_2, and σ_4. Provided that we choose σ_4 so that i^{**} does not get

[70] When we compose two permutations, such as σ and x, we write σx instead of $\sigma(x)$. Note that a permutation is a mapping from N to N, not a permutation matrix.

object i and j^{**} does not get object j, i^{**} and j^{**} also receive different objects in σ_1, σ_2, and σ_4. This is possible because $|\sigma C_n \backslash \{\sigma_1, \theta\sigma_2\}| \geq 3$. Therefore, $\{\sigma_1, \sigma_2, \sigma_4\}$ is a free triple. The pairs $\{\sigma_4, \sigma_1\}$ and $\{\sigma_2, \sigma_3\}$ are connected using the intermediate pair $\{\sigma_1, \sigma_2\}$. Hence, the dictator $d(\sigma)$ on $\{\sigma_4, \sigma_1\}$ must be the same as the dictator on $\{\sigma_2, \sigma_3\}$.

Step 4. Next we show that there exists a $d \in N$ such that $d(\sigma) = d$ for all $\sigma \in \Sigma_n$. Consider any $\sigma \in \Sigma_n$. Any permutation can be written as the composition of transpositions, so there exist $\theta_1, \theta_2, \ldots, \theta_q \in \Theta_n$ such that $\sigma = \theta_1 \theta_2 \cdots \theta_q$. By Step 3, $d(\theta_q) = d(\theta_{q-1}\theta_q)$, $d(\theta_{q-1}\theta_q) = d(\theta_{q-2}\theta_{q-1}\theta_q)$, ..., $d(\theta_1\theta_2 \cdots \theta_q) = d(\theta_2 \cdots \theta_q)$. Hence, the dictator on σC_n is the same as the dictator on $\theta_q C_n$ which, by Step 3, is the same as the dictator on C_n.

Step 5. In this step, we show that for all $\sigma \in \Sigma_n$ and all $\theta \in \Theta_n$, d is a dictator on all pairs $\{\sigma_1, \sigma_2\}$ for which $\sigma_1 \in \sigma C_n$ and $\sigma_2 \in \theta\sigma C_n$.

First, suppose that $\{\sigma_1, \sigma_2\}$ is a free pair. If we identify σ_1 with σx in Step 2, it follows that if $\sigma_2 \in \{\theta\sigma x, \theta\sigma x_{i^*}, \theta\sigma x_{j^*}\}$, then someone receives the same object in σ_1 and σ_2, contradicting the assumption that $\{\sigma_1, \sigma_2\}$ is a free pair. Hence, $\sigma_2 \in E$. By choosing $\sigma_3 \in E$ distinct from σ_2, $\{\sigma_1, \sigma_2, \sigma_3\}$ is a free triple with $\sigma_3 \in \theta\sigma C_n$. By Step 4, d is the dictator on $\{\sigma_2, \sigma_3\}$ and, therefore, d must also be the dictator on the free triple $\{\sigma_1, \sigma_2, \sigma_3\}$.

If $\{\sigma_1, \sigma_2\}$ is not a free pair, d is trivially a dictator on this pair if $\sigma_1(d) = \sigma_2(d)$, so we only need to consider the case in which $\sigma_1(d) \neq \sigma_2(d)$. Consider an arbitrary profile $\mathbf{R} \in \Pi_{i=1}^n \mathcal{R}_{iA}$ for which $\sigma_1 P_d \sigma_2$. By Step 2, there exist $\sigma_3, \sigma_4 \in \theta\sigma C_n$ such that $\{\sigma_1, \sigma_3, \sigma_4\}$ is a free triple. Because someone receives the same object in σ_1 and σ_2, whereas everyone receives different objects in any two assignments in $\theta\sigma C_n$, the fact that $\{\sigma_1, \sigma_3, \sigma_4\}$ is a free triple implies that $\{\sigma_2, \sigma_3, \sigma_4\}$ is also a free triple. Because the two free triples have two alternatives in common, they must have the same dictator. By Step 4, d is the dictator on $\{\sigma_2, \sigma_3, \sigma_4\}$, so d is the common dictator.

Note that our assumptions imply that d receives a different object in each of σ_1, σ_2, σ_3, and σ_4. Hence, there exists a profile $\mathbf{R}' \in \Pi_{i=1}^n \mathcal{R}_{iA}$ for which (i) $R'_i = R_i$ for all $i \neq d$ and (ii) $\sigma_1 P'_d \sigma_3 P'_d \sigma_4 P'_d \sigma_2$. Because d is a dictator on each adjacent pair in this sequence of alternatives, we have $\sigma_1 P' \sigma_3 P' \sigma_4 P' \sigma_2$. Transitivity of R' implies that $\sigma_1 P' \sigma_2$. We then have $\sigma_1 P \sigma_2$ by IIA. Thus, d is a dictator on $\{\sigma_1, \sigma_2\}$.

Step 6. We now show that for all $\sigma, \sigma' \in \Sigma_n$, if d is dictator on all pairs $\{\sigma_1, \sigma_2\}$ such that $\sigma_1 \in \sigma C_n$ and $\sigma_2 \in \sigma' C_n$, then for all $\theta \in \Theta_n$, d is a dictator on all pairs $\{\sigma_1^*, \sigma_2^*\}$ such that $\sigma_1^* \in \sigma C_n$ and $\sigma_2^* \in \theta\sigma' C_n$.

Suppose that for some admissible profile $\mathbf{R}$, $\sigma_1^* P_d \sigma_2^*$. Consider an assignment $\sigma_3^* \in \sigma' C_n$ in which d receives a different object than in either σ_1^* or σ_2^*. There then exists another admissible profile $\mathbf{R}'$ such that (i) $R'_i = R_i$ for all

$i \neq d$ and (ii) $\sigma_1^* P_d' \sigma_3^* P_d' \sigma_2^*$. It follows from the hypothesis of this step and from Step 5 that $\sigma_1^* P' \sigma_3^* P' \sigma_2^*$. Transitivity of P' then implies that $\sigma_1^* P' \sigma_2^*$. Hence, using IIA, we conclude that $\sigma_1^* P \sigma_2^*$.

Step 7. To complete the proof that $\Pi_{i=1}^n \mathcal{R}_{iA}$ is Arrow-inconsistent, we show that d is a dictator on $\{\sigma, \sigma'\}$ for any $\sigma, \sigma' \in \Sigma_n$. The proof is trivial if $\sigma(d) = \sigma'(d)$, so suppose that $\sigma(d) \neq \sigma'(d)$. As in Step 4, there exist $\theta_1, \theta_2, \ldots, \theta_q \in \Theta_n$ such that $\sigma = \theta_1 \theta_2 \cdots \theta_q \sigma'$. From Step 5, d is a dictator on all pairs with one element in $\sigma' C_n$ and the other in $\theta_q \sigma' C_n$. From Step 6, d is therefore a dictator on all pairs with one element in $\sigma' C_n$ and the other in $\theta_{q-1} \theta_q \sigma' C_n$. A repeated application of Step 6 leads to the conclusion that d is a dictator on $\{\sigma, \sigma'\}$. □

Because the domain in the assignment problem is non-Cartesian, we could not analyze individual preference domains separately, as we have done in the Cartesian case. Nevertheless, we were able to group the alternatives in such a way that we could use Arrow's theorem "locally" on each subgroup and then use connection arguments to show that a single individual dictates on the complete set of alternatives. In the set obtained by taking all the circular permutations of an arbitrary assignment, nobody receives the same object in any of these assignments. Thus, these subgroups of alternatives, which partition Σ_n, are free n-tuples. If we take one of these subgroups, say σC_n, and transpose who receives two of the objects, we obtain another one of the subgroups, say $\theta \sigma C_n$. A key step in the proof of Theorem 13 is that there is a free triple that overlaps these two subgroups of alternatives. These free triples play a fundamental role in the connection arguments. This connection argument is illustrated in the following example.

Example 22 There are five indivisible objects to be assigned to five individuals, with each individual receiving one of the objects. The preference domain is $\Pi_{i=1}^5 \mathcal{R}_{iA}$. Let $w = (2,3,4,5,1)$, $x = (1,2,3,4,5)$, $y = (1,4,2,3,5)$, and $z = (4,2,3,5,1)$. We show how to connect the pair $\{w, x\}$ to the pair $\{y, z\}$.

Note that w is in the set of circular permutations generated by x, whereas both y and z are in the set of circular permutations generated by first transposing objects 4 and 5 in x and then transposing objects 1 and 4. To perform the connection argument, we introduce two new alternatives u and v that are in the set of circular permutations generated by transposing objects 4 and 5 in x. We choose u and v so that in each consecutive triple in the sequence w, x, u, v, z, y, each person gets a different object, that is, so that each of these triples is a free triple. The alternatives $u = (5,4,1,2,3)$ and $v = (3,5,4,1,2)$ satisfy these requirements. Thus, $\{w, x\}$ is connected to $\{y, z\}$ using the sequence of nontrivial pairs $\{w, x\}$, $\{x, u\}$, $\{u, v\}$, $\{v, z\}$, $\{z, y\}$.

Bordes and Le Breton (1990a) have used this kind of reasoning to analyze matching and pairing problems. In a *matching problem*, there are two groups of n individuals and each person from one group is matched with a person from the other group. The classic example of a matching problem is the marriage problem in which a group of men and women form married couples. In a *pairing problem*, there is a single set of $2n$ individuals who are grouped in pairs. For example, if college dorm rooms are designed for two people, we have a pairing problem. Provided that individuals only care about who they are matched with, but otherwise have unrestricted preferences, the preference domain in the matching problem is Arrow-inconsistent if $n \geq 4$ and the preference domain in the pairing problem is Arrow-inconsistent if $n \geq 2$. See Bordes and Le Breton (1990a) for the details.

10.2. Exchange Economies

The set of feasible allocations in an exchange economy is another example of a non-Cartesian set of alternatives. In an exchange economy, there is a fixed aggregate endowment $\omega \in \mathbb{R}^m_{++}$ of m goods to be distributed among n individuals. We assume that $m \geq 2$ and $n \geq 2$. When there is no free disposal of goods, the set of *feasible allocations* for this economy is $E(\omega) = \{x \in \mathbb{R}^{mn}_+ \mid \sum_{i=1}^n x^i_j = \omega_j \text{ for all } j = 1, \ldots, m\}$. Let $E^\circ(\omega)$ denote the interior of this set; that is, $E^\circ(\omega)$ is the set of feasible allocations in which everybody's consumption of each good is positive.

Individual preferences are defined over the set of all possible allocations $\mathbb{R}^{mn}_+$, not just the feasible allocations in $E(\omega)$. As a preference domain, we consider the classical private goods preference domain $\mathcal{C}_{pr}$ introduced in Section 7. Recall that this is the set of all profiles of selfish, continuous, strictly monotonic in own consumption, convex individual preferences.

We know from Example 18 that a social welfare function $F\colon \mathcal{C}_{pr} \to \mathcal{R}$ can satisfy all three of the Arrow axioms when $X = \mathbb{R}^{mn}_+$. However, we also know from Theorem 10 and Examples 19 and 20 that the restriction of F to the set of allocations in which everybody has a positive consumption of all goods or to the set of allocations in which everybody has a positive consumption of some good cannot satisfy all of the Arrow axioms. Bordes, Campbell, and Le Breton (1995) have shown that this impossibility also holds for the restriction of F to $E^\circ(\omega)$. Equivalently, if we let $X = E^\circ(\omega)$ and $\mathcal{D}$ be the restriction of $\mathcal{C}_{pr}$ to X, then $\mathcal{D}$ is an Arrow-inconsistent preference domain.[71]

Theorem 14 *If $X = \mathbb{R}^{mn}_+$ with $m \geq 2$ and if $\omega \in \mathbb{R}^m_{++}$, there is no social welfare function with a classical private goods preference domain whose restriction to $E^\circ(\omega)$ satisfies* IIA, WP, *and* ND.[72]

[71] Using a Border-type example (see Example 18), one can show that the restriction of $\mathcal{C}_{pr}$ to $E(\omega)$ is Arrow-consistent. Note that if a preference domain is Arrow-inconsistent, it does not follow that the restriction of the preference domain to a proper subset of the alternatives is also Arrow-inconsistent. See Section 1 of Bordes, Campbell, and Le Breton (1995) for an example of this phenomenon.

[72] Bordes, Campbell, and Le Breton (1995) assumed that preferences are strictly convex. Their arguments also apply to convex preferences because the same pairs and triples of alternatives are strictly free with either convexity assumption.

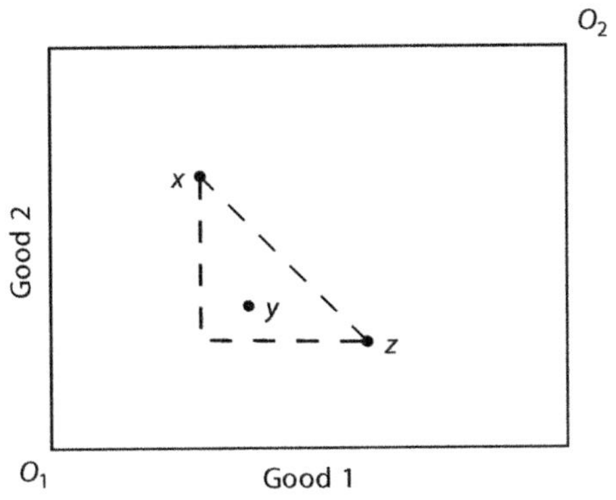

Figure 17.11. A Free Triple for Person One in the Edgeworth Box.

To prove this theorem, Bordes, Campbell, and Le Breton used a version of the local approach, but they had to depart quite significantly from the conventional arguments described in earlier sections. To see why this is necessary, we prove Theorem 14 for the case in which $m = n = 2$; that is, for an Edgeworth box economy.

Proof (for $m = n = 2$)

Step 1. Reasoning as in Examples 8 and 17, $\{x, y\}$ is a free pair for person i if and only if neither $x^i > y^i$ nor $y^i > x^i$.[73] Because of the resource constraint, if a pair is free for one individual, it is also free for the other individual. Any pair that is not free is trivial, with person i having a strict preference for x over y if and only if person j has the reverse strict preference. It is not possible for anyone to be indifferent on a trivial pair.

Step 2. Consider a triple of alternatives $\{x, y, z\}$ in $E^\circ(\omega)$. The discussion in Step 2 of Example 8 shows that for this triple to be free for individual one, the alternatives must be situated as shown in Figure 17.11.[74] This triple is not free for person two because y cannot be ranked last in this triple by this individual. More generally, if $\{x, y, z\}$ is a free triple for person i, then there is an alternative $a \in \{x, y, z\}$ with the property that j can have any preference on this triple in which a is strictly preferred to one of the other two alternatives. In Figure 17.11, $a = y$. If the three alternatives are arranged in increasing order of the consumption of good one, this implies that j has a single-peaked preference on this triple. Thus, there are no free triples in $E^\circ(\omega)$, which is why the local analysis must be modified in order for it to apply to an Edgeworth box economy.

[73] In our discussion of the two-person case, we use i to denote an arbitrary member of $\{1, 2\}$ and j to denote the other person.

[74] In Figures 17.11 and 17.12, O_1 (resp. O_2) is person one's (resp. two's) origin.

Step 3. For any free pair $\{x,y\}$ and any $i \in \{1,2\}$, we can find a third alternative $z \in E^{\circ}(\omega)$ such that $\{x,y,z\}$ is a free triple for i and the alternative a that cannot be ranked last by the other individual is a prespecified member of the triple. For example, if $i=1$, for the x and y depicted in Figure 17.1, z would need to be located in region III if $a=x$, in region IX if $a=y$, and in region VI if $a=z$.

Step 4. Suppose that F is a social welfare function with a classical private goods preference domain whose restriction to $E^{\circ}(\omega)$ satisfies IIA and WP. The next part of the proof is concerned with determining the decisiveness implications of these assumptions. In this two-person economy, individual i is almost decisive for (x,y) if x is socially preferred to y when i prefers x to y and j prefers y to x. Let $AD_i(x,y)$ denote that i is almost decisive for (x,y). Suppose that $\{x,y,z\}$ is a free triple for i and, without loss of generality, that y is the alternative in this triple that cannot be ranked last by j. In this step, we show that either i is almost decisive on all ordered pairs of distinct alternatives in $\{x,y,z\}$ or j is almost decisive on all ordered pairs (a,b) of distinct alternatives in $\{x,y,z\}$ for which $b \neq y$.[75]

Let $\mathbf{R}^1$ be a profile for which $xP_i^1yP_i^1z$ and $yP_j^1zP_j^1x$. By WP, we have yP^1z. If zR^1x and xR^1y, R^1 would not be an ordering. Therefore, either xP^1z or yP^1x. We consider each case in turn.

Case 1. If xP^1z, IIA implies $AD_i(x,z)$. Suppose now that $AD_i(a,b)$ holds for $a,b \in \{x,y,z\}$ with $a \neq y$. Let c be the other alternative in the triple and consider a profile $\mathbf{R}^2$ for which $aP_i^2bP_i^2c$ and $bP_j^2cP_j^2a$. We then have aP^2b by $AD_i(a,b)$ and bP^2c by WP. Transitivity of R^2 then implies that aP^2c and, hence, $AD_i(a,c)$. A similar argument can be used to show that $AD_i(c,b)$ holds. Letting $a=x$ and $b=z$, it then follows from $AD_i(x,z)$ that $AD_i(x,y)$ and $AD_i(y,z)$. Now letting $a=x$ and $b=y$, it follows from $AD_i(x,y)$ that $AD_i(z,y)$. Similarly, it can be shown that $AD_i(z,x)$ and $AD_i(y,x)$ both hold. Therefore, i is almost decisive on all of the distinct ordered pairs in $\{x,y,z\}$.

Case 2. If yP^1x, IIA implies $AD_j(y,x)$. Consider a profile $\mathbf{R}^3$ for which $xP_i^3zP_i^3y$ and $yP_j^3xP_j^3z$. We then have yP^3x by $AD_j(y,x)$ and xP^3z by WP. Thus, yP^3z by the transitivity of R^3, which establishes $AD_j(y,z)$. We can similarly show that $AD_j(z,x)$ and $AD_j(x,z)$ both hold. Therefore, j is almost decisive on all ordered pairs (a,b) of distinct alternatives in $\{x,y,z\}$ for which $b \neq y$.[76]

[75] A more complete proof of this result may be found in the proof of Lemma 1 in Bordes, Campbell, and Le Breton (1995).

[76] Note that none of the profiles used in this demonstration has person j ranking y last in $\{x,y,z\}$.

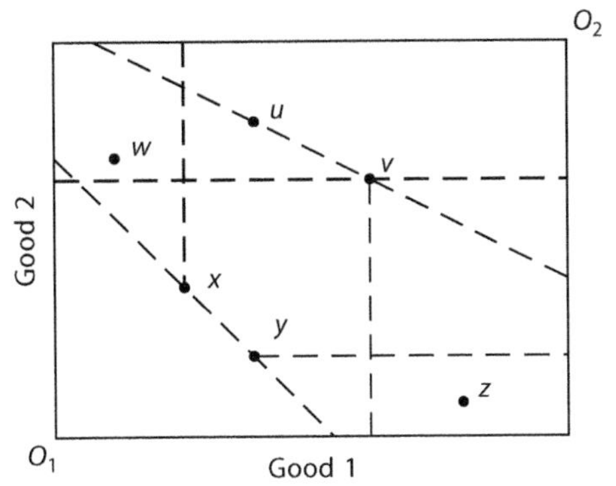

Figure 17.12. The Connection Argument in an Edgeworth Box.

Step 5. Suppose that Case 2 of the preceding step holds. By Step 3, there exists a $w \in E^{\circ}(\omega)$ such that $\{w, x, y\}$ is a free triple for j with w never ranked last by i in this triple. If $AD_i(x, y)$ holds, we would have a contradiction with $AD_j(y, x)$. Hence, by Step 4, j is almost decisive on all of the distinct ordered pairs in $\{w, x, y\}$. In particular, we have $AD_j(x, y)$. A similar argument can be used to show that $AD_j(z, y)$. Thus, Steps 4 and 5 show that if $\{x, y, z\}$ is a free triple for i, then either i or j is almost decisive on every ordered pair of distinct alternatives in $\{x, y, z\}$.

Step 6. For the triple considered in the previous two steps, suppose that $AD_i(x, y)$ holds. Consider a profile $\mathbf{R}^4$ for which $xP_i^4 yP_i^4 z$, $yP_j^4 x$, and $yP_j^4 z$, with x and z ranked arbitrarily by j. We then have $xP^4 y$ by $AD_i(x, y)$ and $yP^4 z$ by WP. Transitivity of R^4 implies that $xP^4 z$, so i is decisive for (x, z). Similar arguments can be used to show that one of the two individuals is decisive on all ordered pairs of distinct alternatives in $\{x, y, z\}$. In other words, there is a dictator on this triple.

Step 7. Because there are no free triples, we cannot connect two nontrivial pairs with a sequence of overlapping free triples, as in the local approach. Nevertheless, it is possible to "connect" these pairs with a sequence of overlapping triples, with each triple in the sequence free for one of the two individuals. As in the local approach, overlapping triples have two alternatives in common. As a consequence, who is the dictator on each triple must be the same. Hence, one individual, say d, dictates on all the nontrivial pairs.

We illustrate the connection argument with the nontrivial pairs $\{u, v\}$ and $\{x, y\}$ shown in Figure 17.12. For the w and z shown in Figure 17.12, the sequence of triples $\{u, v, z\}$, $\{v, z, w\}$, $\{z, w, x\}$, and $\{w, x, y\}$ exhibits the properties we require. The first two triples in this sequence are free for person two, while the other two are free for person one.[77]

Step 8. A separation argument is now used to show that d is also a dictator on the trivial pairs. Suppose that $\{x, y\}$ is a trivial pair and that $xP_d y$. As in our discussion of Example 19, $\{x, y\}$ is separable for d, so there exists a $z \in E^\circ(\omega)$ such that $\{x, z\}$ and $\{y, z\}$ are free for d and there exists a profile $\mathbf{R}'$ in the domain for which $xP'_d zP'_d y$. Because d is a dictator on the two free pairs, we have $xP'z$ and $zP'y$. Hence, $xP'y$ by transitivity. IIA now implies that xPy, which completes the proof. □

The proof of Theorem 14 is completed by first showing that the theorem holds for $n \geq 3$ and $m = 2$, and then proving that the two-good impossibility can be extended to more goods. The proof of the two-good case makes use of Redekop's topological version of the local approach discussed in Section 6. Unlike the two-person case we have considered in detail, when there are at least three individuals, any free pair can be embedded in a free triple. See Bordes, Campbell, and Le Breton (1995) for the details.

In Example 19, we have seen that when $X = (\mathbb{R}^m_+ \backslash \{0_m\})^n$ with $m \geq 2$, the domain of classical private goods preferences $\mathcal{C}_{pr}$ is hypersaturating and, hence, Arrow-inconsistent. Let $\mathcal{C}^=_{pr}$ denote the subset of $\mathcal{C}_{pr}$ in which everyone has the same preference for own consumption in each profile. In Section 9, we noted that Redekop (1993a) has shown that $\mathcal{C}^=_{pr}$ is also Arrow-inconsistent when $X = (\mathbb{R}^m_+ \backslash \{0_m\})^n$. These conclusions also hold if $X = \mathbb{R}^{mn}_{++}$. In view of the impossibility result established in Theorem 14 for classical private goods preferences, one might wonder if the restriction of $\mathcal{C}^=_{pr}$ to the interior of the set of feasible allocations for an exchange economy is also Arrow-inconsistent. Example 23 demonstrates that this is not the case. This example illustrates the importance of the assumption that the set of alternatives is Cartesian for Redekop's impossibility theorem.

Example 23 In this example, the set of alternatives is $E^\circ(\omega)$, where $\omega \in \mathbb{R}^m_{++}$ and $m \geq 2$. Preferences are defined on $\mathbb{R}^{mn}_+$. The domain $\mathcal{D}$ of the social welfare function is the restriction of $\mathcal{C}^=_{pr}$ to $E^\circ(\omega)$. We show that this domain is Arrow-consistent.

A social welfare function $F\colon \mathcal{D} \to \mathcal{R}$ satisfying the three Arrow axioms can be constructed as follows. Let e denote the alternative in which each person receives an equal share of each good. For each profile $\mathbf{R} \in \mathcal{D}$, (i) e is socially preferred to all of the other

[77] Viewed from person one's perspective, u, v, x, and y have the same relative positions as the alternatives used in Figure 17.3. In that diagram, the alternatives w and z were chosen to lie on the axes sufficiently far from the origin so that all the triples in the sequence are free for this individual. That argument is unaffected if w and z are modified slightly so that the consumption of both goods is positive. However, our earlier argument made essential use of the assumption that the set of alternatives is unbounded from above. In Figure 17.12, if z were instead chosen to lie above the line through u and v, but below the horizontal line through y (as in Figure 17.3), z would lie outside the Edgeworth box.

alternatives in $E^\circ(\omega)$ and (ii) for all pairs of alternatives that do not include e, the social ranking coincides with R_1. Because R_1 is an ordering, $F(\mathbf{R})$ is as well. By construction, F satisfies IIA. Person one never ranks e first in $E^\circ(\omega)$, so F satisfies *ND*. Because everyone has the same preferences, e is Pareto optimal for all $\mathbf{R} \in \mathcal{D}$. This observation combined with the way social preferences are defined on pairs that do not include e implies that F satisfies WP.[78]

11. EFFECTIVE SOCIAL WELFARE FUNCTIONS

Determining a social preference is often just the first step of a social choice procedure whose ultimate goal is to choose a set of alternatives. Given a preference profile, the social welfare function first aggregates the individual preferences into a social preference, and then this social preference is used to determine the socially-best alternatives in the feasible set of alternatives. In this section, we consider the implications of requiring socially-best alternatives to exist on some collections of subsets of the universal set of alternatives when there are private alternatives.

For a nonempty set $A \subseteq X$ and an ordering $R \in \mathcal{R}$, the *set of best alternatives* in A according to R is

$$B(A,R) = \{x \in A \mid xRy \text{ for all } y \in A\}.$$

Let $\mathcal{A}$ be a collection of nonempty subsets of X. A social welfare function $F: \mathcal{D} \to \mathcal{R}$ is *effective on* $\mathcal{A}$ if for all $\mathbf{R} \in \mathcal{D}$ and all $A \in \mathcal{A}$, $B(A, F(\mathbf{R})) \neq \emptyset$. For the classical domain of private goods preferences used in Example 17, Campbell (1989a) has shown that there is no social welfare function that is both effective on all compact subsets of X and satisfies the Arrow axioms.

Theorem 15 *If* $X = \mathbb{R}_+^{mn}$ *with* $m \geq 2$, *there is no social welfare function with a classical private goods preference domain that is effective on the nonempty compact subsets of* X *and satisfies* IIA, WP, *and* ND.

Proof. On the contrary, suppose that there exists a social welfare function that satisfies all the assumptions of the theorem. From our discussion of Example 19, we know that there must be a dictator d on $(\mathbb{R}_+^m \setminus \{0_m\})^n$. Given the restrictions on individual preferences, in order for d not to be a dictator on all of X, there must exist $i \in N$, $x, y \in X$ with $x^d \neq 0_m$ and $y^i = 0_m$, and a profile $\mathbf{R} \in \mathcal{D}$ such that $xP_d y$, but yRx. Consider the alternative z

[78] Note that the construction in this example can be used to show that a preference domain is Arrow-consistent whenever there is an alternative that is in the Pareto set for all admissible preference profiles.

obtained by adding $\varepsilon > 0$ to each person's consumption of every good in y. Because R_d is continuous, for sufficiently small ε, we have $xP_d zP_d y$. Let $A = \{x, y, z\}$. Because d is a dictator on $\{x, z\}$, $z \notin B(A, R)$. By WP, $y \notin B(A, R)$. Because the social welfare function is effective on compact sets, we therefore have $B(A, R) = \{x\}$, which contradicts the assumption that yRx. □

The requirement that socially-preferred alternatives exist on all compact subsets of X may be too demanding. For example, we might only need to choose out of compact, comprehensive subsets of X. A set $A \subseteq \mathbb{R}^m_+$ is *comprehensive* if for any $x, y \in \mathbb{R}^m_+$ with $x \geq y$, $x \in A$ implies $y \in A$. For any $x \in \mathbb{R}^m_+$, the *comprehensive set* of x is $x_\downarrow = \{y \in \mathbb{R}^m_+ \mid x \geq y\}$. Following Duggan (1996), for any $x, y \in \mathbb{R}^m_+$, $x_\downarrow \cup y_\downarrow$ is called the *corner set* of $\{x, y\}$.

By strengthening WP to SP in Theorem 15, we obtain an impossibility theorem when the social welfare function is only required to be effective on the compact, comprehensive subsets of X.

Theorem 16 *If $X = \mathbb{R}^{mn}_+$ with $m \geq 2$, there is no social welfare function with a classical private goods preference domain that is effective on the nonempty compact, comprehensive subsets of X and satisfies* IIA, SP, *and* ND.

Proof. The proof of this theorem is similar to the proof of Theorem 15. Instead of letting $A = \{x, y, z\}$, we now let $A = x_\downarrow \cup z_\downarrow$. By SP, $B(A, R) \subseteq \{x, z\}$. As in the earlier proof, $B(A, R) = \{x\}$, which results in a contradiction with the assumption that yRx. □

Donaldson and Weymark (1988) have noted that Border's social welfare function in Example 18 is not effective for standard feasible sets of allocations because there is always a discontinuity in the social preference on the boundary of the allocation space. For example, consider a two-person, two-good exchange economy. Because the social welfare function satisfies WP, we can restrict our search for socially-best alternatives to allocations in the Edgeworth box for this economy. For the social welfare function in Example 18, all points in the Edgeworth box excluding the two origins are socially preferred to person two's origin, which, in turn, is socially preferred to person one's origin. However, for all points other than the two origins, transferring some of any good from person one to person two is a social improvement (provided person one remains with some consumption). Hence, there is no socially-best alternative.

Bone (2003) has shown that effectiveness has strong implications for an exchange economy. As in Section 10.2, let $E(\omega)$ be the feasible allocations in an m-good, n-person exchange economy when there is no free disposal of goods. Suppose that F is a social welfare function with a classical private goods preference domain that is effective on $E(\omega)$ and that satisfies IIA and WP. By Theorem 14, there is a dictator d on $E^\circ(\omega)$ (the interior of $E(\omega)$). Because d has no best alternative in $E^\circ(\omega)$, for any admissible profile, any socially-best alternative in $E(\omega)$ must give someone nothing of at least one good. Bone has shown that, in fact, someone consumes the whole endowment.

Requiring a social welfare function to be effective on the compact subsets of X is less demanding than requiring social preferences to be continuous. Variants of Theorems 15 and 16 can be established quite simply when it is assumed that social preferences are continuous on X.[79] From our discussion of Example 20, we know that there must be a dictator on the interior of $\mathbb{R}^{mn}_{+}$ if the social welfare function satisfies IIA and WP. Continuity of the social preference extends this dictatorial power to all of $\mathbb{R}^{mn}_{+}$.

In view of the largely negative results surveyed in Part I, it is natural to wonder if more satisfactory social choice procedures are possible if we abandon the objective of constructing a social welfare function and, instead, directly determine the socially-best alternatives in an agenda as a function of the individual preferences. This is the subject of Part II.

Part II: Social Choice Correspondences

12. A CHOICE-THEORETIC VERSION OF ARROW'S THEOREM

12.1. The Arrow Choice Axioms

An *agenda* is a nonempty subset of X. The set of admissible agendas, the *agenda domain*, is $\mathcal{A}$, a collection of nonempty subsets of X. Each agenda in the agenda domain is a potential feasible set.

A *social choice correspondence* $C\colon \mathcal{A} \times \mathcal{D} \to X$ is a mapping that assigns a nonempty subset of the agenda to each admissible agenda and admissible profile.[80] That is, for all $A \in \mathcal{A}$ and all $\mathbf{R} \in \mathcal{D}$, $\emptyset \neq C(A,\mathbf{R}) \subseteq A$. The set $C(A,\mathbf{R})$ is called the *choice set*. If, for all agendas and profiles in the domain, the choice set only contains a single alternative, then C is a *social choice function*.

Choice-theoretic versions of Arrow's Theorem employ a choice consistency condition. A *choice consistency* condition for a social choice correspondence places restrictions on how the choices from different agendas are related for a given preference profile. The choice consistency axiom used in Arrow's Theorem is *Arrow's Choice Axiom*.

[79] See, for example, Campbell (1992b, 1996) for discussions of continuity of social preference.

[80] The assumption that the domain of C is the Cartesian product of $\mathcal{A}$ and $\mathcal{D}$ excludes from consideration the possibility that the feasibility of an agenda may depend on the preference profile, as in asymmetric information models with self-selection constraints.

Arrow's Choice Axiom (ACA)
For all $A^1, A^2 \in \mathcal{A}$ and all $\mathbf{R} \in \mathcal{D}$, if $A^1 \subset A^2$ and $C(A^2, \mathbf{R}) \cap A^1 \neq \emptyset$, then $C(A^1, \mathbf{R}) = C(A^2, \mathbf{R}) \cap A^1$.

In words, for a given profile $\mathbf{R}$, if anything that is chosen in A^2 is feasible when the agenda shrinks to A^1, then the choice set for the smaller agenda consists of that part of the original choice set that is still feasible.

The definition of a social welfare function incorporates the social rationality condition that all social rankings of the alternatives are orderings. For the agenda domain used in our version of Arrow's Theorem for social choice correspondences, ACA is the choice-theoretic analogue of this social rationality condition. To see why, we need to take a brief excursion into revealed preference theory.

A social welfare function $F\colon \mathcal{D} \to \mathcal{R}$ *rationalizes* the social choice correspondence C if for all $A \in \mathcal{A}$ and all $\mathbf{R} \in \mathcal{D}$, $C(A, \mathbf{R}) = B(A, F(\mathbf{R}))$. That is, for each agenda A and each profile $\mathbf{R}$ in the domain of C, the choice set consists of the best elements in A according to the social preference relation R assigned to the profile $\mathbf{R}$ by the social welfare function F.

For each $\mathbf{R} \in \mathcal{D}$, the social choice correspondence C defines a choice correspondence $C_{\mathbf{R}}\colon \mathcal{A} \to X$. Revealed preference theory has identified a number of circumstances in which a choice correspondence can be rationalized by an ordering. See, for example, Suzumura (1983). These results can be trivially reformulated as social choice revealed preference theorems.[81]

In the version of Arrow's Theorem that we present in the next section, we assume that the agenda domain is the set of all finite subsets of X.[82]

Complete Finite Agenda Domain
$A \in \mathcal{A}$ if and only if A is a finite subset of X.

For this agenda domain, Arrow (1959) has shown that a social choice correspondence C can be rationalized by a social welfare function if and only if C satisfies ACA. It is this revealed preference theorem that provides the link between ACA and the social rationality condition used in his social welfare function impossibility theorem.

Theorem 17 *On a complete finite agenda domain, a social choice correspondence can be rationalized by a social welfare function if and only if it satisfies* ACA.

[81] The revealed preference results described in what follows were originally established for choice correspondences.
[82] The inclusion of the agendas containing only one alternative is of no consequence because the choice on one-alternative agendas is completely determined by the requirement that the choice sets are nonempty. In all of the agenda domains we consider, it is implicitly assumed that only nonempty sets are in the domain.

With this agenda domain, the social welfare function F that rationalizes a social choice correspondence C satisfying ACA is uniquely determined by the choices made in the binary agendas. That is, for all $x, y \in X$ and all $\mathbf{R} \in \mathcal{D}$, $xF(\mathbf{R})y$ if and only if $x \in C(\{x,y\},\mathbf{R})$. For a fixed profile, the binary relation defined in this way is called the *base relation*.

Arrow's revealed preference theorem is a special case of a theorem due to Hansson (1968) that has played an important role in the development of some of the results described in subsequent sections. In the version of Hansson's Theorem that we consider, the agenda domain is closed under finite unions. An agenda domain $\mathcal{A}$ is *closed under finite unions* if for all $A^1, A^2 \in \mathcal{A}$, $A^1 \cup A^2 \in \mathcal{A}$. A complete finite agenda domain is closed under finite unions.

Theorem 18 *A social choice correspondence whose agenda domain is closed under finite unions can be rationalized by a social welfare function if and only if it satisfies* ACA.[83]

If some of the binary agendas are not feasible, the social welfare function that rationalizes the social choice correspondence need not be unique.[84]

Arrow's choice axiom is closely related to the Weak Axiom of Revealed Preference. For a given profile, this axiom requires that if it is ever the case that x, but not y, is chosen when both x and y are feasible, then y is never chosen when x is in the agenda.

Weak Axiom of Revealed Preference (WARP)

For all $x, y \in X$ and all $\mathbf{R} \in \mathcal{D}$, if there exists an $A^1 \in \mathcal{A}$ such that $x \in C(A^1,\mathbf{R})$ and $y \in A^1 \setminus C(A^1,\mathbf{R})$, then there does not exist an $A^2 \in \mathcal{A}$ such that $y \in C(A^2,\mathbf{R})$ and $x \in A^2$.

If a social choice correspondence satisfies WARP, then it necessarily satisfies ACA. In general, the reverse implication does not hold. However, if the agenda domain is closed under finite unions, WARP is equivalent to ACA (see Suzumura, 1983). Because a complete finite agenda domain is closed under finite unions, it does not matter which of these two axioms is used in the choice-theoretic version of Arrow's Theorem. However, on most of the agenda domains we consider in subsequent sections, these axioms are not equivalent. When this is the case and the domain has an economic interpretation, it has been customary to use ACA rather than WARP.

Choice consistency conditions link the choices made from different agendas for a fixed profile. In contrast, independence conditions link the choices made from a fixed agenda for different profiles. *Independence of Infeasible Alternatives* requires the choice set to be independent of preferences over alternatives not in the agenda.

[83] This theorem is a special case of a more general result established by Hansson (1968).

[84] Arrow (1951, p. 20) has said that even when no binary agendas are in the agenda domain, "under certain plausible conditions" it is nevertheless possible to rationalize a choice correspondence. However, he does not say what these conditions are.

Independence of Infeasible Alternatives (IIF)
For all $A \in \mathcal{A}$ and all $\mathbf{R}^1, \mathbf{R}^2 \in \mathcal{D}$, if $\mathbf{R}^1$ and $\mathbf{R}^2$ coincide on A, then $C(A, \mathbf{R}^1) = C(A, \mathbf{R}^2)$.

It might seem that the natural choice-theoretic analogue to Independence of Irrelevant Alternatives would only place restrictions on the choices from agendas containing only two alternatives. However, a binary version of IIF is vacuous if no binary agendas are in the agenda domain, as is typically the case in economic problems.

Plott (1976) has argued that almost any reasonable social decision procedure satisfies IIF. In essence, his argument is that a necessary condition for a social choice rule to be implementable (using any of the standard cooperative or noncooperative solution concepts) is that the alternatives chosen must only depend on individual preferences for feasible alternatives. In this view, the independence assumption is not a normative principle of social choice, but is, rather, a constraint on what is achievable.[85] However, not everyone believes that implementability is a necessary requirement for a social choice correspondence to be satisfactory. Implementability is a demanding requirement that is not satisfied by, for example, the standard Walrasian competitive equilibrium correspondence on standard economic domains.

We consider weak and strong versions of the Pareto principle. For all $A \in \mathcal{A}$ and all $\mathbf{R} \in \mathcal{D}$, the *weak Pareto set* (the set of weakly Pareto optimal alternatives) is

$$\mathcal{P}^w(A, \mathbf{R}) = \{x \in A \mid \nexists y \in A \text{ such that } yP_ix \text{ for all } i \in N\}$$

and the *strong Pareto set* (the set of strongly Pareto optimal alternatives) is

$$\mathcal{P}^s(A, \mathbf{R}) = \{x \in A \mid \nexists y \in A \text{ such that } yR_ix \text{ for all } i \in N \text{ and } yP_jx \text{ for some } j \in N\}.$$

The *Weak Pareto* (resp. *Strong Pareto*) axiom requires the choice set to be a subset of the weak (resp. strong) Pareto set.[86]

Weak Pareto (WP)
For all $A \in \mathcal{A}$ and all $\mathbf{R} \in \mathcal{D}$, $C(A, \mathbf{R}) \subseteq \mathcal{P}^w(A, \mathbf{R})$.

[85] See Campbell (1992a, 1992c) for further discussion of the relationship between IIF and implementability. As in Plott (1976), Campbell argues that IIF is a necessary condition for the implementabilty of a social choice correspondence. Campbell assumes that the social choice correspondence C is generated from a social welfare function F by setting $C(A, \mathbf{R})$ equal to the set of alternatives that are maximal in A for $F(\mathbf{R})$. He has shown that if the preference domain satisfies a regularity condition and if social preferences are continuous, then C satisfies IIF if and only if F satisfies IIA when the agenda domain consists of all m-element subsets of X, where $m > 1$.

[86] Some of our axioms (and acronyms) for social choice correspondences have the same names as the corresponding axioms for social welfare functions. It is always clear from the context whether a social choice correspondence or a social welfare function axiom is being used.

Strong Pareto (SP)
For all $A \in \mathcal{A}$ and all $\mathbf{R} \in \mathcal{D}$, $C(A,\mathbf{R}) \subseteq \mathcal{P}^s(A,\mathbf{R})$.

Pareto conditions place no cross-profile or cross-agenda restrictions on a social choice correspondence.

A social choice correspondence is *dictatorial* if the choice set is always a subset of some single individual's best alternatives in the agenda. Formally, an individual $d \in N$ is a *dictator* for the social choice correspondence C if $C(A,\mathbf{R}) \subseteq B(A,R_d)$ for all $A \in \mathcal{A}$ and all $\mathbf{R} \in \mathcal{D}$. If $C(A,\mathbf{R}) = B(A,R_d)$ for all $A \in \mathcal{A}$, then d is a *strong dictator* for C. *Nondictatorship* is the requirement that there be no dictator.

Nondictatorship (ND)
There is no dictator.

The *Arrow axioms* for a social choice correspondence are ACA, IIF, WP, and ND.

If it is possible to find a social choice correspondence that satisfies all of the Arrow axioms on the domain $\mathcal{A} \times \mathcal{D}$, it is natural to inquire if there are other desirable properties that can be satisfied on this domain. ND precludes any individual from having complete power to determine the choice set in all circumstances, but it does not rule out having one individual's preferred choices being made in almost all choice situations, nor does it preclude the decision-making power being concentrated in the hands of as few as two individuals. It is therefore of interest to see if it is possible to spread the decision-making power more widely among the population. One way that has been proposed to do this is to require the social choice correspondence to satisfy *Anonymity*, the requirement that the choice set from a given agenda be invariant to permutations of the individual preferences.

Anonymity (ANON)
For all $A \in \mathcal{A}$ and all $\mathbf{R}^1, \mathbf{R}^2 \in \mathcal{D}$, if $\mathbf{R}^1$ is a permutation of $\mathbf{R}^2$, then $C(A,\mathbf{R}^1) = C(A,\mathbf{R}^2)$.

This formulation of an anonymity condition is only appropriate if all of the individual preference domains are the same. If there are private alternatives and everyone is selfish, ANON is vacuous because if we, say, permute i's and j's preferences, i would then only care about j's consumption and vice versa, which takes us outside the preference domain. For Cartesian sets of alternatives and selfish individual preference domains, it is the induced private preferences Q_i on the individual consumptions sets X_i that should be permuted, not the preferences on X.

Private Alternatives Anonymity (PANON)
For all $A \in \mathcal{A}$ and all $\mathbf{R}^1, \mathbf{R}^2 \in \mathcal{D}$, if $\mathbf{Q}^1 = (Q_1^1, \ldots, Q_n^1)$ is a permutation of $\mathbf{Q}^2 = (Q_1^2, \ldots, Q_n^2)$, then $C(A,\mathbf{R}^1) = C(A,\mathbf{R}^2)$.

In the case of public alternatives, provided that the preference domain is not too degenerate, ANON is a strengthening of ND. Similarly, for private alternatives, provided that the induced private preference domain is not too degenerate, PANON is also more demanding than ND.

12.2. Arrow's Theorem

The version of Arrow's Theorem that we consider in this section supposes that the preference domain is unrestricted and that the agenda domain is the set of all nonempty finite subsets of X. With these domain assumptions, the choice-theoretic version of Arrow's Theorem shows that there is no social choice correspondence that satisfies ACA, IIF, WP, and ND if there are at least three alternatives. We provide a proof of this theorem because the proof strategy has proved useful on restricted domains as well.

Theorem 19 *If* $|X| \geq 3$, *there is no social choice correspondence with a complete finite agenda domain and an unrestricted preference domain that satisfies* ACA, IIF, WP, *and* ND.

Proof. On the contrary, suppose that there exists a social correspondence $C\colon \mathcal{A} \times \mathcal{D} \to X$ that satisfies all the assumptions of the theorem. By Theorem 17, C can be rationalized by a social welfare function $F\colon \mathcal{D} \to \mathcal{R}$. Further, for each profile $\mathbf{R}$ in the preference domain, the rationalizing social ordering $F(\mathbf{R})$ is uniquely given by the base relation.

Consider any $x, y \in X$ and any $\mathbf{R}^1, \mathbf{R}^2 \in \mathcal{D}$ that coincide on $\{x, y\}$. By IIF, $C(\{x,y\},\mathbf{R}^1) = C(\{x,y\},\mathbf{R}^2)$ and, hence, because F is constructed from the base relations, $xF(\mathbf{R}^1)y$ if and only if $xF(\mathbf{R}^2)y$. Thus, F satisfies IIA.

Next, consider any $x, y \in X$ and any $\mathbf{R} \in \mathcal{D}$ for which xP_iy for all $i \in N$. Because C satisfies WP, $C(\{x,y\},\mathbf{R}) = \{x\}$. Because $F(\mathbf{R})$ rationalizes C, x is socially preferred to y according to $F(\mathbf{R})$; that is, F satisfies WP.

By the social welfare function version of Arrow's Theorem, F is dictatorial. Let $d \in N$ be this dictator. Because C is nondictatorial, there exist an agenda $A \in \mathcal{A}$, alternatives $x, y \in A$, and a profile $\mathbf{R} \in \mathcal{D}$ such that xP_dy and $y \in C(A,\mathbf{R})$. ACA then implies that $y \in C(\{x,y\},\mathbf{R})$. Thus, $yF(\mathbf{R})x$, contradicting the assumption that d is a dictator for F. □

13. UNRESTRICTED PREFERENCE DOMAINS

Before considering simultaneous restrictions on the preference and agenda domains, it is useful to consider a number of social choice problems in which the preference domain is unrestricted. Unrestricted preference domains do not arise naturally in economic problems, but are often natural in voting problems. In Section 13.1, we discuss a finite-alternative generalization of the choice-theoretic version of Arrow's Theorem due to Grether and Plott (1982). In Section 13.2, we present a theorem due to Dutta, Jackson, and Le Breton (2001) on the impossibility of constructing a Paretian voting procedure that is immune to strategic entry decisions on the part of the candidates. As shown by Ehlers and Weymark (2003), the Grether–Plott Theorem can be used to help prove Dutta, Jackson, and Le Breton's candidate stability theorem. In Section 13.3, we discuss the work of Gibbard, Hylland, and Weymark (1987) on agenda domains in which one or more alternatives are in every agenda. Such agenda domains capture some of the institutional features of committee and legislative decision making.

Some of the agenda domains that we consider in this section have the property that some, or all, of the binary agendas are not admissible. This is the usual framework employed in the theory of nonbinary social choice theory. The literature on nonbinary social choice when the preference domain is unrestricted is quite extensive, but, as noted, it has limited relevance for economic problems. See Deb (2010) for a survey of this literature.

13.1. The Grether–Plott Theorem

The proof of Arrow's Theorem presented in Section 12.2 makes essential use of the assumption that all binary agendas are in the domain. Grether and Plott (1982) noted that economic and political problems typically have agenda domains in which this assumption is violated. To overcome this problem, they relaxed the complete finite agenda domain assumption. Assuming that the universal set of alternatives X is finite, their agenda domain is the set of all agendas containing at least k alternatives, where $k < |X|$.

k-Set Feasibility (KSF)
There exists a finite positive integer $k < |X|$ such that $A \in \mathcal{A}$ if and only if $|A| \geq k$.

The value of k must be strictly less than the number of alternatives in order for ACA to play any role. This domain is appropriate if only the "large" agendas are feasible, with the parameter k being used to identify when an agenda is "large."

For a finite universal set of alternatives, the Grether–Plott Theorem shows that the Arrow axioms are inconsistent when the preference domain is unrestricted and KSF is satisfied.[87]

Theorem 20 *If* $3 \leq |X| < \infty$, *there is no social choice correspondence with an unrestricted preference domain that satisfies* KSF, ACA, IIF, WP, *and* ND.

When KSF is satisfied, the agenda domain is closed under finite unions. Hence, by Hansson's Theorem (Theorem 18), ACA implies that the social choice correspondence

[87] The assumption that there are only a finite number of alternatives limits the relevance of the Grether–Plott Theorem for economic problems with divisible goods.

can be rationalized by a social welfare function. However, if $k > 2$, this rationalization is typically not unique. For example, suppose that $X = \{w, x, y, z\}$, $k = 3$, and $C(X, \mathbf{R}) = \{w, x\}$. For this profile, the choice set for any of the three-alternative agendas is completely determined by ACA. However, the ranking of y and z is arbitrary in any ordering that rationalizes these choices. Because of the possible non-uniqueness of the rationalizing social welfare function, the strategy used to prove Arrow's Theorem in Section 12.2 cannot be used to prove Theorem 20.

Grether and Plott's proof establishes that if a social choice correspondence satisfies all of the assumptions of Theorem 20 with $k \geq 3$, then it is is possible to construct another social choice correspondence with the same preference domain that satisfies $(k-1)$-Set Feasibility and all of the Arrow axioms. An induction argument then shows that the Arrow axioms are consistent when all nonempty finite feasible sets are feasible, which is impossible. Note that if k is 1 or 2, Theorem 20 is simply a finite version of Arrow's Theorem.

It is instructive to consider how Grether and Plott constructed the social choice correspondence used in their proof. For $h = k-1, k$, let $\mathcal{A}^h = \{A \in \mathcal{A} \mid |A| \geq h\}$. Suppose that $3 \leq k < |X|$ and that $C^k \colon \mathcal{A}^k \times \mathcal{R}^n \to X$ satisfies the Arrow axioms. For all $A \in \mathcal{A}^{k-1} \backslash \mathcal{A}^k$, $z \in X \backslash A$, and $\mathbf{R} \in \mathcal{R}^n$, let $\bar{\mathbf{R}}(A, z, \mathbf{R})$ denote the unique profile in $\mathcal{R}^n$ for which, for all $i \in N$,

(i) $\forall x, y \in A$, $xR_i y \leftrightarrow x\bar{R}_i(A, z, \mathbf{R})y$,
(ii) $\forall x \in A$, $x\bar{R}_i(A, z, \mathbf{R})z$ and $\neg[z\bar{R}_i(A, z, \mathbf{R})x]$,
(iii) $\forall x \notin A \cup \{z\}$, $z\bar{R}_i(A, z, \mathbf{R})x$ and $\neg[x\bar{R}_i(A, z, \mathbf{R})z]$,
(iv) $\forall x, y \notin A \cup \{z\}$, $xR_i y \leftrightarrow x\bar{R}_i(A, z, \mathbf{R})y$.

In other words, for each individual i, the alternatives in A have been moved to the top and the alternatives not in $A \cup \{z\}$ have been moved to the bottom of i's preference ordering, preserving the original rankings in each of these groups. The alternatives in A are all preferred to z, which in turn is preferred to all of the remaining alternatives.

The social choice correspondence $C^{k-1} \colon \mathcal{A}^{k-1} \times \mathcal{R}^n \to X$ is defined by setting

$$C^{k-1}(A, \mathbf{R}) = C^k(A, \mathbf{R}), \quad \forall A \in \mathcal{A}^k,\ \forall \mathbf{R} \in \mathcal{R}^n,$$

and

$$C^{k-1}(A, \mathbf{R}) = \bigcup_{z \notin A} C^k(A \cup \{z\}, \bar{R}(A, z, \mathbf{R})), \quad \forall A \in \mathcal{A}^{k-1} \backslash \mathcal{A}^k,\ \forall \mathbf{R} \in \mathcal{R}^n.$$

Because C^k satisfies WP, $\emptyset \neq C^k(A \cup \{z\}, z, \bar{R}(A, z, \mathbf{R})) \subseteq A$, and thus C^{k-1} is a well-defined social choice correspondence.

Because C^k and C^{k-1} agree on agendas in $\mathcal{A}^k$ and C^k satisfies ND, so does C^{k-1}. When $\mathbf{R}^1$ and $\mathbf{R}^2$ coincide on $A \in \mathcal{A}^{k-1}$, $\bar{R}(A,z,\mathbf{R}^1)$ and $\bar{R}(A,z,\mathbf{R}^2)$ coincide on A as well. It thus follows from the assumption that C^k satisfies IIF that C^{k-1} does too. Because C^k satisfies WP, so does C^{k-1}. The proof that C^{k-1} satisfies ACA is quite lengthy. See Grether and Plott (1982) for the details.

In Grether and Plott's proof, it is necessary to move a set of alternatives to the top of each person's preferences, while preserving their relative rankings. The assumption that the preference domain is unrestricted ensures that this is possible. However, in economic problems with divisible goods, preferences are typically assumed to be continuous. With continuous preferences, this kind of construction is not possible, which suggests that the proof strategy used by Grether and Plott is not likely to be applicable to problems with divisible goods and continuous preferences.

13.2. Strategic Candidacy

By interpreting X as a finite set of potential candidates in an election and N as the set of voters, a social choice correspondence can be used to model elections in which the number of candidates is endogenous. Dutta, Jackson, and Le Breton (2001) have used this framework to investigate voting procedures in which the outcome of an election is unaffected by the decision not to stand for office of a candidate who would not win if he or she entered the election. We consider the case in which no candidate is also a voter.

An agenda is now interpreted as the set of candidates who contest the election. Dutta, Jackson, and Le Breton (2001) assumed that there are at least three potential candidates and that any subset of potential candidates could be on the ballot. Thus, the social choice correspondence has a complete finite agenda domain. Voters submit their rankings of the candidates, with no ties permitted. The preference domain is the unrestricted linear preference domain introduced in Section 2.[88] Only one candidate can be elected, so the social choice correspondence is in fact a social choice function.

Single-Valuedness (SV)
For all $A \in \mathcal{A}$ and all $\mathbf{R} \in \mathcal{D}$, $C(A,\mathbf{R})$ is a singleton.

The voting procedure described by the social choice correspondence is assumed to be invulnerable to the withdrawal of a candidate who would lose if all potential candidates stood for office.

[88] The voting rules used by Dutta, Jackson, and Le Breton (2001) choose a candidate from an agenda as a function of the preferences of both voters and candidates. A candidate is assumed to rank him- or herself first, but otherwise can have any linear order. Dutta, Jackson, and Le Breton assumed that the election outcome only depends on the voters' preferences, which permits us to simplify the statement of the problem as we have done here when candidates cannot vote.

Candidate Stability (CS)
For all $x \in X$ and all $\mathbf{R} \in \mathcal{D}$, if $x \notin C(X,\mathbf{R})$, then $C(X,\mathbf{R}) = C(X\backslash\{x\},\mathbf{R})$.

CS is a relatively weak way of requiring a voting procedure to be immune to the strategic entry decisions of the candidates because it only applies when all of the other potential candidates enter the election.[89]

Unanimity requires a candidate to be elected who is ranked first on the ballot by all of the voters.

Unanimity (UNAN)
For all $A \in \mathcal{A}$, $x \in A$, and $\mathbf{R} \in \mathcal{D}$, if for all $i \in N$, xP_iy for all $y \in A\backslash\{x\}$, then $C(A,\mathbf{R}) = \{x\}$.

Dutta, Jackson, and Le Breton (2001) used a strengthened form of the Arrovian nondictatorship condition. An individual is a dictator for large elections if this individual's most-preferred candidate is elected when at least $|X| - 1$ candidates run for office. Formally, an individual $d \in N$ is a *dictator for large elections* for the social choice correspondence C if for all $A \in \mathcal{A}$ with $|A| \geq |X| - 1$ and all $\mathbf{R} \in \mathcal{D}$, $C(A,\mathbf{R}) = \{x\}$ whenever $x \in A$ and xP_dy for all $y \in A\backslash\{x\}$.

Strong Nondictatorship (SND)
There is no dictator for large elections.

Dutta, Jackson, and Le Breton (2001) have shown that no voting procedure can satisfy IIF in addition to the assumptions described above.

Theorem 21 *If* $3 \leq |X| < \infty$, *there is no social choice correspondence with a complete finite agenda domain and an unrestricted linear preference domain that satisfies* SV, IIF, UNAN, CS, *and* SND.[90]

Both Arrow's Theorem and the Grether–Plott Theorem are valid for the preference domain $\mathcal{L}^n$. However, because UNAN is, by itself, a much weaker condition than WP, the Dutta–Jackson–Le Breton Theorem does not follow directly from either of these results. For this reason, they do not exploit either of these theorems in proving Theorem 21.

[89] The candidate stability axiom used here is what Dutta, Jackson, and Le Breton (2001) have called Strong Candidate Stability. They also considered a second candidate stability axiom that requires each candidate to prefer the outcome when all candidates are on the ballot to the outcome that would obtain if he or she withdrew from the election. As Dutta, Jackson, and Le Breton have shown, when the sets of voters and candidates are disjoint, these two candidate stability axioms are equivalent, given their other assumptions. When candidates and voters have individuals in common, this equivalence no longer holds.

[90] When candidates are permitted to vote, Dutta, Jackson, and Le Breton (2001) have shown that if CS is combined with some other reasonable properties of voting procedures, then the distribution of power among voters must be quite unequal.

Ehlers and Weymark (2003) have shown that the Grether–Plott Theorem can be used to help prove Theorem 21. Their proof strategy begins by assuming that the social choice correspondence C satisfies all of the assumptions of Theorem 21 except SND. By then restricting attention to the agendas with at least $|X| - 1$ candidates, the resulting social choice correspondence on the subdomain inherits all of the assumed properties of C. On this domain, CS is equivalent to ACA for single-valued social choice correspondences. In addition, the new agenda domain satisfies k-Set Feasibility for $k = |X| - 1$. On the subdomain, the social choice correspondence also satisfies WP, and, hence, by the Grether–Plott Theorem, it must be dictatorial, which, in terms of the original domain, is equivalent to the existence of a dictator for large elections. The proof that C satisfies WP on the subdomain is somewhat lengthy. See Ehlers and Weymark (2003) for the details.

13.3. Fixed Feasible Alternatives

In Gibbard, Hylland, and Weymark (1987), there is a finite set of alternatives and it is assumed that there is some alternative or set of alternatives that is in every feasible agenda. Examples with a single fixed feasible alternative include (i) allocation problems with fixed endowments in which preserving the initial distribution is always an option and (ii) bargaining problems in which there is a prespecified alternative (the threat point) that is chosen if no agreement is reached on the choice of another alternative. In committee or legislative decision making, the rules of order may specify that the motion and the *status quo* are always under consideration, with various possible amendments generating three-alternative agendas. In this example, there are two fixed alternatives in every admissible agenda.

For a nonempty subset $\bar{A}$ of X, the agenda domain is *$\bar{A}$-restricted* if $\bar{A}$ is in every feasible agenda.

$\bar{A}$-Restricted Agenda Domain
$A \in \mathcal{A}$ implies $\bar{A} \subseteq A$.

This domain restriction does not require that every superset of $\bar{A}$ is a feasible agenda. An agenda domain with this property is called *complete*.

Complete $\bar{A}$-Restricted Agenda Domain
$A \in \mathcal{A}$ if and only if $\bar{A} \subseteq A$.

Gibbard, Hylland, and Weymark (1987) have shown that for any $\bar{x} \in X$, Arrow's axioms, with WP strengthened to SP, are consistent when the agenda domain is $\bar{x}$-restricted and the preference domain is unrestricted.[91]

[91] The Arrow axioms are also consistent for any $\bar{A}$-restricted agenda domain when the preference domain is unrestricted.

Theorem 22 *If* $2 \leq |X| < \infty$, *for any* $\bar{x} \in X$, *there exist social choice correspondences with an* $\{\bar{x}\}$*-restricted agenda domain and an unrestricted preference domain that satisfy* ACA, IIF, SP, *and* ND.

The proof of this theorem is constructive. The social choice correspondence Gibbard, Hylland, and Weymark used to establish Theorem 22 is presented in Example 24.

Example 24 Fix $\bar{x} \in X$ and suppose that $\mathcal{A}$ is $\{\bar{x}\}$-restricted. For all $x \in X$ and $\mathbf{R} \in \mathcal{R}^n$, let $N^+(x,\mathbf{R}) = |\{i \in N \mid xP_i\bar{x}\}|$, $N^-(x,\mathbf{R}) = |\{i \in N \mid \bar{x}P_ix\}|$, and $N(x,\mathbf{R}) = N^+(x,\mathbf{R}) - N^-(x,\mathbf{R})$. If every individual assigns one point to each alternative preferred to $\bar{x}$, zero points to each alternative indifferent to $\bar{x}$, and negative one point to every other alternative, then $N(x,\mathbf{R})$ is the total number of points assigned to x in the profile $\mathbf{R}$.

For all $A \in \mathcal{A}$ and $\mathbf{R} \in \mathcal{R}^n$, let

$$C^R(A,\mathbf{R}) = \{x \in A \mid \forall y \in A, N(x,\mathbf{R}) \geq N(y,\mathbf{R})\},$$

$$C^0(A,\mathbf{R}) = \{x \in C^R(A,\mathbf{R}) \mid \forall y \in C^R(A,\mathbf{R}), N^-(x,\mathbf{R}) \leq N^-(y,\mathbf{R})\},$$

and, for all $i \in N$,

$$C^i(A,\mathbf{R}) = \{x \in C^{i-1}(A,\mathbf{R}) \mid \forall y \in C^{i-1}(A,\mathbf{R}), xR_iy\}.$$

The social choice correspondence C^n satisfies all of the assumptions of Theorem 22.

C^n satisfies ACA because it is rationalized by a lexicographic social welfare function. For a given profile, the alternatives are first ranked by the number of points received. Alternatives that are tied at this stage are then ranked in reverse order of the number of negative votes received. Finally, a serial dictatorial ordering is used as a secondary tie-breaking rule.

Richelson (1984) considered the social choice correspondence C^R. The use of C^R and the first tie-breaking rule ensure that C^n is nondictatorial.[92] C^R violates WP because if everyone prefers x to y to $\bar{x}$ and the agenda contains $\{x, y, \bar{x}\}$, then x and y receive the same number of points, even though they are Pareto ranked. The use of a serial dictatorship as a tie-breaking rule ensures that C^n satisfies SP. Because $C^n(A,\mathbf{R})$ is determined using only information about the individual preferences on A, C^n satisfies IIF.

Gibbard, Hylland, and Weymark (1987) have provided other examples of social choice correspondences that satisfy the Arrow axioms when the agenda domain is $\bar{A}$-restricted. Example 25 requires $\bar{A}$ to include two alternatives.

[92] If the first tie-breaking rule is not included, person one is a dictator when $n = 2$ or $|A| \leq 2$ for all $A \in \mathcal{A}$.

Example 25 Fix $\bar{x}, \bar{y} \in X$ and suppose that $\mathcal{A}$ is $\{\bar{x}, \bar{y}\}$-restricted. There are 3^n possible preference profiles restricted to $\{\bar{x}, \bar{y}\}$, which we number arbitrarily from 1 to 3^n. Let $\mathcal{D}^j$ denote the set of all profiles in $\mathcal{R}^n$ that coincide with the jth of these restricted preference profiles on $\{\bar{x}, \bar{y}\}$. Let $d\colon \{1, \ldots, 3^n\} \to N$ be a surjective function. The social choice correspondence $C\colon \mathcal{A} \times \mathcal{R}^n \to X$ is defined by setting $C(A, \mathbf{R}) = B(A, R_{d(j)})$ for all $A \in \mathcal{A}$, all $j \in \{1, \ldots, 3^n\}$, and all $\mathbf{R} \in \mathcal{D}^j$. In other words, restricted to profiles in $\mathcal{D}^j$, individual $d(j)$ is a strong dictator.

Because, for each profile, the choice sets are determined by maximizing some individual's preference ordering, both ACA and WP are satisfied.[93] Because the agenda domain is $\{\bar{x}, \bar{y}\}$-restricted, if two profiles coincide on a feasible agenda, they coincide on $\{\bar{x}, \bar{y}\}$. As a consequence, the same dictator is used for both profiles, so IIF is satisfied. Each individual is a dictator for some subset of the profiles, so C is nondictatorial.

Restricted to preference profiles in $\mathcal{L}^n$, the lexicographic social welfare function used to construct the social choice correspondence in Example 24 is an example of what Campbell and Kelly (2000) have called a three-layer gateau rule. With a three-layer gateau rule, for each profile $\mathbf{R}$ in the domain $\mathcal{D}$, the alternatives are partitioned into three groups, $T(\mathbf{R})$, $M(\mathbf{R})$, and $B(\mathbf{R})$, with all the alternatives in $T(\mathbf{R})$ socially ranked above the alternatives in $M(\mathbf{R})$, which, in turn, are all socially ranked above the alternatives in $B(\mathbf{R})$ (the three layers of a cake). More precisely, a social welfare function $F\colon \mathcal{D} \to \mathcal{R}$ is a *three-layer gateau rule* if there exists an $\bar{x} \in X$ and two families $\mathbf{N}_1$ and $\mathbf{N}_2$ of subsets of N such that,

(i) $I \cap J \neq \emptyset$ if $I \in \mathbf{N}_1$ and $J \in \mathbf{N}_2$,
(ii) $I \subseteq N$ and $I \notin \mathbf{N}_1 \to \ N \setminus I \in \mathbf{N}_2$,
(iii) $\forall \mathbf{R} \in \mathcal{D},\ T(\mathbf{R}) = \{x \in X \mid \exists I \in \mathbf{N}_1 \text{ such that } \forall i \in I, x P_i \bar{x}\}$,
(iv) $\forall \mathbf{R} \in \mathcal{D},\ B(\mathbf{R}) = \{x \in X \mid \exists J \in \mathbf{N}_2 \text{ such that } \forall i \in J, \bar{x} P_i x\}$,
(v) $\forall \mathbf{R} \in \mathcal{D},\ M(\mathbf{R}) = X \setminus [T(\mathbf{R}) \cup B(\mathbf{R})]$,

where $T(\mathbf{R})$, $M(\mathbf{R})$, and $B(\mathbf{R})$ are socially ranked as described above.

The distinguished alternative $\bar{x}$ is in $M(\mathbf{R})$. It is easy to show that if $\mathbf{R} \in \mathcal{L}^n$, then $\bar{x}$ is the only alternative in $M(\mathbf{R})$. Any group of individuals $I \in \mathbf{N}_1$ forces x to be in the top layer if everyone in this group prefers x to $\bar{x}$ and any group of individuals $J \in \mathbf{N}_2$ forces x to be in the bottom layer if everyone in this group prefers $\bar{x}$ to x. Condition (i) ensures that no alternative is put in more than one layer. Restricted to preference profiles in $\mathcal{L}^n$, the social welfare function used to construct Example 24 is a three-layer gateau rule with the following specification of the families $\mathbf{N}_1$ and $\mathbf{N}_2$: (i) for odd n, $\mathbf{N}_1 = \mathbf{N}_2 = \{I \subseteq N \mid |I| > n/2\}$ and (ii) for even n, $\mathbf{N}_1 = \{I \subseteq N \mid |I| > n/2\}$ and $\mathbf{N}_2 = \{I \subseteq N \mid |I| \geq n/2\}$.

[93] If a serial dictatorship is used for each $\mathcal{D}^j$ to determine the choice sets, SP is satisfied.

Three-layer gateau rules are social welfare functions that satisfy a weaker form of IIA in which the social ranking of a pair of alternatives only depends on the individual rankings of this pair and some prespecified alternative $\bar{x}$.

Independence of Irrelevant Alternatives Relative to $\bar{x}$ (IIA$\bar{x}$)
For all $x, y \in X$ and all $\mathbf{R}^1, \mathbf{R}^2 \in \mathcal{D}$, if $\mathbf{R}^1$ and $\mathbf{R}^2$ coincide on $\{x, y, \bar{x}\}$, then R^1 and R^2 coincide on $\{x, y\}$.

Campbell and Kelly (2000) have shown that if there are at least four alternatives and the preference domain is $\mathcal{L}^n$, then any social welfare function that satisfies this independence condition and is weakly Paretian must be a three-layer gateau rule.[94]

Theorem 23 *If $|X| \geq 4$, for any $\bar{x} \in X$, if a social welfare function with an unrestricted linear preference domain satisfies* IIA$\bar{x}$ *and* WP, *then it is a three-layer gateau rule.*

Consider a social choice correspondence C with a complete $\bar{x}$-restricted agenda domain and the preference domain $\mathcal{L}^n$. This agenda domain is closed under finite unions, so, by Hansson's Theorem, C can be rationalized by a social welfare function F whose domain is $\mathcal{L}^n$. Using this observation, it might seem that the Campbell–Kelly Theorem can be used to characterize the social choice correspondences that satisfy IIF and WP on such domains. However, this is not the case. As we have already noted, when not all the binary agendas are feasible, ACA does not guarantee that there is a unique social welfare function rationalizing the social choice correspondence. This is the case here. For example, consider a profile in which everyone prefers $\bar{x}$ to both x and y. WP implies that $\bar{x}$ is chosen out of $\{x, y, \bar{x}\}$, so the social ranking of x and y is arbitrary. As a consequence, it does not follow from the assumption that C satisfies IIF that F satisfies IIA$\bar{x}$. The non-uniqueness of the rationalizing social welfare function makes it a challenging problem to characterize all of the social choice correspondences that satisfy the Arrow axioms on a complete $\bar{x}$-restricted agenda domain.

Examples 24 and 25 both exhibit dictatorial features. In Example 24, a serial dictatorship is used as a tie-breaking rule, while in Example 25, the preference domain has been partitioned into subsets on which someone is a dictator. For any complete $\bar{A}$-restricted agenda domain, Gibbard, Hylland, and Weymark (1987) have shown that if the preference domain is unrestricted and there are at least three alternatives in X not in $\bar{A}$, then it is not possible to satisfy the Arrow axioms with ND strengthened to ANON. Thus, it is inevitable that any social choice correspondence satisfying the assumptions of Theorem 22 cannot avoid all vestiges of dictatorship on such domains.

[94] Yanovskaya (1994) has investigated the implications of IIA$\bar{x}$ in a framework in which social preferences are merely required to be reflexive and transitive.

Theorem 24 *For any nonempty $\bar{A} \subseteq X$, if $|\bar{A}| + 3 \leq |X| < \infty$, there is no social choice correspondence with a complete $\bar{A}$-restricted agenda domain and an unrestricted preference domain that satisfies* ACA, IIF, WP, *and* ANON.

Proof. Let $C: \mathcal{A} \times \mathcal{R}^n \to X$ satisfy all of the assumptions of the theorem except ANON. Let $\mathcal{D}_{\bar{A}}$ be a subdomain of profiles in which (i) everyone ranks every alternative not in $\bar{A}$ above the alternatives in $\bar{A}$ and (ii) the individual rankings of the alternatives in $\bar{A}$ agree with some fixed set of individual orderings (e.g., have everyone regard these alternatives as being indifferent). Let $Y = X \backslash \bar{A}$ and $\mathbf{R}|_Y$, $\mathcal{D}_{\bar{A}}|_Y$, $A|_Y$, and $\mathcal{A}|_Y$ denote the restrictions of $\mathbf{R}$, $\mathcal{D}_{\bar{A}}$, A, and $\mathcal{A}$, respectively, to Y. Define the social choice correspondence $C^*: \mathcal{A}|_Y \times \mathcal{D}_{\bar{A}}|_Y \to Y$ by setting $C^*(A_Y, \mathbf{R}|_Y) = C(A, \mathbf{R})$ for all $A \in \mathcal{A}$ and all $\mathbf{R} \in \mathcal{D}_{\bar{A}}$. Because C satisfies WP, the alternatives in $\bar{A}$ are never chosen from any agenda when the profile is in $\mathcal{D}_{\bar{A}}$. Hence, C^* is well-defined. Because $\mathcal{A}$ is a complete $\bar{A}$-restricted agenda domain, $\mathcal{A}|_Y$ is a complete finite agenda domain for Y. Further, C^* has an unrestricted preference domain. It is straightforward to confirm that C^* satisfies ACA, IIF, and WP. Because $|Y| \geq 3$ it follows from Arrow's Theorem that C^* is dictatorial, which implies that C does not satisfy ANON. □

The conclusions to be drawn from the results discussed in this section are essentially negative—either the axioms are inconsistent or any social choice correspondence satisfying the axioms necessarily exhibits some dictatorial features. This suggests that restricting the agenda domain while keeping the preference domain unrestricted is not a very promising way of avoiding Arrovian impossibilities.

14. SINGLE-PEAKED PREFERENCES AND INTERVAL AGENDA DOMAINS

We now turn to restricted preference domains. In this section, we suppose that the set of alternatives X is a compact interval $[\underline{x}, \bar{x}]$ of $\mathbb{R}$ with $\underline{x} < \bar{x}$. The agenda domain consists of all the nonempty closed intervals of X, which we denote by $\mathcal{A}_I$. For a preference domain, we consider the unrestricted single-peaked preference domain $\mathcal{S}_P^n$ introduced in Section 3. With these domain assumptions, the Arrow axioms with ND strengthened to ANON are consistent. We describe one class of social choice functions that satisfy all of these axioms, the class of generalized median social choice functions introduced in Moulin (1980), and we present an axiomatization of this class due to Moulin (1984).

We refer to the agenda domain considered in this section as a *complete closed interval agenda domain.*

Complete Closed Interval Agenda Domain
$\mathcal{A} = \mathcal{A}_I$.

Note that $\mathcal{A}_I$ is the set of all nonempty, compact, convex subsets of X.

For all $R \in \mathcal{S}_P$, let $\pi(R)$ denote the *peak* of R. Consider any $A = [a,b] \in \mathcal{A}_I$ and any $R \in \mathcal{S}_P$. The restriction of R to A is single-peaked with peak at $\mathrm{Pr}_A\pi(R)$, the *projection* of $\pi(R)$ on A. Thus, $B(A,R) = \pi(R)$ if $\pi(R) \in A$, $B(A,R) = a$ if $\pi(R) < a$, and $B(A,R) = b$ if $\pi(R) > b$.

Following Moulin (1984), we assume that choice is single-valued. One interpretation of our problem is that we are to locate a public facility on a street. Each individual has a preferred location, with preference declining monotonically from this ideal location. Not all locations may be feasible, but the ones that are form a closed interval.

Moulin (1984) required the alternative chosen to vary continuously with the endpoints of the feasible set for a given preference profile. This continuity axiom presupposes that the social choice correspondence C is single-valued.

Interval Continuity (IC)
For all $\mathbf{R} \in \mathcal{D}$, the function $C(\cdot,\mathbf{R})$ is continuous at $[a,b]$ with respect to a and b for all $\underline{x} \le a < b \le \bar{x}$.

The agenda domain $\mathcal{A}_I$ is not closed under finite unions, so we cannot appeal to Hansson's Theorem (Theorem 18) to conclude that ACA is equivalent to the existence of a social welfare function that rationalizes the social choice correspondence $C\colon \mathcal{A}_I \times \mathcal{S}_P^n \to X$. Nevertheless, Moulin (1984) has shown that this equivalence holds if C is single-valued and satisfies IC. Further, for each profile, the social preference that rationalizes the choice in each agenda can be chosen to be single-peaked.

Lemma 5 *If the social choice correspondence* $C\colon \mathcal{A}_I \times \mathcal{S}_P^n \to X$ *satisfies* SV *and* IC, *then* C *can be rationalized by a social welfare function* $F\colon \mathcal{S}_P^n \to \mathcal{S}_P$ *if and only if* C *satisfies* ACA.

Proof. Suppose that C satisfies ACA. Consider any $\mathbf{R} \in \mathcal{S}_P^n$. Let $\beta = C(X,\mathbf{R})$ and let $R^\beta \in \mathcal{S}_P$ have peak β. Now consider any $[a,b] \in \mathcal{A}_I$. We want to show that $B([a,b],R^\beta) = C([a,b],\mathbf{R})$. If $\beta \in A$, this follows immediately from ACA. If $\beta \notin [a,b]$, we may without loss of generality assume that $\beta < a$, which implies that $B([a,b],R^\beta) = a$. Suppose that $C([a,b],\mathbf{R}) = c > a$. By ACA, $C([\underline{x},b],\mathbf{R}) = \beta$. Because $C([\underline{x},b],\mathbf{R}) = \beta$ and $C([a,b],\mathbf{R}) = c$, by IC, there must exist an $a' \in (\underline{x},a)$ such that $C([a',b],\mathbf{R}) = a$. ACA then implies that $C([a,b],\mathbf{R}) = a$, a contradiction. Hence, $B([a,b],R^\beta) = C([a,b],\mathbf{R})$ in this case as well.

The reverse implication is straightforward to verify.[95] □

Moulin (1980) introduced the following class of *generalized median social choice functions* for the agenda domain in which X is the only feasible set. He extended his definition to the domain $\mathcal{A}_I$ in Moulin (1984).

[95] Our proof of this lemma is based on the proof of Lemma 2.1 in Ehlers (2001). Note that the assumption that individual preferences are single-peaked is not used in the proof.

Generalized Median Social Choice Function

A social choice function $C\colon \mathcal{A}_I \times \mathcal{S}_P^n \to X$ is a generalized median social welfare function if there exists a profile $\mathbf{R}^P = (R_{n+1}^P, \ldots, R_{2n-1}^P) \in \mathcal{S}_P^{n-1}$ such that for all $A \in \mathcal{A}_I$ and all $\mathbf{R} \in \mathcal{S}_P^n$,

$$C(A, \mathbf{R}) = \mathrm{Pr}_A \ \mathrm{median}\{\pi(R_1), \ldots, \pi(R_n), \pi(R_{n+1}^P), \ldots, \pi(R_{2n-1}^P)\}.^{96}$$

As in the construction of a generalized median social welfare function in Example 1, fixed single-peaked preferences for $n-1$ phantom individuals are specified. For each profile $\mathbf{R} \in \mathcal{S}_P^n$, the median of the peaks of the $2n-1$ real and phantom individuals is determined. For any agenda $A \in \mathcal{A}_I$, the choice set $C(A, \mathbf{R})$ is the projection of this median peak to A. Equivalently, $C(A, \mathbf{R})$ is the best alternative in A for the individual (either real or phantom) with the median peak. It is straightforward to verify that $C(A, \mathbf{R})$ can also be determined by first projecting all $2n-1$ peaks onto A and then computing the median of these projected peaks.

Recall from Section 3 that the binary relation $\leq$ (resp. $\geq$) on X declares x to be weakly preferred to y if and only if $x \leq y$ (resp. $x \geq y$). If n is odd, half of the phantoms have the preference $\leq$, and the other half have the preference $\geq$, then the phantom individuals are irrelevant and $C(A, \mathbf{R})$ is obtained by maximizing the preference of the (real) individual with the median peak. If there are $n-k$ phantoms with preference $\leq$ and $k-1$ with preference $\geq$, $C(A, \mathbf{R})$ maximizes the preference of the individual with the kth smallest peak.

Suppose the C is a generalized median social choice function. Because the number of phantom individuals is less than the number of real individuals, the median peak in $(\mathbf{R}, \mathbf{R}^P)$ must lie in the interval defined by the smallest and largest peaks in $\mathbf{R}$. As a consequence, C satisfies SP.[97] For a fixed profile, the choices from different agendas are determined by maximizing the same preference, so C satisfies ACA. If the profiles $\mathbf{R}^1$ and $\mathbf{R}^2$ coincide on the agenda A, then the projections of the individual peaks coincide as well. Hence, C satisfies IIF. It is clear that a generalized median social choice function also satisfies ANON and IC. Moulin (1984) has shown that these five axioms characterize the class of generalized median social choice functions. To facilitate the comparison of this result with the other theorems in Part II, we state Moulin's theorem as a theorem about social choice correspondences.

Theorem 25 *For any $X = [\underline{x}, \bar{x}] \subset \mathbb{R}$ with $\underline{x} < \bar{x}$, if a social choice correspondence has a complete closed interval agenda domain and an unrestricted single-peaked preference domain, then it satisfies* SV, ACA, IIF, SP, ANON, *and* IC *if and only if it is a generalized median social choice function.*

[96] For each $j \in \{n+1, \ldots, 2n-1\}$, it is only necessary to specify the peak, and not the complete preference ordering. Generalized median social choice functions are called *generalized Condorcet-winner* social choice functions in Moulin (1984).

[97] WP and SP are equivalent for the domain $\mathcal{A}_I \times \mathcal{S}_P^n$.

By Lemma 5, SV, ACA, and IC imply that a social choice correspondence $C: \mathcal{A}_I \times \mathcal{S}_P^n \to X$ can be rationalized by a social welfare function $F: \mathcal{S}_P^n \to \mathcal{S}_P$. For $k = 1, \ldots, n-1$, let $\mathbf{R}^k$ be the profile in which $R_i^k = \leq$ for $i = 1, \ldots, k$ and $R_i^k = \geq$ for $i = k+1, \ldots, n$ and let $\beta_k = \pi(F(\mathbf{R}^k))$. The sufficiency part of the proof of Theorem 25 involves showing that C is the generalized median social choice function defined by the profile of phantom preferences $\bar{\mathbf{R}}^P = (F(\mathbf{R}^1), \ldots, F(\mathbf{R}^{n-1}))$. To do this, it is sufficient to show that for all $\mathbf{R} \in \mathcal{S}_P^n$, $\pi(F(\mathbf{R})) = \text{median}\{\pi(R_1), \ldots, \pi(R_n), \beta_1, \ldots, \beta_{n-1}\}$. See Moulin (1984) for the details of the proof.

Moulin (1984) has also considered the domains of single-plateaued and quasiconcave preferences. A preference R on $X = [\underline{x}, \bar{x}]$ is *single-plateaued* if there exist $\beta_1, \beta_2 \in X$ (not necessarily distinct) such that (i) xPy whenever $\beta_1 \geq x > y$ or $\beta_2 \leq x < y$ and (ii) xIy whenever $x, y \in [\beta_1, \beta_2]$. A preference R on $X = [\underline{x}, \bar{x}]$ is *quasiconcave* if there exists a $\beta \in X$ such that xRy whenever $\beta \geq x > y$ or $\beta \leq x < y$.[98] A single-peaked preference is single-plateaued and a single-plateaued preference is quasiconcave. Moulin has shown that a version of Theorem 25 holds for single-plateaued preferences and that his axioms are incompatible when the preference domain includes all profiles of quasiconcave preferences.

For the domain of Theorem 25, Ehlers (2001) has considered the problem of choosing exactly m alternatives from each agenda, where $m < n$ (so that it is not possible always to pick everyone's preferred alternative). Thus, a social alternative consists of m (not necessarily distinct) points in X. Preferences need to be extended from X to the set of subsets of X of cardinality at most m. Ehlers assumes that each individual orders subsets by comparing his or her most-preferrred alternatives in these sets. For $m = 2$, he has shown that the only social choice correspondence satisfying ACA, IIF, SP, and IC is the *extreme peaks social choice correspondence*. For each profile, this solution identifies the individuals with the smallest and largest peaks and then maximizes their preferences on each agenda. For $m > 2$, Ehlers has shown that SP and IC are incompatible.

15. ANALYTIC PREFERENCE DOMAINS

We have seen in Examples 11 and 12 that Arrow's social welfare function axioms are inconsistent for the domain of monotone analytic preferences with no critical points when there are two or more public goods and for the domain of Euclidean spatial preferences. Le Breton and Weymark (2002) have shown that if either of these domains of analytic preferences is combined with an agenda domain consisting of compact sets with nonempty interiors, then IIF is vacuous on the combined agenda and preference

[98] A preference that is strictly quasiconcave according to the definition in Section 3 need not be quasiconcave.

domain, and this permits the construction of social choice correspondences that satisfy the Arrovian axioms. We review their results in this section.

15.1. Euclidean Spatial Preferences

Recall that $\mathcal{E}$ denotes the set of all Euclidean spatial preferences on $\mathbb{R}^m_+$. In the spatial preference domain that we consider in this section, each individual is assumed to have a Euclidean spatial preference.

Euclidean Spatial Preference Domain
$\mathcal{D} \subseteq \mathcal{E}^n$.

The assumptions on the agenda domain are made precise in the following definition.

Full-Dimensional Compact Agenda Domain
For all $A \in \mathcal{A}$, A is a compact set with a nonempty interior.

If we think of the preferences as belonging to legislators who must choose the quantities of various public goods, an agenda can be interpreted as the set of public goods allocations that are feasible given the resources at the legislators' disposal. As these resources are varied, we obtain different agendas.

With these domain assumptions, IIF is vacuous.

Lemma 6 *If* $X = \mathbb{R}^m_+$ *with* $m \geq 2$ *and a social choice correspondence is defined on a full-dimensional compact agenda domain and a Euclidean spatial preference domain, then it satisfies* IIF.

The basic idea of the proof is very simple. A Euclidean spatial preference is completely determined by the location of its ideal point. Further, the ideal point can be identified from a segment of an indifference contour by taking the point of intersection of the lines orthogonal to the indifference surface at two points in the segment. As a consequence, it is not possible to have two profiles coincide on an agenda unless they are identical.

With this result in hand, Le Breton and Weymark (2002) were able to establish the following possibility theorem.

Theorem 26 *If* $X = \mathbb{R}^m_+$ *with* $m \geq 2$, *on any full-dimensional compact agenda domain and any Euclidean spatial preference domain, there exist social choice correspondences that satisfy* ACA, IIF, SP, *and* ANON.

The following example was used to establish Theorem 26.

Example 26 A Bergson–Samuelson social welfare function is a real-valued function defined on n-tuples of utilities. Let W: $\mathbb{R}^n \rightarrow \mathbb{R}$ be any continuous, symmetric, Bergson–Samuelson social welfare function, increasing in each of its arguments. For all

$R \in \mathcal{E}$, a continuous utility function U^R is chosen to represent R. Using the Bergson–Samuelson social welfare function W and these representations of the individual preferences, the social welfare function $F: \mathcal{D} \to \mathcal{R}$ is defined by setting,

$$xF(\mathbf{R})y \leftrightarrow W[U^{R_1}(x), \ldots, U^{R_n}(x)] \geq W[U^{R_1}(y), \ldots, U^{R_n}(y)],$$

for all $\mathbf{R} \in \mathcal{D}$ and all $x, y \in X$. The social choice correspondence $C: \mathcal{A} \times \mathcal{D} \to X$ is defined by letting $C(A, \mathbf{R})$ be the set of best alternatives in A according to the social preference $F(\mathbf{R})$. Formally, $C(A, \mathbf{R}) = B(A, F(\mathbf{R}))$ for all $(A, \mathbf{R}) \in \mathcal{A} \times \mathcal{D}$. Because W and U^{R_i}, $i \in N$, are continuous functions, $F(\mathbf{R})$ is a continuous ordering. Thus, C is well-defined because each agenda is compact.

By Lemma 6, C satisfies IIF. C satisfies *SP* because W is an increasing function. Because W is symmetric in its arguments and the same utility function U^R is used no matter who has the preference R, C satisfies ANON. Because C is rationalized by the social welfare function F, it satisfies ACA.

An attractive feature of Example 26 is that it provides a link between Arrovian social choice theory and traditional Bergson–Samuelson welfare economics.[99] Because none of the binary agendas are feasible, the social welfare function used in this example does not satisfy IIA, thereby circumventing the social welfare function impossibility theorem for Euclidean spatial preferences discussed in Example 12.

15.2. Monotone Analytic Preferences

Le Breton and Weymark (2002) have also used the construction in Example 26 to establish a possibility theorem for monotone analytic preferences. Let $\mathcal{M}$ denote the *set of all monotone analytic preferences preferences with no critical points* on $\mathbb{R}^m_+$. Le Breton and Weymark assumed that the preference domain is any subset of $\mathcal{M}^n$. Thus, further restrictions, such as convexity of preferences, can be imposed on the preference domain.

Monotone Analytic Preference Domain
$\mathcal{D} \subseteq \mathcal{M}^n$.

As in the preceding discussion, each agenda is assumed to be a nonempty compact set with a nonempty interior. An agenda can be interpreted as being the set of feasible allocations of public goods obtainable from the economy's initial resources given the production possibility sets of the firms. Different agendas are obtained by varying the production technologies and/or the resource endowments. The compactness of an agenda follows from standard assumptions on firms' technologies that imply that the

[99] See also the related discussion in Pazner (1979).

aggregate production possibilities set is closed and that only finite amounts of goods may be produced with the economy's resource endowment. Agendas can also be supposed to be convex and comprehensive, as would be the case if firms' technologies are convex and exhibit free disposal. It is important that the agendas are compact. On a noncompact, comprehensive agenda, the Pareto set is typically empty, making it impossible for a social choice correspondence to satisfy WP.

Consider two real-valued monotone analytic functions with no critical points defined on $\mathbb{R}^m_{++}$, with $m \geq 2$. Le Breton and Weymark (2002) have shown that if these functions are ordinally equivalent on an open subset of $\mathbb{R}^m_{++}$, then they are ordinally equivalent on all of $\mathbb{R}^m_{++}$.[100] Because the admissible agendas have nonempty interiors, it then follows that it is impossible for two distinct profiles in $\mathcal{M}^n$ to coincide on an agenda. Hence, IIF is vacuous.

Lemma 7 *If $X = \mathbb{R}^m_+$ with $m \geq 2$ and a social choice correspondence is defined on a full-dimensional compact agenda domain and a monotone analytic preference domain, then it satisfies* IIF.

Using Lemma 7, the social choice correspondence in Example 26 is easily shown to satisfy all the axioms of Theorem 26 on a full-dimensional compact agenda domain and a monotone analytic preference domain.

Theorem 27 *If $X = \mathbb{R}^m_+$ with $m \geq 2$, on any full-dimensional compact agenda domain and any monotone analytic preference domain, there exist social choice correspondences that satisfy* ACA, IIF, SP, *and* ANON.

As noted by Le Breton and Weymark (2002), it is straightforward to construct a private goods version of Theorem 27. With private goods, this theorem is modified by (i) assuming that individuals are selfish and have preferences for own consumption that are monotone and analytic with no critical points and (ii) replacing ANON with PANON.

16. CLASSICAL DOMAINS OF SPATIAL AND ECONOMIC PREFERENCES

The results discussed in the preceding section demonstrate that by combining an Arrow-inconsistent preference domain with natural restrictions on the admissible agendas, it is sometimes possible to obtain a social choice correspondence possibility theorem.

[100] This result is an ordinal version of the Analytic Continuation Principle for monotone analytic functions with no critical points.

However, there are spatial preferences that are not Euclidean and there are classical economic preferences that are not analytic. In this section, we review a number of results for larger domains of spatial and economic preferences. In Sections 16.1 and 16.2, we consider classical domains of economic preferences for exchange and production economies. In Section 16.3, we consider spatial preferences that are not limited to being Euclidean.

16.1. Exchange Economies

Bailey (1979) questioned the relevance of Arrow's Theorem for economic problems on the grounds that economic agendas typically contain an infinite number of alternatives, whereas Arrow's proof of his theorem rests on an implicit assumption that all binary agendas are feasible. Bailey purported to provide an example of a social choice rule that satisfies all of the Arrow axioms for a class of exchange economies. Bailey's discussion of his example is quite informal and confuses the social welfare function and social choice correspondence formulations of Arrow's problem in a rather fundamental way.[101] Below, we argue that Bailey's example is problematic and, as a consequence, misidentifies why Arrow's axioms are consistent for a domain of exchange economies. Nevertheless, Bailey was correct to question the relevance of Arrow's Theorem for exchange economies, as Donaldson and Weymark (1988) have demonstrated.

Consider an economy with $m \geq 2$ private goods. The set of alternatives is $X = \prod_{i=1}^{n} X_i$, where $X_i = \mathbb{R}_+^m$ for all $i \in N$. We consider two domains of economic preferences. The first is the classical private goods preference domain $\mathcal{C}_{pr}$ considered in Example 17. Recall that $\mathcal{C}_{pr}$ is the set of all profiles of selfish, continuous, strictly monotonic in own consumption, convex preference orderings on $\mathbb{R}_+^{mn}$. Our second preference domain strengthens the assumptions on preferences by ruling out the possibility that an individual's induced private preference can have an indifference contour containing a consumption bundle with strictly positive components that intersects an axis.

Strongly Classical Private Goods Preference Domain

For all $i \in N$, $\mathcal{D}_i$ is the set of all selfish, continuous, convex preference orderings on $\mathbb{R}_+^{mn}$ that are strictly monotonic in own consumption on $\mathbb{R}_{++}^m$ for which xP_iy for all $R_i \in \mathcal{D}_i$, all $x \in \mathbb{R}_+^{mn}$ with $x_j^i > 0$ for all $j \in \{1, \ldots, m\}$, and all $y \in \mathbb{R}_+^{mn}$ with $y_j^i = 0$ for some $j \in \{1, \ldots, m\}$.

For each aggregate endowment $\omega \in \mathbb{R}_{++}^m$, the *generalized Edgeworth box* is $A(\omega) = \{x \in X \mid \sum_{i=1}^{n} x_j^i \leq \omega_j \text{ for all } j = 1, \ldots, m\}$. Note that it is not assumed a priori that all of the endowment is consumed. The agenda domain is the set of all generalized Edgeworth boxes.

[101] In fairness to Bailey, we note that some of this confusion is due to the fact that the independence condition stated as an axiom in Arrow (1951) is IIF, even though it is IIA that is used to establish Arrow's Theorem.

Edgeworth Box Agenda Domain
$\mathcal{A} = \{A(\omega) \mid \omega \in \mathbb{R}^m_{++}\}$.[102]

Donaldson and Weymark (1988) claimed that the Walrasian competitive equilibrium correspondence when the endowment is shared equally satisfies all of the Arrow axioms with ND strengthened to PANON on an Edgeworth box agenda domain and a classical private goods preference domain. In order for their argument to be valid, we must use the slightly more restrictive preference domain described above.

Theorem 28 *For a private goods economy with* $X = \mathbb{R}^{mn}_+$ *and* $m \geq 2$, *there exist social choice correspondences with an Edgeworth box agenda domain and a strongly classical private goods preference domain that satisfy* ACA, IIF, SP, *and* PANON.[103]

Example 27 defines the Walrasian correspondence from equal split and shows why it satisfies the assumptions of Theorem 28.

Example 27 Suppose that the set of alternatives X, the agenda domain $\mathcal{A}$, and the preference domain $\mathcal{D}$ are defined as in Theorem 28. For each aggregate endowment and admissible preference profile, the Walrasian correspondence from equal split is the social choice correspondence C defined by setting the choice set equal to the set of all competitive equilibrium allocations obtainable from an initial equal division of the endowments. That is, ω/n is each person's endowment when the agenda is $A(\omega)$.

Because competitive equilibria exist in an exchange economy with classical economic preferences when each person has a positive endowment of every good, C is well-defined. By the first Fundamental Theorem of Welfare Economics, all competitive equilibria are Pareto optimal. Because each person has the same endowment, permuting private preferences among individuals results in an economy that only differs from the original economy in the labeling of individuals, so PANON is also satisfied.

With preferences that are strictly monotonic in own consumption, Pareto optimality requires all of the resources be consumed. In order for $A(\omega^1)$ to be a strict subset of $A(\omega^2)$, it must be the case that $\omega^1_j \leq \omega^2_j$ for all j, with strict inequality for some j. Hence, for a given preference profile $\mathbf{R}$, the strong Pareto sets $\mathcal{P}^s(A(\omega^1), \mathbf{R})$ and $\mathcal{P}^s(A(\omega^2), \mathbf{R})$ do not intersect. Thus, C trivially satisfies ACA.

It remains to show that IIF is satisfied. On the contrary, suppose that there exists an endowment $\omega \in \mathbb{R}^m_{++}$, profiles $\mathbf{R}^1, \mathbf{R}^2 \in \mathcal{D}$ that coincide on $A(\omega)$, and an allocation x for which $x \in C(A(\omega), \mathbf{R}^1)$ and $x \notin C(A(\omega), \mathbf{R}^2)$. Because x is a Walrasian equilibrium from equal split for the profile $\mathbf{R}^1$, there exists a price vector $p \in \mathbb{R}^n_{++}$

[102] Note that in contrast with the exchange economies considered in Section 10.2, free disposal is permitted and consumption of goods is not required to be strictly positive.

[103] The weak and strong Pareto sets coincide in economies with classical economic preferences.

such that for all $i \in N$, $px^i = p\omega/n$ and $py^i > p\omega/n$ if $yP_i x$. The assumptions on preferences imply that $x \in \mathbb{R}^{mn}_{++}$, so x is in the interior of the generalized Edgeworth box $A(\omega)$. Because x is not a Walrasian equilibrium from equal split for the profile $\mathbf{R}^2$, there exists a $k \in N$ and $y \in \mathbb{R}^{mn}_{+}$ such that $yP^2_k x$ and $py^k \leq p\omega/n$. To satisfy our preference domain assumption, we must have $y^k \in \mathbb{R}^m_{++}$. Because preferences are convex and monotone in own consumption, $[\lambda y + (1-\lambda)x]P^2_k x$ for all $\lambda \in (0,1]$. Further, for such λ, $p[\lambda y^k + (1-\lambda)x^k] \leq p\omega/n$. Because x is in the interior of $A(\omega)$, for positive λ sufficiently close to zero, $[\lambda y + (1-\lambda)x]$ is also in the interior of $A(\omega)$. On $A(\omega)$, $\mathbf{R}^1$ and $\mathbf{R}^2$ coincide. Hence, for such λ, we have $[\lambda y + (1-\lambda)x]P^1_k x$ and $p[\lambda y^k + (1-\lambda)x^k] \leq p\omega/n$, which contradicts the assumption that x is a Walrasian equilibrium from equal split for the profile $\mathbf{R}^1$. Thus, C satisfies IIF.[104]

As in Section 15, the consistency of the axioms in Theorem 28 turns on one of the axioms being trivially satisfied. In this case, it is ACA that is vacuous, at least for Paretian social choice correspondences.

A related Arrovian possibility theorem was established by Grether and Plott (1982). They noted that when the preference domain is unrestricted and there are a finite number of alternatives, all of the Arrow axioms can be satisfied by setting each choice set equal to the weak Pareto set if the feasible agendas are pairwise disjoint. In their result, it is the pairwise disjointness of the feasible agendas that renders ACA vacuous. Because the resource constraints are not assumed to hold with equality, this is not the case in Example 27.[105]

There is a fixed aggregate endowment in the main example in Bailey (1979). A government allocates these resources to individuals, with the final allocation of goods determined by the competitive market mechanism. Bailey clearly regarded each distribution of resources as corresponding to a different agenda. However, how the aggregate

[104] With the preference domain used by Donaldson and Weymark (1988), it is possible for an equilibrium allocation to lie on the boundary of a generalized Edgeworth box. For concreteness, suppose that there are just two goods and two individuals. If, for example, only person one receives a positive consumption of all goods at the equilibrium allocation x, person one's indifference curve containing x consists of two linear segments with a kink at x, and the slope of this indifference curve outside the Edgeworth box has the same slope as the budget line, then changing person one's preferences over nonfeasible alternatives can change the Walrasian equilibrium. This is not possible if the equilibrium allocation is in the interior of the Edgeworth box.

This problem does not arise with the *constrained Walrasian correspondence from equal split*. This correspondence is defined in the same way as the Walrasian correspondence from equal split except that, for every price vector, each person's budget set is the intersection of the Walrasian budget set with the set of consumption bundles that do not exceed the aggregate endowment ω. This correspondence satisfies all of the axioms of Theorem 28 on an Edgeworth box agenda domain and a classical private goods preference domain. We are grateful to Marc Fleurbaey for this observation.

[105] The finiteness of the set of alternatives ensures that the Pareto sets in Grether and Plott's construction are nonempty. Nonemptiness of the Pareto sets in Example 27 follows from the compactness of the feasible agendas and the continuity of the individual preferences.

endowment is distributed does not affect what is feasible for the economy, so it would seem that there is only one feasible set in his framework. Because the equilibrium allocations depend on the initial allocation of endowments to individuals, Bailey has not constructed an Arrovian social choice correspondence.

16.2. Production Economies

ACA is not, in general, vacuous in production economies. Nevertheless, Donaldson and Weymark (1988) have shown that the Arrow axioms are consistent in production economies. They considered both public goods and private goods economies.

In the case of private goods, the universal set of alternatives is the same as in the preceding subsection. In the public goods economy, there are $m \geq 2$ public goods and the set of alternatives is $X = \mathbb{R}^m_+$.

Donaldson and Weymark's possibility theorem is not very sensitive to the choice of preference domain, provided that all preferences are continuous. They assumed that the preference domain is the set of all profiles of continuous preferences in the public goods case and the set of all profiles of continuous selfish preferences in the private goods case. They noted that their theorem also holds with classical restrictions on preferences, and we state their result in this form. For private goods, we use the classical private goods preference domain $\mathcal{C}_{pr}$. For public goods, we use the classical public goods preference domain $\mathcal{C}_{pu}$ described in Example 8. Recall that $\mathcal{C}_{pu}$ is the set of all profiles of continuous, strictly monotonic, convex preference orderings on X.

In addition to the assumptions made about the agenda domain in Section 15, it is assumed that all agendas are comprehensive.

Full-Dimensional Compact Comprehensive Agenda Domain

For all $A \in \mathcal{A}$, A is a compact comprehensive set with a nonempty interior.

As in Section 15.2, an agenda is interpreted as being the set of feasible allocations of goods that can be made available to consumers from the economy's initial resources using the production possibility sets of the firms. With this interpretation of an agenda, comprehensiveness corresponds to assuming that goods can be freely disposed. Theorem 29 is valid with further restrictions on the agenda, such as convexity.

For both public and private goods economies, Donaldson and Weymark (1988) have shown that Arrow's axioms are consistent if the preference domain is classical and there is a full-dimensional compact comprehensive agenda domain. It is an open question whether ANON and PANON can be used instead of ND in this theorem.

Theorem 29 *(a) For a public goods economy with $X = \mathbb{R}^m_+$ and $m \geq 2$, there exist social choice correspondences with a full-dimensional compact comprehensive agenda domain and a classical public goods preference domain that satisfy* ACA, IIF, WP, *and* ND. *(b) For a private goods economy* *with* $X = \mathbb{R}_+^{mn}$ *and* $m \geq 2$*, there exist social choice correspondences with a full-dimensional compact comprehensive agenda domain and a classical private goods preference domain that satisfy* ACA, IIF, WP, *and* ND.

As in Example 24, there is a distinguished alternative in every admissible agenda. Here, this distinguished alternative is the origin. However, every admissible preference ranks the origin last and every agenda includes an infinite number of alternatives, so it is not possible to adapt Example 24 to show the consistency of Arrow's axioms in production economies. Although there do not exist more than one distinguished alternative in every admissible agenda, the example Donaldson and Weymark (1988) used to establish Theorem 29 exploits the fact that profiles can be partitioned in such a way that whenever two profiles coincide on an agenda, they must be in the same cell of the partition, as is the case in the construction (Example 25) that Gibbard, Hylland, and Weymark (1987) used to show the consistency of the Arrow axioms when the agenda domain is $\{\bar{x}, \bar{y}\}$-restricted. We present Donaldson and Weymark's public goods example. A private goods version of this example can be used to establish the second part of Theorem 29.

Example 28 Consider a public goods economy with $X = \mathbb{R}_+^m$ and $m \geq 2$ that satisfies the domain restrictions of Theorem 29. Let $\mathbf{R}^*$ be an arbitrary profile in $\mathcal{D}$. The preference domain is partitioned into the sets $\mathcal{D}_1$ and $\mathcal{D}_2$ as follows. For any profile $\mathbf{R} \in \mathcal{D}$, $\mathbf{R} \in \mathcal{D}_1$ if and only if $\mathbf{R}$ coincides with $\mathbf{R}^*$ in some neighborhood of the origin. The social choice correspondence C: $\mathcal{A} \times \mathcal{D} \to X$ is defined by setting, for all $A \in \mathcal{A}$, $C(A,\mathbf{R}) = B(A,R_1)$ for all $\mathbf{R} \in \mathcal{D}_1$ and $C(A,\mathbf{R}) = B(A,R_2)$ for all $\mathbf{R} \in \mathcal{D}_2$. That is, person one is a strong dictator for the profiles in $\mathcal{D}_1$ and person two is a strong dictator for the profiles in $\mathcal{D}_2$.

Using essentially the same reasoning as in Example 25, C satisfies ACA, WP, and ND. Because any admissible agenda A includes a neighborhood of the origin if two profiles agree on A, they must (i) either both agree with $\mathbf{R}^*$ on some neighborhood of the origin or (ii) neither of them agrees with $\mathbf{R}^*$ on any neighborhood of the origin. In either case, the same dictator is used for both profiles, so IIF is satisfied.[106] Note that that C is rationalized by a social welfare function that satisfies all of the Arrow axioms except IIA.[107]

Consider a public goods economy with $X = \mathbb{R}_+^m$ and $m \geq 2$. For all $(p, w) \in \mathbb{R}_{++}^{m+1}$, let $Y(p,w) = \{x \in X \mid px \leq w\}$. $Y(p,w)$ can be interpreted as being the set of feasible allocations for a production economy with a linear production possibility set.

[106] If a serial dictatorship is used for each cell of the partition, SP is also satisfied. Everyone can be a dictator on some cell if more reference profiles are used to partition the preference domain into n or more cells.

[107] Campbell (1995) has shown that the Arrow axioms are inconsistent if the preference domain in this example is combined with an agenda domain that includes all finite subsets of X of cardinalities k and $k+1$ for some $k \geq 2$, but no subset with a smaller cardinality.

Complete Linear Comprehensive Agenda Domain
$A \in \mathcal{A}$ if and only if $A = Y(p, w)$ for some $(p, w) \in \mathbb{R}^{m+1}_{++}$.

With this agenda domain, there is little scope for ACA to play a role if preferences are continuous and monotonic and the social choice correspondence is Paretian. WP implies that all Pareto optimal alternatives are contained in the upper boundary of an agenda. If one "linear" agenda is a strict subset of another, either their upper boundaries do not intersect or, if they do, all the alternatives they have in common lie on the boundary of $\mathbb{R}^m_+$. Thus, if the preference domain is restricted in such a way that weak Pareto sets only include alternatives with positive consumption of all goods, ACA is vacuous. The following preference domain has this feature.

Strongly Convex Classical Public Goods Preference Domain
$\mathcal{D}$ is the set of all profiles of continuous preference orderings on $\mathbb{R}^m_+$ that are strictly monotonic and strictly convex on $\mathbb{R}^m_{++}$ and for which for all $\mathbf{R} \in \mathcal{D}$, xP_iy for all $i \in N$, all $x \in \mathbb{R}^m_{++}$, and all $y \in \mathbb{R}^m_+$ with $y_j = 0$ for some $j \in \{1, \ldots, m\}$.

The last condition in this definition rules out any indifference contour that contains an alternative with strictly positive components from intersecting an axis.

Le Breton (1997) has observed that with this kind of preference domain and a complete linear comprehensive agenda domain, it is possible to construct social choice correspondences that satisfy all of the Arrow axioms, with ND strengthened to ANON.

Theorem 30 *If $X = \mathbb{R}^m_+$ with $m \geq 2$, there exist social choice correspondences with a complete linear comprehensive agenda domain and a strongly convex classical public goods preference domain that satisfy* ACA, IIF, WP, *and* ANON.

Le Breton (1997) did not provide an explicit example of such a social choice correspondence. We provide one in Example 29.

Example 29 Consider a public goods economy with $X = \mathbb{R}^m_+$ and $m \geq 2$ and a social choice correspondence C that satisfies the domain assumptions of Theorem 30. Let C be defined by setting $C(Y(p, w), \mathbf{R}) = \mathcal{P}^w(Y(p, w), \mathbf{R})$ for all $(p, w) \in \mathbb{R}^{m+1}_{++}$ and all $\mathbf{R} \in \mathcal{D}$. In other words, the social choice correspondence always chooses the whole weak Pareto set, as in the Grether–Plott example discussed in Section 16.1.

16.3. General Spatial Preferences

The distinguishing features of a spatial preference are that it is convex and it has a bliss point. Duggan (1996) has shown that the Arrow axioms are inconsistent when the preference domain includes all profiles of spatial preferences and the agenda domain is the set of compact convex subsets of the universal set of alternatives X when X is a multidimensional convex subset of a Euclidean space. We consider Duggan's Theorem in this section.

More precisely, with X as described above, a *spatial preference* R on X is a continuous, strictly convex ordering with a bliss point. Let $\mathcal{S}$ denote the *set of all spatial preferences*.[108] Clearly, $\mathcal{E} \subset \mathcal{S}$. Duggan assumed that all profiles of spatial preferences are admissible.

Unrestricted Spatial Preference Domain
$\mathcal{D} = \mathcal{S}^n$.

Duggan's agenda domain is the set of all compact convex subsets of X.

Complete Compact Convex Agenda Domain
$\mathcal{A}$ is the set of compact convex subsets of X.

Note that any spatial preference in $\mathcal{S}$ has a unique maximum on any compact convex agenda.

Aside from the trivial agendas that contain only one alternative, each admissible agenda contains an infinite number of alternatives. Duggan noted that the proof of his theorem only requires the agenda domain to include the agendas formed by taking the convex hulls of any pair or triple of alternatives. However, it is essential that the domain includes the convex hull of any pair of alternatives, and such sets do not have an interior. In contrast, the possibility theorem for Euclidean spatial preferences presented in Section 15.1 and the possibility theorems for economic preference domains discussed above all assume that every agenda has a nonempty interior. This assumption plays an important role in the proofs of these results.

Theorem 31 is Duggan's impossibility theorem for spatial preferences.

Theorem 31 *If X is a convex subset of a Euclidean space and the dimension of X is at least two, there is no social choice correspondence with a complete compact convex agenda domain and an unrestricted spatial preference domain that satisfies* ACA, IIF, WP, *and* ND.

The proof we presented in Section 12.2 of the choice-theoretic version of Arrow's Theorem begins by rationalizing the social choice correspondence by a social welfare function and then showing that this social welfare function satisfies all of Arrow's original axioms, which is impossible. Because Duggan's agenda domain is not closed under finite unions, Hansson's Theorem does not apply, so ACA does not guarantee that the social

[108] Because a spatial preference is required to be continuous, if X is an interval of the real line, $\mathcal{S}$ is a strict subset of the set of single-peaked preferences $\mathcal{S}p$.

choice correspondence can be rationalized. Thus, a different proof strategy is required to establish Theorem 31. Duggan's proof of this theorem is an ingenious adaptation of the proof strategy described in Section 2 for the social welfare function version of Arrow's Theorem. Duggan's proof is too long to reproduce here, so we limit ourselves to a discussion of its main features.

Let C be a social choice correspondence satisfying Duggan's domain assumptions and all of the Arrow axioms except ND. For any subset Y of X, let $ch(Y)$ denote the *convex hull* of Y. Although no pair of distinct alternatives is an admissible agenda, the convex hull of any pair is. It is these sets that Duggan used to make binary comparisons. Note that any admissible preference is single-peaked on $ch(\{x, y\})$. Duggan defined his decisiveness relations for $\{x, y\}$ in terms of the social choice from $ch(\{x, y\})$ when the individual preference peaks are at the endpoints of this line segment. Specifically, for any ordered pair $(x, y) \in X^2$, (i) $G \subseteq N$ is *almost decisive* for the ordered pair (x, y) if $C(ch(\{x, y\}), \mathbf{R}) = \{x\}$ when $B(ch(\{x, y\}), R_i) = \{x\}$ for all $i \in G$ and $B(ch(\{x, y\}), R_i) = \{y\}$ for all $i \notin G$, and (ii) G is *decisive* for the ordered pair (x, y) if $C(ch(\{x, y\}), \mathbf{R}) = \{x\}$ when $B(ch(\{x, y\}), R_i) = \{x\}$ for all $i \in G$. By IIF, if a group is (almost) decisive for (x, y), then the complement of this group cannot be (almost) decisive for (y, x).

A group $G \subseteq N$ is *proper* if $\emptyset \neq G \neq N$. For any $x, y, z \in X$ that are not colinear, Duggan has shown that if a proper group G is almost decisive for (x, y), then it is also almost decisive for (y, z). This is done by investigating the relationship between the social choice from $ch(\{x, y, z\})$ and the choices from the edges of $ch(\{x, y, z\})$ when the Pareto set of $ch(\{x, y, z\})$ is contained in $ch(\{x, y\})$. A similar argument then shows that G is also almost decisive for (w, z) when x, z, and w are not colinear. Because X is at least two-dimensional, these two results imply that if a proper group G is almost decisive for some pair of distinct alternatives, then it is almost decisive for all pairs. Once this has been established, it is not too difficult to show that G is decisive for all pairs of alternatives.

The preceding argument shows that G has the power to determine the social choice on line segments when the members of G all agree that one end of the line segment is the best feasible alternative. The next step in the argument shows that G also has the power to determine the social choice on any feasible agenda A if the members of G agree about what is best in A. Duggan called a group G for which $C(A, \mathbf{R}) = \{x\}$ whenever $B(A, R_i) = \{x\}$ for all $i \in G$ an *oligarchy*. A dictator is a one-person oligarchy. By WP, N is an oligarchy. The rest of the proof is devoted to showing that the smallest oligarchy contains only one person. Hence, C is dictatorial.

As previously noted, Duggan's proof strategy requires that the line segment joining any two distinct alternatives in X is an admissible agenda. It is an open question whether Arrow's axioms are consistent for the preference domain $\mathcal{S}^n$ when the agenda domain is the set of all compact convex subsets of X that have nonempty interiors.

17. INDEPENDENCE OF PARETO IRRELEVANT ALTERNATIVES

The example (Example 28) that Donaldson and Weymark (1988) used to establish the consistency of Arrow's axioms in their possibility theorem for production economies (Theorem 29) has the property that whose preference is used to determine the choice set depends on properties of the preference profile in an arbitrarily small neighborhood of the origin. With monotone preferences and a full-dimensioned agenda, none of these alternatives are Pareto optimal. Donaldson and Weymark (1988) have suggested that preferences for Pareto dominated alternatives should be irrelevant when determining what to choose from an agenda, a property they call *Independence of Pareto Irrelevant Alternatives*. In this section, we review the theorems Donaldson and Weymark (1988) and Duggan (1996) have established using this independence axiom.

With Independence of Pareto Irrelevant Alternatives, each choice set only depends on the restriction of the preference profile to the Pareto set. There are two versions of this axiom, one based on weak Pareto optimality and one based on strong Pareto optimality.

Independence of Weakly Pareto Irrelevant Alternatives (WPIIA)
For all $A \in \mathcal{A}$ and all $\mathbf{R}^1, \mathbf{R}^2 \in \mathcal{D}$, if $\mathcal{P}^w(A, \mathbf{R}^1) = \mathcal{P}^w(A, \mathbf{R}^2)$ and $\mathbf{R}^1$ and $\mathbf{R}^2$ coincide on this common Pareto set, then $C(A, \mathbf{R}^1) = C(A, \mathbf{R}^2)$.

Independence of Strongly Pareto Irrelevant Alternatives (SPIIA)
For all $A \in \mathcal{A}$ and all $\mathbf{R}^1, \mathbf{R}^2 \in \mathcal{D}$, if $\mathcal{P}^s(A, \mathbf{R}^1) = \mathcal{P}^s(A, \mathbf{R}^2)$ and $\mathbf{R}^1$ and $\mathbf{R}^2$ coincide on this common Pareto set, then $C(A, \mathbf{R}^1) = C(A, \mathbf{R}^2)$.

Note that, in general, the second axiom is more demanding than the first. Both of these axioms imply IIF on any domain for which the Pareto sets are always nonempty.

When the agenda domain consists of the nonempty finite subsets of X, because, for any admissible preference profile and any admissible agenda, each Pareto set is also feasible, ACA, IIF, and WP (resp. SP) imply WPIIA (resp. SPIIA).[109] As a consequence, regardless of the preference domain, with an unrestricted finite feasible set agenda domain, the implications of IIF and WPIIA are the same when combined with Arrow's other axioms. This is not the case in production economies, as Example 28 demonstrates.

17.1. Nonconvex Agendas

For the public goods economy considered in Theorem 29, Donaldson and Weymark (1988) have shown that replacing IIF with WPIIA results in an impossibility theorem if the agenda domain is enlarged to the set of all compact and comprehensive subsets of X.

[109] The finiteness assumption ensures that the Pareto sets are nonempty.

Complete Compact Comprehensive Agenda Domain
$A \in \mathcal{A}$ if and only if A is a compact comprehensive subset of X.

Note that this agenda domain includes sets with an empty interior.

Recall that for any $x, y \in \mathbb{R}^m_+$, their corner set $x_\downarrow \cup y_\downarrow$ is obtained by taking the union of the comprehensive sets of x and y. Because agendas have not been assumed to be convex, the corner set generated by any pair of alternatives is an admissible agenda. It is these agendas that permit Donaldson and Weymark (1988) to make binary comparisons.

Theorem 32 is Donaldson and Weymark's public goods impossibility theorem.

Theorem 32 *If $X = \mathbb{R}^m_+$ with $m \geq 2$, there is no social choice correspondence with a complete compact comprehensive agenda domain and a classical public goods preference domain that satisfies* ACA, WPIIA, WP, *and* ND.

Proof. On the contrary, suppose that there exists a social correspondence $C\colon \mathcal{A} \times \mathcal{D} \to X$ that satisfies all the assumptions of the theorem. The agenda domain is closed under finite unions, so by Hansson's Theorem (Theorem 18), C can be rationalized by a social welfare function $F\colon \mathcal{D} \to \mathcal{R}$.

Consider any $x, y \in X$ and any $\mathbf{R} \in \mathcal{D}$. By the continuity and monotonicity of preferences and the compactness of $x_\downarrow \cup y_\downarrow$, the Pareto set $\mathcal{P}^w(x_\downarrow \cup y_\downarrow, \mathbf{R})$ is a nonempty subset of $\{x, y\}$. Hence, WP implies that $C(x_\downarrow \cup y_\downarrow, \mathbf{R}) \subseteq \{x, y\}$. It follows from this observation that F is uniquely determined from the choices out of corner sets as follows: for all $x, y \in X$ and all $\mathbf{R} \in \mathcal{D}$, $xF(\mathbf{R})y \leftrightarrow x \in C(x_\downarrow \cup y_\downarrow, \mathbf{R})$.

If $\mathbf{R}^1$ and $\mathbf{R}^2$ coincide on $\{x, y\}$, then $\mathcal{P}^w(x_\downarrow \cup y_\downarrow, \mathbf{R}^1) = \mathcal{P}^w(x_\downarrow \cup y_\downarrow, \mathbf{R}^2)$. Hence, by WPIIA, $C(x_\downarrow \cup y_\downarrow, \mathbf{R}^1) = C(x_\downarrow \cup y_\downarrow, \mathbf{R}^2)$. Because F rationalizes C, $F(\mathbf{R}^1)$ and $F(\mathbf{R}^2)$ therefore coincide on $\{x, y\}$; that is, F satisfies IIA.

If xP_iy for all $i \in N$, then x is the unique Pareto optimal alternative in $x_\downarrow \cup y_\downarrow$. Thus, $C(x_\downarrow \cup y_\downarrow, \mathbf{R}) = \{x\}$, from which it follows that F satisfies WP.

Suppose that $d \in N$ is a dictator for F. Because C is nondictatorial, there exist an $A \in \mathcal{A}$, $x, y \in A$, and an $\mathbf{R} \in \mathcal{D}$ such that xP_dy, but $y \in C(A, \mathbf{R})$. By ACA, $y \in C(x_\downarrow \cup y_\downarrow, \mathbf{R})$.[110] Because F rationalizes C, d is a dictator for F, and xP_dy, we must have $C(x_\downarrow \cup y_\downarrow, \mathbf{R}) = \{x\}$, a contradiction. Hence, F satisfies ND.

We have shown that F satisfies all of the assumptions of the Kalai–Muller–Satterthwaite Theorem (Theorem 5), which is impossible. □

This proof strategy is similar to the one used to prove the choice-theoretic version of Arrow's Theorem. The proof begins by assuming that all of the axioms can be satisfied. Using Hansson's Theorem, ACA implies that the social choice correspondence is rationalized by a social welfare function. The choices from corner sets are used to uniquely

[110] Even if A has a nonempty interior, $x_\downarrow \cup y_\downarrow$ need not, which is why the agenda domain is not restricted to sets with nonempty interiors.

identify this function, whereas the choice from pairs of alternatives were used to do this in the proof of Arrow's Theorem. This social welfare function is then shown to satisfy all of the Arrow social welfare function axioms. Finally, a social welfare function impossibility theorem is used to show that this is impossible. Here, it is the Kalai–Muller–Satterthwaite Theorem, not Arrow's original impossibility theorem, that establishes the contradiction.

Donaldson and Weymark (1988) have established the following private goods analogue of Theorem 32.

Theorem 33 *If* $X = \mathbb{R}_+^{mn}$ *with* $m \geq 2$, *there is no social choice correspondence with a complete compact comprehensive agenda domain and a classical private goods preference domain that satisfies* ACA, SPIIA, SP, *and* ND.

Because classical private goods preferences are only strictly monotonic in own consumption, for a profile **R**, one cannot, in general, infer that the weak Pareto set for a corner set $x_\downarrow \cup y_\downarrow$ is contained in $\{x, y\}$. However, the strong Pareto set is. Thus, by strengthening WP to SP and using SPIIA instead of WPIIA, the argument used to prove Theorem 32 shows that a social choice correspondence satisfying the assumptions of Theorem 33 can be rationalized by a social welfare function satisfying the Arrow axioms, which is impossible by Theorem 16 on effective social welfare functions.

17.2. Convex Agendas

Nonconvex agendas play two roles in the proof of Theorem 32. First, if only convex agendas are feasible, it would not be possible to use Hansson's Theorem to show that the social choice correspondence is rationalizable. Second, corner sets are needed to isolate pairs of alternatives, and so make binary comparisons. As a consequence, Donaldson and Weymark's proof strategy is ill-suited to deal with convex agendas.

Donaldson and Weymark (1988) and Duggan (1996) have investigated the consistency of the axioms in Theorem 32 in convex production economies. Donaldson and Weymark have shown that these axioms (with ND strengthened to ANON) are consistent when there are only two public goods, whereas Duggan has shown that they are not consistent when there are more than two goods. Their agenda domains are restricted to include only convex sets, as would be the case if all firms' technologies are convex. Preferences are required to be strictly convex, not merely convex.[111]

Complete Compact Comprehensive Convex Agenda Domain

$A \in \mathcal{A}$ if and only if A is a compact, comprehensive, convex subset of X.

[111] Alternatively, in Donaldson and Weymark's Theorem, preferences need only be assumed to be convex if the agendas are assumed to be strictly convex.

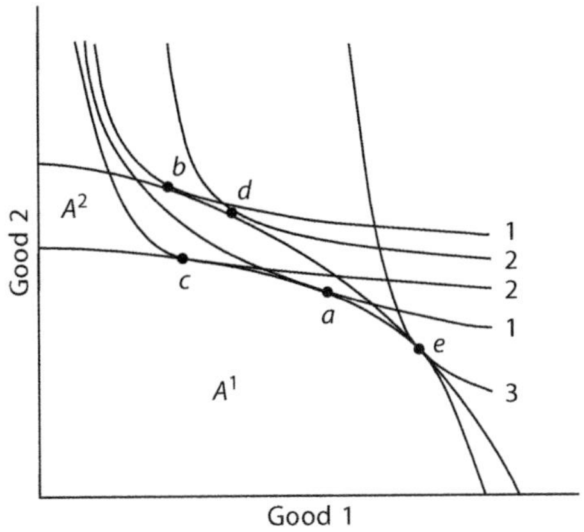

Figure 17.13. The Construction of the Generalized Median Social Choice Function.

Strictly Convex Classical Public Goods Preference Domain
$\mathcal{D}$ is the set of all profiles of continuous, strictly monotonic, strictly convex preference orderings on X.

In Donaldson and Weymark's (1988) possibility theorem, ND is strengthened to ANON.

Theorem 34 *If* $X = \mathbb{R}^2_+$, *there exist social choice correspondences with a complete compact comprehensive convex agenda domain and a strictly convex classical public goods preference domain that satisfy* ACA, WPIIA, WP, *and* ANON.

With these domain restrictions, on the upper boundary of any agenda, everyone has a single-peaked preference. This observation was used by Donaldson and Weymark (1988) to construct the following example satisfying all of the assumptions of Theorem 34.

Example 30 Consider a two-good public goods economy with $X = \mathbb{R}^2_+$ that satisfies the domain restrictions of Theorem 34. The social choice correspondence $C\colon \mathcal{A} \times \mathcal{D} \to X$ is defined by setting, for all $A \in \mathcal{A}$ and all $\mathbf{R} \in \mathcal{D}$, $C(A,\mathbf{R}) = \{x \in A \mid x_1 = \max_{i \in N} B_1(A, R_i)\}$, where $B_1(A, R_i)$ is the first component of the unique alternative that maximizes R_i on A. On the upper boundary of A, everyone has single-peaked preferences. The rightmost of the individual peaks is the social choice. In other words, one of the class of generalized median social choice functions introduced by Moulin (1980) and discussed in Section 3 is used to determine each choice set.

The construction of C for the case of three individuals is illustrated in Figure 17.13. Person one's best choices in the agendas A^1 and A^2 are a and b, respectively. Person two's best choices in the agendas A^1 and A^2 are c and d, respectively. Person three's best choice in both agendas is e. For this profile of preferences, the social choice out of both A^1 and A^2 is e.

It is easy to verify that C satisfies WPIIA, WP, and ANON. For a given profile, suppose that the agenda shrinks from, say, A^2 to A^1, but the original choice remains feasible. Anyone whose peak is still feasible has the same peak on A^1 as on A^2. Because the rightmost of the original peaks remains feasible, the convexity of preferences ensures that nobody's peak moves to the right of the original choice, as illustrated in Figure 17.13. Hence, ACA is satisfied.

Le Breton (1997) has observed that the social choice correspondence in this example can be rationalized by a social welfare function. Using the Hausdorff metric (see Munkres 1975) to measure the distance between sets, for a given profile $\mathbf{R} \in \mathcal{D}$, for any sequence of agendas $A^1, A^2, \ldots$ in $\mathcal{A}$ for which $A^k \to A \in \mathcal{A}$ and $\mathcal{P}^w(A^k, \mathbf{R}) \to \mathcal{P}^w(A, \mathbf{R})$, it can be shown that $C(A^k, \mathbf{R}) \to C(A, \mathbf{R})$. It follows from a theorem of Peters and Wakker (1991) that when this Pareto continuity condition is satisfied on the agenda domain of Example 30, C is rationalized by a social welfare function. Peters and Wakker's rationalizability theorem does not generalize to more goods.[112]

Duggan (1996) has shown that Arrow's axioms are inconsistent on a complete compact comprehensive convex agenda domain and a strictly convex classical public goods preference domain when there are three or more goods. Thus, the restriction to two goods in Theorem 34 is essential.

Theorem 35 *If $X = \mathbb{R}^m_+$ with $m \geq 3$, there does not exist a social choice correspondence with a complete compact comprehensive convex agenda domain and a strictly convex classical public goods preference domain that satisfies* ACA, WPIIA, WP, *and* ND.

Before proving Theorem 35, it is useful to provide an overview of Duggan's proof strategy. First, Duggan's spatial impossibility theorem (Theorem 31) is used to show that there is a dictator for the subdomain of agendas whose upper boundaries all lie in the same hyperplane. A connection argument is then used to show that the same person is a dictator on agendas whose upper boundaries are contained in different hyperplanes. Finally, ACA is used to show that this individual is a dictator on agendas whose upper boundaries are not contained in a hyperplane.

Proof of Theorem 35. Let $C\colon \mathcal{A} \times \mathcal{D} \to X$ be a social choice correspondence satisfying all of the assumptions of the theorem except for ND. For any $x \in \mathbb{R}^m_+$ and any $p \in \mathbb{R}^m_{++}$, let $H_x(p)$ denote the restriction to $\mathbb{R}^m_+$ of the hyperplane containing x that is normal to p. For any compact convex subset A of $H_x(p)$, let $A_\downarrow = \cup_{x \in A} x_\downarrow$. $A_\downarrow$ is an admissible

112 Peters and Wakker's theorem is for single-valued choice correspondences. With single-valuedness, as they show, if the agenda domain is closed under intersections, ACA is a necessary and sufficient condition for a choice correspondence to be rationalized by a binary relation (which need not be an ordering) on A.

agenda and its upper boundary is A. Note that any admissible preference R is spatial when restricted to $H_x(p)$ and that R has a unique maximum on $A_\downarrow$. Person $d \in N$ is a *dictator for* $H_x(p)$ if $C(A_\downarrow, \mathbf{R}) = B(A_\downarrow, R_d)$ for all compact convex $A \subseteq H_x(p)$ and all $\mathbf{R} \in \mathcal{D}$.

Consider any $x \in \mathbb{R}^m_+ \backslash \{0_m\}$ and any $p \in \mathbb{R}^m_{++}$. Let $\mathcal{A}^*$ and $\mathcal{D}^*$ denote the restrictions of the agenda and preference domains to $H_x(p)$. $\mathcal{A}^*$ is a complete compact convex agenda domain and $\mathcal{D}^*$ is an unrestricted spatial preference domain. A social choice correspondence $C^*: \mathcal{A}^* \times \mathcal{D}^* \to H_x(p)$ can be defined by setting $C^*(A, \mathbf{R}^*) = C(A_\downarrow, \mathbf{R})$ for all $A \in \mathcal{A}^*$ and all $\mathbf{R} \in \mathcal{D}$, where $\mathbf{R}^*$ is the restriction of $\mathbf{R}$ to $H_x(p)$. Because the Pareto set $\mathcal{P}^w(A_\downarrow, \mathbf{R})$ is contained in A when $A \subseteq H_x(p)$, WP and WPIIA ensure that C^* is well-defined. It is easy to verify that C^* satisfies ACA, IIF, and WP. Hence, by Theorem 31, C^* is dictatorial, which implies that there is a dictator d for C on $H_x(p)$.

Consider any $x, y \in \mathbb{R}^m_+ \backslash \{0_m\}$ and any $p, q \in \mathbb{R}^m_{++}$. Simple geometry confirms that it is possible to find a $z \in \mathbb{R}^m_+ \backslash \{0_m\}$ and an $r \in \mathbb{R}^m_{++}$ such that $H_z(r)$ intersects both $H_x(p)$ and $H_y(q)$. Further, $H_z(r) \cap H_x(p)$ and $H_z(r) \cap H_y(q)$ are at least one-dimensional. There must be a dictator on each of these three sets and the overlap between $H_x(p)$ and $H_z(r)$ and between $H_z(r)$ and $H_y(q)$ implies that the same person is the dictator in all three cases. Hence, d is a dictator on $H_w(s)$ for all $w \in \mathbb{R}^m_+ \backslash \{0_m\}$ and all $s \in \mathbb{R}^m_{++}$.[113]

Now consider any $A \in \mathcal{A}$ with $A \neq \{0_m\}$ and any $\mathbf{R} \in \mathcal{D}$. Let x be the unique maximum of R_d on A. Because A is compact, convex, and comprehensive and R_d is continuous, strictly monotonic, and convex, there exists a $p \in \mathbb{R}^m_{++}$ such that $H_x(p)$ is a separating hyperplane for A and the upper contour set of R_d at x. Because d has strictly convex preferences and is a dictator for $H_x(p)$, $C(H_x(p)_\downarrow, \mathbf{R}) = \{x\}$. ACA then implies that $C(A, \mathbf{R}) = \{x\}$. Because the choice is trivial when $A = \{0_m\}$, d is therefore a dictator for C. □

WPIIA and SPIIA have not been investigated in private goods economies when only convex agendas are admissible.

Except when there are only two public goods and all agendas are convex, the theorems in this section are all negative. Duggan (1996) and Le Breton (1997) have argued that these results illustrate the undue restrictiveness of WPIIA and SPIIA and they should not be used to conclude that it is impossible to construct satisfactory social choice correspondences for production economies. Le Breton used the following example to make his point.

Example 31 Consider a public goods economy with $X = \mathbb{R}^m_+$ and $m \geq 2$. Suppose that $\mathcal{D}$ is a strictly convex classical public goods preferences domain and that, as in Example 29, there is a complete linear comprehensive agenda domain. If everyone is

[113] Note that it has now been established that the axioms are inconsistent on a complete linear agenda domain and a strictly convex classical public goods preference domain.

given an equal share of the economy's wealth w and given access to the linear technology defined by p, an individual with preference R would choose $B(Y(p, w/n), R)$. Le Breton (1997) has suggested that fairness requires the social choice correspondence to guarantee that no individual is ever worse off than if he or she had an equal right to w. That is, with the agenda $Y(p, w)$ and profile $\mathbf{R}$, the choice set should be contained in $\bigcap_{i \in N} U(p, w, R_i)$, where $U(p, w, R_i) = \{x \in Y(p, w) \mid x R_i B(Y(p, w/n), R_i)\}$. Note that $B(Y(p, w/n), R_i)$ is feasible using $\frac{1}{n}$th of the economy's resources and, hence, $\sum_{i=1}^{n} B(Y(p, w/n), R_i)$ is feasible using all of the economy's endowment. By the strict monotoncity of preferences, this alternative is in $\bigcap_{i \in N} U(p, w, R_i)$, so it is always possible to satisfy Le Breton's fairness criterion.

Define the social choice correspondence C by setting $C(Y(p, w), \mathbf{R}) = B(\bigcap_{i \neq 1} U(p, w, R_i), R_1)$ for all $(p, w) \in \mathbb{R}^{m+1}_{++}$ and all $\mathbf{R} \in \mathcal{D}$. That is, person one's preferences are maximized subject to the constraint that none of the other individuals is worse off than they would be with an equal claim on the resources. C satisfies all of the Arrow axioms and the fairness condition described above, but it does not satisfy WPIIA.

18. CONCLUDING REMARKS

In this survey, we have considered the consistency of Arrow's axioms when his unrestricted domain assumptions are replaced by domain conditions that incorporate the restrictions on agendas and preferences encountered in economic environments. For social welfare functions, we have seen that economic domain restrictions do not provide a satisfactory way of avoiding Arrovian social choice impossibilities, except when the set of alternatives is one-dimensional and preferences are single-peaked. In contrast, for social choice correspondences, a number of economic domains have been identified for which the Arrow axioms are consistent.

With a social welfare function, a domain restriction only specifies what profiles of individual preferences are admissible. A unifying theme of Part I is that if a preference domain is Arrow-inconsistent, then this can generally be established using some version of the local approach introduced by Kalai, Muller, and Satterthwaite (1979). This methodology has been used by Kalai, Muller, and Satterthwaite (1979), Bordes and Le Breton (1989, 1990b), and Redekop (1991, 1993a, 1993c, 1996) to identify sufficient conditions for a preference domain to be Arrow-inconsistent. The exact form of these conditions depends on whether the model being considered has public or private goods (or both). We have illustrated the power of this approach by showing how it can be used to prove that a number of domains of interest are saturating, which is Kalai, Muller, and Satterthwaite's sufficient condition for Arrow-inconsistency for public alternatives. The difficulty of determining whether a particular domain is saturating or not depends on the domain being considered, but the general principles being applied do not.

The local approach involves identifying free pairs and free triples and showing how the free pairs can be connected to each other using a chain of overlapping free triples. Even when not every pair of free pairs can be connected, we have shown that the application of the local approach can sometimes be used to infer a great deal about the structure of an Arrovian social welfare function, as is the case in our ordinal probability example (Example 15). Our discussion of exchange economies in Section 10.2 shows that it is even possible to adapt the local approach to show the Arrow-inconsistency of a specific domain in which free triples fail to exist. Thus, the local approach can be viewed as being the fundamental tool for determining whether a preference domain is Arrow-inconsistent.[114]

The critical assumption that permits the application of the local approach is Independence of Irrelevant Alternatives. Mayston (1980) has noted that this axiom precludes considering individual marginal rates of substitution (when they are well-defined) in deciding how to socially rank a pair of alternatives, as it is not possible to calculate marginal rates of substitution without considering other "irrelevant" alternatives. In economic models, it therefore seems appropriate to consider weaker formulations of Arrow's independence condition, formulations that permit marginal rates of substitution at an alternative x or the indifference surface containing x to be relevant features of x. With the exception of some early work by Inada (1964, 1971) and Pazner (1979), it is only recently that alternative independence conditions have been investigated for economic domains. See, for example, Fleurbaey and Maniquet (2008) and Fleurbaey, Suzumura and Tadenuma (2005a).

Although lengthy, our discussion in Part I is not comprehensive. The results discussed in Part I have been extended in the following directions.

There is a large literature that examines the implications for Arrow's Theorem of weakening the assumption that social preferences are orderings or weakening (or dispensing with) the Pareto principle. On an unrestricted domain, the results obtained from this line of inquiry are rather negative. See Campbell and Kelly (2002). Similar negative results have been obtained for economic domains by, for example, Border (1983), Bordes and Le Breton (1989, 1990a, 1990b), Campbell (1989b, 1990a, 1990b, 1992b, 1992d, 1992e, 1996), and Nagahisa (1991).[115]

In Arrow's Theorem, it is assumed that there is a finite number of individuals. In many applications, such as overlapping generations economies, the society is infinite. With an unrestricted preference domain and an infinite society, social welfare functions exist that satisfy all of Arrow's axioms (although these functions have other unattractive

[114] An alternative to the local approach has been proposed by Saari (1991) to investigate the consistency of axioms for aggregation problems, including preference aggregation problems of the kind considered in Part I. Saari's approach utilizes a discrete version of a calculus argument to identify restrictions on the domain and range of his aggregation function that imply that the aggregation function only depends on one argument. For social welfare functions, this restriction corresponds to the existence of a dictator.

[115] Many of these restricted domain theorems require social preferences to be continuous.

features). Infinite societies with restricted preference domains have been considered by Campbell (1989a, 1989b, 1990b, 1992a, 1992b, 1992d) and Redekop (1995, 1996).

We have only considered alternatives that are either purely public or purely private. The mixed case in which alternatives have both public and private components has been considered by Bordes and Le Breton (1990b) and Redekop (1995, 1996).

A *social welfare functional* aggregates a profile of utility functions into a social preference. The use of a social welfare functional allows for information about interpersonal utility comparisons, when available, to play a role in determining the social ordering of the alternatives. Social welfare functionals on economic domains have been studied by Bordes, Hammond, and Le Breton (2005) and Weymark (1998).

The social choice correspondence framework permits us to consider restrictions on the set of feasible agendas, not just on the set of admissible preference profiles. Unlike with the local approach used to analyze social welfare functions, no single methodology has been identified that can be used to determine the consistency of Arrow's choice-theoretic axioms in a wide variety of economic environments. However, a lesson that does emerge from the results we have surveyed in Part II is that the consistency of the Arrow axioms depends very much on how restrictive Independence of Infeasible Alternatives and Arrow's Choice Axiom are, and this depends on the structure of the agenda and preference domains. In some environments, one of these axioms is vacuous. For example, Independence of Infeasible Alternatives is vacuous for the economies with analytic preference domains and compact agenda domains considered in Section 15, and Arrow's Choice Axiom is vacuous in the exchange economies considered in Section 16.1. In such cases, it is very easy to construct social choice correspondences that satisfy all of the other Arrow axioms. Even when none of the axioms is vacuous, we have seen that possibility theorems emerge when the preference or agenda domains are sufficiently restricted.

Arrovian social choice theory on economic domains has a close affinity to the rapidly growing literature on the axiomatic analysis of resource allocation.[116] As is the case with the literature discussed in Part II, the research on axiomatic models of resource allocation investigates the implications of a set of axioms when both individual preferences and the set of feasible agendas are assumed to satisfy the kinds of restrictions found in microeconomic models. However, it departs from the research discussed here in its choice of axioms and, in some cases, on the kinds of economic problems being considered. Many of the axioms advocated by practitioners of this approach to analyzing resource allocation problems are motivated by fairness considerations, by incentive issues, or by the belief that the choices for different population sizes should be consistent with each other. For the most part, this literature has developed independently of the research we have surveyed and has typically not included all of the Arrow axioms in the set of axioms being investigated.

[116] See Moulin and Thomson (1997) for an introduction to this literature.

Of the four Arrow axioms for social choice correspondences, Arrow's Choice Axiom is the most controversial. We know from the work of Arrow (1959) and Hansson (1968) that, for some agenda domains, this axiom is equivalent to requiring the social choice correspondence to be rationalizable by a social welfare function. This is not true in general. When viewed as a constraint on the consistency of the choices made in different agendas, Arrow's Choice Axiom is a compelling normative property of a choice correspondence. It is interesting to note that, when combined with strong Pareto, a version of the resource monotonicity axiom used in the literature on the axiomatic analysis of resource allocation implies a "welfarist" version of Arrow's Choice Axiom for social choice functions. Applied to abstract agenda domains, *Resource Monotonicity* requires that, for any fixed profile of preferences, nobody should be harmed by an expansion of the feasible set.[117] For the social choice function C, consider a profile $\mathbf{R}$ and two agendas A and B with $A \subset B$ for which $C(B,\mathbf{R}) \in A$. Resource Monotonicity implies that $C(B,\mathbf{R})R_iC(A,\mathbf{R})$ for all $i \in N$. From Strong Pareto and the assumption that $C(B,\mathbf{R}) \in A$, it then follows that $C(B,\mathbf{R})I_iC(A,\mathbf{R})$ for all $i \in N$. Arrow's Choice Axiom is somewhat more demanding, requiring that $C(B,\mathbf{R}) = C(A,\mathbf{R})$. This argument provides indirect support for requiring choices from different agendas to satisfy a choice consistency condition similar to the one used by Arrow. However, Resource Monotonicity is a demanding axiom that often conflicts with other appealing normative criteria. For example, for domains of exchange economies like those studied in Section 16.1, Moulin and Thomson (1988) have shown that any social choice function satisfying Resource Monotonicity and Weak Pareto must violate some very weak fairness axioms.

Our discussion of the theorems of Gibbard, Hylland, and Weymark (1987), Le Breton and Weymark (2002), and Donaldson and Weymark (1988) in Sections 13.3, 15, and 16.2, respectively, demonstrates that when investigating the consistency of the Arrovian axioms on restricted domains, it matters a great deal whether one is dealing with a social welfare function or a social choice correspondence. Preference domains that result in an impossibility theorem using a social welfare function may well yield a possibility theorem using a social choice correspondence when combined with an appropriate agenda domain.[118] It is standard practice in general equilibrium theory and in welfare economics to place a priori restrictions on both preferences and the set of feasible alternatives. For example, assumptions are often made on production technologies and on endowments to ensure that the set of feasible alternatives is compact, comprehensive, and convex. The

[117] This property was introduced in the context of models in which the expansion of the feasible set was achieved by an increase in the economy's resource endowment.

[118] Marchant (2000) has suggested that this comparison is somewhat unfair because we are not comparing comparable objects. In particular, he argued that it would be more appropriate to make this comparison if the independence assumption for social welfare functions was restricted to apply only to a restricted set of agendas, as is the case with the independence assumption for social choice correspondences. Marchant's argument is consistent with our view that agenda domain restrictions can play an important role in the development of Arrovian possibility theorems. See also the discussion in Fleurbaey, Suzumura, and Tadenuma (2005b) of the relative strength of independence axioms in the social welfare function and social choice correspondence frameworks.

literature surveyed here suggests that pursuing a similar strategy in Arrovian social choice theory can be quite promising.

Much has been learned about the compatibility of Arrow's axioms in different economic environments. In our review of this literature, we have identified several open questions. Thus, in spite of the substantial progress that has be made, much more remains to be discovered about Arrovian social choice theory on economic domains.

ACKNOWLEDGMENTS

This chapter incorporates some material that has previously appeared in Le Breton and Weymark (1996). It is reprinted here with the permission of Springer Science+Business Media. We are grateful to Lars Ehlers, Marc Fleurbaey, and Thierry Marchant for their comments. Preliminary versions of this chapter served as the basis for lectures given at EUREQua, Université Paris 1 (Panthéon-Sorbonne); at the 21st Century Center of Excellence Program "Constructing Open Political-Economic Systems," Waseda University; and at the Workshop on Mathematical Models of Individual and Public Choice held at the Institute for Mathematical Behavioral Sciences of the University of California at Irvine.

REFERENCES

Arrow, K. J. (1951). *Social choice and individual values*. New York: Wiley.

Arrow, K. J. (1959). Rational choice functions and orderings. *Economica, 26*, 121–127.

Arrow, K. J. (1963). *Social choice and individual values* (2nd ed.). New York: Wiley.

Austen-Smith, D., & Banks, J. S. (1999). *Positive political theory i: collective preference*. Ann Arbor: University of Michigan Press.

Bailey, M. J. (1979). The possibility of rational social choice in an economy. *Journal of Political Economy, 87*, 37–56.

Black, D. (1948). On the rationale of group decision-making. *Journal of Political Economy, 56*, 23–34.

Blau, J. H. (1957). The existence of social welfare functions. *Econometrica, 25*, 302–313.

Bone, J. (2003). Simple Arrow-type propositions in the Edgeworth domain. *Social Choice and Welfare, 20*, 41–48.

Border, K. C. (1983). Social welfare functions for economic environments with and without the Pareto principle. *Journal of Economic Theory, 29*, 205–216.

Border, K. C. (1984). An impossibility theorem for spatial models. *Public Choice, 43*, 293–305.

Border, K. C., & Jordan, J. S. (1983). Straightforward elections, unanimity and phantom voters. *Review of Economic Studies, 50*, 153–170.

Bordes, G., Campbell, D. E., & Le Breton, M. (1995). Arrow's theorem for economic domains and Edgeworth hyperboxes. *International Economic Review, 36*, 441–454.

Bordes, G., Hammond, P. J., & Le Breton, M. (2005). Social welfare functionals on restricted domains and in economic environments. *Journal of Public Economic Theory, 7*, 1–25.

Bordes, G., & Le Breton, M. (1989). Arrovian theorems with private alternatives domains and selfish individuals. *Journal of Economic Theory, 47*, 257–281.

Bordes, G., & Le Breton, M. (1990a). Arrovian theorems for economic domains: assignments, matchings, and pairings. *Social Choice and Welfare, 7*, 193–208.

Bordes, G., & Le Breton, M. (1990b). Arrovian theorems for economic domains: the case where there are simultaneously private and public goods. *Social Choice and Welfare, 7*, 1–17.

Bossert, W., & Weymark, J. A. (1993). Generalized median social welfare functions. *Social Choice and Welfare, 10*, 17–33.

Campbell, D. E. (1989a). Arrow's theorem for economic environments and effective social preferences. *Social Choice and Welfare, 6*, 325–329.

Campbell, D. E. (1989b). Wilson's theorem for economic environments and continuous social preferences. *Social Choice and Welfare, 7*, 315–323.

Campbell, D. E. (1990a). Can equity be purchased at the expense of efficiency? an axiomatic inquiry. *Journal of Economic Theory, 51*, 32–47.

Campbell, D. E. (1990b). Intergenerational social choice without the Pareto principle. *Journal of Economic Theory, 50*, 414–423.

Campbell, D. E. (1992a). The Arrow and Plott independence conditions. *Economics Letters, 39*, 143–146.

Campbell, D. E. (1992b). *Equity, efficiency, and social choice*. Oxford: Clarendon Press.

Campbell, D. E. (1992c). Implementation of social welfare functions. *International Economic Review, 33*, 525–533.

Campbell, D. E. (1992d). Quasitransitive intergenerational choice for economic environments. *Journal of Mathematical Economics, 21*, 229–247.

Campbell, D. E. (1992e). Transitive social choice in economic environments. *International Economic Review, 33*, 341–352.

Campbell, D. E. (1993). Euclidean individual preference and continuous social preference. *European Journal of Political Economy, 9*, 541–550.

Campbell, D. E. (1995). Nonbinary social choice for economic environments. *Social Choice and Welfare, 12*, 245–254.

Campbell, D. E. (1996). Social ranking of alternatives with and without coalition formation. In N. Schofield (Ed.), *Collective decision-making: social choice and political economy* (pp. 63–78). Boston: Kluwer Academic Publishers.

Campbell, D. E., & Kelly, J. S. (2000). Information and preference aggregation. *Social Choice and Welfare, 17*, 3–24.

Campbell, D. E., & Kelly, J. S. (2002). Impossibility theorems in the Arrovian framework. In K. J. Arrow, A. K. Sen, & K. Suzumura (Eds.), *Handbook of social choice and welfare*, Vol. 1 (pp. 35–94). Amsterdam: North-Holland.

Deb, R. (2010). Non-binary social choice. In K. J. Arrow, A. K. Sen, & K. Suzumura (Eds.), *Handbook of social choice and welfare*, Vol. 2 (pp. 331–362). Amsterdam: North-Holland.

Donaldson, D., & Roemer, J. E. (1987). Social choice in economic environments with dimensional variation. *Social Choice and Welfare, 4*, 253–276.

Donaldson, D., & Weymark, J. A. (1988). Social choice in economic environments. *Journal of Economic Theory, 46*, 291–308.

Duggan, J. (1996). Arrow's theorem in public goods environments with convex technologies. *Journal of Economic Theory, 68*, 303–318.

Dutta, B., Jackson, M., & Le Breton, M. (2001). Strategic candidacy and voting procedures. *Econometrica, 69*, 1013–1037.

Ehlers, L. (2001). Independence axioms for the provision of multiple public goods as options. *Mathematical Social Sciences, 41*, 239–250.

Ehlers, L., & Storcken, T. (2008). Arrow's Possibility Theorem for one-dimensional single-peaked preferences. *Games and Economic Behavior, 64*, 533–547.

Ehlers, L., & Storcken, T. (2009). Oligarchies in spatial environments. *Journal of Mathematical Economics, 45*, 250–256.

Ehlers, L., & Weymark, J. A. (2003). Candidate stability and nonbinary social choice. *Economic Theory, 22*, 233–243.

Fishburn, P. C. (1976). Dictators on blocks: generalization of social choice impossibility theorems. *Journal of Combinatorial Theory, Series B, 20*, 153–170.

Fishburn, P. C., & Kelly, J. S. (1997). Super-Arrovian domains with strict preferences. *SIAM Journal on Discrete Mathematics, 10*, 83–95.

Fleurbaey, M., & Maniquet, F. (2008). Utilitarianism versus fairness in welfare economics. In M. Fleurbaey, M. Salles & J. A. Weymark (Eds.), *Justice, political liberalism, and utilitarianism: themes from Harsanyi and Rawls* (pp. 263–280). Cambridge: Cambridge University Press.

Fleurbaey, M., Suzumura, K., & Tadenuma, K. (2005a). Arrovian aggregation in economic environments: how much should we know about indifference surfaces? *Journal of Economic Theory, 124*, 22–44.

Fleurbaey, M., Suzumura, K., & Tadenuma, K. (2005b). The informational basis of the theory of fair allocation. *Social Choice and Welfare, 24*, 311–341.

Gaertner, W. (2001). *Domain conditions in social choice theory*. Cambridge: Cambridge University Press.

Gaertner, W. (2002). Domain restrictions. In K. J. Arrow, A. K. Sen, & K. Suzumura (Eds.), *Handbook of social choice and welfare*, Vol. 1 (pp. 131–170). Amsterdam: North-Holland.

Gibbard, A., Hylland, A., & Weymark, J. A. (1987). Arrow's theorem with a fixed feasible alternative. *Social Choice and Welfare, 4*, 105–115.

Grether, D. M., & Plott, C. R. (1982). Nonbinary social choice: an impossibility theorem. *Review of Economic Studies, 49*, 143–149.

Hansson, B. (1968). Choice structures and preference relations. *Synthese, 18*, 443–458.

Inada, K. (1964). On the economic welfare function. *Econometrica, 32*, 316–338.

Inada, K. (1971). Social welfare function and social indifference surfaces. *Econometrica, 39*, 599–623.

Kalai, E., Muller, E., & Satterthwaite, M. A. (1979). Social welfare functions when preferences are convex, strictly monotonic, and continuous. *Public Choice, 34*, 87–97.

Kalai, E., & Ritz, Z. (1980). Characterization of the private alternatives domains admitting Arrow social welfare functions. *Journal of Economic Theory, 22*, 23–36.

Kannai, Y. (1970). Continuity properties of the core of a market. *Econometrica, 38*, 791–815.

Kannai, Y. (1974). Approximation of convex preferences. *Journal of Mathematical Economics, 1*, 101–106.

Kelly, J. S. (1994). The Bordes-LeBreton exceptional case. *Social Choice and Welfare, 11*, 273–281.

Lainé, J., Le Breton, M., & Trannoy, A. (1986). Group decision making under uncertainty: a note on the aggregation of 'ordinal probabilities'. *Theory and Decision, 21*, 155–161.

Le Breton, M. (1986). Essais sur les fondements de l'analyse économique de l'inégalité, Thèse pour le Doctorat d'État en Sciences Économiques, Université de Rennes 1.

Le Breton, M. (1997). Arrovian social choice on economic domains. In K. J. Arrow, A. K. Sen, & K. Suzumura (Eds.), *Social choice re-examined*, Vol. 1 (pp. 72–96). London: Macmillan.

Le Breton, M., & Trannoy, A. (1987). Measures of inequality as an aggregation of individual preferences about income distribution: the Arrovian case. *Journal of Economic Theory, 41*, 248–269.

Le Breton, M., & Weymark, J. A. (1996). An introduction to Arrovian social welfare functions on economic and political domains. In N. Schofield (Ed.), *Collective decision-making: social choice and political economy* (pp. 25–61). Boston: Kluwer Academic Publishers.

Le Breton, M., & Weymark, J. A. (1999). Strategy-proof social choice functions with continuous separable preferences. *Journal of Mathematical Economics, 32*, 47–85.

Le Breton, M., & Weymark, J. A. (2002). Social choice with analytic preferences. *Social Choice and Welfare, 19*, 637–657.

Marchant, T. (2000). Is there something more in SWF than in SCW? Unpublished manuscript, Department of Data Analysis, University of Ghent.

Maskin, E. S. (1976). Social welfare functions for economics. Unpublished manuscript, Darwin College, Cambridge University and Department of Economics, Harvard University.

Mayston, D. J. (1980). Where did prescriptive welfare economics go wrong? In D. A. Currie, & W. Peters (Eds.), *Contemporary economic analysis*, Vol. 2, (pp. 175–220). London: Croom Helm.

Moulin, H. (1980). On strategy-proofness and single peakedness. *Public Choice, 35*, 437–455.

Moulin, H. (1984). Generalized Condorcet-winners for single-peaked and single-plateau preferences. *Social Choice and Welfare, 1*, 127–147.

Moulin, H., & Thomson, W. (1988). Can everyone benefit from growth? two difficulties. *Journal of Mathematical Economics, 17*, 339–345.

Moulin, H., & Thomson, W. (1997). Axiomatic analysis of resource allocation problems. In K. J. Arrow, A. K. Sen, & K. Suzumura (Eds.), *Social choice re-examined*, Vol. 1 (pp. 101–120). London: Macmillan.

Munkres, J. R. (1975). *Topology: a first course*. Englewood Cliffs, NJ: Prentice-Hall.

Nagahisa, R. (1991). Acyclic and continuous social choice in T_1 connected spaces: including its application to economic environments. *Social Choice and Welfare, 8*, 319–322.

Nitzan, S. (1976). On linear and lexicographic orders: majority rule and equilibrium. *International Economic Review, 17*, 213–219.

Pazner, E. A. (1979). Equity, nonfeasible alternatives and social choice: a reconsideration of the concept of social welfare. In J.-J. Laffont (Ed.), *Aggregation and revelation of preferences* (pp. 161–173). Amsterdam: North-Holland.

Peters, H., & Wakker, P. (1991). Independence of irrelevant alternatives and revealed group preferences. *Econometrica, 59*, 1787–1801.

Plott, C. R. (1976). Axiomatic social choice theory: an overview and interpretation. *American Journal of Political Science, 20*, 511–596.

Redekop, J. (1991). Social welfare functions on restricted economic domains. *Journal of Economic Theory, 53*, 396–427.

Redekop, J. (1993a). Arrow-inconsistent economic domains. *Social Choice and Welfare, 10*, 107–126.

Redekop, J. (1993b). The questionnaire topology on some spaces of economic preferences. *Journal of Mathematical Economics, 22*, 479–494.

Redekop, J. (1993c). Social welfare functions on parametric domains. *Social Choice and Welfare, 10*, 127–148.

Redekop, J. (1995). Arrow theorems in economic environments. In W. A. Barnett, H. Moulin, M. Salles, & N. J. Schofield (Eds.), *Social choice, welfare, and ethics* (pp. 163–185). Cambridge: Cambridge University Press.

Redekop, J. (1996). Arrow theorems in mixed goods, stochastic, and dynamic economic environments. *Social Choice and Welfare, 13*, 95–112.

Richelson, J. T. (1984). Social choice and the status quo. *Public Choice, 42*, 225–234.

Saari, D. G. (1991). Calculus and extensions of Arrow's theorem. *Journal of Mathematical Economics, 20*, 271–306.

Sen, A. K. (1970). *Collective choice and social welfare*. San Francisco: Holden-Day.

Suzumura, K. (1983). *Rational choice, collective decisions, and social welfare*. Cambridge: Cambridge University Press.

von Neumann, J., & Morgenstern, O. (1947). *Theory of games and economic behavior* (2nd ed.). Princeton: Princeton University Press.

Weymark, J. A. (1997). Aggregating ordinal probabilities on finite sets. *Journal of Economic Theory, 75*, 407–432.

Weymark, J. A. (1998). Welfarism on economic domains. *Mathematical Social Sciences, 36*, 251–268.

Yanovskaya, E. B. (1994). Correspondence between social choice functions and solutions of cooperative games. *Mathematical Social Sciences, 27*, 217–234.

CHAPTER EIGHTEEN

Topological Theories of Social Choice

Nicholas Baigent
Institute of Public Economics, Graz University, Graz, Austria and Department of Philosophy, Logic and Scientific Method, London School of Economics and Political Science, London, UK

Contents

Abstract

This chapter presents a simple introduction to the main results in topological social choice theory. Given a continuous social welfare function, these results show the following: (i) Unanimity and Anonymity are incompatible; (ii) Weak Pareto and No Veto are incompatible; and (iii) Weak Pareto implies the existence of a Strategic Manipulator. Given the role of continuity in all these results, its justification is critically discussed. Finally, a remarkable proof of Arrow's theorem using topological methods is presented.

Keywords:
JEL codes: D71, C02, C65

Handbook of Social Choice and Welfare, Volume II
ISSN: 0169-7218, DOI: 10.1016/S0169-7218(10)00018-3

1. INTRODUCTION

The purpose of this chapter is to survey topological theories of social choice. The original contributions to this area of social choice came in a series of papers by Chichilnisky (1979, 1980, 1982a, 1982b, 1982c, 1983, 1993). Since there are already three excellent surveys, Mehta (1997), Lauwers (2000, 2009), and a useful introduction and overview in Heal (1997),[1] this survey is highly selective. It has two main objectives. One is to give a simplified presentation of the key results for which the prerequisites are minimal. Most sections should be well within reach for senior undergraduates in the field of economics. The other purpose is to offer a critical discussion of the defining property of topological social choice, namely continuity. Footnotes or references to the literature provide further detail. Most of the exposition is limited to the simple case of two agents and two commodities.

Section 2 presents an elementary introduction to Chichilnisky's impossibility theorem, and Section 3 presents a domain restriction that provides a possible escape. Further results are presented in Sections 4 and 5. Section 6 discusses continuity in a critical way since it is the key property in the earlier sections. Section 7 presents a very different sort of result, namely a highly original proof of Arrow's famous impossibility theorem. Finally, Section 8 briefly presents conclusions.

2. CHICHILNISKY'S THEOREM: AN ELEMENTARY INTRODUCTION

This section presents a simple version of the seminal result of topological social choice theory. The mathematical concepts from algebraic topology are explained in an intuitive way before using them in two related proofs of the theorem.

2.1. Linear Preferences

Interpret $\mathbb{R}^2_+$ as a commodity space of bundles of two collective goods. A linear preference on $\mathbb{R}^2_+$ can be represented by straight-line indifference curves, two of which are shown in Figure 18.1, or by a vector of unit length perpendicular to an indifference curve at an arbitrary bundle.

The bundle at which the unit vector is based does not matter, given the linearity of the preferences. Its direction shows the direction of preference, so that two "opposite" linear preferences have the same indifference curves, but their unit vectors go in

[1] Mehta's survey is concise and very good for the technical details of the results it presents. Lauwers (2000) is comprehensive and Lauwers (2009) is more selective but simpler.

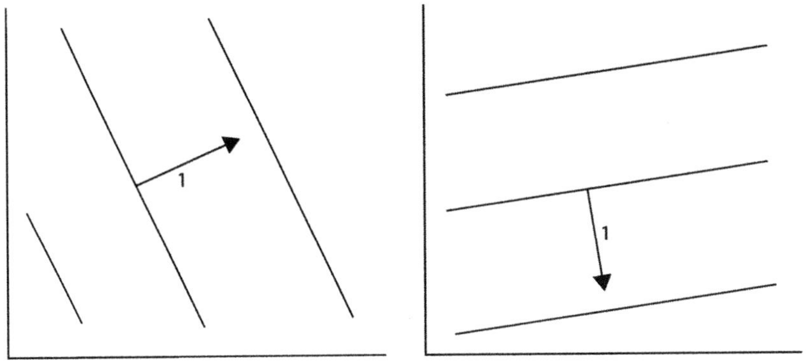

Figure 18.1. Linear Preferences and Their Unit Vectors.

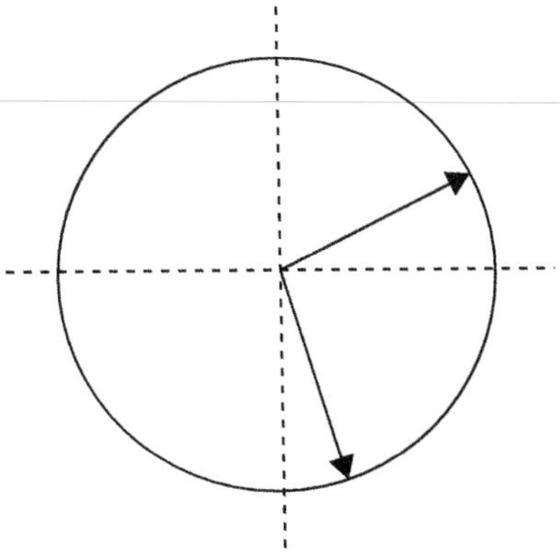

Figure 18.2. The Unit Circle and Unit Vectors of Linear Preferences.

opposite directions. Since vectors are normalized to have unit length, there is no role for preference intensity or interpersonal comparisons.

Now imagine lifting the unit vectors from the diagrams in Figure 18.1 and placing them in a circle of unit radius centered at the origin as shown in Figure 18.2.

Doing this for all possible linear preferences uniquely associates a linear preference with a point on a unit circle and vice versa. Thus, the set of points on S^1, the unit circle, may be taken as the set of all linear preferences.

Identifying linear preferences with points in S^1 is key to all that follows and understanding the simple mathematics of unit circles is therefore crucial. A brief review, easily skipped, covers the only essential prerequisites for understanding simple versions of the main results.[2]

[2] Knowledge of elementary operations on sets and functions between sets is assumed.

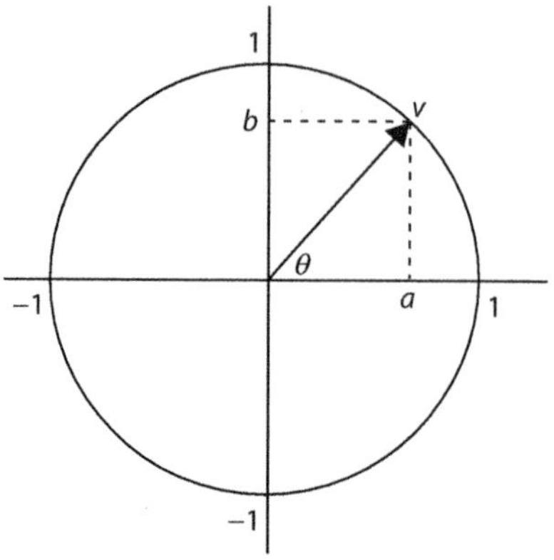

Figure 18.3. The Unit Circle.

Figure 18.3 shows points on the unit circle centered at the origin given by their Cartesian coordinates as follows: $S^1 = \{(a,b) \in \mathbb{R}^2 : (a^2+b^2)^{1/2} = 1\}$. These points may also be considered as the set of unit vectors, v. Each such vector, v, is determined by the angle, θ, between the horizontal axis and v. It is often convenient to specify θ by its "circular," or polar, coordinate given by the length of the arc from point (1,0) to v in a counterclockwise, or positive, direction. Thus, $\theta = 0$ and $(a,b) = (1,0)$ both denote the same point. Cartesian and polar coordinates are related by $a = \cos\theta$ and $b = \sin\theta$. Finally, any point in the unit circle may be thought of as a complex number $e^{\theta i} = \cos\theta + i\sin\theta$. This is particularly useful in considering rotations in the positive direction as θ increases from 0 to 2π, and in the negative, clockwise, direction as θ decreases from 0 to -2π. Usually, points in S^1 will be specified by their polar coordinate $\theta \in [0, 2\pi]$, so care should be taken to remember that $\theta = 0$ and $\theta = 2\pi$ specify the same point.

2.2. Chichilnisky's Impossibility Theorem

Consider the special case of two agents with linear preferences on $\mathbb{R}^2_+$. A *social welfare function* $f : S^1 \times S^1 \to S^1$ then aggregates agents' preferences $(\theta_1, \theta_2) \in S^1 \times S^1$ into a social preference $f(\theta_1, \theta_2) \in S^1$. Thus, a social welfare function is a function from a subset of one Euclidean space to a subset of another Euclidean space, and continuity is defined in the usual way for such functions.[3]

A simple example is given by a *constant function* that assigns the same $\theta^* \in S^1$ to all pairs $(\theta_1, \theta_2) \in S^1 \times S^1$ of agents' preferences. Another example is given by a social welfare function for which the social preference is the same as agent 1's preference as follows.

[3] Imagine agents pointing to a touch screen monitor with an additional monitor showing the social preference. If agents move their fingers around S^1 on their screens without taking fingers off S^1, pointing to the changing social preferences would require keeping a finger not only on the screen but also on S^1.

For all $(\theta_1, \theta_2) \in S^1 \times S^1, f(\theta_1, \theta_2) = \theta_1$. This social welfare function is a *dictatorship* of agent 1. All constant and dictatorial social welfare functions are continuous so that the social preference does not jump from one point to another as agents' preferences change.

For a constant function, social preferences are completely insensitive to the preferences of all agents. For a dictatorial social welfare function, social preferences are completely insensitive to the preferences of all agents except the dictator. Thus, for constant and dictatorial social welfare functions, social preferences are insensitive to agents' preferences.

Two properties of social welfare functions rule out such insensitivities, namely Unanimity and Anonymity. A social welfare function is *Unanimous* (UN) if and only if the social preference is the same as any unanimously held agents' preference. That is, for all $\theta \in S^1, f(\theta, \theta) = \theta$. A social welfare function is *Anonymous* (AN) if and only if it is invariant to reassignments of preferences among agents. That is, for all $\theta, \theta' \in S^1$, $f(\theta, \theta') = f(\theta', \theta)$. Dictatorial social welfare functions are UN but not AN. Constant social welfare functions are AN but not UN. However, both are continuous.

The next example is both UN and AN, but not continuous. This example has the flavor of "averaging" agents' preferences. First, the social preference is defined for agents' preferences that are not given by opposite points on the circle. Thus, for preferences that are not opposites, let the social preference be given by the midpoint of the shortest arc between them, as shown in Figure 18.4. For preferences that are not opposites, this social welfare function is continuous.

It is for opposite preferences that continuity fails. However the social preference is defined for opposite preferences, there must be a discontinuity. To see this, hold θ_2 constant in Figure 18.4 and let θ_1 rotate positively. As θ_1 approaches the point opposite θ_2, the social preference tends to the "North Pole," (0,1), or equivalently, $\pi/2$. Immediately the rotation passes beyond the point opposite θ_2, the social preference jumps to a point close to $(0, -1)$, or equivalently, $3\pi/2$. Thus, this social welfare function is discontinuous at all opposite preferences. It is, however, UN and AN.

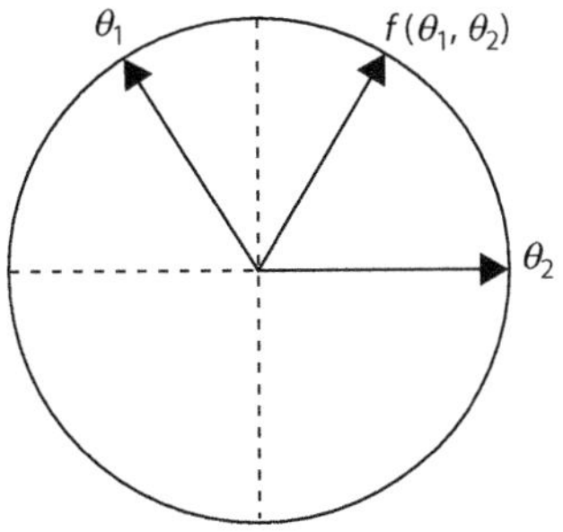

Figure 18.4. Averaging Agents' Preferences.

These examples suggest that it may be difficult to find a continuous social welfare function that is UN and AN. The seminal result in topological social choice theory establishes that such social welfare functions do not exist.

Theorem 1 (Chichilnisky, 1979, 1980, 1982a) *There is no continuous social welfare function* $f : S^1 \times S^1 \to S^1$ *that has the UN and AN properties.*

The proof is postponed until after a few mathematical tools have been developed. This result generalizes straightforwardly from circles S^1 to spheres S^m, $1 \leq m < \infty$, and to any finite number of two or more agents. See Chichilnisky (1982a), Mehta (1997), and Lauwers (2000, 2009).

2.3. Loops

This section offers an informal presentation of the main topological ideas required to prove Theorem 1.

For an arbitrary set X, a *path in* X is a continuous function $\alpha : [0, 1] \to X$ from the unit interval to X. Figure 18.5 shows the image of two paths, α and β, in $\mathbb{R}^2_+$.

Images of paths are orientated in the sense that they "travel" from an initial to a terminal point as shown by the arrows in Figure 18.5. Indeed, reversing the arrows interchanges the initial and terminal points.

Two paths are *homotopic* if one can be continuously deformed into the other. Thus, in Figure 18.5, α and β are homotopic. The homotopy relationship between paths is

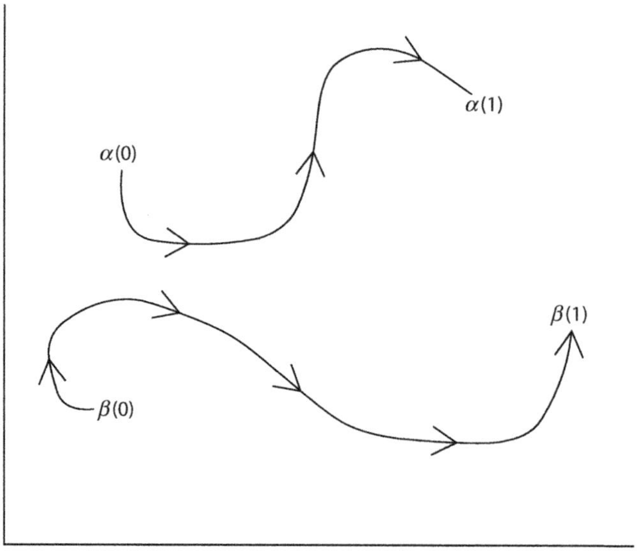

Figure 18.5. Paths in the Plane.

preserved by composition. That is, if paths $\alpha : [0,1] \to X$ and $\beta : [0,1] \to X$ are homotopic, and $\phi : X \to Y$ is a continuous function, *the compositions* $\phi \circ \alpha$ *and* $\phi \circ \beta$ *are also homotopic.*

A *loop in* X is a closed path in X, in the sense that its initial and terminal points are the same. In other words, a path $\alpha : [0,1] \to X$ is a loop in X if and only if $\alpha(0) = \alpha(1)$. It is also convenient to regard a loop in X equivalently as taking a circle continuously into X. That is, a loop in X is a continuous function $\alpha : S^1 \to X$.

Since loops are paths, they may be homotopic, and Figure 18.6 shows two homotopic loops in $\mathbb{R}^2_+$. Indeed, it is easy to see that all loops in $\mathbb{R}^2_+$ may be continuously deformed into each other and are therefore homotopic. This is not the case for sets with "holes" in them, such as the annulus in Figure 18.7 given by the points bounded by two concentric circles. Indeed, loops β and γ are homotopic, but neither is homotopic to α.

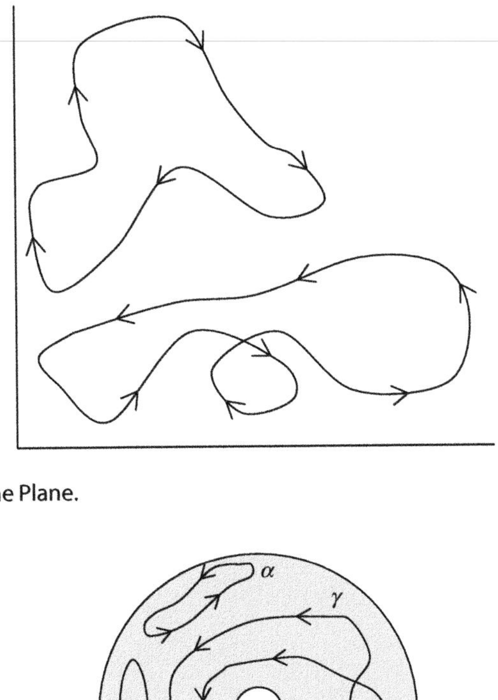

Figure 18.6. Loops in the Plane.

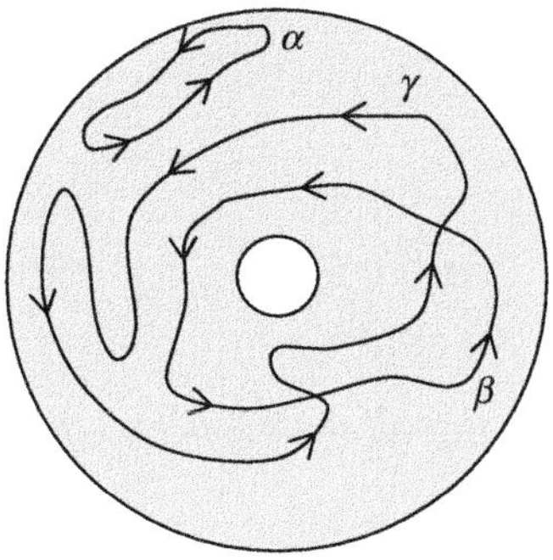

Figure 18.7. Loops in an Annulus.

The reason for these homotopy relations between loops in an annulus is clear. Loop α does not go around the hole while loops β and γ go around the hole once. Note that loops may double back on themselves as shown by γ in Figure 18.7. Even so, it goes around the hole counterclockwise exactly once, as does β. A key intuition is that loops in sets with one hole are homotopic if and only if they go around the hole the same net number of times. While loops in the unit circle will eventually be our main focus of attention, these remarks about loops in an annulus give key intuitions for important facts about loops in the unit circle.

Assume that the circle forming the outer boundary of the annulus in Figure 18.7 is fixed, and imagine the inner circle increasing in radius. As its radius increases the loops are squeezed until eventually they are pressed onto the outer circle. They become loops in the circle, S^1. Squeezed onto S^1, loop α in Figure 18.7 goes part of the way around S^1, but before completing a rotation it returns to its starting point. Loop β when squeezed onto S^1 completes one whole positive rotation as does γ, even though γ temporarily changes to move negatively. Since loops in S^1 cannot be seen directly in diagrams of S^1, a different diagram is required, namely Figure 18.8.

Consider a circle S^1 centered at the origin of the plane, $(0,0) \in \mathbb{R}$. Figure 18.8 shows the behavior of six loops in S^1, taking $(1,0) \in S^1$ as an arbitrary starting point. The vertical axis shows for loop $\alpha: S^1 \to S^1$ how the image $\alpha(\theta) \in S^1$ behaves as θ increases from 0 to 2π along the horizontal axis. For the loop $\alpha_1: S^1 \to S^1$, $\tilde{\alpha}_1$ shows on the vertical axis that the loop α in S^1 first makes four positive rotations, traveling a distance of 8π, then reverses to make two negative rotations, reversing again to make two positive rotations before finally making one positive rotation. The net number of complete counterclockwise rotations made by α is therefore $4-2+2-1=3$. From $\tilde{\alpha}_2$ in Figure 18.8, α_2 in S^1 also makes three net positive rotations, though it first makes one negative rotation followed by four positive rotations.[4]

The definition of a loop requires that it ends where it begins, having the same initial and terminal points. Therefore, in Figure 18.8, the value of all functions given on the vertical axis at 2π on the horizontal axis is either a positive even multiple of π for a positive net number of rotations, or a negative even multiple of π for a negative net number of rotations, or zero. Indeed, calculating $\tilde{\alpha}_1(2\pi)/2\pi = 3$ gives the net number of rotations of α_1.

The net number of rotations of a loop in S^1 is known as its degree. In general, for any loop λ in S^1, represented by a function $\tilde{\lambda}$ as in Figure 18.8, its degree, $\deg(\lambda)$, is given by:

$\deg(\lambda) = \tilde{\lambda}(2\pi)/2\pi$. For the loops described in Figure 18.8: $\deg(\alpha_1) = \deg(\alpha_2) = 3$, $\deg(\beta_1) = \deg(\beta_2) = 1$ and $\deg(\gamma) = -3$.

[4] $\tilde{\alpha}$ is called the *lift* of α. See Armstrong (1983).

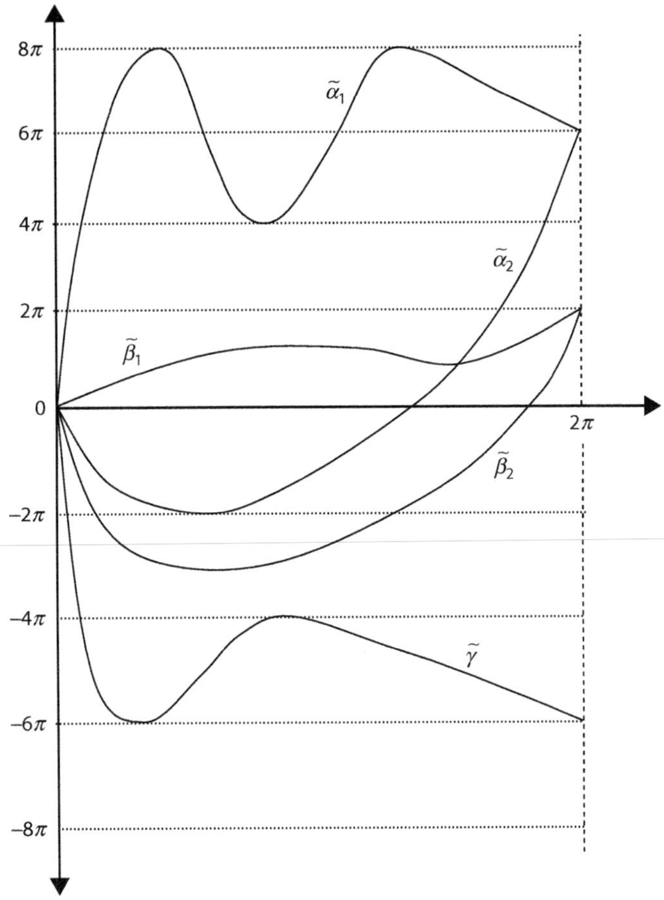

Figure 18.8. Lifts Showing Loops in Circles.

Looking at Figure 18.8, it should be clear that loops having the same degree are homotopic and loops having different degrees are not homotopic. For example, α_1 can clearly be continuously deformed into α_2, but neither of these can be continuously deformed into β_1, β_2 or γ.[5] Preservation of degree by homotopy is a useful result.

Theorem 2 *Let α and β be loops in S^1. Then α and β are homotopic if and only if* $\deg(\alpha) = \deg(\beta)$.

One more construction concerning loops is required, namely the product of loops. The rough idea is that two loops may be joined together to form another loop. For example,

[5] Actually, Figure 18.8 shows the possibilities for continuous deformations between the lift representations of loops used in the diagram, which are paths and not loops, rather than the possibilities for continuous deformations of the loops themselves. However, loops in S^1 are homotopic if and only if their lifts in Figure 18.8 are homotopic.

Figure 18.7 shows loops β and γ in $\mathbb{R}^2_+$. The image of the product, $\beta \cdot \gamma$, of β and γ would begin at one of the intersections of their individual images, go around the image of β first and then around the image of γ.

Consider again any loops α and β in S^1. The net number of times that their product, $\alpha \cdot \beta$, rotates positively in S^1 must be equal to the sum of the net number of positive rotations that each makes individually. After all, roughly speaking, their product first "does what α does" and then "does what β does." In other words: $\deg(\alpha \cdot \beta) = \deg(\alpha) + \deg(\beta)$: *The degree of a product of loops in S^1 is equal to the sum of their degrees.*

The key points for later use are:

- homotopy of paths is preserved by composition;
- degrees of loops are preserved by homotopy (Theorem 2);
- degree of products of loops is equal to the sum of their degrees.

2.4. Fundamental Equation of Topological Social Choice Theory

This section begins by presenting particular loops and some relationships between them. These lead to the fundamental equation of topological social choice theory, an equation that plays a crucial role in all major results, including Theorem 1.

The first loop, λ_1, is agent 1's loop and it shows the social preference as agent 1's preference makes a positive rotation. However, it is useful to consider this loop as a composition of another loop with the social welfare function. The intuition is given in Figure 18.9.

Beginning at the left of Figure 18.9, the first circle shows a positive rotation that determines the same positive rotation of agent 1's preference, shown in the left circle in the center of the diagram. The second of the two central circles shows agent 2's preference held constant at $\theta = 0$. Note that the far left and two central circles show a loop in $S^1 \times S^1$. Each pair of points in the central circles is then taken by the social welfare function, $f : S^1 \times S^1 \to S^1$, into a social preference in the final circle on the right of the diagram. Thus, agent 1's loop, λ_1, does indeed show the social preference for a positive rotation of agent 1's preference.

In the same way, agent 2's loop, λ_2, shows the social preference as agent 2's preference makes a positive rotation, and it too may be considered as the composition of a loop in

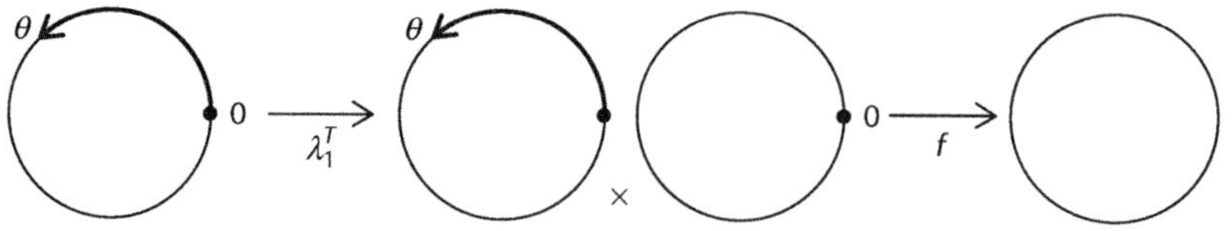

Figure 18.9. Response of the Social Preference to a Positive Rotation in the Preference of Agent 1.

$S^1 \times S^1$ with the social welfare function. Figure 18.9 is easily adapted for this case by exchanging the roles of the two central circles.[6]

Considering this loop for constant and dictatorial social welfare functions may help to clarify the analysis. For a constant social welfare function, consider what happens in Figure 18.9 as θ rotates in the circle on the far left. There is an identical rotation in the left of the two central circles while the point in the right of the central circles remains constant at 0. Finally, the social preference given in the circle on the far right of Figure 18.9 remains constant at some point in S^1 that is determined by the social welfare function. For a dictatorial social welfare function, the only rotation that differs from the constant social welfare function just described is for the rotation in the far right circle in Figure 18.9. This rotation is exactly the same as the rotation in the circle on the far left.

The next loop combines λ_1 and λ_2 into their product, $\lambda_{12} = \lambda_1 \cdot \lambda_2$. This loop shows the social preferences for sequential positive rotations of the preferences of agents 1 and 2. With some care, Figure 18.9 may be adjusted for this case too. First, beginning on the left of the diagram as before, consider half a positive rotation of θ from 0 to π. During this half rotation, there is a positive rotation in the left of the two central circles. That is, agent 1's preference makes one complete positive rotation during half a positive rotation in the far left circle. As the rotation in the far left circle continues to complete a positive rotation, agent 2's preference in the right of the two central circles makes a complete positive rotation. The circle on the far right then shows the response of the social preference. Thus, the loop λ_{12} does indeed show the response of the social preference on the right to sequential positive rotations, first of agent 1's preference and then of agent 2's preference.

The loop λ_U shows the response of the social preference to a unanimous positive rotation in both agents' preferences. In Figure 18.9, as a complete positive rotation takes place in the first circle on the far left, the same rotation simultaneously takes place in both central circles. The circle on the far right then shows the response of the social preference to this unanimous positive rotation in agents' preferences.

The loops λ_{12} and λ_U have more than one thing in common. First, they both show the response of the social preference to complete positive rotations in agents' preferences. The only difference in the rotations in agents' preferences is that in λ_U the rotations are simultaneous while in λ_{12} they are sequential. The other thing they have in common is that they each compose a loop in $S^1 \times S^1$, shown by the left arrow in Figure 18.9, with the social welfare function, shown by the right arrow in Figure 18.9. Since the social welfare function is the same for both λ_{12} and λ_U, they therefore only differ because they use different loops in $S^1 \times S^1$.

[6] Of course, obvious notational changes are also required, namely changing λ_1^T to λ_2^T. Similar notational changes required by subsequent variations in Figure 18.9 are left to the reader.

By considering variations in these loops in $S^1 \times S^1$, it will now be shown that λ_{12} and λ_U can be continuously deformed into each other. That is, they are homotopic. In fact, an explicit homotopy will be constructed using a class of loops λ_δ^T. The intuitive idea is to let agent 1's preference rotate "faster" than agent 2's, so that it rotates ahead of agent 2's preference. The parameter, δ, $0 \leq \delta \leq 1$, determines the extent to which agent 1's preference rotates ahead of agent 2's. The loop λ_δ^T is given in Table 18.1.

The first row shows that as θ, given in the first column, goes through the first half of a positive rotation, agent 1's preference rotates ahead of it by $\delta\theta$ and the rotation of agent 2's preference lags behind it by $-\delta\theta$. This is also shown in Figure 18.10. At the end of the first half of the rotation in column 1, row 2 shows $\theta = \pi$, $\theta_1 = (1+\delta)\pi$ and $\theta_2 = (1-\delta)\pi$. The second half of the rotation then follows and is given in the second row of Table 18.1. In the second row of the table, agent 2's rotation is faster then agent 1's and it just catches it as the rotation is completed. This can be seen by setting $\theta_1 = \theta_2 = 2\pi$ in the second row.

To see that a homotopy has been constructed, consider λ_δ^T for $\delta = 0$ and $\delta = 1$. If $\delta = 0$, $\theta_1 = \theta_2 = \theta$ everywhere in Table 18.1 and this is the loop λ_U^T of unanimous rotations. For $\delta = 1$, the first row of the table shows that $\theta_1 = 2\theta$ and agent 1's preference completes a positive rotation when $\theta = \pi$. Furthermore, agent 2's preference remains constant at $\theta_2 = 0$. Substituting $\delta = 1$ in the second row of Table 18.1 shows agent 1's preference remaining constant at $2\pi = 0$ and agent 2's preference making a complete positive rotation. Thus, if $\delta = 1$, λ_δ^T specifies sequential positive rotations in the agents' preferences, first for 1 and then for 2, just as required by λ_{12}^T. Indeed, as δ varies from 0 to 1, λ_δ^T continuously changes from λ_U^T to λ_{12}^T showing that λ_U^T and λ_{12}^T are homotopic.

Table 18.1 Table for λ_δ^T

θ	θ_1	θ_2
$0 \leq \theta \leq \pi$	$(1+\delta)\theta$	$(1-\delta)\theta$
$\pi \leq \theta \leq 2\pi$	$(1+\delta)\pi + (1-\delta)(\theta - \pi)$	$(1-\delta)\pi + (1+\delta)(\theta - \pi)$

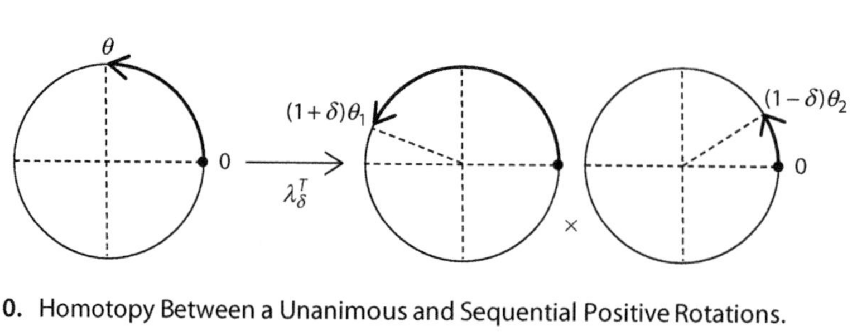

Figure 18.10. Homotopy Between a Unanimous and Sequential Positive Rotations.

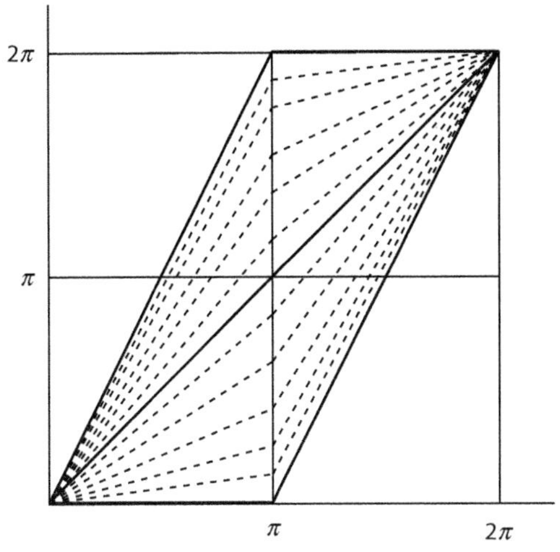

Figure 18.11. An Alternative Diagram for the Homotopy shown in Figure 18.10.

This homotopy is also illustrated in Figure 18.11. Column 1 of Table 18.1 is given on the horizontal axis and columns 2 and 3 are shown on the vertical axis. The upper and lower continuous lines with horizontal segments show the sequential rotations in preferences of agents 1 and 2, respectively. The diagonal shows the unanimous rotation. Dashed lines show the rotations for $0 < \delta < 1$, with the rotation of agent 1's preference above the diagonal and that of agent 2's preference below it. Clearly, the dashed lines show unanimous rotations continuously deforming into sequential rotations.

Since λ_U^T and λ_{12}^T are homotopic, and taking their compositions with a continuous social welfare function giving λ_U and λ_{12}, it follows that λ_U and λ_{12} are also homotopic since homotopy is preserved by composition. From Theorem 2 therefore, it follows that: $\deg(\lambda_U) = \deg(\lambda_{12})$. Substituting $\deg(\lambda_{12}) = \deg(\lambda_1) + \deg(\lambda_2)$ now gives the fundamental equation of topological social choice theory.

$$\deg(\lambda_U) = \deg(\lambda_1) + \deg(\lambda_2) \tag{1}$$

It should be emphasized that Equation (1) is an implication of continuity alone. Neither UN nor AN is used in its derivation.

2.5. Proof of Theorem 1

Consider (1): $\deg(\lambda_U) = \deg(\lambda_1) + \deg(\lambda_2)$. UN and AN yield further restrictions on (1) that quickly lead to a contradiction.

UN requires that a unanimously held preference is also the social preference. Therefore, if agents' preferences make a unanimous (simultaneous) positive rotation, the social preference makes exactly one net positive rotation. That is, $\deg(\lambda_U) = 1$, which substituted in (1) gives:

$$1 = \deg(\lambda_1) + \deg(\lambda_2).$$

AN requires that the number of rotations made by the social preference is exactly the same in response to a rotation in agent 1's preference as it is to a rotation in agent 2's preference. That is, $\deg(\lambda_1) = \deg(\lambda_2) = z$ for some integer z. Substituting into (1) now gives: $1 = 2z$.

However, there is no integer that, when doubled, is equal to 1. Thus, there is no continuous social welfare function that is unanimous and anonymous, and the proof is complete.

Two observations on this proof are worth making. One concerns the distinct roles of the properties. The other concerns the distinctive role played by information that is summarized by integers.

The fundamental equation of topological social choice theory given in (1) is a consequence of continuity alone. The proof proceeds by using the other properties, UN and AN, to obtain restrictions on the terms in (1). These are that the degree of λ_U is equal to one and the degrees of λ_1 and λ_2 are equal. Other major results will be proved in a similar way, by starting with (1) and then obtaining restrictions on it using other properties.

The terms in (1) all count the net number of preference rotations for specific loops. Therefore, these terms must all be integers. Indeed, the problem of proving Theorem 1, as well as other results, can be reduced to an integer problem.[7] It is instructive to give a variation on the proof that makes this reduction explicit.

The first step is to associate the set $\mathbb{Z}$ of integers with loops in S^1 and the set of ordered pairs of integers $\mathbb{Z} \times \mathbb{Z}$ with loops in $S^1 \times S^1$. Since degrees of loops are integers, it is no surprise that degrees of loops are used to establish this association. For example, associate with any loop λ in S^1 its degree, $\deg(\lambda)$. Given the homotopy preservation of degree, this integer is also associated with any loop that is homotopic to λ.

The loop λ_1^T in $S^1 \times S^1$, in which agent 1's preference makes one positive rotation while agent 2's preference is constant, is associated with $(1,0) \in \mathbb{Z} \times \mathbb{Z}$. Similarly, λ_2^T is associated with $(0,1) \in \mathbb{Z} \times \mathbb{Z}$. Associating the loops λ_U^T and λ_{12}^T with ordered pairs in $\mathbb{Z} \times \mathbb{Z}$ will be particularly useful. The sequential positive rotations specified by λ_{12}^T are associated with the sum of the pairs in $Z \times \mathbb{Z}$ associated with λ_1^T and λ_2^T, $(1,0) + (0,1) \in \mathbb{Z} \times \mathbb{Z}$. Finally, the simultaneous positive rotations in agents' preferences specified by λ_U^T are associated with $(1,1) \in \mathbb{Z} \times \mathbb{Z}$.

[7] Lauwers (2009) is particularly successful in highlighting the "integer approach" that follows in this section. Indeed, his paper establishes some unity in topological social choice theory.

Given these associations of loops with points in $\mathbb{Z} \times \mathbb{Z}$, a function $f_* : \mathbb{Z} \times \mathbb{Z} \to \mathbb{Z}$ may be associated with a continuous social welfare function, $f : S^1 \times S^1 \to S^1$. Setting aside some details, consider the following.

(i) $f_*((1,0)+(0,1))$: This gives the number of rotations of social preferences in response to sequential positive rotations in agent 1's preference followed by a sequential positive rotation in agent 2's preference.
(ii) $f_*(2,0)$: This gives the number of rotations of social preferences in response to two positive rotations in agent 1's preference.
(iii) $2f_*(1,0)$: This is double the number of rotations of social preferences in response to one positive rotation in agent 1's preference.

Now, very roughly, AN says that the response of social preferences to rotations in agents' preferences depends on the total number of rotations, not how that total is distributed among agents. It follows that the responses in social preferences in (i), (ii), and (iii) are all equal:

$$f_*((1,0)+(0,1)) = f_*(2,0) = 2f_*(1,0). \tag{2}$$

Since $(1,0)+(0,1)=(1,1)$, it follows from (2) that:

$$f_*(1,1) = 2f_*(1,0). \tag{3}$$

UN requires that $f_*(1,1)=1$, since the social preference must make one positive rotation in response to simultaneous rotations in agents' preferences. Therefore (3) becomes:

$$1 = 2f_*(1,0). \tag{4}$$

Again, this is impossible since there is no integer $f_*(1,0)$ that, when multiplied by 2, is equal to 1.

3. DOMAIN RESTRICTION

This section presents a possibility result for continuous social welfare functions that are Unanimous and Anonymous. Unlike other areas of social choice, the literatugre in topological social choice has focused almost exclusively on domain variations as a way of escaping the impossibility in Theorem 1. The leading result is in Chichilnisky and Heal (1983), where a general class of domains are considered.[8] A rather special case of this class restricts the domain of linear preferences, and this is the topic of this section.

[8] Some members of this class are not domain restrictions and some are not easily interpreted as subsets of preferences.

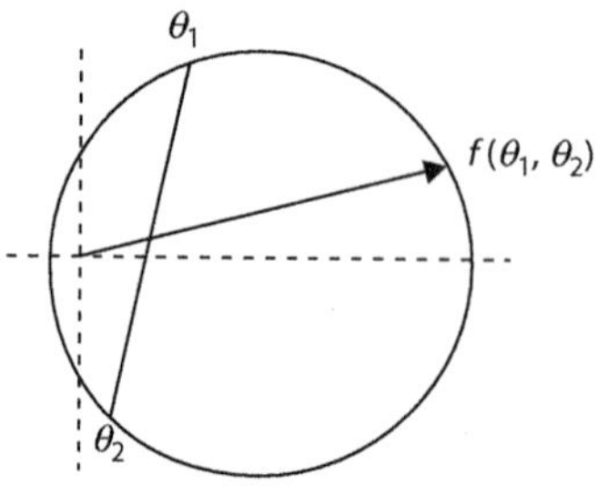

Figure 18.12. Possibility with a Domain Restriction.

3.1. Domain Restriction

In Figure 18.12, the center of the unit circle is no longer at the origin of $\mathbb{R}^2$. It has been shifted horizontally to the right. Assume that the linear preferences given by points in $\mathbb{R}^2$ to the left of the vertical axis cannot be the preferences of any agent. Thus, only points on the circle that are to the right of the vertical axis are subject to aggregation. These points will be called *admissible*.

To aggregate any pair of admissible points, θ_1 and θ_2, project the midpoint of the line, or chord, between them from the origin of $\mathbb{R}^2$ onto the circle. If $\theta_1 = \theta_2 = \theta$, then this construction gives $f(\theta,\theta) = \theta$, so that UN is satisfied. Interchanging θ_1 and θ_2 does not change the chord used for the projection, and therefore AN is satisfied. Finally, this aggregation[9] is clearly continuous. On this restricted domain, therefore, there is a continuous social welfare function that is Unanimous and Anonymous. Since this construction remains possible even if only a single point of the circle is not admissible, the minimal restriction may be very mild.

3.2. Contractibility

There is a topological property of a set that is responsible for the possibility result obtained by restricting the domain to a proper subset of S^1 that is one of its arcs. Intuitively, this property is that a set can be continuously shrunk to one of its points.

Consider the set of points on or inside a circle, known as a disk. Clearly, it is possible to continuously shrink the disk to any of its points. Indeed, the convexity of the disk may be used to obtain a very simple continuous shrinkage to a point. However, such continuous shrinkages may also be possible in nonconvex sets, and the admissible arc in Figure 18.12 is an example. This can be seen by imagining that the arc is made of string and lifted off the circle and laid on the horizontal axis. As such, it would coincide with an interval of real numbers, and this is a convex set. Sets that can be continuously shrunk

[9] This aggregation may be given as follows. Let $C(S^1)$denote the admissible subset of S^1. Then, for all $(\theta_1,\theta_2) \in C(S^1) \times C(S^1), f(\theta_1,\theta_2) = (\theta_1 + \theta_2)/\,\|\theta_1 + \theta_2\|$.

to any of its points are called *contractible*. Arcs are contractible, including an arc equal to a circle with a single point deleted.

Theorem 3 *Let $C(S^1)$ denote an arc of the circle, S^1. Then there exists a continuous function $f : C(S^1) \times C(S^1) \to C(S^1)$ that has the UN and AN properties.*

Before leaving this issue, it should be mentioned that the result in Chichilnisky and Heal (1983) shows that, for a general class of domains, contractibility is necessary and sufficient for the existence of continuous aggregations that are unanimous and anonymous. However, the use of this particular class is controversial, and it is not clear that some of its members can be interpreted as preferences. See Lauwers (2000, 2009) for a discussion and further references.

4. WEAK PARETO AND NO VETO

This section strengthens the Unanimity property of Theorem 1 to a Pareto property, and replaces Anonymity with a No Veto property. With these variations on Theorem 1, another impossibility result is obtained.

4.1. The Cone Property and the No Veto Property

As before, consider commodity bundles in $\mathbb{R}^2_+$ of collective goods and agents with linear preferences on $\mathbb{R}^2_+$ given by unit vectors. The set $A = \{1, \ldots, k\}$, $2 \leq k < \infty$, denotes the set of agents.[10] A social welfare $f : (S^1)^k \to S^1$ now assigns a social preference $f(\theta_1, \ldots, \theta_k) \in S^1$ to all k-tuples $(\theta_1, \ldots, \theta_k) \in (S^1)^k$ of agents' preferences.

Consider Figure 18.13. In the left diagram in Figure 18.13, continuous lines show indifference curves for two agents' linear preferences intersecting at bundle y, and their unit vectors. These are also shown in the center diagram. Dashed lines show indifference curves and unit vectors for different social preferences in the left and center diagrams. All the unit vectors in the left and center diagrams are shown in the unit circle in the right diagram.

In both the center and left diagrams in Figure 18.13, bundles that are strictly preferred to y by both agents' preferences are shown by shaded areas. All these bundles are also strictly preferred to y by the social preference in the left diagram but not in the center diagram. This has implications for the unit vectors as follows. In the right diagram, an arc is determined by the intersection of the cone given by the unit vectors of agents' preferences and the circle. The unit vector of the social preference in the left diagram is contained in this arc, but the unit vector of the social preference in the center diagram is

[10] The proof of the theorem in this section is trivial if there are only two agents.

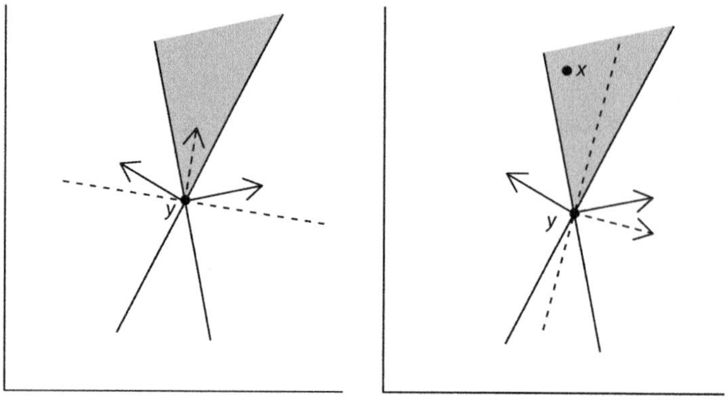

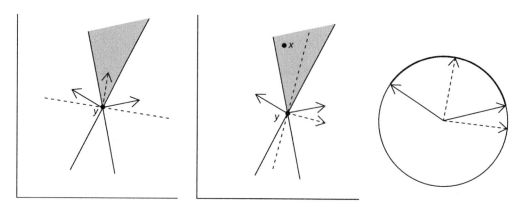

Figure 18.13. Weak Pareto and the Cone Property.

not. In general, all social preferences with unit vectors contained in the arc determined in this way by a pair of agents' preferences will strictly prefer all bundles to y that both agents strictly prefer to y.

A "Cone property" may be now be formulated. A social welfare function $f : (S^1)^k \to S^1$ has the *Cone* property if and only if agents' preferences are given either by $\theta_1 \in S^1$ or $\theta_2 \in S^1$, and the social preference is in the shortest arc between them. In case of unanimity, $\theta_1 = \theta_2 = \theta$, the arc is a single point and the social preference must be θ to satisfy the Cone property. Thus, the Cone property implies UN but not vice versa.

A little more notation is required for the Pareto property. For all $x, y \in \mathbb{R}^2_+$, all $i \in A$ and all $\theta_i \in S^1$, $xP(\theta_i)y$ will be written in case x is strictly preferred to y according to i's linear preference given by θ_i. For any k-tuple of agents' preferences, $(\theta_1, \ldots, \theta_k) \in (S^1)^k$, $xP\left(f(\theta_1, \ldots, \theta_k)\right) y$ will be written in case x is strictly preferred to y by the social preference for this k-tuple of preferences.

The most commonly used Pareto unanimity property is called the weak Pareto property, following Arrow (1951). It requires that if all agents strictly prefer one bundle to another, so must the social preference. This may be expressed a little more formally as follows. A social welfare function $f : (S^1)^k \to S^1$ has the *weak Pareto* (WP) property if and only if, for all $(\theta_1, \ldots, \theta_k) \in (S^1)^k$ and all $x, y \in \mathbb{R}^2_+$: if $xP(\theta_i)y$ for all $i \in A$ then $xP\left(f(\theta_1, \ldots, \theta_k)\right) y$. If there are at most two distinct agents' preferences, as in the discussion of Figure 18.13, WP imposes the same restriction on the social preference as the Cone property. However, WP imposes restrictions on the social preference in many other situations as well, in which agents may have more than two distinct preferences. Therefore, the WP property implies the Cone property, but not vice versa. In fact, Theorem 3 below can be strengthened by replacing WP by the Cone property.

The final property necessary in this section involves situations in which the preference of one agent is the opposite of the preferences of all other agents. Thus, agents' preferences will be called polarized against agent i if all the other agents have exactly the opposite preference that i has. A little more formally: $(\theta_1,\ldots,\theta_k) \in (S^1)^k$ is *polarized against* $i \in A$ if and only if, for some $\theta \in S^1$, $\theta_j = \theta$ for all $j \in A\backslash\{i\}$ and $\theta_i = -\theta$.

Particularly for larger numbers of agents, it seems reasonable that in the case of polarization against an agent, the social preference should not be the same as the preference of the minority agent. That is, this prevents the social preference from being the same as the minority agents' preference whenever this is unanimously opposed with its opposite preference. This property may be expressed as follows. A social welfare function $f : (S^1)^k \to S^1$ has the *No Veto* (NV) property if and only if, for all $i \in A$, all $(\theta_1,\ldots,\theta_k) \in (S^1)^k$ and all $\theta \in S^1$: if $(\theta_1,\ldots,\theta_k)$ is polarized against i and $\theta_i = -\theta$ then $f(\theta_1,\ldots,\theta_k) \neq -\theta$.

Theorem 4 may now be expressed as follows.

Theorem 4 (Chichilnisky 1982c) *There is no continuous social welfare function* $f : (S^1)^k \to S^1$ *that has the WP and NV properties.*

The proof may be easily understood using diagrams similar to the one given in Figure 18.8, Section 2.3. Consider unanimous agents' preferences and, for simplicity, let their unanimous preference be identified with the point $(1,0) \in S^1$ or, equivalently, $\theta = 0 \in S^1$. Now consider the loop λ_i defined as in Section 2.4 showing the response of the social preference to a positive rotation in i's preference, holding the preferences of all other agents constant. This is illustrated by the solid line in Figure 18.14. As i's preference rotates from $\theta_i = 0$ to $\theta_i = 2\pi$, shown on the horizontal axis, the social preference determined by the solid line is shown on the vertical axis.

The shaded areas in Figure 18.14 show the restriction required by the Cone property which is implied by WP. For example, for $0 < \theta_i < \pi$, the social preference must be between 0 and θ_i, and this gives the left shaded area. At $\theta_i = \pi$, i has a preference that is the opposite preference from all other agents. That is, agents are polarized against i.

Therefore, at $\theta_i = \pi$, NV requires that the social preference is not the same as the preference of other agents. That is, the social preference is not equal to π. Continuity of

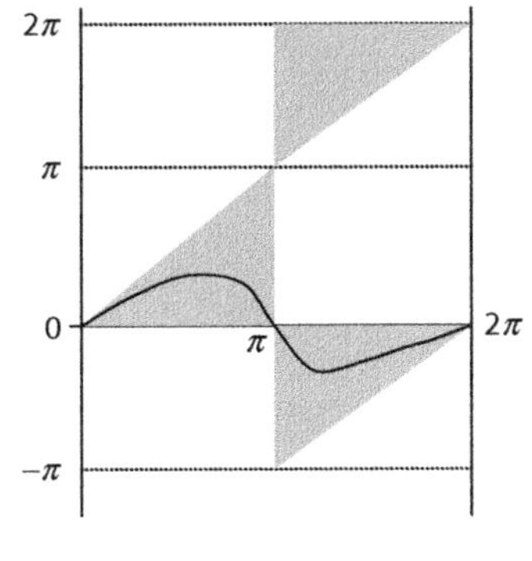

Figure 18.14. Cone and No Veto Properties.

the social welfare function then implies that the social preference in Figure 18.14 enter the lower of the two shaded areas in the right of the diagram. To enter the higher shaded area, the social preference would have to be the same as that of i, namely π, violating NV. Therefore, for $\pi < \theta_i < 2\pi$, continuity of the social welfare function requires that the social preference is in the lower of the shaded areas on the right of Figure 18.14. It follows that at $\theta_i = 2\pi$, the social preference must be 0.

To summarize, as i's preference makes a positive rotation, the net number of times that the social preference rotates is 0. Indeed, in the case illustrated in Figure 18.14, the social preference rotates positively at first, while i's preference makes roughly a quarter of a rotation, after which it reverses direction and rotates negatively for nearly half a rotation before changing direction again and making roughly nearly a quarter of a positive rotation. The important point is that the social preference fails to make a complete rotation. In other words: $\deg(\lambda_i) = 0$. Of course, the argument used for i could be made for all other agents, so that $\deg(\lambda_i) = 0$ for all $i \in A$ and certainly $\deg(\lambda_1) + \cdots + \deg(\lambda_k) = 0$.

Since WP implies UN, and UN implies $\deg(\lambda_U) = 1$, the fundamental equation of topological social choice theory, $\deg(\lambda_U) = \deg(\lambda_1) + \cdots + \deg(\lambda_k)$ therefore requires that $1 = 0$. This contradiction completes the proof.

5. STRATEGIC MANIPULATORS AND HOMOTOPIC DICTATORS

This section presents two closely related results. Both concern continuous social welfare functions that have the weak Pareto property. Section 4 showed that this property, together with the No Veto property, leads to an impossibility result for continuous social welfare functions. This section shows that the only possibilities created by dropping the No Veto property have strategic manipulators that are also homotopic dictators. However, it is the former that is the more signficant.

5.1. Dropping the No Veto Property

Recall that continuity implies the fundamental equation of topological social choice theory:

$$\deg(\lambda_U) = \deg(\lambda_1) + \cdots + \deg(\lambda_k) \tag{1}$$

Recall also that WP implies the Cone property, and consider the implications of this using Figure 18.15.

In Figure 18.15 it is assumed that the linear preferences of all agents except $j \in A$ are given by $\theta = 0$, and j's linear preference makes a positive rotation as θ increases from 0 to 2π on the horizontal axis. The social preferences given by a continuous social welfare

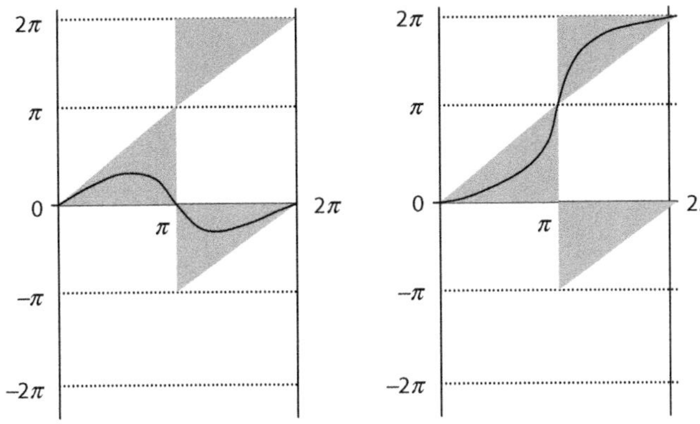

Figure 18.15. Possible Responses of Social Preference to a Positive Rotation in an Agent's Preference, for a Continuous Weakly Paretian Social Welfare Function.

function for this rotation are shown via the solid lines on the vertical axes. That is, the solid lines are an illustration of the loop λ_j as defined in Section 2.3 As in Figure 18.14, Section 4, the Cone property restricts the solid lines to the shaded areas.

For $0 \leq \theta < \pi$ on the horizontal axis, there is a single shaded area. However, at $\theta = \pi$ a transition must be made to one of the two shaded areas on the right. The left diagram in Figure 18.15 shows a transition to the lower shaded area. In this case, the social preference does not complete a rotation. That is, $\deg(\lambda_j) = 0$. In the right-hand diagram, the transition is to the higher of the shaded areas and the social preference makes one positive rotation in response to a positive rotation in agent 1's preference, that is, $\deg(\lambda_j) = 1$.

Substituting $\deg(\lambda_U) = 1$ in equation (1): $1 = \deg(\lambda_1) + \cdots + \deg(\lambda_k)$. Since, as has just been shown, for all $i \in A$, $\deg(\lambda_i) = 0$ or $\deg(\lambda_j) = 1$, it follows that for exactly one agent j, $\deg(\lambda_j) = 1$, and for all other agents i, $\deg(\lambda_i) = 0$. In other words, the right diagram in Figure 18.15 holds for one agent, and it is the left diagram that holds for all the others.

Figure 18.16 repeats the right diagram in Figure 18.15 and illustrates the sense in which that agent is favored by the social welfare function.

In Figure 18.16, if the agent wants θ' to be the social preference the agent can achieve this by expressing θ''. Indeed, for all possible $\theta' \in S^1$ and $\theta \in S^1$, there exists a $\theta'' \in S^1$ such that $f(\theta'', \theta) = \theta$. Such an agent is called a *strategic manipulator.* The following result has therefore been established.

Theorem 5 (Chichilnisky 1983, 1993) *Let the continuous social welfare function* $f : (S^1)^k \rightarrow S^1$ *have the WP property. Then there is a Strategic Manipulator.*

In other words, for a continuous weakly Paretian social welfare function, there is one agent who can get whatever social preference he or she wants, irrespective of the preferences expressed by other agents, and no other agents can do this. It may seem as

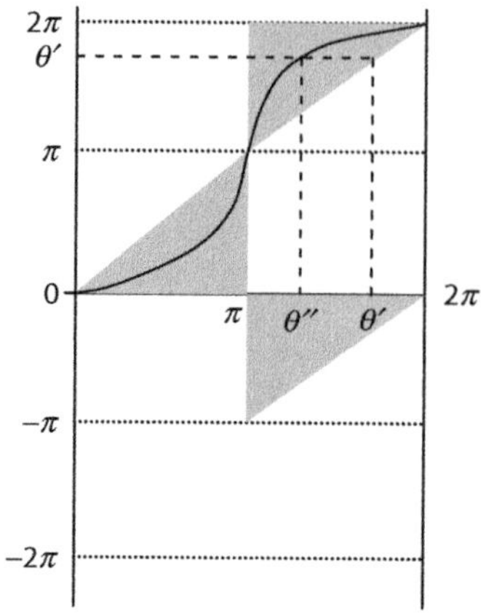

Figure 18.16. Strategic Manipulation.

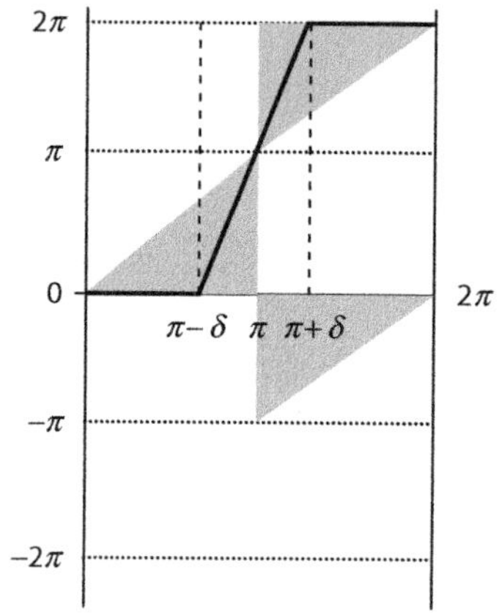

Figure 18.17. Homotopic Dictatorship.

though such an agent has some sort of "dictatorial" power. Indeed, consider Figure 18.16 again. The solid line can be continuously deformed into the diagonal. The diagonal shows the case of a dictator in the sense that the social preference is always the same as that of the agent. Such an agent is called a *Homotopic Dictator*. See Chichilnisky (1982b).

That is, for continuous weakly Paretian social welfare functions, there must be a homotopic dictator. The significance and interpretation of this result has attracted criticism in Baigent (2002, 2009), Saari (1997), and Saari and Kronwetter (2009). The issue is whether a homotopic dictator is favored in some way that it is distinct from being a strategic manipulator. In particular, are Homotopic Dictators necessarily objectionable in a way that is similar to dictators of the type formulated in Arrow (1951)? Critics do not think so, and their argument is illustrated in Figure 18.17.

Assume for simplicity that there are only two agents, one of whom must be a strategic manipulator. Assume this agent is 1. The heavy solid line shows changes in social preference as agent 1's preference makes a positive rotation. For θ close to 0, as the solid line goes along the horizontal axis, the social preference remains the same as agent 2's preference. It does not respond at all to these changes in agent 1's preference. For agent 1's preference θ between $\pi - \delta$ and $\pi + \delta$, the social preference rotates faster than agent 1's preference until, at $\theta = \pi + \delta$, it completes a positive rotation. At this point the social preference is again equal to agent 2's preference. It remains equal to agent 2's preference for the remainder of agent 1's rotation. As δ becomes arbitrarily close to zero, the proportion of the domain on which the social preference is the same as agent 2's preference can be made arbitrarily large.

All this may be summed up as follows: The agent that is not the homotopic dictator may have almost dictatorial power. Yet the homotopic dictator can always get any particular preference to be the social preference by strategically manipulating.

6. CONTINUITY

A social welfare function is continuous if changes in social preference can be bounded to be arbitrarily small by taking sufficiently small changes in agents' preferences. In Section 2.1, "small" is defined using the Euclidean metric.[11] This property defines topological social choice theory and is therefore subjected to critical scrutiny in this section.[12] The main question is the following: What good reasons are there for imposing continuity on a social welfare function? Closely related issues regarding some of the limitations arising from the formulation of continuity are also briefly addressed.

6.1. Justification

The most striking thing about the justification of continuity is how little attention it has received. In Chichilnisky (1982a, p. 337), after claiming that continuity "can be argued to be a natural property," the following justification is offered:

> *One reason for requiring continuity is that it is desirable for the social rule to be relatively insensitive to small changes in individual preferences. This makes mistakes in identifying preferences less*

[11] More generally, a family $\mathscr{T}(X)$ of subsets of a set X containing itself and the empty set is a *topology* on X if and only if it contains arbitrary unions and finite intersection of its members. Members of $\mathscr{T}(X)$ are called *open* sets of this topology on X. One way, but not the only way, to define open sets is by using a metric as follows. A set is open if, for all its members, it also contains all elements sufficiently close to it. Given sets X and Y, both with topologies, a function from X to Y is *continuous* if and only if the inverse images of open sets in Y are open in X. Any book on topology will give further explanation.

[12] See also Lauwers (2000, and especially 2009).

crucial. It also permits one to approximate social preferences on the basis of a sample of individual preferences.

This justification assumes that social choice requires agents' preferences to be known, not just by agents themselves but by others. The reason for this is not clear. Certainly, this is not the case in many formulations of social choice problems. For example, in many descriptions of social choice problems, agents' preferences are widely regarded as private information, and the response to this in social choice theory has been design rather than approximation or estimation. Given this, it is not clear what role "mistakes," estimation, or "approximation" could be. In the design approach, one role of a social welfare function is evaluative. That is, it establishes what the social choice ought to be for different agents' preferences. However, there is no requirement to establish agents' preferences. Rather, the problem is to design mechanisms such that, whatever agents' preferences happen to be, their strategic choices based on their preferences lead to the same outcomes that the social welfare function has determined ought to be chosen. There is no central planner in this account who needs to "find out" what agents' preferences are or who may make mistakes in establishing agents' preferences.

The point here is that if continuity is meant to solve some sort of practical problem, then an explicit description of a social choice problem in which the alleged problem arises would be a welcome addition to the literature.

This point may also be clarified by considering another much discussed discontinuity in the literature, namely the literature on Sen's Poverty Index. This well-known function is not continuous, having a discontinuity at the poverty line. See Sen (1997, Section A.6.4) where the issue of measurement errors is discussed. Sen writes: "In the context of *actual use* of poverty indicators, the possibility of measurement errors is indeed a legitimate and serious concern" (emphasis added). However, as argued in the previous paragraph, it is not clear that social welfare functions have an *actual use* in the same sense as poverty indices or any other sense in which mistakes, approximation, or estimation arise. Social welfare functions have quite different uses for which it is not clear why continuity is desirable.

If, for some social choice problems, agents' preferences do need to be estimated, the emerging area of spherical statistics may seem promising; see, for example, Jammalamadaka and SenGupta (2001). They define versions of the usual descriptive statistics for observations of "directions," given by points on a unit circle. Such data may, for example, record the directions of birds migrating. The "averaging" example in Section 2.1 of this chapter is taken as the definition of the mean for such observations. However, for opposite points on the circle, they write: "We say that no mean direction exists," and "In this case, it is clear that the data do not indicate any preferred or mean direction" (p. 15). This response suggests that the estimation of social preferences may not be a straightforward exercise.

While some may claim that continuity "can be argued to be a natural property," it is not clear what makes it natural. Indeed, in Lauwers (2009) it is observed that discontinuity is also a natural phenomenon. To this, it may be added that discontinuity is sometimes created by human beings where it does not exist in nature. For example, in most countries there are two contrived discontinuities every year when clock time changes between summer and winter time. Discontinuities in clock time also occur moving from one time zone to another. Presumably, some see advantages or benefits in these discontinuities since they are not imposed by nature. Such examples warn against any general presumption that discontinuities are undesirable.

Indeed, it may appear far-fetched, but perhaps discontinuities in social welfare functions can serve a useful purpose. For example, the "averaging" social welfare function used as an example in Section 2 has discontinuities exactly at points at which agents' linear preferences are completely opposed. This fact may be exploitable in a number of ways. For example, instead of lamenting the loss of continuity whenever there is maximum disagreement, perhaps this should be taken as an opportunity to use nonpreference information. Another possible use is that further reflection or discussion is required for a preference to be regarded as representing agents' preferences.

6.2. Limitations of Continuity

Recall that continuity of a function requires images of points that are relatively close in its domain to be relatively close in its codomain. However, there are many contexts in which intuitions about closeness either are absent or are not clear, and this limits the development of topological social choice theory.

Consider the diversity of the development of social choice theory following Arrow (1950, 1951). Among other major areas, it led to characterization results that greatly enhanced the understanding and appreciation of particular aggregation procedures. It also led to the study of aggregation procedures using interpersonal utility comparisons. A major development considered nonbinary social choice. In all of these cases, closeness intuitions are a lot less obvious than they are for the linear preferences required in topological social choice theory.

Consider, for example, nonbinary social choice.[13] This area eventually led to assigning choice functions to agents' preferences rather than social preferences. If a choice function always selects single alternatives for agents' preferences and the alternatives are points in Euclidean space, then closeness may be based on clear intuitions. See Chichilnisky (1993) and Lauwers (2009). However, these intuitions quickly lose their clarity if several alternatives are given as acceptable choices for some agents' preferences, and this less restricted formulation is typical elsewhere in social choice theory (see Deb 2010).

The importance of assigning choice functions rather than preferences to agents' preferences was emphasized early in Buchanan (1954) and much later in Sen (1993). The lack

[13] See Deb (2010) for a survey of nonbinary social choice.

of clear intuitions about closeness at least hinders raising these problems in topological social choice theory. Indeed, many of the developments that followed Arrow (1950) will remain beyond the limits of topological social choice theory unless clear intuitions about the closeness of the relevant objects are developed.

Finally, it is worth emphasizing that the Kemeny metric for preferences on finite sets of alternatives does embody a clear intuition. This is that the more pairs of alternatives on which preferences disagree, and the greater the extent of their disagreement on those pairs, the further they are apart. The use of this metric goes back at least to Dodgson (1893) and has been used for results in Arrow's framework that are in the same spirit as Theorem 1.[14] Finally, in the nontopological framework, there is no limitation on the analysis of nonbinary choice corresponding to the one in topological social choice. See Baigent (1987) for an example.

7. TOPOLOGICAL PROOF OF ARROW'S THEOREM

Baryshnikov (1993) presents a remarkable proof of Arrow's famous theorem that uses topological methods. Some of these have been developed in previous sections, but there is at least one additional concept required. In any case, the topological proof of Arrow's Theorem is probably more challenging than the theorems presented earlier. The purpose of this section is to simplify the presentation of Baryshnikov's important contribution as much as possible. It deserves to be more widely appreciated.

7.1. Nerves[15]

The concept of the "nerve of a covering of a set" is the key concept that facilitates the transformation of Arrow's formulation so that topological arguments can be used. For simplicity, consider the set of all strict preferences[16] on the three alternatives, x, y, and z. There are six such strict preferences as shown in Table 18.2. These preferences are identified subsequently by their numbers in this table. Preferences 1, 2, and 5 are the only preferences for which x is strictly preferred to y. Let $(xy+)$ denote this subset of preferences. Likewise, let $(xy-)$ denote the subset of preferences for which x is ranked strictly below y.[17] Table 18.3 gives the subsets of preferences having a specific strict preference on each pair of alternatives:

[14] Baigent (1997) gives a result in a non binary framework that is analogous to Theorem 1 in Section 2.2.

[15] A slightly different presentation of the material in this section may be found in Baryshnikov (1997) and Lauwers (2000, 2009).

[16] Thus, agents' preferences are complete, reflexive, and antisymmetric binary relations on the set of alternatives.

[17] Of course, $(xy+) = (yx-)$.

Table 18.2 All Strict Preferences on Three Alternatives

1	2	3	4	5	6
x	x	y	y	z	z
y	z	x	z	x	y
z	y	z	x	y	x

Table 18.3 Subsets of Preferences Having a Given Strict Preference on Each Pair of Alternatives

$(xy+)$	$(yx+)$	$(yz+)$	$(zy+)$	$(xz+)$	$(zx+)$
1	3	1	2	1	4
2	4	3	5	2	5
5	6	4	6	3	6

Note that the union of all the subsets of preferences contains the set of all strict preferences on x, y, and z. That is, this collection of subsets of preferences *covers* the set of all strict preferences on these alternatives.

The *nerve* of this cover is a geometrical object called a *simplical complex* constructed from the subsets of preferences given in the previous table. It consists of points called *vertices*, lines called *edges*, and triangular sets of points called *faces*.[18] There are six vertices, each one associated with a subset of preferences given by a column in Table 18.3. A pair of vertices is connected by an edge if and only if their subsets of preferences have at least one preference in common. For example, $(xy+)$ and $(xz+)$ are connected by an edge since they have at least one preference in common. In this case, the intersection of $(xy+)$ and $(xz+)$ contains exactly preferences 1 and 2. See columns 1 and 5 in Table 18.3. However, vertices $(xy+)$ and $(yx+)$ have an empty intersection, having no preference in common. Thus, in the simplical complex under construction there is no edge connecting $(xy+)$ and $(yx+)$. Finally, the triple of vertices $(xy+)$, $(yz+)$, and $(xz+)$ has a nonempty intersection shown by preference 1 in columns 1, 3, and 5 of Table 18.3. Thus, these three vertices give a face of the object under construction. However, there are two triples of vertices whose subsets of preferences have nothing in common. Therefore, there are no faces for these triples. Consideration of the columns in Table 18.3 shows these triples to be firstly, $(xy+)$, $(zx+)$, and $(yz+)$, and secondly, $(xz+)$, $(zy+)$, and $(yx+)$. In Figure 18.19, these are the vertices of the two triangular holes. However, it is instructive to consider Figure 18.18 first and then construct Figure 18.19 from it.

Notation is simplified in Figures 18.18 and 18.19 by writing xy instead of $(xy+)$ and yx instead of $(yx+)$, and similarly for subsets of preferences determined by a specific

[18] It may help to take an early look at the figure that will be constructed. See Figure 18.19.

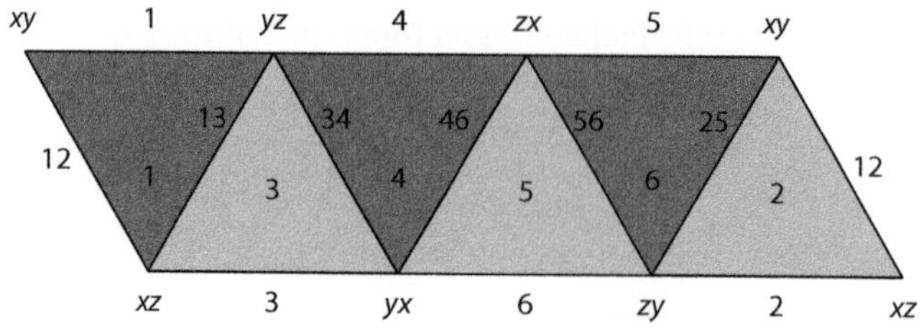

Figure 18.18. Plane Diagram for the Nerve of a Cover of All Strict Preferences on Three Alternatives.

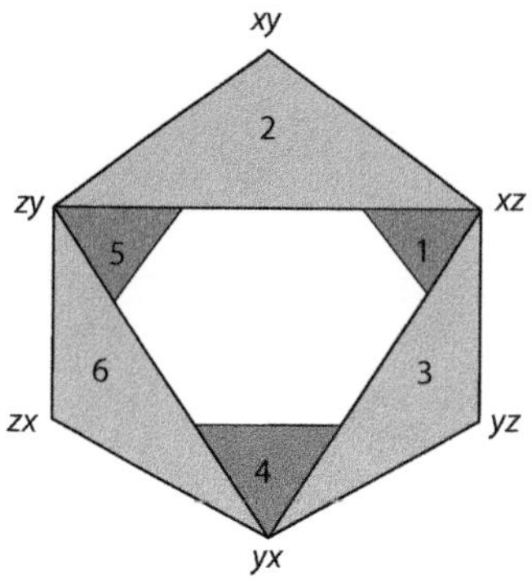

Figure 18.19. The Nerve of a Cover of All Strict Preferences on Three Alternatives as a Simplical Complex.

strict preference on other pairs of alternatives. In Figure 18.18, edges connect vertices for pairs of subsets of preferences having at least one preference in common, and the triangles are shaded for vertices associated with three subsets of preferences having at least one preference in common. As already described, therefore, there is an edge connecting xy and xz, since they have at least one preference in common, but there is no edge connecting xy and yx since no preference can be in both of these subsets. Preference 2 is in the subsets associated with vertices xy, zy, and xz, ensuring that not only are each of the pairwise vertices connected, but also that their triangle is shaded. However, there is no preference in all of the subsets for xy, yx, and xz, so the triangle for these vertices is not shaded. The numbers in Figure 18.18 identify the preferences that are in the intersections of the vertices that give the edges and faces. While edges determine subsets of either one or, in some cases two, preferences, faces determine a unique preference.

To obtain the diagram in Figure 18.19 from Figure 18.18, note that the left and right edges in Figure 18.18 are the same, both connecting xy with xz. It would be possible to cut out Figure 18.18 and glue these two edges together while making folds along the edges that join all of the shaded triangles. The result is a band, or bracelet, with a surface of triangular tiles. In fact, Figure 18.19 illustrates an octahedron with two "opposite" faces deleted.

The figure illustrated in Figure 18.19 has been built up by joining some vertices and edges into triangles and then joining some triangles together along one of their edges as required by the definition of a *simplical complex*. The particular simplical complex shown in Figure 18.19 is the *nerve* $N(\mathcal{P})$ *of* $\mathcal{P}$, where $\mathcal{P}$ denotes the set of all strict preferences on the alternatives. Baryshnikov's proof of Arrow's Theorem also requires the nerve of a cover of another set, namely $\mathcal{P} \times \mathcal{P}$, the set of all pairs of strict preferences.

For any pair of alternatives, x and y, let $(xy++)$ denote the subset of pairs of strict preferences in $\mathcal{P} \times \mathcal{P}$ for which both agents strictly prefer x to y; let $(xy+-)$ denote the subset of pairs of strict preferences in $\mathcal{P} \times \mathcal{P}$ for which agent 1 strictly prefers x to y and agent 2 strictly prefers y to x; let $(xy-+)$ denote the pair of strict preferences in $\mathcal{P} \times \mathcal{P}$ for which agent 1 strictly prefers y to x and agent 2 strictly prefers x to y; and $(xy--)$ denotes the subset of pairs of strict preferences for which both agents strictly prefer y to x. A similar notation is used for the other pairs of alternatives, y and z, and x and z.

The union of all these subsets of ordered pairs of preferences contains the set of all ordered pairs of preferences. Thus, these subsets of ordered pairs of preferences cover the set $\mathcal{P} \times \mathcal{P}$. The previous method of constructing $N(\mathcal{P})$ is easily extended to give the nerve $N(\mathcal{P} \times \mathcal{P})$ of this cover of $\mathcal{P} \times \mathcal{P}$. Each of the subsets, $(xy++)$, $(xy+-)$,..., $(xz-+)$ and $(xz--)$, is associated with a vertex. If any pair of these subsets have an ordered pair of preferences in common then they have an edge connecting them and so on for faces determined by more than two vertices. Since there are 4 vertices for each ordered pair of alternatives and 3 alternatives, there are 12 vertices.

In Table 18.4, each row and column corresponds to the strict preferences shown. It follows that each cell corresponds to an ordered pair of preferences, and the entries in the cells show which of the subsets of ordered pairs of preferences contains that pair of preferences. From this information, it is easy to determine all of the edges and faces of the nerve $N(\mathcal{P} \times \mathcal{P})$ of this cover of ordered pairs of preferences. For example, $(xy--)$ and $(xz++)$ are connected by an edge since both are present in at least one cell in the table. Since there are three vertices given in each cell of the table, the triangular faces are easily determined.

$N(\mathcal{P})$ and $N(\mathcal{P} \times \mathcal{P})$ are the nerves required for Baryshnikov's proof of Arrow's theorem.

7.2. Loops in Nerves

Loops in these nerves may be associated with integers and pairs of integers in the same way as for circles and products of circles in Section 2.3. In Figure 18.19 let a loop that makes a net number of counterclockwise (positive) rotations around $N(\mathcal{P})$ be associated with the integer 1. Similarly, a loop that does not complete a rotation is associated with the integer 0. The following examples will be used.

Table 18.4 The Vertices of the Nerve of a Cover of All Pairs of Strict Preferences on Three Alternatives

	x y z	x z y	y x z	y z x	z x y	z y x
x	$(xy++)$	$(xy++)$	$(xy+-)$	$(xy+-)$	$(xy++)$	$(xy+-)$
y	$(yz++)$	$(yz+-)$	$(yz++)$	$(yz++)$	$(yz+-)$	$(yz+-)$
z	$(xz++)$	$(xz++)$	$(xz++)$	$(xz+-)$	$(xz+-)$	$(xz+-)$
x	$(xy++)$	$(xy++)$	$(xy+-)$	$(xy+-)$	$(xy++)$	$(xy+-)$
z	$(yz-+)$	$(yz--)$	$(yz-+)$	$(yz-+)$	$(yz--)$	$(yz--)$
y	$(xz++)$	$(xz++)$	$(xz++)$	$(xz+-)$	$(xz+-)$	$(xz+-)$
y	$(xy-+)$	$(xy-+)$	$(xy--)$	$(xy--)$	$(xy-+)$	$(xy--)$
x	$(yz++)$	$(yz+-)$	$(yz++)$	$(yz++)$	$(yz+-)$	$(yz+-)$
z	$(xz++)$	$(xz++)$	$(xz++)$	$(xz+-)$	$(xz+-)$	$(xz+-)$
y	$(xy-+)$	$(xy-+)$	$(xy--)$	$(xy--)$	$(xy-+)$	$(xy--)$
z	$(yz++)$	$(yz+-)$	$(yz++)$	$(yz++)$	$(yz+-)$	$(xz+-)$
x	$(xz-+)$	$(xz-+)$	$(xz-+)$	$(xz--)$	$(xz--)$	$(xz--)$
z	$(xy++)$	$(xy++)$	$(xy+-)$	$(xy+-)$	$(xy++)$	$(xy+-)$
x	$(yz-+)$	$(yz--)$	$(yz-+)$	$(yz-+)$	$(yz--)$	$(yz--)$
y	$(xz-+)$	$(xz-+)$	$(xz-+)$	$(xz--)$	$(xz--)$	$(xz--)$
z	$(xy-+)$	$(xy-+)$	$(xy--)$	$(xy--)$	$(xy-+)$	$(xy--)$
y	$(yz-+)$	$(yz--)$	$(xz-+)$	$(xz-+)$	$(yz--)$	$(yz--)$
x	$(xz-+)$	$(xz-+)$	$(xz-+)$	$(xz--)$	$(xz--)$	$(xz--)$

Example 1 This loop goes from $(xz+)$ to $(zy+)$, then to $(yx+)$ before returning to $(xz+)$. This is the loop along the top edges in Figure 18.18. Since it makes one positive rotation it is associated with the integer 1.

Example 2 This loop goes from $(xz+)$ to $(zy+)$, then to $(xy+)$ before returning to $(xz+)$. This loop does not make a complete rotation and it is therefore associated with the integer 0.

The next example is of a loop in $N(\mathcal{P} \times \mathcal{P})$.

Example 3 This loop goes from $(xz++)$ to $(zy++)$ and then to $(yx+-)$ before returning to $(xz++)$.

Since this loop is in $N(\mathcal{P} \times \mathcal{P})$, the sequence of vertices in the image of the loop are subsets of ordered pairs of preferences. However, this loop combines the loops in Examples 1 and 2. Indeed, the only difference between the loops in Examples 1 and 2 involves the alternatives x and y, in which the first preferences strictly prefer y to x and the second preferences are the opposite. Therefore the pair of integers associated with the loop in Example 3 is $(1,0) \in \mathbb{Z} \times \mathbb{Z}$. Other pairs of integers are associated with loops in $N(\mathcal{P} \times \mathcal{P})$ in a similar way. For example, $(1,1) \in \mathbb{Z} \times \mathbb{Z}$ is associated with a loop in

$N(\mathcal{P} \times \mathcal{P})$ that combines both preferences making a loop like the one in Example 1. These associations of loops with integers play a crucial role in the next section.

7.3. Arrow's Theorem

For simplicity, continue to consider a set of three alternatives x, y, and z, and two agents with strict preferences on these alternatives. The social welfare function $f : \mathcal{P} \times \mathcal{P} \to \mathcal{P}$ assigns a social strict preference $f(R_1, R_2)$ to the strict preferences $R_1 \in \mathcal{P}$ for agent 1 and $R_2 \in \mathcal{P}$ for agent 2. The weak Pareto property was introduced in Section 4. It requires that the social preference on any pair of alternatives is the same as any unanimous agents' strict preference on that pair.

The property of Independence of Irrelevant Alternatives (IIA) is also required. IIA requires that the social preference on any pair of alternatives only depend on agents' preferences for that pair. That is, if $R_1 \in \mathcal{P}$ ranks a pair of alternatives in the same way as $R_1' \in \mathcal{P}$, and $R_2 \in \mathcal{P}$ ranks the same pair in the same way as $R_2' \in \mathcal{P}$, then IIA requires that the social preference $f(R_1, R_2)$ ranks this pair in the same way as the social preference $f(R_1', R_2')$. Social welfare functions that have the IIA property may be decomposed into pairwise social welfare functions, each one aggregating agents' rankings of a pair of alternatives.[19] It is IIA that enables the construction of a function $F : (N(\mathcal{P} \times \mathcal{P})) \to N(\mathcal{P})$ corresponding to a social welfare function, $f : \mathcal{P} \times \mathcal{P} \to \mathcal{P}$.

To construct $F : (N(\mathcal{P} \times \mathcal{P})) \to N(\mathcal{P})$, start with the vertices in $N(\mathcal{P} \times \mathcal{P})$ and map them into the vertices of $N(\mathcal{P})$ using the social welfare function $f : \mathcal{P} \times \mathcal{P} \to \mathcal{P}$ as follows. Consider for example the vertex, $(xy+-)$. This is the set of all ordered pairs of preferences such that agent 1 strictly prefers x to y, and agent 2 has the opposite strict preference. From IIA, the social preference on x and y must be the same for all ordered pairs of preferences in $(xy+-)$ since agents 1 and 2 rank x and y in the same way in all of them. If the social preference strictly prefers x to y, then F maps $(xy+-)$ into $(xy+)$, the set of preferences for which x is strictly preferred to y. The assignment of vertices in $N(\mathcal{P})$ to vertices in $N(\mathcal{P} \times \mathcal{P})$ by $F : (N(\mathcal{P} \times \mathcal{P})) \to N(\mathcal{P})$ is done in the same way. It is worth emphasizing that the weak Pareto property restricts the images of $(xy++)$ and $(xy--)$ to be $(xy+)$ and $(xy-)$, respectively, and similarly for the other two pairs of alternatives.

The next step is to extend this mapping of vertices to the edges and faces as well in a way that ensures $F : (N(\mathcal{P} \times \mathcal{P})) \to N(\mathcal{P})$ is continuous. This can be done in the following way: vertices are mapped into vertices; vertices that give edges or faces are mapped into vertices that also do this; and finally, the mapping on edges and faces is linear.[20] Such mappings are called *simplicial*, and they are well-known to be continuous.

[19] See Blau (1971).

[20] For example, a point in the interior of an edge is a convex combination of the vertices that give the edge, and the image of that point must be the same convex combination of the images of these vertices; similarly for interior points of faces. See Maunder (1996) for details.

For Arrow's finite formulation of the social choice problem, all sets are finite, and therefore there is no direct use for topological methods. However, the map $F : (N(\mathcal{P} \times \mathcal{P})) \to N(\mathcal{P})$ just obtained from $f : \mathcal{P} \times \mathcal{P} \to \mathcal{P}$ is a continuous mapping between subsets of Euclidean spaces. The final construction is to use the associations of loops in $N(\mathcal{P})$ and $N(\mathcal{P} \times \mathcal{P})$ with integers in $\mathbb{Z}$ and $\mathbb{Z} \times \mathbb{Z}$, respectively, to associate a function $F_* : \mathbb{Z} \times Z \to \mathbb{Z}$ with $F : (N(\mathcal{P} \times \mathcal{P})) \to N(\mathcal{P})$. It is no accident that this strikingly resembles the association described in Section 2.5.[21]

The function $F_* : \mathbb{Z} \times \mathbb{Z} \to \mathbb{Z}$ will now be used to complete this sketch of the proof of Arrow's Theorem. The three examples of loops described earlier, and the integers associated with them, will also be required. The sequences of vertices for these loops are:

Loop 1: $(xz+)$, $(zy+)$, $(yx+)$ and back to $(xz+)$
Loop 2: $(xz+)$, $(zy+)$, $(yx-)$ and back to $(xz+)$
Loop 3: $(xz++)$, $(zy++)$, $(yx+-)$ and back to $(xz++)$

Recall that Loop 3 is associated with $(1,0) \in \mathbb{Z} \times \mathbb{Z}$. The values that the integer $F_*(1,0)$ may have can be determined by considering first $F(xz++)$, and $F(zy++)$. The weak Pareto property implies $F(xz++) = (xz+)$, and $F(zy++) = (zy+)$. The two loops, 1 and 2, that are combined in Loop 3, only differ for the pair x and y of alternatives. If $F(yx+-) = (yx+)$ then $F_*(1,0) = 1$ and agent 1 is a dictator. If $F(yx+-) = (yx-)$ then $F_*(1,0) = 0$ and $F_*(0,1) = 1$, since $F_*(1,1) = F_*(1,0) + F_*(0,1)$, $F_*(0,1) = 1$ and both terms on the right-hand side are either 0 or 1. In this case, 2 is a dictator. Since either 1 or 2 must be a dictator, this completes the sketch of Baryshnikov's proof of Arrow's Theorem.

Two observations may be made about Baryshnikov's contribution. First, it is unaffected by any of the problems raised in Section 6. Indeed, the way the continuity of the function $F : (N(\mathcal{P} \times \mathcal{P})) \to N(\mathcal{P})$ is defined does not need to be intuitively appealing for the purpose of proving Arrow's Theorem. Second, Baryshnikov's approach, via the nerves of covers, may also be useful for the analysis of domain restrictions as an escape from Arrow's impossibility. Lauwers (2009) contains some suggestive remarks about deleting faces from $N(\mathcal{P} \times \mathcal{P})$ to obtain the single-peaked domain restriction. It may be useful to consider other domain restrictions in a similar way.

8. CONCLUSION

All of the theorems in Sections 2, 3, 4, and 5 present the key theorems of topological social choice. It has been shown (Theorem 1) that continuity is incompatible with

[21] The circle and $N(\mathcal{P})$ both have the same first fundamental groups, namely $\mathbb{Z}$ and the product of two circles, and $N(\mathcal{P} \times \mathcal{P})$ also have the same fundamental group, namely $\mathbb{Z} \times \mathbb{Z}$. See Maunder (1996).

unanimity and anonymity, though a very mild domain restriction, contractibility, leads to a possibility result (Theorem 3). Theorem 4 weakens unanimity to the weak Pareto property or the even weaker Cone property, and shows that this is incompatible with a No Veto property for continuous social welfare functions (Theorem 4). Theorem 5 shows that there exists a Strategic Manipulator for continuous social welfare functions that have the weak Pareto property. These are the main results of topological social choice theory, apart from a very different kind of result, namely Baryshnikov's proof of Arrow's Theorem.

All of the results except that of Baryshnikov require a justification of continuity. The discussion in Section 6 argues that the justifications given in the literature are not completely convincing because they require a different formulation of the social choice problem than any given in the literature. Some remarks on the naturalness of continuity were discussed along with limitations that may account for the absence of developments similar to those that followed Arrow's Theorem. Among these, the absence of a topological analysis of nonbinary social choice was discussed in more detail.

Overall, the view presented is that the justification of continuity requires more attention; its formulation to include nonbinary social choice would be an important contribution; and finally, Baryshnikov's proof of Arrow's Theorem is a major achievement and may yet have other uses.

ACKNOWLEDGMENTS

I am very grateful to Kotaro Suzumura for his encouragement and patience, and to Luc Lauwers for many particularly helpful comments and early access to his work. Several sections of this chapter have been presented in seminars at the Ecole Polytechnique and the Choice Group at the London School of Economics. I am very grateful to all participants and to the London School of Economics for their hospitality and stimulating research environment.

REFERENCES

Armstrong, M. A. (1983). *Basic topology*. New York: Springer-Verlag.

Arrow, K. J. (1950). A difficulty in the concept of social welfare. *Journal of Political Economy, 58*(4), 328–346.

Arrow, K. J. (1951). *Social choice and individual values*. New York: Wiley.

Baigent, N. (1987). Preference proximity and anonymous social choice. *Quarterly Journal of Economics, 102*, 162–169.

Baigent, N. (2002). Topological theories of social choice, mimeo.

Baigent, N. (2008). Harmless homotopic dictators. Chapter 2 in P. K. Pattanaik, K. Tadenuma, Y. Xu & N. Yoshihara (Eds.), *Rational choice and social welfare: theory and applications essays in honor of Kotaro Suzumura*. Berlin & Heidelberg: Springer.

Baryshnikov, Y. M. (1993). Unifying impossibility theorems: a topological approach. *Advances in Mathematics, 14*, 404–415.

Baryshnikov, Y. M. (1997). Topological and discrete social choice: in search of a theory. In G. Heal (Ed.), *Topological social choice* (pp. 53–63). Heidelberg: Springer.

Blau, J. H. (1971). Arrow's theorem with weak independence. *Economica, 38*(152), 413–420.
Buchanan, J. M. (1954). Social choice, democracy, and free markets. *Journal of Political Economy, 62*, 114–123.
Chichilnisky, G. (1979). On fixed point theorems and social choice paradoxes. *Economic Letters, 3*, 347–351.
Chichilnisky, G. (1980). Social choice and the topology of spaces of preferences. *Advances in Mathematics, 37*(2), 165–176.
Chichilnisky, G. (1982a). Social aggregation rules and continuity. *Quarterly Journal of Economics, 97*, 337–352.
Chichilnisky, G. (1982b). The topological equivalence of the Pareto condition and the existence of a dictator. *Journal of Mathematical Economics, 9*, 223–233.
Chichilnisky, G. (1982c). Structural instability of decisive majority rules. *Journal of Mathematical Economics, 9*, 207–221.
Chichilnisky, G. (1983). Social choice and game theory: recent results with a topological approach. Chapter 6 in P. K. Pattanaik & M. Salles (Eds.), *Social choice and welfare* (pp. 103–120). Amsterdam: North-Holland.
Chichilnisky, G. (1993). On strategic control. *Quarterly Journal of Economics, 37*, 165–176.
Chichilnisky, G., & Heal, G. M. (1983). A necessary and sufficient condition for the resolution of the social choice paradox. *Journal of Economic Theory, 31*, 68–87.
Deb, R. (2010). Nonbinary social choice. In K. J. Arrow, A. K. Sen & K. Suzumura, *Handbook of social choice and welfare*, Vol. II, New York: Elsevier.
Dodgson, C. L. (1893). A discussion of various methods of procedure in conducting elections, Oxford.
Heal, G. (1997). Social choice and resource allocation: a topological perspective. In *Topological social choice*, (pp. 1–14). Heidelberg: Springer.
Lauwers, L. (2000). Topological social choice. *Mathematical Social Sciences, 40*(1), 1–39.
Lauwers, L. (2009). The topological approach to the aggregation of preferences. *Social Choice and Welfare, 33*, 449–476.
Maunder, C. R. F. (1996). *Algebraic topology*. New York: Dover Publications.
Mehta, P. (1997). Topological methods in social choice: an overview. In G. Heal (Ed.), *Topological social choice* (pp. 87–97). Heidelberg: Springer.
Rao Jammalamadaka, S., & SenGupta, A. (2001). *Topics in circular statistics*. London: World Scientific Publishing Co.
Saari, D. G. (1997). Informational geometry of social choice. In G. Heal (Ed.), *Topological social choice* (pp. 65–86). Heidelberg: Springer.
Saari, D. G., & Kronwetter, J. (2009). From decision problems to dethroned dictators. *Journal of Mathematical Economics, 44*(7–8), 745–761.
Sen, A. K. (1993). Internal consistency of choice. *Econometrica, 61*(3), 495–521.
Sen, A. K. (1997). *On economic inequality*. Oxford: Oxford University Press.

CHAPTER NINETEEN

Nonbinary Social Choice

Rajat Deb
Department of Economics, Southern Methodist University, Dallas, TX

Contents

Abstract

Economists have used the term "nonbinary" to describe both choice functional nonbinariness (choice functions that cannot be rationalized as the maximizing outcome of a binary preference relation) and structural nonbinariness (the structure of the model dictates that pairs of alternatives do not belong to the domain of the social choice function). Here we have described necessary and sufficient conditions for oligarchy and dictatorship results in social choice models that are nonbinary in both senses.

Keywords: nonbinariness, dictatorship, oligarchy, rationalizability.

JEL codes: D70, D71, D79.

1. INTRODUCTION

Arrow (1963) formulated his General Possibility Theorem in the context of a model in which individual preference profiles are aggregated to yield transitive social preferences. The idea of society having a "preference" and the concept of collective rationality embedded in the transitivity requirement on social preferences immediately raised some serious concerns. Buchanan's (1954, p. 116) argued:

Handbook of Social Choice and Welfare, Volume II
ISSN: 0169-7218, DOI: 10.1016/S0169-7218(10)00019-5

> *The mere introduction of the idea of social rationality suggests the fundamental philosophical issues involved. Rationality or irrationality as an attribute of the social group implies the imputation to the group of an organic existence apart from that of individual components.... We may adopt the philosophical bases of individualism in which the individual is the only entity possessing ends or values. In this case no question of social or collective rationality may be raised.... Alternatively, we may adopt some variant of the organic philosophical assumption in which the collectivity is an independent entity possessing its own value ordering. It is legitimate to test the rationality or irrationality of the entity only against this value ordering.*

It was in response to Buchanan's criticism that Arrow (1963), in the second edition of *Social Choice and Individual Values*, put forward a famous justification of transitive rationality in terms of "path independence":

> *Those familiar with the integrability controversy in the field of consumer's demand theory will observe that the basic problem is the same: the independence of the final choice from the path to it. Transitivity will insure this independence.*

Arrow, however, did not provide a clear analytical formulation of the concept of "path independence" and its relationship to transitivity. Insightful analysis by Plott (1973) revealed that Arrow's requirement of collective rationality while sufficient was not in fact necessary for path independence. Thus, a gap was recognized between Arrow's notion of collective rationality, which was unambiguously binary in nature, and the nonbinary social choice theoretic consistency requirement of "path independence." Thus, a number of economists found it worthwhile to explore the question as to whether "nonbinariness" was a way out of the Arrovian Impossibility result. Some of the early contributions along these lines have been surveyed by Sen (1977).

In these early models, Arrow's model of binary social "preference" was extended to a model of social "choice," with social preference being interpreted as social *revealed* preference. Soon monographs, textbooks, and articles were demonstrating (see, for instance, Blair et al. 1976, Fishburn 1973, Kelly 1978) that results derived in the Arrovian social preference framework could be proved in the social choice framework. It was shown that this could be done by interpreting Arrow's "social preference" as preference that was revealed from "binary" choices (i.e., choices from pairs of alternatives) and by imposing the appropriate type of transitivity condition on this binary revealed preference relation either directly or through suitable consistency conditions embodied in axioms of revealed preference.

What happens to the results proved in Arrow's framework if (a) binary choices are not observed (pairs of alternatives never come up for choice), or (b) if inconsistencies of social choice lead to a model that cannot be rationalized using a binary relation (the social choice function is not "integrable")? Answers to these questions form the basis of the modern theory of nonbinary social choice.

The basic ideas underlying nonbinariness can be formulated in terms of a general choice function model without specifically defining the process of *social* choice. This is done in Sections 2 and 3. Section 2 looks at the notion of *structural* nonbinariness by describing and comparing a number of alternative restrictions that have been proposed for the domain of the choice function when the structure of the model (possibly) precludes choices from pairs. Section 3 looks at *choice functional* nonbinariness by examining the relationship between axioms of revealed preference, consistency conditions and nonbinariness in the sense of not being able to rationalize a choice function as the outcome of a maximizing exercise of some underlying binary preference relation. Section 4 provides the social context and gives a precise definition of nonbinary social choice. Section 5 uses some basic definitions and notations from social choice theory to examine the relationship of Arrow's "social preference" model to the model of a "social choice function." Consistency conditions have no role in a special and "extreme" case of structural nonbinariness where there is a *single* agenda (with more than two alternatives). Section 6 discusses this case. First, some significant results from Denicolò (1993) using Hansson's independence condition (Hansson 1969) are presented. Next, implications of an alternative independence condition proposed by Sen (1993) are used to derive "oligarchy" and "dictatorship" results in this single-agenda context. These core results are used in Section 7 to provide necessary and sufficient conditions for "oligarchy" and "dictatorship" results to hold in a multi-agenda framework that allows for both structural and choice functional nonbinariness. These results are compared to existing results in the literature. Section 8 summarizes our principal conclusions.

2. CHOICE FUNCTIONS AND DOMAIN RESTRICTIONS

Let X, $|X| \geq 3$, be the set of alternatives and let Ω be a nonempty set of nonempty subsets of X. A choice function T on $< X, \Omega >$ is a function that for every $A \in \Omega$ specifies a nonempty subset $T(A)$ of A. Ω is interpreted as the set of potential feasible sets ("budget sets") and $T(A)$ as the set of alternatives selected when A is available. We will assume that Ω contains some set A such that $|A| \geq 3$. In this case we say that the feasibility domain (Fe-domain), Ω, is *nontrivial.*[1]

Restrictions on the Fe-domain of the choice function arise quite naturally in the context of specific choice problems. These restrictions determine which subsets of X may potentially come up for choice. For instance, in the standard models analyzing the behavior of a perfectly competitive consumer, the particular structure of a budget set *rules out* certain subsets of X (such as finite sets and nonconvex sets) from being potential budget sets. In social choice, just as in consumer theory, the particular context determines the set Ω. What Kelly (1978) has referred to as the "standard domain" in social choice consists of *all* nonempty subsets of X. Indeed, in a large class of voting

[1] Without this restriction, one would be dealing with the case of choices from "binary" sets with such choices being easily rationalizable by a binary preference relation and thus ruling out the essence of "nonbinariness" from the very outset.

problems where any subset of the set of eligible individuals may stand for elections, this is a perfectly reasonable condition. However, there are other problems in social choice (such as models for the provision of public goods) where the structure of the model, just like in the study of the perfectly competitive consumer, dictates that some subsets of X be ruled out from being potential budget sets (see for instance Campbell 1995).

A number of authors (Campbell 1995, Denicolò 1987, Grether and Plott 1982, Panda 1983) have used the term "nonbinary social choice" to describe social choice models that rule out "binary choices," in the sense that two alternative sets are not necessarily required to be potential feasible sets or are excluded outright from being potential feasible sets. Certain special Fe-domains have played an important role in the development of this type of nonbinary social choice theory. Two such well-known restrictions (defined for integer values of k) are:

(a) Fishburn's k-domain ($F_{k=}$) (Fishburn 1974): Ω consisting of all subsets of X with *exactly* k elements.[2]

(b) Grether and Plott's k-feasibility restriction ($GP_{k\geq}$) (Grether and Plott 1982): This is a requirement that all nonempty subsets of X with k *or more elements* be included in Ω.

If Ω satisfies $GP_{k\geq}$ with $k=1$, the Fe-domain is *complete*. This is what we have referred to earlier as a part of the "standard domain" in social choice. If $F_{k=}$ domains with $k=1$ and $k=2$ are *subsets* of Ω, then the Fe-domain is *pairwise complete*. If the Fe-domain is not pairwise complete it will be said to be *nonbinary*. If $F_{k=}$ domains with $k=1$ and $k=2$ do not intersect with Ω, the Fe-domain will be said to be *strictly nonbinary*.

The first four parts of Definition 1 below follow Denicolò (1987). The fifth part is a weaker version of the assumption of "finite additivity" (see Suzumura 1983, Chapter 2).

Definition 1

(1.1) Fixed Agenda (FA): Ω *is a singleton (i.e.,* $|\Omega|=1$).

(1.2) Ω *satisfies* universal set feasibility (USF) *if* $X\in\Omega$.

(1.3) Ω *is* minimally binary *if, for all distinct* $x,y\in X$, *there exists a finite sequence of sets* $A_1,A_2,\ldots,A_m\in\Omega$ *such that* $\cap A_j=\{x,y\}$.

(1.4) Ω *is* connected *if, for all* $A,B\in\Omega$, $\min\{|A|,|B|\}\geq 2$, *there exists a finite sequence* $A=A_1,A_2,\ldots,A_m=B\in\Omega$ *such that* $|A_j\cap A_{j+1}|\geq 2$ *for* $j=1,2,\ldots,m-1$.

(1.5) Ω *is* covered *if, for all* $B_1,B_2\in\Omega$, *there exists* $B_3\in\Omega$ *such that* $B_1\cup B_2\subseteq B_3$.

The fixed agenda (Definition 1.1) represents the simplest case whose results can be used to analyze all other cases. *USF* (Definition 1.2) requires that Ω contain the

[2] Fishburn restricts k to be at least three, thus making sure that no binary set belongs to the domain of the choice function. For expositional convenience, here, we impose no such restriction.

universal set, X. Note that if X is "infinite and unbounded" and members of Ω represent resource constraints (as in consumer behavior), then clearly, USF is unlikely to be satisfied. The property of being "covered" (Definition 1.5) is an extension of USF designed to handle this case. The assumption of Ω being covered (somewhat like $GP_{k\geq}$) implies the inclusion of "large" sets in Ω. The condition is also similar in spirit but weaker than the assumption of "finite additivity" (see Suzumura 1983, Chapter 2) requiring that the union of any two sets in Ω also belong to Ω.[3] Ω in the standard theory of the perfectly competitive consumer is not "finitely additive," nor does it satisfy $GP_{k\geq}$; it is, however, covered.

Of the Fe-domain restrictions in Definition 1, the assumptions of minimal binariness (Definition 1.3) and connectedness (Definition 1.4) represent the weakest restrictions. (Both these assumptions are consistent with the Fe-domain being nonbinary.) The intuition behind these assumptions is that elements of Ω need to "overlap" sufficiently. Ω in the fixed agenda problem violates minimal binariness as does the standard model of the perfectly competitive consumer. But, both the fixed agenda model and the standard model of the perfectly competitive consumer satisfy the assumption of being connected.

These interpretations of the intuitions underlying the concepts in Definition 1 (that sufficiently large sets should be included in Ω and sets in Ω should overlap sufficiently) are supported by the results in Proposition 1. Proposition (1.5), for instance, tells us that if large sets (relative to X) are included in Ω they will (at least indirectly) overlap.

The following proposition follows immediately from the definitions of the concepts just given:

Proposition 1

(1.1) *complete* $\mapsto$ *pairwise complete* $\mapsto$ *minimally binary.*

(1.2) *complete* $\mapsto$ *For* $k < |X|$, $GP_{k\geq} \mapsto \Omega$ *is minimally binary.*

(1.3) *complete* $\mapsto$ *For* $k \leq |X|$, $GP_{k\geq} \mapsto USF \mapsto \Omega$ *is covered.*

(1.4) $FA \mapsto \Omega$ *is covered.*

(1.5) Ω *is covered* $\mapsto \Omega$ *is connected.*

(1.6) *For* $k \geq 3$, $F_{k=}$ *domain is connected but not necessarily covered.*

3. CONSISTENCY AND RATIONALIZABILITY

If choices from the feasible sets are in fact based on some underlying preference of the agent making the choices, and if this preference is "well behaved," then the choices made from different feasible sets will satisfy some "consistency" axioms. Furthermore,

[3] "Finite additivity" plays a key role in the theory of revealed preference and rational choice. It is, however, not satisfied by the usual model of a perfectly competitive consumer.

through observation of choices inference may be drawn about the underlying preferences of the agent. This revealed preference approach to the theory of choice can be traced back to classic papers by Samuelson (1938, 1948, 1950). He put forward the famous internal consistency condition that has come to be known as the "weak axiom" of revealed preference. This axiom states that if through the process of choice x is "revealed preferred" to y, then y should never be "revealed preferred" to x. This was further strengthened by Houthakker (1950) by allowing for *indirect* preference revelation through a sequence of choices.

Three "revealed preference" relations (Definition 2) and a few (of the many) internal consistency conditions that have been used in the literature ("axioms of revealed preference") will be of interest to us. (For comprehensive accounts of revealed preference relations and consistency conditions see Aizerman 1985, Arrow 1959, Herzberger 1973, Sen 1971, 1986, and Suzumura 1983).

Definition 2

(2.1) Binary Base Relation: $xR_2^T y$ *iff* $\{x,y\} \in \Omega$ *and* $x \in T(\{x,y\})$.

(2.2) Weak Revealed Preference Relation: $xR^T y$ *iff there exists* $A \in \Omega$ *such that* $x \in T(A)$ *and* $y \in A$.

(2.3) Strict Revealed Preference Relation: $xR_>^T y$ *iff there exists* $A \in \Omega$ *such that* $x \in T(A)$ *and* $y \in (A - T(A))$.

Clearly, $xR_2^T y$ implies $xR^T y$ and $xR_>^T y$ implies $xR^T y$ while the converses are not true. Furthermore, R_2^T and $R_>^T$ are unrelated.

Definition 3

(3.1) Weak Axiom of Revealed Preference (WARP)[4]: $xR_>^T y$ *implies not* $yR^T x$. *(If x is picked and y is rejected then y is never picked when x is present.)*

(3.2) Arrow's Choice Axiom (ACA): *For* $A, B \in \Omega$ *and* $A \subseteq B$, *if* $T(B) \cap A \neq \emptyset$ *then* $T(A) = T(B) \cap A$. *(If any of the elements picked on a larger set are available, then these alone will be picked on a smaller set.)*

(3.3) Chernoff's Axiom (α): *For* $A, B \in \Omega$ *and* $A \subseteq B$, *if* $T(B) \cap A \neq \emptyset$ *then* $(T(B) \cap A) \subseteq T(A)$. *(Anything that is rejected on a smaller set will also be rejected on a larger set.)*

(3.4) Dual Chernoff Axiom (DCA): *For* $A, B \in \Omega$ *and* $A \subseteq B$, *if* $T(B) \cap A \neq \emptyset$ *then* $T(A) \subseteq (T(B) \cap A)$. *(If any of the chosen elements from a larger set are available, then anything rejected on the larger set will also be rejected on a smaller set.)*

(3.5) Weak Dominance Axiom (δ^*): *For* $A, B \in \Omega$ *and* $A \subseteq B$, *if* $T(B) \subseteq A$, *then* $T(A) \subseteq T(B) \cap A$. *(If all of the chosen elements from a larger set are available, then anything rejected on the larger set will also be rejected on a smaller set.)*

[4] This is a version of Samuelson's "weak axiom" of revealed preference.

The relationship between the axioms is shown in the following proposition.

Proposition 2

(2.1) $WARP \mapsto ACA$.
(2.2) $ACA \leftrightarrow \alpha \& DCA$.
(2.3) $DCA \mapsto \delta^*$.

Choice functions generate "revealed preference" relations. Conversely, the process of maximization using a (binary) preference relation can be used to generate a choice function. Whenever a choice function can be "explained" in this way as the outcome of a maximizing exercise,[5] we will say that the choice function is *binary rationalizable*:

Definition 4 (Binary Rationalizable (BR)) *A choice function T is* binary rationalizable (BR) *iff there exists a connected*[6] *binary relation R on X such that for all $A \in \Omega$, $T(A) = C(A, R)$ where $C(A, R) = \{x \in A \;\&\; \text{for all } y \in A, xRy\}$. If T is binary rationalizable using a transitive relation we say that T is* transitive rationalizable (TR). *Similarly, if T is binary rationalizable using a quasi-transitive (respectively, acyclic) relation we say that it is* quasi-transitive rationalizable (QTR) *(resp., acyclic rationalizable (ACR)).*

Proposition 3 $TR \mapsto QTR \mapsto ACR \mapsto BR$.

There is a significant amount of literature in social choice (Batra and Pattanaik 1972, Matsumoto 1985, Phillips and Stevens 1981, Xu 1996) that associates "nonbinary social choice" with the violation of *binary rationalizability* of the (social) choice function (rather than with the nonbinariness of the Fe-domain of the (social) choice function). While consistency of the choice function can imply binary rationalizability of choice, this need not always be the case. The next proposition discusses the relation between consistency of T as represented by the revealed preference axioms that we have introduced already and binary rationalizability. We see that while $WARP$ implies binary rationalizability,[7] even though $WARP$ cannot guarantee acyclic rationalizability.[8] Moreover, for the other consistency axioms described above there is, in general, no relationship between binary rationalizability and these other conditions, in the sense that *by themselves* these consistency axioms are compatible with the *choice function* being "nonbinary."

[5] This is the solution of the so-called "integrability" problem. (See Samuelson 1950.)
[6] A binary relation R on X is connected iff for all $x, y \in X$, either xRy or yRx.
[7] *WARP*, clearly, will not imply transitive rationalizability. For transitive rationalizability in the general domain it is well known that Richter's "Congruence Axiom" must be satisfied (see Richter 1966). Also, note that Suzumura (1977) has shown that a suitable reinterpretation of Houthakker's "strong axiom of revealed preference" (see Houthakker 1950) is necessary and sufficient for transitive rationalizability, and hence that it is equivalent to Richter's Congruence Axiom.
[8] Note that binary rationalizability does not imply acyclic rationalizability, because we are not assuming that every finite subset of alternatives belongs to Ω. If $X = \{x, y, z\}$ and Ω consists of all pairs of alternatives then $T(\{x, y\}) = \{x\}$, $T(\{y, z\}) = \{y\}$ and $T(\{x, z\}) = \{z\}$ is binary rationalizable but not acyclic rationalizable.

Proposition 4

(4.1) $WARP \mapsto BR$.
(4.2) $WARP \nrightarrow ACR$.
(4.3) $ACA \nrightarrow BR$.
(4.4) $BR \nrightarrow \delta^*$.

Just as in the case of "structural" nonbinariness, the nature of the social choice problem may lead to "choice functional" nonbinariness. There are two closely related reasons that both consistency and binary rationalizability may fail for certain types of social choice problems. Firstly, the feasible sets in some problems may have epistemic value (see Sen 1993), in the sense that what is offered up for choice gives us information about the underlying problem. This would lead to the same alternative being valued differently in different feasible sets, making the choice function appear to be "irrational and inconsistent." Secondly, for certain social choice problems the criterion for choice may not be based on the intuition of finding a maximal or extreme value but rather on concepts of moderation and compromise. As I have argued elsewhere (Deb, 1975), if one is trying to select an "average" rather than the "most" or the "least," both consistency and binary rationalizability of the choice function can easily be violated. Both these issues are important in three specific areas of social choice: (a) Models of Rights and Liberties (see Batra and Pattanaik 1972, Sen 1993); (b) Models of Fair Division and Bargaining (in this context see Luce and Raiffa's 1957, p. 133, discussion of Nash's "independence" condition); (c) Models of Justice (see for instance Phillips and Stevens 1981).[9]

4. NONBINARY SOCIAL CHOICE: A DEFINITION

From a general choice functional model of choice we can arrive at a model of *social* choice as follows.

Let the set of social alternatives be X and Ω be a nontrivial set of feasible agendas. $R, \overline{R}, \widetilde{R} \ldots$, etc. will represent binary relations on X, with asymmetric and symmetric factors of the relation being written as P, $\overline{P}$, $\widetilde{P}, \ldots$, etc. and I, $\overline{I}$, $\widetilde{I}, \ldots$, etc., respectively. Let $N = \{1, 2, \ldots, n\}$, $n \geq 3$, be the set of individuals. For $i \in N$, individual i's preference *orderings* on X will be denoted by R_i, $\overline{R}_i, \ldots$, etc. We will use $\pi, \overline{\pi}, \ldots$, etc. to denote individual preference profiles $(R_1, R_2, \ldots, R_n)$, $(\overline{R}_1, \overline{R}_2, \ldots, \overline{R}_n) \ldots$, etc. and $\pi_A, \overline{\pi}_A, \ldots$, etc. for the restrictions of these profiles to the subset A of X.

[9] One way around these types of problems, without having to give up binariness, is to look at "extended" models of social choice (see for instance Pattanaik 1996, Pattanaik and Suzumura 1996). In our case, by interpreting $X \times \Omega$ (instead of what in our model is X) as the set of "social alternatives" provides us with a framework in which the choice function can usually be expected to be both binary rationalizable and consistent. This promising approach needs to be investigated more thoroughly.

A *Social Choice Function (SCF)* is a function F from a nonempty set of preference profiles $\mathcal{P}$ to the set of all choice functions on $< X, \Omega >$. Thus, for every possible preference profile $\pi \in \mathcal{P}$ we get a choice function $T(\pi)$.[10] We will refer to $\mathcal{P}$ as the preference-domain (P-domain) of the choice function.

For any of the axioms and properties described in the previous sections for the choice function, T, we will say that a particular axiom or property is satisfied by the *SCF* if there does not exist a $\pi \in \mathcal{P}$ such that the condition is violated by $T(\pi)$. Thus, for instance we will say that the *SCF* satisfies *WARP* iff there does not exist a $\pi \in \mathcal{P}$ such that the choice function $T(\pi)$ violates *WARP*. In what follows we will follow the traditional terminology of social choice introduced by Fishburn (1973) and (abusing our notation) refer to $T(A, \pi)$ (for $\pi \in \mathcal{P}$ and $A \in \Omega$) rather than to the function F as the *SCF*.

In the last two sections we have identified the two ways in which *SCFs* may be described as being nonbinary:

(a) *Structural Nonbinariness*: the Fe-domain Ω is nonbinary.
(b) *Choice Functional Nonbinariness*: there exists a preference profile $\pi \in \mathcal{P}$ at which the choice function $T(., \pi)$ violates binary rationalizability (*BR*).

We will follow the literature and refer to social choice models with either type of nonbinariness as nonbinary. We will refer to models that are both structurally and choice functionally nonbinary as being *doubly* nonbinary.

5. SOCIAL CHOICE: SOME STANDARD CONCEPTS

The following "standard" terminology will be used to describe the properties of *SCF*s.

Definition 5 *Let T be an SCF with P-domain $\mathcal{P}$ and let A be any element of Ω.*

(5.1) *A coalition $L \subseteq N$ is* decisive *for x against y on the agenda A (denoted by $L \in D(x, y; A)$) iff for all profiles $\pi \in \mathcal{P}$, xP_iy for all $i \in L$ implies $y \notin T(A, \pi)$.*

[10] There are two things that the reader should observe. Firstly, defining an *SCF* as a function from *profiles of individual orderings* to the set of choice functions is just one of many ways of modeling social choice. One could, for instance, define an *SCF* from profiles of quasi-transitive or acyclic individual preferences to the set of choice functions or even more generally from a set of profiles of *individual* choice funtions to the set of social choice functions (see for instance Aleskerov and Duggan 1993). Secondly, just as we have argued earlier that restrictions on the Fe-domain of T may arise naturally as the part of a particular choice problem, one could with just as much justification argue that restrictions on the P-domain of F may also arise as a strutural feature of particular problems. For instance, for social choice problems in economic environments, individual preferences are usually taken to satisfy certain continuity and convexity assumptions, and hence not only may the set of "feasible sets" be restricted to having certain specific forms, but all "logically" possible profiles may, in fact, *also* not be permissible (see Campbell 1995, Donaldson and Weymark 1988). For the sake of keeping this chapter to a reasonable length, these important alternative approaches to nonbinary social choice have not been considered here.

(5.2) *A coalition* $L \subseteq N$ *has a* veto *for* x *against* y *on the agenda* A *(denoted by* $L \in V(x,y;A)$*) iff for all profiles* $\pi \in \mathcal{P}$, xP_iy *for all* $i \in L$ *implies* $\{y\} \neq T(A,\pi)$.

(5.3) *If* $L \in D(x,y;A)$ *(resp.,* $L \in V(x,y;A)$*) for all* $x, y \in A$ *then we say that L is* decisive *(resp., has a* veto*)* on A. *This is denoted by* $L \in D(A)$ *(resp.,* $L \in V(A)$*).*

(5.4) *If* $L \in D(B)$ *(resp.,* $L \in V(B)$*) for all* $B \in \Omega$*, then L is* decisive *(resp., L has a* veto*). A* singleton *decisive coalition (resp., a singleton coalition that has a veto) is a* dictator *(resp.,* vetoer*). If a dictator exists T is* dictatorial.

(5.5) *If a coalition of vetoers is decisive then the coalition is an* oligarchy *and T is* oligarchic.

(5.6) *T is* Paretian *iff N is decisive.*[11]

(5.7) *T satisfies* choice functional independence of irrelevant alternatives *(IIA(C)) iff for all* $B \in \Omega$ *and all profiles* $\pi, \overline{\pi} \in \mathcal{P}$, $\pi_B = \overline{\pi}_B$ *implies* $T(B,\pi) = T(B,\overline{\pi})$.

(5.8) *T has an* unrestricted domain (UD) *iff* $\mathcal{P}$ *consists of all* logically *possible individual preference profiles.*

(5.9) *T has a* maximal individually tractable domain (MIT) *iff* $\mathcal{P}$ *consists of all individual preference profiles* $\pi = (R_1, R_2, \ldots, R_n)$ *for which for all* $A \in \Omega$, $C(A, R_i) \neq \emptyset$ *for all* $i \in N$.

Now, consider Arrow's formulation of the social aggregation problem. In Arrow's model individual preferences are aggregated into a social *preference*. Let a Social Preference Function (*SPF*) f be a function from a domain of profiles $\mathcal{P}$ to the set of all binary relations on X. The Arrovian Social Welfare Function (*SWF*) is an *SPF* which for any π in its domain specifies a binary social preference *ordering* $R(\pi)$ in its range. For Arrow's model, the assumption of unrestricted domain (*UD*) requires that every logically possible profile of individual orderings belong to the domain of the *SPF*; the Pareto condition is the weak Pareto (*WP*) condition requiring that for all profiles $\pi \in \mathcal{P}$, if for all $i \in N$: xP_iy then $xP(\pi)y$; Arrow's Independence of Irrelevant Alternatives condition (*IIA(A)*) requires that if for some $\pi, \overline{\pi} \in \mathcal{P}$ and $x, y \in X$, $\pi_{\{x,y\}} = \overline{\pi}_{\{x,y\}}$ then the social preference relations given by the *SPF* for these two profiles are identical over $\{x,y\}$; and the Arrovian dictator is an individual $\overline{d} \in N$ such that for all profiles $\pi \in \mathcal{P}$, $xP_{\overline{d}}y$ implies $xP(\pi)y$. Using this notation, Arrow's General Possibility Theorem (*GPT*) tells us that there does not exist an *SWF* satisfying *UD*, *IIA(A)*, *WP* such that no Arrovian dictator exists.

In order to understand the relationship between Arrow's model, his assumptions, and the *GPT* and the *SCF* model and the assumptions in Definition 5, consider an *extended version* of Arrow's model in which the ordering R given by the *SWF* is used to generate a Social Choice Function on Ω using binary maximality (i.e., $T(A,\pi) = C(A, R(\pi))$). Now, *if* such an *SCF* exists, then it is easy to check that the conditions *Paretian* and *IIA(C)* are "equivalent" to Arrow's corresponding conditions *WP* and *IIA(A)*; and that

[11] We will only be considering Paretian *SCFs*. For what happens in social choice models when this assumption is relaxed see Aleskerov and Duggan (1993), Campbell and Kelly (1993) and Wilson (1972).

the existence of an Arrovian dictator would be equivalent to having the *SCF* of the extended version of Arrow's model being dictatorial.

However, notice that $R(\pi)$ being an ordering does not guarantee $C(A, R(\pi)) \neq \emptyset$ on infinite sets A. Thus, the presence of infinite sets in Ω creates a tension within *SCF* models (and for the extended choice functional version of Arrow's model) between the Pareto condition and *UD*, that does not arise in Arrow's basic model and has nothing whatsoever to do with Arrow's *GPT*.

Proposition 5 *If there exists $A \in \Omega$ such that A contains an infinite number of elements then there does not exist a Paretian SCF satisfying UD.*[12]

Thus, imposing *UD* has the effect of "trivializing" impossibility results in frameworks permitting infinite sets. In order not to rule out interesting nonbinary social choice models where infinite sets are members of Ω, we will prove our results using *MIT*.[13] The intuitive justification for *MIT* lies in the fact that if social choice is to be based on individual preferences, and if on infinite sets some individual preference orderings are such that individuals are "unable to choose," then under those circumstances one should not expect an *SCF* to exist. Notice that if one uses *MIT* there is an added bonus of being able to tease out the relationship between Arrow's *GPT* and analogous results that may arise in social choice models permitting the possibility of infinite "budget sets" without being distracted by the type of tension between the axioms described in Proposition 5. However, the reader should note that a large number of social choice models deal with finite universal sets and that in such models *UD* and *MIT* are equivalent assumptions.

6. DICTATORSHIP AND OLIGARCHY: THE FIXED AGENDA CASE

In this section we will use two classic methods, that of Hansson (1969) and that of Sen (1993), to analyze dictatorship and oligarchy results in the special case where $\Omega = \{A\}$ and $|A| \geq 3$.[14] We will find it useful to use the following additional notation:

Preference orderings will (also) be described by rows with better elements to the left and indifferent alternatives bracketed together using (...).

$$L\text{: xy(zw)}$$

will indicate that for $L \subseteq N$, for all $i \in L$, $xP_iyP_izI_iw$.

[12] Pick a countably infinite set of alternatives $x_1, x_2 \ldots \infty$ and construct identical individual preferences with $x_{m+1}P_ix_m$ and let the remaining alternatives all be indifferent and strictly worse than the countable set $x_1, x_2 \ldots \infty$.

[13] All the formal "impossibility" results that we prove with *MIT* will also be true if the assumption is replaced with *UD*.

[14] While this clearly represents nonbinariness in the structural sense, the nonbinariness will not be choice functional since it will always be possible to rationalize the choice function using the (binary) ordering $R^T(\pi)$ (where $R^T(\pi)$ is the revealed preference relation at the profile π (see Definition 2).

We will also use the notation [.,.] for unspecified rankings between alternatives and the word "*rest*" for all remaining alternatives. Thus,

$$i\colon [x,y][rest]$$

will denote *all* orderings in which either x or y (or both) are the best alternatives for individual i with the remaining alternatives ranked strictly below both x and y in all possible arbitrary ways.

6.1. Social Choice with a Fixed Agenda: Hansson's Independence Condition

What happens to Arrow's GPT if the agenda is fixed? If Ω is nontrivial and a singleton (i.e., Ω satisfies FA), then for any preference domain that satisfies MIT, a Paretian and nondictatorial SCF satisfying $IIA(C)$[15] exists. Such an SCF can be obtained by simply setting $T(A,\pi)$ equal to the set of Pareto optimal elements of A.[16] To understand this possibility result note that the analogue in the (social) choice function framework of Arrow's assumption of transitivity of (social) preferences are the "revealed preference axioms." These axioms impose consistency conditions on choices from *different* feasible sets. Here, since there is just one feasible set, these revealed preference axioms completely lose their bite. In a pioneering paper, Hansson (1969) suggested an alternative independence condition that builds back into the single agenda choice function framework a notion of "consistency" of social choice:

Definition 6 *(Hansson's Independence Condition) Let T be an SCF.*

(6.1) *T satisfies $IIA(H_0)$ iff for all $A \in \Omega$, all $B \subseteq A$ and all preference profiles $\pi, \overline{\pi}$ in the P-domain of T such that $\pi_B = \overline{\pi}_B$: either $B \cap T(A,\pi) = \emptyset$ or $B \cap T(A,\overline{\pi}) = \emptyset$ or $B \cap T(A,\pi) = B \cap T(A,\overline{\pi})$.*

(6.2) *T satisfies $IIA(H_1)$ iff for all $A \in \Omega$, and all preference profiles, $\pi, \overline{\pi}$ in the P-domain of T such that $\pi_{\{x,y\}} = \overline{\pi}_{\{x,y\}}$: $(x \in T(A,\pi)$ and $y \in (A - T(A,\pi)))$ implies $y \notin T(A,\overline{\pi})$.*

$IIA(H_1)$ clearly has the flavor of an independence condition together with a revealed preference type of consistency axiom of the type "if x is selected and y is rejected then y should not be picked in the presence of x." To appreciate the fact that it is an "independence condition" rather than a true "rationality condition" notice that the difference of $IIA(H_1)$ from "revealed preference axioms" is that revealed preference axioms involve inter-agenda comparisons of choice *at a given preference profile* while $IIA(H_1)$, like

[15] Recall this is the choice functional equivalent of Arrow's $IIA(A)$.
[16] The Pareto optimal set will be a superset of $\cup_{i \in N} C(A, R_i)$ that, by MIT, is nonempty.

other independence axioms, involves only inter-profile comparisons of choice on a *given agenda*. The following result is from Denicolò (2000):[17]

Proposition 6 *(Denicolò) $IIA(H_0)$ is equivalent to $IIA(H_1)$.*

Next, we define two related independence conditions $IIA(H_2)$ and $IIA(H_3)$ that are weaker versions of $IIA(H_1)$. We also describe a special "revealed preference relation" R^+ associated with $IIA(H_3)$. The definitions of $IIA(H_2)$ and R^+ follow Denicolò (1993).[18]

Definition 7

(7.1) *The SCF, T, satisfies $IIA(H_2)$ iff for all $A \in \Omega$, and all preference profiles, $\pi, \overline{\pi}$ in the P-domain of T such that $\pi_{\{x,y\}} = \overline{\pi}_{\{x,y\}}$: $\{x\} = T(A,\pi)$ implies $y \notin T(A,\overline{\pi})$.*

(7.2) *The SCF, T, satisfies $IIA(H_3)$ iff for all $A \in \Omega$, and all preference profiles, $\pi, \overline{\pi}$ in the P-domain of T such that $\pi_{\{x,y\}} = \overline{\pi}_{\{x,y\}}$ if π is such that*

$$N: [x,y][rest],$$

then $\{x\} = T(A,\pi)$ implies $y \notin T(A,\overline{\pi})$.

(7.3) *Let R^+ be a function which for every profile, π and all $A \in \Omega$, specifies a binary relation $R^+(A,\pi)$ on X given as follows: for all $x,y \in X$, $xR^+(A,\pi)y$ iff $\pi^+(x,y)$ belongs to the P-domain of T, $x,y \in A$ and $x \in T(A,\pi^+(x,y))$ where π^+ is obtained from π by raising $\{x,y\}$ to the top of every individual's ordering and is given by: (a) $\pi_{\{x,y\}} = \pi^+_{\{x,y\}}(x,y)$, (b) $\pi_{X-\{x,y\}} = \pi^+_{X-\{x,y\}}(x,y)$, and (c) $N: [x,y][rest]$. In the absence of any ambiguity we will write $R^+(\pi)$ instead of $R^+(A,\pi)$.*

Proposition 7 $IIA(H_1) \mapsto IIA(H_2) \mapsto IIA(H_3)$.

The conclusions in $IIA(H_i)$ $i = 1,2,3$ are all exactly the same: $y \notin T(A,\overline{\pi})$. Furthermore, in all the three conditions the hypothesis requires that $\pi_{\{x,y\}} = \overline{\pi}_{\{x,y\}}$. In addition, for the hypothesis of $IIA(H_1)$ it is required that x be selected when the profile is $\overline{\pi}$; the hypothesis of $IIA(H_2)$ has the stronger requirement that x be uniquely selected, while $IIA(H_3)$ strengthens the hypothesis even further by narrowing down the circumstances under which x is required to be uniquely selected.

[17] Denicoló attributes this result to R. Cagliozzi. To see that $IIA(H_0)$ implies $IIA(H_1)$ let $B = \{x,y\}$. The conclusion of (6.1) becomes either $\{x,y\} \cap T(A,\pi) = \emptyset$ or $\{x,y\} \cap T(A,\overline{\pi}) = \emptyset$ or $\{x,y\} \cap T(A,\pi) = \{x,y\} \cap T(A,\overline{\pi})$. Now, assume to the contrary that $x \in T(A,\pi)$, $y \in (A - T(A,\pi))$ and $y \in T(A,\overline{\pi})$. This implies $x \in \{x,y\} \cap T(A,\pi) \neq \emptyset$, $y \in \{x,y\} \cap T(A,\overline{\pi}) \neq \emptyset$ and, since $y \notin T(A,\pi)$ and $y \in T(A,\overline{\pi})$, $\{x,y\} \cap T(A,\pi) \neq \{x,y\} \cap T(A,\overline{\pi})$: a contradiction to the conclusion of $IIA(H_0)$.

Now, we will argue that $IIA(H_1)$ implies $IIA(H_0)$. Assume to the contrary that $IIA(H_1)$ is satisfied and $B \subseteq A \in \Omega$, $\pi_B = \overline{\pi}_B$, $B \cap T(A,\pi) \neq \emptyset$, $B \cap T(A,\overline{\pi}) \neq \emptyset$ and $B \cap T(A,\pi) \neq B \cap T(A,\overline{\pi})$. Without loss of generality we can assume that there exists $x \in B \cap T(A,\pi)$ such that $x \notin B \cap T(A,\overline{\pi})$. But, $B \cap T(A,\overline{\pi}) \neq \emptyset$. Thus, there exists $y \in B \cap T(A,\overline{\pi})$. Since $\pi_B = \overline{\pi}_B$, we have $\pi_{\{x,y\}} = \overline{\pi}_{\{x,y\}}$ and $y \in T(A,\overline{\pi})$, $x \in B \subseteq A$ and $x \notin T(A,\overline{\pi})$. By $IIA(H_1)$, $x \notin T(A,\pi)$. This contradicts $x \in B \cap T(A,\pi)$.

[18] $IIA(H_1)$ and $IIA(H_2)$ are Denicolò's (1993) independence and weak independence conditions, respectively.

The next two lemmas bring out a special relationship between $IIA(H_3)$ and $R^+(A,\pi)$.

Lemma 1 *Let Ω satisfy FA with $\{A\} = \Omega$ and let the Paretian SCF T satisfy MIT and $IIA(H_3)$. Then, $R^+(A,\pi)$ satisfies IIA (A) (Arrow's Independence of Irrelevant Alternatives).*

Proof. Since there is no ambiguity under *FA*, we will omit the "*A*" in the description of $R^+(A,\pi)$. Without any loss of generality, assume to the contrary that there exist[19] $x,y \in A$ and profiles π and $\overline{\pi}$ such that $\pi_{\{x,y\}} = \overline{\pi}_{\{x,y\}}$, $xP^+(\pi)y$ and $yR^+(\overline{\pi})x$. Now, (using the fact that T is Paretian) $xP^+(\pi)y$ implies that $\{x\} = T(A,\pi^+(x,y))$. By $IIA(H_3)$, since $\pi^+_{\{x,y\}}(x,y) = \pi_{\{x,y\}} = \overline{\pi}_{\{x,y\}} = \overline{\pi}^+_{\{x,y\}}(x,y)$, $y \notin T(A,\overline{\pi}^{\,+}(x,y))$. This contradicts $yR^+(\overline{\pi})x$. □

Lemma 2 *Let Ω satisfy FA with $\{A\} = \Omega$ and let the SCF T be Paretian and satisfy MIT: (2.1) T satisfies $IIA(H_3)$ implies $R^+(\pi)$ satisfies acyclicity.*[20] *(2.2) T satisfies $IIA(H_2)$ implies $R^+(\pi)$ is quasi-transitive. (2.3) T satisfies $IIA(H_1)$ implies $R^+(\pi)$ is transitive.*

Proof. We will prove (2.1). The proofs of (2.2) and (2.3) are similar and can be found in Denicolò (1993).

Assume to the contrary that there exists $B = \{x_1,x_2,\ldots,x_k\} \subseteq A$ and a profile π such that $x_1P^+(\pi)x_2, x_2P^+(\pi)x_3,\ldots,x_{k-1}P^+(\pi)x_k$ and $x_kP^+(\pi)x_1$. Consider a profile $\widetilde{\pi}$ created from π by raising the set of alternatives in B to the top of every individual's ordering as follows: (a) $\widetilde{\pi}_B = \pi_B$, (b) $\widetilde{\pi}_{X-B} = \pi_{X-B}$, (c) N: $[B][rest]$. By the definition of $\widetilde{\pi}$, for any pair of alternatives $x,y \in B$: $\widetilde{\pi}_{\{x,y\}} = \pi_{\{x,y\}} = \pi^+_{\{x,y\}}(x,y)$. Now, using Lemma 1 and the fact that T is Paretian, $x_{m-1}P^+(\pi)x_m$, $m = 2,3\ldots,k$, implies $\{x_{m-1}\} = T(A,\pi^+(x_m,x_{m-1})$ by $IIA(H_3)$, $x_m \notin T(A,\widetilde{\pi})$ for all $m = 2,3,\ldots,k$. Similarly, using $x_kP^+(\pi)x_1$, $x_1 \notin T(A,\widetilde{\pi})$. By our construction of $\widetilde{\pi}$ this contradicts the fact that T is Paretian and selects a non-empty subset of A. □

The next result shows that a Paretian *SCF* model satisfying $IIA(H_1)$ and Arrow's extended model *if it is restricted* to a single agenda are, in the sense described below, "mathematically equivalent."

Proposition 8 *Let Ω be nontrivial and satisfy FA with $\{A\} = \Omega$.*

(i) *For a Paretian SCF T satisfying MIT, if $IIA(H_1)$ holds for T then $R^+(\pi)$ satisfies WP, $IIA(A)$, $R^+(\pi)$ is transitive and connected on A and $T(A) = C(A,R^+(\pi))$.*

[19] If either x or y does not belong to A, then for all profiles the two alternatives would be unrelated under $R^+(A,\pi)$ and thus $IIA(A)$ would not fail.

[20] $IIA(H_3)$ does not in fact imply that $R^+(\pi)$ is quasi-transitive. To see this let $X = A = \{x,y,z\}$, $N = \{1,2,3,4\}$ and define T as follows: $T(A,\pi) = \{x :$ for all $y \in A$, not $yQ(\pi)x\}$ where $Q(\pi)$ is given by $xQ(\pi)y$ iff under the profile π, three out of the four individuals strictly prefer x to y. Similarly, it is possible to construct choice functions to show that $IIA(H_2)$ does not imply the transitivity of $R^+(\pi)$.

(ii) *If $R(\pi)$ is a SPF with MIT such that R satisfies WP, IIA(A), R is transitive and connected on A and if $T(A) = C(A, R)$ then T satisfies $IIA(H_1)$.*

Proof

(i) Since T is Paretian that R^+ satisfies *WP* is immediate. By Lemmas 1 and 2 all that we will need to show is that $IIA(H_1)$ implies $T(A) = C(A, R^+(\pi))$.

First, we show that $C(A, R^+(\pi)) \subseteq T(A, \pi)$. If $x \in C(A, R^+(\pi))$ and $x \notin T(A, \pi)$, then there exist $y \in T(A, \pi)$ and $x \in (A - T(A, \pi))$. Consider $\pi^+(x, y)$ obtained by raising $\{x, y\}$ to the top of all orderings. By the definition of $R^+(\pi)$ and using $x \in C(A, R^+(\pi))$ we get $x \in T(A, \pi^+(x, y))$, but since $\pi^+_{\{x,y\}}(x, y) = \pi_{\{x,y\}}$, using $IIA(H_1)$, this contradicts $y \in T(A, \pi)$ and $x \in (A - T(A, \pi))$. To complete the proof we will show that $T(A, \pi) \subseteq C(A, R^+(\pi))$. Assume to the contrary that $x \in T(A, \pi)$ and there exists some $y \in A$ such that $yP^+(\pi)x$. This implies that $y \in T(A, \pi^+(x, y))$ and $x \in A - T(A, \pi^+(x, y))$. Since $\pi^+_{\{x,y\}}(x, y) = \pi_{\{x,y\}}$, this together with $IIA(H_1)$ contradicts $x \in T(A, \pi)$.

(ii) Consider two profiles π and $\overline{\pi}$ in the P-domain such that $\pi_{\{x,y\}} = \overline{\pi}_{\{x,y\}}$. Assume to the contrary that $x \in T(A, \pi) = C(A, R(\pi))$, $y \in (A - T(A, \pi)) = (A - C(A, R(\pi))$ and $y \in T(A, \overline{\pi}) = C(A, R(\overline{\pi}))$. By $IIA(A)$, since $\pi_{\{x,y\}} = \overline{\pi}_{\{x,y\}}$, since $xR(\pi)y$ iff $xR(\overline{\pi})y$. Thus, $y \in C(A, R(\overline{\pi}))$ implies $yR(\pi)x$. This contradicts that $x \in C(A, R(\pi))$ and $y \in (A - C(A, R(\pi))$ and $R(\pi)$is an ordering. □

Remark 1 *Replacing* $IIA(H_1)$ with $IIA(H_2)$, *transitivity with quasi-transitivity and* $T(.,.) = C(.,.)$ *with* $T(.,.) \subseteq C(.,.)$, *a result similar to Proposition 8 (i) can be proved. The relationship between* $IIA(H_2)$ *and Gibbard's* Oligarchy Theorem *(see Sen 1970) along the lines of Proposition 8 (ii) can also be established.*

It is clear from the last proposition and the remark following it that standard results such as Arrow's *GPT* or Gibbard's *Oligarchy Theorem* (see Sen 1970) should lead us to corresponding results in this fixed agenda structurally nonbinary *SCF* framework.[21] The following results are in Denicolò (1993):

Theorem 1 (Denicolò) *Let Ω be nontrivial and satisfy FA with $\{A\} = \Omega$, and let the SCF T be Paretian and satisfy UD. Then, if T satisfies $IIA(H_1)$, T is dictatorial.*

Theorem 2 (Denicolò) *Let Ω be nontrivial and satisfy FA with $\{A\} = \Omega$, and let the SCF T be Paretian and satisfy UD. Then, if T satisfies $IIA(H_2)$, T is oligarchic.*

6.2. Social Choice with a Fixed Agenda: Sen's Approach to the Independence Condition

We have argued (Proposition 8) that Hansson's (1969) approach to the fixed agenda social choice problem leads to a mathematical structure that is equivalent to an

[21] Clearly, "veto" theorems depending on acyclicity can also be proved. These, however, would entail additional concepts and notation to describe different types of "monotonicity" for the *SCF* and are not pursued here.

"extended version" of Arrow's model. Next, we examine an alternative approach to the "independence" condition proposed by Sen (1993) in the context of a fixed agenda. Additional discussions of this approach can also be found in Denicolò (1998).

Definition 8 *For any set of profiles* $\mathcal{P}$ *and any set of individuals L let the subprofiles representing restrictions of* $\pi \in \mathcal{P}$ *to L and* $(N - L)$ *be represented by* π^L, π^{N-L}, *respectively, so that* $\pi = (\pi^L, \pi^{N-L}) \in \mathcal{P}$.

(8.1) $IIA(S_1)$ *is satisfied if the following condition holds for every* $A \in \Omega$ *and all* $\overline{\mathcal{P}}$ *subset of the P-domain of the choice function such that for all* $\pi \in \overline{\mathcal{P}}$ *and all* $i \in L{:}\, xP_iy$. *If for* every *profile* π *in the P-domain of the choice function there* exists *a profile* $(\overline{\pi}^L, \overline{\pi}^{N-L}) \in \overline{\mathcal{P}}$ *such that* $\overline{\pi}^{N-L}_{\{x,y\}} = \pi^{N-L}_{\{x,y\}}$, $x \in T(A, \overline{\pi})$ *and* $y \in (A - T(A, \overline{\pi}))$, *then L is decisive for x against y on A (i.e.,* $L \in D(x, y; A)$*).*

(8.2) $IIA(S_2)$ *is satisfied if the following conditions hold for every* $A \in \Omega$ *and all* $\overline{\mathcal{P}}$ *subset of the P-domain of the choice function such that for all* $\widehat{\pi} \in \overline{\mathcal{P}}$ *and all* $i \in L{:}\, x\widehat{P}_iy$.

(i) *If for every profile* π *in the P-domain of the choice function there exists a profile* $(\overline{\pi}^L, \overline{\pi}^{N-L}) \in \overline{\mathcal{P}}$ *such that* $\overline{\pi}^{N-L}_{\{x,y\}} = \pi^{N-L}_{\{x,y\}}$, $x \in T(A, \overline{\pi})$ *and* $y \in (A - T(A, \overline{\pi}))$, *then L has a veto for x against y on A (i.e.,* $L \in V(x, y; A)$*).*

and

(ii) *If for every profile* π *in the P-domain of the choice function there exists a profile* $(\overline{\pi}^L, \overline{\pi}^{N-L}) \in \overline{\mathcal{P}}$ *such that* $\overline{\pi}^{N-L}_{\{x,y\}} = \pi^{N-L}_{\{x,y\}}$, $\{x\} = T(A, \overline{\pi})$ *and* $y \in A$, *then L is decisive for x against y on A (i.e.,* $L \in D(x, y; A)$*).*

$IIA(S_1)$ is Sen (1993) "independent decisiveness." Sen explains the intuition underlying the condition on as follows:

> *To explain the requirement in another way, if the ability of members of group G, all of whom prefer x to y, to secure rejection of y in the presence of x in S were to change with the alteration in the individual rankings of alternatives other than x and y, then the power of rejection decisiveness would fail to be independent of irrelevant alternatives. (Sen 1993, p. 511)*

The condition $IIA(S_2)$ is a weaker version of $IIA(S_1)$: under some of the circumstances under which $IIA(S_1)$ would imply "local decisiveness," $IIA(S_2)$ can be satisfied with the weaker implication of "local veto power."

These two conditions $IIA(S_1)$ and $IIA(S_2)$ will be used to prove dictatorship and oligarchy theorems, which are versions of the results in Sen (1993, pp. 511–512).[22]

Theorem 3 *Let* Ω *be nontrivial and satisfy FA, and let T be a Paretian SCF with a P-domain satisfying MIT. Then, T satisfies* $IIA(S_1)$ *iff T is dictatorial.*

[22] As we did with Hansson's (1969) approach, to avoid the burden of additional concepts and complex notation, we choose not to investigate "veto" versions of impossibility theorems using Sen's approach.

Theorem 4 *Let Ω be nontrivial and satisfy FA, and let T be a Paretian SCF with a P-domain satisfying MIT. Then, T satisfies IIA(S_2) iff T is oligarchic.*

For a direct proof of the sufficiency part of Theorem 3 see Sen (1993). Here we provide a proof of Theorem 4 that with a minor modification also becomes, *inter alia*, a proof of Theorem 3 (see Remark 2 following the proof of Theorem 4).

Lemma 3 *Let Ω be nontrivial and satisfy FA, and let T be a Paretian SCF with a P-domain satisfying MIT. If IIA(S_2) is satisfied, then for all $x, y \in A$: (i) $L \in D(x, y; A)$ implies $L \in D(A)$. (ii) $L \in V(x, y; A)$ implies $L \in V(A)$.*

Proof. Let $z \in A - \{x, y\}$ and consider a subset of the P-domain of T given by the set of profiles $\overline{\mathcal{P}}$ as follows:

$$L \quad : \quad xyz[rest]$$
$$N - L \quad : \quad y[zx][rest].$$

T is Paretian implies that for all $\overline{\pi} \in \overline{\mathcal{P}}$: $T(A, \overline{\pi})$ equals either $\{x\}$ or $\{y\}$ or $\{x, y\}$. Using this together with $L \in D(x, y; A)$ (resp., $L \in V(x, y; A)$) we get $\{x\} = T(A, \overline{\pi})$ (resp., $x \in T(A, \overline{\pi})$ and $z \in A - T(A, \overline{\pi})$).

Since the relation between x and z is unspecified, for members of $(N - L)$, for any profile π in the P-domain of T it is possible to find a $\overline{\pi} \in \overline{\mathcal{P}}$ such that $\overline{\pi}^{(N-L)}_{\{x,z\}} = \pi^{(N-L)}_{\{x,z\}}$ and $\{x\} = T(A, \overline{\pi})$ (resp., $x \in T(A, \overline{\pi})$ and $z \in (A - T(A, \overline{\pi}))$. Thus, we can use *IIA*$(S_2)$ to get $L \in D(x, z; A)$ (resp., $L \in V(x, z; A)$).

Similarly, using the profiles:

$$L \quad : \quad zxy[rest]$$
$$N - L \quad : \quad [yz]x[rest]$$

we can conclude that $L \in D(x, y; A)$ (resp., $L \in V(x, y; A)$) implies $L \in D(z, y; A)$ (resp., $L \in V(z, y; A)$).

The standard technique can now be used to prove $L \in D(A)$ (resp., $L \in V(A)$). □

Lemma 4 *Let Ω be nontrivial and satisfy FA, and let T be a Paretian SCF with a P-domain satisfying MIT. If IIA(S_2) is satisfied then, $L_1, L_2 \in D(A)$ implies $L_1 \cap L_2 \in D(A)$.*

Proof. Let x, y, z be distinct alternatives in A. Consider a subset of the P-domain of T given by the set of profiles $\overline{\mathcal{P}}$ as follows:

$$L_1 \cap L_2 \quad : \quad xyz[rest]$$
$$L_1 - (L_1 \cap L_2) \quad : \quad y[zx][rest]$$
$$L_2 - (L_1 \cap L_2) \quad : \quad [xz]y[rest]$$
$$N - (L_1 \cup L_2) \quad : \quad [xyz][rest].$$

For all $\overline{\pi} \in \overline{\mathcal{P}}$, $L_1 \in D(A)$ and $L_2 \in D(A)$ imply $y, z \in A - T(A, \overline{\pi})$. Since T is Paretian, $\{x\} = T(A, \overline{\pi})$. Since, the relationship between z and x is unspecified for members of $N - (L_1 \cap L_2)$, for any profile π in the P-domain of T it is possible to find a $\overline{\pi} \in \overline{\mathcal{P}}$ such that $\overline{\pi}^{N-(L_1 \cap L_2)}_{\{x,z\}} = \pi^{N-(L_1 \cap L_2)}_{\{x,z\}}$ and $T(A, \overline{\pi}) = \{x\}$. By $IIA(S_2)$, $L_1 \cap L_2 \in D(x, z; A)$. By Lemma 3, $L_1 \cap L_2 \in D(A)$. □

Proof of Theorem 4. Let L_0 be given by the intersection of all the sets in $D(A)$. T is Paretian implies $D(A)$ is nonempty, hence, using Lemma 4,[23] L_0 is unique, nonempty, and well-defined. We will argue that L_0 is an oligarchy.

By Lemma 4, it is clear that $L_0 \in D(A)$. If L_0 is a singleton, we are done and the member of L_0 is a dictator. If L_0 is not a singleton, then to establish that L_0 is an oligarchy we need to show that every member $v \in L_0$ is a vetoer on A. Select any $v \in L_0$ (i.e., any v that belongs to every set in $D(A)$) and consider the following subset of the P-domain of T consisting of the profiles $\overline{\mathcal{P}}$ given by:

$$N - \{v\} \quad : \quad x[yz][rest]$$
$$\{v\} \quad : \quad [zx]y[rest].$$

Since T is Paretian, for all $\overline{\pi} \in \overline{\mathcal{P}}$, $T(A, \overline{\pi}) \subseteq \{x, z\}$. Consider the two mutually exclusive and exhaustive possibilities:

A. There exists a profile $\hat{\pi}$ in the P-domain of T such that for every profile $\overline{\pi} \in \overline{\mathcal{P}}$, $\overline{\pi}^{N-\{v\}}_{\{y,z\}} = \hat{\pi}^{N-\{v\}}_{\{y,z\}}$ implies $\{x\} = T(A, \overline{\pi})$.

B. For every profile π in the P-domain of T there exists $\overline{\pi} \in \overline{\mathcal{P}}$ (possibly depending on π) such that $\pi^{N-\{v\}}_{\{y,z\}} = \overline{\pi}^{N-\{v\}}_{\{y,z\}}$ and $z \in T(A, \overline{\pi})$.

A. Since in defining $\overline{\mathcal{P}}$ the relationship between y and z for individuals in $N - \{v\}$ is not specified there exists $\tilde{\pi} \in \overline{\mathcal{P}}$ such that $\tilde{\pi}^{N-\{v\}}_{\{y,z\}} = \hat{\pi}^{N-\{v\}}_{\{y,z\}}$. Consider the subset $\tilde{\mathcal{P}}$ of $\overline{\mathcal{P}}$ given by $\pi \in \overline{\mathcal{P}}$ such that $\tilde{\pi}^{N-\{v\}}_{\{y,z\}} = \hat{\pi}^{N-\{v\}}_{\{y,z\}}$. Since in this case (case **A**) for every profile $\overline{\pi} \in \overline{\mathcal{P}}$, $\overline{\pi}^{N-\{v\}}_{\{y,z\}} = \hat{\pi}^{N-\{v\}}_{\{y,z\}}$ implies $\{x\} = T(A, \overline{\pi})$. In particular, we have:

$$\text{For all } \tilde{\pi} \in \tilde{\mathcal{P}} \subseteq \overline{\mathcal{P}} : \{x\} = T(A, \tilde{\pi}). \tag{1}$$

However, notice that for all $\tilde{\pi} \in \tilde{\mathcal{P}} \subseteq \overline{\mathcal{P}}$: for all $i \in N - \{v\}$, $xP_i z$ and moreover, the relation between x and z is unspecified for individual $\{v\}$ for all $\overline{\pi} \in \tilde{\mathcal{P}} \subseteq \overline{\mathcal{P}}$. It follows that for any π in the P-domain of T there exists $(\tilde{\pi}^{N-\{v\}}, \overline{\pi}^{\{v\}}) \in \tilde{\mathcal{P}}$ such that $\overline{\pi}^{\{v\}}_{\{x,z\}} = \pi^{\{v\}}_{\{x,z\}}$ and by (1): $T(A, (\tilde{\pi}^{N-\{v\}}, \overline{\pi}^{\{v\}})) = \{x\}$. Applying (ii) of $IIA(S_2)$,

[23] We are also using the finiteness of N and hence the finiteness of $D(A)$.

$(N-\{v\}) \in D(x,z;A)$. By Lemma 3 (i), $(N-\{v\}) \in D(A)$. This contradicts the fact that v belongs to the intersection of all the sets in $D(A)$. Thus, **B** must be true.

B. For every profile π in the P-domain of T there exists $\overline{\pi} \in \overline{\mathcal{P}}$ (possibly depending on π) such that $\pi_{\{y,z\}}^{N-\{v\}} = \overline{\pi}_{\{y,z\}}^{N-\{v\}}$ and $z \in T(A,\overline{\pi})$ and $y \in A - T(A,\overline{\pi})$. Since we have $zP_v y$ for all $\pi \in \overline{\mathcal{P}}$ by (i) in $IIA(S_2)$, $\{v\} \in V(z,y;A)$. By Lemma 3 (ii), $\{v\} \in V(A)$. This completes the proof of the "sufficiency" part of the theorem.

To complete the proof of the theorem we still need to show that if L_0 is an oligarchy then $IIA(S_2)$ is satisfied.

Assume to the contrary that some nonempty subset L_0 of N is an oligarchy and $IIA(S_2)$ is violated. This implies that either condition (i) in $IIA(S_2)$ is violated or condition (ii) in $IIA(S_2)$ is violated.

Case 1 If (i) in $IIA(S_2)$ is violated, then there exist an $L \subseteq N$ and a set of profiles $\overline{\mathcal{P}}$ such that for all profiles in $\overline{\mathcal{P}}$ and for all $i \in L$: $xP_i y$ and for every profile π in the P-domain of the choice function there exists a profile $(\overline{\pi}^L, \overline{\pi}^{N-L}) \in \overline{\mathcal{P}}$, such that $\overline{\pi}_{\{x,y\}}^{N-L} = \pi_{\{x,y\}}^{N-L}$, $x \in T(A,\overline{\pi})$ and $y \in (A - T(A,\overline{\pi}))$, and $L \notin V(x,y;A)$.

In particular, this has two implications:

Firstly, since $L \notin V(x,y;A)$, no individual member of L belongs to $V(x,y;A)$. This implies that no member of L is a member of the oligarchy L_0. Thus,

$$L_0 \subseteq (N-L) \tag{2}$$

Secondly, by MIT, there exists $(\overline{\pi}^L, \overline{\pi}^{N-L}) \in \overline{\mathcal{P}}$ such that:

$$\text{for all } i \in N-L,\ y\overline{P}_i x \text{ and } x \in T(A,\overline{\pi}) \text{ and } y \in (A - T(A,\overline{\pi})) \tag{3}$$

Using (2) for all $i \in L_0$, $y\overline{P}_i x$ when (3) is true. But, we also know that since L_0 is an oligarchy, $L_0 \in D(A)$, this contradicts $x \in T(A,\overline{\pi})$ in (3).

Case 2 If (ii) in $IIA(S_2)$ is violated then for some $L \subseteq N$ and a set of profiles $\overline{\mathcal{P}}$ such that for all profiles in $\overline{\mathcal{P}}$ for all $i \in L$: $xP_i y$ and for every profile π in the P-domain of the choice function there exists a profile $(\overline{\pi}^L, \overline{\pi}^{N-L}) \in \overline{\mathcal{P}}$ such that $\overline{\pi}_{\{x,y\}}^{N-L} = \pi_{\{x,y\}}^{N-L}$, $T(A,\overline{\pi}) = \{x\}$ and $L \notin D(x,y;A)$).

Consider two subcases: (a) $(N-L) \cap L_0 = \emptyset$, or (b) $(N-L) \cap L_0 \neq \emptyset$.

(a) implies $L_0 \subseteq L$, and since $L_0 \in D(A)$, this will contradict $L \notin D(x,y;A)$.

(b) This case, too, is impossible, since every member in L_0 is a vetoer and there exists some member of L_0 in $(N-L)$, and by our assumption of MIT on the P-domain, the preference of $i \in (N-L) \cap L_0$ can take the form $yP_i x$ for some $\overline{\pi} \in \overline{\mathcal{P}}$; this contradicts $\{x\} = T(A,\overline{\pi})$ for some such $\overline{\pi}$. □

Remark 2 *Note that in the above proof of Theorem 4, using $IIA(S_1)$ instead of $IIA(S_2)$ would lead to $\{v\} \in D(z,y;A)$ and hence $\{v\} \in D(A)$ (by Lemma 3) establishing the "sufficiency" part of Theorem 3. The proof of necessity of $IIA(S_1)$ in Theorem 3 is similar to that of the case (i) above in the necessity part of the proof of Theorem 4.*

Remark 3 *The two parts, (i) and (ii), of $IIA(S_2)$ are independent of each other, in that neither can be derived from the other. Without either part an oligarchy may fail to exist. This is illustrated in the following examples:*

Example 1 Let $X = A = \{x_1, x_2, x_3\}$, $\Omega = \{A\}$ and $N = \{1,2,3\}$. Let the SCF be given as follows: if individual 1 is indifferent between all three alternatives, then the alternative x_1 picked; otherwise, all Pareto undominated alternatives are chosen. This satisfies $IIA(S_2)$ (ii) but not $IIA(S_2)$ (i).[24] Only individual 1 is a vetoer, but 1 is not decisive. (Only the grand coalition is decisive.) Hence, an oligarchy does not exist.

Example 2 Let $X = A = \{x_1, x_2, x_3\}$, $\Omega = \{A\}$ and $N = \{1,2,3\}$. Let the SCF be given as follows: if individual 1 is not indifferent between all three alternatives, then individual 2's best elements are picked; otherwise, all the alternatives are selected. This satisfies $IIA(S_2)$ (i) but not $IIA(S_2)$ *(ii)*.[25] Only individual 2 is a vetoer, but 2 is not decisive. (Only N and $\{1,2\}$ are decisive.) Thus, an oligarchy does not exist.

Remark 4 *In contrast with Hansson's (1969) approach, which gives us sufficient conditions for impossibility results, the type of independence conditions suggested by Sen (1993) is both necessary and sufficient for dictatorship and oligarchy theorems. In particular, note that Theorems 1 and 3 together imply that for Paretian SCFs that satisfy MIT, $IIA(H_1)$ implies $IIA(S_1)$ and Theorems 2 and 4 together imply that $IIA(H_2)$ implies $IIA(S_2)$. The following example shows that the converse implications are not true.*

Example 3 Let $X = A = \{x_1, x_2, x_3\}$, $\Omega = \{A\}$ and $N = \{1,2,3,4\}$. Consider the rule $T(A,\pi)$, which selects that subset of individual 1's top ranked alternatives that a majority

[24] To see that it violates $IIA(S_2)$ *(i)* consider the profiles:

$$\{2\} \;:\; x_2 x_3 x_1$$

$$\{1,3\} \;:\; x_3 [x_2 x_1].$$

Under our rule, x_2 (and x_3) would be picked and x_1 rejected. Since the preference between x_2 and x_1 is unspecified for $\{1,3\}$ by $IIA(S_2)$ *(i)*, $\{2\}$ should have a veto for x_2 against x_1. However, $\{2\}$ has no such veto, since under the specified rule whenever $\{1\}$ is indifferent between all alternatives the singleton $\{x_1\}$ is selected.

[25] To see that it violates $IIA(S_2)$ (ii) consider the profiles:

$$\{2\} \;:\; x_2 x_3 x_1$$

$$\{1,3\} \;:\; x_3 [x_2 x_1].$$

Under our rule, x_2 alone would be selected. Since the preference between x_2 and x_1 is unspecified for $\{1,3\}$ by $IIA(S_2)$ *(ii)*, $\{2\}$ should be decisive for x_2 against x_1. However, $\{2\}$ is not decisive, since under the specified rule whenever $\{1\}$ is indifferent between all alternatives the $\{x_1, x_2, x_3\}$ is selected.

of the individuals consider to be (weakly) better than all the other best alternatives of individual 1, should such a nonempty subset exist; otherwise, $T(A,\pi)$ consists of all of individual 1's top ranked alternatives. Clearly, individual 1 is a dictator. Now, consider a profile in which individual 1 is indifferent between all elements of X and the standard Latin Square profile over the other three individuals occurs.[26] In this case, it is easy to see that $R^{+}(A,\pi)$(see Definition 7) violates acyclicity. By Lemma 2, $IIA(H_i)$, $i = 1,2,3$ are violated. But, since 1 is a dictator, by Theorems 3 and 4, $IIA(S_1)$ and $IIA(S_2)$ are satisfied.

Theorems 1, 2, 3, and 4 of this section provide the basis of the multi-agenda results discussed in the next section.

7. DICTATORSHIP AND OLIGARCHY: WITH MULTIPLE AGENDAS

Let us now turn to the general case where Ω may contain more than one element. We have seen in the last section how "intra-agenda independence conditions" can be used to show the existence of dictatorial and oligarchic power *on some specific agenda A*. To what extent is this type of asymmetric distribution of power "contagious"? Does this type of dictatorial or oligarchic power necessarily spread to all agendas in Ω? To understand the intuition underlying extensions of dictatorship and oligarchy results to multi-agenda contexts, consider the following example:

Example 4 Let $N = \{1,2,3\}$, $X = \{x_1,x_2,x_3,x_4,x_5\}$, $\Omega = \{A_1,A_2\}$ where $A_1 = \{x_1,x_2,x_3\}$ and $A_2 = \{x_4,x_5\}$. Let $T(A_1,\pi)$ be the set of best elements of individual 1 and let $T(A_2,\pi)$ be the Condorcet winner(s) in A_2.

Clearly, 1 is just a "local" dictator. By "adding" more alternatives to X and more pairs to Ω the example is easily modified where no dictator exists on almost all agendas. Alternatively, one may modify the example where different individuals are only "local" dictators on different agendas.[27] In either case the *SCF* will not be dictatorial. Thus, the oligarchy and dictatorship results can be extended to the multi-agenda case only if additional restrictions are imposed. We will consider two types of conditions:

(a) Inter-agenda "consistency" conditions: conditions requiring choice from different agendas be consistent.

(b) Inter-agenda "relatedness" conditions: the different agendas must in some sense have elements in "common" for one to be able to relate choices from one agenda to choices from another so that the "consistency" conditions have some bite. For

[26] Our rule tells us that in this case X (which is individual 1's set of best elements) is picked.

[27] This, indeed, may be considered to be a good thing. See Sen's formulation of minimal liberty as "local dictatorships" of two individuals in their "personal spheres" (Sen 1970, 1976, 1992).

instance, in Example 4, consistency conditions alone can have little significance because the alternatives in the two agendas do not overlap at all.

We have already introduced the two types of conditions that accomplish (a) and (b). For (a), we have different rationality ("consistency") conditions in the form of different types of revealed preference axioms (*WARP*, α, δ^*, etc.). For (b), we have various Fe-domain conditions (pairwise complete, covered, connected, etc.) imposing restrictions on Ω. Indeed, we have argued that these two types of conditions are closely related to the two basic conceptions of nonbinary social choice. To establish the main results of this section, from the various Fe-domain conditions that we have defined, we will use one of the weakest restrictions consistent with nonbinariness of Ω: connectedness (see Proposition 1). But, what about consistency?

Sen (1993) has argued that the usual rationale that underlies the use of consistency conditions in the theory of consumer behavior in economics may not extend to other contexts. He cites Buchanan's (1954) argument that since society is not an organic entity, "social preference" is an amorphous concept and it (i.e., the notion of social preference) should not be used to justify imposing consistency requirements on social choice. He argues that any such "internal" consistency requirement needs to be justified in terms of an external reference. In what follows we do not try to justify the use of consistency conditions in social choice by using specific external norms, but rather we make explicit the *informational basis* of certain consistency conditions that are not only sufficient but are also *necessary* for proving versions of Arrow's and Gibbard's theorems in the multi-agenda social choice model. Clearly, one's *normative* judgment as to the appropriateness of this informational basis will determine how compelling one finds nonbinary versions of dictatorship and oligarchy results in the multi-agenda case.

Definition 9 *A Paretian SCF, T, satisfies a* Pareto Restricted Weak Axiom of Revealed Preference (P-WARP) *iff for all $x, y \in X$, all $A_1, A_2 \in \Omega$ and all* linear *preference profiles*[28] *π in the P-domain of the choice function such that $\pi = \pi^+(x,y)$, if $x \in T(A_1,\pi)$ and $y \in (A_1 - T(A_1,\pi))$, then $x \in A_2$ implies $y \notin T(A_2,\pi)$.*[29]

The condition tells us that *if x and y are either the best or the second best alternative for all individuals, then which of the two is picked (from any set containing both) by a Paretian SCF should not depend on what other alternatives are contained in the feasibility set.* Clearly, *P-WARP* is implied by *WARP*.[30] However, *P-WARP* is weaker because it uses the

[28] By linear preference profiles we mean preference profiles consisting of linear orderings (i.e., preference orderings that do not permit individual indifference over distinct alternatives).

[29] Notice that in Definition 9, for Paretian *SCF*'s, ($x \in T(A_1,\pi)$ and $y \in (A_1 - T(A_1,\pi))$) is in fact equivalent to $\{x\} = T(A_1,\pi)$.

[30] Recall that *WARP* tells us that for *any* profile in the P-domain of T, if x is picked and y is rejected in some agenda, then at the same profile y is never picked in any other agenda in the presence of x.

Pareto criterion to limit the *WARP*-like consistency requirement by restricting its applicability to only those *linear* profiles where all *other* alternatives are Pareto dominated by the pair of alternatives under consideration.[31] Notice, too, that our condition also has similarities with Hansson's (1969) independence condition (see Definition 6.2). However, unlike typical "independence" conditions, *P-WARP* is a "true" consistency condition in that it entails only inter-agenda choice comparisons for a *fixed* preference profile.

We have shown (see Propositions 2 and 4) that conditions weaker than WARP (such as *ACA*) are consistent with the choice function being nonbinary while *WARP* itself is not. The following result establishes that *P-WARP* is weaker than *ACA* and unlike *WARP* is consistent with nonbinary choice:

The following proposition clarifies the relation between *P-WARP* and the conditions in Definition 10, when Ω is covered.

Proposition 9 *Let Ω be covered. Then, for any Paretian SCF, T,*

$$ACA \to (\alpha \text{ and } \delta^*) \to P\text{-}WARP$$

Proof. The first implication follows from Proposition 2. To complete the proof we need to show that (α and δ^*) imply *P-WARP*. Assume to the contrary that for a Paretian *SCF*, T, there exists a *linear* preference profile π in the P-domain of the choice function such that for some $A_1, A_2 \in \Omega$ and for some $x, y \in X$, $\pi = \pi^+(x, y)$, $x \in T(A_1, \pi)$, $y \in (A_1 - T(A_1, \pi)$, $x \in A_2$, and $y \in T(A_2, \pi)$. Since Ω is covered there exists $B \in \Omega$ such that $A_1 \cup A_2 \subseteq B$. Using α, that $x \in T(A_1, \pi)$, $y \in (A_1 - T(A_1, \pi))$ and the fact that T is Paretian, we get $\{x\} = T(B, \pi)$. But, this together with δ^* implies $y \notin T(A_2, \pi)$. This contradicts $y \in T(A_2, \pi)$. □

We state two results, a dictatorship result and an oligarchy result, that apply in the multiple-agenda context when the Fe-domain is nonbinary (i.e., Ω includes no pairs).

Theorem 5 *Let Ω be nontrivial, strictly nonbinary, and connected and let T be a Paretian SCF with a P-domain satisfying MIT. Then, T satisfies $IIA(S_1)$ and P-WARP iff T is dictatorial.*

Theorem 6 *Let Ω be nontrivial, strictly nonbinary, and connected and let T be a Paretian SCF with a P-domain satisfying MIT. Then, T satisfies $IIA(S_2)$ and P-WARP iff T is oligarchic.*

Lemma 5 *Let Ω be nontrivial and strictly nonbinary, and let T be a Paretian SCF with a P-domain satisfying MIT, $IIA(S_2)$, and P-WARP. If for some $A, B \in \Omega$, $|A \cap B| \geq 2$, $L_0 \in D(A)$, then $L_0 \in D(B)$.*

[31] Pareto modification of a rationality condition is not new. "Pareto-transitivity" conditions have been used very effectively in the context of "contagion" results in Arrow's social preference framework in the elegant work by Bloomfield (1971). Definition (7.3) is an example of a Pareto modified independence condition. For *P-WARP*, additionally, linearity of the preference profile is being required.

Proof. Assume to the contrary that $L_0 \in D(A)$ and $L_0 \notin D(B)$. By Theorem 4 there exists an oligarchy $\overline{L}_0 \subseteq N$, $\overline{L}_0 \neq L_0$ such that $\overline{L}_0 \in D(B)$ and for all $\overline{v} \in \overline{L}_0$, $\{\overline{v}\} \in V(B)$. This together with $L_0 \notin D(B)$ implies that there exists $\overline{v} \in \overline{L}_0 - L_0$ and $\{\overline{v}\} \in V(B)$. Consider a linear preference profile π such that for some distinct $x, y \in A \cap B$ and all $z \in X - \{x, y\}$, both x and y Pareto dominate z, and for all $i \in L_0$, xP_iy and for all $j \in N - L_0$, yP_jx. (In particular this implies $yP_{\overline{v}}x$.) Thus, since $\{\overline{v}\} \in V(B)$ and since T is Paretian, we have $y \in T(B, \pi)$. But, since $L_0 \in D(A)$ and T is Paretian, we have $x \in T(A, \pi)$ and $y \in (A - T(A, \pi))$. This contradicts *P-WARP*. □

Lemma 6 *Let Ω be nontrivial and strictly nonbinary, and let T be a Paretian SCF with a P-domain satisfying MIT, $IIA(S_2)$, and P-WARP. If for some $A, B \in \Omega$, $|A \cap B| \geq 2$, $L_0 \in D(B)$ and for all $v \in L_0$, $\{v\} \in V(B)$, then for all $v \in L_0, \{v\} \in V(A)$.*

Proof. Using Lemma 5, assume to the contrary that $L_0 \in D(A) \cap D(B)$ and there exists $v_0 \in L_0, \{v_0\} \in V(B)$ and $\{v_0\} \notin V(A)$. By Theorem 4 there exists $\overline{L}_0 \subseteq N$, $\overline{L}_0 \neq L_0$ such that $\overline{L}_0 \in D(A)$ and for all $v \in \overline{L}_0$, $\{v\} \in V(A)$. This implies $v_0 \in L_0 - \overline{L}_0$. Consider a linear preference profile π such that for some distinct $x, y \in A \cap B$ and all $z \in X - \{x, y\}$, both x and y Pareto dominate z and for all $i \in \overline{L}_0$, xP_iy and for all $j \in N - \overline{L}_0$, yP_jx. (In particular this implies $yP_{v_0}x$.) Thus, since $\{v_0\} \in V(B)$ and since T is Paretian we have $y \in T(B, \pi)$. But, since $\overline{L}_0 \in D(A)$ and T is Paretian we have $x \in T(A, \pi)$ and $y \in (A - T(A, \pi))$. This contradicts *P-WARP*. □

Proof of Theorem 6. We will first show sufficiency. By nontriviality and Theorem 4 we know that there exists $L_0 \subseteq N$ such that for some $A \in \Omega$, $L_0 \in D(A)$ and for all $v \in L_0$, $\{v\} \in V(A)$. For any $B \in \Omega$, by connectedness of Ω there exists a finite sequence $A = A_1, A_2, \ldots, A_m = B \in \Omega$ such that $|A_j \cap A_{j+1}| \geq 2$ for $j = 1, 2, \ldots, m-1$. Using Lemmas 5 and 6 for the pairs of feasible sets (A_j, A_{j+1}), $j = 1, 2, \ldots, m-1$, it follows that $L_0 \in D(B)$ and for all $v \in L_0$, $\{v\} \in V(B)$. This proves that L_0 is an oligarchy.

Next we turn to establishing necessity. For any $A \in \Omega$, the necessity of $IIA(S_2)$ has already been established in Theorem 4. We need to show that under the hypothesis of the theorem, if an oligarchy L_0 exists, then *P-WARP* is also necessarily satisfied.

Assume to the contrary that L_0 is an oligarchy and for some *linear* preference profile π in the P-domain of the choice function, there exists $A_1, A_2 \in \Omega$ and $x, y \in X$ such that $\pi = \pi^+(x, y)$, $x \in T(A_1, \pi)$ and $y \in (A_1 - T(A_1, \pi)$, $x \in A_2$ and $y \in T(A_2, \pi)$. Since T is Paretian, $\pi = \pi^+(x, y)$, $x \in T(A_1, \pi)$ and $y \in (A_1 - T(A_1, \pi))$ implies $T(A_1, \pi) = \{x\}$. Hence, since each member of L_0 has a veto and the preference profile π is linear, this implies that for all $i \in L_0$, xP_iy. But, since $L_0 \in D(A_2)$, we get $y \notin T(A_2, \pi)$. This contradicts $y \in T(A_2, \pi)$. □

Remark 5 *Slight changes to the argument above give us a proof of Theorem 5. By letting L_0 be a singleton, changing $IIA(S_2)$ to $IIA(S_1)$ in Lemma 5 and applying Theorem 3 instead* *of Theorem 4 in the above proof helps us establish the sufficiency part of Theorem 5. Since a dictatorship is also an oligarchy, the necessity of P-WARP in Theorem 5 follows as a corollary of Theorem 6.*

Next, we will provide two examples. Our first example (Example 5) shows that Theorems 5 and 6 cover some *SCF*s that are *doubly* nonbinary in the sense that the Fe-domain is nonbinary and that the scope of these theorems admit rules that (for some preference profiles) cannot be rationalized using a binary social preference relation. Our second example demonstrates the need for the assumption that the Fe-domain is *strictly* nonbinary in the hypothesis of Theorems 5 and 6. This example (Example 6) shows that if Ω is not restricted to being strictly nonbinary (i.e., if there are pairs in Ω) then the sufficiency parts of Theorems 5 and 6 may not hold.

Example 5 Let $X = \{x_1, x_2, x_3, x_4\}$ and let Ω consist of all sets with three or more alternatives and $N = \{1,2,3,4,5\}$. Let the *SCF* be as follows: if 1is not indifferent between all four alternatives, 1's best alternatives are picked from any feasible set. If 1 is indifferent between all the alternatives in X, then the Condorcet winners among the alternatives in the feasible set are picked (if such Condorcet winners exist). If a Condorcet winner does not exist, everything in the feasible set is selected. The choice function that is generated on Ω when 1 is indifferent between all the alternatives and a Latin Square profile with the four alternatives is used for the other four individuals does not satisfy *BR*.

Example 6 Let $X = \{x_1, x_2, x_3\}$ and let $\Omega = \{X, \{x_1, x_2\}\}$ and $N = \{1,2,3\}$. Let the *SCF* be as follows: on X individual 1's best elements are always picked. On $\{x_1, x_2\}$, individual 1's best elements are picked except in those profiles when $x_1 I_2 x_2$. If this (i.e., $x_1 I_2 x_2$) happens x_1 is selected. The *SCF* is Paretian, it satisfies[32] $IIA(S_1)$ and *P*-WARP but is not oligarchic. No individual has a veto for x_2 against x_1 on $\{x_1, x_2\}$.

Additional consistency conditions can, clearly, be used to get around the "need" for the assumption of strict nonbinariness of the Fe-domain Ω that has been illustrated in Example 6. For instance, by using δ^* we get the following corollary of Theorem 5.

Corollary 1 *Let Ω be nontrivial and connected, and let T be a Paretian SCF with a P-domain satisfying MIT. Then, T satisfies $IIA(S_1)$, P-WARP and δ^* implies T is dictatorial.*

To understand what is happening in the corollary, recall that since δ^* requires that if all of the chosen elements from a larger set are available, then anything rejected on the larger set will also be rejected on a smaller set. This requirement lets us "solve" the "problem" encountered in Example 6 by extending the local dictatorship result that holds for triples and larger sets (using Theorem 5) to agendas with just two elements.

[32] Note that the $IIA(S_1)$ requires that 1 be decisive for x_1 against x_2 but, in this case, cannot be applied to derive decisiveness for x_2 against x_1.

Note that if one of two distinct feasible sets contain *exactly* two elements and these two sets have two elements in common, then one set is a subset of the other and the other set has more than two elements. Hence, using connectedness of Ω, δ^* implies that the "local" dictator on the larger sets of three or more alternatives will also be a dictator in the smaller sets in Ω having two alternatives.

The above corollary will allow us to compare Theorems 5 and 6 to other results in the literature. There are mainly three types of Fe-domain models that have been considered in the literature (see Denicolò 1987): (i) "Grether–Plott" types of domain where Ω is covered (and hence connected); (ii) "Fishburn" type domains (these domains are also connected but not covered); (iii) "Standard" social choice Fe-domains containing all nonempty subsets of X (this domain is necessarily connected).

For each of these types of models we will consider the most general of the dictatorship results that have been reported in the literature and compare these results with those that we have presented above. The following two results in the "Fishburn" and "Grether–Plott" frameworks are from Denicolò (1987):

Theorem A (Denicolò) *Let Ω be nontrivial and connected. There is no nondictatorial Paretian SCF satisfying UD, IIA(C), WARP, and MB.*

Theorem B (Denicolò) *Let Ω be nontrivial and satisfy USF. There is no nondictatorial Paretian SCF satisfying UD, IIA(C), DCA, α, and MB.*

The next result is by Matsumoto (1985) and is proved in the context of the "standard" social choice Fe-domain:

Theorem C (Matsumoto) *Let Ω be nontrivial and complete. There is no nondictatorial Paretian SCF satisfying UD such that the revealed preference relation R^T is transitive and satisfies IIA(A) and WP.*

First, consider Denicolò's results. The major part of Denicolò's proofs of Theorems A and B consists of showing that the hypotheses of these theorems imply $IIA(H_1)$. We already know that $IIA(H_1)$ implies $IIA(S_1)$ (Remark 4) and that *UD* implies *MIT*. Thus, using the fact that *WARP* implies *P*-WARP and δ^* (Proposition 3), it is clear that the conclusion of Theorem A can be derived as a special case of Corollary 1.

Similarly, it is easy to see that *USF* implies Ω is covered and that hence it is connected (Proposition 1), that *DCA* implies δ^* (Proposition 3), and that α and δ^* (when Ω is covered) together imply *P-WARP* (Proposition 9). Thus, the conclusion of Theorem B, too, can be derived from Corollary 1.

Moreover, note that while Corollary 1 allows for *SCF*s that are doubly nonbinary,[33] it is easy to see from Proposition (4.1) and Proposition 8 (i) that this is not true for

[33] For instance, the *SCF* in Example 5 satisfies the hypothesis of Corollary 1.

Theorems A and B: they allow for structural nonbinariness but do not allow rules that are choice functionally nonbinary.

Now, turning to Matsumoto's theorem, notice that it is a straightforward application of Arrow's *GPT*, and there seems to be no obvious relationship with the result in Theorem 5. However, it is clear that Theorem C, like Theorems A and B, does not apply to doubly nonbinary choice functions. This is so because while allowing for choice functional nonbinariness, it rules out structural nonbinariness.

Oligarchy analogues of Theorems A, B, C can be stated (see Denicolò 1996, and Panda 1983) and a similar relationship between these results and Theorem 6 may be shown to exist. More importantly, Theorems A, B, C (and their oligarchy analogues) *and* Corollary 1 (unlike Theorems 3, 4, 5, and 6) are not full characterization results and therefore just provide *sufficiency* conditions for dictatorial and oligarchic social choice. Hence, given Sen's (and Buchanan's) criticism of consistency conditions in the context of social choice, one can ask to what extent are the consistency conditions used really *necessary* for dictatorship and oligarchy results in the (possibly doubly) nonbinary multi-agenda context? To extend the characterization results in Theorems 5 and 6 so as to allow Ω to contain pairs, we will give up all extraneous rationality conditions.

Definition 10

(10.1) *$IIA(S_3)$ is satisfied if the following condition holds for every $A \in \Omega$ and all $\overline{\mathcal{P}}$ subset of the P-domain of the choice function such that for all $\pi \in \overline{\mathcal{P}}$ and all $i \in L$: xP_iy. If for every* linear *profile π in the P-domain of the choice function there* exists *a profile $(\overline{\pi}^L, \overline{\pi}^{N-L}) \in \overline{\mathcal{P}}$ such that $\overline{\pi}^{N-L}_{\{x,y\}} = \pi^{N-L}_{\{x,y\}}$, $x \in T(A, \overline{\pi})$ and $y \in (A - T(A, \overline{\pi}))$, then L is decisive for x against y on A (i.e., $L \in D(x, y; A)$).*

(10.2) *$IIA(S_4)$ is satisfied if the following conditions hold for every $A \in \Omega$ and all $\overline{\mathcal{P}}$ subset of the P-domain of the choice function such that for all $\overline{\pi} \in \overline{\mathcal{P}}$ and all $i \in L$: $x\widehat{P}_iy$.*

(i) *If for every* linear *profile π in the P-domain of the choice function there exists a profile $(\overline{\pi}^L, \overline{\pi}^{N-L}) \in \overline{\mathcal{P}}$ such that $\overline{\pi}^{N-L}_{\{x,y\}} = \pi^{N-L}_{\{x,y\}}$, $x \in T(A, \overline{\pi})$ and $y \in A$ then L has a veto for x against y on A (i.e., $L \in V(x, y; A)$).*

and

(ii) *If for every* linear *profile π in the P-domain of the choice function there exists a profile $(\overline{\pi}^L, \overline{\pi}^{N-L}) \in \overline{\mathcal{P}}$ such that $\overline{\pi}^{N-L}_{\{x,y\}} = \pi^{N-L}_{\{x,y\}}$, $\{x\} = T(A, \overline{\pi})$ and $y \in A$ then L is decisive for x against y on A (i.e., $L \in D(x, y; A)$).*

Remark 6 *$IIA(S_3)$ and $IIA(S_4)$, like $IIA(S_1)$and $IIA(S_2)$, are independence conditions rather than rationality conditions. By comparing Definition 10 and Definition 8 it is easy to verify that the two definitions are different in exactly two respects. Firstly, the word "linear" has been added in (10.1), (10.2) (i), and (10.2) (ii), a word that is absent in Definition 8. Secondly, the hypothesis of Definition (10.2) (i) replaces " $y \in (A - T(A, \overline{\pi}))$" in Definition (8.2) (i) with " $y \in A$." Both these changes weaken the hypotheses in Definition 8, while leaving the conclusions unchanged.*

Hence, $IIA(S_3)$ and $IIA(S_4)$ imply $IIA(S_1)$ and $IIA(S_2)$, respectively. The converse, in general, is not true. For instance, in Example 6, for $A = \{x_1, x_2\}$, while $IIA(S_1)$ and $IIA(S_2)$ are satisfied, $IIA(S_3)$ and $IIA(S_4)$ are not. The following proposition examines the relationship between these assumptions in the special context of the fixed agenda model considered in the last section:

Proposition 10 *Let Ω be nontrivial and satisfy FA and let T be a Paretian SCF with a P-domain satisfying MIT. Then, (i) T satisfies $IIA(S_3)$ iff T satisfies $IIA(S_1)$, and (ii) T satisfies $IIA(S_4)$ iff T satisfies $IIA(S_2)$.*

Proof. We will prove (ii). (The proof of (i) is similar.)

By Remark 6, it is sufficient for us to prove that $IIA(S_2)$ implies $IIA(S_4)$. Using Theorem 4, we know that under our hypothesis, if $IIA(S_2)$ is satisfied, then an oligarchy will exist. Thus, to complete the proof all that we need to show is that the existence of an oligarchy implies that $IIA(S_4)$ is satisfied. Reading through the proof of Theorem 4, showing that the existence of an oligarchy implies $IIA(S_2)$, and replacing $IIA(S_2)$ with $IIA(S_4)$, the reader can verify that exactly the same argument remains valid if one replaces "$y \in (A - T(A))$" with "$y \in A$"; "there exists a profile $(\overline{\pi}^L, \overline{\pi}^{N-L}) \in \overline{\mathcal{P}}$" with "there exists a *linear* profile $(\overline{\pi}^L, \overline{\pi}^{N-L}) \in \overline{\mathcal{P}}$"; and "every profile π in the domain of the choice function" with "every *linear* profile π in the domain of the choice function." □

Remark 7 *Observe that neither the assumption of FA nor that of nontriviality of Ω plays any role in the proof above establishing the property that* if T is oligarchic, $IIA(S_4)$ is satisfied.

Remark 8 *It follows from Proposition 10 that for Paretian SCF's satisfying MIT, in the special case of a (nontrivial) fixed agenda, $IIA(S_1)$ and $IIA(S_2)$ may be appropriately viewed as the fixed agenda "versions" of $IIA(S_3)$ and $IIA(S_4)$, respectively.*

Using $IIA(S_3)$ and $IIA(S_4)$ we can now eliminate the requirement in Theorems 5 and 6 that Ω be strictly nonbinary.

Theorem 5* *Let Ω be nontrivial and connected, and let T be a Paretian SCF with a P-domain satisfying MIT. Then, T satisfies $IIA(S_3)$ and P-WARP iff T is dictatorial.*

Theorem 6* *Let Ω be nontrivial and connected, and let T be a Paretian SCF with a P-domain satisfying MIT. Then, T satisfies $IIA(S_4)$ and P-WARP iff T is oligarchic.*

We will prove Theorem 6*; the argument for Theorem 5* is similar.

Lemma 7 *Let Ω be nontrivial and connected, and let T be a Paretian SCF with a P-domain satisfying MIT. Then, T satisfies $IIA(S_4)$ and P-WARP implies that for all $A, B \in \Omega$, such that $|A \cap B| \geq 2$, for any $x, y \in A \cap B$, $D(x, y; A) = D(x, y; B)$.*

Proof. Without loss of generality let $L \in D(x,y;A)$ and consider the set of profiles

$$L: xy[rest]$$

$$N - L: [xy][rest].$$

Let $\overline{\mathcal{P}}$ be the largest subset of this set of profiles that consist of linear orderings. Since $L \in D(A)$, for every $\pi \in \overline{\mathcal{P}}$, $T(A,\pi) = \{x\}$. By *P-WARP*, $T(B,\pi) = \{x\}$. Since the preferences in $\overline{\mathcal{P}}$ of individuals $N - L$ over the alternatives $\{x,y\}$ are unspecified except for the requirement of being linear, it is clear, that by $IIA(S_4)$ (ii), $L \in D(x,y;B)$. □

*Proof of Theorem 6**. We have already established that the existence of an oligarchy implies *P-WARP* (see Theorem 6). Similarly, Proposition 10 implies that if an oligarchy is present, $IIA(S_4)$ is satisfied for all $A \in \Omega$ (see Remark 7). This establishes that the two conditions are necessary. Thus, we will need to show that $IIA(S_4)$ and *P-WARP* are sufficient for the existence of an oligarchy.

From Theorem 6 we know that there exists a unique set $L_0 \subseteq N$ such that L_0 is decisive over all triples and larger sets in Ω, and that each member of L_0 has a veto on these members of Ω. We will argue that this property extends to all pairs in Ω. Using the fact that Ω is connected, Lemma 5 and Lemma 7 imply that over any $x,y \in X$ such that $\{x,y\} \in \Omega$, $L_0 \in D(\{x,y\})$, and that each member $j_0 \in L_0$ belongs to *every* decisive set for that pair.

To complete the proof, using connectedness of Ω and Theorem 6, all we need to establish is that for any $\{x,y\} \in \Omega$ and any $j_0 \in L_0, j_0 \in V(x,y;\{x,y\})$. If L_0 is a singleton, then since $L_0 \in D(\{x,y\})$, we have a dictatorship and the proof is complete. If not, consider the profiles:

$$j_0 : xy[rest]$$

$$N - \{j_0\} : [yx][rest]$$

and let $\overline{\mathcal{P}}$ be the largest subset of this set of profiles that consist of linear orderings. Assume to the contrary that $j_0 \notin V(x,y;\{x,y\})$. Since T is Paretian, using $IIA(S_4)$, this implies that there exists a linear profile $\overline{\pi}$ in the P-domain of T such that for all $\pi \in \overline{\mathcal{P}}$, $\pi^{N-\{j_0\}}_{\{x,y\}} = \overline{\pi}^{N-\{j_0\}}_{\{x,y\}}$ implies $T(\{x,y\},\pi) = \{y\}$. Let $\widehat{\pi}$ be one such profile, then we would have $T(\{x,y\},\widehat{\pi}) = \{y\}$. However, since Ω is connected there exists some $A \in \Omega$ with three or more elements such that $\{x,y\} \subseteq A$. But, since every member $j_0 \in L_0$ has a veto on any $A \in \Omega$ with three or more alternatives (and using the fact that T is Paretian), we have $x \in T(A,\widehat{\pi})$. But this together with $T(\{x,y\},\widehat{\pi}) = \{y\}$ contradicts *P-WARP*. □

Remark 9 *Theorems 5* and 6* completely characterize dictatorial and oligarchic Social Choice Functions. The results themselves are tight in the sense that none of the (six) conditions in the hypothesis of each theorem are implied by a combination of the others.*[34]

8. CONCLUSION

Economists have used the term "nonbinary" to describe both choice functional nonbinariness (choice functions that cannot be rationalized as the maximizing outcome of a binary preference relation) and structural nonbinariness (the structure of the model dictates that pairs of alternatives do not belong to the domain of the social choice function). We have described necessary and sufficient conditions for oligarchy and dictatorship results in social choice models that are nonbinary in both senses. For Paretian Social Choice Functions with connected nonbinary feasibility domains and maximal individually tractable preference domains, these necessary and sufficient conditions are of two types. The first type of condition is an intra-agenda independence condition of the kind suggested by Sen (1993). Roughly speaking, this type of condition requires that the veto power and/or the power to get an element rejected in the presence of some other alternative in any given feasibility set should be independent of preferences of individuals over the other (irrelevant) alternatives. The second condition that is required is a rationality condition. This condition takes the form of a Pareto "restricted" Weak Axiom of Revealed Preference. The condition can be interpreted as saying that for any fixed profile of linear preferences if two alternatives Pareto dominate all other alternatives, then for this preference profile which of these two alternatives gets picked by the social choice function should be the same for every feasible set containing both alternatives and thus be "independent of" what other alternatives are contained in the feasible set. The framework within which these results hold is fairly general, but whether or not one finds the informational assumptions implicit in these two types of conditions to be acceptable would depend on the *specific* context. Analysis of nonbinary social

[34] For Theorem 5* (resp., Theorem 6*) consider the various assumptions: (i) T is Paretian; (ii) Ω is non-trivial; (iii) Ω is connected; (iv) the P-domain satisfies *MIT*; (v) $IIA(S_3)$ (resp., $IIA(S_4)$; (vi) *P-WARP*.

- A fixed agenda with SCF $T(A, \pi) = A$ for all profiles π can be used to to demonstrate that (i) cannot be derived from the other assumptions.
- A singleton Ω consisting of $\{x, y\}$ with T being the Condorcet winner satisfies all the assumptions excepting (ii).
- A variarion of Example 4 with different local dicatators on unconnected members of Ω (see the discussion in the text immediately following Example 4) can show all the assumptions being satisfied excepting (iii).
- If only a single ordering is permitted in the P-domain, one in which all individuals are indifferent between all alternatives and the *SCF* is given by $T(A, \pi) = A$, all assumptions excepting (iv) would be satisfied.
- Violations of (v) with other assumptions being satisfied are shown in Examples 1 and 2.
- Example 6 satisfies all the assumptions except (vi).

choice for specific problems—public goods, economic environments, rights and liberties, justice—is gradually developing. While some work has been done in these areas, much still remains to be done.

ACKNOWLEDGMENTS

I would like to thank Professor Kotaro Suzumura for his very valuable suggestions. The discussion in the Introduction closely follows his suggestions. Any errors or omissions of course remain my responsibility.

REFERENCES

Aizerman, M. A. (1985). New problems in general choice theory: review of a research trend. *Social Choice and Welfare, 2*, 235–282.

Aleskerov, F., & Duggan, J. (1993). Functional voting operators: the non-monotonic case. *Mathematical Social Sciences, 26*, 175–201.

Arrow, K. J. (1959). Rational choice functions and orderings. *Economica, 26*, 121–127.

Arrow, K. J. (1963). *Social choice and individual values* (2nd ed.). New York: Wiley.

Batra, R., & Pattanaik, P. K. (1972). On some suggestions for having non-binary social choice functions. *Theory and Decision, 3*, 1–11.

Blair, D. H., Bordes, G., Kelly, J., & Suzumura, K. (1976). Impossibility theorems without collective rationality. *Journal of Economic Theory, 13*, 361–379.

Bloomfield, S. (1971). *An axiomatic formulation of constitutional games* (Technical Report No. 71–18). Stanford, CA Stanford University.

Buchanan, J. M. (1954). Social choice, democracy, and free markets. *Journal of Political Economy, 62*, 114–123.

Campbell, D. E. (1995). Nonbinary social choice for economic environments. *Social Choice and Welfare, 12*, 245–254.

Campbell, D. E., & Kelly, J. S. (1993). *t* or 1-*t*. That is the trade-off. *Econometrica, 61*, 1355–1365.

Deb, R. (1975). *Rational choice and cyclic preferences*, Ph.D. dissertation, London School of Economics. London: University of London.

Denicolò, V. (1987). Some further results in nonbinary social choice. *Social Choice and Welfare, 4*, 277–285.

Denicolò, V. (1993). Fixed agenda social choice theory: correspondence theorems for social choice correspondences and social decision functions. *Journal of Economic Theory, 59*, 324–332.

Denicolò, V. (1998). Independent decisiveness and the Arrow theorem. *Social Choice and Welfare, 15*, 563–566.

Denicolò, V. (2000). Independence of irrelevant alternatives and consistency of choice. *Economic Theory, 15*, 221–226.

Donaldson, D., & Weymark, J. A. (1988). Social choice in economic environments. *Journal of Economic Theory, 46*, 291–308.

Fishburn, P. C. (1973). *The theory of social choice*. Princeton, N.J: Princeton University Press.

Fishburn, P. C. (1974). On collective rationality and a generalized impossibility theorem. *Review of Economic Studies, 41*, 445–458.

Grether, D. M., & Plott, C. R. (1982). Nonbinary social choice: an impossibility theorem. *Review of Economic Studies, 49*, 143–149.

Hansson, B. (1969). Voting and group decision functions. *Synthese, 20*, 526–537.

Herzberger, H. G. (1973). Ordinal preference and rational choice. *Econometrica, 41*, 187–237.

Houthakker, H. S. (1950). Revealed preference and the utility function. *Economica, N.S., 17*, 159–174.

Luce, R. D., & Raiffa, H. (1957). *Games and decisions*. New York: Wiley.
Kelly, J. S. (1978). *Arrow impossibility theorems*. New York: Academic Press.
Matsumoto, Y. (1985). Non-binary social choice: revealed preferential interpretation. *Economica, 52,* 185–195.
Panda, S. C. (1983). On non-binary social choice. *Mathematical Social Sciences, 4,* 73–78.
Panda, S. C. (1986). Some impossibility results with domain restrictions. *Journal of Economic Theory, 38,* 21–34.
Pattanaik, P. K. (1996). Modelling individual rights: some conceptual issues. In K. J. Arrow, A. K. Sen & K. Suzumura (Eds.), *Social choice re-examined* (Vol. 2). London: Macmillan.
Pattanaik, P. K., & Suzumura, K. (1996). Individual rights and social evaluation. *Oxford Economic Papers, 48,* 194–212.
Phillips, J., & Stevens, D. (1981). A just, non-binary choice rule. *American Economist, 25,* 44–48.
Richter, M. (1966). Revealed preference theory. *Econometrica, 34,* 987–991.
Plott, C. (1973). Path independence, rationality and social choice. *Econometrica, 41,* 1075–1091.
Samuelson, P. (1938). A note on the pure theory of consumer's behaviour. *Economica, N.S., 5,* 353–354.
Samuelson, P. (1948). Consumption theory in terms of revealed preference. *Economica, N.S., 15,* 243–253.
Samuelson, P. (1950). The problem of integrability in utility theory. *Economica, N.S., 17,* 355–385.
Sen, A. K. (1970). *Collective choice and social welfare*. San Francisco: Holden Day, republished, Amsterdam: North-Holland, 1979.
Sen, A. K. (1971). Choice functions and revealed preference. *Review of Economic Studies, 36,* 381–393.
Sen, A. K. (1976). Liberty, unanimity and rights. *Economica, 43,* 217–241.
Sen, A. K. (1977). Social choice theory: a re-examination. *Econometrica, 45,* 53–89.
Sen, A. K. (1986). Social choice theory. In K. Arrow & M. Intriligator (Eds.), *Handbook of mathematical economics* (Vol. 3). Amsterdam: North-Holland.
Sen, A. K. (1992). Minimal liberty. *Economica, 59,* 139–159.
Sen, A. K. (1993). Internal consistency of choice. *Econometrica, 61,* 495–521.
Suzumura, K. (1977). Houthakker's axiom in the theory of rational choice. *Journal of Economic Theory, 14,* 284–290.
Suzumura, K. (1983). *Rational choice, collective decisions and social welfare*. Cambridge: Cambridge University Press.
Wilson, R. B. (1972). Social choice without the Pareto principle. *Journal of Economic Theory, 5,* 14–20.
Xu, Y. (1996). Non binary social choice: a brief introduction. *Collective decision-making: social choice and political economy* (pp. 79–91.) Published with assistance from Annette Milford, Boston, Dordecht: Kluwer.

CHAPTER TWENTY

Social Choice with Fuzzy Preferences

Richard Barrett* and Maurice Salles**
*Department of Economics, University of Birmingham, United Kingdom
**Université de Caen, Caen Cedex, France, and London School of Economics, London, United Kingdom

Contents

Abstract

Fuzzy set theory has been explicitly introduced to deal with vagueness and ambiguity. One can also use probability theory or techniques borrowed from philosophical logic. In this chapter, we consider fuzzy preferences and we survey the literature on aggregation of fuzzy preferences. We restrict ourselves to "pure aggregation" theory and, accordingly, do not cover strategic aspects of social choice. We present Arrovian aggregation problems in a rather standard framework as well as in a very specific economic environment. We also consider a fuzzy treatment of Sen's impossibility of a Paretian liberal. We distinguish two types of fuzziness: quantitative fuzziness, defined via real numbers, and qualitative fuzziness, defined via linguistic data with a suitable order structure. We outline the thin frontier between impossibility and possibility results.

Keywords: fuzzy sets, fuzzy preferences, aggregation theory, Arrow impossibility theorem, Sen impossibility theorem.

JEL codes: D71 C65 H41

1. INTRODUCTION

The most important concept of social choice theory is probably the concept of preference, be it individual preference or social preference. Typically, preferences are

Handbook of Social Choice and Welfare, Volume II
ISSN: 0169-7218, DOI: 10.1016/S0169-7218(10)00020-1

crisp, that is, given by a binary relation over the set of options (social states, candidates, etc.). Then, for two options, either one is preferred to the other, or there is an indifference between them, or there is no relation between them. In most cases, the possibility that there is no relation between them is excluded. The binary relation is then complete. Several authors, including Sen (1992), have considered that incompleteness was a way to deal with ambiguity. However, when the options are uncertain we must adopt preferences related in some way to probabilities, and when they are complex, for instance when each option has manifold characteristics, we must try to take account of the vagueness this entails. To deal with vagueness, various authors have had recourse to, roughly speaking, three different techniques. The first is *probability theory*. Fishburn (1998, p. 276) writes: "Vague preferences and wavering judgments about better, best, or merely satisfactory alternatives lead naturally to theories based on probabilistic preference and probabilistic choice." The second is *fuzzy set theory*. Each of these two theories has champions that apparently strongly disagree. There are, however, several signs indicating that the scientific war should eventually end (see Ross et al. 2002, and the forewords in that book by Zadeh and Suppes). The third is due to philosophers. Vagueness is an important topic within analytic philosophy (Keefe and Smith 1996, Burns 1991, Williamson 1994, Keefe 2000). Philosophers have mainly been concerned with predicates such as tall, small, red, bald, heap, and solutions to the sorites paradox. For instance, a nice example for the predicate "small" is Wang's paradox discussed by Dummett (1975). Consider the inductive argument: 0 is small; if n is small, $n + 1$ is small: therefore every number is small.) Although there is little agreement among them about the nature of vagueness, a theory has been designed to deal with it: supervaluation theory. In an interesting paper, Broome (1997) has jointly considered vagueness and incompleteness.

As social choice theorists, we are perhaps more interested in vagueness of relations than the kind of predicates mentioned above, and most of the papers dealing with vagueness in choice theory have used fuzzy sets. The purpose of this chapter is to present some of the main results obtained on the aggregation of fuzzy preferences. Regarding the possible interpretations of preferences, it seems to us that we must confine ourselves to what Sen (1983, 2002) calls the *outcome evaluation*. Preference is about the fact that an option is judged to be a better state of affairs than another option. In Sen's typology, the two other interpretations are about choices, normative or descriptive. In particular, our analysis is not well adapted to voting, since the voters' ballot papers are not vague, and the results of the election are not vague either, even if, before designing a crisp preference, each voter had rather fuzzy preferences.

After introducing the concepts of fuzzy preference in Section 2, Section 3 will be devoted to Arrovian aggregation problems and Section 4 to other aspects, including a fuzzy treatment of Sen's impossibility of a Paretian liberal and the first results about fuzzy aggregation in economic environments.

2. FUZZY PREFERENCES

In (naive) set theory, given a set X, a subset A, and an element $x \in X$, either $x \in A$ or $x \notin A$. Belonging to the subset can be defined by a function b from X to $\{0, 1\}$, where $x \in A$ is equivalent to $b(x) = 1$ and $x \notin A$ is equivalent to $b(x) = 0$. If the subset A refers to the description of some semantic concepts (events or phenomena or statements), there might be no clear-cut way to assert that an element is or is not in this subset. Classical examples are the set of tall men, the set of intelligent women, or the set of beautiful spiders. The basic idea of replacing $\{0, 1\}$ by $[0, 1]$ as the set where the membership function takes its values is due to Zadeh. However, the origin of this is probably older, taking us back at least to Łukasiewicz, who introduced many-valued logic in 1920. For excellent mathematical introductions, we recommend Dubois and Prade (1980) and Nguyen and Walker (2000).

For a fuzzy binary relation, the membership function associates a number in $[0, 1]$ to an ordered pair of options (x, y). The interpretation of a number $\alpha \in [0, 1]$ associated to (x, y) can be the degree of intensity with which x is preferred to y is α or the degree of truth that x is preferred to y is α. Though in some cases the first interpretation is possible and amounts to considering strength of preference, the second interpretation is always possible and is compulsory if, at some stage, fuzzy connectives (and, or ...) have been introduced.

The fact that some positive value α is associated to (x, y) does not entail, in general, that the value 0 must be assigned to (y, x). For instance, if we consider two versions of Beethoven's *Grosse Fuge*, say, by the Juilliard Quartet and the Berg Quartet, we may have mixed and conflicting feelings. We may prefer to some extent the Berg version because of its energy but have also some preference for the Juilliard because of its poetry. This will entail that some value $\alpha \in]0, 1]$ be given to the preference for the Berg version over the Juilliard, but also that some value $\beta \in]0, 1]$ be given to the preference for the Juilliard version over the Berg.

Moreover, on the basis of this example, it might seem strange to describe fuzziness by assigning a precise number. The logician Alasdair Urquhart (2001) has rightly observed:

> *One immediate objection that presents itself to this line of approach is the extremely artificial nature of the attaching of precise numerical values to sentences like "73 is a large number" or "Picasso's Guernica is beautiful." In fact, it seems plausible to say that the nature of vague predicates precludes attaching precise numerical values just as much as it precludes attaching precise classical truth values.*

One way to avoid this difficulty is to replace $[0, 1]$ ordered by $\geq$ by some set of qualitative elements ordered by a complete preorder. For instance, to give some intuition in the context of preference, the elements could be interpreted as being "not at all," "insignificantly," "a little," "mildly," "much," "very much," "definitely," and so on. We will consider both cases in the following subsections.

2.1. Fuzzy Preferences: Numerical Values

We will focus in this chapter on the notions and properties used in the fuzzy aggregation literature. There are many notions about transitivity and choice that will not be introduced (see, for instance, Barrett, Pattanaik, and Salles 1990, Basu, Deb, and Pattanaik 1992, Dasgupta and Deb 1991, 1996, 2001, Salles 1998).

Let X be the set of alternatives with $\#X \geq 3$.

We will consider two types of fuzzy binary relations. Strict binary relations as described here were introduced in Barrett, Pattanaik, and Salles (1986), hereafter denoted by BPS, and weak binary relations were introduced by Dutta (1987).

Definition 1 *A* fuzzy binary relation *over* X *is a function* $h : X \times X \to [0,1]$.

Definition 2 *A fuzzy binary relation* p *is a* BPS-fuzzy strict preference *if for all distinct* $x, y, z \in X$,

(i) $p(x,x) = 0$,
(ii) $p(x,y) = 1 \Rightarrow p(y,x) = 0$,
(iii) $p(x,y) > 0$ *and* $p(y,z) > 0 \Rightarrow p(x,z) > 0$.

Definition 3 *A* BPS-*fuzzy strict preference* p *is* BPS-complete *if for all distinct* $x, y \in X$,

$$p(x,y) > 0 \quad or \quad p(y,x) > 0.$$

$p(x,y)$ can be interpreted as the degree of intensity with which x is preferred to y (or, see above, the degree of truth that x is preferred to y): (i) expresses that we consider strict preferences; (ii) means that when strict preferences are definite (in some sense nonfuzzy), they are asymmetric; (iii) is a rather mild transitivity property. It is now well known that many transitivity concepts are available for fuzzy binary relations (Dasgupta and Deb 1996). In particular, the most widely used concept, max-min transitivity, which states that given any $x, y, z \in X$, $p(x,z) \geq \min(p(x,y), p(y,z))$, is stronger than (iii).

Subramanian (1987) uses two different fuzzy strict preferences, one of which is a variant of *BPS*-fuzzy strict preferences.

Definition 4 *A fuzzy strict preference* p^{S_1} *is an* S_1-fuzzy strict preference *if it is a* BPS-*fuzzy strict preference for which for all distinct* $x, y, z \in X$, $p^{S_1}(x,y) = p^{S_1}(y,x) = p^{S_1}(y,z) = p^{S_1}(z,y) = 0 \Rightarrow p^{S_1}(x,z) = p^{S_1}(z,x) = 0$.

A fuzzy strict preference p^{S_2} *is an* S_2-fuzzy strict preference *if it satisfies properties (i) and (ii) of Definition 2, and if for all distinct* $x_1, x_2, \ldots, x_k \in X, p^{S_2}(x_1, \;x_2) >$

$p^{S_2}(x_2, x_1)$ *and* $p^{S_2}(x_2, x_3) > p^{S_2}(x_3, x_2)$ *and* ... *and* $p^{S_2}(x_{k-1}, x_k) > p^{S_2}(x_k, x_{k-1}) \Rightarrow \neg(p^{S_2}(x_k, x_1) = 1$ and $p^{S_2}(x_1, x_k) = 0)$.

Definition 5 *A fuzzy binary relation r is a* fuzzy weak preference *if it is reflexive, that is, if for all* $x \in X$, $r(x,x) = 1$.

The basic idea underlying the concept of fuzzy weak preference is that it will be possible to derive from it two components, viz. a symmetric component, the fuzzy indifference, i,[1] and more importantly a strict component that is in some fuzzy sense asymmetric, p. All the numerical fuzzy weak preferences we are considering in this chapter are connected (or complete) with the following meaning.

Definition 6 *A fuzzy weak preference r is* connected *if for all* $x, y \in X$, $r(x,y) + r(y,x) \geq 1$.

We will present three decompositions of a fuzzy weak preference introduced, respectively, by Dutta (1987), Banerjee (1994), and Richardson (1998) and Dasgupta and Deb (1999). Theoretical results about these decompositions can be found in the cited papers and in Dasgupta and Deb (2001). We will not present these results here since they are not directly connected with the topic of the chapter.

Definition 7 *A fuzzy weak preference* r^D *is a* D-fuzzy weak preference *if for all* $x, y \in X$, $i^D(x,y) = \min(r^D(x,y), r^D(y,x))$ *and*

$$p^D(x,y) = \begin{cases} r^D(x,y) & \text{if } r^D(x,y) > r^D(y,x) \\ 0 & \text{otherwise.} \end{cases} \tag{1}$$

Banerjee objects to this decomposition on the basis that if $i^D(x,y) > 0$, $p^D(x,y)$ should be less than $r^D(x,y)$. It seems strange that when $r^D(x,y) = 1$ and $r^D(y,x) = 0.999$, and when $r^D(x,y) = 1$ and $r^D(y,x) = 0$, $p^D(x,y)$ has the same value *(1)*. Richardson adds that the discontinuity of p^D seems also rather unreasonable. If $r^D(x,y) = 1$ and $r^D(y,x) = 0.999$, $p^D(x,y) = 1$, and if $r^D(x,y) = r^D(y,x) = 1$, $p^D(x,y) = 0$.

Definition 8 *A fuzzy weak preference* r^B *is a* B-fuzzy weak preference *if for all* $x, y \in X$, $i^B(x,y) = \min(r^B(x,y), r^B(y,x))$ *and* $p^B(x,y) = 1 - r^B(y,x)$.

Richardson discusses this decomposition and the role of a property of strong connectedness. In particular, he notes that $p^B(x,y)$ has the same value when $r^B(x,y) = 1$ and $r^B(y,x) = 0.999$, and when $r^B(x,y) = 0.001$ and $r^B(y,x) = 0.999$.

Definition 9 *A fuzzy weak preference r is* strongly connected *if for all* $x, y \in X$, $\max(r(x,y), r(y,x)) = 1$.

[1] Although the letter i is also used as the generic letter for individuals, there will clearly be no confusion possible.

Definition 10 *A fuzzy weak preference* r^{RD^2} *is an* RD^2-fuzzy weak preference *if for all* $x, y \in X$, $i^{RD^2}(x,y) = \min(r^{RD^2}(x,y), r^{RD^2}(y,x))$ *and* $p^{RD^2}(x,y) = \max(r^{RD^2}(x,y) - r^{RD^2}(y,x), 0)$.

In these definitions D is for Dutta (1987), B is for Banerjee (1994), and RD^2 is for both Richardson (1998) and Dasgupta and Deb (1999).

We will now introduce several transitivity properties for fuzzy weak preferences.

Definition 11 *A fuzzy binary relation r is*

(i) max-min transitive *if for all* $x, y, z \in X$, $r(x,z) \geq \min(r(x,y), r(y,z))$,
(ii) max-δ transitive *if for all* $x, y, z \in X$, $r(x,z) \geq r(x,y) + r(y,z) - 1$,
(iii) exactly transitive *if for all* $x, y, z \in X$, $r(x,y) = 1$ *and* $r(y,z) = 1 \Rightarrow r(x,z) = 1$,
(iv) weakly max-min transitive *if for all* $x, y, z \in X$, *if* $r(x,y) \geq r(y,x)$ *and* $r(y,z) \geq r(z,y)$, *then* $r(x,z) \geq \min(r(x,y), r(y,z))$.

Max-min transitivity implies max-δ transitivity, which implies exact transitivity. Also, it is obvious that max-min transitivity implies weak max-min transitivity (see Dasgupta and Deb 1996 for further results). Based on these four transitivities, we will define various social welfare functions in the next section. As mentioned above, there are many transitivity concepts for fuzzy binary relations (in fact, obviously an infinity). A basic requirement is that, when applied to values restricted to be 0 or 1 (i.e., to crisp relations), one must recover the standard notions of transitivity. For instance, if we consider (iii) of Definition 2, we have: $p(x,y) = 1$ and $p(y,z) = 1 \Rightarrow p(x,z) = 1$, which is the transitivity of the standard (strict) preference. But if we consider the following definition:

$$\text{for all distinct } x, y, z \in X, p(x,y) > .05 \text{ and } p(y,z) > .01 \Rightarrow p(x,z) = 1$$

we have a transitivity notion for a fuzzy binary relation that is compatible with its crisp counterpart without being intuitively convincing. It is furthermore independent of (iii) of Definition 2. Of course, if, moreover, the transitivity properties are not independent, then all other things being equal, for impossibility results the weakest notion is the best, and for possibility results the strongest notion the best.

2.2. Fuzzy Preferences: Qualitative Values

We mentioned that assigning precise numbers to elements to describe vagueness could seem paradoxical. Goguen (1967) and Basu, Deb, and Pattanaik (1992) have proposed assigning some qualitative value, the set of these values being subject to some binary relation. We will follow here Barrett, Pattanaik, and Salles (1992) and consider fuzzy strict preferences where fuzziness is given by elements in a finite set L completely preordered by a relation $\succeq$. This is, of course, very similar to Goguen's L-fuzzy sets, the only difference being that in Goguen $\succeq$ is a linear order, that is, an anti-symmetric complete preorder. This means that, with a non-anti-symmetric complete preorder, there might be a non-unique way to define a degree of fuzziness (for instance "a little" and "mildly" can express the same fuzziness, though they are different elements of L).

Let L be a finite set and $\succeq$ a complete preorder on L with a unique $\succeq$-maximum, denoted $d^\star$, and a unique $\succeq$-minimum, denoted $d_\star$.

Definition 12 An ordinally fuzzy binary relation H *is a function* $H : X \times X \to L$.

Definition 13 *An ordinally fuzzy binary relation* P *is a* BPS-ordinally fuzzy strict preference *if for all distinct* $x, y, z \in X$,

(i) $P(x,x) = d_\star$,
(ii) $P(x,y) = d^\star \Rightarrow P(y,x) = d_\star$,
(iii) $P(x,y) = d^\star \Rightarrow P(x,z) \succeq P(y,z)$, *and* $P(y,z) = d^\star \Rightarrow P(x,z) \succeq P(x,y)$.

We will introduce a variety of transitivity conditions. As previously, it might be difficult to say which condition is the most appropriate. It can depend on the context. However, we impose with (iii) a sort of transitivity condition that seems as compelling as (i) (exact irreflexivity) and (ii) (exact asymmetry). According to (iii), if x is definitely (or exactly) better than y, then x must "fare as well" against z as y against z (in terms of preference in favor), and if y is definitely better than z, then x must "fare as well" against z as against y. If one definitely prefers Bartok's concerto for orchestra to Gorecki's third symphony, the degree of this preference for Bartok's concerto over Dutilleux's first symphony (which may be "mild") must be "at least as strong as" the degree of his preference for Gorecki's symphony over Dutilleux's symphony (which may be null).

Definition 14 *Let* P *be a* BPS-*ordinally fuzzy strict preference.* P *is*

(i) weakly max-min transitive *if for all* $x, y, z \in X$, $P(x,y) \succeq P(y,x)$ *and* $P(y,z) \succeq P(z,y) \Rightarrow P(x,z) \succeq P(x,y)$ *or* $P(x,z) \succeq P(y,z)$,

(ii) quasi-transitive *if for all* $x, y, z \in X$, $P(x,y) \succ P(y,x)$ *and* $P(y,z) \succ P(z,y) \Rightarrow P(x,z) \succ P(z,x)$,

(iii) acyclical *if there is no finite set* $\{x_1, \ldots, x_k\} \subseteq X$ $(k > 1)$ *such that* $P(x_1,x_2) \succ P(x_2,x_1)$ *and ... and* $P(x_{k-1},x_k) \succ P(x_k,x_{k-1})$ *and* $P(x_k,x_1) \succ P(x_1,x_k)$,

(iv) simply transitive *if for all* $x, y\ z \in X$, $(P(x,y) \succ d_\star$ *and* $P(y,x) = d_\star)$ *and* $(P(y,z) \succ d_\star$ *and* $P(z,y) = d_\star) \Rightarrow P(x,z) \succ d_\star$ *and* $P(z,x) = d_\star$.

The following example justifies the choice of these transitivity properties as compared with others. Consider three options: a sum of money m, then $m+\delta$ $(\delta > 0)$ and x, which is unspecified. Suppose $P(m+\delta, m) = d^\star$, $P(m,x) = d$, $P(x, m+\delta) = d'$, with $d^\star \succ d \succ d_\star$ and $d^\star \succ d' \succ d_\star$. If we consider the ordinal version of max-min transitivity, that is, if for all $x, y, z \in X$, $P(x,z) \succeq P(x,y)$ or $P(x,z) \succeq P(y,z)$, we should obtain $P(m, m+\delta) \succeq d$ or $P(m, m+\delta) \succeq d'$. Since $P(m+\delta, m) = d^\star$, by (ii) in Definition 13, $P(m, m+\delta) = d_\star$, a contradiction. The same is true if we consider the ordinal version of (iii) in Definition 2, that is, for all x, y, $z \in X$, $P(x,y) \succ d_\star$ and $P(y,z) \succ d_\star \Rightarrow P(x,z) \succ d_\star$. However, this example is compatible with our four transitivity properties.

3. AGGREGATION OF FUZZY PREFERENCES: ARROVIAN THEOREMS

We will introduce in all the cases just defined aggregation procedures and properties that are essentially the fuzzy replicates of Arrow's conditons (see Arrow 1963, Sen 1970).

3.1. The Case of Numerical Values

Let $N = \{1,...,n\}$ be a finite set of individuals ($n \geq 2$).

Definition 15 *A* fuzzy aggregation function *is a function that associates a social fuzzy binary relation over X, denoted h_S, to an n-list of individual fuzzy binary relations over X, denoted $(h_1,...,h_i,...,h_n)$.*

$h_i(x,y)$ can be interpreted as the degree of intensity with which individual i prefers (weakly or strictly) x to y (or the degree of confidence we have that i prefers (weakly or strictly) x to y).

Definition 16 *Let f be a fuzzy aggregation function, h_i, h_S, etc., be fuzzy binary relations, p_i, p_S, etc., be* BPS*-fuzzy strict preferences, or strict components of r_i, r_S of any type (i.e., D, B or RD^2, etc.) f satisfies*

FI (fuzzy independence of irrelevant alternatives) *if for all n-lists $(h_1,...,h_n),(h'_1,...,h'_n)$ and all distinct $x,y \in X$, $h_i(x,y) = h'_i(x,y)$ and $h_i(y,x) = h'_i(y,x)$ for every $i \in N$ implies $h_S(x,y) = h'_S(x,y)$ and $h_S(y,x) = h'_S(y,x)$, where $h_S = f(h_1,...,h_n)$ and $h'_S = f(h'_1,...,h'_n)$;*

FPC (fuzzy Pareto criterion) *if for all $(h_1,...,h_n)$, all distinct $x,y \in X$, $p_S(x,y) \geq \min_i p_i(x,y)$, where $h_S = f(h_1,...,h_n)$;*[2] *and*

FPR (fuzzy positive responsiveness) *if for all $(r_1,...,r_n),(r'_1,...,r'_n)$ and all distinct $x,y \in X$, $r_i = r'_i$ for all $i \neq j$, $r_S(x,y) = r_S(y,x)$, and ($p_j(x,y) = 0$ and $p'_j(x,y) > 0$) or ($p_j(y,x) > 0$ and $p'_j(y,x) = 0$) $\Rightarrow p'_S(x,y) > 0$.*

FI is the natural counterpart of Arrow's independence of irrelevant alternatives, and *FPC* means that if every individual prefers x to y with at least degree t, then the society must reflect this unanimity.

Let $\mathbb{A}_{BPS}$ be the set of *BPS*-fuzzy strict preferences and $\mathbb{A}'_{BPS} \subseteq \mathbb{A}_{BPS}$, $\mathbb{A}'_{BPS} \neq \emptyset$.

[2] $(h_1,...,h_n)$ is either $(p_1,...,p_n)$ in the BPS framework or $(r_1,...,r_n)$, with h_S being respectively p_S or r_S.

Definition 17 *A* BPS-fuzzy social welfare function *is a fuzzy aggregation function* $f : \mathbb{A}'^n_{BPS} \to \mathbb{A}_{BPS}$.

Definition 18 *Let* $f : \mathbb{A}'^n_{BPS} \to \mathbb{A}_{BPS}$ *and* $J_f = \{(t_1, t_2) \in [0,1] \times [0,1]$: *for some* $p \in \mathbb{A}'_{BPS}$ *and some distinct* $a, b \in X$, $p(a,b) = t_1$ *and* $p(b,a) = t_2\}$.

f *is said to have a* non-narrow domain *for distinct* $x, y, z \in X$ *if*
for all $(t_1, t_2) \in J_f$, *there exists* $p \in \mathbb{A}'_{BPS}$ *such that* $p(x,y) = p(x,z) = 1$ *and* $p(y,z) = t_1$ *and* $p(z,y) = t_2$, *and also there exists* $p' \in \mathbb{A}'_{BPS}$ *such that* $p'(y,x) = p'(z,x) = 1$ *and* $p'(y,z) = t_1$ *and* $p'(z,y) = t_2$, *and*
for all $(t_1, t_2) \in [0,1] \times [0,1]$ *for which* $(t_1, 0), (t_2, 0) \in J_f$ *and* $t_2 \geq t_1$, *there exists* $p \in \mathbb{A}'_{BPS}$ *such that* $p(x,y) = t_1, p(y,z) = 1, p(x,z) = t_2$ *and* $p(y,x) = p(z,y) = p(z,x) = 0$, *and also there exists* $p' \in \mathbb{A}'_{BPS}$ *such that* $p'(x,y) = 1, p'(y,z) = t_1, p'(x,z) = t_2$ *and* $p'(y,x) = p'(z,y) = p'(z,x) = 0$.

Of course, if $\mathbb{A}'_{BPS} = \mathbb{A}_{BPS}$, it can be easily seen that the condition defining a non-narrow domain is satisfied for all distinct $x, y, z \in X$. This condition is weaker than a universality condition requiring that $\mathbb{A}'_{BPS} = \mathbb{A}_{BPS}$ and is sufficient to obtain the following theorems. A coalition is a nonempty subset of N.

Theorem 1 *Let* $f : \mathbb{A}'^n_{BPS} \to \mathbb{A}_{BPS}$ *be a BPS-fuzzy social welfare function satisfying FI, FPC, and having a non-narrow domain for all distinct* $x, y, z \in X$. *Then there exists a unique coalition* C *such that*

for all distinct $x, y \in X$ *and all* $(p_1, ..., p_n) \in \mathbb{A}'^n_{BPS}$, *if* $p_i(x,y) > 0$ *and* $p_i(y,x) = 0$ *for every* $i \in C$, *then* $p_S(x,y) > 0$, *where* $p_S = f(p_1, ..., p_n)$; *and*
for all distinct $x, y \in X$ *and all* $(p_1, ..., p_n) \in \mathbb{A}'^n_{BPS}$, *if for some* $j \in C$, $p_j(x,y) > 0$ *and* $p_j(y,x) = 0$, *then* $p_S(y,x) = 0$, *where* $p_S = f(p_1, ..., p_n)$.

This theorem is reminiscent of Gibbard's (1969) oligarchy theorem. If the individuals in coalition C share some agreement in their preferences, they can exert some positive (fuzzy) power. Furthermore, each individual in the coalition has some fuzzy veto power.

One can verify that the fuzzy aggregation function given by $p_S(x,y) = \min_i p_i(x,y)$ is a *BPS*-fuzzy social welfare function. This does not contradict Theorem 1. In this case the unique coalition C is the entire N.

Theorem 2 *Consider the further requirement that if* $p_S \in f(\mathbb{A}'^n_{BPS})$, *then* p_S *is BPS-complete. Then* $\#C = 1$, *that is, the coalition* C *shrinks:*

there exists an individual $i \in N$ *such that for all distinct* $x, y \in X$ *and all* $(p_1, ...p_n) \in \mathbb{A}'^n_{BPS}$, *if* $p_i(x,y) > 0$ *and* $p_i(y,x) = 0$, *then* $p_S(x,y) > 0$ *and* $p_S(y,x) = 0$, *where* $p_S = f(p_1, ..., p_n)$.

This theorem is a fuzzy analog of Arrow's Theorem (1963), and the individual of Theorem 2 could be considered a *BPS-fuzzy dictator.*

We will now consider fuzzy weak preferences.

Let $\mathbb{A}_{D_1}$ be the set of D-fuzzy weak preferences that are max-min transitive.

Definition 19 *A* D_1-fuzzy social welfare function *is a fuzzy aggregation function* $f : \mathbb{A}^n_{D_1} \to \mathbb{A}_{D_1}$.

For such functions, one obtains a result similar to Theorem 1.

Theorem 3 *Let* $f : \mathbb{A}^n_{D_1} \to \mathbb{A}_{D_1}$ *be a* D_1*-fuzzy social welfare function satisfying FI and FPC. Then there exists a unique coalition C such that*

for all distinct $x, y \in X$ *and all* $(r^D_1, ..., r^D_n) \in \mathbb{A}^n_{D_1}$, *if* $p^D_i(x, y) > 0$ *for every* $i \in C$, *then* $p^D_S(x, y) > 0$, *where* $r^D_S = f(r^D_1, ..., r^D_n)$; *and*
for all distinct $x, y \in X$ *and all* $(r^D_1, ..., r^D_n) \in \mathbb{A}^n_{D_1}$, *if for some* $j \in C$, $p^D_j(x, y) > 0$, *then* $p^D_S(y, x) = 0$, *where* $r^D_S = f(r^D_1, ..., r^D_n)$.

Although Dutta (1987) provides an example showing that Theorem 2 cannot be directly extended (take $r_S(x, x) = 1$, and for $x \neq y$ $r_S(x, y) = 1$ if for all $i \in N$ $r_i(x, y) > r_i(y, x)$, and $r_S(x, y) = \alpha \in]1/2, 1]$ otherwise), a result similar to Theorem 2 is possible if one further assumes that f satisfies the positive responsiveness conditon defined in Definition 16.

Theorem 4 *Let* $n \geq 3$ *and* $f : \mathbb{A}^n_{D_1} \to \mathbb{A}_{D_1}$ *be a* D_1*-fuzzy social welfare function satisfying FI, FPC, and FPR. Then there exists an individual* $i \in N$ *such that for all distinct* $x, y \in X$ *and all* $(r^D_1, ...r^D_n) \in \mathbb{A}^n_{D_1}$, *if* $p^D_i(x, y) > 0$, *then* $p^D_S(x, y) > 0$, *where* $r^D_S = f(r^D_1, ..., r^D_n)$.

The result is reminiscent of a result of Mas-Colell and Sonnenschein (1972). The individual shown to exist is a sort of fuzzy dictator. However, if max-min transitivity is replaced by max-δ transitivity, the kind of impossibility of Theorem 4 vanishes.

Let $\mathbb{A}_{D_2}$ be the set of D-fuzzy weak preferences that are max-δ transitive.

Definition 20 *A* D_2-fuzzy social welfare function *is a fuzzy aggregation function* $f : \mathbb{A}^n_{D_2} \to \mathbb{A}_{D_2}$.

Theorem 5 *For all* $(r^D_1, ..., r^D_n) \in \mathbb{A}^n_{D_2}$ *and all* $x, y \in X$, *let* $r_S(x, y) = (1/n)\Sigma_i r^D_i(x, y)$.[3] *Then this function is a* D_2*-fuzzy social welfare function satisfying FI, FPC, and FPR for which there is no individual* $i \in N$ *such that for all distinct* $x, y \in X$ *and all* $(r^D_1, ..., r^D_n) \in \mathbb{A}^n_{D_2}$, *if* $p^D_i(x, y) > 0$, *then* $p^D_S(x, y) > 0$, *where* $r^D_S = f(r^D_1, ..., r^D_n)$.

In fact this rule is also obviously anonymous, with anonymity defined in the usual way as symmetry over individuals (incidentally, it is also symmetric over options).

Banerjee (1994) shows that on substituting fuzzy weak preferences r^B, Theorem 5 is no longer true and a theorem similar to Theorem 4 is obtained. However, as Richardson

[3] This function is sometimes called the mean rule; for extended studies see García-Lapresta and Llamazares (2000) and Ovchinnikov (1991).

(1998) observes, Banerjee uses the hidden fact that two of the sufficient conditions to obtain his decomposition imply that the fuzzy weak preferences r^B are strongly connected. One of these two conditions is in fact imposed by all the mentioned contributors. It is the sort of fuzzy asymmetry mentioned earlier. It says that the strict component p must satisfy $p(x,y) > 0 \Rightarrow p(y,x) = 0$. If it is obviously the case for r^D and r^{RD^2}, it is not for r^B. However, by adding strong connectedness, it also becomes true for r^B.

Let $\mathbb{A}_B$ be the set of B-fuzzy weak preferences that are strongly connected and max-δ transitive.

Definition 21 *An* B-fuzzy social welfare function *is a fuzzy aggregation function* $f : \mathbb{A}_B^n \rightarrow \mathbb{A}_B$.

Theorem 6 *Let* $f : \mathbb{A}_B^n \rightarrow \mathbb{A}_B$ *be a B-fuzzy social welfare function satisfying FI and FPC. Then there exists an individual* $i \in N$ *such that for all distinct* $x, y \in X$ *and all* $(r_1^B, \ldots, r_n^B) \in \mathbb{A}_B^n$, *if* $p_i^B(x,y) > 0$, *then* $p_S^B(x,y) > 0$, *where* $r_S^B = f(r_1^B, \ldots, r_n^B)$.

We will now consider the third decomposition, that is, fuzzy weak preferences r^{RD^2}.

Let $\mathbb{A}_{RD^2}$ be the set of RD^2-fuzzy weak preferences that are strongly connected and exactly transitive.

Definition 22 *An* RD^2-fuzzy social welfare function *is a fuzzy aggregation function* $f : \mathbb{A}_{RD^2}^n \rightarrow \mathbb{A}_{RD^2}$.

We may note that exact transitivity is a very weak condition, so the following theorem due to Richardson is quite interesting even though strong connectedness may appear as rather constraining.

Theorem 7 *Let* $f : \mathbb{A}_{RD^2}^n \rightarrow \mathbb{A}_{RD^2}$ *be an* RD^2*-fuzzy social welfare function satisfying FI and FPC. Then there exists an individual* $i \in N$ *such that for all distinct* $x, y \in X$ *and all* $(r_1^{RD^2}, \ldots, r_n^{RD^2}) \in \mathbb{A}_{RD^2}^n$, *if* $p_i^{RD^2}(x,y) > 0$, *then* $p_S^{RD^2}(x,y) > 0$, *where* $r_S^{RD^2} = f(r_1^{RD^2}, \ldots, r_n^{RD^2})$.

However, if we assume that the RD^2-fuzzy weak preferences are only max-δ transitive, we get again a kind of possibility result.

Let $\mathbb{B}_{RD^2}$ be the set of RD^2-fuzzy weak preferences that are max-δ transitive.

Definition 23 *An* RD_δ^2-fuzzy social welfare function *is a fuzzy aggregation function* $f : \mathbb{B}_{RD^2}^n \rightarrow \mathbb{B}_{RD^2}$.

Theorem 8 *For all* $(r_1^{RD^2}, \ldots, r_n^{RD^2}) \in \mathbb{B}_{RD^2}^n$ *and all* $x, y \in X$, *let* $r_S(x,y) = (1/n)\Sigma_i r_i^{RD^2}(x,y)$. *Then this function is an* RD_δ^2*-fuzzy social welfare function satisfying FI, FPC, and FPR for which there is no individual* $i \in N$ *such that for all distinct* $x, y \in X$ *and all* $(r_1^{RD^2}, \ldots, r_n^{RD^2}) \in \mathbb{B}_{RD^2}^n$, *if* $p_i^{RD^2}(x,y) > 0$, *then* $p_S^{RD^2}(x,y) > 0$, *where* $r_S^{RD^2} = f(r_1^{RD^2}, \ldots, r_n^{RD^2})$.

Weak max-min transitivity is found by Dasgupta and Deb (1996, 2001) to perform well in permitting nontrivial fuzzy preferences and in preventing cycles of strict preferences. By using RD^2 decomposition they obtain again a rather negative result, showing the existence of an individual having disproportionate power.

Let $\mathbb{C}_{RD^2}$ be the set of RD^2-fuzzy weak preferences that are weakly max-min transitive.

Definition 24 *An* RD^2_w-fuzzy social welfare function *is a fuzzy aggregation function* $f: \mathbb{C}^n_{RD^2} \to \mathbb{C}_{RD^2}$.

Theorem 9 *Let* $f: \mathbb{C}^n_{RD^2} \to \mathbb{C}_{RD^2}$ *be an* RD^2_w*-fuzzy social welfare function satisfying FI and FPC. Then there exists an individual* $i \in N$ *such that for all distinct* $x, y \in X$ *and all* $(r_1^{RD^2}, \ldots, r_n^{RD^2}) \in \mathbb{C}^n_{RD^2}$, *if* $p_i^{RD^2}(x,y) = 1$, *then* $p_S^{RD^2}(x,y) > 0$, *where* $r_S^{RD^2} = f(r_1^{RD^2}, \ldots, r_n^{RD^2})$.

The kind of fuzzy dictator we have here, called a weak dictator by Dasgupta and Deb (1999), exerts power only in case he or she exactly prefers one option to another.

Important papers propose generalizations of some of these theorems. Fono and Andjiga (2005) and Duddy, Perote-Peña, and Piggins (2008) consider a generalization of transitivity properties such as max-min transitivity and max-δ transitivity. They use a transitivity called max-$\star$ transitivity based upon a kind of algebraic structure defined via properties of a function (called triangular norm) from $[0,1] \times [0,1]$ into $[0,1]$. Fono and Andjiga (2005) deal with fuzzy weak preferences being decomposed, although Duddy, Perote-Peña, and Piggins (2008) obtain their results without any use of decomposition. In these two papers the frontier between possibility and impossibility is explored. This frontier is also a central topic of a paper by Subramanian (2009). Subramanian introduces a new kind of decomposition (based on Dutta's decomposition) for which the asymmetry of the strict component, p, is weakened, but the symmetric component, i, is necessarily exact, that is, $i(x,y) \in \{0,1\}$.

3.2. The Case of Qualitative Values

This subsection will be entirely based on Barrett, Pattanaik, and Salles (1992). Fuzzy aggregation in an ordinal framework has rarely been explored. The only other work we know is Barrett and Pattanaik (1990), where Barrett, Pattanaik, and Salles (1992) is extended in characterizing rank-based aggregation rules such as the median rule.

Definition 25 *An* ordinally fuzzy aggregation function *is a function that associates a social ordinally fuzzy binary relation over* X, *denoted* H_S, *to an n-list of individual ordinally fuzzy binary relations over* X, *denoted* $(H_1, \ldots, H_i, \ldots, H_n)$.

Definition 26 *Let* f *be an ordinally fuzzy aggregation function;* H_i, H_S, *etc., be ordinally fuzzy binary relations;* P_i, P_S, *etc., be* BPS*-ordinally fuzzy strict preferences.* f *satisfies*

OFI (ordinally fuzzy independence of irrelevant alternatives) *if for all n-lists* $(H_1, \ldots, H_n), (H'_1, \ldots, H'_n)$ *and all* $x, y \in X$, $H_i(x,y) \sim H'_i(x,y)$ *and* $H_i(y,x) \sim H'_i(y,x)$ *for every* $i \in N$ *implies* $H_S(x,y) \sim H'_S(x,y)$ *and* $H_S(y,x) \sim H'_S(y,x)$*; and*
OFU (ordinally fuzzy unanimity) *if for all n-lists* $(P_1, \ldots, P_n)$ *and all* $x, y \in X$, *there exists* $i \in N$ *such that* $P_i(x,y) \succeq P_S(x,y)$ *and there exists* $j \in N$ *such that* $P_S(x,y) \succeq P_j(x,y)$.

Condition *OFU* is a sort of Pareto criterion. Consider $(P_1, \ldots, P_n)$ and $x, y \in X$. The set $\{\max_\ell P_\ell(x,y)\}$ $(\ell = 1, \ldots n)$ contains some element α.[4] Similarly, $\{\min_\ell P_\ell(x,y)\}$ contains some element β. The condition means that the ordinally fuzzy strict social preference $P_S(x,y)$ must be "between" α and β or "at the same level" as α or β, that is, $\alpha \succeq P_S(x,y) \succeq \beta$.

Let $\mathbb{O}$ be the set of *BPS*-ordinally fuzzy strict preferences and $\mathbb{O}_w$, $\mathbb{O}_q$, $\mathbb{O}_a$, and $\mathbb{O}_s$ be, respectively, the set of *BPS*-ordinally fuzzy strict preferences that are weakly max-min transitive, quasi-transitive, acyclical, and simply transitive.

Theorem 10 $\mathbb{O}_w \subseteq \mathbb{O}_q \subseteq \mathbb{O}_a$.

We will now introduce several ordinally fuzzy aggregation functions distinguished according to the set in which these functions take their values. The domains of these functions are identical, viz., the Cartesian product of $\mathbb{O}_w$ (or, of course, the Cartesian product of any superset of $\mathbb{O}_w$, though it will not be indicated).

Definition 27 *A w-* (resp. *q-*, *a-*, *s-*) ordinally fuzzy social welfare function *is an ordinally fuzzy social welfare function* $f : \mathbb{O}^n_w \to \mathbb{O}_w$ *(resp.* $\mathbb{O}^n_w \to \mathbb{O}_q$, $\mathbb{O}^n_w \to \mathbb{O}_a$, $\mathbb{O}^n_w \to \mathbb{O}_s$*).*

According to the different transitivity properties and other conditions imposed, we obtain the five following results.

Theorem 11 *Let* $\#X \geq n$ *and let* $f : \mathbb{O}^n_w \to \mathbb{O}_a$ *be an a-ordinally fuzzy social welfare function satisfying OFI and OFU. Let* $d \in L$, $d \succ d_\star$. *Then there exists an individual j such that for all* $x, y \in X$ *and for all* $(P_1, \ldots, P_n) \in \mathbb{O}^n_w$, $P_j(x,y) \succeq d \succ P_j(y,x)$ *and* $d \succeq P_i(y,x)$ *for all* $i \in N - \{j\} \Rightarrow P_S(x,y) \succeq P_S(y,x)$, *where* $P_S = f(P_1, \ldots, P_n)$.

This is clearly an expression of veto power. This sort of veto power can even be strengthened if the number of options is increased.

Theorem 12 *Let* $\#X \geq 2n$ *and let* $f : \mathbb{O}^n_w \to \mathbb{O}_a$ *be an a-ordinally fuzzy social welfare function satisfying OFI and OFU. Let* $d \in L$, $d \succ d_\star$. *Then there exists an individual j such that for all* $x, y \in X$ *and for all* $(P_1, \ldots, P_n) \in \mathbb{O}^n_w$, $P_j(x,y) \succeq d \succ P_j(y,x) \Rightarrow P_S(x,y) \succeq P_S(y,x)$, *where* $P_S = f(P_1, \ldots, P_n)$.

[4] Since $\succeq$ is a complete preorder, we have not excluded the possibility that two different elements essentially represent the same "degree of preference" (for instance, "a little" and "mildly"). Then $\{\max_\ell P_\ell(x,y)\}$ may contain more than one element.

It is possible to extend these two theorems when no restriction is imposed on the number of elements in X. Regarding Theorem 11, if $\lceil n/\#X \rceil$ is the smallest integer $\geq n/\#X$, N can be partitioned into at most $\#X$ coalitions of size $\leq \lceil n/\#X \rceil$. Then the kind of veto power assigned to individual j will be assigned to some coalition belonging to the partition. For Theorem 12, it is sufficient to replace $\lceil n/\#X \rceil$ by $\lceil 2n/\#X \rceil$.

We will consider now the case of quasi-transitivity.

Theorem 13 *Let $f : \mathbb{O}_w^n \to \mathbb{O}_q$ be a q-ordinally fuzzy social welfare function satisfying OFI and OFU. Let $d \in L$, $d \succ d_\star$. Then there exists a coalition C such that:*

for all $x, y \in X$ and for all $(P_1, ..., P_n) \in \mathbb{O}_w^n$, $P_i(x,y) \succeq d \succ P_i(y,x)$ for all $i \in C \Rightarrow P_S(x,y) \succ P_S(y,x)$, where $P_S = f(P_1, ..., P_n)$; and
for all $i \in C$, for all $x, y \in X$ and for all $(P_1, ..., P_n) \in \mathbb{O}_w^n$, $P_i(x,y) \succeq d \succ P_i(y,x) \Rightarrow P_S(x,y) \succeq P_S(y,x)$, where $P_S = f(P_1, ..., P_n)$.

Replacing $\mathbb{O}_q$ by $\mathbb{O}_w$, we obtain the following theorem.

Theorem 14 *Let $f : \mathbb{O}_w^n \to \mathbb{O}_w$ be a w-ordinally fuzzy social welfare function satisfying OFI and OFU. Let $d \in L$, $d \succ d_\star$. Then there exists a coalition C such that:*

for all $x, y \in X$ and for all $(P_1, ..., P_n) \in \mathbb{O}_w^n$, $P_i(x,y) \succeq d \succ P_i(y,x)$ for all $i \in C \Rightarrow P_S(x,y) \succeq d \succ P_S(y,x)$, where $P_S = f(P_1, ..., P_n)$; and
for all $i \in C$, for all $x, y \in X$ and for all $(P_1, ..., P_n) \in \mathbb{O}_w^n$, $P_i(x,y) \succeq d \succ P_i(y,x) \Rightarrow P_S(x,y) \succeq d$ or $d \succ P_S(y,x)$, where $P_S = f(P_1, ..., P_n)$.

Finally, we consider the case of simple transitivity.

Theorem 15 *Let $f : \mathbb{O}_w^n \to \mathbb{O}_s$ be an s-ordinally fuzzy social welfare function satisfying OFI and OFU. Then there exists a coalition C such that:*

for all $x, y \in X$ and for all $(P_1, ..., P_n) \in \mathbb{O}_w^n$, $P_i(x,y) \succ d_\star$ and $P_i(y,x) = d_\star$ for all $i \in C \Rightarrow P_S(x,y) \succ d_\star$ and $P_S(y,x) = d_\star$, where $P_S = f(P_1, ..., P_n)$; and
for all $i \in C$, for all $x, y \in X$ and for all $(P_1, ..., P_n) \in \mathbb{O}_w^n$, $P_i(x,y) \succ d_\star$ and $P_i(y,x) = d_\star \Rightarrow P_S(x,y) \succ d_\star$ or $P_S(y,x) = d_\star$, where $P_S = f(P_1, ..., P_n)$.

By Theorem 10, one can replace appropriately the transitivity properties in Theorems 11, 12, and 13. Theorem 15 can be compared to Theorem 1. The result of Theorem 15 is slightly weaker regarding the kind of veto power, since we have $P_S(x,y) \succ d_\star$ or $P_S(y,x) = d_\star$ rather than $p_S(y,x) = 0$.

4. OTHER ASPECTS

In this section, we will present two aspects that are heretofore less developed than what can be called Arrovian aspects, viz., fuzzy versions of Sen's impossibility of a Paretian liberal and considerations of some economic types of restriction on fuzzy preferences.

4.1. Aggregation of Fuzzy Preferences and Sen's Impossibility Theorem

This subsection is essentially based upon Subramanian (1987).

Sen's impossibility theorem demonstrates that for some class of aggregation functions (generally called social decision functions) that includes Arrovian social welfare functions, given a sufficiently large domain, there is an inconsistency between unanimity—or the weak Pareto principle (whenever every individual prefers alternative a to alternative b, so does the society)—and a condition called minimal liberalism (there are at least two individuals i and j, and for each of them two alternatives, a_i, b_i for i (resp. a_j, b_j for j), such that the (strict) preference of i (resp. j) over his alternatives is reflected by the social (strict) preference over these alternatives). The intuition is that the alternatives a_i, b_i for i (resp. a_j, b_j for j) belong to i's (resp. j's) personal sphere, or, more precisely, differ on characteristics concerning i (resp. j) only. This condition may appear as being very strong and giving too much power to these two individuals. Rather than describing individual liberty, it can be interpreted as some kind of local dictatorship (Salles 2000). In Subramanian's (1987) fuzzy version, the condition is weakened. Whenever i (resp. j) exactly prefers one of his two alternatives to the other, say a_i to b_i, then the degree of the fuzzy social preference of a_i over b_i must be greater than (or at least as great as) the degree of the fuzzy social preference of b_i over a_i.

Let $\mathbb{S}_1$ be the set of S_1-fuzzy strict preferences, $\mathbb{S}_2$ the set of S_2-fuzzy strict preferences, $\mathbb{S}_{1e}$ the subset of S_1 made up of all exact S_1-fuzzy strict preferences (those for which the only possible values are 0 or 1), $\mathbb{S}_{2e}$ the subset of S_2 made up of all exact S_2-fuzzy strict preferences. (See Definition 4.)

Definition 28 *An* S_1-fuzzy social welfare function *is a fuzzy aggregation function* $f : \mathbb{S}_1^n \to \mathbb{S}_2$. *An* S_{1e}-fuzzy social welfare function *is a fuzzy aggregation function* $f : \mathbb{S}_{1e}^n \to \mathbb{S}_2$. S'_{1e}-fuzzy social welfare function *is a fuzzy aggregation function* $f : \mathbb{S}_{1e}^n \to \mathbb{S}_1$.

In the following definition, f will be any of the fuzzy aggregation functions defined in Definition 28, and we will use generically $(p_1, ..., p_n)$ for any n-list in the domains of these functions.

Definition 29 *Let f be any of the fuzzy aggregation functions of Definition 28. f satisfies*

SFPC (S-fuzzy Pareto criterion) *if for all* $(p_1, ..., p_n)$, *all distinct* $x, y \in X$, $p_i(x, y) = 1$ *and* $p_i(y, x) = 0$ *for all* $i \in N \Rightarrow p_S(x, y) = 1$ *and* $p_S(y, x) = 0$, *where* $p_S = f(p_1, ..., p_n)$; *and*

FML_1 (fuzzy minimal liberalism-1) *if there exist two individuals* $i, j \in N$ *and for each of them two options,* a_i *and* b_i *for* i *and* a_j *and* b_j *for* j, *such that*
for all $(p_1, ..., p_n)$, $p_i(a_i, b_i) = 1$ *and* $p_i(b_i, a_i) = 0 \Rightarrow p_S(a_i, b_i) > p_S(b_i, a_i)$, *and for all* $(p_1, ..., p_n)$, $p_i(b_i, a_i) = 1$ *and* $p_i(a_i, b_i) = 0 \Rightarrow p_S(b_i, a_i) > p_S(a_i, b_i)$; *and*

for all $(p_1,...,p_n)$, $p_j(a_j,b_j)=1$ *and* $p_j(b_j,a_j)=0 \Rightarrow p_S(a_j,b_j) > p_S(b_j,a_j)$, *and for all* $(p_1,...,p_n)$, $p_j(b_j,a_j)=1$ *and* $p_j(a_j,b_j)=0 \Rightarrow p_S(b_j,a_j) > p_S(a_j,b_j)$; *and*
FML_2 (fuzzy minimal liberalism-2) *if there exist two individuals* $i,j \in N$ *and for each of them two options,* a_i *and* b_i *for* i *and* a_j *and* b_j *for* j*, such that*
for all $(p_1,...,p_n)$, $p_i(a_i,b_i)=1$ *and* $p_i(b_i,a_i)=0 \Rightarrow p_S(a_i,b_i) \geq p_S(b_i,a_i)$, *and for all* $(p_1,...,p_n)$, $p_i(b_i,a_i)=1$ *and* $p_i(a_i,b_i)=0 \Rightarrow p_S(b_i,a_i) \geq p_S(a_i,b_i)$; *and*
for all $(p_1,...,p_n)$, $p_j(a_j,b_j)=1$ *and* $p_j(b_j,a_j)=0 \Rightarrow p_S(a_j,b_j) \geq p_S(b_j,a_j)$, *and for all* $(p_1,...,p_n)$, $p_j(b_j,a_j)=1$ *and* $p_j(a_j,b_j)=0 \Rightarrow p_S(b_j,a_j) \geq p_S(a_j,b_j)$.

It should be noted that both liberalism conditions are based on individual exact preferences. The first one is interpreted by Subramanian as the fuzzy counterpart of the condition due to Sen (1970a, 1970b) and the second of the version due to Karni (1978). Also the Pareto criterion (unanimity) is based on individual and social exact preferences.

Theorem 16 *There does not exist a function* $f : \mathbb{S}^n_{1e} \to \mathbb{S}_2$ *satisfying conditions SFPC and* FML_1.

Theorem 17 *There does not exist a function* $f : \mathbb{S}^n_{1e} \to \mathbb{S}_1$ *satisfying conditions SFPC and* FML_2.

Theorem 18 *The fuzzy aggregation function* f *defined by*

for all $x,y \in X$, *all* $(p_1,...,p_n) \in \mathbb{S}^n_1$, $p_S(x,y) = \min_i p_i(x,y)$, *where* $p_S = f(p_1,...,p_n)$, *is an* S_1*-fuzzy social welfare function satisfying SFPC and* FML_2.

The crucial role of exact preferences in these theorems must be underlined. Exact preferences are the only preferences in the domains for Theorems 16 and 17, and furthermore, individual preferences are exact in the definitions of the Pareto condition (*SFPC*) and the fuzzy versions of minimal liberalism conditions.

Dimitrov (2004) uses intuitionistic fuzzy sets introduced by Atanassov (1999). Rather than associating a (unique) number to an ordered pair (x,y), he associates two numbers, the first one expressing the degree to which x is preferred to y and the second the degree to which x is not preferred to y, requiring that the sum of these numbers be ≤ 1. He considers fuzzy weak preferences with a decomposition à la Dutta and obtains a possibility result.

4.2. Aggregation of Fuzzy Preferences and Economic Environments

When social choice theory started its modern development in the 1940s, Black (1958) introduced a condition (in a kind of geometric way), called single-peakedness, restricting the individual preferences. In the exact case, if the individual preferences given by complete preorders are single-peaked, majority rule is a social welfare function (given some mild condition on the number of individuals having these preferences). A number of developments took place from the 1960s. They are excellently surveyed in

Gaertner (2001, 2002). Among the restrictive conditions on individual preferences, those used in standard microeconomic theory are particularly important. For instance, consider exchange economies. Since equilibrium redistributions are Pareto-optimal, it seems crucial to be able to rank these redistributions on the basis of an aggregation function that satisfies some properties related to ethical and social justice considerations. A major difficulty arises about these considerations, because individuals have preferences over their consumption sets but not on redistributions. This can be resolved by assuming selfishness and by identifying an individual's preferences over the redistributions with this individual's preferences over his or her individual bundles. In the case of (pure) public goods, this difficulty disappears as individuals and society have their preferences on the same set of alternatives, which is generally taken to be the positive orthant of a Euclidean space. Then an individual's preference is generally given by a complete preorder that is, furthermore, monotonic, continuous, and (strictly) convex. In a fundamental paper that started the literature on aggregation in an economic environment, Kalai, Muller, and Satterthwaite (1979) dealt with the case of public goods. The excellent overview of this topic by Le Breton and Weymark (2004) is highly recommended. Geslin, Salles, and Ziad (2003) consider the public good case when individual and social preferences are fuzzy. They test the robustness of the results of Barrett, Pattanaik, and Salles (1986) when the set of alternatives is the positive orthant of a Euclidean space (i.e., a pure public good economy where the social and individual preferences are defined over the same set), and when the individuals' fuzzy strict preferences satisfy some monotonicity properties.

Geslin, Salles, and Ziad (GSZ) consider the case where $X = \mathbb{R}^{\ell}_{+}$, the positive orthant of ℓ-dimensional Euclidean space. They introduce two monotonicity properties on individual *BPS*-fuzzy strict preferences. Although the first is probably specific to their paper, the second is an adaptation of the monotonicity of preferences of microeconomics texts.

We will use the standard notation regarding inequalities between vectors in $\mathbb{R}^{\ell}$, that is, given $x = (x_1, \dots, x_\ell)$ and $y = (y_1, \dots, y_\ell)$, $x \geq y$ if $x_h \geq y_h$ for $h = 1, \dots, \ell$; $x > y$ if $x \geq y$ and $x \neq y$; and $x \gg y$ if $x_h > y_h$ for $h = 1, \dots, \ell$. We will consider *BPS*-fuzzy strict preferences (see Definition 2).

Definition 30 *A* BPS-*fuzzy strict preference p satisfies F*–monotonicity *if for any y, x, $x' \in \mathbb{R}^{\ell}_{+}$,*

(1) *if $x \leq y$, $p(x, y) = 0$, and*
(2) *otherwise, $x > x' \Rightarrow p(x, y) > p(x', y)$ if $p(x', y) \neq 1$ and $p(x, y) = 1$ if $p(x', y) = 1$.*[5]

This definition is intuitively appealing. It means that the degree to which x is preferred to y is greater (when it is possible) than the degree to which x' is preferred to y, when x is greater (in the vector sense) than x'.

Let $\mathbb{M}_1$ be the set of F-monotonic *BPS*-fuzzy strict preferences.

[5] This corrects the definition in GSZ that is insufficient to prove Theorem 19.

Definition 31 *An* F-monotonic BPS-social welfare function *is a fuzzy aggregation function* $f : \mathbb{M}_1^n \to \mathbb{A}_{BPS}$.

Theorem 19 *Let* $X = \mathbb{R}_+^\ell$. *The fuzzy aggregation function* f *defined by*

for all $x, y \in \mathbb{R}_+^\ell$ *and all* $(p_1, \ldots, p_n) \in \mathbb{M}_1^n$, $p_S(x,y) = (1/n)\Sigma_i p_i(x,y)$ *is an* F*-monotonic BPS-fuzzy social welfare function satisfying FI and FPC.*

Of course, as previously, one can remark that this fuzzy social welfare function satisfies other properties (in particular, properties of symmetry). In BPS (1986), it is indicated that the mean rule is not a *BPS*-fuzzy social welfare function because (iii) of Definition 3 is not satisfied by the social preference. The preceding result indicates that F-monotonicity is a sufficient condition to obtain (iii). GSZ introduce a second monotonicity property which they call E-monotonicity.

Definition 32 *A* BPS-*fuzzy strict preference* p *satisfies* E-monotonicity *if for all distinct* $x, y \in \mathbb{R}_+^\ell$, $x > y \Rightarrow p(x,y) = 1$ *and* $p(y,x) = 0$.

This is, of course, similar to the standard property of microeconomics. Let $\mathbb{M}_2$ be the set of E-monotonic *BPS*-fuzzy strict preferences.

Definition 33 *An* E-monotonic BPS-social welfare function *is a fuzzy aggregation function* $f : \mathbb{M}_2^n \to \mathbb{A}_{BPS}$.

GSZ show that Theorems 1 and 2 are essentially preserved when individual fuzzy preferences are E-monotonic *BPS*-fuzzy strict preferences.

Theorem 20 *Let* $X = \mathbb{R}_+^\ell$ *and* $f : \mathbb{M}_2'^n \subseteq \mathbb{M}_2^n \to \mathbb{A}_{BPS}$ *be an* E*-monotonic BPS-fuzzy social welfare function satisfying FI and FPC and having a non-narrow domain for all distinct* $x, y, z \in \mathbb{R}_+^\ell$ *such that there is no* $>$*-relation between any two of them. Then there exists a unique coalition* C *such that*

for all distinct $x, y \in \mathbb{R}_+^\ell$ *and all* $(p_1, \ldots, p_n) \in \mathbb{M}_2'^n$, *if* $p_i(x,y) = 1$ *and* $p_i(y,x) = 0$ *for every* $i \in C$, *then* $p_S(x,y) > 0$, *where* $p_S = f(p_1, \ldots, p_n)$; *and*
for all distinct $x, y \in X$ *and all* $(p_1, \ldots, p_n) \in \mathbb{M}_2'^n$, *if for some* $j \in C$, $p_j(x,y) = 1$ *and* $p_j(y,x) = 0$, *then* $p_S(y,x) = 0$, *where* $p_S = f(p_1, \ldots, p_n)$.

The following theorem is a simple corollary (in the same way as Theorem 2 is a corollary of Theorem 1).

Theorem 21 *Let* $X = \mathbb{R}_+^\ell$, $f : \mathbb{M}_2'^n \subseteq \mathbb{M}_2^n \to \mathbb{A}_{BPS}$ *be an* E*-monotonic BPS-fuzzy social welfare function satisfying FI and FPC and having a non-narrow domain for all distinct* $x, y, z \in \mathbb{R}_+^\ell$ *such that there is no* $>$*-relation between any two of them, and* $p_S \in f(\mathbb{M}_2'^n)$ *be BPS-complete. Then* $\#C = 1$: *there exists an individual* $i \in N$ *such that for all distinct* $x, y \in \mathbb{R}_+^\ell$ *and all* $(p_1, \ldots, p_n) \in \mathbb{M}_2'^n$, *if* $p_i(x,y) = 1$ *and* $p_i(y,x) = 0$, *then* $p_S(x,y) > 0$ *and* $p_S(y,x) = 0$, *where* $p_S = f(p_1, \ldots, p_,)$.

These two theorems can be stated and proved in an essentially similar manner for another monotonicity assumption: *$F^\star$-monotonicity*. p is said to be *$F^\star$-monotonic* if for all distinct $x, y \in \mathbb{R}^\ell_+$, $x > y \Rightarrow p(x,y) > 0$ and $p(y,x) = 0$.

GSZ consider another subclass of E-monotonic *BPS*-fuzzy strict preferences, which appears as very restrictive and rather arbitrary. Their purpose, here, is to show that they obtain similar results even in this very restrictive case, which exemplifies the robustness of their quasi-negative results.

Definition 34 *Let $a \in \mathbb{R}^\ell_+$, $a \gg 0$, and $\alpha \in]0,1[$. The strictly positive vector a is said to* α-parametrize *a fuzzy binary relation $p^{a\alpha}$ over $\mathbb{R}^\ell_+$ if for all $x, y \in \mathbb{R}^\ell_+$,*

$$p^{a\alpha}(x,y) = \begin{cases} 1 & \text{if } ax > ay \\ \alpha & \text{if } ax = ay \text{ and } x \neq y \\ 0 & \text{otherwise,} \end{cases} \tag{2}$$

where ax and ay are dot products.

Let $\mathbb{P}$ be the set of fuzzy binary relations over $\mathbb{R}^\ell_+$ that are α-parametrized by some strictly positive vector for some $\alpha \in]0,1[$.

Definition 35 *A* P−BPS-social welfare function *is a fuzzy aggregation function $f : \mathbb{P}^n \to \mathbb{A}_{BPS}$.*

Theorem 22 *If $p \in \mathbb{P}$, then $p \in \mathbb{M}_2$.*

We now show again that Theorems 1 and 2 are essentially preserved when $\mathbb{A}'_{BPS} = \mathbb{P}$.

Theorem 23 *Let $X = \mathbb{R}^\ell_+$ and $f : \mathbb{P}^n \to \mathbb{A}_{BPS}$ be a $P-$ BPS-fuzzy social welfare function satisfying FI and FPC. Then there exists a unique coalition C such that*

> *for all distinct $x, y \in \mathbb{R}^\ell_+$ and all $(p_1, ..., p_n) \in \mathbb{P}^n$, if $p_i(x,y) = 1$ and $p_i(y,x) = 0$ for every $i \in C$, then $p_S(x,y) > 0$, where $p_S = f(p_1, ..., p_n)$,*
> *and for all distinct $x, y \in X$ and all $(p_1, ..., p_n) \in \mathbb{P}^n$, if for some $j \in C$, $p_j(x,y) = 1$ and $p_j(y,x) = 0$, then $p_S(y,x) = 0$, where $p_S = f(p_1, ..., p_n)$.*

The following theorem is a simple corollary (in the same way as Theorem 2 is a corollary of Theorem 1).

Theorem 24 *Let $X = \mathbb{R}^\ell_+$, $f : \mathbb{P}^n \to \mathbb{A}_{BPS}$ be a $P-$ BPS-fuzzy social welfare function satisfying FI and FPC and $p_S \in f(\mathbb{P}^n)$ be BPS-complete. Then $\#C = 1$:*

> *there exists an individual $i \in N$ such that for all distinct $x, y \in \mathbb{R}^\ell_+$ and all $(p_1, ..., p_n) \in \mathbb{P}^n$, if $p_i(x,y) = 1$ and $p_i(y,x) = 0$, then $p_S(x,y) > 0$ and $p_S(y,x) = 0$, where $p_S = f(p_1, ...p_n)$.*

5. CONCLUDING REMARKS

It is clear from this chapter (which we hope is as complete as possible) that there are many routes that have not yet been explored within fuzzy set theory. The most striking feature of this approach is its flexibility. Exploring various assumptions, each with intuitive appeal, one can obtain divergent results. This is true when we consider different ways to decompose fuzzy weak preferences. It is also true, in economic environments, when we consider different monotonicity conditions.

Finally, let us mention that fuzzy sets are only one way to deal with imprecision and vagueness. Other approaches are possible, even though largely unexplored in economic theory. This is the case with *rough sets* theory, which provides a nice way to describe similarities (indifferences). It is also the case with *supervaluation theory*, particularly in vogue among philosophers, as mentioned in the introduction, and with the theory of *interval orders* (Fishburn 1985) and other aspects of measurement theory.

First, let us consider *rough sets*. Given a set X and a partition of X (geometrically, one can imagine some kind of grid), any subset S of X will possibly contain elements of the partition (i.e., entire subsets belonging to the partition). The union of these elements will be considered as an inner approximation of S (it will be included in S). Also, if we consider elements of the partition that have a nonempty intersection with S, one can take the union of these elements. This union will contain S and will be the outer approximation of S. This construction due to Pawlak (1982) (see also Polkowski 2002) has been used by Bavetta and del Seta (2001) to describe problems in the freedom of choice literature, in particular to deal with the difficulty raised by indistinguishable alternatives.

In *supervaluation theory* (a theory pertaining to philosophical logic), a proposition containing a vague term is true if it is true in all sharpenings of the term. A "sharpening" is an "admissible" way in which a vague term can be made precise. Consider, for instance, the term *old*. *Old* can be interpreted as "being over 55 years of age." Alternatively, it can be interpreted as "being over 60 years of age," and so on. None of these "sharpenings" is the actual meaning of *old*, which is vague, but they are ways *old* might be sharpened. On the other hand, "being over 20 years of age" cannot be a "sharpening" of *old* since it is clearly not an "admissible" way of making *old* precise. So the notion of "being admissible" is crucial. For supervaluation theory and the (philosophical) study of vagueness, Williamson (1994), Keefe (2000), and Piggins and Salles (2007) are recommended. We have drawn our presentation from Piggins and Salles (2007), which also included applications to welfare economics.

Finally, in *measurement theory* (Fishburn 1970, 1988, Krantz et al. 1971), a binary relation $\succ_{ST}$ on $X \times X$, where X is the set of alternatives, is interpreted as a comparison of the strengths of preference between ordered pairs, $(x, y) \succ_{ST} (z, w)$, meaning that the strength of preference of x over y exceeds the strength of preference of z over w.

An underlying preference $\succ$ over X is defined by $x \succ y$ if $(x, y) \succ_{ST} (y, y)$. Given a set of axioms, a utility representation for comparable differences, that is, a real-valued function u such that $(x, y) \succ_{ST} (z, w) \Leftrightarrow u(x) - u(y) > u(z) - u(w)$ can be derived. This, of course, is reminiscent of the von Neumann–Morgenstern representation of a complete preorder over lotteries, but despite this the formalization has been, to the best of our knowledge, largely ignored by fuzzy set theorists. A problem is that it is also rather difficult to interpret the notion of strength of preference of y over y. We would need for this to have a notion of (unique) minimum for the strength of preference relation.

ACKNOWLEDGMENTS

We are most grateful to Prasanta Pattanaik for our joint work on this topic over the years. Thanks also to a referee for useful suggestions, and to Dinko Dimitrov for his careful reading and for providing corrections.

REFERENCES

Arrow, K. J. (1963). *Social choice and individual values* (2nd ed.). New York: Wiley.

Atanassov, K. T. (1999). *Intuitionistic fuzzy sets: theory and applications*. Heidelberg: Physica-Verlag.

Banerjee, A. (1994). Fuzzy preferences and Arrow-type problems in social choice. *Social Choice and Welfare, 11*, 121–130.

Barrett, C. R., & Pattanaik, P. K. (1990). Aggregation of fuzzy preferences. In J. Kacprzyk & M. Fedrizzi (Eds.), *Multiperson decision making using fuzzy sets and possibility theory*, pp. 155–162. Dordrecht: Kluwer.

Barrett, C. R., Pattanaik, P. K., & Salles, M. (1986). On the structure of fuzzy social welfare functions. *Fuzzy Sets and Systems, 19*, 1–10.

Barrett, C. R., Pattanaik, P. K., & Salles, M. (1990). On choosing rationally when preferences are fuzzy. *Fuzzy Sets and Systems, 34*, 197–212.

Barrett, C. R., Pattanaik, P. K., & Salles, M. (1992). Rationality and aggregation of preferences in an ordinally fuzzy framework. *Fuzzy Sets and Systems, 49*, 9–13.

Basu, K., Deb, R., & Pattanaik, P. K. (1992). Soft sets: an ordinal formulation of vagueness with some applications to the theory of choice. *Fuzzy Sets and Systems, 45*, 45–58.

Bavetta, S., & del Seta, M. (2001). Constraints and the measurement of freedom of choice. *Theory and Decision, 50*, 213–238.

Black, D. (1958). *The theory of committees and elections*. Cambridge: Cambridge University Press.

Broome, J. (1997). Is incommensurability vagueness? In R. Chang (Ed.), *Incommensurability, incomparability, and practical reason*, pp. 67–89. Cambridge, MA: Harvard University Press.

Burns, L. C. (1991). *Vagueness*. Dordrecht: Kluwer.

Dasgupta, M., & Deb, R. (1991). Fuzzy choice functions. *Social Choice and Welfare, 8*, 171–182.

Dasgupta, M., & Deb, R. (1996). Transitivity and fuzzy preference. *Social Choice and Welfare, 13*, 305–318.

Dasgupta, M., & Deb, R. (1999). An impossibility theorem with fuzzy preferences. In H. de Swart (Ed.), *Logic, game theory and social choice*, pp. 482–490. Tilburg: Tilburg University Press.

Dasgupta, M., & Deb, R. (2001). Factoring fuzzy preferences. *Fuzzy Sets and Systems, 118*, 489–502.

Dimitrov, D. (2004). The Paretian liberal with intuitionistic fuzzy preferences: a result. *Social Choice and Welfare, 21*, 149–156.

Dubois, D., & Prade, H. (1980). *Fuzzy sets and systems: theory and applications*. New York: Academic Press.

Dummett, M. (1975). Wang's paradox. *Synthese, 30*, 325–365.

Duddy, C., Perote-Peña, J., & Piggins, A. (2008). Arrow's theorem and max-star transitivity. Forthcoming, *Social Choice and Welfare*.

Dutta, B. (1987). Fuzzy preferences and social choice. *Mathematical Social Sciences, 13*, 215–229.
Fishburn, P. C. (1970). *Utility theory for decision making*. New York: Wiley.
Fishburn, P. C. (1985). *Interval orders and interval graphs: a study of partially ordered sets*. New York: Wiley.
Fishburn, P. C. (1988). *Nonlinear preference and utility theory*. Wheatsheaf: Brighton.
Fishburn, P. C. (1998). Stochastic utility. In S. Barbera, P. J. Hammond & C. Seidl (Eds.), *Handbook of utility theory* (Vol. 1), pp. 273–319. Dordrecht: Kluwer.
Fono, L. A., & Andjiga, N. (2005). Fuzzy strict preference and social choice. *Fuzzy Sets and Systems, 155*, 372–389.
Gaertner, W. (2001). *Domains conditions in social choice theory*. Cambridge: Cambridge University Press.
Gaertner, W. (2002). Domain restrictions. In K. J. Arrow, A. K. Sen & K. Suzumura (Eds.), *Handbook of social choice and welfare* (Vol. 1), pp. 132–174. Amsterdam: North-Holland.
García-Lapresta, J. L., & Llamazares, B. (2000). Aggregation of fuzzy preferences: some rules of the mean. *Social Choice and Welfare, 17*, 673–690.
Geslin, S., Salles, M., & Ziad, A. (2003). Fuzzy aggregation in economic environments I: quantitative fuzziness, public goods, and monotonicity assumptions. *Mathematical Social Sciences, 45*, 155–166.
Gibbard, A. (1969). Social choice and the Arrow conditions, scanned version. Department of Philosophy, University of Michigan, Ann Arbor, 2010.
Goguen, J. A. (1967). L-fuzzy sets. *Journal of Mathematical Analysis and Applications, 18*, 145–174.
Kalai, E., Muller, E., & Satterthwaite, M. (1979). Social welfare functions when preferences are convex, strictly monotonic, and continuous. *Public Choice, 34*, 87–97.
Karni, E. (1978). Collective rationality, unanimity, and liberal ethics. *Review of Economic Studies, 45*, 571–574.
Keefe, S. (2000). *Theories of vagueness*. Cambridge: Cambridge University Press.
Keefe, S., & Smith, P. (Eds.). (1996). *Vagueness: a reader*. Cambridge, MA: MIT Press.
Krantz, D. H., Luce, R. D., Suppes, P., & Tversky, A. (1971). *Foundations of measurement* (Vol. 1). New York: Academic Press.
Le Breton, M., & Weymark, J. A. (2004). Arrovian social choice theory on economic domains. In K. J. Arrow, A. K. Sen & K. Suzumura (Eds.), *Handbook of social choice and welfare* (Vol. 2). Amsterdam: North-Holland.
Mas-Colell, A., & Sonnenschein, H. F. (1972). General possibility theorems for group decisions. *Review of Economic Studies, 39*, 185–192.
Nguyen, H. T., & Walker, E. A. (2000). *A first course in fuzzy logic* (2nd ed.). Boca Raton, FL: Chapman & Hall.
Ovchinnikov, S. V. (1991). Social choice and Łukasiewicz logic. *Fuzzy Sets and Systems, 43*, 275–289.
Pawlak, Z. (1982). Rough sets. *International Journal of Information and Computer Sciences, 11*, 341–356.
Piggins, A., & Salles, M. (2007). Instances of indeterminacy. *Analyse & Kritik, 29*, 311–328.
Polkowski, L. (2002). *Rough sets, mathematical foundations*. Heidelberg: Physica-Verlag.
Richardson, G. (1998). The structure of fuzzy preferences: social choice implications. *Social Choice and Welfare, 15*, 359–369.
Ross, T. J., Booker, J. M., & Parkinson, W. J. (Eds.). (2002). *Fuzzy logic and probability applications: bridging the gap*. Alexandria, VA: American Statistical Association and Philapelphia: Society for Industrial and Applied Mathematics.
Salles, M. (1998). Fuzzy utility. In S. Barbera, P. J. Hammond & C. Seidl (Eds.), *Handbook of utility theory* (Vol. 1), pp. 321–344. Dordrecht: Kluwer.
Salles, M. (2000). Amartya Sen: droits et choix social. *Revue Economique, 51*, 445–457.
Sen, A. K. (1970a). *Collective choice and social welfare*. San Francisco: Holden-Day.
Sen, A. K. (1970b). The impossibility of a Paretian liberal. *Journal of Political Economy, 78*, 152–157.
Sen, A. K. (1983). Liberty and social choice. *Journal of Philosophy, 80*, 5–28.

Sen, A. K. (1992). *Inequality reexamined*. New York: Russell Sage Foundation and Oxford: Clarendon Press.
Sen, A. K. (2002). *Rationality and freedom*. Cambridge, MA: Harvard University Press.
Subramanian, S. (1987). The liberal paradox with fuzzy preferences. *Social Choice and Welfare*, *4*, 213–218.
Subramanian, S. (2009). The Arrow paradox with fuzzy preferences. *Mathematical Social Sciences*, *58*, 265–271.
Urquhart, A. (2001). Basic many-valued logic. In D. M. Gabbay & F. Guenthner (Eds.), *Handbook of philosophical logic* (2nd ed., Vol. 2), pp. 249–295. Dordrecht: Kluwer.
Williamson, T. (1994). *Vagueness*. London: Routledge.

PART SEVEN

Fairness and Rights

CHAPTER TWENTY-ONE

Fair Allocation Rules

William Thomson
Professor of Economics, University of Rochester, Rochester, NY

Contents

Handbook of Social Choice and Welfare, Volume II
ISSN: 0169-7218, DOI: 10.1016/S0169-7218(10)00021-3

Abstract

We review the theory of fairness as it pertains to concretely specified problems of resource allocations. We present punctual notions designed to evaluate how well individuals, or groups, are treated in relation to one another: no-envy, egalitarian-equivalence, individual and collective lower or upper bounds on welfare, notions of equal or equivalent opportunities, as well as various families extending these notions. We also introduce relational notions specifying how allocation rules should respond to changes in resources (resource monotonicity), technologies (technology monotonicity), preferences (welfare domination under preference replacement), and population (population monotonicity, consistency, converse consistency).

We investigate the implications of these properties, in various combinations, in the context of various models: the "classical" problem of dividing an unproduced bundle, economies with production, economies with public goods, economies with single-peaked preferences, economies with indivisible goods, and economies in which the dividend is a non-homogeneous continuum. We consider economies in which resources are owned collectively, economies in which they are owned privately, and economies in which ownership is mixed. We offer a number of characterizations of particular allocation rules.

Keywords: fairness, no-envy, egalitarian-equivalence, lower bounds on welfares, upper bounds on welfare, equal opportunities, equivalent opportunities, resource monotonicity, technology monotonicity, preference domination under preference replacement, population monotonicity, consistency, converse consistency, classical problem of fair division, production economies, public goods, single-peaked preferences, indivisible goods, non-homogeneous continuum,

JEL Codes: C79, D63, D74.

1. INTRODUCTION

In the last thirty years, a variety of formal criteria of economic justice have been introduced that have broad conceptual appeal as well as significant operational power. Our purpose is to review this literature. Mathematically, the objects of study are mappings associating with each economy in some domain a nonempty subset of its set of feasible allocations. These mappings are called "solutions" or "rules."

The Bergson–Samuelson social welfare functions (Bergson 1938, Samuelson 1938), a central tool in traditional welfare economics, do provide the basis for answers to distributional questions in the form of complete orderings defined on the space of vectors of utilities (see Chapter 14). However, they are in general not ordinal, and in fact they often rely on interpersonal comparisons of utility. The conceptual and practical issues associated with the measurement of an agent's utility, the choice of scales in which to make interpersonal comparisons of utility, and the manner in which to make them, are discussed in Chapter 14.

The formal social choice literature that originated in Arrow's work (1951) (see Part V), partly as a criticism of the Bergson–Samuelson approach, does not require utility information, but it has been argued that its formulation is too abstract to be directly relevant to the understanding of concrete resource allocation problems, such as problems of fair allocation. Indeed, it ignores information that gives such problems their specificity. The mathematical structure of consumption spaces is not retained, so that restrictions on preferences that would be natural to impose cannot be formulated. Rules cannot be defined that take into account that information, nor can requirements on rules that are meaningful for their evaluation in each particular context be expressed.

It is only in 1967 that an ordinal equity criterion designed for the evaluation of choices in concretely specified resource allocation models was first proposed: "no-envy" (Foley 1967). This criterion has since been the object of a large number of studies. Its limitations have been uncovered and alternative notions offered, in part to remedy these limitations. Although it remains important, we will see that the literature has developed much beyond it.

On what basis should we evaluate a solution? First of all, of course, is our intuition about what is "fair." We should also understand when it is compatible with other fundamental requirements, such as efficiency. If certain minimal "rights" or "guarantees" have to be offered to agents, does it protect these rights and does it offer these guarantees? Another consideration is the scope of its applicability. We should ask whether it performs well on "classical" domains of economies with privately appropriable goods, that is, when these goods are infinitely divisible and preferences satisfy standard assumptions of continuity, monotonicity, and convexity, and production sets (when included in the specification of economies) are well-behaved too. But we should also inquire whether it can accommodate wider classes of situations, when public goods or indivisible goods are present, when preferences may be satiated or exhibit consumption externalities, and when technologies are subject to increasing-returns-to-scale or externalities.

How adaptable is the solution to the evaluation of trades, as opposed to that of allocations, and to the evaluation of how fairly groups, as opposed to individuals, are treated? Its informational demands and ease of computation are also relevant issues. Is it appropriately responsive to changes in the parameters defining the economy, such as increases in the resources available, improvements in technology, variations in the population of agents involved, or changes in their preferences? Does it give agents the incentive to exert themselves or to provide accurate information about their tastes or the technologies they are familiar with? How vulnerable is it to manipulation? And can it be implemented by well-chosen game forms? All of these are questions that should be addressed.

This survey deals only with resource allocation models and ordinal solutions. Yet it is undeniable that distributional judgments are often based on utility information, and even involve interpersonal comparisons of utility. And great is the intellectual appeal of the all-encompassing theories of the kind envisioned by Arrow (1951), Sen (1970), Rawls (1971), and others. However, by targeting more narrowly resource allocation problems, a lot more can be said, and without invoking concepts of utility. We will attempt here to find out how far such an approach can take us. The debate about which variables one should focus on when discussing fairness (resources, welfares, utilities, opportunities, functionings) has involved many writers (Dworkin 1981a, 1981b, Cohen 1989, 1990, Sen 1970, Roemer 1996). Here, we center our attention on resources and opportunities, understood in their physical sense.

The scope of our study is limited in another way, to models in which agents' preferences play a central role. Although it is methodologically relevant, we ignore the literature concerning the problem of cost allocation in which demands are taken as fixed data, as it has been the object of another survey in volume 1 (Moulin, Chapter 6), and the literature on the adjudication of conflicting claims, covered in Thomson (2003). Finally, and although we see their study as an integral part of the program under discussion here, we leave strategic issues aside. They too are the subject of other chapters (Barberà, Chapter 25). We only indicate in square brackets how our survey connects with that literature.

Earlier surveys covering some of the same ground as the present one are Thomson and Varian (1985), Young (1985), Arnsperger (1994), and Moulin and Thomson (1997). Book-length treatments are Kolm (1972, 1997), Young (1994), Moulin (1995, 2003), Thomson (1995c), Brams and Taylor (1996), Fleurbaey (1996b), and Roemer (1996).

As far as the search for meaningful social orderings in the context of resource allocation is concerned, we note that an important axiomatic literature has recently been developed (Fleurbaey and Maniquet, Chapter 22). These advances are conceptually related to the program we describe here. A precursor of this work is Goldman and Sussangkarn (1978) and more recent contributions are by Tadenuma (2001, 2005).

2. A NOTE ON THE APPROACH FOLLOWED

We use the classical model to introduce the central concepts. In subsequent sections, we revisit these concepts in the context of several other models. Much of the literature we survey is axiomatic. For a discussion of this approach in this context we refer to Thomson (2001), but a short presentation may be useful at this point.

Our goal is to identify well-behaved solutions and rules. Requirements on these mappings, given the mathematical expressions of **axioms**, are formulated. Their logical relations are clarified and their implications, when imposed singly and in various combinations, are explored. For each such combination, do solutions exist that satisfy all of them? If yes, can one characterize the class of solutions satisfying them?

Requirements can be organized into two main categories: *punctual* requirements apply to each economy separately; *relational* requirements relate choices made across economies. The first category can be subdivided: (1) One subcategory consists of bounds on welfares defined agent-by-agent, in an intrapersonal way; some are lower bounds, offering agents welfare guarantees; others are upper bounds, specifying ceilings on their welfares. (2) The other subcategory consists of concepts based on interpersonal comparisons of bundles, or more abstractly, "opportunities" or "circumstances," involving exchanges of, or other operations performed on, these objects.

The category of relational requirements can also be subdivided. First are various expressions of the central idea of solidarity: when the environment in which agents find themselves changes, and if no one in particular is responsible for the change (or no one in a particular group of agents is responsible for it), the requirement is that the welfares of all agents (or all agents in this particular group) should be affected in the same direction: these agents—we call them the "relevant" agents—should all end up at least as well off as they were initially, or they should all end up at most as well off. In implementing this general idea, the focus of each study is usually on one specific parameter entering the description of the environment under consideration. When this parameter belongs to a space equipped with an order structure, which is often the case, one can speak of the parameter being given a "greater" or "smaller" value in that order. Examples are the resources available (a point in a vector space), the technology (a subset of a vector space), and the population of agents present (a natural number). Then, depending on which assumptions are made on preferences, together with efficiency, the solidarity idea often implies a specific direction in which welfares should be affected. It sometimes tells us that all relevant agents should end up at least as well off as they were initially, and it sometimes tells us that they should all end up at most as well off. Thus, solidarity takes the form of what are usually called "monotonicity" requirements.

The other subcategory of relational requirements are expressions of the idea of robustness. They are motivated less by normative considerations than by the desire to prevent the solution from being too dependent on certain data of the problem. In that family are several notions of conditional invariance under changes in preferences, resources, technology, or populations. A number of those are particularly relevant to the understanding of strategic issues, but, as already mentioned, other contributors to this volume have reviewed the strategic component of the axiomatic literature. For that reason, we only make passing mention of studies involving both normative and strategic principles but in which the latter play a central role.

Although the general principles just discussed are few, for each particular model, some adaptation is often necessary. This is what makes the work interesting and challenging. Also, because models vary in their mathematical structures, the implications of a given principle may differ significantly from one to the other. For instance, monotonicity requirements are very restrictive for the classical model when imposed in conjunction with no-envy and efficiency, but not so in the context of allocation with single-peaked preferences. This survey should help readers gain an appreciation of this twin fact, the great generality of the principles invoked and the specificity of their implications for each model.

Important Remark on Notation and Language We examine in succession several classes of economies, starting with the canonical model, which concerns the allocation of a bundle of unproduced goods among agents equipped with standard preferences. We introduce each issue in the context of this model, and study it in the context of several other models in subsequent sections. We consider economies with public goods, economies with indivisible goods, economies with single-peaked preferences, and economies in which the dividend is a nonhomogenous continuum. When we turn to these models, and in order to save space, we do not rewrite all the definitions, unless the necessary adjustments are not straightforward. We hope that no confusion will result from taking this shortcut.

Our generic notation for an agent set is N and when this set is fixed, $N \equiv \{1, \ldots, n\}$. Some of our relational axioms involve variations of populations. To allow for such variations, we imagine then that agents are drawn from an infinite universe of "potential" agents, the set $\mathbb{N}$ of natural numbers. We denote by $\mathcal{N}$ the class of finite and nonempty subsets of $\mathbb{N}$, and N is now the generic element of $\mathcal{N}$. In the statements of many results, solutions and rules are required to satisfy certain axioms none of which involves changes in populations. Other relational axioms may be invoked, however, specifying how rules should respond to changes in other parameters. In each case, the domain should be understood to be rich enough that changes in these parameters can actually take place.

Our generic notation for solutions is the letter φ. We place statements pertaining to strategic questions within square brackets to help relate our survey to the work reviewed in other chapters in this volume. We always assume preferences to be continuous (when continuity is meaningful), and omit this assumption from the formal statements of the theorems.

A solution is **single-valued**—we refer to it as a **rule**, then—if for each economy in its domain, it selects a single allocation, and **essentially single-valued** if whenever it selects several allocations, these allocations are **Pareto-indifferent**, that is, all agents are indifferent between them. An *essentially single-valued* subsolution of a solution φ is a **selection from φ**.

We often use the same name for a property of an allocation and the mapping that associates with each economy the set of allocations that satisfy the property (e.g., we speak of an envy-free allocation and of the no-envy solution).

3. THE CLASSICAL PROBLEM OF FAIR DIVISION

Here is our first model. There are ℓ privately appropriable and infinitely divisible goods and a set $N \equiv \{1, \ldots, n\}$ of agents. Each agent $i \in N$ is described by means of a (continuous, as indicated previously) **preference relation** R_i defined on $\mathbb{R}^\ell_+$. The strict preference relation associated with R_i is denoted by P_i and the corresponding indifference relation by I_i. Let $R \equiv (R_i)_{i \in N}$ be the profile of preference relations.

Let $\mathcal{R}$ be our generic notation for a **domain of admissible preferences**. A preference relation is **classical** if it is (i) continuous: lower and upper contour sets are closed; (ii) monotonic: if $z'_i > z_i$, then $z'_i \; P_i \; z_i$;[1] and (iii) convex: upper contour sets are convex. On occasions, we assume preferences to be strictly monotonic: if $z'_i \geq z_i$, then $z'_i \; P_i \; z_i$.

Since preferences are continuous, we can represent them by continuous real-valued functions, and it is sometimes convenient to do so. For each $i \in N$, let $u_i : \mathbb{R}^\ell_+ \to \mathbb{R}$ be such a representation of agent i's preferences, and let $u \equiv (u_i)_{i \in N}$. Except in a few places

[1] Vector inequalities: $x \geqq y$ means that for each $i \in N$, $x_i \geq y_i$; $x \geq y$ means that $x \geqq y$ and $x \neq y$; $x > y$ means that for each $i \in N$, $x_i > y_i$.

in this exposition, these representations have no cardinal significance. Indeed, the theory developed here is based only on preferences.

The vector of resources available for distribution, the **social endowment**, is denoted $\Omega \in \mathbb{R}^{\ell}_{+}$.

Altogether, an **economy** is a pair $(R,\Omega) \equiv ((R_i)_{i\in N},\Omega) \in \mathcal{R}^N \times \mathbb{R}^{\ell}_{+}$. Let $\mathcal{E}^N$ be our generic notation for a domain of economies.

In an economy, resources are owned collectively, whereas in an **economy with individual endowments**, each agent starts out with a particular share of society's resources. Agent i's **endowment**, a vector $\omega_i \in \mathbb{R}^{\ell}_{+}$, is usually interpreted as a bundle that he has the right to dispose of as he wishes. However, this interpretation, which strongly suggests that he is entitled to a welfare that is at least the welfare he experiences when consuming his endowment, is not the only possible one.[2] Formally, $\omega \equiv (\omega_i)_{i\in N}$ is simply a reference allocation on which the final choice is allowed, or required, to depend. A generic economy is now a pair $e \equiv (R,\omega)$ with $R \in \mathcal{R}^N$ and $\omega \in \mathbb{R}^{\ell N}_{+}$.

We distinguish between the problem of fairly allocating a social endowment from the problem of fairly **re**allocating individual endowments. A **feasible allocation for** $(\boldsymbol{R},\boldsymbol{\Omega})$ is a list $z \equiv (z_i)_{i\in N} \in \mathbb{R}^{\ell N}_{+}$ such that $\sum z_i = \Omega$,[3] and a **feasible allocation for** $(\boldsymbol{R},\boldsymbol{\omega})$ is a list $z \equiv (z_i)_{i\in N} \in \mathbb{R}^{\ell N}_{+}$ such that $\sum z_i = \sum \omega_i$. The i-th component of a feasible allocation is agent i's **consumption bundle**. The equality sign appearing in the feasibility constraint indicates the absence of free disposal. When preferences are monotonic and efficiency is required, as is mostly the case here, this assumption entails no loss of generality. In Section 11, where we drop monotonicity, the equality takes real significance. Let $\boldsymbol{Z(e)}$ be the set of feasible allocations of $e \in \mathcal{E}^N$. A feasible allocation of particular interest is **equal division,** $\left(\frac{\Omega}{|N|},\ldots,\frac{\Omega}{|N|}\right)$. We designate it as **ed**.

We recall that an allocation is (Pareto)-**efficient** if it is feasible and there is no other feasible allocation that **Pareto-dominates** it, which means that each agent finds it at least as desirable and at least one agent prefers. It is **weakly efficient** if there is no other feasible allocation that each agent prefers. The **Pareto solution** associates with each economy its set of efficient allocations.

Sometimes, we find it notationally convenient to assume that preferences are defined over the cross-product of the consumption spaces. Instead of statements of the form "$z_i\ R_i\ z'_i$," we write "$z\ R_i\ z'$." Also, given $z,z' \in Z(e)$, if for each $i \in N$, $z_i\ R_i\ z'_i$, we write $z\ R\ z'$, the statements $z\ P\ z'$ and $z\ I\ z'$ being understood in a similar way. When externalities in consumption are present, such notation is of course necessary.

[2] This is why we prefer avoiding the phrase "private ownership economy," which is commonly used.

[3] Unless otherwise indicated, a sum without explicit bounds should be understood to be carried out over all agents.

Quasi-linear preference profiles are of particular interest: for such a profile, there is a good whose consumption is usually unrestricted in sign (but sometimes non-negativity is imposed)—we always let it be good 1—such that all preferences can be given representations that are separably additive in good 1 on the one hand, and a function $v_i\colon \mathbb{R}_+^{\ell-1} \to \mathbb{R}$ of the remaining goods on the other. Designating by $x_i \in \mathbb{R}$ agent i's consumption of good 1 and by $y_i \in \mathbb{R}_+^{\ell-1}$ his consumption vector of the other goods, we can write $u_i(x_i, y_i) = x_i + v_i(y_i)$. Quasi-linear economies lend themselves to the application of the solution concepts developed in the rich theory of cooperative games with "transferable utility." Quasi-linearity applies to domains other than the classical domain by appropriately choosing the arguments of the v_i functions.

4. EQUITABLE ALLOCATIONS

The simplest problem of fair division is when there is only one good and preferences are strictly monotonic. Since in this situation, efficiency is automatically satisfied, how we choose to perform the division is a reflection of our position on normative issues only. Indeed, preferences are identical then. Our choice is equal division. This is because, as already announced, we have decided to ignore intensities of satisfaction—we have no "utility" information. When agents differ in the effort they provide, their productive talents, and so on, adjustments may also have to be made, but for the time being, we ignore these complications. An important exception is Section 5.

4.1. Comparisons to Equal Division

If there is more than one good, equal division conflicts with efficiency, so other criteria have to be formulated. Our next proposals are based on comparisons to equal division.[4] The first comparison is expressed in physical terms. **No-domination of, or by, equal division**, says that no agent should receive a bundle that contains at least as much as equal division of each good, and more than equal division of at least one good (Thomson 1995c), or a bundle that contains at most as much as equal division of each good, and less than equal division of at least one good.

The next comparison involves preferences: each agent should find his bundle at least as desirable as equal division. It has been advocated by many authors (see for instance Kolm 1973, and in particular, Pazner 1977).

[4] Pazner and Schmeidler (1976) give several reasons why equal division would emerge in the "original position," and they propose a way of giving operational meaning to the Rawlsian objective of making the worse-off agent as well-off as possible.

Definition *Given* $e \equiv (R, \Omega) \in \mathcal{E}^N$*, the allocation* $z \in \boldsymbol{Z}(e)$ ***meets the equal-division lower bound in e****, written as* $z \in \underline{\boldsymbol{B}}_{ed}(e)$*, if* $z \; R \; (\frac{\Omega}{|N|}, \ldots, \frac{\Omega}{|N|})$.[5]

The existence of efficient allocations meeting the equal-division lower bound is a straightforward consequence of the compactness of the feasible set and continuity of preferences.

We add two elementary requirements on a solution involving comparisons to equal division. First, if equal division is efficient, it should be chosen. Second, if equal division is efficient, any allocation that is Pareto-indifferent to it—these allocations are the ones that meet the equal-division lower bound—should be chosen (Thomson 1987c). This second requirement is stronger but it is satisfied by most of the solutions that we will encounter:

Property $\boldsymbol{\alpha}$ For each $e \equiv (R, \Omega) \in \mathcal{E}^N$, if $(\frac{\Omega}{|N|}, \ldots, \frac{\Omega}{|N|}) \in P(e)$, then $\varphi(e) \supseteq \underline{B}_{ed}(e)$.

4.2. No-Domination

Another natural extension of our choice of equal division for the one-good case, this time involving interpersonal comparisons but again formulated in physical terms, is that no agent should receive at least as much of all goods as, and more of at least one good than, some other agent (Thomson 1983a, Thomson and Varian 1985. The notion appears as a formal solution in Moulin and Thomson 1988):

Definition *Given* $e \equiv (R, \Omega) \in \mathcal{E}^N$*, the allocation* $z \in \boldsymbol{Z}(e)$ ***satisfies no-domination****, written as* $z \in \boldsymbol{D}(e)$*, if there is no pair* $\{i, j\} \subseteq N$ *such that* $z_i \geq z_j$.

The no-domination requirement, which has the practical merit of being verifiable without knowing preferences, is a very weak one, and we will present more powerful ones. Most of them are based on comparisons of bundles involving preferences, and they differ from each other only in the specification of which comparisons are admissible. For no-envy, the admissible comparisons are between the allocation that is being evaluated and the allocations obtained by permuting its components. But we will define solutions based on comparisons that are restricted, for example to only efficient allocations, or extended, for example to certain infeasible allocations.

4.3. No-Envy

Next, we require of an allocation that each agent should find his bundle at least as desirable as that of each other agent (Foley 1967):[6]

[5] These allocations are often referred to as "individually rational from equal division," but we prefer not using this phrase since it implies that agents are entitled to equal division. This may not be a legitimate assumption.

[6] The idea had been formulated by at least one previous writer. Tinbergen (1953) devotes a few pages to a discussion of the no-envy test, explaining that he had developed it in conversations with the Dutch physicist Ehrenfest. However, it is thanks to Foley that the criterion has become known, and this author is usually credited with it.

Definition *Given* $e \equiv (R, \Omega) \in \mathcal{E}^N$, *the allocation* $z \in Z(e)$ ***is envy-free for*** *e, written as* $z \in F(e)$, *if for each pair* $\{i,j\} \subseteq N$, $z_i \; R_i \; z_j$.

This definition can also be stated as follows. Let Π^N denote the class of permutations on N, with generic element π. Given $z \in Z(e)$, let $\pi(z)$ be the allocation whose i-th component is $z_{\pi(i)}$. Then, $z \in F(e)$ if and only if for each $\pi \in \Pi^N$, $z \; R \; \pi(z)$ (in Figure 21.1a, the permutation exchanging agents 1 and 2 is denoted $\bar{\pi}$).

It is clear that if preferences are strictly monotonic, no-envy implies no-domination. Because equal division satisfies the definition, envy-free allocations always exist in the classical model.

Before we address the issue of the existence of envy-free and efficient allocations, a comment on the terminology we have adopted may be useful. As usually understood, "envy" denotes a feeling that reflects negatively not only on the external circumstances in which people find themselves (here, their circumstances are defined by the bundles they receive), but also on preferences themselves. A number of writers have argued that reference to "envy" is justified only if externalities in consumption exist (Archibald and Donaldson 1979). Translating into economic terminology the connotation that referring to an individual, say agent i, as being "envious" has in common language would require specifying his preferences as exhibiting consumption externalities that fail to be monotonic with respect to agent j's consumption, where $j \neq i$. Chaudhuri (1985), following Nozick (1974), formalizes such a notion and relates it to other forms of externalities. He also establishes elementary properties of the binary "envy relation" that one can associate with each allocation, pointing out that it may not be transitive. Sussangkarn and Goldman (1980) suggest plausible specifications of these external effects, and establish various impossibilities in reconciling the standard approach, followed here, with an approach in which external effects are explicitly taken into account.

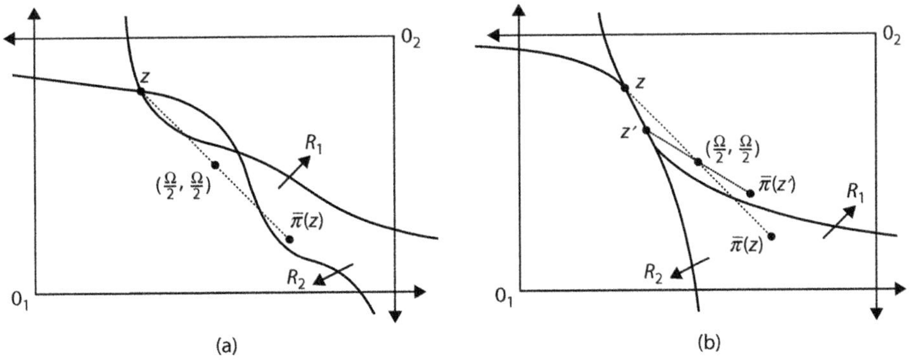

Figure 21.1. No-envy.
In both panels, $N \equiv \{1,2\}$. (a) A simple geometric test tells us that z is envy-free: each agent $i \in N$ finds his bundle z_i at least as desirable as its symmetric image with respect to the center of the Edgeworth box, $\bar{\pi}_i(z)$. (b) The no-envy and Pareto solution violates *Pareto-indifference*: here, z is envy-free and efficient and $z' \; I \; z$; yet, since agent 1 prefers z'_2 to z'_1, z' is not envy-free.

As we use the term, "envy" can occur even if externalities in consumption are not present. More neutral expressions, explicitly referring to the mathematical operation that is being performed in evaluating an allocation (such as "robustness under substitutions," "under transpositions," or "under permutations"),[7] might be more accurate, but we chose to use the term that is common in the literature.[8]

To summarize the various possibilities that could arise when preferences do exhibit consumption externalities, and starting from a given allocation $z \in Z(e)$, we could check whether agent i is better off (i) after his bundle has been *switched* with agent j's bundle; (ii) after his bundle has been *replaced* by a bundle identical to agent j's; (iii) after agent j's bundle has been *replaced* by a bundle identical to agent i's; (iv) after an arbitrary *permutation* of the components of z.

Note that in (ii) and (iii), the list of bundles to which z is compared constitutes a feasible allocation only in the trivial case $z_i = z_j$. Also, a feature of "envy," as the term is commonly understood, is that it is *directed* against a specific individual. Thus, the operation described in (iv), where the i-th components of z and $\pi(z)$ may actually be the same, has nothing to do with envy, although it seems economically relevant: it reflects agent i's view on how the resources assigned to the other agents should be distributed between them.

Whether the feelings suggested in common language by the term "envy" should be acknowledged in the evaluation of an allocation has been the object of an interesting debate (Kolm 1995, 1996, Fleurbaey 1994).

From here on, we return to the standard case of preferences that do not exhibit consumption externalities. In such economies, do envy-free and efficient allocations exist? The answer is yes under classical assumptions.

Theorem 4.1 Domain: private goods; monotonic and convex preferences. *Envy-free and efficient allocations exist.*

The simplest way to prove Theorem 4.1 is to invoke the concept of an equal-division Walrasian allocation. These allocations are obviously envy-free:

Definition *Given* $e \equiv (R, \Omega) \in \mathcal{E}^N$, *the allocation* $z \in Z(e)$ ***is an equal-division Walrasian allocation for e****, written as* $z \in W_{ed}(e)$, *if there is* $p \in \Delta^{\ell-1}$ *such that for each* $i \in N$, z_i *is a maximizer of* R_i *in the budget set* $B_i(p) \equiv \{z'_i \in \mathbb{R}^{\ell}_+ : pz'_i \leq p\frac{\Omega}{|N|}\}$.

Under the assumptions of Theorem 4.1, equal-division Walrasian allocations exist. In fact, any set of assumptions guaranteeing the existence of these allocations also guarantees

7 In Thomson (1983a), we use the phrase "permutation-acceptable" to designate a related concept. Gevers (quoted in Fleurbaey and Maniquet 1996a) suggests the term "permutation-proof."

8 In much of the early literature, the term "fair" was used to designate allocations that are envy-free and efficient (Schmeidler and Yaari 1971). In common language, fairness has no efficiency connotation, and we will express the two requirements separately.

that of envy-free and efficient allocations. Usually, convexity of preferences is included.[9] Although envy-free and efficient allocations may not exist if preferences are not convex (Varian 1974), their existence can actually be derived from substantially weaker assumptions than those known to ensure the existence of Walrasian allocations. It should be noted, however, that in addition to monotonicity of preferences, the main ones concern the structure of the efficient set and not the primitives themselves. We state them in order of increasing generality: if an allocation z is efficient, (i) no other allocation is Pareto-indifferent to z (Varian 1974);[10] (ii) the set of allocations that are Pareto-indifferent to z is convex (Svensson 1983, 1994); (iii) the set of allocations that are Pareto-indifferent to z is contractible (Diamantaras 1992).

At this point, we do not claim any particular merit for the equal-division Walrasian solution except as a convenient means of delivering envy-free and efficient allocations. However, this solution stands out for its informational efficiency, as measured by the dimensionality of message spaces required for what is called in the theory of mechanism design, its "realization": in a formal sense that would require more machinery than is justified for this survey (see Hurwicz 1977, and Mount and Reiter 1974, for the theoretical foundations), the Walrasian mechanism has minimal dimension among all mechanisms realizing envy-free and efficient allocations. Moreover, it is the only such mechanism (Calsamiglia and Kirman 1993). A number of other characterizations bringing out the informational merits of the Walrasian solution, such as the fact that it only depends on local information about preferences, or that it is invariant under certain "monotonic" transformations of preferences (Maskin 1999, Gevers 1986; Section 7.3 in this chapter) are available (Thomson 1985, 1987c, Gevers 1986, Nagahisa 1991, 1992, 1994, Nagahisa and Suh 1995, Yoshihara 1998). Some of these characterizations involve no-envy but we will not elaborate, as the informational considerations on which they are based do not have a strong normative relevance. We only emphasize that by contrast, the no-envy criterion, as well as most of the other fairness notions surveyed here, cannot be checked on the basis of local information only. Marginal analysis, the fundamental tool of modern microeconomics, is often of little use when investigating fairness, although it regains its relevance when efficiency is also required.

Beyond existence, we would like to understand the structure of the set of envy-free and efficient allocations. First, the no-envy and Pareto solution violates a requirement that is satisfied by virtually all solutions commonly discussed. It says that if an allocation is chosen, then so should any allocation that all agents find indifferent to it:[11]

[9] Actually, "constrained" equal-division Walrasian allocations (Hurwicz, Maskin, and Postlewaite 1995) are envy-free as well, and under slightly stronger assumptions, efficient.

[10] Alternatively, one may assume of each preference relation that any non-zero bundle is preferred to the zero bundle, and on the preference profile that the Pareto set coincides with the weak Pareto set.

[11] The usefulness of this condition in the context of the problem of fair division is pointed out by Thomson (1983a) and Gevers (1986). The condition has played an important role in recent literature.

Pareto-Indifference

For each $e \equiv (R, \Omega) \in \mathcal{E}^N$, and each pair $\{z, z'\} \subset Z(e)$, if $z \in \varphi(e)$ and $z' \, I \, z$, then $z' \in \varphi(e)$.

In the economy $e \equiv (R, \Omega)$ depicted in Figure 21.1b, $z \in F(e)$ (in fact, $z \in FP(e)$), and $z' \, I \, z$; yet, since $z'_2 \, P_1 \, z'_2$, $z' \notin F(e)$.[12]

Another basic requirement, obviously satisfied by the no-envy solution but by neither the equal-division lower bound solution nor by the no-domination solution, is that agents with the same preferences should be assigned bundles that are indifferent according to these preferences (not necessarily identical bundles, although, in the presence of efficiency, and if preferences are strictly convex, equality of bundles will result):[13]

Equal Treatment of Equals

For each $e \equiv (R, \Omega) \in \mathcal{E}^N$, each pair $\{i, j\} \subseteq N$, and each $z \in \varphi(e)$, if $R_i = R_j$, then $z_i \, I_i \, z_j$.

To obtain the entire set of envy-free allocations in an Edgeworth box, it suffices to identify for each agent the set of points each of which he finds indifferent to its symmetric image with respect to equal division. This set is (i) a strictly downward-sloping continuous curve that (ii) passes through equal division and is symmetric with respect to that point (Kolm 1972, Baumol 1982, 1986, Thomson 1982, Kolpin 1991a).[14] An allocation is envy-free if it is on or above each agent's envy boundary (Figure 21.2). In general, the envy-free zone is the disconnected union of closed sets, one of which contains the set of allocations meeting the equal-division lower bound.

Let us add efficiency. Under standard assumptions (if preferences are continuous, strictly monotonic, and strictly convex), the efficient set is a continuous curve connecting the two origins, and it intersects the envy-free set along a curvilinear segment. This segment is contained in the component of the envy-free set to which equal division belongs. It often contains allocations that do not meet the equal-division lower bound. In Figure 21.2, these allocations constitute the curvilinear segments from x to z^1 and from y to z^2.

These remarks indicate that the envy-free set does not have a simple structure, even for $|N| = 2$. Unfortunately, if $|N| > 2$, things get worse. In particular, an allocation meeting the equal-division lower bound is not necessarily envy-free.

However, the main limitation of the no-envy concept is that in production economies, envy-free and efficient allocations may not exist, even under very standard assumptions on preferences and technologies. This difficulty occurs as soon as productivities are allowed to differ across agents (see Section 5).

[12] In fact, preferences could be drawn in such a way that z' violates no-domination.

[13] This condition is often referred to as "horizontal equity."

[14] Conversely, any curve with properties (i) and (ii) is the envy boundary of some monotonic and convex preference relation, for instance, one with right-angle indifference curves (Thomson 1995c).

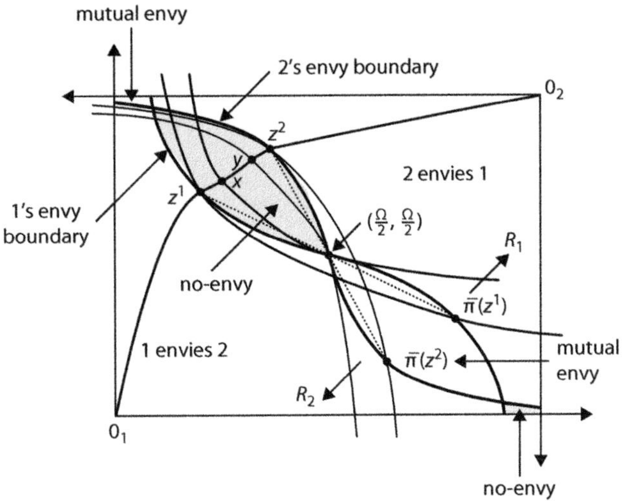

Figure 21.2. Determining the set of envy-free and efficient allocations in an Edgeworth box: It is the set of allocations that are above each agent's envy boundary. In the example, it is the union of two disconnected sets (the two shaded areas).

4.4. Concepts Related to No-Envy

Here, we discuss several variants and extensions of no-envy. First is **average no-envy**: each agent should find his bundle at least as desirable as the average of what the others receive. Indeed, one could argue that how the resources allocated in total to these agents have been distributed among them should be of no concern to him (Thomson 1979, 1982, Baumol 1982, Kolpin 1991b).

If $|N| = 2$, the criterion coincides with no-envy. Under convexity of preferences, it is less restrictive than the equal-division lower bound, but under certain regularity conditions, in a large economy (e.g., in a replica economy), it is "approximately" equivalent to it. An allocation may be envy-free and efficient and yet not average envy-free. Conversely, an allocation may be average envy-free and efficient and yet not envy-free.[15]

A stronger requirement, **strict no-envy**, involves subgroups: each agent should find his bundle at least as desirable as the average of the bundles received by any subgroup of the other agents (Zhou 1992). A further strengthening is obtained by dropping the proviso that the agent not be a member of the comparison group.

[15] For each agent, one can define a boundary above which an agent's consumption should lie for it to pass the average no-envy test. The properties of this boundary are established in Baumol (1986) and Thomson (1982). The boundary is analogous to the envy boundary encountered earlier, but now the construction can be performed for any number of agents.

The following requirement includes all of the above as special cases (Kolm 1973).[16] Given $i \in N$, we specify (i) a subgroup $G_i \subseteq N$ of agents with whose bundles a comparison of agent i's bundle is judged relevant, and (ii) a set Λ_i of admissible vectors of weights $\lambda \in \Delta^{G_i}$ to be used in these comparisons.[17] Let $(\mathcal{G}, \Lambda) \equiv (G_1, \ldots, G_n, \Lambda_1, \ldots, \Lambda_n)$.

Definition (Kolm 1973) *Given* $e \equiv (R, \Omega) \in \mathcal{E}^N$*, the allocation* $z \in Z(e)$ ***is*** $(\mathcal{G}, \Lambda)$***-envy-free for e*** *if for each* $i \in N$ *and each* $\lambda \in \Lambda_i$, $z_i \; R_i \sum_{j \in G_i} \lambda_j z_j$.

Suppose $G_i \equiv N \backslash \{i\}$. Then, if each Λ_i is the set of unit vectors in Δ^{G_i}, the resulting definition coincides with no-envy, and if Λ_i contains only the vector of equal coordinates, we obtain average no-envy. If for each $i \in N$, $G_i = N$ and $\Lambda_i = \Delta^N$, then the requirement is that each agent should find his bundle at least as desirable as any point in the convex hull of all assigned bundles (Kolm 1996).[18] Strictly envy-free allocations are also obtained as a special case. Equal-division Walrasian allocations satisfy the definition no matter what $(\mathcal{G}, \Lambda)$ is (Kolm 1973).

Some solutions are based on comparing across agents the number of agents whom each agent envies and the number of agents who envy him. One such "counting requirement," **balanced envy**, is that for each agent, these two numbers should be equal (Daniel 1975).[19] It is particularly appealing in production economies, where there may be no envy-free and efficient allocations (see Section 5). Indeed, the existence of allocations with balanced envy in such economies can be established more generally than is standard for other concepts (as in the variants of Theorem 4.1 discussed after its statement). In economies without production, the main assumption for existence is not convexity of preferences, but that no two Pareto-efficient allocations be Pareto-indifferent. (A refinement is proposed by Fleurbaey 1994, and proven to be nonempty).

The concept has been criticized because it is theoretically compatible with the existence of a large number of occurrences of envy (Pazner 1977). However, in situations where envy cannot be avoided, it is natural to attempt to distribute it "uniformly" across agents. Other natural ideas are to require of an allocation that all agents should envy the same number of agents, or that all agents should be envied by the same number of agents. But neither will do, as soon as efficiency is imposed, a consequence of the following proposition:

Proposition 4.1 (Varian 1974, Feldman and Kirman 1974) Domain: feasible set is closed under permutations of the components of allocations. *At an efficient allocation, at least one agent envies no one, and at least one agent is envied by no one.*

[16] Kolm uses the phrase "super envy-free."

[17] By the notation $\mathbb{R}^{G_i}$, we mean the cross-product of $|G_i|$ copies of $\mathbb{R}$, indexed by the members of G_i. Kolm actually allows the weights to be negative.

[18] Kolm uses the phrase "super equity."

[19] Daniel uses the term "just."

Proposition 4.1 certainly reinforces the appeal of the balanced-envy criterion, but there are other ways to deal with the nonexistence of envy-free and efficient allocations in production economies (Section 5). Varian 1976 invokes the proposition to render operational the Rawlsian objective of making the worse-off agent as well off as possible, defining a worse-off agent as one whom no one envies, and "making that agent as well off as possible" being interpreted as minimizing the number of agents whom he envies—no one, if that is possible. (Then an envy-free allocation is obtained.)

Other notions have been proposed in which each agent's preference relation is used to compare the bundles received by any two other agents. A suggestion is to require of an allocation that there should not be two agents such that all agents, if consuming the bundle assigned to the first one, would be worse off than if consuming the bundle assigned to the second one (van Parijs 1990, Iturbe-Ormaetxe and Nieto 1996a, and Fleurbaey 1994, generalize the idea.)

4.5. Selections and Rankings

As we have seen, in exchange economies, envy-free and efficient allocations exist very generally, and the set they constitute may even be quite large. In such situations, we would like to be able to identify which allocations are preferable in the envy-free set, that is, to refine the no-envy concept, perhaps to rank all allocations in terms of the extent to which they satisfy no-envy. However, strengthening it will aggravate the nonexistence difficulty that we will encounter in production economies, and unfortunately, the concept does not seem to lead directly to a ranking of all feasible allocations in terms of equity. Of course, we could (i) declare socially indifferent all allocations at which no one envies anyone, (ii) declare socially indifferent all allocations at which someone envies someone else, and (iii) declare any allocation at which no one envies anyone socially preferred to any allocation at which someone envies someone else. But this ranking would have only two indifference classes and thus would provide a trivial answer to our question.[20] Finer rankings would be desirable.

One suggestion has been to measure aggregate envy at an allocation z by the number of pairs $\{i,j\} \subseteq N$ such that $z_j \, P_i \, z_i$ (Feldman and Kirman 1974). Other proposals involve cardinal measurements of welfare differences: after choosing for each agent $i \in N$ a numerical representation of his preferences, u_i, the extent to which agent i is envious is quantified by the sum $e_i(z) \equiv \sum_j \max\{0, u_i(z_j) - u_i(z_i)\}$. (When utility information is available, one may argue that these are the functions that should be used for that purpose.) Aggregate envy is then evaluated by the expression $\sum e_i(z)$ (Feldman and Kirman 1974). Alternatively, we may also want to take into account the extent to which agent

[20] A more limited question is whether one can associate to each allocation an order on the set of agents reflecting how well they are treated. At an efficient allocation, the no-envy relation is acyclic but not transitive unless a strong assumption of similarity of preferences is made (Feldman and Weiman 1979).

i prefers his bundle to the bundles of the agents whom he does not envy. Then, defining $\bar{e}_i(z) \equiv \sum_{j \in N}[u_i(z_j) - u_i(z_i)]$, aggregate envy is evaluated by the expression $\sum \bar{e}_i(z)$. Finally, these individual sums can be weighted. Varian (1976) suggests a particular way in which the weights can be made to depend on the allocation.

These measures all have the advantage of yielding complete rankings of the set of feasible allocations, although the ranking provided by the counting measure still has large indifference classes.[21] The measures of aggregate envy proposed by Feldman and Kirman (1974) do provide fine rankings of the set of allocations at which someone envies someone else, but all allocations at which no one envies anyone belong to the same indifference class.

The extent to which an agent envies another agent can be measured in other ways, and a fine ranking of all allocations derived from this measure, as follows: Given $z \in Z(e)$ for which there is a pair $\{i,j\} \subseteq N$ such that $z_j\ P_i\ z_i$, let $\lambda_{ij}(z) \in \mathbb{R}_+$ be the factor by which z_j should be reduced so as to obtain a bundle that agent i finds indifferent to z_i: $\lambda_{ij}(z)z_j\ I_i\ z_i$. Then we rank allocations at which there is envy as a function of the quantity $\sum_{\{i,j\} \subseteq N; z_j P_i z_i} \lambda_{ij}(z)$ (Chaudhuri 1985, 1986).

Conversely, in order to measure the extent to which an allocation may exceed the no-envy requirement, let $z \in Z(e)$ be an allocation for which there is a pair $\{i,j\} \subseteq N$ such that $z_i\ P_i\ z_j$, but this time, let $\lambda_{ij}(z)$ be the factor by which z_j should be expanded so as to recover indifference, that is, so that once again $\lambda_{ij}(z)z_j\ I_i\ z_i$. This is a natural generalization of the previous idea. We then evaluate z by the sum $\sum \lambda_{ij}(z)$. Alternatively, instead of evaluating an allocation z by summing the terms $\lambda_{ij}(z)$, we could focus on the largest coordinate of the vector $(\lambda_{ij}(z))_{i,j \in N}$. Choosing the allocation at which this coordinate is as small as possible is more likely to produce a fair distribution of envy across agents when envy cannot be avoided, and to even out distance from envy, when envy-free allocations exist. The formal definition is as follows:

Definition (Diamantaras and Thomson 1990) *Given* $e \equiv (R, \Omega) \in \mathcal{E}^N$, *and* $\lambda \in \mathbb{R}$, *let* $F^\lambda(e) \equiv \{z \in Z(e)$: *for each* $\{i,j\} \subseteq N, z_i\ R_i\ \lambda z_j\}$. *Let* $\lambda(e) \equiv \inf\{\lambda\colon F^\lambda P(R) \neq \emptyset\}$ *and* $H(e) \equiv F^{\lambda(e)}P(e)$.

The existence of $\lambda(e)$ is guaranteed if indifference curves are transversal to the axes (and holds for significantly broader domains of economies than the domain considered in this section). This definition both maximally strengthens no-envy when the concept is too permissive without losing existence, and minimally weakens it so as to recover existence when it is too strong. Like the no-envy notion itself, the solution it generates violates *Pareto-indifference*. Although it is quite selective, it is not *essentially single-valued.*

[21] Feldman and Kirman (1974) assess the extent to which these criteria distribute welfare "evenly" across agents. As they have the form of a summation, it is not surprising that the answer may be unsatisfactory, as frequently occurs from maximization of utilitarian objectives. Another relevant contribution is Allingham (1977).

Finally, it is not the case, as one could have hoped, that for each allocation z it selects, and for each $i \in N$, there is $j \in N$ such that $z_i = \lambda(e) z_j$ (Kolpin 1991a).

The contractions and expansions underlying these definitions can be adapted so as to extend, or select from, other equity notions (Thomson 1995c), and from them rankings of the set of feasible allocations can be derived (for the special case of agents with identical and homothetic preferences, Chaudhuri 1986 establishes a relation to rankings based on income inequality). An application to income taxation is developed by Nishimura (2002).[22]

Other geometric operations are conceivable. For instance, if an agent envies some other agent, one could use the distance between that second agent's bundle to the lower contour set of the first agent at his assigned bundle (Chaudhuri 1986).

All of the definitions may have intuitive appeal, but none has axiomatic foundations. It is the chief merit of the Fleurbaey and Maniquet program cited earlier that it shows how rankings of allocations can be derived from axioms.

4.6. Economies with a Large Number of Agents

Next, we turn to economies with a large number of agents modeled as an atomless measure space. An important result for that case concerns no-envy: informally, if preferences are smooth and "sufficiently dispersed," the set of envy-free and efficient allocations is approximately equal to the set of equal-division Walrasian allocations.

We have seen that in economies with finitely many agents, the equal-division Walrasian solution is a subsolution of the no-envy and Pareto solution independently of the number of agents, and of course this inclusion remains true for infinite economies. We will state a theorem on the approximate equivalence of the two solutions in large economies that is reminiscent of the asymptotic equivalence of the core and of the Shapley value (Shapley 1953) with the Walrasian solution. However, it occurs here under less general conditions. In particular, one of the most convenient methods of modeling economies of increasing size, namely replication, does not guarantee convergence of the no-envy and Pareto solution to the equal-division Walrasian solution.

Although the study of variable-population requirements will mainly be discussed in later sections, it is convenient to introduce here a basic one. Given a profile R of preferences, and a natural number $k \in \mathbb{N}$, we denote by $k * R$ a profile obtained by introducing, for each $i \in N$, $k-1$ agents with the same preferences as his. We say that it is a "k-replica of R." The notation $k * z$ designates the corresponding k-replica of z.

[22] Another idea is to formulate iterative procedures to improve the equity "content" of allocations at every step. For the case of two goods and two agents, an attempt at such a formulation is made by Baumol (1982): it consists of identifying the extreme points of the envy-free set and of successively selecting "a middle zone" (in a manner that we will not specify). Philpotts (1983) studies this procedure and shows that it is incompatible with efficiency. A reformulation is proposed by Dominguez and Nicolo (2009).

The requirement is that if an allocation is chosen for some economy, then for each $k \in \mathbb{N}$, and each k-replica economy, its k-replica should be chosen:

Replication-Invariance

For each $N \in \mathcal{N}$, each $(R, \Omega) \in \mathcal{E}^N$, each $z \in \varphi(R, \Omega)$, each $N' \supset N$, each $k \in \mathbb{N}$, and each $(R', \Omega') \in \mathcal{E}^{N'}$, if (R', Ω') is a k-replica of (R, Ω), then $k * z \in \varphi(R', \Omega')$.

The no-envy and Pareto solution is obviously *replication-invariant*. Now, starting from a finite economy admitting an envy-free and efficient allocation that is not an equal-division Walrasian allocation, one can easily construct an atomless economy with the same feature. However, if preferences are smooth and "sufficiently dispersed," any envy-free and efficient allocation is an equal-division Walrasian allocation. The first formal result of this kind is due to Varian (1976). To formalize the idea that preferences are dispersed, we work with a continuum of agents indexed by a parameter $t \in T \equiv]0,1[$, supposing that there is a function $u\colon T \times \mathbb{R}^\ell_+ \to \mathbb{R}$ representing their preferences such that agent t's welfare from consuming the bundle z is $u(t,z)$. The assumption is that the function u is continuous in both arguments and for each $t \in T$, $u(t,\cdot)$ is strictly concave.

Under this assumption, if z is an envy-free allocation and t, t' are close, we expect $z(t)$ and $z(t')$ to be close evaluated by either $u(t,\cdot)$ or $u(t',\cdot)$, that is, agents with similar preferences are treated similarly. If in addition, z is efficient, then the bundles $z(t)$ and $z(t')$ themselves are close: the function $z\colon T \to \mathbb{R}^\ell_+$ is continuous. The next result is based on the stronger assumption that z is in fact differentiable.

Theorem 4.2 (Varian 1976) Domain: private goods; continuum of agents whose preferences can be represented by a function satisfying the above assumption. *If an envy-free and efficient allocation is a differentiable function, it is an equal-division Walrasian allocation.*

The tightness of Varian's assumptions is examined by Kleinberg (1980) and McLennan (1980). Kleinberg (1980) and Champsaur and Laroque (1981) specify assumptions on the primitives of an economy with a continuum of agents guaranteeing the Walrasian conclusion. They require strict monotonicity, strict convexity, and smoothness of preferences, and model an economy as a mapping from some space of parameter values (an open subset of a finite-dimensional Euclidean space) onto a space of preference relations. If this mapping satisfies sufficient continuity properties, the only envy-free and efficient allocations are equal-division Walrasian allocations. Mas-Colell (1987) also identifies conditions on the primitives guaranteeing the implication.

Now, recall that at a strictly envy-free allocation, each agent finds his bundle at least as desirable as the average of the bundles received by any subgroup of the other agents (Section 4.4). An interesting equivalence holds:

Theorem 4.3 (Zhou 1992) Domain: private goods; measure space of agents; preferences are strictly monotonic and differentiable in the interior of commodity space. *An allocation* *is efficient and the set of agents each of whom prefers the average bundle of some group to his own bundle has measure zero, if and only if it is an equal-division Walrasian allocation.*

We also note that under standard assumptions on preferences, the equal-division core and the set of equal-income Walrasian allocations coincide (Vind 1971).

4.7. Equity Criteria for Groups

Next, we propose criteria designed to evaluate the relative treatment of groups. First are extensions of the no-domination requirement. **No-domination of, or by, equal division for groups** says that no group of agents should receive on average at least as much as equal division of each good and more than equal division of at least one good (this is equivalent to requiring that no group should receive on average at most equal division of at least one good and less than equal division of at least one good).

Next is a generalization of the equal-division lower bound: suppose that each agent is given access to an equal share of the social endowment, and require of an allocation that no group of agents should be able, by redistributing among themselves the resources they collectively control, to make each of its members at least as well off, and at least one of them better off:

Definition *Given* $e \equiv (R, \Omega) \in \mathcal{E}^N$*, the allocation* $z \in Z(e)$ ***belongs to the equal-division core of*** e*, written as* $z \in C_{ed}(e)$*, if for each* $G \subseteq N$*, there is no list* $(z'_i)_{i \in G} \in \mathbb{R}_+^{\ell G}$ *such that* $\sum_G z'_i = \frac{|G|}{|N|}\Omega$*;* $z'_G \; R_G \; z_G$*; and for at least one* $i \in G$*,* $z'_i \; P_i \; z_i$*.*

We have seen that if $|N| = 2$, an allocation meeting the equal-division lower bound is envy-free. However, if $|N| > 2$, an allocation in the equal-division core may not be envy-free (Kolm 1972, Feldman and Kirman 1974). In fact, this situation is the rule. Indeed, absence of envy implies that two agents with the same preferences are assigned bundles that are indifferent according to these preferences, but this property is certainly not met at each equal-division core allocation. For economies parameterized by their endowment profiles, the violations are typical (Green 1972, Khan and Polemarchakis 1978). An interesting exception are replica economies. At an equal-division core allocation of such an economy, two agents with the same preferences receive bundles that are indifferent according to these preferences (Debreu and Scarf 1963).

We continue with inter-group requirements. An allocation $z \in Z(e)$ satisfies **no-domination for groups** if there is no pair $\{G, G'\}$ of subsets of N such that $\frac{\sum_G z_i}{|G|} \geq \frac{\sum_{G'} z_i}{|G'|}$: on a *per capita* basis, G should not receive at least as much of each good as G', and more of at least one good. We obtain variants of the definition by requiring $|G'| = |G|$ or $G' = N \setminus G$. Also, in the first case, we can require $G' \subseteq N \setminus G$.

To adapt to groups the no-envy criterion, we have several choices. First, we can consider what a group G could achieve by redistributing among its members what has been assigned to any other group, these resource being adjusted to take account of their relative sizes, and require that no such redistribution should make each member of G at least as well off as he was initially, and at least one of them better off (Vind 1971, Varian 1974). We introduce the formal definition in two steps. Given $e \equiv (R, \Omega) \in \mathcal{E}^N$, $z \in Z(e)$, and $G \subseteq N$, **the list $(z'_i)_{i\in G}$ G-dominates z in e** if $z'_G \, R_G \, z_G$, and for at least one $i \in G$, $z'_i \, P_i \, z_i$.

Definition *Given $e \equiv (R, \Omega) \in \mathcal{E}^N$, the allocation $z \in Z(e)$ **is group envy-free for e** if there is no $(z'_i)_{i\in G} \in B(z)$ that G-dominates z, where*

$$B(z) \equiv \{(z'_i)_{i\in G}: \text{ there is } G' \subseteq N \text{ with } \sum_G z'_i = \frac{|G|}{|G'|} \sum_{G'} z_i\}.$$

Alternatively, we can insist on $|G'| = |G|$ and set $B(z) \equiv \{(z'_i)_{i\in G}:$ there is $G' \subseteq N$ with $|G'| = |G|$ and $\sum_G z'_i = \sum_{G'} z_i\}$ (Varian 1974).[23] If we want $G' = N \setminus G$, we set $B(z) \equiv \{(z'_i)_{i\in G}: \sum_G z'_i = \frac{|G|}{|N|-|G|} \sum_{N\setminus G} z_i\}$. Finally, the first two definitions can be weakened by requiring $G' \subseteq N \setminus G$. (The concept of a strictly envy-free allocation of Section 4.4 can be seen as a step towards the definitions just given.)

Further generalizations, along the lines of Kolm's generalization of no-envy (Section 4.4), can also be formulated. Equal-division Walrasian allocations satisfy all of them. Moreover, under replication, there is a sense in which the set of efficient allocations that are group envy-free converges to the set of equal-division Walrasian allocations (Varian 1974; in this chapter, see Section 8). We also have the following equivalences:

Theorem 4.4 (Kolpin 1991b) Domain: private goods; locally nonsatiated and strictly convex preferences. *In an economy replicated at least twice, any equal-division core allocation is envy-free. If the economy is replicated at least $3|N| - 1$-times, any such allocation is group envy-free. (When, in the definition of group no-envy, comparisons are restricted to groups of the same size, it suffices to replicate three times for this conclusion to hold.)*

For economies with a large number of agents modeled as a continuum, direct equivalence results between several of these definitions hold (Varian 1974). The set of group envy-free (according to our primary definition, but even if only groups of the same size are compared) and efficient allocations coincide with the set of equal-division Walrasian allocations (Varian 1974).

We conclude this subsection with a short discussion of nonconvex preferences. Envy-free and efficient allocations may not exist then, as we saw, and it is natural to ask whether weakening no-envy to no-domination would help. The answer is no:

[23] In the case $|G'| = |G|$, we could simply reallocate among the members of G the specific bundles attributed to the members of that group, but then we would simply recover the no-envy concept.

Theorem 4.5 (Maniquet 1999) Domain: private goods; strictly monotonic, smooth, but not necessarily convex preferences. *There are economies in which all efficient allocations violate no-domination.*

Theorem 4.5 can be proved by means of a two-good and three-agent example. If $|N|=2$, the solution that selects the allocation most preferred by one of the two agents among all allocations that the other finds indifferent to equal division, does satisfy the two requirements of the theorem.

4.8. Egalitarian-Equivalence

Our next criterion is at the center of a family of solutions that constitute the main alternative to the families based on the permutation idea and on the agent-by-agent lower or upper bounds. It involves comparisons to "reference" allocations whose fairness could not be disputed since they are composed of identical bundles:

Definition (Pazner and Schmeidler 1978a) *Given* $e \equiv (R, \Omega) \in \mathcal{E}^N$*, the allocation* $z \in Z(e)$ ***is egalitarian-equivalent for e****, written as* $z \in E(e)$*, if there is* $z_0 \in \mathbb{R}^{\ell}_{+}$ *such that* $z \; I \; (z_0, \ldots, z_0)$.

The fact that $(z_0, \ldots, z_0)$ is not feasible has been at the origin of some opposition to the concept, but the reference to hypothetical situations in the evaluation of an actual alternative is not unreasonable. In abstract social choice theory, axiomatic bargaining theory, apportionment theory, to name just a few examples, the desirability of an outcome for some situation is often evaluated by comparing it to choices made in reference to economies that have a larger or smaller feasible set, involve a greater or smaller number of agents, or exhibit certain symmetries not actually present.

Some critics have also argued that the criterion might lead us to declare desirable an allocation associated with a reference bundle that none of the agents cares for (Daniel 1978). But this criticism is misdirected since such an allocation would in general not be efficient, and we presumably will want to complement the criterion with efficiency. It would be equally easy to identify economies admitting envy-free allocations at which each agent is indifferent between his assignment and the zero bundle. Should we object to the no-envy concept on these grounds?

Nevertheless, objections can indeed be raised against egalitarian-equivalence, and we will present them after a study of its basic features. On the positive side, we will see in later sections that it enjoys a variety of desirable properties not satisfied by the no-envy concept, justifying the important place it has in this exposition.

The existence of egalitarian-equivalent and efficient allocations is obtained under weak assumptions. Note in particular that in the following theorem, no convexity assumption is made:

Theorem 4.6 (Pazner and Schmeidler 1978a) Domain: private goods; strictly monotonic preferences. *Egalitarian-equivalent and efficient allocations exist.*

The egalitarian-equivalence solution and its intersection with the Pareto solution both satisfy *Pareto-indifference* and *equal treatment of equals*. If $|N| = 2$, envy-free allocations are egalitarian-equivalent. This relation, however, fails for $|N| > 2$. In fact, an equal-division Walrasian allocation may then not be egalitarian-equivalent.

Conversely, an egalitarian-equivalent allocation may violate no-domination, and *a fortiori*, no-envy. In fact, extreme violations of no-domination may occur: at an egalitarian-equivalent and efficient allocation, a particular agent may receive the entire social endowment.[24] This suggests that the egalitarian-equivalence and Pareto solution is "too large." Are there selections from it that satisfy no-domination? The following paragraphs clarify the extent to which these various ideas can be reconciled.

Definition *Let $r \in \mathbb{R}^{\ell}_{+}$, $r \neq 0$, be given. Given $e \equiv (R, \Omega) \in \mathcal{E}^N$, the allocation $z \in \boldsymbol{Z(e)}$ is* ***r-egalitarian-equivalent for e****, written as $z \in \boldsymbol{E_r(e)}$, if it is egalitarian-equivalent with a reference bundle proportional to r.*

The existence of r-egalitarian-equivalent and efficient allocations is guaranteed under the assumptions of Theorem 4.6.

For each $r \in \mathbb{R}^{\ell}_{+}\backslash\{0\}$, let $\bar{E}_r P$ be the selection from the egalitarian-equivalence and Pareto solution defined by requiring the reference bundle z_0 to be such that the vector $z_0 - \frac{\Omega}{|N|}$ is proportional to r, and let $\bar{E}P \equiv \bigcup_{r \in \mathbb{R}^{\ell}_{+}\backslash\{0\}} \bar{E}_r P$. The subcorrespondence of the egalitarian-equivalence and Pareto solution so obtained is a subsolution of the equal-division lower bound solution.

Obviously, if r and r' are proportional, $E_r = E_{r'}$. If $|N| = 2$ and r is proportional to Ω (but only then), the solution $E_r P$ satisfies no-domination. In fact, still if $|N| = 2$, if r is proportional to Ω and additionally preferences are convex, any r-egalitarian-equivalent and efficient allocation is envy-free. Without convexity, this inclusion may fail (Figure 21.3a).

If $|N| > 2$, requiring r to be proportional to Ω does not guarantee no-domination, although it obviously guarantees that the equal-division lower bound is met (Figure 21.3b).[25] More seriously, there are economies where all egalitarian-equivalent and efficient allocations violate no-domination.[26] Therefore, egalitarian-equivalence is fundamentally incompatible with no-domination (and therefore no-envy).

To compensate for this limitation, the egalitarian-equivalence correspondence enjoys a variety of appealing properties. In particular, it admits selections that are monotonic with respect to changes in resources, technologies, and other parameters, and we will

[24] Corchón and Iturbe-Ormaetxe (2001) propose a general definition of fairness based on expectations. It covers various notions discussed in the foregoing pages, such as no-envy and egalitarian-equivalence, as special cases.

[25] Pazner and Schmeidler (1978a) provide other reasons for requiring the reference bundle to be proportional to the average bundle.

[26] This follows directly from an example constructed by Postlewaite (1979) and described by Daniel (1978) in order to establish the existence of economies where all egalitarian-equivalent and efficient allocations violate no-envy.

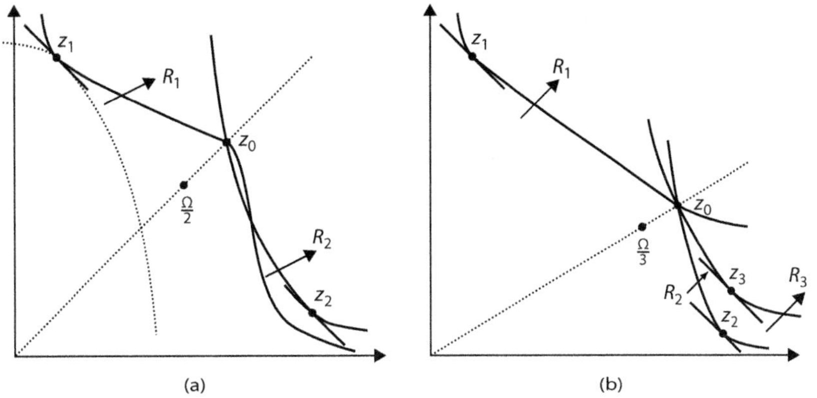

Figure 21.3. Clarifying the relation between no-domination, no-envy, and egalitarian-equivalence.
(a) Here, $N = \{1,2\}$. The dotted concave curve is the symmetric image of agent 2's indifference curve through z_2 with respect to equal division. The allocation z is r-egalitarian-equivalent and efficient for the two-agent economy depicted here, with $r \equiv \Omega$, but since agent 1 prefers z_2 to z_1, z is not-envy-free.
(b) Here, $N = \{1,2,3\}$. The allocation z is r-egalitarian-equivalent and efficient for this three-agent economy, but since $z_3 > z_2$, z violates no-domination.

come back to it on many occasions (for instance, Section 7). Moreover, it can be generalized so as to yield other concepts that also enjoy these properties, as we will discover at various points in this survey.

Conditions are known that guarantee the existence of Ω-egalitarian-equivalent and efficient allocations for economies with a large number of agents modeled either as an infinitely countable set or as a continuum (Sprumont and Zhou 1999).

4.9. Equitable Trades

Consider a society where each agent starts out with a bundle on which he has particular rights. The allocation defined by these individual endowments not being in general efficient, the problem arises as to how to distribute the gains made possible by exchanges among agents. In other words, how should we evaluate the process that takes an economy from its initial position to its final position when it is felt that the possibly uneven rights that agents have on resources should be taken into account?[27] Recall that an economy with individual endowments is a pair $e \equiv (R,\omega) \in \mathcal{R}^N \times \mathbb{R}_+^{\ell N}$. Let $\mathcal{E}_{end}^N$ be a domain of such economies. Given $e \in \mathcal{E}_{end}^N$, let $T(e) \subseteq \mathbb{R}^{\ell N}$ be its set of feasible trade profiles: $T(e) \equiv \{t \in \mathbb{R}^{\ell N} : \sum t_i = 0\}$.

[27] Holcombe (1983) emphasizes this aspect of fairness.

We start with the evaluation of the equity of trades. The simplest idea is formulated in physical terms: the trade of no agent should dominate, good by good, that of any other agent:

Definition *Given* $e \equiv (R, \omega) \in \mathcal{E}^N_{end}$, *the trade profile* $\boldsymbol{t} \in \boldsymbol{T(e)}$ ***satisfies no-domination for e*** *if* $(\omega + t) \in Z(e)$ *and for no pair* $\{i, j\} \subseteq N$, $t_j \geq t_i$.

Next is the counterpart of the equal-division lower bound. It is a standard requirement:

Definition *Given* $e \equiv (R, \omega) \in \mathcal{E}^N_{end}$, *the trade profile* $\boldsymbol{t} \in \boldsymbol{T(e)}$ ***meets the individual-endowments lower bound for e*** *if* $(\omega + t) \in Z(e)$ *and* $(\omega + t)\ R\ \omega$.

The following concept is the counterpart for trades of the no-envy concept introduced earlier for allocations: if given access to any of the trade vectors $(t_j)_{j \in N}$, each agent $i \in N$ would choose the vector t_i intended for him:

Definition (Kolm 1972, Schmeidler and Vind 1972) *Given* $e \equiv (R, \omega) \in \mathcal{E}^N_{end}$, *the trade profile* $\boldsymbol{t} \in \boldsymbol{T(e)}$ ***is envy-free for e*** *if* $(\omega + t) \in Z(e)$ *and for no pair* $\{i, j\} \subseteq N$ *such that* $(\omega_i + t_j) \in \mathbb{R}^\ell_+$, *we have* $(\omega_i + t_j)\ P_i\ (\omega_i + t_i)$.

Obviously, no-envy implies that two agents with the same endowments and the same preferences receive bundles that are indifferent according to these preferences. The Walrasian solution satisfies this requirement, which generalizes *equal treatment of equals*. However, both the "cardinal value" and the "ordinal value," solutions induced on the economies under consideration here by the Shapley value (Shapley 1953) violate it (Yannelis 1985).

Imagine now that agents have repeated access to any of the trades in the list $(t_i)_{i \in N}$. We obtain the following stronger definition, which embodies a requirement of anonymity:

Definition (Schmeidler and Vind 1972) *Given* $e \equiv (R, \omega) \in \mathcal{E}^N_{end}$, *the trade profile* $\boldsymbol{t} \in \boldsymbol{T(e)}$ ***is strongly envy-free for e*** *if* $(\omega + t) \in Z(e)$, *and for no* $i \in N$ *and no* $\alpha \in \mathbb{N}^N$, $(\omega_i + \sum \alpha_j t_j)\ P_i\ (\omega_i + t_i)$.

Walrasian trades are easily seen to be strongly envy-free. More interesting is that under weak conditions on preferences, a converse holds (Schmeidler and Vind 1972).

The no-envy concept can also be adapted to evaluate the trades of groups. Given $z \in Z(e)$, we could require that there should be no pair of groups $\{G, G'\} \subseteq N$ with $G \cap G' = \emptyset$ and a list $t \equiv (t_i)_{i \in G} \in \mathbb{R}^{\ell|G|}$ of trades for the members of G such that $\sum_G t_i = \sum_{G'} (z_j - \omega_j)$; $(\omega + t)\ R_G\ z$; and for at least one $i \in G$, $(\omega_i + t_i)\ P_i\ z_i$. Note that in this definition, the relative sizes of the two groups are not restricted. The set of allocations passing this test is contained in the core and it contains the set of Walrasian allocations (Jaskold-Gabszewicz 1975, Yannelis 1985). The extent to which an allocation obtained through a group envy-free trade differs from a Walrasian allocation can be quantified.

Yannelis (1985) proves the existence of allocations meeting an approximate version of group no-envy in economies with small and large traders in which small traders may not have convex preferences.

Jaskold-Gabszewicz (1975) also considers economies with both atoms and an atomless sector and studies this notion of envy-free trades for groups, when the admissible groups are arbitrary, and alternatively, when they are restricted to be subsets of the two sectors. He relates the sets of allocations satisfying these definitions to the core and to the set of Walrasian allocations. If there are no atoms, the core coincides with the set of group envy-free allocations. Also, at a group envy-free allocation of such a mixed economy, and even if only groups of equal measures are considered in the definition, the value of the trades of all small agents are equal (Shitovitz 1992).

4.10. Towards a Complete Theory of Equity

Suppose that it has been decided that gains from trade should be distributed according to a particular method. One could hope that the equity of the final allocation would be guaranteed if the initial allocation is itself equitable. But how is one to judge the equity of an initial allocation? A complete theory of equity would involve choosing criteria for initial positions, final positions, and trades. Now, the question is whether the criteria chosen for trades and initial allocations should bear any relation to the criterion chosen for allocations, or whether these choices can be made independently. In this subsection, we attempt to lay the foundation for an integrated theory of fairness.[28]

We start with the evaluation of initial allocations. Once again, equal division is an appealing choice. In fact, equal division seems to be a more legitimate initial-state than end-state principle since its (usual) inefficiency will hopefully be removed by any reasonable transition principle. However, the end-state principles discussed in Section 4 can be used as initial-state principles too. For instance, we can certainly define an envy-free *initial* allocation as we defined an envy-free *final* allocation.

Next, we submit that there are good reasons to preserve the conceptual distinction between initial-state and end-state principles. Elaborating on the previous example, the fact that an agent would not want to *consume* anyone else's initial bundle may be thought irrelevant; the initial position matters only to the extent that it affects the final position. In more general situations, preferences may not even be defined on initial positions: for instance, in a production economy, the initial position would commonly be given by the specification of how much of each of the factors of production (machinery,

[28] For a discussion of related issues, see Varian (1975). Yamashige (1997) can be seen as a contribution to this program too, as he proposes the following test on a transition principle φ: if agent j's endowment dominates agent i's endowment, commodity by commodity, then at the allocation chosen by φ, agent j should not envy agent i. For consistency, one could argue that the same test should be performed on initial and final allocations, and for greater generality, base the comparisons on other fairness notions.

land, etc.) each agent controls. These resources cannot be directly consumed, but their initial distribution will in general affect the final allocation.

The following facts, which have been described in the literature as "paradoxes," clearly indicate that certain consistency conditions should indeed be respected.

We have already seen that (i) if $|N| \geq 3$, starting from equal division (an envy-free but typically not efficient allocation), a trade to the core may lead to an allocation that is not envy-free (Kolm 1972, Feldman and Kirman 1974). In fact, starting from equal division, a sequence of envy-free trades may lead to a core allocation that is not envy-free (Sussangkarn and Goldman 1980). (ii) Also, and even if $|N| = 2$, starting from an envy-free (and not efficient) allocation, an envy-free trade profile (even a Walrasian trade profile) may lead to an allocation that is not envy-free (Kolm 1972, Feldman and Kirman 1974). (iii) Moreover, and again even if $|N| = 2$, starting from an envy-free (and nonefficient) allocation, there may be no Pareto-improving trade leading to an envy-free and efficient allocation (Goldman and Sussangkarn 1978). Since, in general, there are envy-free trades that are not Pareto improving, the following fact is even more serious. (iv) Even if $|N| = 2$, starting from an envy-free (and not efficient) allocation, there may be no envy-free trade leading to an envy-free and efficient allocation (Thomson 1982).

The complex structure of the set of envy-free allocations is reflected in its image in utility space, but at least this image is connected, which is not the case for the former set.

The main lesson to be drawn from (i)–(iv) is that it is not legitimate to arbitrarily and independently select initial-state, transition, and end-state principles. These choices should be linked in some way. We will decompose the search for links by first assuming that a transition principle has been selected, and in showing that on the basis of this choice, natural restrictions on both the initial-state and the end-state principles can be formulated. Then, we will suggest how transition principles can in turn be derived from end-state principles. We will conclude by requiring the "consistency" of the two operations. (These developments follow Thomson 1983a, and Thomson and Varian 1985.)

4.10.1. Deriving Initial-State and End-State Principles from Transition Principles

The derivation of initial-state and end-state principles from transition principles is achieved by a simple extension of the permutation idea. Let φ be a transition principle:

Definition *Given* $e \equiv (R, \omega) \in \mathcal{E}^N_{end}$, *the pair* $(\omega, z) \in Z(e) \times Z(e)$ *of an initial allocation and a final allocation is a* ***φ-acceptable pair for e*** *if for each* $\pi \in \Pi^N$, $z \in \varphi(R, \pi(\omega))$.

Here, the initial position is evaluated indirectly, via its effect on the final allocation. Similarly, the final allocation is evaluated indirectly, by checking its independence from permutations of the components of the initial position.

Since equal division is not affected by permutations, it is clear that, as soon as φ is well-defined, φ-acceptable pairs exist. Indeed, any pair of the form $(\bar{\omega}, z)$, where $\bar{\omega} \equiv (\frac{\sum \omega_i}{|N|}, \ldots, \frac{\sum \omega_i}{|N|})$ and $z \in \varphi(R, \bar{\omega})$, satisfies the definition.

However, the free choice of ω may lead to a violation of no-domination, and if we insist on this important requirement, the consistency requirement suggested above should be strengthened. We propose to strengthen it by placing a natural restriction on the class of comparisons in which society engages in order to decide whether an allocation is equitable (and limiting our attention to subsolutions of the Pareto solution). Assuming a commitment to efficiency, and given an efficient allocation whose equity is to be evaluated, we declare its comparison to nonefficient allocations irrelevant. Since the allocation $\pi(z)$ obtained from some z through an arbitrary permutation π is in general not efficient, we ignore it as a possible candidate.

It remains that permuting the components of z is appealing. The question then is whether one could associate with $\pi(z)$ some efficient allocation that is equivalent to it from the viewpoint of equity and to which z could be compared instead. We suggest that if an equitable transition principle has been adopted, this can be done since whatever inequities exist in $\pi(z)$ will presumably be preserved by its operation. This line of thought leads us to the following test: starting from some efficient allocation z, we permute its components to obtain $\pi(z)$, and we reestablish efficiency by operating φ. It is to the resulting allocation(s) that we compare z. We require that this process returns to z, or rather *can* return to z.

Definition *Given* $e \equiv (R, \omega) \in \mathcal{E}^N_{end}$, *the allocation* $z \in Z(e)$ ***is*** $\boldsymbol{\varphi}$***-acceptable for*** *e if for each* $\pi \in \Pi^N$, $z \in \varphi(R, \pi(z))$.

Let us apply the definitions to some examples:

Theorem 4.7 (Thomson 1983a) Domain: private goods; monotonic and convex preferences. *The acceptable allocations relative to (a) the individual-endowments lower bound and Pareto transition correspondence are the envy-free and efficient allocations; (b) the Walrasian transition correspondence are the equal-division Walrasian allocations.*

4.10.2. Deriving Transition Principles from End-State Principles

Summarizing the progress we have made, our problem of selecting initial-state, transition, and end-state principles has been reduced to the selection of a transition principle. In Section 4.9 we already suggested several criteria to evaluate trades, but we would like to be systematic and coherent in our choice.

Could *internal* considerations such as the ones that helped us derive end-state principles from transition principles permit us to achieve this objective? We now argue that indeed such considerations can be brought in to *derive transition principles from end-state principles*. First, recall the definition of an envy-free trade (Section 4.9): this is a feasible trade $t \in \mathbb{R}^{\ell N}$ such that for each $i \in N$ and each $\pi \in \Pi^N$, if $(\omega_i + \pi_i(t)) \in \mathbb{R}^{\ell}_{+}$, then $z_i \equiv (\omega_i + t_i)\ R_i\ (\omega_i + \pi_i(t))$. This transition principle is obtained from the end-state principle of an envy-free allocation by substituting trades for final consumption bundles, and using the preference relations on trades induced in the natural way from the preference relations on final consumption bundles. We propose to apply this transformation generally, thereby defining a mapping from end-state principles to transition principles that mirrors the mapping from transition principles to end-state principles defined in the previous section. Examples of transition principles that can be so obtained are the notion of an **average-envy-free trade for (R,ω)**, that is, a trade $t \in \mathbb{R}^{\ell N}$ such that for no $i \in N$, $\left(\omega_i + \frac{\sum_{N\setminus\{i\}} z_j}{|N|-1}\right)\ P_i\ (\omega_i + t_i)$, and the notion of an **egalitarian-equivalent trade for (R,ω)**, that is, a trade $t \in \mathbb{R}^{\ell N}$ such that for some $t_0 \in \mathbb{R}^{\ell}$, and for each $i \in N$, $(\omega_i + t_i)\ I_i\ (\omega_i + t_0)$.

4.10.3. Consistency between Transition Principles and End-State Principles

We are now ready to close the loop. Starting from some end-state principle, we derive from it a transition principle as just indicated. From this transition principle, we derive the end-state principle as explained earlier; **the consistency test that we suggest is that we get back to where we started.** Are there end-state principles such that the loop closes back on itself?

The answer is yes, and we possess all the elements to provide it. If the end-state principle is the equal-division Walrasian solution, then the transition principle is the (standard) Walrasian solution, which takes us back to the equal-division Walrasian solution as end-state principle.

To give an example of a sequence that does not fold back on itself, suppose that the end-state principle is the equal-division lower bound. Then, the derived transition principle is Pareto-domination, which in turn leads us to the end-state principle of no envy for allocations.

Usually, the loop will indeed not close back on itself. The "fixed point" property satisfied by the pair {Walrasian solution, equal-division Walrasian solution} does not seem to be shared by many other examples.

Another way of relating initial allocations, trades, and final allocations is proposed by Maniquet (2001): the transition principle should be **robust under partial delivery** of the trades it specifies. If a trade $t \in \mathbb{R}^{\ell N}$ is chosen for some economy (R,ω), and an arbitrary proportion α of this trade is carried out, then the remainder of it, $(1-\alpha)t$, should be chosen for the revised economy $(R,\omega + \alpha t)$.[29] On the domain of economies with individual endowments in which preferences are smooth, if a subsolution of the no-envy in trades and Pareto solution is *robust under partial delivery*, then in fact it is a subsolution of the Walrasian solution.

[29] Maniquet calls this invariance property "decomposability."

5. ECONOMIES WITH PRODUCTION

Although we have been concerned up to now only with the fair allocation of a *fixed* bundle of goods among agents with equal rights on them, another fundamental issue is that of fair allocation when agents have contributed differently to the production of these goods, because they have supplied unequal amounts of their time, or because they have unequal productivities, or both.

A number of results described next pertain to this more general situation, in which some inputs are "agent-specific." The consumption bundle of each agent $i \in N$ has a coordinate representing his consumption of leisure, ℓ_i. Through an appropriate normalization, we assume that each agent i's maximal consumption of leisure is 1, so that his labor input is $1 - \ell_i$. If skills differ across agents, labor inputs have to be distinguished according to who supplies them. Then, production possibilities are given as a subset Y of $\mathbb{R}^{n+m}$, where n is the number of labor inputs (equal to the number of agents) and m is the number of produced goods.

Let $\mathcal{Y}$ be a class of admissible production sets. An economy is now a pair $(R, \Omega, Y) \in \mathcal{R}^N \times \mathbb{R}^\ell_+ \times \mathcal{Y}$. Let $\mathcal{E}^N_{pro}$ be our generic notation for a class of such economies.

5.1. Adapting the Basic Concepts

A first way to extend the notion of an envy-free allocation to such economies is by having each agent $i \in N$ compare his *complete* consumption bundle (ℓ_i, x_i) to those of the other agents. Unfortunately, we run into the fundamental incompatibility with efficiency:

Theorem 5.1 (Pazner and Schmeidler 1974) Domain: private goods; strictly monotonic and linear preferences; linear production function with agent-specific inputs. *Envy-free and efficient allocations may not exist.*

Interestingly, at an efficient allocation of an economy with production, two agents may mutually envy each other, a situation that, as the reader may recall, cannot occur in an exchange economy (Proposition 4.1).

We emphasize that in Theorem 5.1, preferences are quite well-behaved. It is true that if either all abilities or all preferences are the same, envy-free and efficient allocations do exist (Varian 1974), but these assumptions are of course overly restrictive. Now, consider a two-good economy, the two goods being time and another good produced from labor. Suppose that agents can be ordered by their productivities and that their preferences satisfy the following Spence–Mirrlees "single-crossing" condition: given any two agents, at each bundle in their common consumption space, the increase in the consumption good required to keep a less productive agent on the same indifference curve when he gives up an arbitrary amount of leisure is greater than the corresponding increase for the more productive agent. Then, if the production technology is linear, envy-free and efficient allocations exist (Piketty 1994).

Finally, in a production economy in which agents differ in their productivities, there may be no efficient allocation at which each agent finds his bundle at least as desirable as the average of the bundles received by all agents (a criterion proposed by Pazner 1977). This can be seen by means of the example Pazner and Schmeidler (1978a) use to prove Theorem 5.1, because in that example preferences are convex.[30]

Faced with the fundamental negative result stated as Theorem 5.1, a number of authors have proposed alternative definitions of equity. We have already encountered egalitarian-equivalence and balanced envy (Section 4.4). Egalitarian-equivalent and efficient allocations exist quite generally (Pazner and Schmeidler 1978a). The main assumption is "welfare-connectedness": if an agent consumes a non-zero bundle, resources can be redistributed away from him so that all other agents are made better off. Under sufficiently strong convexity assumptions on preferences and technologies, the reference bundle in the definition of egalitarian-equivalence can be required to be proportional to the average consumption bundle and existence preserved. The assumption under which balanced-envy and efficient allocations are known to exist are more restrictive (mainly, that the production set is a convex cone, and that no two Pareto-efficient allocations be Pareto-indifferent; Daniel 1975).

The following proposal is another generalization of no-envy. It recognizes the envy of agent $j \in N$ by agent $i \in N$ only after agent i's consumption of leisure is adjusted for him to produce the output produced by agent j:

Definition (Varian 1974) *Given $e \equiv (R, \Omega, Y) \in \mathcal{E}^N_{pro}$, the allocation $z \in Z(e)$ **is productivity-adjusted envy-free**[31] **for e** if for each $i \in N$, $(\ell_i, x_i)\ R_i\ (\ell_i(\bar{x}_j), x_j)$, where $\bar{x}_j$ is the bundle produced by agent $j \in N$, and $1 - \ell_i(\bar{x}_j)$ is the amount of labor that agent $i \in N$ needs to produce $\bar{x}_j$.*

The concept has the technical disadvantage of being well-defined only if the production set is additive, since only then is it possible to identify the share of the total output produced by each agent. Another more fundamental problem with it is that, in a sense, it lets agents with high productivity appropriate the benefits of their greater skills. To the extent that higher productivity is "earned," through a lengthier or costlier education or greater exertion on the job, this may be legitimate (but would be recognized in a model in which all inputs are properly included in the description of an allocation). However, if it is the result of greater innate ability, one may well object to it (Pazner 1977).

[30] Pazner refers to it as "per-capita fairness." Similarly, since average no-envy and the various criteria of group equity coincide with one of these criteria for $|N| = 2$, we conclude that existence also fails for them in production economies with differentially productive agents.

[31] Varian (1974) refers to these allocations as "wealth-fair."

A proof of the existence of productivity-adjusted envy-free and efficient allocations can be given along the lines of the "Walrasian" proof of existence of envy-free and efficient allocations in exchange economies and under the same assumptions. It suffices to operate the Walrasian solution from equal division of the produced goods but leaving to each agent the ownership of his time endowment. At any allocation reached in this manner, each agent produces a bundle whose value at the equilibrium prices is equal to the value of the bundle produced by each other's agent (Varian 1974).

The intent of the next concept is to distribute across agents the benefits derived from the greater productivity of the more productive among them (Pazner and Schmeidler 1978b, Varian 1974, Pazner 1977). The solutions using either equal division as a lower bound on welfares or no-envy are not easily adaptable, because the preferences of an agent are not defined on a space that includes other agents' leisure, but one can at least take advantage of the instrumental value of the Walrasian solution in delivering envy-free allocations when there is no production, and in providing equal opportunities. Let us then operate the Walrasian solution from equal division of all goods, including time endowments.[32] Svensson (1994b) states an existence result for allocations at which implicit incomes are equal, and neither preferences nor technology are necessarily convex. As in the extensions of Theorem 4.1, where the main assumption pertains to the topological structure of the Pareto set, his critical assumption is that the Pareto set be invariant under replication. (Section 8 is devoted to an analysis of properties of this type.)[33]

A concept in the same spirit as that of a productivity-adjusted envy-free allocation, but subject to the same limitations, is formulated by Otsuki (1980). Biswas (1987) also defines an equity notion in production economies with differently productive agents.

Nonconvexities in technologies present another difficulty for the existence of envy-free and efficient allocations:

Proposition 5.1 (Vohra 1992) Domain: private goods; strictly monotonic and convex preferences; no agent-specific inputs; not necessarily convex technologies. *Envy-free and efficient allocations may not exist.*

In the face of this negative result, which in fact can be proved by means of an example in which the only source of nonconvexity in the technology is the presence of a fixed cost, Vohra proposes to weaken no-envy by imposing a certain symmetry among all

[32] These authors speak of the equalization of "implicit incomes," or "potential incomes," or "full incomes," and use the term "income-fairness" for the resulting fairness notion.

[33] As a compromise between the two definitions just discussed, Archibald and Donaldson (1979) propose that each agent be given ownership of a certain fraction of his own time and an equal share of the remaining time of everyone. At equilibrium, budget sets are not related by inclusion, which they suggest is a minimal requirement of "fairness of implicit opportunities" (Section 6 of this chapter).

agents with respect to possible occurrences of envy (a notion related to one suggested by Varian 1974):

Definition (Vohra 1992) *Given* $e \equiv (R, \Omega, Y) \in \mathcal{E}^N_{pro}$, *the allocation* $\boldsymbol{z} \in \boldsymbol{Z(e)}$ ***is essentially envy-free for e*** *if for each* $i \in N$, *there is* $z^i \in Z(e)$ *that is Pareto-indifferent to* z *and at which agent* i *envies no one.*

If preferences are strictly convex, this definition reduces to no-envy. This weakening of the standard definition suffices to recover existence. In fact, existence holds without any convexity assumption on either preferences or technologies. A critical one, however, remains that there be no agent-specific input:

Theorem 5.2 (Vohra 1992) Domain: private goods; strictly monotonic preferences; no agent-specific input; non-empty and compact feasible set. *Essentially envy-free and efficient allocations exist.*

In economies in which no two distinct Pareto-efficient allocations are Pareto-indifferent, an allocation is essentially envy-free as well as efficient if and only if it is envy-free and efficient. In general, if $|N| > 2$, the set of allocations that are Pareto-indifferent to an envy-free and efficient allocation (these allocations may violate no-domination) is a strict subset of the set of essentially envy-free allocations.

5.2. Agent-by-Agent Lower and Upper Bounds

No-envy and egalitarian-equivalence notions are based on interpersonal comparisons of bundles. We now turn to criteria that, by contrast, can be evaluated agent by agent, just like the equal-division lower bound.

First, for each agent, we imagine an economy composed of agents having preferences identical to his, and we identify his welfare under efficiency and *equal treatment of equals*. We take this welfare as a bound. For nowhere-increasing returns-to-scale, the profile of these welfares is feasible, and it can be used to define a lower bound requirement on welfares.

Definition (Gevers 1986, Moulin 1990d) *Given* $e \equiv (R, \Omega, Y) \in \mathcal{E}^N_{pro}$, *the allocation* $z \in Z(e)$ *meets the* ***identical-preferences lower bound for*** e *if for each* $i \in N$, $z_i \; R_i \; z_i^*$, *where* z_i^* *is a bundle that agent* i *would be assigned by any efficient solution satisfying* equal treatment of equals *in the hypothetical economy in which each other agent had preferences identical to his.*[34]

Alternatively, we could imagine each agent in turn to have control of an equal share of the social endowment and unhampered access to the technology:[35]

[34] Gevers uses the phrase "egalitarian lower bound" and Moulin the phrase "unanimity lower bound." The bound proposed by Steinhaus (1948) can also be understood in this way (Section 12 of this chapter).

[35] Yoshihara (1998) proposes an extension of this notion to the case of economies with arbitrarily many goods.

Definition (Moulin 1990d) *Given* $e \equiv (R, \Omega, Y) \in \mathcal{E}^N_{pro}$, *the allocation* $z \in Z(e)$ *meets the* ***equal-division free-access upper bound for e*** *if for each* $i \in N$, $z_i^* \; R_i \; z_i$, *where* z_i^* *is a bundle that maximizes agent i's preferences if given access to* $(\frac{\Omega}{|N|}, Y)$.

This definition can be generalized by imagining each group of agents in turn to have control over a proportion of the social endowment equal to its relative size in the economy and unhampered access to the technology:

Definition (Foley 1967) *Given* $e \equiv (R, \Omega, Y) \in \mathcal{E}^N_{pro}$, *the allocation* $z \in Z(e)$ *is in the* ***equal-division free-access core of e*** *if there is no* $G \subseteq N$ *and no list of bundles* $(z_i^*)_{i \in G} \in \mathbb{R}^{\ell G}_+$ *such that for each* $i \in G$, $z_i^* \; R_i \; z_i$, *and for at least one* $i \in G$, $z_i^* \; P_i \; z_i$, *this list being attainable by the group G if given access to* $(\frac{|G|}{|N|}\Omega, Y)$.

What of the compatibility of these bounds with no-envy? First, we state an incompatibility:

Proposition 5.2 (Moulin 1990c) Domain: one-input one-output production economies; monotonic and convex preferences; concave production function. *There are economies in which no allocation that is envy-free and efficient meets the equal-division free-access upper bound.*

The equal-division free-access upper bound itself is met on the domain specified in the theorem by selections from the Pareto solution, in particular by a solution we find more convenient to define later, the constant-returns-to-scale–equivalent solution (Mas-Colell 1980a, Moulin 1987b). (See the discussion following Theorem 7.3.)

In the case of nowhere-decreasing returns-to-scale, the equal-division free-access bound becomes a lower bound, and an impossibility parallel to that stated in Proposition 5.2 obtains: no subsolution of the Pareto solution satisfies no-envy for trades and meets the equal-division free-access lower bound (Moulin 1987b).

When preferences are quasi-linear, the welfare of a group at an allocation can be defined as the aggregate utility of its members evaluated by means of the quasi-linear representations. Then, the core constraints form a system of inequalities that is familiar in the theory of transferable utility coalitional games.

Next is another bound for one-input one-output production economies. Say that an allocation z is a **proportional allocation for** ***e*** if there are prices such that each agent i maximizes his preferences given these prices at z_i. Let $Pro(e)$ be the set of these allocations. An allocation z satisfies the **constant-returns-to-scale lower bound** if for each $\bar{z} \in Pro(e)$, $z \; R \; \bar{z}$ (Maniquet 1996a, 1996b).[36] Such allocations exist very generally, but on the domain of economies with concave production functions, no solution jointly satisfies the constant-returns-to-scale lower bound and the identical-preferences lower bound.

[36] Maniquet uses the phrase "average-cost lower bound."

A "proportional equilibrium" is a configuration of input contributions that constitute a Nash equilibrium of the game that results when agents are paid for their input contributions according to average cost. The proportional equilibria can be Pareto ranked. We require next that **each agent should find his bundle at least as desirable as what he would receive at the Pareto superior proportional equilibrium**. The existence of allocations satisfying this bound can be established by standard arguments. Unfortunately, there may be no such allocation satisfying no-envy (Maniquet 1996b).

Fleurbaey and Maniquet (1996a, 1999) formulate yet other bounds and study their compatibility with other criteria (Chapter 21 of this volume). They consider a model in which each agent is described in term of his preferences over a two-dimensional commodity space and a productivity parameter. The **constant-returns-to-scale lower bound** is defined for each agent by reference to the best bundle he could achieve if he had access to a constant-returns-to-scale technology, the same for all agents; the **work-alone lower bound** is defined for each agent by reference to the best bundle he could achieve if given unhampered access to the technology but under the obligation to provide bundles to the other agents to which he would not prefer his own.

For another study of the logical relations between bounds in a class of two-good economies with convex production sets, the identical-preferences lower bound and the free-access upper bound, see Watts (1999). She shows that, except in trivial cases, the latter does not imply the former.

A general theory of "aspirations" that encompasses several of the notions discussed above is developed by Corchón and Iturbe-Ormaetxe (2001).

6. EQUAL OPPORTUNITIES AS EQUAL, OR EQUIVALENT, CHOICE SETS

In this section, we switch our focus from allocations to the opportunities that lead to allocations. The notion of equal opportunities is of course central in the theory of economic justice, and many references could be given (Arneson 1989, Cohen 1989, and Fleurbaey 1995a are representative pieces). We are interested here in implementing it in concrete economic environments, and exploring various notions of "equal opportunities as equal, or equivalent, choice sets." These notions formalize and generalize ideas informally discussed by a number of authors.

The phrase "equal opportunities" has been given a variety of meanings. When used in economies affected by uncertainty, it may mean "equal treatment ex-ante"; after the choice of nature is known, agents may end up with bundles that are not necessarily equitable, but redistributions may not be possible. Uncertainty may be endogenously generated by an allocation rule. Anticipating briefly the discussion in Section 10, consider the problem of allocating an indivisible good. A lottery giving all agents equal chances might be deemed equitable ex-ante, although the final allocation may well appear unequitable.

Alternatively, in a context where agents' opportunities today are determined by decisions they made yesterday, equal opportunities may mean having access to the same set of decisions at that early stage. An example here is education. Giving two children with equal talents access to the same educational opportunities ensures that whatever differences exist between them later in life are due to their own decisions, for instance how hard they studied in school. It is often argued that, because of incentive considerations, we should not attempt to equalize end-results but should limit ourselves to giving people equal chances to develop their potential. Then, equal opportunities are provided by the transition mechanism (Section 4.9). Here, we ignore questions of uncertainty and incentives, and focus instead on comparing availability of concrete choices given in commodity space. This section is mainly based on Thomson (1994a).

Other approaches have been taken for the comparative evaluation of opportunity sets. One line of investigation was opened by Barberà, Barrett, and Pattanaik (1984) and pursued by Pattanaik and Xu (1992), Klemisch-Ahlert (1993), Bossert, Pattanaik, and Xu (1994), Kranich (1996), and Bossert (1997), to name a few representative contributions. These authors derive axiomatic characterizations of various rules to rank opportunity sets. (For a survey of this literature, see Peragine 1999).

An initial limitation of this literature is that most of it was written for abstract domains, no account being taken of the natural restrictions on domains and alternatives that characterize concretely specified economic domains. Also, and for the same reason, they ignore restrictions on preferences that are natural on such domains. Recent contributions have addressed these issues however (Kranich 1997, 2009, Xu 2004).

6.1. Equal Opportunities

Another way to give substance to the idea of equal opportunities is to let each agent choose his consumption bundle from a common choice set, as suggested in particular by Kolm (1973).

Although the straight-line choice sets of Walrasian analysis first come to mind, for a number of practical and theoretical reasons, we may want to consider other possibilities. First, even in economies where resources are supposedly allocated by operating the Walrasian mechanism, in practice, agents rarely face linear prices. Quantity discounts, quantity constraints, nonlinear tax rates, welfare payments, all contribute to generating choice sets that depart considerably from standard Walrasian budget sets. Neither convexity of choice sets nor smoothness of their boundaries should be expected. In the theory of revealed preference, generalized notions of choice sets have been discussed and a complete treatment elaborated (Richter 1979). Here, too, we would like to start from abstract choice sets with no a priori restrictions. How generally can this be done?

The difficulty with giving all agents the same choice set is of course that the list of choices they will make from it will in general not constitute a feasible allocation: aggregate feasibility of the profile of choices precludes that the set be specified once and for all, before preferences are determined. Instead, one should have access to a "rich enough" family of choice sets, that is, a family such that, no matter what preferences are, it is guaranteed that for at least one member of the family, the list of chosen bundles constitutes a feasible allocation. In addition, one would prefer efficiency to hold whenever feasibility does. Although experience with the modified Walrasian budget sets agents face in the real world should make us doubt that this will be the case very generally, the search for families for which it does is certainly worthwhile. Let $\mathcal{B}$ be a family of choice sets (subsets of $\mathbb{R}_+^\ell$). We state the definitions for economies with production, $\mathcal{E}_{pro}^N$ being a generic domain of such economies with agent set N.

Definition *Given* $e \equiv (R, \Omega, Y) \in \mathcal{E}_{pro}^N$, *the allocation* $z \in Z(e)$ ***is an equal-opportunity allocation relative to*** $\mathcal{B}$ ***for*** e, *written as* $z \in O_{\mathcal{B}}(e)$, *if there is* $B \in \mathcal{B}$ *such that for each* $i \in N$, z_i *maximizes* R_i *on* B.

Definition ***The family*** $\mathcal{B}$ ***is satisfactory*** *on the domain* $\mathcal{E}_{pro}^N$ *if for each* $e \in \mathcal{E}_{pro}^N$, $\emptyset \neq O_{\mathcal{B}}(e) \subseteq P(e)$.

A satisfactory family is easy to find: the **equal-income Walrasian family,** $\mathcal{W}_{ei}$, is satisfactory on the classical domain.

It turns out that under natural assumptions on preferences and on the family $\mathcal{B}$, if $\mathcal{B}$ is satisfactory, then $O_{\mathcal{B}} \supseteq W_{ei}$. Families $\mathcal{B}$ exist for which $O_{\mathcal{B}} \supset W_{ei}$, however. For instance, if $|N| = 2$, families $\mathcal{B}$ can be defined such that $O_{\mathcal{B}} = \underline{B}_{ed}P$. Of course, for each family $\mathcal{B}$, we have $O_{\mathcal{B}} \subseteq F$. This inclusion is in fact a common justification for no-envy, namely an implication of equal opportunities, some say "equal liberty."

6.2. Equal-Opportunity–Equivalence

Another concept is obtained by generalizing the reasoning underlying the notion of egalitarian–equivalence. It involves checking whether an allocation under consideration is such that, for some member of the family of choice sets, each agent is indifferent between what he receives and the best bundle he could attain. Again, let $\mathcal{B}$ be a family of choice sets:

Definition (Thomson 1994a) *Given* $e \equiv (R, \Omega, Y) \in \mathcal{E}_{pro}^N$, *the allocation* $z \in Z(e)$ ***is equal-opportunity–equivalent relative to*** $\mathcal{B}$ ***for*** e, *written as* $z \in O_{\mathcal{B}}^{\sim}(e)$, *if there is* $B \in \mathcal{B}$ *such that for each* $i \in N$, $z_i \, I_i \, z_i^*$, *where* z_i^* *maximizes* R_i *on* B.

If $\mathcal{B} \equiv \{\{z_0\}: z_0 \in \mathbb{R}^\ell_+\}$, then $O^{\sim}_{\mathcal{B}} = E$ (egalitarian–equivalence). If $|N| = 2$, and $\mathcal{B}$ is the family of all linear choice sets, then $O^{\sim}_{\mathcal{B}} = P$. For $|N| > 2$, there is no containment between $O^{\sim}_{\mathcal{B}}P$ and EP. If $\mathcal{B} \equiv \mathcal{W}_{ei}$, then $O^{\sim}_{\mathcal{B}} = W_{ei}$. Suppose now that preferences satisfy the classical assumptions and that the technology is convex. Then, for a natural subfamily of the linear family of choice sets, if the associated equal-opportunity–equivalence solution is to have an empty intersection with the no-domination solution, then the family should be a subsolution of the equal-income Walrasian family, as noted earlier. The resulting solution is the equal-income Walrasian solution. Here are other examples:

Definition *Let* $p \in \Delta^{\ell-1}$ *be fixed. Given* $M \in \mathbb{R}_+$, *let* $B^p(M) \equiv \{z \in \mathbb{R}^\ell_+ : pz \leq M\}$. *Let* $\mathcal{B}^p \equiv \{B^p(M): M \in \mathbb{R}_+\}$.

Definition *Given* $p \in \Delta^{\ell-1}$, *let* $L(p) \equiv \{z \in \mathbb{R}^\ell_+ : pz = p\frac{\Omega}{|N|}\}$. *Let* $\mathcal{L} \equiv \{L(p): p \in \Delta^{\ell-1}\}$.

Let $p \in \Delta^{\ell-1}$ be fixed. If the family $\mathcal{B}^p$ is used, and when efficiency is imposed, we obtain the solution that selects for each economy the efficient allocations that are Pareto-indifferent to $|N|$-lists of bundles whose values at the prices p (which have nothing to do with the prices of support of z) are equal. For the family $\mathcal{L}$, we obtain any efficient allocation such that each agent finds his component of it indifferent to the best bundle he could achieve if endowed with $\frac{\Omega}{|N|}$ and given access to a constant-returns-to-scale technology, the same for all agents (Mas-Colell 1980a). We describe in Section 7 a characterization of the solution just defined on the basis of a monotonicity requirement (Moulin 1987a; Roemer and Silvestre 1993 also explore the criterion).

Yet other examples of solutions can be obtained by having all agents face a hypothetical technology obtained from the actual one by imagining the productivity of one specific factor of production (alternatively of some subset of the factors of production) to be multiplied by some number, or by introducing a fixed cost of some factor of production (alternatively, introducing a fixed cost proportional to some fixed vector). Radial expansions and contractions of the production set can also be considered. A special case is the ratio solution (Kaneko 1977a, 1977b). A general application of the concept is due to Nicolò and Perea (2005). It covers private good allocations, cost sharing, and location of a public good.

6.3. No Envy of Opportunities

Given $e \equiv (R, \Omega, Y) \in \mathcal{E}^N_{pro}$ and $z \in P(e)$, let us now define the (implicit) opportunity set of agent $i \in N$ at z as the set of bundles whose value at the prices supporting z is no greater than the value of z_i (Varian 1976). Equal opportunities, according to this definition, implies that $z \in W_{ei}(e)$. More generally, define the (once again, implicit) opportunity set of agent $i \in N$ at any $z \in Z(e)$ as the set of bundles whose value at the prices supporting agent i's upper contour set at z_i is no greater than the value of z_i

(Archibald and Donaldson 1979). For this definition to make sense, we should assume that these supporting prices are unique. Now, if the opportunity sets of two agents are not the same, they may not be related by inclusion, in contrast to the situation considered by Varian. In a production economy with differently productive agents, supporting prices need not be the same, so implicit opportunities cannot be equalized. One may require instead that no agent should prefer the implicit opportunities of another. To generalize this idea, let $\mathcal{B}$ be a family of choice sets:

Definition (Thomson 1994a) *Given* $e \equiv (R, \Omega, Y) \in \mathcal{E}^N_{pro}$, *the allocation* $\boldsymbol{z} \in \boldsymbol{Z(e)}$ ***exhibits no envy of opportunities relative to*** $\mathcal{B}$ ***for e****, written as* $\boldsymbol{z} \in \boldsymbol{OF_{\mathcal{B}}(e)}$, *if for each* $i \in N$, *there is* $B_i \in \mathcal{B}$ *such that* $z_i \in B_i$ *and* z_i *maximizes* R_i *on* $\bigcup B_j$.

It is easy to check that if $\mathcal{B}$ is the family $\mathcal{L}$ of linear choice sets, then the resulting solution $OF_{\mathcal{B}}$ coincides with the equal-income Walrasian solution. Also, if $\mathcal{B}$ is the family of $|N|$-lists of bundles, we obtain the following concept, which generalizes both no-envy and egalitarian-equivalence:

Definition (Pazner 1977) *Given* $e \equiv (R, \Omega, Y) \in \mathcal{E}^N_{pro}$, *the allocation* $z \in \boldsymbol{Z(e)}$ ***is envy-free–equivalent for e*** *if there is* $z' \equiv (z'_i)_{i \in N} \in \mathbb{R}^{\ell N}_+$ *such that for each pair* $\{i,j\} \subseteq N$, $z'_i \; R_i \; z'_j$, *and* $z \; I \; z'$. *(Note that* $z' \in Z(e)$ *is not required.)*

A model in which agents have preferences over commodity bundles, preferences over opportunity sets, and preferences over pairs of a commodity bundle and an opportunity set is studied by Tadenuma and Xu (2001). They say that a pair of a profile of an allocation and a profile of opportunity sets is **decentralizable for a profile of preference relations over bundles** if for each agent, his component of the allocation maximizes his preference relation over bundles in his component of the opportunity profile. They relate notions of no-envy according to these different relations, and offer characterizations of the Walrasian solution on the basis of decentralizability, and various forms of independence and no-envy requirements.

7. MONOTONICITY

Throughout most of the preceding sections, we have assumed the social endowment, and the production set when there was one, to be fixed. Here, we imagine changes in these data and study how solutions respond to such changes. We start with the distribution of an unproduced social endowment. If it increases, we require that all agents should end up at least as well off as they were initially. We ask whether this requirement is compatible with our earlier equity criteria. As we will see, the answer depends on which of them is chosen. In economies with production, an appealing requirement is that if the technology improves, all agents should end up at least as well off as they were initially. We also consider a monotonicity requirement pertaining to economies with fixed resources but a variable number of agents. When population increases, we would like everyone initially present to help supporting newcomers.

Each of the parameters just listed, whose possible variations we consider, belongs to a space equipped with an order structure, and the rule is required to respond well to changes that can be evaluated in that order. Under such assumptions, the change can be unambiguously evaluated in terms of welfares. More generally, we could consider simply replacing the initial value taken by the data with another value, and only require that the welfares of all agents should be affected in the same direction, namely that all should end up at least as well off as they were initially or that they all should end up at most as well off. We close with an application of the idea to situations when it is the replacement of the preferences of some agents that has to be faced, thereby obtaining an application of what we call later the "replacement principle."

7.1. Resource-Monotonicity

Our first monotonicity property pertains to variations in resources. (For a survey of the various applications of the idea of monotonicity with respect to resources or opportunities, see Thomson 1999c.) Given a class $\mathcal{R}$ of possible preferences over $\mathbb{R}^{\ell}_{+}$, an economy is a pair $(R,\Omega) \in \mathcal{E}^N \equiv \mathcal{R}^N \times \mathbb{R}^{\ell}_{+}$ and a solution is a mapping defined over $\mathcal{E}^N$ and taking its values in $\mathbb{R}^{\ell N}_{+}$.

Our requirement is that if the social endowment increases, all agents should end up at least as well off as they were initially. It allows for solution correspondences but given the choice of quantifiers, it implies *essential single-valuedness*.

Resource-Monotonicity (Thomson 1978, Roemer 1986a, 1986b, Chun and Thomson 1988) For each $(R,\Omega) \in \mathcal{E}^N$, each $z \in \varphi(R,\Omega)$, each $\Omega' \in \mathbb{R}^{\ell}_{+}$, and each $z' \in \varphi(R,\Omega')$, if $\Omega' \geqq \Omega$, then $z' \; R \; z$.

It is easy to see that the equal-division Walrasian solution violates the property (Figure 21.4a). This is so even on domains on which it is *essentially single-valued*, such as the domain of homothetic preferences (*essential single-valuedness* follows from the fact that in addition, endowments are equal), so writing the definition with existential instead of universal quantifiers for z and z' would not help. Our main result here is that the Walrasian solution is far from being the only one to suffer from this problem. To present it, we need to formally introduce as a solution the correspondence that associates with each economy the set of allocations at which no agent receives at least as much of each good as some other agent and more of at least one good. Let $D\colon \mathcal{E}^N \to \mathbb{R}^{\ell N}_{+}$ be the no-domination solution: $D(R,\Omega) \equiv \{z \in Z(R,\Omega)\colon$ for no pair $\{i,j\} \subseteq N, z_i \geq z_j\}$ (note that the definition does not involve preferences). This is a "large" correspondence. However, even under strong assumptions on preferences, it is not large enough to admit efficient *resource-monotonic* selections.

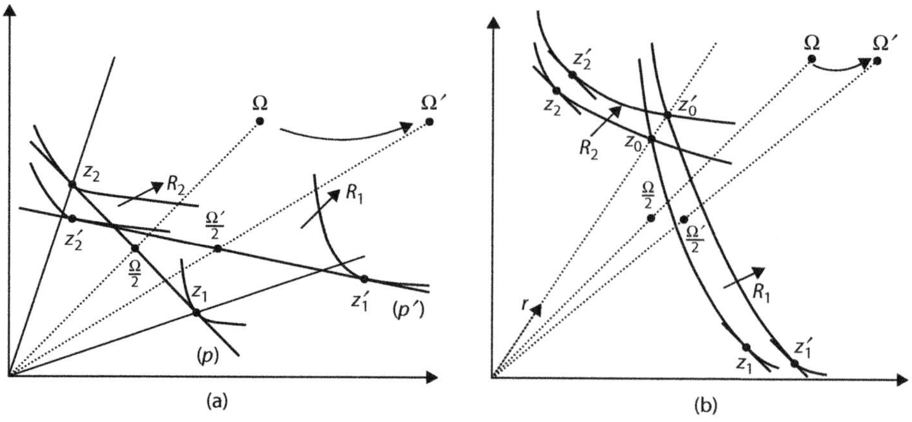

Figure 21.4. Two solutions, one resource-monotonic, the other not.
(a) The equal-division Walrasian solution is not *resource-monotonic*. When the social endowment is Ω, the solution selects z. After the social endowment increases to Ω', it selects z', to which agent 2 prefers z. (b) The r-egalitarian-equivalence and Pareto solution is *resource-monotonic*. As the social endowment increases from Ω to Ω', the reference bundle associated with the allocation chosen by this solution can only move further out on the ray defined by r (it goes from z_0 to z_0'). This implies that both agents end up at least as well off as they were initially.

Theorem 7.1 (Moulin and Thomson 1988) Domain: private goods; strictly monotonic, convex, and homothetic preferences. *No selection from the no-domination and Pareto solution is resource-monotonic.*

Theorem 7.1 is rather disappointing, but unfortunately, the situation is worse. Indeed, given $\varepsilon \geq 0$, let us replace no-domination by the requirement that each agent should be made at least as well off as he would be by consuming ε percent of the social endowment (Moulin and Thomson 1988). The smaller ε is, the weaker the requirement. However, no matter how small ε is, provided it is positive, the incompatibility persists. Alternatively, and here too, for each $\varepsilon > 0$, no-domination could be replaced in this theorem by the requirement that no agent should receive less than ε percent of what each other agent receives.

It is only at the limit, when $\varepsilon = 0$, that is, when no restriction is placed on the extent to which an agent might be discriminated against, that a positive result is obtained. Indeed, all of the egalitarian-type solutions defined as follows are *resource-monotonic*: for each agent, choose a continuous numerical representation of his preferences—a welfare index—and then the allocation(*s*) whose image in welfare space is maximal among all feasible points (the points in that space that are the images of feasible allocations) at which the welfare gains from the image of the allocation consisting entirely of zero bundles are equal. Any such solution is *resource-monotonic* because an increase in the social endowment causes the feasible set to expand. It then becomes possible to move further up along the equal-gains line.[37] More generally, each equal-opportunity–equivalent solution with respect to a family of choice sets satisfying minimal regularity properties is *resource-monotonic.* One can even go beyond this class without losing *resource-monotonicity*: each solution defined by selecting a maximal point of equal welfares, using as welfare index for each agent a function that takes value zero at the zero bundle, will do.

A result related to Theorem 7.1 is that no selection from the Pareto solution satisfies *Property* α (Section 4.1) and *resource-monotonicity* (Maniquet and Sprumont 2000).

A requirement in the spirit of, but weaker than, *resource-monotonicity* is that when the social endowment increases, there should not be an agent whose assignment is dominated, good by good, by the bundle assigned to him initially. No selection from the no-envy and Pareto solution satisfies it (Geanakoplos and Nalebuff 1988).[38]

The proofs of the negative results just described rely on the admissibility of preferences with indifference curves that are close to right angles. In their "ε variants," the smaller ε is, the closer to right angles indifference curves are. Do the results persist if preferences are required to satisfy some minimal degree of substitutability? The answer is no. For instance, it follows from Polterovich and Spivak (1980, 1983) that when preferences satisfy gross substitutability and all goods are normal, the equal-division Walrasian solution is *resource-monotonic* (Moulin and Thomson 1988).

Let $r \in \Delta^{\ell-1} \backslash \{0\}$ be given. By using as each agent i's welfare index the function $t\colon \mathbb{R}^{\ell}_{+} \to \mathbb{R}$ defined by $z_i \; I_i \; t(z_i)r$, we deduce from an earlier observation that the r-egalitarian-equivalence and Pareto solution is *resource-monotonic* (Figure 21.4b). (In fact, the rule is such that the welfares of all agents are affected in the same direction by any variation in the social endowment, whether or not the values it takes are related by domination.) This property of the r-egalitarian-equivalence family of solutions is a very strong point in their favor. In the pages that follow, we will encounter a number of additional arguments of that nature lending them additional support. What is critical is that the reference bundle be independent of the social endowment. We saw that requiring that it be proportional to the social endowment guarantees that the equal-division lower

[37] It is on this fact that Kalai's (1977) well-known characterization of the egalitarian solution to the bargaining problem is based. In economies in which agents are individually endowed, this fact also underlies the proof of existence of rules that are "own-endowment monotonic," that is, such that when an agent's endowment increases, he ends up at least as well off as he was initially. Aumann and Peleg (1974) provide an example of an economy with continuous, strictly monotonic, convex, and homothetic preferences revealing that this rule violates the property. In the example, the Walrasian allocation is in fact unique for each endowment profile. The strategic implication of such a violation is that an agent may benefit from destroying part of his endowment (Hurwicz 1978). The Aumann–Peleg example can also be used to show that the Walrasian solution is such that as one agent transfers some of his endowment to some other agent, both may benefit (Gale 1974), a phenomenon related to the "transfer problem," well-known to international trade theorists.

[38] Geanakoplos and Nalebuff state their result for correspondences, requiring that when the social endowment increases, then for each agent there should be at least one good, one allocation in the initial economy, and one allocation in the final economy, at which he receives more of that good after the enlargement. This choice of quantifiers makes the monotonicity requirement weaker. Their nonexistence proof involves economies with more than two agents.

bound is met. It is an implication of Theorem 7.1 that if efficiency is imposed, this bound is obtained at the price of *resource-monotonicity*. (Without efficiency, the rule that always selects equal division would of course be acceptable.)

For the quasi-linear case, we have good news. Given an economy e in which preferences can be represented by functions that are quasi-linear with respect to a particular good (the same for all agents), and using such representations as welfare indices—the special good is used as an "accounting good," then—consider the coalitional game $w(e)$ defined as follows: set the worth of each coalition to be the maximal aggregate welfare it can reach if given access to the entire social endowment—its "free-access" aggregate welfare, in the terminology of Section 5.2. The next proposition describes additional properties of preferences under which the Shapley value (Shapley 1953) applied to the coalitional game $w(e)$ induces a *resource-monotonic* solution. First, say that **two goods j and k are substitutes for a function $f\colon \mathbb{R}^\ell \to \mathbb{R}$** if the amount by which it increases as its k-th argument increases by some arbitrary amount is a decreasing function of its j-th argument: for each $y_i \in \mathbb{R}^\ell_+$ and each pair $\{a,b\} \subset \mathbb{R}_+$, we have $f(y_i + be^k) - f(y_i) \geq f(y_i + ae^j + be^k) - f(y_i + ae^j)$, where e^j denotes the j-th unit vector. Also, **the function f satisfies substitutability** if any two goods are substitutes for f. (Writing thc condition when $j = k$ is equivalent to saying that f is concave in y_j.) Finally, **the coalitional game $w(e)$ satisfies substitutability** if each of its coordinates does. Now, we have:

Proposition 7.1 (Moulin 1992b) Domain: private goods; quasi-linear preference profiles; free-access coalitional game associated to each economy satisfies substitutability. *The Shapley value, when applied to these games, induces a resource-monotonic solution.*

If there is only one good in addition to the accounting good, substitutability of v_i is equivalent to its concavity. Another application of Proposition 7.1 is when there are only two goods in addition to the accounting good, and for each $i \in N$, the function v_i is concave and submodular over $\mathbb{R}^2_+$. It also applies in the case of many goods if for each $i \in N$, the function v_i is twice continuously differentiable in the interior of $\mathbb{R}^\ell_+$, strictly concave, exhibits gross substitutability, and the marginal utility of each good at 0 is infinite. Studies of monotonicity in abstract settings are due to Moulin (1989, 1990d).

7.2. Welfare-Domination under Preference-Replacement

In the statement of the monotonicity properties discussed above, we focused on one of the parameters defining the economy and considered changes in that parameter that could be unambiguously described as good for a certain group of agents; we required that as a result of the change, all agents should be made at least as well off as they were initially. We could in fact imagine *arbitrary* changes in the parameter and demand that the welfares of all relevant agents should be affected in the same direction: as a result of the replacement, they should all be made at least as well off as they were initially or they should all be made at most as well off. This is the most general way of expressing the idea of solidarity among agents. It is referred to in Thomson (1990c, 1997) as the **replacement principle**. The principle can also be applied to changes in parameters taken from spaces that are not equipped with order structures. A primary example of such a parameter are the preferences of an agent. This consideration leads us to the following requirement. (The literature devoted to its analysis in various models is surveyed by Thomson 1999a.)

Welfare-Domination under Preference-Replacement

For each $(R,\Omega) \in \mathcal{E}^N$, each $z \in \varphi(R,\Omega)$, each $i \in N$, each $R_i' \in \mathcal{R}$, and each $z' \in \varphi(R_i', R_{-i}, \Omega)$, either $z'_{N\setminus\{i\}}\ R_{N\setminus\{i\}}\ z_{N\setminus\{i\}}$ or $z_{N\setminus\{i\}}\ R_{N\setminus\{i\}}\ z'_{N\setminus\{i\}}$.

It is obvious that the equal-division Walrasian solution violates the property, even in the two-good case. In general, a change in some agent's preferences is accompanied by a change in the equilibrium prices, and if at least two of the other agents are initially on opposite sides of the market, any such change will make one of them better off and the other worse off. Unfortunately, this difficulty is widely shared:

Theorem 7.2 (Thomson 1996) Domain: private goods; strictly monotonic and homothetic preferences. *No selection from the no-envy and Pareto solution satisfies welfare-domination under preference-replacement.*

The proof is by means of two-good and three-agent economies. In fact, even if no-envy is weakened to no-domination, an incompatibility with efficiency holds (Kim 2001). It is clear however that selections from the egalitarian-equivalence and Pareto solution exist that satisfy *welfare-domination under preference-replacement.* Simply choose a continuous, unbounded, and monotone path in commodity space and require the reference bundle to belong to the path. If the path goes through equal division, the resulting rule is also a selection from the equal-division lower bound solution. These desirable properties hold whether or not the path is a ray.

The replacement principle can be applied to the joint replacement of resources and preferences. A general result describing its implications then is given by Sprumont (1996). His formulation covers as special cases the classical model but also public good models. Suppose that it is meaningful to compare the relative treatment of agents i and j, when agent i has preferences R_i and is assigned a consumption on a certain indifference curve of R_i and agent j has preferences R_j and is assigned a consumption on a certain indifference curve of R_j, and that in fact a social order exists on the space of all such pairs. The result is that under a richness property of its range, and if there are at least three agents, a rule satisfies what can be called *welfare-domination under resource-and-preference replacement* if and only if there is an ordering of the kind just described such that for each problem, the rule selects an allocation at which all agents are assigned consumptions so that they are all treated equally well according to this ordering.

7.3. Technology-Monotonicity

Another interesting comparison can be made between two economies that differ only in their technologies. Suppose that the technology of one dominates the technology of the other. It seems natural to require that in the first one, all agents should be made at least as well off as they are in the second one. In order to formally state the property, we need to reintroduce production possibilities in the notation. A technology is a subset Y of commodity space $\mathbb{R}^{\ell}$. Let $\mathcal{Y}$ be a class of admissible technologies. Here, an economy is a triple $(R, \Omega, Y) \in \mathcal{R}^N \times \mathbb{R}^{\ell}_{+} \times \mathcal{Y}$. Let $\mathcal{E}^N_{pro}$ be our generic notation for a domain of economies.

Technology-Monotonicity (Roemer 1986a)
For each $(R, \Omega, Y) \in \mathcal{E}^N_{pro}$, each $Y' \in \mathcal{Y}$, each $z \in \varphi(R, \Omega, Y)$, and each $z' \in \varphi(R, \Omega, Y')$, if $Y' \supseteq Y$, then $z' \; R \; z$.

The requirement is satisfied by certain selections from the egalitarian-equivalence and Pareto solution. In the case of two goods, a characterization of a particular one is obtained by imposing it together with a few other minimal requirements, as explained next.

Suppose first that good 1 is used to produce good 2 according to a nowhere-decreasing-returns-to-scale technology Y. Given a group N of agents with preferences defined on $\mathbb{R}^2_{+}$, given some social endowment Ω of good 1, which can be consumed as such or used as input in the production of good 2, and given Y, let $\varphi(R, \Omega, Y)$ be the set of allocations selected by the solution φ. Here, we denote by $\underline{B}_{ed+Y}(R, \Omega, Y)$ the set of allocations such that each agent finds his bundle at least as desirable as the best bundle he could achieve if endowed with $\frac{\Omega}{|N|}$ and given unhampered access to the technology Y: the **equal-division free-access lower bound solution**.

The next solution illustrates the definition of equal-opportunity–equivalence of Section 6.2. The definition is depicted in Figure 21.5 for a nowhere-increasing-returns-to-scale technology.

Definition (Mas-Colell 1980a) *Given $e \equiv (R, \Omega, Y) \in \mathcal{E}^N_{pro}$, the allocation $z \in \boldsymbol{P(e)}$* ***is a constant-returns-to-scale–equivalent allocation for e****, written as $z \in \boldsymbol{CRS^{\simeq}(e)}$, if there is a constant returns-to-scale technology Y such that for each $i \in N$, $z_i \; I_i \; z_i^*$, where z_i^* maximizes agent i's preferences if given access to $\left(\frac{\Omega}{|N|}, Y\right)$.*

Theorem 7.3 (Moulin 1987b, 1990d) Domain: one-input and one-output production economies; social endowment of the input; preferences are strictly monotonic with respect to the input and monotonic with respect to the output; (a) nowhere-decreasing-returns-to-scale technologies; (b) nowhere-increasing-returns-to-scale technologies (alternatively, convex technologies). *(a) The only selection from the equal-division free-access lower bound and Pareto solution satisfying Pareto-indifference and technology-monotonicity is the constant-returns-to-scale–equivalence solution. (b) A parallel statement holds for selections from the equal-division free-access upper bound.*

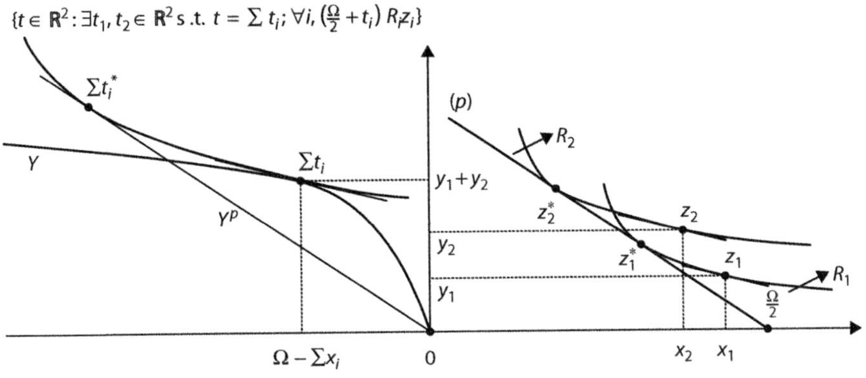

Figure 21.5. Constant-returns-to-scale–equivalence solution.
This solution selects the unique (up to Pareto-indifference) efficient allocation such that, for some reference constant-returns-to-scale technology Y^p, each agent $i \in N$ is indifferent between his bundle z_i and the best bundle he could reach if endowed with an equal share of the social endowment of the input and given access to that reference technology.

Although in part (a) of the theorem, the bounds on welfares are individual bounds, the solution that emerges happens to satisfy the requirement that no group of agents should be able to make each of its members at least as well off, and at least one of them better off, if each of its members is endowed with an equal share of the social endowment and the group is given unhampered access to the technology. A parallel statement holds for part (b).

One could be more demanding and consider simultaneous changes in several of the parameters describing the problem. For instance, suppose that resources and technologies both change. This may or may not lead to an enlargement of opportunities, but Dutta and Vohra (1993), who study this possibility, require of a correspondence that if an enlargement of the set of feasible profiles of welfare levels does occur, each allocation chosen initially should be welfare dominated by some allocation chosen after the change, and that each allocation chosen after the change should welfare dominate some allocation chosen initially. Let us refer to this requirement as **opportunity-monotonicity**. They also require, under the name of ***r*-equity**, that in an exchange economy in which there is only some amount of good r to divide, equal division should be chosen. They consider an invariance requirement that also depends on the choice of a good, say r, so we call it ***r*-invariance**. It is somewhat technical and not motivated by normative considerations, so we do not state it explicitly, only noting that it is a weak version of the invariance requirement shown by Maskin (1999) to be critical to the possibility of implementation. This requirement is usually called "Maskin monotonicity," but we will use the more descriptive expression of **invariance under monotonic transformations of preferences**: if an allocation is chosen for some economy and preferences change in such a way that the restriction of each agent's new lower contour set at his component of the allocation to the set of feasible allocations contains the corresponding set for his initial preferences, then the allocation should still be chosen for the new economy.

Theorem 7.4 (Dutta and Vohra 1993) Domain: private goods; monotonic and convex preferences such that each indifference curve crosses the r-th axis; production set is closed, contains the origin, and exhibits free disposal (nonconvex sets are allowed; exchange economies are included); set of feasible welfare profiles (using arbitrary continuous numerical representations of preferences) is bounded. *Up to Pareto-indifference, (a) the r-egalitarian equivalence and Pareto solution is the only subsolution of the Pareto solution satisfying r-equity and opportunity-monotonicity, and (b) on the subdomain of exchange economies, it is the only subsolution of the Pareto solution satisfying r-equity, r-invariance, and opportunity-monotonicity.*

Another independence condition is **contraction-independence**: if an allocation is chosen for some economy, the technology contracts but the allocation remains feasible, then it should still be chosen.

Several characterizations are available that involve this requirement. For the first one, we need an addition definition, due to Roemer and Silvestre (1993). They consider economies with arbitrarily many goods and identify general conditions under which existence is guaranteed. We limit attention to economies with two goods:

Definition *Given $e \equiv (R, \Omega, Y) \in \mathcal{E}^N_{pro}$, a class of production economies with two goods, one of them being used as an input in the production of the other, the allocation $z \in$* ***P(e) is a proportional allocation for e****, written as $z \in$* ***Pro(e)****, if either $z = 0$ or for each pair $\{i,j\} \subseteq N$, the ratio of agent i's input contribution over his output consumption is equal to the corresponding ratio for agent j.*

Theorem 7.5 (Moulin 1990d) Domain: one-input one-output production economies; monotonic and strictly convex preferences; convex technologies. *(a) If a selection from the identical-preferences lower bound satisfies contraction-independence, then it contains the equal-income Walrasian solution. (b) The proportional rule is the only selection from the Pareto and free-access upper bound solution satisfying contraction-independence and invariance under monotonic transformations of preferences.*

We also have a partial characterization based on the constant-returns-to-scale lower bound:

Theorem 7.6 (Maniquet 1996b) Domain: one-input one-output production economies; monotonic and convex preferences; nowhere-increasing-returns-to-scale technology. *If a subsolution of the constant-returns-to-scale lower bound solution satisfies Pareto indifference and contraction-independence, then it contains the constant-returns-to-scale–equivalence solution.*

The next theorem involves **weak invariance under monotonic transformations of preferences**, obtained from the requirement defined above by using the hypothesis of inclusion of upper contour sets instead of inclusion of restricted upper contour sets (Gevers 1986).

Theorem 7.7 (Maniquet 2002) Domain: one-input one-output production economies; monotonic and convex preferences; convex technologies. *The proportional rule is the only subsolution of the Pareto solution that selects the efficient and proportional allocations when they exist and satisfies weak invariance under monotonic transformations of preferences.*

We close this discussion of production economies with a mention of two other interesting monotonicity requirements. The first one pertains to situations where agents are differentiated by their input contributions. It simply says that if the contribution of an agent increases, he should end up at least as well off as he was initially.

The second one pertains to situations in which agents differ in their productivities. It states the corresponding requirement that if an agent's productivity increases, he should end up at least as well off as he was initially.

Technology-monotonicity is also considered in Moulin and Roemer (1989). They focus on economies with two agents equipped with utility functions, the same for both, but their productivities may differ.

7.4. Population-Monotonicity

Next, and returning to the problem of distributing a fixed bundle of goods, we consider a monotonicity property that pertains to situations in which resources are fixed but the population of agents varies. If it enlarges, we require that all agents initially present should end up at most as well off as they were initially. (The literature devoted to the analysis of this requirement in various models is surveyed in Thomson 1995b.) For a formal statement, recall our notation for solutions that accommodate variable populations (Section 2).

Population-Monotonicity (Thomson 1983b)
For each $N \in \mathcal{N}$, each $(R,\Omega) \in \mathcal{E}^N$, each $z \in \varphi(R,\Omega)$, each $N' \subseteq N$, and each $z' \in \varphi(R_{N'},\Omega)$, we have $z' \; R_{N'} \; z_{N'}$.

It is easy to see that the equal-division Walrasian solution violates this property (Figure 21.6). In fact, it may violate it in economies with monotonic, convex, and homothetic (or quasi-linear) preferences (Chichilnisky and Thomson 1987). More seriously, we have the following general impossibility:[39]

Theorem 7.8 (Kim 2004) Domain: private goods; strictly monotonic, convex, and homothetic preferences. *No selection from the no-envy and Pareto solution is population-monotonic.*

[39] The proof requires that there be at least eight agents.

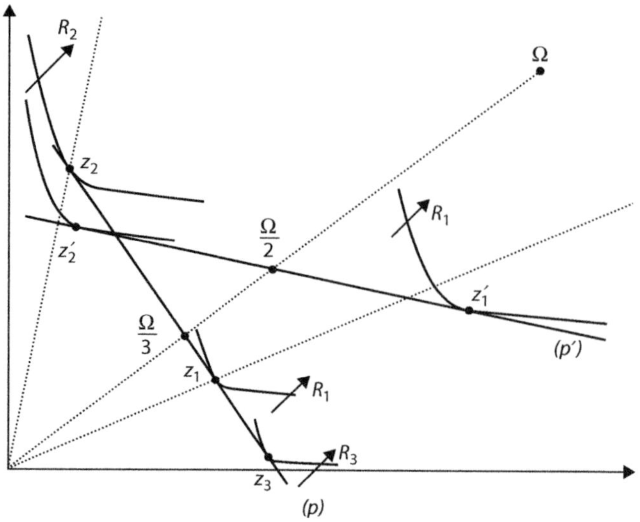

Figure 21.6. The equal-division Walrasian solution is not population-monotonic.
In the example depicted here, when all three agents are present, the solution selects z. If agent 3 is not present, it selects z', to which agent 2 prefers z.

A related result holds for economies with a large number of agents modeled as a continuum (Moulin 1990c, 1991).

Theorem 7.8 can be strengthened in the same manner as Theorem 7.1 was: on the same domain, for each $\varepsilon > 0$, no selection from the ε—no-domination and Pareto solution is *population-monotonic* (Kim 2004) (the smaller ε is, the larger the number of agents required for the proof). Just as was the case for Theorem 7.1 and its "ε variant," Theorem 7.8 and its own "ε variant" rely on the admissibility of preferences whose indifference curves can be chosen arbitrarily close to right angles. Positive results hold for the equal-division Walrasian solution, if preferences satisfy some minimal degree of substitutability. In particular, it follows from Polterovich and Spivak (1980, 1983) that this solution is *population-monotonic* if preferences exhibit the gross-substitutability property and all goods are normal (Fleurbaey 1995c).

There is a connection between *population-monotonicity* being violated by the equal-division Walrasian rule to its being subject to the "transfer paradox": in an economy with individual endowments, a transfer of endowment from one agent to some other agent may make the donor better off and the recipient worse off. The following results pertain to homothetic preferences: In the absence of substitution effects, the Walrasian rule is subject to the transfer paradox if and only if it violates *population-monotonicity*. In the presence of substitution effects, it may violate *population-monotonicity* even in situations where no transfer paradox occurs (Jones 1987).

What if other distributional requirements are imposed? If preferences are strictly monotonic, the Ω-egalitarian-equivalence and Pareto solution is *population-monotonic*

(Thomson 1987a). Recall that this solution also meets the equal-division lower bound. More generally, and still if preferences are strictly monotonic, the equal-opportunity–equivalence and Pareto solutions of Section 6.2 are *population-monotonic.*

For quasi-linear preference profiles, we have a counterpart of Proposition 7.1:

Proposition 7.2 (Moulin 1992b) Domain: private goods with a positive amount of money; quasi-linear preferences; free-access coalitional game associated with each economy satisfies substitutability. *The Shapley value, when applied to these games, induces a population-monotonic solution.*

Selections from the equal-division lower bound and Pareto solution exist that are *population-monotonic.* A constructive algorithm producing such a solution can indeed be defined (Moulin 1990b), but in contrast with the solution induced by the Shapley value, this solution is not *resource-monotonic.*

If we apply the replacement principle of Section 7.2 to the *joint* replacement of preferences and population, then under the additional requirement of *replication-invariance*, only one solution emerges, namely the selection from the egalitarian-equivalence solution for which the reference bundle is proportional to the social endowment.

Theorem 7.9 (Sprumont and Zhou 1999) Domain: private goods; strictly monotonic and convex preferences. *The* Ω*-egalitarian-equivalence and Pareto solution is the only selection from the equal-division lower bound and Pareto solution satisfying replication-invariance and welfare-domination under preference-and-population-replacement.*

Interestingly, this uniqueness result fails if the joint *welfare-domination* requirement is replaced by two separate requirements, one pertaining to changes in preferences and the other pertaining to changes in populations.

In a model with infinitely many agents modeled as a continuum, versions of Theorem 7.9 hold that do not involve *replication-invariance* (Sprumont and Zhou 1999).

7.5. Monotonicity in Economies with Individual Endowments

If the issue is that of allocating gains from trade, other appealing monotonicity requirements can be imposed. One is that if an agent's endowment increases, he should end up at least as well off as he was from the first endowment profile. Another is that under the same hypotheses, nobody else should end up worse off than he was from the first endowment profile. Here are the formal definitions:

Own-Endowment Monotonicity

For each $(R,\omega) \in \mathcal{R}^N \times \mathbb{R}_+^{\ell N}$, each $z \in \varphi(R,\omega)$, each $i \in N$, each $\omega_i' \in \mathbb{R}_+^{\ell}$, and each $z' \in \varphi(R,\omega_i',\omega_{-i})$, if $\omega_i' \geq \omega_i$, then $z_i' \, R_i \, z_i$.

No Negative Effects on Others

Under the hypotheses of the previous definition, $z'_{N\backslash\{i\}} \, R_{N\backslash\{i\}} \, z_{N\backslash\{i\}}$.

It is easy to define selections from the individual-endowments lower-bound and Pareto solution that are *own-endowment monotonic*. However, we also have impossibilities:

Theorem 7.10 (Thomson 1987a) Domain: private goods; strictly monotonic, convex, and homothetic preferences; individual endowments. (a) *No selection from the no-envy in trades and Pareto solution satisfies either own-endowment monotonicity or no negative effect on others.*[40] (b) *No selection from the egalitarian-equivalence and Pareto solution satisfies no negative effect on others.*[41]

When agents have private endowments, the appropriate expression of the idea of *population-monotonicity* is that the welfares of all agents who are present before and after the change should be affected in the same direction. It is easy to see that the Walrasian solution violates the property, even when preferences are homothetic and endowments proportional (assumptions that guarantee its *single-valuedness*).

However, the selections from the egalitarian-equivalence in trades and Pareto solution, obtained by requiring the reference trade to lie on a monotone path, satisfy the requirement (Thomson 1987a). They also meet the individual-endowments lower bound.

8. CONSISTENCY AND RELATED PROPERTIES

Here, we return to situations in which both the population of agents and the resources available may vary, but this time, our focus is on a variety of invariance properties. These properties can be interpreted as formalizing tradeoffs between equity and efficiency objectives with objectives of informational simplicity. Unless otherwise indicated, this section is based on Thomson (1988). (The literature devoted to the analysis of the properties in various models is surveyed in Thomson 1990b, 1995d.)

8.1. Consistency and Converse Consistency

We have already encountered *replication-invariance* (Section 4.6). A converse of this requirement is that if an allocation that is chosen for a replica economy happens to be a replica allocation (of the same order), then the model allocation should be chosen for the model economy:

Division-Invariance

For each $N \in \mathcal{N}$, each $(R,\Omega) \in \mathcal{E}^N$, each $z \in \varphi(R,\Omega)$, each $N' \subset N$, each $(R',\Omega') \in \mathcal{E}^{N'}$, and each $k \in \mathbb{N}$, if (R,Ω) is a k-replica of (R',Ω') and z is the corresponding k-replica of some $z' \in Z(R',\Omega')$, then $z' \in \varphi(R',\Omega')$.

[40] The first part of this statement is an implication of the fact that on this domain no selection from the no-envy in trades and Pareto solution is immune to manipulation through withholding of endowments (Postlewaite 1979).

[41] An ε variant of this result holds, analogous to the ε variant of Theorem 7.1.

Given a group $N \in \mathcal{N}$, and an allocation z chosen for some economy $(R, \Omega) \in \mathcal{E}^N$, consider some subgroup $N' \subset N$, and the problem of allocating among its members the resources that it has received in total. Our next requirement, the central one in this section, is that the restriction of z to the subgroup should be chosen for this economy, $(R_{N'}, \sum_{N'} z_i)$, the **reduced economy of e with respect to N' and z.** Then, a choice made initially need not be revisited after some agents have received their assignments and left:

Consistency

For each $N \in \mathcal{N}$, each $(R, \Omega) \in \mathcal{E}^N$, each $z \in \varphi(R, \Omega)$, and each $N' \subset N$, we have $z_{N'} \in \varphi(R_{N'}, \sum_{N'} z_i)$.

A counterpart of this requirement when the population of agents enlarges is the following: given some allocation z that is feasible for some economy, check whether the restriction of z to each subgroup of two agents is chosen for the problem of allocating between them what they have received in total. If the answer is yes for each such subgroup, then one can say that each agent is in a sense treated fairly in relation to each other agent; then, we require that z itself should be chosen for the initial economy:

Converse Consistency

For each $N \in \mathcal{N}$, each $e \equiv (R, \Omega) \in \mathcal{E}^N$, and each $z \in Z(e)$, if for each $N' \subseteq N$ with $|N'| = 2$, $z_{N'} \in \varphi(R_{N'}, \sum_{N'} z_i)$, then $z \in \varphi(e)$.

An alternative formulation is obtained by writing the hypotheses for all proper subgroups of N, as opposed to all subgroups of two agents, but an easy induction argument shows that this apparently weaker property is equivalent to the one just stated.

Several results below require preferences to be **smooth**: at each $z_i \in \mathbb{R}^{\ell}_{++}$, agent i's upper contour set has a unique hyperplane of support. Let $\mathcal{E}^N_{sm}$ be a class of smooth economies.

It is easy to see that the Pareto solution is *consistent*. Under smoothness of preferences, it is also *conversely consistent*. (Goldman and Starr 1982 establish conditions under which the hypothesis that no group of $t < |N|$ agents can achieve any gain from trade implies that the entire set of agents cannot either.) It is *replication-invariant* in general (convexity of preferences is important here). The no-envy solution satisfies all of the above properties, and the egalitarian-equivalence solution only fails *converse consistency*. This is also the case for the equal-division Walrasian solution. Its *consistency* is illustrated by Figure 21.7a. (The same prices remain equilibrium prices in each reduced economy, but there could be other equilibrium allocations, some of which are supported by prices other than the equilibrium prices of the initial economy.) Figure 21.7b shows that the equal-division Walrasian solution is not *conversely consistent*. However, if preferences are smooth and corners are excluded, the property does hold. The equal-division core satisfies *division-invariance* but none of the other properties.

We will complement the four properties just listed by efficiency and fairness requirements, obtaining characterizations of the equal-division Walrasian solution. The first one

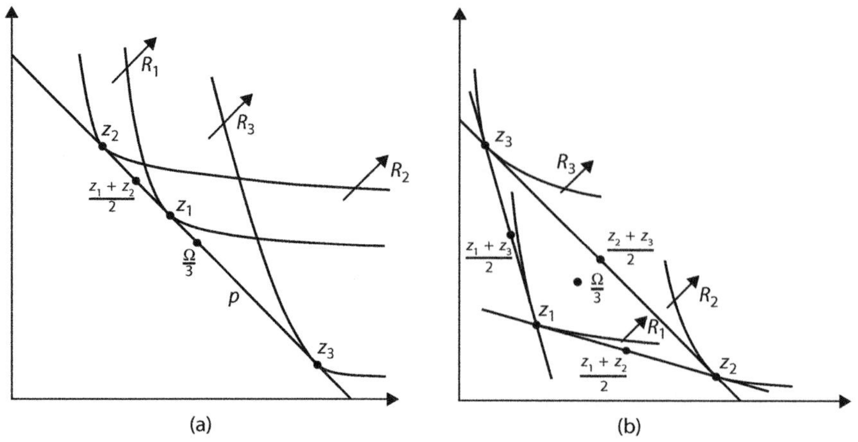

Figure 21.7. The equal-division Walrasian solution is consistent but not conversely consistent. (a) For the three-agent economy represented here, the solution selects the allocation z. For the economy with agent set $\{1,2\}$ in which the amount to divide is $\Omega - z_3$, it selects (z_1, z_2) (the same prices can serve as equilibrium prices). (b) If kinks in indifference curves are permitted, the solution is not *conversely consistent.* We consider the efficient allocation z in the three-agent economy $e \equiv (R_1, R_2, R_3, \Omega)$. It is such that for each pair $\{i,j\}$, $(z_i, z_j) \in W_{ed}(R_i, R_j, z_i + z_j)$. Yet $z \notin W_{ed}(e)$.

is a direct consequence of the well-known fact that under replication, the core shrinks to the set of Walrasian allocations (Debreu and Scarf 1963). Many variants of this theorem have been proved. It is stated in this form in Thomson (1988). Nagahisa (1994) also discusses the issue.

Theorem 8.1 Domain: private goods (strictly positive social endowment); locally nonsatiated and convex preferences. *If a subsolution of the equal-division core is replication-invariant, it is a subsolution of the equal-division Walrasian solution.*

Theorem 8.2 (Varian 1974) Domain: private goods; monotonic and convex preferences. *If a subsolution of the group no-envy solution is replication-invariant, it is a subsolution of the equal-division Walrasian solution.*

Theorem 8.3 (Thomson 1988) Domain: private goods; monotonic, convex, and smooth preferences. *If a subsolution of the equal-division lower bound and Pareto solution is replication-invariant and consistent, it is a subsolution of the equal-division Walrasian solution.*

A characterization of the equal-division Walrasian solution on the basis of the concept of a strictly envy-free allocation (Section 4.4) due to Zhou (1992) is equivalent to Theorem 8.3. Zhou also offers an estimate of the speed of convergence to Walrasian allocations as the order of replication increases.

The issue of *consistency* in economies with a large number of agents modeled as a continuum has also been addressed. For this model, we adapt the definition of a strictly envy-free allocation as one such that the set of agents each of whom prefers the average bundle received by some group to his own bundle has measure zero. Under certain assumptions, a central one being smoothness of preferences, the equal-division Walrasian solution coincides with the strict no-envy and Pareto solution (Zhou 1992). Also, it is the only subsolution of the equal-division lower bound and Pareto solution satisfying *consistency* (Thomson and Zhou 1993). As compared to Theorem 8.3, it is noteworthy that this second result does not involve *replication-invariance*. Also, it extends to economies with possibly satiated preferences, yielding a characterization of the "equal-slack Walrasian solution" (Mas-Colell 1992), a solution that differs from the standard notion in that each agent's income is obtained by adding to the value of his endowment a supplementary income, the same for all agents. Finally, it holds for solutions defined on a domain consisting of a single economy and all of its possible reductions. The case of economies with both atoms and an atomless sector is considered by Zhou (1992). There, a Walrasian conclusion is reached for the members of the atomless sector only.

The following characterization of the equal-division Walrasian solution involves *converse consistency*:

Theorem 8.4 (Thomson 1995d) Domain: private goods; monotonic, convex, and smooth preferences. *(a) If a subsolution of the equal-division lower bound and Pareto solution is anonymous and conversely consistent, then on the subdomain of two-agent economies, it is a subsolution of the equal-division Walrasian solution. (b) If in fact coincidence occurs on that subdomain, it is an arbitrary solution containing the equal-division Walrasian solution for all other cardinalities.*

The next result involves two new axioms. **Uniform treatment of uniforms** says that if all agents have the same preferences, only allocations consisting of bundles that they find indifferent to each other according to these preferences should be chosen (Maniquet 1996a). **Juxtaposition-invariance** says that if an allocation is efficient for some economy and it happens to be obtained by juxtaposing two allocations that are chosen for two subeconomies with equal per-capita social endowments, then it should be chosen (Thomson 1988):

Theorem 8.5 (Maniquet 1996a) Domain: private goods; monotonic, convex, and smooth preferences such that no positive bundle is indifferent to a bundle having at least one zero coordinate. *The equal-division Walrasian solution is the only subsolution of the Pareto solution satisfying uniform treatment of uniforms, juxtaposition-invariance, and consistency.*

The next results pertain to production economies. In formulating *consistency* for a production economy, the issue arises of how to redefine the technology to reflect the fact that agents leave with their consumption bundles. The simplest one is to translate the production set by the sum of the bundles taken with them by the agents who leave. Standard classes of technologies are not closed under this operation, however, and adjustments have to be made to ensure that the "reduced" production set is admissible. Adjustments are also needed for *replication-invariance*.

A requirement related to *invariance under monotonic transformations of preferences* is that if an allocation is chosen for some economy and preferences change in such a way that for each agent, his indifference curve through his assigned bundle remains the same, then the allocation should still be chosen. Let us refer to it as **invariance under restricted monotonic transformations of preferences** (Maniquet 2002).

Theorem 8.6 (Maniquet 2002) Domain: one-input one-output production economies; monotonic and convex preferences; production set is closed under disposal. *If a subsolution of the Pareto and constant-returns-to-scale lower bound solution satisfies invariance under restricted monotonic transformations of preferences, replication-invariance, and consistency, then it is subsolution of the constant-returns-to-scale–equivalent solution.*

Next are characterizations of two essentially single-valued solutions, the **equal-wage–equivalent and Pareto solution**, which selects the allocations for which there is a reference wage such that each agent finds his bundle indifferent to the best bundle he could achieve by maximizing his preferences on a budget set defined by this wage rate. The **output-egalitarian-equivalence and Pareto solution** selects the efficient allocations that each agent finds indifferent to a common consumption consisting of only some amount of the output. We will impose the self-explanatory notion of **equal welfares for equal preferences**.

Theorem 8.7 (Fleurbaey and Maniquet 1999) Domain: private goods; preferences are strictly monotonic with respect to output and monotonic with respect to input, and convex; unrestricted technologies. *The equal-wage–equivalent and Pareto solution is the only* essentially single-valued *selection from the constant-returns-to-scale lower bound solution satisfying Pareto-indifference, equal welfares for equal preferences, contraction-independence, and consistency.*

Note the difference of domains in the next theorem:

Theorem 8.8 (Fleurbaey and Maniquet 1999) Domains: private goods; preferences are strictly monotonic with respect to output and monotonic with respect to input, and convex; technologies are one of the following: (a) they are unrestricted, (b) they exhibit nowhere-increasing-returns-to-scale, or (c) they are concave. *The output-egalitarian-equivalence and Pareto solution is the only essentially single-valued selection from the work-alone lower bound solution satisfying Pareto-indifference, equal welfares for equal preferences, and consistency.*

Roemer (1986a, 1986b, 1988) formulates consistency requirements with respect to changes in the number of goods. We will not review these papers here as they importantly depend on utility information, which we have chosen to ignore in defining the scope of this survey. (Iturbe-Ormaetxe and Nieto 1992 and 1996b provide further results along the same lines.)

8.2. Minimal Consistent Enlargements

When a solution is not *consistent*, one may be interested in evaluating how far it is from satisfying the property. We propose two procedures for doing this.

First, it follows directly from the definitions that the intersection of an arbitrary family of *consistent* solutions, if it constitutes a well-defined solution (i.e., if it is nonempty for each economy in its domain), is *consistent*. Also, for most natural ways of specifying allocation problems, the solution that associates with each economy its entire feasible set is *consistent*. Now, given a solution φ, consider the correspondence that associates with each economy its set of allocations that are selected by all of the *consistent* solutions containing φ. Since this family is nonempty, this correspondence is a well-defined solution, and it is clearly the minimal *consistent* solution containing φ, its **minimal consistent enlargement**.

This definition is proposed and explored by Thomson (1994d), who establishes certain algebraic properties of the concept and applies it to examples. To illustrate, the minimal *consistent* enlargement of the union of two solutions is the union of their minimal *consistent* enlargements. The minimal *consistent* enlargement of their intersection is a subsolution of the intersection of their minimal *consistent* enlargements; the inclusion may be strict.

The enlargement is sometimes considerable. For instance, the minimal *consistent* enlargement of the equal-division lower bound and Pareto solution—recall that this solution is not *consistent*—is "essentially" the Pareto solution. Also, that of the Ω-egalitarian-equivalence and Pareto solution is "essentially" the egalitarian-equivalence and Pareto solution.

A second procedure to evaluate how far a solution is from being *consistent*, provided that it contains at least one *consistent* solution, is to reduce it until the property is recovered (instead of enlarging it). A minimal reduction is possible because *consistency* is preserved under arbitrary unions. Thus, define the **maximal consistent subsolution** of a solution φ as the union of all of its *consistent* subsolutions of φ. Parallel algebraic relations can be established for the maximal *consistent* subsolution of the intersection and the union of two solutions as a function of the maximal *consistent* subsolutions of the two of them.

This concept allows us to relate different notions that have been discussed separately in the literature. To describe an application, let us first observe that *replication-invariance* is preserved under arbitrary unions too, and so by the same logic, one can define the **maximal consistent and replication-invariant subsolution** of a given solution, provided the solution has at least one subsolution with these properties. Now, the maximal *consistent* and *replication-invariant* subsolution of the equal-division lower bound solution is the solution defined by requiring that each agent should find his bundle at least as desirable as any bundle in the convex hull of the bundles received by all agents (one of the formal definitions of Section 4.4). Also, the strict no-envy solution (Section 4.4) is nothing other than the maximal *consistent* and *replication-invariant* subsolution of the average no-envy solution (Section 4.4).

8.3. Consistency in Economies with Individual Endowments

In economies with individual endowments, formulating *consistency* is not straightforward. If we imagine the departure of some agents with their bundles and keep the endowments of the agents who stay as initially specified, the list of bundles assigned to these agents initially will not be feasible given their endowments.

One possible resolution of this feasibility problem is to adjust the endowments of the agents who stay. Dividing equally among them the difference between the sum of the bundles assigned to the agents who left and the sum of the endowments of these agents comes to mind (Dagan 1995, Thomson 1992), but revised endowments may have negative coordinates, which requires further adjustments.

Another resolution is to add to the description of an economy a "gap vector" $T \in \mathbb{R}^{\ell}$: a positive coordinate of T is understood as a surplus of the corresponding good and a negative coordinate as a deficit. A **generalized economy** is a list $(R, \omega, T) \in \mathcal{R}^N \times \mathbb{R}_+^{\ell N} \times \mathbb{R}^{\ell}$ such that $\sum \omega_i + T \geqq 0$, and a feasible allocation for it is a list $(z_i)_{i \in N} \in \mathbb{R}_+^{\ell N}$ such that $\sum z_i = \sum \omega_i + T$. This formulation is proposed by Thomson (1992) and Dagan (1994). Let φ be a solution defined on a domain of generalized economies. To reduce $(R, \omega, T) \in \mathcal{R}^N \times \mathbb{R}_+^{\ell N} \times \mathbb{R}^{\ell}$ with respect to $N' \subset N$ and $z \in \varphi(R, \omega, T)$, we restrict the preference and endowment profiles to the members of N' and adjust the gap vector by the difference between the sum of the consumptions of the departing agents and the sum of their endowments: this yields the list $(R_{N'}, \omega_{N'}, T + \sum_{N \setminus N'}(\omega_i - z_i))$. Equipped with this notion of a reduction, *consistency* takes the usual form: $z_{N'}$ should be chosen by φ for the reduced economy.

Natural examples of *consistent* Walrasian-like solutions can be based on two alternative choices for the distribution of the gap among agents, equal division on the one hand and proportional division on the other (Thomson 1992). Peleg (1996) establishes the existence of an extension of the notion of a Walrasian equilibrium for generalized economies. His notion covers the examples just mentioned. He suggests, for each price vector, to add to each agent's income a share of the value of the gap calculated at these prices, in such a way that the agent's total income be a non-negative and continuous function.

It is fair to say that none of the characterizations obtained for these models are as natural as the ones we presented for the model without individual endowments. Indeed, most of them allow solutions to be empty-valued, and in fact, empty-valuedness is frequent (Dagan 1994, van den Nouweland, Peleg, and Tijs 1996). If not, they involve strong additional requirements (Korthues 1996, 2000).

Serrano and Volij (1998) also explore the issue in the context of production economies, and propose two definitions inspired by concepts of cooperative game theory. Their main results are characterizations of the Pareto solution, the core, and the Walrasian solution.

9. PUBLIC GOODS

The formulation and the study of equity criteria in economies with public goods has been the object of much less attention than economies with only private goods.

9.1. Basic Solutions

Before beginning our discussion of fairness for this model, we refer the reader to the classical marginal conditions for efficiency identified by Samuelson (1955), and subsequently refined by Saijo (1990), Campbell and Truchon (1988), and Conley and Diamantaras (1996). The topological properties (closedness and connectedness) of the set of efficient allocations are studied by Diamantaras and Wilkie (1996). This set coincides with the set of weakly Pareto efficient allocations under significantly stronger assumptions than in private good economies.

We begin our discussion of fairness by considering the case of one private good and one public good, the public good being produced from the private good according to a linear technology that, with an appropriate choice of units of measurement, we can assume to be one-to-one. If $|N| = 2$, the feasible allocations can be identified with the points of an equilateral triangle of appropriate size, as in Figure 21.8 (Kolm 1970; a pedagogical presentation is Thomson 1999b). An allocation is a vector $z \equiv (x_1, x_2, y) \in \mathbb{R}_+^N \times \mathbb{R}_+$ with $x_1 + x_2 + y = \Omega_x$, where the amount $\Omega_x \in \mathbb{R}_+$ of the private good initially available can be consumed as such—this accounts for $x_1 + x_2$ units of it, or used as an input in producing y units of the public good, which requires y units of it. Let $\mathcal{E}_{pub}^N$ denote a class of economies.

Since agents necessarily consume the same amount of the public good, an allocation $z \equiv (x_1, x_2, y)$ is **envy-free** if and only if $x_1 = x_2$. (More generally, as long as there is only one private good, the no-envy and no-domination criteria coincide.) An envy-free allocation can then be equivalently described as an "equal contribution allocation." Thus, the set σ of envy-free allocations is the vertical segment containing the top vertex. It is independent of preferences. (Independence holds whenever there is only one private good.) It intersects the Pareto-optimal set, which typically is a curvilinear segment with endpoints on the slanted axes of the triangle, at a finite number of points. In Figure 21.8a, the Pareto set is "thick," and there is a continuum of envy-free and efficient allocations.

There are many situations in economic theory where the **Lindahl solution** has been found to be the natural counterpart for public good economies of the Walrasian solution. Given the usefulness of the latter, when operated from equal division, in producing envy-free allocations, one may wonder whether the Lindahl mechanism will be equally useful in achieving this goal. However, since the public good can be produced at several alternative levels, there does not exist a unique "point of equal division." In the Kolm

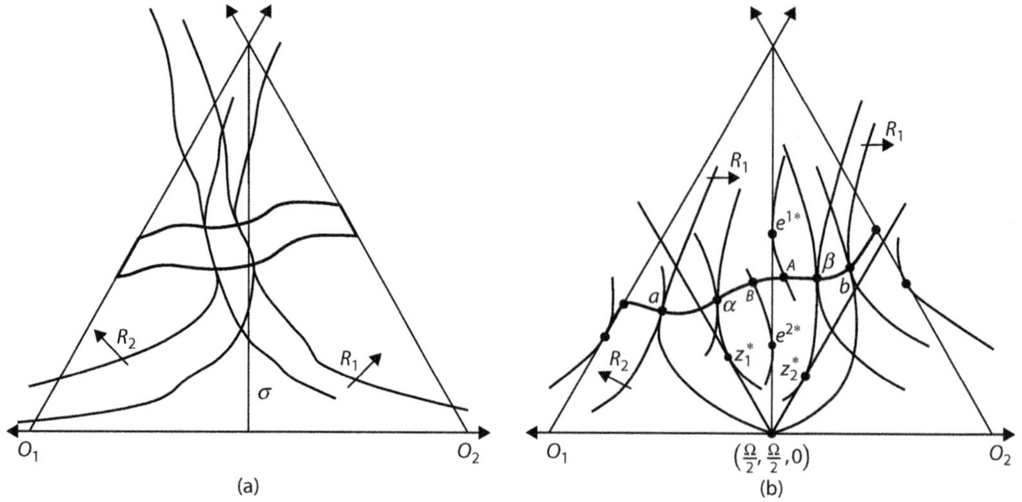

Figure 21.8. Envy-free allocations in the Kolm triangle.
(a) The set of envy-free allocations is the segment σ. The Pareto set is the horizontal wavy band connecting the two slanted sides. (b) The curvilinear segment from α to β is the set of efficient allocations that each agent finds at least as desirable as the best bundle he could achieve if endowed with an equal share of the social endowment of the private good and given unhampered access to the technology. The curvilinear segment from A to B is the set of efficient allocations that each agent finds at most as desirable as the equal-bundle allocation he prefers (e^{1*} for agent 1 and e^{2*} for agent 2).

triangle, any point of σ qualifies. Given $\omega \in \sigma$, operating the Lindahl solution from ω yields an envy-free allocation only accidentally. Also, the Lindahl solution operated from any $\omega \in \sigma$ does not necessarily treat identical agents identically (in contrast with the Walrasian solution); at a Lindahl allocation, two identical agents may receive bundles that are not indifferent to each other according to their common preferences. It is true, however, that there always are Lindahl allocations at which identical agents receive equivalent bundles (Champsaur 1976 studies the continuity properties of the subsolution of the Lindahl solution that selects these allocations).

The above observations indicate that the existence of envy-free and efficient allocations cannot be obtained as a direct corollary of theorems stating the existence of Lindahl allocations (following the pattern we had observed in exchange economics). However, under standard assumptions on preferences and production sets that we will not state in detail, and if for each efficient allocation the set of allocations that are Pareto-indifferent to it is contractible, and if there are no agent-specific input (these are the critical assumptions), envy-free and efficient allocations exist (Diamantaras 1992). Moreover, if envy-free and efficient allocations cannot be reached by operating the Lindahl solution from equal division, they are supported as "public competitive equilibria" when taxation is proportional to incomes and endowments are equal (Foley 1967), because then equal expenditure on the private goods is obtained. That every envy-free and efficient allocation is an equilibrium allocation of this type is proved for an economy with a large set of agents modeled as a continuum by Diamantaras (1991).

The notion of **egalitarian-equivalence** is well defined for public good economies, and egalitarian-equivalent and efficient allocations exist under general conditions. Sato (1985) considers the case when there is only one private good and advocates the selection from the egalitarian-equivalence and Pareto solution obtained by requiring the reference bundle to be the unit vector in the private good direction. This choice provides a natural interpretation of the reference bundle as measuring each "agent's willingness to pay for the public good in terms of the private good."

The case of one public good is of particular interest: Suppose there are ℓ private goods, which can be either consumed directly or used in the production of the public good. Let $Y \subseteq \mathbb{R}_+^{\ell+1}$ be the production set. There is a social endowment $\Omega \in \mathbb{R}_+^{\ell}$ of the private goods, and a set N of agents with preferences defined over $\mathbb{R}_+^{\ell+1}$. The following is the selection from the egalitarian-equivalence and Pareto solution obtained by requiring the reference bundle to be of the form $\left(\frac{\Omega}{|N|}, y_0\right)$ for some $y_0 \geq 0$.

Definition (Mas-Colell 1980b) *Given* $e \equiv (R, \Omega, Y) \in \mathcal{E}_{pub}^N$, *let* $E_y(e) \equiv \{z \in Z(e):$ *there is* $y_0 \geq 0$ *such that for each* $i \in N$, $z_i\ I_i\ (\frac{\Omega}{|N|}, y_0)\}$.

Sato (1987) proposes a notion of equity for which the Lindahl solution plays a role similar to the role played by the Walrasian solution. He also discusses generalizations (1990).

The issue of informational efficiency is addressed by Aizpurua and Manresa (1995) for a general model with arbitrarily many private and public goods, but in which there are no agent-specific inputs. A variant of the Lindahl mechanism that they introduce under the name of "Lindahl egalitarian" (which produces the public competitive equilibria described earlier) has minimal dimensionality among all mechanisms satisfying a regularity condition and realizing envy-free and efficient allocations.

Next, we formulate upper and lower bounds similar to the ones defined earlier for economies with private goods (Section 5.2).

The first bound, the **equal-division lower bound**, is simply that each agent should be made at least as well off as he would be by consuming an equal share of the social endowment of the private good(s). In the example depicted in Figure 21.8, the unique envy-free and efficient allocation meets this bound, but it is easy to modify it to show that there may be no envy-free and efficient allocation that does.

A second lower bound on an agent's welfare is obtained by imagining that he is alone and has to cover the full cost of the public goods.[42]

[42] The previous bound is often called "individual rationality from equal division" and the next one, "strong individual rationality from equal division."

Definition (Moulin 1992c) *Given* $e \equiv (R, \Omega, Y) \in \mathcal{E}^N_{pub}$, *the allocation* $z \in Z(e)$ *meets the* ***equal-division free-access lower bound for*** *e if for each* $i \in N$, $z_i \; R_i \; z_i^*$, *where* z_i^* *is any bundle that would maximize agent i's welfare if endowed with an equal share of the social endowment and given free access to the technology.*

A third bound—this time it is an upper bound—is obtained by first imagining, for each agent, that all others have preferences identical to his, and in this economy of identical agents, imposing efficiency and *equal treatment of equals*. Returning to the actual economy, we require that each agent should be made at most as well off as he would be in this hypothetical economy:

Definition (Moulin 1992c) *Given* $e \equiv (R, \Omega, Y) \in \mathcal{E}^N_{pub}$, *the allocation* $z \in Z(e)$ *meets the* ***identical-preferences upper bound for*** *e if for each* $i \in N$, $z_i^* \; R_i \; z_i$, *where* z_i^* *is any bundle that agent i would be assigned by any efficient solution satisfying* equal treatment of equals *in the hypothetical economy in which each other agent had preferences identical to his.*

The existence of efficient allocations meeting the *identical-preferences upper bound* is guaranteed under general assumptions (Moulin 1992c).

On the domain of one-input one-output economies, the *identical-preferences upper bound* and the *equal-division free-access lower bound* are compatible. Here is an example of an efficient solution satisfying both:

Definition (Moulin 1992c) *Let* $e \equiv (R, \Omega, Y) \in \mathcal{E}^N_{pub}$ *be a one-input one-output economy. The allocation* $z \in Z(e)$ *is an* ***equal-ratio–equivalent allocation for*** *e if there is* $\lambda \in \mathbb{R}_+$ *such that for each* $i \in N$, $z_i \; I_i \; z_i^*$, *where* z_i^* *is any bundle that would maximize agent i's welfare if given access to an equal share of the social endowment and to the technology* $Y^\lambda \equiv \{(x, y) \in \mathbb{R}^2 : (\lambda x, y) \in Y\}$.

The free-access constraints can be generalized to groups:

Definition (Moulin 1992c) *Given* $e \equiv (R, \Omega, Y) \in \mathcal{E}^N_{pub}$, *the allocation* $z \in Z(e)$ *is in the* ***equal-division free-access core of*** *e if for each* $S \subseteq N$, *there is no list* $(z_i^*)_{i \in S}$ *that is feasible for the coalition S (without the contribution of the complementary coalition), if endowed with* $\frac{|G|}{|N|}\Omega$ *and given unhampered access to the technology, and such that for each* $i \in S$, $z_i^* \; R_i \; z_i$, *and for at least one* $i \in S$, $z_i^* \; P_i \; z_i$.

Under general conditions, this solution is nonempty: Indeed, the solution $E_y P$ is a subsolution of the equal-division free-access core. The solution $E_y P$ also happens to satisfy very appealing monotonicity properties in response to improvements in the technology (Section 9.4).

In a class of economies with one private good and one public good produced according to a convex technology, further logical relations between the identical-preferences upper bound and the equal-division free-access lower bound are developed by Watts (1999). She shows that, except in trivial cases, the former does not imply the latter.

9.2. Notions of Equal, or Equivalent, Opportunities

The notions of equal opportunities introduced in Section 6 can be adopted to the current situation, but not all the results established in the private good case extend. In particular, even if $|N| = 2$, there is no family of choice sets whose associated equal-opportunity solution is a subsolution of the Pareto solution. Suppose now that preferences satisfy the classical assumption and that the technology is linear. Then, if $|N| = 2$, the equal-opportunity–equivalence solution associated with the family of linear choice sets is the egalitarian-equivalence solution. If $|N| > 2$, there is no necessary containment between the intersections of these two solutions with the Pareto solution, a result that mirrors one obtained for the private good case. Most importantly, under appropriate assumptions on preferences, the intersection of the equal-opportunity–equivalent and Pareto solution associated with the family of choice sets normal to a fixed price vector is well defined.

9.3. Social Endowment Monotonicity

Monotonicity questions are addressed in the context of public good economies by Thomson (1987c) and Moulin (1992c). The interesting case here is when there is, in addition to the public goods, only one private good. Indeed, as soon as there are two private goods, the impossibility results obtained for exchange economies extend to this more general class of economies. It suffices to consider "degenerate" public good economies in which agents happen to only care about the private goods.

If there is only one private good, and preferences are such that the r-egalitarian-equivalence and Pareto solution E_rP, where r is the unit vector corresponding to that good, is well defined (this requires that all indifference surfaces intersect the axis corresponding to the good), then this solution is *resource-monotonic*. Therefore, *resource-monotonic* selections from the egalitarian-equivalence and Pareto solution exist. However, no such selections from the no-envy and Pareto solution exist:

Theorem 9.1 (Thomson 1987c) Domain: one private good and one public good; strictly monotonic and convex preferences; linear technologies. *No selection from the no-envy and Pareto solution is resource monotonic.*

9.4. Technology-Monotonicity

Here, we address the issue of *technology-monotonicity*. Recall the definition of the selection from the egalitarian-equivalence and Pareto solution obtained by requiring the reference bundle to be of the form $(\frac{\Omega}{|N|}, y_0)$. Given $e \equiv (R, \Omega, Y) \in \mathcal{R}^N \times \mathbb{R}_+ \times \mathcal{Y}$, $E_y(e) \equiv \{z \in Z(e)$: there is y_0 such that for each $i \in N$, $z_i \; I_i \; (\frac{\Omega}{|N|}, y_0)\}$. We have the following characterization of this solution, in which assumptions are made to guarantee that it is well defined:

Theorem 9.2 (Moulin 1987a) Domain: one private good and one public good; the preferences of each agent i, defined over a set of the form $[0, \omega_i] \times \mathbb{R}_+$, are strictly monotonic with respect to the private good, weakly monotonic with respect to the public good, and such that for each $x \geq 0$, there is a unique $z_i \in Y_i$ for which $(x, y_i)\ I_i\ (\omega_i, 0)$; technology exhibits returns-to-scale that are bounded above. *The solution $E_Y P$ is the only selection from the equal-division free-access lower bound and Pareto solution satisfying technology-monotonicity.*

The assumption on the technology can be relaxed. What is important is that production sets be closed under union. However, the assumption that there is only one public good cannot be removed (Ginés and Marhuenda 1996, 1998).

The solution characterized in Theorem 9.2 is applied by Weber and Wiesmeth (1991). These authors identify assumptions on preferences under which it actually coincides with the Lindahl solution (these assumptions are obviously quite strong), and they define a generalization of it in Weber and Wiesmeth (1990).

9.5. Welfare-Domination under Preference-Replacement

Here, we will only note that the selection from the egalitarian-equivalence and Pareto solution characterized in Theorem 9.2 happens to be such that any change in the preferences of one agent affects all other agents in the same direction. Moreover, although we only required that an improvement in the technology should make all agents at least as well off as they are initially, it turns out that any change in the technology affects the welfares of all agents in the same direction (i.e., even when the old and the new technologies cannot be ranked, the welfare levels can).

We omit the formal statement of *welfare-domination under preference-replacement*, and simply note that a counterpart of Theorem 7.2 holds for this domain.

9.6. Monotonicity in Economies with Individual Endowments

Here, we consider economies in which agents may be individually endowed, and discuss properties introduced in Section 7.5. We ask whether it is possible to ensure that an increase in an agent's endowment never hurts any of the others. We have the following:

Theorem 9.3 (Thomson 1987b) Domain: economies one private good and one public good; monotonic and convex preferences; convex technologies. *No selection from (a) the no-envy and Pareto solution, or (b) the egalitarian-equivalence and Pareto solution, satisfies no negative effect on others.*

Under certain properties of preferences, the Lindahl solution is *population-monotonic* (Sertel and Yıldız 1998).

9.7. Population-Monotonicity

Turning now to variable populations with fixed resources, we have a possibility result provided we are satisfied with weak Pareto-optimality. Let $e \equiv (R, \Omega, Y) \in \mathcal{E}^N_{pub}$ and

$\underline{B}_{ed}(e)$ be the set of feasible allocations for e at which each agent is at least as well off as he would be at the best point he could achieve, if endowed with an equal share of the social endowment of the private good and given unhampered access the technology: this is the equal-division free-access lower bound solution.

In situations in which sufficiently strong positive external effects exist, the natural monotonicity requirement to formulate in response to increases in the population is that all agents initially present should be affected positively. Let us refer to this condition as **population-monotonicity$_+$**.

The selection from the egalitarian-equivalence and Pareto solution obtained by requiring the reference bundle to be the unit vector corresponding to the public good is a *population-monotonic$_+$* selection from the Pareto solution.

In the quasi-linear case, the Shapley value (Shapley 1953) when applied to the free-access game associated with each economy induces a *population-monotonic* solution. A *population-monotonic* solution meeting the *identical-preferences upper bound* is constructed by Moulin (1990a). Parallel results hold for the case of bads (Moulin 1992a).

Let us say that a solution is **weakly population-monotonic** if when new agents come in, all agents initially present are affected in the same direction.

Proposition 9.1 (Thomson 1987c) Domain: one private good and possibly multiple public goods; strictly monotonic preferences except that any bundle that is not strictly positive is indifferent to 0. *There are selections from the equal-division free-access lower bound solution satisfying weak population-monotonicity*.

A counterpart of Theorem 7.9 holds for economies with one private good and possibly multiple public goods, the population of agents being modeled as an atomless continuum. It is a characterization of the solution that selects any efficient allocation, such that there is a ratio $a \geq 0$ with the property that each agent is indifferent between his bundle and the best bundle he could reach among all bundles obtained for which he would have to pay the fraction a of the cost of production. Let us call this solution the **equal-factor-equivalence solution**.

Theorem 9.4 (Sprumont 1998) Domain: one private good and possibly multiple public goods; continuum of agents; strictly monotonic and convex preferences; cost function for the public goods is strictly increasing, strictly convex, takes value 0 at 0, and satisfies a mild regularity condition. *The equal-factor–equivalence and Pareto solution is the only selection from the identical-preferences upper bound and Pareto solution satisfying welfare-domination under preference-and-population–replacement*.

As for the private good version of the theorem (Theorem 7.9), uniqueness depends on the possibility of varying preferences and populations jointly. A version of the result holds for finite economies provided a certain form of *replication-invariance* is also imposed.

9.8. Consistency

In a public goods economy, conceptual problems arise in expressing the idea of consistency (Section 8) because one cannot imagine the departing agents to leave with their consumptions. Indeed, the public goods components of their consumptions are also consumed by the agents who stay. Proposals have been made to deal with this problem, but the definitions are not as compelling as in the private goods case.

For a version of the model in which the set of agents is represented as a continuum, Diamantaras (1992) provides a characterization of the public competitive equilibrium solution on the basis of such a notion.

Van den Nouweland, Tijs, and Wooders (2002) characterize the generalization of Lindahl equilibrium proposed by Kaneko (1977a, 1977b) under the name of "ratio equilibrium." In defining a reduced economy, they make adjustments in the cost function as a function of the ratios associated with the allocation that is the point of departure.

10. INDIVISIBLE GOODS

Estate or divorce settlements often involve items that cannot be divided (houses, family heirlooms), or can only be divided at a cost that would make the division undesirable (silverware). Other examples that have been the subject of much discussion recently are positions in schools or organs for transplant patients. In this section, we reconsider the theory of fair allocation in the presence of such indivisible goods, called "objects." We assume that there is also an infinitely divisible good, called "money." At first, we focus on situations in which each agent can consume at most one object. An illustration is the problem of allocating rooms to students in a house they share, and specifying how much each of them should contribute to the rent. The multi-object-per-agent case and the object-only case are discussed in Section 10.7.

Some, but not all, of the concepts introduced earlier can be adapted to this situation, but interestingly, due to the special structure of the model, several equivalences exist that do not hold in general. Consistency properties can be met and characterizations are available based on them. On the other hand, monotonicity properties are quite restrictive and hold only on narrow subdomains.

10.1. The Model

Let Ω be a social endowment consisting of some amount M of money and a set A of objects. This endowment is to be distributed among a set N of agents. Unless specified otherwise, $|N| = |A|$. Each agent $i \in N$ has preferences R_i defined over $\mathbb{R} \times A$ (or over $\mathbb{R}_+ \times A$, but for these introductory paragraphs, we adopt the former specification). They are continuous and strictly monotonic with respect to money, and satisfy the following "possibility of compensation" assumption: for each bundle $(m_i, \alpha) \in \mathbb{R} \times A$, and each object $\beta \in A$, there is $m_i' \in \mathbb{R}$ such that $(m_i', \beta)\ I_i\ (m_i, \alpha)$. Let $\mathcal{R}_{ind}$ be the class of all such preferences. An **economy** is a list $e \equiv (R, M, A)$ as just described, and $\mathcal{E}_{ind}^N$ is our generic notation for a class of economies. A **feasible allocation** for $e \equiv (R, M, A) \in \mathcal{E}_{ind}^N$ is a pair $z \equiv (m, \sigma)$ consisting of a vector $m \in \mathbb{R}^N$ such that $\sum m_i = M$ specifying how much money each agent receives, and a bijection σ: $N \to A$ specifying which object is assigned to each agent. Thus, the bundle received by agent $i \in N$ at z is $z_i \equiv (m_i, \sigma(i))$. Let $Z(e)$ denote the set of feasible allocations of $e \in \mathcal{E}_{ind}^N$.

Situations where there are fewer objects than agents are accommodated by introducing a "null object," denoted ν, the objects in A being then referred to as "real objects" if there is a risk of confusion. There are always enough copies of the null object for each agent to end up with one object. Denoting by A^* the augmented set $A \cup \nu$, preferences are then defined over $\mathbb{R} \times A^*$. A real object α is **desirable** for R_i if for each $m_i \in \mathbb{R}$, $(m_i, \alpha)\ R_i\ (m_i, \nu)$. It is **undesirable** if preference always goes in the other direction. An object may of course be neither desirable nor undesirable. If there are fewer agents than objects, some objects are unassigned. In some applications, it is natural to require that the null object not be assigned until all real objects are, even if these objects are undesirable. For instance, they could be tasks to be assigned to students in the house they share. Some students may find some of these tasks desirable and some other students do not (cooking might be an example here), but all tasks may have to be carried out.

Figure 21.9a gives a convenient graphical representation of the model for $|N| = |A|$. There are $|A|$ axes indexed by the elements of A. Along the axis indexed by each object is measured the amount of the divisible good that comes with that object. The broken line through $z_i \equiv (m_i, \alpha)$ links z_i to two other bundles $z_i' \equiv (m_i', \beta)$ and $z_i'' \equiv (m_i'', \gamma)$ that agent i finds indifferent to z_i; it can be thought of as an indifference curve.

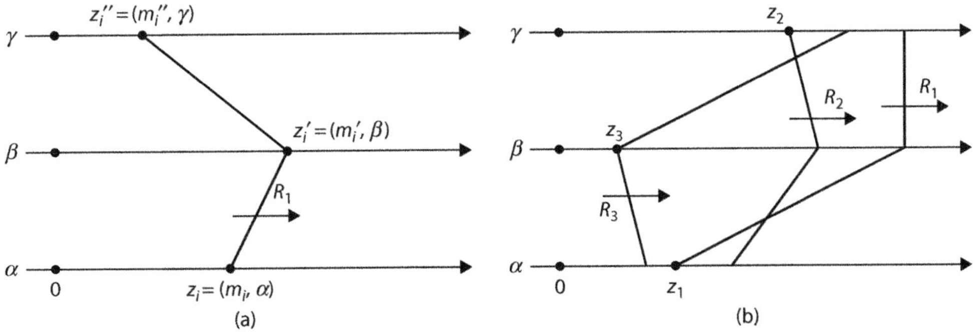

Figure 21.9. The no-envy solution applied to economies with indivisible goods.
(a) Representation of consumption space and of an indifference curve for agent 1. (b) The allocation z is not envy-free since agent 3's indifference curve through z_3 passes to the left of z_1.

Quasi-linearity of preferences means that indifference curves are all obtained from any one of them by horizontal translations.

A variant of the model just described is when the objects in A are identical. For instance, they may be jobs on an assembly line. When there are more workers than jobs, the null object is interpreted as being unemployed. Finally, there is the even more special situation in which $|A| = 1$. In either one of these cases, any recipient of a real object is called a "winner." The others are called "losers."

10.2. Basic Solutions

The **no-envy** concept applies directly to this model. In Figure 21.9b, agent 1 envies no one, agent 2 envies no one, but agent 3 envies agent 1.

For the distribution of multiple copies of the same object, in order for the winners not to envy each other, they should receive equal amounts of money. For the losers not to envy each other, they too should receive equal amounts of money. In addition, each winner should find the "winning bundle" at least as desirable as the "losing bundle," and each loser should find the "losing bundle" at least as desirable as the "winning bundle."'

It is clear that if consumptions of money have to be non-negative, envy-free allocations may not exist. Imagine for instance that all agents have the same preferences and the social endowment of money is 0. Conversely, one may hope that if the social endowment of money is sufficiently large, it is possible to compensate those agents who do not receive the objects they would prefer. This hope is justified:

Theorem 10.1 (Svensson 1983) Domain: one infinitely divisible good, and a set A of objects; equal number of agents; preferences, defined on $\mathbb{R}_+ \times A$, are strictly monotonic with respect to money, and such that for each $i \in N$ and each $\alpha \in A$, there is an allocation at which the bundle containing α is most preferred among all bundles the allocation is composed of. *(a) Envy-free allocations exist. (b) Envy-free allocations are efficient.*

Techniques rather different from Svensson's have been used to prove the existence of envy-free allocations (Maskin 1987, Alkan, Demange, and Gale 1991). When consumptions of money are unbounded below, and if preferences are continuous, monotonic with respect to money, and satisfy the compensation assumption, envy-free allocations exist without any assumption relating preferences and the social endowment of money (Alkan, Demange, and Gale 1991). A constructive proof is possible that covers preferences that need not be monotonic but otherwise satisfy assumptions similar to those of Theorem 10.1 (Su 1999). For a general proof that covers all of the above, see Velez (2007). When the objects are identical, an elementary existence proof is also available (Tadenuma and Thomson 1993). The most general argument is Velez (2008).

The implication stated as part (b) of Theorem 10.1 fails if $|A| > |N|$. It is clear why: no-envy may well be achieved by assigning objects that all agents find inferior to objects that are not assigned. However, the implication can be recovered under a certain strengthening of the definition of no-envy, a definition that is nonvacuous under general conditions (Alkan, Demange, and Gale 1991). The distributional merits of the stronger notion can be questioned however, as it sometimes seems to favor particular agents (Tadenuma 1994).

A variant of the model is when each agent can consume only some of the objects available (Svensson 1988). To illustrate, the objects could be jobs, and not all agents may be qualified for all jobs. Svensson states assumptions guaranteeing the existence of envy-free allocations in this context.

For quasi-linear preferences, several algorithms leading to envy-free allocations have been developed. Under that assumption, and except for degenerate cases, the assignments of objects are the same at all efficient allocations (efficiency is undisturbed by transfers of money among agents), so that one can speak of an "efficient allocation of objects." There are finitely many assignments of objects, so the efficient ones can be identified by exhaustive search. Aragones's (1995) starting point is such an assignment. She considers the case when consumptions of money are non-negative, and her algorithm identifies the smallest social endowment of money M^* guaranteeing the existence of envy-free allocations. This amount depends of course on preferences. The envy-free allocation obtained then is unique up to Pareto-indifference, and it provides the basis for the definition of a selection from the set of envy-free allocations of that economy when the social endowment of money M is at least M^*, by dividing equally among all agents the difference $M - M^*$.

Klijn's algorithm (2000) starts from an arbitrary feasible allocation. Envy cycles are first eliminated. If an envy relation remains, transfers of money from the envied agent to the envious agent are made to eliminate it, but additional transfers to or from other agents are also carried out in order to ensure that no new envy relation is created.[43]

At each step of the market-like algorithm proposed by Abdulkadiroğlu, Sönmez, and Ünver (2004), no-envy is met, as all agents maximize their preferences over a common budget set, but feasibility is not, and convergence is to a feasible allocation. When envy-free allocations exist at which consumptions of money are all non-positive, as might be needed when the social endowment of money is negative, objects are desirable, and each agent is required to pay something for receiving an object (think of the rent division application), the algorithm produces such an allocation. A family of algorithms in that spirit is developed by Ünver (2003).[44]

[43] The algorithm can be modified to produce the extreme points of the set of envy-free allocations.

[44] Another procedure is defined by Brams and Kilgour (2001) that generates an efficient allocation at which agents do not receive money, but it may not be envy-free.

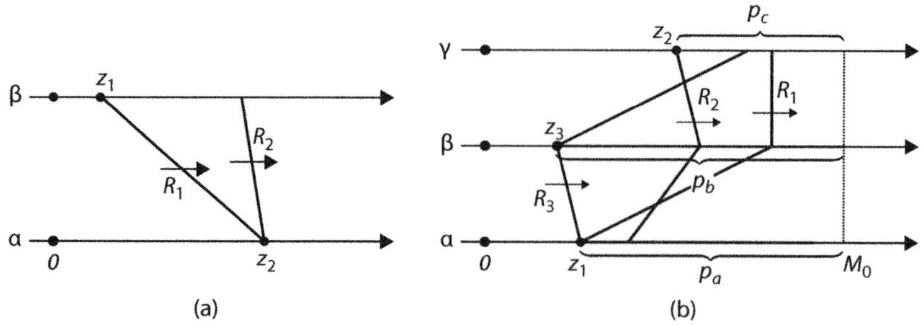

Figure 21.10. Egalitarian-equivalence and the equal-income Walrasian solution in economies with indivisible goods.
(a) For $|N| = 2$, if z is egalitarian-equivalent and efficient, it is envy-free. (b) Independently of the number of objects, if z is an equal-income Walrasian allocation, it is envy-free.

The notion of **egalitarian-equivalence** also applies directly to this model. Egalitarian-equivalent and efficient allocations exist very generally, when consumptions of money are unbounded below and the compensation assumption holds. The proof is similar to that of the existence of r-egalitarian-equivalent and efficient allocations in classical economies. When preferences are defined over $\mathbb{R}_+ \times A$, existence holds under similar assumptions as the ones guaranteeing that of envy-free allocations in Theorem 10.1. In either case, to each object can be associated a reference bundle containing that object to which corresponds an egalitarian-equivalent and efficient allocation (Svensson 1983b). Thus, there are as many egalitarian-equivalent and efficient allocations as objects. Let $e \equiv (R, M, A) \in \mathcal{E}^N$. Figure 21.10a illustrates that if $|N| = 2$ and $z \in EP(e)$, then $z \in F(e)$. If $z \in EP(e)$ with reference bundle z_0, then there is $i \in N$ such that $z_i = z_0$, so that agent i envies no one, but if $|N| \geq 3$, there may be occurrences of envy. Moreover, just as in the classical case, there are economies in which all egalitarian-equivalent and efficient allocations violate no-envy (Thomson 1990a).

If there is only one real object, however, these notions are compatible. Consider the solution $\boldsymbol{F^*}$ that selects the envy-free allocation that is the least favorable to the winner: at this allocation, the winner is indifferent between his bundle and the losers' common bundle. (For some configurations of preferences, there are several—they are Pareto-indifferent—allocations with this property.) This allocation is egalitarian-equivalent, with the losers' bundle serving as reference bundle.

The **Walrasian solution** can be adapted to the present model as follows: for each $\alpha \in A$, let $p_\alpha \in \mathbb{R}_+$. We call p_α the **price** of object α. A **price vector** is a list $p \equiv (p_\alpha)_{\alpha \in A}$.

Definition *Given $e \equiv (R, M, A) \in \mathcal{E}^N_{ind}$, the allocation $z \in Z(e)$ is an **equal-income Walrasian allocation for e**, written as $z \in W_{ei}(e)$, if there are $p \in \mathbb{R}^A_+$ and $M_0 \in \mathbb{R}_+$ such that for each $i \in N$ and each $z'_i \equiv (m'_0, \alpha') \in \mathbb{R} \times A$ satisfying $m'_0 + p_{\alpha'} \leq M_0$, we have $z_i \; R_i \; z'_i$.*

The definition is illustrated in Figure 21.10b. Recall that in classical economies, the equal-income Walrasian allocations constitute a small subset of the set of envy-free and efficient allocations. Here, the two notions coincide. We also have equivalence between no-envy for individuals and **group no-envy** (defined as in the classical case):

Theorem 10.2 (Svensson 1983b) Domain: one infinitely divisible good, and a set A of objects; preferences, defined on $\mathbb{R}_+ \times A$ (or on $\mathbb{R} \times A$), are monotonic with respect to the divisible good. *(a) An allocation is envy-free if and only if it is an equal-income Walrasian allocation. (b) An allocation is envy-free if and only if it is group envy-free.*

A variety of selections from the no-envy solution have been proposed. First, define the worse-off agent at an allocation as the agent who receives the smallest amount of money. The **maximin money** rule selects the envy-free allocation at which this amount is as large as possible. If the null object is present, define the worse-off agent as the one whose money-only equivalent bundle contains the smallest amount of money. The **maximin money-only-equivalent** rule selects the envy-free allocation at which this amount is as large as possible. Two solutions can be defined in a symmetric way based on identifying the agent whose consumption of money is the largest. The **minimax money** rule selects the envy-free allocation at which the agent who receives the largest amount of money receives the smallest such amount. The **minimax money-only-equivalent** rule performs the parallel exercise with the money-only equivalent bundles (Alkan, Demange, and Gale 1991; the first criterion is also studied in the quasi-linear case by Aragones 1995).

Next (and whether or not the null object is available), given any envy-free allocation, for each two-agent subgroup and each agent in the pair, calculate the amount of money that should be added to the other agent's bundle for the first agent to be indifferent between his bundle and the second agent's revised bundle. These $|N|(|N|-1)$ "compensation" terms give a picture of how well each agent is treated in relation to each other agent at the allocation. Then, select the allocation(s) at which all agents are treated "as equally as possible." This can be done in several ways. One is to calculate for each agent the average of his compensation terms over the pairs to which he belongs, and choosing the allocation(s) at which the smallest (across agents) such average is maximal. This **maximin average compensation** rule is *essentially single-valued* (Tadenuma 1989). Criteria based on lexicographic operations are also possible, focused on the agents who are treated the worse according to the size of their compensation terms (Tadenuma and Thomson 1995).

Another idea exploits the fact that if $|N| = 2$, the assignment of objects is the same at all envy-free allocations (except for degenerate cases). Given an envy-free allocation, for each two-agent subgroup, identify the two extreme allocations obtained by transferring money from one agent to the other without violating envy. The difference between the amounts of money received by either one of the two agents at these two allocations can be thought of as an "equity surplus" at the allocation. Calculate the share of this surplus that each agent receives. Then, select the allocation(s) at which these shares are as equal as possible. Again, several choices are possible here depending upon whether an average of these shares is considered, yielding what could be called a **maximin average share** rule, or whether a lexicographic operation is performed on these shares (these last two proposals are developed by Tadenuma and Thomson 1995). In the two-agent case, and when preferences are quasi-linear, several of these proposals agree.

In the model under study here, dividing resources equally is not an option, but an earlier distributional requirement remains meaningful: each agent should be at least as well off as he would be at the (essentially) unique envy-free allocation of the hypothetical economy in which everyone had his preferences. This is the **identical-preferences lower bound**. If $|N| = 2$, meeting this bound is actually equivalent to no-envy, but if $|N| > 2$, the identical-preferences lower bound is weaker (Bevia 1996a). (In particular, it does not imply efficiency.) Thus, this concept gives us another chance of obtaining positive results when no-envy is too demanding. Unfortunately, there are quasi-linear economies with equal numbers of objects and agents in which all egalitarian-equivalent and efficient allocations violate not only no-envy, as we already know, but in fact the identical-preferences lower bound. When there are more objects than agents, an allocation may be envy-free and efficient without meeting the identical-preferences lower bound, but it meets the variant of the lower bound obtained by using only the objects that are assigned. Let us call it the **weak identical-preferences lower bound**. Our earlier result concerning the incompatibility of egalitarian-equivalence and the identical-preferences lower bound persists, however, since it can be proved by means of an example with an equal number of objects and agents, for which the two versions of the bound coincide (Thomson 2003b).

10.3. Resource-Monotonicity

Next, we consider changes in resources. We begin with the requirement that as the amount of money available increases, all agents should end up at least as well off as they were initially:

Money-Monotonicity

For each $(R, M, A) \in \mathcal{E}^N_{ind}$, each $z \in \varphi(R, M, A)$, each $M' > M$, each $z' \in \varphi(R, M', A)$, we have $z' \, R \, z$.

Any selection from the egalitarian-equivalence and Pareto solution obtained by fixing the reference object is *money-monotonic.* If there is only one real object, and if the reference object is chosen to be the null object, we obtain the solution F^*, introduced earlier, which is also a selection from the no-envy solution. This solution enjoys other desirable properties, as we will see.

In the multiple-object case, selections from the no-envy solution exist that are *money-monotonic* (Alkan, Demange, and Gale 1991).

Next, we require that when additional objects become available, all agents should end up at least as well off as they were initially. This property makes sense if the objects are desirable or if they do not have to be assigned. Of course, in specifying an economy, we now have to allow the numbers of objects and agents to differ. Then, an envy-free allocation is not necessarily efficient and we explicitly impose efficiency. Recall that in our basic definition of an economy, preferences are defined over the cross-product of $\mathbb{R}$ with the set of objects. In specifying the economy that results after the disappearance of some objects, we therefore restrict preferences to the cross-product of $\mathbb{R}$ with the set of remaining objects.

Object-Monotonicity

For each $(R, M, A) \in \mathcal{E}^N_{ind}$, each $z \in \varphi(R, M, A)$, each $A' \subset A$, each $z' \in \varphi(R_{|\mathbb{R}\times A'}, M, A')$, we have $z \, R \, z'$.

A negative result holds, even on the quasi-linear domain:

Theorem 10.3 (Alkan 1994) Domain: one infinitely divisible good and a set A of objects and its subsets; preferences, defined on $\mathbb{R} \times A$, are quasi-linear. *No selection from the no-envy and Pareto solution is object-monotonic.*

A weaker monotonicity requirement can be formulated, which says that for each economy, there should be at least one allocation such that, upon the addition of one more object, an improvement in the welfares of all agents can be achieved. A limited sense in which this requirement of **local extendability in an object-monotonic way** can be met within the no-envy solution is discussed by Alkan, Demange, and Gale (1991). The most general result along these lines covers variations in populations as well, and we find it convenient to wait until our discussion of this issue to give a single statement (Section 10.5).

Consider situations in which all real objects have to be assigned before any null object is, independently of whether they are desirable. For instance, objects may be activities that some agents enjoy and others do not, but these activities have to be carried out if there are enough agents for that. Even if preferences are quasi-linear, no selection from the weak identical-preferences lower bound and Pareto solution is **weakly object monotonic**, that is, such that the welfares of all agents are always affected in the same direction by an enlargement of the set of objects (Thomson 2003b).

We have one positive result to report, which is parallel to Theorem 7.1 pertaining to the classical model. Consider the quasi-linear domain when all objects are desirable. The Shapley value (Shapley 1953), when applied to the free-access coalitional game associated with each economy, induces an *object-monotonic* selection from the identical-preferences lower bound and Pareto solution (Moulin 1992a).

10.4. Welfare-Domination under Preference-Replacement

Here, we turn to the requirement introduced in Section 7.2 under the name of *welfare-domination under preference-replacement*, that a change in some agent's preferences should affect all other agents in the same direction.

In the one-object case, the property can be met, but in the presence of no-envy, in a unique way, by the solution F^* of Section 10.2 (which selects the envy-free allocation that is the least favorable to the winner). This solution is also a selection from the egalitarian-equivalence solution (recall that in the one-object case, egalitarian-equivalence and no-envy are compatible). We state this uniqueness result for general preferences, although it also holds on the quasi-linear domain:

Theorem 10.4 (Thomson 1998) Domain: one infinitely divisible good and a set A consisting of a single object; at least three agents; preferences, defined on $\mathbb{R} \times A$, satisfying the compensation assumption. *The solution F^* is the only selection from the no-envy solution satisfying Pareto-indifference and welfare-domination under preference-replacement.*

In the case of more than one object, we have an impossibility, even on the quasi-linear domain:[45]

Theorem 10.5 (Thomson 1998) Domain: one infinitely divisible good and a set A of objects; quasi-linear preferences, defined on $\mathbb{R} \times A$, satisfying the compensation assumption. *No selection from the no-envy solution satisfies welfare-domination under preference-replacement.*

10.5. Population-Monotonicity

Next, we consider variations in populations, generalizing the model and the notation in the following way: an economy is a triple (R, M, A) where $M \in \mathbb{R}$ is an amount of money, A is a list of objects, and $R \equiv (R_i)_{i \in N}$, for some $N \in \mathcal{N}$, is a list of preferences defined on $\mathbb{R} \times A$.

A first requirement in this context is that if the social endowment of money is non-negative and the objects are all desirable, none of the agents initially present should benefit from the arrival of additional agents.

We start with the one-object case. First, even when preferences are quasi-linear, *population-monotonicity* is incompatible with no-envy (Alkan 1994, Moulin 1990b). In fact, an agent could be better off at any envy-free allocation than if he were alone, so that a violation of the *free-access upper bound* (see Section 7) is unavoidable if no-envy is insisted upon.

However, in this model in which there is no lower bound on consumption spaces, requiring agents to end up at most as well off when new agents come in may not be the

[45] This result is proved for any $n \geq 4$. Gordon (2000) shows that it also holds for $n = 3$.

right thing to do. This is because the model is then essentially equivalent to a production model. Receiving the object is similar to being given a chance to produce. When new agents come in with "good" production functions, they may be able to use the input very productively, and the agents originally present may be made to benefit from it. To be ready to deal with that case and with the case where the new agent has a poor production function, we return to *weak population-monotonicity* (the requirement that changes in population should affect the welfares of all agents who are present before and after the change in the same direction.)

It is easy to see that the solution F^* enjoys the property, but it is essentially the only selection from the no-envy solution to do so. To state this characterization formally, we need the following very mild condition of **neutrality**: if an allocation obtained by exchanges of bundles from one that is chosen by the solution leaves unaffected the welfares of all agents, then it should also be chosen by the solution. We also impose **translation invariance**: for each $t \in \mathbb{R}$, if each preference map is translated by t and the social endowment of money is changed by t times the number of agents, then the recommended bundle for each agent should be obtained from his old one by changing its money component by t units.

Theorem 10.6 (Tadenuma and Thomson 1993) Domain: one infinitely divisible good and a set A consisting of a single object; preferences, defined over $\mathbb{R} \times A$, are strictly monotonic with respect to money and satisfy the compensation assumption. *The solution F^* is the only selection from the no-envy solution to be neutral, translation invariant, and weakly population-monotonic.*

The next few results pertain to economies in which the object is desirable: an agent would always need to be compensated to give it up. Then, in economies with quasi-linear preferences in which the amount of money is 0, a *population-monotonic* selection from the identical-preferences lower bound and Pareto solution can be defined that differs from F^* (Moulin 1990b). For each economy, the allocation it recommends is the one obtained by applying the Shapley value to the associated free-access game. When preferences are not necessarily quasi-linear and the amount of money is non-negative, the existence of a solution enjoying these same properties can still be demonstrated (Bevia 1996c). Its restriction to the quasi-linear case is the solution induced by the Shapley-value in the manner just described.

In the multiple-object case, the selection from the egalitarian-equivalence and Pareto solution obtained by requiring the reference bundle to contain a fixed object is *weakly population-monotonic,* but it is not guaranteed to be a selection from the no-envy solution anymore. In fact, if no-envy is imposed, we have the following impossibility, which holds even on the quasi-linear domain:

Theorem 10.7 (Tadenuma and Thomson 1995) Domain: one infinitely divisible good and a set A of objects; preferences, defined over $\mathbb{R} \times A$, are strictly monotonic with respect to money and satisfy the compensation assumption. *No selection from the no-envy solution is weakly population-monotonic.*

The following positive result is available. Consider the quasi-linear domain and suppose that the social endowment of money is 0. The Shapley value, when applied to the free-access coalitional game associated with each economy, induces a *population-monotonic* selection from the identical-preferences lower bound and Pareto solution (Moulin 1992a).

Theorem 10.7 shows that *weak population-monotonicity* is a very strong requirement in the present context, and it is therefore natural to investigate the possibility of satisfying weaker requirements. The following question can be asked (Alkan 1994): for each economy, and when all objects are desirable, *is there an allocation* such that upon the arrival of an additional agent, all agents initially present are made at most as well off as they were initially, and such that upon the departure of an agent, all remaining agents are made at least as well off as they were initially? If yes, the allocation is **locally lower-extendable, and locally upper-extendable (respectively), in a population-monotonic way**. This definition extends a notion introduced in Section 10.3 in connection with variations in the number of objects. Alkan (1994) considers a two-part definition that covers both variations in objects and variations in populations. We refer to it by the shorter phrase **locally upper, or lower, extendability**. It turns out that if no-envy is required, only a limited form of these properties holds:

Theorem 10.8 (Alkan 1994) Domain: one infinitely divisible good and a set A of objects and subsets; preferences, defined over $\mathbb{R} \times A$, are strictly monotonic with respect to money and satisfy the compensation assumption. *(a) When objects are desirable, the minimax money allocation of each economy is an envy-free and locally upper-extendable allocation. (b) The maximin money-only-equivalent allocation of each economy is locally lower-extendable. (c) When objects are desirable and there are at least as many agents as objects, the minimax money allocation is the only locally upper-extendable in an object-monotonic way envy-free allocation.*[46]

Local lower-extendability in a population-monotonic way is a weaker requirement than *local upper-extendability*: indeed there are economies in which all envy-free allocations are *locally lower-extendable in a population-monotonic way* (Alkan 1994).

10.6. Consistency

We now turn to *consistency* and related properties. The concept was first encountered in Section 8.1 in the context of classical economies. Let $\mathcal{A}$ be the family of all finite subsets of a set of "potential" objects, with generic element denoted A. Given $\sigma : N \rightarrow A$ and $N' \subset N$, let $\sigma(N') \equiv \bigcup_{N'} \sigma(i)$:

[46] A version of (a) holds that accommodates objects that are not desirable. The uniqueness result stated in (c) does not persist if variations in populations are considered.

Consistency

For each $N \in \mathcal{N}$, each $(R,M,A) \in \mathcal{E}^N_{ind}$, each $z \equiv (m,\sigma) \in \varphi(R,M,A)$, and each $N' \subset N$, we have $z_{N'} \in \varphi((R'_i)_{i\in N'}, \sum_{N'} m_i, \sigma(N'))$, where $z_{N'}$ is the restriction of z to the group N', and for each $i \in N'$, R'_i is the restriction of R_i to $\mathbb{R} \times \sigma(N')$.

It is clear that both the Pareto solution and the no-envy solution are *consistent*. Are there *consistent* subsolutions of the no-envy solution?

In the one-object case, the solution F^* is a *consistent* selection from the no-envy solution. Moreover, subject to *neutrality*, it is the smallest one, as follows directly from the following theorem:

Theorem 10.9 (Tadenuma and Thomson 1993) Domain: one infinitely divisible good; a set A consisting of at most one object; preferences, defined on $\mathbb{R} \times A$, are monotonic with respect to money and satisfy the compensation assumption. *If a subsolution of the no-envy solution is neutral and consistent, then it contains the solution F^*.*

As a corollary of Theorem 10.9, one easily obtains a complete characterization of all solutions satisfying its hypotheses.

The results in the multiple-object case are quite different:

Theorem 10.10 (Tadenuma and Thomson 1991) Domain: one infinitely divisible good; a set A of objects; equal number of agents; preferences, defined on $\mathbb{R} \times A$, are monotonic with respect to money and satisfy the compensation assumption. *If a subsolution of the no-envy solution is neutral and consistent, then in fact it coincides with the no-envy solution.*

This result is also true when the objects are identical. On the other hand, and here too, whether or not the objects are identical, there are many subsolutions of the no-envy solution satisfying the weakening of *consistency* obtained by applying it only to two-agent subgroups (*bilateral consistency*), but all such solutions coincide with the no-envy solution in the two-agent case.

The next axiom pertains to the arrival of new agents, and it is the counterpart of an axiom of the same name that we encountered first in our study of the classical model (Section 8.1):

Converse Consistency

For each $N \in \mathcal{N}$ with $|N| > 3$, each $e \equiv (R,M,A) \in \mathcal{E}^N_{ind}$, each $z \equiv (m,\sigma) \in Z(e)$, if for each $N' \subset N$ such that $|N'| = 2$, $z_{N'} \in \varphi((R_{i|\mathbb{R}\times\sigma(N')})_{i\in N'}, \sum_{N'} m_i, \sigma(N'))$, then $z \in \varphi(e)$.

Clearly, the no-envy solution is *conversely consistent*, but many proper subsolutions of it are too (as well as *neutral*). On the other hand, the Pareto solution is not, unless the objects are identical. However, we have:

Theorem 10.11 (Tadenuma and Thomson 1991) Domain: one infinitely divisible good; a set A of objects; equal number of agents; preferences, defined on $\mathbb{R} \times A$, are monotonic with respect to money and satisfy the compensation assumption. *If a subsolution of the no-envy solution is neutral, bilaterally consistent, and conversely consistent, then in fact it coincides with the no-envy solution.*

The identical-preferences lower bound solution is *conversely consistent* but not *consistent*. The *minimal consistent enlargement* (Section 8.2) of its intersection with the Pareto solution is the Pareto solution itself. This is true when there is at most one object, when there are multiple identical objects, and when there are multiple and possibly different objects. The maximal *consistent* subsolution of the identical-preferences lower bound and Pareto solution is the no-envy solution (Bevia 1996a).

10.7. Related Models

10.7.1. Several Objects per Agent

Another generalization of the model is when each agent can consume several objects (in addition to the infinitely divisible good). Unless otherwise indicated, all of the results below are due to Bevia (1998). The lesson that emerges from her work is that the situation is quite different from what it is in the one-object-per-person case, unless severe additional restrictions are imposed on preferences. It is true that, under similar assumptions as in the one-object-per-agent case, efficient allocations still exist and that so do envy-free allocations (this is also shown by Tadenuma 1996). Moreover, when preferences are quasi-linear, allocations that are both envy-free and efficient exist too. If consumptions of money are required to be non-negative, existence holds if and only if the social endowment of money is at least as large as a certain amount that can be identified. (This amount depends on the preference profile.) An algorithm is available that leads to envy-free allocations (Haake, Raith, and Su 2002). At each step, it focuses on a pair of agents between whom envy is maximal, as measured in terms of the amount of money that should be added to the bundle of the envious agent so as to make him nonenvious, and adjustments are carried out so as to decrease this maximal envy.

If preferences are not quasi-linear, and even when consumptions of money are unbounded below (or the social endowment of money is sufficiently large), and preferences satisfy the compensation assumption, envy-free and efficient allocations may not exist (Tadenuma 1996, Meertens, Potters, and Reijnierse 2002).

Even if preferences are quasi-linear, no-envy does not imply efficiency any more. Thus, and since by definition group no-envy still implies efficiency, the group no-envy solution may be a proper subsolution of the no-envy solution. There may be no allocation meeting the identical-preferences lower bound, although a necessary and sufficient condition on preferences can be stated guaranteeing existence. The no-envy and identical-preferences lower bound solutions are not related by inclusion. An equal-income Walrasian allocation obviously remains envy-free—in fact, it remains group envy-free—but a group envy-free allocation may not be an equal-income

Walrasian allocation. Equal-income Walrasian allocations exist if preferences have additive numerical representations, a case discussed in the next paragraph. Egalitarian-equivalence applies to this model with no difficulty and existence is guaranteed very generally.

Preferences that have additive representations have been the object of particular attention. For that case, a rule is proposed by Knaster (this attribution is by Steinhaus 1948; also, Kuhn 1967). It consists of first assigning all objects efficiently (this is a meaningful objective because of quasi-linearity), and, using our earlier terminology, assigning consumptions of money so that all agents receive equal amounts of it above their identical-preferences lower bounds. Steinhaus also defines an asymmetric generalization of the solution. An alternative is the selection from the egalitarian-equivalence and Pareto solution obtained by choosing the null object as reference object. Interestingly, this second solution is a selection from the no-envy solution (Willson 2003), showing that for additive preferences, no-envy is compatible with egalitarian-equivalence. Each is *money-monotonic* and each satisfies a form of *object-monotonicity*. Knaster's solution is advocated by Samuelson (1980).

Next, we turn to the implications of relational fairness requirements of monotonicity and consistency. If the social endowment of money is non-negative and all objects are desirable, the natural form of *population-monotonicity* is that upon the arrival of additional agents, each of the agents initially present should end up at most as well off as he was initially. Then, and even if preferences are quasi-linear and no other fairness requirement is imposed, no selection from the Pareto solution is *population-monotonic* (Bevia 1996b). On the other hand, suppose that preferences are further restricted by the requirement that the free-access game associated with each economy satisfies the substitutability assumption described before Proposition 7.1. Then, the Shapley value, when applied for each economy to the free-access game associated with it, induces a rule that satisfies the property (Bevia 1998). Much is known about *consistency*. In contrast to the one-object-per-person case, there are *consistent* subsolutions of the no-envy and Pareto solution, and *converse consistency* becomes a much stronger requirement. Nevertheless, characterizations in the spirit of Theorems 10.10 and 10.11 hold under an additional invariance requirement on solutions (Bevia 1998).

10.7.2. Lotteries

Population-monotonicity of rules based on lotteries is examined by Ehlers and Klaus (2001). [They also consider strategic issues. Lotteries are allowed by Crawford and Heller (1979), but mainly in the context of the strategic analysis of divide-and-choose.]

10.7.3. When Monetary Compensations Are Not Possible

One Object per Agent

Economies in which money is not available to make compensations have recently been much studied, mainly in situations where preferences over objects are strict.

[This literature often considers the implications of fairness conditions in conjunction with the strong requirement of immunity to strategic behavior called *strategy-proofness*, which says that no agent should ever benefit from misrepresenting his preferences.]

It is clear that punctual requirements of fairness such as no-envy and egalitarian-equivalence are not achievable here (think of situations where all agents have the same preferences), and not much can be said about these requirements. However, most of our relational requirements remain meaningful. The main lesson of this literature is that they can be satisfied, but in a rather limited way.

Of course, they are satisfied by the **single-order priority rules** defined as follows. To each order on the set of agents is associated a rule. It is the rule that selects, for each preference profile, the allocation at which the agent ranked first receives his most preferred object, the agent ranked second receives his most preferred object among the remaining objects, and so on. These rules, which are the counterparts for this model of what are usually called "dictatorial rules" or "sequential dictatorial rules," are a little less distasteful than they are in the classical model since here, there is a natural constraint on what an agent consumes. Even if an agent receives his most preferred object, other objects remain that are available for the other agents, and in fact some of these agents may also receive their most preferred objects.

Being first in an order amounts to being given ownership rights over the entire social endowment of objects. Once the agent ranked first has exercised his rights by choosing his most preferred object, the agent ranked second is given ownership rights over the remaining objects, and exercises his rights by choosing his most preferred object among them, and so on. More generally, one can "spread" ownership over agents. For each object, let us specify a priority order over agents. Each agent i is assigned the object he prefers among all objects if he owns it. If agent i owns the best object of the owner of his own best object, they exchange these objects and leave. Suppose there is a cycle starting with agent i such that agent i's best object is owned by the next agent in the cycle, the next agent's best object is owned by the following agent, and so on, until the last agent's best object is owned by agent i. Then these agents trade along the cycle and leave. Each object in the endowment of an agent who leaves is inherited by the first agent in the priority order for that object who does not leave. These "bequests" define revised ownership rights for the remaining agents and the process is repeated with them. Let us call a rule so defined a **multiple-order priority rule**. The collection of the orders indexed by objects (the priority profile), presented as a table, is the **inheritance table** of the rule, which can also be referred to as the **hierarchical exchange rule associated with the inheritance table** (Pápai 2000).

Although envy cannot be avoided in this model, there is a natural way to attempt to limit it. Given a priority order on the set of agents and an allocation, say that agent i's envy of agent j is "justified" if agent i prefers the object agent j receives to the one he receives and he has a higher priority than agent j (Svensson 1994a). More generally, when the priority order may depend on the object, and given an allocation, say that agent i's envy of agent j is "justified" if agent i prefers the object agent j receives to the one he receives and he has a higher priority than agent j for that object. **A rule respects a priority profile** if it always selects an allocation at which there is no justified envy (Balinski and Sönmez 1999). [Svensson 1994a addresses the issue of *strategy-proofness* when agents may be indifferent between objects.]

We also need the notion of an **acyclic priority profile** (one usually speaks of the acyclicity of a single relation, but here the notion applies to a profile of relations). It is defined as follows: If for some object, agent i is ranked above agent j and agent j is ranked above agent k, there is no other object for which agent k is ranked above agent i (Ergin 2002). It turns out that this is equivalent to saying that an ordered partition of the set of agents into singletons and pairs exists, such that each agent in a singleton set appears in an entire row of the inheritance table, and the two agents in each pair appear only in two successive rows (Ergin 2002). By considering ordered partitions in which components would be allowed to have up to three members, then up to four, and so on, we would dilute even more the hierarchical nature of the rule and move further and further away from single-order priority rules. But for a partition with at most two agents in each component, the resulting rule is not far from being a single-order priority rule, so we say that it is **one step away from a single-order priority rule**.[47]

Unfortunately, this is as far as one can go if imposing the requirement that when the set of available objects expands, all agents should end up at least as well off as they were initially, **object-monotonicity** (already encountered in the context of allocating an infinitely divisible good and objects). When the set of objects may vary, the question is whether in defining an economy, one specifies preferences over all potential objects, or only over existing objects. We choose the latter formulation, for which we can state a result that takes a very simple form:[48]

Theorem 10.12 (Ehlers and Klaus 2003) Domain: at least as many potential objects as agents; strict preferences over objects; either one of the following holds: (a) real objects may or may not be preferred to the null object; (b) real objects are always preferred to the null object. *A selection from the Pareto solution is object-monotonic if and only if it is one step away from a single-order priority rule.*

The implications of *consistency* for this model are explored by Ergin (2000). His main theorem involves no efficiency requirement, but we state the corollary obtained by adding efficiency:

[47] These rules are usually referred to as "mixed dictator-pairwise-exchange rules," or "restricted endowment inheritance rules."

[48] Ehlers and Klaus (2003) choose the former formulation and their characterization also involves the requirement that, given two economies for which for each agent, the restrictions of his preferences over the set of existing objects are the same, the rule should make the same choice: how agents rank objects that are not available should not affect the choice.

Theorem 10.13 (Ergin 2000) Domain: a set of objects; strict preferences over individual objects. *A selection from the Pareto solution is neutral and consistent if and only if it is a single-order priority rule.*

For solution correspondences, a characterization is available based on the axioms of Theorem 10.13 together with *converse consistency*. All admissible rules are obtained as certain unions of single-order priority rules.

The following theorem states that within the class of multiple-order priority rules, either one of two important properties implies that the orders are strongly correlated:

Theorem 10.14 (Ergin 2002) Domain: a set of objects; strict preferences over individual objects. *A multiple-order priority rule is a selection from the Pareto solution or satisfies consistency, if and only if it is one step away from a single-order priority rule.*

[Another requirement on a rule for which the conclusion of Theorem 10.14 applies is *group strategyproofness*, that is, immunity to joint misrepresentation of preferences by the agents in any group. The implications for selections from the Pareto solution of *population monotonicity* and *strategyproofness* together are described by Ehlers, Klaus, and Pápai (2002). The only rules passing these tests are one step away from single-order priority rules reformulated so as to apply to this variable-population context. The order used for each population should be induced from a single "reference" order over the entire set of potential agents. The family of selections from the Pareto solution satisfying *consistency* and *strategyproofness* is characterized by Ehlers and Klaus (2005a, 2005b). Kesten (2003, 2008) investigates the implication of *resource monotonicity* and *group strategy proofness*, and Kesten and Yazici (2010) are other contributions to this line of investigation.]

When to Each Object Is Associated an Order Over the Agent Set: School Choice

A richer formulation of the model (Abdulkadiroğlu and Sönmez 2003) is obtained by specifying for each object an order over the agent set, interpreted as a priority order that agents have over the objects. An application is to the assignment to students to schools, named "school choice." Each student (rather, his or her parents) have preferences over the schools, and for each school (schools are the objects here) there is a priority order over the students seeking admission. A school's priority order is derived from the proximity of students' residence to the school and depend on whether the student already has a sibling attending the school. Kesten (2006) studies *resource-monotonic, population-monotonicity*, and *consistency* in this context. [A considerable literature studies strategic issues.]

Several Objects per Agent

Still assuming that money is not available, we now imagine that each agent can receive several objects. Then, preferences are defined over sets of objects. No selection from the

Pareto solution satisfies *welfare-domination under preference replacement* (Klaus and Miyagawa 2001). [The implications of *resource-monotonicity*, *population monotonicity*, and *consistency* have also been studied for this problem, but mainly when imposed in conjunction with *strategyproofness*, so we will not elaborate (Klaus and Miyagawa 2001, Ehlers and Klaus 2003). These combinations of properties mainly result in some form of sequential priority rule.]

The model is also considered by Herreiner and Puppe (2002), who propose the following fairness criterion: For each allocation and each agent, one determines the rank in his preference of the set he receives. An allocation is then evaluated by means of the highest (across agents) such rank. Thus, the focus is on the agent who is treated the worst according to these ranks. An iterative procedure can be defined that produces the efficient allocation that is best according to this criterion among all efficient allocations.[49]

Brams and Fishburn (2000) for $|N| = 2$ and Edelman and Fishburn (2001) for $|N| > 2$ examine the special case when agents have the same preferences over individual objects but possibly different preferences over sets of objects. These preferences are assumed to have additive representations in the second paper and to satisfy a slightly more general property in the first paper. Envy-free allocations may not exist—in fact, the more preferences agree, the less likely such allocations are to exist—so they propose alternative criteria. These studies underscore the importance of the relation between the number of objects and the number of agents. Brams, Edelman, and Fishburn (2003) pursue this analysis without the assumption that preferences over individual objects are the same, and propose, in addition to requirements related to no-envy, some that are based on comparing the numbers of objects received by the various agents. Brams, Edelman, and Fishburn (2001) relate the no-envy condition in the context of this model to efficiency, and to the Rawls (1971) and Borda (1781) choice rules. For one of the examples they exhibit, there is a unique envy-free allocation, but it is not efficient.

Models with Individual Endowments

The possibility that agents are endowed with objects is first considered by Shapley and Scarf (1974). Situations when some objects are initially individually owned and others are commonly owned, as in Section 8.3, are also of interest, residential housing on a university campus being an illustrative example, since current renters are usually allowed to keep the units they occupy from one year to the next. An application to kidney exchange is discussed by Roth, Sönmez, and Ünver (2004). [Abdulkadiroğlu and Sönmez (1999) define a *strategyproof* selection from the Pareto solution that respects individual ownership. See also Sönmez and Ünver (2005).]

[49] Herreiner and Puppe (2002) also discuss variants of this criterion and identify situations (they are quite limited) under which an envy-free allocation may be obtained. See also Ramaekers (2006).

Lotteries

Rules based on lotteries are examined by Hylland and Zeckhauser (1979), Abdulkadiroğlu and Sönmez (1998, 1999), and Bogomolnaia and Moulin (2001, 2002, 2004). Demko and Hill (1988) consider the several-objects-per-agent case in this context.

10.7.4. Compensations

Consider the problem of allocating a single infinitely divisible good, "money," among agents characterized by talent or handicap variables, which cannot be transferred. Preferences are defined over the cross-product of the real line and the set of possible values of these variables. Each agent can be understood as endowed with a particular one of these objects, but no exchange of objects can take place. How should money be divided? This model, formulated by Fleurbaey (1994, 1995b), has been analyzed from a variety of angles (Bossert 1995, Bossert and Fleurbaey 1996, Fleurbaey and Maniquet 1996b, 1998, 1999, Iturbe-Ormaetxe and Nieto 1996a, Otsuki 1996b, Sprumont 1997, Maniquet 1998, Bossert, Fleurbaey, and van de Gaer 1999). Fleurbaey and Maniquet (2003, Chapter 21) survey this work in detail and discuss how it fits in with the literature under discussion here, so we will not elaborate.

11. SINGLE-PEAKED PREFERENCES

Consider a one-commodity model where preferences are single-peaked: up to some critical level, an increase in an agent's consumption increases his welfare, but beyond that level the opposite holds.

An example of a situation of this kind is distribution at disequilibrium prices in a two-good economy with strictly convex preferences; the restrictions of such preferences to budget lines are indeed single-peaked. Alternatively, imagine a task that is to be divided among a group of agents who are jointly responsible for it, and suppose that each agent enjoys performing it up to a point, but that additional time spent at it decreases the agent's welfare. Then, the agent has single-peaked preferences over the time performing the task. If the task has to be completed, the feasibility requirement is that the sum of the amounts of time spent by the agents performing it should be *equal* to the total time needed for completion. Depending upon whether the sum of the preferred amounts is greater or smaller than completion time, each agent may have to supply more than his preferred amount, or each may have to supply less. The formal model is introduced by Sprumont (1991).

The main lesson of the literature concerning this model is that a certain rule, known as the uniform rule, is central in solving this class of problems, independently of the angle from which it is approached; whether we consider changes in the amount to divide, or in the population (here, monotonicity or consistency requirements have been considered), or in the preferences of some agents. [The rule also has very desirable strategic properties, and it is in the context of *strategyproofness* that it first emerged.]

11.1. The Model

Each agent $i \in N$ is equipped with a continuous preference relation R_i defined on $\mathbb{R}_+$ with the property that there is a number, denoted $p(R_i)$ and called his **peak amount**, such that for each pair $\{z_i, z_i'\} \subset \mathbb{R}_+$, if $z_i' < z_i \leq p(R_i)$ or $p(R_i) \leq z_i < z_i'$, then $z_i \; P_i \; z_i'$: the relation is **single-peaked**. Let $\mathcal{R}_{sp}$ denote the class of all such relations. Given $z_i \in \mathbb{R}_+$, let $r_i(z_i)$ be the amount on the other side of his peak amount that agent i finds indifferent to z_i, if there is such an amount. If there is no such amount and $z_i < p(R_i)$, let $r_i(z_i) \equiv \infty$, and otherwise, let $r_i(z_i) \equiv 0$. Let $\Omega \in \mathbb{R}_+$ denote the social endowment. An **economy** is a pair $e \equiv (R, \Omega) \in \mathcal{R}_{sp}^N \times \mathbb{R}_+$ and $\mathcal{E}_{sp}^N$ is the domain of all economies. The commodity is not freely disposable. Thus, a **feasible allocation** for $e \equiv (R, \Omega) \in \mathcal{E}_{sp}^N$ is a list $z \equiv (z_i)_{i \in N} \in \mathbb{R}_+^N$ such that $\sum z_i = \Omega$. Let $\boldsymbol{Z(e)}$ denote the set of feasible allocations of e.

11.2. Basic Solutions

It is easy to check that an allocation $z \in Z(e)$ is **efficient** for $e \equiv (R, \Omega) \in \mathcal{E}_{sp}^N$ if and only if (i) when $\Omega \leq \sum p(R_i)$, then for each $i \in N$, $z_i \leq p(R_i)$, and (ii) when $\Omega \geq \sum p(R_i)$, then for each $i \in N$, $z_i \geq p(R_i)$: all consumptions should be "on the same side" of the peak amounts (Sprumont 1991). In the first case, we can say that "there is too little of the commodity" (too little because everyone has to receive at most his peak amount), and in the second case, that "there is too much" (too much because everyone has to receive at least his peak amount).

Figure 21.11 illustrates an **envy-free** and efficient allocation for $N \equiv \{1, \ldots, 7\}$ and $e \equiv (R, \Omega) \in \mathcal{E}_{sp}^N$ such that $\sum p(R_i) > \Omega$. In the example, agents are ordered by their peak amounts: $p(R_1) \leq \cdots \leq p(R_7)$. As we just saw, by efficiency, no one receives more than his peak amount. By no-envy, agents are partitioned into groups—in the example, they are $\{1,2,3\}$, $\{4\}$, $\{5\}$, and $\{6,7\}$—with all agents in each group receiving equal amounts. For each group G, the common consumption of the members of the group receiving the next greatest amount is at least $\max_{i \in G} r_i(z_i)$.

The question of existence of envy-free and efficient allocations is given a very simple positive answer later on. In fact, the set of these allocations is usually quite large, and one of our objectives is to identify well-behaved selections from the no-envy and Pareto solution.

The **equal-division lower bound** is defined as in classical economies, and so is the **equal-division core**. There always are allocations meeting the equal-division lower bound, but the equal-division core may be empty. However, if the blocking requirement for each group is strengthened by insisting that each agent in the group should be made

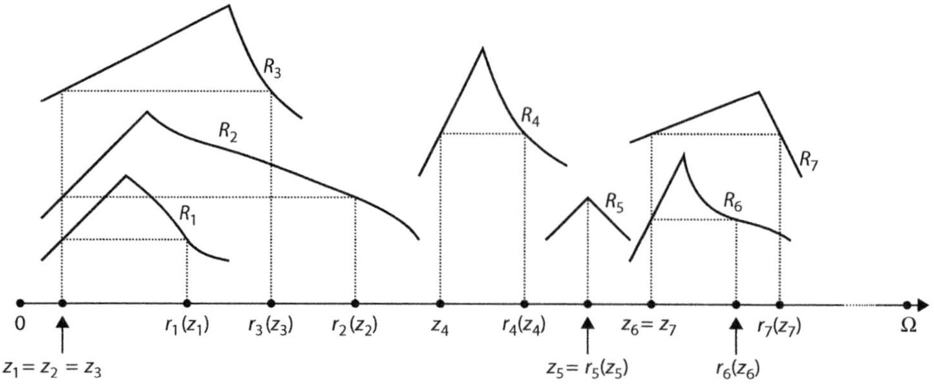

Figure 21.11. An envy-free and efficient allocation in an economy with single-peaked preferences.
When there is not enough of the commodity, efficiency requires that each agent should receive at most his peak amount. For no-envy, no agent's consumption should fall in the interval of peak consumptions of any other agent at his consumption. All of these requirements are met here.

better off by redistribution of the resources the group controls, then nonemptiness is recovered, as we will see.[50]

A number of interesting solutions can be defined for this model by taking advantage of its special features. Quite a few are *single-valued.* Here are some of them. The first one is the most frequent suggestion in the context of rationing: Given $e \equiv (R, \Omega) \in \mathcal{E}_{sp}^N$, the allocation $z \in Z(e)$ is the **proportional allocation of *e*** if, when at least one peak amount is positive, there is $\lambda \in \mathbb{R}_+$ such that for each $i \in N$, $z_i = \lambda p(R_i)$. If all peak amounts are zero, $z \equiv \left(\frac{\Omega}{|N|}, \ldots, \frac{\Omega}{|N|}\right)$. It is its **equal-distance allocation** if there is $\lambda \in \mathbb{R}_+$ such that for each $i \in N$, $z_i = \max\{p(R_i) - \lambda, 0\}$. It is its **equal-preferred-sets allocation** if (i) when $\Omega \leq \sum p(R_i)$, then for each $\{i,j\} \subseteq N$, $z_i - r_i(z_i) = z_j - r_j(z_j)$, or $z_i = 0$, and (ii) when $\Omega \geq \sum p(R_i)$, then for each $\{i,j\} \subseteq N$, $z_i - r_i(z_i) = z_j - r_j(z_j)$.

The following rule will turn out to be most central in our analysis:

Definition (Bénassy 1982) *Given $e \equiv (R, \Omega) \in \mathcal{E}_{sp}^N$, the allocation $z \in Z(e)$ is the* ***uniform allocation of e*** *if (i) when $\Omega \leq \sum p(R_i)$, there is $\lambda \in \mathbb{R}_+$ such that for each $i \in N$, $z_i = \min\{p(R_i), \lambda\}$, (ii) when $\Omega \geq \sum p(R_i)$, there is $\lambda \in \mathbb{R}_+$ such that for each $i \in N$, $z_i = \max\{p(R_i), \lambda\}$.*

The proportional, equal-distance, and equal-preferred-sets rules are motivated by the desire to distribute "evenly" across agents deficits or surpluses (the difference $\Omega - \sum p(R_i)$ when it is negative or positive, respectively). The uniform rule does not

[50] The notion of egalitarian-equivalence cannot be directly applied in this context, but a reformulation is possible that produces a well-defined solution (Chun 2000).

seem to achieve this objective since it assigns to some agents their peak amounts, and it assigns to the others equal amounts (it ignores differences in the peak amounts of the members of the latter group). However, it does select an allocation that is envy-free (this solves the existence question for these allocations, as announced earlier), and it meets the equal-division lower bound, in contrast with the proportional, equal-distance, and equal-preferred-sets rules.

The uniform rule depends only on the profile of peak amounts—we say that it satisfies **peak-only**. This property is satisfied by many other solutions such as the Pareto solution, and by the equal-distance and proportional rules. However, we have the following characterization:

Theorem 11.1 (Thomson 1994c) Domain: one good; single-peaked preferences. *The uniform rule is the only subsolution of the no-envy and Pareto solution satisfying peak-only.*

The uniform allocation of an economy is also its only efficient allocation at which each agent receives an amount that he finds at least as desirable as any convex combination of the amounts received by all agents (recall Kolm's generalization of no-envy; Chun 2000). When there is too little of the commodity, it is also the only allocation maximizing the factor α such that each agent finds the amount he receives at least as desirable as the proportion α of the social endowment. When there is too much, replace "maximizing" by "minimizing." Finally, the uniform rule is the only selection from the Pareto solution minimizing either one of the following two alternative ways of measuring the disparity among the amounts received by the various agents: (i) the difference between the smallest amount anyone receives and the greatest amount anyone receives; (ii) the variance of the amounts they all receive (Schummer and Thomson 1997). Parallel results can be obtained if the Pareto requirement is replaced by *peak-only* (Kesten 2006a).

The **group no-envy** solution, defined as in the classical case, is sometimes empty, but the uniform allocation satisfies the weaker requirement on an allocation that no group of agents can make all of its members better off, assuming that each of them is given access to an equal share of the social endowment, by redistributing the resources it controls in total.

11.3. Resource-Monotonicity

We begin our study of relational requirements for this model by considering changes in the social endowment. Since preferences are not monotonic, it would of course make no sense to ask that when it increases, all agents should be made at least as well off as they were initially. Instead, a natural expression of the idea of solidarity is that *either* all agents should be made at least as well off as they were initially *or* that they should all be made at most as well off. In the presence of efficiency, the first case applies in particular if all agents initially receive at most as much as their peak amounts and the social endowment does not increase too much, and the second case if initially they already receive at least as much as their peak amounts. Unfortunately, none of the rules defined above satisfies this requirement, as can be seen by means of simple examples. Although it is met on a large subdomain of our primary domain by variants of the equal-preferred-sets rule, it turns out to be incompatible with no-envy as well as with the equal-division lower bound, even if efficiency is dropped. The reason is that the increase can be so disruptive that it turns an economy in which there is too little to one in which there is too much. The relevance of this distinction to the possibility of monotonicity should not be surprising, and it suggests limiting the application of the requirement to situations in which no such switches occur. We write this weaker property for *single-valued* solutions:

One-Sided Resource-Monotonicity
For each $(R, \Omega) \in \mathcal{E}_{sp}^N$ and each $\Omega' \in \mathbb{R}_+$, if either $\Omega' \leq \Omega \leq \sum p(R_i)$ or $\sum p(R_i) \leq \Omega \leq \Omega'$, then $\varphi(R, \Omega)\ R\ \varphi(R, \Omega')$.

This property is satisfied by all the rules mentioned earlier. Yet, when imposed in conjunction with no-envy and efficiency, it essentially singles out the uniform rule. The "essentially" is a reference to a restriction on the domain: for each $i \in N$, 0 should have a finite equivalent ($r_i(0) < \infty$). If the restriction is not imposed, generalizations of the uniform rule become admissible. The class they constitute can be characterized, but we omit their formal description.

Theorem 11.2 (Thomson 1994b) Domain: one good; single-peaked preferences for which 0 has a finite equivalent. *The uniform rule is the only selection from the no-envy and Pareto solution satisfying one-sided resource-monotonicity.*

In this characterization, the Pareto requirement can be replaced by *peak-only* (Kesten 2006a), or by **resource-continuity**, which says that small changes in the resource should not lead to large changes in the selected allocation (Ehlers 2002d).

11.4. Welfare-Domination under Preference-Replacement

Next, we consider the replacement of the preferences of some agents by some other preferences, and require that the welfares of all other agents should be affected in the same direction by the replacement (Section 7.2). This property of **welfare-domination under preference-replacement** is also quite strong: once again, no selection from the no-envy and Pareto solution satisfies it. The reason is that here, too, the change may turn an economy in which there is too little to one in which there is too much, or conversely. So, let us consider the weaker property of **one-sided welfare-domination under preference-replacement**, obtained by limiting attention to changes in preferences that do not reverse the direction of the inequality between the amount to divide and the sum of the peak amounts.

Many rules satisfy this property, including the uniform, proportional, equal-distance, and equal-preferred-sets rules, but here, too, we have a uniqueness result. It is another characterization of the uniform rule, based on this property. It also involves *replication-invariance*. This requirement is very weak, being met by the Pareto solution, the no-envy solution, their intersection, the uniform rule, and the equal-division lower bound solution. Nevertheless, we have:

Theorem 11.3 (Thomson 1997) Domain: one good; single-peaked preferences for which 0 has a finite equivalent. *The uniform rule is the only selection from the no-envy and Pareto solution satisfying replication-invariance and one-sided welfare-domination under preference-replacement.*

The independence of *replication-invariance* from the other axioms in Theorem 11.3 is established by Klaus (1999).

There are selections from the equal-division lower bound and Pareto solution satisfying *welfare-domination under preference-replacement* other than the uniform rule. They constitute a convex class.

11.5. Separability

Here, we consider the requirement that, given any two economies having a group of agents in common, if the agents in this group receive the same aggregate amount in both, then each of them should receive the same amount in both (Chun 2006c). Note that the economies that are compared may have different social endowments:

Separability
For each $N \subset \mathcal{N}$, each $e \equiv (R, \Omega) \in \mathcal{E}_{sp}^{N}$, each $N' \subset N$, and each $e' \equiv (R', \Omega') \in \mathcal{E}_{sp}^{N'}$, if $R_{N'} = R'_{N'}$ and $\sum_{N'} \varphi_i(e) = \sum_{N'} \varphi_i(e')$, then $\varphi_{N'}(e) = \varphi_{N'}(e')$.

We have the following characterizations:

Theorem 11.4 (Chun 2006c) Domain: one good; single-peaked preferences. *The uniform rule is the only selection* (i) *from the no-envy and Pareto solution satisfying resource-continuity and separability;* (ii) *from the equal-division lower bound and Pareto solution satisfying resource-continuity and separability;*[51] (iii) *from the equal-division lower bound solution satisfying one-sided resource monotonicity and separability.*

In (i), the conclusion persists if *replication-invariance* is imposed instead of *resource-continuity* (Klaus 2006).

11.6. Population-Monotonicity

Turning now to variations of population, we first note that here, too, it would make no sense to require as we did for classical economies, that the departure of some agents, resources being kept fixed, should make all of the remaining agents at least as well off

[51] We do not include *replication invariance*, which Chun had imposed, as Klaus (2006) showed that it is redundant.

as they were initially. Indeed, when there is initially too much of the commodity, this departure is bad news for the remaining agents. Therefore, we require instead that their welfares should all be affected in the same direction.

This requirement is incompatible with no-envy as well as with the equal-division lower bound. However, as was the case in our examination of the impact of changes in the social endowment, on important subdomains of our primary domain, there are selections from the Pareto solution that do satisfy it, namely, variants of the equal-preferred-sets rule.

Just as was the case there, the reason why *population-monotonicity* is so strong is that it sometimes forces comparisons between economies in which there is too little to divide and economies in which there is too much. We therefore weaken it by excluding from its coverage changes in populations that reverse the direction of the inequality between the amount to divide and the sum of the peak amounts, thereby obtaining **one-sided population-monotonicity**. We have the following uniqueness result:

Theorem 11.5 (Thomson 1995a) Domain: one good; single-peaked preferences for which 0 has a finite equivalent. *The uniform rule is the only selection from the no-envy and Pareto solution satisfying replication-invariance and one-sided population-monotonicity.*

The independence of *replication-invariance* from the other axioms in Theorem 11.5 is established by Klaus (1999). Also, the Pareto requirement can be replaced by *peak-only* without affecting the conclusion (Kesten 2006a). Other characterizations of the uniform rule not involving efficiency are available (Chun 2003). The distributional requirements are either no-envy or the equal-division lower bound and the relational requirements are *replication-invariance, one-sided population-monotonicity*, and *separability*. Additional properties involving simultaneous changes in several parameters can be formulated (Chun 2006c discusses their logical relations).

11.7. Consistency

Recall that a (possibly multivalued) solution is **consistent** (Section 8) if the desirability of an allocation it selects for some economy is not affected by the departure of some agents with their assigned consumptions:

Consistency
For each $N \in \mathcal{N}$, each $(R,\Omega) \in \mathcal{E}_{sp}^N$, each $z \in \varphi(R,\Omega)$, and each $N' \subset N$, we have $z_{N'} \in \varphi(R_{N'}, \sum_{N'} z_i)$.

Quite a few solutions are *consistent*, including the Pareto solution, the no-envy solution, and the uniform and proportional rules. The equal-division lower bound solution is not. However, *consistency*, together with the mild and self-explanatory requirement of **resource upper hemi-continuity**, when imposed on a subsolution of the no-envy and Pareto solution, implies that this solution contains the uniform rule:

Theorem 11.6 (Thomson 1994c) Domain: one good; single-peaked preferences. *If a subsolution of the no-envy and Pareto solution satisfies resource upper hemi-continuity and consistency, then it contains the uniform rule.*

From this theorem we can easily derive a complete characterization of the class of solutions satisfying the hypotheses. A corollary of that characterization is that if the solution is in addition required to be *single-valued*, then in fact, it coincides with the uniform rule. A similar result holds when the equal-division lower bound is imposed instead of no-envy.

A direct proof of this corollary, exploiting more completely the *single-valuedness* requirement, is possible (Dagan 1996). The main step is showing that if a *single-valued* selection from the no-envy and Pareto solution is *consistent*, then it satisfies *peak-only*. The conclusion follows then by Theorem 11.1. This characterization involves no continuity requirement.

The uniform rule is also the only *single-valued* selection from the equal-division lower bound and Pareto solution to be *replication-invariant* and *consistent* (a counterpart of Theorem 8.3), and to be *anonymous* and *conversely consistent* (see Section 8 for a formulation of this property, whose adaptation to the current model is straightforward) (Thomson 1994c).

When the set of agents is modeled as a nonatomic measure space, the uniform rule is the only subsolution of the equal-division lower bound and Pareto solution to be *consistent* (this is an application of a result due to Thomson and Zhou 1993, and mentioned in Section 8.1).

11.8. Extensions and Related Models

11.8.1. Other Characterizations of the Uniform Rule

Sönmez (1994) strengthens *one-sided resource-monotonicity*—let us call the stronger requirement *strong one-sided resource-monotonicity*—and characterizes the uniform rule as the only selection from the equal-division lower bound solution to satisfy this property and to be *consistent*. For a parallel strengthening of *one-sided population-monotonicity*, he characterizes the rule as the only selection from the equal-division lower-bound solution to satisfy in addition *replication-invariance* and *consistency* (or *converse consistency*). He does not impose efficiency. It turns out that in fact, *one-sided resource-monotonicity* could have been imposed instead. When consumption spaces are bounded above, *strong one-sided resource-monotonicity* by itself implies efficiency (Ehlers 2002a). Uniqueness still holds with *bilateral consistency* instead of *consistency* Kesten (2006a).

In this model, the idea of resource monotonicity can also be formulated in physical terms: when the amount to divide increases, each agent should receive at least as much as he did initially (Otten, Peters, and Volij 1996 consider variants of the idea; Moulin 1999). Otten, Peters, and Volij (1996) require that two agents with the same preferences should receive amounts that are indifferent according to these common preferences, and impose a monotonicity property with respect to simultaneous changes in the social endowment and preferences. Their main result is a characterization of the uniform rule.

It is easy to see that in the presence of efficiency, the various notions of *resource-monotonicity* that have been proposed for the model are equivalent (Ehlers 2002a). The implications of several combinations of solidarity requirements with respect to changes in several of the parameters of the problem, as well as *consistency*, are explored by Chun (2003). Additional results, which are also characterizations of the uniform rule, involve no efficiency. [For the variant of the model in which consumption spaces are bounded above, a family of "fixed path" rules that can be seen as generalizations of the uniform rule emerge as the only selections from the Pareto solution to satisfy *resource-monotonicity* expressed in physical terms, *consistency*, and *strategyproofness*; Moulin 1999. Ehlers 2002a and 2002b establishes a variety of related results, some not involving efficiency.]

11.8.2. Economies with Individual Endowments and Economies with a Social Endowment and Individual Endowments

All of the rules we have discussed can be easily extended to the variant of the model obtained by introducing individual endowments. Various fairness issues for this model are considered by Moreno (2002), Klaus (1997, 2001b), and Klaus, Peters, and Storcken (1997a). [*Strategyproofness* is studied by Klaus, Peters, and Storcken 1997a, 1997b, and Barberà, Jackson, and Neme 1997, the latter invoking it in conjunction with *one-sided welfare-domination under preference-replacement.*]

Even more general are situations where, in addition to individual endowments, we specify an amount interpreted as a collective obligation to or from the outside world (recall the "generalized" economies of Section 8.3). Various ways of generalizing the punctual fairness requirements that have been central in this survey, and issues of *monotonicity*, with respect to the individual endowments, the collective obligation, in addition to *consistency* and *population-monotonicity*, have been addressed (Thomson 1996, Herrero 2002).

In these studies, a rule that is the natural extension of the uniform rule has most frequently emerged. Like the uniform rule, it gives all agents equal opportunities, but this time, for changes in consumptions. For each $i \in N$, let $\omega_i \in \mathbb{R}_+$ be agent i's endowment, and let $T \in \mathbb{R}$ be the collective obligation. Assume that $\sum \omega_i + T \geq 0$, since otherwise there would be no feasible allocation. Now, given $\lambda \in \mathbb{R}$, if $\sum \omega_i + T \leq \sum p(R_i)$, assign to each agent $i \in N$ the maximizer of his preferences among all amounts at most as large as $\omega_i + \lambda$ if such amounts exist. Assign him 0 otherwise. If $\sum \omega_i + T \geq \sum p(R_i)$, give to each agent $i \in N$ the maximizer of his preferences among all amounts at least as large as $\omega_i + \lambda$. In each case, choose λ so that the list of maximizers defines a feasible allocation. (To apply the definition to economies in which there is no collective obligation, just set $T = 0$.)

11.8.3. Multicommodity Generalization

A multicommodity version of the single-peaked assumption is easily defined. For such a model, a generalization of the "equal-slacks Walrasian solution" (Mas-Colell 1992) is axiomatized along the lines of Schummer and Thomson's (1997) axiomatization of the uniform rule (Amoros 1999). [Amoros 2002 defines an extension of the uniform rule that remains a *strategyproof* selection from the no-envy solution, but it only satisfies a weak form of efficiency. Sasaki 2003 also focuses on *strategyproofness*.]

11.8.4. Lotteries

A probabilistic version of the uniform rule is defined and characterized by Sasaki (1997). [Probabilistic rules are studied for a version of the model in which the dividend comes in discrete units by Ehlers and Klaus 2003b, who focus on *strategyproofness*. Their main result is a characterization of a probabilistic version of the uniform rule.]

11.8.5. An Application to a Pollution-Control Problem

The problem of allocating pollution permits can be seen as a variant of the present model, and characterizations of a counterpart of the uniform rule for it have been developed (Kıbrıs 2003).

11.8.6. Single-Troughed Preferences

Concerning the "dual" case of single-troughed preferences, not much can be said about fairness. Preferences not being convex, there may be no efficient allocation that is also envy-free or meets the equal-division lower bound. [The model has mainly been studied in the context of strategic issues, by Klaus, Peters, and Storcken 1997b, Klaus 2001a, Ehlers 2002c.]

12. NONHOMOGENEOUS CONTINUUM

Here, we consider another nonclassical problem, that of dividing a heterogeneous commodity, such as land or time. In such situations, equal division has no economic meaning, even when it can be defined in physical terms (length or surface area, say). However, our central criteria (no-envy, egalitarian-equivalence) remain applicable. A large literature concerns the case when preferences can be represented by atomless measures, and additional criteria can be formulated for that case. Representability by measures means that the value to an agent of measurable subset of the dividend, or "parcel," is independent of which other parcels he may already consume. It precludes complementarity or substitutability between parcels.

This literature has addressed several issues: (i) The existence of partitions satisfying various criteria of fairness as well as certain topological and geometric requirements, for instance whether each agent's component of the partition is connected; whether it is connected to a preexisting parcel that the agent already consumes (and that is added to the specification of the problem); when the dividend is a subset of a Euclidean space, whether the boundaries between components of the partitions are hyperplanes, or perhaps parallel hyperplanes. (ii) The construction of iterative procedures leading to such partitions, the distinction being made between continuous procedures ("moving knife" procedures, in the terminology of Brams and Taylor 1995, or "moving knives" procedures, as there may be more than one knife moving at once) or discrete; the number of steps required, and whether the fairness criterion ends up being met exactly or only in some approximate sense. [The strategic properties of the procedures, that is, whether, when agents behave strategically, it produces the desired partitions, have also been examined. Here, the answer depends on which behavioral assumptions are made, but most writers have assumed that agents follow a maximin criterion. The implementation literature, which we do not review here, has focused on Nash and related behaviors.] The existential part of this program often relies on tools of measure theory, and mathematicians have been the main contributors.

If no restrictions are imposed on preferences apart from continuity and monotonicity (of two parcels related by inclusion, the larger one is preferred to the smaller one), it is easy to show that envy-free and efficient partitions may not exist (Berliant, Dunz, and Thomson 1992). Indeed, there is a sense in which economies with homogeneous goods but nonconvex preferences can be seen as a special case of the economies considered here, and for these economies, there may be no such partition (Section 4.3). However, if preferences can be represented by measures, envy-free partitions exist:

Theorem 12.1 (Weller 1985) Domain: measurable space; preferences representable by finite and atomless measures. *Envy-free and efficient partitions exist.*

An existence result that pertains to the notion of a group envy-free partition is available:

Theorem 12.2 (Berliant, Dunz, and Thomson 1992) Domain: measurable subset of a finite-dimensional Euclidean space; strictly monotonic preferences that are representable by atomless measures. *Group envy-free partitions exist.*

An interesting special case is the one-dimensional case when the continuum has to be divided into intervals, each agent receiving one. It has many applications: division of an interval of time, a length of road, etc. The existence of envy-free partitions when preferences are represented by measures is proved by Woodall (1980). A more general existence result holds, however. It only relies on continuity of preferences and a very weak monotonicity assumption:

Theorem 12.3 (Stromquist 1980) Domain: interval in $\mathbb{R}_+$; preferences, defined over intervals, are such that each interval is at least as desirable as the empty set. *Envy-free partitions into intervals exist.*

An even stronger result holds for preferences that may exhibit a certain form of consumption externalities, no-envy being appropriately reformulated. The proof is existential. Under essentially the same assumptions, Su (1999) gives an algorithmic proof for the existence of partitions satisfying no-envy—not exactly but up to any degree of approximation.

If the one-dimensional continuum is a closed curve, there may be no envy-free partition (Thomson 2007) unless $|N| = 2$, in which case existence holds as soon as the preferences of at least one agent are representable by a measure.

Under monotonicity of preferences, no-envy implies efficiency (Berliant, Dunz, and Thomson 1992). This implication is reminiscent of an earlier result pertaining to the assignment of objects when monetary compensations are possible (Theorem 10.1). These authors describe a class of models for which no-envy implies efficiency, and in fact group no-envy.

As far as egalitarian-equivalent and efficient allocations are concerned, existence is guaranteed under continuity and strict monotonicity of preferences (Berliant, Dunz, and Thomson 1992).

An extensive literature pertains to the case when preferences can be represented by countably additive and atomless measures,[52] and the requirement is that for each agent, the value to him of his assignment should be at least $\frac{1}{n}$ times his value of the dividend. Let us refer to it as the **$\frac{1}{n}$–lower-bound**. It is the form taken by the identical-preferences lower bound for this model. Some of the early literature searched for partitions such that for each agent, the value to him of his assignment should be equal to $\frac{1}{n}$ times his value of the dividend (which is of course in violation of efficiency). A more demanding requirement than the $\frac{1}{n}$–lower-bound is that in addition and when possible, the inequality be strict for each agent. Given a list $\alpha \in \Delta^N$ of "shares," chosen so as to reflect the relative importance to be given to the various agents—asymmetric treatment may be important in some circumstances—the notion can be modified by requiring that each agent i should receive at least α_i times his value of the dividend. Let us refer to it as the **α–lower-bound**. The existence of partitions satisfying these notions and generalizations is an easy implication of the Dvoretsky, Wald, and Wolfovitz (1951) theorem (Barbanel and Zwicker 1995). Barbanel (1996b) proposes yet more general criteria. No-envy remains of course applicable for this model and we have already cited Weller's (1985) existence result. Until relatively recently and except for that paper,

[52] Properties of preferences guaranteeing representability by such measures are given by Barbanel and Taylor (1995).

efficiency issues had been ignored in this literature—this is the case in the papers just cited—computational and algorithmic aspects of the problem being given a central place instead.

The existence of partitions meeting the α–lower-bound, for each $\alpha \in \Delta^N$, is in fact guaranteed under a more general assumption than in Theorem 12.1, namely that preferences be representable by an integrable function h with two arguments, the points of the dividend, and measurable subsets of it, and such that for each pair $\{B, B'\}$ of such subsets with $B' \subset B$, and each $x \in B \setminus B'$, we have $h(x, B') \geq h(x, B)$ (Berliant, Dunz, and Thomson 1992; related sufficient conditions for existence are stated by these authors). Efficiency is obtained in some approximate sense. An existence result for preferences representable by atomless concave capacities is given by Maccheroni and Marinacci (2003). Akin (1995) also goes beyond Theorem 12.1 by proving the existence of envy-free partitions for a more general notion of a partition (where agents receive "fractional" consumptions of each point of the dividend).

A succession of attempts at generalizing to more than two agents the classical two-person divide-and-choose scheme (one agent divides and the other chooses one of the two pieces; the divider receives the other) have been made over the years that generate partitions that are either envy-free or meet the $\frac{1}{n}$–lower-bound, two properties that the scheme satisfies (as noted earlier, some authors have required that each agent's own measure of his share be exactly $\frac{1}{n}$ of his measure of the dividend) (Knaster 1946, Steinhaus 1948, 1949, Dubins and Spanier 1961, Singer 1962, Kuhn 1967, Austin 1982, Sobel 1981, Woodall 1986). Some of these papers also cover the case when the monotonicity assumption on preferences is reversed (of two parcels related by inclusion, the smaller one is at least as desirable as the larger one), which describes situations when the dividend is a "bad." Several of these procedures yield partitions satisfying the $\frac{1}{n}$–lower-bound. It took many years until an algorithm that produces an envy-free partition in the n-person case, for arbitrary n, was discovered (Brams and Taylor 1995). In none of these algorithmic papers is efficiency necessarily attained.

Other contributors are Hill (1983), Legut (1985, 1990), Barbanel (1995, 1996a, 1996b), Brams, Taylor, and Zwicker (1997), Reijnierse and Potters (1998), Ichiishi and Idzik (1999), Zeng (2000), and Barbanel and Brams (2004). Brams and Taylor (1996) offer a detailed review of the literature. Robertson and Webb (1998) focus on algorithms and pay little attention to efficiency. On the other hand, Barbanel (2005) provides an in-depth analysis of the shape of the image of the set of feasible partitions in a Euclidean space of dimension equal to the number of agents, using their measures as representations of their preferences. It offers characterizations of its subset of efficient points. It also gives existence results for efficient and envy-free partitions.

13. OTHER DOMAINS AND ISSUES

We began this survey by specifying its scope as being limited to resource allocation in concretely specified economic models. We conclude by tying it to literatures concerning other models.

- Arrovian model of extended sympathy. The no-envy concept has been studied in this context (Goldman and Sussangkarn 1978, Suzumura 1981a, 1981b, 1983, Denicoló 1999).
- Rights assignments. Here too, the no-envy concept has been the object of several studies (Austen-Smith 1979, Suzumura 1982).
- Quasi-linear model of social choice. This model is somewhat more structured, although physical resource constraints do not explicitly appear. A number of bounds on welfares have been defined, and relational fairness requirements investigated (Moulin 1987c, Chun 1986).
- Intertemporal allocation. Models of allocation across generations are usually formulated in utility space (Diamond 1965 is a precursor; Svensson 1980 is the closest in spirit to the literature we reviewed).
- Choosing a point from an interval or a closed curve when agents have single-peaked preferences. Since all agents consume the same thing, punctual fairness requirements provide little help here, but relational requirements of monotonicity are still meaningful (Thomson 1993, Ching and Thomson 1992, Ehlers and Klaus 2006, Gordon 2007b). [Moulin 1980 is the classic reference for *strategyproofness*.]
- Strategic issues (the implementability of solutions, in particular *strategyproofness*) have been the object of a considerable literature, reviewed in Chapter 5. A number of authors have considered implementation in the special context of fairness (Crawford 1979, Demange 1984, van Damme 1986, 1992, Maniquet 1994, 2002, Thomson 2005).
- Cost sharing. This literature is reviewed in Chapter 6 (Moulin, and various coauthors).
- Queueing, scheduling, and sequencing. This is a very new literature (Crès and Moulin 2001, Maniquet 2003, Chun 2006a, 2006b).
- Matching. A background reference here is Roth and Sotomayor (1990).

14. CONCLUSION

When normative issues are being addressed, the likelihood of a resolution that satisfies everyone is even more remote than when only issues of efficiency are at stake.

In addition, several approaches to the problem of fair allocation can be taken, and we have deliberately followed only an ordinal approach, without attempting to survey the literature based on utility information. Our objective was simply to see how far this approach could take us, and to explore its potential and limitations.

We now have available a well-developed theory of fair allocation that is unified in its conceptual apparatus, and well integrated with theoretical developments that have taken place in other areas of economic theory, such as the theory of mechanism design and implementation.

At this point, it might therefore be appropriate to attempt some preliminary assessment, and we close with a few general remarks intended to highlight what we think are particularly important developments.

Punctual Fairness Requirements. Although we have encountered a great variety of concepts, they can all be roughly divided into criteria compatible with, or in the spirit of, no-envy, and a class of "egalitarian" criteria, which we have discussed under the name of egalitarian-equivalence. In each family, noteworthy solutions have been identified. The most prominent member of the first family is the equal-division Walrasian solution. For the second family, various selections obtained by imposing some restriction on the reference bundle have proved most useful.

Relational Requirements. As far as these types of axioms are concerned, and in spite of their apparent diversity, we should return to the notion of solidarity to emphasize it as a major unifying theme. Its general expression is that when a parameter entering the description of a problem changes (simultaneous changes in several parameters can be considered too), the welfares of what we call the "relevant" agents should be affected in the same direction. When efficiency is imposed as well, it is often known what that direction has to be. For instance, in a private good economy with monotonic preferences, an increase in the social endowment is required to benefit everyone (the scope of the axiom covers everyone), a requirement that we have studied under the name of *resource monotonicity*. When some agents leave, the relevant agents are the agents who stay. Together with efficiency, we derive our condition of *population monotonicity*. Sometimes it is not clear whether the change permits a Pareto improvement or whether it forces a Pareto deterioration, so solidarity takes the weaker form of a uniform change in the direction of the welfares of the relevant agents. This is the case in a private good economy when the amount available of some commodity goes up and that of another commodity goes down (once again, everyone is a relevant agent), or when the preferences of some agents change (here, the relevant agents are all the agents whose preferences are fixed). The requirement of *consistency* can also be seen in that light. This time, we imagine some agents leaving, not empty-handed but with the bundles assigned to them by the rule. Together with efficiency, the solidarity idea tells us that for the remaining agents, the rule should choose the same bundles as initially, or a Pareto-indifferent distribution of these bundles.

Solutions. Given the prominence of the Walrasian solution throughout modern economic theory, we should emphasize that the equal-division Walrasian solution has a priori no greater intrinsic merit than others do. Yet, the recommendation is often made to use this solution. Explicit reasons are rarely given, although the fact that it treats agents anonymously seems to be an important underlying motivation. However, most of the other solutions commonly discussed also have this property when operated from equal division, and much more is needed to justify focusing on the Walrasian solution.

One lesson to be drawn from the work we have reviewed is that the solution does have a number of remarkable features that indeed justify that special attention be paid to it. First, as noted earlier, it is compatible with no-envy, but as opposed to this concept itself, which is satisfied by a continuum of allocations, Walrasian allocations typically are few in number; it often makes much more precise recommendations. Equal-division Walrasian allocations satisfy various notions related to no-envy, as well as criteria, adapted from no-envy, designed to deal with the fair treatment of groups. In large economies in which the set of agents is modeled as a continuum, if preferences are smooth and sufficiently dispersed, any envy-free and efficient allocation is in fact equal-division Walrasian. Moreover, together with the concept of a Walrasian trade, that of an equal-division Walrasian allocation can form the basis for a complete and coherent theory of fair allocation, free of the conceptual difficulties encountered with some of the other solutions. When more general formulations are examined, in particular, in situations where it is deemed desirable to give agents equal opportunities to choose from a common choice set, we found that requiring the choice set to have a straight-line boundary, that is, to be a Walrasian choice set, has a number of advantages. In a model with variable populations, the equal-division Walrasian solution is the only solution to satisfy a number of appealing consistency requirements. In economies with indivisible goods, it coincides with the no-envy solution. In economies with single-peaked preferences, the special form it takes, which is known under the name of the uniform rule, was also found to be best-behaved from a number of viewpoints. [The equal-division Walrasian solution plays a prominent role in the analysis of incentive and informational issues.] These findings contribute to creating an overall picture in which the star solution is the equal-division Walrasian solution.

On the negative side, we should recognize that the equal-division Walrasian solution fails a number of important relational tests of solidarity. In particular, it fails all monotonicity tests with respect to any of the data describing an economy (resources, technology, number of agents). Moreover, better-behaved solutions exist. These solutions are various selections from egalitarian-equivalence, as well as some generalizations. If increases in the social endowment may hurt some agents when the Walrasian solution is operated from equal division, selections from the egalitarian-equivalence and Pareto solution exist that behave well in response to such changes. Similarly, in public good economies, selections from the correspondence exist that respond well to improvements in the technology, whereas in private good economies with increasing returns, an extension of the concept is shown to provide the only way to select efficient allocations that satisfy a natural individual rationality condition: this solution is such that each agent finds his bundle indifferent to the best bundle he could reach if given access to a constant-returns-to-scale economy, this reference technology being the same for all.

It would serve no purpose at this point to commit oneself to a particular concept. Certainly the recent literature has shown that no concept uniformly dominates the other, but some reassessment of the existing concepts has certainly taken place, and at the same time a variety of new concepts have been proposed and exciting results established.

ACKNOWLEDGMENTS

I thank Dimitrios Diamantaras, Diego Dominguez, Yoichi Kasajima, Çağatay Kayı, Onur Kesten, Bettina Klaus, Van Kolpin, Eve Ramaekers, Joachim Silvestre, and Rajiv Vohra for their comments and the National Science Foundation for its support under grant SBR-9731431.

REFERENCES

Abdulkadiroğlu, A., & Sönmez, T. (1998). Random serial dictatorship and the core from random endowments in house allocation problems. *Econometrica, 66*, 689–701.

Abdulkadiroğlu, A., & Sönmez, T. (1999). House allocation with existing tenants. *Journal of Economic Theory, 88*, 233–260.

Abdulkadiroğlu, A., & Sönmez, T. (2003). School choice: a mechanism design approach. *American Economic Review, 93*, 729–747.

Abdulkadiroğlu, A., Sönmez, T., & Ünver, U. (2004). Room assignment-rent division: a market approach. *Social Choice and Welfare, 22*, 515–538.

Aizpurua, J., & Manresa, A. (1995). A decentralized and informationally efficient mechanism realizing fair outcomes in economies with public goods. *Economic Design, 1*, 141–158.

Akin, E. (1995). Vilfredo Pareto cuts the cake. *Journal of Mathematical Economics, 24*, 23–44.

Alkan, A. (1994). Monotonicity and envyfree assignments. *Economic Theory, 4*, 605–616.

Alkan, A., Demange, G., & Gale, D. (1991). Fair allocation of indivisible goods and criteria of justice. *Econometrica, 59*, 1023–1039.

Allingham, M. (1977). Fairness and utility. *Economie Appliquée, 29*, 257–266.

Amoros, P. (1999). Efficiency and income redistribution in the single-peaked preference model with several commodities. *Economics Letters, 63*, 341–349.

Amoros, P. (2002). Single-peaked preferences with several commodities. *Social Choice and Welfare, 19*, 57–67.

Andersson, T., Svensson, L.-G., & Yang, Z. Constrainedly fair job assignments under minimum wages. *Games and Economic Behavior*, forthcoming, 2010.

Aragones, E. (1995). A derivation of the money Rawlsian solution. *Social Choice and Welfare, 12*, 267–276.

Archibald, P., & Donaldson, D. (1979). Notes on economic inequality. *Journal of Public Economics, 12*, 205–214.

Arneson, R. J. (1989). Equality and equal opportunity for welfare. *Philosophical Studies, 56*, 77–93.

Arnsperger, C. (1994). Envy-freeness and distributive justice. *Journal of Economic Surveys, 8*, 155–186.

Arnsperger, C. (1997). Reformulating equality of resources. *Economics and Philosophy, 13*, 61–77.

Arrow, K. (1951). *Social choice and individual values* (2nd ed., 1963). New York: John Wiley.

Austen-Smith, D. (1979). Fair rights. *Economics Letters, 4*, 29–32.

Austin, A. K. (1982). Sharing a cake. *Mathematical Gazette, 66*, 212–215.

Aumann, R., & Peleg, B. (1974). A note on Gale's example. *Journal of Mathematical Economics, 1*, 209–211.

Balinski, M., & Sönmez, T. (1999). A tale of two mechanisms: student placement. *Journal of Economic Theory, 84*, 73–94.

Barbanel, J. (1995). Game-theoretic algorithms for fair and strongly fair cake division with entitlements. *Colloquium Mathematicum, 69*, 59–73.

Barbanel, J. (1996a). Super envy-free cake division: and independence of measures. *Journal of Mathematical Analysis and Applications, 197*, 54–60.

Barbanel, J. (1996b). On the possibilities for partitioning a cake. *Proceedings of the American Mathematical Society, 124*, 3443–3451.

Barbanel, J. (2005). *The geometry of efficient fair division*. Cambridge: Cambridge University Press.

Barbanel, J., & Brams, S. (2004). Cake division with minimal cuts: envy-free procedures for 3 persons, 4 persons, and beyond. *Mathematical Social Sciences, 48*, 251–269.

Barbanel, J., & Brams, S. (2009). Cutting a pie is not a piece of cake. *American Mathematical Monthly, 116*, 496–514.

Barbanel, J., & Taylor, A. (1995). Preference relations and measures in the context of fair division. *Proceedings of the American Mathematical Society, 123*, 2061–2070.

Barbanel, J., & Zwicker, W. (2001). Two applications of a theorem of Dvoretsky, Wald, and Wolfovitz to cake division. *Theory and Decision, 43*, 639–650.

Barberà, S., Barrett, C. R., & Pattanaik, P. K. (1984). On some axioms for ranking sets of alternatives. *Journal of Economic Theory, 33*, 301–308.

Barberà, S., Jackson, M., & Neme, A. (1997). Strategy-proof allotment rules. *Games and Economic Behavior, 18*, 1–21.

Baumol, W. (1982). Applied fairness theory and rationing policy. *American Economic Review, 72*, 639–651.

Baumol, W. (1986). *Superfairness*. Cambridge, MA: MIT Press.

Bénassy, J.-P. (1982). *The economics of market disequilibrium*. New York: Academic Press.

Bergson, A. (1938). A reformulation of certain aspects of welfare economics. *Quarterly Journal of Economics, 52*, 310–334.

Berliant, M., Dunz, K., & Thomson, W. (1992). On the fair division of a heterogeneous commodity. *Journal of Mathematical Economics, 21*, 201–216.

Bevia, C. (1996a). Identical preferences lower bound and consistency in economies with indivisible goods. *Social Choice and Welfare, 13*, 113–126.

Bevia, C. (1996b). Population monotonicity in a general model with indivisible goods. *Economics Letters, 50*, 91–97.

Bevia, C. (1996c). Population monotonicity in economies with one indivisible good. *Mathematical Social Sciences, 32*, 125–137.

Bevia, C. (1998). Fair allocation in a general model with indivisible goods. *Review of Economic Design, 3*, 195–213.

Biswas, T. (1987). Distributive justice and allocation by the market: on the characterization of a fair market economy. *Mathematical Social Sciences, 14*, 225–237.

Bogomolnaia, A., & Moulin, H. (2001). A new solution to the random assignment problem. *Journal of Economic Theory, 100*, 295–328.

Bogomolnaia, A., & Moulin, H. (2002). A simple random assignment problem with a unique solution. *Economic Theory, 19*, 298–317.

Bogomolnaia, A., & Moulin, H. (2004). Random matching under dichotomous preferences. *Econometrica, 72*, 257–279.

Borda, J.C. de (1781). *Memoire sur les elections au scrutin*. Paris: Histoire de l'Academie des Sciences.

Bossert, W. (1995). Redistribution mechanisms based on individual characteristics. *Mathematical Social Sciences, 29*, 1–17.

Bossert, W. (1997). Opportunity sets and individual well-being. *Social Choice and Welfare, 14*, 97–112.

Bossert, W., & Fleurbaey, M. (1996). Redistribution and compensation. *Social Choice and Welfare, 13*, 343–355.

Bossert, W., Fleurbaey, M., & Van de Gaer, D. (1999). Responsibility, talent, and compensation: a second best analysis. *Review of Economic Design, 4*, 35–55.

Bossert, W., Pattanaik, P. K., & Xu, Y. (1994). Ranking opportunity sets: an axiomatic approach. *Journal of Economic Theory, 63*, 326–345.

Brams, S., Edelman, P., & Fishburn, P. (2002). Paradoxes of fair division. *Journal of Philosophy, 98*, 300–314.

Brams, S., Edelman, P., & Fishburn, P. (2003). Fair division of indivisible items. *Theory and Decision, 55*, 147–180.

Brams, S., & Fishburn, P. (2000). Fair division of indivisible items between two people with identical preferences: envy-freeness, Pareto-optimality, and equity. *Social Choice and Welfare, 17*, 247–267.

Brams, S., Jones, M. A., & Klamler, C. (2006). Better ways to cut a cake. *Notices to the American Mathematical Monthly, 53*, 1314–1321.

Brams, S., Jones, M. A., & Klamler, C. (2008). Proportional pie-cutting. *International Journal of Game Theory, 36*, 353–367.

Brams, S., & Kilgour, M. (2001). Competitive fair division. *Journal of Political Economy, 109*, 418–443.

Brams, S., & Taylor, A. D. (1995). An envy-free cake division protocol. *American Mathematical Monthly, 102*, 9–18.

Brams, S., & Taylor, A. D. (1996). *Fair division: from cake-cutting to dispute resolution*. Cambridge: Cambridge University Press.

Brams, S., Taylor, A.D., & Zwicker, W. (1997). A moving-knife solution to the four-person envy-free cake-division problem. *Proceedings of the American Mathematical Society, 125*, 547–554.

Calsamiglia, X., & Kirman, A. (1993). A unique informationally efficient and decentralized mechanism with fair outcomes. *Econometrica, 61*, 1147–1172.

Campbell, D., & Truchon, M. (1988). Boundary optima and the theory of public goods supply. *Journal of Public Economics, 35*, 241–249.

Champsaur, P. (1976). Symmetry and continuity properties of Lindahl equilibria. *Journal of Mathematical Economics, 3*, 19–36.

Champsaur, P., & Laroque, G. (1981). Fair allocations in large economies. *Journal of Economic Theory, 25*, 269–282.

Chaudhuri, A. (1985). Formal properties of interpersonal envy. *Theory and Decision, 18*, 301–312.

Chaudhuri, A. (1986). Some implications of an intensity measure of envy. *Social Choice and Welfare, 3*, 255–270.

Chichilnisky, G., & Thomson, W. (1987). The Walrasian mechanism from equal division is not monotonic with respect to variations in the number of consumers. *Journal of Public Economics, 32*, 119–124.

Ching, S., & Thomson, W. (1992). Population monotonic solutions in public good economies with single-peaked preferences. mimeo, *Social Choice and Welfare*, forthcoming.

Chun, Y. (1986). The solidarity axiom for quasi-linear social choice problems. *Social Choice and Welfare, 3*, 297–310.

Chun, Y. (2000). Distributional properties of the uniform rule in economies with single-peaked preferences. *Economics Letters, 67*, 23–27.

Chun, Y. (2003). One-sided population-monotonicity, separability, and the uniform rule. *Economics Letters, 78*, 343–349.

Chun, Y. (2006a). A pessimistic approach to the queueing problem. *Mathematical Social Sciences, 51*, 171–181.

Chun, Y. (2006b). No-envy in queueing problems. *Economic Theory, 29*, 151–162.

Chun, Y. (2006c). The separability principle in economies with single-peaked preferences. mimeo. *Social Choice and Welfare, 26*, 239–253.

Chun, Y., & Thomson, W. (1988). Monotonicity properties of bargaining solutions when applied to economics. *Mathematical Social Sciences, 15*, 11–27.

Cohen, G. A. (1989). On the currency of egalitarian justice. *Ethics, 99*, 906–944.

Cohen, G. A. (1990). Equality of what? On welfare, goods and capabilities. *Recherches Economiques de Louvain, 56*, 357–382.

Conley, J., & Diamantaras, D. (1996). Generalized Samuelson conditions and welfare theorems for nonsmooth economies. *Journal of Public Economics, 59*, 137–152.

Corchón, L., & Iturbe-Ormaetxe, I. (2001). A proposal to unify some concepts in the theory of fairness. *Journal of Economic Theory, 101*, 540–571.

Crawford, V. (1979). A procedure for generating Pareto efficient egalitarian equivalent allocations. *Econometrica, 47*, 49–60.

Crawford, V., & Heller, W. (1979). Fair division with indivisible commodities. *Journal of Economic Theory, 21*, 10–27.

Crès, H., & Moulin, H. (2001). Scheduling with opting out: improving upon random priority. *Operations Research, 49*, 565–577.

Dagan, N. (1992). Consistency and the Walrasian allocation correspondence. mimeo.

Dagan, N. (1995). Consistent solutions in exchange economies: a characterization of the price mechanism. mimeo.

Dagan, N. (1996). A note on Thomson's characterization of the uniform rule. *Journal of Economic Theory, 69*, 255–261.

Daniel, T. (1975). A revised concept of distributional equity. *Journal of Economic Theory, 11*, 94–109.

Daniel, T. (1978). Pitfalls in the theory of fairness comment. *Journal of Economic Theory, 19*, 561–564.

Debreu, G., & Scarf, H. (1963). A limit theorem on the core of an economy. *International Economic Review, 4*, 235–246.

Demange, G. (1984). Implementing efficient egalitarian equivalent allocations. *Econometrica, 52*, 1167–1177.

Demko, S., & Hill, T. (1988). Equitable distribution of indivisible objects. *Mathematical Social Sciences, 16*, 145–158.

Denicoló, V. (1999). No-envy and Arrow's conditions. *Social Choice and Welfare, 16*, 585–597.

Diamantaras, D. (1991). Envy-free and efficient allocations in large public good economies. *Economics Letters, 36*, 227–232.

Diamantaras, D. (1992). On equity with public goods. *Social Choice and Welfare, 9*, 141–157.

Diamantaras, D., & Thomson, W. (1990). An extension and refinement of the no-envy concept. *Economics Letters, 33*, 217–222.

Diamantaras, D., & Wilkie, S. (1994). A generalization of Kaneko's ratio equilibrium for economies with public and private goods. *Journal of Economic Theory, 62*, 499–512.

Diamantaras, D., & Wilkie, S. (1996). On the set of Pareto-efficient allocations in economies with public goods. *Economic Theory, 7*, 371–379.

Diamond, P. (1965). The evaluation of infinite utility streams. *Econometrica, 33*, 170–177.

Dominguez, D., & Nicolo, A. (2009). Envy-free and efficient minimal rights: recursive no-envy. *The B.E. Journal of Theoretical Economics, 9*, 27–45.

Dubins, L. E., & Spanier, E. H. (1961). How to cut a cake fairly. *American Mathematical Monthly, 68*, 1–17.

Dutta, B., & Vohra, R. (1993). A characterization of egalitarian equivalence. *Economic Theory, 4*, 465–479.

Dvoretsky, A., Wald, A., & Wolfovitz, J. (1951). Relations among certain ranges of vector measures. *Pacific Journal of Mathematics, 1*, 59–74.

Dworkin, R. (1981a). What is equality? Part I: equality of welfare. *Philosophy and Public Affairs, 10*, 185–246.

Dworkin, R. (1981b). What is equality? Part II: equality of resources. *Philosophy and Public Affairs, 10*, 283–345.
Edelman, P., & Fishburn, P. (2001). Fair division of indivisible items among people with similar preferences. *Mathematical Social Sciences, 41*, 327–347.
Ehlers, L. (2002a). Resource-monotonic allocation when preferences are single-peaked. *Economic Theory, 20*, 113–131.
Ehlers, L. (2002b). On fixed-path rationing methods. *Journal of Economic Theory, 106*, 472–477.
Ehlers, L. (2002c). Probabilistic allocation rules and single-dipped preferences. *Social Choice and Welfare, 19*, 325–348.
Ehlers, L. (2002d). A characterization of the uniform rule without Pareto-optimality. mimeo.
Ehlers, L., & Klaus, B. (2003a). Coalitional strategy-proofness and resource-monotonicity for multiple assignment problems. *Social Choice and Welfare, 21*, 265–280.
Ehlers, L., & Klaus, B. (2003b). Probabilistic assignments of identical indivisible objects and the probabilistic uniform correspondence. *Review of Economic Design, 8*, 249–268.
Ehlers, L., & Klaus, B. (2003c). Resource-monotonicity for house allocation problems. *International Journal of Game Theory, 32*, 545–560.
Ehlers, L., & Klaus, B. (2006). Efficient priority rules. *Games and Economic Behavior, 55*, 372–384.
Ehlers, L., & Klaus, B. (2007). Consistent house allocation. *Economic Theory, 30*, 561–574.
Ehlers, L., Klaus, B., & Pápai, S. (2002). Strategy-proofness and population-monotonicity for house allocation problems. *Journal of Mathematical Economics, 38*, 329–339.
Ergin, H. (2000). Consistency in house allocation problems. *Journal of Mathematical Economics, 34*, 77–97.
Ergin, H. (2002). Efficient resource allocation on the basis of priorities. *Econometrica, 70*, 2489–2497.
Feldman, A., & Kirman, A. (1974). Fairness and envy. *American Economic Review, 64*, 995–1005.
Feldman, A., & Weiman, D. (1979). Envy, wealth and class hierarchies. *Journal of Public Economics, 11*, 81–91.
Fleurbaey, M. (1994). On fair compensation. *Theory and Decision, 36*, 277–307.
Fleurbaey, M. (1995a). The requisites of equal opportunity. In W. A. Barnett, H. Moulin, M. Salles & N. Schofield (Eds.), Chapter 2 of *Social choice, welfare, and ethics* (pp. 37—53). Cambridge: Cambridge University Press.
Fleurbaey, M. (1995b). Three solutions for the compensation problem. *Journal of Economic Theory, 65*, 505–521.
Fleurbaey, M. (1995c). Equal opportunity or equal social outcomes. *Economics and Philosophy, 11*, 25–55.
Fleurbaey, M. (1996a). Rewards patterns of fair solutions. *Journal of Public Economics, 59*, 365–395.
Fleurbaey, M. (1996b). *Théories economiques de la justice*. Paris: Economica.
Fleurbaey, M., & Maniquet, F. (1996a). Cooperative production: a comparison of welfare bounds. *Games and Economic Behavior, 17*, 200–208.
Fleurbaey, M., & Maniquet, F. (1996b). Fair allocation with unequal production skills: the no-envy approach to compensation. *Mathematical Social Sciences, 32*, 71–93.
Fleurbaey, M., & Maniquet, F. (1998). An equal-right solution to the compensation-responsibility dilemma. *Mathematical Social Sciences, 35*, 185–201.
Fleurbaey, M., & Maniquet, F. (1999). Cooperative production with unequal skills: the solidarity approach to compensation. *Social Choice and Welfare, 16*, 569–583.
Fleurbaey, M., & Maniquet, F. (2000). Utilitarianism versus fairness in welfare economics. In M. Salles & J. A. Weymark (Eds.), *Justice, political liberalism and utilitarianism: themes from Harsanyi and Rawls*. Cambridge: Cambridge University Press, 2008.
Foley, D. (1967). Resource allocation and the public sector. *Yale Economic Essays, 7*, 45–98.
Gale, D. (1974). Exchange equilibrium and coalitions: an example. *Journal of Mathematical Economics, 1*, 63–66.

Gaspart, F. (1998). Objective measures of well-being and the cooperative production problem. *Social Choice and Welfare, 15*, 95–112.

Geanakoplos, J., & Nalebuff, B. (1998). On a fundamental conflict between equity and efficiency. mimeo.

Gevers, L. (1986). Walrasian social choice: some simple axiomatic approaches. In W. P. Heller, R. M. Starr & D. A. Starrett (Eds.), *Social choice and public decision making, essays in honor of K. J. Arrow* (pp. 97—114). Cambridge: Cambridge University Press.

Ginés, M. (1997). Core selection in economies with increasing returns and public goods. University of Alicante mimeo.

Ginés, M., & Marhuenda, F. (1996). Cost monotonic mechanisms. *Investigaciones Economicas, 20*, 89–103.

Ginés, M., & Marhuenda, F. (1998). Efficiency, monotonicity, and rationality in public goods mechanisms. *Economic Theory, 12*, 423–432.

Goldman, S., & Starr, R. (1982). Pairwise, t-wise and Pareto-optimality. *Econometrica, 50*, 593–606.

Goldman, S., & Sussangkarn, C. (1978). On the concept of fairness. *Journal of Economic Theory, 19*, 210–216.

Goldman, S., & Sussangkarn, C. (1980). On equity and efficiency. *Economics Letters, 5*, 29–31.

Gordon, S. (2000). No-envy and solidarity in economies with indivisible goods. mimeo.

Gordon, S. (2007a). Solidarity in choosing a location on a cycle. *Social Choice and Welfare, 29*, 125–147.

Gordon, S. (2007b). Public decisions: solidarity and the status quo. *Games and Economic Behavior, 61*, 225–241.

Green, J. (1972). On the inequitable nature of core allocations. *Journal of Economic Theory, 4*, 132–143.

Haake, C.-J., Raith, M., & Su, F. (2002). Bidding for envy-freeness: a procedural approach to n-player fair-division problems. *Social Choice and Welfare, 19*, 723–749.

Herreiner, D., & Puppe, C. (2002). A simple procedure for finding equitable allocations of indivisible goods. *Social Choice and Welfare, 19*, 415–430.

Herrero, C. (2002). General allocation problems with single-peaked preferences: path-independence and related topics. *Spanish Economic Review, 4*, 19–40.

Herrero, C., & Villar, A. (1998). The equal-distance rule in allocation problems with single-peaked preferences. In R. Aliprantis & N. Yannelis (Eds.), *Current trends in economic theory and applications* (pp. 215–223). Berlin: Springer-Verlag.

Herrero, C., & Villar, A. (2000). An alternative characterization of the equal-distance rule for allocation problems with single-peaked preferences. *Economics Letters, 66*, 311–317.

Hill, T. P. (1983). Determining a fair border. *American Mathematical Monthly, 90*, 438–442.

Hill, T. (2009). Cutting cakes correctly. mimeo.

Holcombe, R. (1983). Applied fairness theory: comment. *American Economic Review, 73*, 1153–1156.

Hurwicz, L. (1977). On the dimensional requirements of informationally decentralized Pareto satisfactory processes. In K. Arrow & L. Hurwicz (Eds.), *Studies in resource allocation processes* (pp. 413–424). Cambridge: Cambridge University Press.

Hurwicz, L. (1978). On the interaction between information and incentives in organizations. In K. Krippendorff (Ed.), *Communication and control in society* (pp. 123–147). New York: Scientific Publishers Inc.

Hurwicz, L., Maskin, E., & Postlewaite, A. (1995). Feasible Nash implementation of social choice rules when the designer does not know endowments or production sets. In J. O. Ledyard (Ed.), *The economics of informational decentralization: complexity, efficiency and stability: essays in the honor of Stanley Reiter* (pp. 367–433). Dordrecht: Kluwer Academic Publishers.

Hylland, A., & Zeckhauser, R. (1979). The efficient allocations of individual to positions. *Journal of Political Economy, 87*, 293–314.

Iturbe-Ormaetxe, I., & Nieto, J. (1992). The lexicographic egalitarian solution on economic environments. *Social Choice and Welfare, 9*, 203–212.

Iturbe-Ormaetxe, I., & Nieto, J. (1996a). On fair allocation and monetary compensations. *Economic Theory, 7*, 125–138.

Iturbe-Ormaetxe, I., & Nieto, J. (1996b). A stable and consistent solution to distribution problems. *Economics Letters, 50*, 243–249.

Ichiishi, T., & Idzik, A. (1999). Equitable allocation of divisible goods. *Journal of Mathematical Economics, 32*, 389–400.

Jaskold-Gabszewicz, J.-J. (1975). Coalitional fairness of allocations in pure exchange. *Econometrica, 43*, 661–668.

Jones, R. (1987). The population monotonicity property and the transfer paradox. *Journal of Public Economics, 32*, 125–132.

Kalai, E. (1977). Proportional solutions to bargaining situations: interpersonal comparisons of utility. *Econometrica, 45*, 1623–1630.

Kaneko, M. (1977a). The ratio equilibrium and a voting game in a public good economy. *Journal of Economic Theory, 16*, 123–136.

Kaneko, M. (1977b). The ratio equilibria and core of a voting game $G(N, W)$ in a public goods economy. *Econometrica, 45*, 1589–1594.

Keiding, H., & Moulin, H. (1991). The solidarity axiom in parametric surplus sharing problems. *Journal of Mathematical Economics, 20*, 249–270.

Kesten, O. (2006a). More on the uniform rule: characterizations without Pareto-optimality. *Mathematical Social Sciences, 51*, 192–200.

Kesten, O. (2006b). On two competing mechanisms for priority-based allocation problems. *Journal of Economic Theory, 127*, 155–171.

Kesten, O. (2007). A new principle for indivisible good allocation problems. mimeo.

Kesten, O. (2009). Coalition strategy-proofness and resource monotonicity for house allocation problems. *International Journal of Game Theory, 38*, 17–21.

Kesten, O., & Yazici, A. (2009). The Pareto dominant strategy-proof and equitable rule for problems with indivisible goods. mimeo.

Khan, A., & Polemarchakis, H. (1978). Unequal treatment in the core. *Econometrica, 46*, 1475–1481.

Kıbrıs, O. (2003). Permit allocation problems. *Social Choice and Welfare*, 20, 353–362.

Kim, H. (2001). Essays on fair allocations. Ph.D. Thesis.

Kim, H. (2004). Population monotonicity for fair allocation problems. *Social Choice and Welfare, 23*, 59–70.

Klaus, B. (1997). The characterization of the uniform reallocation rule without side-payments. In T. Parthasarathy, B. Dutta, J. A. M. Potters, T. E. S. Raghavan, D. Ray & A. Sen (Eds.), *Game theoretic applications to economics and operations research* (pp. 239–255). Dordrecht: Kluwer Academic Publishers.

Klaus, B. (1998). *Fair allocation and reallocation: an axiomatic study*. Maastricht University Ph.D. Thesis.

Klaus, B. (1999). The role of replication-invariance: two answers concerning the problem of fair division when preferences are single-peaked. mimeo.

Klaus, B. (2001a). Population-monotonicity and separability for economies with single-dipped preferences and the assignment of an indivisible object. *Economic Theory, 17*, 675–692.

Klaus, B. (2001b). Uniform allocation and reallocation revisited. *Review of Economic Design, 6*, 85–98.

Klaus, B. (2006). A note on the separability principle in economies with single-peaked preferences. *Social Choice and Welfare, 26*, 255–261.

Klaus, B., & Miyagawa, E. (2001). Strategy-proofness, solidarity, and consistency for multiple assignment problems. *International Journal of Game Theory, 30*, 421–435.

Klaus, B., Peters, H., & Storcken, T. (1997a). Reallocation of an infinitely divisible good. *Economic Theory, 10*, 305–333.

Klaus, B., Peters, H., & Storcken, T. (1997b). Strategy-proof division of a private good when preferences are single-dipped. *Economics Letters, 55*, 339–346.

Kleinberg, N. (1980). Fair allocations and equal incomes. *Journal of Economic Theory, 23*, 189–200.

Klemisch-Ahlert, M. (1993). Freedom of choice: a comparison of different rankings of opportunity sets. *Social Choice and Welfare, 10*, 189–207.

Klijn, F. (2000). An algorithm for envy-free allocations in an economy with indivisible objects and money. *Social Choice and Welfare, 17*, 201–215.

Kolm, S. (1970). *La valeur publique*. Paris: Dunod.

Kolm, S. (1972). *Justice et Equité*. Paris: Editions du Centre National de la Recherche Scientifique. English Edition, Cambridge, MA: M.I.T. Press, 1988.

Kolm, S. (1973). Super-equité. *Kyklos, 26*, 841–843.

Kolm, S. (1987). Adequation, equity, and fundamental analysis. mimeo.

Kolm, S. (1995). The economics of social sentiments: the case of envy. *The Japanese Economic Review, 46*, 63–87.

Kolm, S. (1996). The theory of justice. *Social Choice and Welfare, 13*, 151–182.

Kolm, S. (1997). *Modern theories of justice*. Cambridge, MA: M.I.T. Press.

Knaster, B. (1946). Sur le problème du partage pragmatique de H. Steinhaus. *Annales de la Société Polonaise de Mathématique, 19*, 228–230.

Kolpin, V. (1991a). Resolving open questions on the $\lambda *$-envy-free criterion. *Economics Letters, 36*, 17–20.

Kolpin, V. (1991b). Equity and the core. *Mathematical Social Sciences, 22*, 137–150.

Korthues, B. (1996). Consistency and its converse. An approach for economies. mimeo.

Korthues, B. (2000). Characterization of an extended Walrasian concept for open economies. *Journal of Mathematical Economics, 33*, 449–461.

Kranich, L. (1996). Equitable opportunities: an axiomatic approach. *Journal of Economic Theory, 71*, 131–147.

Kranich, L. (1997). Equitable opportunities in economic environments. *Social Choice and Welfare, 14*, 57–64.

Kranich, L. (2009). Measuring opportunity inequality with monetary transfers. *Journal of Economic Inequality, 7*, 371–385.

Kuhn, H. (1967). On games of fair division. In M. Shubik (Ed.), *Essays in honor of Oskar Morgenstern* (pp. 29–37). Princeton: Princeton University Press.

Legut, J. (1985). The problem of fair division for countably many participants. *Journal of Mathematical Analysis and Application, 109*, 83–89.

Legut, J. (1990). On totally balanced games arising from cooperation in fair division. *Games and Economic Behavior, 2*, 47–60.

Maccheroni, F., & Marinacci, M. (2003). How to cut a pizza fairly: fair division with decreasing marginal evaluations. *Social Choice and Welfare, 20*, 457–465.

Maniquet, F. (1994). On the Nash and coalition-proof implementation of the Pareto and no-envy correspondence. Ph.D. Dissertation, University of Namur.

Maniquet, F. (1996a). Horizontal equity and stability when the number of agents is variable in the fair division problem. *Economics Letters, 50*, 85–90.

Maniquet, F. (1996b). Allocation rules for a commonly owned technology: the average cost lower bound. *Journal of Economic Theory, 69*, 490–508.

Maniquet, F. (1998). An equal right solution to the compensation-responsibility dilemma. *Mathematical Social Sciences, 35*, 185–202.

Maniquet, F. (1999). A strong incompatibility between efficiency and equity in non-convex economies. *Journal of Mathematical Economics, 32*, 467–474.

Maniquet, F. (2001). On decomposable exchange rules. *Economics Letters, 70*, 375–380.

Maniquet, F. (2002). A study of proportionality and simplicity in the cooperative production problem. *Review of Economic Design, 7*, 1–15.

Maniquet, F. (2003). A characterization of the Shapley value in queueing problems. *Journal of Economic Theory, 109*, 90–103.

Maniquet, F., & Sprumont, Y. (2000). On resource-monotonicity in the fair division problem. *Economics Letters, 68*, 299–302.

Mas-Colell, A. (1980a). Remarks on the game theoretic analysis of a simple distribution of surplus problems. *International Journal of Game Theory, 9*, 125–140.

Mas-Colell, A. (1980b). Efficiency and decentralization in the pure theory of public goods. *Quarterly Journal of Economics, 94*, 625–641.

Mas-Colell, A. (1987). On the second welfare theorem for anonymous net trades in exchange economies with many agents. In T. Groves, R. Radner & S. Reiter (Eds.), *Information, incentives and economic mechanisms* (pp. 267–292). Minneapolis: University of Minnesota Press.

Mas-Colell, A. (1992). Equilibrium theory with possibly satiated preferences. In M. Majumdar (Ed.), *Equilibrium and dynamics; essays in honor of D. Gale* (pp. 201–213). London: MacMillan.

Maskin, E. (1987). On the fair allocation of indivisible goods. In G. Feiwel (Ed.), Chapter 11 of *Arrow and the foundations of the theory of economic policy* (pp. 341–349). London: MacMillan.

Maskin, E. (1999). Nash equilibrium and welfare optimality. *Review of Economic Studies, 66*, 83–114.

McLennan, A. (1980). Fair allocations. Ph.D. Thesis, Princeton University.

Meertens, M., Potters, J., & Reijnierse, H. (2002). Envy-free and Pareto efficient allocations in economies with indivisible goods and money. *Mathematical Social Sciences, 44*, 223–233.

Moreno, B. (2002). Single-peaked preferences, population-monotonicity and endowments. *Economics Letters, 75*, 87–95.

Moulin, H. (1980). On strategy-proofness and single peakedness. *Public Choice, 35*, 437–455.

Moulin, H. (1987a). Egalitarian equivalent cost sharing of a public good. *Econometrica, 55*, 963–977.

Moulin, H. (1987b). A core selection for pricing a single-output monopoly. *Rand Journal of Economics, 18*, 397–407.

Moulin, H. (1987c). The pure compensation problem: egalitarianism versus laissez-fairism. *Quarterly Journal of Economics, 101*, 769–783.

Moulin, H. (1989). Monotonic surplus sharing: characterization results. *Games and Economic Behavior, 1*, 250–277.

Moulin, H. (1990a). Uniform preference externalities: two axioms for fair allocation. *Journal of Public Economics, 43*, 305–326.

Moulin, H. (1990b). Monotonic surplus-sharing and the utilization of common property resources. In T. Ichiishi, A. Neyman & Y. Tauman (Eds.), *Game theory and applications* (pp. 282–299). Academic Press.

Moulin, H. (1990c). Fair division under joint ownership: recent results and open problems. *Social Choice and Welfare, 7*, 149–170.

Moulin, H. (1990d). Joint ownership of a convex technology: comparisons of three solutions. *Review of Economic Studies, 57*, 439–452.

Moulin, H. (1990e). Interpreting common ownership. *Recherches Economiques de Louvain, 56*, 303–326.

Moulin, H. (1991). Welfare bounds in the fair division problem. *Journal of Economic Theory, 54*, 321–337.

Moulin, H. (1992a). An application of the Shapley value to fair division with money. *Econometrica, 60*, 1331–1349.

Moulin, H. (1992b). Welfare bounds in the cooperative production problem. *Games and Economic Behavior, 4*, 373–401.

Moulin, H. (1992c). All sorry to disagree: a general principle for the provision of non-rival goods. *Scandinavian Journal of Economics, 94*, 37–51.

Moulin, H. (1993). On the fair and coalitionproof allocation of private goods. In K. Binmore, A. Kirman & P. Tani (Eds.), *Frontiers of game theory* (pp. 151–163). Cambridge, MA: M.I.T. Press.

Moulin, H. (1995). *Cooperative microeconomics: a game-theoretic introduction*. Princeton: Princeton University Press.

Moulin, H. (1996). Cost sharing under increasing returns: a comparison of simple mechanisms. *Journal of Economic Theory, 13*, 225–251.

Moulin, H. (1999). Rationing a commodity along fixed paths. *Journal of Economic Theory, 84*, 41–72.
Moulin, H. (2003). *Fair division and collective welfare*. Cambridge, MA: M.I.T. Press.
Moulin, H., & Roemer, J. (1989). Public ownership of the external world and private ownership of self. *Journal of Political Economy, 97*, 347–367.
Moulin, H., & Shenker, S. (1994). Average cost pricing versus serial cost sharing: an axiomatic comparison. *Journal of Economic Theory, 64*, 178–207.
Moulin, H., & Thomson, W. (1988). Can everyone benefit from growth? Two difficulties. *Journal of Mathematical Economics, 17*, 339–345.
Moulin, H., & Thomson, W. (1997). Axiomatic models of resource allocation. In K. Arrow, A. Sen & K. Suzumura (Eds.), *Social choice reexamined* (Vol. I, pp. 101–120). London: MacMillan.
Mount, K., & Reiter, S. (1974). The informational size of message spaces. *Journal of Economic Theory, 8*, 161–192.
Nagahisa, R. (1991). A local independence condition for characterization of Walrasian allocations rule. *Journal of Economic Theory, 54*, 106–123.
Nagahisa, R. (1992). Walrasian social choice in a large economy. *Mathematical Social Sciences, 24*, 73–78.
Nagahisa, R. (1994). A necessary and sufficient condition for Walrasian social choice. *Journal of Economic Theory, 62*, 186–208.
Nagahisa, R., & Suh, S.-C. (1995). A characterization of the Walras rule. *Social Choice and Welfare, 12*, 335–352.
Nicolò, A., & Perea, A. (2005). Monotonicity and equal-opportunity equivalence in bargaining. *Mathematical Social Sciences, 49*, 221–243.
Nishimura, Y. (2002). Envy minimization in the optimal tax context. mimeo.
Nozick, R. (1974). *Anarchy, state, and utopia*. New York: Basic Books.
Otsuki, M. (1980). On distribution according to labor a concept of fairness in production. *Review of Economic Studies, 47*, 945–958.
Otsuki, M. (1992). Surplus from publicness in consumption and its equitable distribution. *Journal of Public Economics, 47*, 107–124.
Otsuki, M. (1993). Equity criteria in value terms. Tohoku University Discussion Paper.
Otsuki, M. (1996a). Criteria for distributive equity: characterization in terms of share value. *Journal of Economic Theory, 71*, 532–557.
Otsuki, M. (1996b). Choice of compensation policy for disabilities. Tohoku University.
Otten, G.-J., Peters, H., & Volij, O. (1996). Two characterizations of the uniform rule. *Economic Theory, 7*, 291–306.
Pápai, S. (2000). Strategy-proof assignment by hierarchical exchange. *Econometrica, 68*, 1403–1433.
Pattanaik, P. K., & Xu, Y. (1990). On ranking opportunity sets in terms of freedom of choice. *Recherches Economiques de Louvain, 56*, 383–390.
Pazner, E. (1977). Pitfalls in the theory of fairness. *Journal of Economic Theory, 14*, 458–466.
Pazner, E., & Schmeidler, D. (1974). A difficulty in the concept of fairness. *Review of Economic Studies, 41*, 441–443.
Pazner, E., & Schmeidler, D. (1976). Social contract theory and ordinal distributive equity. *Journal of Public Economics, 5*, 261–268.
Pazner, E., & Schmeidler, D. (1978a). Egalitarian equivalent allocations: a new concept of economic equity. *Quarterly Journal of Economics, 92*, 671–687.
Pazner, E., & Schmeidler, D. (1978b). Decentralization and income distribution in socialist economies. *Economic Inquiry*, 57–264.
Peleg, B. (1996). A note on existence of equilibria in generalized economies. mimeo.
Peragine, V. (1999). The distribution and redistribution of opportunity. *Journal of Economic Surveys, 13*, 37–69.
Philpotts, G. (1983). Applied fairness theory. *American Economic Review, 73*, 1157–1160.

Piketty, T. (1994). Existence of fair allocations in economies with production. *Journal of Public Economics, 55*, 391–405.

Polterovich, V., & Spivak, V. (1980). The budgetary paradox in the model of economic equilibrium. *Matekon, 16*, 3–22.

Polterovich, V., & Spivak, V. (1983). Gross substitutability of point to set correspondences. *Journal of Mathematical Economics, 11*, 116–140.

Postlewaite, A. (1979). Manipulation via endowments. *Review of Economic Studies, 46*, 255–262.

Ramaekers, E. (2006). Fair allocation of indivisible goods without monetary compensations. mimeo.

Rawls, J. (1971). *A theory of justice*. Cambridge, MA: Harvard University Press.

Reijnierse, J. H., & Potters, J. A. M. (1998). On finding an envy-free Pareto-optimal division. *Mathematical Programming, 83*, 291–311.

Richter, M. (1979). Duality and rationality. *Journal of Economic Theory, 20*, 131–181.

Robertson, J., & Webb, W. (1998). *Cake-cutting algorithms*. Natick, MA: A.K. Peters.

Roemer, J. (1986a). The mismarriage of bargaining theory and distributive justice. *Ethics, 97*, 88–110.

Roemer, J. (1986b). Equality of resources implies equality of welfare. *Quarterly Journal of Economics, 101*, 751–784.

Roemer, J. (1988). Axiomatic bargaining on economic environments. *Journal of Economic Theory, 45*, 1–35.

Roemer, J. (1996). *Theories of distributive justice*. Cambridge, MA: Harvard University Press.

Roemer, J., & Silvestre, J. (1993). The proportional solution for economies with both private and public ownership. *Journal of Economic Theory, 59*, 426–444.

Roth, A., Sönmez, T., & Ünver, U. (2004). Kidney exchange. *Quarterly Journal of Economics, 119*, 457–488.

Roth, A. E., & Sotomayor, M. (1990). *Two-sided matching: a study in game-theoretic modeling and analysis*. Econometric Society Monograph Series. New York: Cambridge University Press.

Saijo, T. (1990). Boundary optima and the theory of public good supply. *Journal of Economic Theory, 42*, 213–217.

Samuelson, P. (1955). The pure theory of public expenditure. *Review of Economic Studies, 46*, 387–389.

Samuelson, W. (1980). The object distribution problem revisited. *Quarterly Journal of Economics, 94*, 85–98.

Sasaki, H. (1997). Randomized uniform allocation mechanism and single-peaked preferences of indivisible good. Waseda University.

Sasaki, H. (2003). Limitation of efficiency: strategy-proofness and single-peaked preferences with many commodities. mimeo.

Sato, T. (1985). Equity and fairness in an economy with public goods. *The Economic Review, 30*, 364–373.

Sato, T. (1987). Equity, fairness, and Lindahl equilibria. *Journal of Public Economics, 33*, 261–271.

Sato, T. (1990). On equity criteria which are compatible with Lindahl's equilibrium concept. *Economic Studies Quaterly, 41*.

Schmeidler, D., & Vind, K. (1972). Fair net trades. *Econometrica, 40*, 637–642.

Schmeidler, D., & Yaari, M. (1971). Fair allocations. mimeo.

Schummer, J., & Thomson, W. (1997). Two derivations of the uniform rule. *Economics Letters, 55*, 333–337.

Sen, A. (1970). *Collective choice and social welfare*. San Francisco: Holden Day.

Serrano, R., & Volij, O. (1998). Axiomatizations of neoclassical concepts for economies. *Journal of Mathematical Economics, 30*, 87–108.

Sertel, M., & Yıldız, M. (1998). The Lindahl solution with changing population and resources. *Mathematical Social Sciences, 35*, 151–163.

Shapley, L. (1953). A value for *n*-person games. In H. W. Kuhn & A. W. Tucker (Eds.), *Contributions to the theory of games II* (Annals of mathematics studies 28) (pp. 307–317). Princeton: Princeton University Press.

Shapley, L., & Scarf, H. (1974). On cores and indivisibility. *Journal of Mathematical Economics, 1*, 23–37.

Shimomura, K.-I. (1993). Individual rationality and collective optimality. mimeo.

Shitovitz, B. (1992). Coalitional fair allocations in smooth mixed markets with an atomless sector. *Mathematical Social Sciences, 25*, 27–40.

Singer, E. (1962). Extension of the classical rule of "Divide and Choose". *Southern Economic Journal, 38*, 391–394.

Sobel, J. (1981). Proportional distribution schemes. *Journal of Mathematical Economics, 8*, 147–157.

Sönmez, T. (1994). Consistency, monotonicity and the uniform rule. *Economics Letters, 46*, 229–235.

Sönmez, T., & Ünver, U. (2005). House allocation with existing tenants: an equivalence. *Games and Economic Behavior, 52*, 153–185.

Sprumont, Y. (1991). The division problem with single-peaked preferences: a characterization of the uniform allocation rule. *Econometrica, 59*, 509–519.

Sprumont, Y. (1996). Axiomatizing ordinal welfare egalitarianism when preferences vary. *Journal of Economic Theory, 68*, 77–110.

Sprumont, Y. (1997). Balanced egalitarian redistribution of income. *Mathematical Social Sciences, 33*, 185–201.

Sprumont, Y. (1998). Equal factor equivalence in economies with multiple public goods. *Social Choice and Welfare, 15*, 543–558.

Sprumont, Y., & Zhou, L. (1999). Pazner-Schmeidler rules in large society. *Journal of Mathematical Economics, 31*, 321–339.

Steinhaus, H. (1948). The problem of fair division. *Econometrica, 16*, 101–104.

Steinhaus, H. (1949). Sur la division pragmatique. *Econometrica, 17*, 315–319.

Stromquist, N. (1980). How to cut a cake fairly. *American Mathematics Monthly, 87*, 640–644.

Su, F. (1999). Rental harmony: Sperner's lemma in fair division. *American Mathematical Monthly, 106*, 930–942.

Sussangkarn, C., & Goldman, S. (1983). Dealing with envy. *Journal of Economic Theory, 23*, 189–200.

Suzumura, K. (1981a). On Pareto-efficiency and the no-envy concept of equity. *Journal of Economic Theory, 25*, 267–379.

Suzumura, K. (1981b). On the possibility of "fair" collective choice rule. *International Economic Review, 22*, 351–364.

Suzumura, K. (1982). Equity, efficiency and rights in social choice. *Mathematical Social Sciences, 3*, 131–155.

Suzumura, K. (1983). Resolving conflicting views of justice in social choice. In P. K. Pattanaik & M. Salles (Eds.), Chapter 8 of *Social choice and welfare* (pp. 125–149). Amsterdam: North-Holland.

Suzumura, K. (1997). Interpersonal comparisons and the possibility of social choice. In K. Arrow, A. Sen & K. Suzumura (Eds.), *Social choice reexamined* (Vol. I, pp. 202—229). London: MacMillan.

Svensson, L.-G. (1980). Equity among generations. *Econometrica, 48*, 1251–1256.

Svensson, L.-G. (1983a). On the existence of fair allocations. *Zeitschrift für National Oekonomie, 43*, 301–308.

Svensson, L.-G. (1983b). Large indivisibilities: an analysis with respect to price equilibrium and fairness. *Econometrica, 51*, 939–954.

Svensson, L.-G. (1988). Fair wages when individual choice sets are incomplete. An application of a model with indivisibilities. *Scandinavian Journal of Economies, 90*, 563–573.

Svensson, L.-G. (1994a). Queue allocation of indivisible goods. *Social Choice and Welfare, 11*, 323–330.

Svensson, L.-G. (1994b). σ-optimality and fairness. *International Economic Review, 35*, 527–531.

Tadenuma, K. (1989). On the single-valuedness of a solution for the problem of fair allocation in economies with indivisibilities. mimeo.

Tadenuma, K. (1994). On strongly envy-free allocations in economies with indivisible goods. mimeo.

Tadenuma, K. (1996). Trade-off between equity and efficiency in a general model with indivisible goods. *Social Choice and Welfare, 13*, 445–450.

Tadenuma, K. (2002). Efficiency first or equity first? Two principles and rationality of social choice. *Journal of Economic Theory, 104*, 462–472.
Tadenuma, K. (2005). Egalitarian-equivalence and the Pareto principle for social preferences. *Social Choice and Welfare, 24*, 455–473.
Tadenuma, K., & Thomson, W. (1991). No-envy and consistency in economies with indivisible goods. *Econometrica, 59*, 1755–1767.
Tadenuma, K., & Thomson, W. (1993). The fair allocation of an indivisible good when monetary compensations are possible. *Mathematical Social Sciences, 25*, 117–132.
Tadenuma, K., & Thomson, W. (1995). Refinements of the no-envy solution in economies with indivisible goods. *Theory and Decision, 39*, 189–206.
Tadenuma, K., & Xu, Y. (2001). Envy-free configurations in the market economy. mimeo.
Thomson, W. (1978). Monotonic allocation mechanisms: preliminary results. mimeo.
Thomson, W. (1982). An informationally efficient equity criterion. *Journal of Public Economics, 18*, 243–263.
Thomson, W. (1983a). Equity in exchange economies. *Journal of Economic Theory, 29*, 217–244.
Thomson, W. (1983b). The fair division of a fixed supply among a growing population. *Mathematics of Operations Research, 8*, 319–326.
Thomson, W. (1985). Manipulation and implementation in economics. mimeo.
Thomson, W. (1987a). Monotonic allocation rules. revised 1989.
Thomson, W. (1987b). Monotonic allocation rules in public good economies. revised 1989.
Thomson, W. (1987c). The vulnerability to manipulative behavior of economic mechanisms designed to select equitable and efficient outcomes. In T. Groves, R. Radner & S. Reiter (Eds.), Chapter 14 of *Information, incentives and economic mechanisms* (pp. 375–396). Minneapolis: University of Minnesota Press.
Thomson, W. (1988). A study of choice correspondences in economies with a variable number of agents. *Journal of Economic Theory, 46*, 237–254.
Thomson, W. (1990a). On the non-existence of envy-free and egalitarian allocations in economies with indivisibilities. *Economics Letters, 34*, 227–229.
Thomson, W. (1990b). The consistency principle. In T. Ichiishi, A. Neyman & Y. Tauman (Eds.), *Game theory and applications* (pp. 187–215). New York: Academic Press.
Thomson, W. (1990c). A replacement principle. mimeo.
Thomson, W. (1992). Consistency in exchange economies. mimeo.
Thomson, W. (1993). The replacement principle in public good economies with single-peaked preferences. *Economics Letters, 42*, 31–36.
Thomson, W. (1994a). Notions of equal, and equivalent, opportunities. *Social Choice and Welfare, 11*, 137–156.
Thomson, W. (1994b). Resource-monotonic solutions to the problem of fair division when preferences are single-peaked. *Social Choice and Welfare, 11*, 205–223.
Thomson, W. (1994c). Consistent solutions to the problem of fair division when preferences are single-peaked. *Journal of Economic Theory, 63*, 219–245.
Thomson, W. (1994d). Consistent extensions. *Mathematical Social Sciences, 28*, 35–49.
Thomson, W. (1995a). Population-monotonic solutions to the problem of fair division when preferences are single-peaked. *Economic Theory, 5*, 229–246.
Thomson, W. (1995b). Population-monotonic allocation rules. In W. A. Barnett, H. Moulin, M. Salles & N. Schofield (Eds.). Chapter 4 of *Social choice, welfare and ethics* (pp. 79–124). Cambridge: Cambridge University Press.
Thomson, W. (1995c). *The theory of fair allocation*. book manuscript. Princeton University Press, forthcoming.
Thomson, W. (1995d). Consistent allocation rules. mimeo.
Thomson, W. (1996). The replacement principle in classical economies with private goods. mimeo.

Thomson, W. (1997). The replacement principle in private good economies with single-peaked preferences. *Journal of Economic Theory, 76*, 145–168.
Thomson, W. (1998). The replacement principle in economies with indivisible goods. *Social Choice and Welfare, 15*, 57–66.
Thomson, W. (1999a). Welfare-domination and preference-replacement: a survey and open questions. *Social Choice and Welfare, 16*, 373–394.
Thomson, W. (1999b). Economies with public goods: an elementary geometric exposition. *Journal of Public Economic Theory, 1*, 139–176.
Thomson, W. (1999c). Option monotonicity. mimeo.
Thomson, W. (2001). On the axiomatic method and its recent applications to game theory and resource allocation. *Social Choice and Welfare, 18*, 327–387.
Thomson, W. (2003a). The axiomatic and game-theoretic analysis of bankruptcy and taxation problems: a survey. *Mathematical Social Sciences, 45*, 249–297.
Thomson, W. (2003b). On monotonicity in economies with indivisible goods. *Social Choice and Welfare, 21*, 195–205.
Thomson, W. (2005). Divide and permute. *Games and Economic Behavior, 52*, 186–2000.
Thomson, W. (2007). Children crying at birthday parties; Why? *Economic Theory, 31*, 501–521.
Thomson, W., & Varian, H. (1985). Theories of justice based on symmetry. In L. Hurwicz, D. Schmeidler & H. Sonnenschein (Eds.), Chapter 4 of *Social goals and social organization* (pp. 107–129). Cambridge: Cambridge University Press.
Thomson, W., & Zhou, L. (1993). Consistent allocation rules in atomless economies. *Econometrica, 61*, 575–587.
Tinbergen, J. (1953). *Redelijke inkomensverdeling* (2nd ed.). Haarlem: N.V. DeGulden Pers.
Ünver, M.U. (2003). Market mechanisms for fair division with indivisible objects and money. mimeo.
van Damme, E. (1986). Fair allocation of an indivisible object. mimeo.
van Damme, E. (1992). Fair division under asymmetric information. In R. Selten (Ed.), *Rational interaction* (pp. 121–144). Berlin: Springer-Verlag.
van den Nouweland, A., Peleg, B., & Tijs, S. (1996). Axiomatic characterizations of the Walras correspondence for generalized economies. *Journal of Mathematical Economics, 25*, 355–372.
van den Nouweland, A., Peleg, B., & Tijs, S. (2002). Axiomatization of ratio equilibria in public good economies. *Social Choice and Welfare, 19*, 627–636.
van Parijs, P. (1990). Equal endowments as undominated diversity. *Recherches Economiques de Louvain, 56*, 327–355.
Varian, H. (1974). Equity, envy, and efficiency. *Journal of Economic Theory, 9*, 63–91.
Varian, H. (1975). Distributive justice, welfare economics, and the theory of fairness. *Philosophy and Public Affairs, 4*, 223–247.
Varian, H. (1976). Two problems in the theory of fairness. *Journal of Public Economics, 5*, 249–260.
Velez, R. (2007). A unifying theory of fair allocation. mimeo.
Vind, K. (1971). Lecture notes in mathematical economics. mimeo.
Vohra, R. (1992). Equity and efficiency in non-convex economies. *Social Choice and Welfare, 9*, 185–202.
Watts, A. (1999). Cooperative production: a comparison of lower and upper bounds. *Journal of Mathematical Economics, 32*, 317–331.
Weber, S., & Wiesmeth, H. (1990). On the theory of cost sharing. *Journal of Economics, 52*, 71–82.
Weber, S., & Wiesmeth, H. (1991). Economic models of NATO. *Journal of Public Economics, 46*, 181–197.
Weller, D. (1985). Fair division of measurable space. *Journal of Mathematical Economics, 14*, 5–17.
Willson, S. (2003). Money-egalitarian-equivalent and gain-maximin allocations of indivisible items with monetary compensation. *Social Choice and Welfare, 20*, 247–259.
Woodall, J. R. (1980). Dividing a cake fairly. *Journal of Mathematical Analysis and Applications, 78*, 233–247.

Woodall, J. R. (1986). A note on the cake-division problem. *Journal of Combinatorial Theory, Series A, 42*, 300–301.

Xu, Y. (2004). On ranking linear budget sets in terms of freedom of choice. *Social Choice and Welfare, 22*, 281–289.

Yamashige, S. (1997). Fairness in markets and government policies: a weak equity criterion for allocation mechanisms. *Hitotsubashi Journal of Economics, 38*, 61–77.

Yannelis, N. (1983). Existence and fairness of value allocation without convex preferences. *Journal of Economic Theory, 31*, 283–292.

Yannelis, N. (1985). Value and fairness. In C. D. Aliprantis, O. Burkinshaw & N. J. Rothman (Eds.), Lecture notes in economics and mathematical systems (Vol. 244), *Advances in equilibrium theory* (pp. 205–235). Berlin: Springer-Verlag.

Yoshihara, N. (1998). Characterizations of public and private ownership solutions. *Mathematical Social Sciences, 35*, 165–184.

Young, P. (ed.). (1985). *Fair allocation*. Providence: American Mathematical Society.

Young, P. (ed.). (1994). *Equity: how groups divide goods and burdens among their members*. Princeton: Princeton University Press.

Zeng, D. Z. (2000). Approximate envy-free procedures. In F. Patrone, I. García-Jurado & S. Tijs (Eds.), Chapter 17 of *Game practice: contributions from applied game theory* (pp. 259–271). Dordrecht: Kluwer Academic Publishers.

Zhou, L. (1992). Strictly fair allocations and Walrasian equilibria in large exchange economies. *Journal of Economic Theory, 57*, 158–175.

CHAPTER TWENTY-TWO

Compensation and Responsibility[1]

Marc Fleurbaey* and François Maniquet**
*CNRS, Université Paris-Descartes, CORE (Université Catholique de Louvain), Sciences-Po and IDEP.
**CORE, Université Catholique de Louvain, and University of Warwick.

Contents

Abstract

Many distributive issues involve situations in which initial characteristics make individuals unequal. In view of prevailing moral sentiments, some of these characteristics call for compensating transfers, and some do not. We study the literature on this problem of compensation. This literature follows the

[1] The last substantial revision of this survey was made in 2005. Some new works on compensation and responsibility have been done since then. We refer the reader to Fleurbaey (2008) for updates.

Handbook of Social Choice and Welfare, Volume II
ISSN: 0169-7218, DOI: 10.1016/S0169-7218(10)00022-5

distinction between the ethical principle of compensation and that of responsibility. According to the former, a good resource allocation system should neutralize the differential influence over agents' outcomes of the characteristics that elicit compensation. According to the latter, a good resource allocation system should remain neutral with respect to inequality arising from the influence of characteristics that do not elicit compensation. The principle of responsibility can be interpreted as a libertarian principle of natural reward, or as a principle of utilitarian reward. Depending on whether the emphasis is put on the principle of compensation or of responsibility, and depending on how the latter is interpreted, there exist four main families of solutions to compensation problems. We review the axiomatic analyses of these four families of solutions in the different models in which they have been studied. We also review the applications that have been made of these solutions to problems of income taxation, education investment, social mobility and health insurance systems.

Keywords: compensation, responsibility, equal opportunity, natural reward, utilitarian reward, conditional equality, egalitarian equivalence.

JEL codes: D63, D71, H21, I18, I22.

1. INTRODUCTION

Many distributive issues involve situations of unequal endowments that call for compensating transfers. When the endowments themselves are transferable, things are relatively simple, at least in the first-best context, because transfers can remove the initial inequality. But in other situations endowments are not transferable, or are only transferable at a prohibitive cost, because of the available technology or because of prevailing moral constraints. For instance, between individuals, features of human capital like education, social background, genetic endowment, health, or bodily characteristics are seldom considered as being transferable. Between regions or countries features like natural environment, landscape, population characteristics, even industry, are, in many decision contexts, not modifiable. In such cases, transfers will not remove all the inequalities but will compensate endowment inequality by a countervailing resource inequality. Sometimes things are still simple because there is an obvious index of performance that measures how much compensation is achieved. For instance, if equality of weight between racers is sought, it is easy to put artificial weight on lighter racers so as to achieve the desired equality, even though transferring weight is in itself impossible. If equality of welfare between individuals is the social objective, and there is an accepted measure of welfare with interpersonal comparability, then it is relatively easy to devise transfers of resources in the direction of such equality, and if full equality is not possible because initial inequalities are too great (or because of second-best impediments), resorting to the maximin criterion seems reasonable.

In many contexts such an undisputed index of compensation is not available. There may be for instance different evaluations of the unequal endowments, leading to a preference aggregation problem. Moreover, it is often the case that among initial characteristics that make individuals (or groups, regions, countries, etc.) unequal, some do not call for compensation, in view of the prevailing moral sentiment. For instance, a non-negligible part of welfare inequalities comes from bodily beauty and attractiveness, although it is seldom argued that such inequalities should induce transfers. Whatever the reason (e.g., organizing transfers on this basis might be damaging to self-respect), this entails that individuals bear the consequences of such inequalities. Similarly, the exercise of responsibility is often thought to generate legitimate inequalities. The classical example of expensive tastes (Arrow 1973, Dworkin 1981a) is a case in point. An expensive taste for rare food or extravagant activities is a kind of handicap in view of achieving happiness, although it may be argued that such a handicap is less of an urgency than bodily disability, because individuals must somehow assume responsibility for their goals. When the disputed characteristic is fully chosen by individuals, it is also often argued that they should bear the consequences, even disregarding the obvious underlying moral hazard issue. The ideal of "equal opportunities" is invoked in this context, with the double requirement of compensating the unequal circumstances in which the individuals are placed and of letting them reap the benefits, or bear the costs, of their choices. Similar considerations arise in the case of other entities like regions or countries. It may sometimes be defended that federal or national subsidies to a region should not cater to inequalities due to consumption patterns, pollution behavior, religious practices, and so on. In all such cases, the scale of compensation for illegitimate inequalities is difficult to assess because the individual index of performance typically mixes the effects of the various characteristics, those that justify compensation and those that do not.

The literature under review in this chapter deals with this problem of compensation. The origins of this literature can be traced back to four different sources. First, the utilitarian approach to this issue has been studied by Arrow (1971) and Sen (1973), who pointed out the paradox that a handicapped individual is likely to have a lower marginal utility and therefore, by application of the utilitarian criterion, to receive less resources than a better-off individual. As an antidote to this unappealing consequence, Sen proposed the *Weak Equity Axiom*, requiring that when an individual has a lower level of utility than another at all levels of income, the optimal allocation must not give less income to him than to the other.

Second, the theory of social choice, as early as in Arrow's seminal monograph (Arrow 1963), has called attention to the issue of inequalities due to personal characteristics, and the notion of extended sympathy was coined to make it possible to evaluate such inequalities. But it did not clearly identify tools to deal with the separation between characteristics that call for compensation and other characteristics, and that was indeed a difficult exercise in the purely abstract framework of social choice, in which transfers of resources are not even explicitly described.

The third origin of the literature presented here is the theory of equity, which was formulated in economic models and therefore was equipped with more precise concepts to evaluate inequalities. In Kolm (1972), a general approach to the assessment of equity based on partial sets of individual characteristics was already proposed, with a full range of criteria going from the most restrictive, equity as No-Envy on resources, to the most comprehensive, justice as equal utility. But this first step was largely ignored, although the related issue of compensating for productivity handicaps was raised by Pazner and Schmeidler (1974) in the model of production with unequal skills, and their negative result about the general existence of efficient and envy-free allocations triggered some research effort, but the resulting literature simply tried to define weaker notions of equity, without relating this difficulty to the general compensation problem.

The fourth source of inspiration was the Rawlsian tradition in political philosophy, initiated by Rawls (1971) and developed by Dworkin (1981a, 1981b), Arneson (1989), Cohen (1989), Sen (1985), and van Parijs (1995), and also commented upon by Roemer (1985a, 1986). This philosophical literature gave a strong endorsement to egalitarian goals, but under the various names of "equality of opportunities," "equal access," or "equal resources," it made the point that it may be reasonable to deny compensation for some welfare deficits, laying the stress on the importance of compensating individuals only for handicaps for which they should not be deemed responsible.

We now briefly summarize the main insights obtained in the more recent theory of compensation, and introduce some basic concepts. One first contribution of the literature reviewed here is a distinction of several relevant ethical issues in the problem of compensation. At first glance, it may appear that the goal of compensating for handicaps, or equalizing opportunities, is a simple goal. But consider the following example.

Example 1 Suppose that individual welfare is determined by the formula

$$u = (x + y)\,z,$$

where x, y, and z are real numbers. The quantity x denotes an external resource allocated by redistributive policies, y is social background, and z is a measure of personal effort and merit. Assume that y and z are independently distributed, and that each of these two variables takes on the values 1 and 3 in equal proportions. The population is then partitioned into four subgroups of equal size, as depicted in the following table:

$y \backslash z$	1	3
1	*the "undeserving poor"*	*the "deserving poor"*
3	*the "undeserving rich"*	*the "deserving rich"*

We assume that the *per capita* amount of available external resource is 4, and that it can be freely allocated among the four subgroups. Let us consider that the goal of redistributive policy is to compensate for inequalities in social background y, whereas inequalities due to personal merit z are deemed acceptable. What kind of policy is adequate in this perspective? A natural candidate is to seek equality of $x+y$ across all individuals. This is achieved by policy A described in the following table:

Policy A

$y \backslash z$	1	3
1	$x=5$ $u=6$	$x=5$ $u=18$
3	$x=3$ $u=6$	$x=3$ $u=18$

Assuming that individuals are in control of variable z, one can consider in this case that equality of opportunity is perfectly achieved, since every individual, after transfer, has a welfare function equal to $u=6z$.

But the simplicity of this solution hides several different underlying ethical values. In order to see this, consider an alternative policy:

Policy B

$y \backslash z$	1	3
1	$x=2$ $u=3$	$x=8$ $u=27$
3	$x=0$ $u=3$	$x=6$ $u=27$

This alternative policy no longer equalizes $x+y$ across individuals, and displays a strong bias in favor of the "deserving" subpopulation. But one can still argue that it compensates for social background y, and even that it equalizes opportunities. Indeed, in any subpopulation with equal z, social background is not a source of welfare inequality under policy B, and every individual, after transfer, faces the same welfare function: $u=3$ if $z=1$; $u=27$ if $z=3$.

These examples of policies show that compensating for inequalities in variable y does not require equalizing $x+y$ over the whole population, but only within the "deserving" subpopulation and within the "undeserving" subpopulation, separately. This, by itself, is generally insufficient to determine fully what redistributive policy is the best. Additional ethical principles are needed to determine how to allocate resources between the "deserving" and the "undeserving" subpopulations. These additional principles will define the appropriate relationship between merit (z) and welfare (u) over the population. In brief, they will decide how merit should be rewarded. The two policies proposed in this example illustrate two different "reward principles." Policy A illustrates an approach that is prominent in the philosophical literature as well as in the literature surveyed in the beginning of this chapter. It expresses a desire of neutrality by avoiding any redistribution on the basis of merit. If, as expressed above, inequalities due to personal merit z are deemed acceptable, it may seem quite reasonable not to interfere with the consequences of such inequalities. The population is then left to bear the consequences of differential merit, without any bias in favor of a subpopulation. Policy B, in contrast, does display a bias in favor of the deserving subpopulation, and such a bias may be justified by a sum-utilitarian view of social welfare. Indeed, policy B maximizes the sum of individual utilities, under the constraint that social background inequalities be fully neutralized. The deserving subpopulation is favored under this policy because, by its own effort and merit, it is more able to transform resources into welfare. Measuring social welfare by the sum is usually considered appropriate when one has no preference for equality in the distribution of welfare, and since inequalities due to differential merit are deemed acceptable it may seem reasonable to adopt a utilitarian approach toward such inequalities.

This example highlights the main ethical principles that will be relevant in this chapter. First, there is a "*principle of compensation*" (Barry 1991, Fleurbaey 1995a), whose limited and separate scope is to neutralize the differential influence over agents' outcomes of the characteristics that elicit compensation.[2] Informally, it is expressed in terms of making sure that such characteristics do not entail by themselves inequalities in final outcomes, or simply that opportunities are made equal. This may be translated into the requirement that any pair of agents who differ only in characteristics to be compensated should obtain equal outcomes. It is also present in the idea that if all unequal characteristics were to be compensated, full equality of outcomes should be the goal. And it will also be shown to underlie the idea that changes in the population profile of characteristics to be compensated should benefit or harm all individuals, in solidarity.

Then, there are various independent reward principles, and two of them are significant in the literature. The first principle, illustrated by policy A in Example 1, is to neutrally respect inequalities entailed by other characteristics. It is usually introduced through the argument that differences in such characteristics should not entail any compensatory redistribution, or that agents who differ only in such characteristics should be submitted to equal treatment in terms of resource allocation or transfers. It is also behind the idea that if all agents were identical in the characteristics that elicit compensation, there would be no reason to make any transfer between the agents. It may also be shown to underlie various requirements that the redistributive policy should be independent in some way of the population profile of characteristics that do not elicit compensation. This reward principle was called the "*principle of natural reward*" in Fleurbaey (1995a), in reference to the fact that by taking a neutral attitude one does not advocate any

[2] This is to be distinguished from the Kaldor–Hicks "Compensation Principle," which has to do with the gains of a subpopulation compensating the losses of the rest of the population.

"artificial" reward favoring the agents who exercise their responsibility in a particular way.[3] This principle receives a strong backing in the philosophical literature. In particular, Rawls's and Dworkin's theories of equality of resources[4] are built around the core principle that once resources are properly equalized, just institutions may let individual welfare be freely determined by the exercise of individual responsibility in the formation of one's view of life, personal ambitions, and goals. No favor should be granted to any subpopulation in virtue of how it exercises its responsibility in this respect. Although Arneson and Cohen disagree with Rawls's and Dworkin's definition of the sphere of individual responsibility,[5] they also endorse a similar reward principle.[6]

The alternative, *utilitarian*, reward principle (illustrated by policy B in Example 1) is adopted by a few authors in the literature on equality of opportunities.[7] The idea is that, since inequalities due to characteristics of responsibility are acceptable, the social objective should simply be to maximize the sum of individual outcomes, once the undue influence of characteristics calling for compensation has properly been taken into account. There are different ways in which this undue influence can be reckoned, and

[3] Barry (1991) proposed calling it "the principle of responsibility," and a similar terminology is retained in part of the literature reviewed here, e.g., Fleurbaey and Maniquet (1998), Maniquet (2004). This raises the issue of deciding whether "artificial" rewards really impede the exercise of responsibility. Imagine that transfers are made so as to make the reward scheme steeper than it would naturally be (effort is rewarded more than naturally). This is exemplified by policy B in Example 1. It is dubious that this diminishes the degree of responsibility that agents can exercise, although this violates the principle of natural reward.

[4] See in particular Rawls (1982) and Dworkin (1981b, 2000).

[5] Instead of considering that individuals should be responsible for their ambitions and use of resources, they argue that individuals should be deemed responsible only for their genuine choices (ambitions and preferences may be influenced in various ways, in which case, according to Arneson and Cohen, individuals should not be held responsible for such characteristics).

[6] "We should ... compensate only for those welfare deficits which are not in some way traceable to the individual's choices" (Cohen 1989, p. 914). "Distributive justice does not recommend any intervention by society to correct inequalities that arise through the voluntary choice or fault of those who end up with less, so long as it is proper to hold the individuals responsible for the voluntary choice or faulty behavior that gives rise to the inequalities" (Arneson 1990, p. 176—see, however, Arneson 2000, p. 344 for a more nuanced view). These authors do not seem to consider the possibility of a policy like policy B in Example 1, which actually *widens* inequalities due to responsibility characteristics. Consider a modified version of Example 1, with $u = 20 - 100/(x + y)z$. In this modified example, a low utility now implies a high marginal utility. Then policy A, in which only inequalities due to y are corrected, leads to $u = 3.33$ for $z = 1$ and $u = 14.44$ for $z = 3$. In contrast, a utilitarian planner maximizing the sum of utilities under the constraint that a poor receives two units more of x than a rich (compensation for y) would choose policy B′:

Policy B′

$y \backslash z$	1	3
1	$x = 6.61$ $u = 6.86$	$x = 3.39$ $u = 12.41$
3	$x = 4.61$ $u = 6.86$	$x = 1.39$ $u = 12.41$

partially correcting inequalities due to z as well because the undeserving have a high marginal utility.

[7] See in particular Roemer (1993, 1998), Van de gaer (1993), and Vallentyne (2002).

therefore different *modified utilitarian social welfare functions* in this branch of the literature, to be presented. Interestingly, the thesis that it would be legitimate to make transfers not only toward those with characteristics to be compensated, but also in favor of those who exercise responsibility in a "good" way (i.e., in such a way as to increase their marginal utility), seems never to have been supported explicitly in the philosophical literature that has been quoted here. The contrast between the natural reward principle and the utilitarian reward principle reflects a deep opposition, in welfare economics and political philosophy, between two views of what it means to be indifferent to inequalities. One view, which inspires the natural reward principle, is based on the libertarian principle that the state should then remain neutral and refrain from tampering with the distribution. The alternative view, based on the utilitarian doctrine, is that the state may intervene and possibly alter the distribution, in order to promote the global good.

The literature to be reviewed here has clarified the distinctions and logical independence between the principle of compensation and the reward principles. In addition, it has also revealed that there exist tensions between the principle of compensation and the reward principles. In particular, as will be explained in various contexts, one often finds logical incompatibility between axioms representing the principle of compensation and axioms representing the natural reward principle. Roughly, the reason is that transfers designed to fully compensate for undue inequalities may sometimes automatically alter the distribution in a way that is clearly non-neutral. This happens when the influence of characteristics that elicit compensation is not separable from the influence of the other individual characteristics. This raises an interesting ethical dilemma, because when the incompatibility arises, the social allocation of resources has to reflect one of the two ethical principles (compensation or natural reward) more than the other one. One might think that the principle of compensation, largely endorsed in the literature, is obviously the one that should be given priority in such a conflict. But this is far from obvious, as illustrated in the following example.

Example 2 This example retains the main data of Example 1, but the welfare function is now modified into

$$u = xz + y.$$

One interpretation of this function is that personal effort z makes one more sensitive to external resources x. For instance, the deserving poor ($y = 1$, $z = 3$) respond very well to transfers of resources ($u = 3x + 1$), whereas such transfers are rather ineffective for the undeserving poor (for whom $y = z = 1$, so that $u = x + 1$).

Here is a policy that fully achieves compensation, so that inequalities in y do not create welfare differences, and every individual faces the same ex post welfare function: $u = 6$ if $z = 1$; $u = 14$ if $z = 3$.

This policy is not strongly biased in favor of the deserving or the undeserving, since both subpopulations receive half of the total resources. Nonetheless, within the poor

Policy A1

$y \backslash z$	1	3
1	$x = 5$ $u = 6$	$x = 4.333$ $u = 14$
3	$x = 3$ $u = 6$	$x = 3.666$ $u = 14$

subpopulation ($y = 1$), a bias seems to be expressed in favor of the undeserving (who receive a larger x than the deserving), whereas the reverse occurs within the rich subpopulation. Moreover, one may object to fully compensating the undeserving poor. Indeed, if such people are responsible for the low $z = 1$, which makes their welfare little sensitive to transfers, one may question compensating them not only for a low y, but also, indirectly, for a low z. Similarly, one may object to full compensation among the deserving, and consider that the remarkable effort made by the deserving poor is not a reason to give them a smaller differential of resources (the differential of x between poor and rich is 2 among the undeserving, and only 2/3 among the deserving).

A similar objection could be made under a different interpretation of the variables. Suppose that the welfare function $xz + y$ reflects subjective preferences about combinations of external and internal resources (x, y). Under this new interpretation, the undeserving are simply y-lovers, whereas the deserving are x-lovers. The undeserving poor consider that they have a deep handicap, whereas the deserving poor consider that their handicap is mild. A full compensation policy such as A1 tries to cater to both opinions at the same time, giving a strong transfer to poor y-lovers, and a small one to poor x-lovers. One may object that there is no reason to accept two different evaluations of the handicap of having a low y, and that society should define its transfer policy on the basis of a consistent evaluation of handicaps.[8]

Whatever the interpretation of the example, such objections to full compensation may lead to an alternative policy like the following one, which is more in line with the natural reward principle.

Policy A2

$y \backslash z$	1	3
1	$x = 4.5$ $u = 5.5$	$x = 4.5$ $u = 14.5$
3	$x = 3.5$ $u = 6.5$	$x = 3.5$ $u = 13.5$

[8] For such a criticism of the principle of compensation, see van Parijs (1997).

In this policy, the poor receive the same differential amount of x, independently of their merit (or preference, under the alternative interpretation). This particular policy performs compensation under the assumption that everyone could have $z = 2$. Indeed with this value of z, a poor would get $u = 2 \times 4.5 + 1 = 10$, just like a rich, for whom $u = 2 \times 3.5 + 3 = 10$. As a consequence, of course, compensation is no longer achieved within each subpopulation. The undeserving poor are not fully compensated, and the deserving poor are more than compensated.

Notice that policy A1 is not the only one to achieve compensation, and similarly, policy A2 is not the only one to comply with the idea of natural reward. As explained in the next section, one may narrow the set of admissible policies by combining one of the two principles with axioms expressing mild versions of the other principle.

There appears also to be a dilemma between the principle of compensation and the utilitarian reward principle, since the modified utilitarian social welfare functions often fail to select allocations that achieve full compensation. This is explained below.

Finally, the contribution of the theory of compensation is not only a clarification of the concepts and an analysis of ethical dilemmas and conflicts of values. It has produced a variety of solutions, allocation rules, and social objectives, which embody the relevant ethical principles and determine precise ways of defining appropriate compensatory policies. Many results take the form of axiomatic characterizations, which are helpful in showing the logical links between some basic ethical principles, expressed in various axioms, and possible redistributive solutions. Some of these solutions are actually observed in various institutions and policies, and this literature contributes to enlarging the set of options available to policy-makers confronted with compensation issues.

This chapter is organized as follows. The next section, Section 2, reviews the results obtained in the basic model describing the case when there is no production, and only one good (such as money) is transferable in order to compensate for handicaps (as in Examples 1 and 2 above). Section 3 is devoted to the Mirrlees–Pazner–Schmeidler model of cooperative production in which the individual characteristics to be compensated are unequal productive skills. Section 4 is devoted to the literature that adopts the utilitarian kind of reward or, more generally, deals with an abstract social choice framework. Section 5 reviews other related parts of the literature.[9]

The main mathematical conventions and notations in this chapter are as follows. The set of real (resp. non-negative, positive) numbers is $\mathbb{R}$ (resp. $\mathbb{R}_+$, $\mathbb{R}_{++}$). Vector inequalities are denoted $\geq, >, \gg$, and set inclusion is denoted $\subseteq$, $\subset$. The symbol $\geq_{\text{lex}}$ denotes the leximin (lexicographic maximin) criterion applied to vectors of real numbers. Namely, $x \geq_{\text{lex}} x'$ if the smallest component of x is greater than the smallest component of x', or they are equal and the second smallest component of x is greater than the second

[9] In Fleurbaey (1998) one can find another survey that emphasizes the link between the economic and the philosophical literatures. See also Peragine (1999), for a survey focused on the notion of opportunity, and Suzumura and Yoshihara (2000).

smallest component of x', and so on. A function $f : A^n \to A$ is said to be idempotent if for all $a \in A, f(a, \ldots, a) = a$. For any set N, let Π_N denote the set of permutations over N (i.e., bijections from N to N). For any function $f : A \to B$, let $f(A) \subseteq B$ denote the range of f. An ordering is a binary relation that is reflexive and transitive. For any set A, $\#A$ denotes its cardinality.

2. FAIR MONETARY COMPENSATION

This section deals with the case when the transferable resource by which compensation of handicaps is performed is not produced and is one-dimensional.[10] This is relevant to various practical problems of compensation, especially the allocation of a central budget to several agencies or administrative units with some autonomy in management. It may be applied to social assistance toward disabled individuals when the impact of redistribution on earning incentives is null (e.g., the population under consideration does not work) or may be ignored (fixed labor supply). Such impact on incentives is taken into account in the model studied in the next section.

This section starts with a description of the model. We then list the various solutions that have been proposed for the compensation problem, and review the axiomatic analysis of the relevant ethical principles. The last subsection focuses on the particular case of quasi-linear utilities, which has attracted much attention in the literature.

2.1. The Model

There are several ways of modeling this problem, which are almost equivalent. One possibility is to have an ordering $\succeq$ defined over triples (x, y, z), where x is an amount of transferable resource, y is a characteristic that elicits compensation, and z a characteristic that does not elicit compensation. This ordering describes the agents' performances, and

$$(x_i, y_i, z_i) \succeq (x_j, y_j, z_j)$$

means that agent i is at least as well-off as agent j. One may also use a function representing this ordering: $f(x_i, y_i, z_i)$ is then agent i's outcome or performance (well-being, income, etc.). One may also simply write this function as $u_i(x_i, y_i)$, where the mapping $u_i(.,.)$ itself incorporates the influence of parameter z_i.

Another approach, adopted by Fleurbaey (1994, 1995d) and Iturbe-Ormaetxe and Nieto (1996), simply endows every agent with preferences over pairs (x, y). This

[10] The literature reviewed in this section includes Bossert (1995), Bossert and Fleurbaey (1996), Bossert, Fleurbaey, and Van de gaer (1999), Cappelen and Tungodden (2002, 2003), Fleurbaey (1994, 1995c, 1995d), Iturbe-Ormaetxe (1997), Iturbe-Ormaetxe and Nieto (1996), Maniquet (2004), Moulin (1994), Sprumont (1997), and Tungodden (2005).

approach is more parsimonious in terms of information, because no interpersonal comparison of outcome is made in this case. Notice, however, that preferences over (x, y) contain more than the usual consumer preferences over commodities, since y is a nontransferable personal characteristic.

It turns out that whatever the approach, the main solutions to this problem do not use more information than these personal, ordinal noncomparable, preferences over pairs (x, y). Since this can be viewed as an interesting ethical conclusion in itself, we adopt here the richer framework with fully interpersonally comparable utilities $u_i(x_i, y_i)$ so as to highlight the way in which interpersonal comparisons of well-being are eventually ruled out, somewhat paradoxically, in the compensation problem.

An *economy* is denoted $e = (y_N, u_N, \Omega)$, where $N = \{1, \ldots, n\}$ is a finite population of size n, $y_N = (y_1, \ldots, y_n)$ is the profile of characteristics to be compensated (hereafter called *talents*), $u_N = (u_1, \ldots, u_n)$ is the profile of *utility functions*, and $\Omega \in \mathbb{R}_{++}$ is the amount of *resource* to be allocated among the population. An agent's utility function u_i, for $i \in N$, is defined over pairs (x, y), where x is a quantity of resource and y a personal talent, and, since utilities are assumed to be fully interpersonally comparable, we can, for instance, say that agent i is at least as well-off as agent j if

$$u_i(x_i, y_i) \geq u_j(x_j, y_j).$$

A pair (x_i, y_i) will be called hereafter a bundle of "extended resources."

An *allocation* is a vector $x_N = (x_1, \ldots, x_n) \in \mathbb{R}^n_+$. It is *feasible* if $\sum_{i \in N} x_i = \Omega$. The set of feasible allocations for the economy e is denoted $F(e)$. Notice that, when utility functions are increasing in x, all feasible allocations are Pareto-optimal in this setting (since we did not assume free disposal in the definition of feasibility).

An *allocation rule* is a correspondence S such that for every e in a given domain, $S(e)$ is a subset of feasible allocations in e. Although the literature reviewed in this section has almost exclusively dealt with allocation rules,[11] we will here make allusions to social ordering functions as well. A *social ordering function* is a mapping R such that for every e in a given domain, $R(e)$ is a complete ordering over the set of allocations $\mathbb{R}^n_+$. We write $x_N R(e) x'_N$ (resp., $x_N P(e) x'_N$, $x_N I(e) x'_N$) to mean that x_N is weakly better than x'_N (resp., strictly better than, indifferent to). The social ordering function R is said to *rationalize* the allocation rule S on some domain if for every e in this domain,

$$S(e) = \{x_N \in F(e) \mid \forall x'_N \in F(e),\ x_N R(e) x'_N\}.$$

The main domain of economies considered here, denoted $\mathcal{E}$, is the set of economies such that: $n \geq 2$; $y_N \in Y^n$, where Y is a given set with at least two elements; for all

[11] The exceptions are Bossert, Fleurbaey, and Van de gaer (1999) and Maniquet (2004).

i, $u_i : \mathbb{R}_+ \times Y \to \mathbb{R}$ is continuous and strictly increasing in the first argument. Let $\mathcal{U}$ denote the set of such utility functions.

This model bears a strong similarity with the model of fair allocation of indivisible goods with money, studied by Svensson (1983) and others. The current model studies what would happen in that model if indivisible goods were already allocated arbitrarily, and only money could still be transferred. The current model also bears some similarity with the bankruptcy model (Aumann and Maschler 1985, O'Neill 1982, Young 1987), in which some money must be allocated on the basis of claims. The current model represents the claims not as simple and fixed demands of money, but as expressions of needs and preferences. On these two related models, see Thomson (Chapter 21 in this volume).

2.2. Fairness as No-Envy, and Related Solutions

A central notion in the literature on fair allocations[12] is No-Envy, suggested by Foley (1967) and analyzed by Kolm (1972), Pazner and Schmeidler (1974), and Varian (1974). In brief, No-Envy is obtained when no agent would rather have another's bundle of resources. This notion appears to be very relevant to the problem of compensation, but some precautions must be taken in its application. Indeed, in the current model one can apply the No-Envy requirement in two ways, either on external resources only:

$$\forall i,j,\ u_i(x_i, y_i) \geq u_i(x_j, y_i),$$

or on extended bundles:[13]

$$\forall i,j,\ u_i(x_i, y_i) \geq u_i(x_j, y_j).$$

The first option is inappropriate, since in this model it is equivalent to

$$\forall i,j,\ x_i \geq x_j,$$

and therefore entails $x_i = \Omega/n$ for all i, which prevents any compensation of inequalities in y. In contrast, the second option is quite reasonable as an expression of the principle of

[12] This literature is surveyed in Thomson (see Chapter 21).

[13] Under the alternative formulation $u_i = f(x_i, y_i, z_i)$, one can think of a third kind of application:

$$\forall i,j, f(x_i, y_i, z_i) \geq f(x_j, y_j, z_j),$$

which directly implies full equality of utilities over the population.

compensation as well as of the principle of natural reward.[14] In line with compensation, two agents i,j with the same utility function $u_i = u_j$ will end up with equal utility levels:

$$\left.\begin{array}{r} u_i(x_i, y_i) \geq u_i(x_j, y_j) \\ u_j(x_j, y_j) \geq u_j(x_i, y_i) \end{array}\right\} \Rightarrow u_i(x_i, y_i) = u_j(x_j, y_j),$$

implying full compensation between them. And in line with natural reward, two agents with the same talent $y_i = y_j$ will receive the same resource:

$$\left.\begin{array}{r} u_i(x_i, y_i) \geq u_i(x_j, y_j) \\ u_j(x_j, y_j) \geq u_j(x_i, y_i) \end{array}\right\} \Rightarrow \left.\begin{array}{r} x_i \geq x_j \\ x_j \geq x_i \end{array}\right\} \Rightarrow x_i = x_j,$$

which prevents any biased transfer between agents who differ only in their utility function. This can be illustrated with Example 1.

Example 1 (pursued) When agent i has a utility function $u_i(x, y) = (x + y)\, z_i$, the No-Envy condition applied to extended resources implies

$$\forall i,j,\ x_i + y_i \geq x_j + y_j,$$

which entails equality of $x + y$ over the whole population, as performed by policy A. This policy is the only one to comply with the No-Envy condition.

In summary, No-Envy is a test of equality of resources, and can be used as a test of compensation provided it bears on extended resources.

No-Envy Allocation Rule (S_{NE}, Foley 1967, Roemer 1985b, Fleurbaey 1994)
$\forall e \in \mathcal{E}$, $\forall x_N \in F(e)$,

$$x_N \in S_{NE}(e) \Leftrightarrow \forall i,j \in N,\ u_i(x_i, y_i) \geq u_i(x_j, y_j).$$

It is immediate to see in simple examples that this allocation rule is likely to be empty in many nonpathological economies. Assume for instance that for any given x, agent i prefers agent j's talent to her own, and conversely. Then any transfer will just increase the envy of one of them. With Example 2 one has a less extreme illustration of this difficulty.

[14] Apart from Kolm (1972), in which No-Envy is considered for any combination of external resources and personal characteristics, early attempts to apply the notion of No-Envy to the compensation of handicaps were problematic. Champsaur and Laroque (1981) limited the No-Envy test to external resources and concluded negatively but unsurprisingly the impossibility of making income transfers in favor of handicapped agents. Roemer (1985b) applied the No-Envy test to extended resources but failed to allow people to feel envy for others' personal characteristics, therefore concluding also negatively about the compensation performed through application of the No-Envy test (see Fleurbaey 1994 for a discussion).

Example 2 (pursued) When agent i has a utility function $u_i(x,y) = xz_i + y$, the No-Envy condition applied to extended resources entails

$$\forall i,j,\ x_i z_i + y_i \geq x_j z_i + y_j,$$

For instance, take i among the undeserving poor, and j among the deserving rich. One then must have

$$\begin{cases} x_i + 1 \geq x_j + 3 \\ 3x_j + 3 \geq 3x_i + 1 \end{cases} \Leftrightarrow x_j + 2 \leq x_i \leq x_j + 2/3,$$

which is impossible. Agent i requires a large transfer not to be envious, which renders agent j envious.

This problem is similar to that encountered by Pazner and Schmeidler (1974) in the model of production with unequal skills (see Section 3), and a line of research is to look for nice weakenings of the No-Envy condition that reduce the nonexistence problem.

Here are three examples of allocation rules derived from this idea. The first one combines two ideas separately proposed by Feldman and Kirman (1974), who suggested to choose allocations with the minimal number of occurrences of envy, and by Daniel (1975), who suggested to choose allocations where the number of agents envying any given agent is equal to the number of agents this agent envies. For any economy e, let $B(e)$ be the set of such "balanced" allocations: $x_N \in B(e)$ if and only if $x_N \in F(e)$ and for all $i \in N$,

$$\#\{j \in N \mid u_j(x_i, y_i) > u_j(x_j, y_j)\} = \#\{j \in N \mid u_i(x_i, y_i) < u_i(x_j, y_j)\},$$

and let $E(e, x_N)$ denote the number of envy occurrences in allocation x_N:

$$E(e, x_N) = \#\{(i,j) \in N^2 \mid u_i(x_i, y_i) < u_i(x_j, y_j)\}.$$

Balanced and Minimal Envy (S_{BME}, Fleurbaey 1994)
$\forall e \in \mathcal{E}$, $\forall x_N \in F(e)$,

$$x_N \in S_{BME}(e) \Leftrightarrow x_N \in B(e) \text{ and } \forall x'_N \in B(e),\ E(e, x'_N) \geq E(e, x_N).$$

Fleurbaey (1994) shows that a sufficient condition for $S_{BME}(e)$ to be nonempty is:[15]

$$\exists \delta > 0, \forall x_N \in F(e), \exists i \in N, x_i > 0,$$
$$\#\{j \in N \mid u_i(x_i, y_i) < u_i(x_j, y_j)\} \leq \#\{j \in N \mid u_j(x_i, y_i) \geq u_j(x_j + \delta, y_j)\}.$$

[15] As shown in Fleurbaey (1994), this condition is logically weaker than the conditions given in Daniel (1975).

The second solution was proposed in a more general context by Diamantaras and Thomson (1990). It tries to minimize the intensity of envy, this intensity being measured for every agent by the resource needed to make this agent non-envious. An advantage of this rule is that it is single-valued.

Minimax Envy Intensity (S_{MEI}, **Diamantaras and Thomson 1990, Fleurbaey 1994)**
$\forall e \in \mathcal{E}, \forall x_N \in F(e)$,

$$x_N \in S_{MEI}(e) \Leftrightarrow \forall x'_N \in F(e), \max_{i \in N} EI_i(e, x'_N) \geq \max_{i \in N} EI_i(e, x_N),$$

where $EI_i(e,x_N) = \min\{\delta \in \mathbb{R} \mid \forall j \in N \setminus \{i\}, u_i(x_i + \delta, y_i) \geq u_i(x_j, y_j)\}$.[16]

The third solution makes use of all agents' opinions about the relative well-being of two agents. It tries to minimize the size of subsets of agents thinking that one agent is worse-off than another agent. It takes inspiration from van Parijs' scheme of "undominated diversity" (van Parijs 1990), which seeks to avoid situations in which one agent is deemed unanimously worse-off than another one, and from the family of solutions put forth by Iturbe-Ormaetxe and Nieto (1996), which generalizes van Parijs' idea and seeks to avoid such a unanimity among a subgroup of a given size and containing the worse-off agent. The following solution selects the allocations that, across pairs of agents (i,j), minimize the size of the groups of agents who find that agent j is strictly better off than agent i. Let

$$I_i^m = \{G \subset N \mid \#G = m, i \in G\}.$$

Minimal Unanimous Domination (S_{MUD}, **Fleurbaey 1994, Iturbe-Ormaetxe and Nieto 1996)**
$\forall e \in \mathcal{E}, \forall x_N \in F(e)$,

$$x_N \in S_{MUD}(e) \Leftrightarrow \exists m \in \{1, \ldots, n\},$$
$$\begin{cases} \text{(i) } \forall i,j \in N, \forall G \in I_i^m, \exists k \in G, u_k(x_i, y_i) \geq u_k(x_j, y_j), \\ \text{(ii) } \forall p < m, \forall x'_N \in F(e), \exists i,j \in N, \exists G \in I_i^p, \\ \qquad \forall k \in G, u_k(x'_i, y_i) < u_k(x'_j, y_j). \end{cases}$$

Fleurbaey (1994) states that $S_{MUD}(e)$ is nonempty if

$$\forall i,j \in N, \exists k \in N, u_k\left(\frac{\Omega}{n-1}, y_i\right) \geq u_k(0, y_j),$$

[16] This rule is well-defined only in economies where $EI_i(e, x_N)$ is bounded from above, namely, in economies where

$$\forall i,j \in N, \exists x \in \mathbb{R}_+, u_i(x, y_i) \geq u_i(\Omega, y_j).$$

and Iturbe-Ormaetxe and Nieto (1996) give an alternative sufficient condition:

$$\forall x_N \in F(e), \exists i, k \in N, x_i > 0, \forall j \in N,\ u_k(x_i, y_i) \geq u_k(x_j, y_j).$$

This rule makes a very indirect use of the No-Envy test, and can be viewed as aggregating the opinions of the population over the transfers of resources to be made between two given agents. Along this line another kind of allocation rule has been proposed, which makes use of one preference relation at a time in order to look for equality of extended resources. Aggregation of opinions can then be made in two ways. Either the preference relation used in the computation of the allocation can be based on the profile of preferences in the population, as in an Arrovian social choice problem. Or aggregation can be made at the level of allocations, for instance by averaging the allocations obtained by taking every agent's preferences in turn as the reference. This suggests two different sorts of allocation rules. Let Φ be a mapping from $\bigcup_{n\geq 1} \mathcal{U}^n$ to $\mathcal{U}$.

Φ-Conditional Equality ($S_{\Phi CE}$, Fleurbaey 1995d)
$\forall e \in \mathcal{E},\ \forall x_N \in F(e)$,

$$x_N \in S_{\Phi CE}(e) \Leftrightarrow \forall i, j \in N,\ \tilde{u}(x_i, y_i) = \tilde{u}(x_j, y_j) \text{ or } \left[\tilde{u}(x_j, y_j) > \tilde{u}(x_i, y_i) \text{ and } x_j = 0\right],$$

where $\tilde{u} = \Phi(u_1, \ldots, u_n)$.

Notice that equality of extended resources is performed here on the basis of the maximin criterion, because it may be impossible to fully compensate some inequalities in personal characteristics with the available resources. In that case some inequalities in well-being persist and the better-off agents are left with no external resource, while only disadvantaged agents receive positive resources (and all of them have the same well-being according to the reference preferences).

Average Conditional Equality (S_{ACE}, Fleurbaey 1995d)
$\forall e \in \mathcal{E},\ \forall x_N \in F(e)$,

$$x_N \in S_{ACE}(e) \Leftrightarrow x_N = \frac{1}{n}\sum_{k=1}^{n} x^k,$$

where

$$\forall i, j, k \in N,\ u_k(x_i^k, y_i) = u_k(x_j^k, y_j) \text{ or } \left[u_k(x_i^k, y_i) < u_k(x_j^k, y_j) \text{ and } x_j^k = 0\right].$$

The Average Conditional Equality rule can be generalized by allowing the weights between the n proposed allocations x^k to differ. This can be done without violating anonymity. For instance, one could argue that allocations based on minority preferences should be overweighted, or, on the contrary, underweighted, or that certain talents should entail a greater weight.

By construction, these two allocation rules are nonempty on the whole domain $\mathcal{E}$ of economies considered here, and they are single-valued. Moreover, the Conditional Equality rule can be immediately interpreted as derived from a social ordering function that rationalizes it,[17] and is defined as follows.

Φ-Conditional Equality ($R_{\Phi CE}$, **Roemer 1993, Bossert, Fleurbaey, and Van de gaer 1999**)
$\forall e \in \mathcal{E}, \forall x_N, x'_N \in \mathbb{R}^n_+,$

$$x_N R_{\Phi CE}(e) x'_N \Leftrightarrow (\tilde{u}(x_i, y_i))_{i\in N} \geq_{\text{lex}} \left(\tilde{u}(x'_i, y_i)\right)_{i\in N},$$

where $\tilde{u} = \Phi(u_1, \ldots, u_n)$.

A rather different approach is inspired by the Egalitarian Equivalence criterion proposed by Pazner and Schmeidler (1978a), which can be easily adapted to the current framework. The idea is to render all agents indifferent between their current bundle of extended resources (x_i, y_i) and a reference bundle that is the same for all. Again this suggests two (families of) allocation rules, depending on whether some unique reference talent $\tilde{y}$ is used to compute Egalitarian Equivalent allocations, or the reference $\tilde{y}$ varies and the average of the resulting allocations is retained. Let Ψ be a mapping from $\bigcup_{n\geq 1} Y^n$ to Y.

Ψ-Egalitarian Equivalence ($S_{\Psi EE}$, **Pazner and Schmeidler 1978a, Fleurbaey 1995d**)
$\forall e \in \mathcal{E}, \forall x_N \in F(e),$

$$\begin{aligned} &x_N \in S_{\Psi EE}(e) \Leftrightarrow \exists \tilde{x} \in \mathbb{R}_+,\\ &\forall i,j \in N, u_i(x_i, y_i) = u_i(\tilde{x}, \tilde{y}) \text{ or } \left[u_i(x_i, y_i) > u_i(\tilde{x}, \tilde{y}) \text{ and } x_i = 0\right], \end{aligned}$$

where $\tilde{y} = \Psi(y_1, \ldots, y_n)$.

Average Egalitarian Equivalence (S_{AEE}, **Moulin 1994**)
$\forall e \in \mathcal{E}, \forall x_N \in F(e),$

$$x_N \in S_{AEE}(e) \Leftrightarrow x_N = \frac{1}{n}\sum_{k=1}^{n} x^k,$$

[17] The Minimax Envy Intensity allocation rule is also rationalized by a social ordering function, defined as follows.

Minimax Envy Intensity (R_{MEI})
$\forall e \in \mathcal{E}, \forall x_N, x'_N \in \mathbb{R}^n_+,$

$$x_N R_{MEI}(e) x'_N \Leftrightarrow (-IE_i(e, x_N))_{i\in N} \geq_{\text{lex}} \left(-IE_i(e, x'_N)\right)_{i\in N}.$$

But this social ordering function does not satisfy the Pareto criterion, since one may have $x_N R_{MEI}(e) x'_N$ and $x'_N \gg x_N$. In particular, it would no longer rationalize S_{MEI} under a free disposal assumption.

where

$$\forall k \in N, \exists \tilde{x} \in \mathbb{R}_+, \forall i \in N,$$
$$u_i(x_i^k, y_i) = u_i(\tilde{x}, y_k) \text{ or } \left[u_i(x_i^k, y_i) > u_i(\tilde{x}, y_k) \text{ and } x_i^k = 0\right].$$

These allocation rules are single-valued but may be empty over the domain $\mathcal{E}$. For convenience we will consider here the subdomain $\mathcal{E}'$ of economies with utility functions such that

$$\forall y \in Y,\ u(0, y) = 0$$

and

$$\forall y, y' \in Y, \forall x \in \mathbb{R}_+, \exists x' \in \mathbb{R}_+,\ u(x', y') \geq u(x, y).$$

On this subdomain these two allocation rules are nonempty.[18] The Egalitarian Equivalent allocation rule is rationalized on $\mathcal{E}'$ by the following social ordering function. This social ordering function applies the leximin criterion to the individual levels of resource x^*, which would make the agents accept the reference talent $\tilde{y}$ instead of their current situation (x_i, y_i). This gives priority to the agents with a low x^*, that is, agents who either have a low x_i or dislike their talent y_i.

Ψ-Egalitarian Equivalence ($R_{\Psi EE}$, Pazner and Schmeidler 1978a, Bossert, Fleurbaey, and Van de gaer 1999)
$\forall e \in \mathcal{E}', \forall x_N, x'_N \in \mathbb{R}^n_+,$

$$x_N R_{\Psi EE}(e) x'_N \Leftrightarrow (\hat{x}(x_i, y_i, u_i, \tilde{y}))_{i \in N} \geq_{\text{lex}} (\hat{x}(x'_i, y_i, u_i, \tilde{y}))_{i \in N},$$

where $\tilde{y} = \Psi(y_1, \ldots, y_n)$, and $\hat{x}(x_i, y_i, u_i, \tilde{y})$ is defined as the solution x^* of

$$u_i(x_i, y_i) = u_i(x^*, \tilde{y}).$$

It is worth stressing that all these allocation rules (and social ordering functions) avoid interpersonal comparisons of utilities. The only information they need is the profile of preferences over (x, y) represented by u_N. This can be intuitively understood as resulting from the fact that what is sought here is equality of extended bundles (x_i, y_i), not of utilities. Therefore utilities are essentially irrelevant. This idea will be made more precise below.[19]

[18] See Fleurbaey (1995d) for an exact definition of the largest domain over which Egalitarian Equivalent allocations exist.
[19] This does not imply that this theory takes sides in the philosophical debate about whether individuals should be held responsible for their utilities and preferences (Cohen 1989, Dworkin 2000). Indeed, we have assumed nothing about the concrete meaning of the variable y, so that y may contain any trait related to subjective satisfaction. The concrete content of the separation between y and u (or z) has to be decided outside the model.

In conclusion, it seems relatively easy to define reasonable allocation rules (or social ordering functions) for the current problem. Is it the case that all of the above solutions are equally appealing? The axiomatic analysis of the model has shown that the answer is no. In the next subsection, we review the main axioms proposed in the literature.

2.3. Axioms and Ethical Principles

Following the literature, we focus on allocation rules, and all axioms presented in this subsection bear on allocation rules defined over some domain $\mathcal{D}$ (either $\mathcal{E}$ or $\mathcal{E}'$).

A basic axiom, satisfied by all reasonable allocation rules, is that names of agents are irrelevant.

Anonymity

$\forall e = (y_N, u_N, \Omega) \in \mathcal{D}$, $\forall x_N \in S(e)$, $\forall \pi \in \Pi_N$,

$$x_{\pi(N)} \in S(y_{\pi(N)}, u_{\pi(N)}, \Omega).$$

A related axiom, which is implied by ***Anonymity*** when the allocation rule is single-valued, is the following horizontal equity requirement, which says that agents who have identical characteristics should receive the same quantity of resources.

Equal Treatment of Equals

$\forall e \in \mathcal{D}$, $\forall x_N \in S(e)$, $\forall i,j \in N$,

$$\left[y_i = y_j \text{ and } u_i = u_j\right] \Rightarrow x_i = x_j.$$

The No-Envy condition can be used to define not only an allocation rule, but also an axiom bearing on allocation rules.

No-Envy Axiom (NE)

$\forall e \in \mathcal{D}$, $S(e) \subset S_{NE}(e)$.

Since $S_{NE}(e)$ is empty for some e in $\mathcal{E}$, this axiom cannot be satisfied. One must therefore weaken the requirement. As explained above, this axiom embodies the principle of compensation as well as the principle of natural reward, because it implies a substantial degree of equality in extended bundles. The axiomatic analysis reviewed here has studied how to weaken this axiom in the dimension of either compensation or natural reward. Most of the axioms presented below are actually sufficiently weak so as to express only one of these two ethical principles.

We begin by listing axioms that express the *principle of compensation*, namely, the goal of neutralizing the impact of unequal characteristics over utilities. The first axiom is inspired by the intuitive requirement that agents with the same utility function, who therefore differ only in characteristics to be compensated, should obtain equal utility after transfer (unless the better-off has a zero resource). Full compensation among such agents can be obtained only when their difference in y does not entail any inequality in utility. The fact that agents with identical utility functions are considered eliminates any problem of separating the influence of y from the influence of $u(.,.)$ in the production of inequalities in utility levels.

Equal Utility for Equal Function (EUEF, Fleurbaey 1994)
$\forall e \in \mathcal{D}, \forall x_N \in S(e), \forall i,j \in N,$

$$u_i = u_j \Rightarrow u_i(x_i, y_i) = u_j(x_j, y_j) \text{ or } [u_i(x_i, y_i) < u_j(x_j, y_j) \text{ and } x_j = 0].$$

Notice that since $u_i = u_j$, this axiom is a direct weakening of ***No-Envy*** and says that no envy should occur among agents with identical utility functions, except when the envied agent has a zero resource. One also sees that it is only when all agents with identical utility function obtain the same utility level that every agent faces one and the same set of opportunities, defining an opportunity as a pair (*utility function, utility level*). Any agent who adopts a particular utility function is then assured of getting the same utility level as the others who adopted the same function. On the other hand, recall that, as explained in Example 2, this axiom is not totally uncontroversial and may be rejected as displaying too much faith in the agents i and j's own (identical but possibly idiosyncratic) evaluation of the impact of y.

The next axiom makes the same requirement, but only when all agents have identical utility functions, which can be interpreted as the case when all characteristics that differ among agents are to be compensated.

Equal Utility for Uniform Function (EUUF, Fleurbaey 1994, Bossert 1995)
$\forall e \in \mathcal{D}, \forall x_N \in S(e),$

$$\begin{aligned}[\forall i, j \in N,\ u_i = u_j] \Rightarrow \forall i,j \in N, \\ u_i(x_i, y_i) = u_j(x_j, y_j) \text{ or } [u_i(x_i, y_i) < u_j(x_j, y_j) \text{ and } x_j = 0].\end{aligned}$$

The next axiom is even weaker, because it requires equality of utilities (or No-Envy) only when utility functions are not only identical, but also belong to some specified subset which may be arbitrarily small.

Equal Utility for Reference Function (EURF, Fleurbaey 1995d)
$\exists \tilde{u} \in \mathcal{U}, \forall e \in \mathcal{D}, \forall x_N \in S(e)$, if $\forall i \in N,\ u_i = \tilde{u}$, then

$$\forall i,j \in N,\ u_i(x_i, y_i) = u_j(x_j, y_j) \text{ or } [u_i(x_i, y_i) < u_j(x_j, y_j) \text{ and } x_j = 0].$$

The next axiom is somewhat different and deals with changes in the profile of characteristics. It says that a change in this profile should affect all agents' final utilities in the same way. The rationale for this condition is that since those characteristics elicit compensation, there is no reason to make some agents benefit while others would lose. This may be related to Rawls's idea "to regard the distribution of natural talents as a common asset and to share in the benefits of this distribution whatever it turns out to be" (Rawls 1971, p.101). In the current model it makes sense to apply this solidarity requirement only to agents who receive positive resources, because agents who do not receive resources will have their utility level depend only on the change in their own talent, independently of changes in the whole profile.

Solidarity (S, Fleurbaey and Maniquet 1999)
$\forall e = (y_N, u_N, \Omega),\ e' = (y'_N, u_N, \Omega) \in \mathcal{D},\ \forall x_N \in S(e),\ \forall x'_N \in S(e')$,

$$\forall i \in N \text{ such that } x'_i > 0,\ u_i(x_i, y_i) \geq u_i(x'_i, y'_i) \text{ or}$$

$$\forall i \in N \text{ such that } x_i > 0,\ u_i(x_i, y_i) \leq u_i(x'_i, y'_i).$$

It is easy to illustrate why these axioms express the principle of compensation and not at all the principle of natural reward, by observing that they are all satisfied by the following welfare egalitarian allocation rule (based on the maximin criterion applied to utilities):

Maximin Utility (S_{MU})
$\forall e \in \mathcal{E},\ \forall x_N \in F(e)$,

$$x_N \in S_{MU}(e) \Leftrightarrow \forall x'_N \in F(e),\ \min_{i \in N} u_i(x_i, y_i) \geq \min_{i \in N} u_i(x'_i, y_i).$$

This allocation rule does not satisfy the principle of natural reward in any sense because it does not seek equality of extended bundles.

We now turn to axioms reflecting the *principle of natural reward*, namely, the goal of compensating only talents and not other characteristics like utility functions. The first axiom says that an agent unanimously considered as more talented than another one should not receive more resources.

Protection of Handicapped (PH, Fleurbaey 1994)
$\forall e \in \mathcal{D}, \forall i,j \in N,$

$$[\forall x \in \mathbb{R}_+, \forall k \in N,\ u_k(x, y_i) \leq u_k(x, y_j)] \Rightarrow [\forall x_N \in S(e),\ x_i \geq x_j].$$

This axiom is similar to Sen's *Weak Equity Axiom*,[20] and boils down to it when all utility functions are identical. When utility functions are heterogeneous, this axiom only applies when unanimity is obtained, which means that it is quite weak in this respect. However, most of the axioms of a similar vein studied here are actually even weaker than it.

It is tempting to view this axiom as expressing the principle of compensation rather than the principle of natural reward. But this would be a mistake. The protection granted to handicapped agents is only minimal, and the allocation rule that always divides Ω equally ($x_i = \Omega/n$ for all i) does satisfy this axiom, without performing any kind of compensation. This axiom never requires any kind of compensation, even when all agents have identical utility functions. On the other hand, it does requires giving equal resources to agents having identical talents y, and therefore prevents any biased transfer in favor of some agents just because they have "good" utility functions. This is why this axiom directly, and rather strongly, expresses the principle of natural reward.

The second, weaker axiom is, precisely, formulating the requirement that agents with equal talents should receive the same treatment in terms of resources.

Equal Resource for Equal Talent (ERET, Fleurbaey 1994)
$\forall e \in \mathcal{D}, \forall x_N \in S(e), \forall i,j \in N,$

$$y_i = y_j \Rightarrow x_i = x_j.$$

The motivation for this requirement has been discussed in Examples 1 and 2, in the Introduction. It guarantees a neutral treatment of different utility functions.

On the other hand, it may be criticized for failing to take account of the fact that different values of talent y may alter the opportunity set and then require a sensitivity of transfers to utility functions. This criticism is illustrated in the following example.

Example 3 This example retains the main data of Examples 1 and 2, except that the utility function is now defined as

$$u = x + yz.$$

With this function, a greater talent y makes one more able to benefit from one's effort. One possible policy respecting the condition formulated in the **E**qual **R**esource for **E**qual

[20] As recalled from Section 1, this axiom says that when an individual has a lower level of utility than another at all levels of income, the optimal allocation must not give him less income.

Talent axiom is the following. It is based on the idea that any agent (rich or poor) who would have $z = 2$ would obtain $u = 8 = 6 + 2 \times 1 = 2 + 2 \times 3$.

Policy AA2

$y \backslash z$	1	3
1	$x = 6$ $u = 7$	$x = 6$ $u = 9$
3	$x = 2$ $u = 5$	$x = 2$ $u = 11$

This policy, like policy A2 in Example 2, fails to compensate in one subpopulation (here, the deserving) and overcompensates in the other (here, the undeserving). Here, one may complain that giving the same transfer to all poor fails to take account of the fact that by exerting effort they are less able to improve their lot than the rich, and since this is due to a low endowment in y they should not suffer from this. Compensation should then take account not only of the fact that they have a lower talent, but also of the fact that this low talent makes them less able to benefit from their own effort. As a consequence, x should depend on z as well as on y.[21]

In essence, this criticism is pointing at a conflict between this ***Equal Resource for Equal Talent*** axiom and the principle of compensation (in particular, the ***Equal Utility for Equal Function*** axiom). This conflict will be formally delineated below.

A weaker requirement than ***Equal Resource for Equal Talent***, in the natural reward line of inspiration, is that the relative position of x_i with respect to the mean resource Ω/n should depend only on talent.

Fair Relative Resource for Equal Talent (FRRET, Sprumont 1997)
$\forall e \in \mathcal{D}, \forall x_N \in S(e), \forall i,j \in N,$

$$y_i = y_j \Rightarrow \left(x_i - \frac{\Omega}{n}\right)\left(x_j - \frac{\Omega}{n}\right) \geq 0.$$

Notice that this formulation is relatively weak since no constraint bears on x_j when $x_i = \Omega/n$.

[21] An argument along these lines is made in Tungodden (2005). A defender of natural reward may reply that agents, being responsible for their effort, cannot complain if by choosing an especially low or high effort they obtain more or less than others. This kind of defense is even more convincing when, in an alternative interpretation, $u = x + yz$ simply represents preferences about bundles (x, y). The deserving poor are then just y-lovers who happen to have a low endowment in y, so that one may object to accepting their view that this is a great handicap. See Fleurbaey (1995b, 2001), Vallentyne (2002), and Vandenbroucke (2001) for critical discussions of natural reward, and Cappelen and Tungodden (2009) for an in-depth study of reward schemes.

The next axiom weakens ***Equal Resource for Equal Talent*** again by applying the requirement only to economies with a uniform talent.

Equal Resource for Uniform Talent (ERUT, Fleurbaey 1994, Bossert 1995)
$\forall e \in \mathcal{D}, \forall x_N \in S(e),$

$$\forall i,j \in N,\ y_i = y_j \Rightarrow \forall i \in N,\ x_i = \frac{\Omega}{n}.$$

And a further weakening[22] goes by applying this only to economies with a uniform talent in a certain, arbitrarily small, subset.

Equal Resource for Reference Talent (ERRT, Fleurbaey 1995d)
$\exists \tilde{y} \in Y, \forall e \in \mathcal{D}, \forall x_N \in S(e)$, if $\forall i \in N,\ y_i = \tilde{y}$, then

$$\forall i \in N,\ x_i = \frac{\Omega}{n}.$$

Another kind of condition relies on the idea that if utilities as such are not to elicit any compensation, the allocation rule should be essentially independent of utilities.

Independence of Utilities (IU, Bossert 1995)
$\forall e = (y_N, u_N, \Omega),\ e' = (y_N, u'_N, \Omega) \in \mathcal{D},$

$$S(e) = S(e').$$

This axiom is very strong because it forbids any use of the agents' preferences in the measurement of talent differentials and in determining the scale of compensation. A weaker requirement is ordinalism, which is satisfied by all allocation rules presented in the previous subsection.

Ordinalism (O)
$\forall e = (y_N, u_N, \Omega),\ e' = (y_N, u'_N, \Omega) \in \mathcal{D},$

$$R_N = R'_N \Rightarrow S(e) = S(e'),$$

where R_N (resp. R'_N) is the profile of preferences represented by u_N (resp. u'_N).

[22] Another weak condition of natural reward has been proposed in Boadway *et al.* (2002). In the current model, it would say that every subpopulation with a given utility function should receive its per capita share of Ω. In other words, there should be no transfers among subpopulations of different utility functions. In the subdomain of economies where talents and utility functions are independently distributed, this condition is implied by ***Equal Resource for Equal Talent***, and (under ***Equal Treatment of Equals***) implies ***Equal Resource for Uniform Talent***. It is logically independent of ***Fair Relative Resource for Equal Talent***. Outside this subdomain it is not reasonable (e.g., if there are more poor among the deserving, it is acceptable to give more resources to the deserving subpopulation than its per capita share).

Finally, we turn to another classical notion of fairness, namely, that equal division should be a minimum right guaranteed to every agent (Steinhaus 1948). Moulin (1991) has shown how to extend this notion by devising lower bounds and upper bounds suitable for division problems. In the current context of compensation, Moulin (1994) suggests to define a bound based on what an agent would obtain if others shared his responsibility characteristics (utility function here). Let $EUUF(y_N, \Omega, u)$ denote the allocation resulting from the application of ***Equal Utility for Uniform Function*** (maximin of utilities) to the economy where all agents have the same utility function u. This defines a bound that cannot operate on all economies as a lower bound, and Moulin suggests to use it as an upper bound when this happens.

Egalitarian Bound (EB, Moulin 1994)
$\forall e = (y_N, u_N, \Omega) \in \mathcal{D}$, $\forall x_N \in S(e)$,

$$\forall i \in N,\ x_i \geq EUUF_i(y_N, \Omega, u_i) \text{ or } \forall i \in N,\ x_i \leq EUUF_i(y_N, \Omega, u_i).$$

Although this axiom clearly has a flavor of compensation (it implies ***Equal Utility for Uniform Function***), one can argue that it also contains a pint of natural reward, because it forbids excessive compensation as performed for instance by the welfare egalitarian allocation rule S_{MU}. In fact it also implies ***Equal Resource for Uniform Talent***, as indicated in the following proposition.

Proposition 1 *The following table describes the logical implications between axioms (for $\mathcal{D} = \mathcal{E}$ or $\mathcal{E}'$).*

Compensation		Natural	Reward
S		O$\Leftarrow$	IU
$\Downarrow^{(1)}$			$\Downarrow^{(2)}$
EUEF	$\Leftarrow$ NE$^{(3)}$ $\Rightarrow$	PH$\Rightarrow$	ERET
			$\Downarrow$
$\Downarrow$	$\Downarrow$		FRRET
			$\Downarrow$
EUUF	$\Leftarrow$ EB $\Rightarrow$		ERUT
$\Downarrow$			$\Downarrow$
EURF			ERRT

(1) *Assuming that S satisfies* **Anonymity**.
(2) *Assuming that S satisfies* **Equal Treatment of Equals**.
(3) *Considered on the subdomain where it can be satisfied.*

Proof. We focus only on the nonobvious implications.

S⇒EUEF, under Anonymity. Consider $e = (y_N, u_N, \Omega)$ with $u_i = u_j = u$. Let $e' = (y'_N, u_N, \Omega)$ be such that $y'_i = y_j$, $y'_j = y_i$, and $y'_k = y_k$ for all $k \neq i, j$. By Anonymity, if $x_N \in S(e)$, then $x'_N \in S(e')$, with $x'_i = x_j$, $x'_j = x_i$, and $x'_k = x_k$ for all $k \neq i, j$. First case: if $x_i = x_j = 0$, then EUEF is satisfied. Second case: $x_i > 0 = x_j$. By Solidarity, either $u(x_j, y_j) \geq u(x'_j, y'_j)$ or $u(x_i, y_i) \leq u(x'_i, y'_i)$, which is the same, and this implies either $u(x_i, y_i) = u(x_j, y_j)$ or $[u(x_i, y_i) < u(x_j, y_j)$ and $x_j = 0]$, as EUEF requires. Third case: $x_i x_j > 0$. By Solidarity, either $u(x_j, y_j) \geq u(x'_j, y'_j)$ and $u(x_i, y_i) \geq u(x'_i, y'_i)$, or $u(x_j, y_j) \leq u(x'_j, y'_j)$ and $u(x_i, y_i) \leq u(x'_i, y'_i)$. Both mean $u(x_i, y_i) = u(x_j, y_j)$, and EUEF is satisfied.

NE⇒EB. Consider an allocation x_N such that there exists i such that $x_i < EUUF_i(y_N, \Omega, u_i)$. This implies that $EUUF_i(y_N, \Omega, u_i) > 0$ and therefore, for all $j \in N$,

$$u_i(EUUF_i(y_N, \Omega, u_i), y_i) \leq u_i(EUUF_j(y_N, \Omega, u_i), y_j).$$

Since $\sum_{j \in N} EUUF_j(y_N, \Omega, u_i) = \sum_{j \in N} x_j = \Omega$, necessarily there is j such that $x_j > EUUF_j(y_N, \Omega, u_i)$. This implies that $u_i(x_i, y_i) < u_i(x_j, y_j)$, and thus x_N is not envy-free. As a consequence, any envy-free allocation is such that for all $i \in N$, $x_i \geq EUUF_i(y_N, \Omega, u_i)$. Therefore EB is satisfied in such an allocation. □

The pattern of incompatibilities displayed in the next table graphically shows that there is a tension between the principle of compensation and the principle of natural reward. It is impossible to fully satisfy both principles at the same time.

Proposition 2 *The following table describes the incompatibilities (marked by ⊗) between the main axioms of compensation and natural reward (for $\mathcal{D} = \mathcal{E}$ or $\mathcal{E}'$), and shows what axioms are satisfied by the various solutions (on their respective domain).*

	IU	ERET	FRRET	ERUT	ERRT
S	⊗	⊗	⊗	⊗	$S_{\Psi EE}$ (Ψ const.)
EUEF	⊗	⊗	⊗	$S_{\Psi EE}$ (Ψ idempot.)	
EUUF	⊗	$S_{\Phi CE}, S_{MUD}, S_{ACE}$ (Φ idempotent)		$S_{AEE}, S_{BME}, S_{MEI}$	
EURF	$S_{\Phi CE}$ (Φ const.)				

Proof. We omit the easy proof of the incompatibility between S and ERUT, and between EUUF and IU, and focus on the proof that EUEF and FRRET are incompatible on $\mathcal{E}'$

(and therefore on $\mathcal{E}$ as well). Assume the utility function is defined by $u = x\left(yz + \hat{y}\hat{z}\right)$, where $(z, \hat{z})$ are preference parameters. Consider an economy with $\Omega = 4$, and four agents, described in the following table:

i	y_i	$\hat{y}_i$	z_i	$\hat{z}_i$
1	1	2	1	2
2	1	2	2	1
3	2	1	1	2
4	2	1	2	1

FRRET requires

$$\begin{cases} (x_1 - 1)(x_2 - 1) \geq 0 \\ (x_3 - 1)(x_4 - 1) \geq 0, \end{cases}$$

and EUEF, in this particular case, simply requires

$$\begin{cases} 5x_1 = 4x_3 \\ 4x_2 = 5x_4. \end{cases}$$

First possibility: $x_1 > 1$. Then $x_2 \geq 1$ by FRRET and $x_3 > 1$ by EUEF, the latter implying $x_4 \geq 1$ by FRRET. All this is incompatible with $x_1 + x_2 + x_3 + x_4 = 4$.

Second possibility: $x_1 < 1$. Then $x_2 \leq 1$ by FRRET, which implies $x_4 < 1$ by EUEF, implying in turn $x_3 \leq 1$ by FRRET. This is again impossible.

Third possibility: $x_1 = 1$. Then $x_3 = 5/4$ by EUEF, implying $x_4 \geq 1$ by FRRET. The latter entails $x_2 > 1$ by EUEF. And again it is impossible to have $x_1 + x_2 + x_3 + x_4 = 4$. □

The axiom ***Protection of Handicapped*** is satisfied by S_{ACE}, by $S_{\Phi CE}$ for some Φ, and by S_{MUD}. The axiom ***Egalitarian Bound*** is satisfied by none of the above solutions.[23]

The literature provides few characterizations of allocation rules for this model. It is first necessary to provide the definition of an ancillary axiom, capturing the idea that the reallocation problem over a subpopulation should be correctly dealt with by the allocation rule applied to the whole population. ***Consistency*** says that a suballocation of a selected allocation must also be selected in the subeconomy defined by the corresponding subgroup of agents and the total amount of money they receive in this suballocation.

[23] Here is an example of a solution satisfying ***Egalitarian Bound*** as well as ***Equal Utility for Equal Function*** and ***Ordinalism***. In $e = (y_N, u_N, \Omega)$, it chooses some $\tilde{y}$ and it selects allocations x_N such that: $\exists \tilde{x} \in \mathbb{R}$, $\forall i \in N$,

$$u_i(x_i, y_i) = u_i(\tilde{x} + \hat{x}_i, \tilde{y}) \text{ or } [u_i(x_i, y_i) > u_i(\tilde{x} + \hat{x}_i, \tilde{y}) \text{ and } x_i = 0],$$

where $\hat{x}_i$ is defined by $u_i(\hat{x}_i, \tilde{y}) = u_i(EUUF_i(y_N, \Omega, u_i), y_i)$.

Consistency (C, Thomson 1988)
$\forall e = (y_N, u_N, \Omega) \in \mathcal{D}, \forall G \subset N, \forall x_N \in S(e),$

$$x_G \in S(y_G, u_G, \sum_{i \in G} x_i).$$

Proposition 3 (Fleurbaey 1995d, Bossert and Fleurbaey 1996) *An allocation rule S defined on $\mathcal{E}$ is single-valued and either satisfies* Independence of Utilities and Equal Utility for Reference Function, *or satisfies* Consistency, Equal Resource for Uniform Talent, *and* Equal Utility for Reference Function *if and only if $S = S_{\Phi CE}$ for some constant function Φ.*

Proof. Assume S satisfies IU and EURF. Take $\tilde{u} \in \mathcal{U}$, as posited in EURF. Consider an economy such that for all i, $u_i = \tilde{u}$. In this economy, EURF requires selecting the only allocation such that

$$\forall i, j \in N, \quad \tilde{u}(x_i, y_i) = \tilde{u}(x_j, y_j) \text{ or } [\tilde{u}(x_i, y_i) < \tilde{u}(x_j, y_j) \text{ and } x_j = 0].$$

By IU, this allocation must be selected in any economy with the same profile y_N, whatever u_N. Therefore $S = S_{\Phi CE}$ with $\Phi(u_N) \equiv \tilde{u}$.

Now, one easily checks that C and ERUT imply IU for a single-valued allocation rule. Hence the second result.[24] □

Proposition 4 (Fleurbaey 1995d) *An allocation rule S defined on $\mathcal{E}'$ is single-valued and satisfies* Consistency, Equal Resource for Reference Talent, *and* Equal Utility for Uniform Function *if and only if $S = S_{\Psi EE}$ for some constant function Ψ.*

Proof. On $\mathcal{E}'$, Egalitarian Equivalent allocations are such that for all i, $u_i(x_i, y_i) = u_i(\tilde{x}, \tilde{y})$, with $\tilde{x} > 0$ whenever $\Omega > 0$. Assume S satisfies C, ERRT, and EUUF. Take some $\tilde{y} \in Y$, as posited in ERRT, and some $e = (y_N, u_N, \Omega) \in \mathcal{E}'$. Let x_N be an Egalitarian Equivalent allocation in e, such that $u_i(x_i, y_i) = u_i(\tilde{x}, \tilde{y})$ for all i. Construct the $2n$-agent economy $e' = ((y_N, \tilde{y}, \ldots, \tilde{y}), (u_N, u_N), \Omega + n\tilde{x})$. By C and EUUF, one must have for all $i \leq n$, $u_i(S_i(e'), y_i) = u_i(S_{i+n}(e'), \tilde{y})$. By C and ERRT, one must have for all $i, j > n$, $S_i(e') = S_j(e')$. These two conditions imply that for all $i > n$, $S_i(e') = \tilde{x}$, and that for all $i \leq n$, $u_i(S_i(e'), y_i) = u_i(\tilde{x}, \tilde{y})$. By C, therefore, $S(e) = x_N$. This implies that $S = S_{\Psi EE}$ with $\Psi(y_N) \equiv \tilde{y}$. □

[24] Fleurbaey (1995d) also characterizes S_{ACE} on the basis of EUUF and an axiom expressing that the allocation rule aggregates opinions about the individual talents. The result in Fleurbaey (1995d) is actually incorrect as stated, because under the guise of ***Anonymity*** the proof makes an implicit use of a third axiom saying that permutations of preferences only do not affect the selected allocation. This third axiom is independent of the others.

A noticeable feature of these results is that the characterized allocation rules satisfy ***Ordinalism*** while the axioms ***Equal Resource for Uniform Talent*** and ***Equal Resource for Reference Talent*** do not by themselves imply it. It is an interesting feature of this literature that it gives an ethical justification to ordinalism, in addition to the traditional positivist justification underlying New Welfare Economics.[25]

There is no axiomatic study of social ordering functions for this model, with the exception of Maniquet (2004), who studies some weak axioms of compensation and natural reward and their consequences about how to measure individual welfare. For instance, the Φ-Conditional Equality ordering function $R_{\Phi CE}$ defined above relies on the leximin criterion applied to individual indices measured by $\tilde{u}(x_i, y_i)$. Maniquet shows that, when combined with a consistency property, compensation and natural reward requirements imply that the social ordering function has the structure of a classical "welfarist" criterion applied to vectors of individual indices of well-being.

2.4. The Quasi-Linear Case

The case when utility functions are quasi-linear is particularly simple and has been the topic of many papers.[26] It is assumed that utility functions are as follows:

$$u_i(x_i, y_i) = x_i + v_i(y_i).$$

As usual in the quasi-linear case, negative quantities of consumption x are allowed, and for simplification the total amount to be distributed is $\Omega = 0$. The quasi-linear case is particularly relevant to applications where u_i measures a monetary outcome. This version of the model is due to Bossert (1995), who described $v_i(y_i)$ as individual pre-tax income, x_i as an income transfer, and $u_i(x_i, y_i)$ as final income. This model is also relevant to other applications, for instance when agents are administrative units (local administrations, local branches of a national organization, etc.) and $v_i(y_i)$ is their initial budget balance, to be corrected by transfers x_i between units. See Section 4.7 for examples of applications.

Bossert (1995), and the subsequent literature, actually adopted a parameterized description of the utility functions:

$$u_i(x_i, y_i) = x_i + v(y_i, z_i).$$

This formulation is mathematically convenient, and also graphical in order to understand that the ethical goal is to neutralize inequalities due to y (principle of compensation) and

[25] In a similar analysis focused on social ordering functions, Maniquet (2004) shows how natural reward axioms entail ordinalism, under a consistency requirement.

[26] See Bossert (1995), Bossert and Fleurbaey (1996), Bossert, Fleurbaey, and Van de gaer (1999), Cappelen and Tungodden (2002, 2003), Iturbe-Ormaetxe (1997), Moulin (1994), Sprumont (1997), and Tungodden (2005).

to preserve inequalities due to z (principle of natural reward). We retain it in the sequel. It is then convenient to describe an economy by the pair of profiles $e = (y_N, z_N)$.

The domain of definition of allocation rules studied here is the set of economies with $n \geq 2$, $y_N \in Y^n$, $z_N \in Z^n$, where Y and Z are subsets of Euclidean spaces, and v is a mapping from $Y \times Z$ to $\mathbb{R}$. Let $\mathcal{E}_{ql}$ denote this domain, $\mathcal{E}_{ql}^{Y}$ the same domain when Y is an interval of $\mathbb{R}$ and v is continuous and increasing in y, and $\mathcal{E}_{ql}^{Z}$ the same domain when Z is an interval of $\mathbb{R}$ and v is continuous and increasing in z. Let $\mathcal{E}_{ql}^{YZc}$ denote the subdomain of $\mathcal{E}_{ql}^{Y} \cap \mathcal{E}_{ql}^{Z}$ such that y and z are complementary, that is, such that $v(y,z) - v(y',z)$ is nondecreasing in z for any given $y > y'$.[27]

The quasi-linear case provides a simpler framework for the formulation of many axioms and solutions. It also sheds more light on the trade-off between compensation and natural reward, and in particular reveals that the root of the problem, in this case, is the nonseparability of v in y and z. When v is additively separable in y and z, then all the main solutions coincide and the tension between compensation and natural reward disappears. This is explained in the following subsection.

2.4.1. *Allocation Rules*

There are a few facts and notions specific to this particular domain.

First, the subdomain in which the No-Envy allocation rule is nonempty now has a precise definition.

Proposition 5 (Svensson 1983) *For all $e \in \mathcal{E}_{ql}$, $S_{NE}(e)$ is nonempty if and only if*

$$\forall \pi \in \Pi_N, \sum_{i \in N} v(y_i, z_i) \geq \sum_{i \in N} v(y_{\pi(i)}, z_i).$$

Second, the definitions of the allocation rules can be simplified because zero is no longer a lower bound to resources. We only provide here a sample of these more explicit definitions.

Φ-Conditional Equality ($S_{\Phi CE}$)
$\forall e \in \mathcal{E}_{ql}$,

$$(S_{\Phi CE})_i(e) = -v(y_i, \tilde{z}) + \frac{1}{n} \sum_{j=1}^{n} v(y_j, \tilde{z}),$$

where $\tilde{z} = \Phi(z_1, \ldots, z_n)$.

[27] This assumption corresponds to the idea that the productivity of talent increases with effort, or equivalently that the productivity of effort increases with talent.

Ψ-Egalitarian Equivalent ($S_{\Psi EE}$)
$\forall e \in \mathcal{E}_{ql}$,

$$(S_{\Psi EE})_i(e) = -v(y_i, z_i) + v(\tilde{y}, z_i) + \frac{1}{n}\sum_{j=1}^{n}(v(y_j, z_j) - v(\tilde{y}, z_j)),$$

where $\tilde{y} = \Psi(y_1, \ldots, y_n)$.

Third, new allocation rules can be defined. The next one is similar to $S_{\Psi EE}$ in that it refers to a benchmark level of pretransfer utility, $v(\tilde{y}, z_i)$, but instead of giving this level of utility to agent i plus an increment, it applies a proportional adjustment so as to meet the resource constraint. Notice that the idea of egalitarian-equivalence is lost in this operation.

Ψ-Proportionally Adjusted Equivalent ($S_{\Psi PAE}$, Iturbe-Ormaetxe 1997)
$\forall e \in \mathcal{E}_{ql}$,

$$(S_{\Psi PAE})_i(e) = -v(y_i, z_i) + \frac{\sum_{j=1}^{n} v(y_j, z_j)}{\sum_{j=1}^{n} v(\tilde{y}, z_j)} v(\tilde{y}, z_i),$$

where $\tilde{y} = \Psi(y_1, \ldots, y_n)$.

Bossert (1995) proposes an average version of this allocation rule. The *Average Proportionally Adjusted Equivalent* (S_{APAE}) allocation rule is constructed by computing the average of $S_{\Psi PAE}$ allocations with $\tilde{y} = y_j$ for every j, successively.

Finally, when the variable y or z is one-dimensional, it is possible to define the following allocation rules.

Balanced Egalitarian (S_{BE}, Sprumont 1997)
$\forall e \in \mathcal{E}_{ql}^{Y}$,

$$(S_{BE})_i(e) = -v(y_i, z_i) + v(\hat{y}, z_i),$$

where $\hat{y}$ is defined as the solution to

$$\sum_{j=1}^{n} v(y_j, z_j) = \sum_{j=1}^{n} v(\hat{y}, z_j).$$

Notice that this solution would belong to the family of $S_{\Psi EE}$ if the function Ψ could have (y_N, z_N) as its argument. The next solution is dual to this one, and similarly, it would belong to the family of $S_{\Phi CE}$ if the function Φ could have (y_N, z_N) as its argument.

Balanced Conditionally Egalitarian (S_{BCE}, Sprumont 1997)
$\forall e \in \mathcal{E}_{ql}^{Z}$,

$$(S_{BE})_i(e) = -v(y_i, \hat{z}) + \frac{1}{n}\sum_{j=1}^{n} v(y_j, z_j),$$

where $\hat{z}$ is defined as the solution to

$$\sum_{j=1}^{n} v(y_j, z_j) = \sum_{j=1}^{n} v(y_j, \hat{z}).$$

Cappelen and Tungodden (2002, 2003) propose an allocation rule that splits the proceeds among agents with similar values of z. First rank the agents in such a way that $z_1 \leq \cdots \leq z_n$. The first agent then receives an equal split of the total v that would be obtained if all agents had the same z_1. The second agent also receives this plus an equal split of the additional v that would be obtained if all agents $i = 2, \ldots, n$ had the same z_2. And so on.

Serially Egalitarian (S_{SE}, Cappelen and Tungodden 2002)[28]
$\forall e \in \mathcal{E}_{ql}^{Z}$,

$$(S_{BE})_i(e) = -v(y_i, z_i) + \frac{1}{n}\sum_{j=1}^{n} v(y_j, z_1) + \sum_{j=2}^{i} \frac{1}{n-j+1}\sum_{k=j}^{n}[v(y_k, z_j) - v(y_k, z_{j-1})].$$

All of these allocation rules are based on complex computations of $v(y, z)$ for combinations of characteristics that are not necessarily observed in the population. One can define adapted versions of some of these allocation rules so as to rely only on the observed $v_i = v(y_i, z_i)$. Define the sets $N_y = \{i \in N \mid y_i = y\}$ and $N_z = \{i \in N \mid z_i = z\}$.

Observable Average Conditional Egalitarian (S_{OACE}, Bossert, Fleurbaey, and Van de gaer 1999)
$\forall e \in \mathcal{E}_{ql}$,

$$(S_{OACE})_i(e) = -\frac{1}{\#N_{y_i}} \sum_{j \in N_{y_i}} v_j + \frac{1}{n}\sum_{j=1}^{n} v_j.$$

[28] Cappelen and Tungodden (2003) also introduce the symmetric rule that starts from z_n. There is also a dual to S_{SE}, which they do not consider, and which taxes agents in proportion to the v that would be obtained if individuals adopted $y_1 \leq \cdots \leq y_i$ in sequence.

Observable Average Egalitarian Equivalent (S_{OAEE}, Bossert, Fleurbaey, and Van de gaer 1999)
$\forall e \in \mathcal{E}_{ql}$,

$$(S_{OAEE})_i(e) = -v_i + \frac{1}{\# N_{z_i}} \sum_{j \in N_{z_i}} v_j.$$

2.4.2. Axioms

The definitions of some of the axioms can be simplified, since zero is no longer a lower bound to resources. Moreover, quasi-linearity entails a property that is not generally true in the previous model (it served to define $\mathcal{E}'$ in the previous subsection):

$$\forall y, y' \in Y, \forall u \in U, \forall x \in \mathbb{R}, \exists x' \in \mathbb{R},\ u(x', y') \geq u(x, y),$$

and these two features guarantee that full equality of utilities is always possible. This simplifies the axioms of compensation. For instance, ***E**qual **U**tility for **E**qual **F**unction* now reads as follows:

Equal Utility for Equal Function (EUEF)
$\forall e \in \mathcal{E}_{ql}$, $\forall x_N \in S(e)$, $\forall i, j \in N$,

$$z_i = z_j \Rightarrow x_i + v(y_i, z_i) = x_j + v(y_j, z_j).$$

A similar simplification applies to ***E**qual **U**tility for **U**niform **F**unction* and ***E**qual **U**tility for **R**eference **F**unction*. The ***S**olidarity* axiom is also simplified somewhat.

Solidarity (S)
$\forall e = (y_N, z_N)$, $e' = (y'_N, z_N) \in \mathcal{E}_{ql}$, $\forall x_N \in S(e)$, $\forall x'_N \in S(e')$,

$$\forall i \in N,\ x_i + v(y_i, z_i) \geq x'_i + v(y'_i, z_i) \text{ or}$$
$$\forall i \in N,\ x_i + v(y_i, z_i) \leq x'_i + v(y'_i, z_i).$$

The literature has also introduced new, specific axioms. One of these, which is the dual counterpart of ***F**air **R**elative **R**esource for **E**qual **T**alent*, refers to the mean utility defined as: $\bar{v}(e) = (1/n) \sum_{i \in N} v(y_i, z_i)$, and requires that two agents with the same utility function should be similarly ranked with respect to the mean utility.

Fair Ranking for Equal Function (FREF, Sprumont 1997)
$\forall e \in \mathcal{E}_{ql}$, $\forall x_N \in S(e)$, $\forall i, j \in N$,

$$z_i = z_j \Rightarrow (x_i + v(y_i, z_i) - \bar{v}(e))\,(x_j + v(y_j, z_j) - \bar{v}(e)) \geq 0.$$

The next axiom is a strengthening of ***Solidarity***, based on the argument that there is no reason to make some agents benefit unequally from variations in the profile; in particular, it would be undesirable to let an agent whose characteristics are improved to benefit more than other agents.

Additive Solidarity (AS, Bossert 1995)[29]
$\forall e=(y_N,z_N),\ e'=(y'_N,z_N)\in\mathcal{E}_{ql},\ \forall x_N\in S(e),\ \forall x'_N\in S(e'),$

$$\forall i,j\in N,\ x_i+v(y_i,z_i)-(x'_i+v(y'_i,z_i))=x_j+v(y_j,z_j)-(x'_j+v(y'_j,z_j)).$$

At the opposite, a weaker version of the ***Solidarity*** axiom applies only when mean utility is unchanged.

Weak Solidarity (WS, Iturbe-Ormaetxe 1997)
$\forall e=(y_N,z_N),\ e'=(y'_N,z_N)\in\mathcal{E}_{ql},\ \forall x_N\in S(e),\ \forall x'_N\in S(e'),$

$$\bar{v}(e)=\bar{v}(e')\Rightarrow\forall i\in N,\ x_i+v(y_i,z_i)=x'_i+v(y'_i,z_i).$$

Another kind of solidarity requires proportional moves of the agents' final utilities:

Multiplicative Solidarity (MS, Iturbe-Ormaetxe 1997)
$\forall e=(y_N,z_N),\ e'=(y'_N,z_N)\in\mathcal{E}_{ql},\ \forall x_N\in S(e),\ \forall x'_N\in S(e'),$

$$\forall i,j\in N,\ [x_i+v(y_i,z_i)][x'_j+v(y'_j,z_j)]=[x'_i+v(y'_i,z_i)][x_j+v(y_j,z_j)].$$[30]

The axioms of natural reward defined in the previous model do not need any adaptation here. Notice that Ordinalism is built in the model, since we make use only of the quasi-linear representation of the quasi-linear preferences.

The axiom of ***Egalitarian Bound*** can be given a more explicit definition.

Egalitarian Bound (EB)
$\forall e=(y_N,z_N)\in\mathcal{E}_{ql},\ \forall x_N\in S(e),$

$$\forall i\in N,\ x_i\geq EUUF_i(y_N,z_i)\quad\text{or}\quad\forall i\in N,\ x_i\leq EUUF_i(y_N,z_i),$$

[29] An equivalent formulation of this axiom, adopted by Bossert (1995), refers to the change of only one agent's characteristics.

[30] When this product is different from zero, one then obtains that the agents' utilities change in the same proportion:

$$\frac{x_i+v(y_i,z_i)}{x'_i+v(y'_i,z_i)}=\frac{x_j+v(y_j,z_j)}{x'_j+v(y'_j,z_j)}.$$

where

$$EUUF_i(y_N, z_i) = -v(y_i, z_i) + \frac{1}{n}\sum_{j=1}^{n} v(y_j, z_i).$$

We now study the modified relationships between the axioms. One sees that the quasi-linear case displays a fuller duality between the axioms and solutions related to the principles of compensation on the one hand, natural reward on the other hand.

Proposition 6 *The following table describes the logical implications between the axioms.*

Compensation			Natural Reward
AS⇒S⇐MS			IU
⇓			
WS			⇓$^{(2)}$
⇓$^{(1)}$			
EUEF	⇐ NE$^{(3)}$ ⇒	PH⇒	ERET
⇓			⇓
FREF	⇓		FRRET
⇓			⇓
EUUF	⇐ EB ⇒		ERUT
⇓			⇓
EURF			ERRT

$^{(1)}$ *Assuming that S satisfies* **A**nonymity.
$^{(2)}$ *Assuming that S satisfies* **E**qual **T**reatment of **E**quals.
$^{(3)}$ *Considered on the subdomain where it can be satisfied.*

The proof is similar to that of Proposition 1.[31]

Proposition 7 *The following table describes the incompatibilities (marked by ⊗) between the main axioms of compensation and natural reward, and shows what axioms are satisfied by the various solutions. The pairs of axioms* AS *and* ERUT, EUEF *and* ERET, EUUF *and* IU *are compatible if and only if v is additively separable in y and z.*[32]

[31] Notice that a weak version of ***Independence of Utilities***, limited to changes of z_N that do not change $\bar{v}(e)$, could play a dual role to ***Weak Solidarity*** in the table.

[32] See also Cappelen and Tungodden (2006) for another perspective on the conflict between compensation and natural reward.

	IU	ERET	FRRET	ERUT	ERRT
AS	⊗	⊗	⊗	⊗	$S_{\Psi EE}$ (Ψ *const.*)
MS	⊗	⊗	⊗	⊗	$S_{\Psi PAE}$ (Ψ *const.*)
S,WS	⊗	⊗	⊗ (S_{BE} *on* E_{ql}^{Y})	⊗	
EUEF	⊗	⊗	⊗	S_{AEE}, S_{APAE} S_{OAEE}, S_{SE} $S_{\Psi EE}$(Ψ *idemp.*)	
FREF	⊗	⊗ (S_{BCE} *on* $\mathcal{E}_{ql}^{Z}$)	⊗		
EUUF	⊗	S_{ACE}, S_{OACE} S_{MUD}, $S_{\Phi CE}$ (Φ *idempotent*)			
EURF	$S_{\Phi CE}$ (Φ *const.*)				

Proof. If v is not additively separable, there exist y, y', z, z' such that

$$v(y', z) - v(y, z) \neq v(y', z') - v(y, z').$$

These values will be used in various examples below.

AS and ERUT are incompatible if v is not additively separable. Consider an economy e with two agents 1 and 2 with profile, respectively, $(y, z), (y, z')$. By ERUT, one must have $x_1 = x_2 = 0$. Consider another economy e' with two agents and a new profile $(y', z), (y', z')$. By ERUT again, one must have $x_1' = x_2' = 0$. And by AS, one must have

$$x_1' + v(y', z) - x_1 - v(y, z) = x_2' + v(y', z') - x_2 - v(y, z'),$$

which is impossible.

EUUF and IU are incompatible if v is not additively separable. Consider an economy e with two agents 1 and 2 with profile, respectively, $(y, z), (y', z)$. By EUUF, one must have $x_1 + v(y, z) = x_2 + v(y', z)$. Consider another economy e' with two agents and a new profile $(y, z'), (y', z')$. By EUUF again, one must have $x_1' + v(y, z') = x_2' + v(y', z')$. And by IU, one must have $x_1' = x_1$ and $x_2' = x_2$, which is impossible.

EUEF and ERET are incompatible if v is not additively separable. Consider an economy with four agents 1 through 4 with profile, respectively, (y,z), (y,z'), (y',z) and (y',z'). By EUEF, one must have

$$x_1 + v(y,z) = x_3 + v(y',z),$$
$$x_2 + v(y,z') = x_4 + v(y',z').$$

By ERET, one must have $x_1 = x_2$ and $x_3 = x_4$. This is again impossible.

FREF and FRRET are incompatible (unlike the previous pairs of axioms, they may be compatible in some cases of nonseparable v). Take an economy with four agents, a function $v((y,\hat{y}),(z,\hat{z})) = yz + \hat{y}\cdot\hat{z}$. The profile of the parameters $y,\hat{y},z,\hat{z}$ is as in the proof of Proposition 2. One computes $\bar{v}(e) = 4.5$. FREF then requires

$$\begin{cases}(x_1+0.5)(x_3-0.5)\geq 0\\(x_2-0.5)(x_4+0.5)\geq 0,\end{cases}$$

while FRRET requires

$$\begin{cases}x_1x_2\geq 0\\x_3x_4\geq 0.\end{cases}$$

Try $x_1 \geq 0$. This implies $x_3 \geq 0.5$, and $x_4 \geq 0$ (from $x_3x_4 \geq 0$), and therefore $x_2 \geq 0.5$. This makes it impossible to achieve $x_1+x_2+x_3+x_4 = 0$.

Try $x_1 < 0$. This implies $x_2 \leq 0$, and therefore $x_4 \leq -0.5$, and therefore $x_3 \leq 0$. Same contradiction. □

In the domain $\mathcal{E}_{ql}$, the axiom ***Egalitarian Bound*** is now satisfied by S_{AEE}.

Characterizations specific to this model have been provided. In Bossert and Fleurbaey (1996) it is shown that S_{ACE} is the only single-valued anonymous allocation rule defined on $\mathcal{E}_{ql}$ and satisfying ***Equal Resource for Equal Talent***, ***Equal Utility for Uniform Function***, and an additional axiom stipulating that, when one agent k's characteristic z_k changes, the change in x_i registered by any i should not depend on the value of z_j for $j \neq i,k$. One motivation for such an axiom, which is logically weaker than ***Independence of Utilities***, is that resource transfers for any agent should not be sensitive to how this agent's characteristic z is compared to the rest of the population. Similarly, S_{AEE} is the only single-valued anonymous allocation rule defined on $\mathcal{E}_{ql}$ and satisfying ***Equal Resource for Uniform Talent***, ***Equal Utility for Equal Function***, and an additional axiom in the vein of ***Solidarity*** (and implied by it), stipulating that, when one agent k's characteristic y_k changes, the change in u_i registered by any i should not depend on the value of y_j for $j \neq i,k$.

It is also easy to check that an allocation rule satisfies ***Additive Solidarity*** (resp. ***Multiplicative Solidarity***) and ***Equal Resource for Reference Talent*** if and only if it is an $S_{\Psi EE}$ (resp. $S_{\Psi PAE}$) with a constant Ψ (Bossert and Fleurbaey 1996, resp. Iturbe-Ormaetxe 1997), and that S_{BE} is the only allocation rule defined on $\mathcal{E}_{ql}^{Y}$ and satisfying ***Weak Solidarity*** and ***Equal Resource for Uniform Talent*** (Iturbe-Ormaetxe 1997).

Bossert (1995) characterizes S_{APAE} as the only allocation rule satisfying ***Equal Resource for Uniform Talent*** and an axiom saying that, when one agent k's characteristic y_k changes to y_k', the change in u_i registered by any i should be equal to the difference $v(y_k', z_i) - v(y_k, z_i)$, up to a multiplicative term depending on the profile and incorporating the feasibility constraint. The difference $v(y_k', z_i) - v(y_k, z_i)$ represents the change in pretax income that would be obtained by i if this agent was submitted to the same change of characteristic as agent k. This axiom is logically stronger than ***Equal Utility for Uniform Function*** and may be viewed as expressing an idea of solidarity, although it is not compatible with ***Weak Solidarity***.

Characterizations of S_{OACE} and S_{OAEE} are provided in Bossert, Fleurbaey, and Van de gaer (1999).

In a model with a continuum of agents, Sprumont (1997) characterizes S_{BE} as the only single-valued allocation rule defined on a domain similar to $\mathcal{E}_{ql}^{Y}$ and satisfying ***Equal Utility for Equal Function*** and ***Fair Relative Resource for Equal Talent***, and he dually characterizes S_{BCE} as the only single-valued allocation rule defined on a domain like $\mathcal{E}_{ql}^{Z}$ and satisfying ***Equal Resource for Equal Talent*** and ***Fair Ranking for Equal Function***.

Tungodden (2005) and Cappelen and Tungodden (2002, 2003) study weak variants of ***Independence of Utilities***, focusing on the issue of how other agents may be affected when an agent j changes his z_j. One variant says that ***Independence of Utilities*** applies only when the agent j changing z_j has $y_j = \tilde{y}$. Combined with ***Equal Utility for Equal Function***, this immediately characterizes $S_{\Psi EE}$ with $\Psi \equiv \tilde{y}$ on a subdomain with fixed y_N (see Tungodden 2005, and Cappelen and Tungodden 2003). Another variant says that when an agent j changes z_j, all other agents i have their transfer x_i changed by the same amount (so that their differential outcomes do not change). This can be justified as an application of a solidarity principle, the other agents not being responsible for the change in z_j.[33] Yet another variant says that when z_j increases, then x_i does not decrease for any $i \neq j$, the idea being that an increase in effort should not hurt others. Among

[33] With this axiom and ***Equal Utility for Equal Function***, Cappelen and Tungodden (2009) characterize a generalized version of egalitarian-equivalence, on a subdomain of $\mathcal{E}_{ql}^{Z}$ with fixed y_N:

$$(S_{GEE})_i(e) = -v(y_i, z_i) + r(z_i) + \frac{1}{n}\sum_{j=1}^{n}\left(v(y_j, z_j) - r(z_j)\right),$$

where $r : Z \to \mathbb{R}$ is an arbitrary function.

the $S_{\Psi EE}$ allocation rules, and on the domain $\mathcal{E}_{ql}^{YZc}$, this axiom is satisfied only by $S_{\Psi EE}$ with $\Psi(y_N) = \min_i y_i$, and Cappelen and Tungodden (2002) characterize it with this axiom, the previous one, ***Equal Utility for Equal Function***, and an ancillary condition restricting the outcome gap between any pair of agents to lie between the maximal and minimal productivity.[34] They also characterize $S_{\Psi EE}$ with $\Psi(y_N) = \max_i y_i$ with the symmetric axiom saying that when z_j increases, then x_i does not increase for any $i \neq j$. Finally, on the domain $\mathcal{E}_{ql}^{YZc}$ they characterize the serial rule S_{SE} with ***Equal Utility for Equal Function*** and an axiom saying that an increase in an agent's z_j does not affect the agents with $z_i \leq z_j$. Interestingly, these various axioms are all logically weaker than ***Independence of Utilities,*** so that they are satisfied by $S_{\Phi CE}$ for constant Φ, but turn out to be also compatible with a high degree of compensation, as shown in the quoted results.

If v is additively separable so that $v(y,z) = v_1(y) + v_2(z)$, then ***Independence of Utilities*** and ***Additive Solidarity*** (and all weaker axioms) are compatible. They are satisfied by the "canonical" allocation rule defined by

$$x_i = -v_1(y_i) + \frac{1}{n}\sum_{j=1}^{n} v_1(y_j),$$

which then coincides with $S_{\Phi CE}$, S_{ACE}, $S_{\Psi EE}$, S_{AEE}, S_{APAE}, S_{BE}, and S_{BCE}.[35] Notice that the characterizations mentioned in this subsection and the previous one are still valid in this particular context of additive separability.

3. UNEQUAL PRODUCTIVE SKILLS

The second environment where properties of compensation and responsibility have been studied is the production environment.[36] It is defined with respect to a group of agents sharing a technology transforming one input (typically their labor) into one

[34] This condition is: if $z_i > z_j$, then

$$v(\min y, z_i) - v(\min y, z_j) \leq S_i(e) + v(y_i, z_i) - S_j(e) - v(y_j, z_j) \leq v(\max y, z_i) - v(\max y, z_j).$$

[35] It coincides with $S_{\Psi PAE}$ for

$$\Psi(y_1, \ldots, y_n) = v_1^{-1}\left(\frac{1}{n}\sum_{i=1}^{n} v_1(y_i)\right).$$

[36] This model has been introduced by Mirrlees (1971) and Pazner and Schmeidler (1974). The problem of compensation as such has been studied in this model by Bossert, Fleurbaey, and Van de gaer (1999), Fleurbaey and Maniquet (1996, 1998, 1999, 2005, 2006, 2007), Gaspart (1996, 1998), Kolm (1996a, 2004a, 2004b), and Maniquet (1998).

output. Agents may differ by their production skill and by their preferences toward labor-time-consumption bundles.[37]

The common ethical premise of the literature surveyed in this section is that the principle of compensation applies to skills (e.g., skills are due to innate or inherited physical or intellectual abilities), whereas preferences are under the agents' responsibility.[38] In addition, it is also considered that different preferences do not justify any differential treatment, which is in line with the principle of natural reward.

We begin by defining the production model. Then, we define the basic compensation and natural reward axioms. As in the pure distribution problem examined a earlier, incompatibilities between axioms reflecting the two principles arise. The remainder of the section is devoted to analyzing several ways out of these negative results. Compared to the previous section, substantially different concepts and results are presented, due to the particular structure of the production problem.

3.1. The Model

There are two goods, an input contribution (labor time) ℓ and a consumption good c. An *economy* is a list $e = (s_N, u_N, f)$, where $N = \{1, \ldots, n\}$ is a finite population, s_i denotes agent i's production skill, u_i denotes agent i's utility function defined on bundles $x = (\ell, c)$, and $f : \mathbb{R}_+ \to \mathbb{R}_+$ is a one-input–one-output production function yielding a total production equal to $f\left(\sum_{i \in N} s_i \ell_i\right)$. The agents' consumption set is $X = [0, \overline{\ell}] \times \mathbb{R}_+$, where $\overline{\ell}$ is the maximal labor time that an agent can provide.

The relevant domain, denoted $\mathcal{E}$, consists of economies $e = (s_N, u_N, f)$ such that $n \geq 2$; for all $i \in N$, $s_i \geq 0$, and u_i is a continuous and quasi-concave function on X, nonincreasing in ℓ and increasing in c; f is increasing and concave. Let $\mathcal{U}$ denote the set of utility functions satisfying the above conditions.

In an economy $e = (s_N, u_N, f) \in \mathcal{E}$, an *allocation* is a vector of bundles $x_N = (x_1, \ldots, x_n) \in X^n$. It is *feasible* for e if and only if

$$\sum_{i \in N} c_i \leq f\left(\sum_{i \in N} s_i \ell_i\right).$$

We denote by $F(e)$ the set of feasible allocations for $e \in \mathcal{E}$, and by $F_i(e)$ the projection of $F(e)$ on agent i's consumption set, for every $i \in N$. The literature has concentrated

[37] In a similar model, Moulin and Roemer (1989) study the very different problem of sharing a technology without compensation for any individual characteristic (self-ownership), but their result is akin to results in Fleurbaey and Maniquet (1999) because one of their axioms actually implies some compensation (see Fleurbaey and Maniquet 1999 for details).

[38] Contrary to the previous model that was more abstract, this model is unambiguously in line with Rawls's and Dworkin's view that individuals should assume responsibility for their preferences, even when such preferences are not under their control.

initially on allocation rules. As in the model studied in Section 2, however, most allocation rules obtained here can be rationalized by social ordering functions. Moreover, axioms directly bearing on social ordering functions have also been proposed, in the special case where the production function is linear. Let $\mathcal{E}^L \subset \mathcal{E}$ denote the subdomain of economies such that $f(q) = q$ for all $q \in \mathbb{R}_+$ (since skills s_N can always be renormalized this covers the more general case of linear production functions).

An *allocation rule* is a correspondence S that associates to every $e \in \mathcal{E}$ a nonempty subset of its feasible allocations $S(e) \subset F(e)$. A *social ordering function* is a mapping R associating every $e \in \mathcal{E}^L$ with a complete ordering $R(e)$ over the set of allocations X^n (and $P(e)$, resp. $I(e)$, denotes the related strict preference, resp. indifference, relation).

At this point, we may introduce some basic requirements that will be used repeatedly in the sequel. First, we have the usual (strong) Pareto efficiency requirement.

Pareto-Efficiency (PE)
$\forall e = (s_N, u_N, f) \in \mathcal{E}$, $\forall x_N \in S(e)$, $\forall x'_N \in F(e)$,

$$[\forall i \in N,\ u_i(x'_i) \geq u_i(x_i)] \Rightarrow [\forall i \in N,\ u_i(x'_i) = u_i(x_i)].$$

For all $e \in \mathcal{E}$, let $PE(e)$ denote the set of Pareto-efficient allocations for e. Let us define the budget set $B(s, w, x) \subset X$ by

$$B(s, w, (\ell, c)) = \{(\ell', c') \in X \mid c' - ws\ell' \leq c - ws\ell\}.$$

This is the budget of an agent with skill s, who is just able to get bundle $x = (\ell, c)$ when w is the relative price of efficient labor. We will say that w is a supporting price for a Pareto-efficient allocation $x_N \in PE(e)$ when:

$$\begin{cases} \forall i \in N,\ x_i \in \arg\max_{x \in B(s_i, w, x_i)} u_i(x), \\ \left(\sum_{i \in N} c_i, \sum_{i \in N} s_i \ell_i\right) \in \arg\max_{(Y,L): Y \leq f(L)} Y - wL. \end{cases}$$

Let $W(x_N)$ denote the set of supporting prices for x_N.

A second basic requirement is that the replica of a selected allocation be a selected allocation for the replicated economy.

Replication Invariance
$\forall e = (s_N, u_N, f) \in \mathcal{E}$, $\forall x_N \in S(e)$, $\forall \nu$ positive integer,

$$\nu x_N \in S(\nu s_N, \nu u_N, f^\nu),$$

where νx_N means that x_N is replicated ν times (and similarly for νs_N and νu_N), and $f^\nu \in \mathcal{F}$ is defined by $f^\nu(q) = \nu f\left(\frac{q}{\nu}\right)$.

Third, we retain the simple horizontal equity requirement that two identical agents always reach the same welfare level.

Equal Treatment of Equals
$\forall e = (s_N, u_N, f) \in \mathcal{E}$, $\forall x_N \in S(e)$, $\forall i, j \in N$,

$$[s_i = s_j \text{ and } u_i = u_j] \Rightarrow [u_i(x_i) = u_j(x_j)].$$

Fourth, there is the requirement that a selected allocation remains selected after a contraction in the production set which leaves this allocation feasible.

Contraction Independence (CI, Moulin 1990)
$\forall e = (s_N, u_N, f), e' = (s_N, u_N, g) \in \mathcal{E}$, $\forall x_N \in S(e)$,

$$[\forall q \in \mathbb{R}_+,\ g(q) \leq f(q) \text{ and } x_N \in F(e')] \Rightarrow [x_N \in S(e')].$$

Finally, we have the requirement that if an allocation is selected, then all the allocations that are Pareto-indifferent to this allocation are also selected.

No Discrimination (ND, Thomson 1983)
$\forall e = (s_N, u_N, f) \in \mathcal{E}$, $\forall x_N \in S(e)$, $\forall x'_N \in F(e)$,

$$[\forall i \in N,\ u_i(x'_i) = u_i(x_i)] \Rightarrow [x'_N \in S(e)].$$

Like most of the literature on fair allocation, the literature reviewed here has focused on a restricted informational basis with ordinal noncomparable preferences. As in Section 2, we depart from it and retain utility functions here, in order to make it more transparent that this informational limitation is not arbitrary and is a consequence of the ethical requirements posited in this context, in particular those pertaining to the natural reward principle. All allocation rules presented below do satisfy the ***Ordinalism*** axiom (defined similarly as in Section 2).

3.2. Fairness in Compensation and Reward

In the model just defined, the skill parameter, for which agents should be compensated, is not an argument of preferences. But this is actually not a fundamental difference with the model of the previous section. Indeed, the current model may equivalently be written in terms of efficient labor $\hat{\ell}_i = s_i \ell_i$. The feasibility constraint is then simply $\sum_{i \in N} c_i \leq f\left(\sum_{i \in N} \hat{\ell}_i\right)$. More importantly, individual utility is then computed as

$$u_i(\ell_i, c_i) = u_i(\hat{\ell}_i / s_i, c_i),$$

where one sees that the parameter s_i does enter the utility function.[39] The most relevant differences between the current model and the previous one are, actually, the following. First, the parameter s_i enters preferences in a special way (as a denominator to $\hat{\ell}_i$), and in particular, the fact that s_i is a real number, and that utility is always nondecreasing in it (in the domain $\mathcal{E}$), excludes any disagreement problem about how to rank individual talents. Second, transferable resources $(\hat{\ell}_i, c_i)$ are two-dimensional, which entails that Pareto-efficiency is no longer trivially satisfied. Third, resources can be transformed by production. The presence of production gives this model a particular structure with specific moral issues. For instance, several notions described in this section are based on the idea that consumption should be somehow proportional to labor, or minimally, that nobody should work for nothing.[40]

As a guide to the definition of proper conditions reflecting the principles of compensation and of natural reward, it is then convenient to apply the No-Envy condition to extended bundles $(\hat{\ell}_i, c_i, s_i)$. This yields:

$$\forall i,j \in N,\ u_i(\hat{\ell}_i/s_i, c_i) \geq u_i(\hat{\ell}_j/s_j, c_j).$$

Since $u_i(\hat{\ell}_j/s_j, c_j) = u_i(\ell_j, c_j)$, one obtains the ordinary No-Envy condition as it was applied by Pazner and Schmeidler (1974) in this context:

No-Envy (NE)
$\forall e = (s_N, u_N, f) \in \mathcal{E},\ \forall x_N \in S(e),\ \forall i,j \in N,\ u_i(x_i) \geq u_i(x_j).$

Pazner and Schmeidler (1974) showed that in some economies of the domain $\mathcal{E}$, there does not exist any Pareto-efficient allocation satisfying the No-Envy condition. In other words, no allocation rule S satisfies the above ***No-Envy*** axiom and the ***Pareto-Efficiency*** axiom.[41] Again, it appears that this negative result is just a consequence of the tension between the principle of compensation and the principle of natural reward, which are both embodied in the No-Envy condition.

First, let us list basic axioms that weaken the ***No-Envy*** requirement and focus on only one of the two conflicting principles. In line with the compensation principle, one would like to compensate for differences in skills, so that two agents having the same utility functions reach the same welfare level. The axioms of ***Equal Utility for Equal Function***, ***Equal Utility for Uniform Function***, and ***Equal Utility for Reference Function*** can

[39] For agents with $s_i = 0$, this reasoning is extended by considering that they are infinitely averse to $\hat{\ell}_i$.

[40] Another difference with the model of Section 2 is that one resource $(\hat{\ell}_i)$ is a bad. Besides, the consumption range for efficient labor differs between agents: $[0, s_i\bar{\ell}]$. This reduces the transferability of $\hat{\ell}$.

[41] In contrast with the model of the previous section, the ***No-Envy*** axiom is not empty. This is due to the fact that s_i enters the utility function $u_i(\hat{\ell}_i/s_i, y_i)$ in a special way. For instance, No-Envy is satisfied by giving the bundle $(\ell, c) = (0, 0)$ to all agents.

be immediately adapted from the previous setting. We present one of them, in order to avoid any ambiguity.

Equal Utility for Equal Function (EUEF)[41]

$\forall e = (s_N, u_N, f) \in \mathcal{E}$, $\forall x_N \in S(e)$, $\forall i,j \in N$,

$$[u_i = u_j] \Rightarrow [u_i(x_i) = u_j(x_j)].$$

Since external resources are multidimensional in this model, the natural reward principle can no longer be formulated in terms of a simple equality of resources between equally talented agents. But the No-Envy condition does express an idea of equality of multidimensional resources.[43] Therefore, weakening No-Envy by applying it only to equally skilled agents seems a good way of adapting the natural reward principle to the current setting.

No-Envy among Equally Skilled (NEES, Fleurbaey and Maniquet 1996)

$\forall e = (s_N, u_N, f) \in \mathcal{E}$, $\forall x_N \in S(e)$, $\forall i,j \in N$,

$$[s_i = s_j] \Rightarrow [u_i(x_i) \geq u_i(x_j)].$$

In the same vein, one can then define an axiom of ***No-Envy among Uniformly Skilled*** (NEUS).

Interestingly, however, there is a problem with defining an axiom based on some arbitrary reference skill. For any economy with a uniform strictly positive skill s, indeed, it is possible to rescale the production function in such a way that the set of feasible bundles is the same as in another economy with any other uniform skill s'.[44] Presumably,

[42] Working only with ordinal noncomparable preferences, Fleurbaey and Maniquet (1996, 1999) actually used the following axiom, which says that agents with identical preferences should have bundles on the same indifference curve (R_i denotes agent i's preference relation, I_i denotes indifference):

Equal Welfare for Equal Preferences

$\forall e \in \mathcal{E}$, $\forall x_N \in S(e)$, $\forall i,j \in N$,

$$[R_i = R_j] \Rightarrow [x_i \, I_i \, x_j].$$

The "Equal Welfare" label is a little misleading, since it suggests that interpersonal comparisons of utilities are smuggled in the analysis. Actually, this axiom is a direct consequence of ***Equal Utility for Equal Function*** and of the ***Ordinalism*** axiom. Indeed, two agents with identical preferences could have the same utility function, in which case ***Equal Utility for Equal Function*** would require giving them equal utilities, that is, in this case, giving them bundles on the same indifference curve. Under ***Ordinalism***, this latter consequence must still hold when the agents have identical preferences but different utility functions. Therefore, this axiom of ***Equal Welfare for Equal Preferences*** is the correct translation of ***Equal Utility for Equal Function*** to a setting with ordinal noncomparable preferences.

[43] In addition, as noticed by Kolm (1972, 1996b), requiring No-Envy among agents is equivalent to requiring that there must be some common opportunity set over which these agents could choose their preferred bundles.

[44] Define $g(q) = f(qs/s')$. Then $g(\sum_i s'\ell_i) = f(\sum_i s\ell_i)$ for all ℓ_N. An allocation x_N is feasible in $e = ((s, \ldots, s), u_N, f)$ if and only if it is feasible in $e' = ((s', \ldots, s'), u_N, g)$.

we are interested only in allocation rules which are neutral to such rescaling. Under such a scale invariance constraint, an axiom of No-Envy among agents with a reference skill, similar to ***Equal Resource for Reference Talent*** of the previous section, would actually be equivalent to ***No-Envy among Uniformly Skilled***, for any strictly positive reference skill. It has not been noted in the literature, however, that if the reference skill is equal to zero, the requirement is independent of any rescaling of skills and production function.[45] In addition, one may argue that the case when all agents have zero skill is particularly telling. If no agent is productive, then we have a pure distribution economy as in the previous model, and it seems clear that an equal sharing of the unproduced resource $f(0)$ is the only reasonable allocation, as recommended by ***No-Envy***, when none of them works, as will be the case in Pareto-efficient allocations (when labor has some disutility). It would be very strange to discriminate between agents on the basis of their preferences over labor, when they do not work.

No-Envy among Zero Skilled (NEZS)
$\forall e = (s_N, R_N, f) \in \mathcal{E},\ x_N \in S(e),$

$$[\forall i \in N,\ s_i = 0] \Rightarrow [\forall i,j \in N,\ x_i R_i x_j].$$

One may also define stronger compensation and natural reward properties. The ***Solidarity*** axiom of the previous section can be applied here rather directly. ***Skill Solidarity*** is consistent with the idea of a collective sharing in the benefits of skills. It requires that all the agents be affected in the same direction if the profile of personal skills changes.

Skill Solidarity (SS, Fleurbaey and Maniquet 1999)
$\forall e = (s_N, u_N, f), e' = (s'_N, u_N, f) \in \mathcal{E},\ \forall x_N \in S(e),\ \forall x'_N \in S(e'),$

$$\forall i \in N,\ u_i(x_i) \geq u_i(x'_i) \quad \text{or} \quad \forall i \in N,\ u_i(x'_i) \geq u_i(x_i).$$

Strong natural reward axioms like ***Independence of Utilities*** cannot be directly transposed to the current model, because with multidimensional external resources such axioms would conflict with ***Pareto-Efficiency***. But some independence of changes in the profile of utility functions is achievable under ***Pareto-Efficiency***. This is done in particular by the ***Monotonicity*** axiom. This axiom, introduced in Maskin (1977), requires that

[45] An alternative solution to this difficulty is to limit application of the No-Envy condition to agents with a reference value of "wage rate" ws_i, where w is a supporting price. This is particularly natural in the subdomain $\mathcal{E}^L$, where, in any given economy, the supporting price is the same for all Pareto-efficient allocations. See Fleurbaey and Maniquet (2005), and the definition of $S\Psi_{EE}$ later in this section.

a selected allocation remain in the selection after a change in one agent's preferences whenever this change enlarges her lower contour set at her assigned bundle. ***Monotonicity*** has played an important role in the implementation literature. It is quite interesting to find a connection between incentive compatibility conditions, which require the allocation rule not to be sensitive to personal characteristics that the agents can easily conceal or misrepresent, and natural reward conditions, which justify a disregard of personal characteristics for which the agents are responsible.

Monotonicity (M, Maskin 1977)
$\forall e = (s_N, u_N, f) \in \mathcal{E}, \forall x_N \in S(e), \forall i \in N, \forall u'_i \in \mathcal{U},$

$$[\forall x \in F_i(e),\ u_i(x_i) \geq u_i(x) \Rightarrow u'_i(x_i) \geq u'_i(x)] \Rightarrow x_N \in S\left(s_N, (u_{N\setminus\{i\}}, u'_i), f\right).$$

When the allocation rule satisfies ***Equal Treatment of Equals***, ***Monotonicity*** implies ***No-Envy among Equally Skilled***.[46] ***Monotonicity*** also implies ***Ordinalism***, as shown by Maskin.

Several properties have been studied in the literature that are even stronger than ***Monotonicity*** (see, e.g., Nagahisa 1991). The following property, introduced in Gaspart (1996), requires that a selected allocation remain in the selection after a change in the agents' utility functions and in the skill profile whenever the allocation is Pareto-efficient in the new economy. This axiom implies ***Monotonicity*** for Pareto-efficient allocation rules. Interestingly, this axiom also has a flavor of compensation, since the selection is also required to be independent, in some cases, of changes in the skill profile.[47]

Pareto Preserving Independence (PPI, Gaspart 1996, 1998)
$\forall e = (s_N, u_N, f),\ e' = (s'_N, u'_N, f) \in \mathcal{E}, \forall x_N \in S(e),$

$$[x_N \in PE(e')] \Rightarrow [x_N \in S(e')].$$

We may now present the general structure of this set of axioms.

[46] This is a consequence of a result in Moulin (1994) and Fleurbaey and Maniquet (1997). The intuition for the proof is as follows. Let $e = (s_N, u_N, f)$. Suppose $s_i = s_j$ and $x_N \in S(e)$ is such that $u_i(x_i) < u_i(x_j)$, i.e., i envies j. Then one can find a function $u^* \in \mathcal{U}$ such that $u^*(x_i) < u^*(x_j)$ and:

$$\forall x \in X,\ u_i(x_i) = u_i(x) \Rightarrow u^*(x_i) = u^*(x),$$

$$\forall x \in X,\ u_j(x_j) \geq u_j(x) \Rightarrow u^*(x_j) \geq u^*(x).$$

By monotonicity, $x_N \in S(s_N, (u_{N\setminus\{i,j\}}, u^*, u^*), f)$. Since $u^*(x_i) \neq u^*(x_j)$, this violates ***Equal Treatment of Equals***. By a similar argument, one can show that ***Monotonicity*** and ***Equal Utility for Equal Function*** imply ***No-Envy***.

[47] An axiom of independence of skill levels is used in Yoshihara (2003). This axiom says that $S(e) = S(e')$ whenever $F(e) = F(e')$ and e, e' differ only in the skill profile. The condition $F(e) = F(e')$ is never obtained when f is increasing, and the axiom is used by Yoshihara only for cases of constant f. Closer to Gaspart's axiom, Yamada and Yoshihara (2007) introduce an axiom that says that a selected allocation remains selected whenever the skills of nonworking agents change without altering the Pareto-efficiency of the allocation.

Proposition 8 *The following table describes the logical implications between axioms:*

Compensation		**Natural Reward**
		PPI
		$\Downarrow^{(3)}$
SS		M $\Rightarrow$ O
$\Downarrow^{(1)}$		$\Downarrow^{(2)}$
EUEF	$\Leftarrow$ NE $\Rightarrow$	NEES
$\Downarrow$		$\Downarrow$
EUUF		NEUS
$\Downarrow$		$\Downarrow$
EURF		NEZS

(1) *Assuming that S satisfies* **A**nonymity.
(2) *Assuming that S satisfies* **E**qual **T**reatment of **E**quals.
(3) *Assuming that S satisfies* **P**areto-**E**fficiency.

The following allocation rules, studied in Fleurbaey and Maniquet (1996, 1999) and Gaspart (1996, 1998), are important when studying the possible combinations of compensation and natural reward properties. First, the Egalitarian Equivalent rule selects Pareto-efficient allocations having the property that there is some consumption level c_0 such that all agents are indifferent between their assigned bundle and consuming c_0 without working at all.

Egalitarian Equivalence (S_{EE}, Kolm 1968,[48] Pazner and Schmeidler 1978a)
$\forall e = (s_N, u_N, f) \in \mathcal{E}$,

$$S_{EE}(e) = \{x_N \in PE(e) \mid \forall i \in N, \exists c_0 \in \mathbb{R}_+,\ u_i(x_i) = u_i(0, c_0)\}.$$

This rule is just a member of more general family, defined as follows. An allocation is selected if it is Pareto-efficient and every agent's utility is equal to her indirect utility over a reference budget (the same for all agents).

[48] Kolm (1968) attributes this idea to Lange (1936), who proposed to compensate workers for the disutility of their particular jobs in his scheme of market socialism. But it is not clear in Lange's writings that such compensation would render all workers indifferent to one and the same bundle $(0, c_0)$.

Budget Egalitarian Equivalence ($S_{\Psi EE}$)
$\forall e = (s_N, R_N, f) \in \mathcal{E}$,

$$S_{\Psi EE}(e) = \left\{ \begin{array}{c} x_N \in PE(e) \mid \exists w \in W(x_N), \exists x_0 \in X, \\ \forall i \in N,\ u_i(x_i) = \max u_i\left(B(\tilde{s}, w, x_0)\right) \end{array} \right\},$$

where $\tilde{s}$ is such that $w\tilde{s} = \Psi(ws_1, \ldots, ws_n)$.[49]

One has $S_{\Psi EE} = S_{EE}$ when $\Psi \equiv 0$. Among the $S_{\Psi EE}$ family, S_{EE} is the most favorable to agents who have a strong aversion to labor, by making all indifference curves cross at a point $(0, c_0)$. This automatically entails envy on behalf of "hardworking" agents toward "lazy" agents (whose indifference curve will lie everywhere above the "hardworking" agents' curve, except at $(0, c_0)$). The other $S_{\Psi EE}$ rules favor other preferences, depending on Ψ. Since $w\tilde{s}$ is the slope of the reference budget in the (ℓ, c)-space, the greater $w\tilde{s}$ the better it is for agents who are willing to work. These allocation rules are therefore not very neutral with respect to preferences.

Second, the Conditional Equality rule selects Pareto-efficient allocations having the property that an agent with reference preferences would be indifferent between having to choose among any of the budget sets of all the agents. This is a rather immediate adaptation of the similar solution from the previous section.

Conditional Equality ($S_{\Phi CE}$, Fleurbaey and Maniquet 1996)
$\forall e = (s_N, R_N, f) \in \mathcal{E}$,

$$S_{\Phi CE}(e) = \left\{ \begin{array}{c} x_N \in PE(e) \mid \exists w \in W(x_N), \forall i,j \in N, \\ \max \tilde{u}\left(B(s_i, w, x_i)\right) = \max \tilde{u}\left(B(s_j, w, x_j)\right) \end{array} \right\},$$

where $\tilde{u} = \Phi(u_1, \ldots, u_n)$.

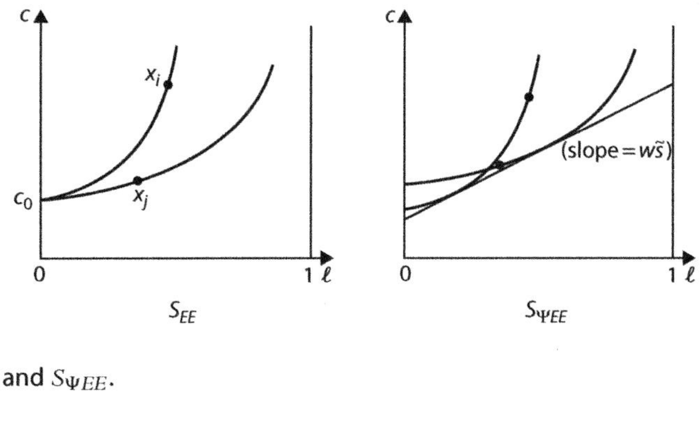

Figure 22.1. S_{EE} and $S_{\Psi EE}$.

[49] The function Ψ bears on the ws_i, because these values are independent of any joint rescaling of the skills and the production function that leaves unchanged the set of feasible allocations.

Third, Objective Egalitarianism selects Pareto-efficient allocations having the property that an agent with reference preferences would be indifferent between the bundles assigned to all agents. This is another possible adaptation of the Conditional Equality rule of the previous section.

Objective Egalitarianism ($S_{\Phi OE}$, Gaspart 1996, 1998)
$\forall e = (s_N, R_N, f) \in \mathcal{E}$,

$$S_{\Phi OE}(e) = \left\{x_N \in PE(e) \mid \forall i, j \in N,\ \tilde{u}(x_i) = \tilde{u}(x_j)\right\},$$

where $\tilde{u} = \Phi(u_1, \ldots, u_n)$.

It is worth examining the redistributive consequences of the choice of $\tilde{u}$ in $S_{\Phi CE}$ and $S_{\Phi OE}$. With a function $\tilde{u}$ displaying a strong aversion to labor, $S_{\Phi CE}$ selects allocations that perform little redistribution from high-skilled to low-skilled. Indeed, all individual budget sets being equivalent for $\tilde{u}$, they must then be similar at low levels of labor, which corresponds to a situation where profits of the firm are approximately equally divided, and no compensation is made for differential skills. Conversely, with a $\tilde{u}$ displaying a very low aversion to labor, $S_{\Phi CE}$ selects allocations that are very favorable to the low-skilled, and quite unfavorable to the high-skilled.

For $S_{\Phi OE}$ the consequences are not exactly the same. With a $\tilde{u}$ displaying a very low aversion to labor, for instance, consumption levels in selected allocations will be substantially equalized, which is favorable to low-skilled agents, but also, among equally skilled agents of any skill level, favorable to agents with a strong aversion to labor (they will work less, without being penalized in terms of consumption). Conversely, a $\tilde{u}$ displaying a strong aversion to labor is favorable to the high-skilled but also to the hardworking agents. This shows that Objective Egalitarianism is not really neutral.

All the rules satisfy ***Pareto-Efficiency***, ***Replication Invariance***, and ***Contraction Independence***, and all but $S_{\Phi OE}$ satisfy ***Equal Treatment of Equals*** and **No Discrimination**.

The following proposition examines how these rules fare in terms of compensation and natural reward, and also depicts the conflict between these two principles.

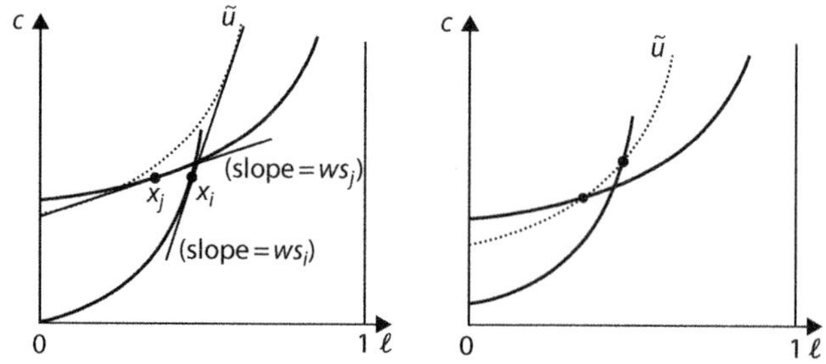

Figure 22.2. $S_{\Phi CE}$.

Proposition 9 *The following table describes the incompatibilities (marked by $\otimes$) between the main axioms of compensation and natural reward, under the assumption that the allocation rule satisfies* Pareto-Efficiency. *The table also shows what axioms are satisfied by the various solutions. Rule* $S_{\Phi OE}$ *does not satisfy* NEES, NEUS, *or* NEZS.[50]

	PPI	M	NEES	NEUS	NEZS
SS	$\otimes$	$\otimes$	$\otimes$	$\otimes$	S_{EE}
EUEF	$\otimes$	$\otimes$	$\otimes$	$S_{\Psi EE}$ (Ψ *idempotent*)	
EUUF	$\otimes$	$\otimes$	$S_{\Phi CE}$ (Φ *idempotent*)		
EURF	$S_{\Phi OE}$ (Φ *constant*)	$S_{\Phi CE}$ (Φ *constant*)			

Proof. We focus on the impossibilities and omit the rest.

SS and NEUS are incompatible. Let $e = ((1,1,1),(u_1,u_2,u_3),f) \in \mathcal{E}$ be defined as follows: $u_1(\ell,c) = c - \ell/10$, $u_2(\ell,c) = c - 9\ell/10$, $u_3(\ell,c) = c - \ell, f(q) = \min\{q,2\}$, and $\overline{\ell} = 1$. Let S satisfy the axioms. Let $x_N \in S(e)$. By PE, $\ell_1 = \ell_2 = 1$, $\ell_3 = 0$, and $c_1 + c_2 + c_3 = 2$. By NEUS, $c_1 = c_2$ and $c_3 \leq c_2 - 9/10$. Therefore $c_1 \geq c_3 + 9/10$, and replacing c_3 by $2 - 2c_1$, one obtains $c_1 \geq 29/30$. Now, consider $e' = ((20,20,20),(u_1,u_2,u_3),f) \in \mathcal{E}$ and $x'_N \in S(e')$. By PE, $\ell'_1 = 1/10$, $\ell'_2 = \ell'_3 = 0$, and $c'_1 + c'_2 + c'_3 = 2$. By NEUS, $c'_2 = c'_3$ and $c'_2 \geq c'_1 - 9/100$. Replacing c'_2 by $1 - c'_1/2$, one obtains $c'_1 \leq 218/300$. The problem is that $u_1(1/10, 218/300) < u_1(1, 29/30)$, which implies that $u_1(x'_1) < u_1(x_1)$, in contradiction with SS (by PE, at least one of the agents is better off in x'_N).

EUEF and NEES are incompatible. Let $e = ((s_1,s_2,s_3,s_4),(u_1,u_2,u_3,u_4),f) \in \mathcal{E}$ be defined as follows: $s_1 = s_2 = 0$, $s_3 = s_4 = 1$, $u_1(\ell,c) = u_3(\ell,c) = c - \ell/4$ and $u_2(\ell,c) = u_4(\ell,c) = c - \ell/2, f(q) = q$ and $\overline{\ell} = 1$. Let S satisfy the axioms. Let $x_N \in S(e)$. By PE, $\ell_1 = \ell_2 = 0$ and $\ell_3 = \ell_4 = 1$; by EUEF, $c_1 = c_3 - 1/4$ and $c_2 = c_4 - 1/2$. By NEES, $c_1 = c_2$ and $c_3 = c_4$, which is incompatible with the previous equalities.

M and EUUF are incompatible. Let $e = ((s_1,s_2),(u_1,u_2),f) \in \mathcal{E}$ be defined as follows: $s_1 = 0$, $s_2 = 1$, $u_1(\ell,c) = c - \ell/4$ and $u_2(\ell,c) = c - \ell/2, f(q) = q$ and $\overline{\ell} = 1$. Let S satisfy the axioms. Let $x_N \in S(e)$. By PE, $\ell_1 = 0$ and $\ell_3 = 1$. Therefore, by M, $x_N \in S(s_N,(u_1,u_1),f)$ and $x_N \in S(s_N,(u_2,u_2),f)$. By EUUF, in $(s_N,(u_1,u_1),f)$ one must have $c_1 = c_2 - 1/4$, whereas in $(s_N,(u_2,u_2),f)$ one must have $c_1 = c_2 - 1/2$. These two equalities cannot be satisfied simultaneously by x_N. □

[50] Notice that since it does not satisfy ***Equal Treatment of Equals***, the fact that it satisfies ***Monotonicity*** does not guarantee that it satisfies these other axioms.

In the above proof of the incompatibility between ***Equal Utility for Equal Function*** and ***No-Envy among Equally Skilled***, a very weak part of ***No-Envy among Equally Skilled*** has been used, namely, the condition that among two equally skilled agents, no one must have more consumption than the other, when they work the same. This shows how strong the incompatibility with ***Equal Utility for Equal Function*** is. Since the ***Equal Utility for Equal Function*** and ***No-Envy among Equally Skilled*** axioms involved in this theorem are logical consequences of the No-Envy axiom, the negative result obtained by Pazner and Schmeidler (1974) about the existence of Pareto-efficient and envy-free allocations is just a corollary of this proposition, and the difficulties with No-Envy can be explained by the fact that this requirement combines compensation and natural reward in a too-demanding way.[51]

The lack of neutrality of S_{EE}, $S_{\Psi EE}$, and $S_{\Phi OE}$ with respect to individual preferences, which has been noticed above, can be explained by the fact that these rules fail to satisfy important natural reward axioms, as stated in the proposition.

Characterization results have been provided for some of these rules. Some of them involve a Consistency axiom that is the proper adaptation of the Consistency defined above to the current framework. Its precise definition is somewhat technical and is omitted here.[52]

Proposition 10 (Fleurbaey and Maniquet 1999) *The* Egalitarian Equivalent rule S_{EE} *is the smallest rule, with respect to inclusion, satisfying* **P**areto **E**fficiency, **E**qual **U**tility for **E**qual **F**unction, **N**o-**E**nvy among **Z**ero **S**killed, **N**o **D**iscrimination, *and* **C**onsistency.[53]

Proposition 11 (Fleurbaey and Maniquet 1996) *If S satisfies* **P**areto **E**fficiency, **E**qual **U**tility for **R**eference **F**unction, **M**onotonicity, **N**o **D**iscrimination, *and* **C**ontraction **I**ndependence, *then there is a constant* Φ *such that for all* $e \in E$, $S_{\Phi CE}(e) \subseteq S(e)$. *The same result is obtained if* **M**onotonicity *is replaced by* **N**o-**E**nvy among **E**qually **S**killed *and* **C**onsistency.

[51] As an alternative direction of research, one can also try and identify subdomains of economies where the incompatibilities presented above do not hold. For instance, Piketty (1994) identified a domain restriction under which ***No-Envy*** and ***Pareto-Efficiency*** are compatible. Any $e = (s_N, u_N, f) \in \mathcal{E}^L$ satisfies this domain restriction if and only if for all $i, j \in N$ such that $s_i \leq s_j$, for all $x, x' \in X$ such that $u_i(x) = u_i(x')$, $x' < x \Rightarrow u_j(x) \geq u_j(x')$.

This condition, which says that the less productive agents have a lower willingness to work as well, is quite strong. It implies the Spence–Mirrlees single-crossing condition (usually defined on earnings-consumption bundles), but it is much stronger.

[52] When one considers a subeconomy, one has to delete the consumption and labor of the rest of the population. This deletion may render the resulting production function nonconcave. The consistency condition can then only be applied when the reduced economy is still in the domain $\mathcal{E}$. See Fleurbaey and Maniquet (1996, 1999) for details, and also Thomson (1988), and Moulin and Shenker (1994).

[53] See Fleurbaey and Maniquet (1999), Proposition 7. This proposition relies, instead of ***No-Envy among Zero Skilled***, on ***Work Alone Lower Bound***, an axiom defined in Section 3.4. But ***No-Envy among Zero Skilled*** would play the same role in the proof as ***Work Alone Lower Bound***.

Proof. The structure of the proofs of the results involving Consistency is very similar to that of Propositions 3 and 4 earlier. We only provide the proof of the first part of the latter proposition.

Let S satisfy PE, EURF, M, ND, and CI. Let $e \in \mathcal{E}$. Let $\tilde{u} \in \mathcal{U}$ be such that EURF is satisfied for it, and consider the constant function $\Phi \equiv \tilde{u}$. Let $x_N \in S_{\Phi CE}(e)$ with a supporting price $w \in W(x_N)$. Let $e' = (s_N, u'_N, g) \in \mathcal{E}$ be defined by: for all $i \in N$, $u'_i(\ell, c) = c - s_i w\ell$, and $g(q) = \sum_{i \in N}(c_i - s_i w\ell_i) + wq$.

We claim that $S(e') = S_{\Phi CE}(e')$. Suppose not. Let $x'_N \in S(e') \setminus S_{\Phi CE}(e')$. Let x''_N be defined by: for all $i \in N$, $x''_i \in \arg\max_{x \in B(s_i, w, x'_i)} \tilde{u}(x)$. One has $x''_N \in F(e')$. By ND, $x''_N \in S(e')$. By M, $x''_N \in S(s_N, (\tilde{u}, \ldots, \tilde{u}), g)$, violating EURF because by construction $x''_N \notin S_{\Phi CE}(s_N, (\tilde{u}, \ldots, \tilde{u}), g)$, so that there are i, j such that $\tilde{u}(x''_i) \neq \tilde{u}(x''_j)$. Therefore $S(e') \subseteq S_{\Phi CE}(e')$. By ND again, one actually has $S(e') = S_{\Phi CE}(e')$.

By ND, $x_N \in S(e')$ as well. By M, $x_N \in S(s_N, u_N, g)$. By CI, one finally concludes that $x_N \in S(e)$. □

As in the monetary compensation problem, the allocation rules can be interpreted as derived from social ordering functions that rationalize them. In particular, the following social ordering function rationalizes the Egalitarian Equivalent rule S_{EE}. It applies the leximin criterion to numerical representations of preferences that are constructed by measuring the distance between the $(0,0)$ bundle and the intersection of an indifference curve with the axes.

Egalitarian Equivalent Ordering Function (R_{EE}, Fleurbaey and Maniquet 2005)
$\forall e \in \mathcal{E}$, $\forall x_N, x'_N \in X^n$,

$$x_N \, R_{EE}(e) \, x'_N \Leftrightarrow (v_i(x_i))_{i \in N} \geq_{\text{lex}} \left(v_i(x'_i)\right)_{i \in N},$$

where for all $i \in N$, $v_i(x)$ is defined by $u_i(x) = u_i(0, v_i(x))$ or $u_i(x) = u_i(-v_i(x), 0)$.

The definition of the appropriate social ordering functions rationalizing $S_{\Phi CE}$ and $S_{\Phi OE}$ over $\mathcal{E}$ is yet an open question, but things are easier for $S_{\Phi CE}$ on the domain $\mathcal{E}^L$. For this domain, one can rely on the notion of implicit budget $IB(s, u, x)$, which is the smallest budget set that enables an agent with skill s and utility function u to obtain the utility level $u(x)$. For $s \in \mathbb{R}_+$, $u \in \mathcal{U}$, $x \in X$, the implicit budget $IB(s, u, x)$ is defined by

$$IB(s, u, x) = \left\{(\ell', c') \in X \mid c' - s\ell' \leq e_u(s, u(x))\right\},$$

where $e_u(.,.)$ is the expenditure function

$$e_u(s, v) = \min\{c - s\ell \mid (\ell, c) \in X, \; u(\ell, c) \geq v\}.$$

Notice that the bundle x need not belong to the implicit budget $IB(s,u,x)$. Then, we have the following social ordering function, which rationalizes $S_{\Phi CE}$ by applying the leximin criterion to the implicit budgets of the agents evaluated with the reference utility function.

Conditional Equality Ordering Function ($R_{\Phi CE}$, **Fleurbaey and Maniquet 2005**)
$\forall e \in \mathcal{E}^L$, $\forall x_N, x'_N \in X^n$,

$$[x_N \, R_{\Phi CE}(e) \, x'_N] \Leftrightarrow (\max \tilde{u}(IB(s_i,u_i,x_i)))_{i\in N} \geq_{\text{lex}} \left(\max \tilde{u}\left(IB(s_i,u_i,x'_i)\right)\right)_{i\in N},$$

where $\tilde{u} = \Phi(u_1,\ldots,u_n)$.

Fleurbaey and Maniquet (2005) provide characterizations of these and other social ordering functions in the domain $\mathcal{E}^L$, relying on axioms that are inspired by the above axioms of compensation and natural reward. We do not go into details here, and only explain how the idea of compensation can suggest various axioms, which bear interesting relations with other parts of the literature.

The ***Equal Utility for Equal Function*** axiom, for allocation rules, requires that equalizing utilities of agents having the same utility function. A social ordering function, similarly, may be required to be averse to welfare inequality among agents having the same utility functions. This may be captured by the following property, which is essentially an application of Hammond's equity axiom (Hammond 1976), expressing an infinite degree of inequality aversion. The difference with Hammond's equity axiom is the restriction to agents with identical utility functions.

Hammond Compensation (Fleurbaey and Maniquet 2005)
$\forall e = (s_N, u_N, f) \in \mathcal{E}^L$, $\forall x_N, x'_N \in X^n$, if there exist $i,j \in N$ such that:

(i) $\forall k \in N,\ k \neq i,j \Rightarrow x_k = x'_k$,
(ii) $u_i = u_j$,
(iii) $u_j(x_j) > u_j(x'_j) > u_i(x'_i) > u_i(x_i)$,

then $x'_N \, P(e) \, x_N$.

As shown in Fleurbaey and Maniquet (2006), one can also rely on the Pigou–Dalton principle of transfer in order to express the same idea, albeit with a milder (arbitrarily small) degree of inequality aversion. The Pigou–Dalton principle is usually applied in studies of one-dimensional inequalities in income.[54] Here income (c) inequality is also reduced, but the principle is applied only to agents with identical utility functions and with identical and unchanged labor (ℓ).[55]

Pigou–Dalton Compensation (Fleurbaey and Maniquet 2006)
$\forall e = (s_N, u_N, f) \in \mathcal{E}^L$, $\forall x_N, x'_N \in X^n$, if there exist $i,j \in N$ and $\delta > 0$ such that:

[54] See, e.g., Sen (1973).
[55] With less restrictions, this axiom would clash with the Pareto principle. See, e.g., Fleurbaey and Trannoy (2003).

(i) $\forall k \in N,\ k \neq i,j \Rightarrow x_k = x'_k$,
(ii) $u_i = u_j$,
(iii) $\ell_i = \ell'_i = \ell_j = \ell'_j$,
(iv) $c'_j = c_j - \delta > c_i + \delta = c'_i$,

then $x'_N\, P(e)\, x_N$.

The study of social ordering functions is particularly relevant for applications of the ethical principles of compensation and natural reward to contexts where the Pareto-efficient allocation rules cannot be implemented. The most important case for applications is income taxation, when neither s_i nor ℓ_i is observed by the redistributive agencies and redistribution must be made only on the basis of earned income $s_i\ell_i$. Such applications are discussed in the next section.

3.3. Bundle Equality and Welfare Lower Bounds

The incompatibility between compensation and natural reward has been dealt with in Section 3.2 by weakening the requirements. One may find, however, that the weakenings of the main axioms ***E****qual* ***U****tility for* ***E****qual* ***F****unction* and ***N****o-****E****nvy among* ***E****qually* ***S****killed* are unsatisfactory. For instance, ***E****qual* ***U****tility for* ***E****qual* ***F****unction* requires welfare equality, that is, an infinite inequality aversion, whenever two agents have identical utility functions. By weakening it into either ***E****qual* ***U****tility for* ***U****niform* ***F****unction* or ***E****qual* ***U****tility for* ***R****eference* ***F****unction*, we have kept the infinite inequality requirement but restricted its application in a sharp way. In two approaches presented now, the infinite inequality aversion is dropped. In the first approach, developed by Gaspart (1996), the emphasis is put on bundle equality. In the second approach, developed by Maniquet (1998), the emphasis is put on opportunity sets of bundles. The two approaches also have in common that each axiom is now intended to simultaneously capture (imperfect) compensation and natural reward requisites.

We begin with two examples of properties in the first approach. These properties are consistent with the idea that bundles should be equalized (though not at the expense of efficiency). ***N****o* ***D****omination by the* ***A****verage* ***B****undle* requires that no bundle be composed of both a larger labor time than the average labor time and a lower consumption than the average consumption. The idea is that no agent should be so badly treated (e.g., because of a low skill—compensation—or a particular utility function—natural reward) that he must work more than average for a lower than average consumption.

No Domination by the Average Bundle (Gaspart 1996)
$\forall e = (s_N, u_N, f) \in \mathcal{E}$, $\forall x_N \in S(e)$, $\forall i \in N$,

$$\ell_i \leq \frac{\sum_{j \in N} \ell_j}{\#N} \text{ or } c_i \geq \frac{\sum_{j \in N} c_j}{\#N}.$$

The axiom of ***S****election of* ***E****fficient* ***E****galitarian* ***A****llocations* requires that whenever a Pareto-efficient allocation composed of equal bundles exists, it is selected. When all agents have the same bundle, it seems clear that no advantage is given to anyone on the basis of his skill (compensation) or utility function (natural reward). Equality of resources and No-Envy cannot be more simply and clearly satisfied.

Selection of Efficient Egalitarian Allocations (Gaspart 1996)
$\forall e = (s_N, u_N, f) \in \mathcal{E}$, $\forall x_N \in F(e)$, $\forall x \in X$,

$$[\forall i \in N,\ x_i = x \text{ and } x_N \in PE(e)] \Rightarrow [x_N \in S(e)].$$

As explained, bundle equality is consistent with responsibility for one's utility function and the principle of natural reward. In addition, by considering labor time-consumption bundles (ℓ, c) rather than efficient labor-consumption bundles $(\hat{\ell}, c)$, the two axioms above also convey an idea of skill compensation.

It is interesting to examine the compatibility scheme between these axioms and the compensation and responsibility properties previously presented. The results are presented in the following theorem. Two main lessons may be drawn from those results. First, axioms based on the desirability of material equality are more easily combined with responsibility and reward properties than with compensation properties. Second, they highlight a new solution, the proportional allocation rule.

Proposition 12 (Gaspart 1996, 1998) *There exist* Pareto-efficient *allocation rules satisfying* **R**eplication **I**nvariance, **C**ontraction **I**ndependence, *and each of the following lists of axioms:*

1. **N**o **D**omination by the **A**verage **B**undle, **S**election of **E**fficient **E**galitarian **A**llocations, *and* **P**areto **P**reserving **I**ndependence*;*
2. **S**election of **E**fficient **E**galitarian **A**llocations *and* ***E**qual **U**tility for **E**qual **F**unction.*

On the other hand, no Pareto-efficient *allocation rule can satisfy any of the following pairs of axioms:*

1. **N**o **D**omination by the **A**verage **B**undle *and* **E**qual **U**tility for **R**eference **F**unction*;*
2. **S**election of **E**fficient **E**galitarian **A**llocations *and* **S**kill **S**olidarity.

The first statement of the theorem is proved by an example. The Proportional rule selects Pareto-efficient allocations having the property that the consumption-labor ratio c_i/ℓ_i is identical among agents.

The Proportional Rule (S_P, Roemer and Silvestre 1989, Gaspart 1998)
$\forall e = (s_N, u_N, f) \in \mathcal{E}$,

$$S_P(e) = \{x_N \in PE(e) \mid \exists r \geq 0, \forall i \in N,\ c_i = r\ell_i\}.$$

The Proportional rule satisfies ***No Domination by the Average Bundle***, ***Selection of Efficient Egalitarian Allocations***, and ***Pareto Preserving Independence***. This rule fails to satisfy ***No Discrimination*** and ***Equal Treatment of Equals***. It is given axiomatic characterizations, on the basis of ***Pareto Preserving Independence*** but also by reference to the family of solutions belonging to Objective Egalitarianism (defined in the previous subsection), in Gaspart (1998).

The compatibility between ***Selection of Efficient Egalitarian Allocations*** and ***Equal Utility for Equal Function*** is an immediate consequence of the fact that a Pareto-efficient egalitarian allocation often fails to exist in economies where two agents have equal preferences but unequal skills. Therefore, these two requirements bear on two essentially disjoint sets of economies.[56]

Now, we turn to the second approach, due to Maniquet (1998), in which allocation rules are required to guarantee *equal rights*. The idea is to grant all agents an identical opportunity set in X, and to require the allocation rule to give every agent a bundle that she weakly prefers to her best choice in the opportunity set. The common opportunity set in X is called an equal *right*, since every agent has a definite right to be as well-off as if her choice was really to be made in this opportunity set.

This equal right is, formally, a compact subset of X. Moreover, Maniquet (1998) suggests that, as an unconditional right, this opportunity set should not depend on the profile u_N. Feasibility constraints impose, however, to take account of s_N and f. In an economy, $e = (s_N, u_N, f)$, an equal right must then be a subset $E(s_N, f) \subset X$ such that $E(s_N, f)^n \in F(e)$.

The guarantee of equal right then takes the form of the following axiom. Following Maniquet (1998), we restrict the domain to the set $\mathcal{E}_+ \subset \mathcal{E}$ of economies where agents have a strictly positive skill.[57]

Guarantee of Equal Right E (Maniquet 1998)
$\forall e = (s_N, u_N, f) \in \mathcal{E}_+$, $\forall x_N \in S(e)$,

$$\forall i \in N, \ u_i(x_i) \geq \max u_i(E(s_N, f)).$$

Let us note that if an equal right E does not satisfy the feasibility constraint $E(s_N, f)^n \in F(e)$, then it cannot be guaranteed by any allocation rule.

[56] As an example, consider the rule that selects egalitarian allocations whenever they are efficient, and coincides with S_{EE} otherwise. This rule satisfies ***Selection of Efficient Egalitarian Allocations*** and ***Equal Utility for Equal Function***, in addition to ***Pareto Efficiency***, ***Replication Invariance***, and ***Contraction Independence***.

[57] This additional assumption simplifies the analysis, since it implies that the sets of weak and strong Pareto-efficient allocations coincide. Moreover, the two last results mentioned in this subsection hold true only if this assumption is made.

An equal right is compensating low-skilled agents, since the lower bound levels $\max u_i(E(s_N,f))$ guaranteed to two agents having the same utility function are the same. Moreover, in line with natural reward, it leaves the agents responsible for their choice over the opportunity set, so that the difference between the minimal welfare levels guaranteed to two agents having the same skill only reflects their different utility function. The compensation it carries out, however, may be rather low, if the equal right itself is small. This suggests trying to find large equal rights.

Let us summarize the main results obtained by this approach. First, an equal right cannot be very large. In other words, we come back here to the fundamental trade-off between compensation and natural reward. Second, an equal right can easily be combined with strong requirements of either skill compensation or natural reward. Third, when combining equal rights with skill compensation or natural reward properties, we come back, essentially, to standard allocation rules.

Looking for an equal right that is as large as possible, Maniquet (1998) shows that a prominent family of equal right correspondences $E(.,.)$ is the following. Let $\ell^\star \in [0,\overline{\ell}]$ be given.

$\ell^\star$-Equal Right (Maniquet 1998)

$$E_{\ell^\star}(s_N,f) = \left\{(\ell,c) \in X \mid \ell \geq \ell^\star,\ c \leq \frac{1}{n} f\left(\sum_i s_i \ell^\star\right)\right\}.$$

Imposing some $\ell^\star$-equal right is compatible with almost any compensation or natural reward requirement. Let $\mathcal{E}_+^{\overline{\ell}} \subset \mathcal{E}_+$ be the subdomain such that for every $e = (s_N, u_N, f) \in \mathcal{E}_+^{\overline{\ell}}$, every $i \in N$, every $x \in X$, there exists $c' \in \mathbb{R}_+$ such that $u_i(\overline{\ell}, c') \geq u(x)$, that is, working maximal time $\overline{\ell}$ can always be compensated by enough consumption.

Proposition 13 (Maniquet 1998) *Let $\ell^\star \in [0,\overline{\ell}]$ be given. There exist allocation rules guaranteeing the* $\ell^\star$-equal right *that satisfy* **P**areto-**E**fficiency, **R**eplication **I**nvariance, **E**qual **T**reatment of **E**quals, **C**ontraction **I**ndependence, *and each one of the following axioms or lists of axioms:*

1. **S**kill **S**olidarity *over $\mathcal{E}_+^{\overline{\ell}}$;*
2. ***E**qual **U**tility for **E**qual **F**unction and* **N**o-**E**nvy among **U**niformly **S**killed*;*
3. **E**qual **U**tility for **U**niform **F**unction *and* **N**o-**E**nvy among **E**qually **S**killed *over $\mathcal{E}_+^{\overline{\ell}}$;*
4. **M**onotonicity.

We restrict our attention to examples of compatibility 1 and 4. The $\ell^\star$-Egalitarian Equivalent rule $S_{\ell^\star EE}$ selects Pareto-efficient allocations having the property that there is some consumption level c_0 such that all agents are indifferent between their assigned bundle and the $(\ell^\star, c_0)$ bundle.

$\ell^\star$-Egalitarian Equivalent Rule ($S_{\ell^\star EE}$, Maniquet 1998)
$\forall e = (s_N, R_N, f) \in \mathcal{E}_+^{\bar{\ell}}$,

$$S_{\ell^\star EE} = \left\{x_N \in PE(e) \mid \exists c_0 \in \mathbb{R}_+, \forall i \in N,\ u_i(x_i) = u_i(\ell^\star, c_0)\right\}.$$

The Egalitarian Equivalent rule S_{EE} is obviously an element of the $S_{\ell^\star EE}$ family of rules. For a given $\ell^\star$, the $S_{\ell^\star EE}$ rule satisfies ***Pareto-Efficiency***, ***Skill Solidarity***, ***Consistency***, ***Replication Invariance***, and ***No Discrimination***, and guarantees the *$\ell^\star$-Equal Right*. Moreover, Maniquet (1998) shows that it is the only one to satisfy such properties on a relevant domain (extended to nonconcave production functions). The argument is similar to the proof of Proposition 10.

The $\ell^\star$-equal budget rules select Pareto-efficient allocations having the property that all budget lines cross at a point of abscissa $\ell^\star$.

$\ell^\star$-Equal Budget Rule ($S_{\ell^\star EB}$, Kolm 1996a, Maniquet 1998)
$\forall e = (s_N, R_N, f) \in \mathcal{E}_+$,

$$S_{\ell^\star EB}(e) = \left\{ \begin{array}{c} x_N \in PE(e) \mid \exists w \in W(x_N), \forall i,j \in N, \\ c_i - s_i w(\ell_i - \ell^\star) = c_j - s_j w(\ell_j - \ell^\star) \end{array} \right\}.$$

Notice that for any e, there is Φ such that $S_{\ell^\star EB}(e) = S_{\Phi CE}(e)$. Therefore $S_{\ell^\star EB}$ can almost be seen as a member of the Conditional Equality family of allocation rules. This rule satisfies ***Pareto-Efficiency***, ***Monotonicity***, ***Consistency***, ***Replication Invariance***, and ***No Discrimination***, and guarantees the *$\ell^\star$-Equal Right*. Moreover, Maniquet (1998) shows that it is the smallest one, with respect to inclusion, to satisfy this list of axioms, on the subdomain of $\mathcal{E}_+$ with differentiable production functions. The argument is similar to the proof of Proposition 11.

Kolm (1996a, 2004a, 2004b) defends the $\ell^\star$-Equal Budget rule as intuitively appealing, since it corresponds to an equal sharing of the agents' earnings $s_i\ell_i$ on the first $\ell^\star$ units of labor, the rest being left to every agent. Kolm suggests that $\ell^\star/\bar{\ell}$ can be interpreted as the degree of egalitarianism of the allocation rule, with respect to earnings. With $\ell^\star/\bar{\ell} = 0$, the $\ell^\star$-Equal Budget rule coincides with Varian's (1974) Equal Wealth rule, consisting of an equal sharing of profits and no sharing of earnings. With $\ell^\star/\bar{\ell} = 1$, the allocation coincides with Pazner and Schmeidler's (1978b) Full-Income-Fair rule, with all budget lines crossing at $\ell = \bar{\ell}$.

The choice of $\ell^\star$ for the $\ell^\star$-Egalitarian Equivalent rule has radically different implications. Whatever $\ell^\star$, this rule performs a substantial compensation at the benefit of low-skilled agents. But with a low $\ell^\star$, $S_{\ell^\star EE}(e)$ is more favorable to the agents who have a strong aversion to labor, and conversely with a high $\ell^\star$. For instance, it is clearly better for an agent with strong aversion to labor to have all indifference curves crossing at $\ell^\star = 0$ than at a greater $\ell^\star$. Unsurprisingly, this rule therefore fails to be neutral with respect to various kinds of individual preferences. This is just a consequence of the fact that, by being good at compensation, this rule is not so good in terms of natural reward.

3.4. Limited Self-Ownership

The compensation principle may be criticized for contradicting the idea that agents, in particular high-skilled agents, should be free to take advantage of their skill, at least to the extent that society should not force them to work to the benefit of low-skilled agents. We will show that some of the proposed solutions pass some reasonable tests of self-ownership.

Pazner and Schmeidler's (1978b) Full-Income-Fair rule, which is at the same time an $\ell^\star$-Equal Budget rule with $\ell^\star = \overline{\ell}$ and a Conditional Equality rule with $\tilde{u}$ defined by: $\tilde{u}(\ell, c) = c$, has been criticized by Varian (1974) and Dworkin (1981b), on the basis that this rule is very hard for the skilled agents, since they are heavily taxed, and may actually be forced to work in order to be just able to pay taxes and have a zero consumption (the "slavery of the talented"). On the other hand, Varian's (1974) Equal Wealth rule, which is the $\ell^\star$-Equal Budget rule with $\ell^\star = 0$, does not display the same shortcoming, but as noticed above, does not perform any compensation of skill inequalities.

We can formalize the criticism by noting that the Full-Income-Fair rule does not satisfy the following participation property.

Participation
$\forall e = (s_N, u_N, f) \in \mathcal{E}$, $\forall x_N \in S(e)$, $\forall i \in N$, $u_i(x_i) \geq u_i(0,0)$.

Actually, this criticism can be addressed to almost all members of the Conditional Equality and $\ell^\star$-Equal Budget families. Moreover, a similar criticism can be addressed to almost all $\ell^\star$-Egalitarian Equivalent rules, even if in this case agents who are likely to be worse off than at $(0,0)$ are the "lazy" agents (i.e., agents with a low willingness to work), rather than the talented.

Proposition 14 (Fleurbaey and Maniquet 1996, Maniquet 1998) *The* Equal Wealth *rule is the only* Conditional Equality *rule and the only* ℓ^*-Equal Budget *rule satisfying* **P**articipation. *The* Egalitarian Equivalent *rule is the only* $\ell^\star$-Egalitarian Equivalent *rule satisfying* **P**articipation.

Since the Equal Wealth rule simply selects the equal-dividend laissez-faire allocations and does not perform any compensation for skill inequalities, this result is quite negative for the families of Conditional Equality rules and $\ell^\star$-Equal Budget rules. In contrast, the Egalitarian Equivalent rule does satisfy substantial compensation axioms.

The participation welfare level is quite low, and ***Participation*** is consistent with a very limited idea of self-ownership. A higher guarantee is provided by the following property.

Work Alone Lower Bound (WALB, Fleurbaey and Maniquet 1999)
$\forall e = (s_N, u_N, f) \in \mathcal{E}$, $\forall x_N \in S(e)$,

$$u_i(x_i) \geq EUUF_i(e),$$

where

$$EUUF_i(e) = \max\left\{\bar{u} \mid \exists x'_N \in F(e), \forall j \neq i, \ell_j = 0,\ \bar{u} = u_i(x'_i) = u_i(x'_j)\right\}.$$

This axiom guarantees that no agent is worse off than in the hypothetical situation in which he alone works and feeds the other agents just enough to be indifferent between his bundle and theirs. The two rules identified in the previous theorem satisfy this individual rationality constraint. Moreover, we have the following results.

Proposition 15 (Fleurbaey and Maniquet 1999) *The* Egalitarian Equivalent *rule is the only rule satisfying* Pareto-Efficiency, **N**o **D**iscrimination, **S**kill **S**olidarity, *and* **W**ork **A**lone **L**ower **B**ound.

Proof. Let S satisfy the axioms. First, we prove that for all $e \in \mathcal{E}$, $S(e) \subseteq S_{EE}(e)$. Suppose not. Then there is $e \in \mathcal{E}$, $x_N \in S(e) \setminus S_{EE}(e)$. Recall v_i from the definition of the Egalitarian Equivalent ordering function R_{EE}. By PE, $\max_{i \in N} v_i(x_i) \geq 0$. Since $x_N \notin S_{EE}(e)$, for some $j \in N$, $u_j(0, \max_{i\in N} v_i(x_i)) > u_j(x_j)$. Let $s'_j \in \mathbb{R}_+$ and $e' = ((0, \ldots, s'_j, \ldots, 0), u_N, f)$ be chosen so that there is $x'_N \in PE(e')$ such that for all $i \in N$, $u_i(x'_i) = u_i(x_i)$ (such an s'_j can be found, by continuity of the u_i and of f). By PE, SS, and ND, $x'_N \in S(e')$, violating WALB for j.

Second, we prove that $S(e) = S_{EE}(e)$. By SS, S is single-valued in utility. Therefore, by ND, $S(e) = S_{EE}(e)$. □

Proposition 16 *The* Equal Wealth *rule is the smallest allocation rule satisfying* **C**ontraction **I**ndependence, **N**o **D**iscrimination, **M**onotonicity, *and* **W**ork **A**lone **L**ower **B**ound.

The proof is similar to that of Proposition 11, noting that in a linear economy like $e' = (s_N, u'_N, g)$ defined there, ***Work Alone Lower Bound*** imposes that for all $j \in N$, $u'_j(x'_j) \geq u'_j(0, \frac{1}{\#N} \sum_{i\in N}(c_i - s_i w \ell_i))$.

4. THE UTILITARIAN APPROACH TO RESPONSIBILITY

We now turn to the literature that has adopted a radically different approach, based on the utilitarian reward principle.[58] This literature combines egalitarian and utilitarian social welfare functions in the construction of a new kind of complex social welfare functions. Such social welfare functions display inequality aversion only in the dimensions of differential talents and circumstances that call for compensation.[59]

4.1. Framework

A distinctive feature of this approach is that it disregards the economic structure of the allocation problem and even the functional form of the function $u(x, y, z)$, in order to focus on the outcomes eventually obtained by agents with different characteristics (y, z). The objects of evaluation are, typically, functions or matrices $(u_{yz})_{y\in Y, z\in Z}$ where u_{yz} is the outcome (an index of utility, or functionings, etc.) achieved by agents with talent y and effort z. For simplicity we will assume that y and z are independently distributed.[60] Let p_y (resp. p_z) be the proportion of the population with talent y (resp. effort z). Let $u_y = (u_{yz})_{z\in Z}$ (a row-vector) and $u_z = (u_{yz})_{y\in Y}$ (a column-vector). One can interpret u_y as describing the "opportunities" open to agents with talent y, and one can even think of a related opportunity set as defined by (assuming non-negative values for outcomes)

$$O_y = \{u \in \mathbb{R}_+^Z \mid u \leq u_y\}.$$

A graphical representation of such a set, that takes account of the distribution of z in the population, is presented in Figure 22.3.

In this setting, the compensation principle remains applicable and implies that inequalities within vectors u_z are bad. On the other hand, in this abstract framework it is impossible to formulate the idea of equal resources or of neutrality with respect to z, so that natural reward cannot even be conceived. It is then understandable that most of the literature has adopted a utilitarian kind of reward, translating the idea that

[58] As mentioned in the Introduction in Section 1, an early application of an unmodified utilitarian criterion to the issue of compensation has been made by Arrow (1971), and Sen (1973) emphasized the fact that this can lead to transfers in the wrong direction, because handicapped agents are likely to have a lower marginal utility. A more egalitarian approach, but still with comparable welfare, has been studied by Otsuki (1996).

[59] The literature reviewed in this section includes Bossert, Fleurbaey, and Van de gaer (1999), Goux and Maurin (2002), Hild and Voorhoeve (2004), Mariotti (2003), Ooghe and Lauwers (2005), Ooghe, Schokkaert, and Van de gaer (2007), Peragine (2002, 2004), Roemer (1993, 1998, 2002b), Schokkaert and Van de gaer (1994), and Van de gaer (1993). A somewhat different analysis of the utilitarian approach can be found in Fleurbaey (2008, ch. 6).

[60] Roemer constructs z so that this always holds. See Subsection 5.7.

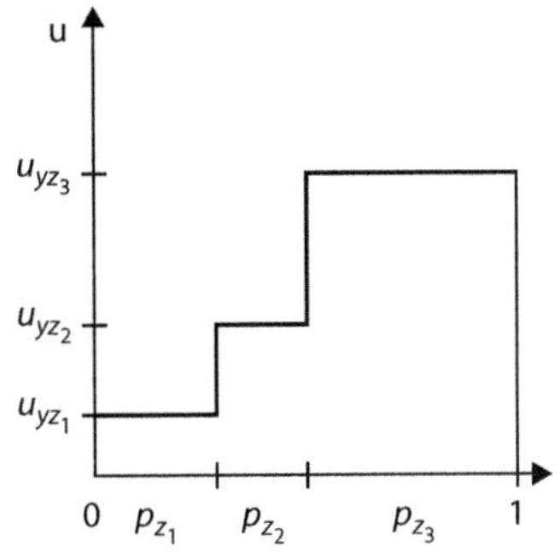

Figure 22.3. Opportunity sets.

inequalities within vectors u_y are acceptable into the idea that the social evaluation may have no aversion to inequality over such vectors.

Recall that one consequence of natural reward was ordinalism, discarding information about utilities as distinct from purely ordinal preferences. Another distinctive feature of the approach reviewed here is that individual preferences are no longer sufficient information, and a cardinally measurable and interpersonally comparable index of achievement u is needed and plays a key role in the evaluation of social situations.

One may wonder whether this framework should be described as welfarist (in the formal sense).[61] It occupies a sort of middle position. A pure welfarist approach would simply rank vectors $(u_i)_{i \in N}$ and would take account neither of individual characteristics y_i, z_i nor of resource allocation. This framework ranks matrices $\left(u_{yz}\right)_{y \in Y, z \in Z}$ but still ignores how the individuals are treated in terms of resources. These differences can be illustrated with Example 1.

Example 1 (pursued) Recall that $u = (x + y)z$, where x, y, and z are real numbers. Suppose that each category of individuals contains only one person and that the four individuals have the following characteristics in two different situations:

$y \backslash z$	1	3
1	*individual 1*	*individual 2*
3	*individual 3*	*individual 4*

Situation S1

$y \backslash z$	1	3
1	*individual 1*	*individual 3*
3	*individual 2*	*individual 4*

Situation S2

[61] Welfarism of the formal sort is compatible with any subjective or objective interpretation of the utility index u. A more substantive (or philosophical) brand of welfarism focuses on subjective utility. On this distinction, see Mongin and d'Aspremont (1998), and d'Aspremont and Gevers (2002).

Suppose that one declares policy B to be better than policy A in situation S1. Then, under pure welfarism, one should also declare policy $\bar{B}$ to be better than policy $\bar{A}$ in situation S2 (if they were feasible), because they yield the same distribution of utilities as policies B and A, respectively:

Policy $\bar{A}$

i	x and u
1	$x=5$, $u=6$
2	$x=15$, $u=18$
3	$x=1$, $u=6$
4	$x=3$, $u=18$

Policy $\bar{B}$

i	x and u
1	$x=2$, $u=3$
2	$x=24$, $u=27$
3	$x=0$, $u=3$
4	$x=5$, $u=27$

In contrast, by looking at the distribution of u_{yz} one is able to say that policy $\bar{B}$ is worse than $\bar{A}$ in situation S2, because it offers individuals with a low y the grim opportunities $(3,3)$ instead of $(6,6)$ with $\bar{A}$.

Now, consider the alternative technology $u=(x+y)z^2/2$. Under this technology, the same distributions of u_{yz} as with policies A and B can be obtained with the following policies:

Policy $\hat{A}$

$y\backslash z$	1	3
1	$x=11$, $u=6$	$x=3$, $u=18$
3	$x=9$, $u=6$	$x=1$, $u=18$

Policy $\hat{B}$

$y\backslash z$	1	3
1	$x=5$, $u=3$	$x=5$, $u=27$
3	$x=3$, $u=3$	$x=3$, $u=27$

If one looks only at the distributions of u_{yz}, one is forced to rank $\hat{A}$ and $\hat{B}$ in the same way as A and B. In contrast, a nonwelfarist criterion can prefer A to B and $\hat{B}$ to $\hat{A}$, because A and $\hat{B}$ are more neutral with respect to individuals' exercise of responsibility. One has to look at the allocation of x in order to see that B strongly rewards a high z, while $\hat{A}$ strongly punishes it.

4.2. Social Welfare Functions

Two prominent social welfare functions have been proposed in order to rank distributions of u_{yz}. Van de gaer (1993) introduced the following:

$$\sum_{y\in Y} p_y\,\varphi\left(\sum_{z\in Z} p_z u_{yz}\right),$$

where φ is a concave function. The idea is to compute the average outcome for each class of y, which can also be interpreted as the population-weighted area of the opportunity set O_y:

$$\sum_{z\in Z} p_z u_{yz}$$

(this is the area delineated in Figure 22.3) and the concavity of φ is meant to embody a social aversion to inequality of such average outcomes. Schokkaert and Van de gaer (1994) and Peragine (2002, 2004)[62] rely on this criterion in order to study various types of Lorenz dominance of distributions of characteristics.

Here we will focus on the maximin version of Van de gaer's social welfare function, which exhibits an infinite aversion to inequalities across y, which is better in line with the compensation principle. We will call it the "min of means" social welfare function:

$$W_{\min M} = \min_{y\in Y}\left(\sum_{z\in Z} p_z u_{yz}\right).$$

The second prominent social welfare function, due to Roemer (1993, 1998), is computed as

$$W_{M\min} = \sum_{z\in Z} p_z \min_{y\in Y} u_{yz}.$$

[62] Van de gaer (1993) actually considered a continuum, so that his social welfare function reads

$$\int_Y \varphi\left(\int_Z u_{yz} g(z)dz\right) f(y)dy,$$

where $f(y)$ and $g(z)$ are the density functions of y and z. Peragine considers a population with a finite number of y, a continuum of z, and a linearized version of the criterion:

$$\sum_y \frac{n_y}{n}\alpha_y \int_Z u_{yz} g(z)dz,$$

where α_y is an ethical weight expressing priority for subpopulations with a "low" y.

One sees that it inverts the position of min and mean, so that we may call it the "mean of mins" social welfare function. It still applies an infinite inequality aversion across y and no inequality aversion across z.[63] Interestingly, it can be interpreted as the population-weighted area of the intersection of opportunity sets

$$\bigcap_{y \in Y} O_y.$$

The two social welfare functions are illustrated in Figure 22.4. Both criteria boil down to ordinary utilitarianism

$$W_U = \sum_{y,z} p_y p_z u_{yz}$$

if all agents in the population have the same y. They may therefore advocate transferring resources to agents with parameter z, inducing higher marginal utility.[64] This illustrates the contrast with the solutions relying on the natural reward principle, which would advocate equal resources in this case.

It is also worth noting that the summation over z featured in these social welfare functions tends to enter in conflict with the principle of compensation, even though the maximin criterion is applied over y. This conflict can be shown in Example 1.

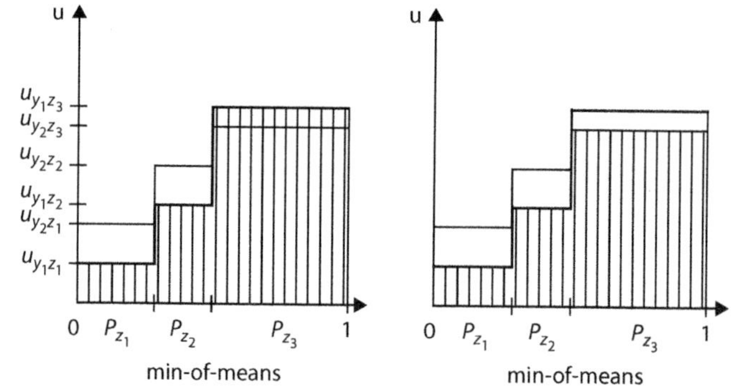

Figure 22.4. Illustration of the Two Social Welfare Functions.

[63] Roemer actually focused on the case of a discrete y and continuous z, so that

$$W_{M\min} = \int_Z \left(\min_{y \in Y} u_{yz} \right) g(z) dz.$$

This has to do with his particular statistical measurement of z, which is explained in Subsection 5.7.

[64] In the production model of Section 3, when agents have identical utility functions $u_i(\ell, c)$, a utilitarian planner would choose a Pareto-efficient allocation such that agents with higher skill obtain a lower utility, as shown by Mirrlees (1974). In Roemer (1998, p. 68), in an example dealing with unemployment insurance, the optimal policy for $W_{M\min}$ produces more inequalities than the laissez-faire.

Example 1 (pursued) The utilitarian-like policy B presented in Example 1 is actually not the best according to the min-of-means and mean-of-mins social welfare functions. One computes that, under policy B, $W_{\min M} = W_{M \min} = 15$ (recall that y and z are independently distributed, with equal population size for each value). An alternative policy can do better for both criteria:

Policy BB

$y \backslash z$	1	3
1	$x = 0$ $u = 1$	$x = 9$ $u = 30$
3	$x = 0$ $u = 3$	$x = 7$ $u = 30$

Under policy BB, one obtains $W_{\min M} = W_{M \min} = 15.5$. What happens is that it is better to sacrifice the undeserving poor and redistribute the two units of resources they receive in policy B to deserving agents, who are able to transform one unit of resource into three units of utility. This is done at the cost of forgoing compensation among the undeserving subpopulation.

In the quasi-linear case of Section 2.4, marginal utility is always equal to one, independently of the agent's characteristics y and z. Then the opposition between natural reward and utilitarian reward is diminished and the conflict between utilitarian reward and compensation is also reduced, as the utilitarian criteria tend to entail a large indifference between allocations (ordinary utilitarianism is then indifferent between all feasible allocations).[65] Bossert, Fleurbaey, and Van de gaer (1999) notice that, in this particular framework, the S_{OACE} rule, which satisfies ***Equal Resource for Equal Talent***, always selects a best allocation for $W_{\min M}$, which shows a relative compatibility between natural reward and utilitarian reward in this case. On the other hand, all egalitarian-equivalent rules $S_{\Psi EE}$, $S_{\Psi PAE}$, S_{AEE}, S_{APAE}, and S_{OAEE} select best allocations for $W_{M \min}$. Actually, the only thing that $W_{M \min}$ then requires is that agents with equal z obtain equal utilities, proving a compatibility between compensation and utilitarian reward in this particular case.

4.3. Min-of-Means or Mean-of-Mins?

The last paragraph in the previous subsection, and related analysis in an optimal taxation problem by Schokkaert *et al.* (2004), suggest that $W_{M \min}$ is somehow stronger in compensation, and therefore more egalitarian, than $W_{\min M}$. This is not always true, however, as the following example shows.

[65] Recall that we assumed no free disposal in Section 2.

Example 4 Consider the following two policies.

Policy B1			Policy B2		
$y\backslash z$	1	3	$y\backslash z$	1	3
1	$u=2$	$u=30$	1	$u=1$	$u=29$
3	$u=20$	$u=26$	3	$u=25$	$u=29$

One computes $W_{\min M}(B1)=16>W_{\min M}(B2)=15$, whereas $W_{M\min}(B1)=14<W_{M\min}(B2)=15$. One sees that $W_{M\min}$ prefers B2, even though it worsens the opportunities of the worst-off group, $y=1$, and hurts the worst-off among the worst-off. This paradox occurs because the mean-of-mins criterion may seek to improve the situation of high-effort agents even when they belong to well-off groups of talents, just because they happen to have the (relatively) smallest outcome in their subgroup of effort level.

Ooghe, Schokkaert, and Van de gaer (2007) have provided axiomatic characterizations of (leximin versions of) $W_{\min M}$ and $W_{M\min}$ that clarify the ethical underpinnings of these criteria.[66] Their framework deals with matrices $(u_{yz})_{y\in Y,z\in Z}$, as defined above. The domain $\mathcal{D}$ of such matrices is the unrestricted domain $\mathbb{R}^{YZ}$. Let $\mathcal{D}^Y$ be the subdomain of $\mathcal{D}$ such that $u_{yz}=u_{yz'}$ for all y,z,z' (flat reward for all talents, effort has no effect); and $\mathcal{D}^Z$ be the subdomain of $\mathcal{D}$ such that $u_{yz}=u_{y'z}$ for all y,y',z (equal prospects for all talents, talent has no effect). The problem is to find a complete ordering R over the domain $\mathcal{D}$. They focus on the particular case when $p_yp_z=p_{y'}p_{z'}$ for all y,y',z,z' (i.e., each component of the matrix $(u_{yz})_{y\in Y,z\in Z}$ represents the same number of individuals)—this simplifies the formulation and justification of permutation axioms presented below.[67]

The leximin extensions of the min-of-means and mean-of-mins criteria are defined as follows:

Leximin of Means ($R^L_{\min M}$)
$\forall u,v\in\mathcal{D}$, $u\,R\,v$ if and only if

$$\left(\sum_{z\in Z}p_zu_{yz}\right)_{y\in Y}\geq_{lex}\left(\sum_{z\in Z}p_zv_{yz}\right)_{y\in Y}.$$

[66] Ooghe and Lauwers (2005) also provide a slightly different axiomatization of a leximin version of $W_{M\min}$.
[67] With a finite number of individuals and an independent distribution of y and z, a matrix with cells of unequal population sizes can always be expanded into a matrix with one individual in each cell (some columns may have the same value of z, and some lines the same value of y). Therefore, it is not really restrictive to consider matrices with the same number of individuals for each cell.

Mean of Leximins ($R^L_{M\min}$)
$\forall u, v \in \mathcal{D}$, $u\ R\ v$ if and only if

$$\left(\sum_{z\in Z} p_z u_{(y)z}\right)_{y\in Y} \geq_{lex} \left(\sum_{z\in Z} p_z v_{(y)z}\right)_{y\in Y},$$

where $\left(u_{(y)z}\right)_{y\in Y}$ is a reranked u_z such that $u_{(1)z} \leq u_{(2)z} \leq \dots$

Let us briefly introduce the main axioms in Ooghe *et al.* (2007). There is a standard strong Pareto axiom, satisfied by both orderings.[68]

Strong Pareto
$\forall u, v \in \mathcal{D}$,

$$u \geq v \Rightarrow u\ R\ v;\ u > v \Rightarrow u\ P\ v.$$

They obtain the utilitarian feature of these orderings by an axiom of translation-scale invariance saying that changing u_{yz} into $u_{yz} + w_z$ for an arbitrary vector $(w_z)_{z\in Z}$ does not change the ranking of matrices. This kind of axiom is common in characterizations of utilitarianism (see, e.g., d'Aspremont and Gevers 1977, and Bossert and Weymark 2004).

Translation-Scale Invariance in z (Ooghe *et al.* 2007)
$\forall u, v \in \mathcal{D}$, $\forall w \in \mathcal{D}^Z$,

$$u\ R\ v \Leftrightarrow u + w\ R\ v + w.$$

Both orderings also satisfy the following egalitarian axiom, which embodies the compensation principle in a mild way. It says that when a type of talent has prospects that dominate another, it is not bad to reduce the gap between them.

Dominance Compensation (Ooghe *et al.* 2007)
$\forall u, v \in \mathcal{D}$, $\forall y, y' \in Y$,

$$\left.\begin{array}{l} v_y > u_y \geq u_{y'} > v_{y'} \\ \forall y'' \neq y, y',\ u_{y''} = v_{y''} \end{array}\right\} \Rightarrow u\ R\ v.$$

We now introduce permutation axioms, referred to as "Suppes indifference." The first two are rather weak and permute the prospects of talents and the achievements of effort. They are satisfied by both orderings. The first axiom simply permutes the whole opportunities of the various talents.

[68] Hild and Voorhoeve (2004) explain, however, that the mean-of-mins social welfare function may violate the (weak) Pareto principle when agents change their z in response to policy.

Suppes Indifference for Talent (Ooghe *et al.* 2007)
$\forall u, v \in \mathcal{D}$, $\forall \sigma$ permutation on Y,

$$\forall y,\ v_y = u_{\sigma(y)} \Rightarrow u\ I\ v.$$

The second axiom is more complex and applies different permutations of outcomes for different y subgroups, but it does so only for matrices in which prospects for different talents are dominated, that is, for any y, y', $u_y \leq u_{y'}$ or $u_y \geq u_{y'}$ (before and after permutations). For such matrices $R^L_{\min M}$ and $R^L_{M\min}$ coincide.

Suppes Indifference for Effort (Ooghe *et al.* 2007)
$\forall u, v \in \mathcal{D}$ such that $\forall y, z,\ u_{yz} = u_{(y)z}$ and $v_{yz} = v_{(y)z}$, $\forall \left(\sigma_y\right)_{y \in Y}$ permutations on Z,

$$\forall y, z,\ v_{yz} = u_{y\sigma_y(z)} \Rightarrow u\ I\ v.$$

The most interesting part of this axiomatic analysis lies in the distinction between the two orderings, which is deciphered through stronger versions of these axioms performing separate permutations for every effort level or every talent.

Strong Suppes Indifference for Talent (Ooghe *et al.* 2007)
$\forall u, v \in \mathcal{D}$, $\forall (\sigma_z)_{z \in Z}$ permutations on Y,

$$\forall y, z,\ v_{yz} = u_{\sigma_z(y)z} \Rightarrow u\ I\ v.$$

Strong Suppes Indifference for Effort (Ooghe *et al.* 2007)
$\forall u, v \in \mathcal{D}$, $\forall \left(\sigma_y\right)_{y \in Y}$ permutations on Z,

$$\forall y, z,\ v_{yz} = u_{y\sigma_y(z)} \Rightarrow u\ I\ v.$$

These axioms are better explained and critically assessed with examples.

Example 5 The first of these axioms, satisfied by the mean-of-leximins ordering, says that permuting the outcomes obtained by a subgroup of given effort level does not change the evaluation. For instance, the following social situations are deemed equivalent, even though the prospects for the two groups of y are comparable in one case and in clear domination in the other.

Policy ML1

$y \backslash z$	1	3
1	$u = 2$	$u = 30$
3	$u = 6$	$u = 26$

Policy ML2

$y \backslash z$	1	3
1	$u = 2$	$u = 26$
3	$u = 6$	$u = 30$

In contrast, the leximin-of-means ordering prefers policy ML1.

The second axiom, satisfied by $R^L_{\min M}$, says that permuting the outcomes obtained by a subgroup of given talent does not change the evaluation. For instance, the following social situations are deemed equivalent, even though the prospects for the two groups of y are equal in one case and very different in the other.

Policy LM1

$y \backslash z$	1	3
1	$u = 2$	$u = 30$
3	$u = 2$	$u = 30$

Policy LM2

$y \backslash z$	1	3
1	$u = 2$	$u = 30$
3	$u = 30$	$u = 2$

In contrast, $R^L_{M\min}$ strongly prefers policy LM1. In other words, it seems that each of these axioms deletes a relevant part of information, and as a result each of the orderings may be criticized for ignoring the respective part.

We may now state the result.

Proposition 17 (Ooghe, Schokkaert, and Van de gaer 2007) *Let R be a complete ordering over $\mathcal{D}$, satisfying* **S**trong **P**areto, **T**ranslation-**S**cale **I**nvariance in z, *and* **D**ominance **C**ompensation. *If, in addition, it satisfies* **S**uppes **I**ndifference for **T**alent *and* **S**trong **S**uppes **I**ndifference for **E**ffort, *then $R = R^L_{\min M}$. On the other hand, if in addition, it satisfies* **S**uppes **I**ndifference for **E**ffort *and* **S**trong **S**uppes **I**ndifference for **T**alent, *then $R = R^L_{M\min}$.*

The same authors also study variants of these orderings. For instance, they consider CES versions, which can be defined as follows.[69]

$$W^{CES}_{\min M} = \left(\sum_{y \in Y} p_y \left(\sum_{z \in Z} p_z \left(u_{yz}\right)^{\mu} \right)^{\frac{\rho}{\mu}} \right)^{\frac{1}{\rho}},$$

$$W^{CES}_{M\min} = \left(\sum_{z \in Z} p_z \left(\sum_{y \in Y} p_y \left(u_{yz}\right)^{\rho} \right)^{\frac{\mu}{\rho}} \right)^{\frac{1}{\mu}}.$$

Hild and Voorhoeve (2004) try to avoid the utilitarian reward and adopt a dominance criterion that covers various possible reward approaches (although the abstract framework itself makes it impossible to apply the natural reward approach). Their criterion may be formulated as an axiom, saying that if for every effort level, the observed outcome distribution is better (according to the leximin criterion), then the overall matrix is better.

[69] Kolm (2001) and Martinez (2004) made similar proposals.

Opportunity Dominance (Hild and Voorhoeve 2004)
$\forall u, v \in \mathcal{D}$,

$$\left.\begin{array}{l}\forall z,\ u_z \geq_{lex} v_z \\ \exists z,\ u_z >_{lex} v_z\end{array}\right\} \Rightarrow u\ P\ v.$$

This axiom is satisfied by $R^L_{M\min}$, but not by $R^L_{\min M}$, as shown in the following example.

Example 5 (pursued) This axiom imposes to prefer MLL2 to ML1 in the following example, even though, as in ML1 vs. ML2, the prospects for the two groups are comparable in ML1 and in clear domination in MLL2, as recognized by $R^L_{\min M}$.

Policy ML1

$y\backslash z$	1	3
1	$u=2$	$u=30$
3	$u=6$	$u=26$

Policy MLL2

$y\backslash z$	1	3
1	$u=2$	$u=27$
3	$u=6$	$u=30$

In other words, the Opportunity Dominance criterion is agnostic about reward but clearly sides with the mean-of-mins approach and against the min-of-means approach on whether the evaluation should be on ex ante opportunities for various y or on ex post inequalities within z subgroups. It can therefore also be criticized for ignoring some relevant information.

The discussions in Example 5 strongly suggest that it would be better to take account of the two kinds of considerations (ex ante and ex post), instead of ignoring one of them totally. Goux and Maurin (2002) address this issue and propose an interesting partial criterion, according to which a matrix u is at least as good as another matrix u' if $W_{M\min}(u) \geq W_{\min M}(u')$. This criterion itself does not yield the desired strict preference in the above examples. But their results suggest a refined criterion, according to which a matrix u is strictly better than u' if[70]

$$\begin{aligned} & W_{M\min}(u) > W_{\min M}(u') \\ \text{or } & W_{\min M}(u) > W_{M\min}(u) \geq W_{\min M}(u') \\ \text{or } & W_{M\min}(u) \geq W_{\min M}(u') > W_{M\min}(u'). \end{aligned}$$

In Example 5, this partial criterion enables us to rank LM1 above LM2, since

$$W_{M\min}(LM1) = W_{\min M}(LM2) = 16 > W_{M\min}(LM2) = 2;$$

[70] Notice that one always has $W_{M\min}(u) \leq W_{\min M}(u)$.

and ML1 above ML2, since

$$W_{\min M}(ML1) = 16 > W_{M\min}(ML1) = 14 = W_{\min M}(ML2).$$

Let us briefly present their axiomatic results underlying this proposal. The domain they deal with is that of non-negative matrices $\mathcal{D} = \mathbb{R}_{+}^{YZ}$. They rely on a weak Pareto axiom.

Weak Pareto
$\forall u, v \in \mathcal{D}$,

$$u \gg v \Rightarrow u \, P \, v.$$

They use a scale invariance axiom, which is satisfied by both $R_{\min M}^{L}$ and $R_{M\min}^{L}$.

Scale Invariance
$\forall u, v \in \mathcal{D}$, $\forall \alpha \in \mathbb{R}_{++}$,

$$u \, R \, v \Leftrightarrow \alpha u \, R \, \alpha v.$$

They also invoke a separability axiom that has to do with decomposing the effect of talent and effort. It says that if the effect of talent remains the same, a change in the multiplicative effect of effort does not alter the ranking of two matrices. This axiom is also satisfied by both $R_{\min M}^{L}$ and $R_{M\min}^{L}$.

Fixed Effort Effect Separability (Goux and Maurin 2002)
$\forall u, v, u', v' \in \mathcal{D}$, if $\forall y, z$, $u_{yz} = \alpha_y \beta_z$, $v_{yz} = \gamma_y \beta_z$, $u'_{yz} = \alpha_y \beta'_z$, $v'_{yz} = \gamma_y \beta'_z$, then

$$u \, R \, v \Leftrightarrow u' \, R \, v'.$$

The most relevant axiom they introduce is meant to force R to take account of ex ante prospects and ex post inequalities at the same time, because it says that if prospects are better for every talent, and outcomes are better for every effort, then the matrix is better overall.

Talent-Effort Dominance (Goux and Maurin 2002)
$\forall u, v \in \mathcal{D}$,

$$\left.\begin{array}{l} \forall y \in Y, \begin{pmatrix} u_y \\ \vdots \\ u_y \end{pmatrix} R \begin{pmatrix} v_y \\ \vdots \\ v_y \end{pmatrix} \\ \forall z \in Z, (u_z, \ldots, u_z) \, R \, (v_z, \ldots, v_z) \end{array}\right\} \Rightarrow u \, R \, v$$

(with strict preference in case of strict preference for some y or some z).

This axiom is not satisfied by $R^L_{\min M}$, and this can be illustrated by the following example.

Example 6 Consider the two policies:

Policy LMM1

$y \backslash z$	1	3
1	$u=4$	$u=18$
3	$u=8$	$u=14$

Policy LMM2

$y \backslash z$	1	3
1	$u=2$	$u=20$
3	$u=10$	$u=12$

The ordering $R^L_{\min M}$ is indifferent between LMM1 and LMM2. But one sees that

$$\begin{array}{|c|c|} \hline 4 & 18 \\ \hline 4 & 18 \\ \hline \end{array} \; I^L_{\min M} \; \begin{array}{|c|c|} \hline 2 & 20 \\ \hline 2 & 20 \\ \hline \end{array}$$

$$\begin{array}{|c|c|} \hline 8 & 14 \\ \hline 8 & 14 \\ \hline \end{array} \; I^L_{\min M} \; \begin{array}{|c|c|} \hline 10 & 12 \\ \hline 10 & 12 \\ \hline \end{array}$$

$$\begin{array}{|c|c|} \hline 4 & 4 \\ \hline 8 & 8 \\ \hline \end{array} \; P^L_{\min M} \; \begin{array}{|c|c|} \hline 2 & 2 \\ \hline 10 & 10 \\ \hline \end{array}$$

$$\begin{array}{|c|c|} \hline 18 & 18 \\ \hline 14 & 14 \\ \hline \end{array} \; P^L_{\min M} \; \begin{array}{|c|c|} \hline 20 & 20 \\ \hline 12 & 12 \\ \hline \end{array}$$

which should imply, by **T**alent-**E**ffort **D**ominance, that LMM1 is strictly better, as it indeed seems obvious, since inequalities ex post are reduced for every level of effort.

Somewhat surprisingly, however, the ***T**alent-**E**ffort **D**ominance* axiom is satisfied by $R^L_{M\min}$, and this suggests that this axiom fails to fully capture the concern for the relevance of ex ante evaluations. In other words, this axiom is compatible with indifference between ML1 and ML2, and with ***S**trong **S**uppes **I**ndifference for **T**alent*, which appears questionable. The $R^L_{M\min}$ ordering is excluded from the theorem below only by an additional continuity condition.

Proposition 18 (Goux and Maurin 2002, Gajdos and Maurin 2004) *If the ordering R, defined on domain $\mathcal{D} = \mathbb{R}^{YZ}_+$, is continuous and satisfies* **W**eak **P**areto, **T**alent-**E**ffort **D**ominance, *and* **F**ixed **E**ffort **E**ffect **S**eparability, *then there exist three continuous, increasing, homogeneous functions $I : \mathcal{D} \to \mathbb{R}_+$, $I_y : \mathbb{R}^Y_+ \to \mathbb{R}_+$, and $I_z : \mathbb{R}^Z_+ \to \mathbb{R}_+$ such that:*

1. *I represents R;*
2. *If $I_y\left(I_z(u_y)_{y\in Y}\right) = I_z\left(I_y(u_z)_{z\in Z}\right)$ then $I(u) = I_y\left(I_z(u_y)_{y\in Y}\right)$;*
3. *If $I_y\left(I_z(u_y)_{y\in Y}\right) \neq I_z\left(I_y(u_z)_{z\in Z}\right)$ then $I(u)$ is strictly in between.*

Relevant examples of such functions are $I_z(u_y) = \sum_{z\in Z} p_z u_{yz}$ and $I_y(u_z) = \min_y u_{yz}$, yielding

$$I_y\left(I_z(u_y)_{y\in Y}\right) = \min_{y\in Y}\left(\sum_{z\in Z} p_z u_{yz}\right) = W_{\min M}(u)$$

$$I_z\left(I_y(u_z)_{z\in Z}\right) = \sum_{z\in Z} p_z\left(\min_{y\in Y} u_{yz}\right) = W_{M\min}(u).$$

Other examples are $I_z(u_y) = \left(\sum_{z\in Z} p_z\left(u_{yz}\right)^{\mu}\right)^{\frac{1}{\mu}}$ and $I_y(u_z) = \left(\sum_{y\in Y} p_y\left(u_{yz}\right)^{\rho}\right)^{\frac{1}{\rho}}$, which then lead to combining the CES versions of the min-of-means and mean-of-mins social welfare functions. One limitation of this theorem is that it implies very little about the functions, and for instance utilitarianism W_U does satisfy all the axioms (with related I_y and I_z which both compute the mean).

Goux and Maurin (2002) emphasize the formal similarity between this issue and the well-known social choice problem of combining ex ante and ex post social evaluations of risky prospects.[71] Assume that z is unknown ex ante. Then the min-of-means criterion may be viewed as focusing on ex ante prospects for y subgroups, while the mean-of-mins criterion focuses on ex post inequalities for various possible realizations of z. From the literature on risky social choice, a simple combination of the two approaches would simply add the two criteria:

$$W_C = W_{\min M} + W_{M\min}.$$

Whether this can be given a convincing justification in the context of opportunities remains to be seen.[72]

Mariotti (2003) also exploits the similarity with the risk context in a different way, and examines the particular case in which an opportunity for agent i is defined as a probability π_i of success. In other words, there are only two possible outcomes, success and failure.[73] If success is valued a unit (1) and failure is valued zero (0), then π_i also measures the expected value of the outcome for i. In this context, and interpreting i as a talent subgroup with a proportion π_i of success, both $R^L_{\min M}$ and $R^L_{M\min}$ would

[71] On this problem, see Gajdos and Maurin (2004), Broome (1991), Deschamps and Gevers (1979), and Ben Porath, Gilboa and Schmeidler (1997). The "min-of-means" and "mean-of-mins" terminology used here is inspired by this literature.

[72] There seem to be significant differences in the two problems. In the risk problem, only one value of z will eventually be realized, and its determination is outside the agents' control, whereas in the opportunity context, all values of z will eventually be observed in the population, and every agent is responsible for his own value of z. These differences may limit the transposition of ethical principles from one problem to the other.

[73] Vallentyne (2002) adopts a similar probabilistic interpretation of opportunity sets, but with more than two possible outcomes.

apply the leximin to the π vector. Instead of the leximin criterion, Mariotti advocates the Nash-product criterion

$$W_N = \pi_1, \ldots, \pi_n.$$

He excludes the maximin by requiring the ranking to obey an independence condition.[74]

5. RELATED LITERATURE

In this section we present some related literature that studies similar issues in different ways, or which applies or extends some of the ideas reviewed thus far.

5.1. Ranking Distributions of Opportunity Sets

In many contexts it is considered that the characteristics that the agents are responsible for are chosen by them, and that compensating for the nonresponsible characteristics is tantamount to providing agents with "equal opportunities." As recalled from the Introduction, this is actually the way some philosophers have introduced these general egalitarian principles.

Thomson (1994) has studied the idea of equal opportunities in the simple fair division model, and has made an important distinction between actual opportunities (the consumed bundle belongs to the opportunity set) and "equivalent" opportunities (the consumed bundle yields the same satisfaction as the best bundle in the opportunity set).

Kranich (1996) has initiated an important branch of the literature that studies how to rank distributions of opportunity sets $(O_1, \ldots, O_n)$, where O_i denotes individual i's opportunity set, in terms of inequality. Kranich (1996) characterizes inequality measures that are linear, such as, in the case of two agents, the absolute value of the cardinality difference, $|\#O_1 - \#O_2|$.

Kranich (1997a) extends this analysis to opportunity sets that are not finite, such as compact subsets of the Euclidean space, for instance budget sets in a market economy. Ok (1997) and Ok and Kranich (1998) analyze the possibility to adapt the basic results of the theory of income inequality, which connect Lorenz dominance to Pigou–Dalton transfers, to this new framework where income is replaced by opportunity sets. They show that the difficulty lies in adapting the notion of transfer, and their results suggest that it is hard to avoid relying on cardinality-based evaluations of opportunity sets if one wants to replicate the classical theorems of income inequality. See also Arlegi and Nieto (1999) and Weymark (2003), the latter revisiting the results of Kranich (1996) with a

[74] For two agents, this condition says that if $(\pi_1, \pi_2)\, R\, (\pi_1', \pi_2')$ and $(\pi_1'', \pi_2)\, R\, (\pi_1''', \pi_2')$, then $(\alpha\pi_1 + (1-\alpha)\pi_1'', \pi_2)$ $R\, (\alpha\pi_1' + (1-\alpha)\pi_1''', \pi_2')$ for all $0 < \alpha < 1$.

version of the Pigou–Dalton transfer principle that only applies when the opportunity sets are nested.

Other parts of this literature simply assume that there is a given measure of the value of sets (Herrero 1997 proposes to measure inequality by the difference between the greatest and the smallest value of the individual sets in the considered distribution, and Herrero 1996 defines social welfare in terms of capability indices) or a given preordering over opportunity sets (Bossert, Fleurbaey, and Van de gaer 1999, Herrero, Iturbe-Ormaetxe, and Nieto 1998). In particular, the last two references provide characterizations of social preorderings, which rank distributions of opportunity sets on the basis of the intersection of individual sets, $\bigcap_{i=1}^{n} O_i$, a notion that has been already encountered in the discussion of the mean-of-mins criterion. This intersection criterion is also axiomatically defended, in an economic model and in terms of "common capabilities," by Gotoh and Yoshihara (1999, 2003).[75]

The earlier parts of the literature presented in the previous sections seldom explicitly referred to opportunity sets but, as emphasized by Bossert *et al.* (1999), it is sometimes easy to interpret the solutions in terms of equalizing some appropriately defined opportunity sets. One can even argue that this literature provides ethical justifications for specific and concrete definitions of opportunity sets in economic contexts. Consider for instance the model of Section 2. The Egalitarian Equivalent allocation rule can be interpreted as equalizing the virtual opportunity sets:

$$\{(x, y) \mid x \leq \tilde{x}, y = \tilde{y}\}.$$

In general, most Egalitarian Equivalent allocation rules can be interpreted as applying the maximin criterion to "equivalent" opportunity sets that individuals would accept to choose from. This is clear, for instance, with the Budget Egalitarian Equivalent rules in Section 3.

The conditional egalitarian allocation rule, again in the model of Section 2, can be read in terms of opportunity sets

$$\{(x, y) \mid x \leq x_i, y = y_i\},$$

and equality is sought between these heterogeneous sets by referring to a particular utility function $\tilde{u}$: The value of an opportunity set is the value taken by the indirect utility function on this set. A similar interpretation can be made of the Conditional Equality allocation rule in the model of Section 3.

If one refers to the philosophical theories, however, it seems more relevant to define opportunity sets in terms of pairs (responsibility variable, achievement). This is actually

[75] More detailed surveys of this literature can be found in Peragine (1999), and Barberà, Bossert, and Pattanaik (2004).

how we proceeded in Example 1 in the Introduction. In the setting of Section 2, this suggests defining the opportunity set of an agent as:

$$\{(u,\bar{u}) \mid u \in \mathcal{U},\ \bar{u} = u(x_i, y_i)\}$$

or in the quasi-linear case:

$$\{(z,\bar{u}) \mid z \in Z,\ \bar{u} = x_i + v(y_i, z)\}.$$

It might be desirable to take account of the potential dependence of x_i on u_i (or z_i) via the allocation rule, in these definitions.[76] Notice that the conditional egalitarian allocation rule amounts to equalizing the sections of these opportunity sets taken at $u = \tilde{u}$, or $z = \tilde{z}$.

5.2. Extended Insurance

As explained in Sections 2.2 and 3.2, the No-Envy condition is too demanding in the context of compensation for nontransferable internal resources, because it is often impossible to find allocations satisfying it. Whereas most of the economic literature tried to escape this difficulty by imagining weaker requirements, Dworkin (1981b) suggested to retain the No-Envy condition but to apply it to a modified framework, namely, imagining a hypothetical insurance market in which agents could insure themselves, ex ante, against the prospect of ending up with a handicap. No-Envy could easily be satisfied ex ante by granting all agents the same income in this hypothetical market. Ex post, the resource transfers performed between agents would just reflect their free choices of insurance. Obviously, this extended insurance market would have to operate under a veil of ignorance, the agents ignoring their personal talents.[77] A similar device was considered by Kolm (1985), and it is rather natural to consider that the extended insurance is just an extension of ordinary insurance markets and social insurance schemes, in the direction of increasing the scope of redistribution from the "lucky" toward the "unlucky."

Roemer (1985a) showed that this intuition is likely to be incorrect, and provided several examples showing that an extended insurance may behave like ordinary utilitarianism and entail the same paradoxical antiredistribution from the unlucky (handicapped)

[76] But then one runs into the following problem. In a small economy, the opportunities for a given agent depend on the values of the responsibility variables chosen by the other agents, so that opportunities become interdependent and there is no way to define them ex ante. See Kolm (1993), Fleurbaey (1995b), Barberà *et al.* (2004) for brief explorations of this matter.

[77] Unlike Rawls's veil of ignorance, the agents would know their preferences and ambitions. Someone with musical ambitions, for instance, could then take a special insurance against short fingers or unperfect pitch. The fact that preferences are often influenced by actual talents makes Dworkin consider the possibility of having agents know their talents but still ignore the market value of their talents.

to the lucky (talented).[78] The reason for this paradox is simple. First, an agent who maximizes his expected utility ex ante is doing a similar formal computation as a utilitarian planner maximizing a weighted sum of utilities. Insurance markets therefore generally produce results that bear a close relationship to a utilitarian allocation of resources. When agents have similar utility functions, with decreasing marginal utility of income, utilitarianism produces egalitarian consequences in the allocation of resources. Similarly, insurance against ordinary damages that reduce income or wealth enables agents to transfer resources from the states where they are rich to the states where they are poor.

Now, contrary to ordinary damages, personal talents typically alter utility functions. When describing agents in an extended insurance market, one then has to deal with state-dependent utility functions. In such a market, if a damage (low talent, handicap) reduces the marginal utility of income, then agents will typically want to transfer resources from states with damage toward states without damage, and will therefore want to insure against the more favorable state, in order to obtain more resources in this state, thereby sacrificing their welfare in the unlucky state.

As Roemer (1985a) shows, in the case of extended insurance for production skills, one also gets unpalatable consequences. We have seen that when all agents have the same utility functions, the principle of compensation calls for an equalization of utility levels. This will generally not happen with the extended insurance market, precisely for the same reason that leads a utilitarian planner to choose allocations with unequal utility levels in such a case.[79]

5.3. Extended Sympathy and Interpersonal Comparisons of Utility

The notion of envy-freeness that is central to the approach presented in this chapter can be considered as intermediate between ordinary envy-freeness, which bears only on external resources, and a more extensive egalitarian criterion, which encompasses all personal characteristics and essentially seeks equality of utilities. This range of possibilities was identified by Kolm (1972), who later argued (Kolm 1996a, 1996b) that the location of the cut between characteristics submitted to compensation and other characteristics is a central feature of various theories of justice. More precisely, assume that individual utility is a function of m personal characteristics: $u_i(x_i, \theta_{i1}, \ldots, \theta_{im})$. Deciding to compensate for

[78] In addition, it is not obvious that the hypothetical choices made in a virtual ex ante state are relevant to justify transfers of resources between individuals who have never lived in this ex ante state. Consider someone who belongs to the unlucky 2% of the population with a genetic disease. Is it an acceptable consolation for him to be told that, if given the possibility, he would have taken the 2% risk of getting those bad genes and ending up with his current share of resources? It is far from clear that trade-offs made by an individual over his possible future selves are relevant to trading-off the conflicting interests of separate individuals who have to share resources. See Kolm (1996b, 1998).

[79] More discussions of the extended insurance scheme can be found in Kolm (1996b, 1998), Roemer (1996, 2002a), Fleurbaey (2002), Dworkin (2002).

the first k characteristics can be enforced, for instance, by applying the No-Envy test in the following way:

$$u_i(x_i,\theta_{i1},\ldots,\theta_{ik},\theta_{ik+1},\ldots,\theta_{im}) \geq u_i(x_j,\theta_{j1},\ldots,\theta_{jk},\theta_{ik+1},\ldots,\theta_{im}).$$

Notice that, as shown in the previous section, this general scheme is also relevant for such characteristics as productive skills, which are not a direct argument of the ordinary utility function but are an argument of a suitably defined utility function.

This generalized envy test seems to introduce a kind of interpersonal comparison of utility, although, as stressed in Section 2, it is perfectly immune to any increasing transformation of the individual utility functions. Only ordinal preferences over vectors of "extended resources" $(x,\theta_1,\ldots,\theta_k)$ do matter. When all characteristics are subject to compensation, the No-Envy test reads like equalizing utilities if the individual utility functions are identical and interpersonally comparable, that is, if there is a unique function $u(x_i,\theta_{i1},\ldots,\theta_{im})$ that describes all individuals' utilities in an interpersonally comparable way.

A related notion is that of extended sympathy, and a joint use of the concepts of extended sympathy and No-Envy has been made in particular by Suzumura (1981a, 1981b, 1983). In the extended sympathy framework, every individual is endowed with preferences over extended pairs (x,i), where x describes the social alternative (say, an allocation) and i is the name of an individual. In order to compare this with our formalism, assume that every agent has a utility function $v_i(x_j,j)$, where x_j is simply agent j's consumption (preferences are self-centered). With this convention, the No-Envy test as applied by Suzumura corresponds to

$$v_i(x_i,i) \geq v_i(x_j,j).$$

This suggests that it is equivalent to the test

$$u_i(x_i,\theta_{i1},\ldots,\theta_{ik},\theta_{ik+1},\ldots,\theta_{im}) \geq u_i(x_j,\theta_{j1},\ldots,\theta_{jk},\theta_{ik+1},\ldots,\theta_{im})$$

if in $v_i(x_j,j)$, the second argument depends only on $(\theta_{j1},\ldots,\theta_{jk})$, and if the shape of the function v_i is molded by $(\theta_{ik+1},\ldots,\theta_{im})$. Therefore the extended sympathy framework is equivalent to ours, albeit with a less explicit description of individual characteristics.

But there remains an important difference. A standard axiom, which is often relied upon in the extended sympathy framework, is the ***Axiom of Identity***, meaning that every agent's extended preferences respect others' tastes over ordinary resources:

Axiom of Identity (Sen 1970)
$\forall i,j \in N, \forall x,x',\ v_i(x,j) \geq v_i(x',j) \Leftrightarrow v_j(x,j) \geq v_j(x',j).$

Translated into our notations, this axiom would mean

$$u_i(x,\theta_{j1},\ldots,\theta_{jk},\theta_{ik+1},\ldots,\theta_{im}) \geq u_i(x',\theta_{j1},\ldots,\theta_{jk},\theta_{ik+1},\ldots,\theta_{im}) \Leftrightarrow$$
$$u_j(x,\theta_{j1},\ldots,\theta_{jk},\theta_{jk+1},\ldots,\theta_{jm}) \geq u_j(x',\theta_{j1},\ldots,\theta_{jk},\theta_{jk+1},\ldots,\theta_{jm}),$$

and it is clear that this condition has little appeal in our framework,[80] even if we assume that $u_i = u_j$, since the difference between characteristics $(\theta_{ik+1},\ldots,\theta_{im})$ and $(\theta_{jk+1},\ldots,\theta_{jm})$ may plausibly entail different preferences over x. For instance, in the production model of Section 3, the ***Axiom of Identity*** would require that all agents have identical preferences over (ℓ,c). Indeed, for this model the equivalence in the ***Axiom of Identity*** translates into

$$u_i(\hat{\ell}/s_j,c) \geq u_i(\hat{\ell}'/s_j,c') \Leftrightarrow u_j(\hat{\ell}/s_j,c) \geq u_j(\hat{\ell}'/s_j,c'),$$

or equivalently,

$$u_i(\ell,c) \geq u_i(\ell',c') \Leftrightarrow u_j(\ell,c) \geq u_j(\ell',c').$$

The ***Axiom of Identity*** seems reasonable only in the case when all characteristics are subject to compensation. Therefore it is probably a safer reading of the extended sympathy approach that it usually deals with the extreme case of full compensation for all individual characteristics.

5.4. Bargaining

Yoshihara (2003) studies a variant of the production model of Section 3, with several goods being produced with unequal skills, and focuses on bargaining solutions (which, unlike allocation rules, select a single utility vector for any given utility possibility set). He provides characterizations of three bargaining solutions (egalitarian, Nash, Kalai–Smorodinsky) and highlights the interpretation of some of the axioms in terms of responsibility and compensation. Unlike the solutions presented thus far, the bargaining solutions violate Ordinalism and rely on utility figures. However, the Nash and Kalai–Smorodinsky solutions do exhibit some independence with respect to rescaling of utilities, which can be interpreted as reflecting some ascription of responsibility to individuals for their utility functions. Conversely, the egalitarian solution satisfies stronger solidarity properties (such as Skill Solidarity). Yoshihara shows that no bargaining solution satisfies Skill Solidarity and an independence axiom with respect to utility rescaling, in addition to Pareto efficiency and Equal Treatment of Equals. Since the Egalitarian-Equivalent allocation rule S_{EE} satisfies all of these axioms, this suggests that bargaining solutions suffer from a stronger dilemma between compensation and responsibility than allocation rules.

[80] Except, trivially, when x is one-dimensional, as in Section 2.

5.5. Surplus-Sharing and Cost-Sharing Approach

The literature presented in Section 3 studies allocation rules that define a subset of first-best allocations for every economy, or social ordering functions that rank all allocations. Another interesting object is a surplus-sharing rule, which defines a sharing of the product for any vector of input contributions. More precisely, consider an economy $e = (s_N, u_N, f) \in \mathcal{E}$. A surplus-sharing rule is a function $\psi : [0, \overline{\ell}]^n \to \mathbb{R}^n_+$ such that for all $\ell_N \in [0, \overline{\ell}]^n$,

$$\sum_{i=1}^{n} \psi_i(\ell_N) = f\left(\sum_{i \in N} s_i \ell_i\right).$$

A surplus-sharing rule defines a game form, in which input contributions are the strategies, and consumptions (paired with input contributions) are the payoffs.

Kranich (1994) studies how to make the rule ψ perform some kind of compensation by considering the following axiom:

Equal Share for Equal Work (Kranich 1994)
$\forall \ell_N \in [0, \overline{\ell}]^n$, $\forall i, j \in N$,

$$\ell_i = \ell_j \Rightarrow \psi_i(\ell_N) = \psi_j(\ell_N).$$

He studies the case of a two-person economy, and gives sufficient conditions for a Pareto-efficient allocation to be obtainable as a Nash equilibrium of the game defined by a surplus-sharing rule satisfying ***Equal Share for Equal Work***. Notice that in this result the choice of the surplus-sharing rule must be tailored to the particular profile of preferences in the economy.

Gotoh and Yoshihara (1999, 2003) study a variant of the same model in which leisure and consumption are used by the agents in order to construct capability sets. In their model the agents have different productive skills but also different skills in the making of capability sets. These authors rely on compensation axioms similar to ***Equal Share for Equal Work***, and on axioms of solidarity with respect to changes in input contributions and changes in capability skills, in order to characterize a family of surplus-sharing rules that maximizes the (appropriately defined) value of the common capability set of the agents.[81]

Moulin and Sprumont (2006) study the cost-sharing problem, which is dual to the surplus-sharing problem and consists of choosing a function $\phi : \mathbb{R}^n_+ \to \mathbb{R}^n_+$ such that for

[81] Extending this analysis, Gotoh, Suzumura, and Yoshihara (2005) study the construction of extended social ordering functions that rank pairs of game forms and allocations on the basis of principles of procedural fairness, capability egalitarianism, and efficiency.

all $c_N \in \mathbb{R}^n_+$,

$$\sum_{i=1}^{n} \phi_i(c_N) = C(c_N),$$

where $C : \mathbb{R}^n_+ \to \mathbb{R}_+$ is a cost function. The problem of compensation may arise in this setting when the cost function is asymmetric in the individual demands c_i (some individuals are more costly to serve than others), and one considers that agents are responsible for the quantities demanded but not for the fact that serving them is more or less costly. Moulin and Sprumont study the following axiom, whose connection with the principle of compensation and ***E**qual **U**tility for **E**qual **F**unction* is quite transparent:

Strong Ranking (Moulin and Sprumont 2006)
$\forall c_N \in \mathbb{R}^n_+$, $\forall i,j \in N$,

$$c_i \geq c_j \Rightarrow \phi_i(c_N) \geq \phi_j(c_N).$$

In particular, this axiom entails that when two agents formulate the same demand, they pay the same share, irrespectively of the differential cost induced by their demands. This equity principle is actually a cornerstone of the pricing policy of some public monopolies (post services, for instance).

Focusing on the case of demands expressed in discrete units ($c_i \in \mathbb{N}$), Moulin and Sprumont (2006) show that many reasonable sharing rules satisfy this axiom, but their axiomatic analysis singles out the *cross-subsidizing serial method* defined as follows, when individuals are re-ranked so that $c_1 \leq \cdots \leq c_n$:

$$\begin{cases} \phi_1(c_N) = \frac{1}{n} C(c_1, \ldots, c_1) \\ \phi_2(c_N) = \phi_1(c_N) + \frac{1}{n-1}[C(c_1, c_2, \ldots, c_2) - C(c_1, \ldots, c_1)] \\ \vdots \\ \phi_i(c_N) = \phi_{i-1}(c_N) + \frac{1}{n-i+1}[C(c_1, c_2, \ldots, c_i, \ldots, c_i) - C(c_1, c_2, \ldots, c_{i-1}, \ldots, c_{i-1})]. \end{cases}$$

To the best of our knowledge, these three works are the only exceptions to a rather intriguing general neglect of the compensation problem in the surplus-sharing and cost-sharing literature. The tradition in this literature is to assign full responsibility to the agents for their demands and for the induced cost. This is expressed in particular in a dummy axiom, according to which any agent i who generates no cost (the cost function is constant with respect to y_i) should pay nothing. This axiom is incompatible with the ***Strong Ranking*** (SR) axiom. For a general survey of the cost-sharing literature, see Moulin (2002).

5.6. Opinions

Although the layman should not necessarily dictate the exact list of equity principles that ought to be studied in political philosophy and in normative economics, it is nonetheless interesting to submit our axioms to the test of questionnaires in which simple situations are presented to uninformed people in order to see what basic principles are spontaneously accepted or rejected.

A number of empirical works have to do with the ethical principles mentioned here. First, the classical paper by Yaari and Bar-Hillel (1984) is well known as showing that the traditional welfarist solutions perform badly because different contexts seem to call for different choices of allocation rules. It turns out the principles of compensation and of natural reward provide a simple explanation of the pattern of answers in that work. Let us briefly recall the setting. A bundle of two goods $(\overline{x_1}, \overline{x_2}) = (12, 12)$ has to be shared between Jones, whose utility function is $u_J(x_1, x_2) = 100x_1$, and Smith, whose utility function is $u_S(x_1, x_2) = 20x_1 + 20x_2$. The main result obtained by Yaari and Bar-Hillel is that when the utility function describes the nutritional metabolism of the individuals, the answers are mostly in favor of the allocation $(4, 0)$ for Jones, $(8, 12)$ for Smith, which yields equal utilities, whereas when it is a matter of tastes, the answers shift to the allocation $(12, 0)$ for Jones, $(0, 12)$ for Smith, which corresponds to either utilitarianism, the Nash bargaining solution, or the equal-income Walrasian equilibrium.

Now, suppose that individuals are not deemed responsible for their metabolism but are deemed responsible for their tastes. When they are not responsible for the difference in the utility functions, then application of the compensation principle requires equalizing the utilities. When they are responsible for the difference, then the principle of natural reward would be satisfied by applying the equal-income Walrasian equilibrium. The answers are perfectly compatible with this pattern. They are also compatible with adopting a utilitarian reward in the latter case.

The simple examples in this case involve only two agents and therefore do not raise the issue of the incompatibility between compensation and natural reward, or between compensation and utilitarian reward. The first incompatibility has been studied by Schokkaert and Devooght (1998). They study examples in the quasi-linear case. In the first subcase, the function is separable in the two parameters y and z (resp., nonresponsible and responsible parameters): $v(y, z) = 50y + 150z$; while in the second subcase it is not separable: $v(y, z) = 200y + 150z + 100yz$. Two different contexts are proposed to the respondents, each with four individuals. The first one deals with health expenditures (y describes medical needs, z describes choosing an expensive doctor), and the second one with income redistribution (y is an innate talent, z measures effort). In the context of health expenditures, and in the separable subcase, the answers are very much in favor of application of the "canonical" allocation rule (which, as described in Section 2, coincides in the separable case with the main allocation rules)

$$x_i = -50y_i + \frac{1}{4}\sum_{j=1}^{4} 50y_j,$$

while in the nonseparable subcase, the respondents tend to favor allocations respecting the natural reward principle (more precisely, the ***Equal Resource for Equal Talent*** axiom), at the expense of compensation.[82]

In the context of income redistribution, the answers are much less attuned to the compensation and natural reward principles, and show an exaggerated willingness to reward less talented agents who make a high effort and to punish more talented agents who exert little effort, but may also be interpreted as expressing a desire to maintain a remuneration of talent itself, especially under effort. One may suspect that respondents bring in incentive considerations that are absent in the model of Section 2.4.

5.7. Applications

Applications of social ordering functions and social welfare functions to the design of optimal income tax have been numerous. The setting is the classical optimal taxation problem, as formulated by Mirrlees (1971). Assuming the planner knows the distribution of types (skills and preferences) in the population, but does not observe individuals' types, they study income tax schemes leading to allocations that maximize a social ordering function, under the usual incentive compatibility constraints (these constraints amount here to letting agents freely choose their labor time on the budget set defined by the tax scheme). Bossert, Fleurbaey, and Van de gaer (1999) and Fleurbaey and Maniquet (1998, 2006, 2007) use the social ordering functions introduced in Section 3, and a few others of a similar kind. Roemer (1998), Roemer *et al.* (2003), Vandenbroucke (2001), and Schokkaert *et al.* (2004) rely on various versions of the min-of-means and mean-of-mins social welfare functions. Van der Veen (2004) directly compares budget sets, viewed as opportunity sets. Most of these works focus on the linear tax, with the exception of the papers by Fleurbaey and Maniquet.[83] Vandenbroucke (2001) and van der Veen (2004) consider the combination of labor subsidies with income tax. In a different vein, the implementation problem (in which the planner does not know the distribution of types) for economies with unequal skills is studied in Yamada and Yoshihara (2007).

[82] An experimental analysis about dental expenditures has also been made by Clément and Serra (2001), and similarly shows some acceptance of the idea of responsibility. See also Schokkaert and Devooght (2003) for an international comparison of opinions on compensation and responsibility.

[83] In a related work, Boadway *et al.* (2002) study an ordinary weighted utilitarian objective on the same model, considering various possible weights for agents with different utility functions, with the idea of spanning diverse reward principles.

Under richness assumptions on the distribution of types (in particular, the smallest skill is 0), and considering nonlinear taxes, Fleurbaey and Maniquet (1998) show that maximizing any social ordering functions satisfying weak Pareto[84] and ***Hammond Compensation*** entails maximizing the minimum income.[85] On the other hand, the tax scheme obtained by maximization of a Conditional Equality ordering function $R_{\Phi CE}$ depends on the choice of the reference function $\tilde{u}$. For some $\tilde{u}$ (corresponding to hardworking preferences), the result is, again, to maximize the minimum income. This shows that the compensation–natural reward conflict may disappear in second-best problems, in the sense that different social objectives based on these two principles may lead to the same allocations.[86] However, Fleurbaey and Maniquet (2006, 2007) show that when the minimum wage is positive, a slight dose of natural reward in social ordering functions based on compensation leads to the conclusion that the marginal tax rate for incomes below the minimum wage must be zero or even negative on average. The reason is that the social ordering function then advocates maximization of the net income of agents who work full-time at the minimum wage (the working poor).

Roemer *et al.* (2003) and Vandenbroucke (2001) study the application of the mean-of-mins and/or min-of-means criteria, with a measure of individual "advantage" $u(x, y, z)$ that is objective. For instance, in a study of various Western countries with the purpose of comparing actual tax rates with the optimal tax rate for Roemer's criterion, Roemer *et al.* (2003) take individual advantage to be the logarithm[87] of income, disregarding the disutility of labor. The idea is to measure inequalities of opportunity for income. But with such an objective approach, they obtain the possibility of choosing linear taxes that are Pareto-inefficient (tax rates beyond 80% are advocated in this paper for some European countries).

Schokkaert *et al.* (2004) make a thorough comparison of the results obtained with various objective and subjective measures of individual utility, and with the two social welfare functions. They show in particular that mean-of-mins generally leads to higher tax rates than min-of-means. Vandenbroucke (2001) shows that the results are bound to change substantially when the possibility of subsidizing labor (assuming labor hours are observable) at a fixed rate is introduced in supplement to the linear income tax.

[84] Weak Pareto requires an allocation to be socially preferred if it is preferred by all agents to another allocation.

[85] An analysis of the basic income proposal in terms of similar considerations is made in Gotoh and Yoshihara (2004).

[86] Another connection between the taxation setting and the ethical principles deserves to be noted. Recall that in the study of allocation rules, a link between incentive conditions (***Independence of Utilities***, ***Monotonicity***) and natural reward axioms already suggested a congruence, noted in Subsection 3.2, between natural reward and incentives. Similarly, in a context of taxation, it appears that the allocations that are achievable under incentive constraints do satisfy significant features of natural reward. For instance, in the linear version of the model of Section 3 (domain $\mathcal{E}^L$), all allocations that are achievable by a redistributive tax on earnings $s_i\ell_i$ do satisfy ***No-Envy among Equally Skilled***, because agents with equal skills automatically have the same budget set in this setting.

[87] Recall that these criteria do not satisfy ***Ordinalism*** and are sensitive to the particular cardinal utility function adopted to measure individual outcomes.

Under the specific assumptions on the distribution of skills and on agents' utility functions used by Roemer (1998), Bossert, Fleurbaey, and Van de gaer (1999) compute the optimal linear tax associated to different social ordering functions, including those presented in Section 3,[88] as well as the min-of-means and mean-of-mins social welfare functions (with a subjective measure of individual utility, avoiding Pareto-inefficient results). Their result is that the highest income tax rate, and therefore the largest redistribution, follows from maximizing the Egalitarian Equivalent ordering function R_{EE}.

Kranich (1997b) studies a slightly different model where tax revenues are used by the government to finance education policies. An education policy consists of allocating different amounts of money to the schooling of agents, thereby enhancing their ability to earn income. Under several assumptions (in particular the assumption that each agent is capable of achieving any earning ability level ex post), this model has the interesting feature that, under complete information, an education policy exists such that the resulting Pareto-efficient allocation satisfies both ***Equal Utility for Equal Function*** and ***Equal Resource for Equal Talent***. Kranich proves, however, that even in this context but under incomplete information, information–incentive constraints also prevent the planner from achieving full compensation, so that ***Equal Utility for Equal Function*** is no longer achievable. This negative outcome also holds, obviously, in ordinary taxation models.

In Roemer (1998, 2002b), an empirical computation of the mean-of-mins criterion is made for the allocation of educational resources in the United States, considering only race as a nonresponsible parameter, and measuring the achievement of individuals by the logarithm of earnings, econometrically estimated as a function of educational resources and "effort" (measured by the percentile of the number of years of attendance in a subgroup of agents with the same race and similar amount of educational resources—see the next paragraph). Policy is described simply by two instruments, the average amount of educational resources given to each of the two types of pupils. The optimal allocation of resources obtained by this computation implies a high transfer, since resources devoted to black pupils should be about ten times as much as resources allotted to white pupils. Llavador and Roemer (2001) also apply the same criterion to the issue of the allocation of international aid across countries.

Roemer (1993, 1998) also makes a specific proposal about how to construct a measure of a responsibility variable for a given population. First, the variables representing talent have to be chosen, and by sample surveys or any statistical means the joint distribution of the talent variables and the other characteristics that influence people's outcomes must be estimated. Then two agents in the population are considered as identical in terms of "responsibility" (or "effort") if their other characteristics are at the same percentile of the conditional distribution of these characteristics in the respective class of talent of these

[88] Actually, they use a different variant of Conditional Equality.

two agents. Of course, this method essentially requires that the other characteristics can be ranked on the real line and are a monotonic function of the underlying "effort" variable that one tries to estimate.[89] An interesting consequence of this method is that the distribution of the responsibility variable is then automatically independent of talent.

This method has been applied by Van de gaer, Martinez, and Schokkaert (2001) in order to define new measures of social mobility. The idea is that social mobility can be viewed as congruent to equality of opportunities, when opportunities are measured on the basis of the conditional distribution of a given generation's outcomes (e.g., income), for a given level of parental outcome.

Similarly, O'Neill, Sweetman, and Van de gaer (2000) make a nonparametric estimation of the distribution of the earnings in the United States, conditional on parental earnings.[90] They draw "opportunity sets" by representing the graph of the inverse of the cumulative distribution function, which gives the income obtained at any percentile in this distribution. In their analysis the only nonresponsible variable that serves to compute the conditional distribution is parental income. Their results show that different parents' incomes entail unequal opportunities to achieve a given income. For instance, the same level of income is obtained by children of poor families who are at the 65th percentile of their conditional distribution, but is obtained by children of rich families who are only at the 40th percentile of their conditional distribution.[91]

A different empirical application of the axioms of compensation has been made by Schokkaert, Dhaene, and Voorde (1998) and Schokkaert and Van de Voorde (2004). It deals with the joint management of health insurance agencies (such as the allocation of budget allowances to regional mutual insurances in Belgium). A basic distinction is made, in the set of variables explaining the level of medical expenditures, between those for which the insurer should be held responsible, and those which do elicit compensation. Compensation in this setting has implications in terms of incentives for risk selection: Full compensation should prevent insurers from selecting among their potential customers those who display favorable risks. Natural reward, on the other hand, has a direct effect on incentives for efficient management of resources. Therefore the axioms of compensation and natural reward seem relevant in this application, albeit with a reinterpretation. The authors show how to rely on an econometric estimation of the equations of medical expenditures in order to choose the allocation rule for the global budget. They discuss the problem of possible nonseparability of the exogenous variables in the equation, and

[89] For a discussion of assumptions underlying this method, see Fleurbaey (1998), Roemer (1998, 2002b), Kolm (2001), and Hild and Voorhoeve (2004).

[90] See Lefranc, Pistolesi, and Trannoy (2008, 2009) for similar applications to French and other data, and Goux and Maurin (2002) for an application combining the Van de gaer and Roemer criteria.

[91] For a general comparison of mobility measures with measures based on the idea of equal opportunities, see Van de gaer, Martinez, and Schokkaert (2001), and Schluter and Van de gaer (2002). See also Roemer (2004) and Fields *et al.* (2005).

show the unavoidable ethical choices that must be made by the public decision-maker in this respect.

A similar kind of application has been made, for the problem of interregional budget transfers, by Cappelen and Tungodden (2007).[92] The idea is that regions are responsible for their policy, in particular their tax rate, but not for characteristics of the region influencing the tax base. They show that two prominent transfer schemes in the fiscal federalism literature, namely the foundation grant and the power equalization grant, can be related to conditional equality and egalitarian-equivalence, respectively. Calsamiglia (2009) studies how policies that attempt to achieve equality of opportunity separately in various sectors of individual life (e.g., health, labor market, education) may ultimately achieve equality of opportunity globally. She shows that, for some contexts, this obtains if and only if rewards to effort are equalized across individuals in each sector. The issue of intergenerational equity and compensation across generations is addressed in Tadenuma and Suzumura (2008).

6. CONCLUSION

Let us put the various approaches described in this chapter in perspective. One of the lessons from the surveyed literature is that anyone who embarks in social evaluations in the compensation-responsibility context must make two key decisions: (1) How should responsibility be rewarded (the two prominent options being liberal neutrality—natural reward—or zero inequality aversion—utilitarian reward)? (2) Is compensation or reward the priority? This second question is inseparable from, and in some contexts equivalent to, a third one: (3) Is the focus on ex post inequalities or on ex ante prospects? The following table places the main evaluation criteria that have been presented in their respective positions with respect to these questions.

	Natural reward	**Utilitarian reward**
Priority on compensation (ex post)	egalitarian-equivalent	mean-of-mins
Priority on reward (ex ante)	conditional equality	min-of-means

In the rest of this conclusion, we highlight a few open questions. The distinction between various reward principles is not clearly made in many parts of the literature: some authors spontaneously adopt a natural reward approach, while other authors choose a utilitarian reward without much justification. Initially, the different approaches were linked to the fact that some authors studied allocation rules and Pareto-efficient

92 This is also the main motivating topic in Iturbe-Ormaetxe and Nieto (1996).

redistribution, while other authors, interested in inequality measurement and dominance analysis or in taxation and redistribution under incentive constraints, looked for social welfare functions and therefore took welfarist social welfare functions as their point of departure. In the theory of fair allocation rules, the Walrasian equilibrium and the general idea of equality of resources (as expressed, e.g., in the No-Envy condition) are absolutely preeminent, and this led authors toward natural reward. In contrast, the theory of social welfare functions identifies neutrality about welfare inequalities with a zero inequality aversion as displayed by a utilitarian social welfare function. Now that social welfare functions embodying natural reward and geared toward Walrasian allocations have been produced,[93] such as the Conditional Equality ordering function $R_{\Phi CE}$ (see Section 3.2), it is possible to compare natural reward and utilitarian reward not only in the field of first-best redistribution, but also in the field of second-best redistribution. A preliminary comparative study is made in Bossert, Fleurbaey, and Van de gaer (1999), but a general confrontation between natural reward and utilitarian reward remains to be done.

Propositions 3 and 4 in Section 2.3 are typical of many results in this literature, in which a family of allocation rules (or social ordering functions) is characterized, but this family contains an infinity of very different solutions, which differ by some crucial parameter (such as $\tilde{y}$ or $\tilde{u}$). The choice of a precise member in such a family presumably requires invoking additional ethical principles, such as more precise reward principles[94] or totally different notions. For instance, self-ownership as studied in Section 3.4 was shown to restrict the range of admissible parameters. But a theory about the choice of the reference parameters remains to be elaborated. In addition, it is rather disturbing when the Consistency axiom forces solutions to stick to one and the same reference parameter, whatever the profile of the population. It would seem more sensible to have the reference parameter depend on the profile, and this has been shown to be important in order to satisfy some compensation or natural reward axioms (e.g., it is necessary, as stated in Proposition 2, that Φ be idempotent so that $S_{\Phi CE}$ may satisfy ***Equal Utility for Uniform Function***).[95] There exist alternative solutions, such as the average rules S_{AEE}, S_{ACE} or the balanced rules S_{BE}, S_{BCE} presented in Section 2.2 or Section 2.4.1. But such solutions have their limitations, since they can be computed only in special contexts (and their characterizations rely either on contrived axioms or on special domain assumptions).

[93] A general study of the construction of social ordering functions that are oriented toward equalizing resources and only rely on individual ordinal noncomparable preferences is made in Fleurbaey and Maniquet (2008), in relation to the theory of allocation rules and also in relation to the presumed impossibility of social choice without interpersonal comparisons of utility.

[94] For instance, Tungodden (2005) argues in favor of the flattest (most egalitarian) reward, advocating a particular $S_{\Psi EE}$ rule. In the production model, Fleurbaey and Maniquet (2005) give related arguments in favor of R_{EE} (and an ordering function rationalizing $S_{\Psi EE}$ in $\mathcal{E}^L$, with $\Psi(ws_N) = w\min_i s_i$), which can also be interpreted as the most egalitarian in a similar sense.

[95] A proposal along this line is made by Valletta (2010).

More generally, we conjecture that in the future a more refined theory will make a distinction between different contexts. For instance, in $u(x, y, z)$, z may be an effort or merit variable, or simply a taste parameter, and the discussions of Examples 2 and 3 have shown that moral intuition may be sensitive to this. Moreover, Examples 1 through 3 rely on different utility functions. In Example 1, x and y are perfect substitutes, which makes the principle of compensation and the principle of natural reward not only compatible, but also equally attractive. Example 2, in which agents are totally responsible for their sensitivity to transfers, has been chosen to criticize the principle of compensation. Example 3, in which talent, but not transfers, affects the productivity of effort, was cooked to criticize the principle of natural reward. The shape of the utility function may then be relevant to the choice of ethical principles.

Another drawback of all the solutions that are not direct extensions of the No-Envy allocation rule S_{NE} is that they may fail to select envy-free allocations when some exist. In other words, axioms like ***Equal Utility for Equal Function*** and ***Equal Resource for Equal Talent*** (or ***No-Envy among Equally Skilled***) are too weak to guarantee that whenever envy-free (and Pareto-efficient) allocations exist, some of them must be selected. On the other hand, the direct extensions of S_{NE} presented in Section 2.2 do not have clear ethical properties in terms of compensation and reward outside the subdomain of economies in which ***No-Envy*** can be satisfied (although Proposition 2 does provide some answers), and do not have any axiomatic justification. In brief, some work remains to be done around ***No-Envy*** in the compensation problem.

The literature has focused on the two models presented here, and therefore has neglected issues that are not described in these models. In particular, it remains to study the general problem of talents and handicaps that simultaneously alter an individual's productive abilities, her quality of life, and her preferences over consumption goods. The model of Section 3 deals only with the first dimension; the model in Section 2 deals with the second dimension and may be considered to cover the third dimension only when x is interpreted as income, u as indirect utility, and when consumption prices are fixed. In-kind transfers cannot be studied in this setting. In a different direction, one may also want to study more specific problems such as spatial inequalities (living somewhere may be seen as a handicap in terms of living cost, access to public goods, etc.), family size, and so on. The production model could also be refined so as to take account of the fact that agents may be deemed responsible for some of their skill parameters, or the fact that they may not be responsible for some of their preference parameters.

ACKNOWLEDGMENTS

We thank K. Suzumura for helpful advice in the preparation of this chapter and detailed comments on a first draft, and L. Kranich for helpful suggestions. We are also grateful to R. Arneson, R. Gary-Bobo, F. Gaspart, M. Le Breton, H. Moulin, E. Ooghe, J. Roemer, E. Schokkaert, Y. Sprumont, K. Tadenuma, W. Thomson, A. Trannoy, B. Tungodden, P. Vallentyne, D. Van de gaer, and N. Yoshihara for comments or discussions, and to participants at a Summer School in Namur.

REFERENCES

Arlegi, R., & Nieto, J. (1999). Equality of opportunity: Cardinality-based criteria. In H. de Swart (Ed.), *Logic, game theory, and social choice*. Tilburg: Tilburg University Press.

Arneson, R. J. (1989). Equality and equal opportunity for welfare. *Philosophical Studies, 56*, 77–93.

Arneson, R. J. (1990). Liberalism, distributive subjectivism, and equal opportunity for welfare. *Philosophy and Public Affairs, 19*, 158–194.

Arneson, R. J. (2000). Luck, egalitarianism, and prioritarianism. *Ethics, 110*, 339–349.

Arrow, K. J. (1963). *Social choice and individual values*. New York: John Wiley.

Arrow, K. J. (1971). A utilitarian approach to the concept of equality in public expenditures. *Quarterly Journal of Economics, 85*, 409–415.

Arrow, K. J. (1973). Some ordinalist-utilitarian notes on Rawls's theory of justice. *Journal of Philosophy, 70*, 245–263.

Aumann, R. J., & Maschler, M. (1985). Game-theoretic analysis of a bankruptcy problem from the Talmud. *Journal of Economic Theory, 36*, 195–213.

Barberà, S., Bossert, W., & Pattanaik, P. K. (2004). Ranking sets of objects. In S. Barberà, P. J. Hammond & C. Seidl (Eds.), *Handbook of utility theory* (Vol. 2). Dordrecht: Kluwer.

Barry, B. (1991). *Liberty and justice: essays in political theory* (Vol. 2), 893–977. Oxford: Oxford University Press.

Ben Porath, E., Gilboa, I., & Schmeidler, D. (1997). On the measurement of inequality under uncertainty. *Journal of Economic Theory, 75*, 194–204.

Boadway, R., Marchand, M., Pestieau, P., & del Mar Racionero, M. (2002). Optimal redistribution with heterogeneous preferences for leisure. *Journal of Public Economic Theory, 4*, 475–498.

Bossert, W. (1995). Redistribution mechanisms based on individual characteristics. *Mathematical Social Sciences, 29*, 1–17.

Bossert, W., & Fleurbaey, M. (1996). Redistribution and compensation. *Social Choice and Welfare, 13*, 343–355.

Bossert, W., Fleurbaey, M., & Van de gaer, D. (1999). Responsibility, talent, and compensation: a second-best analysis. *Review of Economic Design, 4*, 35–56.

Bossert, W., & Weymark, J. A. (2004). Utility theory in social choice. In S. Barberà, P. J. Hammond & C. Seidl (Eds.), *Handbook of utility theory* (Vol. 2), 1099–1177. Dordrecht: Kluwer.

Broome, J. (1991). *Weighing goods*. Oxford: Basil Blackwell.

Calsamiglia, C. (2009). Decentralizing equality of opportunity. *International Economic Review, 50*, 273–290.

Cappelen, A. W., & Tungodden, B. (2002). Responsibility and reward. *Finanz Archiv, 59*, 120–140.

Cappelen, A. W., & Tungodden, B. (2003). Reward and responsibility: how should we be affected when others change their effort? *Politics, Philosophy & Economics, 2*, 191–211.

Cappelen, A. W., & Tungodden, B. (2006). A liberal egalitarian paradox. *Economics and Philosophy, 22*, 393–408.

Cappelen, A. W., & Tungodden, B. (2007). Local autonomy and interregional equality. Fiscal equalization with balanced budgets. *Social Choice and Welfare, 28*, 443–460.

Cappelen, A. W., & Tungodden, B. (2009). Rewarding effort. *Economic Theory, 39*, 425–441.

Champsaur, P., & Laroque, G. (1981). Fair allocations in large economies. *Journal of Economic Theory, 25*, 269–282.

Clément, V., & Serra, D. (2001). Egalitarisme et responsabilité: Une investigation expérimentale. *Revue d'Economie Politique, 111*, 173–193.

Cohen, G. A. (1989). On the currency of egalitarian justice. *Ethics, 99*, 906–944.

Daniel, T. E. (1975). A revised concept of distributional equity. *Journal of Economic Theory, 11*, 94–109.

d'Aspremont, C., & Gevers, L. (1977). Equity and the informational basis of collective choice. *Review of Economic Studies, 44*, 199–209.

d'Aspremont, C., & Gevers, L. (2002). Social welfare functionals and interpersonal comparability. In K. J. Arrow, A. K. Sen & K. Suzumura (Eds.), *Handbook of social choice and welfare* (Vol. 1), 459–541. Amsterdam: North-Holland.

Deschamps, R., & Gevers, L. (1979). Separability, risk-bearing, and social welfare judgments. In J. J. Laffont (Ed.), *Aggregation and revelation of preferences*, 145–160. Amsterdam: North-Holland.

Diamantaras, D., & Thomson, W. (1990). A refinement and extension of the no-envy concept. *Economics Letters, 33*, 217–222.

Dworkin, R. (1981a). What is equality? Part 1: equality of welfare. *Philosophy & Public Affairs, 10*, 185–246.

Dworkin, R. (1981b). What is equality? Part 2: equality of resources. *Philosophy & Public Affairs, 10*, 283–345.

Dworkin, R. (2000). *Sovereign virtue. The theory and practice of equality*. Cambridge, MA: Harvard University Press.

Dworkin, R. (2002). Sovereign virtue revisited. *Ethics, 113*, 106–143.

Feldman, A., & Kirman, A. (1974). Fairness and envy. *American Economic Review, 64*(6), 995–1005.

Fields, G., Dardononi, V., Sanchez, L., & Roemer, J. E. (2005). How demanding should equality of opportunity be, and how much have we achieved? In G. Fields, D. Grusky & S. Morgan (Eds.), *Mobility and inequality: frontiers of research from sociology and economics*, 59–83. Palo Alto: Stanford University Press.

Fleurbaey, M. (1994). On fair compensation. *Theory and Decision, 36*, 277–307.

Fleurbaey, M. (1995a). Equality and responsibility. *European Economic Review, 39*, 683–689.

Fleurbaey, M. (1995b). Equal opportunity or equal social outcome? *Economics and Philosophy, 11*, 25–56.

Fleurbaey, M. (1995c). The requisites of equal opportunity. In W. A. Barnett, H. Moulin, M. Salles & N. J. Schofield (Eds.), *Social choice, welfare, and ethics*, 37–53. Cambridge: Cambridge University Press.

Fleurbaey, M. (1995d). Three solutions for the compensation problem. *Journal of Economic Theory, 65*, 505–521.

Fleurbaey, M. (1998). Equality among responsible individuals. In J. F. Laslier, M. Fleurbaey, N. Gravel & A. Trannoy (Eds.), *Freedom in economics. New perspectives in normative analysis*, 206–234. London: Routledge.

Fleurbaey, M. (2001). Egalitarian opportunities. *Law and Philosophy, 20*, 499–530.

Fleurbaey, M. (2002). Equality of resources revisited. *Ethics, 113*, 82–105.

Fleurbaey, M. (2008). *Fairness, responsibility, and welfare*. Oxford: Oxford University Press.

Fleurbaey, M., & Maniquet, F. (1996). Fair allocation with unequal production skills: the no-envy approach to compensation. *Mathematical Social Sciences, 32*, 71–93.

Fleurbaey, M., & Maniquet, F. (1997). Implementability and horizontal equity imply no-envy. *Econometrica, 65*, 1215–1219.

Fleurbaey, M., & Maniquet, F. (1998). Optimal income taxation: an ordinal approach. CORE D.P. #9865.

Fleurbaey, M., & Maniquet, F. (1999). Fair allocation with unequal production skills: the solidarity approach to compensation. *Social Choice and Welfare, 16*, 569–583.

Fleurbaey, M., & Maniquet, F. (2005). Fair orderings when agents have unequal production skills. *Social Choice and Welfare, 24*, 93–127.

Fleurbaey, M., & Maniquet, F. (2006). Fair income tax. *Review of Economic Studies, 73*, 55–83.

Fleurbaey, M., & Maniquet, F. (2007). Help the low-skilled or let the hard-working thrive? A study of fairness in optimal income taxation. *Journal of Public Economic Theory, 9*, 467–500.

Fleurbaey, M., & Maniquet, F. (2008). Utilitarianism versus fairness in welfare economics. In M. Salles & J. A. Weymark (Eds.), *Justice, political liberalism and utilitarianism: Themes from Harsanyi and Rawls*, 263–280. Cambridge: Cambridge University Press.

Fleurbaey, M., & Trannoy, A. (2003). The impossibility of a Paretian egalitarian. *Social Choice and Welfare, 21*, 243–264.

Foley, D. (1967). Resource allocation and the public sector. *Yale Economic Essays, 7*, 45–98.

Gajdos, T., & Maurin, E. (2004). Unequal uncertainties and uncertain inequalities: an axiomatic approach. *Journal of Economic Theory, 116*, 93–118.

Gaspart, F. (1996). *A contribution to the theory of distributive justice.* Ph.D. thesis, Facultés Universitaires Notre Dame de la Paix, Namur.

Gaspart, F. (1998). Objective measures of well-being and the cooperative production problem. *Social Choice and Welfare, 15*, 95–112.

Gotoh, R., & Yoshihara, N. (1999). A game form approach to theories of distributive justice. Formalizing needs principle. In H. de Swart (Ed.), *Logic, game theory and social choice*, 168–183. Tilburg: Tilburg University Press.

Gotoh, R., & Yoshihara, N. (2003). A class of fair distribution rules à la Rawls and Sen. *Economic Theory, 22*, 63–88.

Gotoh, R., & Yoshihara, N. (2004). Normative foundation of the "basic income" policy: towards welfare economics of welfare states. *Economic Review, 55*, 230–244 (in Japanese).

Gotoh, R., Suzumura, K., & Yoshihara, N. (2005). Extended social ordering function for rationalizing fair allocation rules as game forms in the sense of Rawls and Sen. *International Journal of Economic Theory, 1*, 21–41.

Goux, D., & Maurin, E. (2002). On the evaluation of equality of opportunity for income: axioms and evidence. mimeo, Institut National de la Statistique et des Etudes Economiques, Paris.

Hammond, P. J. (1976). Equity, Arrow's conditions and Rawls' difference principle. *Econometrica, 44*, 793–804.

Herrero, C. (1996). Capabilities and utilities. *Economic Design, 2*, 69–88.

Herrero, C. (1997). Equitable opportunities: an extension. *Economics Letters, 55*, 91–95.

Herrero, C., Iturbe-Ormaetxe, I., & Nieto, J. (1998). Ranking opportunity profiles on the basis of the common opportunities. *Mathematical Social Sciences, 35*, 273–289.

Hild, M., & Voorhoeve, A. (2004). Equality of opportunity and opportunity dominance. *Economics and Philosophy, 20*, 117–146.

Iturbe-Ormaetxe, I. (1997). Redistribution and individual characteristics. *Review of Economic Design, 3*, 45–55.

Iturbe-Ormaetxe, I., & Nieto, J. (1996). On fair allocations and monetary compensations. *Economic Theory, 7*, 125–138.

Kolm, S. C. (1968). The optimal production of social justice. In H. Guitton & J. Margolis (Eds.), *Economie publique*, 145–200. Paris: Editions du CNRS.

Kolm, S. C. (1972). *Justice et équité.* Paris: Editions du CNRS. Rep. and transl. as *Justice and equity*. Cambridge, MA: MIT Press, 1999.

Kolm, S. C. (1985). *Le contrat social libéral.* Paris: PUF.

Kolm, S. C. (1993). *Equal liberty.* mimeo Paris: Conseil Général des Ponts et Chaussées.

Kolm, S. C. (1996a). The theory of justice. *Social Choice and Welfare, 13*, 151–182.

Kolm, S. C. (1996b). *Modern theories of justice.* Cambridge, MA: MIT Press.

Kolm, S. C. (1998). Chance and justice: social policies and the Harsanyi-Vickrey-Rawls problem. *European Economic Review, 42*, 1393–1416.

Kolm, S. C. (2001). To each according to her work? Just entitlement from action: desert, merit, responsibility, and equal opportunities. A review of John Roemer's equality of opportunity. mimeo, EHESS Paris.

Kolm, S. C. (2004a). Liberty and distribution: macrojustice from social freedom. *Social Choice and Welfare, 22*, 113–146.

Kolm, S. C. (2004b). *Macrojustice. The political economy of fairness.* New York: Cambridge University Press.

Kranich, L. (1994). Equal division, efficiency, and the sovereign supply of labor. *American Economic Review, 84*(1), 178–189.

Kranich, L. (1996). Equitable opportunities: an axiomatic approach. *Journal of Economic Theory, 71*, 131–147.

Kranich, L. (1997a). Equitable opportunities in economic environments. *Social Choice and Welfare, 14*, 57–64.

Kranich, L. (1997b). Equalizing opportunities through public education when innate abilities are unobservable. Universidad Carlos III de Madrid WP #97-17.

Lange, O. (1936). On the economic theory of socialism. In B. E. Lippincott (Ed.), *On the economic theory of socialism*, 57–142. Minneapolis: University of Minneapolis Press.

Lefranc, A., Pistolesi, N., & Trannoy, A. (2008). Inequality of opportunities vs. inequality of outcomes: are Western societies all alike? *Review of Income and Wealth, 54*, 513–546.

Lefranc, A., Pistolesi, N., & Trannoy, A. (2009). Equality of opportunity and luck: definitions and testable conditions, with an application to income in France. *Journal of Public Economics, 93*, 1189–1207.

Llavador, H. G., & Roemer, J. E. (2001). An equal-opportunity approach to the allocation of international aid. *Journal of Development Economics, 64*, 147–171.

Maniquet, F. (1998). An equal-right solution to the compensation-responsibility dilemma. *Mathematical Social Sciences, 35*, 185–202.

Maniquet, F. (2004). On the equivalence between welfarism and equality of opportunity. *Social Choice and Welfare, 23*, 127–148.

Mariotti, M. (2003). Opportunities, chances in life and inequality. mimeo, University of London.

Martinez, M. (2004). Une contribution à la mesure de la mobilité intergénérationnelle. Ph.D thesis, EHESS, Paris.

Maskin, E. (1977). Nash equilibrium and welfare optimality. mimeo, University of Harvard. (pub. in 1999, *Review of Economic Studies, 66*, 23–38.)

Mirrlees, J. (1971). An exploration in the theory of optimum income taxation. *Review of Economic Studies, 38*, 175–208.

Mirrlees, J. (1974). Notes on welfare economics, information and uncertainty. In M. S. Balch, D. McFadden & S. Y. Wu (Eds.), *Essays on economic behaviour under uncertainty*, 243–257. Amsterdam: North-Holland.

Mongin, P., & d'Aspremont, C. (1998). Utility theory and ethics. In S. Barberà, P. Hammond & C. Seidl (Eds.), *Handbook of utility theory* (Vol. 1), 371–482. Dordrecht: Kluwer.

Moulin, H. (1990). Joint ownership of a convex technology: comparison of three solutions. *Review of Economic Studies, 57*, 439–452.

Moulin, H. (1991). Welfare bounds in the fair division problem. *Journal of Economic Theory, 54*, 321–337.

Moulin, H. (1993). On the fair and coalition strategy-proof allocation of private goods. In K. Binmore, A. P. Kirman & P. Tani (Eds.), *Frontiers in game theory*, 151–163. Cambridge, MA: MIT Press.

Moulin, H. (1994). La présence d'envie: comment s'en accommoder? *Recherches Economiques de Louvain, 60*, 63–72.

Moulin, H. (2002). Axiomatic cost and surplus sharing. In K. J. Arrow, A. K. Sen & K. Suzumura (Eds.), *Handbook of social choice and welfare* (Vol. 1), 289–357. Amsterdam: North-Holland.

Moulin, H., & Roemer, J. E. (1989). Public ownership of the external world and private ownership of self. *Journal of Political Economy, 97*, 347–367.

Moulin, H., & Shenker, S. (1994). Average cost pricing vs. serial cost sharing: an axiomatic comparison. *Journal of Economic Theory, 64*, 178–201.

Moulin, H., & Sprumont, Y. (2006). Responsibility and cross-subsidization in cost sharing. *Games and Economic Behavior, 55*, 152–188.

Nagahisa, R. (1991). A local independence condition for characterization of the Walras rule. *Journal of Economic Theory, 54*, 106–123.

Ok, E. (1997). On opportunity inequality measurement. *Journal of Economic Theory, 77*, 300–329.

Ok, E., & Kranich, L. (1998). The measurement of opportunity inequality: a cardinality-based approach. *Social Choice and Welfare, 15*, 263–287.

O'Neill, B. (1982). A problem of rights arbitration in the Talmud. *Mathematical Social Sciences, 2*, 345–371.

O'Neill, D., Sweetman, O., & Van de gaer, D. (2000). Equality of opportunity and kernel density estimation: an application to intergenerational mobility. In T. B. Fomby & R. C. Hill (Eds.), *Applying kernel and nonparametric estimation to economic topics. Advances in econometrics* (Vol. 14), 259–274. Stamford, CT: JAI Press.

Ooghe, E., & Lauwers, L. (2005). Non-dictatorial extensive social choice. *Economic Theory, 25*, 721–743.

Ooghe, E., Schokkaert, E., & Van de gaer, D. (2007). Equality of opportunity versus equality of opportunity sets. *Social Choice and Welfare, 28*, 209–230.

Otsuki, M. (1996). Choice of compensation policy for disabilities. W.P. #131, TERG.

Pazner, E., & Schmeidler, D. (1974). A difficulty in the concept of fairness. *Review of Economic Studies, 41*, 441–443.

Pazner, E., & Schmeidler, D. (1978a). Egalitarian equivalent allocations: a new concept of economic equity. *Quarterly Journal of Economics, 92*, 671–687.

Pazner, E., & Schmeidler, D. (1978b). Decentralization and income distribution in socialist economies. *Economic Inquiry, 16*, 257–264.

Peragine, V. (1999). The distribution and redistribution of opportunity. *Journal of Economic Surveys, 13*, 37–69.

Peragine, V. (2002). Opportunity egalitarianism and income inequality. *Mathematical Social Sciences, 44*, 45–64.

Peragine, V. (2004). Measuring and implementing equality of opportunity for income. *Social Choice and Welfare, 22*, 187–210.

Piketty, T. (1994). Existence of fair allocations in economies with production. *Journal of Public Economics, 55*, 391–405.

Rawls, J. (1971). *A theory of justice*. Cambridge, MA: Harvard University Press.

Rawls, J. (1982). Social unity and primary goods. In A. K. Sen & B. Williams (Eds.), *Utilitarianism and beyond*, 159–186. Cambridge: Cambridge University Press.

Roemer, J. E. (1985a). Equality of talent. *Economics and Philosophy, 1*, 151–187.

Roemer, J. E. (1985b). A note on interpersonal comparability and the theory of fairness. W. P. #261, Dep. of Economics, U. C. Davis.

Roemer, J. E. (1986). Equality of resources implies equality of welfare. *Quarterly Journal of Economics, 101*, 751–784.

Roemer, J. E. (1993). A pragmatic theory of responsibility for the egalitarian planner. *Philosophy & Public Affairs, 22*, 146–166.

Roemer, J. E. (1998). *Equality of opportunity*. Cambridge, MA: Harvard University Press.

Roemer, J. E. (2002a). Egalitarianism against the veil of ignorance. *Journal of Philosophy, 99*, 167–184.

Roemer, J. E. (2002b). Equality of opportunity: a progress report. *Social Choice and Welfare, 19*, 455–471.

Roemer, J. E. (2004). Equal opportunity and intergenerational mobility: going beyond intergenerational income transition matrices. In M. Corak (Ed.), *Generational income mobility in North America and Europe*, 48–57. Cambridge: Cambridge University Press.

Roemer, J. E., Aaberge, R., Colombino, U., Fritzell, J., Jenkins, S., & Lefranc, A., *et al.* (2003). To what extent do fiscal regimes equalize opportunities for income acquisition among citizens? *Journal of Public Economics, 87*, 539–565.

Roemer, J. E., & Silvestre, J. (1989). Public ownership: three proposals for resource allocation. W.P. #307, Dep. of Economics, U. C. Davis.

Schluter, C., & Van de gaer, D. (2002). Mobility as distributional difference. mimeo, University of Bristol.

Schokkaert, E., & Devooght, K. (1998). The empirical acceptance of compensation axioms. In J. F. Laslier, M. Fleurbaey, N. Gravel & A. Trannoy (Eds.), *Freedom in economics. New perspectives in normative analysis*. London: Routledge.

Schokkaert, E., & Devooght, K. (2003). Responsibility-sensitive fair compensation in different cultures. *Social Choice and Welfare*, *21*, 207–242.

Schokkaert, E., Dhaene, G., & Van de Voorde, C. (1998). Risk adjustment and the trade-off between efficiency and risk selection: an application of the theory of fair compensation. *Health Economics*, 7, 465–480.

Schokkaert, E., & Van de gaer, D. (1994). Equality of opportunity and intergenerational transmission processes. Center for Economic Studies, K. U. Leuven, Public Economics Research Paper #35.

Schokkaert, E., Van de gaer, D., Vandenbroucke, F., & Luttens, R. (2004). Responsibility-sensitive egalitarianism and optimal linear income taxation. *Mathematical Social Sciences*, *48*, 151–182.

Schokkaert, E., & Van de Voorde, C. (2004). Risk selection and the specification of the conventional risk adjustment formula. *Journal of Health Economics*, *23*, 1237–1259.

Sen, A. K. (1970). *Collective choice and social welfare*. San Francisco: Holden-Day.

Sen, A. K. (1973). *On economic inequality*. Oxford: Clarendon Press.

Sen, A. K. (1985). *Commodities and capabilities*. Amsterdam: North-Holland.

Sprumont, Y. (1997). Balanced egalitarian redistribution of income. *Mathematical Social Sciences*, *33*, 185–202.

Steinhaus, H. (1948). The problem of fair division. *Econometrica*, *16*, 101–104.

Suzumura, K. (1981a). On Pareto-efficiency and the no-envy concept of equity. *Journal of Economic Theory*, *25*, 367–379.

Suzumura, K. (1981b). On the possibility of fair collective choice rule. *International Economic Review*, *22*, 351–364.

Suzumura, K. (1983). *Rational choice, collective decisions, and social welfare*. Cambridge: Cambridge University Press.

Suzumura, K., & Yoshihara, N. (2000). Responsibility and compensation: a new paradigm in welfare economics. *Economic Review*, *51*(2), 162–184 (in Japanese).

Svensson, L. G. (1983). Large indivisibles: an analysis with respect to price equilibrium and fairness. *Econometrica*, *51*, 939–954.

Tadenuma, K., & Suzumura, K. (2008). Normative approaches to the problem of global warming: responsibility, compensation and the Golden-Rule. In J. E. Roemer & K. Suzumura (Eds.), *Intergenerational equity and sustainability*, IEA Conference Proceeding, London: Palgrave.

Thomson, W. (1983). Equity in exchange economies. *Journal of Economic Theory*, *29*, 217–244.

Thomson, W. (1988). A study of choice correspondences in economies with a variable number of agents. *Journal of Economic Theory*, *46*, 237–254.

Thomson, W. (1994). Notions of equal, or equivalent, opportunities. *Social Choice and Welfare*, *11*, 137–156.

Thomson, W. (chapter 21, this volume) Fair allocation rules.

Tungodden, B. (2005). Responsibility and redistribution: the case of first best taxation. *Social Choice and Welfare*, *24*, 33–44.

Vallentyne, P. (2002). Brute luck, option luck, and equality of initial opportunities. *Ethics*, *112*, 529–587.

Valletta, G. (2009). Health, fairness and taxation. mimeo, University of Maastricht.

Van de gaer, D. (1993). Equality of opportunity and investment in human capital. Ph.D. thesis, K. U. Leuven.

Van de gaer, D., Martinez, M., & Schokkaert, E. (2001). Three meanings of intergenerational mobility. *Economica*, *68*, 519–538.

Vandenbroucke, F. (2001). *Social justice and individual ethics in an open society. Equality, responsibility, and incentives*. Berlin: Springer-Verlag.

van der Veen, R. (2004). Basic income versus wage subsidies: competing instruments in an optimal tax model with a maximin objective. *Economics and Philosophy*, *20*, 147–184.

van Parijs, P. (1990). Equal endowments as undominated diversity. *Recherches Economiques de Louvain, 56*, 327–355.

van Parijs, P. (1995). *Real freedom for all*. Oxford: Oxford University Press.

van Parijs, P. (1997). Social justice as real freedom for all: a reply to Arneson, Fleurbaey, Melnyk and Selznick. *The Good Society*, 7(1), 42–48.

Varian, H. (1974). Equity, envy and efficiency. *Journal of Economic Theory, 9*, 63–91.

Weymark, J. A. (2003). Generalized Gini indices of equality of opportunity. *Journal of Economic Inequality, 1*, 5–24.

Yaari, M. E., & Bar-Hillel, M. (1984). On dividing justly. *Social Choice and Welfare, 1*, 1–24.

Yamada, A., & Yoshihara, N. (2007). Triple implementation in production economies with unequal skills by sharing mechanisms. *International Journal of Game Theory, 36*, 85–106.

Yoshihara, N. (2003). Characterizations of bargaining solutions in production economies with unequal skills. *Journal of Economic Theory, 108*, 256–285.

Young, H. P. (1987). On dividing an amount according to individual claims or liabilities. *Mathematics of Operations Research, 12*, 398–414.

CHAPTER TWENTY-THREE

Welfarism, Individual Rights, and Procedural Fairness

Kotaro Suzumura
Professor of Economics, School of Political Science and Economics, Waseda University, Tokyo, Japan

Contents

Abstract

Ever since Sen crystallized the logical conflict between the welfaristic value of the Pareto principle and the nonwelfaristic value of individual libertarian rights into what he christened the *impossibility of a Paretian liberal*, there have been many attempts in social choice theory to generalize, or to repudiate, the conflict between welfare and rights. This chapter focuses on this logical conflict and tries to find a way of balancing these two important values in human well-being. We will identify three issues in this line of research, viz., the *formal articulation of rights*, the *social realization of rights*, and the *initial conferment of rights*. We will also examine the sustainability of Sen's concept of individual rights and examine the game form articulation of individual rights as a viable alternative to Sen's proposed concept.

Keywords: individual rights, welfarism, normal game form, procedural fairness.

JEL codes: D02, D63, D71.

Handbook of Social Choice and Welfare, Volume II
ISSN: 0169-7218, DOI: 10.1016/S0169-7218(10)00023-7

1. INTRODUCTION

A remarkable fact about social choice theory is that the two distinguished precursors of this intellectual discipline, Marie-Jean de Condorcet and Jeremy Bentham, worked in the sharply contrasting intellectual atmosphere on the perennial issue of welfare and rights. Condorcet worked in the intellectual atmosphere of the European Enlightenment, which emphasized inviolable natural rights and rational social design à la Jean-Jacques Rousseau. In conspicuous contrast, Bentham was a harsh critic of the concept of inviolable natural rights, and is known for his famous criticism: "[N]atural rights is simple nonsense: natural and imprescriptible rights, rhetorical nonsense—nonsense upon stilts" (Bentham 1843, p. 501). Instead of inviolable natural rights, Bentham took recourse to the ultimate principle throughout his intellectual discourse that the good social system or rational economic policy should be able to bring about the "greatest happiness of the greatest number." It is true that Bentham, a legal scholar, had every reason to emphasize the importance of rights, but their importance was recognized only in their instrumental role in promoting social welfare rather than their intrinsic value. Not only was social choice theory given birth by these precursors who had sharply contrasting intellectual backgrounds regarding the priority between social welfare and individual rights, but also the tension between welfare and rights has persisted ever since, which has been exerting strong influence on the evolution of social choice theory. This chapter focuses on the logical conflict between welfare and rights, and examines the possibility of finding a proper niche for each one of these two aspects of human life in the fully-fledged theory of social choice and welfare economics.

The structure of this chapter is as follows. In Section 2, we put forward a schematic summary of the informational bases of normative welfare judgments to facilitate understanding and cross-references. Section 3 explains how the potential conflict between welfare and rights made its first appearance within the formal framework of social choice theory when Kenneth Arrow presented his justly famous *general impossibility theorem* in the 1949 Meeting of the Econometric Society. This conflict was subsequently crystallized by Sen (1970a/1979, Chapter 6; 1970b) into the *impossibility of a Paretian liberal.* A related but distinct paradox uncovered by Gibbard (1974) is also identified in Section 3. Section 4 is devoted to the critical examination of some of the proposed resolution schemes for Sen's Paretian liberal paradox. Section 5 turns to the criticisms and reservations in the voluminous literature on Sen's social choice theoretic formulation of individual rights. It is with the purpose of coping with these criticisms and reservations at the conceptual level that Section 6 identifies three distinct issues, to which we should address ourselves in the fully-fledged theory of welfare and rights, viz., the *formulation of rights*, the *realization of rights*, and the *initial conferment of rights*. It is also in Section 6 that we introduce the game form formulation of individual rights as a viable alternative to Sen's social choice theoretic formulation. The proponents of the game form formulation of rights did not necessarily claim that their alternative formulation per se would resolve Sen's and Gibbard's paradoxes. However, it is all too natural that many subsequent scholars tried to examine how these paradoxes would fare if the alternative game form formulation were adopted. Section 7 is devoted to these examinations. Section 8 illustrates how the theory of initial conferment of rights can be constructed in terms of the two-stage model of social choice theory. Section 9 briefly discusses some broader implications of Paretianism, which capitalizes on Sen's (1976) generalization of the Paretian liberal paradox into what he christened the *Paretian epidemic*, on the one hand, and on the other, the recent assertion by Kaplow and Shavell (2001, 2002) that any nonwelfaristic methods of policy assessment cannot but violate the Pareto principle. Section 10 concludes this chapter with some final remarks.

2. INFORMATIONAL BASES OF NORMATIVE WELFARE JUDGMENTS

According to Arrow (1987, p. 124), "[e]conomic or any other social policy has consequences for the many and diverse individuals who make up the society or economy. It has been taken for granted in virtually all economic policy discussions since the time of Adam Smith, if not before, that alternative policies should be judged on the basis of their consequences for individuals." As a matter of fact, the informational basis of traditional normative economics is even more exacting than *consequentialism* as such, since the standard approach in normative economics captures the value of consequences only through individual utilities, or more broadly individual welfares, experienced from these culmination outcomes by individuals who constitute the society or economy.

To facilitate our subsequent analysis, Figure 23.1 summarizes the possible informational bases of normative economics in evaluating the goodness of alternative economic policies or social systems. The point of departure is whether we judge the goodness of alternative policies or systems exclusively on the basis of their consequences, or we go beyond their consequences pure and simple, and take some nonconsequential features of alternative policies or systems properly into consideration. The examples of nonconsequential features of alternative policies or systems abound, and include their *procedural fairness*, as well as the *richness of opportunities* thereby opened up. If the former option of focusing exclusively on consequences is chosen, we are moving from the initial node n_0 toward the node n_1 of *consequentialism*, whereas if the latter option of going beyond consequences pure and simple is chosen, we are moving from the node n_0 toward the node n_1^* of *nonconsequentialism*. In the former case, we are paying no attention whatsoever to the intrinsic value of nonconsequential features of alternative policies or systems. In the latter case, our evaluative perspective goes beyond consequences of alternative

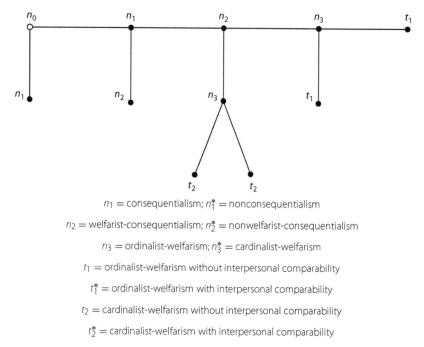

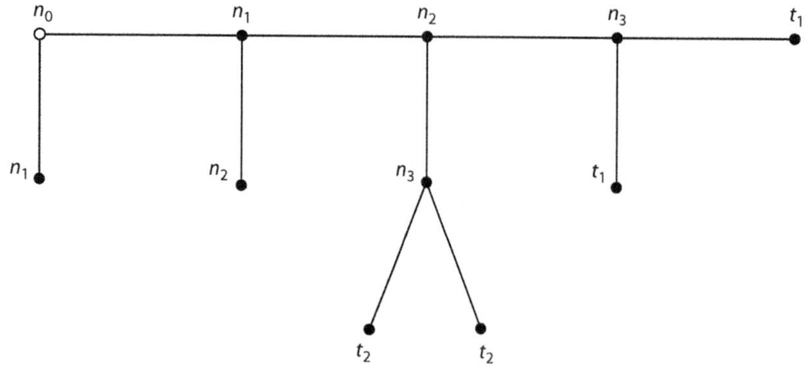

n_1 = consequentialism; n_1^* = nonconsequentialism

n_2 = welfarist-consequentialism; n_2^* = nonwelfarist-consequentialism

n_3 = ordinalist-welfarism; n_3^* = cardinalist-welfarism

t_1 = ordinalist-welfarism without interpersonal comparability

t_1^* = ordinalist-welfarism with interpersonal comparability

t_2 = cardinalist-welfarism without interpersonal comparability

t_2^* = cardinalist-welfarism with interpersonal comparability

Figure 23.1. Informational Bases of Normative Welfare Judgments.

policies or systems. Note, however, that the nonconsequentialist method of evaluation is not necessarily insensitive to the consequences of alternative policies or systems altogether. If our evaluative method depends exclusively on the nonconsequential features of alternative policies or systems in complete neglect of their consequential outcomes, we are in fact relying on the extreme subclass of nonconsequential methods of normative evaluation, which is known as the *deontological method of evaluation.* Any other nonconsequential method of evaluation represents the viewpoint that would weigh the value of consequential outcomes against the intrinsic value of nonconsequential features of alternative policies or systems in forming the fully-fledged judgments on their comparative goodness.[1]

Within the class of consequentialism, we may identify the second point of bifurcation in accordance with whether we value the consequential outcomes of alternative policies or systems only through the looking glass of individual utilities, or more broadly individual welfares, or we also take the nonwelfaristic features of consequences into consideration. If the former option is taken, we are moving from the consequentialist node n_1 toward the node n_2 of *welfarist-consequentialism*, or *welfarism* for short, whereas

[1] The structure of consequential methods of evaluation vis-à-vis that of nonconsequential methods of evaluation is clarified by Suzumura and Xu (2001, 2003, 2009), who provided the axiomatic characterizations of consequentialism and nonconsequentialism.

if the latter option is taken, we are moving from the node n_1 toward the node n_2^* of *nonwelfarist-consequentialism*, or *nonwelfarism* for short.[2] In this case too, the evaluative method of nonwelfarism need not be completely insensitive to the welfaristic features of consequential outcomes. What is at stake is whether or not due attention is paid to the nonwelfaristic features of consequences, and this attention need not be secured at the full sacrifice of attention to the welfaristic features of consequences.

The examples of nonwelfaristic evaluation of consequences abound. For example, in the context of evaluating alternative methods of personal distribution of income and wealth, we may value one method vis-à-vis another method in terms of the consequential changes of individual happiness. In this case, more often than not, the required informational basis of social evaluation may be welfaristic in nature. However, we may alternatively invoke the evaluative method of the Lorenz curve or the Gini coefficient in the space of income and wealth. In this case, the required informational basis of social evaluation cannot but be nonwelfaristic in nature.

Welfarism lies at the heart of normative analysis in general, and normative economics in particular. It was Pigou (1920) who synthesized the long Cambridge tradition of moral philosophy into what he christened the *Economics of Welfare*. The epistemological basis of Pigou's synthesis was Benthamite utilitarianism, which is a typical example of the welfarist method of evaluation.[3] When Robbins (1932/1935) raised his famous criticism against Pigou's "old" welfare economics, so-called, the target of his critical axe was focused on the "unscientific" nature of interpersonal comparability of individual utilities, or more broadly individual welfares, which the utilitarian method of evaluation presupposed as a matter of course. However, there are reasons to believe that Robbins was a thoroughgoing welfarist who cared for nothing other than individual utilities. For him, what was to be criticized and ostracized from economic science was not the welfaristic method of evaluation per se, but the interpersonal comparability of individual utilities, or more broadly individual welfares, underlying utilitarianism, which is nothing but a typical if a special case of welfarism.

Almost simultaneously with Robbins's devastating criticism against the "old" welfare economics, another demolition activity, or an exercise of Ockham's razor to be more precise, took place in the mainstream economics. This time, what was at stake was

[2] There is a subtlety in the use of the concept of *welfarism*, the discussion of which had better be relegated to Section 9.2, where we discuss nonwelfaristic methods of policy evaluation and the Pareto principle.

[3] It is interesting to observe that Pigou (1920; 1952 edition, p. 759), a devoted utilitarian, called our attention to people's legitimate claim to "a minimum standard of real income," which "must be conceived, not as a subjective minimum of satisfaction, but as an objective minimum of conditions." As a matter of fact, his characterization of "an objective minimum of conditions" is close to what is now called "basic needs," which consists of "some defined quantity and quality of house accommodation, of medical care, of education, of food, of leisure, of the apparatus of sanitary convenience and safety where work is carried on ...." Presumably, Pigou would have believed that such a claim right could be justified on the utilitarian grounds in the Benthamite tradition of regarding rights as intrinsically unimportant but instrumentally crucial. However, *Economics of Welfare* is completely reticent on the utilitarian justification of such a claim right, and we are left in the dark as to how central was the consideration of claim rights in Pigou's "old" welfare economics.

whether we should attach any cardinal significance to the concept of utilities, or more broadly welfares, or we should do with the ordinal meaning of these concepts, and the latter stance soon became dominant in the profession. This is what Samuelson (1974) named the *Hicks–Allen revolution in demand theory*. It started in the realm of positive economics under the leadership of Hicks and Allen (1934), but it soon permeated into the realm of normative economics as the "new" welfare economics of Lerner (1934), Kaldor (1939), Hicks (1939, 1940), Bergson (1938), Samuelson (1947, 1950a), and Scitovsky (1941), which is ordinalist in nature and began to fill in the void left open by the Robbinsian demolition activity against the "old" welfare economics.

Taking these evolutions of historical importance into due consideration, let us identify further points of bifurcation within the broad class of welfarism. To begin with, even when two persons agree on the welfaristic approach to social evaluation, they may well disagree on the nature of utilities, or more broadly welfares, to be used in their evaluative exercises. If a person takes the ordinalist (resp. cardinalist) view, he is moving from the welfarist node n_2 toward the node n_3 (resp. n_3^*) of *ordinalist-welfarism* (resp. *cardinalist-welfarism*). In the second place, within the approach of ordinalist-welfarism (resp. cardinalist-welfarism), we can identify a further bifurcation in accordance with the possibility of interpersonal comparisons of utilities, or more broadly welfares. Thus, we may identify four terminal nodes, viz., t_1, t_1^*, t_2, and t_2^*, which are called the *ordinalist-welfarism without interpersonal comparability*, the *ordinalist-welfarism with interpersonal comparability*, the *cardinalist-welfarism without interpersonal comparability*, and the *cardinalist-welfarism with interpersonal comparability*, respectively.

Most if not all informational bases of standard normative economics can be neatly accommodated in the informational framework of Figure 23.1. For example, it should be clear that the "new" welfare economics of the hypothetical compensation school à la Kaldor, Hicks, Scitovsky, and Samuelson, as well as the social welfare functionist school thereof based on the Bergson–Samuelson social welfare function of the individualistic type, belong to the terminal node t_1, viz., the ordinalist-welfarism without interpersonal comparability.[4]

The status of the Arrovian social choice theory within the informational framework of Figure 23.1 is less straightforward. This is because the *Pareto principle* to the effect that *a social state should be judged socially better than another state if all individuals judge the former*

[4] Both Bergson (1938) and Samuelson (1947, Chapter VIII) were careful enough not to make premature commitment to welfarism in their initial exposition of the concept of social welfare function. However, Samuelson's famous Chapter VIII on welfare economics in the *Foundations of Economic Analysis* has a passage where an explicitly welfaristic formulation of the concept of social welfare function is presented. To be more specific, on p. 228 of the *Foundations*, there is an expression for social welfare W as a function of the profile of individual utilities: $W = F(U_1, U_2, \ldots)$. It is precisely this formulation that is often cited, e.g., by Sen (1979b), as a sure-fire proof that the Bergson-Samuelson social welfare function is unambiguously welfaristic in nature. However, for the sake of fairness, it should be pointed out that Samuelson used this special class of social welfare functions purely for the sake of illustration and not as the characterizing feature of the Bergson–Samuelson social welfare functions in general. On this point, see Suzumura (2005, p. 347).

state to be better than the latter state falls short of implying the welfarism in full, even in combination with Arrow's other axioms of *unrestricted domain* and *independence of irrelevant alternatives*. However, it imples what Sen (1977a, 1979b) christened the *strict ranking welfarism*.[5] Furthermore, the welfarism in full is implied if the Pareto principle is replaced by the *Pareto indifference principle* to the effect that *two social states should be judged socially indifferent if all individuals judge them to be indifferent*. For all practical purposes, therefore, we may be able to think that Arrow's social choice theory can be sensibly accommodated within the class of ordinalist-welfarism without interpersonal comparability. Given Arrow's purpose of critically examining the logical consequences of welfaristic "new" welfare economics, this seems to be a legitimate procedure to follow.

To illustrate the evaluative methods that correspond to the other three terminal nodes t_1^*, t_2, and t_2^* in Figure 23.1, we have only to cite just one example for each category. To begin with, the ordinalist-welfarism with interpersonal comparability is exemplified by the *welfarist version of the Rawlsian difference principle*, which judges a policy or a system to be the best among feasible alternatives if the worst-off individual (in the sense of receiving the lowest welfare level among individuals who constitute the society) under this policy or system is best-off among the worst-off individuals under alternative feasible policies or systems. To illustrate the cardinalist-welfarism without interpersonal comparability, we have only to cite the *Nash social welfare function*, which is defined by the product over all individuals of the differences between the individual utilities, or more generally individual welfares, under the policy or system in question and those at the status quo. Finally, the cardinalist-welfarism with interpersonal comparability is best illustrated by nothing other than the Benthamite utilitarianism.

We are now ready to proceed to the social choice theoretic analysis of individual rights with special emphasis on the potential conflict between social welfare and individual rights.

3. SOCIAL WELFARE, INDIVIDUAL RIGHTS, AND LIBERAL PARADOX

It was in the session chaired by Lawrence Klein at the 1948 Cleveland Meeting of the Econometric Society that Arrow made his first presentation of the celebrated general impossibility theorem. According to his recollection: "[I]n the audience was this

[5] Recollect that welfarism means that social welfare is a function of individual utilities, or more broadly individual welfares, and nothing else, so that any two social states are ranked entirely on the basis of individual utilities, or more broadly individual welfares, in respective social states. Strict ranking welfarism is a constrained version of welfarism, which requires that, if individual utility, or more broadly individual welfare, rankings happen to be strict, then any two social states must be ranked entirely on the basis of individual utilities, or more broadly individual welfares, in respective social states.

contentious Canadian, David McCord Wright, who objected because among the objectives, [Arrow] hadn't mentioned freedom as one of the essential values in social choice, and apparently he went out of the room saying that Klein and Arrow were communists" (see Chapter 13, p. 18, in this volume). It goes without saying that this objection was rather misplaced, as it could have been answered easily by pointing out that we might include freedom in whatever form we wished it to take among the essential values in social choice theory, and yet we would end up with the same logical impossibility for a stronger reason. Nevertheless, this episode is not altogether without interest, as it clearly testifies to the fact that the value of freedom as one of the respectable individual rights had to be confronted with Arrow's impossibility theorem on the existence of a democratic social welfare function within the welfaristic framework of social choice theory at the very moment of its first public appearance. However, it was not until much later that the formal attempt was made by Sen (1970a/1979, Chapter 6; 1970b) to introduce the value of freedom as one of the respectable individual rights among other essential values in social choice theory. In so doing, Sen could get rid of the two most controversial and much debated axioms from Arrow's set of values, viz., *collective rationality* and *independence of irrelevant alternatives*, and yet he could crystallize a serious logical conflict between the mild libertarian claim of rights and a weak welfaristic value of social efficiency in the form of the Pareto principle into his justly famous *impossibility of a Paretian liberal.* It is all too natural that his short paper caused a long-lasting stir in the professional circle.

The basic intuition, which Sen (1970a/1979, Chapter 6; 1970b) tried to capture within Arrow's conceptual framework of social choice theory, can be traced back to John Locke and John Stuart Mill in England, and Benjamin Constant and Alexis de Tocqueville in France. This intuition was lucidly expressed in his characteristic parlance by Mill (1848; 1965, pp. 937–938) as follows:

> *Whatever theory we adopt respecting the foundation of the social union, and under whatever political institutions we live, there is a circle around every individual human being, which no government, be it that of one, of a few, or of the many, ought to be permitted to overstep: there is a part of the life of every person who has come to years of discretion, within which the individuality of that person ought to reign uncontrolled either by any other individual or by the public collectively. That there is, or ought to be, some space in human existence thus entrenched around, and sacred from authoritative intrusion, no one who professes the smallest regard to human freedom or dignity will call in question....*

To illustrate how this intuitive conception may conflict with welfarism in the least controversial form of the Pareto principle, Sen constructed the following neat example, which has been cited and debated ever since in the social choice theoretic analysis of social welfare and individual rights.

Example 1 (Lady Chatterley's Lover Case) There is a single copy of *Lady Chatterley's Lover*, which is available to one of Mr. P (the prude) and Mr. L (the lude), but not to both, for reading. Everything else being the same, there are only three social alternatives: Mr. P reading it (r_P), Mr. L reading it (r_L), and no one reading it (r_0). Mr. P prefers

r_0 most ("This is an awful book; it should not be read by anybody"), next r_P ("I will take the damage upon myself rather than exposing the lascivious Mr. L to the imminent danger of reading such a book"), and lastly r_L ("What a terrible mistake to let him face such a muck!"). Mr. L, on his part, prefers r_P most ("That would be useful to open Mr. P's obstinate mind to the reality of human life"), next r_L ("I will enjoy it for sure"), and lastly r_0 ("What a terrible waste of a great literary work!"). How, then, should the society decide on the disposition of the single copy of this book?

If the society respects Mr. P's libertarian right of reading or not reading a book in private, r_P should not be socially chosen in the presence of r_0, since the only difference between r_P and r_0 is whether Mr. P reads it or not, and Mr. P himself prefers not to read it. Likewise, if the society respects Mr. L's libertarian right of reading or not reading a book in private, r_0 should not be socially chosen in the presence of r_L, since the only difference between r_0 and r_L is whether Mr. L reads it or not, and Mr. L himself prefers to read it. Finally, if the society respects the Pareto principle, r_L should not be socially chosen in the presence of r_P, since both Mr. P and Mr. L prefer r_P to r_L. We are then led to the logical impasse, as there is nothing left for the society to choose from the set of alternatives $S := \{r_P, r_L, r_0\}$.

To generalize the moral of this example, let $N := \{1,2,\ldots,n\}$ $(2 \leq n < +\infty)$ be the set of all individuals constituting the society, and let X be the set of all social states, where each social state is defined to be "a complete description of society including every individual's position in it" (Sen 1970b, p. 152). For each $i \in N$, a binary relation $R_i \subseteq X \times X$ denotes the *preference ordering* held by individual i, together forming a profile $\mathbf{R} = (R_1, R_2, \ldots, R_n)$ of individual preference orderings.[6] $\mathcal{R}$ stands for the set of all logically possible profiles. For each $i \in N$ and each $x, y \in X$, the intended interpretation of $(x, y) \in R_i$, or xR_iy for short, is that i judges x to be at least as good as y.

A *social choice rule* is a function f that maps each profile $\mathbf{R} \in \mathcal{R}$ into a *social choice function* $C^{\mathbf{R}} = f(\mathbf{R})$. When a feasible set of social alternatives $S \subseteq X$ is specified from outside, $C^{\mathbf{R}}(S)$ stands for the set of social states that the society chooses from S reflecting individual wishes embodied in the profile $\mathbf{R} \in \mathcal{R}$. Let $\mathcal{S}$ be the family of all feasible sets of social alternatives. In what follows, we assume that $\mathcal{S}$ consists of all nonempty finite subsets of X. Since we do not know at the stage of designing a social choice rule which specific profile $\mathbf{R} \in \mathcal{R}$ will prevail, and which specific feasible set $S \in \mathcal{S}$ will become available in the future, we cannot but assume that f is defined over the full domain $\mathcal{R}$, and $C^{\mathbf{R}}$ is defined, for each $\mathbf{R} \in \mathcal{R}$, over the full domain $\mathcal{S}$. For the sake of later reference, let us state formally the following axiom.

[6] An *ordering* R on the set X is a binary relation that satisfies (a) *completeness*, viz., $(x, y) \in R$ or $(y, x) \in R$ holds for all $x, y \in X$ such that $x \neq y$, (b) *reflexivity*, viz., $(x, x) \in R$ holds for all $x \in X$, and (c) *transitivity*, viz., $(x, y) \in R$ and $(y, z) \in R$ imply $(x, z) \in R$ for all $x, y, z \in X$.

Condition U: Unrestricted Domain The social choice rule f must be able to determine a social choice function $C^{\boldsymbol{R}} = f(\boldsymbol{R})$ with the full domain $\mathscr{S}$ for each and every profile $\boldsymbol{R} \in \mathscr{R}$.

To give analytical substance to the intuitive idea that someone has an individual right to be respected, suppose that the two social states, say x and y, are identical except for some features that are private to someone, say $i \in N$. Suppose that the relevant individual i prefers x to y, yet the society chooses y from some opportunity set $S \in \mathscr{S}$ that contains x. In Sen's perception, this is a clear infringement on i's individual libertarian right, as the society does not seem to be respecting i's preference for x against y, even when the only difference between x and y is a feature that belongs to i's private sphere. To convert this intuitive observation into the formal requirement of social respect for individual rights, define, for each $i \in N$, a subset $D_i \subseteq X \times X$ such that the only difference that exists between x and y, where $(x, y) \in D_i$, is i's private features of the world. Then the social choice rule f is said to respect i's *individual libertarian right* over his *protected sphere* D_i if and only if

$$(x, y) \in D_i \cap P(R_i) \Rightarrow [x \in S \Rightarrow y \notin C^{\boldsymbol{R}}(S)] \text{ for all } S \in \mathscr{S} \quad (1)$$

holds for all $\boldsymbol{R} \in \mathscr{R}$, where $C^{\boldsymbol{R}} = f(\boldsymbol{R})$.[7]

Observe that the social choice rule f that satisfies (1) bestows on $i \in N$ a privilege over $(x, y) \in D_i$, because by simply expressing his personal preference for x against y, i can reject the social choice of his dispreferred social alternative y from any feasible set of social alternatives $S \in \mathscr{S}$ that contains his preferred social alternative x. In what follows, it is assumed that the protected sphere D_i for any $i \in N$ is *symmetric* in the sense that $(x, y) \in D_i$ holds for some $x, y \in D_i$ if and only if $(y, x) \in D_i$ also holds. In view of the intuition behind the concept of individual libertarian rights, this assumption seems to be noncontroversial.

Within this conceptual framework, Sen (1970a, Chapter 6; 1970b) introduced two essential values in social choice, one nonwelfaristic and another welfaristic in nature, which can be formally expressed as follows.

Condition SML: Sen's Minimal Libertarianism There exist at least two individuals, say j and k, each being endowed with a nonempty protected sphere D_j and D_k, respectively, such that f bestows on j and k the libertarian rights in the sense of Sen over D_j and D_k, respectively.

Condition P: Pareto Principle For any $x, y \in X$ and any $\boldsymbol{R} \in \mathscr{R}$,

$$(x, y) \in \cap_{i \in N} P(R_i) \Rightarrow [x \in S \Rightarrow y \notin C^{\boldsymbol{R}}(S)] \text{ for all } S \in \mathscr{S} \quad (2)$$

holds, where $C^{\boldsymbol{R}} = f(\boldsymbol{R})$.

[7] For each binary relation $R \subseteq X \times X$, $P(R)$ and $I(R)$ denote, respectively, the *asymmetric part* and *symmetric part* of R, which are defined by $(x, y) \in P(R)$ if and only if $[(x, y) \in R \ \& \ (y, x) \notin R]$ and $(x, y) \in I(R)$ if and only if $[(x, y) \in R \ \& \ (y, x) \in R]$ for all $x, y \in X$. If R stands for a weak preference ("at least as good as") relation, $P(R)$ and $I(R)$ denote, respectively, the strict preference relation and the indifference relation.

Considered in isolation, both conditions seem to be noncontroversial, yet in combination they bring about the following impossibility result, which is the first formal vindication that the requirement of social welfare, even in the weak form of the Pareto principle, is logically incompatible with the minimal requirement of inviolable individual rights.

Theorem 1 (Impossibility of a Paretian Liberal) *There exists no social choice rule f that satisfies the unrestricted domain* **U**, *Sen's minimal libertarianism* **SML**, *and the Pareto principle* **P**.

As an auxiliary step in proving this theorem, let us introduce the crucial concept of *coherent rights-system*, which is due originally to Farrell (1976) and Suzumura (1978). Let $\boldsymbol{D} = (D_1, D_2, \ldots, D_n)$, where $D_i \subseteq X \times X$ for each $i \in N$, denote the profile of individual protected spheres, which we will call the *rights-system* for mnemonic convenience. A *critical loop* in the rights-system $\boldsymbol{D}$ of the order t, where $2 \leq t < +\infty$, is defined to be a sequence $\{(x^\mu, y^\mu)\}_{\mu=1}^t$ of ordered pairs such that

(α) $(x^\mu, y^\mu) \in \cup_{i=1}^n D_i$ holds for all $\mu \in \{1, 2, \ldots, t\}$;
(β) there exists no $i^* \in N$ such that $(x^\mu, y^\mu) \in D_{i^*}$ holds for all $\mu \in \{1, 2, \ldots, t\}$; and
(γ) $x^1 = y^t$ and $x^\mu = y^{\mu-1}$ hold for all $\mu \in \{1, 2, \ldots, t\}$.

We say that the rights-system $\boldsymbol{D} = (D_1, D_2, \ldots, D_n)$ is *coherent* if and only if there exists no critical loop in $\boldsymbol{D}$ of any order.

We are now ready to present the following:

Proof of Theorem 1

Case 1: $\boldsymbol{D}$ is coherent.

Without loss of generality, suppose that $(x, y) \in D_j$ and $(z, w) \in D_k$, where $x \neq y$ and $z \neq w$. D_j and D_k being symmetric by assumption, we also have $(y, x) \in D_j$ and $(w, z) \in D_k$.

Subcase 1.1: $\{x, y\} = \{z, w\}$.

If $x = w$ and $y = z$, $(x, y), (y, x)$ is a critical loop in $\boldsymbol{D}$ of the order 2. $\boldsymbol{D}$ being coherent by assumption, this is a clear contradiction. The case where $x = z$ and $y = w$ cannot happen either.

Subcase 1.2: $\{x, y\} \cap \{z, w\} = \{z\}$ or $\{w\}$.

To begin with, suppose that $x = z$, and consider a profile $\boldsymbol{R}^1 = (R_1^1, R_2^1, \ldots, R_n^1) \in \mathscr{R}$ such that $(x, y) \in P(R_j^1), (y, w) \in P(R_j^1) \cap P(R_k^1)$, $(w, x) \in P(R_k^1)$ and $(y, w) \in P(R_i^1)$ for all $i \in N - \{j, k\}$. This profile is admissible by virtue of Condition **U**. We now examine $C^{\boldsymbol{R}^1}(\{x, y, w\})$, where $C^{\boldsymbol{R}^1} = f(\boldsymbol{R}^1)$. Condition **SML** entails that $x, y \notin C^{\boldsymbol{R}^1}(\{x, y, w\})$, whereas Condition **P** entails that $w \notin C^{\boldsymbol{R}^1}(\{x, y, w\})$. Thus, $C^{\boldsymbol{R}^1}(\{x, y, w\}) = \emptyset$, which is a contradiction. Other situations within this subcase can be treated similarly.

Subcase 1.3: $\{x,y\} \cap \{z,w\} = \emptyset$.

Consider a profile $\boldsymbol{R}^2 = (R_1^2, R_2^2, \ldots, R_n^2) \in \mathscr{R}$ such that $(w,x), (x,y), (y,z) \in P(R_j^2), (y,z), (z,w), (w,x) \in P(R_k^2)$, and $(w,x), (y,z) \in P(R_i^2)$ for all $i \in N - \{j,k\}$. This profile is admissible by virtue of Condition **U**. We now examine $C^{\boldsymbol{R}^2}(\{x,y,z,w\})$, where $C^{\boldsymbol{R}^2} = f(\boldsymbol{R}^2)$. Condition **P** entails that $x, z \notin C^{\boldsymbol{R}^2}(\{x,y,z,w\})$, whereas y and w must be excluded from $C^{\boldsymbol{R}^2}(\{x,y,z,w\})$ by virtue of the libertarian rights conferred to j and k. Thus, we must have $C^{\boldsymbol{R}^2}(\{x,y,z,w\}) = \emptyset$, which is a contradiction.

Case 2: $\boldsymbol{D}$ is incoherent.

$\boldsymbol{D}$ being incoherent, there exists a critical loop $\{(x^\mu, y^\mu)\}_{\mu=1}^t$ in $\boldsymbol{D}$ of some finite order t such that there exists a mapping, say κ, from $\{1, 2, \ldots, t\}$ into N which satisfies

$$(x^\mu, y^\mu) \in D_{\kappa(\mu)} \text{ for all } \mu \in \{1,2,\ldots,t\} \tag{3}$$

and

$$\kappa(\mu^1) \neq \kappa(\mu^2) \text{ for some } \mu^1, \mu^2 \in \{1,2,\ldots,t\}. \tag{4}$$

Consider now a profile $\boldsymbol{R}^3 = (R_1^3, R_2^3, \ldots, R_n^3) \in \mathscr{R}$ such that $(x^1, x^2) \in P(R_{\kappa(1)}^3), (x^2, x^3) \in P(R_{\kappa(2)}^3), \ldots, (x^t, x^1) \in P(R_{\kappa(t)}^3)$. By virtue of (4), $\boldsymbol{R}^3$ is consistent with the transitivity of R_i^3 for all $i \in N$, so that it must be admissible by virtue of Condition **U**. It follows from $(x^\mu, x^{\mu+1}) \in D_{\kappa(\mu)} \cap P(R_{\kappa(\mu)}^3)$ that $x^{\mu+1} \notin C^{\boldsymbol{R}^3}(S)$, where $S := \{x^1, x^2, \ldots, x^t\}$, for all $\mu \in \{1,2,\ldots,t-1\}$, whereas $(x^t, x^1) \in D_{\kappa(t)} \cap P(R_{\kappa(t)}^3)$ implies that $x^1 \notin C^{\boldsymbol{R}^3}(S)$. Thus, we obtain $C^{\boldsymbol{R}^3}(S) = \emptyset$, which is a contradiction.

□

Several observations may be in order at this juncture. To begin with, as we observed before, Sen's impossibility of a Paretian liberal does not invoke Arrow's axiom of collective rationality, nor does it hinge on Arrow's axiom of independence of irrelevant alternatives.[8] Since these Arrovian axioms have been singled out rather frequently as the

[8] Arrow's axiom of independence of irrelevant alternatives plays an indispensable role in the proof of his general impossibility theorem by diffusing the information about social choice from the binary choice environment $\{x,y\}$ when the profile $\boldsymbol{R}^1$ of individual preference orderings prevails, to social choice from the same binary choice environment $\{x,y\}$ when the different profile $\boldsymbol{R}^2$ of individual preference orderings prevails, as long as $\boldsymbol{R}^1$ and $\boldsymbol{R}^2$ coincide on $\{x,y\}$. To the extent that Sen's impossibility theorem does not invoke the axiom of independence of irrelevant alternatives, it belongs to the class of single-profile impossibility theorems, so-called, in contrast with the class of multiple-profile impossibility theorems such as Arrow's theorem. As Blau (1975) aptly pointed out, however, the Pareto principle has a remnant of the independence property. By making acute use of this implication of the Pareto principle, Sen (1976; 1982c, Chapter 14, p. 295) established what he named the "Paretian epidemic" to the effect that "[t]he limited element of 'independence' implicit in the Pareto principle, combined with the inter-pair consistency requirement of always avoiding preference cycles, is sufficient to spread decisiveness of a person from one pair to every pair, albeit in a weakened form." We will have more to say on Sen's Paretian epidemic in Section 9.1.

major culprits of Arrow's impossibility theorem, it is remarkable that Sen's impossibility theorem is independent of these axioms altogether. Secondly, Sen's theorem is the cornerstone of his devastating criticism against the welfaristic foundations of traditional welfare economics and social choice theory. The Pareto principle is a particular case of welfarism, which asserts the exclusive adequacy of individual welfare information in the special context where everyone's welfare ranking of alternative social states happens to coincide with each other. By showing that the Pareto principle goes squarely counter to the nonwelfaristic principle of social respect for individual libertarian rights, Sen's impossibility theorem constitutes a basic argument that goes squarely against the unexceptional acceptance of welfaristic principles in the traditional welfare economics and Arrovian social choice theory. In the third place, Sen's libertarian right is formulated in terms of the relevant individual's power of decisiveness, which he is conferred by the social choice rule, to prevent some alternatives from being socially chosen. This power is conditional on the relevant individual's preferences over the complete descriptions of social states. For the sake of mnemonic convenience, this crucial feature will be christened as the *preference-contingent power of rejection*. Since Sen's impossibility theorem is presented as a criticism against the welfaristic foundations of normative economics, it is all too natural that this formulation of libertarian rights in terms of the preference-contingent power of rejection has been singled out as the main target in the subsequent critical scrutinies of Sen's argument. These critiques on Sen's formulation will be examined in Section 5.

Once we accept the basic idea of individual rights in the sense of Sen, it may lead us to accept an extended version thereof, which was originally formulated by Gibbard (1974). For each $i \in N$, let X_i denote the set of i's *private decision variables*. It is assumed that X_i contains at least two elements for each and every $i \in N$. There is also a set X_0 of *public decision variables*. Then, each social state is described by specifying a public decision variable $x_0 \in X_0$ and a private decision variable $x_i \in X_i$ for each and every $i \in N$, viz., $x := (x_0, x_1, \ldots, x_n)$. Accordingly, the set of all social states is specified by the product $X := X_0 \times (\Pi_{i \in N} X_i)$. More often than not, we will pick one element $x_0 \in X_0$ and fix it most of the time. To the extent that this is in fact done, we may do so without explicitly specifying the public decision variable.

For each $i \in N$ and each $x = (x_0, x_1, \ldots, x_n) \in X$, let $x_{-i} := (x_0, x_1, \ldots, x_{i-1}, x_{i+1}, \ldots, x_n)$ and define the set

$$\Delta_i := \{(x, y) \in X \times X \mid x_{-i} = y_{-i}\}. \tag{5}$$

Thus, the only potential difference between x and y, where $(x, y) \in \Delta_i$, is the specification of i's private decision variables. It follows that the private sphere D_i of $i \in N$ must be such that $D_i \subseteq \Delta_i$ holds for all $i \in N$.

Once we accept the basic idea of individual libertarian rights in the sense of Sen, it may not be easy to construct a plausible argument that supports Sen's Condition **SML** and yet goes against the following stronger variant thereof that is due to Gibbard (1974).

Condition GL: Gibbard's Libertarianism For each $i \in N$, f bestows on i the libertarian rights in the sense of Sen over the protected sphere $D_i = \Delta_i$.

The transition from Sen's Condition **SML** to Gibbard's Condition **GL**, however small and natural it may seem at first sight, is in fact quite insidious. This fact is vindicated by the following impossibility theorem due to Gibbard (1974). For mnemonic convenience, this impossibility theorem may be referred to as *Gibbard's paradox*.

Theorem 2 (Gibbard's Paradox) *There exists no social choice rule f that satisfies the unrestricted domain* **U** *as well as Gibbard's libertarianism* **GL**.

A conspicuous feature of this impossibility theorem is that no mention is made of the Pareto Principle **P** in its statement. In other words, a seemingly small jump from Sen's Condition **SML** to Gibbard's Condition **GL** is rewarded with a huge logical gain in the sense of getting rid of the welfaristic Pareto Principle **P** altogether without losing the impossibility result. This seems to be a devastating implication of Gibbard's extension of the concept of individual libertarian rights in the sense of Sen. Indeed, unlike Sen's impossibility theorem, Gibbard's impossibility theorem per se does not serve as a forceful criticism against welfarism.

Proof of Theorem 2. We prove **Theorem 2** by reducing it to a special case of **Theorem 1**. Let us pick two distinct individuals, say $j, k \in N$, and suppose that $x_j, x_j^* \in X_j$ and $x_k, x_k^* \in X_k$ are given, where $x_j \neq x_j^*$ and $x_k \neq x_k^*$. Suppose further that $a_0 \in X_0$ and $a_i \in X_i$ for all $i \in N - \{j, k\}$ are given. We now define $x, y, z, w \in X$ by

$$\begin{aligned}
x &= (a_0, a_1, \ldots, a_{j-1}, x_j, a_{j+1}, \ldots, a_{k-1}, x_k, a_{k+1}, \ldots, a_n) \\
y &= (a_0, a_1, \ldots, a_{j-1}, x_j^*, a_{j+1}, \ldots, a_{k-1}, x_k, a_{k+1}, \ldots, a_n) \\
z &= (a_0, a_1, \ldots, a_{j-1}, x_j, a_{j+1}, \ldots, a_{k-1}, x_k^*, a_{k+1}, \ldots, a_n) \\
w &= (a_0, a_1, \ldots, a_{j-1}, x_j^*, a_{j+1}, \ldots, a_{k-1}, x_k^*, a_{k+1}, \ldots, a_n),
\end{aligned}$$

where it is assumed, without loss of generality, that $j < k$. Clearly, $(x, y) \in \Delta_j$, $(y, w) \in \Delta_k$, $(w, z) \in \Delta_j$, and $(z, x) \in \Delta_k$, which imply that $\boldsymbol{D} = \boldsymbol{\Delta} := (\Delta_1, \Delta_2, \ldots, \Delta_n)$ contains a critical loop of the order 4, hence $\boldsymbol{D}$ is incoherent in this case. Recollect that the Case 2 in the Proof of **Theorem 1** did not in fact invoke Condition **P** at all, so that the assertion of **Theorem 2** follows from the Case 2 in the Proof of **Theorem 1** as a special case. □

4. PROPOSED RESOLUTION SCHEMES FOR PARETIAN LIBERAL PARADOX

There exist, by now, substantial literature on Sen's impossibility theorem and related results on the logical conflict between social welfare and individual rights. Many attempts have been made to resolve Sen's Paretian liberal paradox, so-called, accepting the formulation that Sen first invented to give substance to the concept of libertarian claim of rights in the conceptual framework of social choice theory, by weakening *either* the libertarian claim of rights à la Sen, *or* the weak welfaristic claim of the Pareto principle, *or* both.[9] Some others have tried to generalize Sen's impossibility theorem toward various directions, including the extension thereof toward the analysis of group rights.[10] However, by far the most heated response to Sen came from the critics who posed serious doubts on the legitimacy of his articulation of libertarian rights in terms of the preference-contingent power of rejection.[11] Sen (1976, 1979a, 1979b, 1982b, 1983, 1992, 1996a) has painstakingly tried to answer most if not all of these criticisms, but the arena is still in need for conceptual clarifications and further analyses. In the following two sections, we will provide a succinct overview and concise evaluation of some of these attempts to resolve, extend, or exorcise the Pareto libertarian paradox along various lines. The rest of this section will be devoted to the critical examination of some of the proposed resolution schemes without trying to be exhaustive, whereas the next section will try to summarize the most important conceptual criticisms on Sen's formulation of individual rights.

Before coming to the proper task of this section, however, a few words on the relevance of Sen's impossibility theorem may be in order. Note that the concern with this class of impossibility theorems is not just a hairsplitting exercise in the abstract logic of social choice theory. What is at stake is the theoretical possibility of liberal democracy, viz., the logical compatibility between the social protection of the minimum sphere of individual liberty and the establishment of the rule by majority, whose minimum requirement may be the acceptance of the Pareto principle. This is a nontrivial question of substantial importance, as

> *the connexion between democracy and individual liberty is a good deal more tenuous than it seemed to many advocates of both. The desire to be governed by myself, or at any rate to participate*

[9] Important contributions along this line include Austen-Smith (1979, 1982), Basu (1984), Blau (1975), Breyer (1977), Breyer and Gigliotti (1980), Coughlin (1986), Craven (1982), Farrell (1976), Gaertner (1982, 1985), Gaertner and Krüger (1981, 1982), Gekker (1991), Gibbard (1974), Hammond (1982), Harel and Nitzan (1987), Karni (1978), Kelly (1976a, 1976b, 1978), Krüger and Gaertner (1983), MacIntyre (1988), Riley (1989/1990), Saari (1998), Suzumura (1978, 1979, 1980, 1982, 1983a, Chapter 7), and Wriglesworth (1982a, 1985a, 1985b), among many others.

[10] The attempts to generalize the impossibility of a Paretian liberal include Kelsey (1985, 1988), MacIntyre (1987), and Xu (1990), whereas the attempts to extend the impossibility of a Paretian liberal so as to accommodate group rights include Batra and Pattanaik (1972), Hammond (1995), Pattanaik (1988), Stevens and Foster (1978), and Wriglesworth (1982b), among many others.

[11] See Barry (1986), Bernholz (1974), Buchanan (1976/1996), Campbell (1994), Deb (1994, 2004), Deb, Pattanaik, and Razzolini (1997), Farrell (1976), Fleurbaey and van Hees (2000), Gaertner, Pattanaik, and Suzumura (1992), Gärdenfors (1981), Gibbard (1982), Hammond (1996a), Hansson (1988), Pattanaik (1996a, 1996b), Pattanaik and Suzumura (1994, 1996), Peleg (1998, 2004), Peleg, Peters, and Storcken (2002), Rowley (1978), Samet and Schmeidler (2003), Sen (1976, 1982b, 1992, 1996a), Sugden (1978, 1981, 1985, 1993, 1994), Suzumura (1990, 1996), Valentine (1989), and van Hees (1995a, 1995b, 1999), among many others.

in the process by which my life is to be controlled, may be as deep a wish as that of a free area for action, and perhaps historically older. But it is not a desire for the same thing. So different is it, indeed, as to have led in the end to the great clash of ideologies that dominates our world. (Berlin 1969, pp. 130–131)

Nor is the concern about the Pareto libertarian paradox purely theoretical, as the question it poses has substantial relevance not only to the issue of individual freedom and democratic reform in many parts of the world, but also to the issue of designing welfare state policies in the mixed market economies.

How, then, should we cope with the impossibility of a Paretian liberal? From among many proposed resolution schemes existing in the literature, we will choose and discuss only a few schemes. Each of these schemes will shed further light on the nature and significance of this class of social choice impossibility theorems. Many other schemes of importance are critically examined by Sen (1976, 1982b, 1983, 1992), Suzumura (1983a, Chapter 7; 1990, 1996), and Wriglesworth (1985b). Those who are eager to know further variety of proposed resolution schemes for the Pareto libertarian paradox are cordially invited to these other sources for additional information.

4.1. Voluntary Alienation of Conferred Libertarian Rights

In his penetrating analysis of the Pareto libertarian paradox, Gibbard (1974, p. 397) called our attention to "a strong libertarian tradition of free contract," according to which "a person's rights are his to use or bargain away as he sees fit." The pursuit of this tradition in the context of Sen's paradox led Gibbard to what he christened the *alienable rights-system*. The gist of Gibbard's edifice is to make libertarian rights *alienable* if the blind exercise of these conferred rights brings out the conflict with another person's rights to the detriment of his own welfare, or with the Pareto principle, or with the combination of both.

Recollect that a salient common feature of Sen's Condition **SML** and Gibbard's Condition **GL** is that each individual is supposed to be guided exclusively by his isolated rational calculus, and exercises his conferred rights in full neglect of possible repurcussions from the rest of the society. The gist of Gibbard's resolution scheme is to rectify this rigid rule of conduct by making an individual's libertarian rights alienable in cases where the exercise of one's right would bring him into a situation he likes no better than the situation that would otherwise be brought about. To formalize this idea, suppose that the profile $\boldsymbol{R} = (R_1, R_2, \ldots, R_n) \in \mathscr{R}$ and the opportunity set $S \in \mathscr{S}$ are such that $x \in S$ and $(x, y) \in D_i \cap P(R_i)$ are satisfied for some $i \in N$, where $D_i = \Delta_i$. Then i has the will as well as the right to exclude y from $C^{\boldsymbol{R}}(S)$, where $C^{\boldsymbol{R}} = f(\boldsymbol{R})$, by exercising his right for (x, y), but his right had better be waived if there exists a sequence $\{y_1, y_2, \ldots, y_\lambda\}$ in

S such that

$$y_\lambda = x, (y, y_1) \in R_i \;\&\; y \neq y_1, \tag{6}$$

and

$$(\forall t \in \{1,2,\ldots,\lambda-1\}): (y_t, y_{t+1}) \in (\cap_{j\in N} P(R_j)) \cup (\cup_{j\in N-\{i\}}[D_j \cap P(R_j)]). \tag{7}$$

Let us define a subset $W_i(\mathbf{R}|S)$ of D_i, to be called the *waiver set* of $i \in N$ at $(\mathbf{R}|S)$, by $(x,y) \in W_i(\mathbf{R}|S)$ if and only if (6) and (7) hold for some sequence $\{y_1, y_2, \ldots, y_\lambda\}$ in S. We are now ready to introduce the following modified libertarian claim à la Gibbard and his possibility theorem, which holds if Condition **SML** or Condition **GL** is replaced by the modified libertarian claim.

Condition GAL: Gibbard's Alienable Libertarianism For any profile $\mathbf{R} = (R_1, R_2, \ldots, R_n) \in \mathscr{R}$, any opportunity set $S \in \mathscr{S}$, any $i \in N$, and any $x, y \in X$, if $(x,y) \in D_i \cap P(R_i)$ and $(x,y) \notin W_i(\mathbf{R}|S)$, then $[x \in S \Rightarrow y \notin C^{\mathbf{R}}(S)]$, where $C^{\mathbf{R}} = f(\mathbf{R})$.

Theorem 3 (Pareto-Consistency of Gibbard's Alienable Libertarianism) *There exists a social choice rule f that satisfies the unrestricted domain* **U**, *the Pareto principle* **P**, *and Gibbard's alienable libertarianism* **GAL**.

Proof. See Gibbard (1974, Theorem 4, pp. 401–402). □

To illustrate the working of this resolution scheme and clarify the intuition which lies behind Gibbard's rights-waiving rule, let us check how it copes with the Lady Chatterley's Lover Case. It is easy to verify that

$$(r_0, r_P) \in D_P \cap P(R_P), \tag{8.1}$$

$$(r_L, r_0) \in D_L \cap P(R_L), \tag{8.2}$$

and

$$(r_P, r_L) \in P(R_P) \cap P(R_L) \tag{8.3}$$

hold in this case. By virtue of (8.1), Mr. P is able to exclude r_P from $C^{\mathbf{R}}(S)$, where $C^{\mathbf{R}} = f(\mathbf{R}), \mathbf{R} = (R_P, R_L)$ and $S := \{r_P, r_L, r_0\}$, if he decides to exercise his right for r_0 against r_P. If Mr. L counter-exercises his right for r_L against r_0 in view of (8.2) and excludes r_0 from $C^{\mathbf{R}}(S)$, however, the only alternative left for social choice from S is r_L, and Mr. P strictly prefers r_P to r_L as (8.3) testifies. Thus, by exercising his right for $(r_0, r_P) \in D_P$, Mr. P gets something that he likes no better, so that Mr. P would be better off by alienating his right $(r_0, r_P) \in D_P$ in this context. Thus, "[l]eft freely to bargain away their rights... [Mr. P and Mr. L] would agree to the outcome [r_P]. ... Hence, a libertarian may well hold that—deplorable though [Mr. L's] motives be—[r_P] is a *just* outcome under the circumstances" (Gibbard 1974, p. 398). It must be clear now that Gibbard's rights-waiving rule defined in terms of (6) and (7) is nothing other than a natural generalization of this resolution of the Lady Chatterley's Lover case.

A great merit of Gibbard's rights-waiving rule is that it resolves the Pareto libertarian paradox by introducing the voluntary alienation of individual rights, which is motivated by the rational calculus of the relevant individual himself. Nevertheless, a basic fact remains that it is an essentially arbitrary rule, and its success in resolving Sen's paradox hinges squarely on the subtle definition of the waiver set. Indeed, the logical possibility captured by **Theorem 3** stands on the sharp knife-edge, which could be easily annihilated if we would modify the definition of Gibbard's waiver set even to the minimal extent.

To expose this fact unambiguously, consider a slight modification of Gibbard's waiver set, which was proposed by Kelly (1976b; 1978, Chapter 9). An individual $i \in N$ is said to waive his conferred right for $(x,y) \in D_i$ at $(\mathbf{R}|S)$, to be denoted by $(x,y) \in W_i^*(\mathbf{R}|S)$, if and only if there exists a sequence $\{y_1, y_2, \ldots, y_\lambda\}$ in S such that

$$y_\lambda = x \;\&\; (y, y_1) \in P(R_i) \tag{9}$$

and (7). Based on this alternative definition of the waiver set, Kelly proposed the following simple variant of Gibbard's alienable libertarian claim.

Condition KAL: Kelly's Alienable Libertarianism For any profile $\boldsymbol{R} = (R_1, R_2, \ldots, R_n) \in \mathscr{R}$, any opportunity set $S \in \mathscr{S}$, any $i \in N$, and any $x, y \in X$, if $(x,y) \in D_i \cap P(R_i)$ and $(x,y) \notin W_i^*(\mathbf{R}|S)$, then $[x \in S \Rightarrow y \notin C^{\mathbf{R}}(S)]$, where $C^{\mathbf{R}} = f(\mathbf{R})$.

The only difference between Condition **GAL** and Condition **KAL** lies in the contrast between (6) and (9). This revision is motivated by Kelly in the following manner:

> *[I]n forcing the move from y to x by exercising* $[(x,y) \in D_i$, *the individual i*] *does not seem to have gotten into trouble if he is forced in the end to take a* y_1 *where he is indifferent between* y_1 *and y. Waiving might be appropriate for a cautious exerciser if* $[(y, y_1) \in P(R_i)]$ *for some* $[\{y_1, y_2, \ldots, y_\lambda\}]$*, but not if only* $[(y, y_1) \in R_i \;\&\; y \neq y_1]$. *(Kelly 1976b, p. 141; 1978, pp. 146–147)*

This may sound reasonable, and Kelly himself believed that the escape route secured by Gibbard by means of Condition **GAL** would not be closed by his fine-tuning of the rights-waiving rule when he asserted that it would bring about "no significant changes in the theorems that make up Gibbard's libertarian claim" (Kelly 1976b, p. 144; 1978, p. 148). As a matter of fact, however, not only Condition **KAL** but also *all* other modified alienable libertarian claims proposed by Kelly (1976b, 1978) change Condition **GAL** into the standard for individual liberty that cannot possibly be satisfied by any social choice rule whatsoever. Since Kelly's other modifications boil down to the stronger libertarian claims than Condition **KAL**, we have only to show the following:

Theorem 4 (Return of the Gibbard Paradox) (Suzumura 1980; 1983a, Chapter 7) *There exists no social choice rule f that satisfies the unrestricted domain* **U** *as well as Kelly's alienable libertarianism* **KAL**.

Proof. Suppose that a social choice rule f satisfies Condition **U** and Condition **KAL**. Define x, y, z and w as in the proof of **Theorem 2**, and let $S := \{x, y, z, w\}$. Assume that a profile $\boldsymbol{R} = (R_1, R_2, \ldots, R_n) \in \mathscr{R}$ is such that[12]

$$R_k(S)\colon x, w, [y, z] \qquad R_j(S)\colon z, y, [x, w],$$

where $R_i(S) := R_i \cap (S \times S)$ for $i = j, k$; otherwise there is no restriction on $\boldsymbol{R}$. Clearly,

$$(x, z) \in D_k, (w, y) \in D_k, (z, w) \in D_j, (y, x) \in D_j.$$

No other individual has a right over these pairs of social states. Consider the pair $(x, z) \in D_k \cap P(R_k)$. The worst contingency that could happen to k after his exercise of conferred right for (x, z) is the counter-exercise by j of his right for $(y, x) \in D_j$ in view of $(y, x) \in P(R_j)$. Note that there is no state in S that Pareto-dominates x. Since k regards y and z to be indifferent and $y \neq z$, Condition **GAL** would let k waive his right for (x, z), but Condition **KAL** enables him to exercise his right for (x, z), viz., $(x, z) \in W_k(\boldsymbol{R}|S) - W_k^*(\boldsymbol{R}|S)$. Similar reasoning allows us to conclude that $(w, y) \in W_k(\boldsymbol{R}|S) - W_k^*(\boldsymbol{R}|S)$ and $(z, w), (w, y) \in W_j(\boldsymbol{R}|S) - W_j^*(\boldsymbol{R}|S)$. In view of Condition **KAL**, it then follows that $C^{\boldsymbol{R}}(S) = \emptyset$, a contradiction. □

According to **Theorem 3** and **Theorem 4**, the success of the Gibbardian alienable rights-system hinges squarely on the subtle difference between Condition **GAL** and Condition **KAL**, and Kelly's argument in favor of Condition **KAL** sounds reasonable enough at least until we are exposed to its logical consequences. As a matter of fact, the problem with the Gibbardian alienable rights system does not end there; there is another serious difficulty, which Kelly (1976b; 1978, Chapter 9) christened the *correctable miscalculation*. Let us illustrate this problem in terms of the following example constructed by Sen (1976; 1982c, pp. 297–298).

Example 2 (Work Choice Case) There are two persons, 1 and 2, each having a part-time job. The possibility arises of a full-time job. Each prefers more of a job

[12] Preference orderings can be represented by arranging alternatives horizontally with the more preferred alternative being arranged to the left of the less prefererd, and the indifferent alternatives being embraced within square brackets.

to less, viz., prefers 1 (full-time job) to 1/2 (half-time job) to 0 (no job), given the job specification of the other. However, they are spoilt by the competitive society so much that they not only prefer that the other gets less job, but also attach greater importance to the other being left jobless than to their own job situation. Consider the following alternative job possibilities: (1, 1/2), (0, 1/2), (1/2, 1), and (1/2, 0), where the first (resp. the second) number stands for person 1's (resp. 2's) job situation. Let $S := \{(1,1/2),(0,1/2),(1/2,1),(1/2,0)\}$, and let a profile $\boldsymbol{R} = (R_1, R_2)$ and a rights-system $\boldsymbol{D} = (D_1, D_2)$ be defined by:

$$R_1(S)\text{: } (1/2,0),(1,1/2),(0,1/2),(1/2,1)$$
$$R_2(S)\text{: } (0,1/2),(1/2,1),(1/2,0),(1,1/2)$$

and

$$D_1 = \{((1,1/2),(0,1/2)),((0,1/2),(1,1/2))\}$$
$$D_2 = \{((1/2,1),(1/2,0)),((1/2,0),(1/2,1))\}.$$

Consider $C^{\boldsymbol{R}}(S)$, where $C^{\boldsymbol{R}} = f(\boldsymbol{R})$. Suppose that the rights-system $\boldsymbol{D}$ is respected, and the Pareto principle **P** is enforced. Then, $((1,1/2),(0,1/2)) \in D_1 \cap P(R_1)$ and $((1/2,1),(1/2,0)) \in D_2 \cap P(R_2)$ lead us to $(0,1/2) \notin C^{\boldsymbol{R}}(S)$ and $(1/2,0) \notin C^{\boldsymbol{R}}(S)$, whereas $(1,1/2) \notin C^{\boldsymbol{R}}(S)$ and $(1/2,1) \notin C^{\boldsymbol{R}}(S)$ follow from the Pareto principle **P**. Thus, we are forced to conclude that $C^{\boldsymbol{R}}(S) = \emptyset$, a contradiction.

The impasse of the Work Choice Case can be broken by Gibbard's rights-waiving rule. Indeed, since $((1/2,0),(1,1/2)) \in P(R_1) \cap P(R_2)$, $((1/2,1),(1/2,0)) \in D_2 \cap P(R_2)$ and $((0,1/2),(1/2,1)) \in P(R_1)$, 1 will waive his right for $((1,1/2),(0,1/2)) \in D_1$, whereas $((0,1/2),(1/2,1)) \in P(R_1) \cap P(R_2)$, $((1,1/2),(0,1/2)) \in D_1 \cap P(R_1)$ and $((1/2,0),(1,1/2)) \in P(R_2)$ will induce 2 to waive his right for $((1/2,1),(1/2,0)) \in D_2$. As both 1 and 2 will waive their rights, two Pareto-efficient social states $(1/2,0)$ and $(0,1/2)$ will become eligible for social choice, thereby breaking the impasse of social choice impossibility.

Note, however, that 1 (resp. 2) waives his right on the supposition that 2 (resp. 1) will exercise his right, so that the foregoing resolution procedure works on the miscalculations that individuals commit on other's rights-exercising. It is true that people do sometimes commit mistakes, and the committed mistakes may turn out to be socially good after all. However, to count on this phenomenon as a pivotal part of the scheme for resolving the conflict between several moral values does not seem to be an attractive feature of Gibbard's proposed resolution scheme.

How serious are these problems that seem to cast doubts on the workability of the Gibbardian alienable rights-system? Are they specific to the Gibbardian rights-waiving rules, or are they intrinsic to a wide class of voluntary rights-waiving rules? As a matter of fact, it may be the case that the latter verdict is closer to the truth than the former. Indeed, it was shown by Basu (1984) that "if individuals are allowed to waive their rights *voluntarily*, then there is no guarantee that they will do so in a way that resolves the liberty paradox" (Basu 1984, p. 413). In view of this general observation, it seems in vain to seek further sophisticated variants of the alienable rights-system that are free from the difficulties surrounding the Gibbardian alienable rights-system. No way out seems to be open in this direction that helps us to escape from Sen's impossibility of a Paretian liberal.

4.2. Voluntary Exchange of Conferred Libertarian Rights

"[A] strong libertarian tradition of free contract," according to which "a person's rights are his to use or bargain away as he sees fit" (Gibbard 1974, p. 397), admits a different interpretation from Gibbard's own in terms of the alienable rights-system. Instead of capturing this tradition by means of the *voluntary waiving of rights-exercises* by the original holders of the rights, an alternative interpretation tries to capture the same tradition by means of a scheme in which libertarian rights-conferments actually change hands among individuals through the *voluntary exchange of rights-conferments.* This idea seems to have floated in the air over many years ever since the advent of Sen's impossibility of a Paretian liberal. However, the attempt to formulate this idea in sufficient analytical detail, thereby enabling us to examine the logical workability of this resolution scheme, was first conducted by Harel and Nitzan (1987). According to Harel and Nitzan (1987, p. 338), the genesis of this resolution scheme can be traced back to Buchanan (1976/1996), Barry (1986), and Bernholz (1974), with a due proviso that "[u]nlike Buchanan, Bernholz, and Barry's studies, [the Harel–Nitzan] resolution ... is based on a well-defined, explicit, non ad hoc concept of beneficial exchange of rights." It was Seidl (1990, p. 72) who praised the Harel–Nitzan scheme as "a resolution of the Paretian Liberal Paradox [that] is wholly consistent with libertarian principles." In view of this strong word in favor of the Harel–Nitzan resolution scheme, we should carefully examine the performance of this resolution scheme from the viewpoint of its logical coherence as well as its ethical appeal.[13]

To begin with, a succinct recapitulation of the Harel–Nitzan resolution scheme is in order. Take any profile $\boldsymbol{R} = (R_1, R_2, \ldots, R_n) \in \mathscr{R}$, any $i \in N$, and any $x, y, z \in X$. If it so happens that $xP(R_i)z$ and $zP(R_i)y$, then i's preference for x against y is *ordinally*

[13] The following critical examination of the Harel–Nitzan resolution scheme capitalizes on Suzumura (1991). See Breyer (1990), who also criticized the Harel–Nitzan resolution scheme along somewhat related lines.

stronger than his preference for x against z in the sense introduced by Luce and Raiffa (1957, p. 336) and resurged in the context of welfare and rights by Blau (1975). This fact will be denoted by $(x,y)P^*(R_i)(x,z)$. Likewise, we also have $(x,y)P^*(R_i)(z,y)$. In this case, Harel and Nitzan claim that i will be better served by having a right to exclude y from social choice in the presence of x than having a right to exclude z (resp. y) from social choice in the presence of x (resp. z). Capitalizing on this concept, we are now in the position of defining the voluntary exchange of rights-conferments in the sense of Harel and Nitzan.

Suppose that the profile $\boldsymbol{R} = (R_1, R_2, \ldots, R_n)$ and the rights-system $\boldsymbol{D} = (D_1, D_2, \ldots, D_n)$ are such that there exist $i, j \in N$, $(x,y) \in D_i$ and $(z,w) \in D_j$ satisfying

$$(x,z)P^*(R_i)(x,y) \quad \text{and} \quad (y,w)P^*(R_j)(z,w).$$

Then, Harel and Nitzan say that a *potentially advantageous exchange of rights* exists under $\boldsymbol{D}$ at $\boldsymbol{R}$ between i and j, since i and j can realize a more favorable rights-conferment, viz., (x,z) for i and (y,w) for j, by exchanging y (over which i has a right) and z (over which j has a right). A rights-conferment $\boldsymbol{D}^\tau = (D_1^\tau, D_2^\tau, \ldots, D_n^\tau)$ is said to be an *advantageous reallocation* of $\boldsymbol{D}^{\tau-1} = (D_1^{\tau-1}, D_2^{\tau-1}, \ldots, D_n^{\tau-1})$ at $\boldsymbol{R}$, where $\tau \geq 1$ and $\boldsymbol{D}^0 = \boldsymbol{D}$, if $\boldsymbol{D}^\tau$ is obtained through the realization of some potentially advantageous exchanges of rights under $\boldsymbol{D}^{\tau-1}$ at $\boldsymbol{R}$. Finally, a rights-conferment $\boldsymbol{D}^t$ is said to be an *efficient reallocation* of $\boldsymbol{D}^0$ at $\boldsymbol{R}$ if (i) $\boldsymbol{D}^{\tau+1}$ is an advantageous reallocation of $\boldsymbol{D}^\tau$ at $\boldsymbol{R}$, where $\tau \in \{1, 2, \ldots, t-1\}$ $(t \geq 1)$; and (ii) there is no further advantageous reallocation of $\boldsymbol{D}^t$ at $\boldsymbol{R}$.

Condition HNL: Harel-Nitzan Libertarianism Suppose that the rights-conferment $\boldsymbol{D}^t$ is an efficient reallocation of the initial rights-conferment $\boldsymbol{D} = \boldsymbol{D}^0$ at the profile $\boldsymbol{R} \in \mathscr{R}$. Then each $i \in N$ can exclude y from social choice in the presence of x if $(x,y) \in D_i^t \cap P(R_i)$.

The first logical difficulty with this resolution scheme lies in its internal inconsistency. Consider the case with only two individuals, 1 and 2, and the initial rights-conferment $\boldsymbol{D} = (D_1, D_2)$, which is given in the LHS of Figure 23.2. It is clear that this right-conferment $\boldsymbol{D}$ is coherent. Suppose that the profile $\boldsymbol{R} = (R_1, R_2) \in \mathscr{R}$ is such that

$$R_1\colon x, v, w, y, z \qquad R_2\colon v, y, z, x, w.$$

Since $(x,y) \in D_1$, $(z,w) \in D_2$, $(x,z)P^*(R_1)(x,y)$, and $(y,w)P^*(R_2)(z,w)$, there exists a potentially advantageous exchange of rights under $\boldsymbol{D}$ at $\boldsymbol{R}$ between 1 and 2. By realizing this potentiality, a new rights-conferment $\boldsymbol{D}^*$ is created, which is described in the RHS of Figure 23.2. Clearly, $\boldsymbol{D}^*$ is an efficient reallocation of $\boldsymbol{D}$ that, however, is incoherent.

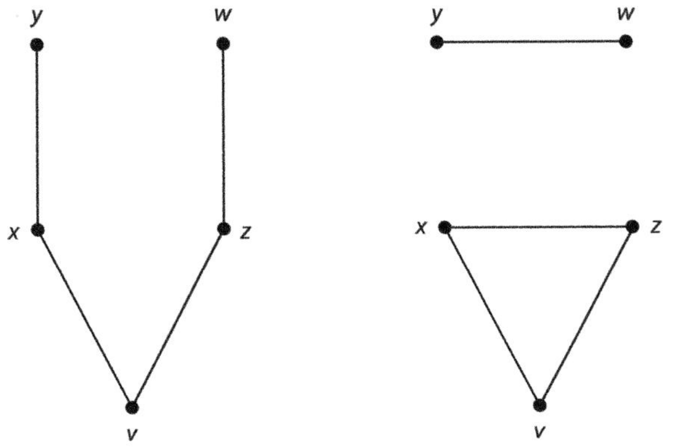

$D_1 = \{(x, y), (y, x), (z, v), (v, z)\}$ $\quad$ $D_1^* = \{(x, z), (z, x), (z, v), (v, z)\}$

$D_2 = \{(z, w), (w, z), (v, x), (x, v)\}$ $\quad$ $D_2^* = \{(y, w), (w, y), (v, x), (x, v)\}$

Figure 23.2. Internal Inconsistency of the Harel–Nitzan Scheme.

Thus, there is no social choice rule that satisfies the unrestricted domain and the Harel–Nitzan libertarian claim.

The second difficulty with this scheme is related to the problem of enforceability of the exchange contract in the realm of libertarian rights. To illustrate this difficulty, consider the Lady Chatterley's Lover Case once again, where the initial rights-conferment $\boldsymbol{D} = (D_P, D_L)$ is as follows:

$$D_P = \{(r_P, r_0), (r_0, r_P)\} \quad D_L = \{(r_L, r_0), (r_0, r_L)\}.$$

Since we have

$$(r_0, r_L)P^*(R_P)(r_0, r_P), (r_0, r_P) \in D_P; (r_P, r_0)P^*(R_L)(r_L, r_0), (r_L, r_0) \in D_L,$$

there exists a potentially advantageous exchange of rights under $\boldsymbol{D}$ at $\boldsymbol{R}$ between Mr. P and Mr. L. By realizing this potentiality, we arrive at an efficient reallocation $\boldsymbol{D}^* = (D_P^*, D_L^*)$ of $\boldsymbol{D}$, where Mr. P (resp. Mr. L) is empowered to decide for r_0 (resp. r_P) against r_L (resp. r_0). It is true that this exchange of decision-making entitlements formally resolves Sen's example of the Lady Chatterley's Lover Case, and r_P emerges as the Harel–Nitzan solution. However, this voluntary exchange of rights, so-called, empowers Mr. P (resp. Mr. L) to decide that Mr. L should not read the book (resp. Mr. P should read the book) against his own preferences. Not only are these ex post decision-making entitlements extremely meddlesome and illiberal, but also "[t]here are far-reaching (and in my view, chilling) implications of trying to enforce contracts of this kind—involving the conduct of personal life. One cannot help remarking that those who see in such contracts a method of ensuring the full exercise of individual liberty must have missed something about the nature of liberty" (Sen 1982b, p. 213).

The third difficulty with this scheme lies in its ethically unappealing nature. To bring this difficulty into clear relief, consider the following example.

Example 3 (Monarchy versus Democracy) Mr. m is the "monarch" and Mr. d is the "dreamer of the restoration." Let x, y, z, and w be such that $x_0 = y_0 =$ "monarchy," $x_d = y_d$, $x_m =$ "to sleep on the belly," $y_m =$ "to sleep on the back," $z_0 = w_0 =$ "democracy," $z_m = w_m$, $z_d =$ "to paint d's bedroom walls pink," and $w_d =$ "to paint d's bedroom walls blue." Since the only difference between x and y is whether Mr. m sleeps on his belly or on his back, it makes sense as the libertarian rights-conferment in the spirit of Sen to require that $(x, y) \in D_m$. Likewise, it makes sense to require that $(w, z) \in D_d$, the only difference between w and z being whether Mr. d paints his bedroom walls blue or pink.

Suppose now that Mr. m and Mr. d have the following preferences:

$$xP(R_m)y \text{ and } yP(R_m)w; \; yP(R_d)w \text{ and } wP(R_d)z.$$

It follows that

$$(x, w)P^*(R_m)(x, y) \text{ and } (x, y) \in D_m; \; (y, z)P^*(R_d)(w, z) \text{ and } (w, z) \in D_d,$$

so that there exists a potentially advantageous exchange of rights under $\boldsymbol{D}$ at $\boldsymbol{R}$ between Mr. m and Mr. d. By realizing this potentiality, Mr. m is empowered to exclude a type of "democracy" with Mr. d's bedroom walls being blue from social choice when "monarchy" with Mr. m sleeping on his belly is available.

The gist of this example is that the ex post rights-conferment in the Harel–Nitzan resolution scheme can be far from being libertarian even in the weakest sense of the word. These difficulties with the Harel–Nitzan scheme, taken together, seem to force us into the inevitable conclusion that it cannot be supported as a libertarian resolution scheme for the impossibility of a Paretian liberal. No escape route from Sen's impossibility theorem can be secured in this direction either.

4.3. Liberal Individual as the Base of the Liberal Society

Recollect that the Gibbard–Kelly resolution scheme based on the voluntary alienation of conferred libertarian rights and the Harel-Nitzan scheme based on the voluntary exchange of conferred libertarian rights have a crucial feature in common: whenener the claim of rights and the Pareto principle come into a conflict with each other, these schemes make the accusing axe fall unfailingly on individual rights, keeping the Pareto principle intact. As a matter of fact, this common feature is also shared by many other resolution schemes in the literature. In contrast, the resolution scheme proposed by Sen (1976; 1982c, Chapter 14) and elaborated further by Suzumura (1978; 1983a, Chapter 7) starts from a doubt on the mechanical use of the Pareto principle in a situation like the Lady Chatterley's Lover Case. Since Mr. P as well as Mr. L prefers r_P to r_L, the Pareto principle entails that r_L should not be socially chosen in the presence of r_P. Observe, however, that the motivation behind Mr. P's preference for r_P against r_L is to prevent Mr. L from being exposed to what Mr. P recognizes as a "dangerous" book. Mr. L, in his turn, prefers r_P to r_L so as to wake the naive Mr. P to what Mr. L perceives to be the reality of human nature. We cannot but feel that such busybody motivations, which lie behind both individual preferences, work to abate the appeal of the Pareto principle in this context.

To illustrate the nature of the Sen–Suzumura resolution scheme, consider the following monologue: "What a terrible necktie he is wearing! He would look much nicer if he were to wear something more decent. However, I am keenly aware that to choose a necktie of his own is his personal matter and none of my business. Thus, my meddlesome concern—no matter how strong it may be—should not count in socially deciding what necktie he should wear." Let us christen an individual having this attitude toward others' personal matters a *liberal individual.* The gist of the Sen–Suzumura resolution scheme is that the liberal society can be sustained in the presence of widespread meddlesomeness if there exists at least one liberal individual in the society.

To make this pivotal concept of a liberal individual operational, consider a profile $\mathbf{R} = (R_1, R_2, \ldots, R_n) \in \mathcal{R}$ and let R_i^0 for each $i \in N$ be the transitive subrelation of R_i that i wants to be counted in social choice. Thus, $(x, y) \in P(R_i)$ holds if i prefers x to y personally, without necessarily requiring this preference to be counted in the procedure of social choice, whereas $(x, y) \in P(R_i^0)$ holds if i wants his preference for x against y to be counted in social choice.

We are now ready to introduce the following modified version of the Pareto principle.

Condition CP: Conditional Pareto Principle For all $x, y \in X$ and $\mathbf{R} \in \mathcal{R}$,

(a) $(x, y) \in R_N^0 \Rightarrow [x \in S - C^{\mathbf{R}}(S) \Rightarrow y \notin C^{\mathbf{R}}(S)]$, and
(b) $(x, y) \in P(R_N^0) \Rightarrow [x \in S \Rightarrow y \notin C^{\mathbf{R}}(S)]$,

where $R_N^0 := \cap_{i \in N} R_i^0$ and $C^{\mathbf{R}} = f(\mathbf{R})$.

What remains to be done is the specification of the analytical definition of R_i^0 for each $i \in N$. Let $\mathbf{D} = (D_1, D_2, \ldots, D_n)$ be the given rights-system. The following lemma, which is due to Suzumura (1978; 1983a, Chapter 7), plays a crucial role in operationalizing the Sen–Suzumura resolution scheme. Recollect that a binary relation Q^* is said to be an *extension* of another binary relation Q if and only if

$$Q \subseteq Q^*; \quad P(Q) \subseteq P(Q^*) \tag{10}$$

hold true. In particular, Q^* is said to be an *ordering extension* of Q if and only if Q^* is an extension of Q, and Q^* satisfies the axiom of an ordering, viz., completeness, reflexivity, and transitivity.

Coherence Lemma (Suzumura 1983a, Theorem 7.2) *There exists an ordering extension R of $Q := \cup_{i \in N}(D_i \cap R_i)$ if and only if the rights-system $\boldsymbol{D}$ is coherent.*

Proof. See Suzumura (1978; 1983a, pp. 194–195). □

In view of the **Coherence Lemma**, let us assume, unless otherwise stated, that the rights-system $\boldsymbol{D}$ is coherent. Given any profile $\boldsymbol{R} \in \mathscr{R}$, let $E(\boldsymbol{D}:\boldsymbol{R})$ be the set of all ordering extensions of $Q := \cup_{i \in N}(D_i \cap R_i)$, which is nonempty by virtue of the **Coherence Lemma**. We then define the restricted preferences of a liberal individual by $R_i^0 := R \cap R_i$ for some $R \in E(\boldsymbol{D}:\boldsymbol{R})$, whereas the "restricted" preferences of an illiberal individual is defined by $R_i^0 = R_i$. Thus, an individual is liberal if and only if he claims only those parts of his preferences, which are compatible with others' preferences over their respective protected spheres, to be counted in social choice. We are now ready to state a possibility theorem established by Sen (1976; 1982b, Chapter 12) and Suzumura (1978, 1979; 1983a, Chapter 7), which reads as follows.

Theorem 5 (Possibility Theorem in the Presence of a Liberal Individual) *There exists a rational social choice rule with unrestricted domain* **U**, *which satisfies the conditional Pareto principle* **CP** *and realizes the initially conferred coherent rights-system* $\boldsymbol{D}$ *with respect to the restricted preference profile* $\boldsymbol{R}^0$, *if there exists at least one liberal individual in the society.*[14,15]

Leaving the formal proof of workability of the Sen–Suzumura resolution scheme to Suzumura (1983a, pp. 197–199), let us illustrate how it works by means of **Example 1**, viz., the Lady Chatterley's Lover Case. The rights-system in this example being $\boldsymbol{D} = (D_P, D_L)$, where $D_P = \{(r_0, r_P), (r_P, r_0)\}$ and $D_L = \{(r_0, r_L), (r_L, r_0)\}$, it is clear that $\boldsymbol{D}$ is coherent. Since $D_P \cap R_P = \{(r_0, r_P)\}$ and $D_L \cap R_L = \{(r_L, r_0)\}$, it is easy to verify

[14] Recollect that a social choice function is said to be *rational* if the choices it describes can be construed to be motivated by the optimization of an underlying preference relation. This concept of rationality can be traced back to the theory of revealed preference à la Samuelson (1938; 1947, Chapter V; 1948, 1950b) and Houthakker (1950). The axiomatic characterization of rational choice functions is developed by Arrow (1959), Bossert, Sprumont and Suzumura (2005), Bossert and Suzumura (2009a, 2009b), Hansson (1968), Richter (1966, 1971), Sen (1971), and Suzumura (1976, 1977; 1983a, Chapter 2), among others.

[15] This resolution scheme, which culminates in **Theorem 5**, can be neatly adapted so as to make it applicable to the incoherent Gibbardian rights-system. The gist of this adaptation is to make the individual's libertarian right contingent on his unconditional preferences for his personal feature alternatives. To be precise, an individual $i \in N$ is said to have an unconditional preference for his feature alternative $x_i \in X_i$ against another feature alternative $y_i \in X_i$ if and only if

$$((x_i; z), (y_i; z)) \in P(R_i) \text{ holds for all } z \in X_{-i}, \tag{1*}$$

where $X_{-i} := \Pi_{j \neq i} X_j$ and $(x_i; z) := (z_1, \ldots, z_{i-1}, x_i, z_{i+1}, \ldots, z_n)$. See Suzumura (1978; 1983a, Chapter 7) for more precise details on this adaptation.

that the ordering extension of $Q := (D_P \cap R_P) \cup (D_L \cap R_L)$ uniquely exists, which is given by $Q^* = \Delta_X \cup \{(r_L, r_0), (r_0, r_P), (r_L, r_P)\}$, where $\Delta_X = \{(r_P, r_P), (r_L, r_L), (r_0, r_0)\}$. Suppose that Mr. P is liberal and Mr. L is not. Then $R_P^0 = R_P \cap Q^* = \Delta_X \cup \{(r_0, r_P)\}$ and $R_L^0 = R_L$. We now define $R^0 = R_P^0 \cup R_L^0 = \Delta_X \cup \{(r_L, r_0), (r_0, r_P), (r_L, r_P)\}$. The social choice that is compatible with the requirements of minimal liberty and the conditional Pareto principle is given by the R^0-greatest point in S, viz., r_L. Thus, the resolution through the Sen–Suzumura scheme for the Lady Chatterley's Lover Case is: "Give the single copy of this book to the willing Mr. L."

The gist of this resolution scheme is very simple and intuitive. The Pareto principle is enforced only by unanimous agreement, so that its use can be vetoed by any one individual. The liberal individual may well serve as a vetoer without sacrificing the requirement of minimal liberty. Indeed, a liberal individual is one who always exercises the veto in favor of every expressed claim of rights, and of every logical consequences of all these requirements. In the parlance of Austen-Smith (1982, p. 90), "a liberal in the Sen/Suzumura sense is giving primacy to the exercising of personal rights over the general right of veto invested by the (unconstrained) Pareto principle. Libertarianism, that is, is perceived as a higher-order value relative to Paretianism."

An insidious aspect of the Sen–Suzumura resolution scheme may be worthwhile to crystallize. For that purpose, let us begin with the observation that the resolution for the Lady Chatterley's Lover Case according to this scheme does not hinge on the supposition that it is Mr. P who is liberal. Indeed, Mr. L being liberal instead of Mr. P brings about the same resolution. Now a natural question suggests itself.

(a) Is it generally true that the resolution according to the Sen–Suzumura scheme is invariant with respect to the distribution of libertarianism among individuals?

It is also natural to ask the following further questions:

(b) Is it generally true that there exists a unique and common ordering extension of each and every individual's preferences over their respective protected spheres?

(c) If the answer to question (b) is in the negative, would the resolution by the Sen–Suzumura scheme remain the same when the liberal individual switched from one ordering extension to the other in deciding which part of his preferences he should claim to be counted in social choice?

These questions were indeed raised and answered in the negative by Suzumura (1978; 1983a, Chapter 7). To verify these negative verdicts, let us apply the Sen–Suzumura resolution scheme to the Work Choice Case, viz., **Example 2**. It is easy to see that the rights-system $\boldsymbol{D} = (D_1, D_2)$ in this example is coherent and that

$$Q := (D_1 \cap R_1) \cup (D_2 \cap R_2) = \{((1, 1/2), (0, 1/2)), ((1/2, 1), (1/2, 0))\}$$

holds true. Clearly, there are multiple ordering extensions of this Q, thirteen altogether, among which we pick out the following three ordering extensions for further illustration:

$$R^{\alpha} = \Delta_X \cup \{((1,1/2),(0,1/2)),((1,1/2),(1/2,1)),((1,1/2),(1/2,0)), ((0,1/2),(1/2,1)),((0,1/2),(1/2,0)),((1/2,1),(1/2,0))\}$$

$$R^{\beta} = \Delta_X \cup \{((1/2,1),(1/2,0)),((1/2,1),(1,1/2)),((1/2,1),(0,1/2)), ((1/2,0),(1,1/2)),((1/2,0),(0,1/2)),((1,1/2),(0,1/2))\}$$

and

$$R^{\gamma} = \Delta_X \cup \{((1,1/2),(1/2,1)),((1/2,1),(1,1/2)),((1,1/2),(0,1/2)), ((1,1/2),(1/2,0)),((1/2,1),(0,1/2)),((1/2,1),(1/2,0)),((0,1/2),(1/2,0))\},$$

where

$$\Delta_X = \{((1,1/2),(1,1/2)),((0,1/2),(0,1/2)),((1/2,1),(1/2,1)),((1/2,0),(1/2,0))\}.$$

Depending on who is liberal and which ordering extension is used, there are different resolution scenarios. Let the scenario where individual 1 is liberal and the ordering extension α is used be denoted by $(1,\alpha)$, and so forth. It is easy, if tedious, to verify that the solution in the scenario $(1,\alpha)$ is (1, 1/2), that in the scenario $(1,\beta)$ or the scenario $(2,\beta)$ is (1/2, 1), and that in the scenario $(\{1,2\},\gamma)$ is $\{(1, 1/2), (1/2, 1)\}$.

How serious is this feature of the Sen–Suzumura resolution scheme? In an article devoted to the elaboration of the Sen–Suzumura resolution scheme, Austen-Smith (1982, p. 98) took this feature seriously when he stated that "social choice derived using the Sen/Suzumura decision making process was ... sensitive to which individuals were liberal and (more seriously) how these individuals manifested their libertarianism." We are not so sure about this verdict. In our view, the major message of Sen's impossibility of a Paretian liberal is that there is a logical conflict between the nonwelfaristic value of social protection of individual rights and the welfaristic value of the Pareto principle. The gist of the Sen–Suzumura resolution scheme, which is crystallized in **Theorem 5**, is that this conflict can be resolved if there exists at least one liberal individual in the society. The dependence of final social choice on the identity of liberal individual as well as on the choice of ordering extension is not really a weakness of this resolution scheme, but is a manifestation of the rich possibilities of social choice that are left open even after we satisfy the minimal conditions for resolving Sen's impossibility theorem along the line of the Sen–Suzumura resolution scheme. If it is so desired, as Austen-Smith (1982) apparently desired in his sophistication of the Sen–Suzumura resolution scheme, we may go further and introduce other axiom(s) to narrow down the residual possibilities left open by their resolution scheme. Those who are interested in articulating in concrete terms how this further exercise can be performed are cordially invited to Austen-Smith (1982).

4.4. Ethical Constraints on the Exercise of Conferred Libertarian Rights

The last class of resolution schemes for Sen's impossibility of a Paretian liberal tries to find an escape route therefrom by imposing some ethical constraints on the exercise of conferred libertarian rights. The underlying idea of this class of resolution schemes may be briefly expressed as follows:

> *I do not want to say that individual freedom is, even in the most liberal societies, the sole, or even the dominant, criterion of social action.... The extent of a man's or a people's liberty to choose to live as they desire must be weighed against the claims of many other values, of which equality, or justice, or happiness, or security, or public order are perhaps the most obvious examples. For this reason, it cannot be unlimited....[Respect] for the principles of justice, or shame at gross inequality of treatment, is as basic in man as the desire for liberty. (Berlin 1958, pp. 54–55)*

As an auxiliary step in formulating this essential idea, assume that information is now available about individual's preferences of the extended sympathy type: It is better (or worse) for me to be in individual i's position in one social state x than to be in individual j's position in another social state y. Extended preferences that embody the welfare comparisons of the extended sympathy type may be operationalized by an *extended preference ordering* E defined on the Cartesian product $X \times N$. Let $\mathscr{E}$ be the set of all extended preference orderings. Given $E \in \mathscr{E}$, $x, y \in X$ and $i, j \in N$, $((x,i),(y,j)) \in E$, or $(x,i)E(y,j)$ for short, means that it is no worse (in the evaluator's judgments) to be an individual i in a social state x than to be an individual j in another social state y. It is assumed that each individual $i \in N$ has an extended preference ordering $E_i \in \mathscr{E}$ of his own, which represents his intrapersonal and intersituational comparisons of welfare, together forming a profile $\boldsymbol{E} = (E_1, E_2, \ldots, E_n) \in \mathscr{E}^n$ of extended preference orderings. In so doing, "in effect, we are asking each agent to put himself in the position of each other agents to determine if that is a better or worse position than the one he is now in" (Varian 1975, p. 240).[16]

Corresponding to a given profile $\boldsymbol{E} = (E_1, E_2, \ldots, E_n) \in \mathscr{E}^n$ of extended preference orderings, we may define two associated individual preference orderings over X.[17] On the one hand, for each $i \in N$, let individual i's *subjective preference ordering* $R_i(E_i)$ be defined by

$$R_i(E_i) = \{(x,y) \in X \times X \mid (x,i)E_i(y,i)\}, \tag{11}$$

[16] The extended sympathy social choice framework is due originally to Arrow (1963, pp. 114–115) and Sen (1970a/1979, Chapter 9), which capitalizes on the highly suggestive work by Suppes (1966).

[17] The nomenclature of subjective preferences and ethical preferences is due to Harsanyi (1955).

which expresses what i actually prefers, whether on the basis of his private interests, or on any other basis. On the other hand, individual i has his *ethical preference ordering*, which expresses "what this individual prefers (or, rather, would prefer) on the basis of impersonal social considerations alone" (Harsanyi 1955, p. 315). To give analytical substance to the concept of ethical preference ordering, let us introduce the concept of a *principle of justice*, which is a rule in terms of which the intrapersonal and intersituational comparisons of the extended sympathy type are mapped into an ethical preference ordering on X. Let ω_i stand for a principle of justice that embodies the moral sense of justice held by individual i. Then, for any profile $\mathbf{E} = (E_1, E_2, \ldots, E_n) \in \mathscr{E}^n$ of extended preference orderings, $\omega_i(E_i)$ denotes a quasi-ordering on X such that $(x, y) \in \omega_i(E_i)$ holds if and only if $x \in X$ is judged by i, whose moral sense of justice is captured by the principle of justice ω_i, to be at least as just as $y \in X$. In particular, if $\omega_i(E_i)$ satisfies the axiom of completeness on X for each and every $E_i \in \mathscr{E}$, ω_i is said to be a *complete principle of justice.* In order to secure that the ethical preference $\omega_i(E_i)$ judges "on the basis of impersonal social considerations alone," the principle of justice ω_i must satisfy the *axiom of impersonality* to be defined as follows. Let Π_N be the set of all permutations over N. For any extended preference ordering $E \in \mathscr{E}$, Suppes's *grading principle of justice* $\omega_S(E)$ is defined by $(x, y) \in \omega_S(E)$ if and only if

$$\exists \pi \in \Pi_N\colon \{\forall i \in N\colon (x, i)E(y, \pi(i))\} \ \& \ \{\exists j \in N\colon (x, j)P(E)(y, \pi(j))\} \tag{12}$$

holds for all $x, y \in X$, where $P(E)$ is the asymmetric part of E. Thus, x is judged more just in the sense of Suppes than y if and only if we may start from the welfare distribution under y and arrive at that under x in the following two steps: (i) interpersonal permutation of welfare levels at y, and (ii) making a Pareto-wise improvement. By making interpersonal permutations of welfare levels ethically irrelevant, the welfare judgments embodied in $\omega_S(E)$ crystallize the intuitive idea of impersonality in a simple operational way. We may now introduce the following axiom that serves us as a litmus paper for checking the ethical qualification of the principles of justice held by individuals.

Axiom IM: Impersonality *For any profile $\mathbf{E} \in \mathscr{E}^n$ of extended preference orderings, the admissible principle of justice ω_i held by each individual $i \in N$ must satisfy $\omega_S(E_i) \subseteq P(\omega_i(E_i))$.*

As a slight generalization of our social choice theoretic framework, an *extended social choice rule* is defined as a function f^* that maps each profile $\mathbf{E} \in \mathscr{E}^n$ of extended preference orderings into a social choice function defined on the set $\mathscr{S}$ of all nonempty finite subsets of X, viz., $C^{\mathbf{E}} = f^*(\mathbf{E})$. The following four conditions on the extended social choice rule are nothing other than the unanimity rule with respect to the two profiles of individual preference orderings associated with each profile of extended preference orderings.

Condition EP: Pareto Principle for Extended Social Choice Rule For any $x, y \in X$ and any $\mathbf{E} \in \mathscr{E}^n$,

$$(x, y) \in \cap_{i \in N} P(R_i(E_i)) \Rightarrow [x \in S \Rightarrow y \notin C^{\mathbf{E}}(S)] \text{ for all } S \in \mathscr{S} \quad (13)$$

holds, where $C^{\mathbf{E}} = f^*(\mathbf{E})$.

Condition ESP: Strong Pareto Principle for Extended Social Choice Rule For any $x, y \in X$ and any $\mathbf{E} \in \mathscr{E}^n$,

$$(x, y) \in P(\cap_{i \in N} R_i(E_i)) \Rightarrow [x \in S \Rightarrow y \notin C^{\mathbf{E}}(S)] \text{ for all } S \in \mathscr{S} \quad (14)$$

holds, where $C^{\mathbf{E}} = f^*(\mathbf{E})$.

Condition JU: Justice Unanimity Principle For any $x, y \in X$ and any $\mathbf{E} \in \mathscr{E}^n$,

$$(x, y) \in \cap_{i \in N} P(\omega_i(E_i)) \Rightarrow [x \in S \Rightarrow y \notin C^{\mathbf{E}}(S)] \text{ for all } S \in \mathscr{S} \quad (15)$$

holds, where $C^{\mathbf{E}} = f^*(\mathbf{E})$.

Condition SJU: Strong Justice Unanimity Principle For any $x, y \in X$ and any $\mathbf{E} \in \mathscr{E}^n$,

$$(x, y) \in P(\cap_{i \in N} \omega_i(E_i)) \Rightarrow [x \in S \Rightarrow y \notin C^{\mathbf{E}}(S)] \text{ for all } S \in \mathscr{S} \quad (16)$$

holds, where $C^{\mathbf{E}} = f^*(\mathbf{E})$.

Even when we impose Axiom **IM** on the principles of justice ω_i for all $i \in N$, there still remains a serious possibility of conflict between the two versions of the unanimity rule, one for the profile of subjective preference orderings and the other for the profile of ethical preference orderings. This conflict may be illustrated in terms of a cute example due to Sen (1970a/1979, pp. 149–150).

Example 4 (Pareto versus Suppes) There are two individuals, viz., a devout Muslim (Mr. 1) and a devout Hindu (Mr. 2). There are two states x and y, where x is a state in which the Muslim receives 2 units of pork and 0 units of beef and the Hindu receives 0 units of pork and 2 units of beef, whereas y is a state in which the Muslim receives 0 units of pork and 1 unit of beef and the Hindu receives 1 unit of pork and 0 units of beef. It is assumed that the Muslim likes beef and is disgusted by pork, whereas the Hindu enjoys pork but cannot bear the thought of eating beef. Assuming free disposal, the Muslim is indifferent between different amounts of pork, and the Hindu is indifferent between different amounts of beef. It is clear that y is Pareto better than x, as the Muslim prefers 1 unit of beef to 2 units of pork, and the Hindu prefers 1 unit of pork to 2 units of beef.

However, both individuals find x to be more just than y in terms of the Suppes principle of justice. This verdict follows from the fact that the Muslim prefers $(x, 2)$ to $(y, 1)$ and is indifferent between $(x, 1)$ and $(y, 2)$, whereas the Hindu prefers $(x, 1)$ to $(y, 2)$ and is indifferent between $(x, 2)$ and $(y, 1)$.

The culprit of **Example 4** seems easy to detect. For any profile $\mathbf{E} \in \mathcal{E}^n$ of extended preference orderings, and for any $i,\ j \in N$, let a binary relation $R_{ij}(E_i)$ on X be defined by

$$\forall\, x, y \in X: (x, y) \in R_{ij}(E_i) \iff (x,j)E_i(y,j). \tag{17}$$

By construction, $(x, y) \in R_{ij}(E_i)$ means that, according to individual i's judgments, it is no worse for individual j to be in x rather than in y, whereas $(x, y) \in R_j(E_j)$ means that j himself feels to be no worse in x rather than in y. By definition, $R_i(E_i) = R_{ii}(E_i)$ holds true for all $i \in N$. Observe that the profile of extended preference orderings used in **Example 4** is such that $(y, x) \in P(R_1(E_1))$, $(x, y) \in P(R_{21}(E_2))$, $(y, x) \in P(R_2(E_2))$, and $(x, y) \in P(R_{12}(E_1))$. What is conspicuous in this configuration is the clear lack of sympathetic identification between individuals. As soon as we recognize this fact, a natural solution to the conflict between Pareto and Suppes suggests itself. Following Sen (1970a, p. 156), we now introduce the following axiom.

Axiom SID: Sympathetic Identification *The admissible profile* $\mathbf{E} \in \mathcal{E}^n$ *of extended preference orderings must be such that*

$$\forall\, i,j \in N: R_{ij}(E_i) = R_j(E_j) \tag{18}$$

holds true.

Axiom **SID** has a strong intuitive appeal; it requires that "[p]lacing oneself in the position of the other should involve not merely having the latter's objective circumstances but also identifying oneself with the other in terms of his subjective features" (Sen 1970a/1979, p. 150). **Example 4** is nothing other than a reflection of the well-known fact that "without sympathetic identification or some such assumption, the analysis may lead to some odd results" (Pattanaik 1968, p. 157). Thus, the necessity of Axiom **SID** was to be expected. Indeed, if Axiom **SID** is imposed on the profile $\mathbf{E} \in \mathcal{E}^n$ of extended preference orderings, the incompatibility between Pareto and Suppes disappears, and we obtain the following amiable property due to Sen (1970a/1979, p. 156):

$$\forall\, i \in N: P(\cap_{j \in N} R_j(E_j)) \subseteq \omega_i(E_i). \tag{19}$$

Note, however, that the introduction of Axiom **SID** accompanies some real change in the informational nature of the whole analysis. Unless and until we impose Axiom **SID**, what is involved in the extended preference ordering is no more than the *intrapersonal* and *intersituational* comparisons of welfare. However, Axiom **SID** forces us to change our informational basis substantially, and allow *interpersonal* comparability of welfare.[18,19] This insidious nature of Axiom **SID** notwithstanding, it is much

[18] The extended sympathy approach without the axiom of sympathetic identification, viz., without interpersonal comparability of welfares, has been invoked extensively in the literature on "fairness-as-no-envy" approach in the theory of resource allocation mechanisms. See, among many others, Foley (1967), Kolm (1972), Varian (1974, 1975), Thomson and Varian (1985), and more recently, Fleurbaey, Suzumura, and Tadenuma (2005). The social choice theoretic implications of fairness-as-no-envy approach were explored by Gärdenfors (1978), Suzumura, (1981a, 1981b, 1982, 1983a, Chapters 5–7; 1983b), and Tadenuma (2002). In particular, Suzumura (1982; 1983a, Chapter 7) examined the effectiveness of fairness-as-no-envy approach in the attempt to resolve the Pareto libertarian paradox and obtained several impossibility theorems.

[19] There is an attempt in the literature to introduce an ethical constraint on the libertarian rights-conferment per se by making use of the concept of equity-as-no-envy without invoking even intrapersonal and intersituational comparisons of welfare, to say nothing of interpersonal comparisons of welfare. This line of research was kicked off by Austen-Smith (1979), which was subsequently followed by Gaertner (1982) and Gekker (1991). Given a profile $\boldsymbol{R} \in \mathscr{R}$ of individual preference orderings over X and a rights-system $\boldsymbol{D} = (D_1, D_2, \ldots, D_n)$, Austen-Smith defined an ordering $Q(R_i)$ on $\{D_1, D_2, \ldots, D_n\}$ for all $i \in N$ by

$$(D_j, D_k) \in Q(R_i) \Leftrightarrow \exists\, x \in \sigma(D_j), \forall y \in \sigma(D_k)\colon (x, y) \in R_i,$$

where $\sigma(D_i) = \{x \in X \mid \exists\, y \in X\colon (x, y) \in D_i \text{ or } (y, x) \in D_i\}$ for all $i \in N$. The rights-system $\boldsymbol{D} = (D_1, D_2, \ldots, D_n)$ is said to be *K-fair* if and only if

$$\forall i, j \in N: (D_i, D_j) \in Q(R_i)$$

and

$$\exists K \subseteq N \cup \{\emptyset\}, \forall k \in K, \exists\, l(k) \in N: (D_k, D_{l(k)}) \in P(Q(R_k)).$$

For example, $\boldsymbol{D}$ is N-fair if, for all $i \in N$, there is an element of $\sigma(D_i)$ that i prefers to any element in $\cup_{j \in N - \{i\}} \sigma(D_j)$. Austen-Smith showed that, if $\#\sigma(D_i) = 2$ for all $i \in N$, and $\boldsymbol{D}$ is K-fair for all $K \subseteq N \cup \{\emptyset\}$, then the Pareto libertarian paradox never surfaces. On the basis of this result, it is claimed that "the use of a fairness criterion in allocating rights to individuals admits the existence of a libertarian social choice rule" (Austen-Smith 1979, p. 29). Whether or not this claim is sustainable seems to be a matter of dispute. For one thing, the assumption that $\#\sigma(D_i) = 2$ for all $i \in N$ is obviously very restrictive, but the main problem with the fair rights-system à la Austen-Smith seems to lie elsewhere. Note that i does not have any right over the set of social states $\sigma(D_j)$ per se; what he is indeed endowed by the libertarian right in the sense of Sen is the power to exclude the social choice of $y \in \sigma(D_j)$ in the presence of $x \in \sigma(D_j)$ when he expresses his preference for x against y, but not otherwise. In other words, the very fact that $x \in \sigma(D_j)$ in isolation means very little, if any at all, from the point of view of rights. In this sense, even in the case where $\#\sigma(D_i) = 2$ for all $i \in N$, the intuitive appeal of Austen-Smith's no-envy fairness approach to the fair conferment of libertarian rights seems to be seriously in dispute. Careful readers may have noticed that the problem with the Austen-Smith resolution scheme has something in common with the problem with the Harel–Nitzan resolution scheme that we discussed in Section 4.2. To bring this point unambiguously home, we have only to consider the following example due to Suzumura (1990, p. 232).

Example 1* (Fairness in the Presence of Spiteful Preferences) Ian has a good job in a social state $x(\mathrm{I})$, but is jobless in another social state $y(\mathrm{I})$, everything else being the same. John sleeps on his belly (resp. back) in the social state $x(\mathrm{J})$ (resp. $y(\mathrm{J})$), everything else being the same. Let the profile of individual preference orderings $\boldsymbol{R} = (R_{\text{Ian}}, R_{\text{John}})$ and the rights-system $\boldsymbol{D} = (D_{\text{Ian}}, D_{\text{John}})$ satisfy $(y(\mathrm{I}), x(\mathrm{J})) \in P(R_{\text{John}})$, $(y(\mathrm{I}), y(\mathrm{J})) \in P(R_{\text{John}})$, $D_{\text{Ian}} = \{(x(\mathrm{I}), y(\mathrm{I})), (y(\mathrm{I}), x(\mathrm{I}))\}$ and $D_{\text{John}} = \{(x(\mathrm{J}), y(\mathrm{J})), (y(\mathrm{J}), x(\mathrm{J}))\}$. John holds these preferences out of his pure spite toward Ian: "I would rather like to see his distress from being jobless, even if I must give up my favorite sleeping position for that." In the presence of such spiteful preferences on the part of John, the need to protect Ian's right seems to be much stronger, not weaker, than otherwise. However, according to Austen-Smith, the rights-system $\boldsymbol{D}$ is judged unfair, and the realization of Ian's right is not recognized as a legitimate claim on the social choice rule.

weaker than the following axiom, which is often used in the literature, for example by Hammond (1976) and Sen (1977b).

Axiom CID: Complete Identification *The admissible profile* $\mathbf{E} \in \mathscr{E}^n$ *of extended preference orderings must be such that*

$$\forall\, i,j \in N\colon E_i = E_j \tag{20}$$

holds true.

Unlike Axiom **SID**, Axiom **CID** does not allow the observer relativity of ordinal interpersonal comparisons of welfare. Nevertheless, it does not impose any restriction on the subsumed profile $\{R_i(E_i) \mid i \in N\}$ of individual preference orderings over the set X of social states. What Axiom **CID** does is to insert "objective"—in the sense of being free from observer relativity—interpersonal welfare comparisons to supplement ordinal and intrapersonal information provided by Arrovian profile of individual preference orderings. In what follows, the set of all profiles of extended preference orderings satisfying Axiom **SID** (resp. **CID**) will be represented by $\mathscr{E}^n_{\mathrm{SID}}$ (resp. $\mathscr{E}^n_{\mathrm{CID}}$). By definition, it is clear that $\mathscr{E}^n_{\mathrm{CID}} \subseteq \mathscr{E}^n_{\mathrm{SID}} \subseteq \mathscr{E}^n$.

The first attempt to invoke the extended sympathy approach with interpersonal comparability in the context of welfare and rights was made by Kelly (1976a), who introduced the following justice-constrained libertarianism.

Condition JCL(1): Justice-Constrained Libertarianism (1) For every admissible profile $\mathbf{E} \in \mathscr{E}^n$ of extended preference orderings, every $i \in N$ with nonempty protected sphere D_i, and every $x, y \in X$,

$$(x,y) \in D_i \cap P(R_i) \,\&\, (y,x) \notin \cup_{j\in N} P(\omega_j(E_j)) \Rightarrow [x \in S \Rightarrow y \notin C^{\mathbf{E}}(S)] \text{ for all } S \in \mathscr{S} \tag{21}$$

holds, where $C^{\mathbf{E}} = f^*(\mathbf{E})$.

Thus, even if a pair of social states belongs to the protected sphere of some individual, he is unable to get his own way under Condition **JCL(1)** if there is someone in the society who protests to the exercise of his right over this pair in the name of justice. However, Kelly has shown that even this restricted version of the claim of rights is still incompatible with the Pareto principle even when the admissible profile of extended preference orderings is confined to $\mathscr{E}^n_{\mathrm{CID}}$.

Theorem 6 (Kelly 1976a) *Suppose that* $\omega_i = \omega_S$ *holds for all* $i \in N$. *Suppose also that there exist at least two individuals, say* j *and* k, *each being endowed with a nonempty protected sphere* D_j *and* D_k, *respectively. Then there exists no extended social choice rule* f^* *on* $\mathscr{E}^n_{\mathrm{CID}}$ *that satisfies Condition* **EP** *and bestows on* j *and* k *the restricted libertarian rights in the sense of Condition* **JCL(1)**.

It was in view of Kelly's "impossibility of a just liberal" that Sen (1976, p. 228) concluded in the context of an impossibility of a Paretian liberal that "introducing interpersonal comparisons is not much of a cure (in contrast with the impossibility results of the Arrow type)." With the purpose of checking whether this sweeping negative verdict is inevitable, let us introduce another principle of justice, which is nothing other than the welfarist version of the Rawlsian principle of justice ω_R, as follows.

Given an extended preference ordering $E \in \mathscr{E}$ and for any $x \in X$ and any $i \in N$, let $i(x)$ be the i-th worst position at x, which is defined as the i-th worst individual in social state x identified by ranking $(x,1),(x,2),\ldots,(x,n)$ in terms of the ordering E, ties, if any, being broken arbitrarily. We may now define ω_R as follows: For all $x,y \in X$,

$$(x,y) \in P(\omega_R(E)) \Leftrightarrow \begin{cases} \exists\, r \in N\colon ((x,r(x)),(y,r(y))) \in P(E) \\ \forall i \in \{1,2,\ldots,r-1\}\colon ((x,i(x)),(y,i(y))) \in I(E) \end{cases} \tag{22}$$

and

$$(x,y) \in I(\omega_R(E)) \Leftrightarrow \forall i \in N: ((x,i(x)),(y,i(y))) \in I(E). \tag{23}$$

Finally,

$$\forall\, x,y \in X\colon (x,y) \in \omega_R(E) \Leftrightarrow (x,y) \in P(\omega_R(E)) \text{ or } (x,y) \in I(\omega_R(E)). \tag{24}$$

We are now ready to state the following possibility theorem, which is in sharp contrast with Kelly's impossibility theorem.

Theorem 7 (Suzumura 1978, Theorem 3) *Suppose that $\omega_i = \omega_R$ holds for all $i \in N$. Suppose also that the rights-system $\mathbf{D} = (D_1, D_2, \ldots, D_n)$ is coherent. Then there exists a rational extended social choice rule f^* on $\mathscr{E}^n_{\text{CID}}$ that satisfies Condition* **EP** *and Condition* **JCL(1)**.

To identify the factor that is responsible for the contrast between **Theorem 6** and **Theorem 7**, a useful step seems to be the reexamination of the Lady Chatterley's Lover Case within the extended sympathy framework. Suppose that Mr. L is universally recognized to be socially unfavored vis-à-vis Mr. P, and the following extended preference ordering E is commonly shared:

$$(r_0,P)P(E)(r_P,P)P(E)(r_L,P)P(E)(r_P,L)P(E)(r_L,L)P(E)(r_0,L). \tag{25}$$

Note that the subsumed profile of subjective preference orderings $(R_P(E), R_L(E))$ coincides with the original profile specified in the Lady Chatterley's Lover Case. It is easy to check that the incomplete Suppesian principle of justice and the complete Rawlsian principle of justice yield, respectively, the following justice rankings over the set of alternatives $S = \{r_0, r_P, r_L\}$ for the extended preference ordering (25):

$$\omega_S(E): r_P, r_L \qquad \omega_R(E): r_P, r_L, r_0. \tag{26}$$

It is clear that Condition **JCL(1)** with the incomplete principle of justice $\omega_S(E)$ does not impose any restriction on anyone's exercise of right and the impossibility result goes through. Hence **Theorem 6**. In contrast, Condition **JCL(1)** with the complete principle of justice $\omega_R(E)$ does prevent Mr. P from exercising his conferred right for r_0 against r_P, thus securing the possibility result **Theorem 7**.

Although **Theorem 7** is useful in suggesting that interpersonal comparisons may be of some help in securing an escape route from the impossibility of a Paretian liberal, it is only a frail possibility theorem; it presupposes that not only complete identification prevails among individuals when they make interpersonal welfare comparisons of the extended sympathy type, but also individuals are in full agreement on the legitimacy of the Rawlsian principle of justice. To gauge how much extra mileage we can gain along the line of **Theorem 7**, consider the following generalization thereof.

Theorem 8 (Suzumura 1982, Theorem 4.3) *Suppose that each and every individual's principle of justice ω_i is complete and that it satisfies Axiom* **IM** *for all $i \in N$. Suppose also that the rights-system $\mathbf{D} = (D_1, D_2, \ldots, D_n)$ is coherent. Then there exists a rational extended social choice rule f^* on $\mathcal{E}^n_{\mathrm{SID}}$ that satisfies Condition* **ESP** *and Condition* **JCL(1)**.[20,21,22]

Some may well think, as Wulf Gaertner (1985) apparently did, that Condition **JCL(1)** is too weak as a libertarian claim, which requires that the exercise of any right should be withheld if there is at least one individual in the society who cries injustice thereof. It is not clear, however, whether this charge is as forceful as the critics thought. As long as each individual's principle of justice satisfies the axiom of impersonality and each

[20] As in the case of **Theorem 5**, this theorem can be modified so as to accommodate the case where the incoherent Gibbardian rights-system prevails. See Suzumura (1982, pp. 153–154) for details.

[21] The domain of the extended social choice rule satisfying Condition **ESP** and Condition **JCL(1)** cannot be expanded beyond $\mathcal{E}^n_{\mathrm{SID}}$. Indeed, we obtain the following impossibility theorem:

Theorem 1* (Suzumura 1982, pp. 148–150) *Suppose that the rights-system $\mathbf{D} = (D_1, D_2, \ldots, D_n)$ is coherent and that, for at least two individuals, say 1 and 2, $D_1 \supseteq \{(x, y), (y, x)\}$ and $D_2 \supseteq \{(z, w), (w, z)\}$ hold with $x \neq y$ and $z \neq w$. Then there exists no extended social choice rule f^* on $\mathcal{E}^n$ satisfying Condition* **EP** *and Condition* **JCL(1)**.

[22] Wriglesworth (1982a; 1985b, p. 55), made a surprising claim that **Theorem 8** holds without the coherence of the rights-system. This claim is emphatically false. The source of his mistake is easy to detect; he is imposing the justice-oriented restriction, not only on the exercise of individual libertarian rights, but also on the Pareto principle. It is true that the justice-constrained rights-exercising can be made compatible with the justice-constrained Pareto principle without imposing coherence of the rights-system. However, to jump from this trivial result to the claim that **Theorem 8**, which is totally different in nature, can likewise be true without imposing coherence of the rights-system is an obvious logical mistake.

individual's interpersonal welfare comparisons is made in accordance with the extended preference ordering satisfying the axiom of sympathetic identification, Condition **JCL(1)** seems rather reasonable. However, we need not settle this problem at this juncture of our argument. Consider the following strengthening of Condition **JCL(1)**.

Condition JCL(2): Justice-Constrained Libertarianism (2) For every admissible profile $\boldsymbol{E} \in \mathscr{E}^n$ of extended preference orderings, every $i \in N$ with nonempty protected sphere D_i, and every $x, y \in X$,

$$(x,y) \in D_i \cap P(R_i) \;\&\; (y,x) \notin \cap_{j \in N} P(\omega_j(E_j)) \Rightarrow [x \in S \Rightarrow y \notin C^{\boldsymbol{E}}(S)] \text{ for all } S \in \mathscr{S} \tag{27}$$

holds, where $C^{\boldsymbol{E}} = f^*(\boldsymbol{E})$.

Those who are critical to Condition **JCL(1)** may be happy with Condition **JCL(2)**. However, Condition **JCL(2)** represents in fact a standard of justice-constrained libertarian claim that is unsustainable in the presence of other conditions appearing in **Theorem 8**, as the following impossibility theorem testifies.

Theorem 9 (Suzumura 1982, Theorem 4.5(b)) *Suppose that the rights-system* $\boldsymbol{D} = (D_1, D_2, \ldots, D_n)$ *is coherent and there exist* $x, y, z, w \in X$ *such that* $\{(x,y),(y,x)\} \subseteq D_1, x \neq y$, $\{(z,w),(w,z)\} \subseteq D_2$, *and* $z \neq w$. *Suppose also that* $\omega_i = \omega_R$ *holds for all* $i \in N$. *Then there exists no extended social choice rule* f^* *on* $\mathscr{E}^n_{\mathrm{SID}}$ *that satisfies Condition* **ESP** *and Condition* **JCL(2)**.

Gathering all the pieces together, we may safely conclude that interpersonal welfare comparisons of the extended sympathy type can in fact help us identify several reasonable ways of resolving the impossibility of a Paretian liberal. For the sake of fairness, however, we should remind ourselves of Immanuel Kant's categorical refutation of the idea of pragmatically conditioning rights in view of other utility-related considerations. Suffice it to quote the following passage:

> *The rights of man must be held sacred, however great a sacrifice the ruling power may have to take. There can be no half measures here; it is no use devising hybrid solutions such as a pragmatically conditioned right halfway between right and utility. For all politics must bend the knee before right, although politics may hope in return to arrive, however slowly, at a stage of lasting brilliance. (Reiss 1970, p. 125)*

This quotation from Kant may be construed to vindicate that he is an uncompromisingly anticonsequential deontologist. However, we should not forget that Kant also showed a strong interest in the nature of actual consequences of following such rules of conduct as "categorical imperatives." It is not clear whether Kant would have refuted the justice-constrained libertarian claim, particularly when the claim was subject to impersonality and sympathetic identification.

5. CRITIQUES ON SEN'S FORMULATION OF INDIVIDUAL RIGHTS

So much for the critical examinations of some of the proposed resolution schemes for Sen's impossibility theorem, which basically accept Sen's formulation of individual rights in terms of the preference-contingent power of rejection. The next order of our business is the critical scrutinies of Sen's formulation of individual libertarian rights per se.

The first criticism to be examined is due to Arrow, whose critical remarks on Sen's formulation of rights are reported in the interview conducted by Kelly on behalf of *Social Choice and Welfare* (and reprinted in Chapter 13 of this volume). They are focused squarely on the *raison d'être of rights*. When Arrow was asked of his first response to Sen's impossibility of a Paretian liberal, he recalled as follows:

> *I thought that [Sen's theorem] was stunning and penetrating to a very important issue. But … why do we have rights? … [T]he one thing I retain from utilitarianism is that, basically, judgments are based on consequences.… I view rights as arrangements that may help you in achieving a higher utility level. For example, if you are much better informed about a certain choice, because it's personal to you and not to me, I don't really know anything about it, I should delegate the choice to you.… [But] who settles what rights are legitimate? The consequentialist view—I won't say that fully settles it either, but at least you have something to argue about. So this is why I'm a little unsympathetic to the rights issue—everybody just multiplies the rights all over the place and you get total paralysis.… Unless somebody produces a logic of rights in terms of which we can argue, I really find the whole issue is unfocused. (Chapter 13, pp. 21–23)*

In essence, what worried Arrow was the conspicuous lack of the reasons for individual rights in the social choice theoretic framework. Why on earth should the society confer rights à la Sen in the first place? Unless we may produce a logic that explains the *raison d'être* of rights, Arrow remains less than convinced by Sen's criticism against the welfaristic foundations of normative economics based on his impossibility of a Paretian liberal.

The second criticism to be examined is actually one of the earliest criticisms raised against Sen's formulation of rights, which was put forward by Nozick in his influential book, *Anarchy, State, and Utopia* (1974). Both Sen and Nozick would agree with John Stuart Mill that each individual should be warranted a personal protected sphere with which the rest of the society should not be permitted to interfere. Substantial differences inevitably surface, however, when they seek to provide a precise formulation of this personal protected sphere and of how the recognition of the personal protected spheres of different individuals get reflected in the choices made by the society. According to Nozick,

> *[a] more appropriate view of individual rights [than Sen's social choice theoretic formulation in terms of the preference-contingent power of rejection] goes as follows. Individual rights are co-possible; each person may exercise his rights as he chooses. The exercise of these rights fixes some features of the world. Within the constraints of these fixed features, a choice may be made by a social choice mechanism based upon a social ordering; if there are any choices left to make! Rights do not determine a social ordering but instead set the constraints within which a social choice is to be made, by excluding certain alternatives, fixing others, and so on. (If I have a right to choose to live in New York or in Massachusetts, and I choose Massachusetts, then alternatives involving my living in New York are not appropriate objects to be entered in a social ordering.)* ... How else can one cope with Sen's result? *(1974, p. 166)*

Thus, instead of formulating rights on a par with the weak welfaristic value such as the Pareto principle, as the preference-contingent power of rejection along the line of Sen indeed does, Nozick proposes to assign rights a completely different role of specifying some personal features of the world before the social choice rule starts its proper function as a preference amalgamation mechanism at the social level. In sharp contrast with Sen's view, which formulates rights in terms of the relevant individual's preferences over the complete descriptions of the society, Nozick's formulation has nothing to do with individual preferences over social states. Instead, his own formulation is based on the relevant individual's choice of personal options. It should be recognised that Nozick's view is deeply rooted in the libertarian tradition of respecting the freedom of choice in private spheres along the line of John Stuart Mill. As such, Nozick's criticism on Sen seems to carry heavy weight in the context of libertarian rights.

The third criticism to be examined was expressd by Farrell (1976) in his last published article, which goes as follows.

> *[T]he attempt to insert "Liberalism" by means of individual decisiveness [as Sen's social choice theoretic formulation does] is ... an unnatural and artificial device, introduced as an afterthought. Suppose two states, x and y, differ only in a matter purely private to individual j. Would a Liberal say that individual j should be decisive between x and y, so as to have a modicum of individual liberty? He is much more likely to say that there is no social choice to be made between x and y, since they differ in a matter private to individual j. (1976, p. 9)*

Pursuing this point of view more formally, Farrell proposed a novel approach that he christened the *liberal partition*.

> *To say that the choice between two elements of S [that is the set of possible social states] is not a social one may be formalized by saying that they are "socially equivalent," where the relation of being socially equivalent is an equivalence relation on the set S. It defines a collection of subsets of S which are nonempty, disjoint, and collectively exhaustive—that is, a partition [$\mathscr{P}$] of S. ... [T]he problem of social choice is that of choosing among elements of [$\mathscr{P}$], not elements of S; once a socially equivalent subset has been selected, the choice of an element from this subset ... is not a social choice, but will be determined by the private decisions.*

Within Farrell's conceptual framework, once the liberal partition is promulgated, the problem of social choice and that of individual choices are sharply separated from each other, and Sen's impossibility of a Paretian liberal disappears once and for all. However, Farrell himself admits that this proposal is plagued with a problem of its own.

> *[T]he determination of a Liberal Partition sounds purely formal, but in practice may be anything but formal. The battle between those who want a very coarse partition and those who want a very fine one—between those who wish to leave a good deal to individual decision and those who would leave very little—has been, is, and is likely to remain a major political issue. Thus, no Liberal Partition can be determined without value judgements and political disputation, perhaps on a large scale.*

The recognition that "a frontier must be drawn between the area of private life and that of public authority" (Berlin 1969, p. 124) is certainly not new. Indeed, it goes back at least to Mill (1859/1977, p. 276) who posed this problem unambiguously:

> *What... is the rightful limit to the sovereignty of the individual over himself? Where does the authority of society begin? How much of human life should be assigned to individuality, and how much to society?*

Mill's answer to his own question was a famous, but deceptively simple, principle.

> *Each will receive its proper share, if each has that which more particularly concerns it. To individuality should belong the part of life in which it is chiefly the individual that is interested; to society, the part which chiefly interests society.*

Unfortunately, Mill's "simple principle" posed more problems than it settled, as

> *[m]en are largely interdependent, and no man's activity is so completely private as never to obstruct the lives of others in any way. "Freedom for the pike is death for the minnows"; the liberty of some must depend on the restraint of others. (Berlin 1969, p. 124)*

The fourth criticism on the social choice theoretic formulation of individual rights, which was expressed by Pattanaik and Suzumura (1994) and Suzumura (1996), focuses on whether or not the social choice rule conveys enough information for the fully-fledged analysis of individual rights. Recollect that the informational basis of a social choice rule consists solely of (a) the information contained in the description of culmination outcomes of the individual as well as social actions, which constitute the social states; (b) individual orderings over the set of social states; and (c) the feasibility and infeasibility of different social states. As long as the social states are interpreted in a conventional way, none of (a), (b), and (c) includes information about the social procedure through which the culmination social outcome is brought about. To illustrate the difficulty that may emerge from the conspicuous lack of procedural information, consider the following example due to Suzumura (1996, 1999).

Example 5 (Dividing a Cake Fairly) A father is to divide a cake among three children fairly. There are two methods to be examined. Method I is that the father himself divides this cake into three equal pieces, and tells the children to take a piece each, or leave it. Method II is that the children are given the opportunity to discuss how this cake should be divided fairly among them, and cut it into three pieces in accordance with the conclusion they agree on. If they happen to conclude that the equal division is the fair outcome, and if we are informed only of the culmination outcomes, we cannot but conclude that these two methods of decision making are the same. It is clear, however, that this is certainly inappropriate in the context where we care about individual rights. Indeed, in the case of Method I, children are not provided with any right whatsoever to participate in the process through which their distributive shares are determined, whereas in the case of Method II, they are indeed endowed with such an important right of participation.

The gist of this example is that the right to participate is an important procedural feature that we are unable to capture if our informational basis is narrowly confined to consist solely of culmination social outcomes and individual orderings defined thereupon. To bring this point into relief, let us consider the following example due to Pattanaik and Suzumura (1994).

Example 6 (Voluntary Exchange versus Central Rationing) Consider an economy endowed with a fixed bundle of commodities. Suppose that individuals are entitled to engage in voluntary exchange among themselves, and the outcome in the core is socially chosen. For simplicity, it is assumed that the core is always nonempty and consists of a single outcome. Suppose now that the social decision-making procedure is changed into the one where the central planning board assigns to each individual a consumption bundle that he would have chosen if the previous voluntary procedure were followed. As long as the culmination outcomes of social decision-making procedures are concerned, the two situations are the same, yet the structure of individual freedom and rights are substantially different between these two situations.

In order to rectify the defects uncovered by **Example 5** and **Example 6**, we should enlarge the description of social states in such a way that, not only the culmination social outcomes, but also the procedures or mechanisms through which such outcomes are chosen, are included. On reflection, Arrow (1963, pp. 90–91) made an early suggestion to this effect:[23]

> *[A]mong the variables which taken together define the social state, one is the very process by which the society makes its choice. This is especially important if the mechanism of choice itself has a*

[23] See, also, Sandmo (1990, p. 58) who made the following insightful observation:

> *Judging allocation mechanisms either by results or by the allocation processes themselves may not be a very fruitful contrast.... One problem with this approach is that it is not always clear how one should draw the distinction between outcomes and processes, because the individuals in the economy may have preferences that are partly defined over the processes themselves. Thus, one may prefer competitive markets to central planning because markets result in more consumption goods for everybody, but one may also have a preference for having one's consumption goods delivered by the market rather than by the central planning bureau.*

value to the individuals in the society. For example, an individual may have a positive preference for achieving a given distribution through the free market mechanism over achieving the same distribution through rationing by the government.

However, the use and usefulness of this extended social choice framework with the comprehensive description of social states have never been formally explored in the context of welfare and rights.[24,25]

In view of these serious criticisms on Sen's original formulation of rights and related problems, we should develop a general conceptual framework that enables us to identify and separate several distinct issues within the theory of social welfare and individual rights including the *raison d'être* of rights, the alternative formulations of rights based on the classical idea of freedom of choice in the protected personal spheres, and the initial conferment of rights. To this crucial task we should now turn.

6. FORMULATION, REALIZATION, AND INITIAL CONFERMENT OF RIGHTS

Let us begin by identifying three distinct issues, to which we should address ourselves in the fully-fledged analysis of welfare and rights. The first issue is the *formulation of rights*; the second issue is the *realization of conferred rights*; and the third issue is the *initial conferment of rights.*

It was Nozick's (1974) criticism of Sen's social choice theoretic formulation of rights that opened the gate toward several game theoretic alternatives to Sen's path-breaking attempt. Throughout the rest of this chapter, our attention will be mostly focused on

[24] Pattanaik and Suzumura (1994, 1996) made an early preliminary exploration of the new vista opened by the extended approach.

[25] It may well be thought that the clear separation between culmination outcomes and procedures through which culmination outcomes are brought about is somewhat misplaced, as we may expand the description of outcomes to include procedures through which culmination outcomes are brought about. It is true that the conceptual expansion of outcomes along this line is indeed conceivable, but doing so may accompany a substantial change of the structure of social choice theory using such an expanded concept of outcomes. To bring this point clearly home, let X be the set of narrowly defined culmination outcomes, over which each individual $i \in N$ has a preference ordering R_i, thereby forming a profile $\boldsymbol{R} = (R_1, R_2, \ldots, R_n)$ of individual preference orderings, and let $\gamma = (N, \boldsymbol{M}, g)$ be a *normal game form* that represents the procedure through which a culmination outcome is determined, where $\boldsymbol{M} := \prod_{i \in N} M_i$, M_i denotes the set of *admissible strategies* for $i \in N$, and $g : \boldsymbol{M} \to X$ denotes the *outcome function*. The pair (x, γ), where $x \in X$, may then be christened the *expanded outcome,* if we like. In order to construct a social choice theory on the basis of the concept of expanded outcomes, we need a definition of feasibility of an expanded outcome. It seems to us that the sensible definition of feasibility of an expanded outcome (x, γ) should be such that, given a profile $\boldsymbol{R}$ of individual preference orderings over the set of culmination outcomes, (x, γ) is feasible if and only if $x = g(\boldsymbol{m}^*)$ holds for some $\boldsymbol{m}^* = (m_1^*, m_2^*, \ldots, m_n^*) \in E(\gamma, \boldsymbol{R})$, where $E(\gamma, \boldsymbol{R})$ denotes the set of *equilibrium strategy profiles*. Thus, the definition of feasibility hinges squarely on the concept of an equilibrium concept as well as on the profile of individual preference orderings on the set of narrowly-defined culmination outcomes. In other words, the conceptual expansion of outcomes is surely possible, but it cannot but accompany a substantial change in the analytical framework of social choice theory.

one of these game theoretic approaches to rights, viz., the *normal game form approach* to rights, which is due to Sugden (1981, pp. 193–195; 1985), Gaertner, Pattanaik, and Suzumura (1992), Deb (1994, 1997, 2004), Deb, Pattanaik, and Razzolini (1997), Peleg (1998, 2004), van Hees (1999), and many others.[26] To motivate this approach intuitively and bring its contrast with Sen's seminal approach into clear relief, let us examine the following modified version of the Lady Chatterley's Lover Case.

Example 7 (First Variant of Lady Chatterley's Lover Case) Mr. P and Mr. L both own a copy of *Lady Chatterley's Lover.* Everything else being the same, there exist four social states, viz., $(r,r),(r,n),(n,r)$, and (n,n), where r (resp. n) denotes "to read the book" (resp. "not to read the book"). Their preference orderings over $S := \{(r,r),(r,n),(n,r),(n,n)\}$ are given as follows:

$$R_P\colon (n,n),(r,r),(r,n),(n,r)$$
$$R_L\colon (n,r),(r,n),(n,n),(r,r).$$

Following the classical libertarian tradition à la Mill of the freedom of choice within one's protected personal sphere, suppose that individuals are free to choose either to read the book or not to read it in full accordance with their respective preferences. By choosing r (resp. n), Mr. P may secure that the final social outcome will be in the subset $\{(r,r),(r,n)\}$ (resp. $\{(n,r),(n,n)\}$) of S, but he is not within his right to decide which one of these two outcomes will eventually materialize. Likewise, by choosing r (resp. n), Mr. L may secure that the final social outcome will be in the subset $\{(r,r),(n,r)\}$ (resp. $\{(r,n),(n,n)\}$) of S, but he is not within his right to decide which one of these two outcomes will eventually emerge. Thus, both Mr. P and Mr. L are facing the problem of choice under uncertainty.

Suppose, for the sake of simplicity, that both individuals follow the rationality postulate of maximin behavior under uncertainty.[27] It is straightforward to check that the

[26] An early attempt of the game theoretic formulation of rights was made in an important paper by Gärdenfors (1981). Capitalizing on the cooperative games in effectivity functional form due to Rosenthal (1972), Moulin and Peleg (1982), Moulin (1983, 1986), Peleg (1984), and many others, Deb (1994, 2004), Hammond (1996a), and Peleg (1998) explored the analysis of individual and group rights by means of effectivity function, which is used to measure the power of coalitions within a game form. At the outset of the next section, we will briefly analyze the effectivity functional approach to individual rights vis-à-vis the normal game form approach to individual rights.

[27] Given the complete ignorance about each other's preferences, there is no compelling reason why the two individuals should not follow the maximin principle of choice under uncertainty. Note, however, that the assumption of maximin behavior is not crucial in our reasoning. Indeed, given any rule of choice under uncertainty, we can modify the features of our example suitably if necessary and obtain the same inconsistency between Sen's preference-contingent formulation of rights and our intuition about individual rights under consideration. To illustrate this point, consider **Example 7** once again, and suppose that both Mr. P and Mr. L follow the rationality postulate of *maximax behavior* under uncertainty. It is easy to check that the maximax choice of Mr. P (resp. Mr. L) is n (resp. r), so that (n,r) is the maximax equilibrium outcome in **Example 7**. Note, however, that (r,r) and (n,r) differ only in Mr. P's choice of either r or n, and that Mr. P himself prefers (r,r) to (n,r). Thus, the realization of the maximax equilibrium outcome (n,r) cannot but be construed to violate Mr. P's libertarian right in the sense of Sen.

maximin choice of Mr. P (resp. Mr. L) is r (resp. n), so that (r, n) is the maximin equilibrium outcome of this game theoretic situation. Note that, intuitively speaking, there is no violation of freedom of choice in this social outcome. However, this is a clear instance of the violation of Mr. P's rights in accordance with Sen's social choice theoretic formulation of rights. To verify this observation, we have only to note that (n, n) and (r, n) differ only in Mr. P's choice of either n or r, and Mr. P himself prefers (n, n) to (r, n).

According to **Example 7**, Sen's social choice theoretic formulation of rights yields an implication that is inconsistent with the rational prediction based on the classical freedom-of-choice approach to rights. In other words, it exemplifies a prima facie violation of libertarian rights in the sense of Sen, even when there is no real violation of anyone's liberty if we follow the freedom-of-choice approach to rights.[28]

The origin of this difficulty seems easy to track down. Under our intuitive conception of the right to choose whether to read a book or not in private, the individual enjoys the power of determining a particular aspect or feature of the complete description of the society; when he makes his choice with respect to this particular aspect or feature, his choice imposes restriction on the final social outcome to the effect that this particular aspect or feature must be exactly as he chooses it to be. In contrast, Sen's approach formulates rights in terms of the complete descriptions of all aspects of the society. This contrast seems to lie at the heart of the problem.

The freedom-of-choice approach to rights may be traced back to Nozick (1974), according to which individuals directly control the matters belonging to their protected personal spheres through their actual choices. Sen (1983, 1986a, 1986b, 1992) has argued, convincingly in our judgments, against recognizing rights exclusively in terms of the exercise of such direct and actual controls. If Mr. A is a Buddhist, it may be thought that Mr. A has a right to be cremated after his death in accordance with the Buddhist rituals. However, Mr. A can hardly control this aspect of the social state directly through his actual choice, even though it may be considered to be within his protected personal sphere. To cope with this criticism, however, we have only to expand the framework so that the individual should be empowered to determine matters within his protected personal sphere *either* by his direct and actual choice of an aspect or feature of the society, *or* by entrusting some other agent to

[28] An insidious feature of the preference profile $\boldsymbol{R} = (R_P, R_L)$ appearing in **Example 7** may deserve to be identified. Observe that Mr. P prefers n to r if Mr. L chooses n, whereas Mr. P prefers r to n if Mr. L chooses r. Likewise, Mr. L prefers r to n if Mr. P chooses n, whereas Mr. L prefers n to r if Mr. P chooses r. It follows that both Mr. P and Mr. L have individual preferences that are not "privately unconditional" in the terminology of Hammond (1982). It is true that the crush between the social choice theoretic articulation of individual rights and the classical articulation of individual rights in terms of the freedom of choice will not surface if we are prepared to exclude the possibility of profiles of individual preference orderings that are not "privately unconditional." However, "it may not be very realistic to rule out altogether individual preferences [that] are not privately unconditional. Nor does it seem analytically satisfactory to use a formulation of rights [that] needs the assumption of privately unconditional individual preferences for its intuitive plausibility" (Pattanaik 1996b, p. 110).

act on his behalf in accordance with his hypothetical choice of an aspect or feature of the society. In fact, this is in full agreement with Sen's (1986a, p. 232) own assertion.

> *There is a danger that in crudely identifying liberty with direct control—overlooking the counterfactual exercises involved in individual liberty—a lot that is important might be lost.... [I]t would be a mistake to assume that considerations of liberty of a person are irrelevant in a particular choice if he himself is not making the choice.... What a person* would have chosen *if he had control is an important consideration in judging the person's liberty.*

Sen (1986a, p. 232) posed another argument against the freedom-of-choice approach to rights with due emphasis on the socially interactive nature of individual choices in the society.

> *Given the complex interdependence that operate in a society, tying together the lives of different people, it may be impossible to isolate their environment sufficiently to guarantee that each has all the controls over his or her personal life. The nature of physical and social environment makes parceling out controls into self-contained bits deeply problematic....*

To illustrate Sen's legitimate concern, let us consider the following example.[29]

Example 8 (Secondary Smoking Case) There are two passengers, Ann and Fred, in the same compartment of the train. Ann cannot stand cigarette smoke, whereas Fred is a cigarette lover. In the compartment is an authorized notice by the train company that "if your fellow-passengers object, please do not smoke." The set of feasible social outcomes is then given by $X = \{x, y, z\}$, where $x =$ "Ann objects and Fred does not smoke," $y =$ "Ann does not object and Fred smokes," and $z =$ "Ann does not object and Fred does not smoke." In the situation like this, if the decision making is completely decentralized and the individuals are left free to choose their private options directly, nothing prevents a culmination outcome, where Ann objects and Fred smokes, from occurring.

It is straightforward, however, to introduce a natural conceptual framework, which is game theoretic in nature, to accommodate socially interactive situations such as **Example 8** well within the freedom-of-choice paradigm of individual rights. To illustrate this possibility in the concrete context of **Example 8**, let us define the following normal game form:

(a) a set of players $N = \{\text{Ann, Fred}\}$;

(b) a set of admissible strategies for each player, viz., $M_{Ann} = \{s, s^*\}$ for Ann and $M_{Fred} = \{t, t^*\}$ for Fred, where $s =$ "to object," $s^* =$ "not to object," $t =$ "to smoke if not objected, not to smoke if objected," and $t^* =$ "not to smoke no matter what";

(c) a set of culmination outcomes $X = \{x, y, z\}$;

(d) an outcome function $g : M_{Ann} \times M_{Fred} \to X$ such that $g(s,t) = x$, $g(s,t^*) = x$, $g(s^*,t) = y$, and $g(s^*,t^*) = z$.

[29] This example was communicated to the author by Sen.

We may now allow Ann and Fred to have full freedom in choosing their respective admissible strategies, thereby faithfully accommodating what the freedom-of-choice approach to rights should claim in the present context of secondary smoking.

Capitalizing on the moral of **Example 8** as well as on the intuitive appeal of the classical idea of the freedom of choice in protected private spheres, let us now introduce the normal game form approach to individual rights in general terms. Formally speaking, a *normal game form* is a specification of

(a) a set N of n *players*, $N = \{1, 2, \ldots, n\}$, where $2 \leq n < +\infty$;
(b) a set M_i of *admissible strategies* for each player $i \in N$;
(c) a set X of all *feasible culmination outcomes*; and
(d) an *outcome function* g that specifies exactly one outcome $g(\boldsymbol{m}) \in X$ for each n-tuple $\boldsymbol{m} = (m_1, \ldots, m_i, \ldots, m_n)$ of admissible strategies, one admissible strategy $m_i \in M_i$ for each and every player $i \in N$.

The formal contents of normal game form rights are nothing other than the complete freedom of each and every individual to choose his/her admissible strategy, and the obligation of all individuals not to choose inadmissible strategies. If we accept the game form formulation of rights, the formal contents of rights are completely independent of individual preferences over culmination outcomes. This is in sharp contrast with Sen's social choice theoretic formulation of rights in terms of the preference-contingent power of rejection. Indeed, if a game form $\gamma = (N, \boldsymbol{M}, g)$ captures the formal contents of rights, where $\boldsymbol{M} = \Pi_{i \in N} M_i$ is the set of admissible strategy profiles, there is no role whatsoever to be assigned to the profile of individual preference orderings over culmination outcomes as far as the formal contents of rights are concerned.

Needless to say, the concept of individual preferences over culmination outcomes plays an indispensable role in the *realization of conferred game form rights*. Indeed, when the profile $\boldsymbol{R} = (R_1, R_2, \ldots, R_n) \in \mathcal{R}$ of individual preference orderings on the set X of culmination outcomes is revealed, and the game form γ represents the description of rights conferred in the society, we obtain a fully-fledged *game* $(\gamma, \boldsymbol{R})$. The realization of conferred rights in the game form approach is formally described by the equilibrium of this game.

At this juncture of our discourse, further clarifying remarks on the game form formulation of rights may be in order. In the first place, it should be obvious that the notion of game forms, by itself, has very little to do with rights. What we are asserting is that rights are best described as normal game forms, where the admissible strategy set of each player is construed to be the set of legally or socially admissible action plans for him, and the outcome function embodies the rule through which the culmination outcome corresponding to the profile of admissible strategies is determined.[30] As a matter of fact, there are numerous game forms in various social contexts in which the question of rights does not arise at all. This being the case, it is the specific *interpretation* of the set of admissible strategies and the outcome function that determines whether the normal game form properly captures some rights or not.[31]

In the second place, it is *not* our claim that the switch from Sen's preference-contingent formulation of rights to the game form formulation of rights, by itself, can resolve Sen's impossibility of a Paretian liberal. In our judgments, Sen's impossibility theorem captures a deep conflict between social welfare and individual rights, which cannot be dissipated simply by replacing Sen's social choice theoretic approach to rights with the game form approach to rights. To bring this important point unambiguously home, consider the following further variant of the Lady Chatterley's Lover Case. Incidentally, this example serves to reveal that Sen's impossibility of a Paretian liberal has a close connection with the classical *prisoners' dilemma*.[32]

Example 9 (Second Variant of Lady Chatterley's Lover Case) Mr. P and Mr. L both own a copy of *Lady Chatterley's Lover*. Everything else being the same, there exist four social states, viz., $(r,r),(r,n),(n,r)$, and (n,n), where r (resp. n) denotes "to read the book" (resp. "not to read the book"). Their preference orderings over $S := \{(r,r),(r,n),(n,r),(n,n)\}$ are given as follows:

$$R_P: (n,n),(r,n),(n,r),(r,r)$$

$$R_L: (r,r),(r,n),(n,r),(n,n).$$

Individuals are free to choose either to read the book or not to read it in full accordance with their respective preferences. A salient feature of this profile is that there exists a

[30] At the risk of emphasizing what may be obvious, let us remind ourselves that the game form formulation should not be construed as recognizing the rights of an individual simply as a matter of his freedom of choice from his own set of admissible strategies. This is because an individual's rights might sometimes be secured only through an appropriate specification of admissible strategies of other individuals. For example, if an individual's right involves his immunity from certain invasive actions of other individuals, the game form formulation should capture such immunity through an appropriate specification of admissible strategies of these other individuals. See Sen (1992), Gaertner, Pattanaik, and Suzumura (1992), and Pattanaik (1996a) for discussions on this and related issues.

[31] In Sen's social choice theoretic formulation of rights as well, it is not the formal specification of decisive power of individuals as such, but the specific interpretation of the intuitive basis of such decisive power, which brings rights into the picture. Sen (1970a/1979, p. 89) was careful enough to point out that the acceptability of his formulation of rights will "depend on the nature of the alternatives that are offered for choice," and "if the choices are all non-personal, e.g., whether or not to outlaw untouchability, to declare war against another country," his formulation "should not have much appeal." It is only when two social alternatives are interpreted as differing solely with respect to someone's personal life that his formulation of rights was intended to be of relevance.

[32] The close relationship between the prisoners' dilemma and the Paretian liberal paradox was first pointed out in print by Fine (1975). Sen informed me that it was Thomas Schelling who first pointed it out verbally in the first seminar presentation of Sen (1970a) at Harvard University.

dominant strategy for each of Mr. P and Mr. L. Thus, whatever Mr. L's (resp. Mr. P's) choice may happen to be, Mr. P (resp. Mr. L) prefers n (resp. r) to r (resp. n), so that n (resp. r) constitutes Mr. P's (resp. Mr. L's) dominant strategy. Thus, (n, r) is the dominant strategy equilibrium of this game. Note, however, that this dominant strategy equilibrium is Pareto dominated by (r, n), which is another vindication of the impossibility of a Paretian liberal.

Thus, the main thrust of the impossibility of a Paretian liberal does not disappear simply by replacing Sen's social choice theoretic formulation of rights by the normal game form formulation thereof. As Arrow (1951/1963, p. 109) acutely observed in the context of his own general impossibility theorem, "[t]he paradox of social choice cannot be so easily exorcized." Indeed, Deb, Pattanaik, and Razzolini (1997) examined systematically the possible recurrence of the impossibility of a Paretian liberal within the game form approach to rights. We will have more to say on this issue in the next section.

In the third place, we must specify an equilibrium concept if we want to predict the equilibrium outcome of the libertarian game. Riley (1989, p. 143) claimed that the selection of an appropriate equilibrium concept for libertarian game is "an important issue." In his perception, if the Nash equilibrium in pure strategy is adopted as the equilibrium concept, and if no such equilibrium exists, it is a sure-fire proof that the game form formulation of rights is defective, as it "is unable to explain or justify a particular outcome" (Riley 1989, p. 147). As was aptly emphasized by Sugden (1993), however, the game form approach to rights "is not intended to explain or justify outcomes: it is intended to explain or justify procedures. From the viewpoint of the procedural approach, respect for rights is a property of the rules of the decision-making procedure used in the society.... [W]hatever problems there may be in predicting the outcome of the game, there is no incoherence in the underlying conception of rights" (1993, p. 134).

In the fourth place, the game form approach can shed light on the fact that the informational basis of social choice rules is altogether ill-suited for the articulation of individual rights. To illustrate this difficulty, we have only to consider **Example 7** once again. It was shown that the maximin behavior adopted by Mr. P and Mr. L leads us into the maximin equilibrium outcome (r, n). In this case, the rights-respecting society must settle for (r, n). As we have done in footnote 26, suppose that Mr. P and Mr. L change their risk attitude and adopt instead the maximax behavior. Even if the feasible set of social alternatives remains the same at $S := \{(r, r), (r, n), (n, r), (n, n)\}$ and the profile of individual preference orderings remains the same at $\boldsymbol{R} = (R_P, R_L)$, the culmination outcome will change in accordance with this change in the individual behavior into the maximax equilibrium outcome (n, r). In this case, the rights-respecting society must settle for (n, r). It should be clear that this rights-respecting social choice procedure cannot be captured in terms of a social choice rule whose informational basis consists solely of individual preference orderings and the set of socially feasible outcomes.

In the fifth and last place, how does the society decide which strategies should or should not be admitted to a specific player, and how should the society decide on a culmination outcome that would prevail under a specified profile of admissible strategies? In other words, how should rights be conferred to individuals in the first place within the game form formulation of rights? This problem was posed by Gaertner, Pattanaik, and Suzumura (1992), but they did not pursue it to the logical end. Sen (1992, p. 155) responded to their suggestion by saying that

> *Gaertner* et al. *(1992) do, in fact, pose the question, "How does the society decide which strategies should or should not be admissible for a specific player in a given context?" This, as they rightly note, is "an important question."... [I]t is precisely on the answer to this further question that the relationship between the game form formulations and social choice formulations depend... We must not be too impressed by the "form" of the "game forms." We have to examine its contents and its rationale. The correspondence with social choice formulations becomes transparent precisely there.*

It is to this important question of initial conferment of normal game form rights that we will turn in Section 8. Before coming to this task, however, we should examine how Gibbard's paradox and Sen's paradox will fare in the game form approach to rights. Section 7 will be devoted to this examination.

7. LIBERAL PARADOXES WITH GAME FORM RIGHTS

7.1. Power Structure Generated by Game Form Rights

Recollect that the essence of Sen's formulation of individual rights lies in the preference-contingent power of rejection that is conferred to each individual, according to which a culmination outcome $y \in X$ is prohibited to be socially chosen from the opportunity set S such that $\emptyset \neq S \subseteq X$ if only there exists a social alternative $x \in S$ such that (a) x and y differ only in some individual's personal feature, and (b) this individual himself prefers x to y. In contrast, the definition of normal game form rights has nothing to do with individual preferences on the set of culmination outcomes. It follows that each individual, who is endowed with the normal game form rights, is incapable of exercising any such preference-contingent power of rejection. Note, however, that those individuals with the normal game form rights have some definite power that is not contingent on their individual preferences on the set of culmination outcomes. To bring this simple point clearly home, consider the normal game form $\gamma = (N, \boldsymbol{M}, g)$, where $\boldsymbol{M} = \prod_{i \in N} M_i$. For each $i \in N$ and each $m_i \in M_i$, let a subset $g(m_i; \boldsymbol{M}_{-i})$ of X be defined by

$$g(m_i; \boldsymbol{M}_{-i}) = \{g(m_i; \boldsymbol{m}_{-i}) \in X | \boldsymbol{m}_{-i} \in \boldsymbol{M}_{-i}\},$$

where $\boldsymbol{M}_{-i} = \prod_{j \neq i} M_j$. Note that, subject to the condition that nobody ever adopts any inadmissible strategy, the individual $i \in N$ is capable of restricting the realizable culmination outcomes to the set $g(m_i; \boldsymbol{M}_{-i}) \subseteq X$ by choosing his own admissible strategy $m_i \in M_i$, no matter how the other individuals choose their admissible strategies. It is in this sense that each individual is said to be endowed with the power under the normal game form formulation of individual rights. It is clear that such a power of each individual is not contingent on individual preferences on the set of culmination outcomes.

Before proceeding any further, several remarks on the nature of normal game form rights and the power these normal game forms confer to individuals may be in order. To begin with, one of the potential drawbacks of normal game form formulation of individual rights is that it may be placing too much emphasis on the procedural details of how a culmination outcome is brought about when we are in fact focusing on the relevant individual's capability to secure some features of culmination outcomes. For example, we may be interested in whether each individual is capable of getting back some objects from another individual, to whom the relevant individual has rented these objects in the past, no matter what procedure is invoked in the process of securing the desired culmination outcome as long as nobody uses an inadmissible strategy en route. In the case such as this, we may focus on the power that each individual is conferred under the specified normal game form rather than on the procedural details of the normal game form itself.

In the second place, there are several methods to measure the *power to control* and the *power to delegate* held by coalitions of individuals under the normal game form. The former can be captured by means of the *effectivity function*, which is due to Moulin and Peleg (1982), Moulin (1983, 1986), and Peleg (1984, 1998, 2004), whereas the latter can be captured by means of the *waiver function*, which is due to Deb (1994, 2004). To make matters precise, consider the normal game form $\gamma = (N, \boldsymbol{M}, g)$, where $\boldsymbol{M} = \prod_{i \in N} M_i$ and, for each $L \subseteq N, \boldsymbol{M}_L = \prod_{i \in L} M_i$. An individual or a group of individuals is said to be *effective* for a subset $S \subseteq X$ if the individual or the group of individuals can choose the respective admissible strategies in such a way as to restrict the culmination outcomes into the set S.[33] To be precise, the effectivity function E^{γ} of the normal game form γ assigns to each and every coalition $L \subseteq N$ a family of subsets of the set $g(\boldsymbol{M}) = A \subseteq X$ of culmination outcomes, to be denoted by $E^{\gamma}(L)$, such that for any set $S \in E^{\gamma}(L)$ there exists $\boldsymbol{m}_L \in \boldsymbol{M}_L$ that is capable of ensuring that $g(\boldsymbol{m}_L; \boldsymbol{m}_{N-L}) \in S$ for all $\boldsymbol{m}_{N-L} \in \boldsymbol{M}_{N-L}$. As a matter of fact, to capture the essence of such a power, it is sufficient to identify the minimal elements of $E^{\gamma}(L)$ for each $L \subseteq N$. Let the *basis* of E^{γ}, to be denoted by E^{γ}_*, be defined as the function that identifies the minimal elements of E^{γ} in the set-inclusion sense. It should be clear that E^{γ} can be derived from E^{γ}_* by adding all the subsets of $g(\boldsymbol{M}) = A \subseteq X$ that are supersets of elements in $E^{\gamma}_*(L)$ for each $L \subseteq N$. As an alternative way to capture the power of an individual or a group of individuals under the normal game form γ, let us introduce the concept of a waiver function W^{γ} that assigns to every

[33] The concept of effectivity used in the text is that of *alpha-effectivity*. See Moulin (1983) and Peleg (1984).

coalition $L \subseteq N$ a family of subsets of the set $g(\boldsymbol{M}) = A \subseteq X$ of culmination outcomes, to be denoted by $W^{\gamma}(L)$ such that, for any set $S \in W^{\gamma}(L)$, there exists $\boldsymbol{m}_L \in \boldsymbol{M}_L$, such that, for every $x \in S$, there exists $\boldsymbol{m}_{N-L} \in \boldsymbol{M}_{N-L}$ that satisfies $g(\boldsymbol{m}_L; \boldsymbol{m}_{N-L}) = x$.

Although the effectivity function E^{γ} as well as the waiver function W^{γ} captures some aspects of the power of individuals under the normal game form γ, they are, in general, different from each other. Indeed, it was shown by Deb (1994, Proposition 1) that there exists a coalition L satisfying $\emptyset \subset L \subset N$ such that $E^{\gamma}(L) \neq W^{\gamma}(L)$. To dig deeper into the concept of power under the normal game form, let us begin by exemplifying the use and usefulness of E_*^{γ} and W_*^{γ} in terms of the following example.

Example 10 (The State versus Nozick (Nozick 1974, Sen 1976, Deb 1994)**)** Consider the normal game form $\gamma = (N, \boldsymbol{M}, g)$, where $N = \{\text{State, Nozick}\}$ and $\boldsymbol{M} = M_{State} \times M_{Nozick}$. The state has three strategies, viz., $M_{State} = \{m_1^S, m_2^S, m_3^S\}$, where m_1^S = "to force Nozick to live in Boston," m_2^S = "to force Nozick to live in New York," and m_3^S = "to allow Nozick to choose between living in Boston and living in New York," whereas Nozick has two strategies, viz., $M_{Nozick} = \{m_1^N, m_2^N\}$, where m_1^N = "to live in Boston if the state does not prevent him from doing so; to live in New York if the state forces him to do so," and m_2^N = "to live in New York if the state does not prevent him from doing so; to live in Boston if the state forces him to do so." The outcome function g is defined as follows:

$$g(m_1^S, m_1^N) = g(m_1^S, m_2^N) = g(m_3^S, m_1^N) = \{B\};$$
$$g(m_2^S, m_1^N) = g(m_2^S, m_2^N) = g(m_3^S, m_2^N) = \{NY\}.$$

The basis E_*^{γ} of the effectivity function E^{γ} and the basis W_*^{γ} of the waiver function W^{γ} are as follows:

$$E_*^{\gamma}(\{\text{Nozick}\}) = \{\{B, NY\}\}; E_*^{\gamma}(\{\text{State}\}) = \{\{B\}, \{NY\}\};$$
$$W_*^{\gamma}(\{\text{Nozick}\}) = W_*^{\gamma}(\{\text{State}\}) = \{\{B, NY\}\}.$$

It follows from $E_*^{\gamma}(\{\text{Nozick}\}) = \{\{B, NY\}\}$ that Nozick is powerless under the normal game form γ. The fact that Nozick's right to waive is trivial arises from this lack of power, but it cannot be captured if we observe only the basis W_*^{γ} of the waiver function W^{γ}. Although the fact that the state is all-powerful within the normal game form γ can be understood from the basis E_*^{γ} of the effectivity function E^{γ}, we need the assistance of the basis W_*^{γ} of the waiver function W^{γ} in order to confirm that the state's power to assign Nozick to Boston or to New York is not the state's obligation but the state's right. This observation should be sufficient to conclude that E_*^{γ} and W_*^{γ} are not only different in general, but they are complementary with each other for the purpose of describing rights under the normal game form.

If the basis of the effectivity function, E_*^{γ}, and the basis of the waiver function, W_*^{γ}, are identical, then the effectivity function E^{γ} and the waiver function W^{γ} contain the same information about rights in the normal game form γ. Deb (1994) identified a necessary and sufficient condition for this identity to hold, which reads as follows.

Condition SD: Sufficient Distinctness For any individual $i \in N$, any two strategies m_i and m_i^* are sufficiently distinct in the sense that some culmination outcome that is possible under m_i is ruled out by m_i^*, and some culmination outcome that is possible under m_i^* is ruled out by m_i.

It is shown that the following proposition holds true.

Theorem 10 (Deb 1994, Proposition 3) *The following statements are mutually equivalent:*

(a) *Condition* **SD** *is satisfied.*
(b) *For any $i \in N$, there exists a one-to-one onto mapping between $E_*^\gamma(\{i\})$ and M_i and between $W_*^\gamma(\{i\})$ and M_i.*
(c) *For any $L \subseteq N$, $E_*^\gamma(L) = W_*^\gamma(L)$.*

According to **Theorem 10**, $E_*^\gamma = W_*^\gamma$ holds if and only if Condition **SD** is satisfied, and one of the important aspects of the normal game form, viz., the strategy sets, can be identified by virtue of (b), in the sense that the number of admissible strategies is known to us for each and every individual. However, this important fact falls short of identifying the various culmination outcomes that arise from any strategy profile. Those readers who are interested in knowing if and when the full recoverability of normal game form from the bases $E_*^\gamma = W_*^\gamma$ is guaranteed are cordinally invited to consult Deb (1994). See also Deb (2004).

To pose a more general problem of representing an effectivity function by a normal game form, a general effectivity function $E : 2^N \to 2^X$ is defined as a correspondence that satisfies the following four conditions:

$$(i)\ E(\emptyset) = X; (ii)\ E(N) = 2^X - \{\emptyset\}; (iii)\ \forall L \subseteq N : \emptyset \notin E(L); (iv)\ \forall L \subseteq N : X \in E(L).$$

If there exists a normal game form $\gamma = (N, \boldsymbol{M}, g)$, where $g(\boldsymbol{M}) = X$, such that $E^\gamma(L) = E(L)$ holds for all $L \subseteq N$, the effectivity function E is said to be representable by the normal game form γ. Alternatively, the normal game form γ is said to be a representation of the effectivity function E. The following proposition identifies a set of necessary and sufficient conditions for an effectivity function to be representable by a normal game form.

Theorem 11 (Moulin 1983, Peleg 1998) *The effectivity function E is representable by the normal game form γ if and only if the following conditions are satisfied:*

(a) ***Super Additivity***: *For every $L_1, L_2 \subseteq N$, every $B_1 \in E(L_1)$, and every $B_2 \in E(L_2)$, $L_1 \cap L_2 = \emptyset$ implies $B_1 \cap B_2 \in E(L_1 \cup L_2)$;*
(b) ***Monotonicity***: *For every $L \subseteq N$ and every $B \in E(L), B \subseteq C \subseteq X$ implies $C \in E(L)$.*

According to **Theorem 11**, the concept of rights defined in terms of the effectivity functions corresponds precisely to the concept of rights defined in terms of the normal game forms under the natural conditions of super additivity and monotonicity. It is true that there is no guarantee that the normal game form representation of the effectivity function is unique, but the multiple normal game form representations of the same effectivity function are *equivalent* in the sense defined in precise terms by Hammond (1996a). In other words, as long as we are ready to accept super additivity and monotonicity as natural constraints on the admissible class of effectivity functions, we may essentially identify the normal game form articulation of rights and the articulation of rights by means of effectivity functions.

In the third place, there exists a conspicuous claim in the literature to the effect that Sen's formulation of individual rights and normal game form formulation of individual rights are equivalent. To highlight the contrast between Sen's formulation and game form formulation in view of this claim, which is due to Riley (1989/1990) and Hammond (1995), let us consider the following canonical example.

Example 11 (Color Choice Case) There are two individuals, viz., $N = \{1,2\}$, and four feasible social alternatives, viz., $X = \{(b,b),(b,w),(w,b),(w,w)\}$. For mnemonic convenience, let b (resp. w) stand for "blue shirt" (resp. "white shirt"). Thus, the social alternative (b,w) is the one where individual 1 wears blue shirt and individual 2 wears white shirt, everything else remaining the same. Similarly for social alternatives (b,b), (w,b), and (w,w). Consider the following profile $\boldsymbol{R} = (R_1, R_2)$ of individual preference orderings:

$$R_1\colon (b,b),(w,w),(b,w),(w,b),$$

$$R_2\colon (b,w),(w,b),(w,w),(b,b).$$

The problem of libertarian rights involved in this situation can be neatly analyzed along the line of Sen's formulation of individual rights as well as the normal game form formulation of individual rights.

To begin with, let f be the social choice rule embodying Sen's requirement of libertarian rights, and define $C^{\boldsymbol{R}} = f(\boldsymbol{R})$. Applying the social choice function $C^{\boldsymbol{R}}$ to the opportunity set $S = X$, we may easily confirm that $C^{\boldsymbol{R}}(S)$ cannot but be empty in view of Sen's requirement of libertarian rights, thereby vindicating the Gibbard paradox. Turning to the normal game form formulation of individual rights, the essential feature of libertarianism in the context of color choice case can be captured by means of the game form $\gamma = (N, \boldsymbol{M}, g)$, where $M_i = \{b, w\}$ denotes individual i's set of admissible strategies $(i = 1,2)$, $\boldsymbol{M} = M_1 \times M_2$, and g denotes the outcome function satisfying $g(s,t) = (s,t)$ for all $(s,t) \in \boldsymbol{M}$. Since the full content of libertarianism captured by means of the normal game form γ is exhausted by the complete freedom of each and every individual to choose his admissible strategy, and the obligation of all individuals not to choose inadmissible strategies, there is no counterpart of the Gibbard paradox in the normal game form approach to individual rights. In view of this substantial difference between the two conceptions of individual rights, the Riley–Hammond claim of the equivalence between Sen's conception of individual rights and the game form conception of individual rights seems to be hard to sustain from an intuitive point of view.

It is true that the fully fledged two-person game $G = (\gamma, \boldsymbol{R})$ in **Example 11** does not have any Nash equilibrium outcome. Thus, a game theorist might find it hard to predict what outcome would emerge through the game theoretic interactions between the two individuals. However, the nonexistence of a Nash equilibrium for the game G has no relevance for judging whether or not the two individuals are assured of their libertarian rights. This is the claim made by the initial proponents of the normal game form approach to rights. See Gaertner, Pattanaik, and Suzumura (1992), and Sugden (1985, 1993, 1994), among others.

7.2. Gibbard Paradox with Game Form Rights

Let us remind ourselves that our verdict in the previous subsection on the Gibbard paradox within the normal game form approach to rights, to the effect that *there exists no counterpart of the Gibbard paradox in the context of normal game form rights*, hinges squarely on one specific interpretation of the Gibbard paradox. According to this interpretation, which is commonly held by most, if not all, proponents of game form rights, the essence of game form rights lies in its procedural nature in conspicuous contrast with the preference-contingent Sen rights that focus on the culmination outcomes. As long as all individuals are entitled to choose their admissible strategies without outside prohibition or interference, there is no violation of conferred normal game form rights. This remains true even in the case where the realized profile of individual preference orderings on the set of culmination outcomes is such that the normal game form embodying rights results in the fully-fledged game without any Nash equilibrium in pure strategies whatsoever.[34] However, there are several scholars who construe the Gibbard paradox differently. For these scholars, the essence of the Gibbard paradox is nothing other than the nonexistence of culmination outcome for social choice after the exercise of conferred individual rights *without invoking anything else such as the welfaristic Pareto principle.* If we subscribe to this alternative interpretation of the Gibbard paradox, the nonexistence of the Nash equilibrium in pure strategies for the game, the rules of which being

[34] The use of mixed strategies will solve the problem of this nonexistence of Nash equilibrium, but the use of mixed strategies does not seem to be appealing in the context of the consistency of normal game form rights. The use of alternative equilibrium concepts may have some relevance in this salvage operation, but we will not go into this potentially fruitful territory in the rest of this chapter.

prescribed by the normal game form embodying procedural rights along the line of game form approach to individual rights, is the sure-fire manifestation of the Gibbard paradox. The task of this subsection is to have a brief overview of works pursued along this alternative interpretation of the Gibbard paradox.

To prepare for this overview, let us say that a normal game form $\gamma = (N, \boldsymbol{M}, g)$ is *Nash solvable* if and only if, for any profile $\boldsymbol{R} = (R_1, R_2, \ldots, R_n)$ of individual preference orderings on the set of culmination outcomes, the corresponding noncooperative game $G = (\gamma, \boldsymbol{R})$ has at least one Nash equilibrium in pure strategies. We may then assert that, in order for the normal game form γ to represent rights, which are free from the Gibbard paradox, it is necessary and sufficient that γ is Nash solvable. In the special case where $n = \#N = 2$, a necessary and sufficient condition for γ to be Nash solvable is known to be as follows:[35]

Condition T: Tightness For any $L \subseteq N$ and any $\emptyset \subset B \subseteq X$, if $B \notin E^{\gamma}(L)$, then $X - B \in E^{\gamma}(N - L)$.

In the case where $3 \leq n = \#N$, however, Condition **T** is neither necessary nor sufficient for Nash solvability of the normal game form γ. Thus, the task for those who want to identify the escape route from the Gibbard paradox is precisely to find the condition for the Nash solvability of the normal game form γ in the case where $3 \leq n = \#N$.

As a preliminary step, let a subset $\boldsymbol{A}_i^{\gamma}$ of X be defined for each $i \in N$ by

$$\boldsymbol{A}_i^{\gamma} = \{g(m_i; \boldsymbol{M}_{-i}) | m_i \in M_i\}$$

and let $\boldsymbol{A}^{\gamma}$ be defined by $\boldsymbol{A}^{\gamma} = \prod_{i \in N} \boldsymbol{A}_i^{\gamma}$. A normal game form γ is said to be *rectangular* if the following conditions are satisfied:

(a) For all $(A_1, A_2, \ldots, A_n) \in \boldsymbol{A}^{\gamma}$: $\#(\cap_{i \in N} A_i) = 1$; and
(b) For all $x \in X$, there exists some $(A_1, A_2, \ldots, A_n) \in \boldsymbol{A}^{\gamma}$ such that $\{x\} = \cap_{i \in N} A_i$.

The importance of the concept of rectangular normal game form lies in the following theorem:[36]

Theorem 12 (Gurvich 1978, Abdou 1998a) *Within the class of rectangular normal game forms, Condition* **T** *on* γ *is necessary and sufficient for Nash solvability of* γ.

As long as the class of rectangular normal game forms is concerned, **Theorem 12** provides us with a complete characterization of Nash solvability of each and every admissible normal game form γ by means of the tightness thereof. This is theoretically satisfying, but

35 See Gurvich (1978, 1989). See also Abdou and Keiding (1991), Moulin (1983), and Peleg (1984, 1998, 2004).
36 See also Abdou (1998b) for this and other conditions for Nash solvability of normal game forms.

the implication of the crucial condition of rectangularity in terms of individual libertarian rights is not clear, to say the least.

There is yet another attempt to characterize the Nash solvability of normal game forms, which is due to Peleg *et al.* (2002). A crucial difference from the approach due to Gurvich (1978, 1989) and Abdou (1998a, 1998b) is that Peleg *et al.* (2002) take off from the admissible class of effectivity functions rather than the admissible class of normal game forms, where the conditions for admissibility are specified by Condition **SA** (super additivity) and Condition **M** (monotonicity), and identify the condition for each admissible effectivity function to have a Nash solvable normal game form representation. To the extent that the specified admissibility conditions may make intuitive sense in terms of the power conferred to the coalitions of individuals, the characterization by Peleg *et al.* (2002) may be of much relevance in the context of the Gibbard paradox on the consistency of game-theoretic articulation of libertarianism. As a preliminary step, the *polar* of the effectivity function E is defined as an effectivity function E^P such that:

(a) $E^P(\emptyset) = \emptyset$; and
(b) $\forall L$ s.t. $\emptyset \subset L \subseteq N$: $E^P(L) = \{\emptyset \subset S \subseteq X | \forall S^* \in E(N-L): S \cap S^* \neq \emptyset\}$.

It is then asserted that:

Theorem 13 (Peleg *et al.* 2002) *A necessary and sufficient condition for a super additive and monotone effectivity function E to have a representation by a Nash solvable normal game form* γ^E *is that the following condition holds true:*

$$(\mathbf{NS})[\forall i \in N: A_i \in E^P(\{i\})] \Rightarrow [\cap_{i \in N} A_i \neq \emptyset].$$

Furthermore, the Nash solvable normal game form representation γ^E *of E is such that, for each profile* $\mathbf{R}$ *of individual preference orderings, the game* $G^E = (\gamma^E, \mathbf{R})$ *has a Pareto efficient Nash equilibrium culmination outcome.*

Note that the second part of **Theorem 13** has strong relevance to the issue of Pareto libertarian paradox in the context of normal game form rights. To this issue we now turn.

7.3. Pareto Libertarian Paradox with Game Form Rights

Although the normal game form rights are proposed as a viable alternative to the Sen rights defined by means of preference-contingent power of rejection, there is no claim that the Pareto libertarian paradox will disappear just by replacing the Sen rights with the normal game form rights. To confirm this crucial fact, the best way seems to have another look at **Example 9**.

Example 9* (Pareto Libertarian Paradox with Normal Game Form Rights (1)) A normal game form $\gamma = (N, \boldsymbol{M}, g)$ is defined by $N = \{\text{Mr. P, Mr. L}\}$, $\boldsymbol{M} = M_P \times M_L$, where $M_P = M_L = \{n, r\}$, is the set of admissible profiles of strategies, and the outcome function g is defined by $g(m_P, m_L) = (m_P, m_L)$ for all $(m_P, m_L) \in \boldsymbol{M}$. Suppose that the profile $\boldsymbol{R}$ of individual preference orderings is given by $\boldsymbol{R} = (R_P, R_L)$, where

$$R_P\colon (n,n), (r,n), (n,r), (r,r),$$
$$R_L\colon (r,r), (r,n), (n,r), (n,n)$$

as in **Example 9**. Then the set $NE(G)$ of all Nash equilibrium outomes of the non-cooperative game $G = (\gamma, \boldsymbol{R})$ is given by $NE(G) = \{(n,r)\}$, and the unique Nash equilibrium outcome (n,r) is Pareto-dominated by (r,n). This is the clear manifestation of the Pareto libertarian paradox in the present context of normal game form rights.

Thus, the normal game form rights is not a sure-fire antidote against the Pareto libertarian paradox. Note that the situation given by **Example 9*** is such that *all* the Nash equilibrium outcomes are Pareto-dominated by other admissible culmination outcome. To see that this feature is not intrinsic to the Pareto libertarian paradox within the normal game form rights, consider the following another variant of **Example 9**:

Example 9 (Pareto Libertarian Paradox with Normal Game Form Rights (2))** *Suppose that a normal game form* $\gamma = (N, \boldsymbol{M}, g)$ *is the same as that in* **Example 9***. *Let the profile* $\boldsymbol{R}^*$ *of individual preference orderings be given by* $\boldsymbol{R}^* = (R_P^*, R_L^*)$, *where*

$$R_P^*\colon (n,r), (r,r), (r,n), (n,n),$$
$$R_L^*\colon (n,r), (n,n), (r,n), (r,r).$$

Then the set $NE(G^*)$ *of all Nash equilibriunm outcomes of the noncooperative game* $G^* = (\gamma, \boldsymbol{R}^*)$ *is given by* $NE(G^*) = \{(n,r), (r,n)\}$. *Note that one of the Nash equilibrium outcomes* (r,n) *is Pareto-dominated by* (n,r), *whereas the other Nash equilibrium outcome* (n,r) *is Pareto undominated by any other feasible culmination outcome.*

It is with the contrast between the situation such as **Example 9*** and the situation such as **Example 9**** in mind that Deb, Pattanaik, and Razzolini (1997) set about classifying the instances of Pareto libertarian paradox with the normal game form rights.

There are two senses in which a conflict surfaces between the welfaristic principle of Pareto efficiency and the normal game form rights conferred to individuals.

Pareto Libertarian Paradox in the Weak Sense

Given a normal game form γ that embodies conferred individual rights, the normal game form rights are in conflict with the Pareto principle in the *weak* sense if and only if there exists some profile $\boldsymbol{R} = (R_1, R_2, \ldots, R_n)$ of individual preference orderings such that the set of Nash equilibrium outcomes of the game $G = (\gamma, \boldsymbol{R})$ to be denoted by $NE(G)$ is nonempty, and there exists *some* $x \in NE(G)$ that is Pareto dominated by some other feasible culmination outcome.

Pareto Libertarian Paradox in the Strong Sense
Given a normal game form γ that embodies conferred individual rights, the normal game form rights are in conflict with the Pareto principle in the *strong* sense if and only if there exists some profile $\boldsymbol{R} = (R_1, R_2, \ldots, R_n)$ of individual preference ordering such that the set of Nash equilibrium outcomes of the game $G = (\gamma, \boldsymbol{R})$ is nonempty, and *every* $x \in NE(G)$ is Pareto dominated by some other feasible culmination outcome.

Within this conceptual framework, Deb, Pattanaik, and Razzolini (1997) identified the conditions in terms of the nature of the normal game form, under which the weak and strong versions of the Pareto libertarian paradox surface. Let us begin with the weak version of the Pareto libertarian paradox. For our present purpose, it suffices if we state a simple special case of the general theorem established by Deb, Pattanaik, and Razzolini:[37]

Theorem 14 *Let γ be a normal game form. Then there exists a profile $\boldsymbol{R} = (R_1, R_2, \ldots, R_n)$ of individual preference orderings such that the game $G = (\gamma, \boldsymbol{R})$ has a Nash equilibrium outcome $x \in NE(G)$, where x is Pareto dominated by some other feasible outcome if there exist a culmination outcome $y \in g(\boldsymbol{M}) = A \subseteq X$ and a strategy profile $\boldsymbol{m} \in \boldsymbol{M}$ such that $y \notin g(M_i; \boldsymbol{m}_{-i})$ holds for all $i \in N$.*

Let us conclude this discussion of the weak libertarian paradox by observing that the sufficiency condition identified by **Theorem 14** is indeed satisfied by **Example 9****. To verify this fact, let $y \in g(\boldsymbol{M}) = X$ and $\boldsymbol{m} \in \boldsymbol{M}$ be defined by $y = g(n, r) = (n, r)$ and $\boldsymbol{m} = (r, n)$. Then we have $y \notin g(M_P, m_L) = \{(r, n), (n, n)\}$ and $y \notin g(m_P, M_L) = \{(r, r), (r, n)\}$, so that the condition identified by **Theorem 14** is satisfied. This is satisfying to some reasonable extent, but the identified condition does not seem to have any appealing interpretation from the viewpoint of libertarianism.

Turn now to the strong version of the Pareto libertarian paradox. As an auxiliary step, let us define, for every individual $i \in N$ and every strategy $m_i \in M_i$, the set $A(m_i)$ of all $x \in g(\boldsymbol{M}) = A \subseteq X$ such that, for some $\boldsymbol{m}_{-i} \in \boldsymbol{M}_{-i}$, $x = g(m_i; \boldsymbol{m}_{-i})$, viz., $A(m_i) = g(m_i; \boldsymbol{M}_{-i})$ for every $i \in N$ and every $m_i \in M_i$. We may then define the following:

Condition DVP: Dichotomous Veto Power The normal game form $\gamma = (N, \boldsymbol{M}, g)$ confers dichotomous veto power on every individual in the sense that, for every $i \in N$, the set A of culmination outcomes can be partitioned into two nonempty subsets A_i^* and A_i^{**} of A such that [for every $m_i \in M_i : \{(A(m_i) \subseteq A_i^*) \vee (A(m_i) \subseteq A_i^{**})\}$], [for some $m_i \in M_i : A(m_i) \subseteq A_i^*$], and [for some $m_i \in M_i : A(m_i) \subseteq A_i^{**}$].

This condition, which was introduced by Deb, Pattanaik, and Razzolini (1997), is demonstrably sufficient to ensure that the strong Pareto libertarian paradox holds.[38]

[37] Proposition 1 of Deb *et al.* (1997) identified a necessary and sufficient condition for the weak Pareto libertarian paradox to hold, where the relevant equilibrium concept is that of *dominant strategy equilibrium*.
[38] See Deb, Pattanaik, and Razzolini (1997, Proposition 5) for a generalization of this theorem.

Theorem 15 *Let γ be a normal game form that satisfies Condition* **DVP**. *Then there exists a profile* $\boldsymbol{R} = (R_1, R_2, \ldots, R_n)$ *of individual preference orderings such that the game* $G = (\gamma, \boldsymbol{R})$ *has nonempty set* $NE(G)$ *of Nash equilibrium outcomes such that any outcome* $x \in NE(G)$ *is Pareto dominated by a feasible culmination outcome.*

Let us conclude this discussion of the strong libertarian paradox by observing that the crucial Condition **DVP** is indeed satisfied by the game form in **Example 9***. To verify this fact, define $M_P = \{m_P, m_P^*\}$ and $M_L = \{m_L, m_L^*\}$ by $m_P = m_L = n$ and $m_P^* = m_L^* = r$. Furthermore, define A_P^*, A_P^{**}, A_L^* and A_L^{**} by $A_P^* = A(m_P) = \{(n,n),(n,r)\}, A_P^{**} = A(m_P^*) = \{(r,n),(r,r)\}, A_L^* = A(m_L) = \{(n,n),(n,r)\}$ and $A_L^{**} = A(m_L^*) = \{(n,r),(r,r)\}$. It is clear, then, that Condition **DVP** is satisfied by γ.

Observe that **Theorem 14** as well as **Theorem 15** identifies a condition on the normal game form γ that guarantees the existence of a profile $\boldsymbol{R} = (R_1, R_2, \ldots, R_n)$ of individual preference orderings such that the game $G = (\gamma, \boldsymbol{R})$ has a nonempty set $NE(G)$ of Nash equilibrium outcomes. The game in **Theorem 14** has at least one Pareto inefficient Nash equilibrium outcome, whereas the game in **Theorem 15** is such that all Nash equilibrium outcomes are Pareto inefficient. Thus, these theorems vindicate the weak or strong Pareto libertarian paradox in the context of normal game form rights. In contrast, the research program pursued by van Hees (1999) is diagonally opposite to that pursued by Deb, Pattanaik, and Razzolini (1997), which is to identify a condition on the game theoretic formulation of rights that ensures the existence of a Pareto efficient Nash equilibrium outcome. In other words, van Hees intends to find a game-theoretic condition that is effective to resolve the Pareto libertarian paradox.[39] The starting point of the game theoretic analysis of libertarian rights by van Hees is "the (classic liberal) perspective according to which liberalism demands a maximization of individual freedom, subject to the constraints imposed by the freedom of others" (van Hees 1999, p. 295). This sounds reasonable enough, but it remains vacuous unless and until the meaning of individual freedom and the maximization thereof are made precise.

Following Nozick (1974, p. 166), van Hees studies the two-stage decision procedure. In the first stage, individuals exercise their conferred rights. If there remain multiple outcomes after the first stage, a social decision mechanism is used to determine the unique culmination outcome. A right is formalized in terms of "the permission to adopt a strategy that reduces the set of possible outcomes.... Thus a right is simply ... the set of alternatives to which an individual can reduce the final outcome" (van Hees 1999, pp. 296–297). This perception of rights, together with the basic requirement that rights are allocated consistently, is formulated as follows: A *rights structure* is an n-tuple $\Sigma =$

[39] The formulation of rights due to van Hees can be neatly translated into the terminology of effectivity functions. I owe this observation to Naoki Yoshihara.

$(\Sigma_1, \Sigma_2, \ldots, \Sigma_n)$ such that (a) for every $i \in N$, Σ_i is a family of nonempty subsets of X, and (b) for all $(S_1, S_2, \ldots, S_n) \in \prod_{i \in N} \Sigma_i$, we have $\cap_{i \in N} S_i \neq \emptyset$. A *right* $S_i \in \Sigma_i$ is said to be a *strong right* if Σ_i does not contain a proper subset of S_i. Given the rights structure Σ, the family of strong rights of $i \in N$ is denoted by Σ_i^*. As in the scenario described by Nozick (1974), the set of alternatives that remain feasible after the exercise of rights constitutes the *agenda* of the subsequent application of collective choice procedure. It is in this context of collective choice that individual preference orderings on the set of culmination outcomes become relevant.

Let $c(S, \boldsymbol{R})$, where S satisfying $\emptyset \subset S \subseteq X$ is the agenda and $\boldsymbol{R} = (R_1, R_2, \ldots, R_n)$ is the profile of individual preference orderings, be an element of S that is collectively chosen from S in reflection of individual wishes represented by $\boldsymbol{R}$. A condition imposed on the collective choice procedure c is that of *nonimposition* to the effect that, for every agenda S such that $\emptyset \subset S \subseteq X$ and every alternative $x \in S$, $x = c(S, \boldsymbol{R})$ holds for some profile $\boldsymbol{R}$. A game $G^{\Sigma} = (\gamma, \boldsymbol{R})$, where $\gamma = (N, \boldsymbol{M}, g)$ with $\boldsymbol{M} = \prod_{i \in N} M_i$, is induced by a rights structure Σ and a collective choice procedure c by (a) for all $i \in N$, the strategy set M_i consists of all pairs (S_i, h_i), where $S_i \in \Sigma_i$ and h_i is a mapping from $\prod_{j \in N} \Sigma_j$ into the family of all preference orderings over X, and (b) for all $\boldsymbol{m} = ((S_1, h_1), (S_2, h_2), \ldots, (S_n, h_n))$, $g(\boldsymbol{m}) = c(S, \boldsymbol{R})$, where $S = \cap_{j \in N} S_j$ and $\boldsymbol{R} = (h_1(S_1, S_2, \ldots, S_n), h_2(S_1, S_2, \ldots, S_n), \ldots, h_n(S_1, S_2, \ldots, S_n))$. The focus of this analysis of the game G^{Σ} is on the Nash equilibrium outcome thereof. The resolution of the Pareto libertarian paradox will be sought through the identification of a condition of the rights structure Σ, such that the induced game G^{Σ} has at least one Nash equilibrium outcome that is Pareto efficient.

The relevant condition on the rights structure that serves to this end is given by:

Condition MF: Maximal Freedom The rights structure Σ^{max} realizes maximal freedom if (a) there is no rights structure Σ such that $\Sigma_i^{\max}$ is a subset of Σ_i for all $i \in N$, and a proper subset for at least one $i \in N$, and (b) for all $(S_1, S_2, \ldots, S_n) \in \prod_{i \in N} \Sigma_i^{\max}$, it holds that $\# \mid \cap_{i \in N} S_i \mid = 1$.

Observe that part (a) requires that we cannot confer on any individual an extra right without violating any right of any other individual, whereas part (b) requires that if each and every individual exercises one of his strong rights, the outcome is uniquely determined without leaving any room for the application of collective choice procedure.

We are now ready to state the following theorem due to van Hees, leaving the discussion on the reasonableness of Condition **MF** for later examination.

Theorem 16 (van Hees 1999, Theorem 3.1) *Any game G^{Σ} induced by the conferred rights structure Σ satisfying Condition* **MF** *has a Pareto efficient Nash equilibrium outcome.*

It is satisfying that a condition on the rights structure is thereby neatly identified, which (1) has a meaningful sense as a reasonable requirement in the spirit of classical liberalism, and (2) induces a game whose set of Nash equilibrium outcomes contains at least one Pareto efficient culmination outcome. However, we should also point out that (1*) in van Hees's own admission, the crucial condition of "[m]aximal freedom is a rather strong demand..., and the resulting games are extreme" van Hees (1999, p. 303) and that (2*) although **Theorem 16** succeeds in resolving the strong Pareto libertarian paradox in the sense that not all Nash equilibrium outcomes of the libertarian game are Pareto inefficient, it falls short of resolving the weak libertarian paradox. It is true that van Hees (1999, pp. 302–303) tried to respond to the critical observation (1*) by allowing the possibility that individuals may abstain from exercising their libertarian rights by their own, and decide to settle their private issues through a collective choice procedure. It is not clear, however, if this compromised use of libertarian rights makes a reasonable sense from the viewpoint of liberalism. In addition, this compromised version of libertarian rights à la van Hees does not seem to be effective against the other reservation, viz., (2*).

As a matter of fact, any game form that resolves the Pareto libertarian paradox in the weak sense and realizes the maximal freedom is in fact confined to a narrow class of game forms that includes the dictatorial game form, but excludes the *King-maker mechanism* due to Hurwicz and Schmeidler (1978). To state this result due to Peleg (2004), let us introduce the class of *acceptable* game forms, which is defined by means of the following two properties: (i) any game form in this class is Nash solvable, and (ii) for any profile of individual preference orderings, any game form in this class generates a game such that every Nash equilibrium outcome thereof is weakly Pareto efficient. It is shown that

Theorem 17 (Peleg 2004) *A necessary and sufficient condition for a super additive and monotone effectivity function E to have a representation by an acceptable game form is that E satisfies the two conditions listed below:*

(a) *E satisfies the condition* (**NS**) *in* **Theorem 13**; *and*
(b) $[L, L^* \in 2^N - \{\emptyset\}, B \in E(L), B^* \in E(L^*)\ \&\ L \cap L^* = \emptyset]$ *implies* $B \cup B^* = A$.

Recollect that, by virtue of **Theorem 13**, the condition (**NS**) is necessary and sufficient for E to have a Nash solvable representation. Thus, the crucial condition for the Nash solvable representation of E to be acceptable is condition (b). It should be clear that condition (b) is quite strong and can be satisfied by the dictatorial game form, but not by the Hurwicz–Schmeidler King-maker mechanism.

The best way to conclude this section on the liberal paradoxes with game form rights seems to be with one more theorem due to Peleg (1998, 2004). As an auxiliary step, we define the condition of *minimal liberalism* à la Peleg as follows:

Condition ML: Minimal Liberalism An effectivity function E satisfies the condition of minimal liberalism if and only if there exist two individuals $i, j \in N$ and $B^i, B^j \subseteq A$ such that $B^i \neq \emptyset$, $B^j \neq \emptyset$, $B^i \neq A \neq B^j$ and $B^i \in E(\{i\})$ and $B^j \in E(\{j\})$.

We are now ready to state the following theorem due to Peleg.

Theorem 18 (Peleg 1998, 2004) *Suppose that an effectivity function E satisfies Condition* **ML**. *Then there exists no acceptable game form that serves as a representation of E.*

8. INITIAL CONFERMENT OF GAME FORM RIGHTS

Let us turn back, then, to the question of initial conferment of normal game form rights. Although this crucial problem has been occasionally mentioned in the literature by, for example, Gaertner, Pattanaik, and Suzumura (1992), Sen (1992), Pattanaik and Suzumura (1994, 1996), and Suzumura (1996), a fully-fledged analytical framework has not been developed as of now. To exemplify the problems to be faced in this arena, let us expound briefly an attempt by Suzumura and Yoshihara (2008).

To illustrate the nature of the problem of initial conferment of normal game form rights, consider the following example.

Example 12 (Secondary Smoking Case Revisited) There are two passengers 1 and 2 in the compartment of a train, where 1 is a smoker and 2 is a nonsmoker. The train company is to decide either to respect the smoker's desire to smoke freely, or to respect the nonsmoker's desire not to be imposed with secondary smoking. The company's problem is to choose from the set of various game forms, which includes the following two game forms.

The first game form is $\gamma = (N, \boldsymbol{M}^{\gamma}, g^{\gamma})$, where $N = \{1,2\}$, $\boldsymbol{M}^{\gamma} = M_1^{\gamma} \times M_2^{\gamma}, M_i^{\gamma}$ is the set of player i's strategies $(i = 1,2)$ and g^{γ} is the outcome function, viz., $g^{\gamma}(m_1, m_2)$ is the culmination outcome corresponding to the strategy profile $(m_1, m_2) \in \boldsymbol{M}^{\gamma}$. It is assumed that $M_1^{\gamma} = \{s, ns\}$, where $s =$ "to smoke" and $ns =$ "not to smoke," $M_2^{\gamma} = \{(l|s, r|ns), r\}$, where $(l|s, r|ns) =$ "to leave the compartment if the smoker smokes, to remain in the compartment if the smoker does not smoke," and $r =$ "to remain in the compartment no matter what," and g^{γ} is defined by

1 \ 2	$(l\|s, r\|ns)$	r
s	(s, l)	(s, r)
ns	(ns, r)	(ns, r)

where (s, l) is the culmination outcome such that the smoker smokes and the nonsmoker leaves the compartment. The culmination outcomes (ns, r) and (s, r) may be interpreted similarly.

The second game form $\gamma^* = (N, \boldsymbol{M}^{\gamma^*}, g^{\gamma^*})$ is defined by $N = \{1,2\}$, $\boldsymbol{M}^{\gamma^*} = M_1^{\gamma^*} \times M_2^{\gamma^*}$, $M_1^{\gamma^*} = \{(s|p, ns|np), ns\}$, where $(s|p, ns|np) =$ "to smoke if the nonsmoker permits it, not to smoke if the nonsmoker does not permit it" and $ns =$ "not to smoke no matter what," $M_2^{\gamma^*} = \{p \cdot r, p \cdot l, np\}$, where $p \cdot r =$ "to permit the smoker to smoke and remain in the compartment," $p \cdot l =$ "to permit the smoker to smoke and leave the compartment if and only if the smoker indeed smokes," and $np =$ "not to permit the smoker to smoke no matter what," and g^{γ^*} is defined by

1 \ 2	$p \cdot r$	$p \cdot l$	np
$(s \mid p, ns \mid np)$	(s, r)	(s, l)	(ns, r)
ns	(ns, r)	(ns, r)	(ns, r)

Observe that the set of culmination outcomes is given by $A = \{(s,l), (ns,r), (s,r)\}$. It should be clear that the company confers on the smoker (resp. the nonsmoker) the right for free smoking (resp. the right for clean air) if it chooses the game form γ (resp. γ^*).

The gist of this example is that *the social choice of a normal game form is tantamount to the initial conferment of individual rights.* This social choice issue should be solved by designing and implementing a democratic social decision procedure for initial conferment of individual rights.

This analysis can be based on the conceptual framework developed by Pattanaik and Suzumura (1994, 1996), which proposed to capture the intuitive conception of decision-making procedure as a carrier of intrinsic value beyond the instrumental usefulness thereof in realizing valuable culmination outcomes. In the conceptual framework of Pattanaik and Suzumura, the model of social decision-making consists of two stages. In the first stage, the society decides on the game form rights to be promulgated. In the second stage, the promulgated game form rights, coupled with the revealed profile of individual preference orderings over the set of culmination outcomes, determine a fully-fledged game, and the play of this game determines a culmination outcome as the Nash equilibrium outcome.[40]

[40] We may illustrate this two-stage framework by means of **Example 12**. Suppose that the two passengers have their own preference orderings over the set of culmination outcomes A, together forming the following profile $\boldsymbol{R} = (R_1, R_2)$ of individual preference orderings:

$$R_1 : (s,l), (s,r), (ns,r), \quad R_2 : (ns,r), (s,l), (s,r).$$

Given this profile $\boldsymbol{R}$, (s,l) is the unique pure strategy Nash equilibrium outcome of the game $(\gamma, \boldsymbol{R})$, whereas (ns,r) is the unique pure strategy Nash equilibrium outcome of the game $(\gamma^*, \boldsymbol{R})$. For the sake of further argument, let us assume that γ^* is the socially chosen game form. Since γ^* is chosen in the first stage before the profile $\boldsymbol{R}$ is revealed, the two individuals play the game $(\gamma^*, \boldsymbol{R})$ in the second stage, and the unique pure strategy Nash equilibrium outcome (ns,r) will emerge as a consequence.

In order to formulate the first stage of social decision-making procedure, each individual is assumed to have an *ordering function* Q_i, which assigns an extended ordering $Q_i(\boldsymbol{R})$ over the set of pairs of normal game forms and realized culmination outcomes corresponding to each profile $\boldsymbol{R} = (R_1, R_2, \ldots, R_n)$ of individual preference orderings on the set A of feasible culmination outcomes.[41]

Let Ψ be the social aggregator, to be called the *extended constitution function*, which maps each admissible profile $\mathbf{Q} = (Q_1, Q_2, \ldots, Q_n)$ of individual ordering functions into a social ordering function: $Q = \Psi(\mathbf{Q})$. It is this social ordering function that determines the game form rights-system to be socially chosen and promulgated as the rule of the game to be played in the second stage. Within this conceptual framework, the crucial task is to show the existence of a "reasonable" extended constitution function Ψ. In what follows, we will introduce several axioms on Ψ to identify a "reasonable" extended constitution function. We will also introduce several conditions that identify the class of "liberal" game forms. To sum up, the purpose of this analysis is to investigate the existence of a "reasonable" extended constitution function, by means of which a "liberal" game form can be rationally chosen.[42]

Let us describe the two-stage model of initial conferment of normal game form rights. Let $\boldsymbol{\Gamma}$ be the universal set of normal game forms. Let $\mathcal{R}$ be the family of profiles of individual preference orderings over the set of culmination outcomes. Given a game form $\gamma = (N, \boldsymbol{M}, g) \in \boldsymbol{\Gamma}$ and a profile $\boldsymbol{R} \in \mathcal{R}$ of individual preference orderings, let $\mathcal{E}(\gamma, \boldsymbol{R})$ be the set of all Nash equilibria of the game $(\gamma, \boldsymbol{R})$. Thus, a culmination outcome $x^* \in A$, where A denotes the set of attainable culmination outcomes, is a Nash equilibrium outcome of the game $(\gamma, \boldsymbol{R})$ if and only if there exists a Nash equilibrium $\boldsymbol{m}^* \in \mathcal{E}(\gamma, \boldsymbol{R})$ such that $x^* = g(\boldsymbol{m}^*)$. For each $x \in A$ and each $\gamma \in \boldsymbol{\Gamma}$, a pair (x, γ) is an *extended social alternative*. Given an $\boldsymbol{R} \in \mathcal{R}$, an extended social alternative $(x, \gamma) \in A \times \boldsymbol{\Gamma}$ is *realizable at* $\boldsymbol{R}$ if and only if $x \in g(\mathcal{E}(\gamma, \boldsymbol{R}))$ holds.[43] $\Lambda(\boldsymbol{R})$ denotes the set of all realizable extended social alternatives at $\boldsymbol{R}$, viz., $(x, \gamma) \in \Lambda(\boldsymbol{R})$ if and only if $x \in g(\mathcal{E}(\gamma, \boldsymbol{R}))$.

What we have christened the extended constitution function is a mapping Ψ that sends each profile $\mathbf{Q} = (Q_1, Q_2, \ldots, Q_n)$ of individual ordering functions into a social ordering function Q, viz., $Q = \Psi(\mathbf{Q})$. Note that the present framework of analyzing

[41] In **Example 12**, $((ns, r), \gamma^*)\, Q_i(\boldsymbol{R})\, ((s, l), \gamma)$ means that the situation where (ns, r) is realized as a Nash equilibrium outcome of the game $(\gamma^*, \boldsymbol{R})$ is at least as desirable for i as the situation where (s, l) is realized as a Nash equilibrium outcome of the game $(\gamma, \boldsymbol{R})$. This should suffice to suggest the intended interpretation of the extended ordering $Q_i(\boldsymbol{R})$.

[42] A scheme similar to the present one is pursued by Koray (2000) in the sense that Koray also addresses himself to the social choice of social decision rules. One of the crucial differences is that the social decision rules envisaged by Koray are the conventional social choice functions, whereas the scheme presented here focuses on the social decision rules as game forms. Another difference is that Koray was concerned only about the consequential values of social decision rules, whereas the present scheme is focused on the consequential values as well as nonconsequential values of social decision rules as game forms.

[43] In Section 7, we used $NE(G)$ as the set of Nash equilibrium outcomes. If $G = (\gamma, \boldsymbol{R})$ and $\gamma = (N, \boldsymbol{M}, g)$, we have $NE((\gamma, \boldsymbol{R})) = g(\mathcal{E}(\gamma, \boldsymbol{R}))$.

social welfare and individual rights makes use of two distinct types of individual preferences. The first is an individual's preferences over the set of culmination outcomes, which represents his subjective tastes. The second is his ordering function, which represents his value judgments on the set of pairs of procedures and consequences. This dual use of the concept of individual preferences is due originally to Harsanyi (1955). See also Pattanaik and Suzumura (1996). Given an extended constitution function Ψ, the associated *rational social choice function* C is defined for each profile $\mathbf{Q}$ of individual ordering functions and each profile $\boldsymbol{R}$ of individual preferences orderings on the set of culmination outcomes by $\gamma \in C(\Psi(\mathbf{Q});\boldsymbol{R})$ if and only if (1) $\gamma \in \boldsymbol{\Gamma}$, and (2) there exists an $x \in A$ such that $(x,\gamma) \in \Lambda(\boldsymbol{R})$ and $(x,\gamma)Q(\boldsymbol{R})(y,\delta)$ holds for all $(y,\delta) \in \Lambda(\boldsymbol{R})$, where $Q = \Psi(\mathbf{Q})$.

What qualifies an extended constitution function to be "reasonable"? In what follows, let us enumerate three distinct types of conditions, which characterize a reasonable extended constitution function. The first type of conditions are Arrovian in nature, which require that an extended constitution satisfies Condition **SP** (**Strong Pareto Principle**), Condition **PI** (**Pareto Indifference Principle**), Condition **I** (**Independence**), and Condition **ND** (**Nondictatorship**).[44] The second requirement is that the extended constitution function Ψ should generate *uniformly rational* social choice functions in the following sense:

Condition UR (Uniform Rationality) For each admissible profile $\mathbf{Q}$ of individual ordering functions,

$$\cap_{\boldsymbol{R}\in\mathcal{R}} C(\Psi(\mathbf{Q});\boldsymbol{R}) \neq \emptyset$$

holds.

To understand the meaning of Condition **UR**, suppose that the normal game form γ^* is chosen from the nonempty set $\cap_{\boldsymbol{R}\in\mathcal{R}} C(\Psi(\mathbf{Q});\boldsymbol{R})$. Then γ^*, which embodies the normal game form rights, applies *uniformly* to every future realization of the profile $\boldsymbol{R} \in \mathcal{R}$. Since the choice of normal game form is the formal method of specifying the initial conferment of rights in the society prior to the realization of the profile of individual preference orderings on the set of culmination outcomes, it seems desirable to design the extended constitution function satisfying Condition **UR**. Indeed, if we implement a normal game form $\gamma^* \in \cap_{\boldsymbol{R}\in\mathcal{R}} C(Q;\boldsymbol{R})$, γ^* prevails as the rights-system no matter how frivolously $\boldsymbol{R}$ may change.[45]

[44] Since these conditions are simple adaptation of the well-known Arrovian conditions in the present context, we may safely skip their formal statement. Those who need a formal statement of these conditions are cordially invited to see the relevant part of Suzumura and Yoshihara (2008).

[45] It is true that Condition **UR** is strong, as it requires that the promulgated rules of the game remain insensitive to the unforeseen changes in $\boldsymbol{R} \in \mathcal{R}$. It follows that the conditions which guarantee the satisfaction of **UR** cannot but be stringent and go beyond the consequentialist border of informational constraints. See Suzumura and Yoshihara (2008) for more details.

In the third place, we must introduce three requirements on the class of normal game forms. The first requirement is the Nash solvability of the normal game forms. Let $\Gamma_{\mathbf{NS}} \subseteq \Gamma$ be the family of the Nash solvable normal game forms. The second requirement is that the normal game form $\gamma \in \Gamma$ is *liberal* in the sense that there exists $B^i \in E^{\gamma}(\{i\})$ with $B^i \subsetneq A$ for every $i \in N$. Let $\Gamma_{\mathbf{L}} \subseteq \Gamma$ be the family of the liberal normal game forms. The third requirement is that the normal game form $\gamma = (N, \boldsymbol{M}, g) \in \Gamma$ is *efficient* in the sense that there exists a Pareto efficient Nash equilibrium outcome in A for every profile $\boldsymbol{R} \in \mathcal{R}$ whenever $\mathcal{E}(\gamma, \boldsymbol{R})$ is nonempty. Let $\Gamma_{\mathbf{PE}} \subseteq \Gamma$ be the family of the Pareto efficient normal game forms.

We are now ready to state the problem of searching for a *satisfactory* mechanism for initial conferment of *reasonable* normal game form as follows: Under what domain restrictions on the acceptable family of profiles of individual ordering functions, can we ensure the existence of an extended constitution function, which is not only consistent with Arrovian conditions of **SP** (Strong Pareto), **PI** (Pareto Indifference), **I** (Independence), and **ND** (Nondictatorship), but also capable of generating uniformly rational choice function that may choose a normal game form $\gamma^* \in \Gamma_{\mathbf{NS}} \cap \Gamma_{\mathbf{L}} \cap \Gamma_{\mathbf{PE}}$, viz., a Nash solvable, liberal, and Pareto efficient normal game form?

An attempt to answer the problem of initial conferment of normal game form rights along this line in the affirmative was made by Suzumura and Yoshihara (2008), to which we cordially request the interested readers to refer.[46]

9. SOME FURTHER REMARKS ON PARETIANISM

9.1. The Paretian Epidemic and Its Implications

Back, then, to the impossibility of a Paretian liberal with the preference-contingent concept of individual rights à la Sen. For the purpose of this subsection, it is more convenient to use the *relational social choice rule* h rather than the (choice functional) social choice rule f used in earlier sections of this chapter, which specifies a social preference relation R for each profile $\boldsymbol{R} = (R_1, R_2, \ldots, R_n)$ of individual preference orderings: $R = h(\boldsymbol{R})$. If h generates a social preference ordering R for each profile $\boldsymbol{R} = (R_1, R_2, \ldots, R_n)$ of individual preference orderings, viz., $R = h(\boldsymbol{R})$ satisfies the three requirements of reflexivity, completeness, and transitivity for every profile $\boldsymbol{R} = (R_1, R_2, \ldots, R_n)$ of individual preference orderings, then h is a *social welfare function* introduced by Arrow (1951/1963). If

[46] Since the extended constitution function is required to satisfy the essentially Arrovian conditions, the existence of a reasonable Ψ cannot be assured if we impose the condition of unrestricted domain. Thus, the task to be faced is to identify an appropriate domain restriction under which we can secure the existence of an extended constitution function that is capable of generating a reasonable game form rights-system. This is essentially what was pursued by Suzumura and Yoshihara (2008).

h is such that the social preference relation $R = h(\mathbf{R})$ satisfies the three requirements of reflexivity, completeness, and acyclicity for every profile $\mathbf{R} = (R_1, R_2, \ldots, R_n)$ of individual preference orderings, then h is a *relational social decision function* introduced by Sen (1970a/1979). Let us now follow Sen (1976/1982c, Chapter 14) and define several variants of the Arrovian concept of decisiveness.[47]

Decisiveness
An individual $i^* \in N$ is *decisive* over an ordered pair $(x, y) \in X \times X$ if and only if, for any profile $\mathbf{R} = (R_1, R_2, \ldots, R_n)$ of individual preference orderings in the domain of h, $xP(R_{i^*})y$ cannot but imply $xP(R)y$, where $R = h(\mathbf{R})$.

Semidecisiveness
An individual $i^* \in N$ is *semidecisive* over an ordered pair $(x, y) \in X \times X$ if and only if, for any profile $\mathbf{R} = (R_1, R_2, \ldots, R_n)$ of individual preference orderings in the domain of h, $xP(R_{i^*})y$ cannot but imply xRy, where $R = h(\mathbf{R})$.

Potential Decisiveness and Semidecisiveness
An individual $i^* \in N$ is *potentially decisive* (resp. *potentially semidecisive*) over an ordered pair $(x, y) \in X \times X$ if and only if, for any profile $\mathbf{R} = (R_1, R_2, \ldots, R_n)$ of individual preference orderings in the domain of h satisfying some specified restrictions on the rankings of pairs other than (x, y), which leaves the rankings of (x, y) by all individuals $i \in N - \{i^*\}$ completely unrestricted, $xP(R_{i^*})y$ cannot but imply $xP(R)y$ (resp. xRy), where $R = h(\mathbf{R})$.

The *impossibility of a Paretian liberal* in terms of a relational social choice rule uses the following conditions.

Condition RU: Relational Unrestricted Domain The domain of h consists of all logically possible profiles $\mathbf{R} = (R_1, R_2, \ldots, R_n)$ of individual preference orderings over the set X of culmination outcomes.

Condition RU: Relational Pareto Principle For each $x, y \in X$, if $xP(R_i)y$ for all $i \in N$, then $xP(R)y$, where $R = h(\mathbf{R})$.

Condition RML: Relational Minimal Libertarianism There exist at least two individuals, say $k, l \in N$, who are decisive both ways over at least one pair of alternatives each, viz., $\{x^k, y^k\}$ for individual k and $\{x^l, y^l\}$ for individual l, respectively.

Then we obtain the following impossibility theorem due to Sen.

47 Note that the concept of decisiveness used in the previous sections of this chapter was defined by means of choice functional social choice rule rather than relational social choice rule. However, the correspondence between these concepts should be clear to the reader and require no further elucidation.

Theorem 19 (Sen 1970a/1979, 1970b) *There exists no relational social decision function h that satisfies Condition* **RU**, *Condition* **RP**, *and Condition* **RML**.

Sen found the essence of this impossibility theorem in some insidious implications of the Pareto principle. Capitalizing on this theorem and its implications, he went on to crystallize his critical observations on the welfaristic Pareto principle by means of what he christened the *Paretian epidemic.*[48] It shows that, for a relational social decision function satisfying Condition **RU**, Condition **RP** is sufficient to spread decisiveness over a single pair of alternatives to all pairs of alternatives in the weaker form of potential semidecisiveness.

Theorem 20 (Sen 1976/1982, Appendix A2) *For any relational social decision function satisfying Condition* **RU**, *Condition* **RP** *implies that an individual $i^* \in N$, who is decisive both ways over any one pair of alternatives in X, must be potentially semidecisive over every ordered pair in X.*

If quasi-transitivity rather than acyclicity of social preference relations generated by relational social decision function is required, the spread of decisive power of individual $i^* \in N$ turns out to be even more conspicuous.

Theorem 21 (Sen 1976/1982, Appendix A2) *For any relational social decision function satisfying Condition* **RU** *and generating quasi-transitive social preference relations, Condition* **RP** *implies that an individual $i^* \in N$, who is decisive both ways over any one pair of alternatives in X, must be potentially decisive over every ordered pair in X.*

It deserves emphasis that the impossibility of a Paretian liberal in the form of **Theorem 1** and **Theorem 19** does not invoke the Arrovian condition of independence of irrelevant alternatives. In the present context of relational social decision functions, this condition reads as follows.

Condition RI: Relational Independence of Irrelevant Alternatives For any profile $\boldsymbol{R} = (R_1, R_2, \ldots, R_n)$ of individual preference orderings, the restriction $R(\{x,y\})$ of social preference relation $R = h(\boldsymbol{R})$ over any pair $\{x,y\} \subset X \times X$ depends only on the profile $\boldsymbol{R}(\{x,y\}) = (R_1(\{x,y\}), R_2(\{x,y\}), \ldots, R_n(\{x,y\}))$ of restriction $R_i(\{x,y\})$ of individual preference ordering R_i for every $i \in N$.

It is also true that **Theorem 20** and **Theorem 21** do not hinge on Condition **RI**, but nothing prevents us from asking how the introduction of an additional requirement of Condition **RI** modifies the crucial message of the Paretian epidemic. It was in this spirit

[48] Although **Theorem 19** does not make an explicit use of the Arrovian axiom of independence of irrelevant alternatives, it was pointed out by Blau (1975) that *the Pareto principle contains an important element of independence axiom.* Sen's Paretian epidemic extracts this independence element of the Pareto principle and shows that this vestigal element of independence is sufficient to bring about insidious consequences that crystallize the message of the impossibility of a Paretian liberal.

that Sen (1976/1982), Appendix A2) established the following interesting implications of Condition **RI** in the context of his Paretian epidemic.

Theorem 22 (Sen 1976/1982, Appendix A2) *For any relational social decision function satisfying Condition* **RU**, *Condition* **RP** *and Condition* **RI** *together imply that an individual* $i^* \in N$, *who is decisive both ways over any pair of alternatives in* X, *is semidecisive over every ordered pair of alternatives in* X.

Theorem 23 (Sen 1976/1982, Appendix A2) *For any relational social decision function satisfying Condition* **RU** *and generating quasi-transitive social preference relations, Condition* **RP** *and Condition* **RI** *together imply that an individual* $i^* \in N$, *who is decisive over any ordered pair of alternatives in* X, *must be decisive over every ordered pair of alternatives in* X.

Gathering all pieces together, the summary verdicts on the role played by the Pareto principle in the relational social decision function satisfying Condition **RU** can be stated as follows. Suppose that an individual $i^* \in N$ is decisive both ways over some pair in X, then

(a) Condition **RP** implies that i^* is potentially semidecisive everywhere,
(b) Condition **RP**, coupled with quasi-transitivity of social preference relations, implies that i^* is potentially decisive everywhere, and
(c) Condition **RP**, coupled with Condition **RI**, implies that i^* is semidecisive everywhere.

Besides, if $i^* \in N$ is decisive over some ordered pair of alternatives in X, then

(d) Condition **RP**, coupled with quasi-transitivity of social preference relations and Condition **RI**, implies that i^* is a dictator.

Recollect that Sen's impossibility of a Paretian liberal was meant to cast a serious doubt on the universal acceptance of welfarism, the classical Pareto principle being a salient example thereof. Sen's Paretian epidemic is an even more conspicuous way of bringing the insidious implications of the Pareto principle, hence of welfarism, into clearer relief. As a research strategy for attacking the universal acceptance of welfarism in the arena of welfare economics and social choice theory, Sen's strategic focus on the insidious implications of the Pareto principle is effective as well as understandable. However, if a scissor cuts a paper, both blades are to be equally held responsible for the act of cutting. Likewise, if there exists no relational social decision function satisfying Condition **A** and Condition **B**, not only Condition **A** but also Condition **B** should be equally held responsible as the culprit of the logical conflict. Furthermore, even if Condition **A** (resp. Condition **B**) has a special reason to be held responsible for these logical difficulties, it is always a possibility that Condition **A** (resp. Condition **B**) can be decomposed into two nonvacuous, mutually exclusive, and jointly exhaustive components $\mathbf{A}^*$ and

A** (resp. **B*** and **B****) in such a way that the full force of Condition **A** (resp. Condition **B**) is not needed for the occurrence of the logical difficulty in question in the sense that Condition **A*** (resp. Condition **B***) can replace Condition **A** (resp. Condition **B**) without upsetting the logical conflict between conditions. It was in this spirit that Kelsey (1985, 1988) and Xu (1990) tried to factorize the conditions that jointly lead to the impossibility of a Paretian liberal and/or the Paretian epidemic. Those who are interested in knowing the crucial part of the Pareto principle that is responsible for these logical difficulties are invited to the examination of these subsequent work.

9.2. Nonwelfaristic Policy Assessment and the Pareto Principle

Another attempt to uncover the insidious implications of the Pareto principle was developed by Kaplow and Shavell, according to whom "for any nonwelfarist[ic] method of policy assessment (i.e., for any [nonindividualistic] social welfare function), there always exist circumstances in which the Pareto principle is violated." This is a rather devastating verdict on the Paretian welfare economics, as it implies that "any conceivable notion of social welfare that does not depend solely on individuals' utilities will sometimes require adoption of a policy that makes every person worse off." (Kaplow and Shavell, 2001, p. 282)

The first point to be clarified is how Kaplow and Shavell could arrive at their important conclusion. Let X be the set of all conceivable states of the world. A *social welfare function* F is a function that maps X into the set of all real numbers, so is an individual i's utility function U_i for each and every $i \in N$. An *individualistic* social welfare function F is *welfaristic* in the sense that it takes the special form $F(x) = W(U_1(x), U_2(x), \ldots, U_n(x))$, where x is a typical element of X. By definition, a social welfare function F is nonindividualistic, hence *nonwelfaristic*, if and only if there exist $x, y \in X$ such that we have $U_i(x) = U_i(y)$ for all $i \in N$, and yet we also have $F(x) \neq F(y)$. Within this framework, the weak Pareto principle asserts that if $x, y \in X$ are such that $U_i(x) > U_i(y)$ for all $i \in N$, we must conclude that $F(x) > F(y)$. Under fairly weak assumptions on the society's economic environment, Kaplow and Shavell could prove that *a nonindividualistic, hence nonwelfaristic, social welfare function violates the weak Pareto principle*. No wonder this conclusion caused a stir in the profession.[49]

[49] Capitalizing on Kaplow and Shavell (2002) and bringing a somewhat different implication of their original analysis into clear relief, Suzumura (2001) showed that the following distinct versions of the Pareto principle turn out to be logically equivalent to each other under similar conditions on the society's economic environment:

Pareto Indifference Principle: For all $x, y \in X$, if $xI(R_i)y$ holds for all $i \in N$, then $xI(R)y$ holds.
Weak Pareto Principle: For all $x, y \in X$, if $xP(R_i)y$ holds for all $i \in N$, then $xP(R)y$ holds.
Strong Pareto Principle: For all $x, y \in X$, if xR_iy holds for all $i \in N$, and $xP(R_j)y$ holds for some $j \in N$, then $xP(R)y$ holds.
Full Pareto Principle: The strong Pareto principle and the Pareto indifference principle hold.

Although the formal result of Kaplow and Shavell (2002) is logically impeccable, the method of interpreting their formal result to the effect that *any method of policy assessment, which is not purely welfaristic, violates the Pareto principle* seems to leave a room for criticisms. Indeed, Fleurbaey, Tungodden, and Chang (2003) criticized Kaplow and Shavell (2002) for identifying welfarism and the Pareto indifference principle, because "no Pareto condition by itself entails welfarism" (Fleurbaey *et al.*, 2003, p. 1383) in the standard sense widely accepted among the circle of social choice theorists, which is defined, for example, by d'Aspremont and Gevers (1977) and Sen (1979a, 1986a). The source of this seeming contradiction is in fact easy to identify. While Kaplow and Shavell (2002, p. 283) base their verdict on the observation that *welfarism in their sense and the Pareto indifference principle are equivalent for a fixed profile of individual utility functions*, d'Aspremont and Gevers (1977) invoke welfarism in the sense used widely in social choice theory to the effect that

> *the social preference relation in utility space (represented by the [social welfare] function W) be the same for all possible profiles of individual utility functions. To derive this strong neutrality property, we must combine Pareto indifference and transitivity conditions with an independence condition requiring the social ordering over any pair of alternatives to be independent of information about other alternatives. (Fleurbaey, Tungodden, and Chang 2003, p. 1383)*

Thus, it is clear that the difference of opinions between Kaplow and Shavell (2002), on the one hand, and Fleurbaey, Tungodden, and Chang (2003), on the other hand, has much to do with the old controversy between the single-profile approach to normative issues, which is widely supported by the traditional theorists along the line of new welfare economics à la Bergson (1938), Samuelson (1947/1983, 1967, 1981), and Little (1952), and the multiprofile approach to normative issues, which is widely adopted in social choice theory along the line of Arrow (1951/1963) and Sen (1970a/1979, 1986a). Those who are in need of a brief account of this controversy are cordially requested to refer back to Suzumura (2002, Section 2).

10. CONCLUDING REMARKS

In concluding this chapter, let us go back to where we started, viz., the informational bases of normative economics. Recollect that Sen's *impossibility of a Paretian liberal* was meant to cast serious doubt on the prevalent use of welfaristic informational basis. On reflection, it was Hicks (1959) who first declared that welfarism is too narrow as the informational basis of normative economics in his farewell to the traditional approach in welfare economics, which is welfaristic in nature:

> *The view which, now, I do not hold I propose ... to call "Economic Welfarism": for it is one of the tendencies which has taken its origin from that great and immensely influential work, the* Economics

> of Welfare *of Pigou. But the distinction which I am about to make has little to do with the multifarious theoretical disputes to which the notion of Welfare Economics has given rise. One can take any view one likes about measurability, or additivity, or comparability of utilities; and yet it remains undetermined whether one is to come down on one side or other of the Welfarist fence. The line between Economic Welfarism and its opposite is not concerned with what economists call utilities; it is concerned with the transition from Utility to the more general good . . . . (Hicks 1959, pp. viii–ix)*

Hicks was led to dissociate himself from "Economic Welfarism," because he came to the strong belief that "when the economist makes a recommendation, he is responsible for it in the round; all aspects of that recommendation, whether he chooses to label them economic or not, are his concern" (Hicks 1959, pp. x–xi). However, Hicks was not ready to jump to the other polar extreme:

> *I have . . . no intention, in abandoning Economic Welfarism, of falling into the "fiat libertas, ruat caelum" which some later-day liberals seem to see as the only alternative. What I do maintain is that the liberal goods are goods; that they are values which, however, must be weighed up against other values. The freedom and the justice that are possible of attainment are not the same in all societies, at all times, and in all places; they are themselves conditioned by external environment, and (in the short period at least) by what has occurred in the past. Yet we can recognize these limitations, and still feel that these ends are worthier ends than those which are represented in a production index. It is better to think of economic activity as means to these ends, than as means to different ends, which are entirely its own. (Hicks 1959, p. xiv)*

Within this arena prepared by Hicks, Sen vindicated Hicks's apprehension about the use of welfaristic informational basis by establishing that the welfaristic value in the weakest form of the Pareto principle is logically incompatible with the weakest form of libertarian value. It should be clear that the Pareto principle and the Sen principle of minimal liberty belong to the informational bases of welfarist-consequentialism and the nonwelfarist-consequentialism, respectively. In contrast, the requirement of social respect for normal game form rights is a principle of libertarianism that is expressed on the informational basis of nonconsequentialism.

The second point to be emphasized is that the nonwelfaristic approach, which focuses on the intrinsic value of procedures as well as the instrumental value thereof, may call for a radical reformulation of the research program of social choice theory. According to the contribution of Hammond in this volume (see Chapter 15, p. 50), "[s]ocial choice theory concerns itself with the proper choice of a social state from a given feasible set of social states. The main question the theory addresses is how that social choice should depend on the profile of individual preferences." Note, however, that the tripartite classification of the issues of individual rights, viz., the formulation of rights, the realization of conferred rights, and the initial conferment of rights, within the context of the normal game form formulation of rights, leads us to an alternative perspective of the theory of social choice. According to this alternative view, social choice theory is concerned with the proper or fair choice of a normal game form or mechanism from a given feasible set of normal game forms or mechanisms, and the proper or fair choice of a social state is delegated to the decentralized play of the fully-fledged game after the profile of individual preference orderings over culmination outcomes is revealed. Needless to say, this chapter could at best be a preliminary study of this alternative scenario, and much depends on the future exploration of the new vista in several theoretical and empirical frontiers.

In the third and last place, we are keenly aware that the issues of rights could be captured exhaustively neither by social choice rules, nor by normal or any other game forms. Our concentration on the social choice theoretic formulation of rights or the normal game form formulation of rights is nothing other than the reflection of how and where the current theory stands, and not the reflection of our deliberate judgments on the potential reach of these two approaches vis-à-vis others. Concerning their relative merits, a wide and clear consensus seems to have emerged. Suffice it to quote Sen's (2002, p. 643) summary evaluation to the following effect:

> *At the level of form-specification of many types of rights, there are clear advantages in using game-form formulations. Indeed, the common-sense understanding of many acknowledged rights takes this form, focusing on what people are free to do (including the permission and the ability to do certain things), rather than examining the results that the people involved can actually achieve (as would be included in the characterization of a "social state").*

However, Sen (2002, p. 645) was also careful enough to observe that "[the fact that] a class of rights exists that concentrates primarily on outcomes—even culmination outcomes—and not on the freedom to undertake actions can scarcely be disputed .... It is, however, not exactly easy to characterize fully the entire membership of this class of rights." The exploration of these other rights with special reference to their implications for social welfare is beyond the scope of the present chapter and must be left for future explorations.

ACKNOWLEDGMENTS

My sincere gratitude goes to Professors Kenneth Arrow, Walter Bossert, Rajat Deb, Allan Gibbard, Peter Hammond, Prasanta Pattanaik, Bezalel Peleg, Amartya Sen, Robert Sugden, Naoki Yoshihara, and Yongsheng Xu, with whom I had several opportunities to discuss some of the issues examined in this chapter over the years. I am particularly grateful to the coeditors of this *Handbook* for their helpful editorial advice. Needless to say, nobody other than myself should be held responsible for any remaining defect of this chapter.

REFERENCES

Abdou, J. (1998a). Rectangularity and tightness: a normal form characterization of perfect information extensive game forms. *Mathematics of Operations Research*, *23*, 553–567.

Abdou, J. (1998b). Tight and effectively rectangular game forms: a Nash solvable class. *Games and Economic Behavior*, *23*, 1–11.

Abdou, J., & Keiding, H. (1991). *Effectivity functions in social choice*. Dordrecht: Kluwer Academic Publishing.

Arrow, K. J. (1951/1963). *Social choice and individual values* (1st ed. 1951; expanded 2nd ed. 1963). New York: John Wiley & Sons.

Arrow, K. J. (1959). Rational choice functions and orderings. *Economica, 26*, 121–127.

Arrow, K. J. (1984). *Social choice and justice* (Vol. 1) of *collected papers of Kenneth J. Arrow*. Oxford: Basil Blackwell.

Arrow, K. J. (1987). Arrow's theorem. In J. Eatwell, M. Milgate & P. Newman (Eds.), *The New Palgrave: a dictionary of economics* (Vol. 1, pp. 124–126). London: Macmillan.

Arrow, K. J., Sen, A. K., & Suzumura, K. (Eds.). (1996/1997). *Social choice reexamined* (Vol. 2). London: Macmillan.

Austen-Smith, D. (1979). Fair rights. *Economics Letters, 4*, 29–32.

Austen-Smith, D. (1982). Restricted Pareto and rights. *Journal of Economic Theory, 10*, 89–99.

Baigent, N. (1981). Decompositions of minimal liberalism. *Economics Letters*, 7, 29–32.

Barry, B. (1965/1990). *Political argument*. London: Routledge & Kegan Paul. (A re-issue with a new introduction. London: Harvester-Wheatsheaf, 1990).

Barry, B. (1986). Lady Chatterley's Lover and Doctor Fisher's Bomb Party: liberalism, Pareto optimality, and the problem of objectionable preferences. In J. Elster & A. Hylland (Eds.), *Foundations of social choice theory* (pp. 11–43). Cambridge, MA: Cambridge University Press.

Barry, B. (1989). *Theories of justice*. London: Harvester-Wheastsheaf.

Basu, K. (1984). The right to give up rights. *Economica, 15*, 413–422.

Batra, R. N., & Pattanaik, P. K. (1972). On some suggestions for having non-binary social choice functions. *Theory and Decision, 3*, 1–11.

Bentham, J. (1843). Anarchical fallacies. First published in English in J. Bowring (Ed.), *The works of Jeremy Bentham* (Vol. II). Edinburgh: William Tait. (Republished in 1955, (pp. 489–534). Bristol: Theommes Press.)

Bergson, A. (1938). A reformulation of certain aspects of welfare economics. *Quarterly Journal of Economics, 52*, 310–334.

Bergson, A. (1954). On the concept of social welfare. *Quarterly Journal of Economics, 68*, 233–252.

Berlin, I. (1958). *Two concepts of liberty*. Oxford: Clarendon Press.

Berlin, I. (1969). *Four essays on liberty*. Oxford: Clarendon Press.

Bernholz, P. (1974). Is a Paretian liberal really impossible? *Public Choice, 19*, 99–107.

Blau, J. H. (1975). Liberal values and independence. *Review of Economic Studies, 42*, 395–402.

Bossert, W., Sprumont, Y., & Suzumura, K. (2005). Consistent rationalizability. *Economica, 72*, 185–200.

Bossert, W., & Suzumura, K. (2009). Rational choice on general domains. In K. Basu & R. Kambur (Eds.), *Argument for a better world: essays in honor of Amartya Sen, Vol. I, ethics, welfare, and measurement* (pp. 103–135). Oxford: Oxford University Press.

Bossert, W., & Suzumura, K. (2010). *Consistency, choice, and rationality*. Cambridge, MA: Harvard University Press.

Breyer, F. (1977). The liberal paradox, decisiveness over issues, and domain restrictions. *Zeitschrift für Nationalökonomie, 37*, 45–60.

Breyer, F. (1990). Can reallocation of rights help to avoid the Paretian liberal paradox? *Public Choice, 65*, 469–481.

Breyer, F., & Gardner, G. (1980). Liberal paradox, game equilibrium, and Gibbard optimum. *Public Choice, 35*, 469–481.

Breyer, F., & Gigliotti, G. A. (1980). Empathy and respect for the rights of others. *Zeitschrift für Nationalökonomie, 40*, 59–64.

Buchanan, J. (1976/1996). An ambiguity in Sen's alleged proof of the impossibility of the Paretian liberal, mimeograph, Virginia Polytechnic Institute and State University, 1976. 1996, *Analyse & Kritik, 18*, 118–125.

Campbell, D. (1994). A power structure version of Sen's Paretian liberal theorem. *Seoul Journal of Economics, 7*, 269–278.
Campbell, D. E., & Kelly, J. S. (1997). Sen's theorem and externalities. *Economica, 64*, 375–386.
Cohen, L. J., Loś, J., Pfeiffer, H., & Podewski, K.-P. (Eds.). (1982). *Logic, methodology and philosophy of science.* Amsterdam: North-Holland.
Coughlin, P. J. (1986). Rights and the private Pareto principle. *Economica, 53*, 303–320.
Craven, J. (1982). Liberalism and individual preferences. *Theory and Decision, 14*, 351–360.
d'Aspremont, C., & Gevers, L. (1977). Equity and the informational basis of collective choice. *Review of Economic Studies, 46*, 199–209.
d'Aspremont, C., & Gevers, L. (2002). Social welfare functionals and interpersonal comparability. In K. J. Arrow, A. K. Sen & K. Suzumura (Eds.), *Handbook of social choice and welfare* (Vol. I, pp. 459–541). Amsterdam: Elsevier.
Dasgupta, P. (1980). Decentralization and rights. *Economica, 47*, 107–123.
Dasgupta, P. (2001). *Human well-being and the natural environment.* Oxford: Oxford University Press.
Deb, R. (1994). Waiver, effectivity and rights as game forms. *Economica, 61*, 167–178.
Deb, R. (1997). Discussion of Hammond's paper, in Arrow, Sen, & Suzumura (1997), 96–99.
Deb, R. (2004). Rights as alternative game forms. *Social Choice and Welfare, 22*, 83–111.
Deb, R., Pattanaik, P. K., & Razzolini, L. (1997). Game forms, rights, and the efficiency of social outcomes. *Journal of Economic Theory, 72*, 74–95.
Dutta, B. (1984). Effectivity functions and acceptable game forms. *Econometrica, 52*, 1151–1166.
Farrell, M. J. (1976). Liberalism in the theory of social choice. *Review of Economic Studies, 43*, 3–10.
Feinberg, J. (1973). *Social philosophy.* Englewood Cliffs, NJ: Prentice-Hall.
Feinberg, J. (1980). *Rights, justice, and the bounds of liberty.* Princeton: Princeton University Press.
Feinberg, J. (1992). In defense of moral rights. *Oxford Journal of Legal Studies, 12*, 149–169.
Fine, B. (1975). Individual liberalism in Paretian society. *Journal of Political Economy, 83*, 1277–1281.
Fleurbaey, M., & van Hees, M. (2000). On rights in game forms. *Synthese, 123*, 295–326.
Fleurbaey, M., Suzumura, K., & Tadenuma, K. (2005). The informational basis of the theory of fair allocation. *Social Choice and Welfare, 24*, 311–341.
Fleurbaey, M., Tungodden, B., & Chang, H. F. (2003). Any non-welfarist method of policy assessment violates the Pareto principle: a comment. *Journal of Political Economy, 111*, 1382–1385.
Foley, D. K. (1967). Resource allocation and the public sector. *Yale Economic Essays, 7*, 45–98.
Gaertner, W. (1982). Envy-free rights assignments and self-oriented preferences. *Mathematical Social Sciences, 2*, 199–208.
Gaertner, W. (1985). Justice constrained libertarian claims and Pareto efficient collective decisions. *Erkenntnis, 23*, 1–17.
Gaertner, W., & Krüger, L. (1981). Self-supporting preferences and individual rights: the possibility of Paretian liberalism. *Economica, 48*, 17–28.
Gaertner, W., & Krüger, L. (1982). Envy-free rights assignments and self-oriented preferences. *Mathematical Social Sciences, 2*, 199–208.
Gaertner, W., & Pattanaik, P. K. (1988). An interview with Amartya Sen. *Social Choice and Welfare, 5*, 69–79.
Gaertner, W., Pattanaik, P. K., & Suzumura, K. (1992). Individual rights revisited. *Economica, 59*, 161–177.
Gärdenfors, P. (1978). Fairness without interpersonal comparisons. *Theoria, 44*, 57–74.
Gärdenfors, P. (1981). Rights, games and social choice. *Noûs, 15*, 341–356.
Gärdenfors, P. (1983). On the information about individual utilities used in social choice. *Mathematical Social Sciences, 4*, 219–228.
Gekker, R. (1991). On the impossibility of an envy-free Paretian liberal. *Journal of Economics (Zeitschrift für Nationalökonomie), 53*, 75–82.
Gibbard, A. (1973). Manipulation of voting schemes: a general result. *Econometrica, 41*, 587–601.

Gibbard, A. (1974). A Pareto-consistent libertarian claim. *Journal of Economic Theory, 7*, 388–410.

Gibbard, A. (1982). Rights and the theory of social choice, in Cohen, Loś, Pfeiffer, & Podewski (1982), 595–605.

Gurvich, V. A. (1978). *Application of Boolean functions and contact schemes in game theory*. Candidate's dissertation, Moskow, Fiz-Tekn. Inst., in Russian.

Gurvich, V. A. (1989). Equilibrium in pure strategies. *Soviet Mathematics Doklady, 38*, 597–602.

Hammond, P. J. (1976). Equity, Arrow's conditions, and Rawls's difference principle. *Econometrica, 44*, 793–804.

Hammond, P. J. (1982). Liberalism, independence of rights and the Pareto principle, in Cohen, Loś, Pfeiffer, & Podewski (1982), 607–620.

Hammond, P. J. (1986). Consequentialist social norms for public decisions. In W. P. Heller, R. M. Starr & D. A. Starrett (Eds.), *Essays in honor of Kenneth J. Arrow* (pp. 3–27). Cambridge: Cambridge University Press.

Hammond, P. J. (1988). Consequentialism and the independence axiom. In B. R. Munier (Ed.), *Risk, decision and rationality* (pp. 503–515). Dordrecht: Kluwer Academic.

Hammond, P. J. (1995). Social choice of individual and group rights. In W. Barnett, H. Moulin, M. Salles & N. Schofield (Eds.), *Social choice, welfare, and ethics* (pp. 55–77). Cambridge: Cambridge University Press.

Hammond, P. J. (1996a). Game forms versus social choice rules as models of rights, in Arrow, Sen, & Suzumura (Eds.). (1996/1997), *2*, 82–95.

Hammond, P. J. (1996b). Consequentialist decision theory and utilitarian ethics. In F. Farina, F. Hahn & S. Vannucci (Eds.), *Ethics, rationality and economic behaviour* (pp. 92–118). Oxford: Clarendon Press.

Hammond, P. J. (2010). Competitive market mechanisms as social choice procedures. In K. J. Arrow, A. K. Sen & K. Suzumura (Eds.), *Handbook of social choice and welfare* (Vol. II, Ch. 15). Amsterdam: Elsevier.

Hansson, B. (1968). Choice structures and preference relations. *Synthese, 18*, 443–458.

Hansson, S. O. (1986). A note on the typology of rights. In P. Needham & J. Odelstad (Eds.), *Changing positions* (pp. 47–57). Uppsala: University of Uppsala.

Hansson, S. O. (1988). Rights and the liberal paradoxes. *Social Choice and Welfare, 5*, 287–302.

Hansson, S. O. (1996). Social choice with procedural preferences. *Social Choice and Welfare, 13*, 215–230.

Harel, A., & Nitzan, S. (1987). The libertarian resolution of the Paretian liberal paradox. *Zeitschrift für Nationalökonomie, 47*, 337–352.

Harsanyi, J. C. (1955). Cardinal welfare, individualistic ethics, and interpersonal comparisons of utility. *Journal of Political Economy, 63*, 309–321.

Hicks, J. R. (1939). The foundations of welfare economics. *Economic Journal, 49*, 696–712.

Hicks, J. R. (1940). The valuation of social income. *Economica, 7*, 105–124.

Hicks, J. R. (1959). *Essays in world economics*. Oxford: Clarendon Press.

Hicks, J. R. (1975). The scope and status of welfare economics. *Oxford Economic Papers, 27*, 307–326.

Hicks, J. R. (1981). *Collected essays in economic theory, Vol. 1, wealth and welfare*. Oxford: Basil Blackwell.

Hicks, J. R., & Allen, R. G. D. (1934). A reconsideration of the theory of value, I and II. *Economica, 1*, 52–75, 196–219.

Houthakker, H. S. (1950). Revealed preference and the utility function. *Economica, 17*, 159–174.

Hurwicz, L. (1996). Institutions as families of game forms. *Japanese Economic Review, 47*, 113–131.

Hurwicz, L., & Schmeidler, D. (1978). Construction of outcome functions guaranteeing existence and Pareto optimality of Nash equilibria. *Econometrica, 46*, 1447–1474.

Kaldor, N. (1939). Welfare propositions in economics and interpersonal comparisons of utility. *Economic Journal, 49*, 549–552.

Kanger, S. (1985). On realization of human rights. In G. Holmström & A. J. I. Jones (Eds.), *Action, logic and social theory, Acta Philosophica Fennica* (Vol. 38, pp. 71–78).

Kanger, S., & Kanger, H. (1966/1972). Rights and parliamentalism. *Theoria, 32*, 85–115. (Reprinted with changes in R. E. Olson & A. M. Paul (Eds.). (1972). *Contemporary philosophy in Scandinavia* (pp. 213–236). Baltimore, MD: The Johns Hopkins Press.)

Kaplow, L., & Shavell, S. (2001). Any non-welfarist method of policy assessment violates the Pareto principle. *Journal of Political Economy, 109*, 281–286.

Kaplow, L., & Shavell, S. (2002). *Fairness versus welfare*. Cambridge, MA: Harvard University Press.

Kaplow, L., & Shavell, S. (2004). Any non-welfarist method of policy assessment violates the Pareto principle: reply. *Journal of Political Economy, 112*, 249–251.

Karni, E. (1978). Collective rationality, unanimity and liberal ethics. *Review of Economic Studies, 45*, 571–574.

Keiding, H. (1986). Stability of effectivity functions with an infinite set of alternatives. *Methods of Operations Research, 50*, 519–530.

Kelly, J. S. (1976a). The impossibility of a just liberal. *Economica, 43*, 67–76.

Kelly, J. S. (1976b). Rights exercising and a Pareto-consistent libertarian claim. *Journal of Economic Theory, 13*, 138–153.

Kelly, J. S. (1978). *Arrow impossibility theorems*. New York: Academic Press.

Kelly, J. S. (1987). An interview with Kenneth J. Arrow. *Social Choice and Welfare, 4*, 43–62. (Reprinted in K. J. Arrow, A. K. Sen & K. Suzumura (Eds.). *Handbook of social choice and welfare* (Vol. II, Ch. 13). Amsterdam: Elsevier.)

Kelsey, D. (1985). The liberal paradox: a generalization. *Social Choice and Welfare, 1*, 245–250.

Kelsey, D. (1987). The role of information in social welfare judgements. *Oxford Economic Papers, 39*, 301–317.

Kelsey, D. (1988). What is responsible for the "Paretian epidemic"? *Social Choice and Welfare, 5*, 303–306.

Kolm, S.-C. (1972). *Justice et équité*. Paris: Editions du CNRS.

Kolpin, V. (1978). A note on tight extensive game forms. *International Journal of Game Theory, 17*, 187–191.

Koray, S. (2000). Self-selective social choice functions verify Arrow and Gibbard-Satterthwaite theorems. *Econometrica, 68*, 981–995.

Kreps, D. (1990). *A course in microeconomic theory*. Princeton: Princeton University Press.

Krüger, L., & Gaertner, W. (1983). Alternative libertarian claims and Sen's paradox. *Theory and Decision, 15*, 211–229.

Lerner, A. P. (1934). The concept of monopoly and the measurement of monopoly power. *Review of Economic Studies, 1*, 157–175.

Levi, I. (1982). Liberty and welfare. In A. Sen & B. Williams (Eds.), *Utilitarianism and beyond* (pp. 239–249). Cambridge: Cambridge University Press.

Li, S. (1994). Strongly consistent game forms. *Social Choice and Welfare, 11*, 177–192.

Little, I. M. D. (1952). Social choice and individual values. *Journal of Political Economy, 60*, 422–432.

Luce, R. D., & Raiffa, H. (1957). *Games and decisions*. New York: John Wiley & Sons.

Lyons, D. (1982). Utility and rights. *Nomos, 24*, 107–138.

MacIntyre, I. D. (1987). "The liberal paradox: a generalization" by D. Kelsey. *Social Choice and Welfare, 4*, 219–223.

MacIntyre, I. D. (1988). Justice, liberty, unanimity and the axiom of identity. *Theory and Decision, 24*, 225–237.

Mariotti, M., & Veneziani, R. (2009). Non-interference implies equality. *Social Choice and Welfare, 32*, 123–128.

Maskin, E. (1995). Majority rule, social welfare functions, and game forms. In K. Basu, P. K. Pattanaik & K. Suzumura (Eds.), *Choice, welfare, and development: a Festschrift in honour of Amartya K. Sen* (pp. 100–109). Oxford: Clarendon Press.

Mill, J. S. (1848/1965). *Principles of political economy with some of their applications to social philosophy*. London: Parker. (Reprinted in Robson, J. M. (Ed.). (1965). *Collected works of John Stuart Mill* (Vol. III). Toronto: University of Toronto Press.)

Mill, J. S. (1859/1977). *On liberty*. London: Parker. (Reprinted in Robson, J. M. (Ed.). (1977). *The collected works of John Stuart Mill* (Vol. XVIII). Toronto: University of Toronto Press.)

Moulin, H. (1983). *The strategy of social choice*. Amsterdam: North-Holland.

Moulin, H. (1986). *Game theory for the social sciences*. New York: New York University Press.

Moulin, H., & Peleg, B. (1982). Cores of effectivity functions and implementation theory. *Journal of Mathematical Economics, 10*, 115–145.

Nozick, R. (1974). *Anarchy, state and Utopia*. Oxford: Basil Blackwell.

Osborne, D. K. (1975). On liberalism and the Pareto principle. *Journal of Political Economy, 83*, 1283–1287.

Pareto, V. (1906). *Manuel di economia politica*. Milan: Societa Editrice Libraria. (French translation (revised), 1909, *Manual d'économie politique*. Paris: M. Giard. English translation, 1927, *Manual of political economy*. New York: A. M. Kelley.)

Pattanaik, P. K. (1968). Risk, impersonality, and the social welfare function. *Journal of Political Economy, 76*, 1152–1169.

Pattanaik, P. K. (1988). On the consistency of libertarian values. *Economica, 55*, 517–524.

Pattanaik, P. K. (1994). Rights and freedom in welfare economics. *European Economic Review, 38*, 731–738.

Pattanaik, P. K. (1996a). On modeling individual rights: some conceptual issues, in Arrow, Sen, & Suzumura (1996/1997), *I*, 100–128.

Pattanaik, P. K. (1996b). The liberal paradox: some interpretations when rights are represented as game forms. *Analyse & Kritik, 18*, 38–53.

Pattanaik, P. K., & Suzumura, K. (1994). Rights, welfarism and social choice. *American Economic Review: Papers and Proceedings, 84*, 435–439.

Pattanaik, P. K., & Suzumura, K. (1996). Individual rights and social evaluation: a conceptual framework. *Oxford Economic Papers, 48*, 194–212.

Pattanaik, P. K., & Xu, Y. (2003). Non-welfaristic policy assessment and the Pareto principle, mimeograph, University of California at Riverside.

Peleg, B. (1984). *Game theoretic analysis of voting in committees*. Cambridge: Cambridge University Press.

Peleg, B. (1998). Effectivity functions, game forms, games, and rights. *Social Choice and Welfare, 15*, 67–80.

Peleg, B. (2004). Representation of effectivity functions by acceptable game forms: a complete characterization. *Mathematical Social Sciences, 47*, 275–287.

Peleg, B., Peters, H., & Storcken, T. (2002). Nash consistent representation of constitutions: a reaction to the Gibbard paradox. *Mathematical Social Sciences, 43*, 267–287.

Pettit, P. (1988). The consequentialist can recognize rights. *Philosophical Quarterly, 38*, 42–55.

Pigou, A. C. (1920/1932). *The economics of welfare*. London: Macmillan (4th ed. 1932).

Rawls, J. (1958). Justice as fairness. *Philosophical Review, 67*, 164–194.

Rawls, J. (1971). *A theory of justice*. Cambridge, MA: Harvard University Press.

Reiss, H. (Ed.). (1970). *Kant's political writings*. Cambridge: Cambridge University Press.

Richter, M. K. (1966). Revealed preference theory. *Econometrica, 41*, 1075–1091.

Richter, M. K. (1971). Rational choice. In J. S. Chipman, L. Hurwicz, M. K. Richter & H. F. Sonnenschein (Eds.), *Preferences, utility, and demand* (pp. 29–58). New York: Harcourt Brace Jovanovich.

Riley, J. M. (1989/1990). Rights to liberty in purely private matters, Part I and Part II. *Economics and Philosophy, 5*, 121–166; *6*, 27–64.

Robbins, L. (1932/1935). *An essay on the nature and significance of economic science* (1st ed.). London: Macmillan (2nd ed., 1935).

Robbins, L. (1961). Hayek on liberty. *Economica, 28*, 66–81.

Rosenthal, R. W. (1972). Cooperative games in effectiveness form. *Journal of Economic Theory, 5*, 88–101.

Rowley, C. K. (1978). Liberalism and collective choice: a return to reality? *Manchester School of Economics and Social Studies, 46*, 224–251.

Saari, D. G. (1997). Are individual rights possible? *Mathematics Magazine, 70*, 83–92.

Saari, D. G. (1998). Connecting and resolving Sen's and Arrow's theorems. *Social Choice and Welfare, 15*, 239–261.

Samet, D., & Schmeidler, D. (2003). Between liberalism and democracy. *Journal of Economic Theory, 110*, 213–233.

Samuelson, P. A. (1938). A note on the pure theory of consumer's behaviour. *Economica, 5*, 61–71.

Samuelson, P. A. (1947/1983). *Foundations of economic analysis*. Cambridge, MA: Harvard University Press (enlarged ed., 1983).

Samuelson, P. A. (1948). Consumption theory in terms of revealed preference. *Economica, 15*, 243–253.

Samuelson, P. A. (1950a). Evaluation of real national income. *Oxford Economic Papers, 2*, 1–29.

Samuelson, P. A. (1950b). The problem of integrability in utility theory. *Economica, 17*, 355–385.

Samuelson, P. A. (1967). Arrow's mathematical politics. In S. Hook (Ed.), *Human values and economic policy* (pp. 41–52). New York: New York University Press.

Samuelson, P. A. (1974). Complementarity: an essay on the 40th anniversary of the Hicks-Allen revolution in demand theory. *Journal of Economic Literature, 12*, 1255–1289.

Samuelson, P. A. (1981). Bergsonian welfare economics. In S. Rosenfielde (Ed.), *Economic welfare and the economics of Soviet socialism: essays in honor of Abram Bergson* (pp. 223–266). Cambridge: Cambridge University Press.

Sandmo, A. (1990). Buchanan on political economy: a review article. *Journal of Economic Literature, 28*, 50–65.

Scitovsky, T. (1941). A note on welfare propositions in economics. *Review of Economic Studies, 9*, 77–88.

Seidl, C. (1975). On liberal values. *Zeitschrift für Nationalökonomie, 35*, 257–292.

Seidl, C. (1990). On the impossibility of a generalization of the libertarian resolution of the liberal paradox. *Public Choice, 51*, 71–88.

Sen, A. K. (1970a/1979). *Collective choice and social welfare*. San Francisco: Holden-Day, and Edinburgh: Oliver & Boyd. (Republished, Amsterdam: North-Holland, 1979.)

Sen, A. K. (1970b). The impossibility of a Paretian liberal. *Journal of Political Economy, 78*, 152–157.

Sen, A. K. (1971). Choice functions and revealed preference. *Review of Economic Studies, 38*, 307–317.

Sen, A. K. (1975). Is a Paretian liberal really impossible? a reply. *Public Choice, 21*, 111–113.

Sen, A. K. (1976). Liberty, unanimity and rights. *Economica, 43*, 217–245.

Sen, A. K. (1977a). Social choice theory: a re-examination. *Econometrica, 45*, 53–89.

Sen, A. K. (1977b). On weights and measures: informational constraints in social welfare analysis. *Econometrica, 45*, 1539–1573.

Sen, A. K. (1979a). Personal utilities and public judgements: or what's wrong with welfare economics? *Economic Journal, 89*, 537–558.

Sen, A. K. (1979b). Utilitarianism and welfarism. *Journal of Philosophy, 76*, 463–489.

Sen, A. K. (1982a). Rights and agency. *Philosophy and Public Affairs, 11*, 3–39.

Sen, A. K. (1982b). Liberty as control: an appraisal. *Midwest Studies in Philosophy*, 7, 207–221.

Sen, A. K. (1982c). *Choice, welfare and measurement*. Oxford: Basil Blackwell.

Sen, A. K. (1983). Liberty and social choice. *Journal of Philosophy, 80*, 5–28.

Sen, A. K. (1985). Well-being, agency and freedom: the Dewey Lecture 1984. *Journal of Philosophy, 82*, 169–221.

Sen, A. K. (1986a). Foundations of social choice theory: an epilogue. In J. Elster & A. Hylland (Eds.), *Foundations of social choice theory* (pp. 213–248). Cambridge: Cambridge University Press.

Sen, A. K. (1986b). Social choice theory. In K. J. Arrow & M. Intrilligator (Eds.), *Handbook of mathematical economics* (pp. 1073–1181). Amsterdam: North-Holland.
Sen, A. K. (1988). Freedom of choice: concept and content. *European Economic Review, 32*, 269–294.
Sen, A. K. (1992). Minimal liberty. *Economica, 59*, 139–159.
Sen, A. K. (1996a). Rights: formulation and consequences. *Analyse & Kritik, 18*, 153–170.
Sen, A. K. (1996b). Legal rights and moral rights: old questions and new problems. *Ratio Juris, 9*, 153–167.
Sen, A. K. (2002). *Rationality and freedom*. Cambridge, MA: The Belknap Press of Harvard University Press.
Stevens, D. N., & Foster, J. E. (1978). The possibility of democratic pluralism. *Economica, 45*, 401–406.
Sugden, R. (1978). Social choice and individual liberty. In M. J. Artis & A. R. Nobay (Eds.), *Contemporary economic analysis* (pp. 243–271). London: Croom Helm.
Sugden, R. (1981). *The political economy of public choice*. Oxford: Martin Robertson.
Sugden, R. (1985). Liberty, preference, and choice. *Economics and Philosophy, 1*, 213–229.
Sugden, R. (1993). Rights: why do they matter, and to whom? *Constitutional Political Economy, 4*, 127–152.
Sugden, R. (1994). The theory of rights. In H. Siebert (Ed.), *The ethical foundations of the market economy* (pp. 31–53). Tübingen: J. C. B. Mohr.
Suzumura, K. (1976). Remarks on the theory of collective choice. *Economica, 43*, 381–390.
Suzumura, K. (1977). Houthakker's axiom in the theory of rational choice. *Journal of Economic Theory, 14*, 284–290.
Suzumura, K. (1978). On the consistency of libertarian claims. *Review of Economic Studies, 45*, 329–342.
Suzumura, K. (1979). On the consistency of libertarian claims: a correction. *Review of Economic Studies, 46*, 743.
Suzumura, K. (1980). Liberal paradox and the voluntary exchange of rights exercising. *Journal of Economic Theory, 22*, 407–422.
Suzumura, K. (1981a). On Pareto-efficiency and the no-envy concept of equity. *Journal of Economic Theory, 25*, 367–379.
Suzumura, K. (1981b). On the possibility of "fair" collective choice rule. *International Economic Review, 22*, 351–364.
Suzumura, K. (1982). Equity, efficiency and rights in social choice. *Mathematical Social Sciences, 3*, 131–155.
Suzumura, K. (1983a). *Rational choice, collective decisions, and social welfare*. New York: Cambridge University Press.
Suzumura, K. (1983b). Resolving conflicting views of justice in social choice. In P. K. Pattanaik & M. Salles (Eds.), *Social choice and welfare* (pp. 125–149). Amsterdam: North-Holland.
Suzumura, K. (1990). Alternative approaches to libertarian rights in the theory of social choice. In K. J. Arrow (Ed.), *Markets and welfare: issues in contemporary economics* (Vol. 1, pp. 215–242). London.
Suzumura, K. (1991). On the voluntary exchange of libertarian rights. *Social Choice and Welfare, 8*, 199–206.
Suzumura, K. (1996). Welfare, rights, and social choice procedure: a perspective. *Analyse & Kritik, 18*, 20–37.
Suzumura, K. (1999). Consequences, opportunities, and procedures. *Social Choice and Welfare, 16*, 17–40.
Suzumura, K. (2000). Welfare economics beyond welfarist-consequentialism. *Japanese Economic Review, 50*, 1–32.
Suzumura, K. (2001). Pareto principles from Inch to Ell. *Economics Letters, 70*, 95–98.
Suzumura, K. (2002). Introduction. In K. J. Arrow, A. K. Sen & K. Suzumura (Eds.), *Handbook of social choice and welfare* (Vol. I, pp. 1–32). Amsterdam: Elsevier.
Suzumura, K. (2005). An interview with Paul Samuelson: welfare economics, "old" and "new", and social choice theory. *Social Choice and Welfare, 25*, 327–356.
Suzumura, K. (2010). *Choice, opportunities, and procedures: selected papers on social choice and welfare*, forthcoming.
Suzumura, K., & Suga, K. (1986). Gibbardian libertarian claims revisited. *Social Choice and Welfare, 3*, 61–74.

Suzumura, K., & Xu, Y. (2001). Characterizations of consequentialism and non-consequentialism. *Journal of Economic Theory, 101*, 423–436.

Suzumura, K., & Xu, Y. (2003). Consequences, opportunities, and generalized consequentialism and non-consequentialism. *Journal of Economic Theory, 111*, 293–304.

Suzumura, K., & Xu, Y. (2004). Welfarist-consequentialism, similarity of attitudes, and Arrow's general impossibility theorem. *Social Choice and Welfare, 22*, 237–251.

Suzumura, K., & Xu, Y. (2009). Consequentialism and non-consequentialism: the axiomatic approach. In P. Anand, P. K. Pattanaik, & C. Puppe (Eds.), *Handbook of decision theory and social choice* (pp. 346–373). Oxford: Oxford University Press.

Suzumura, K., & Yoshihara, N. (2008). On initial conferment of individual rights. Working paper, Institute of Economic Research, Hitotsubashi University.

Tadenuma, K. (2002). Efficiency first or equity first? Two principles and rationality of social choice. *Journal of Economic Theory, 104*, 462–472.

Thomson, W., & Varian, H. R. (1985). Theories of justice based on symmetry. In L. Hurwicz, D. Schmeidler & H. Sonnenschein (Eds.), *Social goals and social organization: essays in memory of Elisha Pazner* (pp. 107–129). Cambridge: Cambridge University Press.

Valentine, P. (1989). How to combine Pareto optimality with liberty considerations. *Theory and Decision, 27*, 217–240.

van Hees, M. (1995a). *Rights and decisions: formal models of law and liberalism.* Dordrecht: Kluwer Academic.

van Hees, M. (1995b). Libertarian collective decision-making: a new framework. *Social Choice and Welfare, 12*, 155–164.

van Hees, M. (1999). Liberalism, efficiency, and stability: some possibility results. *Journal of Economic Theory, 88*, 294–309.

Varian, H. R. (1974). Equity, envy, and efficiency. *Journal of Economic Theory, 9*, 63–91.

Varian, H. R. (1975). Distributive justice, welfare economics, and the theory of fairness. *Philosophy and Public Affairs, 4*, 223–247.

Wriglesworth, J. L. (1982a). Using justice principles to resolve the "impossibility of a Paretian liberal." *Economics Letters, 10*, 217–221.

Wriglesworth, J. L. (1982b). The possibility of democratic pluralism. A comment. *Economica, 49*, 43–48.

Wriglesworth, J. L. (1985a). Respecting individual rights in social choice. *Oxford Economic Papers, 37*, 100–117.

Wriglesworth, J. L. (1985b). *Libertarian conflicts in social choice.* Cambridge: Cambridge University Press.

Xu, Y. (1990). The libertarian paradox: some further observations. *Social Choice and Welfare*, 7, 343–351.

CHAPTER TWENTY-FOUR

Freedom, Opportunity, and Well-Being

James E. Foster
The George Washington University and Oxford Poverty and Human Development Initiative, Oxford, UK

Contents

Abstract

This paper reexamines key results from the measurement of *opportunity freedom,* or the extent to which a set of options offers a decision maker real opportunities to achieve. Three cases are investigated: no preferences, a single preference, and plural preferences. The three corresponding evaluation methods—the cardinality relation, the indirect utility relation, and the effective freedom relation—and their variations are considered within a common axiomatic framework. Special attention is given to representations of freedom rankings, with the goal of providing practical approaches for measuring opportunity freedom and the extent of people's capabilities.

Keywords: freedom, individual choices, welfare, capabilities, axiomatic approach, orderings.
JEL codes: D63, D03, Z13, I31

ISSN: 0169-7218, DOI: 10.1016/S0169-7218(10)00024-9

1. INTRODUCTION

Choice is a central feature of economic models, and the evaluation of choice outcomes is fundamental to welfare economics and to the development of policies for improving welfare. Traditional evaluation methods focus purely on the outcome—say, the bundle of goods or the occupation—selected by the decision maker. Yet a compelling case can be made for broadening the basis of evaluation to include other factors, such as the *process* by which the choice was made and the number and characteristics of *unchosen* alternatives (Sen 1988, 2002). This is the fundamental concern of the *freedom* approach to welfare economics, which argues that broader contextual features of choice may have normative value beyond their impact on the specific alternative selected.

The relevant issues can be illustrated by the case of Jill, a newly minted graduate who has just chosen teaching as her life's vocation. An evaluation of Jill's life chances and well-being might consider the salary, benefits and other characteristics of this profession, and the lifestyle that it might entail. However, suppose that it were revealed that the process by which Jill "chose" her occupation included a preliminary stage in which most other occupations, including the one she preferred—civil engineering—were simply removed from her choice set by a society that regarded them as inappropriate for women. Or alternatively, suppose her home was a small village and significant pressure was brought to bear on her to adhere to the expressed preferences of, say, a local chieftain. Or suppose that the actual choice was made on her behalf by some nameless government functionary. It seems reasonable that an evaluation of the choice outcome should not be indifferent to the process that led to that outcome—particularly when the process can stray so far from the idealized, traditional view of choice.

All of these scenarios involve a compromised choice process—the first in which the option set is artificially limited (agenda manipulation), the second in which the chooser's preferences are distorted (preference manipulation), and the final in which the selection is made by another person (choice manipulation). Each likely delivers an outcome that is different to one that would arise in the absence of manipulation. But even if the selected option—Jill's vocation in the above scenarios—were identical to the one obtained under autonomous, free choice, the fact that the process is deeply flawed may well change our evaluation of the outcome. The low level of personal autonomy and the clear vulnerability to luck and the whims of others detract from an otherwise agreeable conclusion to the decision process.

Sen (2002) has discussed at some length the "process aspect of freedom" whose roots are found in many classic works in economics and philosophy (Kant 1788, Mill 1848, 1859, Smith 1759). Contemporary works in economics and related fields have stressed the importance of human agency and process freedom (Agarwal, Humphries, and Robeyns 2007, Frank 1988, Nagel 1970, Nozick 1974, Rawls 1971, Scitovsky

1986, Sugden 1981, 1998, van Hees 1998) and much effort is being devoted to developing empirically relevant measures (Alkire 2008). Additional applications to the study of corruption, competition policy, law and economics, and behavioral economics can be readily envisioned.

This chapter focuses on a second way that freedom enters into the analysis of choice and welfare that is called by Sen (2002) the "opportunity aspect of freedom." Suppose that the agent has free choice from a naturally occurring set of options (and hence unrestricted process freedom). A larger set of options offers the decision maker a greater opportunity to obtain a more favorable selection.[1] The usual method of evaluation, however, ignores all available options apart from the chosen one. In the case of Jill, this would amount to saying that a setting in which her *only* option available is to become a civil engineer (her favorite choice) is equivalent to the setting in which she has before her a broad array of plausible and desirable occupations, from which she selects civil engineering. In contrast to this standard view, the wider range of real opportunities is seen to enhance the opportunity aspect of freedom even when the final choice is the same.

Much of the literature on opportunity freedom has been concerned with identifying a source of value for unchosen options, and providing a way of measuring this value. One approach posits that there is an intrinsic value to having a greater number of options, irrespective of the qualities the extra options bring. This naturally leads to an emphasis on the *quantity* of options and hence to a *counting* or *cardinality* approach to measuring opportunity freedom (Pattanaik and Xu 1990). Alternatively, one can consider the *quality* of options as indicated by the preferences or utility of the decision maker. The key example, known as the *indirect utility* approach, evaluates an opportunity set by the value of its best element. Other methods take into account both the quantity and quality of alternatives (Sen 1991, Bossert, Pattanaik, and Xu 1993).

There is yet another route by which unchosen options are seen to be valuable. Let us return to the example of Jill at the moment of decision and ask: If the preference relation were fixed and known, so that the choice could be predicted with certainty, why should the other options in the opportunity set matter at all? A traditional indirect utility view would conclude that they have no value. However, the situation would be different if, when we approached Jill, she were of two minds about her preferences. If Jill thought that she *might* prefer teaching over civil engineering, but also might have the *opposite* preferences, then there may be value to having additional options due to Jill's uncertainty regarding her preferences. The situation is analogous to an analysis of flexibility by Kreps (1979) in which the value of having more options originates from the presence of unresolved uncertainty, and is also similar to Weisbrod's (1964) notion of

[1] This presumes that the options being added are desirable; and that the additional costs of decision making with more options are not so large as to outweigh the benefits.

"option value." This gives rise to a third approach to evaluating opportunity freedom—the *plural preference* approach.

The most important contemporary exponent of the analysis of freedom and choice is Amartya Sen, who through a series of books and papers has argued forcefully for broadening the informational bases of welfare economics to include the opportunity freedoms we have. He defines *capabilities* to be the real freedoms people have to achieve beings and doings they value and have reason to value (Sen 1980, 1985, 1992). The *capability set* is "a set of vectors of functionings, reflecting the person's freedom to lead one type of life or another . . . to choose from possible livings" (Sen 1992, p. 40).[2] The capability approach evaluates social and economic outcomes in the space of human lives and yet maintains a substantive role for opportunity freedom. A key question is how to measure the extent of choice in a given capability set, or how to measure opportunity freedom. The work presented in this chapter can be viewed as providing a theoretical basis for empirical measures of capabilities.

One noteworthy feature of the capability approach is that it does not reduce well-being into a single dimension (such as income or utility) but instead is inherently multidimensional. For example, a person's capability set might include capabilities related to nutrition, to knowledge, to friendship, or other dimensions. The capability approach would suggest that an adequate measure of well-being (or poverty) must reflect the conditions in multiple dimensions simultaneously. For example, the Human Development Index (HDI), to which Sen contributed (UNDP 1990), measures well-being with respect to health, education, and income. More recently, the capability approach has provided the conceptual framework for a substantial literature on multidimensional poverty measurement (Alkire and Foster 2007, Anand and Sen 1997, Atkinson 2003, Bourguignon and Chakravarty 2003) designed to supplement or replace traditional income-based poverty measures.[3]

This chapter reviews the literature on the evaluation of opportunity freedom, intuitively defined as the extent to which a set of options, or an opportunity set, offers an agent a range of meaningful choices.[4] The basic objects of study are *rankings* of opportunity sets, *measures* of freedom, and the *axioms* they satisfy. We survey some of the main approaches to constructing freedom rankings and explore combinations of axioms

[2] See also Foster and Sen (1997) and Basu and López-Calva (2010). Sen's 2009 book *The Idea of Justice* restates the importance of considering human advantage in the space of capabilities.

[3] See Sen (1976), Foster, Greer, and Thorbecke (1984, 2010), and Foster and Sen (1997) for discussions of income poverty measurement. Note that the multidimensional measures, though motivated by the capability approach, use data on achieved functionings rather than capabilities.

[4] This is by no means an exhaustive account of the existing literature on freedom evaluation. Instead, the goal here is to highlight some of the key results, and several new findings, within a coherent overarching framework. More extensive presentations may be found in the surveys of Barberà, Bossert, and Pattanaik (2004), Gaertner (2006), and Dowding and van Hees (2009), as well as in collections such as Laslier *et al.* (1998).

that characterize specific freedom rankings. We reinterpret several axiomatic characterizations of rankings as representation theorems. Since many freedom rankings are incomplete, we often use a vector-valued function to represent the underlying ranking, with noncomparable vectors indicating situations where two sets cannot be ranked.[5] We also explore extensions of the resulting quasi-orderings to complete orderings and note the common structure of the various measures of freedom.

A key tension in the measurement of freedom arises between the quantity and quality of available alternatives, and different evaluation strategies emphasize one of these aspects exclusively or attempt to include them both. Of critical importance is whether the agent has a preference ordering over *alternatives* that may be invoked in constructing a freedom ranking over *sets*. Three cases are investigated in this chapter: (1) where there is no preference ordering, (2) where there is a single preference ordering, and (3) where there is a collection of potential orderings. In the first case, the absence of preference information means that a freedom measure can only reflect quantitative aspects of opportunity sets. This can lead to the most basic kind of freedom ranking—set inclusion—or, under additional axioms (e.g., Pattanaik and Xu 1990), to a complete ordering where freedom is measured by the cardinality of a given set. The severe incompleteness of the former and the profound arbitrariness of the latter provide a strong incentive to incorporate additional information on the relative desirability of alternatives.

In the second case, where a preference relation or a utility function over individual alternatives is provided, the quality of the elements in a given set can be incorporated into the measurement of freedom. The traditional economic model of decision making leads us to identify the value of a given set with the utility of its best element. The resulting indirect utility criterion for measuring freedom ignores the number and characteristics of unchosen alternatives in the set, instead viewing greater freedom purely in terms of the ability to achieve a better outcome. It can be axiomatically characterized and has an intuitive representation in terms of the size of the set of alternatives that the best element dominates.

The indirect utility freedom measure, like the cardinality measures of freedom, generates a complete ordering of opportunity sets by focusing exclusively on one aspect of freedom (in this case quality instead of quantity). If both aspects are deemed to have salience, new rankings can be constructed by either *aggregating* the cardinality and indirect utility measures of freedom or by taking their *intersection*, wherein an increase in freedom requires an increase in both. We present these approaches and explore the properties of the resulting combination freedom rankings.

[5] On incompleteness see Majumdar and Sen (1976), Putnam (2002), or Sen (2002). Vector-valued representations of incomplete relations abound in economics, and include Pareto dominance, mean variance analysis, stochastic dominance, among other well-known examples. See Foster (1993) or Ok (2002).

The indirect utility approach depends entirely on the utility of a best alternative in a set and ignores the unchosen alternatives in the set and the unavailable alternatives outside the set. One could augment this informational basis by including the second best utility level, the third, and so forth, resulting in many dimensions of quality. Once again the multidimensionality might be dealt with by aggregation (yielding a freedom measure and a complete ordering) or by intersection (yielding a quasi-ordering with a vector-valued representation). The resulting freedom rankings are presented and their properties are also discussed.

In the third case of *plural preferences*, the agent has a set of potential preference relations, each of which may be the agent's actual preference when it comes time to select an alternative from the opportunity set. However, the agent must rank sets *before* it is known which preference will obtain. A natural way of dealing with this uncertainty is to rank sets according to the intersection of the indirect utility orderings of the potential preferences. The resulting *effective freedom* ranking judges one set to have greater than or equal freedom to another if all indirect utility orderings agree this is so (Foster 1993). As with the indirect utility approach, it is the quality rather than the number of alternatives in a set that determines its ranking. If preferences are very similar, then one very good alternative may do the trick, and the freedom ranking would resemble an indirect utility ranking; but if preferences vary dramatically, then a variety of good alternatives may be needed for a set to be highly ranked. This is the sense in which the multiple preference approach can favor greater numbers of alternatives. We present the effective freedom relation, its properties, and several representations, and then provide an interesting extension of this quasi-ordering to a complete ordering based on a count of options in the associated *effective opportunity set*. As the collection of potential preferences varies from a single preference ordering to all possible orderings, the effective freedom relation varies from the indirect utility ordering to set inclusion, while the counting ordering varies from the indirect utility ordering to the cardinality ordering of Pattanaik and Xu (1990).

Sen (2002) considers a subrelation of the effective freedom quasi-ordering in which the order of intersecting and evaluating indirect utility is reversed: preferences are intersected to obtain a quasi-ordering of alternatives which then is used to construct a generalized indirect utility relation. The altered order ensures that Sen's freedom relation is generally less complete than the effective freedom quasi-ordering; however, when the Sen relation applies, it conveys additional information that is especially useful in a model where the timing of events reversed. Arrow (1995) extends the effective freedom quasi-ordering to a complete ordering by assigning probabilities to the various preferences—now given as utility functions—and aggregating over indirect utility levels. We note that when all logically possible preference orderings are possible and equally likely, Arrow's extension can be reduced to Pattanaik and Xu's (1990) cardinality measure once again.

2. NOTATION

In what follows, the (finite) universal set of n alternatives will be denoted by X. An *opportunity set* or *menu* is any nonempty subset of X, with the set of all such menus being denoted by Z. Freedom is evaluated using a binary relation R on Z, with ARB indicating that the level of freedom offered by $A \in Z$ is as great as the level offered by $B \in Z$. R is typically assumed to be a *quasi-ordering,* which means that R is reflexive and transitive. Notice that completeness (requiring the relation to rank any two opportunity sets) is not being assumed; it is entirely possible that neither ARA' nor $A'RA$ holds for any given pair A and A' in Z.

The asymmetric part of R, denoted P, and the symmetric part of R, denoted I, decompose this relation in such a way that APB indicates that A has strictly more freedom than B, while AIB ensures that the two opportunity sets have the same level of freedom. It is easily shown that both I and P are transitive relations. The cardinality of menu A, denoted $|A|$, will play an important role in the first approach to measuring freedom. The *cardinality freedom ranking* R^C is defined by AR^CB if and only if $|A| \geq |B|$; it judges freedom on the basis of the number of elements in a menu. The second approach will make use of a preference ordering R_1 on X, whose ranking over individual alternatives will be used in constructing the freedom ranking R over menus of alternatives. The *indirect utility freedom ranking* R^U is defined by AR^UB if and only if there exists $x \in A$ such that $xR_1\,y$ for all $y \in B$; it judges freedom on the basis of the best alternatives in the menus. The third approach constructs R with the help of a finite number m of preference orderings $R_1, \ldots, R_m$ on X; the collection of preference orderings will be denoted by $\mathfrak{R} = \{R_1, \ldots, R_m\}$.

3. FREEDOM COUNTS

Our first approach to measuring freedom follows the old saw that certain academic officials can count but can't read; in other words, quantity is observable, but quality is not easily ascertained. Regardless of the accuracy of this observation, it provides a handy place to begin our discussion of the measurement of freedom viewed as the number of available choices. Our focus is the approach of Pattanaik and Xu (1990), whose axiomatic result characterizing the cardinality measure of freedom has produced much discussion.[6] We provide an intuitive proof of the characterization theorem, and then subject it to a sensitivity analysis in which the axioms are progressively relaxed until the essential source

[6] See also Suppes (1987), Sen (1990, 1991, 2002), and Puppe (1996), among others.

of the result is revealed.[7] We also translate the theorem into a vector space structure, to show that it has the form of a traditional additive representation theorem.

3.1. Rankings and Axioms

To frame their analysis, Pattanaik and Xu (1990) take as their primary concern the *intrinsic* value of freedom, not its instrumental use in achieving utility or some other end. They provide a series of axioms to help define their notion of freedom. The first of these axioms requires the freedom ranking to have a rather strong form of consistency: that the relative ranking of a pair of opportunity sets is unchanged when an additional alternative is added to, or when a common alternative is removed from, both sets.

Simple Independence Let A, B, and C be elements of Z for which $A \cap C = \emptyset = B \cap C$ and $|C| = 1$. Then ARB if and only if $(A \cup C)R(B \cup C)$.

Notice that this axiom actually comprises two separate conditional requirements. The first requires that if A is comparable to B by the freedom ranking, then the enlarged set $(A \cup C)$ is *comparable* to the enlarged set $(B \cup C)$, and moreover, the ranking of these sets should be the *same* as the ranking of A versus B. The second requires that if $(A \cup C)$ can be compared to $(B \cup C)$, then the smaller sets A and B must be comparable and have a ranking that corresponds to the ranking over the larger sets. The latter requirement can be problematic for certain notions of freedom. In particular, if A and B are initially noncomparable or one is strictly preferred to the other, and both are dominated by a third set C, then we might expect $(A \cup C)$ to be indifferent to $(B \cup C)$. But this is not allowed under the second part of this axiom.

A basic requirement for a freedom ranking is for the expansion of an opportunity set to enhance its freedom or at least leave it unchanged. Pattanaik and Xu (1990) focus on the special case where the initial set under consideration is singleton and then strengthen the requirement to demand a *strict* increase in freedom when a second alternative becomes available.

Simple Strict Monotonicity Let A and B be elements of Z with $|B| = 1$ and $|A| = 2$. If $B \subset A$ then APB.

Note that under this version of monotonicity, indifference between a two-element menu and a singleton subset is ruled out—regardless of the characteristics or quality of the extra alternative.

The final axiom assumes that all singleton sets are comparable and specifies a particular ranking for them.

[7] In this way we extend the line of discussion in Sen (2002).

Simple Anonymity Let A and B be elements of Z with $|A| = 1$. If $|A| = |B|$ then AIB.

This axiom ensures that the singleton opportunity sets all have the same level of freedom, irrespective of the characteristics or quality of the alternative each happens to contain.

Now which freedom rankings satisfy all three of these properties, as well as the maintained assumption that R is a quasi-ordering? Pattanaik and Xu (1990) provide the answer as follows:

Theorem 1 *R is a quasi-ordering satisfying simple independence, simple strict monotonicity, and simple anonymity, if and only if R is the cardinality ordering R^C.*

Thus, the only quasi-ordering consistent with this collection of properties is the one that is based on a simple counting of alternatives in the respective sets.

We will presently provide an additional interpretation of this theorem, but first let us explore some direct implications of the Pattanaik and Xu (1990) axioms. Notice that the three axioms are stated with restrictions on the sizes of sets (hence the term "simple"). Consider the following counterparts in which these restrictions have been removed.[8]

Independence Let A, B, and C be elements of Z for which $A \cap C = \emptyset = B \cap C$. Then ARB if and only if $(A \cup C)R(B \cup C)$.

Strict Monotonicity Let A and B be elements of Z. If $B \subset A$ then APB.

Anonymity Let A and B be elements of Z. If $|A| = |B|$ then AIB.

The next result shows that this collection of axioms is entirely as general as the three simple counterparts.[9]

Lemma 1 *Let R be a quasi-ordering. Then independence, strict monotonicity, and anonymity are equivalent to simple independence, simple strict independence, and simple anonymity.*

Proof. If R satisfies the unrestricted versions of the three axioms, then it clearly satisfies the simple versions. Conversely, suppose that R satisfies the simple versions. It is immediately clear that R must satisfy independence. To see this, let $A \cap C = \emptyset = B \cap C$ where C contains more than one alternative. Rather than adding all the elements of C at once to A and B, we can do this one element of C at a time to obtain a series of pairs of sets beginning with A and B and ending with $A \cup C$ and $B \cup C$. Applying simple

[8] The three simple versions were originally called Independence (IND), Strict Monotonicity (SM), and Indifference between No-choice Situations (INS), by Pattanaik and Xu. The Sen (2002) terminology for the latter two is Superiority of Some Choice and Principle of No Choice, while the three stronger versions are called Suppes Additivity, Strict Set Dominance, and Equi-cardinality Indifference, respectively. Note that $\subset$ indicates strict set inclusion throughout.

[9] Related results are found in Sen (2002, p. 688).

independence to adjacent pairs in this series yields a string of equivalences from ARB to $(A \cup C)R(B \cup C)$, and hence independence.

Next we show that R satisfies strict monotonicity. Suppose that $A \supset B$ where $|A| - |B| = 1$. Select any subset C of B such that $B' = B \backslash C$ has cardinality $|B'| = 1$ and $A' = A \backslash C$ has cardinality $|A'| = 2$. Then by simple strict monotonicity it follows that $A'PB'$ and hence by independence we have APB. Now let $k > 1$ and suppose that $A \supset B$ entails APB for all A and B satisfying $|A| - |B| < k$. We will show that this is also true for $|A| - |B| = k$. Let $A \supset B$ with $|A| - |B| = k$, and pick any B'' such that $A \supset B''$ and $B'' \supset B$. Then by the induction hypothesis APB'' and $B''PB$, and hence we obtain APB by the transitivity of P. This establishes strict monotonicity.

Finally, to show that R satisfies anonymity, let $k > 1$ and suppose that $|A| = |B|$ entails AIB for all A and B satisfying $|A| < k$. We will show this is also true for $|A| = k$. So let $|A| = |B| = k$. Pick c in $A \cap B$ if this set is nonempty and denote $A' = A \backslash \{c\}$ and $B' = B \backslash \{c\}$. By independence and the induction hypothesis we have AIB. If $A \cap B = \emptyset$, then pick any a in A and b in B, and denote $A' = A \backslash \{a\}$ and $B' = B \backslash \{b\}$. By the induction hypothesis, we have $A'IB'$ and hence $(A' \cup \{a\})I(B' \cup \{a\})$ by independence, and moreover $(B' \cup \{a\})I(B' \cup \{b\})$ by simple anonymity and independence. Hence, by the transitivity of I, we have AIB. This verifies that anonymity holds. □

This result shows that the unrestricted versions of the axioms are collectively equivalent to the original simple versions. Armed with this observation, the proof of the Pattanaik and Xu (1990) theorem is immediate.

Proof (Theorem 1). It is clear that the cardinality ordering R^C satisfies all three axioms. Now let us begin with any quasi-ordering R satisfying all three axioms. We want to show that R is R^C. Suppose that AR^CB or, equivalently, $|A| \geq |B|$. Pick any $C \subseteq A$ with $|C| = |B|$. By strict monotonicity (or reflexivity) we know that ARC, while anonymity ensures that CIB. Hence by transitivity we conclude that ARB. Conversely, suppose that it is not the case that AR^CB or, equivalently, that we have $|A| < |B|$. Select $C \supset A$ with $|C| = |B|$. By anonymity we have BIC while by strict monotonicity we know CPA. By transitivity we cannot have ARB. Therefore, AR^CB if and only if ARB. □

The simple anonymity axiom is transformed by the independence axiom into anonymity, which in turn implies that the indifference class associated with a given opportunity set includes all sets having the same number of alternatives. By independence, the characteristics of R are dependent on how it compares opportunity sets with cardinality 1 and 2. What role does simple strict monotonicity play in the proof of the characterization result? First, it ensures that there is *comparability* across opportunity sets of sizes 1 and 2. This fact alone (along with independence) leaves open three possibilities for R: either it is represented by $|A|$, it is represented by $-|A|$, or it is constant across all opportunity sets A. The second role that simple strict monotonicity plays is to determine the particular *orientation* for this ranking, thus ensuring that the first of these possibilities—the cardinality ordering—is the only one that applies.

We noted earlier that the strict forms of monotonicity are not unambiguously acceptable, since they require that the addition of an alternative must lead to a strictly higher level of freedom, irrespective of the alternative's characteristics. On the other hand, few would argue that the addition of an alternative would not lead to a weakly higher (higher or the same) level of freedom. The following weaker monotonicity axioms allow freedom to remain the same when a new alternative is added, and hence are arguably more natural requirements for a freedom ranking.[10]

Simple Monotonicity Let A and B be elements of Z with $|B| = 1$ and $|A| = 2$. If $B \subseteq A$ then ARB.

Monotonicity Let A and B be elements of Z. If $B \subseteq A$ then ARB.

Each of these two axioms is implied by its strict counterpart. Moreover, simple monotonicity and monotonicity are clearly equivalent for a quasi-ordering R satisfying independence. To see the marginal importance of the strictness of the monotonicity axiom, we explore what happens to the Pattanaik and Xu (1990) result when the strict form of monotonicity is replaced by the weaker version. Consider the *trivial* freedom ranking R^T defined by AR^TB for all $A, B \in Z$, so that R^T regards all opportunity sets as having the same level of freedom. It turns out that there are *two* freedom rankings consistent with the previous two axioms and the less restrictive monotonicity axiom.

Theorem 2 *R is a quasi-ordering satisfying simple independence, simple monotonicity and simple anonymity if and only if R is the cardinality ordering R^C or the trivial ordering R^T.*

Proof. It is clear that the orderings R^C and R^T satisfy the three axioms. Now let us suppose that R is any quasi-ordering satisfying the three, hence independence and anonymity by an argument analogous to Lemma 1. We want to show that R is either R^C or R^T. So let x and y be any two distinct alternatives in X. By simple monotonicity, we obtain $\{x, y\}R\{y\}$. Suppose first that $\{x, y\}P\{y\}$ for this particular x and y. Then by anonymity and transitivity it follows that APB for any A and B in Z with $|A| = 2$ and $|B| = 1$. Hence R must satisfy simple strict monotonicity, and so by Theorem 1 we know that R is R^C. Alternatively, suppose that $\{x, y\}I\{y\}$ for the given x and y. Then by anonymity and transitivity we obtain AIB for any A and B in Z with $|A| = 2$ and $|B| = 1$. Independence extends this conclusion to any A and B with $|A| - |B| = 1$, and hence, by transitivity, to all A and B in Z. Consequently, R is R^T. □

This result offers strong evidence that strict monotonicity is not the driving force behind the Pattanaik and Xu theorem. Even when simple strict monotonicity is replaced by

[10] Monotonicity is called Weak Set Dominance in Sen (2002).

simple monotonicity—an innocuous requirement that augmenting a singleton set by an additional alternative either increases freedom or leaves it unchanged—the simple independence and simple anonymity axioms conspire to ensure that the resulting ordering is either the cardinality ordering or the trivial ordering (that considers all opportunity sets to have the same level of freedom). The "strictness" of the monotonicity in the Pattanaik and Xu theorem only serves to remove the trivial ranking.

As mentioned, the independence axioms are made up of two parts: an implication from smaller sets (ARB) to larger sets ($(A \cup C)R(B \cup C)$); and a converse implication from the larger sets to the smaller. The first of these is fundamental to the notion of freedom: adding the same alternatives to two ranked sets cannot render the sets unrankable, nor can it strictly reverse the ranking. The second component, by which removing the same alternatives from the two sets preserves the ranking, is quite restrictive and, indeed, is inconsistent with many plausible conceptions of freedom. We now explore the implications of removing the objectionable part of this axiom. Consider the following requirements for freedom rankings:

Simple Semi-Independence Let A, B, and C be elements of Z for which $A \cap C = \emptyset = B \cap C$ and $|C| = 1$. Then ARB implies $(A \cup C)R(B \cup C)$.

Semi-Independence Let A, B, and C be elements of Z for which $A \cap C = \emptyset = B \cap C$. Then ARB implies $(A \cup C)R(B \cup C)$.

These axioms retain the unambiguous part of the original independence axioms, which requires the addition of elements to A and B not to disrupt the original ranking of A and B. It is easy to show by a proof entirely analogous to the one given above for the independence axioms that the two forms of semi-independence are equivalent. Moreover, this more limited form of independence is all that is needed to show that simple monotonicity is equivalent to monotonicity and simple anonymity is equivalent to anonymity.

Now what is the impact of relaxing simple independence in Theorem 2 to simple semi-independence? For $k = 1, \ldots, n$, define the *censored cardinality measure* $|A|^k$ by: $|A|^k = |A|$ for $|A| < k$ and $|A|^k = k$ for $|A| \geq k$. Consider the *censored freedom ranking* R^k defined by AR^kB if and only if $|A|^k \geq |B|^k$. Notice that R^n is simply R^C, the cardinality ranking, which measures freedom in terms of the number of elements in the set; while R^1 is R^T, the trivial ranking for which all sets have equal freedom. For k between 1 and n the freedom ranking R^k orders sets on the basis of their cardinality censored at k. Freedom is augmented by an additional alternative so long as the total number of alternatives remains below k; thereafter, adding an alternative has no effect on freedom. We have the following result.

Theorem 3 *R is a quasi-ordering satisfying simple semi-independence, simple monotonicity, and simple anonymity if and only if R is R^k for some $k = 1, \ldots, n$.*

Proof. It is obvious that each R^k is a quasi-ordering that satisfies simple monotonicity and simple anonymity. Moreover, suppose that A, B, and C are elements of Z

for which $A \cap C = \emptyset = B \cap C$ and $|C| = 1$, and suppose that AR^kB, or equivalently, $|A|^k \geq |B|^k$. There are three possibilities. First, if $|A| < k$, then $|A \cup C|^k = |A| + 1 \geq |B| + 1 = |B \cup C|^k$ and hence $(A \cup C)R^k(B \cup C)$. Second, if $|A| \geq k > |B|$, then $|A \cup C|^k = |A| \geq |B| + 1 = |B \cup C|^k$ and hence $(A \cup C)R^k(B \cup C)$. Third, if $|B| \geq k$, then $|A \cup C|^k = |A| = |B| = |B \cup C|^k$ and hence $(A \cup C)R^k(B \cup C)$. Thus, R^k satisfies simple semi-independence.

Now, suppose that R is any quasi-ordering satisfying simple semi-independence, simple monotonicity, and simple anonymity. By the above discussion, R satisfies semi-independence, monotonicity, and anonymity. Monotonicity ensures that all sets can be compared and that $|A| \geq |B|$ implies that ARB. Pick a menu C with the lowest cardinality such that XIC, that is, C has maximal freedom. Let $k = |C|$ and note that for any sets A and B in Z with $|A|^k = |B|^k$ we must have AIB. Further, it is clear by definition of C that any set, say C', satisfying $|C| = |C'| + 1$ would have to satisfy CPC'. Indeed, any pair of sets D' and D satisfying $k > |D| = |D'| + 1$ would have to satisfy DPD'; otherwise, if DID' then semi-independence, anonymity, and transitivity would imply that CIC', contrary to the above. Hence, for any A and B in Z with $|A|^k > |B|^k$ we must have APB. It follows immediately that R is R^k. □

Theorem 3 provides convincing evidence that simple anonymity is the key axiom underlying the Pattanaik and Xu (1990) result. Even in the presence of the unambiguous simple semi-independence axiom (which requires that adding a new alternative to a weakly ranked pair of menus preserves the ranking) and the equally justifiable simple monotonicity axiom (which ensures that adding a new alternative to a singleton set results in a set with greater or equal freedom), the simple anonymity axiom restricts consideration to the family of censored cardinality freedom rankings R^k, including the cardinality ordering R^C and the trivial ordering R^T. Strengthening the monotonicity axiom removes the trivial freedom ordering from consideration, but leaves all R^k with $k > 1$; strengthening the independence axiom removes the intermediate censored cardinality rankings with $1 < k < n$, leaving the two extremes of R^T and R^C. Simple anonymity along with both of the more demanding axioms then reduces the possibilities to the cardinality ranking R^C.

3.2. Additive Representations and Cardinality Freedom

The theorem of Pattanaik and Xu (1990) not only offers a characterization of a freedom ranking, it provides a function that represents the relation (namely $|A|$). The interpretaton of their theorem as a representation theorem has not been emphasized in the literature. However, this perspective reveals a close relationship to traditional additive representation results and suggests other theorems including an extension to "fuzzy" opportunity sets. We now present this reinterpretation and its potential implications.

Select an arbitrary enumeration of the n elements of X. Every opportunity set in Z can be represented by a vector v from the set $V = \{v \epsilon \mathrm{R}^n \backslash \{0\} : v_i = 0,\ 1 \text{ for all } i\}$, where $v_i = 1$ indicates that the ith element of X is present in the given set while $v_i = 0$ indicates that the ith element is absent. So, for example, given a three-element set X with elements enumerated as a, b, c, the vector $v = (1, 0, 1)$ corresponds to the set $\{a, c\}$. With this reinterpretation of sets as vectors, each of the above axioms can be directly translated to the new environment. In what follows e_i denotes the ith basis vector, and v, w, v', and w' are elements of V.

Quasi-Ordering The relation R on V is reflexive and transitive.

Simple Anonymity $e_i I e_k$ for all i, k.

Simple Strict Monotonicity $(e_i + e_k)Pe_i$ for all $i \neq k$.

Simple Independence Let $k \epsilon \{1, \ldots, n\}$. Suppose that $v_i = v'_i$ and $w_i = w'_i$ for all $i \neq k$, while $v_k = w_k$ and $v'_k = w'_k$. Then vRw if and only if $v'Rw'$.

Anonymity $vI(\Pi v)$ for all v and every $n \times n$ permutation matrix Π.

Strict Monotonicity $v > w$ implies vPw.

Independence Let $K \subset \{1, \ldots, n\}$. Suppose that $v_i = v'_i$ and $w_i = w'_i$ for all $i \notin K$, while $v_k = w_k$ and $v'_k = w'_k$ for all $k \epsilon K$. Then vRw if and only if $v'Rw'$.

It is an easy exercise to verify that each axiom corresponds exactly to its previously defined twin. However, the properties are now much more familiar. For example, simple anonymity becomes a requirement that any two usual basis vectors are ranked identically by the relation, while full anonymity requires the same conclusion to hold for any two vectors that are permutations of one another. Strict monotonicity is the standard version that requires an increase in one dimension, and no decrease in any other, to lead to a strict increase in the ranking; the simple version requires the sum of any two basis vectors to be ranked strictly higher than either of them. Independence is indeed a standard separability axiom used in additive representations, while simple independence is a more limited form of the same.[11]

It is straightforward to show that the Pattanaik and Xu (1990) result is equivalent to the following theorem.

Theorem 4 *Let R be any quasi-ordering on the set V satisfying simple anonymity, simple strict monotonicity, and simple independence. Then vRv' if and only if $\sum_{i=1}^{n} v_i \geq \sum_{i=1}^{n} v'_i$.*

In other words, the three axioms are sufficient to ensure that the quasi-ordering R has an unweighted *additive representation*.

[11] See, for example, Blackorby, Primont, and Russell (1978) for a standard treatment of separability.

One notable aspect of this result is that the completeness of R is not being assumed a priori, but rather falls out as an implication of the other axioms. But if we knew a priori that R were a complete ordering, the theorem would seem very natural indeed—even intuitive. The independence requirement is entirely analogous to traditional separability. Combined with strict monotonicity—not an unusual property for an ordering—we could well expect there to be an additive representation $\Sigma_i f_i(v_i)$ for R with increasing component functions f_i. Anonymity then acts to ensure that all the f_i are identical and equal to a single increasing function f. Normalizing f such that $f(0) = 0$ and $f(1) = 1$ then yields the given representation, a function that adds up the v_i's or, equivalently, counts the number of dimensions for which $v_i = 1$.

This reinterpretation of the Pattanaik and Xu (1990) theorem suggests some interesting generalizations. First, if R is an ordering satisfying simple monotonicity and simple independence, might there exist an additive representation $\Sigma_i f_i(v_i)$ where each f_i is increasing and normalized to $f_i(0) = 0$ or, equivalently, an additive representation of the form $\Sigma_i \alpha_i v_i$ where each alternative has a weight or value $\alpha_i > 0$? This would lead to a weighted cardinality rule where instead of counting the number of alternatives in a given set, one would add up the weights associated with its members to indicate the aggregate desirability of the given set.

Second, suppose that we allow v_i to range continuously between 0 and 1, and interpret v_i as the *degree of membership* of the ith element in the given *fuzzy set* associated with the membership vector v (Zadeh 1965). Let R be an ordering on the domain of fuzzy set vectors $V' = \{v \in R^n : 0 < v_i \leq 1 \text{ for all } i\}$. We can directly extend the anonymity, strict monotonicity, and independence axioms to the larger domain of fuzzy sets. It would be interesting to investigate whether the following conjecture is true: R is an (continuous) ordering on V' satisfying anonymity, strict monotonicity, and independence if and only if R is represented by $F(v) = \Sigma_i f(v_i)$ for some strictly increasing function f: $[0, 1] \to [0, 1]$ with $f(0) = 0$ and $f(1) = 1$. If it were true, then interpreting $f(v_i)$ as the "subjective" degree of membership where v_i is the "objective" level, this would provide a justification for a freedom ranking that is represented by a simple sum of subjective degrees of membership across all possible alternatives.

3.3. Reflections on Counting as a Measure of Freedom

The intriguing result of Pattanaik and Xu (1990) has given rise to a secondary literature that critiques this result and suggests alternatives.[12] Perhaps the most natural interpretation of the result (and its general approach) is that it is confronting the problem of

[12] For example, Bossert (2000) points out that Pattanaik and Xu presume that there is no uncertainty; that individuals completely control their choices and no undesirable option has the slightest chance of being implemented unintentionally. Klemisch-Ahlert's (1993) spatial approach argues that what should be counted are not the actual number of options, but rather the characteristics of the options in the set, or the dissimilarity between sets. Pattanaik and Xu (2000) also extend their result beyond the finite case.

measuring freedom when the informational basis for doing so is unrealistically thin. More specifically, if individual alternatives are indistinguishable from one another (as embodied in simple anonymity), it shows that the possibilities for constructing useful freedom rankings are rather limited, namely, the cardinality ranking (which identifies greater freedom with a greater number of alternatives), the trivial ranking (which is indifference between all sets), or some censored cardinality rule in between (which counts numbers of alternatives up to a certain level). Given the general acceptability of the monotonicity and semi-independence axioms, there is little ambiguity in this result. The criticism that these measures ignore other aspects important to freedom is valid but has little salience if we truly believe no other aspects are available.

However, the situation is rather different if we take the empirically defensible view that information on the quality of alternatives *is* readily available in the form of the agent's preference ordering. Then the onus would be on supporters of simple anonymity to explain why the agent's preferences should be entirely ignored in measuring the freedom of singleton sets. To be sure, all singleton sets have the same cardinality; but since the quality of the elements can vary widely, requiring simple anonymity is tantamount to assuming that quality does not matter at all. The next section explores freedom rankings that take into account the quality of alternatives as represented by a preference relation. Interestingly, counting procedures will play a role in the preference-based approaches, but as part of a method of representing preferences and their associated freedom rankings.

4. PREFERENCE AND INDIRECT UTILITY

The previous section focused on several possibilities for measuring freedom when there is no basis for discerning the quality of alternatives, and hence they are treated symmetrically. This section assumes that an agent can distinguish between alternatives with the help of a preference ordering. The presumption is that the agent will select a best element from a given opportunity set and hence the comparison of sets entails a comparison of their respective best elements. We alter the Pattanaik and Xu (1990) axioms to obtain a set of properties satisfied by the resulting indirect utility freedom ranking R^U and then note that the ranking is axiomatically characterized by these properties. We explore the relationship between R^U and the cardinality ranking R^C, and construct a series of freedom rankings by combining the two components of freedom rankings—quality and quantity—in various ways.

4.1. Rankings and Axioms

Let R_1 denote the agent's preference relation over X. How does the existence of a preference ordering impact the resulting freedom ranking? The precise way that R_1 figures into the construction of R will depend crucially on the structure of the selection process that eventually converts a set of alternatives into a specific alternative. For example, suppose that the process is one in which, subsequent to the agent's choice of opportunity set, an alternative is randomly selected by nature and presented to the agent. In this case, the agent cannot predict which outcome will be selected and may wish to choose the menu with the highest expected utility level (for some utility representation of R_1). This would not be much of a freedom ranking, since adding an element with below average utility could lower one's ability to achieve a preferred outcome. Alternatively, suppose that while the agent has the power to determine the menu of alternatives, the selection process consists of, say, a mortal enemy picking an alternative from the menu. The agent can certainly predict the outcome that would be selected (the worst) and would likely want to choose a set to maximize the minimum utility. Once again, monotonicity would be forfeited and greater freedom of choice would only hurt the agent—all due to the assumed selection process.

In contrast to the above examples, the selection process assumed here provides an agent with the full measure of information and control in selecting an alternative from the set. When a given opportunity set is considered, the agent knows that a best alternative will be selected, and judges the set accordingly. The indirect utility freedom ranking R^U compares sets in terms of their best elements: the one with the better best element has greater freedom. Since the underlying preference relation R_1 is an ordering, it follows that the derived freedom ranking R^U is also an ordering. Note that the addition of an alternative will either increase freedom or leave it unchanged, hence the indirect utility ordering satisfies monotonicity (but not necessarily strict monotonicity). The addition of one or more new alternatives to any sets A and B satisfying $AR^U B$ will not reverse the ranking, and so the indirect utility ordering also satisfies semi-independence (but not necessarily independence). On the other hand, so long as R_1 is not completely indifferent across alternatives, simple anonymity will be violated. Instead, the indirect utility ordering satisfies the following natural axiom:

Extension For any a, b in X, we have $\{a\}R\{b\}$ if and only if aR_1b.

This axiom requires that in comparisons of singleton sets, the freedom ranking R must echo the judgments of the preference ordering R_1.

There is an additional axiom satisfied by the indirect utility ranking, namely, if a set A has as much freedom as either B or D, then A has as much freedom as the union of B and D. This is due to the fact that if A has an element that is weakly preferred to the best that either B or D has to offer, then its best element will surely weakly dominate the best alternative in $B \cup D$. We also define a restricted version of this requirement that restricts A and D to be singleton sets. In symbols, the two axioms are as follows:

Simple Composition Let A, B, and D be elements of Z such that $|A| = |D| = 1$. If ARB and ARD then $AR(B \cup D)$.

Composition Let A, B, and D be elements of Z. If ARB and ARD then $AR(B \cup D)$.

Notice that this type of axiom is violated by the cardinality ranking, since even if A is considered to have more freedom than B and D individually, the act of combining the two will force the ranking to be reversed if the combined number of elements exceeds the number in A. The exclusive focus on quantity and not quality is what allows this to occur. On the other hand, the indirect utility ranking ignores all but the best alternatives in a given set, and this ensures that A will have greater freedom than $B \cup D$.

We have listed four axioms satisfied by R^U: two that were part of the previous axiomatic framework developed for the cardinality freedom ranking; one that is a natural replacement for simple anonymity when information on the quality of alternatives is provided by a preference relation; and a composition property that makes sense in the present context where the quality of options is paramount. We have the following result.

Theorem 5 *R is a quasi-ordering satisfying simple semi-independence, simple monotonicity, simple composition, and extension if and only if R is R^U.*

Proof. It is clear that R^U satisfies each of the required axioms. Now suppose that R is any quasi-ordering satisfying simple semi-independence, simple monotonicity, simple composition, and extension. Notice that by previous arguments R must satisfy semi-independence and monotonicity. Now consider any A and B in Z and let a be a best element of A under ordering R_1 so that aR_1a' for all $a' \in A$. By repeated application of simple composition and extension we have $\{a\}RA$. A similar argument for any best element b of B yields $\{b\}RB$. By monotonicity it follows that $\{a\}IA$ and $\{b\}IB$. By transitivity, then, ARB if and only if $\{a\}R\{b\}$, or equivalently aR_1b. It follows, then, that R is simply R^U. □

This theorem implies that the indirect utility ordering is the only quasi-ordering that satisfies the preference-based extension axiom and the intuitive semi-independence, monotonicity, and composition axioms. Notice that this result, like the characterizations of R^C above, does not assume that the freedom ranking is complete. Rather, it derives completeness from the combination of the axioms, none of which individually demands it. The theorem differs from Kreps (1979, p. 566) in that it posits a preference ordering rather than deriving it.

It is instructive to analyze this theorem in the special case where the preference relation R_1 is complete indifference. Under this specification for R_1, the extension axiom is tantamount to simple anonymity, and Theorem 5 would entail all the axioms from Theorem 3. Consequently, the latter result would imply that R would have to be a censored cardinality ranking R^k for some $k = 1, \ldots, n$. But it is clear that none of the rankings R^k with $k > 1$ satisfies the simple composition axiom; indeed, we know that

$\{a\}R^k\{c\}$ and $\{a\}R^k\{d\}$ for any distinct a, c, d in X, and yet $\{c, d\}P^k\{a\}$ for every $k > 1$. Hence this additional requirement rules out all possibilities apart from $R = R^k$ with $k = 1$, or equivalently, the trivial freedom ranking R^T. And this is indeed the ranking that Theorem 5 would yield in the special case where the preference relation regards all alternatives as being indifferent to one another.

It is straightforward to show that R^U also satisfies the following axiom.

Consistency Let A, B, C and D be elements of Z. Then ARB and CRD imply $(A \cup C)R(B \cup D)$.

In other words, if the freedom ranking registers an increase (or stays the same) when B is replaced by A, and D becomes C, then it must also register an increase (or stay the same) when the two higher freedom sets (and the two lower freedom sets) are combined. This requirement is not dissimilar to subgroup consistency requirements used in the measurement of inequality, poverty, and welfare (Foster and Sen 1997) and directly implies composition and (under reflexivity) semi-independence. It is easy to show the following result.

Corollary R is a quasi-ordering satisfying consistency, monotonicity, and extension if and only if R is R^U.

The characterization of the cardinality freedom ranking R^C relied on independence, strict monotonicity, and anonymity; this result shows that the indirect utility ranking R^U for the posited preference relation R_1 is obtained when strict monotonicity is relaxed to monotonicity, independence is altered to consistency, and anonymity is transformed into extension, which ensures that the ranking over singleton sets follows R_1.

4.2. Representations of Indirect Utility Freedom

The usual indirect utility function from consumer theory can be interpreted as a measure of freedom that ranks budget sets according to their maximum attainable utility levels.[13] We can follow this intuition to obtain a natural counting representation for R^U. For any alternative a in X, let $L_1(a) = \{a' \in X | aR_1a'\}$ denote the *lower contour set* of a. Define the utility function $u: X \to R$ by $u(a) = |L_1(a)|$, the number of alternatives in the lower contour set. It is a simple matter to show that u represents the preference ordering R_1, that is, aR_1b if and only if $u(a) \geq u(b)$. Indeed, in a world where the only information that is available about R_1 is ordinal, the utility representation u is an especially intuitive indicator

[13] For an interesting application of the indirect utility approach, see the aggregate social preference relation of Chipman and Moore (1979).

of the desirability or quality of an alternative in terms of the number of alternatives it beats or ties.[14]

One can extend this function to obtain a representation of the ordering R^U on opportunity sets as follows. For any A in Z, define $L_1(A)$ to be the lower contour set of a best alternative in A, that is, $L_1(A) = L_1(a)$ for some best element a in A. $L_1(A)$ is the "free disposal hull" of A found by taking the union of the lower contour sets of its elements. Extend u to Z by setting $u(A) = |L_1(A)|$, so that the "utility" of a set is simply the number of alternatives in the free disposal hull of A. We claim that $u(A)$ represents the indirect utility ordering R^U on Z. Indeed, suppose that AR^UB. Then, by the definition of R^U, we know that any best element a of A is weakly preferred to any best element b of B. Hence $L_1(B) \subseteq L_1(A)$ and so $u(B) = |L_1(B)| \leq |L_1(A)| = u(A)$. Alternatively, if it is not the case that AR^UB, then by completeness, any best element of A must be strictly dominated by any best element of B, and so $L_1(A) \subset L_1(B)$, which implies that $u(A) = |L_1(A)| < |L_1(B)| = u(B)$. Consequently AR^UB if and only if $u(A) \geq u(B)$, and so u represents R^U.

This representation of R^U is similar to the one presented above for R^C in that it is based on a simple counting of alternatives. However, instead of ignoring the quality dimension of freedom (as R^C does by using $|A|$) it focuses on the quality or "effective freedom" of a set by including all alternatives that are weakly dominated by its best element, and then measuring freedom as the size of this more expansive set. The result is an indirect utility evaluation of freedom based on the above utility representation of R_1 (which interprets the utility of an option as the number of alternatives it weakly dominates). Note that the difference $u(A) - |A|$ gives the number of alternatives that are "effectively," but not actually, in the set. This margin can be interpreted as the error with which quality is measured by a set's cardinality measure, and its value can range from 0 to $n - |A|$.

4.3. Combining Cardinality and Indirect Utility

The freedom orderings R^C and R^U often present conflicting judgments due to their different emphases on the quantity and quality dimensions of freedom. For example, an additional alternative always has a positive marginal impact on freedom under R^C, but it increases freedom under R^U only if the alternative has high enough quality (and otherwise has no impact). Singleton sets exhibit the lowest level of freedom under R^C, while they range from the lowest to the highest levels of freedom under R^U. Many authors have suggested that a synthetic approach might be preferable to a single-minded concentration on quantity or quality alone, and we present the two principal candidates

[14] See the related representation of Rader (1963). Note that we are not endowing u with a special normative significance. It is a convenient representation of R_1.

below. The first is a traditional *aggregation* exercise, which combines the two freedom measures into a single indicator that balances the effects of the two components when they disagree. The second is a standard *intersection* approach, which creates an unambiguous ranking where the two measures agree, with gaps of incompleteness where they disagree.

Perhaps the simplest method of obtaining a new freedom ranking from R^C and R^U is to aggregate the functions that represent the two orderings. Let $u(A) = |L_1(A)|$ and $c(A) = |A|$ be the functions representing orderings R^U and R^C, respectively, and let $g: R^2_+ \to R$ be any function that is strictly increasing in each argument. Then the aggregate freedom measure $g(u(A), c(A))$ and its associate ordering R_g takes both quantity and quality into account when it evaluates menus of alternatives and satisfies strict monotonicity. For example, if $g(u,c) = (u+c)/2$, then the freedom measure would be a simple average of the number of alternatives in A and the number of alternatives dominated by the best element of A (under the preference ordering R_1). Note, though, that even though both constituent orderings satisfy semi-independence, R_g need not.[15]

While the general aggregation approach has not been explicitly studied in the literature, special cases have been investigated. Bossert, Pattanaik, and Xu (1994) consider the freedom rankings obtained by applying the two lexicographic orderings on the space of (u,c) pairs, namely

$$AR_uB \text{ if and only if } u(A) > u(B) \text{ or } [u(A) = u(B) \text{ and } c(A) \geq c(B)]$$

$$AR_cB \text{ if and only if } c(A) > c(B) \text{ or } [c(A) = c(B) \text{ and } u(A) \geq u(B)].$$

The first of these is the "utility first" lexicographic ordering, which primarily relies on the quality indicator to make judgments, but when two sets have the same quality level, it uses the quantity indicator to break the tie. The "cardinality first" ranking proceeds in the opposite order, with the quantity indicator as the primary basis for making comparisons, but with quality being used to break the ties. As an example, suppose X contains three alternatives, x, y, z, with xP_1yP_1z. Then $\{x\}P_u\{y,z\}$, illustrating R_u's overriding emphasis on quality, while R_c's contrary focus on quantity yields $\{y,z\}P_c\{x\}$; and yet $\{x,z\}P_u\{x\}$ and $\{x\}P_c\{y\}$, which indicates the sensitivity of each to its secondary measure when the primary measure is held fixed. It is also not difficult to see that R_u and R_c are examples of orderings R_g generated by an aggregator function g. Indeed, $g_u(u,c) = nu + c$ represents R_u (since the large weight on the u ensures that an increase in u cannot be counteracted

[15] For example, suppose that A has $c = 3$ and its best alternative has $u = 7$, while B has $c = 4$ with $u = 5$, so that the $g(u,c) = (u+c)/2$ is larger for A. If an alternative with utility of 8 is added to both, then the order is reversed, violating semi-independence.

by a lower level of c, while if u is unchanged the ranking depends entirely on c); similarly, $g_c(u,c) = nc + u$ represents R_c (by the same reasoning).[16]

At the other end of the spectrum is the intersection approach, which instead of balancing the gains and losses of the two components when they disagree, reaches no decision at all. Bossert, Pattanaik, and Xu (1994) apply the vector dominance quasi-ordering in the space of (u,c) pairs, to obtain the dominance quasi-ordering R_d that is defined by

$$AR_dB \text{ if and only if } (u(A), c(A)) \geq (u(B), c(B))$$

or, equivalently, AR_dB holds if and only if both AR^UB and AR^CB hold. To be sure, conflicts between the two freedom orderings will occur, for example, when one of the sets has just a few elements, but they are high-ranking, while the other has many elements and they are low-ranking. The resulting quasi-ordering is not complete, but since it is more likely for the two components $u(A)$ and $c(A)$ to move weakly in tandem than it is for them to move strictly contrary to one another, it is not disastrously incomplete.

The characteristics of the three freedom rankings R_u, R_c, and R_d, and the interrelationships among them, are well known from analogous discussions of the lexicographic and dominance rankings in two-dimensional space. Obviously, the lexicographic relations are orderings, whose singleton indifference sets in (u,c) space correspond to equal-sized opportunity sets whose best elements under R_1 are indifferent under R_1. Note that the quasi-ordering R_d is a subrelation of both R_u and R_c, and indeed corresponds to their intersection quasi-ordering (so that AR_dB holds if and only if AR_uB and AR_cB). Similarly, R_d is a subrelation of any freedom relation R_g generated by an aggregation function g, and indeed R_d is also the intersection quasi-ordering across all such R_g. This holds true even in the extreme case where the preference relation R_1 is completely indifferent between alternatives, so that the indirect utility ordering R^U is the trivial freedom ranking R^T and each of the composite rankings is identical to the cardinality ordering R^C. To rule out this unusual case, and to simplify the subsequent discussion, let us assume that there are distinct alternatives x, y, and z in X such that xR_1y and yP_1z.

It is easy to show that all three of these composite rankings satisfy the same subset of the previously defined properties, namely, extension, semi-independence, monotonicity, and strict monotonicity. They all violate anonymity and its simple version (by Theorem 3), composition and its simple version (by Theorem 5), consistency (by the Corollary), and independence and its simple version, which can be shown directly by example. They inherit semi-independence and monotonicity from both component orderings R^U and

[16] The lexicographic orderings are representable here due to the discrete nature of u and c.

R^C. Unlike R^U, which only satisfies monotonicity, each composite ranking satisfies strict monotonicity through its sensitivity to R^C. Unlike R^C, which satisfies simple anonymity, each composite ranking satisfies the extension axiom through its sensitivity to R^U. Bossert, Pattanaik, and Xu (1994) find additional axioms that allow the three composite rankings to be uniquely characterized from among all freedom rankings.

4.4. Other Views of Quality

The last section illustrated how quality (as represented by the utility of the best element) can be combined with quantity (the number of elements in a set) to create freedom rankings with various desirable characteristics. Other authors drop quantity as an explicit dimension of freedom and consider alternative notions of quality that take into account the entire distribution of utilities from elements in the set, not just the maximum utility. We now present various proposals that proceed along this line.

Once again, we represent every set A by a vector v of 0's and 1's, where $v_i = 1$ indicates that the corresponding alternative x_i is in the set A, while $v_i = 0$ indicates that x_i is not. Let q be the corresponding utility vector defined by $q_i = v_i u(x_i) = v_i |L_1(x_i)|$ for $i = 1, \ldots, n$, so that q_i is the utility of x_i in set A (or 0 if it is not). Reordering the entries of q from highest to lowest, we obtain the *ordered version* of q, formally defined as the vector $\hat{q}$ satisfying $\hat{q}_1 \geq \hat{q}_2 \geq \ldots \geq \hat{q}_n$ and $\hat{q} = \Pi q$ for some $n \times n$ permutation matrix Π. We will call $\hat{q}$ the *(ordered) quality vector*, since $\hat{q}_i > 0$ is the quality of the ith best alternative in A, while $\hat{q}_i = 0$ indicates that A has no ith best element.[17]

Note that the first entry $\hat{q}_1 = \max_i \hat{q}_i = u(A)$ is the quality or utility of the best element of A, which is our measure of indirect utility freedom. The approaches discussed in this section extend consideration to the entire quality vector $\hat{q}$ in evaluating the freedom of A. Once again there will be two main candidates for combining the n dimensions of $\hat{q}$ to obtain a freedom ranking: *aggregation* and *intersection*.

One natural approach to aggregation would be to use a strictly increasing, real valued function h to combine the dimensions of $\hat{q}$ into an overall measure of freedom $F(A) = h(\hat{q})$. For example, the measure $F(A)$ obtained when $h(\hat{q}) = \Sigma_i \hat{q}_i$, or more generally $h(\hat{q}) = \Sigma_i w_i \hat{q}_i$ for some weights w_i that are weakly decreasing in i to capture the intuition that the first best should have at least as much weight as the second best, and so on. Now the resulting ranking clearly satisfies monotonicity; however, as before, there may be problems with semi-independence. On the other hand, if the weights w_i decrease abruptly enough in i, then the resulting measure would represent the *leximax*, a semi-independent ordering R_x discussed by Bossert, Pattanaik, and Xu (1994).[18] This ranking first compares

[17] There may be ambiguity in defining a unique ith best element when R_1 is indifferent between two elements of A; however, since the respective quality levels would then be the same, we may arbitrarily select one of the two without loss of generality.

[18] One such representation of R_x would be $h(\hat{q}) = n^{n-1}\hat{q}_1 + n^{n-2}\hat{q}_2 + \cdots + n\hat{q}_{n-1} + \hat{q}_n$.

the quality of the best elements from each set and, if equal, compares the quality of the next best elements and so on until a lexicographic comparison of quality vectors is obtained. Where L is the standard "earlier is better" lexicographical ordering, R_x can be defined by

$$AR_xB \text{ if and only if } \hat{q}L\hat{q}'$$

given that $\hat{q}$ is the quality vector of A and $\hat{q}'$ is the quality vector of B. Note that AP^UB implies AP_xB, in which case both rankings ignore the quality and quantity of lower-quality alternatives. But when AI^UB we could have either AP_xB or BP_xA depending on whether the inequality is $\hat{q}_i > \hat{q}_i{}'$ or $\hat{q}_i < \hat{q}_i{}'$ the first time that $\hat{q}_i$ departs from $\hat{q}_i{}'$. Again, once a strict inequality is obtained one way or the other, the remaining elements have no impact.

Sen (1991) applies the intersection approach to obtain a freedom ranking R_s that is equivalent to comparing sets A and B using vector dominance over their respective ordered quality vectors, that is,

$$AR_sB \text{ if and only if } \hat{q} \geq \hat{q}'.$$

There are three cases (and hence interpretations) of the constituent inequality $\hat{q}_i \geq \hat{q}_i'$:

1. If $\hat{q}_i' > 0$, then $\hat{q}_i \geq \hat{q}_i'$ indicates that ith best member of A is as good as the ith best member of B;
2. if $\hat{q}_i > 0 = \hat{q}_i'$, then A contains an ith best element, but B does not; and
3. if $\hat{q}_i = 0 = \hat{q}_i'$, then neither A nor B has an ith best element.

Sen's (1991) original definition has AR_sB holding whenever there exists a one-to-one correspondence from B to A, with each element of B being weakly dominated by its corresponding element from A (according to R_1). However, it is clear that this is equivalent to the definition via quality vectors, since (1) above implicitly defines a correspondence meeting Sen's requirements.

Through the first entry of the quality vector, it is easy to see that AR_sB implies AR^UB for any opportunity sets A and B. The remaining $n-1$ requirements act to ensure that the original ranking over best elements is robust to the other dimensional comparisons. If there is some ith order comparison that strictly disagrees with the original judgment, then the two sets are declared to be noncomparable. On the other hand, A and B can be indifferent according to R^U, and yet AP_sB through a strict inequality for some higher-order comparison.[19] It is also clear that AR_sB implies that AR^CB, and hence AR_dB, where R_d is the quality/quantity dominance ranking defined above. It is interesting to note that since the quality vectors are ordered, the degree of incompleteness of quasi-ordering R_s is quite low, and certainly not much worse than R_d; indeed, for

[19] This uses the standard definition of P_s as the asymmetric part of R_s. Sen (1991) presents an alternative strict freedom ranking requiring *every* nonzero entry of A's quality vector (including the first entry) to be strictly higher.

the case of five strictly ordered elements, R_d has approximately 10% of set comparisons being noncomparable, while R_s has about 15%.

To discuss the properties satisfied by R_x, and R_s, let us once again assume that there are three alternatives x, y, and z, such that xR_1yP_1z. Both freedom rankings satisfy the fundamental properties of monotonicity and semi-independence as well as strict monotonicity and the extension axiom. At the same time, we know from the above theorems that both rankings violate anonymity and its simple version, composition and its simple version, and consistency. Curiously, both also satisfy independence. Bossert, Pattanaik, and Xu (1994) find additional axioms that uniquely characterize the leximax ordering from among all freedom rankings.

4.5. Reflections on Indirect Utility as a Measure of Freedom

In the traditional economic setting where a decision maker has a fixed preference ordering and can freely select a most preferred element from a menu, the indirect utility measure is the natural method for comparing opportunity sets, and one that is clear in its priorities. It takes the utility of the best alternative as the basis of all comparisons. It regards an opportunity set as having the same freedom level as a singleton set containing its best element. The quantity and quality of other options are not relevant, and there is no scope for sacrificing indirect utility to improve the quantity or quality of the unchosen options. Given the decision maker's unchanging preferences and complete process freedom, it is not surprising that the resulting notion of freedom is quite narrow.

As we have seen, there is scope within this setting for constructing freedom rankings that incorporate additional information on the quantity and quality of options in a set, and their axiomatic descriptions go some distance in revealing the features of these methods and discerning among them. However, the value they accord unchosen alternatives is essentially ad hoc and ungrounded in the current model of decision-making. We now consider a new setting and several associated freedom rankings whose values for unchosen options can be intuitively justified.

5. PLURAL PREFERENCES AND EFFECTIVE FREEDOM

The previous sections have presented one setting in which information on preferences is not available and a second in which the agent has a single, fixed preference relation. This section considers a model in which the agent has several potential preference relations, one of which will eventually become relevant. In the resulting *plural preference* environment, where the agent's choice depends on the realized preference ordering, unchosen options can add value to an opportunity set by providing the agent with greater flexibility until the uncertainty has been resolved. This approach is motivated by the literature on *preference for flexibility* as presented by Kreps (1979) and

Koopmans (1964); it has close conceptual links to the key notion of option value in economics and finance (Weisbrod 1964; Malkiel and Quandt 1969).[20] There are many ways of incorporating the new information on preferences into a freedom ranking. This section presents several plural preference methods that are based on the *intersection* or *aggregation* of preferences.

We begin with the *effective freedom* approach of Foster (1993), which constructs a freedom ranking by taking the intersection of the indirect utility rankings arising from a set of preferences. Under this approach, one set will have greater freedom than another if, no matter the preference relation, it has at least as high indirect utility and, for some preference relation, it is strictly higher. At one extreme (where there is a single preference ordering), this approach yields an indirect utility ordering; at the other (where all preferences are possible) it tends toward the set inclusion quasi-ordering. The properties of the freedom ranking are explored, and several natural representations are given. One partial representation based on a counting of alternatives in "effective opportunity sets" extends the effective freedom ranking to a complete ordering that is the indirect utility ordering at one extreme and the Pattanaik and Xu (1990) cardinality ordering at the other.

The alternative intersection approach by Sen (2002) is then discussed, which first applies the intersection approach to the collection of preference orderings and then extends the resulting quasi-ordering over alternatives to a relation over opportunity sets. It is noted that the resulting freedom ranking is generally more incomplete than the effective freedom ranking, but when it does hold, stronger statements about the freedom levels of the two sets can be made. Note that neither of these approaches requires the agent to make an assessment of the likelihood of the various possible preferences. Arrow (1995) follows more closely the lead of Kreps (1979) in assuming that each preference relation (as represented by a utility function) has a given probability of arising, and hence the expected indirect utility may be used in evaluating opportunity sets. Under this aggregation approach, greater freedom means that a weighted average of the indirect utility levels is higher, where the weights are the respective probabilities. We note that Arrow's approach reduces to an indirect utility freedom ordering when a particular utility function has probability 1; and it can generate the cardinality freedom ordering in the special case when all preferences are possible and equally likely.

5.1. Rankings and Axioms

The effective freedom approach of Foster (1993) begins with a collection $\mathfrak{R} = \{R_1, \ldots, R_m\}$ of complete orderings over X, where m can vary from 1 to the number of all logically possible preference orderings. $\mathfrak{R}$ is interpreted here as the set of all *potential*

[20] See also Jones and Sugden (1982). In his Plural Utility article, Sen (1980/1981, p. 207) suggests an analogous two-stage evaluation process.

preferences that the agent may have when making a selection from an opportunity set, although other interpretations are possible and are consistent with the formal implications of the approach.[21] The *actual* preference relation will be revealed to the agent before it is time to select an alternative and, indeed, from this point on the resulting process is entirely analogous to the indirect utility approach: the agent selects a best element from the opportunity set according to the preference relation. However, at the time that the opportunity sets are being evaluated, the agent only knows the collection $\mathfrak{R}$ of possible preferences and *not* the one that eventually obtains. So long as there is unresolved uncertainty, the agent can derive value from extra options even if in the course of time the extra options are not chosen.

Now when does adding an alternative offer strictly greater freedom? Let us return to the occupational choice problem facing the recent graduate Jill to find an intuitive answer. If Jill has a menu containing a single alternative (say civil engineering) which for all of her possible preferences in $\mathfrak{R}$ is considered to be at least as good as the new alternative (say teaching), then it could be argued that adding this alternative would have no impact on freedom. Under all potential realizations of preferences, Jill will do just as well with the singleton set as with the two-vocation set. In contrast, suppose that Jill has at least one preference ordering in her set that ranks teaching strictly above civil engineering. Then adding teaching to the civil engineering menu would certainly expand Jill's freedom since she would now be able to select a strictly preferable vocation if that preference ordering happened to emerge.[22]

We now formalize this general approach. For any given preference ordering R_j in $\mathfrak{R}$, let R_j^U denote the associated indirect utility ranking on Z. One opportunity set A is said to have as much *effective freedom* as a second opportunity set B, written AR^*B, if A has as much indirect utility freedom as B for all allowable preferences; that is,

$$AR^*B \text{ if and only if } AR_j^U B \text{ for all } R_j \in \mathfrak{R}.$$

This means that no matter which preference ordering R_j in $\mathfrak{R}$ happens to arise, the opportunity set A has an element that is at least as good as all the elements of B according to R_j (although this option may vary with R_j). Note that since R^* is the intersection of a collection of complete orderings over opportunity sets (namely, the indirect utility

21 See for example Jones and Sugden (1982), Sugden (1998), and Pattanaik and Xu (1998).

22 Note that this discussion is entirely dependent on the assumption that the process aspect of freedom has not been compromised so that Jill can freely select from the opportunity set once her preferences have been realized. Also, we are not restricting the mechanism by which preferences are realized, apart from the requirements that all preferences in $\mathfrak{R}$ are considered to be relevant at the time an opportunity set is being evaluated; and only one preference ordering will be relevant when an alternative is selected from the set. Nature could select the preference ordering, or the person's mother, or the person. Which of these is correct may well impact our evaluation of process freedom of the final choice; but our procedure is designed to measure only the opportunity freedom across sets, and abstracts from the way the resolution of preference uncertainty can directly impact process freedom.

rankings), it must be a quasi-ordering (i.e., transitive and reflexive, but not necessarily complete). As is typical of quasi-orderings, the symmetric part I^* requires I_j^U to hold for all constituent preference orderings, while the asymmetric part P^* requires R^* in conjunction with P_j^U for some preference ordering in $\mathfrak{R}$.

It is easy to see that R^* will generally violate the Pattanaik and Xu (1990) axioms: independence, since removing an unambiguously best option from both sets may convert I^* to P^*; strict monotonicity, since adding a dominated option leads to I^* and not P^*; and anonymity, since P^* or noncomparability across singleton sets can easily arise. On the other hand, R^* inherits semi-independence, monotonicity, composition, and consistency from its constituent indirect utility orderings. The extension property is no longer applicable since there are now many potential preference relations, and no one of them determines the freedom ranking over singleton sets. However, the property can be generalized to apply to the plural preference environment as follows:

Plural Extension For any a, b in X, we have $\{a\}R\{b\}$ if and only if aR_jb for all $R_j \in \mathfrak{R}$.

This axiom posits that if all preference orderings in $\mathfrak{R}$ agree that one alternative is at least as good as another, then the freedom ranking over the associated singleton sets must be consistent with this consensus opinion. Moreover, in the case where two preference orderings disagree, the associated singleton sets are unable to be compared using the freedom ranking.

A second property concerns the role of sets of options that are noncomparable under R^* in creating sets that have strictly greater freedom. As in the example where Jill is not sure how to rank teaching and civil engineering, let us consider opportunity sets A and B that cannot be compared using R^*. By monotonicity we know that $(A \cup B)R^*B$ and hence $(A \cup B)R_j^UB$ for all $R_j \in \mathfrak{R}$. Since A and B are not comparable this implies that $BP_{j'}^UA$ for some $R_{j'} \in \mathfrak{R}$. But by the transitivity of ordering $R_{j'}^U$ we have $(A \cup B)P_{j'}^UA$, and hence $(A \cup B)P^*A$ by the definition of P^*. It follows that R^* satisfies the following property:

Semi-Strict Monotonicity Let A and B be elements of Z. If $B \subseteq A$ then ARB; and in addition if B and $A \backslash B \neq \emptyset$ are noncomparable under R, then APB.

In addition to monotonicity, this axiom requires that whenever an opportunity set B is merged with a second, noncomparable opportunity set $A \backslash B$, we obtain a new set A having strictly greater freedom. So if Jill is unable to rank the singleton options of teaching and civil engineering, having both options is strictly freedom enhancing. It would be interesting to explore whether these latter two axioms could characterize R^* among all freedom quasi-orderings satisfying consistency.

The effective freedom ranking R^* is generally incomplete, and its ability to make comparisons depends on the extent to which the preferences in $\mathfrak{R}$ (or more precisely the indirect utility orderings) agree. If $\mathfrak{R}$ has only a single preference ordering, then R^* will be an indirect utility ranking and hence complete. If $\mathfrak{R}$ contains all logically possible preference orderings on X, then R^* becomes set inclusion ranking, so that $A \supseteq B$ if and only if AR^*B. This is the most incomplete quasi-ordering consistent with monotonicity. An intermediate, six-alternative example based on Sen (1990) shows how agreement across preference orderings expands the reach of R^* beyond set inclusion. Suppose $C = \{g, t, w\}$ contains "great," "terrific," and "wonderful" alternatives while $D = \{b, a, d\}$ contains "bad," "awful," and "dismal" alternatives wherein each option in C is regarded by every $R_i \in \mathfrak{R}$ as strictly preferable to each option in D. Preferences in $\mathfrak{R}$ are otherwise unconstrained. Then the associated effective freedom ranking goes beyond set inclusion in two ways: (1) if A contains an alternative from C while B does not, then AP^*B; (2) if both contain alternatives from C, then the ranking depends only on these alternatives, with AR^*B following from $(A \cap C) \supseteq (B \cap C)$. Of course, CP^*D as expected.

A second example based on Foster (1993) shows that the effective freedom ranking R^* can compare opportunity sets even when the underlying preferences in $\mathfrak{R}$ are incompatible. Kamala is a Bollywood aficionado who judges movies by the number of dance scenes and number of fight scenes. For her, a movie is represented as a vector of the two values, so that $x = (3, 5)$ is a movie with three dance and five fight scenes. On some nights, Kamala has a strong hankering for choreography and would rather avoid the punch-ups: her "dance-loving" ordering R_1 is represented by $u_1(x) = x_1 - x_2$. On others, she looks forward to rampant fisticuffs but could do without the Bhangra: her "fight-loving" ordering R_2 is represented by $u_1(x) = x_2 - x_1$. The set $X = \{w, x, y, z\}$ of all possible movies is depicted in Figure 24.1. Notice that her two preferences never agree: R_1 ranks the elements as $wP_1xP_1yP_1z$, while R_2 ranks them as $zP_2yP_2xP_2w$. The intersection quasi-ordering generated by R_1 and R_2 on X is empty—there is no hope for consensus. In contrast the effective freedom ranking R^* on Z, which is the intersection

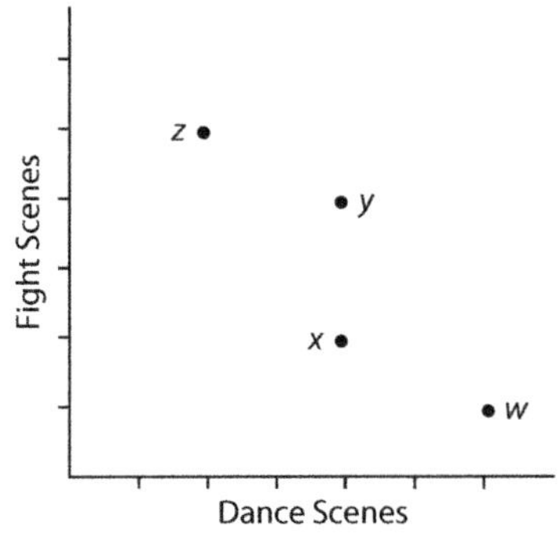

Figure 24.1. Choosing Movies.

of the indirect utility rankings R_1^U and R_2^U, can make many nontrivial comparisons. For example, consider $\{w, z\}$ and $\{x, y\}$. Clearly $\{w, z\}$ offers dance-loving Kamala her best element (namely w) and also offers fight-loving Kamala her best alternative (namely z). Consequently, both indirect utility rankings R_1^U and R_2^U agree on the superiority of $\{w, z\}$ over $\{x, y\}$, so $\{w, z\}P^*\{x, y\}$. Moreover, since singleton sets are noncomparable, any two-alternative opportunity set has greater effective freedom than either of its singleton components (as required by semi-strict monotonicity). We will return to this example when we discuss Sen (2002).

5.2. Representations and Measures

The effective freedom ranking R^* has several representations that help in interpreting the ranking and linking it to other approaches. The first is a natural representation in terms of utility vectors. Recall the discussion of indirect utility freedom in which the elements in the effective opportunity set $L_1(A)$ are counted to obtain a utility representation $u(A) = |L_1(A)|$ of R^U. In the plural preference case we can construct the analogous utility representation $u_j(A) = |L_j(A)|$ for each R_j^U and then define the vector-valued utility function $u(A) = (u_1(A), \ldots, u_m(A))$. It is clear from the definition of R^* that

$$AR^*B \text{ if and only if } u(A) \geq u(B)$$

and hence u is a vector-valued representation of R^*. The function u maps from Z to the space of utility vectors ordered by vector dominance and is entirely analogous to how Pareto dominance is viewed in utility space.

The second representation uses transformed opportunity sets to indicate when R^* holds. For any opportunity set A, define the *effective opportunity set* $D(A) = \cup_{AR^*B} B$ to be the set containing all elements that are found in any set B weakly dominated by A according to R^*. $D(A)$ is equivalently seen as the set of all $y \in X$ having the property that no matter which preference ordering $R_j \in \Re$ is selected, there is some $x_j \in A$ for which $x_j R_j y$.[23] It can be shown that $AI^*D(A)$, and that AR^*B holds exactly when $D(A) \supseteq D(B)$. In other words, A has the same level of effective freedom as its associated effective opportunity set $D(A)$, and furthermore R^* is represented by D where effective opportunity sets are ordered by set inclusion. Note that unlike the indirect utility case (which yields a complete freedom ranking R^U), it is possible for two sets A and B to be unranked by R^*, which corresponds to the case where neither $D(A)$ nor $D(B)$ contains the other.

A third representation uses the enumeration methodology of Section 3.2 by which an opportunity set A is described as a vector $v(A)$ of 0's and 1's (where 1 indicates an alternative's presence while 0 indicates its absence). Let $v_D(A) = v(D(A))$ denote the

[23] Hence $D(A)$ is intersection of $L_j(A)$ across all j.

vector corresponding to A's effective opportunity set $D(A)$, and similarly define $v_D(B)$. Then it is immediate that

$$AR^*B \text{ if and only if } v_D(A) \geq v_D(B)$$

so that v_D is a second vector-valued representation of the effective freedom ranking. If $\mathfrak{R}$ includes all logically possible orderings, then $D(A) = A$ so that v itself is a vector-valued representation of the effective freedom ranking R^* (which in this case is set inclusion). In the special case where $\mathfrak{R}$ has a single ordering, every pair of vectors $v_D(A)$ and $v_D(B)$ can be ranked by vector dominance and R^* (or the indirect utility freedom ranking) is complete. This representation is the vector-valued version of the previous representation based on effective opportunity sets.

Define the *counting representation* $u^{\#}(A) = |D(A)|$ to be the cardinality of the effective opportunity set $D(A)$ or, equivalently, the sum of the entries of the vector $v_D(A)$. This is an intuitive numerical measure of freedom that uses information on preferences from $\mathfrak{R}$ to assess the quality and range of choices in A. It does so by counting the number of elements in X that are dominated by A, and hence the number that A effectively includes (given $\mathfrak{R}$). It is clear that $u^{\#}$ *partially* represents R^* in the sense that

1. AI^*B implies $u^{\#}(A) = u^{\#}(B)$, and
2. AP^*B implies $u^{\#}(A) > u^{\#}(B)$.

This means that the measure $u^{\#}$ follows the quasi-ordering R^* when it applies, and hence is never inconsistent with its rankings.[24]

The counting representation $u^{\#}$ induces a complete ordering, say $R^{\#}$, that extends R^* in a natural way and is of some independent interest. If A and B are comparable by R^*, then $D(A)$ and $D(B)$ are ranked by set inclusion, and hence the counting representation ensures that $R^{\#}$ ranks A and B in the same way; if A and B are not comparable under R^*, so that neither $D(A)$ nor $D(B)$ lies within the other, $R^{\#}$ makes the comparison by counting alternatives in the respective effective opportunity sets and ranking accordingly.[25] $R^{\#}$ thus bases its rankings on information about the quality of options as interpreted by the preferences in $\mathfrak{R}$ and uses counting methods when preference information is not available to make the comparison.

It is instructive to examine the freedom rankings R^* and $R^{\#}$ in two extreme cases: first, where $\mathfrak{R}$ has a single element, so that the decision maker's preference ordering is known with certainty; and second, where $\mathfrak{R}$ contains all logically possible preferences,

[24] See Aumann (1962, p. 450), who uses (1) and (2), and Majumdar and Sen (1976), who provide a general discussion of the representation of incomplete rankings. Note that a full representation (with "if and only if") of R^* is out of the question as $u^{\#}$ can compare any two sets; this is why the implications are only required in one direction. Of course a partial representation is less informative than a full one, since there are typically many quasi-orderings consistent with a complete ordering.

[25] This extension is not unlike the way that the Gini coefficient inequality measure extends the Lorenz ranking.

which may be interpreted as having no information on the decision maker's preferences. In the first case, the effective freedom approach is identical to the indirect utility approach, generating the complete ranking R^U that is based on the given preference ordering. And since R^* is complete, there is no scope for extending the quasi-ordering by counting, and hence $R^U = R^* = R^\#$. The counting measure $u^\#$ represents each of the three freedom orderings; it aggregates all the available information on preferences and nothing else. In the second case, the lack of effective information on preferences reduces each effective opportunity set $D(A)$ to A itself. Consequently, R^* is reduced to set inclusion, a minimal freedom quasi-ordering, while the counting ordering becomes R^C, the cardinality ordering presented by Pattanaik and Xu (1990). With so little information to go on, the effective freedom ranking R^* is squeezed down to the most incomplete freedom quasi-ordering; the counting measure $u^\#$, then, must perform much of the heavy lifting in extending R^* to $R^\# = R^C$.

Pattanaik and Xu's (1990) cardinality approach to freedom and the traditional indirect utility approach to freedom thus arise as two polar cases of the same method, where freedom is measured as the number of options in the effective opportunity set. The cardinality ranking is located at one extreme where preference information is essentially absent, while indirect utility is at the other where preference information is exact. The effective freedom approach and its associated counting measure based on the size of effective opportunity sets can go well beyond these two informational extremes, since all intermediate degrees of information in $\mathfrak{R}$ can be accommodated and incorporated into this framework for evaluating freedom.

5.3. Sen's Subrelation and Arrow's Extension

The effective freedom relation is one natural way of evaluating opportunity freedom in the plural preference model. In his *Arrow Lectures*, published in 2002, Sen presents a more stringent criterion that ranks opportunity sets whenever an element can be found in one set that is weakly preferred to every element from the second set, irrespective of the preference ordering. In symbols, the Sen freedom ranking R^S is defined by

$$AR^SB \text{ if and only if there exists } a \in A \text{ such that } aR_jb \text{ for all } R_j \in \mathfrak{R} \text{ and all } b \in B,$$

By contrast, the effective freedom ranking can be defined as

$$AR^*B \text{ if and only if for each } R_j \in \mathfrak{R} \text{ there exist } a_j \in A \text{ such that } a_jR_jb \text{ for all } b \in B,$$

and hence R^S is a subrelation of R^* (i.e, AR^SB implies AR^*B). Under R^* the dominating alternatives a_j can vary with the preference relation R_j, while R^S requires all the a_j to be the same—an additional restriction that might be called Sen's *uniformity requirement*.[26] Sen (2002) justifies R^S within a model that has an altered timeline for uncertainty resolution, and this argument will be reviewed below. We begin with a discussion of the coverage, representations and properties of the resulting freedom relation R^S.

To see how the uniformity requirement affects the coverage of the freedom relation, let us revisit our previous examples. In Sen's classic example with sets $C = \{g, t, w\}$ and $D = \{b, a, d\}$, the ranking $CP^S D$ follows immediately from the definition of R^S, since any element of C dominates any element of D for all possible preferences. However, R^S cannot compare C to *itself*, nor even to the menu $\{g, t\} \subset C$, since by assumption no one element dominates g and t for all preferences. This, of course, means that R^S is neither reflexive nor monotonic, in contrast to R^* and the other relations we have discussed. In the second example, where the effective freedom relation concludes $\{w, z\}P^*\{x, y\}$, the Sen relation is powerless to compare $\{w, z\}$ and $\{x, y\}$: no *one* alternative in $\{w, z\}$ is better than each element of $\{x, y\}$ for both preference orderings. Clearly, R^S is more incomplete than R^* in this key example as well.

Since R^S is a subrelation of R^*, it follows that each representation for R^* constitutes a *partial* representation for R^S. In general, though, since R^S is not a quasi-ordering, it is impossible to find a *full* representation for R^S analogous to the ones found for the other freedom rankings. It *is* possible to restate the definition of R^S in terms of R^* and its effective opportunity set representation. Indeed, $AR^S B$ holds if and only if there exists $a \in A$ such that $\{a\}R^* B$ and, consequently,

$$AR^S B \text{ if and only if } D(\{a\}) \supseteq D(B) \text{ for some } a \in A.$$

Testing for $AR^* B$ requires a single comparison of $D(B)$ and $D(A)$, while $AR^S B$ entails a series of comparisons between $D(B)$ and *every* $D(\{a\})$ for $a \in A$.

As for the properties of this relation, it is immediate that R^S satisfies transitivity, simple monotonicity, simple composition, and plural extension. It is likewise clear that R^S follows R^* in generally violating the Pattanaik and Xu (1990) axioms of simple anonymity, simple independence, and simple strict monotonicity (and their stronger versions). However, apart from simple composition, it can be verified that the other properties that were shown to be satisfied by R^* are not generally satisfied by R^S.[27] Using R^S instead of R^* can mean foregoing these intuitive properties.

[26] To be precise, it requires that among all such dominating collections of a_j there must be at least one set with a_j constant across all j. Note that there is no presumption that the resulting uniform a is in any sense a best choice from set A; it could be strictly worse than some a_j' in A according to R_j, or even dominated by some a' uniformly across *all* preferences.

[27] For example, to show semi-independence can be violated, consider $X = \{a, b, c\}$ and $\Re = \{R_1, R_2\}$ with $aP_1 bP_1 c$ and $cP_2 aP_2 b$. Then $\{a\}R^S\{b\}$, and yet we do not have $\{a, c\}R^S\{b, c\}$. To see that composition can be violated, let $X = \{a, a', b, d\}$ and suppose $\Re = \{R_1, R_2\}$ has $aP_1 bP_1 a' P_1 d$ and $a' P_2 dP_2 aP_2 b$. Then $\{a, a'\}R^S\{b\}$ and $\{a, a'\}R^S\{d\}$, and yet we do not have $\{a, a'\}R^S\{b, d\}$.

Sen (2002) has emphasized that the appropriateness of a given freedom ranking can depend upon the "sequence of events" in the underlying model. Recall that in the original effective freedom model, the preference uncertainty is resolved *after* the choice of opportunity sets but *before* the selection of a specific alternative from the set. Given this "sequencing," the effective freedom ranking R^* is the natural ranking to use.[28] A different ranking may arise, though, if resolution of the uncertainty is pushed up or back. For example, if the resolution occurs *before* either choice has to be made, this yields the special case of a single preference ordering and suggests the use of the indirect utility freedom relation R^U. Alternatively, suppose that the resolution takes place *after* both choices, so that one would have to select a menu *and* an element without knowing which of the preferences would actually obtain. Sen suggests that R^S would be more natural than R^* in this plural preference model.

In principle, even with the new order of events we could still rank sets according to R^*; however, the original justification for that ranking (that a preference-contingent set of choices from A can be found that dominates any such preference-contingent set of choices from B) would have no force. Preference-contingent choices are no longer feasible and their relative desirability has no relevance. Under the new scenario, a single choice must be selected from each set without knowing which preference ordering will eventually obtain, and since R^* offers no such guidance it is clearly out of place. In contrast, Sen's uniformity requirement ensures that there is some alternative a in A uniformly better than every element in B, and this helps make the case that A is the preferred menu in the new scenario. But even when an alternative like a exists, it will not necessarily be the *choice* from A (another a' could dominate a) nor does the ranking R^S provide guidance on how such a choice might be made (there may be several better alternatives with no clear winner). Sen's ranking may well be more natural than R^* in this environment, but whether it fully responds to the challenges laid out in the scenario is not entirely clear.

The new order of events moves us away from the sequential "preference for flexibility" view of freedom to a more challenging "all-at-once" problem of choice under uncertainty that is arguably less grounded in considerations of freedom. Problems of this type have been the subject of much investigation in decision theory, with standard solutions often requiring further assumptions on the comparability of preferences and the resolution of uncertainty. Sen (2002, p. 614) uses the logic of one well-known solution to scrutinize the decisions of R^* and we now turn to a fuller discussion of this approach. Imagine a scenario in which preferences are given by level comparable utility functions and uncertainty is resolved by an "unfriendly" agent once an option

[28] See Sen (2002, p. 677). To be sure, subrelation R^S might *also* be applied in this environment to distinguish between certain R^* comparisons; however, it may not make sense to rule out a given R^* comparison just because the uniformity requirement fails.

is chosen. This pessimistic scenario naturally gives rise to the *maxmin criterion*, which selects the "safest" option (whose vector of utilities has the highest minimum entry) and ranks opportunity sets accordingly.[29] Return once again to the Bollywood example, and consider the vectors of utility pairs that the three elements w, y, and z generate:

	u_1	u_2	min
w	5	-5	-5
y	0	0	0
z	-3	3	-3

In the third column we have listed the minimum utility across the option's two utility levels. Now let us compare the opportunity sets $\{w, y, z\}$ and $\{w, z\}$ first for R^* and then for the maxmin criterion. Recall that R^* ranks both sets the same: option y is never a best element and its absence leaves effective freedom unaffected. For the maxmin, we see that the option in $\{w, z\}$ with the highest minimum utility level is z with -3, while the maxmin choice from $\{w, y, z\}$ is y with 0 and hence $\{w, y, z\}$, which contains the safe alternative y, is strictly superior to $\{w, z\}$, which does not.

Sen considers each ranking to be appropriate in its own setting, but argues that the all-at-once scenario may drive out the freedom-as-flexibility scenario if the agent develops doubts about the resolution of uncertainty. Should this bring joy to lovers of freedom? Perhaps not since, by its very definition, this scenario necessarily denies value to unchosen elements: In the minmax example, we find that $\{w, y, z]$ is equivalent to $\{y\}$, so that elements w and z add nothing. In contrast, R^* reduces $\{w, y, z]$ to $\{w, z\}$, where both remaining elements irreducibly provide value, and yet only one is eventually chosen.

Arrow (1995, p. 8–9) argues that "the notion of freedom must be grounded in a multiplicity of preferences" but contends that "if the concept of freedom is to have any operational meaning, it must lead to a complete ordering." Drawing upon a stream of literature in economics reaching back to Hart (1942), Arrow provides a simple framework for evaluating opportunity freedom as *flexibility*. This view mirrors the framework of Kreps (1979) in relying upon two traditional constructs that convert plural preferences over options into a complete ordering over sets of options. Each preference relation R_j is represented by a utility function u_j; and utility levels from the various functions are aggregated up using a probability vector $p = (p_1, \ldots, p_m)$. The order of events coincides with the effective freedom model in which the agent first decides between opportunity sets and then, after the preference ordering is revealed, selects the best alternative from the chosen set. Let $u_j(A) = \max_{a \in A} u_j(a)$ denote the indirect utility function that extends

[29] See for example Gilboa (2009).

u_j to sets of alternatives by associating with each set the utility level of its best element. The *expected indirect utility* of a set is defined as $U_p(A) = p_1u_1(A) + \cdots + p_mu_m(A)$; this is the numerical measure of opportunity freedom employed by Arrow (1995). We will denote the associated freedom ordering by R_p.

Since each R_j is represented by u_j, it follows that the relation R^* has a vector-valued representation using $u(A) = (u_1(A), \ldots, u_m(A))$, the vector of Arrow's indirect utilities. It is immediately clear that so long as p assigns positive probability $p_j > 0$ to each u_j, the resulting freedom ordering R_p is an extension of the effective freedom relation R^* (and hence R^* is a subrelation of R_p). Moreover, the freedom measure $U_p(A) = pu(A)$ partially represents R^*.

To illustrate how the Arrow approach expands the comparisons offered by R^*, let us return to the utility version of the Bollywood example and set $p = (1/2, 1/2)$. Since $u(\{w,y,z\}) = u(\{w,z\}) = (5,3)$, it follows that $U_p(\{w,y,z\}) = U_p(\{w,z\}) = 4$; both $\{w,y,z\}I^*\{w,z\}$ and $\{w,y,z\}I_p\{w,z\}$ hold, as we would expect, since y would never be selected under either realization. As for the singleton sets, the indirect utility vectors associated with $\{w\}, \{y\}$, and $\{z\}$ are, respectively, $(5,-5), (0,0)$, and $(-3,3)$, and are not ranked by R^*; the freedom measure U_p takes a value of 0 for each, and so $\{w\}I_p\{y\}I_p\{z\}$. Finally, adding an alternative to a singleton set always raises its vector and hence its freedom measure in this example. For instance $u(\{w,y\}) = (5,0) > (5,-5) = u(\{w\})$, while $U_p(\{w,y\}) = 2.5 > 0 = U_p(\{w\})$, and so both rankings are in agreement.

As for the properties of this relation, Arrow (1995) notes that R_p is a complete ordering satisfying monotonicity. In general, though, R_p does not satisfy any of the other axioms discussed above. R_p generally violates the Pattanaik and Xu (1990) properties since its subrelation R^* can violate them. However, it may be less obvious why properties satisfied by R^* can be violated by R_p, so we will reexamine the Bollywood example to illustrate why this occurs. Let $A = \{z\}, B = \{w\}$, and $C = \{y\}$ so that AR_pB and the other requirements of simple semi-independence hold. Now consider $A \cup C$. When the utility is known to be u_1, option y would be chosen, yielding a utility level of 0; when utility is u_2 the choice would be z and the level would be 3. Consequently, $u(A \cup C) = (0,3)$, which leads to $U_p(A \cup C) = 1.5$. In contrast, $B \cup C$ has the best element w for utility u_1 and the best element y for utility u_2, yielding $u(B \cup C) = (5,0)$ and hence $U_p(B \cup C) = 2.5 > U_p(A \cup C)$. This goes against the conclusions of simple semi-independence. For simple composition, select $A = \{y\}, B = \{w\}$, and $D = \{z\}$. Since all singleton sets have an expected indirect utility of 0, it follows that AR_pB, AR_pD, and all the other conditions for simple composition are met. Yet $U_p(B \cup D) = 4 > U_p(A)$ and hence $B \cup DP_pA$, violating the conclusions of simple composition. In this example, we see how Arrow's requirement of completeness has forced a ranking (e.g., indifference) among singleton opportunity sets that have very different preference-contingent utility levels and hence are unranked by R^*. With this key information aggregated away, it is impossible to predict the combined value of a set of alternatives since this depends on the precise way that the utility vectors match up.[30] As a result the intuitive composition property satisfied by R^* is violated by R_p.

At the same time, the structure underlying R_p agrees with the constructs standardly used in modeling an agent facing some form of uncertainty. The resulting expected indirect utility freedom measure carries with it a significant amount of meaning and is readily computed, so long as the utility representations and probability vector underlying it can be agreed upon.[31] In addition, the structure itself can represent a surprisingly wide range of conceptions of freedom. At one extreme, when there is a single preference ordering in $\mathfrak{R}$ (or the probability vector over plural preferences is degenerate so that a single preference ordering has all the weight), R_p becomes the indirect utility freedom ordering associated with that preference ordering. Alternatively, suppose that each preference relation is represented by $u_j(x) = |L_j(x)|$, so that utility is the number of elements in the lower contour set of x. Suppose further that $\mathfrak{R}$ is the set of all logically possible preference orderings and each is considered to be equally likely by p. If opportunity sets A and B satisfy $|A| = |B|$, then by the symmetry of the situation, their indirect utility vectors must be permutations of one another and, hence, $U_p(A) = U_p(B)$. Moreover, if $x \in X$ is an option that is not in A, then for the assumed set of preferences, A and $\{x\}$ cannot be ranked by R^* and so $A \cup \{x\} P^* A$. This means that $u(A \cup \{x\}) > u(A)$ and thus $U_p(A \cup \{x\}) > U_p(A)$. It follows that R_p is simply the cardinality ranking R^C. Hence, Pattanaik and Xu's (1990) freedom ranking R^C can arise in the Arrow framework when the decision maker has maximal uncertainty about preferences (in that all logically possible preferences are equally probable) and utilities take a particularly simple form (the number of weakly dominated alternatives). This shows both the flexibility of the Arrow framework and the unrealistic assumptions that are implicit in the cardinality freedom ranking.

5.4. Reflections on Plural Preferences and Effective Freedom

When a decision maker has several preference orderings, any one of which *may* become relevant for a choice situation, this can create value for certain options that, in the course of events, were not chosen. This view of freedom (as the range of options that might have value in potential choice situations) relies upon multiple futures to construct value today. If resolution of all uncertainty occurs up front, leading to the single preference model and the indirect utility ranking, the value from unchosen options is lost. If the resolution is in the distant future, with all actions being taken under the same cloud of uncertainty, then the ability to respond and make particular use of valuable options is muted. The two serial choice problems (namely, set-choice and element-choice) become

[30] The negative correlation of u_1 and u_2 would appear to have played a pivotal role in this example.

[31] The fact that the approach requires agreement on these elements can be a drawback in practical applications.

a single and essentially static decision problem, and the focus once again is the chosen elements (not the unchosen). In contrast, the effective freedom model embodies the perspective of "freedom as flexibility"—the ability to react and do well in the face of changing circumstances.

If uncertainty and preferences can be quantified into probabilities and utilities, the toolkit of expected utility can be brought to bear, resulting in a precise freedom measure and complete ordering of freedom. However, now it is the robustness of the measure (and the comparisons it makes) that is in doubt. As a remedy we might begin with a *set* of possible probability vectors and inquire whether the original comparison obtained with p would be preserved *for all probability vectors* in the set. This is analogous to the Bewley (2002) model of Knightian uncertainty, and several other related constructs for modeling ambiguity.[32] Various sets might be considered, but one interesting case is where it is the entire simplex of probability vectors, and where *full robustness* is being required. This may be viewed as a case of maximal ambiguity, where one's confidence in the initial probability vector is small. It is easy to see that Arrovian comparisons of freedom are fully robust to changes in the probability vector exactly when the effective freedom ranking R^* holds. Thus, R_p and R^* are two extremes of a model with varying levels of ambiguity: with the complete ordering R_p arising when there is no ambiguity concerning p; and the quasi-ordering R^* arising when ambiguity concerning p is greatest.

6. CONCLUSIONS

The traditional economic model of decision making leaves little room for valuing options that are not chosen by the decision maker. Yet as noted by Arrow (1995), the idea that increased flexibility—"keeping your options open"—can have value in a variety of contexts has been understood by economists for many years. The work on opportunity freedom has been exploring related insights in the context of normative economics, with the ultimate goal of enriching the basis for evaluating well-being and providing practical measurement tools for the capability approach.

In this chapter, we have reviewed three main approaches to evaluating and measuring opportunity freedom. The first takes the untenable position that there is simply no way of determining the relative desirability of options. Left with a minimal informational base for evaluation, the cardinality approach equates greater freedom with greater numbers of options. The Pattanaik and Xu (1990) characterization of the cardinality ranking formally captures this lack of information in its axioms, including one that requires all singleton sets to have equal levels of opportunity freedom.

[32] For example, see Gilboa (2009) and Foster, McGillivray, and Seth (2009).

The second approach brings into the discussion exactly the sort of preference information needed to evaluate the quality of the various options. But once the agent's preference information has been introduced into the model, it is natural to ignore all but the very best option in a set and hence to use an indirect utility approach—which equates opportunity freedom with the level of utility of the chosen alternative (and ignores the other "unchosen" alternatives). The indirect utility approach to freedom likewise can be characterized with the help of a key axiom that extends the preference ordering of alternatives to the freedom ranking of singleton sets. Using the two building blocks of cardinality freedom (representing a concern for quantity) and indirect utility freedom (embodying the concern for quality), many hybrid measures of freedom can be constructed.

The third approach to evaluating freedom assumes the decision maker has multiple preference orderings, each of which could be the relevant one when a choice is made from an opportunity set. Each element generates a vector of possible utility levels, while a set generates a vector of maximum achievable (or indirect) utility levels, one for each realized preference. The effective freedom quasi-ordering is vector dominance over these contingent indirect utility levels, which means that the best element of one set is as good as the best element of the other, for all possible preference orderings. A set's effective freedom level is unchanged when a dominated option is added to the set. However, the level rises if the added option is strictly better than a best element for at least one of the possible preferences. The effective freedom ranking can be represented in several ways, and a subrelation and an extension have been constructed to fit alternative models of choice. The taxonomy of the chapter was constructed to readily allow a comparison of properties and characteristics of the various freedom rankings, and to reveal the hidden relationships among the different approaches. It is hoped that this structure will help future researchers formulate practical ways of measuring the freedoms that constitute our well-being.

ACKNOWLEDGMENTS

The author wishes to thank Sabina Alkire, Prasanta Pattanaik, Amartya Sen, Suman Seth, Shabana Singh, Kotaro Suzumura, and John Weymark for helpful comments and assistance with this chapter. Any remaining errors are the author's alone.

REFERENCES

Agarwal, B., Humphries, J., & Robeyns, I. (Eds.). (2007). *Capabilities, freedom, and equality: Amartya Sen's work from a gender perspective*. Oxford: Oxford University Press.

Alkire, S. (2008). Concepts and measures of agency. In Basu, Kaushik, & R. Kanbur (Eds.), *Arguments for a better world: essays in honor of Amartya Sen, Vol. I: ethics, welfare and measurement* (pp. 455–474). Oxford: Oxford University Press.

Alkire, S., & Foster, J. (2007). Counting and multidimensional poverty measurement. OPHI working paper series No. 7. http://ophi.qeh.ox.ac.uk.

Anand, S., & Sen, A. K. (1997). Concepts of human development and poverty: a multidimensional perspective. In *Poverty and human development: human development papers 1997* (pp. 1–20). New York: United Nations Development Programme.

Arlegi, R., & Nieto, J. (1990). Equality of opportunity: cardinality-based criteria. In H. de Swart (Ed.), *Logic, game theory and social choice* (pp. 458–481). Tilburg: Tilburg University Press.

Arlegi, R., & Nieto, J. (2001). Ranking opportunity sets: an approach based on the preference for flexibility. *Social Choice and Welfare, 18*, 23–36.

Arrow, K. J. (1995). A note on freedom and flexibility. In K. Basu, P. K. Pattanaik, & K. Suzumura (Eds.), *Choice, welfare, and development. A festschrift in honor of Amartya K. Sen* (pp. 7–16). Oxford: Clarendon Press.

Arrow, K. J. (2006). Freedom and social choice: notes in the margin. *Utilitas, 18*(1), 52–60.

Atkinson, A. B. (2003). Multidimensional deprivation: contrasting social welfare and counting approaches. *Journal of Economic Inequality, 1*(1), 51–65.

Aumann, R. (1962). Utility theory without the completeness axiom. *Econometrica, 30*, 445–462.

Barberà, S., Bossert, W. & Pattanaik, P. K. (2004). Ranking sets of objects. In S. Barberà, P. J. Hammond, & Ch. Seidl (Eds.), *Handbook of utility theory*. Boston, MA: Kluwer Academic Publishers.

Basu, K., & Lopez-Calva, L. F. (2010). Functionings and capabilities. In K. Arrow, A. Sen, & K. Suzumura (Eds.), *Handbook of social choice and welfare, Vol. II*. Amsterdam: Elsevier Science-North Holland Publishers.

Bewley, T. F. (2002). Knightian decision theory: part I. *Decisions in Economics and Finance, 25*(2), 79–110.

Blackorby, C., Primont, D., & Russell, R. (1978). *Duality, separability, and functional structure: theory and economic applications*. New York: North-Holland.

Bossert, W. (2000). Opportunity sets and uncertain consequences. *Journal of Mathematical Economics, 33*, 475–496.

Bossert, W., Pattanaik, P. K., & Xu, Y. (1994). Ranking opportunity sets: an axiomatic approach. *Journal of Economic Theory, 63*(2), 326–345.

Bourguignon, F., & Chakravarty, S. R. (2003). The measurement of multidimensional poverty. *Journal of Economic Inequality, 1*(1), 25–49.

Buchanan, J. M. (1954). Social choice, democracy and free markets. *Journal of Political Economy, 62*, 114–123.

Chipman, J. S., & Moore, J. C. (1979). On social welfare functions and the aggregation of preferences. *Journal of Economic Theory, 21*, 111–139.

Dowding, K., & van Hees, M. (2009). Freedom of choice. In P. Anand, P. K. Pattanaik, & C. Puppe (Eds.), *Oxford handbook of individual and social choice* (pp. 374–392). Oxford: Oxford University Press.

Foster, J. (1993). Notes on effective freedom. Paper presented at the Stanford workshop on economic theories of inequalty, sponsored by the MacArthur foundation, March 11–13, 1993. Mimeographed, Vanderbilt University.

Foster, J., Greer, J., & Thorbecke, E. (1984). A class of decomposable poverty measures. *Econometrica, 42*, 761–766.

Foster, J., Greer, J., & Thorbecke, E. (2010). The Foster-Greer-Thorbecke poverty measures: twenty-five years later, Forthcoming. *Journal of Economic Inequality*.

Foster, J., & Sen, A. (1997). On economic inequality: after a quarter century. Annex to the enlarged edition of *on economic inequality*, by A Sen. Oxford: Clarendon Press.

Foster, J. E., McGillivray, M., & Seth, S. (2009). Rank robustness of composite indicators. OPHI Working Paper 26, Oxford University.

Frank, R. (1988). *Passions within reason*. New York: Norton.

Gaertner, W. (2006). *A primer in social choice theory*. Oxford: Oxford University Press.

Gilboa, I. (2009). *Theory of decision under uncertainty*. Cambridge: Cambridge University Press.

Hart, A. G. (1942). Risk, uncertainty and the unprofitability of compounding probabilities. In O. Lange, F. McIntyre, & T. O. Yntema (Eds.), *Studies in Mathematical Economics and Econometrics* (pp. 110–118). Chicago: University of Chicago Press.

Jones, P., & Sugden, R. (1982). Evaluating choice. *International Review of Law and Economics, 2*, 47–65.

Kant, I. (1788). *Critique of practical reason*, trans L. W. Beck. New York: Bobbs-Merrill 1956.

Klemisch-Ahlert, M. (1993). Freedom of choice—a comparison of different rankings of opportunity sets. *Social Choice and Welfare, 10*, 189–207.

Koopmans, T. (1964). On flexibility of future preferences. In M. W. Shelley & G. L. Bryan (Eds.), *Human judgments and optimality*. New York: Wiley and Sons.

Kreps, D. M. (1979). A representation theorem for "preference for flexibility." *Econometrica, 47*(3), 565–577.

Laslier, J., Fleurbaey, M., Gravel, N., & Trannoy, A. (1998). *Freedom in economics: new perspectives in normative analysis.* Routledge studies in social and political thought. London: Routledge.

Majumdar, M., & Sen, A. K. (1976). A note on representing partial orderings. *Review of Economic Studies, 43*(3), 543–545.

Malkiel, B. G., & Quandt, R. E. (1969). *Strategies and rational decisions in the securities options market.* Cambridge, MA: MIT Press.

Mill, J. S. (1848). *Principles of political economy*. New York: Prometheus Books, 2004.

Mill, J. S. (1859). *On liberty* (London); republished in J. S. Mill, *Utilitarianism; on liberty; representative government*. London: Everyman's Library, Dent, 1972.

Nagel, T. (1970). *The possibility of altruism*. Oxford: Clarendon Press.

Nozick, R. (1974). *Anarchy, State and Utopia*. Oxford: Blackwell.

Ok, E. A. (2002). Utility representation of an incomplete preference relation. *Journal of Economic Theory, 104*(2), 429–449.

Pattanaik, P. K., & Xu, Y. (1990). On ranking opportunity sets in terms of freedom of choice. *Récherches Economiques de Louvain, 56*, 383–390.

Pattanaik, P. K., & Xu, Y. (1998). On preference and freedom. *Theory and Decision, 14*(4), 173–198.

Pattanaik, P. K., & Xu, Y. (2000). On ranking opportunity sets in economic environments. *Journal of Economic Theory, 93*, 48–71

Perragine, V. (1999). The distribution and redistribution of opportunity. *Journal of Economic Surveys, 13*, 37–70.

Puppe, C. (1996). An axiomatic approach to "preferences for freedom of choice". *Journal of Economic Theory, 68*(1), 174–199.

Putnam, H. (2002). On the rationality of preferences. In H. Putnam, *The collapse of the fact/value dichotomy and other essays*. 79–95. Cambridge, MA: Harvard University Press.

Rader, J. T. (1963). The existence of a utility function to represent preferences. *Review of Economic Studies, 30*, 229–232.

Rawls, J. (1971). *Theory of justice*. Cambridge, MA : Harvard University Press.

Scitovsky, T. (1986). *Human desire and economic satisfaction*. Brighton: Wheatsheaf Books.

Sen, A. K. (1976). Poverty: an ordinal approach to measurement. *Econometrica, 46*, 219–232.

Sen, A. K. (1980). Equality of what? In S. McMurrin (Ed.), *Tanner lectures on human values* (Vol. 1). Cambridge, UK: Cambridge University Press.

Sen, A. K. (1980/1981). Plural utility. *Proceedings of the Aristotelian Society*, New Series *81*, 193–215.

Sen, A. K. (1985). Well-being, agency and freedom: the Dewey lectures 1984. *The Journal of Philosophy, 82*(4), 169–221.

Sen, A. K. (1988). Freedom of choice: concept and content. *European Economic Review, 32*, 269–294.

Sen, A. K. (1990). Welfare, freedom and social choice: a reply. *Récherches Economiques de Louvain, 56*, 451–485.

Sen, A. K. (1991). Welfare, preference and freedom. *Journal of Econometrics, 50,* 15–29.
Sen, A. K. (1992). *Inequality re-examined.* Oxford: Clarendon Press.
Sen, A. K. (2002). *Rationality and freedom.* Cambridge, MA: The Belknap Press of Harvard University Press.
Sen, A. K. (2009). *The idea of justice.* London: Penguin.
Smith, A. (1759). *The theory of moral sentiments.* London: Printed for A. Millar, A. Kincaid, & J. Bell.
Sugden, R. (1981). *The political economy of public choice.* Oxford: Martin Robertson.
Sugden, R. (1998). The metric of opportunity. *Economics and Philosophy, 14,* 307–337.
Suppes, P. (1987). Maximizing freedom of decision: an axiomatic approach. In G. Feiwel (Ed.), *Arrow and the foundations of the theory of economic policy.* Dordrecht: Reidel.
UNDP (1990). *Human development report 1990: concept and measurement of human development.* New York: Oxford University Press.
van Hees, M. (1998). On the analysis of negative freedom. *Theory and Decision, 45*(2), 175–197.
van Hees, M., & Wissenburg, M. (1999). Freedom and opportunity. *Political Studies, 47*(1), 67–82.
Weisbrod, B. A. (1964). Collective-consumption services of individual-consumption goods. *Quarterly Journal of Economics, 78,* 471–477.
Weymark, J. A. (2003). Generalized Gini indices of equality of opportunity. *Journal of Economic Inequality, 1*(1), 5–24.
Zadeh, L. (1965). Fuzzy sets. *Information and Control, 8,* 338–353.

PART EIGHT

Voting and Manipulation

CHAPTER TWENTY-FIVE

Strategyproof Social Choice

Salvador Barberà
MOVE, Universitat Autònoma de Barcelona and Barcelona GSE, Bellaterra, Spain

Contents

Handbook of Social Choice and Welfare, Volume II
ISSN: 0169-7218, DOI: 10.1016/S0169-7218(10)00025-0

Abstract

This chapter surveys the literature on strategy proofness from a historical perspective. While I discuss the connections with other works on incentives in mechanism design, the main emphasis is on social choice models.

Keywords: strategyproofness, social choice, dominant strategies, domain restrictions, voting.
JEL codes: D7, D51, C7, H41.

1. THE PURPOSE AND LIMITATIONS OF THIS SURVEY

Surveys may have many different uses. I hope this survey on strategyproofness in social choice is able to fulfill some of them.

A possible use is informing the general reader about the type of questions that are addressed by the experts in the area, and the kind of answers that they look for. In trying to meet this objective I have provided a narrative that may be read as an introduction to the topic.[1] It also suggests to the reader some "boxes" in which to classify the many papers on the subject. The examples used to illustrate this narrative are treated more extensively than the rest of the articles that are also mentioned. This, I hope, allows for this chapter to be more than a list of papers. But the choice of illustrations is largely personal, includes some of my own work along with other contributions, and is not meant to signal that the results in question are more important than others that receive a more succinct treatment.

A second use for a survey is, I think, to provide a perspective of what has been done in the past. How did the topic come to be attractive to enough people as to deserve special attention, when and why did this happen, and how did this interest evolve? Every generation may need to rediscover some themes that were already treated by earlier ones, and this is surely a guarantee that important issues are not forgotten and get to be analyzed from new angles. But there is also a tendency to forget earlier works, and economics at large suffers, I believe, from an inability to accumulate established knowledge. In that respect, I provide an account of how an old remark that voting methods were manipulable was picked up in the early 1970s and became part of a very successful move to incorporate the analysis of incentives as an essential part in the study of economic mechanisms. The attention here will be essentially restricted to the issue of strategyproofness in the context of social choice, but I hope it becomes clear that the subject is part of a larger picture, and an important part indeed. I hope that this survey provides the reader with a good overview of the path followed until the beginning of the twenty-first century.

[1] Part of this narrative is borrowed from my previous paper "An Introduction to Strategy-proof Social Choice Functions" (2001a).

A third important use of a survey is to suggest important directions for future work. In that respect, I must admit that the contributions of the last years are treated here in much less detail than those of the preceding decades, and that the survey is not a good substitute for reading the latest news on the topic, even if I mention enough recent references to provide the hungry reader with a good start. In fact, there are new developments that receive only slight mention. I will go back and refer to them in the final remarks (Section 11). I have even left out some essential work on mechanism design that was born and grew in parallel to the contributions in social choice theory that I emphasize here. Again, the reader will find some comments on this literature in the text, and some more at the end. My only confort when admitting these limitations is that any survey gets old, and therefore this last role is more ephemeral than the other two that I tried to serve primarily.

2. INTRODUCTION: A FEW HISTORICAL NOTES

Voting rules have been used since ancient times, and the actors involved (candidates, voters, and designers) have certainly been aware ever since of the many possibilities that arise to affect their results through strategic behavior, even when the rules are formally respected. We have evidence of this awareness through the writings of those thinkers who discussed and analyzed voting systems in the past, and I shall mention a few, following the historical materials contained in Black (1958) and in McLean and Urken (1995).

Already in Roman times Pliny the Younger (CE 105) discussed beautifully the possibility of what we would call today agenda manipulation: it may be that the sequence in which different proposals are put to vote has an impact on the vote's outcome, thus giving the chairman, or whoever chooses the order of votes, a clear occasion to act strategically to his advantage.[2]

The organization of the Church gave rise to many occasions to vote (see, for example, Gaudemet 1979), and one of the contributions of Ramon Llull (1283, 1299) was to propose, in separate texts, the use of those rules that have come to be known as Borda's and Condorcet's methods. While not elaborating on the strategic aspects, Llull's remarks offer evidence of his awareness of the possibility that agents might not behave straightforwardly, and also of the possibility of influencing the behavior of voters through the design of appropriate rules and procedures. When describing the method to nominate candidates to become abbess, McLean and Urken (1995, p. 71) requires from the participants that, before voting secretly, they "all ... should take an oath to tell the truth."

[2] In fact, as noted by McLean and Urken, the case described by Pliny is one where the order of vote does not actually matter.

Likewise, in a later writing, where McLean and Urken (1995, pp. 73–74) proposes open, public voting, he demands that "all voters take an oath that they will elect the better and more suitable candidate." Yet, even then he insists that one of the virtues of the method is that if the voters "do not choose the best, it will be obvious to everyone in the chapter that they are choosing the worse candidate and perjuring themselves without any color of an excuse" (p. 73). To add, later on that "those who choose openly are so placed as to be in disgrace with their colleagues if they choose badly. Those who elect in secret are not" (p. 74).

In spite of having required his voters to "strip themselves of all sins" and "swearing an oath in the Lord's altar to elect the person that their free conscience shall duly judge best," McLean and Urken (1995, pp. 77–78) had to qualify his enthusiastic defense of the method he proposes. He said that no other method "can be conceived which is more holy, just, honest or free. For, by this procedure, no other outcome is possible, *if the electors act according to conscience* [my italics], than the choice of that candidate adjudged best by the collective judgement of all present."

More than three hundred years later, Jean-Charles de Borda (1784) also defended the method that took his name under the assumption that voters would sincerely express their preferences, and when criticized for that assumption retorted that his election method was only meant to be used by honest men (see McLean and Urken 1995, Chapter 1, footnote 10). Joseph Isidoro Morales (1797, LXXXIX, XC, pp. 220–221 in McLean and Urken), who proposed the same method as Borda just a few years later, discussed much more explicitly the possibility of strategic behavior under different voting rules:

> *In the methods of election currently in use . . . an area lies open to private or personal injustice by the electors, as, depending on the situation, one, two, three or more of them can prevent the election of the most deserving candidate if they thus wish to contravene the course of justice. This system is so well known and occurs so often that an explanation of it is redundant.*

Morales then defended Borda's proposed method along the lines that were already expressed in Llull but at much greater length:

> *In such an election, merit and justice are safeguarded by censorship of other electors in the case of a public election, and pangs of conscience if it is secret. Even if men's passions cause them to lean toward injustice, their pride will lead them to conceal it (Morales 1797).*

In spite of Morales' arguments, which run along a different line, Borda's rule is manipulable, in the sense to be used in this survey, which is standard in the contemporary literature. This had already been argued by Daunou (1803), who pointed at the possibility of voters abusing the method by ranking the most dangerous opponents to their favorite candidate as being the worst candidates.

The most important predecessor of modern social choice theory, M. J. A. N. de Caritat, Marquis de Condorcet, wrote on the matter from two different perspectives. One is associated with the point of view that we now use in developments related to the Condorcet Jury Theorem (Condorcet 1785). That is indeed the perspective that better explains the writings of his predecessors as well. In this perspective, it makes sense to speak about the "true" or "correct" social ordering,[3] to refer to malicious deviations from it, and to consider the possibility of costs for those who are discovered to act maliciously (either imposed socially or by their own conscience). In other writings, Condorcet did propose the use of specific rules, and adopted a point of view much closer to that underlying the Arrovian Tradition, where there is no room for such a thing as the "true" social order, as a separate entity from individual preferences. Condorcet was aware of the possibilities of manipulation arising from the simultaneous consideration of more than two alternatives, and that his insistence on the use of pairwise comparisons responds to this concern, at least in part. This, coupled with his awareness that these majority comparisons can lead to no conclusion, leads him to accept imperfect but operational methods. Take, for example, Condorcet (1792), where he actually accepts a second best, after arguing that a first best might not be attained, which brings us very close to what a modern social choice theorist could end up presenting as an impossibility theorem. In his ideal method, and once all candidates are nominated,

> *Each voter would then express his complete will, by making a comparative judgement between all the candidates taken two by two, and from the majority will on each comparison, we could deduce its general will. However, this method will often give an unsatisfactory result and will not always reveal which candidate the majority prefers, since there may sometimes be no such thing as a majority preference.... Now, since we cannot choose the only method which usually reveals the candidates considered most worthy by a majority... we have had to choose the simplest and most practical one, the one that is least susceptible to factions and intrigue. (Condorcet 1792, pp. 145–146 in McLean and Urken)*

I will take here a huge leap in time, since it took almost two hundred years after the first golden age of social choice theory[4] to have a general and precise statement confirming the extended suspicion that all rules are subject to some form of strategic manipulation. The sparse nineteenth-century authors that worked on electoral systems concentrated on other topics. Likewise, the emphasis of contemporary social choice theory, as initiated by Arrow (1951, second edition 1963) was not on the strategic aspects. Even then, all major authors in the 1950s, 1960s, and early 1970s were aware of the relevance of the issue, and elaborated on it to some extent.

Arrow devotes Section 2 of Chapter 1 in *Social Choice and Individual Values* to discuss some limitations of his analysis, and says that

[3] In the setup of the Condorcet Jury Theorem, there is not only a "true" ranking, but also all voters are assumed to share it as a common goal, while having different information and perceptions regarding what the common ranking is. Voting rules must then be viewed as estimators of the common good, given the voters' revealed information. Even in this version of Condorcet's setup there is room for strategic behavior, this time directed to enhance the common interest (Austen-Smith and Banks 1996, Coughland 2000, Feddersen and Pesendorfer 1998, and Rata 2002).

[4] This is how McLean and Urken (1995) qualify the times of Borda and Condorcet.

The aspects not discussed may be conveniently described as the game aspects.... Once a machinery for making social choices is established, individuals will find it profitable, from a rational point of view, to misrepresent their tastes by their actions, either because such misrepresentation is somehow directly profitable or, more usually, because some other individual will be made so much better off by the first individual's misrepresentation that he could compensate the first individual in such a way that both are better off than if everyone really acted in direct accordance with his tastes.... Even in a case where it is possible to construct a procedure showing how to aggregate individual tastes into a consistent social preference pattern, there still remains the problem of devising rules of the game so that individuals will actually express their true tastes even when they are acting rationally. (Arrow 1963, p. 7)[5]

Contemporary to Arrow's first writings were those of Black (1948a, 1948b, 1958c). He explicitly stated that under majority rule, no agent or group could clearly gain from preference misrepresentation when agent's preferences are single-peaked, but he also pointed out that some misrepresentations could lead to cycles, even if this restriction holds. This is because Black and most of the authors in the period were trying to reason about manipulability as a characteristic of binary decision processes, where the chosen outcome is not directly a function of the preference profile but arises as the maximal element of a social binary relation. Moreover, Black's statement assumes that agents, when called to vote in sequence, can reveal preferences that are not single-peaked.[6] As a result, Black's defense of the strategic properties of majority under single-peakedness is less optimistic than that of later writers. But his contribution is essential. As we shall see, single-peakedness and similar conditions have played an important role in defining domains that admit strategyproof rules.

Without yet proving any theorem, Vickrey (1960, p. 518) expressed a neat conjecture about the structure of rules that might be strategyproof. In a section devoted to "Strategic Misrepresentations of Preferences," he stated that

social welfare functions that satisfy the nonperversity and the independence postulates and are limited to rankings as arguments are ... mmune to strategy. It can be plausibly conjectured that the converse is also true, that is, that if a function is to be immune to strategy and be defined over a comprehensive range of admissible rankings, it must satisfy the independence criterion, although it is not quite so easy to provide a formal proof for this.

Luce and Raiffa's encyclopedic work *Games and Decisions* (1957 pp. 359–362) also touched at the issue of strategic voting (Section 14.8, pp. 359–362), though concentrated

[5] Even after excluding the subject explicitly, Arrow referred to it in the text, by discussing the possibility of strategic voting in elections based on pairwise sequential contests. He cites the following example: "Let individual 1 have ordering x, y, z; individual 2, y, x, z; and individual 3, z, y, x. Suppose that the motions come up in the order y, z, x. If all individuals voted according to their orderings, y would be chosen over z and then over x. However, individual 1 could vote for z the first time, insuring its victory; then, in the choice between z and x, x would win if individuals 2 and 3 voted according to their orderings, so that individual 1 would have a definite incentive to misrepresent" (Arrow 1951, pp. 80–81). The problem treated here is similar to, though not identical with, the majority game, and the complicated analysis needed to arrive at rational solutions there suggests strongly the difficulties of this more general problem of voting.

[6] This point was taken up later by Blin and Satterthwaite (1976).

only on the manipulation of decisions made by majority rule when alternatives are eliminated sequentially and majority is not transitive, as already discussed by Arrow. Their remarks point out that transitivity may also be necessary for nonmanipulability and are thus nicely complementary to those of Vickrey (1960).

The most elaborate analysis of strategic issues in voting at that early period was due to Farquharson (1969). Actually, this monograph was published longer after it was written, in the mid-1950s, and part of Farquharson's ideas were transmitted to the profession through his joint work with Dummett (Dummett and Farquharson 1962). Much of Farquharson's monograph is devoted to the analysis of game theoretic equilibria of voting games, using in particular the noncooperative notion of sophisticated equilibrium and a more cooperative notion of collective equilibrium. But before engaging in such analysis, he discusses the possibility of what are now called strategyproof rules, ones for which expressing truthful preferences is always a dominant strategy for all players. He uses the term "straightforward" to refer to such rules. I quote:

> *The only circumstance in which a voter can make his choice of strategy with absolute confidence are those in which he can be sure that, whatever contingency eventuates, his strategy will give at least as desirable an outcome as any other strategy would have done.... We adopt the term "straightforward" to describe a strategy which is thus unconditionally best.... If a procedure affords a voter a straightforward strategy, we may transfer the epithet and say that the procedure itself is straightforward for him. (Farquharson 1969, p. 30)*

Farquharson studied, in his Chapter 7, the conditions on individual preferences under which binary procedures, based on the sequential elimination of alternatives by pairwise comparison, may be straightforward. And he concluded that "if there are three or more outcomes, no binary procedure can be straightforward for all possibility scales" (p. 32). This is already a strong and rigorous statement, even if it only covers a particular class of procedures. In a more recent article, Dummett (2005) has described the circumstances of his cooperation with Farquharson and how close they had been on proving the result that was later attained by Gibbard (1973) and Satterthwaite (1975).

Murakami (1968, Chapter 4, Section 10) also discussed the issue of stability along similar lines as Dummett and Farquharson (1961). He took one step in the direction conjectured by Vickrey, showing that satisfying a monotonicity property is necessary and sufficient for a social decision function based on pairwise comparisons to be stable.

A fundamental text in the development of social choice theory was Sen's *Collective Choice and Social Welfare* (1970). There again, the author was perfectly aware of the issues, and in fact devoted a section (Section 11.3, p. 192 and on) to discuss the specific question of sincere preference revelation. Sen's discussion is in line with those authors, such as Vickrey (1960) and Murakami (1968), who discussed the importance of specific requirements on social choice procedures in order to control the extent of manipulation.

Sen was aware of the technical difficulty involved in finding conditions that eliminate all possibilities for manipulation. He pointed out that "non-negative response or even positive responsiveness is no guarantee against insincere voting being an efficient strategy" (p. 194), and provided an example involving manipulation by groups. But he also qualified the importance of the issue. While admitting that "honest voting" is often not in a person's best interest, he added that: "this is a perfectly general difficulty, but its relevance will vary greatly with the system of collective choice. As Murakami has argued, with those collective choice systems that are non-negatively responsive to individual preferences the scope of what voters can achieve by distorting their preferences is very limited."

Another important book from that period was Fishburn's *The Theory of Social Choice* (1973). It also discusses the issue of voting strategy, again in the specific context of sequential voting methods (pp. 97–99), but mostly concentrates on other topics.

By this time Allan Gibbard came up with a framework and a result that gave new strength to all preceding remarks on strategic voting, and started a much more systematic study of the issue. We turn now to this fundamental contribution.

3. STRATEGYPROOF SOCIAL CHOICE FUNCTIONS FOR UNRESTRICTED DOMAINS: THE GIBBARD–SATTERTHWAITE THEOREM

3.1. Statement

It was Gibbard (1973) who first published a precise theorem within a framework that allowed for a sharp and unambiguous statement that all nontrivial social decision functions are manipulable. The same result was proved independently by Satterthwaite (1973) in his doctoral dissertation, and has thus come to be known as the Gibbard–Satterthwaite Theorem.

Let us begin by a statement of this celebrated result.[7]

A will be a set of *alternatives* (finite or infinite). $I = \{1, 2, \ldots, n\}$ will be a finite set of *agents*. Agents in I will be assumed to have *preferences* on A. Preferences will be always complete, reflexive, transitive binary relations on A. We denote individual preferences by $\succcurlyeq$, $\succcurlyeq'$, $\succcurlyeq_i$, etc. The corresponding symbols $\succ$, $\succ'$, $\succ_i$ will stand for the strict part of the relation. $\mathcal{R}$ will stand for the set of all possible preferences on A. *Preference profiles* are n-tuples of preferences, one for each agent in $I = \{1, 2, \ldots, n\}$.

[7] Unfortunately, social choice theory has not developed a unified notation or a unified set of denominations for its basic constructs. Terms like voting schemes, social decision functions, social choice functions, and the like are often used to name the same construct, and each one may be used to denote a different one in some other article. I will not try to use the words of each of the authors, but try instead to be somewhat consistent within the survey.

A *social choice function* on the domain $D_1 \times \cdots \times D_n \subset \mathcal{R}^n$ is a function $f: D_1 \times \cdots \times D_n \to A$, where each D_i is considered to represent the set of preferences that are admissible for agent i.

What preferences are admissible, or interesting, or relevant, will change with the interpretation of A, the set of alternatives. Different economic situations will give rise to alternative setups, some of which will be considered along this paper.

We shall focus on social choice functions that are strategyproof, or nonmanipulable. A *social choice function* $f : D_1 \times \cdots \times D_n \to A$ *is manipulable* iff there exist some preference profile $(\succcurlyeq_1, \ldots, \succcurlyeq_n) \in D_1 \times \cdots \times D_n$, an agent i and some preference $\succcurlyeq_i \in D_i$, such that

$$f(\succcurlyeq_1, \ldots, \succcurlyeq_i', \ldots, \succcurlyeq_n) \succ_i f(\succcurlyeq_1, \ldots, \succcurlyeq_i, \ldots, \succcurlyeq_n)$$

The function f *is strategyproof* on $D_1 \times \cdots \times D_n$ iff it is not manipulable.

Different reasons for why this is an interesting property of social choice mechanisms will be discussed along the text. Let us first introduce a few comments here. As already noted by Gibbard, "to call a voting scheme manipulable is not to say that, given the actual circumstances, someone is really in a position to manipulate it. It is merely to say that, given some possible circumstances, someone could manipulate" (1973). From the point of view of voters, it may pay to learn about others under a manipulable social choice function but not under a strategyproof one. As for the consequences of manipulation, if they occur, there may be many, but the possible loss of efficiency is particularly worrisome from the point of view of the designer. Social choice functions that would always select an efficient outcome if voters provide truthful information may end up recommending an inefficient alternative after voters distort their preferences in order to manipulate.

Given a social choice function f, denote by r_f the *range* of f. Given a complete preference relation $\succcurlyeq$ on the set A of alternatives, and a subset B of A, let $C(\succcurlyeq, B) = \{b \in B \mid \text{for all } c \in B, b \succcurlyeq c\}$. The set $C(\succcurlyeq, B)$ denotes the $\succcurlyeq$-maximal elements in B, and is interpreted as the set of alternatives that an agent endowed with preferences $\succcurlyeq$ would consider best out of those in B.

A social choice function f is *dictatorial* iff there exists a fixed agent i such that, for all preference profiles in its domain,

$$f(\succcurlyeq_1, \ldots, \succcurlyeq_n) \in C(\succcurlyeq_i, r_f).$$

Hence, a dictatorial social choice function is trivial, in that it does not really aggregate preferences of agents, but simply chooses one of the best elements of one and the same agent (when it is unique, this fully describes the rule; otherwise complementary criteria to break ties are allowed, but this hardly allows us to consider the rule anything but trivial).

The following theorem establishes that all nontrivial social choice functions on the universal domain of preferences are manipulable. We informally bunch up, under the term "trivial," two types of rules: those that are dictatorial, and those that only choose between two alternatives. Indeed, for the simple case where society must decide between only two alternatives, the majority rule, or any reasonable variant of it, are strategyproof. But these rules break down dramatically when more than two choices are at stake, as expressed by the following.

Theorem 1 (Gibbard 1973, Satterthwaite 1975) *Any social choice function* $f : \mathcal{R}^n \rightarrow A$, *whose range contains more than two alternatives, is either dictatorial or manipulable.*

Notice that choosing by majority over two alternatives (with an appropriate tie-breaking rule) is a nondictatorial and nonmanipulable social choice function. Because of this and other similar examples, Theorem 1 must be explicit about the requirement that there are at least three alternatives in the range. Another essential assumption of this theorem is that the social choice function is defined on the universal set of preferences over A. Much of the work surveyed here consists of examining how this conclusion may change when the domain of preferences is restricted in different ways.

Let me briefly comment on the definition of manipulability and on the implications of the Gibbard–Satterthwaite Theorem. Since I elaborate on the topic at different points, these initial remarks are just introductory, with a warning about being too simplistic a reading of the result.

First of all, notice that the definition of manipulability assumes that one agent could gain from misrepresenting his preferences if (1) he knew for sure how others would vote, and (2) that their vote would not change as a result of the misrepresentation. Moreover, the definition predicates that such an opportunity for gain would arise at some profile. Therefore, there are many qualifications to make about the actual implications of manipulability. Certainly, the fact that a social choice function is manipulable does in no way imply that agents will engage extensively in changing their declared preferences. This is because they cannot always gain: either because they may not know whether they can at any given situation, either for ignorance about the other agent's preferences, actions, or strategies; and, as different authors have pointed out, also because the potential beneficiary of a manipulation may have difficulties in determining/computing the implications of his actions under complex rules. Yet, as soon as an agent understands that a social choice function is manipulable, he has an interest in knowing whether the conditions to take advantage from it do hold. It may be to his benefit to know about the other agent's preferences, intentions, or strategies, as well as about the intricacies of the rule. By contrast, a rational agent who was aware of operating under a strategyproof rule would know that there is no point in wasting resources in such quests, since the added knowledge would not yield any potential gain. Agents under strategyproof rules will derive no advantage from acting strategically, that is, from conditioning their behavior on that of others. By contrast, the possibility of manipulation is an invitation to attach value to all the considerations above, even in those cases where, in the final analysis, agents could decide not to misrepresent their preferences for one reason or other.

3.2. The Impact of the Gibbard–Satterthwaite Theorem

In fact, this statement, which is standard today, did not appear in this exact form in the initial work of either of the two authors after whom it is named. Gibbard's Theorem was presented as a corollary of a more general statement, regarding game forms. We shall elaborate further on that larger framework. Satterthwaite's original work used a different but equivalent notion of manipulability (Satterthwaite, 1975, footnote 5). A statement and proof of the result in the terms that became more widely known was due to Schmeidler and Sonnenschein (1976), who also used the term Gibbard–Satterthwaite Theorem for the first time.

Gibbard's proof was based on connecting the structure of strategyproof social choice functions and that of Arrovian social welfare functions. We shall elaborate on this connection later on, but point out here how ripe the situation was for the theorem to appear, after the different conjectures and results by authors like Vickrey (1960), Sen (1970) and Murakami (1968), along with the negative partial statements already proved by Farquharson (1969). Gibbard (1973, pp. 587–588) remarks that

> *The theorems in that paper should come as no surprise. ... Since many voting schemes in common use are known to be subject to manipulation, writers on the subject have conjectured, in effect, that all voting schemes are manipulable. ... A result such as the one given here, then, was to be expected. It does not, however, turn out to be easy to prove from known results.*

In fact, two important articles on the subject also appeared in 1973, both written independently from Gibbard's article and Satterthwaite's thesis. One is due to Pattanaik (1973), entitled "On the Stability of Sincere Voting Situations." This work, and subsequent articles on the subject, qualify Pattanaik's contributions to be among the most salient in the study of manipulation, as he essentially proved the impossibility of non-manipulable rules within the Arrovian framework. Yet, by concentrating on group decision rules, rather than the simplest framework of social choice functions, Pattanaik had to face different technical problems, including the need to break ties in case of social indifferences, which made his results harder to communicate to larger audiences. Another important paper was Zeckhauser's "Voting Systems, Honest Preferences, and Pareto Optimality" (1973). That paper considers a different framework than Gibbard and Satterthwaite's, by allowing lotteries as outcomes and letting individuals state their preferences over lotteries. We shall refer to it later, along with other results in this framework. What I want to stress here is that Zeckhauser's paper elaborates on the connections between voting and economic systems, and explicitly discusses the trade-off between strategyproofness and efficiency, two conditions that we shall see to be very hard to encompass with nontrivial decision rules.[8]

This insistence that the time was ripe for such a result is not to minimize the importance of the Gibbard–Satterthwaite Theorem. Rather, it is to wonder about how important it is for a good result to appear in the right form, at the right moment.

The moment was right not only because of the internal developments in social choice theory that I have outlined, but also because of the larger trends in economics. The popularization of the Gibbard–Satterthwaite Theorem coincided with other important discoveries in public economics: the Clarke–Groves mechanisms (Clarke 1971, Groves 1973, Groves and Loeb 1975); Green and Laffont (1979), which provided a sharp solution to the free rider problem as stated by Samuelson (1954); and Hurwicz's (1973, 1977) analysis of the incentives dimension within his general framework for the study of mechanism design. It also coincided with a renewal in the ability of game theory to provide sharp analytical tools to analyze the strategic behavior of agents. All of a sudden, the incentives for agents to behave according to the set rules of the economic and political game became a matter of priority in the research agendas of economists and political scientists. A clear picture of this state of affairs is provided by J. J. Laffont's introduction to his book *Aggregation and Revelation of Preferences* (1979).

The form of the Gibbard–Satterthwaite Theorem was also crucial for its instant popularity. It is a sharp statement, formulated within a simple but general framework, and refers to a single type of strategic behavior, leaving aside other complications. Previous authors had been getting close to state that all social decision rules were manipulable, and to connect the condition of strategyproofness with some of Arrow's conditions. But many of these statements were marred by the fact that authors had in mind a framework where social aggregation resulted in a social binary relation, which might in turn lead to social cycles (with ill-defined choices), or to social indifference (with more than one choice). The simpler framework used by Gibbard and Satterthwaite allowed a focus on essentials.[9]

Gibbard (1973, p. 592) had to express the difference with great force: "Neither voting schemes nor game forms allow ties. Both take single outcomes as values, and for a good reason. In questions of manipulability, the final outcome is what matters.... In this respect, a voting scheme differs from an Arrow 'constitution,' which it resembles in all other aspects."

By concentrating on social decision functions, that initial result gained in transparency and conveyed its message with maximal effectivity. Likewise, considering manipulability

[8] For further comments, see Section 6.5.3.

[9] In fact, this framework had already been proposed by Farquharson (1969), who then did not spend too much time on the issue of straightforwardness and moved to the analysis of more game-theoretical questions.

only, and leaving aside other important forms of strategic behavior, contributed to sharpening the results. And stating the theorem for functions defined on a universal domain was also essential to obtain its strong negative conclusion.

Much of the literature that followed can be seen as a sequence of qualifications regarding Gibbard and Satterthwaite's choice of framework. These results will sometimes show the robustness of the theorem, and sometimes show that it does not hold under certain alternative frameworks. But there is no doubt that this theorem marks the start of several important lines of research. I will point at several of these directions in the next section, and will concentrate mostly on those more closely related to social choice theory in the rest of the chapter.

Before anything else, we should look into the different proofs of that seminal result.

3.3. Proofs of the Theorem

Because the theorem is important, it has been the object of much attention, and many alternative proofs of it have been offered. We shall briefly outline several of them. To unify the discussion, we concentrate on the case where the set of alternatives is finite.

3.3.1. Proofs Based on the Connection with Arrovian Social Welfare Functions

The earliest proof is due to Gibbard (1973), and it relies heavily on Arrow's impossibility theorem (1951). The latter refers to social welfare functions: that is, to rules that assign a transitive preference relation to each preference profile. It states that a social welfare function over the universal domain satisfying the properties of Pareto (P) and Independence of Irrelevant Alternatives (IIA) must be dictatorial (when there are at least three alternatives).

Gibbard's proof referred to a wide framework, involving game forms. We concentrate here on its adaptation to social choice functions. In its simple form, the argument we provide, which captures Gibbard's essential insight, was popularized by Schmeidler and Sonnenschein (1974, 1978), and it runs as follows.

Start from a strategyproof social choice function f with at least three alternatives of its range. Construct (in a way to be described) an auxiliary rule, based on f, that assigns to each profile a binary relation on the alternatives in the range of f. Prove that, under the given construction, this binary relation is transitive (if f is strategyproof), and that the auxiliary rule w_f is thus a social welfare function. Show that, again due to f's strategyproofness, w_f must also satisfy the conditions of Pareto and IIA. Conclude (from Arrow's theorem) that w_f is dictatorial and (from the construction) that f must also be.

Different ways to define w_f from f can be used to make the above argument. Gibbard's (1973) is as follows: for any profile $(\succcurlyeq_1, \ldots, \succcurlyeq_n)$, and any two alternatives x and y in the range, construct a new profile $\left(\succcurlyeq_1^{xy}, \ldots, \succcurlyeq_n^{xy}\right)$, where each agent i places x and y on the top of his ranking, while keeping the relative order of x and y as in $\succcurlyeq_i$, and also respecting the relative orders of any pair not involving x and y; calculate the outcome $f\left(\succcurlyeq_1^{xy},\ldots,\succcurlyeq_n^{xy}\right)$; if f is strategyproof, we must get either x or y (this takes an easy proof); then, declare x socially preferred to y under profile $(\succcurlyeq_1,\ldots,\succcurlyeq_n)$ if x is the outcome of f for $\left(\succcurlyeq_1^{xy},\ldots,\succcurlyeq_n^{xy}\right)$, or y preferred to x if y comes out.

A similar proof is due to Gärdenfors (1977, also see 1976). Instead of using Arrow's theorem, he resorted to an analogous result of social choice functions for multiple agendas due to Hanson (1969).

Batteau, Blin, and Monjardet (1981) provided a proof that stresses the connection between strategyproof rules and Arrovian social welfare functions, by showing that the distribution of power underlying both types of rules must have the same structure. Specifically, the family of "preventing sets" underlying a strategyproof rule must be an ultrafilter, which is the structure of "decisive sets" in Arrovian functions.

3.3.2. Proofs by Inspection and Further Induction

A second interesting approach to prove the Gibbard–Satterthwaite Theorem is based on a close examination of strategyproof social choice rules for three alternatives and two persons with linear preferences, followed by an extension to weak orders and by a double induction on the number of agents and alternatives. Induction had already been used by Satterthwaite (1973) in his dissertation. Schmeidler and Sonnenschein (1978) provided a simple and elegant proof along these lines. Concentrating first on the 6×6 matrix corresponding to the combinations of strict preferences for the two agents, a number of short but subtle arguments lead to the conclusion that strategyproofness only allows for social outcomes that always coincide with the preferred alternative of one of the two agents. Then, a simple reasoning extends the conclusion to general preferences (admitting indifferences), and induction does the rest (Sen, 2001). This proof emphasizes that the two-person, three-alternative case contains all the essential elements of the theorem, in a nutshell. Another proof along similar lines, but limited to the two-person, three-alternative case, is provided by Feldman (1980).

The use of induction on the number of alternatives is limitative, as it does not allow extending the result to cases with an infinity of alternatives. On the other hand, the use of induction on the number of agents is quite suggestive of a fact that arises in many contexts: solving the problem of strategyproofness for two-individual societies is a long step toward solving it for any society with a finite number of agents.[10]

3.3.3. Proofs Based on the Necessity of Strong Monotonicity

Monotonicity properties can be predicated from social choice functions, social choice correspondences, social welfare functions, or other models of social choice. They all try to

[10] This is not the case, for example, for different forms of implementability, where the two-person case needs to be handled separately than that with more people.

reflect the idea that, if an alternative is chosen at some profile, then it must also be chosen at other profiles where that alternative has improved its position. Because the notion of "improving the position" is subject to different qualifications, there are several versions of monotonicity. A strong form of it turns out to be necessary for the strategyproofness of social choice function. Moreover, social choice functions whose range has more than two alternatives can only satisfy strong monotonicity if they are dictatorial. This is the line of argument developed by Muller and Satterthwaite (1977, 1985). See also Peleg (1984, p. 33) and Moulin (1988, Section 9.1).

3.3.4. Proofs That Emphasize the Role of Pivots

In two separate papers, Barberà (1980a, 1983a) provided new proofs of Arrow's and Gibbard and Satterthwaite's theorems, which focused on the role of pivotal voters in collective decision making. Essentially, an agent is a pivot at a preference profile if she can change the social outcome just by changing her preferences. The proofs consist, both for Arrow and for Gibbard-Satterthwaite, in first proving that only one agent can be pivotal at each preference profile (otherwise, a contradiction to Arrow's conditions would arise, or a manipulation would be possible). Then, it proceeds to show that the agent who is eventually pivotal at some profiles is always the same, and always pivotal: the dictator. By a very different type of reasoning than that of Satterthwaite (1975), these early papers also pointed at the strong connections between both theorems, in the context of unrestricted domains.[11]

3.3.5. Proofs That Build on the Structure of Strategyproof Rules and Option Sets

I would like to sketch a proof that was presented in Barberà and Peleg (1990), and has its roots in Barberà (1983a). While the preceding proofs only apply when the number of alternatives is finite, the proof I am about to present, although it is sketched here for the finite set of alternatives, two-voter case, can be adapted to cover the case with a continuum of alternatives.[12] It is also a good starting point for the analysis of strategyproof rules operating under restricted domains. Because of that, many of the results to be surveyed later are proven with techniques similar to those I will now present. As Sprumont (1995, pp. 98–99) pointed out, this "proof technique has been successfully applied to other domains of preferences over public alternatives.... Moreover, the bulk of the recent literature on strategyproofness in private commodity environments also follows (this) approach."As we shall see, the crucial notion in this approach is that of

[11] When domains are restricted, Arrow's conditions need not lead to the same conflicts as Gibbard–Satterthwaite's, and vice versa. See Barberà (1996).

[12] The reader will see that the version I provide for a finite set of alternatives involves the use of concepts, like that of the second best alternative, that would not be well defined for the continuum and need adaptation. For a careful analysis about the implications on the range and on the shape of option sets in the continuum case, see Le Breton and Weymark (1999).

an option set. The role of this concept had been noticed by Laffond (1980), and by Chichilnisky and Heal (1981).

To be concise, I will consider two-agent social choice functions and assume that agents have strict preferences. We denote the set of all strict preferences by $\mathcal{P}$ (here again, the extensions to general preferences and to n agents are quite straightforward). The argument runs as follows.

- Let $f : \mathcal{P} \times \mathcal{P} \rightarrow A$ be strategyproof
- Given f, define the notion of an option set. This will be key to our proof. The options left for 2, given a preference P_1 for agent 1, are defined by

$$o_2(P_1) = \{x \mid \exists P_2,\ \ f(P_1, P_2) = x\}.$$

Notice that this definition is relative to f. We should write $o_{2f}(P_1)$, but we omit the f for simplicity. These are the outcomes that 2 could obtain, by some declaration of preferences (truthful or not), should 1 declare preferences P_1.

The proof now proceeds along five elementary remarks.

- The first remark is that, *if f is strategyproof, then for all preference profiles* $f(P_1, P_2) = C(P_2, o_2(P_1))$. This is just a rewording of the strategyproofness condition, but it allows us to think of functions satisfying this property as generated by a two-stage process: agent 1, by declaring her preferences P_1, narrows down 2's options to $o_2(P_1)$; then, agent 2 chooses her best alternative out of the options left by 1. (Clearly, the argument is symmetric; the roles of 1 and 2 could be reversed all along.) Notice that, if agent 1 was a dictator, then $o_2(P_1)$ would be a singleton and coincide with $1'$s preferred alternative. On the other hand if 2 is a dictator $o_2(P_1) = r_f$ for any P_1, since 1's declaration is irrelevant to the function's outcome, and fixing it does in no way restrict the possible choice of 2.

Given this first remark, the proof of the Gibbard–Satterthwaite Theorem consists of showing that a strategyproof social choice function must generate option sets $o_2(P_1)$ that always select a singleton (1's best alternative) or always leave all of r_f for 2 to choose from. This is easily proven through a sequence of additional remarks, which shed light on the structure of strategyproof functions, and whose proofs are really simple. (The reader can try to prove them directly. If in need, turn to Barberà and Peleg 1990, Section 2.)

- The second remark is that, for any P_1, $o_2(P_1)$ must contain the best element of P_1 in r_f. That is, agent 1 should always leave room for 2 to choose, eventually, 1's favorite outcome.
- The third remark establishes that whenever $C(P_1, r_f) = C(P_1', r_f)$, then $o_2(P_1) = o_2(P_1')$. That is, only the "top" alternative for agent 1 in r_f can be relevant in determining the options that 1 leaves for 2.

- The fourth remark is that, whenever the range of f contains at least three alternatives, then $o_2(P_1)$ must either be, for each P_1, equal to r_f or to $C(P_1, r_f)$.
- The fifth and last remark concludes the proof by showing that, in fact, only one of the two possibilities above can hold. Either $o_2(P_1)$ is always equal to r_f, or it is always equal to $C(P_1, r_f)$. Hence, f must be dictatorial if it is strategyproof, has at least three alternatives in its range (this plays a role in proving the fourth remark), and is defined on a universal domain (this is used to prove the last three remarks).

To end this section, let me insist that strategyproofness has implications on the structure of option sets. In the case where preferences are defined on a continuum, it also has implications on the structure of the range. On that, see Le Breton and Weymark (1999).

3.3.6. The Gibbard–Satterthwaite Theorem as a Corollary

In spite of its generality, the Gibbard–Satterthwaite Theorem does appear as a corollary of even more general results, in different frameworks.

We shall see later that one can embed any finite set of alternatives into a multi-dimensional Euclidean space. General results describing the structure of strategyproof rules under different range structures and preference domains induce the Gibbard–Satterthwaite Theorem as a special case (Barberà, Massó, and Neme 1997, Barberà, Massó, and Serizawa 1998, Nehring and Puppe 2002).

An important model in mechanism design is the one where compensations via money transfers are allowed. This framework, which was introduced in the research on strategyproof allocation initiated by Clarke (1971) and Groves (1973), also provides a way toward the Gibbard–Satterthwaite Theorem. This is based on the remark that no nonimposed decisive rule be implemented in dominant strategies without the use of transfers, which at some point violate the global feasibility constraints. This argument was made in an early and important paper of Roberts (1979), which is a starting point for many recent developments in the literature on rules involving compensation.

One of the intriguing aspects in the Gibbard–Satterthwaite result is that, even before it was formally proven, some authors did establish its close connection with Arrow's impossibility theorem (Vickrey 1960). Satterthwaite (1975) and Kalai and Muller (1977) went a long way in establishing this connection (I elaborate further on this point in Section 10.1.)

Recently, different authors (Geanakoplos 2005, Reny 2001), insisted on the strong parallels between some of the proofs of these two results. Two papers by Eliaz (2004) and Barberà (2001b) have provided results that surpass this approach, by proving both results to be specific instances of larger, more abstract theorems on preference aggregation.

4. GAME FORMS AND THE QUESTION OF IMPLEMENTATION

4.1. Strategyproofness in a Larger Picture

As I already pointed out, Gibbard's (1973) statement and proof of his results about manipulation do not only refer to social choice functions (which he called voting schemes), but to a more general framework. As he writes:

> *A voting scheme is a special case of what I will call a game form. A game form ... is a system which allows each individual his choice among a set of strategies, and makes an outcome depend, on a determinate way, on the strategy each individual chooses. A "strategy" here is the same as a pure strategy in game theory, and indeed a game form is a game with no individual utilities yet attached to the possible outcomes. Formally, then, a game form is a function g with a domain of the following sort. To each player 1 to n is assigned a nonempty set, $S_1, \ldots, S_n$ respectively of strategies. It does not matter, for purposes of the definition, what a strategy is. The domain of the function g consists of all n-tuples $<s_1, \ldots, s_n>$, where $s_1 \in S_1, s_2 \in S_2, \ldots, s_n \in S_n$. The values of the function g are called outcomes. A voting scheme, it follows, is a game form such that, for each player, his set of strategies is the set of all orderings of a set Z of available alternatives, where Z includes the set X of outcomes. ... For game forms alone ... there is no such thing as manipulation. To manipulate a system, a voter must misrepresent his preferences. To talk about manipulation, then, we must specify not only a game form, but for each voter and preference ordering P we must specify the strategy which "honestly represents" P. Manipulability, then, is a property of a game form $g(s_1, \ldots, s_n)$ plus n functions $\sigma_1, \ldots, \sigma_n$ where for each individual k and preference ordering P, $\sigma k(P)$ is the strategy for k which honestly represents P. ... What we can show is this: however we characterize honest voting in a system, the system, as characterized, will be manipulable. ... Here is the result. ... A strategy s^* is dominant for player k and preference ordering P of the set of outcomes if, for each fixed assignment of strategies to players other than k, strategy s^* for k produces an outcome at least as high in preference ordering P of the set of outcomes if, for each fixed assignment of strategies to players other than k, strategy s^* for k produces an outcome at least as high in preference ordering P as does any other strategy open to k. ... A game form is straightforward if for every player k and preference ordering P of the outcomes, some strategy is dominant for k and P. The theorem on game forms says that no non-trivial game form is straightforward. (Gibbard, pp. 588–591)*

I quoted extensively from Gibbard to show that, indeed, his formulation was very broad and opened the way to consider, with very small changes of framework, general issues of incentive compatibility and implementation. For comparison and perspective, I will provide a framework for implementation theory, as described by Moore (1992)[13] in a brilliant survey, written some twenty years later:

> *Consider an environment with a finite set $\{1, \ldots, i, \ldots, I\}$ of* agents, *and a set A of feasible* outcomes, *with typical element a.*
>
> *The profile of the agents' preferences over outcomes is indexed by the* state *θ, agent i has preference ordering $R_i(\theta)$ on the set A. Let $P_i(\theta)$ and $I_i(\theta)$ respectively denote the strict preference relation and the indifference relation corresponding to $R_i(\theta)$.*

[13] I excerpt liberally from Moore's exposition (pp. 214–217), which has become the standard.

Each of the agents is assumed to observe the state θ, so there is complete information *among the agents about their preferences over A.*

The above formulation allows for any degree of correlation across the agents' preferences. Θ may, for example, comprise all possible vectors of preference orderings over A: the universal domain. *Or there may be perfect correlation, in which case knowing one agent's preference ordering over A would be enough to deduce all the other agents'. We shall say that preferences in Θ have* independent domains *if agent i's set of possible preference orderings over A is fixed—independent of how the other agents $j \neq i$ happen to rank A.*

A choice rule is a correspondence $f : \Theta \twoheadrightarrow A$ that specifies a nonempty choice set $f(\theta) \subseteq A$ for each state θ.

The implementation problem is as follows: does there exist a mechanism, *or game form, g such that in any state θ, the set of equilibrium outcomes of g coincides with $f(\theta)$? If so, then g (fully)* implements *f. This is a general notion of implementation, in that we have left open the choice of equilibrium concept.*

A natural place to start is with a revelation mechanism, *g^*, in which each agent i's strategy set comprises his set of possible preference orderings, $\{R_i(\theta) \mid \theta \in \Theta\}$: that is, each agent simply announces what are his preferences over A. (Arguably, revelation mechanisms make most sense if preferences in Θ have independent domains, because then any vector of preferences reported by the agents could in principle be the truth.) If, in each state θ truth-telling is an equilibrium, whose outcome is in $f(\theta)$, then g^* truthfully implements f. Notice that this is weaker than (full) implementation, because there may be other, untruthful equilibria in state θ whose outcomes are not in $f(\theta)$.*

The most appealing notion of implementation is the one that makes the weakest assumptions about the agents' behavior: implementation in dominant strategy *equilibrium.*

To discover what can be implemented in dominant strategy equilibrium (and other equilibrium concepts), a useful ground-clearing result comes from the Revelation Principle. *This provides a set of necessary conditions—in effect, incentive constraints—which a choice rule must satisfy if it is to be (fully) implementable. In particular, consider the case where preferences in Θ have independent domains, and where the choice rule f is* single-valued *(i.e., where $f(\theta)$ is a single outcome for all θ). Then if f is (fully) implementable in dominant strategy equilibrium, it must also be truthfully implementable in dominant strategy equilibrium. To see why, replace the non-revelation mechanism g which (fully) implements f in dominant strategies by a revelation mechanism g^* which mimics it. That is, if, in state θ, the I agents choose the vector of (dominant) strategies $(s_1(\theta))$, say, in g, then announcing the truth in g^* leads to the same outcome: $g^*[R_1(\theta), \ldots, R_I(\theta)] \equiv g[s_1(\theta), \ldots, s_I(\theta)]$. Clearly, for each agent i, announcing the truth $R_i(\theta)$ in g^* must be a dominant strategy, because $s_i(\theta)$ is a dominant strategy in g—hence g^* truthfully implements f in dominant strategy equilibrium, as required. However, in moving from g to g^*, we may admit new, unwanted, untruthful dominant strategy equilibria: g^* need not (fully) implement f.*

Nevertheless, one senses that for a rich enough choice rule and associated mechanism g^*, there is unlikely to be a multiplicity of dominant strategy equilibria. In particular, there will only be a gap between (full) implementation and truthful implementation in dominant strategy equilibrium if there are indifferences in the agents' preference orderings. If Θ only contains *strict preference orderings, then dominant strategies are essentially unique: it can easily be shown that a choice rule f is (fully) implementable in dominant strategy equilibrium if and only if it is single-valued and truthfully implementable in dominant strategies. Laffont and Maskin (1982, pp. 42–43) present other conditions guaranteeing that if truth-telling is a dominant strategy equilibrium of the revelation mechanism g^*, then it is the only one.*

Unfortunately, for dominant strategy implementation, the necessary conditions (the incentive constraints) provided by the Revelation Principle are very demanding. For a single-valued choice rule f to be truthfully implementable in dominant strategy equilibrium, it must be strategyproof*: for any agent i, if $\theta,\phi \in \Theta$ are such that $R_j(\theta) = R_j(\phi)$ for all $j \neq i$, then $f(\theta) R_i(\theta) f(\phi)$ and, symmetrically, $f(\phi) R_i(\phi) f(\theta)$.*

This follows straight from the definition: if f is truthfully implementable, then in state θ agent i cannot gain from misreporting his preferences as $R_i(\phi)$, thereby changing the outcome from $f(\theta)$ to $f(\phi)$. Moreover, it is clear that, if preferences in Θ have independent domain, then strategyproofness is also sufficient for f to be truthfully implementable in dominant strategy equilibrium: simply use the revelation mechanism $g^*[R_1(\theta),\ldots,R_I(\theta)] \equiv f(\theta)$.

Under this general framework, the Gibbard–Satterthwaite Theorem takes the following form:

Theorem 2 (Gibbard 1973, Satterthwaite 1975) *Suppose Θ includes all possible strict preference orderings over A. Then no single-valued choice rule f, whose range contains at least three distinct outcomes, can be truthfully implemented in dominant strategy equilibrium unless it is dictatorial.*[14]

It should be apparent from this formulation that the question of strategyproofness is a limited one. The question of implementation can be asked with reference to many other equilibrium concepts, and that is what implementation theory has done, while also allowing for multivalued choice functions and restricted domains. There exist many expository articles and a vast literature on the issue. Three good references are Moore (1992), Jackson (2001), and Maskin and Sjostrom (2002).

4.2. Strengthenings, Weakenings, and Related Definitions

Although I will not review results in implementation theory that are the outcome of substituting the requirement of dominant strategies for other standard game theoretic equilibrium concepts, I need to mention some variants of the notion of manipulation, and some definitions close to that of manipulation that have appeared in the literature, in close connection to the basic ideas we analyze here.

As we have already seen, Farquharson (1969), and Dummett and Farquharson (1961) did analyze the concept of stability. A modified version of stability was used by Murakami (1968), and criticized by Sen (1970) and by Pattanaik (1973, 1974). The latter author provided a new definition, which applies to group decision rules, resulting in a social preference relation for every preference profile, and allowing for the (weak) social preference to select more than one alternative. Besides the fact that stability is defined for a different class of objects than social choice functions, its main difference with strategyproofness is that it contemplates the possibility of joint deviations by groups of agents. Similar possibilities of cooperative manipulation can be defined for social choice functions, and rules avoiding them are termed "group strategyproof."

[14] This is the end of my extensive quote from Moore.

In those contexts where only trivial strategyproof social choice functions exist, there is little point insisting on stronger requirements. However, there are contexts where the strategyproofness of attractive rules can be attained, and then group strategyproofness becomes an additional standard.

Let us provide some formal definitions, in the vein of those we used when presenting the notion of (individual) strategyproofness.

A social choice function $f : D_1 \times \cdots \times D_n \to A$ is *group manipulable* iff there exist some preference profile $(\succcurlyeq_1, \ldots, \succcurlyeq_n) \in D_1 \times \cdots \times D_n$, a group of agents $S \subset I$ and preferences $\succcurlyeq_i' \in D_i$ for all agents $i \in S$, such that

$$f\left(\succcurlyeq_{I\setminus S}, \succcurlyeq_S'\right) \succ_i f\left(\succcurlyeq_1, \ldots, \succcurlyeq_i, \ldots, \succcurlyeq_n\right)$$

for all $i \in S$.[15]

The function f is *group strategyproof* iff it is not group manipulable.

Clearly, this definition allows for many qualifications. A social choice function may be strategyproof but manipulable by groups, and in this case the size of the groups can be relevant. Intuitively, rules that are manipulable by large groups only can be seen as more robust than others that can be manipulated by small groups. The extreme case where two agents alone could manipulate rules that are (individually) strategyproof occurs in several instances (Barberà 1979a, Barberà, Sonnenschein, and Zhou 1991). Serizawa (2006) has studied the issue specifically, and has explored the consequences of imposing the requirement of pairwise strategyproofness, which explicitly avoids this extreme form of group manipulability. The requirement of group strategyproofness, even if very strong, turns out to be compatible with other interesting properties in different domains, motivated by a variety of economic interpretations. Although we shall mention them later, let us announce some here: house allocation (Ehlers 2002, Takamiya 2001), allocation of other indivisible goods (Ehlers and Klaus 2003a, 2003b), excludable public goods (Olszewski 2004), and matching models (Martínez *et al.* 2004). A similar requirement is that of bribe-proofness, introduced by Schummer (2000), where again two agents can manipulate through mutually beneficial strategies. This same author, as well as Shenker (1993), discussed different variants that represent additional demands above that of strategyproofness.

Another interesting fact, that was first remarked by Blair and Muller (1983), is that in different domains the (nontrivial) satisfaction of individual strategyproofness precipitates that of group strategyproofness as well. This is the case, for example, when preferences are single-peaked (see Moulin's 1980a, 1980b characterization in Section 5), or single-dipped (Peremans and Storcken 1999), among other cases. I have already mentioned that

[15] We use the notation $f\left(\succcurlyeq_{I\setminus S}, \succcurlyeq_S'\right)$ to denote the profile where all agents in $I\setminus S$ retain the preferences in the original profile $(\succcurlyeq_1, \ldots, \succcurlyeq_n)$ and those in S change preferences to those $\succcurlyeq_i'$ specified in the definition.

this connection does not always hold. Le Breton and Zaporozhets (2009), and Barberà, Berga, and Moreno (2009) establish conditions on the domains that actually do guarantee that rules satisfying the weaker (individual) version about them will also meet the stronger (group) requirement.

Pattanaik (1976a, 1976b) also considered interesting weakenings of the notion of strategyproofness, both in the Arrovian context of group decision rules and in that of social choice functions. These weakenings were based on the possibility that some threats of manipulation (either by a single voter or by a coalition) might be diffused by the existence of counterthreats. Then, one might only be concerned with (relevant) threats that are not met by (adequate) counterthreats.[16] This idea is very natural and has its roots in cooperative game theory, where it is incorporated into different solution concepts, like that of the bargaining set (be it the version of Maschler, Mas-Colell, or Zhou). Unfortunately, Pattanaik's results did prove that weakenings of stability or strategyproofness along these lines do not significantly improve upon the negative result of the Gibbard–Satterthwaite Theorem, for most cases (see also Barberà 1980b). Maximin behavior of agents has also been analyzed, in different versions, within the context of strategic behavior. See, for example, Moulin (1981a, 1981b). Thomson (1979), and Barberà and Dutta (1982).

The general theory of implementation is interested in achieving desirable outcomes (as expressed by a given social choice function, or by a correspondence), through the agent's interplay within a mechanism (or game form). A more specific formulation would not allow for any game form to implement a given function, but rather examine the equilibria of the game that is implicitly defined by some given voting rule, and see whether, in spite of violating strategyproofness, the rule may be expected to give rise to interesting outcomes. This led several authors to analyze different issues regarding the equilibria associated to certain types of voting methods. Following Farquharson (1969), Moulin (1980b, 1981b, 1983) developed an elaborate theory of sophisticated voting, showing that some families of voting rules based on sequential voting would lead to attractive outcomes. Dutta and Pattanaik (1978; see also Dutta 1980a), developed an idea of consistency, which was later followed up by Moulin and Peleg (1982; see also Peleg 2002). A good overview of these developments from a game theoretic angle is found in Moulin (1994a).

4.3. Other Forms of Strategic Behavior in Voting

The notion of manipulation is quite general. Under appropriate interpretations, it formalizes many form of strategic behavior that will not literally consist of misrepresenting preferences. Yet voting methods are subject to other possible types of strategic behavior,

[16] Notice that this vague expression leaves room for many different definitions in a similar spirit, depending on what threats are defined to be relevant, and what counterthreats are considered adequate to difuse them.

which exceed the limited framework within which the notion of strategyproofness is formulated. We should just mention some of these aspects, as a sample. Blin and Satterthwaite (1977) pointed out the possibility of an agent manipulating a voting procedure by inducing false beliefs in other agents about his/her true preferences. Dutta, Jackson, and Le Breton (2001, 2002) have analyzed the influence of strategic candidacy over the outcomes of single-valued voting procedures. Their work has been extended by Carmelo Rodríguez-Álvarez (2004, 2006) to the case of correspondences and probabilistic rules.

One important strategic question arises in connection with the choice of rules that society will use. Different authors have studied the possibility of guaranteeing the stability in the choice of rules. Koray (2000) proved its impossibility under a very demanding definition. His proof builds on the notion of strategyproofness in an interesting way. Barberà and Jackson (2006), Messner and Polborn (2004), and others have also investigated the issue for restricted situations and a less demanding definition of stability.

Berga *et al.* (2006) have studied the strategies of entry and exit to and from a voting body whose decisions affect the voters' satisfaction. Cantalá (2004) considers the case of voluntary consumption of public strategic goods, which also induces additional strategic considerations. This is an incomplete list of issues that I mention because they are close to the standard social choice literature, but there are many others, and with a long tradition. Luce and Raiffa's (1957) wonderful book *Games and Decisions* already listed a number.

Other subjects are so important in political economy and political science, that I will just mention them without references: a very important issue in practical terms is that of agenda manipulation; another is logrolling; and a third is participation and abstention. A fourth is the issue of candidacy: who participates in an election is an extremely relevant strategic decision. The issue of platforms is also important, and whether agents want to look like others, or rather differentiate. Unfortunately, these issues exceed the present essay.

4.4. The Analysis of Specific Social Choice Rules

Since no voting rule is strategyproof in the universal domain, authors interested in the strategic performance of specific voting rules must look into their somewhat more limited properties. Their analysis often suggests properties that may be specific to the rule in question, or sometimes extend to others. Brams and Fishburn (2002) contains a complete account of voting procedures analyzed from different points of view. As an example, consider the study of approval voting, a method proposed by Brams and Fishburn (1978). Approval voting is part of a more general class of procedures, called nonranked voting systems. Fishburn (1978) did also study issues of preference revelation in that context. While obviously not strategyproof in large enough domains, the method satisfies some weaker properties of interest (Brams and Fishburn 1993). Moreover, under appropriate domain restrictions, it can not only attain strategyproofness but in fact be the only symmetric neutral and efficient rules to do so (Vorsatz 2007). Another example is given by plurality rule. Early work by Pazner and Wesley (1977, 1978) emphasized that this and other rules, which are obviously manipulable, become less so when the number of voters grows large. Notions of "asymptotic" strategyproofness, or others related to the size of society, have emerged in other contexts (see Section 9.2). More recent work by Slinko (2002) addresses the asymptotic manipulability of other rules. Another approach to evaluate rules that fail to satisfy strategyproofness consists of defining some degree of approximate satisfaction of the property. An example is provided by Schummer's (2004) notion of Almost-Dominant strategy implementation. Another example is given by the notion of threshold strategyproofness, which bounds the gains from manipulation (Ehlers, Peters, and Storcken 2004). Other authors are more interested in comparing different rules among themselves, rather than highlighting any specific one. Then, again, it is useful for them to have a standard different than manipulability, for which all nontrivial rules would fail to meet. One of the concepts that have been used is that of susceptibility to manipulation. In fact, the idea that one can measure the degree of manipulability of different rules was developed by Kelly (1993) and further studied by Aleskerov and Kurbanov (1999). These works concentrate on the relative size of the subdomains where the rules do satisfy the exact version of strategyproofness. Another way to measure departures is in Campbell and Kelly (2002a, 2003b). These authors have also analyzed the gains to manipulators and the losses that these can impose on others by manipulating different types of rules (Campbell and Kelly 2009, and forthcoming). One can also investigate the minimal size of profiles where manipulation possibilities will arise: Maus, Peters, and Storcken (2007) have established lower bounds on this size.

Work by Campbell and Kelly (2003a, 2006) and Merrill (2007) has also explored the limits of the intuition that choosing Condorcet winners would be an individual or even group strategyproof rule if it was always well defined. Saari (1990, 2000) has argued that the Borda count is the one member of the general class of scoring rules that has the best relative performance in terms of incentives. The Borda count can be strategyproof for adequately restricted domains, as shown in Vorsatz (2007) and more generally in Puppe and Tasnádi (2008) and Barbie, Puppe, and Tasnádi (2006). Another measure related to manipulation is the degree of complexity required in order to compute a manipulative misrepresentation, which varies from rule to rule. Bartholdi *et al.* (1989) initiated a literature that has now, years later, become extremely popular among computer scientists. I will not attempt to survey this recent and important literature here.

5. THE SEARCH FOR STRATEGYPROOFNESS: AN OUTLINE

In spite of the limited scope of the issue as compared with the broader question of implementation, this survey concentrates on strategyproofness. We shall see that there is much to say on the subject, beyond the most abstract results, when one concentrates on specific concepts, models, and interpretations.

It is important to ask under what circumstances it would be possible to design nontrivial strategyproof decision rules, because strategyproofness, when attainable, is an extremely robust and attractive property.

The clear-cut conclusion of the Gibbard–Satterthwaite Theorem is obtained at some costs. One of them is the assumption of universal domain, according to which all possible preferences over alternatives are admissible for all agents. The other is to assume that there are more than two alternatives to choose from, and that at least three of them will eventually be chosen for some admissible state of opinion.

In many cases, the nature of the social decision problem induces a specific structure on the set of alternatives, and this structure suggests, in turn, some restrictions on the set of admissible individual preferences. It is then natural to investigate how much does the negative conclusion of the Gibbard–Satterthwaite Theorem change, when social choice functions are only required to operate on restricted domains of preferences.

Much of the research on strategyproofness can be seen as an investigation on the structure of alternatives, the existence of domain restrictions on such alternatives which allow for nontrivial strategyproof social choice functions, and the characterization of such functions, when possible. There are many domain restrictions that had been studied for purposes other than the analysis of strategyproofness, especially in the context of public decision making, and that also turn out to be interesting for our purpose. For example, domains where preferences are single-peaked, single-plateau, single-dipped, single-crossing, or others where individual preferences are expected to exhibit indifferences between certain alternatives. Let me mention some other types of natural restrictions: that of representability in terms of von Neumann–Morgenstern utility functions become natural when alternatives are lotteries; or strict convexity that may be appropriate as a preference restriction when dealing with exchange economies, and so on. In these and many other cases the restriction of preferences to such classical domains, or to others arising from different models and their interpretations may allow for the existence of nontrivial strategyproof social choice functions.

Much of what we have learned about strategyproofness responds to the following pattern.

First, consider some wide class of social decision problems, and formulate a model that formalizes them. We survey work that addresses, among others, the following issues: how to choose the levels of provision of one or several public goods, elect candidates or locations characterized by a variety of characteristics, ration the usage of different production factors, match students to colleges, or allocate private goods through markets.

Second, discuss under what domain restrictions, defined within each specific model, would it be possible to design nontrivial strategyproof social decision rules. Notice that there are several levels at which such a discussion may be set and resolved. Impossibility results may be attained, even in specific contexts, if meaningful and stringent enough domain restrictions cannot be found. Partial possibility results may be attained, describing rules that are strategyproof for specific domains. But the ideal result would be one that jointly characterizes domains that admit strategyproof rules, and the family of rules that have this property for such domains. When such knowledge can be attained, it is very informative, and it allows for further inquiries. Take, for example, the question of efficiency. If we know that strategyproof rules exist under some restrictions, and how they look, then one may ask whether some of these rules can guarantee efficiency. Even if none can achieve it, one can study how far from efficiency they are, and thus measure the efficiency costs of strategyproofness under specific circumstances. Eventually, such costs should be compared with those arising from incorrect preference revelation under alternative rules not satisfying strategyproofness.

In addition to strategyproofness, there are several other requirements of interest that one may impose on social choice rules. One is coverage: rules are interesting only to the extent that they operate on rich enough preference domains. Another is nondictatorship: although within the scope of conceivable mechanisms, dictatorial procedures are formally trivial and normatively unattractive. A third requirement is efficiency, which I have already mentioned. It is worth referring to two related conditions that may help understand why strategyproof rules may fail to be efficient. One is the extent of their range. Social choice functions may or may not have the whole set of alternatives as their images. Some functions may become strategyproof at the expense of never choosing some a priori feasible alternatives, regardless of individual preferences. An extreme case is that of functions whose range has two alternatives only, but for restricted domains there may be others. Hence, the flexibility of a social choice function, as measured by the extension of its range, will be an important property to check.[17]

Feasibility of the social choices is another concern. Some rules may be focused on partial decisions, and one should then worry about the compatibility between these decisions and the overall resources held by society. For example, the traditional problem of choosing an optimal level for a public decision, along with some transfers of a private good, as studied by Clarke (1971), Groves (1973), and so many other authors, does not a priori require that such transfers should balance. In this survey I will briefly comment on this important line of work, but I will mostly concentrate on studying rules that always guarantee that the recommended outcome is feasible.

[17] For example, when the domain of preferences contains all those that are single-dipped relative to a given order, the range of strategyproof rules can only consist of two alternatives, regardless of the number of those on which agents can express their preferences. Other bounds apply for any subdomain of single-dipped preferences (see Peremans and Storcken 1999, Barberà, Berga, and Moreno 2009, Manjunath 2009). This is in sharp contrast with the case where the range consists of single-peaked preferences, where the functions can be on the set of alternatives under very mild assumptions on the domains.

In what follows, I will describe different groups of articles. All of them deal, in some way, with the trade-offs between strategyproofness, domain extension, nondictatorship, efficiency, range dimensionality, or other similar properties of social choice rules. In order to classify them, I adopt a double criterion.

On the one hand, I distinguish between the case of "common preferences," and that of "personalized preferences." In some social choice situations, it is natural to assume that if a ranking of alternatives is admissible for one agent, then it is also admissible for all others. This is the case, for example, when voters have to rank a number of candidates for office, or if they all have to indicate their desired level for a single variable (the amount of a public good, say). I classify problems where all agents are entitled to have the same preferences into the "common preferences" case. In other cases, the nature of the alternatives and of agent's preferences are such that what is admissible for an agent is not for others. For example, alternatives may be feasible allocations of private goods, and under the assumption of selfishness each of the agents will contemplate these allocations from their own perspective. What is an admissible preference on the alternatives for one agent is not admissible for others. But the same happens when alternatives consist of allocations involving some public and some private goods. Even the classical model where decisions consist in determining one level for a public good and a transfer of a private good for each agent belong to this second class, because each agent evaluates transfers to herself differently than transfers to others. I call these the "personalized preferences" cases.[18]

Probably the most important limitation of this survey is that it does not include a systematic treatment of the very important family of models where the objects of choice are combinations of allocation decisions involving the allocation of goods and of money transfers, and where typically (though not always) the preferences of agents are quasi-linear in money. I had to establish some bounds for this survey on social choice, and I decided to concentrate on models where money transfers among agents do not play a fundamental, explicit role (although the definition of alternatives may include them implicitly). There will still be some mention of them in specific contexts where the boundaries are hard to establish, as in the analysis of assignment and cost-sharing models (see Sections 9.3 and 9.4). But I exclude very important and extensive work on public goods allocation, in the line of Vickrey (1960), Groves (1973), Groves and Loeb (1975), Green and Laffont (1979), or Roberts (1979), and also ignore the very relevant subject of auctions, where economists, and more recently computer scientists as well, have examined a host of questions related to incentives in general and to strategyproofness in particular.

[18] These cases are often referred to as the public good case and the private good case, but it should be clear from my discussion that I consider this a misnomer.

The second criterion I use to organize the rest of the survey has to do with formal models and with the leading interpretation that each model is given.

I will start Section 6 with an exhaustive description of models involving sets of alternatives defined by a finite combination of attributes, on which agents hold strict preferences satisfying some form of generalized single-peakedness. These models can be viewed as formalization situations where alternatives can be described in terms of a finite set of characteristics, measured in units on which individual preferences are not necessarily monotonic. Although these models were mostly developed in the 1990s, and were preceded by many other studies on strategyproofness, their sequence will provide me with a good example of how a family of questions relating to strategyproofness can be thoroughly analyzed. These models cover the case where agents must choose among public projects, or establish the level of one or several public goods, but no money transfers are envisaged.

Sections 7 and 8 turn to models where the outcomes of the social choice process adopt special structures. In Section 7, I consider rules whose outcomes are lotteries. In Section 8, I consider outcomes to be sets of alternatives. This formulation takes us away from the realm of social choice functions to that of social choice correspondences, and will requires a detour regarding the framework and the interpretation of these models, as well as the definition of strategyproofness within them.

Then, in Section 9, I will describe different models where preferences are definitely personalized and that arise in economic contexts: division problems, exchange, matching, and cost-sharing. These are examples of setups where the question of strategyproofness gives rise to interesting analysis and conclusions.

In Section 10, I turn to more abstract domain restrictions, which were explored quite soon after the Gibbard–Satterthwaite Theorem was formulated, in order to tie the new result with the traditional Arrovian framework in which many of the developments of social choice theory had taken place. Some of these restrictions applied to the common preference case, while others examined similar questions for personalized preferences. I also refer to the technical but important question of maximality.

6. COMMON DOMAINS: STRATEGYPROOF RULES FOR THE CHOICE OF MULTI-ATTRIBUTE ALTERNATIVES

In this section I will thoroughly review the progress in understanding the domain restrictions allowing for nontrivial strategyproof rules, and the type of rules that preserve this property in such domains, for a specific class of models. The models arise naturally as one considers the problem of deciding among the possible levels for k public goods, the location of facilities on the nodes of a grid, the choice of candidates who can be described by their performance regarding k different criteria. As we shall see, a natural twist in the model does allow one to see it as a canonical way to formalize any collective decision-making problem involving a finite set of alternatives. Because of this, and since many of the ideas and techniques that have been developed in analyzing the issue of strategyproofness within this model are also extensible to other cases, I will describe the results in this section at length.

6.1. Two Alternatives

Although rather special, the case of choice between two alternatives 0 and 1 *is* important and well studied.[19] Strategyproof rules can be described as choosing 1 unless there is enough support for the opposite, in which case 0 will be selected. What do we mean by "enough support"? We could establish the list of coalitions that will get 0 if all their members prefer it to 1; and it is natural to require that, if a coalition can enforce 0, then its supersets are also able to. Such a family of "winning" coalitions will fully describe the rule; it corresponds to what is called a *monotonic simple game.*[20,21]

6.2. Linearly Ordered Sets of Alternatives

We now consider situations where a finite set of alternatives can be linearly ordered, according to some criterion (from "left" to "right" in political applications, from smaller to greater according to some quantitative index, etc.). In this context, it makes sense to say that one alternative x is between two others, z and w, say. And it is sometimes natural to assume that the preference of agents over alternatives is single-peaked, meaning that (1) each agent has a single preferred alternative $\mathcal{T}(\succcurlyeq_i)$, and (2) if alternative z is between x and $\mathcal{T}(\succcurlyeq_i)$, then z is preferred to x (intuitively, this is because z can be considered closer than x to the ideal $\mathcal{T}(\succcurlyeq_1)$). Single-peaked preferences were first discussed by Black (1948a, 1948b), and they arise naturally in many contexts. As we shall see later, the same basic idea can be extended to more complex cases, where the betweenness relation does not necessarily arise from a linear order. But we start from this simple case.[22]

To be specific, we will concentrate on the case where the number of alternatives is finite, and identify them with the integers in an interval $[a, b] = \{a, a+1, a+2, \ldots, b\} \equiv A$. (All the results we describe also apply to the case where A is the real line, ordered by the

[19] Part 1 of Fishburn's book (1972) is devoted to "Social Choice with Two Alternatives"; Murakami (1968) devoted a chapter to study "Democracy in a World of Two Alternatives"; many recent works on voting start from the analysis of choices between two alternatives, in order to avoid some of the problems we deal with here and to concentrate on others.

[20] References on simple games and their use in social choice theory are Peleg (1984, 2002), and Abdou and Keiding (1991).

[21] Campbell and Kelly (2002b) analyze the case where more than two alternatives exist, but individual preferences always rank them into m indifference classes. They show that when $m = 2$, there still exist strategyproof and nondictatorial rules, while this is not the case when $m \geq 3$.

[22] Another important domain restriction in many types of analysis is that of single-crossing. An analysis of its consequences for the existence of strategyproof rules is found in Saporiti and Tohmé (2003) and Saporiti (2009).

$\succcurlyeq$ relation. In fact, that is the context of Moulin 1980a, whose results we adapt here.) We assume throughout that the preferences of all agents are single-peaked.

Under these assumptions, there exist nontrivial strategyproof social choice functions. Here are some examples:

Example 1 There are three agents. Allow each one to vote for her preferred alternative. Choose the median of the three voters.

To see that the rule is not manipulable, consider the options of one agent, say 1, when the other two have already voted for some alternatives c and d (without loss of generality, let $c \leq d$). Then, 1 can determine any outcome between c and d, and none other (if $c = d$, then this is the outcome regardless of 1's vote). If 1's top alternative is in the integer interval $[c, d]$, then 1 gets her best without manipulating. If her top alternative is below c, then c is the outcome and, by single-peakedness, this is better for 1 than any outcome in $[c, d]$. Similarly, if the top for 1 is above d, d is 1's best option. Notice that the same rule would not be strategyproof for larger domains, allowing preferences not to be single-peaked.

Example 2 There are two agents. We fix an alternative p in $[a, b]$. Agents are asked to vote for their best alternatives, and the median of p, T_1 and T_2 is the outcome.

Again, the median is well defined, because it is taken from an odd number of values: two of them are the agent's votes, while the third one is a fixed value. We will call this value a phantom.

Example 3 For any number of agents, ask each one for their preferred alternative and choose the smallest.

This is another strategyproof rule. Notice that the options left to any agent are those smaller than or equal to the smallest vote of others. Hence, if this agent's ideal is still lower, she can choose it. Otherwise, the outcome of voting for her best (which is the lowest vote of others) cannot be improved either.

Remark that this rule, which might appear to be quite different from the preceding ones, can in fact also be written as a median. To do so, when there are n agents, place $n - 1$ phantoms and n alternatives on the lowest alternative a. Then the function can be described as choosing the median between these $n - 1$ phantoms and the n alternatives supported by actual voters.

Up to here, those rules are anonymous: interchanging the roles of agents (along their votes) does not change the outcome. The following and last example describes a strategyproof rule where different agents play different roles.

Example 4 There are two agents. Fix two alternatives w_1 and w_2 ($w_1 \leq w_2$). If agent 1 votes for any alternative in $[w_1, w_2]$, the outcome is 1's vote. If 1 votes for an alternative larger than w_2, the outcome is the median of w_2 and the votes of both agents. If 1 votes below w_1, then the outcome is the median of w_1 and the votes of both agents.

Notice that this rule can also be described in other ways.

One way is the following. Assign values on the extended real line to the sets $\{1\},\{2\},\{1,2\}$. Specifically, let $a_1 = w_1$, $a_2 = w_2$, $a_{1,2} = a$ (the lowest value in the range). Now, define the rule as choosing

$$f(\succcurlyeq_1, \succcurlyeq_2) = \inf_{S \in \{\{1,2\},\{1\}\{2\}\}} \left[\sup_{i \in S} (a_S, \mathcal{T}(\succcurlyeq_i)) \right].$$

We shall state immediately that this formula generalizes. There are also other ways to write the same rule. These are described in the following pages.

Moulin (1980a) characterized the class of all strategyproof social choice functions on single-peaked domains. Actually, he worked on the extended real line. He also assumed that the rules were only based on the preferred elements for each voter. This is an unnecessary assumption, because strategyproof social choice rules in these (and in many other) domains are restricted to only use information on what each agent considers best. This was proven in Barberà and Jackson (1994) in a context of public goods, and also in Sprumont (1991) in a context of allocation rules. As a result, we can express the structure of all strategyproof social choice functions (defined on the full set of single-peaked preference profiles), even if the actual rules we discuss only use information about the peaks. An adaptation of Moulin's characterization is as follows.

Construction

For each coalition $S \in 2^N \backslash \emptyset$, fix an alternative a_S. Define a social choice function in such a way that, for each preference profile $(\succcurlyeq_1, \ldots, \succcurlyeq_n)$,

$$f(\succcurlyeq_1, \ldots, \succcurlyeq_n) = \inf_{S \subset N} \left[\sup_{i \in S} (a_S, \mathcal{T}(\succcurlyeq_i)) \right].$$

The functions so defined will be called *generalized median voter schemes.*

The values a_S appear here just as parameters defining functions in this class. Their role becomes more clear under the alternative definition of generalized median voter schemes that will be proposed in Definition 2.

Theorem 3 (Moulin 1980a) *A social choice function on profiles of single-peaked preferences over a totally ordered set is strategyproof if and only if it is a generalized median voter scheme.*

This characterization can be sharpened if we restrict attention to anonymous social choice functions. In this case, the only strategyproof rules are those that are indeed based in calculating the medians of agents' votes and some fixed collection of phantoms.

Theorem 4 (Moulin 1980a) *An anonymous social choice function on profiles of single-peaked preferences over a totally ordered set is strategyproof if and only if there exist* $n+1$ *points* $p_1, \ldots, p_{n+1}$ *in* A *(called the phantom voters), such that, for all profiles,*

$$f(\succcurlyeq_1, \ldots, \succcurlyeq_n) = med\left(p_1, \ldots, p_{n+1}; \mathcal{T}(\succcurlyeq_1), \ldots, \mathcal{T}(\succcurlyeq_n)\right).$$

(A similar statement, with f defined with only $n-1$ phantoms, characterizes strategyproof and efficient social choice functions).[23]

Generalized median voter schemes are an important class of voting rules, and it will prove useful to provide a second definition of that class. This second definition is equivalent to the one given above. It is useful when stating and proving some results. It also provides an alternative view on how these rules operate.

To motivate this new definition, let us remember the case when we must choose among only two alternatives, 0 and 1. Strategyproof rules can be described as choosing 1 unless there is enough support for the opposite, in which case 0 will be selected, where "enough support" is given by the list of those coalitions that will get 0 if all their members prefer it to 1. If that list defines a monotonic simple game, then the rule is strategyproof.

This same idea can be extended to cases where we must select among a finite set of values on the real line (as opposed to only two). Without loss of generality, we can identify these values with a list of integers, from a to b. Let each voter declare her preferred value. Now, we can start by asking whether a should be chosen. If "enough" people have voted for a, then let us choose a. To determine what we mean by "enough," we can give a list of coalitions $C(a)$. If all agents in one of these coalitions support a, then a is chosen. If not, go to $a+1$. Now ask the question whether "enough" agents support values up to $a+1$. That is, look at all agents who support either a or $a+1$, and check whether they form a group in the list $C(a+1)$. If they do, then choose $a+1$. If not, go to $a+2$, and check whether the agents who support a, $a+1$ and $a+2$ form a group in $C(a+2)$. If so, choose $a+2$; if not, proceed to $a+3$, etc. Given appropriate lists of coalitions $C(a)$, $C(a+1), \ldots, C(b-1)$, $C(b)$, the rules described above should lead us to choose some value between a and b, for each list of the agents' preferred values. These lists of coalitions will be called left coalition systems, because the first

[23] The statement of this result by Moulin without his tops-only requirement must be carefully qualified in the case of a continuum of preferences. The version we provide for expository purposes should be finessed. Two ways to do it would be either to assume a further condition that the range is connected, or a unanimity requirement on f. See Barberà and Jackson (1994) and Le Breton and Weymark (1999).

value to the left of the interval to get enough support is declared to be the choice. (One can similarly describe the rules by a set of right coalition systems, and then start by checking first whether b has enough support, then $b-1$, then $b-2$, etc. In this description, the first value to the right which gets enough support should be chosen.) To complete the description of a left coalition system, we need to add a few requirements on the lists of values for $C(.)$, in order to guarantee that the above description makes sense. These requirements are that (1) if a coalition is "strong enough" to support an outcome, so are its supersets; (2) if a coalition is "strong enough" to support the choice of a given value, it is also "strong enough" to support any higher value; and (3) any coalition is "strong enough" to guarantee that the choice will not exceed the maximum possible value b. (Similar requirements must hold for right coalition systems.) All of this is summarized by the following formal definitions. Definition 1 formalizes the description of left (resp. right) coalition systems. Definition 2 describes how each of these coalition systems can be applied to produce a generalized median voter scheme. Notice that the parameters, as in Moulin's definition of a generalized median voter scheme (Section 5.3.1), correspond to the minimum (or maximum) value of a at which coalition S appears in $C(a)$.

Definition 1 *A left (resp. right) coalition system on the integer interval $B=[a,b]$ is a correspondence $\mathcal{C}$ assigning to every $\alpha \in B$ a collection of nonempty coalitions $\mathcal{C}(\alpha)$, satisfying the following requirements:*

(1) if $c \in \mathcal{C}(\alpha)$ and $c \subset c'$, then $c' \in \mathcal{C}(\alpha)$;
(2) if $\beta > \alpha$ (resp. $\beta < \alpha$) and $c \in \mathcal{C}(\alpha)$, then $c \in \mathcal{C}(\beta)$; and
(3) $\mathcal{C}(b) = 2^N \backslash \emptyset$ (resp. $\mathcal{C}(a) = 2^N \backslash \emptyset$).

We will denote left coalition systems by $\mathcal{L}$, and right coalition systems by $\mathcal{R}$. Elements of $\mathcal{L}$ will be denoted by $l(\cdot)$, and those in $\mathcal{R}$ by $r(\cdot)$.

We can now proceed with our definition of generalized median voter schemes.

Definition 2 *Given a left (resp. right) coalition system $\mathcal{L}$ (resp. $\mathcal{R}$) on $B=[a,b]$, its associated generalized median voter scheme is defined so that, for all profiles $(\succcurlyeq_1, \ldots, \succcurlyeq_n)$*

$$f(\succcurlyeq_1, \ldots, \succcurlyeq_n) = \beta \text{ iff } \{i \mid \mathcal{T}(\succcurlyeq_i) \leq \beta\} \in \mathcal{L}(\beta)$$

and

$$\{i \mid \mathcal{T}(\succcurlyeq_i) \leq \beta - 1\} \notin \mathcal{L}(\beta - 1)$$

(respectively,

$$f(\succcurlyeq_1, \ldots, \succcurlyeq_n) = \beta \text{ iff } \{i \mid \mathcal{T}(\succcurlyeq_i) > \beta\} \in \mathcal{R}(\beta)$$

and

$$\{i \mid \mathcal{T}(\succcurlyeq_i) > \beta + 1\} \notin \mathscr{R}(\beta + 1)).$$

Clearly, we could have just referred to either left (or right) coalition system as the primitives in our definitions. To every generalized median voter scheme we can associate one system of each type. Referring to both simultaneously will be useful later on.

Notice that, in order for these rules to be well defined, we only need the alternatives to be linearly ordered and the agents to have a unique maximal alternative. Whether or not the rules have good properties depends, then, on the domain of preferences over which they operate.

The description of generalized median voter schemes was first proposed by Barberà, Gul, and Stacchetti (1993). It is easily extended to the case where the choices must be made not on a finite ordered set, but on the real line (Barberà, Massó, and Serizawa 1998).

These two expressions of the form of strategypoof rules on the real line (or on integer intervals) are not the only ones. Others are due to Kim and Roush (1984), and to Ching (1997), who provided another representation of the same object. He maintained Moulin's idea of using medians and defined "augmented median rules," which allow for variable phantoms and can thus relax the anonymity that is implicit in the original version.

For clarification, I propose a couple of simple examples

Example 5 Let $B = [1,2,3]$, $N = \{1,2,3\}$. Let $\mathcal{L}(1) = \mathcal{L}(2) = \{S \in 2^N \backslash \emptyset : \#S \geq 2\}$.

Define f to be the generalized median voter scheme associated with $\mathcal{L}$. Then, for example

$$f(1,2,3) = 2$$

$$f(3,2,3) = 3$$

$$f(1,3,1) = 1.$$

This is, in fact, the median voter rule.

Example 6 Let now $B = [1,2,3,4]$, $N = \{1,2,3\}$. Consider the right coalition system given by

$$\mathscr{R}(4) = \mathscr{R}(3) = \mathscr{R}(2) = \{C \in 2^N \setminus \emptyset : 1 \in C \text{ and } 2 \in C\}.$$

In that case, both 1 and 2 are essential to determine the outcome. Let g be the generalized median voting scheme associated with $\mathscr{R}$. Here are some of the values of g:

$$g(1,4,4) = 1$$

$$g(3,3,1) = 3$$

$$g(3,2,2) = 2.$$

Other, earlier authors, had also introduced alternative descriptions of the rules leading to strategyproof choices on the line. These were less constructive and relied on the properties that actually characterize the rules. Chichilnisky and Heal (1981, 1997) proved that these rules must be "locally simple," that is, they must be locally constant or locally dictatorial. Border and Jordan (1981, 1983), and then Peters, van der Stel, and Storken (1991), identified another property that is common and exclusive to such rules. They named it "uncompromisingness": this means that no changes in the peak of any agent has any impact on the value of the function unless that agent's peak changes from the right of this value to its left (or vice versa).

A few authors have considered how to extend the results to the case where alternatives can be assumed to be located on a graph, and preferences on the voters of this graph satisfy an extended notion of single-peakedness due to Demange (1982). Results are positive when the graph is a tree, and become negative when loops are allowed. See Schummer and Vohra (2002) and Danilov (1994).

Notice that although single-peaked preferences do not preclude indifferences among other alternatives, they are defined so that there is a unique maximal element for each agent.

As it turns out, allowing for indifferences in this and other models tends to complicate the analysis of strategyproof rules. In the present case, the basic result of Moulin is essentially preserved if one allows for "single-plateaued" preferences, having several contiguous maximal elements, in addition to single-peaked ones. Berga's (1998) careful discussion of this extension clearly illustrates how indifferences complicate the essential picture, even in such a simple model.

An interesting extension of the model we have discussed arises when agents must choose more than one point in the line. This problem was first described by Miyagawa (1998, 2001) and it accommodates, among other possible interpretations, the idea that the location (and modes of use) of several public facilities have to be jointly decided upon. Miyagawa (2001) characterizes a class of rules that are coalitionally strategyproof, under the assumption that preferences over simple facilities are single-peaked, no congestion effects, and there is the use of only one facility. Bogomolnaia and Nicolò (1999) characterize rules that are strategyproof, efficient, and stable for the case where facilities congestion affects individual preferences.

6.3. *n*-Dimensional Grids

6.3.1. *Strategyproofness for Generalized Single-Peaked Domains*

The assumption that social alternatives can be represented by a set of linearly ordered values is a very fruitful one. But a multidimensional representation of social alternatives would allow for a much richer representation of the choices open to society. You can think of those characteristics that are crucial to distinguish among alternatives. For example, when choosing among political candidates, you may decide that they can be fully described by their stand on economic, human rights, and foreign policy issues, say. Then, candidates could be described by a three-dimensional vector, whose first component would describe the candidate's position on the economic dimension, with the second and third standing for the candidate's stand on the other two issues. On each issue, that is, on each of the three dimensions, you should decide how the candidates' stands can be attached to a value, from lowest to highest. The same formalism applies to the more classical problem of choosing simultaneously the level of provision of k different public goods. And many other interpretations are possible, including location decisions. Yet each particular interpretation may suggest what are "natural" or relevant restrictions on the agents' preferences of these k-dimensional objects. At some levels, generality prevails while, at others the particulars derived from interpretation of the model do matter.

The following framework will allow us to formalize multidimensional social choices of a rather general sort.

Let K be a number of dimensions. Each dimension will stand for one characteristic that is relevant to the description of social alternatives. Allow for a finite set of admissible $B_k = [a_k, b_k]$ on each dimension $k \in K$. Now the set of alternatives can be represented as the Cartesian product $B = \Pi_{k=1}^{K} B_k$. Sets like this B are called K-dimensional boxes. Representing the set of social alternatives as the set of elements in a K-dimensional box allows us to describe many interesting situations. With two dimensions, we can describe location problems in a plane. We can describe political candidates by their positions on different issues. We can describe alternative plans for a municipality, by specifying which projects could be chosen in each of the different dimensions of concern: schools, safety, sanitation, etc.

There still remains a number of limitations in this specification. One is that we keep assuming that the projects are linearly ordered within each dimension. Another one is that, by assuming that any point in the Cartesian product is a possible choice for society, we are implicitly saying that there are no further constraints on the choices faced by society. We shall later comment on how to relax these assumptions. But the multidimensional model can represent a variety of interesting situations. We first consider what can be said about strategyproof rules in this setting and will then proceed to other perhaps more realistic ones. Again, we start with a specification that assumes a finite set of alternatives.

Similar results can be expressed in a continuous setting and will be discussed in parallel. But the continuous setting also allows for new questions, regarding the connection of the model with the standard economic treatment of preferences on public goods. We shall consider these additional questions in the next section.

Before we proceed, we must be specific about the type of restrictions to impose on preferences over such sets of alternatives. We shall maintain the spirit of single-peakedness by requiring every preference to have a unique top (or ideal) and then assuming that, if z is between x and $\mathcal{T}(\succcurlyeq_i)$, then z is preferred to x. But in order to make the "betweenness" relationship precise, we must take a stand. Following Barberà, Gul, and Stacchetti (1993), we endow the set B with the L_1 norm (the "city block" metric), letting, for each $\alpha \in B$, $\|\alpha\| = \sum_{k=1}^{K} |\alpha_k|$. Then, the minimal box containing two alternatives α and β is defined as $MB(\alpha,\beta) = \{\gamma \in B \mid \|\alpha - \beta\| = \|\alpha - \gamma\| + \|\gamma - \beta\|\}$.

We can interpret that z is "between" alternatives x and $\mathcal{T}(\succcurlyeq_i)$, if $z \in MB(x, \mathcal{T}(\succcurlyeq_i))$. Under this interpretation, the following is a natural extension of single-peakedness.

Definition 3 *A preference $\succcurlyeq_i$ on B is generalized single-peaked iff for all distinct $\beta, \gamma \in B$, $\beta \in MB(\mathcal{T}(\succcurlyeq_i), \gamma)$ implies that $\beta \succ_i \gamma$.*

This definition collapses to that of standard single-peakedness when the set of alternatives is one-dimensional. It implies, and it is in fact equivalent to, the following two conditions: (a) the restriction of generalized single-peaked preference to sets of alternatives that only differ on one dimension is single-peaked, and (b) the projection of the best element on each of these sets is the best element within them.

One possible way to choose from K-dimensional boxes consists of using K (possibly different) generalized median voter schemes, one for each dimension. Then, if each agent is asked for her best alternative, the kth component of her ideal can be combined with the kth component corresponding to other agents, and used to determine a choice, by means of the specific generalized median voter scheme that is attached to this kth component. Similarly, the values for any other component can also be computed, and the resulting K-tuple of values be taken as social outcome.

Formally, we can define (K-dimensional) generalized median voter schemes on $B = \Pi_{k=1}^{K} B_k = \Pi_{k=1}^{K} [a_k, b_k]$, as follows:

Let $\mathcal{L}$ (resp. $\mathcal{R}$) be a family of K left (resp. right) coalition systems, where each $\mathcal{L}_k$ (resp. $\mathcal{R}_k$) is defined on $[a_k, b_k]$. The corresponding k-dimensional generalized median voter scheme is the one that, for all profiles of preferences on B, chooses

$$f(\succcurlyeq_1, \ldots, \succcurlyeq_n) = \beta \text{ iff } \{i \mid \mathcal{T}(\succcurlyeq_i) \leq \beta_k\} \in \mathcal{L}_k(\beta_k)$$

and

$$\{i \mid \mathcal{T}(\succcurlyeq_i) \leq \beta_{k-1}\} \notin \mathcal{L}(\beta_{k-1}),$$

for all $k = 1, \ldots, K$
(or respectively,

$$f(\succcurlyeq_1, \ldots, \succcurlyeq_n) = \beta \text{ iff } \{i \mid \mathcal{T}(\succcurlyeq_i) \leq \beta_k\} \in \mathcal{R}_k(\beta_k)$$

and

$$\{i \mid \mathcal{T}(\succcurlyeq_i) \leq \beta_{k-1}\} \notin \mathscr{R}(\beta_{k-1})).$$

Example 7 We can combine Examples 5 and 6 in Section 6.2 and give an example of a generalized median voter scheme.

Let $B = [1,2,3] \times [1,2,3,4]$, $N = (1,2,3)$. Let $\mathcal{L}_1$ be as $\mathcal{L}$ in Example 5. Let $\mathscr{R}_2$ be as $\mathscr{R}$ in Example 6. Let h be the two-dimensional generalized median voter scheme associated to this coalition system. Then, for example,

$$h((1,1),(2,4),(3,4)) = (2,1)$$
$$h((3,3),(2,3),(3,1)) = (3,3)$$
$$h((1,3),(3,2),(1,2)) = (1,2).$$

Moulin's theorem generalizes nicely to this context. We just need to add a condition on the social choice function, which is usually referred to as voters' sovereignty. This condition requires that each one of the alternatives should be chosen by the function, for some preference profile.

Theorem 5 (Barberà, Gul, and Stacchetti 1993) *A social choice function f defined on the set of generalized single-peaked preferences over a K-dimensional box, and respecting voters' sovereignty, is strategyproof iff it is a (K-dimensional) generalized median voter scheme.*

Results in the same vein had been obtained by previous authors for a variety of contexts and under different assumptions regarding individual preferences.

Border and Jordan (1981, 1983)[24] did characterize strategyproof rules for the k-dimensional problem with a continuum of choices on each dimension, under different assumptions regarding the preferences of agents. They got positive results, close in spirit to that of Theorem 5, for narrow and symmetric enough classes of preferences, which they call separable star-shaped, and include the quadratic case. Their characterization is in terms of the properties they had discovered to be required for one-dimensional rules to be strategyproof under single-peakedness. It is based on the fact that the projections of these highly symmetric preferences on each of the axes do in fact induce a subclass of (symmetric) single-peaked preferences.[25]

[24] I mention the working paper, as well as its published version, because the latter is quite incomplete and requires constant reference to the original version.

[25] Notice that in k-dimensional settings with continous preferences, these will systematically contain indifference classes. I have already remarked that indifferences may introduce complications in the analysis. Such complications do not arise in these contexts, because only the projections of the general preference on the axis matters, and these projections are single-peaked for restricted enough domains.

A similar extension to k-dimensional spaces, but expressed in terms of the local simplicity of the rules to be used on each of the axis, was obtained by Chichilnisky and Heal (1981, 1997).[26]

In that same context, a very special case arises if one restricts attention to Euclidean preferences, whose indifference classes are hyperspheres. In that case, the choice of axis on which to project the different preferences becomes an additional issue. Laffond (1980) gave an early treatment of this case, which was also tackled by Kim and Roush (1984), van der Stel (2000), and Peters, van der Stel, and Storken (1991). Additional results on preferences generated by strictly convex norms are contained in van der Stel (2000), and Peters, van der Stel, and Storken (1992, 1993).[27]

6.3.2. A Special Case: Voting by Committees

Theorem 5 above applies to the general case where alternatives are elements of any K-dimensional box and voters' preferences are generalized single-peaked. A specific instance of this general setup can help us to describe what we have learned. The example is interesting on its own, and it was studied in Barberà, Sonnenschein, and Zhou (1991). Consider a club composed of N members, who are facing the possibility of choosing new members out of a set of K candidates. Are there any strategyproof rules that the club can use?

We consider that the club has no capacity constraints, nor any obligation to choose any prespecified number of candidates. Hence, the set of alternatives faced by the present members consists of all possible subsets of candidates: they can admit any subset. Because of that, it is natural to assume that the preferences of voters will be defined on these subsets: every member of the club should be able to say whether she prefers to add S, rather than S', to the current membership, or the other way around.

What is the connection between this example and our n-dimensional model? Observe that given K candidates, we can represent any subset S of candidates by its characteristic vector: that is, by a K-dimensional vector of zeros and ones, where a one in the Ith component would mean that the Ith candidate is in S, while a zero in the Jth component indicates that the Jth candidate is not in S. Hence, the set of all subsets of K candidates can be expressed as the Cartesian product of K integer intervals. Each of these intervals would only allow for two values now: $a = 0$, and $b = 1$. The "characteristics" of the alternatives are known once we know what candidates are in and what candidates are out. Therefore, choosing members for a club can be seen as a particular problem within our general class of K-dimensional choice problems.

What about strategyproofness? We certainly should not expect a general positive answer unless we assume some restriction on preferences. Consider, for example, that

[26] Their 1981 paper remained unpublished until 1997, when an improved version appeared in *Social Choice and Welfare*.
[27] For a more complete treatment of this point, see Sprumont (1995).

there are two candidates x and y, and that I am a voter. I prefer x to y, but since these two candidates would always be fighting if both were elected, I prefer nobody to be elected rather than both being in: the latter is my worst alternative. Suppose that, under some voting rule, y will be elected even if I don't support him or her, while x would only be elected if I add my support to that of other voters. Then, I might not support x, whom I like, in order to avoid the bad outcome that both candidates are in! This type of manipulation is almost unavoidable, unless the preferences of voters are restricted in such a way that these strong externalities from having several candidates can be ruled out. One way to do it is by restricting attention to separable preferences.

To check whether a given preference order on sets of candidates is separable, say that a candidate is "good" if it is better to choose this candidate alone than choosing no candidate at all; otherwise, call the candidate "bad" (this, of course, refers to the given preference order). Now, we'll say that the overall order is separable, if whenever we add a "good" candidate g to any set S of candidates, the enlarged set is better than S, and whenever we add a bad candidate b to S, then the enlarged set is worse than S.

In Barberà, Sonnenschein, and Zhou (1991), it is shown that there exists a wide class of strategyproof social choice rules when the preferences of club members over sets of candidates are separable. In fact, this is a corollary of Theorem 5 above. This is because, when there are only two possible values for each dimension, the separability assumption we just stated is equivalent to the assumption of generalized single-peakedness for the general case. Then the class of strategyproof rules we are looking for is the one formed by all possible generalized median voter schemes. But, as we already remarked at the beginning of Section 6.1, the left coalition systems corresponding to the case with only two possible values are given by committees, that is, by monotonic families of winning coalitions. As a result, here is the way to guarantee strategyproofness in our clubs. For each candidate, determine what sets of voters will have enough strength to bring in that candidate, if they agree to do so. Make sure that if a set is strong enough, so are its supersets. Then, ask each voter to list all the candidates who she likes. Choose all candidates who are supported by a coalition that is strong enough to bring him in. This is a full characterization. In particular, it contains a family of very simple rules, called the quota rules. Fix a number q between 1 and N. Let each agent support as many candidates as she likes. Elect all candidates that receive at least q supporting votes. These rules are not only strategyproof under separable preferences: They are also the only ones to treat all candidates alike (neutrality) and all voters alike (anonymity).

Taking up from this particular model, where each proposal takes two possible values in each dimension, Ju (2003) considered the case with three possible valuations of an object: "good," "bad," or "null"; notice that this is a way to introduce indifferences in that simple model. He provides a characterization of strategyproof rules satisfying some additional properties. Larsson and Svensson (2006) have also elaborated on the consequences of indifference in this and other contexts.

6.3.3. The Issue of Strategyproofness for Broader Domains

As I already pointed out, Moulin's (1980a) seminal paper was written for a general framework where agents could have preferences on, and choose from, a one-dimensional continuum of possible values. These can be interpreted in many ways. A leading interpretation is that agents must choose the level of a public good. Because of this, different authors soon tried to extend Moulin's analysis to k-dimensional spaces.

I started to describe these extensions in Section 6.3.2, with the analysis of results on generalized single-peakedness. By doing that, I have given precedence to positive results that are possible in these restricted domains, and not in larger ones. But I have not respected the temporal sequence of the literature on the subject. It is now time to refer to earlier attempts to explore the issue of strategyproofness on broader domains, which led to different negative results.

An early paper on strategyproof choice in environments where preferences satisfy standard economic assumptions was due to Satterthwaite and Sonnenschein (1981). They examined the issue for different types of goods, and in the case of public goods they came up with an analog of the Gibbard–Satterthwaite Theorem. Their analysis was based on some additional restrictions regarding the smoothness of allocation rules under consideration, and it only established that these rules should be locally dictatorial, a property that does not imply global dictatorship.

Several of the papers I will refer to did also contain some positive results for particular subclasses of preferences. To that extent, they have already been mentioned in the preceding section, and I will only emphasize their impossibility results here.

Border and Jordan (1981, 1983) was a major article in this direction. They explored different classes of saturated preferences and proved that an impossibility arises as soon as the domain includes some that are not separable. Another early paper by Chichilnisky and Heal (1981, 1997) also proved negative results for large domains of preferences.

These papers had assumed that preferences satisfied some k-dimensional version of single-peakedness, and showed that the route to avoid impossibilities was to use preferences satisfying, in addition, some strong form of separability. This additional property, whose essence we have already discussed in Section 6.3.2, was later proven to be essential in establishing the borders between possibility and impossibility results. This is addressed in the following section.

More generally, one could wonder about the possibility to extend Gibbard and Satterthwaite's result to environments where preferences satisfied some of the assumptions that are standard in economics. A paper by Barberà and Peleg (1990) tackled this issue in a larger setting that contains our k-dimensional spaces as a particular case.

Letting the set of alternatives be any metric space, and the admissible preferences be the set of all continuous utility functions on such alternatives, they proved that all nondictatorial rules whose range has more than three alternatives will be manipulable. This result opened the door to many others, since it had to develop new techniques of proof: indeed, prior proofs of the Gibbard–Satterthwaite result were based on arguments requiring the use of discontinuous utilities and were not applicable. As we have already mentioned in Section 2.3.5, these new techniques are quite useful in proving that classical result as well. Yet, Barberà and Peleg's result on continuous preferences is neither implied by nor implies Gibbard and Satterthwaite's. As soon as we have continuous preferences and an infinity of alternatives on a multidimensional space, more work is needed to attain results.

A paper by Zhou (1991a) continued the same line of research. He considered the set of alternatives to be any convex (nonempty) subset of the k-dimensional real space. The admissible preferences were those satisfying continuity and convexity. The latter is a strong requirement missing in Barberà and Peleg (1990). Hence, Zhou's result is stronger to that extent, though it needs of some additional requirements. He established that the only strategyproof nondictatorial rules on such a domain had to operate on an extremely rigid range, whose dimension had to be less than two. This dimensionality condition is closely related to the condition that the range contains at least three alternatives: here, the only way in which three or more alternatives belong to a space of dimension less than two is by all lying on the same line.

Bordes, Laffond, and Le Breton (1990) also obtained impossibility results in the k-dimensional setting. Interesting variants of Zhou's results were attained by Moreno (1999) and Moscoso (2001), who used different domains, more amenable to economic interpretations.

Barberà and Jackson (1994) looked for a more constructive approach. They built on Zhou's remark on the special form of ranges that allow for strategyproof rules in k-dimensional spaces and did provide their characterization for convex preferences. Essentially, they are rules that only use the restriction of these convex preferences on the linear range. Because these restrictions are typically single-peaked, Moulin's characterization for one-dimensional ranges and single-peaked preferences applies, with some technical qualifications.

6.4. Constraints: A First Approach

Many social decisions are subject to political or economic feasibility constraints. Different feasible alternatives may fulfill different requirements to degrees that are not necessarily compatible among themselves. A community may have enough talent to separately run a great program for the fine arts, or a top-quality kindergarten, but not to maintain both programs simultaneously at the same level of excellence. We can still model these constraints within our model, where alternatives are described by K-tuples of integer values, as long as we do no longer require the set of alternatives to be a Cartesian product. For example, if a firm must choose a set of new employees out of $K = \{1, 2, \ldots, k\}$ candidates, the alternative sets can be identified with the elements in the box $B = \Pi_{j=1}^{k} [0, 1]$.

But if only three positions are open, and at least one of them must be filled, the feasible set—consisting of K-tuples with at least a nonzero and at most three nonzero components—is no longer a Cartesian product. Similarly, the location of two facilities in some pair of sites out of a set of five municipal plots $(p_1, p_2, \ldots, p_5)$ can be formalized as a choice from $[1,5] \times [1,5]$, excluding (by feasibility) the elements with the same first and second component.

Here is how I will formalize the distinction between feasible and conceivable alternatives. Start from any set Z. Let B be the minimal box containing Z. Identify Z with the set of feasible alternatives. Restrict attention to functions whose range is Z. Then by exclusion, interpret the elements of $B \backslash Z$ as those alternatives that are conceivable but not feasible. Let the agents' preferences be defined on the set Z. Specifically, consider domains of preferences that are restrictions to Z of multidimensional single-peaked preferences on B, with the added requirement that the unconstrained maximal element of these preferences belongs to Z. (This is a limitation, since it rules out interpretations of our model under which preferences would be monotonic on the levels of characteristics. For example, these levels cannot be such that, for all agents, the higher is always the better.)

Two major facts can be established in this context (see Barberà, Massó, and Neme 1997; also Barberà, Massó, and Serizawa 1998 for a version with a continuum of alternatives). One is that, regardless of the exact shape of the set of feasible alternatives, any strategyproof social choice function must still be a generalized median voter scheme. Notice, then, that not all generalized median voter schemes will now give rise to well-defined social choice functions, because some of these schemes, by choosing the values on different dimensions in a decentralized way, could recommend the choice of nonfeasible alternatives. Our second result characterizes the set of all generalized median voter schemes that are proper social choice functions, for any $Z \subset B$. This characterization is based on the intersection property, a condition that states that the decision rules operating on different dimensions will be coordinated to always guarantee the choice of a feasible alternative. Before stating it, let us remark that it is not a simple condition, but it provides a full characterization, and it can orient our research for strategyproof rules for any specification of feasibility constraints.

All of the above is expressed in the following results (Barberà, Massó, and Neme 1997):

Definition 4 *A generalized median voter scheme f on B respects feasibility on $Z \subset B$ if $f(\succcurlyeq_1, \ldots, \succcurlyeq_n) \subset Z$ for all $(\succcurlyeq_1, \ldots, \succcurlyeq_n)$ such that $T(\succcurlyeq_i) \in Z$.*

Definition 5 *Let $Z \subset B$ and let f be a generalized median voter scheme on B, defined by the left coalition system $\mathcal{L}$ or, alternatively by the right coalition system $\mathcal{R}$. Let $\alpha \notin Z$ and $S \subset Z$. We say that f has the intersection property for (α, S) iff for every selection $r(\alpha_k)$ and $l(\alpha_k)$ from* *the sets* $\mathcal{R}(\alpha_k)$ *and* $\mathcal{L}(\alpha_k)$, *respectively, we have*

$$\cap_{\beta \in S}\left[\left(\cup_{k \in M^+(\alpha,\beta)} l(\alpha_k)\right) \cup \left(\cup_{k \in M^-(\alpha,\beta)} r(\alpha_k)\right)\right] \neq \emptyset$$

where $M^+(\alpha,\beta) = \{k \in K \mid \beta_k > \alpha_k\}$ *and* $M^-(\alpha,\beta) = \{k \in K \mid \beta_k < \alpha_k\}$.

We will say that f *satisfies the intersection property if it is does for every* $(\alpha, S) \in \left(B - Z, 2^K\right)$.

Theorem 6 (Barberà, Massó, and Neme 1997) *Let* f *be a generalized median voter scheme on* B, *let* $Z \subset B$, *and* f *respect voters' sovereignty on* Z. *Then* f *preserves feasibility on* Z *if and only if satisfies the intersection property.*

Denote by $\mathcal{S}_Z$ the set of all single-peaked preferences with top on $Z \subset B$. Let f be an onto social choice function with domain $\mathcal{S}_Z^n$ and range Z.

Theorem 7 (Barberà, Massó, and Neme 1997) *If* $f : \mathcal{S}_Z^n \to Z$ *is strategyproof, then* f *is a generalized median voter scheme.*

Theorem 8 (Barberà, Massó, and Neme 1997) *Let* $f : \mathcal{S}_Z^n \to Z$ *be an onto social choice function. Then* f *is strategyproof on* $\mathcal{S}_Z^n$ *iff it is a generalized median voter scheme satisfying the intersection property.*

6.5. The Structure of Strategyproof Rules

6.5.1. A Surprising Twist: Back to the Gibbard–Satterthwaite Theorem

One may by now feel to be walking on very narrow grounds. We have specified the alternatives to be a subset of K-dimensional space. We have required the preferences to be single-peaked with their top on the prespecified subset. We have seen that strategyproofness requires using very specific voting rules, and satisfying a general and not always easy to interpret condition (the intersection property). The Gibbard–Satterthwaite Theorem is an elegant result, even if it only applies to a specific situation, where all conceivable preferences are admissible. Our last theorem can be interpreted either as a possibility or an impossibility theorem, depending on the range restriction. Indeed, when the set of alternatives is Cartesian, our theorems are quite positive. True, respecting strategyproofness restricts us to choose among generalized median voter schemes, but these are quite versatile, and different ones can be chosen for different dimensions. On the other hand, for some special shapes of the range, the intersection property becomes highly restrictive, and only very special rules are eligible. Moreover, our theorems apply to preferences that are restrictions to feasible sets of more general preferences, which in turn we assumed to be single-peaked on the minimal box containing our feasible alternatives, and to have their best element within this set. Hence, while the universal domain assumption is quite invariant to the specification of alternatives (modulo their total number), our domain restrictions are specific for each set of alternatives under consideration.

Because of all these ifs and buts, it is particularly pleasant to remark that our theorem is, in fact, a very general one, and includes the Gibbard–Satterthwaite Theorem as a corollary. The apparent specificity can be otherwise interpreted as a source of versatility, as allowing us to cover many different environments, and the one envisaged by the Gibbard–Satterthwaite Theorem in particular.

Consider any finite set of alternatives, with no particular structure. We can always identify them with the k unit vectors in a k-dimensional space. The minimal box containing them is the set $B = \Pi_{k=1}^{K} [0, 1]$. Since no third element in the set of unit vectors U is "between" any other two, any arbitrary order of these unit vectors can be obtained as the restriction to U of a preference with peak on U which is single-peaked on B. Hence, our last theorem applies to social choice functions defined on all preferences over U, with range U. Any strategyproof social choice function must be a generalized median voter scheme satisfying the implications of the intersection property. These implications are that the same scheme must be used for all dimensions, and that it must be dictatorial. This is the Gibbard–Satterthwaite Theorem. It is not a separate entity, but the consequence of a much larger characterization involving special shapes for the range, specific domain restrictions, and the general structure of the strategyproof rules.

The paper by Barberà, Massó, and Neme (1997), which contains the general results, is also specific about this specific application.

6.5.2. Embedding Alternatives in a Grid

In the preceding subsection we have seen how an appropriate identification of any abstract set of k alternatives as k points in a k-dimensional grid could precipitate the Gibbard–Satterthwaite Theorem. The theorem can be obtained as a corollary of results we already know regarding the structure of strategyproof rules on grids when preferences are single-peaked and feasibility constraints may be required. This is just an example of a larger set of questions that one may ask regarding strategyproof rules with the aid of our previous knowledge.

To see what is the more general nature of these questions, let us recapitulate. Essentially, we have learned that, whenever the domain of preferences for a strategyproof social choice rule includes all the single-peaked preferences on the range of this rule having their top on that range, then the rule in question must be a generalized median voting scheme satisfying the intersection property.

One could boldly state the following converse of the statement: "Take any strategyproof social choice function. There will always exist a method that identifies the alternatives in its range with some points in a grid, in such a way that: (a) the rule is a generalized voter scheme, and (b) the preferences in the domain of the rule are single-peaked for that embedding." As far as I know, Faruk Gul stated this conjecture for the first time in the late 1980s, and attempts to make it precise have been quite productive even if, as I shall comment, it cannot be exact. But I like to comment on this conjecture, even if only because it introduces a new point of view, connecting results on "abstract" alternatives with others regarding rather structured environments. In the context of grids, each alternative can be viewed as the conjunction of certain characteristics (one for each dimension of the grid) satisfied at some level of performance (determined by the position of the alternative on the scale that refers to that characteristic in particular).

Hence, in some way each strategyproof rule would be associated with an appropriate embedding in a grid, and that embedding would reveal the structural characteristics around which one should organize the choice of alternatives.

In fact, as we shall see, the conjecture is not exact but inspiring. Even getting close to an appropriate statement needs many qualifications, each of which provides some insights. Let us consider them in turn. To do that, assume we are given a strategyproof social choice function. First of all, can we always embed into a grid the set of abstract alternatives belonging to the range of this function? The answer is obviously yes, unless we impose any further restrictions on the embedding. So, let us formulate the question in a way that is closer to Gul's conjecture. Can we embed the range of the function in such a way that all the preferences in the domain are single-peaked? Again, the answer is trivial: yes we can. Just identify each alternative, as suggested in the previous section, with the unit vectors in a grid where each alternative accounts for one dimension. Since any preferences are single-peaked in that space, then all preferences in the domain, however small it is, should be single-peaked. Of course, this identification would be a dead end, because our characterization results require not only that some single-peaked preferences should belong to the domain, but that all single-peaked preferences should be admissible. So let us start again. Can we embed the range of the function in such a way that all the preferences in the domain are single-peaked, and so that all single-peaked preferences with top on one of the alternatives (relative to the embedding) are in the range? Now, we are closer. Because if the answer is yes, we know that the rule will be a generalized median voter scheme. Moreover, we know that it will have to satisfy the intersection property.

Gul's conjecture cannot be completely true. We have no guarantee that the set of preferences in the range of strategyproof social choice function will coincide with a rich enough set of single-peaked preferences, relative to any embedding, let alone with the whole set of them. And yet some richness of domain is needed to guarantee that only median voting rules can satisfy strategyproofness. Even so, Gul's conjecture has driven research by different authors, some of whose partial results are indeed enlightening.

For example, even when an embedding guarantees that preferences in the domain are single-peaked, it will seldom be the case that the set of alternatives consists of a full box. (Not, for example, if the number of alternatives is a prime, except for the most favorable case when they can be embedded on a line.) Therefore, the discovery of the intersection property by Barberà, Massó, and Neme (1997) was essential in allowing the very statement of the conjecture to have some meaning. Bogomolnaia (1998) studied carefully conditions under which one could properly speak of median voting (after an appropriate embedding of alternatives) when the initial setup lacks structure. The interest of the approach was indicated in Barberà (1996), along with several examples. Two recent papers by Nehring and Puppe (2005, 2007a) have made a systematic search of several aspects related to the conjecture. Nehring and Puppe (2007b) extend the notion of generalized single-peakedness to cover a variety of structures, based on abstract notions of "betweenness." They also provide useful procedures that one could try when attempting to actually "construct" an appropriate space in which to embed the alternatives in the range of a function. Nehring and Puppe (2002) exploit the requirements imposed by the intersection property in order to characterize the shapes of ranges that allow for "nice" strategyproof rules, and to set them apart from other range forms that precipitate dictatorship.

6.5.3. The General Structure of Strategyproof Rules

Some essential features of strategyproof rules emerge again and again in different contexts. Although they are not necessarily held by all such rules in all possible contexts, I find it convenient to discuss them here, because the results we just discussed regarding rules on K-dimensional grids are paradigmatic.

One first characteristic of strategyproof rules in several contexts is that they are only responsive to a limited amount of the information contained in the preferences of agents. Specifically, rules that only use the information regarding what is the preferred alternative of each one of the agents emerge as the only candidates to respect strategyproofness in many different cases. Remember that proving this "tops only" requirement (Weymark 1999a calls it "nontop-insensitivity") is the first step in one of the proofs of the Gibbard–Satterthwaite Theorem (Barberà and Peleg 1990). The same requirement is proved to be necessary for strategyproof rules defined over single-peaked preferences in k-dimensional grids. Sprumont (1991) and Barberà and Jackson (1994) showed that it was necessary in the one-dimensional case (Moulin 1980a had a priori restricted attention to the class of rules satisfying the property). The different papers involving the use of generalized median voter schemes start by showing some version of the "tops only property," even if the same basic idea may require slight additional qualifications depending on the context. For example, in those contexts where the best alternatives of agents might not be feasible (see Barberà, Massó, and Neme 1997, or Weymark 1999a), then the condition still holds but now requires that the rules should process information about those feasible alternatives that are best. In other terms, the rules should only use information about those alternatives that are top on their range. Weymark (2006) explores the possibility of finding general conditions under which the "tops only" condition is a necessary condition for strategyproofness.

A second important property of strategyproof rules operating on k-dimensional alternative spaces is that they must be decomposable: that is, they should be possible to express as the combination of k rules, each one operating on one of these dimensions, each one being itself strategyproof. This decomposability is quite independent of the particular set of preferences that are admissible in each of these dimensions. When preferences on each dimension are single-peaked, then the rules can be decomposed in k rules, each one of them being of the type described by Moulin (1980a). But if the set of admissible preferences on each dimension is broad enough, then only dictatorships on each dimension may be strategyproof, and only compositions of dictatorial rules may emerge. The bottom line is that, although decomposability comes along with single-peakedness in positive results, it is a more general requirement for strategyproof rules operating on k-dimensional spaces.

Decomposable rules must be such that the combination of characteristics chosen in each dimension generates a feasible outcome. This is no problem when the ranges of functions are full k-dimensional boxes: any combination of choices, dimension by dimension, generate an element in the box. No coordination is needed between what are the choices in one dimension and what emerges in another. However, in contexts where the ranges are not full boxes (due to constraints, e.g.), then decomposability is not the final requirement. The rules in each one of the dimensions must be "coordinated" enough to ensure that they will never recommend the choice of unfeasible combinations of characteristics. This is the role played by the intersection property.

These are basic features that appear in all their neatness under special conditions. Specifically, they require the existence of a single top alternative in each of the relevant dimensions of the problem, and the possibility to identify these "partial" tops from just knowing what the global top alternative is for an agent. Thus, complications arise in contexts when agents may be indifferent among several possible top alternatives. Even then, and sometimes using additional restrictions (like non-bossiness), results regarding the simplicity of inputs and the decomposability of strategyproof rules may still hold for these more complex environments. Another aspect to watch for, because it is determinant for these general features to arise, is that the domains of definition of the functions should be rich enough.

The first results on decomposability were due to Border and Jordan (1983) and Chichilnisky and Heal (1977, 1981). Different papers developed their own separability results as they worked along to get specific results. A systematic application of the principles evoked here appear in Barberà, Sonnenschein, and Zhou (1991) and in Barberà, Massó, and Neme (1997).

More specifically, different authors have carefully studied the general conditions under which each of these properties become necessary for strategyproofness. Le Breton and Sen (1995, 1999) and Le Breton and Weymark (1999) studied separately the cases when preferences are strict and the additional complications induced by the presence of indifferences. Weymark (1999a) concentrated on decomposability and obtained additional results based on a variety of domain conditions. A superb account of these structural features and their discovery is found in Sprumont (1995).

A major issue we have already hinted at in Section 3.2 is that of the difficult compatibility between efficiency and strategyproofness. Two well-known domains where these two conditions can be jointly satisfied by non-trivial rules involve extensions of the notion of single-peakedness to appropriate sets of alternatives. One is the case when one candidate or one location has to be elected, and preferences are single-peaked (Moulin 1980). Another case arises when one good must be rationed and the agent's preferences over shares are single-peaked (Sprumont 1991). See Sections 6 and 9.1. A third case, this time in a two-dimensional space, is considered in Kim and Roush (1984). Nehring and Puppe (2007a) discuss the trade-off between efficiency and strategyproofness in a very constructive way, by concentrating on a large class of preference domains and characterizing the rules that can meet both requirements. The analysis of these rules proves that compatibility requires either a low-dimensional space of alternatives (as in the above-mentioned references) or the rule to be "near" dictatorial.

6.6. Constraints Revisited

Until now, the papers I have described on the issue of constrained ranges were based on the assumption that the domain of preferences only included those satisfying two conditions:

(1) That the preferences on the range were the restriction on the alternatives in the range of some single-peaked preferences on the minimal box containing them.
(2) And that the preferences on the range had their top in the range.

I will now discuss the consequences of dropping this second condition. Before I do, let me briefly argue that it is sometimes appropriate to use it, while in other cases it seems unnecessarily restrictive.

We have mentioned two scenarios under which it seems natural to concentrate on social choice functions whose range is not a box. One such scenario comes from considering any social choice function on abstract sets of alternatives and then embedding them in a k-dimensional space. In that case, it is perfectly natural to think of the preferences on alternatives in the range as the primitives, and assumption 2 just assumes that there is one best feasible alternative. We can then see assumption 1 as a restriction on the domain that is sufficiently rich to provide characterization results, and sufficiently restrictive to allow for nontrivial strategyproof rules.

The second scenario is one where the structure of the set of alternatives comes naturally with the k-dimensional model, so that in principle preferences can be defined on all alternatives, feasible or not. In that context, we may study the consequences of additional constraints, precluding some alternatives from being chosen. Under this interpretation, assumption 1 is still perfectly acceptable, but it seems unnatural to exclude the possibility that agents might prefer most some alternative that happens to be unfeasible.

Barberà, Massó, and Neme (2004) studied the impact of feasibility constraints when the top of agent's preferences may be out of the range. They provide a characterization of all possible strategyproof rules for all conceivable constraints. Since this is a complex task, they do it for the simplified world that was first described in Barberà, Sonnenschein, and Zhou (1991), as described in Section 6.3.2. This is the world where each alternative can be described by a collection of characteristics, each of which is binary.

In that context, rules that satisfy strategyproofness are still voting by committees, with ballots indicating the best feasible alternative for each agent. Yet the committees for different objects (or combinations of characteristics, depending on the interpretation that we give to vectors of values) must now be interrelated, in precise ways that depend on what alternatives are feasible. Specifically, each family of feasible subsets (in one of the interpretations) will admit a unique decomposition, which in turn dictates the exact form of the strategyproof and onto social choice functions that can be defined on it. One important feature arising in that context is that results are more sensitive to the domain of admissible preferences than they are in all the contexts we have described up to now. Specifically, the class of rules that can be strategyproof when preferences are additively representable is substantially larger than the set of rules having that property when all separable single-peaked preferences are allowed. This is in contrast with the results in the preceding literature on k-dimensional grids, where the same characterizations obtain for both sets of restricted preferences.

The characterization of strategyproof rules for the case where all separable preferences are allowed is quite negative. The decomposition result implies that, except for very special cases, nondictatorial rules will be manipulable. In contrast, the result for additively representable preferences leaves a wider slack. Depending on the shapes of feasible alternatives, results with a positive flavor may arise, and strategyproof nondictatorial rules may exist.

The contrast between these results, allowing for restricted preferences whose best element need not be feasible, and the preceding results, is quite striking. The result in Barberà, Massó, and Neme (2004) is complex, even if restricted to the case where each dimension admits two values only. Not much could be gained by considering the more general case where multiple levels are allowed for in each of the relevant dimensions of an alternative. An exploration in this direction is to be found in Svensson and Torstensson (2008).

7. COMMON DOMAINS: PROBABILISTIC VOTING SCHEMES

Voting and chance have been combined as collective decision devices since ancient times. At one extreme, certain public officials were in the past and are even now chosen at random among those eligible for office. At the other, voting determines the outcome of the election to the last detail. But there are many variants in between, where agents vote and chance also plays a role in determining the final choice. In this section I will review work that explicitly models the outcomes of voting as lotteries. In the next section I will review social choice correspondences: while these admit different interpretations, many authors have actually analyzed them under the implicit or explicit assumption that the final choices among the different alternatives preselected by the correspondence will eventually be made by resorting to chance.[28]

The study of methods that combine voting with chance has a long tradition, but I shall restrict my account relating to incentive theory and start with the pioneering work of Zeckhauser (1973). The author provides a framework where agents are endowed with von Neumann–Morgenstern preferences over lotteries, and rules determine a lottery over alternatives as a function of preference profiles. He proposes a good definition of strategyproofness and discusses some of the characteristics of his proposed methods. His results on strategyproofness are partial and not fully correct (as shown years later by other authors), but the paper is inspiring and generated a number of follow-ups in different directions.

In fact, when modeling the interaction between voting and chance, one must be specific about the range of objects that will result from the interaction among voters, and also on the domain of preferences that the rule will elicit. In my opinion, the neatest choice for a range is to describe the outcomes of the voting process as lotteries (probability distributions) over outcomes. And the most natural choice for a domain, in that case, is to allow voters to express their preferences on such lotteries. This was Zeckhauser's initial proposal, and one that we shall explore.

Of course, not much mileage is to be gained from such a model unless some domain restrictions are predicated. Notice that, in the case of lotteries, it is natural to assume that their range contains a continuum of alternatives, even if they are based on a finite number of prizes, and this case is not fully covered by the Gibbard–Satterthwaite Theorem. Yet other results in the same spirit suggest that models that do not restrict the agent's preferences over lotteries would simply fall into the same kind of impossibility that is announced by the theorem.

Yet a very natural restriction arises in that context, and it is to assume that agents' preferences over lotteries satisfy the von Neumann–Morgenstern axioms (or some variant of them) and are therefore representable by utility functions satisfying the expected utility property.

To make things simpler, we will deal with *lotteries over a finite set of alternatives* A, and denote their set by $L(A)$.

[28] There is a substantial literature where social preferences are modeled as fuzzy relations. We shall not survey it here, especially because not much of it addresses the issue of strategyproofness. An exception is Perote and Piggins (2007).

Utility representations of preferences over $L(A)$ will be denoted by $u, v, \ldots$, and their set by U. We will assume that they are normalized in such a way that each preference is represented by one and only one function. In order to fix ideas, we will assume that the normalization is such that the most preferred alternative is assigned utility 1, the worse alternative has utility 0, and that not all alternatives can be indifferent to all others.

Then, our first object of study will be functions of the form $f : U^n \to L(A)$, where n stands for the number of voters.

I shall call them probabilistic rules. As for a definition of strategyproofness in that context, it is just a rewriting of the same notion we have discussed until now. Namely, a probabilistic rule f is strategyproof iff, for all utility profiles all $(u_1, \ldots, u_i, \ldots, u_n) \in U^n$, all $i \in \{1, \ldots, n\}$ and all $u_i' \in U$ we have that

$$u_i \cdot f(u_1, \ldots, u_i, \ldots, u_n) \geqslant u_i \cdot f(u_1, \ldots, u_i', \ldots, u_n).$$

Notice that this is, in a different notation, the same definition we have been using all along: the lottery resulting from any agent declaring his/her true preferences is at least as preferred (i.e., provides as much expected utility) as any one attainable by declaring any other preference (i.e., any other admissible utility function).

Even if this is a very natural setup, some early literature departed from this general model and considered an alternative scenario (which can in fact be reinterpreted as a particular case), where the outcomes are lotteries over outcomes and preferences are rankings of these outcomes.

According to the logic underlying this survey, these models appear to be poorly specified, since the preferences expressed by the voters do not refer directly to the objects to be chosen. Yet the models are attractive from a less formal point of view, since they can be considered the natural expression of voting rules that rely on the ordinal preferences of voters over outcomes, but introduce a chance element by determining that the result of the process is a lottery over these outcomes. Formally, they take the form

$$g : \mathcal{R}^n \to L(A)$$

where $\mathcal{R}$ stands for the set of preorders over A (alternatively, in some cases, for the set of strict orders).

This was the setup of a pioneering contribution by Gibbard (1977), who gave these functions the name of "decision schemes." He also proposed the following definition of strategyproofness in that context.

A decision scheme $g : \mathcal{R}^n \to L(A)$ is strategyproof iff, for all preferences profiles $(R_1, \ldots, R_i, \ldots, R_n)$, all $i \in \{1, \ldots, n\}$, all $R_i' \in \mathcal{R}$, and all "$u_i \in U$ *fitting* R_i,"

$$u_i \cdot g(R_1, \ldots, R_i, \ldots, R_n) \geqslant u_i \cdot g(R_1, \ldots, R_i', \ldots, R_n).$$

This definition may seem to incorporate an additional and somewhat extraneous element in the definition of strategyproofness. Indeed, the expression "u_i *fitting* R_i" refers to any $VN - M$ utility function that respects the ranking of alternatives established by R_i and it appears as an added element in the valuation of outcomes.

However, as I already mentioned, there is a way to reinterpret voting schemes as a particular subclass of probabilistic rules. And Gibbard's definition will become equivalent to the standard one under this reinterpretation, which I now offer.

Notice that, given preferences over lotteries ($v \in U$), they determine uniquely a pre-order over outcomes ($R \in \mathcal{R}$). Conversely, each order over outcomes can be identified with an equivalence class in U, naturally defined as the set of utility functions that give rise to the some order or even with a single one, if we accept the normalization suggested for the preceding class of models. In fact, given a v, the elements in its class are all the (normalized) utility functions that result from a monotone transformation of it. With this in view, we can consider that a voting scheme g is a particular probabilistic rule satisfying the following invariance property:

Invariance

For all n-tuples of monotonic transforms

$$\varphi i : U \rightarrow U, \text{ and all } (v_i, \ldots, v_n) \in U^n,$$
$$g(v_i, \ldots, v_n) = g(\varphi_i(v_i), \ldots, \varphi_n(v_n)).$$

This is equivalent to saying that such functions do not process any cardinal features of the $VN - M$ utility functions, but just the order of final outcomes.

Under this identification, Gibbard's definition becomes standard, if we think that the image of a scheme g will be the same for all of the utilities belonging to a given class, and yet it will suffice that one of the preferences over lotteries within the class recommends manipulation in order to violate the condition of strategyproofness class function.

We now turn to the known results about decision schemes. Even if the more general framework is that of probabilistic rules, it is good to start with Gibbard's (1977) results, since his characterization of strategyproof decision schemes is particularly elegant, and its knowledge will facilitate the presentation of other facts. Gibbard provides the following definitions, which I present somewhat informally.

- A decision scheme is *unilateral* if its image is exclusively determined by the preferences of one agent alone. Notice that a dictatorial rule, where the dictator's preferred outcome gets probability one, is unilateral. But another example is the rule where an agent's favorite alternative gets $\frac{2}{3}$, her second best gets $\frac{1}{6}$, and her third best another $\frac{1}{6}$.
- A decision scheme is *duple* if its image always consists of a lottery that attaches positive probability to at most two alternatives, which are always the same. An example of a duple scheme is one that preselects two alternatives x and y, never attaches any

probability to any other, and determines the choice probability of each of these two alternatives as a function of the support that agents give to one of them over the other.

- A decision scheme is *nonperverse* if switching the place of an alternative upward in an agent's ranking never decreases the weight attached to that alternative.
- A set X of alternatives *heads a ranking* P_k if all alternatives in X are preferred to those in $V - X$ according to P_k. A decision scheme d is *localized* iff for any agent k and any pair of preference profiles $(P_i, \dots, P_k, \dots, P_n)$ and $(P_i, \dots, P_k^{'}, \dots, P_n)$, which only differ in k's preference, if X heads both P_k and $P_k^{'}$, the total weight attached by the scheme to alternatives in X is the same for both profiles.

We can now state Gibbard's elegant characterization of strategyproof decision schemes.

Theorem 9 (Gibbard 1977) *A decision scheme is strategyproof if and only if it is a probability mixture of decision schemes, each of which is nonperverse, localized, and either unilateral or duple.*

The above statement uses the term "probability mixture" to describe the combination of rules attaching to each profile a convex combination of the lotteries obtained by each of the decision scheme that would be "mixed." Since the outcomes of each of these decisions are lotteries over the same set of alternatives, convex combinations of these lotteries are well defined.

An important corollary of the above characterization is due to Sonnenschein (cited in Gibbard).

Corollary 1 *A decision scheme is strategyproof and ex post efficient if and only if it is a random dictatorship (for* $\#A \succcurlyeq 3$).

Ex post efficiency requires that no alternative that is Pareto dominated ever gets a chance of being chosen. Clearly, ex post efficiency rules out the possibility of duple schemes being part of the decomposition of a strategyproof scheme. It also rules out the possibility of unilateral schemes allowing for a positive probability to dominated alternatives. What is left is random dictatorship: the probability mixture of dictatorial schemes.

Gibbard's characterization, and its corollary, have been usually interpreted as rather negative, but this involves some fallacy of composition. While unilateral and duple schemes are certainly unattractive, their probability mixtures need not be. In fact, Barberà (1979b) provides a number of results proving that Gibbard's class contains rather attractive methods, which result from the natural extensions to a probabilistic framework of the two basic properties used in making deterministic choices: majority and positional (or point) voting. These positive results, in turn, must be taken with a grain of salt, since all these schemes could be manipulated to the benefit of two-agent coalitions (Barberà 1979a, Dutta 1980b).

A necessary qualification to Gibbard's characterization result is that it only applies when individual preferences over alternatives are strict. When indifferences are allowed, the same general idea still applies, but hierarchies of agents enter the picture in a complex manner (see Gibbard 1978, and Benoît 2002).

Gibbard's proof is constructive and elegant but complicated. Nandeibam (1998) and Duggan (1996) provided simpler proofs of the main corollary of the result, for the special case where efficiency is also required.

I have already noted in Sections 1 and 2 that the connections between Arrow's and Gibbard and Satterthwaite's results were the subject of a lot of attention. An analog parallel was established by Pattanaik and Peleg (1986) and by McLennan (1980) among Gibbard's strategyproof decision schemes and the probabilistic analogs of Arrow's social welfare functions studied in Barberà and Sonnenschein (1978).

A few papers have investigated the properties of rules that choose lotteries over more structured alternatives. Ehlers, Peters, and Storcken (2002) studied rules that choose lotteries over the real line, when the ordinal preferences of agents are single-peaked. They proved that an extension of Moulin's results for social choice functions does characterize the decision schemes satisfying strategyproofness. In this extension, fixed probability distributions play the role that phantom voters (or fixed ballots) play in the deterministic case.

A further extension is due to Dutta, Peters, and Sen (2002). In that case, lotteries are defined over a convex set of Euclidean spaces, and agents are endowed with strictly convex, continuous single-peaked preferences on that set. Their main result is that all unanimous mechanisms satisfying strategyproofness in the sense of Gibbard (1977) must be random dictatorships. Ehlers (2002) analyzes probablilistic methods when preferences are single-dipped. In this work, and also in Ehlers and Klaus (2003b), applications of probabilistic rules to assignment problems are discussed.

I now turn to the study of probabilistic rules, which assign a lottery to any profile of preferences over lotteries satisfying the axioms of expected utility. To my knowledge, a full characterization of strategyproof probabilistic rules is not available, but it is possible to go a long way in the understanding of such rules by following the path of the previous results by Gibbard (1977), and adapting its definitions to the present (and larger) framework.

Let us first extend the notion of a unilateral rule.

Select any subset of lotteries, and consider the function obtained by letting a single fixed agent select the best lottery from that set (given any profile). Such a function (if well defined) will be a unilateral probabilistic rule, and it will obviously be strategyproof. Depending on the set's characteristics, the chosen agent's best set may contain several lotteries. In that case, we may extend the notion to that of *hierarchically unilateral* rules. These are defined by some fixed set of alternatives and a given order of agents, in such a way that, for any profile, the first agent in the list selects her best lotteries, the second chooses her best among those, the third agent picks her best among those still left, and so on. Eventually, a fixed tie-breaking rule may be appended to guarantee that a unique choice is finally made.

Gibbard's notion of a duple scheme can also be extended. Now, one can fix any two lotteries[29] and declare that a probabilistic rule is *duple* if it always selects a convex combination of the two. Clearly, if the choice is made in such a way that the probabilities attached to each of the basic lotteries responds "adequately" to the preferences of agents over them, this gives rise to strategyproof rules. For the purpose of the following statement, we incorporate into the definition of a duple the notion that it properly responds to agent's preferences.

Proposition 1 (Barberà, Bogomolnaia, and van der Stel 1998) *All probabilistic mixtures of (hierarchically) unilateral and duple probabilistic (social choice) functions are strategyproof.*

Notice that this falls short of a characterization à la Gibbard, because the converse is not present. Proving that all strategyproof rules are in that shape is a hard task. To begin with, the set of alternatives in this context is a continuum, and the type of constructive proof provided by Gibbard is a nonstarter. Moreover, hierarchical versions of duples are also strategyproof and hard to describe. At any rate, the proposition above allows for a number of interesting qualifications. One is that, in this context, it makes sense to extend the notion of probabilistic mixtures even to consider integrals of probabilistic rules. Another one is that some rules may now be expressed as combinations of duples and also as combinations of unilaterals (an added difficulty for a full characterization). Most importantly, it allows us to prove a partial result that explains the difficulties to design well-behaved strategyproof functions, even when they exist.

Proposition 2 (Barberà, Bogomolnaia, and van der Stel 1998) *If a strategyproof probabilistic social choice function is twice continuously differentiable, then it is a convex combination of unilaterals.*

This result was improved by Bogomolnaia (1998), who relaxed the continuity requirement. It shows that strategyproofness requires, in a deep sense, some form of discontinuity, as also shown in other contexts. In fact, early results by Freixas (1984) had already bumped into this kind of difficulty, when applying the standard techniques developed by Laffont and Maskin (1979).

Again, if one requires efficiency, the only possible rules to satisfy strategyproofness collapse to random dictatorship, as in the case of decision schemes. This was proven by Hylland (1980). For a new proof and some additional results in this context, see Dutta, Peters, and Sen (2007).

[29] Notice that duples, in Gibbard's sense, can only be based on degenerate lotteries.

8. COMMON DOMAINS: SOCIAL CHOICE CORRESPONDENCES

The Gibbard–Satterthwaite Theorem, and many of the results that ensued, apply to social choice functions—that is, to rules that select one alternative, and only one, for each preference profile. Yet in many cases, collective decision processes are formalized by means of correspondences. These allow for nonempty sets of alternatives, not necessarily singletons, to be associated with each preference profile. That formalization may be natural under different interpretations. If we view social choices as the maximal elements of some social preference relation, then sets will be chosen if more than one alternative is best. If we seek some symmetry in the treatment of voters and/or alternatives, sets should be chosen under preference profiles that are highly symmetric. But this formalization also requires an appropriate interpretation. Since alternatives are mutually exclusive, the images of a social choice correspondence cannot be interpreted as giving a final social outcome. Some different interpretation must be provided, to connect the choice of a set of alternatives with the choice of a single social outcome, and the most common is as follows. The set is interpreted as the result of a first screening process, after which every alternative in the set, and no other, is still a candidate to be the final choice. Different assumptions about the process to be used for the final selection will result in different methods to evaluate the individual preference for sets. And, as we shall see immediately, these evaluations are crucial to make sense of the notions of manipulation and strategyproofness, when applied to correspondences.

Many models in economics and in politics formalize collective decision making by means of multivalued rules, or correspondences. The Walrasian correspondence assigns to each economy the set of allocations that are sustained as equilibria of this economy, for some price vector. Typically, there will be several such allocations for the same economy. Similarly, the core correspondence in economic or political games assigns to each relevant game the set of imputations in its core. Again, this set is seldom a singleton. Arrovian social welfare functions assign a social preference to each profile of individual preferences, and it is usually understood that the social preference will be used to choose the socially preferred among the feasible alternatives. Once more, there may be several of them, once we accept that the social preference might be a preorder.

As a matter of fact, most of the analysis of incentives in public decision making does benefit from formalizing such processes by means of correspondences, rather than functions. Implementation theory, with its multiple possibility results, would collapse to little if one restricted attention to social choice functions alone.

Yet, the study of strategyproofness for social choice correspondences has been quite problematic, especially because different authors interpret these objects in different manners. In social choice theory, alternatives are defined as being mutually exclusive: if an alternative a occurs, then any other alternative b cannot occur. Hence, the meaning of having more than one alternative socially chosen must be clarified. In general terms, there is agreement to interpret the set of alternatives resulting at a given preference profile as the result of some screening process: alternatives not selected do not qualify as adequate. But it is unusual to specify how a final choice is to be made among those that pass the screening.

In many cases, being silent about the resolution of this indeterminacy does not pose any problems. Which competitive allocation or what core allocation will prevail when there are several are not essential issues in economic analysis. But this silence becomes a problem when trying to define strategyproofness.

Consider social choice correspondences, of the form

$$c : \mathcal{R}^n \to 2^A \backslash \emptyset.$$

Intuitively, this correspondence is manipulable iff for some profile of preferences some agent can obtain a better result by misrepresenting her preferences than by declaring them truthfully. Yet the outcomes at the truthful and the nontruthful profile may both be sets of alternatives, and who knows when a set is better than another? Certainly not the analyst who studies the model, unless additional assumptions are made, allowing the extension of the voter's preferences from the set of alternatives to its power set.

A possible reaction to this difficulty is to declare social choice correspondences as being poorly specified. If agents choose sets of alternatives, they should be asked about preferences on sets, not on alternatives in isolation. I shall go back to this point of view when describing the work of Barberà, Dutta, and Sen (2000). However, the use of social choice correspondences is pervasive, and it is worth pursuing the issue as we have formulated it. One should keep in mind, though, that all the literature on strategy-proof correspondences must include some implicit or explicit assumption about the way in which agents rank sets of alternatives, even if this information is extraneous to the description of the correspondence, when its domain simply contains rankings of alternatives.

Because of the instant success of the Gibbard–Satterthwaite result, there was an early literature concerning the possibility of extending it to the case of correspondences. Different authors took different paths in doing it. The essential difference among them was in regard to their assumptions about preferences over sets. Clearly, there was no need to be specific about the complete extension of preferences R from alternatives to their power set. It was enough to allow for some partial comparisons among sets in order to get manipulability of correspondences.

To illustrate the nature of these assumptions, let us consider three of the routes taken by early papers in this field. They can be expressed as assumptions on the connections between the preferences R on alternatives and the preferences $\mathfrak{R}$ on sets.

Gärdenfors (1976) based his analysis on the following assumption on how these preferences were connected:

Gärdenfors' Partial Extension

For all nonempty subsets A and B of X, $A\mathfrak{R}_G B$ iff one of the following conditions is satisfied:

(i) $A \subset B$, and for all $x \in A$ and $y \in B - A$, xRy.
(ii) $B \subset A$, and for all $x \in A - B$ and $y \in B$, xRy.
(iii) Neither $A \subset B$ nor $B \subset A$, and for all $x \in A - B$ and $y \in B - A$, xRy.

From the general definition of the strict relation it follows that $A\mathfrak{P}_G B$ iff either (i) and there exist $x \in A$ and $y \in B - A$ such that xPy or (ii) and there exist $x \in A - B$ and $y \in B$ such that xPy or (iii) and there exist $x \in A - B$ and $y \in B - A$ such that xPy.

Another early proposal was due to Kelly (1977):

Kelly's Partial Extension

For all nonempty subsets A and B of X, $A\mathfrak{R}_K B$ iff xRy for all $x \in A$ and $y \in B$.

From this definition it is easy to show that $A\mathfrak{P}_K B$ iff $A\mathfrak{R}_K B$ and there exist $x \in A$ and $y \in B$ such that xPy.

A third proposal was made by Barberà (1977a):

Barberà's Partial Extension

If xPy, then $\{x\}\mathfrak{P}_B\{x, y\}\mathfrak{P}_B\{y\}$.

Notice that these three criteria imply that some comparisons among sets are possible, once we know the agent's preferences, while they do not assume all sets to be comparable. Each one of them was used to obtain an impossibility result that was analogous to the one by Gibbard and Satterthwaite, under some additional conditions.

Before turning to the rest of the literature, let me mention some of the difficulties associated with these early attempts, and with many later ones.

First of all, how should one judge the merits of some suggested extension vis-à-vis those of another proposal? From a formal point of view, the weaker the extension, the stronger the impossibility result that one would obtain. In that respect, *cæteris paribus*, an impossibility obtained under Barberà's extension would be stronger than one obtained by using any of the other two, since it would require less assumptions about the voter's way to rank sets. However, the results in any of these three papers are not strictly comparable. This is because each of the authors had to introduce some additional assumption in order to get an impossibility result: Gärdenfors assumed anonymity and neutrality conditions on its rules; Barberà assumed a positive response property; Kelly imposed a consistency requirement across the choices that the rule would make if some alternatives were dropped.

In balance, the literature on strategyproof social choice correspondences confirms the robustness of the Gibbard–Satterthwaite impossibility result. Although some additional requirements are needed, and technical problems tend to mar the sharpness of their statements, most contributions end up proving some analog of the classic result for functions in the multivalued case. From that point of view, the different results reinforce each other: any combination of conditions that induces an impossibility is informative, and all of them taken together establish that there is not significant room for strategyproofness that results from relaxing the single-valuedness assumption.

In spite of that, some authors have explored the general issue from a more relativistic viewpoint. Alan Feldman (1979a, 1979b, 1980), in a series of interesting articles, investigated the extent to which different definitions of strategyproofness for social choice correspondences would precipitate impossibilities or rather allow for some possibility results. In particular, he examined the question for the Pareto rule under a variety of definitions. He concluded that this important rule would be considered manipulable under some definitions, and not for others.

One author who deserves special mention again is Pattanaik. As I have already pointed out, he was close to the same result that Gibbard and Satterthwaite attained, but his results were not as neat because he was working in a context similar to that of Arrow: he considered rules whose outcomes were binary relations, and this led him also to deal with the connections between the choices that such relations would induce under different agendas, or subsets of alternatives. One of the questions that arises naturally in that context, if one follows Arrow's tradition to allow for social preorders, is that social choices are often multivalued. Hence, Pattanaik (1973, 1974, 1978) usually assumed that when comparing different sets, agents would use some form of the maximin rule. Another issue in that context is the consistency of choices across agendas, an issue that Gibbard and Satterthwaite did avoid only by dealing with functions that choose an alternative from the complete agenda, and being silent about choices when not all alternatives are available. Part of the early literature on strategyproofness of social choice correspondences inherited from Arrow and Pattanaik's formulation in requiring some consistency conditions. See Kelly (1977) and Barberà (1977b), for example, as well as many of the results surveyed in Muller and Satterthwaite (1985). We will go back to this issue in Section 10.1.

Until now I have referred to different proposals on how to make assumptions regarding preferences of sets that are not explicit in the model, but described them as purely formal. A richer point of view is to discuss the merits of each of these extension proposals by referring to specific interpretation of correspondences. In fact, people may rank sets of alternatives in many different ways, depending on the meaning of such sets. Barberà, Bossert, and Pattanaik (2004) contains an extensive review of several strands of literature about set rankings and their connections with underlying rankings of singletons. Parts of that literature are of interest to those attempting to define strategyproofness for correspondences.

What are the leading interpretations for a correspondence? Not all authors are explicit about it, but one very common assumption is that some random device will eventually be used to "break the ties" and choose one of the alternatives in the image of the correspondence. In an early survey of different criteria to partially rank sets, Gärdenfors (1976) was quite explicit about the fact that many of the proposals had this interpretation in the background. However, other authors insist that this interpretation is only one among several.

After a period when the issue was not much under discussion, the question of manipulation of social choice correspondences made a comeback. As we shall see, the interpretation of sets of alternatives as the basis for some unspecified lottery was quite explicit in that later work.

But there were exceptions. As I already mentioned, some authors reject quite explicitly the interpretation that the images of social choice correspondences are the basis for lotteries. Campbell and Kelly (2002a, 2003b) propose other alternative interpretations and define manipulability under set comparisons that are justified by other means. Specifically, leximin orderings of sets are used to establish a number of impossibility results regarding the existence of strategyproof nonresolute social choice procedures. In a similar spirit, see also Sato (2008); his results are extended by Rodríguez-Álvarez (2009). Nehring (2000) discusses the relationship between the properties of monotonicity and a generalized version of strategyproofness for correspondences. Özyurt and Sanver (2009) provide a general impossibility result when preferences over sets are based on lexicographic orderings. Other variants of the topic include the analysis of group strategyproof correspondences (Umezawa 2009), or the study of the consequences of imposing restrictions on the size of the chosen sets of alternatives (Campbell and Kelly 2000, Özyurt and Sanver 2008). The latter is connected with the analysis of multidimensional alternatives discussed in Section 6.3.

Duggan and Schwartz (2000) worked within the classical framework of social choice correspondences. They define a correspondence to be manipulable if there exist an individual, a "true" preference, and a "false" ranking, such that for every lottery over the set obtained by lying, and for every lottery obtained from telling the truth, there is an expected utility function consistent with the voter's true ranking of basic alternatives for which the expected utility of the first lottery exceeds the expected utility of the second.

This definition is quite demanding, and it is not easy to prove an impossibility result without, again, some additional conditions. Duggan and Schwartz manage to keep such conditions at a minimum, by showing that there will always be such types of manipulation when there are at least three alternatives, for all correspondences satisfying citizen sovereignty, nondictatorship, and what they call residual resoluteness. This last-named condition requires the correspondence to choose singletons for some special profiles. Rodríguez-Álvarez (2007) provide an alternative proof and extension of the result.

Ching and Zhou (2002, p. 571) also consider social choice correspondences. Their definition is also based on interpreting their images as the basis for some lottery, and on the explicit assumption that individuals will be "Bayesian rational," in the following sense:

> *He has a priori a subjective probability measure μ_i over A as well as a von Neumann–Morgenstern utility function u_i over A. Then for any subsets X and Y of A, he can compare X and Y by calculating the expected values of u_i conditional on X and Y: he ranks X over Y if and only if $E_{\mu|X}u_i \geq E_{\mu|Y}u_i$. This actually induces a complete ranking of subsets of A. Of course, this ranking depends on both μ_i and u_i, and information of neither is contained in R_i. Hence, if only R_i is known, then X might be ranked above Y for one particular set of choices of μ_i and u_i, consistent with R_i, but below Y for some different choices of μ_i and u_i also consistent with R_i. Nonetheless, for some pairs of subsets X and Y, such comparisons always lead to the same ranking.*

In fact, Ching and Zhou proceed to characterize the cases where the comparisons of sets are unambiguous, in that the ranking of one above the other is independent of the chosen expectation and utility. A subset X of alternatives will always be preferred in that sense to a subset Y if and only if

(i) aR_ib for all $a \in X\backslash Y$ and $a \in Y$ if $X\backslash Y \neq 0$, and
(ii) cR_id for all $c \in X$ and $d \in Y\backslash X$ if $Y\backslash X \neq 0$.

After this observation, they define a correspondence to be strategyproof if it is not unambiguously manipulable by a Bayesian rational voter.

With this definition in hand, they prove that any social choice correspondence is either dictatorial or constant (of course, when there are at least three alternatives).

Ching and Zhou's paper avoids the need for any further assumptions regarding the correspondence, and it is thus one of the closest in spirit to the Gibbard–Satterthwaite result. This neat result is obtained with a definition of manipulation that is less stringent than the one used by Duggan and Schwartz.

The analysis of strategyproofnessness for social choice correspondences that we have reported departs a bit from the standard approach, where the preferences of agents are defined over the classes of objects to be socially elected. Barberà, Dutta, and Sen (2000) did propose a framework that tackles the same issues within a framework that is closer to that of the rest of the literature. The starting point is that if social choices are sets, then one may want to study those functions where agent's inputs are preferences over sets. This is in line with the approach in the preceding section, where social choice functions whose outcomes are lotteries are defined on preferences over lotteries. Hence, they study functions of the form $f : D \rightarrow A$, where D is the family of nonempty subsets of A and D is some collection of preferences over A. Notice that, because of this change in domain, we are back to the realm of social choice functions, with the explicit specification that their outcomes are sets of basic objects.

Because of that, it is unnecessary to redefine strategyproofness: the standard notion applies.

Obviously, the Gibbard–Satterthwaite impossibility applies if no domain restriction is assumed. But again, the special structure of the outcomes, the fact that they are sets of objects, allows for specific interpretations of the model, and these in turn suggest that some domain restrictions become relevant.

I feel that this approach opens the door for many different inquiries regarding rules that choose among sets. Each interpretation will suggest some natural restriction for preferences over sets. This will allow a study of the possibility of designing procedures that satisfy strategyproofness, or some other properties, within such domains.

In particular, Barberà, Dutta, and Sen (2000) explored the consequences of adopting the interpretation that these sets are the basis for some lottery, and assuming different degrees of information on the part of voters regarding the random device to be used in selecting the final result.

They define a preference over sets to be conditionally expected utility consistent if there is a utility function over basic objects and a lottery on these objects, with the following property: the expected utility of each set, calculated over the given distribution, conditional to this set being chosen, generates the same given preference ranking.

They also consider a narrower domain of preferences, called conditionally expected utility consistent with equal probabilities, where the above expected utility calculations are always made with respect to equal chance lotteries.

These two domains are important per se. Specifically, restricting the domain of definition to the first class of preferences over sets, and then applying the standard definition of strategyproofness for social choice functions, is equivalent to applying Ching and Zhou's (2002) definition of strategyproofness for social choice correspondences. In both cases it is assumed that an agent can manipulate when forming preferences over sets by attributing a given lottery to this set and a given utility to its elements. The further restriction to even-chance lotteries conforms with an old tradition, for which the natural way to resolve the uncertainty among the alternatives chosen by a correspondence is to give all of them the same chance to be elected.

The results of Barberà, Dutta, and Sen (2000) refer to social choice functions that respect unanimity. Under the first domain restriction, only dictatorial rules can be strategyproof. Under the second domain, a new but very restricted set of nondictatorial rules can also emerge: those where the chosen set consists of the best elements of two predetermined agents. These functions are called bi-dictatorial.

The first result is very close to Ching and Zhou's (2002). But these authors do not impose unanimity, and this is why they do not rule out constant functions. As for bi-dictatorial rules, Feldman (1979b) had already referred to them in one of his extensive analyses of different rules under different definitions of strategyproofness.

Benoît (1999) also studied the manipulation of rules where agents reveal preferences over sets in order to choose sets. But his assumptions on individual preferences are not based on expected utility maximization. He requires that certain orderings should be within the domain: he calls them "top" and "bottom" orderings, because they are based on the value of their best (or worst) alternative. With the help of a strong unanimity assumption, he also obtains an impossibility result. It is worth noting that these domain restrictions are completely different than those considered by Barberà, Dutta, and Sen: different interpretations suggest different restrictions on the same models.

Since the basic conclusion of this analysis is that no attractive rules emerge, I also take this line of research as further confirmation of the robustness of the basic impossibility result.

9. STRATEGYPROOFNESS IN PERSONALIZED DOMAINS

In the case of common preferences we have modeled situations where agents do care for alternatives in ways that are potentially the same for all. The same preferences on A can be held by all agents; unanimity is not required, but nor is it precluded.

In other cases, the views of agents are necessarily conflictive. When we must split a dollar, distribute a bunch of desirable objects, decide who will perform an indivisible and unpleasant task, alternatives have to specify how much each one of us may get, or who is to work. Then, alternatives that are best for an agent will typically rank low for others, and unanimity is not to be expected. The sets of admissible preferences for agents over alternatives will not be common, but specific to each agent. In addition it will often be natural to assume that different alternatives assigning the same consequences to one agent are indifferent to her, even if they affect others in quite varied forms. This is the assumption of selfishness, which involves a particular form of specific preferences. Many different collective choice situations are well described by models where the set of agent's preferences over alternatives are specific. The analysis of strategyproof social choice functions in these contexts is more intricate than for those cases considered until now. This is partly due to the fact that unanimity can play a much weaker role in proofs. Another added complication, which we have skipped until now, is that strict preferences over the whole set of alternatives may not be admissible.

I will illustrate the analysis of strategyproof rules in the personalized preferences case by describing results referring to four types of allocation problems.

9.1. Strategyproof Rationing

We will now consider cases where a group of agents must share a task or a good. Examples include division of a job among individuals who have collectively agreed to complete it, distributing assets among creditors in a bankruptcy, sharing the cost of a public project or the surplus of a joint venture, or rationing goods traded at fixed prices. Since shares of the total task, or of the total amount of good, are the specific objects of choice, individuals are assumed to have preferences on shares.[30]

Notice here that the alternatives are the distributions of the total among all agents. Since we will be modeling situations where each agent only cares about her share of the total, preferences will not be common. Agent i will be indifferent about any two alternatives that give her the same share, but j will not be, if these two alternatives give her different amounts. We shall not be insisting on this, and just refer to agents' preferences over their own shares, rather than over complete alternatives. But it is worth making the point here, since the fact will make a difference on the results. We will examine the class of problems where preferences of agents are selfish and single-peaked over their own shares. This is well justified if we think of a reduced model, where the task assignment carries some reward, or the share of one good obtained must be paid for. It is then perfectly natural to prefer some amount of the task or good over all other amounts (and their accompanying rewards/costs), and to consider other amounts better the closer to their ideal. In fact, this would be a consequence of assuming convex, increasing preferences in the effort/reward on good/cost space, and of having the agent choose her share on a convex bounded set.

Formally, for finite set of agents $N = \{1, \ldots, n\}$, allotments will be n-tuples a in the set $A = \left\{a \in [0,1]^n \mid \sum_{i \in N} a_i = 1\right\}$. Preferences being selfish and continuous, they can be identified with continuous utility functions on $[0,1]$, denoted by $u_i, u_i', u_j, \ldots$. These utility functions will represent single-peaked preferences. That is, for each u_i there will be some $x^* \in [0,1]$ such that, for any $y, z \in [0,1]$,

$$x^* < y < z \Rightarrow u_i\left(x^*\right) > u_i(y) > u_i(z),$$

and

$$x^* > y > z \Rightarrow u_i\left(x^*\right) > u_i(y) > u_i(z).$$

Denote by S the set of all continuous single-peaked utility functions on $[0,1]$. We will be interested in allotment rules of the form

$$f : S^n \to [0,1]^n$$

with

$$\sum_{i \in N} f_i(u) = 1 \text{ for all } u \in S^n.$$

[30] An analysis of a similar problem when the good to share is not homogeneous can be found in Thomson (2007).

Notice that u stands for a profile of preferences, $(u_1, \ldots, u_n)$. The value of $f_i(u)$ is the share that goes to i under preference profile u, given rule f.

Some standard requirements, like efficiency and anonymity, can be applied to allotment rules. Efficiency requires that the selected allotment be Pareto efficient at each preference profile. When coupled with the requirement that preferences are single-peaked it is equivalent to the following: at each preferences profile, agents that do not get exactly their ideal point must either all get less than what they wished, or all get more.

Anonymity is a property of symmetric treatment for all agents: for all permutations π of N (π is a function from N onto N) and $u \in S^n$, $f_{\pi(i)}(u^\pi) = f_i(u)$, where $u^\pi = (u_{\pi^{-1}(1)}, \ldots, u_{\pi^{-1}(n)})$. As we shall discuss, anonymity may or may not be an attractive property of allotment rules, depending on the a priori rights of the agents involved.

Finally, in our context, strategyproofness can be written as the requirement that, for all $i \in N$, $u \in S^n$ and $v_i \in S$,

$$u_i(f_i(u)) \geq u_i(f_i(u_{-i}, v_i)).$$

An elegant result due to Sprumont (1991) provides a full characterization of allotment rules satisfying the three requirements of efficiency, anonymity, and strategy-proofness. Actually, only one rule can satisfy all three simultaneously.

Theorem 10 (Sprumont 1991) *An allotment rule is efficient, strategyproof, and anonymous if and only if it is the uniform rule f^* defined by*

$$f_i^*(u) = \begin{cases} \min\left[x^*(u_i), \lambda(u)\right] & \text{if } \sum_{i \in N} x^*(u_i) \geq 1 \\ \max\left[x^*(u_i), \mu(u)\right] & \text{if } \sum_{i \in N} x^*(u_i) \leq 1 \end{cases}$$

where $\lambda(u)$ solves $\Sigma_{i\in N}\min[x^*(u_i), \lambda(u)] = 1$ and $\mu(u)$ solves $\Sigma_{i\in N}\max[x^*(u_i), \mu(u)] = 1$.

Notice that Ching (1992, 1994), Schummer and Thomson (1997), Thomson (2003), and Weymark (1999b) have provided alternative characterizations of this rule. Ehlers (2000) has extended the analysis to the case of single-plateau preferences.

In order to relate this result to previous ones, as well as to understand its possible extensions to the nonanonymous case, let us take a second look at the case where only two individuals must share. This case does not capture all the features of the problem, but gives us some interesting hints. With two agents, the allotment is fully described by a_1 since $a_2 = 1 - a_1$. Hence, the preferences of agent 2 can be expressed as preferences on a_1 as well, by letting $\tilde{u}_2(a_1) = u_2(1 - a_1)$. Clearly, $\tilde{u}_2$ is continuous and single-peaked whenever u_2 is. The allotment problem is now reduced to choosing a single point in $[0, 1]$ when both agents have preferences which are single-peaked over the same variable. We have already seen that anonymity and strategyproofness force us to use the rule that chooses medians among the agents' peaks and one phantom. By symmetry, this phantom must be at $\frac{1}{2}$ in our case. It is easily seen that this is exactly the uniform rule for this simple case.

We can interpret the rule as giving each agent the implicit right to guarantee herself the (one half–one half) distribution. From this guaranteed level, mutually desired improvements can be achieved. A similar interpretation for the n-person case would start by guaranteeing the egalitarian share ($\frac{1}{n}$ of the total) to each agent. Changing these guaranteed levels, while keeping the possibility of mutually consented changes away from them, would be a natural way to eliminate anonymity while keeping efficiency and strategyproofness. In particular, for the two-person case, this would be equivalent to maintaining the median rule, but having a phantom at any point $p \in [0,1]$ different than $\frac{1}{2}$, thus guaranteeing agent 1 the share of p, and for agent 2 the share $1-p$.

But why drop anonymity at all? The reason is that in many situations people may have different rights or entitlements: these may be respected, while allowing agents who do not want to use them to pass on their rights and allow others to enjoy what they do not need. Age, seniority, previous contribution are all examples of criteria calling for possibly nonsymmetric treatment of agents, while efficiency and strategyproofness are still desirable. Surprisingly, there is only one anonymous rule satisfying efficiency and strategyproofness, but there is a continuum of nonanonymous rules with the two latter properties. One of the apparent reasons is that implicit rights can vary; moreover, they can change quite independently in the cases of excess demand from these of excess supply. To see this, let us take a final look at the uniform allotment rule, and at its possible modifications. This time we can look at an example, with $n=5$ agents with ideal points $x_1^*=\frac{3}{20}$, $x_2^*=\frac{2}{20}$, $x_3^*=\frac{5}{20}$, $x_4^*=\frac{6}{20}$, $x_5^*=\frac{14}{20}$. The outcome prescribed by the uniform rule can be reached through the following algorithm (see Sönmez 1994):

Step 1. Determine whether $\Sigma_{i\in N}x^*(u_i)$ equals, exceeds, or falls short of 1. If $\Sigma_{i\in N}x^*(u_i)=1$, then allot shares equal to the ideal points. If $\Sigma_{i\in N}x^*(u_i)>1$, allot their ideal points to those agents who demand no more than $\frac{1}{n}$. If $\Sigma_{i\in N}x^*(u_i)<1$, allot their ideal point to those agents who demand at least $\frac{1}{n}$. In our case, $\Sigma_{i\in N}x^*(u_i)>1$, and agent 1 and 3's ideal points are less than $\frac{1}{5}$. Thus, $a_1=\frac{3}{20}$ and $a_3=\frac{2}{20}$.

Step 2. Determine the remaining number of agents to be allotted and the remaining share to be allotted. Say there are k agents and an amount s to be shared. Perform the same procedure as in Step 1, letting s replace 1 and considering only the k agents. Iterate this step until all the k' remaining agents have ideal points exceeding (or falling short of) $\frac{s'}{k'}$.

In our case, $k=3$ and $s=\frac{15}{20}$. Agent 2 is allotted $a_2=\frac{5}{20}$. There are now $k'=2$ agents remaining with $s'=\frac{10}{20}$. Each has an ideal point that exceeds $\frac{s'}{k'}=\frac{5}{20}$.

Step 3. Allot the remaining $\frac{s'}{k'}$ each.

In our case $a_4 = a_5 = \frac{5}{20}$.

We conclude that agents are allotted the shares $\left(\frac{3}{20}, \frac{5}{20}, \frac{2}{20}, \frac{5}{20}, \frac{5}{20}\right)$, which corresponds to the outcome of the uniform rule with $\lambda(u) = \frac{5}{20} = \frac{1}{4}$.

The above description suggests possible ways to create new nonanonymous allotment rules in similar ways (and thus with good chances to still buy strategyproofness and efficiency).

(1) Rather than have $\frac{1}{n}$ as a starting reference point, choose any collection of shares q_i such that $\Sigma_{i \in N} q_i = 1$.
(2) Rather than having the same reference point for the cases of $\Sigma_{i \in N} x^* (u_i) < 1$ and $\Sigma_{i \in N} x^* (u_i) > 1$, choose different reference points q_i^L and q_i^H.
(3) Let the reference levels depend on the share remaining in each iteration of Step 2 (with enough qualifications on the form of this dependence, in order to preserve strategyproofness).

The above remarks can lead to a characterization of wide classes of efficient and strategyproof allotment rules. This is done in Barberà, Jackson, and Neme (1997), although the article also presents examples that indicate the need for qualifications of the suggested steps for technical reasons. But the essence is in what we have described: there are many reasonable and quite satisfactory ways to design allotment rules, if we can expect preferences on shares to be single-peaked.

Several extensions of the model allow for the use of probabilistic procedures in order to allocate indivisible goods, and provide characterizations that combine strategyproofness and additional properties. Ehlers and Klaus (2003b) establish the connection between this probabilistic framework and Sprumont's results. Other papers in this vein are Kureishi (2000) and Sasaki (1997).

The same positive message is conveyed by Moulin (1999). He proves that strategyproof rationing schemes can be defined, satisfying three other desirable conditions: efficiency, resource monotonicity, and efficiency. Moreover, he shows that these four properties characterize the family of fixed path mechanisms. These procedures are defined by certain pairs of monotonic paths, and they include the uniform rule, the priority rule, and many possible combinations of them.

Unfortunately, this property cannot be expected to hold for agent's preferences on richer types of alternatives, and in particular in the traditional case of exchange economies, where more than one good is to be distributed. We discuss this in the next section.

9.2. Strategyproof Exchange

One of the most classical models in economics is that of an exchange economy. Typically, there are n consumers holding initial endowments of l private goods (however, some models keep silent about the distribution of endowments to the extent that some negative results arise even when this is unspecified). No production takes place. Consumers can exchange among themselves and reallocate the existing amounts of goods. This model emphasizes that preference diversity is an important basis for the existence of mutually advantageous trade among economic agents. Because of that, it is also an important testing ground for questions on preference revelation.

The cost of strategyproofness in exchange economies is efficiency. It has been shown that in exchange economies strategyproof social choice functions that are efficient are also dictatorial. Hurwicz (1972) proved that result for two agents and two goods, for functions satisfying the added requirement of individual rationality with respect to the initial endowment. The result was largely extended in Hurwicz and Walker (1990), who identify classes of preferences for which efficiency and strategyproofness do conflict. Zhou (1991b) proved that this negative result holds for two people even without the assumption of individual rationality. Some of his further conjectures in this paper have been qualified by Kato and Ohseto (2002). Serizawa (2002) extended Hurwicz's result to economies with any finite number of agents.

Zhou's theorem has been extended by Schummer (1997), Ju (2003, 2004), and Hashimoto (2008) to more restrictive domain. These *small domain* results are especially interesting methodologically, because they exhibit very clearly what are the essential features that precipitate impossibilities. Ju considers several domains of interest, including the linear and the CES preference domain, and also risk averse preferences in the context of risk sharing. Schummer's impossibility obtains for the domain of homothetic, strictly convex preferences.

This is in apparent contrast, but in fact nicely complementary, with the results of Nicolò (2004). Under the assumption that individual preferences are only of the generalized Leontieff form, he produces possibility results that are, however, very useful in understanding the difficulties of extending them to larger classes.

When there are at least three individuals, Satterthwaite and Sonnenschein (1981) provided examples on how to construct efficient, nondictatorial social choice functions for the domain of classical preferences. But in their examples someone is bossy: that individual can change the consumption bundle of someone else by misrepresenting her preferences, yet without affecting her own consumption bundle. In fact, this is one of the few papers we know of that can accommodate results on economies with production. Another example of this scarce literature is a paper by Shenker (1993b).

Again, to the extent that bossiness implies a costless interference of some agents on the allocations of others, one may inquire about what rules are left once nonbossiness is required. And a new impossibility arises.

Serizawa and Weymark (2003) have refined these findings. They prove that for an exchange economy with classical preferences, an efficient, strategyproof social choice function must generate unacceptable distributions of the goods on some circumstances.

Specifically, under such rules there must be someone who must sometime be allocated a consumption bundle arbitrarily close to zero.

Papers by Moreno (1994) and Moreno and Walker (1991) also attain impossibility results without resorting to the condition of nonbossiness, and by simply requiring a responsiveness property or a weak unanimity condition. Notice that these authors do not work only in a private good setting, but also admit a mix of public and private goods. This is enough to introduce the personalized preference domains that I use in this survey for taxonomic purposes.

These negative results are important, because they point at some unavoidable trade-offs between efficiency, strategyproofness, and the use of rules providing some minimal guarantees to agents. But if we now want to go beyond and perform any kind of second best analysis, it is worth pursuing matters a little further. Suppose we can characterize all the social choice functions that are strategyproof in exchange economies, as we already have done in voting contexts. Clearly, no reasonable rule within this class will be efficient (we exclude dictatorial rules as unreasonable). But some may be more efficient than others, or less inefficient. This may also be qualified in reference to some additional information, regarding the number of agents, the distribution of preferences, or any other relevant parameters. There is a subtle difference between strategyproofness and implementability in dominant strategies, related to the existence of multiple equilibria. I do not take the route of implementation theory here, but let me mention Mizukami and Wakayama (2007) as an example of a paper bridging this gap in the context of exchange economies. See also Yi (2007). Cason *et al.* (2006) also consider the consequences of multiplicity of equilibria in a theoretical and experimental analysis.

I will report on some of the existing characterization results for strategyproof social choice rules in exchange economies. They are important because they give us a catalog of those mechanisms that can satisfy strategyproofness in full. Then, we may want to choose among them those that satisfy other interesting properties to some extent. Of course, one could start by characterizing the set of rules that satisfy some alternative properties, and then select among them those that are "closest" to strategyproofness. While this is also possible, it raises the question of what we mean by "approximate strategyproofness." We shall not go deeply into that topic, but this is a good moment to mention that the issue arises in connection with the incentives provided by the Walrasian mechanism. There is a generalized feeling that mechanisms that choose Walrasian equilibrium allocations will have good incentive properties, especially for economies with a large number of agents. Roberts and Postlewaite (1976) provide conditions under which the gains from manipulating the Walrasian mechanism become small as the economy grows large. Other comments in the same line include Hammond (1979) or Dasgupta, Hammond, and Maskin (1979). However, small gains will still justify deviations by maximizing agents, and these deviations may have meaningful impacts when aggregated across a large population. Jackson (1992) and Jackson and Manelli (1997) investigate the size and impact of these deviations on the final equilibrium outcome, relative to the truthful one. They show that, under general conditions, each agent's deviations, as well as their aggregate impact, will again become small as the economy grows large. Let me also mention two related papers, one by Cordoba and Hammond (1998), the other by Kovalenkov (2002). Rather than concentrate on the Walrasian mechanism, which is manipulable for any finite economy, these papers describe variants of this mechanism that would be strategyproof (although not always balanced) for finite economies. Then, each of these strategyproof mechanisms is shown to be "approximately balanced" and "approximately Walrasian" when the number of agents is large. These papers nicely complement the previous ones in their attempt to capture the incentive properties of the Walrasian mechanism. One set of papers tends to support the statement that, for large economies, the Walrasian mechanism will perform approximately as if it were strategyproof. The other set supports the statement that, again for large enough economies, some strategyproof mechanisms will become approximately Walrasian.

Makowski, Ostroy, and Segal (1999) have established the equivalence between efficient and dominant strategy incentive compatible mechanisms, on the one hand, and what they call perfectly competitive mechanisms on the other. They refer by this expression to mechanisms where no agent is able to influence prices or anyone's wealth. What they prove is that perfectly competitive incentive compatible mechanisms are nongeneric (although they form a nonvacuous set), while they are generic (yet not universal) in continuum economies. This result about conditions for exact price-taking behavior contrasts with Satterthwaite's (2001) discussion of strategyproofness in markets. Rather than insisting on the Walrasian mechanism, he studies the consequences of operationalizing the supply and demand interactions as a double auction market with Bayesian players under incomplete information. He proves that the ensuing mechanism is approximately strategyproof, and he interprets this result as providing a possible rationale for the fact that price theory seems to approximate real markets quite well, in spite of the negative results we reported above.

As announced, we will consider economies with l private goods and n consumers. The endowment of goods is denoted by $e = \left(e^1, \ldots, e^n\right) \in \mathbb{R}_+^{nl}$. An allocation is a list $x = \left(x^1, \ldots, x^n\right)$ of goods received by each agent, and the set of balanced allocations constitutes the set of alternatives to choose from

$$A = \left\{ x \in \mathbb{R}_+^{nl} \mid \sum_i x^i = \sum_i e^i \right\}.$$

To keep within our general framework, agents should be endowed with preferences over the set of alternatives, that is, on the set of full allocations. But since we will limit ourselves to the analysis of situations when preferences are selfish, we will resort to the traditional formulation in general equilibrium theory, where agents are attributed preferences over the set of admissible consumption vectors (elements in $\mathbb{R}_+^l$, in our case). We assume that the preferences satisfy some further restrictions of convexity and monotonicity. But selfishness itself is also a restriction: all together, these conditions on preferences define the restricted domain for which we will discuss the possibility of strategyproof social choice functions. The preferences of agent i are represented by a utility function $u^i : \mathbb{R}^l_+ \to \mathbb{R}$. U denotes the set of all continuous, strictly quasi-concave and increasing $u^{i\prime}s$.

9.2.1. Two-Agent, Two-Goods Exchange Economies

This is a particular case that turns out to be quite easy to analyze completely, and ties together the specific preference case with the common preference one.

To get a feeling for the general results, let us first consider a specific set of rules that will result in a strategyproof social choice function (the rules define a game under which declaring the truthful preferences is a dominant strategy; the social choice rule is then the one assigning to each preference profile the outcome of this game under truthful strategies).

Example 8 Fix a positive price p, and allow each agent i to select her best alternative out of the set $B(p, e_i) = \{(x_{i1}, x_{i2}) \mid px_{i1} + x_{i2} = pe_{i1} + e_{i2}\}$. This describes the supply/demand of both the agents for both goods. If both agents have excess demand/supply of the same good, the final allocation is e. If the excess demand/supply allows for mutually advantageous trade at price p, then the prescribed allocation is the one where the agent who is less inclined to trade maximizes her utility.

This rule of voluntary trading at fixed prices and with rationing on the short side offers no advantage to manipulation. Since prices are fixed and the rationing rule is not sensitive to the size of unsatisfied demands, it is best for all agents to express what they want. The associated social choice rule is clearly strategyproof. In what follows, we will describe other strategyproof rules for exchange economies. But the essential insights can always be referred back to this simple example.

Remark that, in this simple case, we can identify the exchange economies problem with one of choosing the level of a public good (hence connecting the problem of common preferences with those of specific preferences). This is because, once we have fixed a price ratio p and endowments e, choosing the level of one good for one agent, say x_1^1, fully determines the levels of x_2^1, x_1^2, x_2^2. Moreover, the preferences of agent 1 over values of x_1^1 compatible with allocation on the budget line are single-peaked (because u^1 is quasi-concave and monotonic), and so are the preferences of agent 2 over the same x_1^1 values (which automatically determine $2's$ consumptions). Therefore, our allocation problem reduces to the choice of one value on a totally ordered set, with two agents and single-peaked preferences. Our rule above can be simply rewritten as one picking the median between the best values of x_1^1 for 1 and 2 and the value e_{11} of 1's endowment for good 1. With e_{11} as phantom voter, this is one of the median voter rules we have already identified in Section 5.

Trading at one fixed price has some features that are essential to any strategyproof rule. Others can be dispensed with, to get a some general result. Remark that any budget line corresponding to a positive price ratio defines a diagonal set within the set of allocations, in the following sense:

Definition 6 *A set $D \subset A$ is diagonal iff for each agent i and for all $x, y \in D, (x \neq y), x^i \not\geq y^i$ and $y^i \not\geq x^i$.*

Diagonality of the range rules out the possibility of some agent i getting more of all the goods in one allocation in the range than i would get at another allocation also in the range.

In our case, the budget line corresponding to the fixed price is, indeed, the range of our social choice function. Diagonality of the range is necessary for a social choice function on 2×2 exchange economies to be strategyproof. The use of only one price is not, as shown by the following examples.

We begin by a numerical example.

Example 9 (See Figure 25.1) Agent 1 is endowed with ten units of each of the two goods and agent 2 is endowed with five units of each of the two goods. Agent 1 may offer to buy good one at a price of 2 (units of good two per unit of good one) and sell good one at a price of $\frac{1}{2}$. If, for instance, agent 1 finds buying 3 units of good one most preferred (u^1 in Figure 25.1), then agent 1's dominant strategy is to offer to buy up to 3 units of good one. If agent 2 has the utility function u^2 in Figure 25.1, then his or her dominant strategy is to offer to sell up to 2 units of good one (at a price of 2) and buy up to 1 unit of good one (at a price of $\frac{1}{2}$). In this case, the outcome of the fixed-price

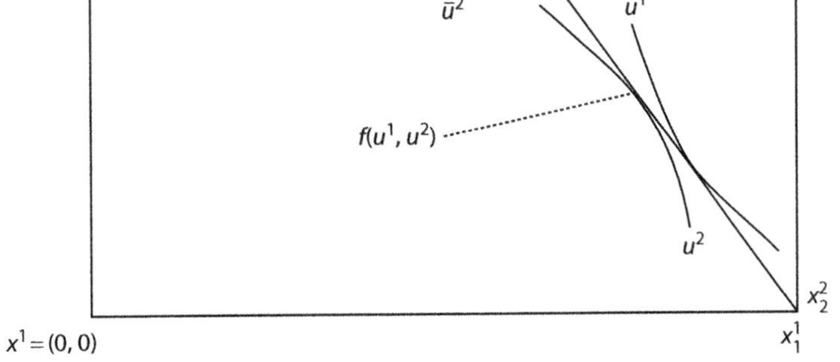

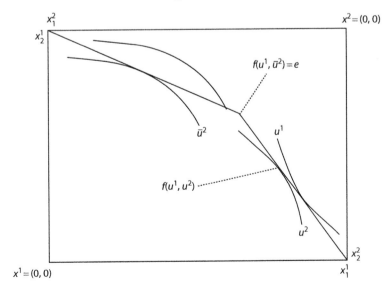

Figure 25.1. A Strategy-proof Mechanism for a 2×2 Exchange Economy.

procedure would be that agent 2 sells 2 units of good one to agent 1 at a price of 2. The final allocation for u is (12,6) for agent 1 and (3,9) for agent 2. If instead, agent 2 has the utility function $\bar{u}^2$ (see Figure 25.1 again), then he or she will not offer to sell good one, but will offer to buy up to 2 units of good one. In this case, no goods are exchanged and the final allocation is the initial endowment.

The principles underlying the case above can be rewritten in a more general form. This is the purpose of our next example.

Example 10 A two-price rule. Endow agents with any initial endowments e^i. Select one of the two agents, say 1. Choose two prices for the first good in terms of the second good. Interpret the first (and lowest) as the price at which agent 1 can offer to sell good 1; the second (and highest) as the price at which he can offer to buy the same good. Given her preferences, agent 1 can then choose to offer some amount of the first good (up to her endowment), or else post an offer to buy some amount (only one of these choices will be optimal, given that preferences are quasi-concave and the selling price is not higher than the lower one; agent 2, given these prices, might have had two best strategies—one of them selling and the other buying—but we do not allow this to be relevant). If agent 1 has made an offer to buy and agent 2 is ready to sell at the buying price, exchange takes place to the extent of the lowest willingness to transact (and up to agent 2's endowment). The same occurs if agent 1 wants to sell and agent 2 is ready to buy.

Examples 9 and 10 implicitly describe, again, a strategyproof social choice function. Their ranges are still diagonal. Also, the preferences of each agent over their option sets (given the declared preferences of the others) are single-peaked (our previous remark on two maxima already hinted that overall preferences of agent 2 on the whole range may no longer be single-peaked). In these two examples, as well as in Example 8, each agent can guarantee herself, by declaring the true preferences, that the social outcome will be at least as good as her initial endowment. The rules are individually rational. Subject to this qualification, the second class of rules we just described through Examples 9 and 10 (to be called the double fixed-price rules) are the only ones to guarantee strategyproofness in 2×2 exchange economies. Example 8, which is a special case where the selling and the buying prices coincide (to be called the single fixed-price rule), constitutes the subclass which, in addition, respects anonymity (i.e., allows both agents to play symmetric roles), provided the initial endowments of both agents are also identical.

Theorem 11 (Barberà and Jackson 1995) *A social choice function on a two-good, two-agent economy is strategyproof and individually rational iff it is the outcome of a double fixed-price exchange mechanism. If, in addition, the function is anonymous, then it is the outcome of a single fixed-price mechanism from the egalitarian endowment.*

The above theorem would need some qualifications to be rigorously stated (a more precise statement of the next theorem will cover this one as a special case). Some bounds on the traded amounts can be exogenously fixed, and a formal definition of what we have presented informally as examples would be in order. The interested reader is referred to Barberà and Jackson (1995), but the essentials are laid down here.

Notice that all the functions covered by the theorem have very narrow ranges, and that these are formed by linear prices. This is a consequence of the fact that the domain of preferences includes all strictly quasi-concave utility functions and that both agents play a role in determining the outcome. Dictatorship is excluded by individual rationality. Since dictatorial rules are obviously strategyproof, a full characterization of rules satisfying this property would require dropping the individual rationality assumption (for this, refer again to Barberà and Jackson 1995).

9.2.2. Two Agents, *l* Goods

Having learned about the 2 × 2 case, we can now ask whether the same basic ideas extend to exchange economies with more than two goods. We still retain the case of two agents, since this (plus our focus on distributing all the resources) allows us to describe the full allocation once we know what one agent gets.

Fixed prices were the key to strategyproof exchange with two goods: the range is a line. But fixed prices, when there are more than two goods, describe budget sets whose boundaries are hyperplanes. However restrictive, these rules allow too much flexibility. Strategyproofness cannot be satisfied if agents are allowed to express their preferences on such large sets. What happens is that, for two goods, the notion of fixed prices and fixed proportions are equivalent. For more than two goods, strategyproof social choice functions can be based on limited trades, along some collection of fixed proportions satisfying some additional properties. In fact, they must be of this particular form if they are to satisfy individual rationality.

Let us express these ideas more formally, after an example.

Example 11 There are two agents and three goods. Endowments are $e^1 = e^2 = (5,5,5)$, for a total $(10,10,10)$ resource vector. Agent 1 can buy units of any of the goods from agent 2, provided she pays one unit of each of the remaining two goods. Hence, agent 1 can offer multiples (but not combinations) of the trades $(1,-1,-1)$, $(-1,-1,1)$, $(-1,1,-1)$. The range of f in terms of $1's$ final allocation is $r_f = \{x \mid \exists \gamma \in [0,1]$ s.t. $x' = \gamma(5,5,5) + (1-\gamma)(10,0,0)$, or $x' = \gamma(5,5,5) + (1-\gamma)(0,10,0)$, or $x' = \gamma(5,5,5) + (1-\gamma)(0,0,10)\}$. If agent 1's most preferred point in the range is, say, $(7,3,3)$, then the allocation is agent 2's most preferred point from the convex combination of $(5,5,5)$ and $(7,3,3)$ (allocations are expressed in terms of what agent 1 gets. Then agent 2 gets $(10,10,10) - x'$).

Notice that, given the structure of the range, agent 1 always has a unique most preferred point, and that all convex combinations of that point and the endowment are preferred to all other points on any other segment. It is this property, that the agent who actually chooses the possible trades actually prefers these trades to any other, that makes fixed proportion trading strategyproof.

We now provide, after some preliminaries, a more formal definition of fixed proportion trading.

Preliminaries

Given points a and b in A, we write ab to denote the set of points lying on the segment with endpoints a and b, so $ab = \{x \mid \exists \gamma \in [0,1],\ x = \gamma a + (1-\gamma)b\}$. We write $c \geq_i^* ab$ if $c^i \geq \gamma a^i + (1-\gamma)b^i$ for some $\gamma \in [0,1]$. Then $c \geq_i^* ab$ indicates that c lies above the segment ab from agent $i's$ perspective.

Given a set $B \subset A$ and a utility profile $u \in U^2$, let $T^i(B,u)$ denote the set of allocations in B that maximize u^i. This set is nonempty if B is closed. A function t^i, which is a selection from T^i, is called a tie-breaking rule. A tie-breaking rule t^i is j–favorable at $B \in r_f$ if for any u, $t^i(B,u) \neq t^i\left(B, u^{-j}, v^j\right)$ only if $v^j\left(t^i\left(B, u^{-j}, v^j\right)\right) \geq v^j\left(t^i(B,u)\right)$.

Definition 7 *A social choice function f defined on a two-agent exchange economy is the result of fixed proportion trading if r_f, the range of f, is closed, diagonal, and contains e, and there exists an agent i such that the following holds:*

(1) *for all distinct x and y in r_f either $x \in ey$, $y \in ex$ or $e \geq_i^* xy$;*
(2) *there exist tie-breaking rules t^i and t^j such that t^i is j–favorable at r_f and t^j is i–favorable at $ea \cap r_f$, for all $e \in r_f$*
(3) *$f(u) = t^j\left(ea \cap r_f, u\right)$, where $a = t^i\left(r_f, u\right)$.*

Condition (1) assures that r_f lies along $k \leq l$ diagonal line segments, each having the endowment as an endpoint. If one chooses x from one segment and y from another segment, then $e \geq_i^* xy$. Condition (2) states that tie-breaking rules either are constant or choose in favor of the other agent. This condition only comes into play if the range is not connected, since then agents might have two possible utility maximizing choices. (This is an aspect that we have not emphasized in our previous informal discussion; it is needed for complete characterization and certainly complicates matters, but does not change anything essential.) Condition (3) states that the outcome of f is agent j's most preferred point in the range, which lies between the endowment and agent $i's$ most preferred point in the range. We can now state

Theorem 12 (Barberà and Jackson 1995) *A two-person social choice function is strategyproof and individually rational iff it is the result of fixed proportion trading.*

9.2.3. Three or More Agents

With three or more agents, it is no longer the case that what one of them gets is determinant of the global allocation. This opens up new possibilities for strategyproof rules, some of which are not necessarily attractive. For example, agent 1 might be offered to choose her best among some feasible baskets of goods. Then, either agent 2 or agent 3 might get the remaining resources, with the beneficiary being determined, say, according to which one of the rejected baskets agent 1 declares to be her worst. This rule is clearly strategyproof, since agent 1 guarantees herself the best attainable basket, and does not care who gets the rest; while the other two agents cannot help agent 1's choice of who will be the lucky one.

This is an example of a bossy social choice function, that is, one where some essential part of the allocation is trusted to an agent who is unaffected by the choice while affecting the utility of the others. Bossy functions were described by Satterthwaite and Sonnenschein (1981). They are usually considered unattractive, and efforts to characterize strategyproof social choice functions have concentrated on finding rules not in this class, called nonbossy.

Barberà and Jackson (1995) provide a characterization of nonbossy strategyproof social choice functions satisfying a version of anonymity and some additional technical conditions. Although the characterization becomes rather involved, it is in the spirit of the results we have described for two-agent exchange economies: strategyproofness requires a limited range of possible exchanges, and thus enters into conflict with efficiency.

9.3. Strategyproof Matching and Assignment

Gale and Shapley (1962) and Shapley and Scraf (1974) proposed a number of fascinating allocation problems and provided initial solutions for each one of them. We shall comment on two of them, the matching problem and the house assignment problem, and on some extensions.

Although these authors were perfectly aware that their proposed solutions to the problems were open to strategic manipulation, they did not concentrate on eliminating such behavior. Thus, it was left for others to establish results on the possibility of designing strategyproof rules in these contexts.

The simplest matching problem is one where pairs must be formed, involving one element in a given set, and one element in another set. These two sets are called the two sides of the matching market, and the problem is usually known as the marriage problem. This is because one can think of elements on one side of the market as men, elements on the other side as women. It is assumed that men have preferences over the women to whom they might be assigned, and also on the possibility of remaining unmatched. Likewise, women have preferences regarding men as possible partners, and also about remaining single. A matching is given by a set of pairs, each composed of a man and a woman, and by a list of those agents who are unmatched. Each agent is listed once and only once, either as part of a pair or in the list of singles.

A matching is stable if it is individually rational (each agent who is matched to someone prefers his or her partner to remaining alone) and no pair could be formed whose members would both prefer their partner in that pair to those they have in the given matching. Gale and Shapley (1962) established many important results concerning the marriage market for a given set of preferences. Stable matchings always exist. They are the members of the core of the market. They form a lattice. The extreme elements of that lattice can be computed through simple algorithms called the men's optimal and the women's optimal algorithm.

Given the number of agents on each side of the market, the notion of a social choice function in that context arises naturally, as a rule that assigns one matching to each specification of the preferences of all the agents involved. Clearly, these social choice rules operate on personalized domains, since different agents value the final outcomes, that is, the resulting matchings, on the basis of what partner they get. Examples of social choice rules for a marriage market are those that choose, for each preference profile, the outcome computed by the men's optimal (or by the women's optimal) algorithm. These rules are obviously manipulable by elements on one side of the market yet the agents on the other side have the truth as a dominant strategy.

One may ask, then, whether there exists any strategyproof social choice rules for matching markets. Without further requirements, the obvious answer is yes. Different quasi-dictatorial methods satisfy this requirement. For example, consider the following rule based on serial dictatorship. Order one side of the market. Then, let the first agent choose his or her preferred element on the other side. After that, let the second ranked agent choose his or her preferred match among the remaining agents on the other side, and so on. It is obvious that such a method is both strategyproof and highly uninteresting. Notice that the negative flavor is maintained, but that the Gibbard–Satterthwaite Theorem does not apply directly, because the model implies clear restrictions on the preference domain.

Hence, one should inquire whether there are strategyproof social choice rules for matching markets satisfying additional conditions.

Given the importance of stability in the matching literature, the first question is whether there is some rule guaranteeing strategyproofness and stability under the standard domain restrictions implicit in Gale and Shapley's formulation of the problem. This question was answered in the negative by Roth (1982). It is also the case that all strategyproof social choice functions on this standard domain violate the milder requirements of efficiency and individual rationality, as proven in Barberà and Alcalde (1994).

These two authors then turned to a formulation that should by now be very familiar to the reader: Is it possible to identify domains of preferences admitting strategyproof stable social choice functions in the context of marriage problems? They identified different families of preferences allowing for a positive answer to that question. These are the families of preferences that satisfy a "top dominance" condition. Barberà and Alcalde proved that the men's optimal and women's optimal algorithms, when applied within these restricted classes of preferences, do indeed define stable and strategyproof rules. Moreover, they showed that these domains are maximal, in a precise sense. More recent work on matching has studied more specific models and established many different conditions under which strategyproofness holds. See Alcalde and Revilla (2004) on team formation; Martínez *et al.* (2004) on many-to-one matchings; Roth, Sönmez, and Ünver (2005) and Hatfield (2005) on kidney exchange; Abdulkadiroglu and Sönmez (2003) and Abdulkadiroglu, Pathak, and Roth (2009) on school choice; among many others.

An analysis of the men's optimal and women's optimal algorithm, and of the possibilities they open to manipulation, easily reveals that these possibilities never arise at profiles where there is a unique stable matching. That is, to use the more general language of game theory, when the core of the matching game is a singleton.

Ledyard (1977) had already remarked and exploited the fact that environments with a single-valued core allow for mechanisms that perform well from the point of view of incentives. Using the language of that early literature, he started from the remark, due to Hurwicz (1972, 1973), that "no organization which selects Pareto optimal allocations and which allows for a 'no trade'option to the participants can be both incentive compatible and decentralized" (Ledyard 1977, p. xx). Then he added a conjecture: that core-selecting organizations are incentive compatible in particular environments if and only if the core of that environment is single-valued (in utility terms). He finally proved that such a conjecture is true in one direction, but needs an additional condition on that single allocation to be exact. Given a set of technical assumptions, Ledyard proves that a core-selecting organization is incentive compatible if and only if the environment possesses an allocation that is the unilaterally best unblocked allocation for all participants.

Sönmez (1999) exploited a similar fact to provide a simple and general result that applies to matching models and to many other cases, including housing markets, roommate problems, indivisible goods exchange economies, coalition formation problems, and networks. He showed that for any model in these classes, there exists a Pareto efficient, individually rational, and strategyproof solution only if all allocations in the core are Pareto indifferent (i.e., unique in utility space, when they exist) for all problems. In fact, any such solution selects an allocation in the core whenever the core is nonempty. This result precipitates the negative results we have discussed for matching markets, and it is at the same time compatible with more positive results in other cases. Takamiya (2003) has provided a converse of this result.

A set of circumstances allowing for positive results arise in the context of housing markets and other assignment problems involving the allocation of heterogeneous indivisible goods to individuals without any possibility of monetary compensations.

Let us begin with a description of Gale's top trading cycle procedure, which was first described by Shapley and Scarf (1974), who introduced the housing market. Each individual owns an indivisible object (a house) initially, and objects may be reallocated. Gale's procedure gives a constructive way of finding a core allocation for such markets. Let all individuals point to the person who owns their favorite home. A top trading cycle consists of individuals such that each one in the cycle points to the next one. A single person may also constitute a cycle, by pointing to herself, if the top choice is the house she owns. Since there are a finite number of individuals, there always is at least one top cycle. Give each individual in a top cycle their favorite choice, and remove them from the market with their assigned houses. Repeat the process until each individual receives her assignment. The resulting allocation is unique if preferences are strict (Roth and Postlewaite 1977), and it is the core allocation. Roth (1982) proved that the core solution, and thus the rule assigning to each profile of preferences the outcome of the top trading cycle procedure, is strategyproof. Furthermore, Ma (1994), Sönmez (1996), Svensson (1999a), and Takamiya (2001) have provided different characterizations of this rule in terms of natural requirements. Bird (1984) and Moulin (1995b) proved that the core solution is also group strategyproof. Ehlers (2002) explores the maximal domains that allow for the definition of strategyproof rules for housing markets. Miyagawa (2001) and Schummer (2000) consider strategyproofness in variants of the problem for the case where monetary transfers would be allowed.

Papai (2000a) considers a family of rules for assignment problems where no individual has any property right; the number of objects is not necessarily the same as the number of individuals. She characterizes the set of group strategyproof, Pareto optimal, and reallocation-proof rules that provide each individual with at most one indivisible object. The method she identifies is called the hierarchical exchange rule, and it is described as the result of a recursive process. Individuals have an initial individual "endowment" of objects such that each object is exactly one individual's endowment. Otherwise, the initial distribution of these endowments is arbitrary, and some individuals may not be endowed with any objects. Apply the top trading cycle procedure to this market. Agents who leave the market and held more than one object as endowment leave the rest of their endowment. That "inheritance" is redistributed among individuals who have not yet received their assignment, and then the top trading procedure is started again. The procedure converges in finite steps, and the resulting allocation is unique if individual preferences are strict. Different hierarchical rules are therefore defined by the original assignment and by the rules to distribute the inheritance. It is interesting to remark that some proxy for initial endowments emerge as a necessary component of these assignment rules, even when property rights are not assumed to exist.

Papai extended her analysis to general markets with indivisible goods, where agents may be endowed with several goods. She defines an extension of the preceding rules, now requiring that not all conceivable trades are allowed, and shows that under her trade restrictions markets arise with a unique core allocation. Then she proves that the fixed deal exchange rules that select this unique allocation are the only exchange rules that satisfy strategyproofness, individual rationality and a weak form of efficiency. These results are reminiscent of the restrictions to trade that need to be imposed on more general markets in order to obtain strategyproofness, as discussed in Section 9.2.1. They also point at the housing market as a very particular case where trade restrictions become unnecessary, and where better general properties can be attained.

Papai (2003) also proves that, under additional assumptions on individual preferences, it is possible to identify new allocation rules, called the segmented trading cycle rules, that provide some additional flexibility for exchange. Other papers on this topic are Miyagawa (2002), Konishi, Quint, and Wako (2001), Svensson and Larsson (2005)

Papai (2000b, 2003, 2007), Klaus and Miyagawa (2002), Ehlers and Klaus (2003a), Ehlers, Klaus, and Papai (2002), and Amorós (2002) have studied strategyproof rules for assignment problems where no individual has any property right, the number of objects is not necessarily the same as the number of individuals, and these individuals may desire to consume more than one object. They have provided characterizations under different domains and for different additional sets of conditions. A general result about consistent strategyproof assignment rules is given in Ehlers and Klaus (2007).

I conclude this section by mentioning other related subjects that I will not review. One involves the use of random procedures in assigning indivisibles, and it has been extensively treated by Moulin (2000), Crès and Moulin (2001), Bogomolnaia and Moulin (2001), Abdulkadiroglu and Sönmez (1998). Another refers to the assignment of heterogeneous individuals to different tasks. An example in this direction is Barberà and Dutta (2000).

9.4. Strategyproof Cost Sharing

As I already explained in previous sections, Clarke and Groves (1991) identified the class of strategyproof mechanisms for a particularly interesting family of problems, involving a public decision and the possibility of monetary transfers among agents. Their model did not restrict attention to procedures that guarantee the feasibility of outcomes, because it allowed for transfers of varying size, making no explicit reference to the availability of resources necessary to make these contributions. This modeling choice makes their work a bit difficult to fit within a social choice framework. Because of this, I will not review the literature that ensued. However, I will describe other related work, also involving economies where decisions about levels of private and public goods are combined. These works explicitly consider feasibility constraints.

Consider the simple context where a single public good can be produced with a single private good according to a given cost function. Assume that each agent cares about the level of the public good and the amount of private good that she is assigned. Let preferences satisfy standard conditions of continuity, strict convexity, and strict monotonicity.

In this simple world, a mechanism determines how much of the public good must be produced, and how much of the private good unused for production goes to each one of the agents. When individuals are assumed to hold some initial amounts of the private good, then the mechanism implicitly determines the contributions of each agent to the production of the public good. Or, in others words, closer to the language used in the literature, the mechanism determines the amount of public good to produce, and how agents share its cost.

It is useful to consider the partial problem faced by each agent if she knows exactly the cost-sharing rule, and thus the amount of private good that she will have to pay for each level of public good, which we can call her "individual" cost function. In that case, the agent knows her ex post holding of private good for each potential level of production for the private good. Therefore, her preferences on the two-dimensional space of public and private goods translates into a preference on one dimension, say that of the public good decision. Thus, we can refer to the preferences of each agent for the amount of the public good, given the sharing rule. The shape of these preferences will depend on the initial cost function, on the specific sharing rule and, of course, on the preferences of each agent for combinations of the two goods.

Notice that if the preferences over the amount of the public good were single-peaked for each of the agents, then we would know how to choose it in a strategyproof manner. These are the rules I discussed extensively in Section 6.2.

Also notice that there are simple conditions under which single-peakedness will hold. This happens if the "individual" cost functions of agents and their preferences are both strictly convex on the range of values that the rule may choose from.

It should by now be clear what is the role of the cost-sharing rule and of the method to choose the level of the public good. The sharing rules alter the "individual" cost functions and thus the preferences for the amount of the public good. Therefore, they determine whether we are at all in a world where designing strategyproof rules to choose the level of a public good is possible. Then, when there is room for such possibility, that choice must be made through some of the methods that we know to be strategyproof.

In that context, Moulin (1994b) defined and characterized what he called the "conservative equal-costs mechanism." The mechanism recommends sharing the costs of production equally, and to produce at the lowest level demanded by some agent. He proved that the rule enjoys, among others, the very strong property of coalitional strategyproofness. I will state his characterization result shortly.

Before that, let me refer to Serizawa (1999). This paper contains several characterizations of rules that satisfy strategyproofness. The author takes care of several complications derived from relaxing strict convexity to convexity. This weakening allows for agents to be indifferent between several levels of provision, and requires a careful treatment of the sharing and decision rule when ties arise. Rather than being precise in all details, I will reproduce Serizawa's informal description of the main terms he uses, state Moulin's and Serizawa's theorems, and provide some comments on each one.

I quote from Serizawa (pp. 122–123):

The production range of a social choice function is the set of the production levels that can be obtained as the outcome of the function for some preference profile. A cost sharing scheme is a social choice function under which agents share the cost of the public good according to predetermined cost share functions depending only on the production level of the public good. A cost sharing scheme is equal if all the agents always pay an equal cost share. A cost sharing scheme is convex if its cost share functions are all convex on the scheme's production range. Given the cost sharing functions, agents are faced with nonlinear budget constraints, from which their demands of the public goods are derived. We consider cost sharing schemes which select the production levels of the public good depending on such demands of agents. The median voter rule is the decision rule on production level such that the public good is produced as much as the median value of the demands. In the median voter rule, given any level of the public good, say Y_0*, a coalition of agents whose cardinality is greater than* $\frac{n}{2}$ *has the power to push the production level higher than* Y_0 *by unanimously demanding higher than* Y_0*. A coalition owning such power is said to be winning at* Y_0*. A quota rule, or simply a* q*-rule, is an anonymous generalization of the median voter rule. In a* q*-rule, for each production level of the public good, an integer is assigned such that a coalition is winning at* Y_0 *if and only if the cardinality of the coalition is not less than the assigned number. Minimax rules (Moulin 1980a, Barberà and Jackson 1994) are nonanonymous generalizations of* q*-rules. In a minimax rule, for each production level* Y_0 *a class of coalitions is specified, all of which are winning at* Y_0*. A minimum demand rule is a public good production rule such that the minimum amount demanded for the public good is produced, that is, it is a* q*-rule such that the assigned level is* n *for all production levels.*

The reader will notice that these are rules falling in the general classes discussed in Section 6.2. With this terminology at hand, we start by stating Moulin's early characterization result.

Theorem 13 (Moulin 1994) *Let the cost function be convex and the production range of the social choice function be equal to the set of possible production levels. Then, the social choice function is group strategyproof, budget balancing, symmetric, and individually rational if and only if it is an equal, convex, cost-sharing scheme determined by a minimum demand rule.*

Notice that the incentives for individuals to reveal their preferences under this rule will be very strong. Not only will they not find any advantage in misrepresenting their preferences individually, but they also cannot find any in coalescing for joint manipulations.

The first result in Serizawa's paper includes Moulin's method and many others, by enlarging the class of methods that can be used to select the level of the public good.

Theorem 14 (Serizawa 1999) *Let the cost function of the public good be convex. A social choice function is strategyproof, budget balancing, and symmetric if and only if it is an equal and convex cost-sharing scheme determined by a minimax rule.*

Notice that Serizawa uses as part of his characterization an equal-treatment property that he calls symmetry. The latter requires that, if two agents declare the same willingness to pay for the public good, they should be assigned the same share of its cost.

In the next result, the requirement of symmetry is substituted by the stronger condition of anonymity, while the assumptions on the cost function are weakened. (For a definition of regularity, see Serizawa 1999a.)

Theorem 15 (Serizawa 1999) *Let the cost function of the public good be increasing, continuous, and regular. A social choice function is strategyproof, budget balancing, and anonymous if and only if it is an equal and convex cost-sharing scheme determined by a q-rule with anonymous tie-breaking rules.*

Serizawa's third result is an extension of Moulin's:

Theorem 16 (Serizawa 1999) *Let the cost function of the public good be increasing, continuous, and regular. A social choice function is strategyproof, budget balancing, symmetric, and individually rational if and only if it is an equal and convex cost-sharing scheme determined by a minimum demand rule.*

Notice that requiring strategyproofness only does not change the fact that Moulin's method is also coalitionally strategyproof. But it reinforces the strength of the characterization, and shows that coalitional strategyproofness is a "bonus" that we may get for free, once we are ready to require the weaker property.

Other results for the same model are obtained in Serizawa (1996a, 1996b).

I have spent time in the simplest versions of the public good production model because they tie neatly with what we have learned about choosing the level of one public good when costs are not considered explicitly, as in Section 6. The condition for this link to work is to control for conditions under which the preferences induced by the cost-sharing rules bring us back to some version of the simplest model for choosing in a linear space.

Characterization results are explicit about the properties that one can guarantee by using a given class of rules, but keep silent about their drawbacks. The important condition of efficiency is not satisfied by the rules we have described. Schummer (1999) has proven that even when agents are restricted to have linear preferences over one private good and one public good produced from the private good (the Kolm triangle), strategyproof rules cannot be efficient. This result is in line with this author's strategy of proving the strength of some impossibility results by showing that they hold on small domains.

Another closely related problem to the one considered until now is that of deciding the levels of production of an excludable public good. The previous results referred to the case where all agents do necessarily participate in the financing of the public good and cannot be excluded from its enjoyment. When agents can be excluded from the consumption of the good, then new mechanisms arise satisfying strategyproofness, and even coalitional strategyproofness. Moulin (1994b) first described the remarkable properties of serial cost-sharing, and then continued the exploration of the incentive properties of cost-sharing mechanisms in different contexts, when agents use a common technology but may consume different amounts of the produced good. Contributions to this literature include Moulin and Shenker (1999, 2001), Mutsuwami (2000, 2005), Yu (2007), Jackson and Nicoló (2004), and Ohseto (2000, 2005). Cantalá (2004) analyzes a related model where agents may excude themselves due to the existence of outside options. This literature is too large to be thoroughly surveyed here. Moulin (1995a, 2002) are good starting points.

10. FURTHER COMMENTS ON PREFERENCE DOMAINS

10.1. Some Special Domains

We have now examined a wide gallery of models. Each one carries, along with one or several economic and political interpretations, some strong hints of what might be reasonable restrictions on the preferences of individuals. Just to mention some, we have studied the consequences of assuming that preferences are single-peaked, that they satisfy the axioms of expected utility, or that they are defined over sets of alternatives, for the common preference case. We have also examined the implications of several classical economic assumptions, like continuity, additivity, (weak or strong) convexity, or monotonicity in different contexts involving common as well as personalized preferences. All these are examples of domain restrictions suggested by particular models and by their interpretations.

Another quest for domain restrictions did start from more abstract considerations and led to a good number of papers. It was motivated by the strong parallel between the contexts where Arrow's impossibility theorems obtain, and those where the negative results à la Gibbard–Satterthwaite arise. Notice that strategyproofness has been defined in most of the works considered here as a property of rules that choose one alternative for each profile of preferences, given a fixed set of alternatives. Yet Arrow's social welfare functions are equipped to choose one (or several) alternatives out of each possible subset of a given universal set. In order to emphasize this parallelism, it is convenient to think of strategyproofness as a property that can also be held by rules defined on all such subsets, requiring that the standard requirement does hold for any restriction of the rule to any of the subsets. This was the point of view that allowed Satterthwaite (1975) to put a strong emphasis on the correspondence between Arrow's theorem and his own results. Under this definition, strategyproofness applies to mechanisms that may also be required to satisfy some form of consistency, or rationality (in the sense that the choices over different subsets may be required to be rationalizable by some order).

Muller and Satterthwaite (1985) describe in detail the literature that explores the following question. Without fixing a priori any domain, nor any specific rule, investigate the necessary and sufficient conditions on preferences such that the resulting domain permits the construction of a strategyproof mechanism satisfying the Pareto criterion, nondictatorship (and, eventually, some additional requirements).

A characterization of this type was provided by Kalai and Muller (1977). It involves a requirement that restricts the distribution of decisive power of different sets of agents over different combinations of alternatives. I will not describe the condition, which leads them to define a concept of decomposability (quite unrelated with other uses of this word in the present survey). But in order to get the flavor of their result, I will provide its statement.

Theorem 17 *For $n \geqslant 2$, the following three statements are equivalent for every domain of admissible preferences Ω.*

(a) *Ω is decomposable.*
(b) *The equivalence class of Ω permits construction of an n-person weakly nondictatorial, rational, strategyproof mechanism that satisfies the Pareto criterion.*
(c) *The equivalence class of Ω permits construction of an n-person weakly nondictatorial, social welfare function that satisfies the Pareto criterion and IIA.*

The preceding theorem applies to environments where the common domain assumption holds. For the case of private goods, results in a similar vein, but requiring combinations with further properties, were obtained by Kalai and Ritz (1980) and Ritz (1981, 1983). Again, without entering into the details about its exact meaning, they identify a new condition regarding decisiveness implications and attain the following result.

Theorem 18 *For the private goods case, when $n \geqslant 2$, the following three statements are equivalent for every domain of admissible preferences Ω:*

(a) *Ω is decomposable over private alternatives.*
(b) *The equivalence class of Ω permits construction of an n-person, weakly nondictatorial, social welfare function that satisfies the strong Pareto criterion and IIA.*
(c) *The equivalence class of Ω permits construction of an n-person, weakly nondictatorial, rational, noncorruptible strategyproof mechanism that satisfies the strong Pareto criterion.*

Notice that in both theorems, attention is restricted to strategyproof mechanisms satisfying rationality. Another early analysis of alternative structures for domains admitting nondictatorial strategyproof rules is found in Kim and Roush (1980). Their domains are defined by structures that are different than those in Kalai and Muller (1977), and their results do not depend on the rationality requirement imposed by these previous authors. An overview of domain restrictions of this and other sorts can be found in Chapter 4 of Gaertner (2001).

10.2. Maximal Domains

In Section 6, I discussed the characterization of all strategyproof social choice functions when alternatives can be described as K-tuples of integer numbers and agents' preferences are single-peaked. What if we allow for a richer class of preferences? Certainly no new rules will arise, but will all generalized median voter schemes still be strategyproof? If not, we could claim single-peakedness to be a maximal domain admitting nontrivial, strategyproof rules (notice that we can always express dictatorship as an extreme example within the class; hence our reference to nontriviality). In fact single-peakedness does not exactly fit the requirement (see Berga 2002, Barberà, Massó, and Neme 1998). But the sharper results on the subject are remarks on fine points, and the basic message one can derive from them is that the hunch that single-peakedness provides a maximal domain is not far off the mark.

Similar questions can be posed in many other contexts. To the extent that any positive results (however weak) regarding strategyproofness must be obtained under some kind of domain restriction, it is important to discuss, for every specific restriction, whether or not it could be relaxed. Research on the maximality of specific domains represent attempts to deal with this issue. In general, they start from some class of preferences that must be included among the admissible ones, and then try to push the restrictions in order to characterize the largest set of preferences that include the originally specified class and still allow for strategyproofness. Results in this vein have been obtained in different contexts. An important initial contribution was due to Serizawa (1995), in the context of voting by committees, following some remarks on the issue in Barberà, Sonnenschein, and Zhou (1991). Also in the context of common domains, but referring to public goods, see Berga and Serizawa (2000). An interesting approach to the question is found in Bochet and Storcken (2008). Maximality results can also be obtained for special rules, like the Borda rule (Puppe and Tasnádi 2008), or even combining the study of special rules with special domains, as in Vorsatz (2007).

The issue of maximality also arises as one way to test the robustness of the results obtained for some classes of preferences, in those contexts where these preferences are personalized. For the case of rationing and division, maximality results have been obtained by Ching and Serizawa (1998), and extended by Massó and Neme (2004), and also by Mizobuchi and Serizawa (2006). In a different framework Ehlers (2000) explores the maximal domains that allow for the definition of strategyproof rules for housing markets.

11. SOME FINAL REMARKS

As announced in the Introduction, I have attempted to depict the process by which the subject of strategic voting, that was known for centuries but had never been central in social choice, became a very relevant one in the 1970s, continued to grow in importance for the rest of the twentieth century, and has become a major object of active attention not only by economists and political scientists but also by philosophers, mathematicians, and computer scientists.

My analysis has been limited, in different ways. I did not consider in depth the economic literature involving money transfers, notably the work on auctions and public goods allocation involving compensations or taxes. I also touched very lightly on developments in other important areas of application. I did not attempt to cover the literature generated by computer scientists in connection with mechanism design, or the recent progress in judgment aggregation, where the issue of strategyproofness is still at an early stage of study. The latter ties in very naturally with a line of research on abstract aggregation introduced by Wilson (1975), whose most recent expression is Nehring and Puppe (2010). In this paper, the link between judgment aggregation theory and more traditional social choice is lucidly discussed, and the issue of strategyproofness is presented as a part of a larger set of results. Nehring and Puppe's treatment ties in well with the contributions (including their own) that are discussed in our Section 6.

At any rate, the description of the literature in the most recent years is sketchy, for the reasons I discussed in my initial remarks on the purposes of the survey. Yet the reader can see that the works I have reviewed are still abundant. I hope they provide a fair account of what has been done in the first thirty years following Gibbard's seminal paper, with enough hints for the reader to draw a personal study guide.

Massive interest in strategyproofness within the economics profession was prompted by a fundamental negative result, but its development has been increasingly associated with the analysis of restricted domains admitting nontrivial strategyproof rules, and the study of interesting economic problems that give rise to them. Much has been learned over the years about the general structure of strategyproof rules and about the specific forms that they take for different environments.

Specific rules have been analyzed, properties different than strategyproofness but related to the general issue of incentives have been proposed, alternative interpretations of formal models have arisen, and different techniques of analysis have developed. All of this knowledge is part of what we have learned about incentives and mechanism design. Maybe a small part but a solid part, as it refers to the most compelling form of incentive compatibility.

ACKNOWLEDGMENTS

Many people have helped, directly and indirectly, to write this survey, and my coauthors in particular. Some colleagues and friends read it at some point and provided advice and criticism. They include Matt Jackson, Michel Le Breton, Jordi Massó, Hervé Moulin, Klaus Nehring, Szilvia Pappai, Clemens Puppe, and John Weymark. None of them is responsible for the final shape and contents of this chapter, as I could only very partially take their comments into account. I received very valuable assistance from Conxa Iglesias, Miguel Angel Alcobendas, and Diego Caramuta at different stages of the project.

Salvador Barberà gratefully acknowledges support from the Spanish Ministry of Science and Innovation through grant "Consolidated Group-C" ECO2008-04756, from the Generalitat de Catalunya, Departament d'Universitats, Recerca i Societat de la Informació through the Distinció per a la Promoció de la Recerca Universitària and grant SGR2009-0419 and from the Barcelona GSE Research Network.

REFERENCES

Abdou, J., & Keiding, H. (1991). *Effectivity functions in social choice*. Dordrecht: Kluwer Academic Publishers.

Abdulkadiroglu, A., Pathak, P. A., & Roth, A. E. (2009). Strategy-proofness versus efficiency in matching with indifferences: redesigning the NYC high school match. *American Economic Review, 99*(5), 1954–1978.

Abdulkadiroglu, A., & Sönmez, T. (2003). School choice: a mechanism design approach. *American Economic Review, 93*(3), 729–747.

Abdulkadiroglu, A., & Sönmez, T. (1998). Random serial dictatorship and the core from random endowments in house allocation problems. *Econometrica, 66*, 689–701.

Alcalde, J., & Barberà, S. (1994). Top dominance and the possibility of strategy-proof stable solutions to matching problems. *Economic Theory, 4*(3), 417–435.

Alcalde, J., & Revilla, P. (2004). Researching with whom? Stability and manipulation. *Journal of Mathematical Economics, 40*(8), 869–887.

Aleskerov, F., & Kurbanov, E. (1999). Degree of manipulability of social choice procedures. In A. Alkan, C. D. Aliprantis & N. C. Yannelis (Eds.), *Current trends in economics* (pp. 13–27). New York: Springer-Verlag.

Amorós, P. (2002). Single-peaked preferences with several commodities. *Social Choice and Welfare, 19*(1), 57–67.

Arrow, K. (1951). *Social choice and individual values*. Cowles Foundation Monograph, Yale University Press. 2nd ed. New York: Wiley, 1963.

Austen-Smith, D., & Banks, J. (1996). Information aggregation, rationality and the Condorcet jury theorem. *American Political Science Review, 90*(1), 34–45.

Baigent, N. (1992). Manipulability of choice aggregations. *Economic Letters, 38*(2), 195–198.

Barberà, S. (1977a). The manipulation of social choice mechanisms that do not leave too much to chance. *Econometrica, 45*(7), 1573–1588.

Barberà, S. (1977b). Manipulation of social decision functions. *Journal of Economic Theory, 15*(2), 266–278.

Barberà, S. (1979a). A note on group strategy-proof decision schemes. *Econometrica, 47*(3), 637–640.

Barberà, S. (1979b). Majority and positionalist voting in a probabilistic framework. *Review of Economic Studies, 46*(2), 379–389.

Barberà, S. (1980a). Pivotal voters: a new proof of Arrow's theorem. *Economics Letters, 6*, 13–16.

Barberà, S. (1980b). Stable voting schemes. *Journal of Economic Theory, 23*(2), 267–274.

Barberà, S. (1983a). Strategy-proofness and pivotal voters: a direct proof of the Gibbard-Satterthwaite theorem. *International Economic Review, 24*(2), 413–418.

Barberà, S. (1983b). Pivotal voters: a simple proof of Arrow's theorem. In P. K. Pattanaik & M. Salles (Eds.), *Social choice and welfare* (pp. 31–35). Amsterdam: North-Holland.

Barberà, S. (1996). Notes on strategy-proof social choice functions. In K. Arrow, A. Sen & K. Suzumura (Eds.), *Social choice re-examined*. London: Macmillan. French version: Sur les fonctions de choix non manipulables. *Revue d'Économie Politique, 106*(1), 1996.

Barberà, S. (2001a). An introduction to strategy-proof social choice functions. *Social Choice and Welfare, 18*(4), 619–653.

Barberà, S. (2001b). A theorem on preference aggregation, WP166 CREA-Barcelona economics.

Barberà, S., Berga, D., & Moreno, B. (2009). Individual versus group strategy-proofness: when do they coincide?, Barcelona economics working paper series WP#372.

Barberà, S., Bogomolnaia, A., & van der Stel, H. (1998). Strategy-proof probabilistic rules for expected utility maximizers. *Mathematical Social Sciences, 35*(2), 89–103.

Barberà, S., Bossert, W., & Pattanaik, P. K. (2004). Ranking sets of objects. In S. Barberà, P. J. Hammond, & C. Seidl (Eds.), *Handbook of utility theory* (Vol. II extensions, pp. 893–977). Amsterdam: Kluwer.

Barberà, S., & Dutta, B. (1982). Implementability via protective equilibria. *Journal of Mathematical Economics, 10*(1), 49–65.

Barberà, S., & Dutta, B. (2000). Incentive compatible reward schemes for labour-managed firms. *Review of Economic Design, 5*(2), 111–127.

Barberà, S., Dutta, B., & Sen, A. (2000). Strategy-proof social choice correspondences. *Journal of Economic Theory, 101*(2), 374–394.

Barberà, S., Gul, F., & Stacchetti, E. (1993). Generalized median voter schemes and committees. *Journal of Economic Theory, 61*, 262–289.

Barberà, S., & Jackson, M. O. (1994). A characterization of strategy-proof social choice functions for economies with pure public goods. *Social Choice and Welfare, 11*, 241–252.

Barberà, S., & Jackson, M. O. (1995). Strategy-proof exchange. *Econometrica, 63*, 51–87.

Barberà, S., Jackson, M. O., & Neme, A. (1997). Strategy-proof allotment rules. *Games and Economic Behavior, 18*(1), 1–21.

Barberà, S., & Jackson, M. O. (2004). Choosing how to choose: self-stable majority rules and constitutions. *Quarterly Journal of Economics, 119*(3), 1011–1048.

Barberà, S., & Peleg, B. (1990). Strategy-proof voting schemes with continuous preferences. *Social Choice and Welfare, 7*, 31–38.

Barberà, S., & Sonnenschein, H. F. (1978). Preference aggregation with randomized social orderings. *Journal of Economic Theory, 18*(2), 244–254.

Barberà, S., Massó, J., & Neme, A. (1997). Voting under constraints. *Journal of Economic Theory, 76*(2), 298–321.

Barberà, S., Massó, J., & Neme, A. (1998). Maximal domains of preferences preserving strategy-proofness for generalized median voter schemes. *Social Choice and Welfare, 16*, 321–336.

Barberà, S., Massó, J., & Neme, A. (2005). Voting by committees under constraints. *Journal of Economic Theory, 122*, 185–205.

Barberà, S., Massó, J., & Serizawa, S. (1998). Strategy-proof voting on compact ranges. *Games and Economic Behavior, 25*, 272–291.

Barberà, S., Sonnenschein, H. F., & Zhou, L. (1991). Voting by committees. *Econometrica, 59*, 595–609.

Barbie, M., Puppe, C., & Tasnádi, A. (2006). Non-manipulable domains for the Borda count. *Economic Theory, 27*(2), 411–430.

Bartholdi, J. J., Tovey, C. A., & Trick, M. A. (1989). The computational difficulty of manipulating an election. *Social Choice and Welfare, 6*(3), 227–241.

Batteau, P., Blin, J. M., & Monjardet, B. (1981). Stability of aggregation procedures, ultrafilters and simple games. *Econometrica, 40*, 527–534.

Benoît, J.-P. (1999). *Strategyproofness for correspondences and lotteries*. Mimeo, New York University.

Benoît, J.-P. (2002). Strategic manipulation in voting games when lotteries and ties are permitted. *Journal of Economic Theory, 102*(2), 421–436.

Berga, D. (1998). Strategy-proofness and single-plateaued preferences. *Mathematical Social Sciences, 35*, 105–120.

Berga, D. (2002). Single-peakedness and strategy-proofness of generalized median voter schemes. *Social Choice and Welfare, 19*(1), 175–192.

Berga, D., Bergantiños, G., Massó, J., & Neme, A. (2006). On exiting after voting. *International Journal of Game Theory, 34*(1), 33–54.

Berga, D., & Serizawa, S. (2000). Maximal domain for strategy-proof rules with one public good. *Journal of Economic Theory, 90*, 39–61.

Bird, C. G. (1984). Group incentive compatibility in a market with indivisible goods. *Economics Letters, 14*, 309–313.

Black, D. (1948a). On the rationale of group decision making. *Journal of Political Economy, 56*, 23–34.

Black, D. (1948b). The decisions of a commitee using a special majority. *Econometrica, 16*, 245–261.

Black, D. (1958). *The theory of committees and elections*. Cambridge University Press, 1958.

Blair, D. H., & Muller, E. (1983). Essential aggregation procedures on restricted domains of preferences. *Journal of Economic Theory, 30*(1), 34–53.

Blin, J. M., & Satterthwaite, M. A. (1976). Strategy-proofness and single peakedness. *Public Choice, 26*, 51–58.

Blin, J. M., & Satterthwaite, M. A. (1977). On preferences, beliefs, and manipulation within voting situations. *Econometrica, 45*(4), 881–888.

Bochet, O., & Storcken, T. (2008). *Maximal domains for strategy-proof or Maskin monotonic choice rules*. Mimeo.

Bogomolnaia, A. (1998). *Medians and lotteries: strategy-proof social choice rules for restricted domains*. Ph.D. Dissertation, Universitat Autònoma de Barcelona.

Bogomolnaia, A., & Moulin, H. (2001). A new solution to the random assignment problem. *Journal of Economic Theory, 100*, 295–328.

Bogomolnaia, A., & Nicolò, A. (1999). Multiple locations with congestion: normative solutions. In H. de Swart (Ed.), *Logic, game theory and social choice. Proceedings of the international conference LGS 99* (pp. 92–103). Tilburg University Press.

Borda, J. C. (1784). *Mémoire sur les élections au scrutiny*. Histoire de l'Académie Royale des Sciences; Paris 1781; translated by Alfred de Grazia as *Mathematical derivation of an election system*; Isis; Vol. 44, Parts 1 & 2; June, 1953; 42–51. Also in I. McLean & A. B. Urken (Eds.), *Classics of social choice*. Ann Arbor, MI: University of Michigan Press, 1995.

Border, K., & Jordan, J. S. (1981). Straightforward elections, unanimity and phantom voters, social science WP#376, California Institute of Technology.

Border, K., & Jordan, J. S. (1983). Straightforward elections, unanimity and phantom voters. *Review of Economic Studies, 50*, 153–170.

Bordes, G., Laffond, G., & Le Breton, M. (1990). *Strategy proofness issues in economic and political domains*. Mimeo.

Brams, S. J., & Fishburn, P. C. (1978). Approval voting. *American Political Science Review, 72*(3), 831–847.

Brams, S. J., & Fishburn, P. C. (1993). Yes-no voting. *Social Choice and Welfare, 10*, 35–50.

Brams, S. J., & Fishburn, P. C. (2002). Voting procedures. In K. J. Arrow, A. K. Sen & K. Suzumura (Eds.), *Handbook of social choice and welfare* (Vol. 1, pp. 173–236). Amsterdam: North-Holland.

Campbell, D. E., & Kelly, J. S. (2000). A trade-off result for preference revelation. *Journal of Mathematical Economics, 34*(1), 129–141.

Campbell, D. E., & Kelly, J. S. (2002a). A leximin characterization of strategy-proof and non-resolute social choice procedures. *Economic Theory, 20*(4), 809–829.

Campbell, D. E., & Kelly, J. S. (2002b). Preference revelation with a limited number of indifference classes. *Spanish Economic Review, 4*(2), 151–158.

Campbell, D. E., & Kelly, J. S. (2003a). A strategy-proofness characterization of majority rule. *Economic Theory, 22*(3), 557–568.

Campbell, D. E., & Kelly, J. S. (2003b). Are serial Condorcet rules strategy-proof? *Review of Economic Design*, 7(4), 385–410.

Campbell, D. E., & Kelly, J. S. (2006). Social welfare functions generating social choice rules that are invulnerable to manipulation. *Mathematical Social Sciences, 51*(1), 81–89.
Campbell, D. E., & Kelly, J. S. (2009). Gains from manipulating social choice rules. *Economic Theory, 40*(3), 349–371.
Campbell, D. E., & Kelly, J. S. Losses due to manipulation of social choice rules. *Economic Theory*, forthcoming.
Cantalá, D. (2004). Choosing the level of a public good when agents have an outside option. *Social Choice and Welfare, 22*(3), 491–514.
Cason, T. N., Saijo, T., Sjöstrom, T., & Yamato, T. (2006). Secure Implementation Experiments: Do strategy-proof mechanisms really work? *Games and Economic Behavior, 57*(2), 206–235.
Chichilnisky, G., & Heal, G. M. (1981). *Incentive compatibility and local simplicity*. University of Essex, Mimeo.
Chichilnisky, G., & Heal, G. M. (1997). The geometry of implementation: a necessary and sufficient condition for straightforward games. *Social Choice and Welfare, 14*(2), 259–294.
Ching, S. (1992). A simple characterization of the uniform rule. *Economics Letters, 40*(1), 57–60.
Ching, S. (1994). An alternative characterization of the uniform rule. *Social Choice and Welfare, 11*(2), 131–136.
Ching, S. (1996). A simple characterization of plurality rule. *Journal of Economic Theory, 71*(1), 298–302.
Ching, S. (1997). Strategy-proofness and "median voters." *International Journal of Game Theory, 26*(4), 473–490.
Ching, S., & Serizawa, S. (1998). A maximal domain for the existence of strategy-proof rules. *Journal of Economic Theory, 78*(1), 157–166.
Ching, S., & Zhou, L. (2002). Multi-valued strategy-proof social choice rules. *Social Choice and Welfare, 19*(3), 569–580.
Clarke, E. (1971). Multipart pricing of public goods. *Public Choice, 11*, 17–33.
Clarke, E., & Groves, T. (1991). A new characterization of the Groves-Clarke mechanism. *Economics Letters, 36*(3), 263–267.
de Condorcet, M. (1785). *Essai sur l'Application de l'Analyse a la Probabilité des Decisions Rendues a la Probabilité des Voix*. Paris: Imprimerie Royale.
de Condorcet, M. (1792). A survey of the principles underlying the draft constitution. In I. McLean & A. B. Urken (Eds.), *Classics of social choice* (pp. 145–146, 1995). Ann Arbor, MI: The University of Michigan Press.
Cordoba, J. M., & Hammond, P. J. (1998). Asymptotically strategy-proof Walrasian exchange. *Mathematical Social Sciences, 36*, 185–212.
Coughlan, P. J. (2000). In defense of unanimous jury verdicts: mistrials, communication and strategic voting. *American Political Science Review, 94*(2), 375–393.
Crès, H., & Moulin, H. (2001). Scheduling with opting out: improving upon random priority. *Operations Research, 49*(4), 565–577.
Cusanus, N. (1434). *De concordantia catholica*. In G. Kallen (Ed.), *Nicolai de Cusa opera omnia, XIV*. Hamburg: Felix Meiner.
Danilov, V. I., & Sotskov, A. I. (2002). *Social choice mechanisms*. Berlin: Springer
Dasgupta, P., Hammond, P., & Maskin, E. (1979). The implementation of social choice rules: some general results on incentive compatibility. *The Review of Economic Studies, 46*(2), 185–216.
Daunou, P. C. F. (1803). A paper on elections by ballot. In I. McLean & A. B. Urken (Eds.), *Classics of social choice*. The University of Michigan Press, 1995.
Demage, G., & Gale, D. (1985). The strategy structure of two sided matching markets. *Econometrica, 53*(4), 873–888.
Demange, G. (1982). Single-peaked orders on a tree. *Mathematical Social Sciences, 3*(4), 389–396.
Dodgson, C. L. (1876). *A method of taking votes on more than two issues*. Oxford: Clarendon Press.

Duggan, J. (1996). A geometric proof of Gibbard's random dictatorship theorem. *Economic Theory, 7*(2), 365–369.
Duggan, J., & Schwartz, T. (2000). Strategic manipulability without resoluteness or shared beliefs: Gibbard-Satterthwaite generalized. *Social Choice and Welfare, 17*(1), 85–93.
Dummett, M. (2005). The work and life of Robert Farquharson. *Social Choice and Welfare, 25*, 475–483.
Dummett, M., & Farquharson, R. (1961). Stability in voting. *Econometrica, 29*(1), 33–44.
Dutta, B. (1980a). On the possibility of consistent voting procedures. *Review of Economic Studies, 47*(3), 603–616.
Dutta, B. (1980b). Strategic voting in a probabilistic framework. *Econometrica, 48*(2), 447–456.
Dutta, B., Jackson, M. O., & Le Breton, M. (2001). Strategic candidacy and voting rules. *Econometrica, 69*(4), 1013–1038.
Dutta, B., Jackson, M. O., & Le Breton, M. (2002). Voting by successive elimination and strategic candidacy. *Journal of Economic Theory, 103*(1), 190–218.
Dutta, B., & Pattanaik, P. K. (1978). On nicely consistent voting systems. *Econometrica, 46*(1), *163–170.*
Dutta, B., Peters, H., & Sen, A. (2002). Strategy-proof probabilistic mechanisms in economies with pure public goods. *Journal of Economic Theory, 106*(2), 392–416.
Dutta, B., Peters, H., & Sen, A. (2007). Strategy-proof cardinal decision schemes. *Social Choice and Welfare, 28*(1), 163–179.
Ehlers, L. (2002). Coalitional strategy-proof house allocation. *Journal of Economic Theory, 105*, 298–317.
Ehlers, L., & Klaus, B. (2003a). Coalitional strategy-proof and resource-monotonic solutions for multiple assignment problems. *Social Choice and Welfare, 21*(2), 265–280.
Ehlers, L., & Klaus, B. (2003b). Probabilistic assignments of identical indivisible objects and the probabilistic uniform correspondence. *Review of Economic Design, 8*, 249–268.
Ehlers, L., & Klaus, B. (2007). Consistent house allocation. *Economic Theory, 30*(3), 561–574.
Ehlers, L., Klaus, B., & Pápai, S. (2002). Strategy-proofness and population-monotonicity for house allocation problems. *Journal of Mathematical Economics, 38*(3), 329–339.
Ehlers, L., Peters, H., & Storcken, T. (2002). Strategy-proof probablistic decision schemes for one-dimensional single-peaked preferences. *Journal of Economic Theory, 10*(2), 408–434.
Ehlers, L., Peters, H., & Storcken, T. (2004). Threshold strategy-proofness: on manipulability in large voting problems. *Games and Economic Behavior, 49*(1), 103–116.
Eliaz, K. (2004). Social aggregators. *Social Choice and Welfare, 22*(2), 317–330.
Farquharson, R. (1969). *Theory of voting*. New Haven, CT: Yale University Press.
Feddersen, T., & Pesendorfer, W. (1998). Convicting the innocent: the inferiority of unanimous jury verdicts under strategic voting. *American Political Science Review, 92*(1), 23–35.
Feldman, A. M. (1979a). Manipulation and the Pareto rule. *Journal of Economic Theory, 21*(3), 473–482.
Feldman, A. M. (1979b). Manipulating voting procedures. *Economic Inquiry, 17*(3), 452–474.
Feldman, A. M. (1980). *Welfare economics and social choice theory*. Boston: Martinus Nijhoff Publishing.
Fishburn, P. C. (1972). *The theory of social choice*. Princeton: Princeton University Press.
Fishburn, P. C. (1978). A strategic analysis of nonranked voting systems. SIAM. *Journal on Applied Mathematics, 35*(3), 488–495.
Fishburn, P. C., & Brams, S. J. (1984). Manipulability of voting by sincere truncation of preferences. *Public Choice, 44*, 397–410.
Freixas, X. (1974). A cardinal approach to straightforward probabilistic mechanisms. *Journal of Economic Theory, 34*(2), 227–251.
Gaertner, W. (2001). *Domain conditions in social choice theory*. Cambridge University Press.
Gale, D., & Shapley, L. S. (1962). College admissions and the stability of marriage. *American Mathematical Monthly, 69*(1), 9–15.

Gärdenfors, P. (1976). Manipulation of social choice functions. *Journal of Economic Theory, 13*(2), 217–228.
Gärdenfors, P. (1977). A concise proof of theorem on manipulation of social choice functions. *Public Choice, 32*, 137–142.
Gärdenfors, P. (1979). On definitions of manipulation of social choice functions. In J. J. Laffont (Ed.), *Aggregation and revelation of preferences* (pp. 29–36). Amsterdam: North-Holland.
Gardner, R. (1974). *Two theories of misrevealed preference for representable elections*. Mimeo.
Gaudemet, J. (1979). *Le gouvernement de l'église à l'époque classique*, tome VIII, Vol. 2: *Le Gouvernement local*, IIe partie. Paris: Cujas.
Geanakoplos, J. (2005). Three brief proofs of arrow's impossibility theorem. *Economic Theory, 26*(1), 211–215.
Gibbard, A. (1973). Manipulation of voting schemes: a general result. *Econometrica, 41*, 587–601.
Gibbard, A. (1977). Manipulation of schemes that mix voting with chance. *Econometrica, 45*(3), 665–681.
Gibbard, A. (1978). Straightforwardness of game forms with lotteries on outcomes. *Econometrica, 46*(3), 595–614.
Green, J., & Laffont, J. J. (1979). *Incentives in public decision-making*. Amsterdam: North-Holland.
Groves, T. (1973). Incentives in teams. *Econometrica, 41*, 617–631.
Groves, T., & Ledyard, J. (1987). Incentive compatibility since 1972. In T. Groves & R. Radner (Eds.), *Essays in honor of Leonid Hurwicz*. Minneapolis, MN: University of Minnesota Press.
Groves, T., & Loeb, M. (1975). Incentives and public inputs. *Journal of Public Economics, 41*, 211–226.
Hammond, P. J. (1979). Straightforward individual incentive compatibility in large economies. *Review of Economic Studies (Symposium on Incentive Compatibility), 46*, 263–282.
Hanson, B. (1969). Voting and group decision functions. *Synthese, 20*, 526–537.
Hashimoto, K. (2008). Strategy-proofness versus efficiency on the Cobb-Douglas domain of exchange economies. *Social Choice and Welfare, 31*(3), 457–473.
Hatfield, J. W. (2005). Pairwise kidney exchange: comment. *Journal of Economic Theory, 125*(2), 189–193.
Hurwicz, L. (1972). On informationally decentralized systems. In G. B. McGuire & R. Radner (Eds.), *Decision and organization*. Amsterdam: North-Holland.
Hurwicz, L. (1973). The design of mechanisms for resource allocation. *American Economic Review, 63*(2), 1–30.
Hurwicz, L., & Walker, M. (1990). On the generic nonoptimality of dominant-strategy allocation mechanisms: a general theorem that includes pure exchange economies. *Econometrica, 58*(3), 683–704.
Hylland, A. (1980). *Strategyproofness of voting procedures with lotteries as outcomes and infinite sets of strategies*. WP Institute of Economics, University of Oslo.
Jackson, M. O. (1992). Incentive compatibility and competitive allocation. *Economic Letters, 40*, 299–302.
Jackson, M. O. (2001). A crash course in implementation theory. *Social Choice and Welfare, 18*(4), 655–708.
Jackson, M. O., & Manelli, A. (1997). Approximately competitive equilibria in large finite economies. *Journal of Economic Theory*, 77, 354–376.
Jackson, M. O., & Nicolò, A. (2004). The strategy-proof provision of public goods under congestion and crowding preferences. *Journal of Economic Theory, 115*(2), 278–308.
Ju, B.-G. (2003). A characterization of strategy-proof voting rules for separable weak orderings. *Social Choice and Welfare, 21*(3), 469–499.
Ju, B.-G. (2003). Strategy-proofness versus efficiency in exchange economies: general domain properties and applications. *Social Choice and Welfare, 21*(1), 73–93.
Ju, B.-G. (2004). Continuous selections from the Pareto correspondence and non-manipulability in exchange economies. *Journal of Mathematical Economics, 40*(5), 573–592.
Ju, B.-G. (2005a). Strategy-proof risk sharing. *Games and Economic Behavior, 50*(2), 225–254.
Ju, B.-G. (2005b). A characterization of plurality-like rules based on non-manipulability, restricted efficiency, and anonymity. *International Journal of Game Theory, 33*(3), 335–354.

Kalai, E., & Muller, E. (1977). Characterization of domains admitting nondictatorial social welfare functions and nonmanipulable voting procedures. *Journal of Economic Theory, 16*(2), 457–469.

Kalai, E., & Ritz, Z. (1980). Characterization of the private alternatives domains admitting Arrow social welfare functions. *Journal of Economic Theory, 22*(1), 23–36.

Kato, M., & Ohseto, S. (2002). Toward general impossibility theorems in pure exchange economies. *Social Choice and Welfare, 19*(3), 659–664.

Kelly, J. S. (1977). Strategy-proofness and social welfare functions without single-valuedness. *Econometrica, 45*(2), 439–446.

Kelly, J. S. (1993). Almost all social choice rules are highly manipulable, but few aren't. *Social Choice and Welfare, 10,* 161–175.

Kim, K. H., & Roush, F. W. (1980). Special domains and nonmanipulability. *Mathematical Social Sciences, 1*(1), 85–92.

Kim, K. H., & Roush, F. W. (1984). Nonmanipulability in two dimensions. *Mathematical Social Sciences, 8*(1), 29–43.

Klaus, B., & Miyagawa, E. (2002). Strategy-proofness, solidarity, and consistency for multiple assignment problems. *International Journal of Game Theory, 30*(3), 421–435.

Koray, S. (2000). Self-selective social choice functions verify Arrow and Gibbard-Satterthwaite theorems. *Econometrica, 68,* 981–995.

Konishi, H., Quint, T., & Wako, J. (2001). On the shapley–scarf economy: the case of multiple types of indivisible goods. *Journal of Mathematical Economics, 35*(1), 1–15.

Kovalenkov, A. (2002). Simple strategy-proof approximately Walrasian mechanisms. *Journal of Economic Theory, 103*(2), 475–487.

Kureishi, W., & Mizukami, H. (2005). A characterization of the randomized uniform rule. Mimeo.

Laffond, G. (1980). *Révélation des Préférences et Utilités Unimodales.* Paris: Conservatoire National des Arts et Métiers.

Laffont, J. J. (1979). *Aggregation and revelation of preferences.* Amsterdam: North-Holland.

Laffont, J. J., & Maskin, E. (1979). A differentiable approach to expected utility maximizing mechanisms. In J. J. Laffont (Ed.), *Aggregation and revelation of preferences.* Amsterdam: North-Holland.

Laffont, J. J., & Maskin, E. (1982). The theory of incentives: an overview. In W. Hildenbrand (Ed.), *Advances in economic theory: invited papers for the Fourth World Congress of Econometric Society* (pp. 31–94). Cambridge University Press.

Larsson, B., & Svensson, L.-G. (2006). Strategy-proof voting on the full preference domain. *Mathematical Social Sciences, 52*(3), 272–287.

Le Breton, M., & Sen, A. (1999). Separable preferences, strategyproofness and decomposability. *Econometrica, 67*(3), 605–628.

Le Breton, M., & Weymark, J. A. (1999). Strategyproof social choice with continuous separable preferences. *Journal of Mathematical Economics, 32*(1), 47–85.

Le Breton, M., & Zaporozhets, V. (2009). On the equivalence of coalitional and individual strategy-proofness properties. *Social Choice and Welfare, 33*(2), 287–309.

Ledyard, J. O. (1977). Incentive compatible behavior in core-selecting organizations. *Econometrica, 45*(7), 1607–1621.

Llull, R. (1283). Blanquera. In I. McLean & A. B. Urken (Eds.), *Classics of social choice.* Ann Arbor, MI: University of Michigan Press, 1995.

Llull, R. (1299). The art of elections. In I. McLean & A. B. Urken (Eds.), *Classics of social choice.* Ann Arbor, MI: University of Michigan Press, 1995.

Luce, R. D., & Raiffa, H. (1957). *Games and decisions.* New York: Wiley.

Ma, J. (1994). Strategy-proofness and the strict core in a market with indivisibilities. *International Journal of Game Theory, 23,* 75–83.

Makowski, L., Ostroy, J., & Segal, U. (1999). Efficient incentive compatible economies are perfectly competitive. *Journal of Economic Theory, 85*(2), 169–225.

Manjunath, V. (2009). *Efficient and strategy-proof social choice when preferences are single-dipped.* Mimeo.

Martínez, R., Massó, J., Neme, A., & Oviedo, J. (2004). On group strategy-proof mechanisms for a many-to-one matching model. *International Journal of Game Theory, 33*(1), 89–106.

Maskin, E., & Sjostrom, T. (2002). Implementation theory. In K. J. Arrow, A. K. Sen & K. Suzumura (Eds.), *Handbook of social choice and welfare* (Vol. 1, pp. 237–288). North-Holland.

Massó, J., & Neme, A. (2004). A maximal domain of preferences for strategy-proof, efficient, and simple rules in the division problem. *Social Choice and Welfare, 23*(2), 187–206.

Maus, S., Peters, H., & Storcken, T. (2007). Anonymous voting and minimal manipulability. *Journal of Economic Theory, 135*(1), 533–544.

McLean, I., & Urken, A. B. (1995). *Classics of social choice.* Ann Arbor, MI: University of Michigan Press.

McLennan, A. (1980). Randomized preference aggregation: additivity of power and strategyproofness. *Journal of Economic Theory, 22*(1), 1–11.

Merrill, L. (2007). *A characterization of strategy-proof rules over the Condorcet domain with an even number of individuals.* Mimeo.

Messner, M., & Polborn, M. K. (2004). Voting on majority rules. *Review of Economic Studies, 71*(1), 115–132.

Miyagama, E. (1998). Mechanisms for providing a menu of public goods. Ph.D. Dissertation. New York: University of Rochester.

Miyagawa, E. (2001). Locating libraries on a street. *Social Choice and Welfare, 18*(3), 527–541.

Miyagawa, E. (2002). Strategy-proofness and the core in house allocation problems. *Games and Economic Behavior, 38*(2), 347–361.

Mizobuchi, H., & Serizawa, S. (2006). Maximal domain for strategy-proof rules in allotment economies. *Social Choice and Welfare, 27*(1), 195–210.

Mizukami, H., & Wakayama, T. (2007). Dominant strategy implementation in economic environments. *Games and Economic Behavior, 60*(2), 307–325.

Moore, J. (1992). Implementation, contracts, and renegotiation in environments with complete information. In J. J. Laffont (Ed.), *Advances in economic theory.* Cambridge University Press.

Morales, J. I. (1797). *Memoria matemática sobre el cálculo de la opinion en las elecciones.* Madrid: Imprenta Real. Reprinted in Martínez-Panero, M., & García-Lapresta, J. L. (2003). José Isidoro Morales, precursor ilustrado de la teoría de la elección social. Valladolid: Foreword of Salvador Barberà. Secretariado de Publicaciones e Intercambio Editorial de la Universidad de Valladolid. Translated in English (1995) as Mathematical memoir on the calculation of opinión in elections. In I. McLean & A. B. Urken (Eds.). *Classics of social choice.* Ann Arbor, MI: University of Michigan Press.

Moreno, D. (1994). Nonmanipulable decision mechanisms for economic environments. *Social Choice and Welfare, 11*, 225–240.

Moreno, D. (1999). Strategy-proof allocation mechanisms for pure public good economies when preferences are monotonic. *Economic Theory, 13*, 183–197.

Moreno, D., & Walker, M. (1991). Nonmanipulable voting schemes when participants' interests are partially decomposable. *Social Choice and Welfare, 8*, 221–233.

Moscoso, M. J. (2001). Mecanismos de asignación no manipulables. Ph.D. Dissertation. Universidad Carlos III de Madrid.

Moulin, H. (1980a). On strategyproofness and single-peakedness. *Public Choice, 35*(4), 437–455.

Moulin, H. (1980b). Implementing efficient, anonymous and neutral social choice functions. *Journal of Mathematical Economics*, 7(3), 249–269.

Moulin, H. (1981a). The proportional veto principle. *Review of Economic Studies, 48*(3), 407–416.

Moulin, H. (1981b). Prudence vs. sophistication in voting strategy. *Journal of Economic Theory, 24*(3), 398–412.

Moulin, H. (1983). *The strategy of social choice*. Amsterdam: North-Holland.

Moulin, H. (1988). *Axioms of cooperative decision making*. Cambridge University Press.

Moulin, H. (1994a). Social choice. In R. J. Aumann & S. Hart (Eds.), *Handbook of game theory with economic applications* (Vol. 2, pp. 1091–1125). Elsevier.

Moulin, H. (1994b). Serial cost-sharing of excludable public goods. *Review of Economic Studies, 61*, 305–325.

Moulin, H. (1995a). *Cooperative micro-economics: a game theoretic introduction*. Princeton: Princeton University Press and London: Prentice Hall.

Moulin, H. (1995b). On additive methods to share joint costs. *Japanese Economic Review, 46*(4), 303–332.

Moulin, H. (1997). *Procedural cum endstate justice: an implementation viewpoint*. WP#97-17, Duke University, Department of Economics.

Moulin, H. (1999). Incremental cost sharing: characterization by coalition strategy-proofness. *Social Choice and Welfare, 16*(2), 279–320.

Moulin, H. (1999). Rationing a commodity along fixed paths. *Journal of Economic Theory, 84*(1), 41–72.

Moulin, H. (2000). Priority rules and other asymmetric rationing methods. *Econometrica, 68*(3), 643–684.

Moulin, H. (2002). Axiomatic cost and surplus sharing. In K. J. Arrow, A. K. Sen & K. Suzumura (Eds.), *Handbook of social choice and welfare* (Vol. 1, pp. 289–360). Amsterdam: North-Holland.

Moulin, H., & Peleg, B. (1982). Cores of effectivity functions and implementation theory. *Journal of Mathematical Economics, 10*(1), 115–145.

Moulin, H., & Shenker, S. (1999). Distributive and additive cost sharing of an homogeneous good. *Games and Economic Behavior, 27*, 299–330.

Moulin, H., & Shenker, S. (2001). Strategyproof sharing of submodular costs: budget balance versus efficiency. *Economic Theory, 18*, 511–533.

Muller, E., & Satterthwaite, M. (1977). The equivalence of strong positive association and strategy-proofness. *Journal of Economic Theory, 14*, 412–418.

Muller, E., & Satterthwaite, M. (1985). Strategy-proofness: the existence of dominant strategy mechanisms. In L. Hurwicz, D. Schmeidler & H. Sonnenschein (Eds.), *Social goals and social organization. Essays in memory of Elisha Pazner*. Cambridge: Cambridge University Press.

Murakami, Y. (1968). *Logic and social choice*. London: Routledge & Kegan Paul.

Mutuswami, S. (1997). *Strategyproof mechanisms for cost sharing*. Mimeo, Indian Statistical Institute.

Mutuswami, S. (2000). *Strategyproof mechanisms for cost sharing*. WP#520 University of Essex discussion.

Mutuswami, S. (2005). Strategyproofness, non-bossiness and group strategyproofness in a cost sharing model. *Economics Letters, 89*(1), 83–88.

Nandeibam, S. (1998). An alternative proof of Gibbard's random dictatorship result. *Social Choice and Welfare, 15*(4), 509–519.

Nehring, K. (2000). Monotonicity implies generalized strategy-proofness for correspondences. *Social Choice and Welfare, 17*(2), 367–375.

Nehring, K., & Puppe, C. (2002). *Strategyproof social choice on single-peaked domains: possibility, impossibility and the space between*. Mimeo.

Nehring, K., & Puppe, C. (2005). *The structure of strategy-proof social choice. Part II: non-dictatorship, anonymity and neutrality*. Mimeo.

Nehring, K., & Puppe, C. (2007a). Efficient and strategy-proof voting rules: a characterization. *Games and Economic Behavior, 59*(1), 132–153.

Nehring, K., & Puppe, C. (2007b). The structure of strategy-proof social choice: general characterization and possibility results on median spaces. *Journal of Economic Theory, 135*(1), 269–305.

Nehring, K., & Puppe, C. (2010). *Abstract Arrowian aggregation*. Mimeo.

Nicolò, A. (1999). *Efficient and strategy-proof exchange with leontief preferences*. Mimeo, Universitat Autonoma de Barcelona.

Nicolò, A. (2004). Efficiency and truthfulness with leontief preferences. A note on two-agent, two-good economies. *Review of Economic Design, 8*(4), 373–382.

Ohseto, S. (2000). Characterizations of strategy-proof mechanisms for excludable versus nonexcludable public projects. *Games and Economic Behavior, 32*(1), 51–66.

Ohseto, S. (2005). Augmented serial rules for an excludable public good. *Economic Theory, 26*(3), 589–606.

Olszewski, W. (2004). Coalition strategy-proof mechanisms for provision of excludable public goods. *Games and Economic Behavior, 46*(1), 88–114.

Özyurt, S., & Sanver, M. R. (2008). Strategy-proof resolute social choice correspondences. *Social Choice and Welfare, 30*(1), 89–101.

Özyurt, S., & Sanver, M. R. (2009). A general impossibility result on strategy-proof social choice hyperfunctions. *Games and Economic Behavior, 66*(2), 880–892.

Papai, S. (2000a). Strategyproof assignment by hierarchical exchange. *Econometrica, 68*, 1403–1433.

Papai, S. (2000b). Strategyproof multiple assignment using quotas. *Review of Economic Design, 5*, 91–105.

Papai, S. (2003). Strategyproof exchange of indivisible goods. *Journal of Mathematical Economics, 39*, 931–959.

Papai, S. (2007). Exchange in a general market with indivisible goods. *Journal of Economic Theory, 132*(1), 208–235.

Pattanaik, P. K. (1973). On the stability of sincere voting situations. *Journal of Economic Theory, 6*, 558–574.

Pattanaik, P. K. (1974). Stability of sincere voting under some classes of non-binary group decision procedures. *Journal of Economic Theory, 8*, 206–224.

Pattanaik, P. K. (1976a). Counterthreats and strategic manipulation under voting schemes. *Review of Economic Studies, 43*, 11–18.

Pattanaik, P. K. (1976b). Threats, counterthreats and strategic voting. *Econometrica, 44*, 91–103.

Pattanaik, P. K. (1978). *Strategy and group choice.* Amsterdam: North-Holland.

Pattanaik, P. K., & Peleg, B. (1986). Distribution of power under stochastic social choice rules. *Econometrica, 54*(4), 909–921.

Pattanaik, P. K., & Sengupta, M. (1980). Restricted preferences and strategyproofness of a class of group decision functions. *Review of Economic Studies, 47*, 965–973.

Pazner, E. A., & Wesley, E. (1977). Stability of social choices in infinitely large societies. *Journal of Economic Theory, 14*(2), 252–262.

Pazner, E. A., & Wesley, E. (1978). Cheatproofness properties of the plurality rule in large societies. *Review of Economic Studies, 45*(1), 85–91.

Peleg, B. (1984). *Game theoretic analysis of voting in committees.* Cambridge: Cambridge University Press.

Peleg, B. (2002). Game-theoretic analysis of voting in committees. In K. J. Arrow, A. K. Sen & K. Suzumura (Eds.), *Handbook of social choice and welfare* (Vol. 1, pp. 395–424). Amsterdam: North-Holland.

Peremans, W., & Storcken, T. (1999). Strategy-proofness on single-dipped preferences domains. *Proceedings of the International Conference, Logic, Game Theory, and Social Choice*, pp. 296–313.

Perote-Peña, J., & Piggins, A. (2007). Strategy-proof fuzzy aggregation rules. *Journal of Mathematical Economics, 43*(5), 564–580.

Peters, H., van der Stel, H., & Storken, T. (1991). On uncompromisingness and strategy-proofness. *Reports in Operations Research and Systems Theory-Report M*, 91–15.

Peters, H., van der Stel, H., & Storken, T. (1992). Pareto optimality, anonymity, and strategy-proofness in location problems. *International Journal of Game Theory, 21*, 221–235.

Peters, H., van der Stel, H., & Storken, T. (1993). Generalized median solutions, strategy-proofness and strictly convex norms. *ZOR-Methods and Models of Operations Research, 38*, 19–53.

Pliny the Younger, A. D. (1995). Letter to Titius Aristo. In I. McLean & A. B. Urken (Eds.), *Classics of social choice.* Ann Arbor, MI: University of Michigan Press.

Puppe, C., & Tasnádi, A. (2008). Nash implementable domains for the Borda count. *Social Choice and Welfare, 31*(3), 367–392.
Rata, C. (2002). Voting and information aggregation. Ph.D. Dissertation, Universitat Autònoma de Barcelona.
Reny, P. (2001). Arrow's theorem and the Gibbard-Satterthwaite theorem: A unified approach. *Economics Letters, 70*, 99–105.
Ritz, Z. On Arrow social welfare functions and on nonmanipulable and noncorruptible socila choice function. Unpublished Ph.D. Dissertation. Evanston, IL: Northwestern University.
Ritz, Z. (1983). Restricted domains, Arrow social welfare functions, and noncorruptible and nonmanipulable social choice correspondences: the case of private alternatives. *Mathematical Social Sciences, 4*(2), 155–179.
Roberts, D. J., & Postlewaite, A. (1976). The incentives for price-taking behavior in large exchange economies. *Econometrica, 44*(1), 115–127.
Roberts, K. (1979). The characterization of implementable choice rules. In J. J. Laffont (Ed.), *Aggregation and revelation of preferences*. North-Holland.
Rodríguez-Álvarez, C. (2004). Candidate stability and probabilistic voting procedures. *Economic Theory, 27*(3), 657–677.
Rodríguez-Álvarez, C. (2006). Candidate stability and voting correspondences. *Social Choice and Welfare, 27*(3), 545–570.
Rodríguez-Álvarez, C. (2007). On the manipulation of social choice correspondences. *Social Choice and Welfare, 29*(2), 175–199.
Rodríguez-Álvarez, C. (2009). On strategy-proof social choice correspondences: a comment. *Social Choice and Welfare, 32*(1), 29–35.
Roth, A. E., & Postlewaite, A. (1977). Weak vs Strong domination in a market with indivisible goods. *Journal of Mathematical Economics, 4*(2), 131–137.
Roth, A. E. (1982). The economics of matching: stability and incentives. *Mathematics of Operations Research*, 7, 617–628.
Roth, A. E., Sönmez, T., & Ünever, M. U. (2005). Pairwise kidney exchange. *Journal of Economic Theory, 125*(2), 151–188.
Saari, D. G. (1990). Susceptibility to manipulation. *Public Choice, 64*(1), 21–41.
Saari, D. G. (2000). Mathematical structure of voting paradoxes. II. Positional voting. *EconomicTheory, 15*(1), 1–53.
Samuelson, P. A. (1954). The pure theory of public expenditure. *Review of Economics and Statistics, 36*, 387–389.
Saporiti, A. (2009). Strategy-proofness and single crossing. *Theoretical Economics, 4*, 127–163.
Saporiti, A., & Tohmé, F. (2006). Strategy-proofness and single crossing. *Social Choice and Welfare, 26*(2), 363–383.
Sasaki, H. (1997). *Randomized uniform allocation mechanism and single-peaked preferences of indivisible good.* Mimeo.
Sato, S. (2008). On strategy-proof social choice correspondences. *Social Choice and Welfare, 31*(2), 331–343.
Satterthwaite, M. A. (1973). The existence of strategy proof voting procedures. Ph.D. dissertation. University of Wisconsin-Madison.
Satterthwaite, M. A. (1975). Strategy-proofness and Arrow's conditions: existence and correspondence theorems for voting procedures and social welfare functions. *Journal of Economic Theory, 10*, 187–217.
Satterthwaite, M. A. (2001). Strategy-proofness and markets. *Social Choice and Welfare, 18*(1), 37–58.
Satterthwaite, M. A., & Sonnenschein, H. (1981). Strategy-proof allocation mechanisms at differentiable points. *Review of Economic Studies, 48*, 587–597.

Schmeidler, D., & Sonnenschein, H. (1974). The possibility of a cheat proof social choice function: a theorem of Gibbard and Satterthwaite. WP#69, The Center for Mathematical Studies in Economics and Management Science, Northwestern University.

Schmeidler, D., & Sonnenschein, H. (1978). Two proofs of the Gibbard-Satterthwaite theorem on the possibility of a strategy-proof social choice function. In H. Gottinger & W. Leinfellner (Eds.), *Decision theory and social ethics*. Dordrecht: Reidel Publishing Company.

Schummer, J. P. (1977a). Strategy-proof allocation for restricted economic domains. Ph.D. Dissertation, at the University of Rochester, under the supervision of William Thomson.

Schummer, J. P. (1977b). Strategy-proofness versus efficiency on restricted domains of exchange economies. *Social Choice and Welfare*, *14*(1), 47–56.

Schummer, J. P. (1999). Strategy-proofness versus efficiency for small domains of preferences over public goods. *Economic Theory*, *13*, 709–722.

Schummer, J. P. (2000). Manipulation through bribes. *Journal of Economic Theory*, *91*, 180–198.

Schummer, J. P. (2004). Almost-dominant strategy implementation. *Games and Economic Behavior*, *48*, 154–170.

Schummer, J. P., & Thomson, W. (1997). Two derivations of the uniform rule and an application to bankruptcy. *Economics Letters*, *55*, 333–337.

Schummer, J. P., & Vohra, R. (2002). Strategy-proof location on a network. *Journal of Economic Theory*, *104*(2), 405–428.

Sen, A. K. (1970). *Collective choice and social welfare*. San Francisco: Holden-Day.

Sen, A. (2001). Another direct proof of the Gibbard-Satterthwaite theorem. *Economics Letters*, *70*(3), 381–385.

Serizawa, S. (1993). Strategy-proof social choice functions in public goods economies. Ph.D. Dissertation, University of Rochester.

Serizawa, S. (1995). Power of voters and domain of preferences where voting by committees is strategy-proof. *Journal of Economic Theory*, *67*(2), 599–608.

Serizawa, S. (1996a). Strategy-proof and individually rational social choice functions for public good economies. *Economic Theory*, *7*, 501–12.

Serizawa, S. (1996b). An impossibility theorem in public goods economies with feasibility constraints. *Japanese Economic Review*, *47*(4), 368–383.

Serizawa, S. (1999). Strategy-proof and symmetric social choice functions for public good economies. *Econometrica*, *67*(1), 121–145.

Serizawa, S. (2002). Inefficiency of strategy-proof rules for pure exchange economies. *Journal of Economic Theory*, *106*(2), 219–241.

Serizawa, S. (2006). Pairwise strategy-proofness and self-enforcing manipulation. *Social Choice and Welfare*, *26*(2), 305–331.

Serizawa, S., & Weymark, J. A. (2003). Efficient strategy-proof exchange and minimum consumption guarantees. *Journal of Economic Theory*, *109*(2), 246–263.

Serrano, R. (2004). The theory of implementation of social choice rules. *SIAM Review*, *46*(3), 377–414.

Shapley, L., & Scarf, H. (1974). On cores and indivisibility. *Journal of Mathematical Economics*, *1*, 23–27.

Shenker, S. (1993a). *Some technical results on continuity, strategy-proofness, and related strategic concepts*. Mimeo.

Shenker, S. (1993b). *On the strategy-proof and smooth allocation of private goods in a production economy*. Mimeo.

Sjostrom, T. (1991). A new characterization of the Groves-Clarke mechanism. *Economics Letters*, *36*(3), 263–267.

Slinko, A. (2002). The asymptotic strategy-proofness of the plurality and the run-off rules. *Social Choice and Welfare*, *19*, 313–324.

Sönmez, T. (1994). Consistency, monotonicity, and the uniform rule. *Economics Letters*, *46*, 229–235.

Sönmez, T. (1996). Implementation in generalized matching problems. *Journal of Mathematical Economics, 26*, 429–439.

Sönmez, T. (1999). Strategy-proofness and essentially single-valued cores. *Econometrica, 67*, 677–689.

Sprumont, Y. (1991). The division problem with single-peaked preferences: a characterization of the uniform allocation rule. *Econometrica, 59*, 509–519.

Sprumont, Y. (1995). Strategy-proof collective choice in economic and political environments. *Canadian Journal of Economics, XXVIII*(I), 68–107.

Svensson, L.-G. (1999a). Strategy-proof allocation of indivisible goods. *Social Choice and Welfare, 16*(4), 557–567.

Svensson, L.-G. (1999b). *The proof of the Gibbard-Satterthwaite theorem revisited.* WP#1999:1, Lund University.

Svensson, L.-G., & Larsson, B. (2005). Strategy-proofness, core, and sequential trade. *Review of Economic Design, 9*(2), 167–190.

Svensson, L.-G., & Torstensson, P. (2008). Strategy-proof allocation of multiple public goods. *Social Choice and Welfare, 30*(2), 181–196.

Takamiya, K. (2001). Coalition strategy-proofness and monotonicity in Shapley–Scarf housing markets. *Mathematical Social Sciences, 41*(2), 201–213.

Takamiya, K. (2003). On strategy-proofness and essentially single-valued cores: a converse result. *Social Choice and Welfare, 20*(1), 77–83.

Thomson, W. (1979). Maximin strategies and elicitation of preferences. In J. J. Laffont (Ed.), *Aggregation and revelation of preferences* (pp. 245–268). North-Holland.

Thomson, W. (2003). Axiomatic and game-theoretic analysis of bankruptcy and taxation problems: a survey. *Mathematical Social Sciences, 45*, 249–297.

Umezawa, M. (2009). Coalitionally strategy-proof social choice correspondences and the Pareto rule. *Social Choice and Welfare, 33*(1), 151–158.

van der Stel, H. (2000). Strategy-proofness, Pareto optimality and strictly convex norms. *Mathematical Social Sciences, 39*(3), 277–301.

Vickrey, W. (1960). Utility, strategy and social decision rules. *Quarterly Journal of Economics, 74*, 507–535.

Vorsatz, M. (2007). Approval voting on dichotomous preferences. *Social Choice and Welfare, 28*(1), 127–141.

Weymark, J. A. (1999a). Decomposable strategy-proof social choice functions. *Japanese Economic Review, 50*(3), 343–355.

Weymark, J. A. (1999b). Sprumont's characterization of the uniform rule when all single-peaked preferences are admissible. *Review of Economic Design, 4*(4), 389–393.

Weymark, J. A. (2006). *Strategy-proofness and the tops-only property*. Mimeo.

Wilson, R. (1975). On the theory of aggregation. *Journal of Economic Theory, 10*(1), 89–99.

Yi, J. (2007). Monotonicity, implementation and generalized strategy-proofness. *Economics Letters, 97*(2), 124–127.

Yu, Y. (2007). Serial cost sharing of an excludable public good available in multiple units. *Social Choice and Welfare, 29*(3), 539–555.

Zeckhauser, R. (1973). Voting systems, honest preferences and Pareto optimality. *The American Political Science Review, 67*, 934–946.

Zhou, L. (1991a). Impossibility of strategy-proof mechanisms in economies with pure public goods. *Review of Economic Studies, 58*, 107–119.

Zhou, L. (1991b). Inefficiency of strategy-proof allocation mechanisms in pure exchange economies. *Social Choice and Welfare, 8*, 247–257.

CHAPTER TWENTY-SIX

Probabilistic and Spatial Models of Voting

Peter Coughlin
Department of Economics, University of Maryland, College Park, MD

Contents

Handbook of Social Choice and Welfare, Volume II
ISSN: 0169-7218, DOI: 10.1016/S0169-7218(10)00026-2

Abstract

This chapter discusses results about committees that use majority rule, some related results about majority rule as a social choice rule (that is, without referring to a specific context where majority rule is used), and results about electoral competitions where the winner is selected by majority rule.

1. BLACK'S ANALYSIS OF COMMITTEES AND RELATED RESULTS ABOUT MAJORITY RULE

An appealing approach to social choice is to select an alternative only if it cannot be beaten in pairwise comparisons made with simple majority rule. However, as Condorcet (1785) first discovered, there is a serious problem with this approach: When there are three or more alternatives, there exist preference orderings for voters where each alternative can be beaten.

Black (1948a, 1948b, 1958) developed a model of a committee that uses simple majority rule, and identified assumptions about the committee members' preferences that imply that there is an unbeaten alternative in that context. He also characterized the unbeaten alternatives. One of the things this section does is summarize the key elements of Black's model of committees and describe important results he derived in that context.

A number of subsequent references (see, for instance, Mas-Colell, Whinston, and Green 1995 and the references they cite) have used the more general approach of (1) considering a model that does not specify the context where simple majority rule will be used, and (2) identifying results for the model that follow from Black's reasoning. A second thing this section does is illustrate this approach with one such model. Results obtained this way are ones that can be applied to committees *and* other settings where simple majority rule is used.

Black (1948a, 1949, 1958) and Bowen (1943) are early sources that identified other settings that are relevant. Black pointed out that results similar to the ones he obtained for committees hold for an analogous model of multicandidate elections where (1) each pair of candidates is compared using simple majority rule, and (2) the characteristics of the candidates that matter to the voters (e.g., policies embodied by a candidate) are exogenous to the model. In independent work, Bowen developed a model of a community that uses referenda to determine the value of one variable: how much public education will be provided (with tax-sharing rules being given). In his model, he used standard assumptions about an individual's trade-off between public education and private consumption. Bowen assumed that the outcome of the referendum is determined by simple majority rule—and (within the specific context of his model) obtained results that are similar to Black's results for committees.

1.1. Voters, Alternatives, and Preferences

Black defined a "committee" to be a group of people who arrive at a decision by means of voting. In addition, he assumed that the number of committee members is finite. Black defined a "motion" to be a proposal before a committee, which it may adopt or reject by a method of voting. Black assumed that there is a set of motions that have been put forward. Black also assumed that each committee member has a preference ordering on the set of motions.

For the general model: Assume there is a finite set of voters. Ω will be an index set for these voters. The elements of Ω will be the successive integers $1,\ldots,\#\Omega$. Assume there is a set of alternatives. This set will be denoted by X. Assume that each voter has a preference ordering on X. More specifically, for each $\omega \in \Omega$, there is a preference relation, $\succeq_\omega$, on X that is (i) complete (for all distinct $x, y \in X$: $x \succeq_\omega y$ or $y \succeq_\omega x$), (ii) reflexive (for all $x \in X$: $x \succeq_\omega x$), and (iii) transitive (for all $x, y, z \in X$: $[x \succeq_\omega y$ and $y \succeq_\omega z] \Rightarrow [x \succeq_\omega z]$). The asymmetric part of $\succeq_\omega$ will be denoted by $\succ_\omega$. The symmetric part of $\succeq_\omega$ will be denoted by $\sim_\omega$. $x \succeq_\omega y$ will be interpreted as "For voter ω, x is at least as good as y"; $x \succ_\omega y$ will be interpreted as "voter ω prefers x to y"; $x \sim_\omega y$ will be interpreted as "voter ω is indifferent between x and y." A set of alternatives and the preferences for a set of voters will be summarized by $(X,(\succeq_1,\ldots,\succeq_{\#\Omega}))$.

1.2. Simple Majority Rule

Black considered a committee that places each of the motions against every other motion in a vote—comparing each pair with simple majority rule.

For any given $(X,(\succeq_1,\ldots,\succeq_{\#\Omega}))$, the relation "beats or ties" for simple majority rule will be denoted by $\succeq^S$. More specifically: For each $x, y \in X$, $x \succeq^S y$ means $\#\{\omega \in \Omega\colon x \succeq_\omega y\} \geq \#\{\omega \in \Omega\colon y \succeq_\omega x\}$. The asymmetric part of $\succeq^S$ will be denoted by $\succ^S$. The symmetric part will be denoted by $\sim^S$. $x \succ^S y$ means x beats y (when simple majority rule is used); $x \sim^S y$ means x ties y (when simple majority rule is used). The definition of $\succeq^S$ clearly implies: (i) For each $x, y \in X$, $x \succ^S y$ if and only if $\#\{\omega \in \Omega\colon x \succ_\omega y\} > \#\{\omega \in \Omega\colon y \succ_\omega x\}$; (ii) for each $x, y \in X, x \sim^S y$ if and only if $\#\{\omega \in \Omega\colon x \succ_\omega y\} = \#\{\omega \in \Omega\colon y \succ_\omega x\}$.

For any given $(X,(\succeq_1,\ldots,\succeq_{\#\Omega}))$, saying that $x \in X$ is a "(weak) simple majority Condorcet winner" means x is a greatest element for $\succeq^S$ on X (that is, $x \succeq^S y, \forall y \in X$).

[Note: This is equivalent to saying x is a maximal element for $\succ^S$ on X (i.e., $\nexists y \in X$ such that $y \succ^S x$).] Saying that $x \in X$ is a "(strong) simple majority Condorcet winner" means $x \succ^S y, \forall y \in X - \{x\}$. [Note: This is equivalent to saying $\nexists y \in X - \{x\}$ such that $y \succeq^S x$).)] Using this terminology, the observation at the end of the first paragraph in Section 1 can be restated as: If $\#X \geq 3$, then $\exists$ $(\succeq_1, \ldots, \succeq_{\#\Omega})$ where there is no (weak) simple majority Condorcet winner. Of course (*a fortiori*): If $\#X \geq 3$, then $\exists$ $(\succeq_1, \ldots, \succeq_{\#\Omega})$ where there is no (strong) simple majority Condorcet winner.

1.3. Single-Peakedness and Median Alternatives

Black assumed each committee member's preference ordering is represented by an ordinal utility function. In addition, he considered a setting where there is a one-to-one function from the motions to points on a horizontal axis and there is a vertical axis for ordinal utility.

Black considered committees where either (i) the set of motions is finite, or (ii) the set of points assigned to motions is a segment of the horizontal axis. For (i) a piecewise-linear curve was obtained for a utility function by putting a dot at every point in a plane where the horizontal coordinate is the number for a point on the horizontal axis assigned to a motion and the vertical coordinate is the utility number for that motion—and joining the dots for consecutive motions with segments. For (ii) he assumed the graph for a utility function is a smooth curve.

Black defined a "single-peaked curve" to be a curve that is always upward-sloping, always downward-sloping, or upward-sloping to a particular point and downward-sloping beyond it. He assumed the one-to-one function from the motions to a horizontal axis to be a function where the resulting curves for the committee members' utility functions are single-peaked curves.

For the general model: The alternatives will be "lined up" by using a type of ordering relation on X that Rubin (1967) and Denzau and Parks (1975) have called a "linear order." More specifically, a relation, $\leq_o$, on X that is (i) complete (for all distinct $x, y \in X : x \leq_o y$ or $y \leq_o x$), (ii) transitive (for all $x, y, z \in X$: $[x \leq_o y$ and $y \leq_o z] \Rightarrow [x \leq_o z]$), and (iii) anti-symmetric (for all $x, y \in X$, $[x \leq_o y$ and $y \leq_o x] \Rightarrow [x$ and y are not distinct$]$). The asymmetric part of $\leq_o$ will be denoted by $<_o$. Black's function (from the motions to points on a horizontal axis), which has the utility functions be single-peaked curves, provides a "natural linear order" for the motions—where, for each pair of motions, $[x \leq_o y] \Leftrightarrow$ [the point on the horizontal axis assigned to x *is the same as or to the left of* the point on the horizontal axis assigned to motion y].

In Black's model, each committee member has a motion that he prefers to every other motion. When each voter in the general model has a unique most-preferred alternative, it will be called a "regular model." More precisely, any given $(X, (\succeq_1, \ldots, \succeq_{\#\Omega}))$ is a "regular model" if and only if there exists a function

$$m\colon \Omega \to X$$

where, for each $\omega \in \Omega$, we have $[m(\omega) \succ_\omega y, \forall y \in X - \{m(\omega)\}]$.

The term "single-peaked" will be used for a property that a voter's preferences can have in a regular model. In particular, for any given $\omega \in \Omega$, saying "$\succeq_\omega$ is single-peaked (with respect to $\leq_o$)" will mean that, for each pair $y, z \in X$,

$$[[z <_o y \text{ and } y <_o m(\omega)] \quad \text{or} \quad [m(\omega) <_o y \text{ and } y <_o z]] \Rightarrow [y \succ_\omega z].$$

In some contexts, X is taken to be a segment of the real line (e.g., when the alternative to be selected is the level of expenditure for a publicly-provided good and that level is modeled as a continuous variable) and a regular model is used. In these contexts, it is natural to consider the ordering relation "is less than or equal to" for real numbers. Under these assumptions, saying that $\succeq_\omega$ is single-peaked (with respect to $\leq$) means that, for each $y, z \in X$, we have $y \succ_\omega z$ whenever either $[z < y < m(\omega)]$ or $[z > y > m(\omega)]$. In these contexts, it is also common to assume that $\succeq_\omega$ is continuous. When these assumptions hold: $[\succeq_\omega$ is single-peaked with respect to $\leq] \Leftrightarrow [\succeq_\omega$ is strictly convex$] \Leftrightarrow [\succeq_\omega$ can be represented by a strictly quasi-concave utility function] (see, for instance, Mas-Colell, Whinston, and Green 1995, p. 801).

When a given $(X, (\succeq_1, \ldots, \succeq_{\#\Omega}))$ is a regular model, the term "distribution of most-preferred alternatives" will be used for the probability distribution on X where

$$\Pr(y) = \#\{\omega \in \Omega\colon m(\omega) = y\}/\#\Omega, \ \forall y \in X.$$

Saying that $x \in X$ is a median for this distribution (*with respect to* a particular ordering relation, $\leq_o$) means

$$\Pr(\{y \in X\colon y \leq_o x\}) \geq \frac{1}{2} \quad \text{and} \quad \Pr(\{y \in X\colon x \leq_o y\}) \geq \frac{1}{2}.$$

Straightforward applications of these concepts will also be used in stating results that Black proved for his committee model.

1.4. Results for Committees and for the General Model

Black (1948a, pp. 27–28; 1948b, pp. 249–251; 1958, pp. 16–18) proved the following results under the assumptions for his committee model, which are stated above. First, a particular motion cannot beaten (i.e., no motion gets a simple majority over that particular motion) if and only if that particular motion is *a* median for the distribution of most-preferred motions (*with respect to* the natural linear order). Second, a particular motion gets a simple majority over every other motion if and only if that particular motion is *the unique* median for the distribution of most-preferred motions (*with respect to* the natural linear order).

The following (analogous) theorem holds under the assumptions for the general model (see, for instance, Denzau and Parks 1975, Theorem 4).

Theorem 1 *Suppose* $(X, (\succeq_1, \ldots, \succeq_{\#\Omega}))$ *is a regular model and there is an ordering relation* $\leq_o$ *that is such that, for each* $\omega \in \Omega$*, the preference ordering* $\succeq_\omega$ *is single-peaked* (with respect to $\leq_o$)*. Then*

(1) $x \in X$ *is a (weak) simple majority Condorcet winner if and only if* x *is a median for the distribution of most-preferred alternatives* (with respect to $\leq_o$)*;*

(2) $x \in X$ *is a (strong) simple majority Condorcet winner if and only if* x *is the unique median for the distribution of most-preferred alternatives* (with respect to $\leq_o$).

For some committees, an absolute majority (i.e., more than half of the entire set of voters) is required for social preference—instead of a simple majority being required. More specifically, for some committees: (i) one alternative beats another one if and only if an absolute majority prefer it, and (ii) otherwise, the two alternatives tie one another.

For any given $(X, (\succeq_1, \ldots, \succeq_{\#\Omega}))$, the relation "beats or ties" for absolute majority rule will be denoted by $\succeq^A$. More specifically, for each $x, y \in X$, $x \succeq^A y$ means $\#\{\omega \in \Omega\colon x \succeq_\omega y\} \geq \#\Omega/2$. The asymmetric part of $\succeq^A$ will be denoted by $\succ^A$. The symmetric part will be denoted by $\sim^A$. The definition of $\succeq^A$ implies (i) for each $x, y \in X$, $x \succ^A y$ if and only if $\#\{\omega \in \Omega\colon x \succ_\omega y\} > \#\Omega/2$; (ii) for each $x, y \in X$, $x \sim^A y$ if and only if $\#\{\omega \in \Omega\colon x \succ_\omega y\} \leq \#\Omega/2$ and $\#\{\omega \in \Omega\colon y \succ_\omega x\} \leq \#\Omega/2$. For any given $(X, (\succeq_1, \ldots, \succeq_{\#\Omega}))$, saying that $x \in X$ is a "(weak) absolute majority Condorcet winner" means $x \succeq^A y, \forall y \in X$. Saying that $x \in X$ is a "(strong) absolute majority Condorcet winner" means $x \succ^A y$, $\forall y \in X - \{x\}$.

The definitions clearly imply the following: (1) if an alternative is a (strong) absolute majority Condorcet winner, then it is a (strong) simple majority Condorcet winner; (2) if an alternative is a (weak) absolute majority Condorcet winner, then it is a (weak) simple majority Condorcet winner. The definitions also clearly imply that the converses of those statements are not true *in general.* So, *in general*, results for simple majority Condorcet winners cannot be expected to hold for absolute majority Condorcet winners. Nonetheless, the following variation on the previous theorem does hold (see, for instance, Denzau and Parks 1975, Theorem 4).

Theorem 2 *Suppose* $(X, (\succeq_1, \ldots, \succeq_{\#\Omega}))$ *is a regular model and there is an ordering relation* $\leq_o$ *that is such that, for each* $\omega \in \Omega$*, the preference ordering* $\succeq_\omega$ *is single-peaked* (with respect to $\leq_o$)*. Then*

(1) *$x \in X$ is a (strong) absolute majority Condorcet winner if and only if x is the unique median for the distribution of most-preferred alternatives* (with respect to $\leq_O$);
(2) *$x \in X$ is a (weak) absolute majority Condorcet winner if and only if x is a median for the distribution of most-preferred alternatives* (with respect to $\leq_O$).

It should be noted that there is an important connection between (a) the set of (weak) absolute majority Condorcet winners, and (b) a solution concept that has been applied when committee decisions have been modeled as cooperative games, as in the models developed by Kramer and Klevorick (1974), and Nakamura (1979). If a committee uses absolute majority rule, then a "winning coalition" is a set of voters that contains more than half of the committee members. Saying that alternative x "dominates" alternative y means there exists a winning coalition, W, where $x \succ_\omega y$, $\forall \omega \in W$. Using this dominance relation, we can now easily state the definition of the relevant solution concept: The "core" is the set $\{y \in X: \nexists x \in X$ such that x dominates $y\}$. Using this definition, it follows that when a committee uses absolute majority rule, an alternative is in the core if and only if it is a (weak) absolute majority Condorcet winner. Discussions of part 2 of the above theorem in terms of the core are in McKelvey (1990, Sections 2 and 3.1), Straffin (1994, Section 6), Saari (2004, Sections 3.1 and 4.1) and other references.

Theorems 1 and 2 (stated above) are very significant for settings where either simple majority rule or absolute majority rule is used *and* the supposition for the theorems is satisfied.

To begin with, the theorems are *positive* results for social choice. More specifically, there is at least one median—so there is at least one (weak) Condorcet winner. So it is *possible* to select an alternative that cannot be beaten.

If $\#\Omega$ is *odd*, there is a unique median. Hence, if $\#\Omega$ is *odd*, there is a (strong) Condorcet winner—which, by definition, is also a unique (weak) Condorcet winner. For the cases where $\#\Omega$ is *even*: (1) if there is a unique median for the distribution of most-preferred alternatives (*with respect to* $\leq_O$), then there is a unique (weak) Condorcet winner *and* it is also a (strong) Condorcet winner; (2) if there is not a unique median for the distribution of most-preferred alternatives (*with respect to* $\leq_O$), then there is more than one (weak) Condorcet winner *and* there is no (strong) Condorcet winner.

The ordering relation referred to in the theorems reflects "a similar attitude toward the alternatives" among the voters, since when this ordering relation is used, every voter has the view that moving away from his most-preferred alternative in either "direction" leads to worse and worse alternatives. Therefore, since the Condorcet winners are medians with respect to that ordering relation, they match with a reasonable measure for the center of the distribution of most-preferred alternatives. Hence they are, in this sense, "centrist" social choices.

The theorems also tell us that one would not have to actually make all the majority rule comparisons to find the appropriate choice(s). Instead, one could find the appropriate choice(s) by finding the median(s) of the distribution of most-preferred alternatives.

An individual whose most-preferred alternative is a median for the distribution of most-preferred alternatives (with respect to a given ordering relation $\leq_o$) is called a "median voter" (with respect to $\leq_o$). When there is a unique median for the distribution of most-preferred alternatives (with respect to $\leq_o$), there will be at least one median voter—and there will be more than one if and only if the median is the most-preferred alternative for more than one individual. In the cases where there is a unique median, the theorems imply that an alternative is a Condorcet winner *if and only if* it is a median voter's most-preferred alternative.

When there is more than one median for the distribution of most-preferred alternatives (with respect to $\leq_o$), there will be at least two median voters—and there will be more than two if and only if there is a median that is the most-preferred alternative for more than one individual. In the cases where there is more than one median, the theorems imply that an alternative is a (weak) Condorcet winner *if* it is a median voter's most-preferred alternative. In these cases, there will always be two distinct (weak) Condorcet winners that are most-preferred alternatives for median voters. In addition, in some instances, there will also be at least one (weak) Condorcet winner that is not anyone's most-preferred alternative. More specifically, let α be the index number for an individual who has *one* of the two distinct most-preferred alternatives that are (weak) Condorcet winners as his most-preferred alternative, let β be the index number for an individual who has the *other* of the two alternatives as his most-preferred alternative, and have the index numbers be such that $m(\alpha) <_o m(\beta)$: the theorems imply that any alternative, y, that satisfies $m(\alpha) <_o y <_o m(\beta)$ will be a (weak) Condorcet winner.

Related discussions of single-peakedness and majority rule are in Arrow (1963, Section 2 in Chapter VII), Fishburn (1973, Sections 9.1–9.3), Denzau and Parks (1975, Sections 1 and 2), Enelow and Hinich (1984, Sections 2.1 and 2.2), Mueller (2003, the last paragraph in Section 5.2 and all of Section 5.3), Mas-Colell, Whinston, and Green (1995, Section 21.D), Shepsle and Bonchek (1997, pp. 83–90 in the section "The Simple Geometry of Voting") and other references.

2. HOTELLING, DOWNS, AND ELECTORAL COMPETITION

An electoral competition has voters with preferences on alternatives, like the models discussed in Section 1. In addition, it has political candidates (or parties) who *compete* with each other by choosing alternatives. After each candidate chooses an alternative, which will become the social choice if he is elected, the voters vote on the candidates, and those votes determine the outcome of the election. One important feature of an electoral competition is that unlike the treatment of voting in Section 1, the voters do not vote directly on the elements in the set of alternatives—instead, they vote directly on candidates. Another important feature is, the characteristics of a candidate that matter to voters (e.g., policies embodied by a candidate) are endogenous.

The literature on electoral competition began with Hotelling (1929). In that paper, Hotelling introduced an influential model for duopolists, which includes as a special case a locational model. Near the end, he briefly described how his locational model could be reinterpreted as a model of competition between two political parties. He then concluded that, in his reinterpreted model, there is a tendency for the competing parties to imitate each other.

Downs (1957) also played a crucial role in the development of the literature on electoral competition, by taking the step of stating *explicit assumptions* that correspond to Hotelling's brief description of his reinterpreted model. The explicit model he specified will be called the "Hotelling–Downs model."

Section 2.1 will describe Hotelling's model for duopolists. Section 2.2 will discuss how Hotelling's locational duopoly model has been reinterpreted as a model of electoral competition.

2.1. Hotelling's Model for Duopolists

Hotelling (1929) considered duopolists who offer an identical commodity, which comes in indivisible units. For each of the two sellers, production is costless. There is also a set of buyers. Each buyer will purchase one unit of the product. A buyer must purchase his unit from one of the duopolists.

Each buyer has a home. The location of a home is modeled as a point in a segment of the real line, which could be, for instance, Main Street in a town or a transcontinental railroad. It is assumed that there is a continuous uniform distribution of buyers' homes along the segment. Each duopolist has one store, and every purchase must be made at one of these stores. The possible locations for a store are modeled as the points in the segment.

Each duopolist's objective is to maximize its profits. Each buyer will pay a price for the unit he purchases, and will transport it home at a constant per-unit-traveled cost. The per-unit-traveled cost is the same for each buyer. Each buyer's objective is to minimize the total of price plus transportation cost.

In his paper, Hotelling devoted a lot of attention to situations where each duopolist can choose a price that it charges its own customers. In addition, he considered situations where the duopolists do not have any control over the price in their industry, but the stores are thought of as movable. The resulting locational model (which has locational competition, but no price competition) is relevant for this chapter, because this is the specific model that Hotelling suggested reinterpreting as a model of electoral competition.

In Hotelling's locational model for duopolists, both duopolists charge their customers the same price (with the price being exogenous to the model), but each duopolist can choose the location for its store before the buyers make their purchases. Under the assumptions for the locational model, (1) a duopolist will achieve its objective by choosing a location (for its store) that maximizes its market share, and (2) a buyer will achieve his objective by purchasing his unit of the product at a store that minimizes his transportation cost.

In Hotelling's locational model, the firms can "look ahead" and determine how the buyers would respond to their possible choices of store locations. When they do, the duopolists' decisions define a two-person game. The unique pure-strategy equilibrium for this game is this: Both duopolists locate at the center of the segment.

Hotelling also identified an important welfare property of the equilibrium, by comparing the equilibrium locations with the locations that will minimize the total of transportation charges paid by the consumers. He concluded that the social objective of minimizing the total transportation charges is achieved if and only if the sellers occupy symmetrical positions at the quartiles—instead of locating at the center of the segment. So, in equilibrium, this social objective is *not* achieved by the duopolistic competition.

2.2. Interpretation as a Model of Electoral Competition

This section will discuss how the various parts of Hotelling's locational model for duopolists have been interpreted in a model of electoral competition.

In the Hotelling–Downs model of electoral competition, the duopolists are relabeled as two political candidates. The buyers are interpreted as voters. A duopolist offering a commodity to buyers is reinterpreted as the corresponding candidate giving voters an opportunity to vote for him. A buyer purchasing a unit of the product from a duopolist is interpreted as a voter casting a vote for the corresponding candidate. Accordingly, each voter must cast one (and only one) vote *and* he must cast it for one of the two candidates.

The locations in the line segment become the alternatives. As in Section 1, the set of alternatives will be denoted by X. A buyer's home is relabeled as the corresponding voter's most-preferred alternative. It is assumed that there is a continuous uniform distribution of voters' most-preferred alternatives along the segment.

Downs suggested that, under certain circumstances, one could think about the possible "locations" for the political candidates as positions on a left-right political spectrum, where, starting at any point in the interior, (1) the more you move to the left the more liberal the position, and (2) the more you move to the right the more conservative the position.

Downs also suggested that, in some of these cases, the set of possible locations (or candidate positions) could be taken to be the segment on the real number line from zero to 100, with a candidate's position indicating the percentage of the economy it wants left in private hands. He argued that this particular interpretation would be plausible if, for instance, voters are solely concerned about the amount of government intervention in the economy.

A firm's store location is relabeled as the alternative that the corresponding candidate chooses. A candidate, c, can choose any point, s_c in the line segment. In Hotelling's locational model for duopolists, a firm maximizes profits if and only if it maximizes the percentage of the buyers who purchase its product (i.e., its market share). Each firm's objective is, accordingly, reinterpreted as the corresponding candidate maximizing the percentage of the voters who vote for him (i.e., his vote share).

Hotelling (1929) assumed that the transportation cost to a buyer from making his purchase at a firm's store is the following product: (per-unit-traveled cost) · (the distance *from* the firm's store *to* the buyer's location). For the political interpretation suggested by Hotelling, one is substituting costs of distance in the segment of alternatives *for* transportation costs. So the total cost to a voter for voting for a political candidate is the following product: (per-unit cost) · (the distance *from* the candidate's position *to* the voter's most-preferred alternative). Since a voter's most-preferred alternative is fixed and the per-unit cost is fixed, this defines a "total cost function" (for a voter) on the set of possible candidate positions.

Using notation that is similar to what was used in Section 1: For any given ω, the corresponding most-preferred alternative can be written as $m(\omega)$. *If* we also let κ denote the (positive and constant) per-unit cost and let $TC_\omega(x)$ denote the total cost to ω from voting for a candidate with position x, *then* the total cost function for ω can be written as $TC_\omega(x) = (\kappa) \cdot | x - m(\omega) |$. For the political interpretation (of the locational model for duopolists) suggested by Hotelling: For any given $\omega \in \Omega$, $U_\omega(x) = -TC_\omega(x)$ can be thought of as a utility function on X. References that have *translated* Hotelling's assumption about buyer preferences *into* this assumption about voter preferences include Davis and Hinich (1966), Stokes (1966), Buchanan (1968), Myerson (1995), and Osborne (1995).

In the duopoly model that Hotelling suggested reinterpreting, a buyer will minimize his transportation cost. So each firm will expect a particular buyer to select a particular firm's store *if* (for that buyer) the transportation cost from buying his unit quantity at that firm's store *is less than* the transportation cost from buying his unit quantity at the other firm's store. When the transportation costs are equal, the buyer will be indifferent between the two firms. In this case, the firms could expect the buyer's choice to be equivalent to the toss of a fair coin.

For the political interpretation suggested by Hotelling, these assumptions can be restated as each party having the following expectations (for any given ω): *If* $TC_\omega(s_1) < TC_\omega(s_2)$, *then* the probability that ω will vote for party 1 is one; *if* $TC_\omega(s_1) > TC_\omega(s_2)$, *then* the probability that ω will vote for party 2 is one; *if* $TC_\omega(s_1) = TC_\omega(s_2)$, *then* the probability for each of ω's two possible choices is one-half.

Under these assumptions, the candidates' decisions define a two-person game (which will be analyzed in more detail in Section 5). The unique pure-strategy equilibrium for this game is that both candidates choose the alternative that is at the center of the segment.

The equilibrium behavior of the candidates is directly analogous to the equilibrium behavior of the duopolists. However, the welfare properties of the equilibria are *not* the same. The next paragraph discusses the candidates' equilibrium from a welfare perspective.

Each voter ends up with the social alternative of the winning candidate rather than the social alternative of whichever candidate he votes for (in contrast to each buyer making his purchase at the specific store that he chooses, instead of all of the buyers making their purchases at the store that a majority prefers). So Buchanan (1968, p. 329) and Myerson (1995, p. 78) have argued that an appropriate social objective is to minimize the total cost of distance *from* the voters' most-preferred alternatives *to* the position of the winning candidate. They have concluded that this social objective is achieved if and only if the candidates locate at the center of the segment. So, in equilibrium, this social objective *is* accomplished by the electoral competition.

3. A FRAMEWORK FOR MODELS OF ELECTORAL COMPETITION

This section provides a framework that will (in subsequent sections) be useful for stating results from the literature on electoral competition.

3.1. Basic Assumptions and Notation

3.1.1. Electorates

Some electorates are very large, and (as in the work of Hotelling and Downs) it is useful to model the voters as an infinite set. Other electorates are relatively small, and it is appropriate to model the voters as a finite set. The following assumptions allow for both possibilities.

There is a set of voters. Ω will be an index set for the voters. $\mathcal{F}(\Omega)$ will be a σ-field of subsets of Ω. $(\Omega, \mathcal{F}(\Omega), \mu_\Omega)$ will be a finite measure space. As (for instance) in McKelvey, Ordeshook, and Ungar (1980, p. 162), for each $B \in \mathcal{F}(\Omega)$, $\mu_\Omega(B)$ "represents the size of the coalition B." The same approach is also used in McKelvey and Ordeshook (1976, p. 1173), where they (similarly) state that the finite measure of a set of voters "represents the 'number' of voters in the set."

π_Ω will denote the probability measure on $(\Omega, \mathcal{F}(\Omega))$, which is obtained when we normalize μ_Ω. As for instance in Davis, DeGroot, and Hinich (1972, p. 149), Sloss (1973, p. 23), McKelvey (1975, pp. 817–818), Grandmont (1978, p. 324), or Calvert (1986, p. 9), for each $B \in \mathcal{F}(\Omega)$, $\pi_\Omega(B)$ is the proportion of the voters with an index in B. π_Ω will be called the "distribution of voter indices."

These assumptions can be illustrated with the Hotelling–Downs model. For that model, Ω can be a closed interval $[\alpha,\beta]$ on the real line. With $\Omega=[\alpha,\beta]$, we can have $\mathscr{F}(\Omega)$ be the collection of Borel sets in $[\alpha,\beta]$. For each $B\in\mathscr{F}(\Omega)$, we can then have $\mu_\Omega(B)=\lambda(B)$ (where λ denotes Lebesgue measure). This gives us $\pi_\Omega(B)=\lambda(B)/(\beta-\alpha)$, for each $B\in\mathscr{F}(\Omega)$. This implies (among other things) that, when we consider a subinterval of the index set for the voters, the proportion of the voters in that subinterval *equals* [the length of that subinterval]/[the length of the index set for the voters]. Since this is a continuous uniform distribution on $[\alpha,\beta]$, we could alternatively use the continuous distribution function $F(\omega)=(\omega-\alpha)/(\beta-\alpha)$ on the set Ω or the continuous density function $f(\omega)=1/(\beta-\alpha)$ on the set Ω.

When there is a finite set of voters, the index set will be $\Omega=\{1,\ldots,\#\Omega\}$, $\mathscr{F}(\Omega)$ will be the power set of Ω, and μ_Ω will be the counting measure on $(\Omega,\mathscr{F}(\Omega))$. These assumptions imply that, for each $W\subseteq\Omega$, we have $\pi_\Omega(W)=\mu_\Omega(W)/\#\Omega$. Since this is a discrete uniform distribution on Ω, we could alternatively use the discrete distribution function $F(\omega)=\omega/\#\Omega$ on the set Ω or the discrete density function (or probability function) $f(\omega)=1/\#\Omega$ on the set Ω.

3.1.2. Regular Models

As in the model in Section 1, there is a set of alternatives, X, and each voter has a preference ordering on X. For each $\omega\in\Omega$, the preference ordering is denoted by $\succsim_\omega$. The asymmetric part of $\succsim_\omega$ is denoted by $\succ_\omega$, and the symmetric part of $\succsim_\omega$ is denoted by $\sim_\omega$.

Within this framework, saying we have a regular model will mean there is a function

$$m:\Omega\rightarrow X$$

where (1) for each ω, $x=m(\omega)$ is the most-preferred alternative in X for the voter whose index is ω *and*, (2) m is measurable on $(\Omega,\mathscr{F}(\Omega))$. With a regular model, one can go from the measures for the indices to corresponding measures for the most-preferred elements. Let $(X,\mathscr{F}(X))$ be a measurable space where, for each $A\in\mathscr{F}(X)$, the set $\{\omega\in\Omega : m(\omega)\in A\}$ is in $\mathscr{F}(\Omega)$. The finite measure on $(X,\mathscr{F}(X))$ induced by μ_Ω will be denoted by μ_X. The probability measure on $(X,\mathscr{F}(X))$ induced by π_Ω will be denoted by π_X. The measure π_X will be called the "distribution of most-preferred alternatives."

These features of the framework can also be illustrated with the Hotelling–Downs model. In that model, X is a segment of the real line. The segment will be denoted by $[a,b]$. We can start with the formulation for the index set described above, where, as we have already seen, π_Ω is a continuous uniform distribution of voter indices. We can let $\mathscr{F}(X)$ be the collection of Borel sets in $[a,b]$. To go from the distribution of voter indices to the distribution of most-preferred alternatives, we can use

$$m(\omega)=[(a\beta-b\alpha)+(b-a)\omega]/(\beta-\alpha)].$$

Then, for each $A \in \mathscr{F}(X)$, we would have $\pi_X(A) = \lambda(A)/(b-a)$. This is a continuous uniform distribution on $[a,b]$. So the distribution of most-preferred alternatives will have the distribution function $F(x) = x/(b-a)$ on the set X and the density function $f(x) = 1/(b-a)$ on the set X.

For the Hotelling–Downs model, the uniform distribution of voter indices is transformed into a uniform distribution of most-preferred alternatives. However, the framework also lets us consider other mappings from Ω to X. So the framework clearly allows for many other possible distributions of most-preferred alternatives.

When there is a finite set of voters, going from the measures for the indices to the measures for the most-preferred alternatives will give us the same distribution of most-preferred alternatives as was used in Section 1. That is, using the notation used in this framework, the distribution of most-preferred alternatives will be the probability distribution on X where

$$\pi_X(\{y\}) = \#\{\omega \in \Omega : m(\omega) = y\}/\#\Omega, \forall y \in X.$$

3.1.3. Candidates and their Strategy Sets

Mueller (2003, p. 180) argues that, in the Hotelling–Downs model, "the words 'candidate' or 'party' can be used interchangeably ... for the implicit assumption when discussing parties is that they take a single position in the voter's eyes." In what follows, I will use these two terms interchangeably.

There will be two political candidates. $C = \{1,2\}$ is an index set for them. For each $c \in C$, there is a pure strategy set, S_c. It will be assumed that $S_1 = S_2 = X$. s_c denotes a strategy for a particular $c \in C$.

In this framework, the candidates' "common strategy set" will not have to satisfy the specific assumptions about the possible candidate choices that are in the Hotelling–Downs model. Rather, those assumptions illustrate *one* (influential) way in which candidates' strategy sets have been formulated. This flexibility is being included in the framework because the subsequent literature has considered a variety of assumptions about the candidates' common strategy set.

Downs (1957) interpreted the possible "locations" for political parties as "party ideologies" (see pp. 114–115). Selecting a party ideology is clearly one way in which a party can potentially embody policies, since a party ideology can indicate (to a voter) the policies that a party plans to implement. Some references have adopted this approach and have explicitly assumed that a strategy for a candidate is something that *indirectly* indicates policies that a party plans to implement. See, for instance, Enelow and Hinich (1984) or Hinich and Munger (1997).

A second approach has been to assume that a party's strategy *directly* identifies the policies it plans to implement. When this approach has been used, the candidates' "common strategy set" has usually been a set of possible policies. See, for instance,

Davis and Hinich (1966, 1968, 1971), Davis, Hinich, and Ordeshook (1970), Riker and Ordeshook (1973), or Ordeshook (1986).

A third approach has been to assume that a candidate might want "to augment his alternative platforms to include obfuscation of the policies that he will adopt if he wins the election" (Ordeshook 1986, p. 180). When a candidate uses this type of strategy, which Ordeshook (1986) calls a "risky strategy," he selects a lottery on a set of possible policies and communicates that lottery to the voters—with the voters then being uncertain about what policies will be implemented. So, when this third approach has been used, the candidates' "common strategy set" has been a set of lotteries. See, for instance, Enelow and Hinich (1984, Section 7.3) or Ordeshook (1986).

With each of these approaches, the candidates' "common strategy set" has been taken to be a pure strategy set. In this framework, I am (similarly) assuming that the elements of X are pure strategies. (Section 11.2 will discuss work that has considered mixed extensions of two-candidate games.)

3.1.4. The Probability that Voter ω will Vote for Candidate c

Arrow (1987, p. 124) has observed that for an "election to an office ... the candidates ... are evaluated by each voter, and the evaluations lead to messages in the form of votes." Each voter will cast one vote. The voters learn s_1 and s_2 *before* they vote. For each $\omega \in \Omega$, there will be a function

$$\mathrm{Pr}^1_\omega\colon S_1 \times S_2 \to [0,1]$$

where the value assigned to a particular $(s_1,s_2) \in S_1 \times S_2$ by Pr^1_ω is the probability that ω will vote for candidate 1 when candidate 1 chooses s_1 and candidate 2 chooses s_2. The probability that ω will vote for candidate 2 when candidate 1 chooses s_1 and candidate 2 chooses s_2 will be

$$\mathrm{Pr}^2_\omega(s_1,s_2) = 1 - \mathrm{Pr}^1_\omega(s_1,s_2).$$

These probabilities could be objective probabilities, or they could be subjective probabilities (with each candidate having the same expectations).

For each $c \in C$ and $\omega \in \Omega$, $V^c_\omega(s_1, s_2)$ will be the Bernoulli random variable where (1) a "success" is a vote for c from ω, and (2) the probability of "success" is $\mathrm{Pr}^c_\omega(s_1,s_2)$ [i.e., $V^c_\omega(s_1, s_2)$ equals 1 with probability $\mathrm{Pr}^c_\omega(s_1,s_2)$ and $V^c_\omega(s_1,s_2)$ equals 0 with probability $1 - \mathrm{Pr}^c_\omega(s_1,s_2)$].

3.1.5. The Voting Scheme

Arrow (1987, p. 124) has pointed out that "for the election to an office ... the social decision, which candidate to elect ..., is made by aggregating the votes according to the particular voting scheme used."

In describing the voting scheme for the Hotelling–Downs model, Downs stated that, as is common in democratic nations, when there are two candidates running for an office, a "single party ... is chosen by popular election to run the government apparatus" (p. 23), and a "party ... receiving the support of a majority of those voting is entitled to take over the powers of government" (p. 24).

For this chapter's framework I will use B_c to denote the set of voters who vote for c, and I will assume that for each $c \in C$, we have $B_c \in \mathcal{F}(\Omega)$. The voting scheme will be (1) if $\mu_\Omega(B_1) > \mu_\Omega(B_2)$, then party 1 wins; (2) if $\mu_\Omega(B_1) < \mu_\Omega(B_2)$, then party 2 wins; (3) if $\mu_\Omega(B_1) = \mu_\Omega(B_2)$, then the two parties tie. When the set of voters is finite, the voting scheme can be stated as (i) if one of the parties gets more votes than the other party, then the party with more votes wins; (ii) if each party gets the same number of votes, then the two parties tie.

This voting scheme, of course, corresponds to an important collective choice rule—the "method of majority decision," as defined by Arrow (1963, p. 46). Theorem 1 (Possibility Theorem for Two Alternatives) in Arrow (1963, p. 48) established that when there are two alternatives (as in the two-party elections that are under consideration), the method of majority decision satisfies all of his conditions—and, as he pointed out, "Theorem 1 is, in a sense, the logical foundation of the Anglo-American two-party system."

3.2. Possible Objectives

To specify a strategic form game, one has to identify the set of players, the strategy set for each player, and the payoff function for each player. In a model of electoral competition, the players are the political candidates. The framework in Section 3.1 provides us with both a set of candidates and a strategy set for each candidate. Hence the framework in Section 3.1 together with an objective for each candidate that defines a payoff function on $S_1 \times S_2$ will specify a strategic form game. There are various objectives for the candidates that have been considered in the literature on electoral competition. This section will discuss the most important objectives that have been considered.

A number of references have also considered whether replacing one objective with another would affect the candidates' decisions, so this section will additionally compare some of the objectives, using the game-theoretic notion of strategic equivalence for noncompetitive games used in Vorobev (1977).

The first two objectives will be based on the number of votes that a candidate gets. The nature of a candidate's vote total in an electoral competition model will be illustrated in the following discussion, which will focus on models with a finite set of voters. A more general treatment will follow.

By definition, when there is a finite set of voters, the total vote for a candidate will just be the sum of the votes cast for him by the individual voters. One (simple) case occurs when, for a given $c \in C$ and $(s_1, s_2) \in S_1 \times S_2$, $V_\omega^c(s_1, s_2)$ is a constant random variable for each $\omega \in \Omega$. In this case, the total vote for c will simply be the number of voters with $\Pr^c_\omega(s_1, s_2) = 1$.

In other cases, we can make use of the fact that for any given $\omega \in \Omega$, $c \in C$, and $(s_1, s_2) \in S_1 \times S_2$, the random variable $V^c_\omega(s_1, s_2)$ can be thought of as one Bernoulli trial (where a success is a vote for c from ω and the probability of a success is $\Pr^c_\omega(s_1, s_2)$) in a sequence of trials—in particular, a sequence where there is one trial in the sequence for each voter.

A relatively simple case occurs when for a given $c \in C$ and $(s_1, s_2) \in S_1 \times S_2$ we have $\Pr^c_\omega(s_1, s_2) \in (0, 1)$, $\forall \omega \in \Omega$ and $\Pr^c_\omega(s_1, s_2)$ has the same value for each $\omega \in \Omega$. In this case, the total vote for c is an ordinary binomial random variable (where the number of trials is equal to the number of voters and the probability of success for each trial is $\Pr^c_\omega(s_1, s_2)$). For instance, suppose that both candidates choose the same strategy and we have $\Pr^c_\omega(s_1, s_2) = 1/2$, $\forall \omega \in \Omega$. Then the resulting binomial random variable for c's total vote has $\#\Omega$ trials and the probability of success for each trial is $1/2$.

The assumptions for the framework in Section 3.1 also clearly allow the values for the $\Pr^c_\omega(s_1, s_2)$ to vary from one voter to another. When $\Pr^c_\omega(s_1, s_2) \in (0, 1)$, $\forall \omega \in \Omega$, but $\Pr^c_\omega(s_1, s_2)$ does *not* have the same value for all voters, the total vote for c is a Poisson binomial random variable, using, for instance, the definition in Section 12.2 of Johnson, Kotz, and Kemp (1992).

Since a candidate can be uncertain about which candidate a particular voter will vote for, he can be uncertain about the total number of votes he will get. Because of this potential uncertainty, "theories of election competition frequently use maximizing expected vote" (Aranson, Hinich, and Ordeshook 1973, p. 205). The expected vote for candidate c (when candidate 1 chooses s_1 and candidate 2 chooses s_2) will be denoted by $EV^c(s_1, s_2)$.

When the set of voters is finite, the expected vote for c will be the sum of the expected votes from the individual voters. Applying the definition of expected value to the random variable $V^c_\omega(s_1, s_2)$, we get

$$EV^c_\omega(s_1, s_2) = (1) \cdot \Pr^c_\omega(s_1, s_2) + (0) \cdot \Pr^k_\omega(s_1, s_2). \tag{1}$$

Therefore, the expected vote for c from ω (when candidate 1 chooses s_1 and candidate 2 chooses s_2) will be $\Pr^c_\omega(s_1, s_2)$. So, when the set of voters is finite, at any given $(s_1, s_2) \in S_1 \times S_2$ the expected vote for c can be written as

$$EV^c(s_1, s_2) = \sum_{\omega=1}^{\#\Omega} \Pr^c_\omega(s_1, s_2). \tag{2}$$

It was noted above that, in the case where (for a given $c \in C$ and $(s_1, s_2) \in S_1 \times S_2$) we have $\Pr^c_\omega(s_1, s_2) \in (0, 1)$, $\forall \omega \in \Omega$ and $\Pr^c_\omega(s_1, s_2)$ has the same value for each $\omega \in \Omega$, the total vote for c is an ordinary binomial random variable. In this case, (2) reduces to $(\mathrm{Pr}^c_\omega(s_1, s_2))\#\Omega$.

When considering objectives for the more general framework in Section 3.1, I will assume that, for each $(s_1, s_2) \in S_1 \times S_2$, $\mathrm{Pr}^1_\omega(s_1, s_2)$ is measurable with respect to $(\Omega, \mathscr{F}(\Omega))$. Using the fact that $\mathrm{Pr}^1_\omega(s_1, s_2)$ is bounded below by 0 and bounded above by 1, it follows that for each $(s_1, s_2) \in S_1 \times S_2$, $\mathrm{Pr}^1_\omega(s_1, s_2)$ is integrable with respect to $(\Omega, \mathcal{F}(\Omega), \pi_\Omega)$. So, for all of the cases covered by the framework in Section 3.1, the expected vote for $c = 1$ is (using the finite measure μ_Ω):

$$\mathrm{EV}^1(s_1, s_2) = \int_\Omega \mathrm{Pr}^1_\omega(s_1, s_2) \mathrm{d}\mu_\Omega(\omega); \tag{3}$$

(3) implies

$$\mathrm{EV}^2(s_1, s_2) = \mu_\Omega(\Omega) - \mathrm{EV}^1(s_1, s_2) = \int_\Omega \mathrm{Pr}^2_\omega(s_1, s_2) \mathrm{d}\mu_\Omega(\omega). \tag{4}$$

When each candidate's objective is to maximize his expected vote, we have the strategic form game where (1) the players are the two candidates; (2) for each $c \in C$, the strategy set is S_c; (3) for each $c \in C$, the payoff function is $\mathrm{EV}^c(s_1, s_2)$. This game will be denoted by $(S_1, S_2;\ \mathrm{EV}^1,\ \mathrm{EV}^2)$.

In the Hotelling–Downs model (and in a number of subsequent models), each c's objective is to maximize his vote share. Within the framework in Section 3.1, this can be generalized to expected vote share. The expected vote share for a particular c (when candidate 1 chooses s_1 and candidate 2 chooses s_2) will be denoted by $\mathrm{VS}^c(s_1, s_2)$. The expected vote share for $c = 1$ is (using the distribution of voter indices, π_Ω):

$$\mathrm{VS}^1(s_1, s_2) = \int_\Omega \mathrm{Pr}^1_\omega(s_1, s_2) \mathrm{d}\pi_\Omega(\omega); \tag{5}$$

(5) implies

$$\mathrm{VS}^2(s_1, s_2) = 1 - \mathrm{VS}^1(s_1, s_2) = \int_\Omega \mathrm{Pr}^2{}_\omega(s_1, s_2) \mathrm{d}\pi_\Omega(\omega). \tag{6}$$

When each candidate's objective is to maximize his expected vote share: (1) the players are the two candidates; (2) for each $c \in C$, the strategy set is S_c; (3) for each $c \in C$, the payoff function is $\mathrm{VS}^c(s_1, s_2)$. This game will be denoted by $(S_1, S_2;\ \mathrm{VS}^1,\ \mathrm{VS}^2)$.

The game-theoretic notion of strategic equivalence can be used with models of electoral competition as follows. Any pair of relevant games for the candidates can, by definition, differ at most in their payoffs. Consider any such pair of games, $(S_1, S_2; a^1, a^2)$ and $(S_1, S_2; b^1, b^2)$. Applying the standard definition of strategically equivalent games (see, for instance, Vorobev 1977, p. 3) in this context, saying that $(S_1, S_2; a^1, a^2)$ and $(S_1, S_2; b^1, b^2)$ are strategically equivalent means $\exists$ a positive real number ρ and real numbers γ_1, γ_2 such that, for each, $(s_1, s_2) \in S_1 \times S_2$,

$$a^1(s_1, s_2) = \gamma_1 + \rho \cdot b^1(s_1, s_2) \quad \text{and} \quad a^2(s_1, s_2) = \gamma_2 + \rho \cdot b^2(s_1, s_2). \tag{7}$$

Using the definition of strategically equivalent games along with (3)–(6), it follows that $(S_1, S_2;\ \mathrm{VS}^1,\ \mathrm{VS}^2)$ and $(S_1, S_2;\ \mathrm{EV}^1,\ \mathrm{EV}^2)$ are strategically equivalent.

One important implication of the definition of strategically equivalent games is the following: The games have the same equilibria (see, for instance, Vorobev 1977, p. 3). So (1) a pair of strategies, $(s_1^*, s_2^*) \in S_1 \times S_2$, is a pure-strategy equilibrium in the game $(S_1, S_2;\ \mathrm{VS}^1,\ \mathrm{VS}^2)$ if and only if (s_1^*, s_2^*) is a pure-strategy equilibrium in the game $(S_1, S_2;\ \mathrm{EV}^1,\ \mathrm{EV}^2)$, and (2) a pair of probability distributions on X is an equilibrium in the mixed extension of $(S_1, S_2;\ \mathrm{VS}^1,\ \mathrm{VS}^2)$ if and only if it is an equilibrium in the mixed extension of $(S_1, S_2;\ \mathrm{EV}^1, \mathrm{EV}^2)$.

A second important implication of the definition of strategically equivalent games is that for any constant-sum game, there exists a zero-sum game that is strategically equivalent to it (see, for instance, Vorobev 1977, p. 5). Since the total vote is always $\mu_\Omega(\Omega)$, the expected votes for the two candidates always sum to $\mu_\Omega(\Omega)$. Therefore, $(S_1, S_2; \mathrm{EV}^1, \mathrm{EV}^2)$ is constant-sum. Since the expected vote shares (by definition) always sum to 1, $(S_1, S_2; \mathrm{VS}^1, \mathrm{VS}^2)$ is also constant-sum. The next game is one that has been studied in the literature and that is strategically equivalent to the games specified above.

In some references, it is assumed that each candidate's objective is to maximize his expected plurality. The expected plurality for candidate c at a particular pair of candidate strategies, $(s_1, s_2) \in S_1 \times S_2$, will be denoted by $P\ell^c(s_1, s_2)$. Within the framework in Section 3.1, the expected plurality for $c = 1$ is:

$$\mathrm{P}\ell^1(s_1, s_2) = \int_\Omega \left[\mathrm{Pr}^1_\omega(s_1, s_2) - \mathrm{Pr}^2_\omega(s_1, s_2)\right] \mathrm{d}\mu_\Omega(\omega); \tag{8}$$

(8) implies

$$P\ell^2(s_1, s_2) = -P\ell^1(s_1, s_2). \tag{9}$$

When each candidate's objective is to maximize his expected plurality, (1) the players are the two candidates; (2) for each $c \in C$, the strategy set is S_c; (3) for each $c \in C$, the payoff function is $P\ell^c(s_1, s_2)$. This game will be denoted by $(S_1, S_2; P\ell^1, P\ell^2)$.

The fact that $(S_1, S_2; P\ell^1, P\ell^2)$ is zero-sum follows from (9). The fact that $(S_1, S_2; P\ell^1, P\ell^2)$ is strategically equivalent to $(S_1, S_2; \mathrm{VS}^1, \mathrm{VS}^2)$ and $(S_1, S_2; \mathrm{EV}^1, \mathrm{EV}^2)$ follows from the definition of strategic equivalence and the payoff functions.

For the voting scheme specified at the end of Section 3.1, one can also specify the probability of a candidate winning. Some references that have used this voting scheme have considered *both* what happens when each candidate is assumed to maximize his expected plurality *and* what happens under the alternative assumption that each candidate maximizes his probability of winning. There are games that differ by having these two different payoff functions where the candidates will definitely make different decisions (which, of course, implies that they are not strategically equivalent). However, assumptions that imply the same candidate decisions under these two payoff functions have been identified by Aranson, Hinich, and Ordeshook (1973), Hinich (1977), Samuelson (1984), Ordeshook (1986), Lindbeck and Weibull (1987), Patty (2002), and others.

Each objective discussed above is a function of votes. Some other assumptions about the objectives of a political candidate have also been considered. For instance, Wittman (1977), Calvert (1985), Roemer (2001), and others have analyzed models where candidates either are solely interested in an election's policy outcome or are willing to make a tradeoff between an election's policy outcome and the margin of victory. For these models, Calvert (1985) has established that in most of the cases that have been studied in the literature, "candidate policy motivations don't affect the conclusions of the spatial model" (p. 73). Similar results are in Wittman (1977, Proposition 5) and Roemer (2001, Theorem 2.1). As a consequence, nothing of significance is lost if one assumes that each candidate's objective is to maximize his expected vote (or, equivalently, his expected vote share or expected plurality).

4. DETERMINISTIC VOTING AND SIMPLE MAJORITY RULE

4.1. Definitions

The Hotelling–Downs model and some of the other models in the electoral competition literature have assumed that a voter's choices are determined by his preferences on the set of alternatives. More precisely, they have assumed, for each $\omega \in \Omega$,

$$\mathrm{Pr}^1_\omega(s_1, s_2) = \begin{cases} 1 & \text{if} \quad s_1 \succ_\omega s_2 \\ \dfrac{1}{2} & \text{if} \quad s_1 \sim_\omega s_2 \\ 0 & \text{if} \quad s_2 \succ_\omega s_1 \end{cases} \tag{10}$$

at each $(s_1, s_2) \in S_1 \times S_2$—which, in the framework set out in Section 3.1, implies a similar equation for $\mathrm{Pr}^2_\omega(s_1, s_2)$. This assumption is commonly called "deterministic voting" (see, for instance, Mueller 2003, Chapter 11).

For the finite measure space of voters specified in Section 3.1, the simple majority rule relation can be defined as follows (as in McKelvey and Ordeshook 1976, Grandmont 1978, or McKelvey, Ordeshook, and Ungar 1980). First, assume

$$\{\omega \in \Omega : x \succeq_\omega y\} \in \mathscr{F}(\Omega), \forall x, y \in X. \tag{11}$$

Then the pairwise comparisons for the simple majority rule relation are, for each $x, y \in X$,

$$x \succeq^S y \quad \text{if and only if} \quad \mu_\Omega(\{\omega \in \Omega : x \succeq_\omega y\}) \geq \mu_\Omega(\{\omega \in \Omega : y \succeq_\omega x\}). \tag{12}$$

As in Section 1, saying that $x \in X$ is a "(weak) simple majority Condorcet winner" will mean $x \succeq^S y$, $\forall y \in X$; the asymmetric part of $\succeq^S$ will be denoted by $\succ^S$; saying that $x \in X$ is a "(strong) simple majority Condorcet winner" will mean $x \succ^S y$, $\forall y \in X - \{x\}$.

4.2. Pure-Strategy Equilibria and Condorcet Winners

When there is deterministic voting and the assumptions in Section 3.1 are satisfied, the objective functions based on votes that were discussed in Section 3.2 can be rewritten as functions of sets of voters with common preferences. For instance, a candidate's expected vote function can be written as

$$\text{EV}^c(s_1, s_2) = \mu_\Omega(\{\omega \in \Omega : s_c \succ_\omega s_k\}) + \left(\frac{1}{2}\right) \cdot \mu_\Omega(\{\omega \in \Omega : s_c \sim_\omega s_k\}) \tag{13}$$

where k is the index for the "other candidate" (that is, k is the element in $C - \{c\}$). (The measurability of $\{\omega \in \Omega : s_c \succ_\omega s_k\}$ and $\{\omega \in \Omega : s_c \sim_\omega s_k\}$ follows from (11) and the fact that $\mathscr{F}$ is a σ-field.)

Using (13), it is easy to see that, when the assumptions in Section 3.1 are satisfied *and* there is deterministic voting, the following two connections hold between the simple majority Condorcet winners for the relation defined by (12) and the pure-strategy equilibria for $(S_1, S_2; \text{EV}^1, \text{EV}^2)$: (1) (s_1^*, s_2^*) is a pure-strategy equilibrium if and only if s_1^* and s_2^* are weak Condorcet winners; (2) if there is a strong Condorcet winner, then (s_1^*, s_2^*) is a pure-strategy equilibrium if and only if $s_1^* = s_2^*$ *and* their common strategy (i.e., $s \equiv s_1^* = s_2^*$) is the strong Condorcet winner.

For the game $(S_1, S_2; \text{EV}^1, \text{EV}^2)$, an "equilibrium strategy" for candidate c is an element of S_c that c chooses in at least one pure-strategy equilibrium this game (using, for instance, the definition of an equilibrium strategy for a player in a noncooperative game in Vorobev 1977, p. 3). Since $(S_1, S_2; \text{EV}^1, \text{EV}^2)$ is constant-sum, (s_1^*, s_2^*) is a pure-strategy equilibrium if and only if s_1^* is an "equilibrium strategy" for candidate 1 and s_2^* is an "equilibrium strategy" for candidate 2. So the result in the previous paragraph can be restated as (1) for each $c \in C$, s_c^* is an equilibrium strategy for c if and only if s_c^* is a weak

Condorcet winner; (2) when there is a strong Condorcet winner, for each $c \in C$, s_c^* is an equilibrium strategy for c if and only if s_c^* is the strong Condorcet winner.

Since the game $(S_1, S_2; \mathrm{EV}^1, \mathrm{EV}^2)$ is strategically equivalent to both $(S_1, S_2; \mathrm{VS}^1, \mathrm{VS}^2)$ and $(S_1, S_2; P\ell^1, P\ell^2)$, it follows that the results in the two previous paragraphs also hold for these two games.

These connections (and variations on them) have been discussed in Shubik (1968), Riker and Ordeshook (1973), Kramer (1977a, 1977b), McKelvey and Ordeshook (1990), Laffond, Laslier, and Le Breton (1994), Laslier (1997), Ordeshook (1997), and other sources. The models of electoral competition discussed in Sections 5 and 6 will be ones where there is deterministic voting. In discussing those models, I will make use of these connections.

5. UNIDIMENSIONAL MODELS WITH DETERMINISTIC VOTING

The first unidimensional model that will be considered is the Hotelling–Downs model. In the formulation of the candidates' expectations about the voters' choices in Section 3.1, for any given c and (s_1, s_2), the expectations are a function of the voters' indexes. However, using the function m for the Hotelling–Downs model specified in Section 3.1, the expectations can be rewritten as a function of the voters' most-preferred alternatives.

Since the function m for the Hotelling–Downs model is a linear function of ω, it is invertible. Therefore (for any given c and (s_1, s_2)), for a voter who has s as his most-preferred alternative, the probability that he will vote for c is given by the $\mathrm{Pr}_\omega^c(s_1, s_2)$ where $\omega = m^{-1}(s)$. This probability will be denoted by $\mathrm{Pr}^c(s_1, s_2 \mid s)$. That is, for any given c and (s_1, s_2), $\mathrm{Pr}^c(s_1, s_2 \mid s) \equiv \mathrm{Pr}_\omega^c(s_1, s_2)$ at the s assigned to ω by m. $\mathrm{Pr}^c(s_1, s_2 \mid s)$ gives us the candidates' expectations about the voters' choices as a function of the most-preferred alternatives. In what follows, an explicit equation for $\mathrm{Pr}^c(s_1, s_2 \mid s)$ will be stated.

In Section 2.2, it was noted that in the political reinterpretation of Hotelling's model, for any given $\omega \in \Omega$, $U_\omega(s) = -TC_\omega(s) = -(\kappa) \cdot | s - m(\omega) |$ will be a utility function on X. In addition, it was noted that each party will have the following expectations (for any given ω): *if* $TC_\omega(s_1) < TC_\omega(s_2)$, *then* the probability that ω will vote for party 1 is one; *if* $TC_\omega(s_1) > TC_\omega(s_2)$, *then* the probability that ω will vote for party 2 is one; *if* $TC_\omega(s_1) = TC_\omega(s_2)$, *then* the probability for each of ω's two possible choices is one-half. Using the definition of the voter's total cost function, this implies that the parties have the following expectations: *if* $|s_1 - m(\omega)| < |s_2 - m(\omega)|$, *then* the probability that ω will vote for party 1 is one; *if* $|s_1 - m(\omega)| > |s_2 - m(\omega)|$, *then* the probability that ω will vote for party 2 is one; *if* $|s_1 - m(\omega)| = |s_2 - m(\omega)|$, *then* the probability for each of ω's two possible choices is one-half. That is, if the alternative selected by one party is closer (when measured with Euclidean distance) to a voter's most-preferred alternative, then the parties are certain he will vote for the closer party—and, if the alternatives selected by the parties are equidistant from a voter's most-preferred ideology, then they consider his two possible choices to be equiprobable.

This conclusion enables us to state the following explicit equation for the candidates' expectations about the voters' choices, as a function of the most-preferred alternatives. More specifically, for any given c and (s_1, s_2),

$$\Pr^c(s_1, s_2 \mid s) = \begin{cases} 1 & \text{if} \quad |s_c - s| < |s_k - s| \\ \dfrac{1}{2} & \text{if} \quad |s_c - s| = |s_k - s| \\ 0 & \text{if} \quad |s_c - s| > |s_k - s| \end{cases} \tag{14}$$

(where k is the index for the other candidate).

I will illustrate how (14) can be applied, using the special case for the Hotelling–Downs model where $X = [0, 100]$. Using the distribution of most-preferred alternatives in the model,

$$EV^c(s_1, s_2) = \int_0^{100} \Pr^c(s_1, s_2 \mid s) ds. \tag{15}$$

Using (14), we can solve the integral in (15)—thereby obtaining a different equation for $EV^c(s_1, s_2)$. In particular, using the fact that $\Pr^c(s_1, s_2 \mid s) = 1/2$, $\forall s$ for any particular (s_1, s_2) where $s_1 = s_2$ and using the function (of s) that is obtained from (14) for any particular (s_1, s_2) where $s_1 \neq s_2$, it follows that (for each $(s_1, s_2) \in S_1 \times S_2$)

$$EV^c(s_1, s_2) = \begin{cases} s_c + [(s_k - s_c)/2] & \text{if } s_c < s_k \\ 50 \quad \text{if} & s_c = s_k \\ [100 - s_c] + [(s_c - s_k)/2] & \text{if } s_c > s_k. \end{cases} \tag{16}$$

Therefore, using (16), for each $(s_1, s_2) \in S_1 \times S_2$,

$$EV^c(s_1, s_2) = \begin{cases} (s_c + s_k)/2 & \text{if } s_c < s_k \\ 50 \quad \text{if} & s_c = s_k \\ 100 - [(s_c + s_k)/2] & \text{if } s_c > s_k. \end{cases} \tag{17}$$

An explicit equation like (17) can be used to learn some of the properties of a party's payoff function. For instance, (17) implies that for any given $s'_k \in [0, 100]$,

(1) when $s_c < s'_k$, party c's payoff is the value assigned by the linear equation

$$f_c(s_c) = \left[s'_k/2\right] + (1/2) \cdot s_c; \tag{18}$$

(2) when $s_c > s'_k$, party c's payoff is the value assigned by the linear equation

$$g_c(s_c) = \left[100 - (s'_k/2)\right] - (1/2) \cdot s_c. \tag{19}$$

(17) also implies that, for any given $s'_k \neq 50$, there is a particular type of "discontinuity" in party c's payoff at $s_c = s'_k$. More specifically (for any given $s'_k \neq 50$), (i) the left-hand limit for party c's payoff at $s_c = s'_k$ is s'_k, (ii) the right-hand limit for party c's payoff at $s_c = s'_k$ is $100 - s'_k$, and (iii) party c's payoff at $s_c = s'_k$ is 50—so these are three different numbers.

In the framework specified in Section 3.1, the Hotelling–Downs model corresponds to the supposition in the following theorem.

Theorem 3 *Suppose* $\Gamma = (S_1, S_2; \mathrm{EV}^1, \mathrm{EV}^2)$ *satisfies the following assumptions: (i)* $X = [a,b] \subset \mathbb{R}^1$, *(ii)* Γ *is a regular model with a continuous uniform distribution of most-preferred alternatives on* X, *(iii) there is deterministic voting, and (iv) for each* $\omega \in \Omega$, *the preference ordering* $\succsim_\omega$ *satisfies*

$$\begin{aligned} s_1 \succ_\omega s_2 \quad &\textit{if and only if} \quad |s_1 - m(\omega)| < |s_2 - m(\omega)| \\ s_1 \sim_\omega s_2 \quad &\textit{if and only if} \quad |s_1 - m(\omega)| = |s_2 - m(\omega)| \\ s_2 \succ_\omega s_1 \quad &\textit{if and only if} \quad |s_1 - m(\omega)| > |s_2 - m(\omega)| \end{aligned}$$

for each $(s_1, s_2) \in S_1 \times S_2$. *Then* x *is an equilibrium strategy for a candidate if and only if* x *is the midpoint of the segment* $[a,b]$.

Since each candidate has a unique equilibrium strategy, a unique pure strategy equilibrium exists. Both Hotelling (1929) and Downs (1957) indicated a way in which each party might adjust its location in response to a location selected by the other party, and concluded that the parties "will converge on the same location" (Downs, p. 117). In the game-theoretic literature on electoral competition, for a given equilibrium, (s_1^*, s_2^*), saying that the parties "converge" at that equilibrium means that $s_1^* = s_2^*$ (see, for instance, McKelvey 1975, p. 820). The theorem clearly implies that the parties converge in this sense. For other discussions of the Hotelling–Downs model, see Shepsle and Bonchek (1997, pp. 104–109, in the section "Spatial Elections") and Aliprantis and Chakrabarti (2000, Example 2.11 on pp. 56–58).

Downs (1957) suggested the idea of considering other regular models with $X \subset \mathbb{R}^1$ where (1) "voters preferences are single-peaked... [but] the slope downward from the apex need not be identical on both sides" (pp. 115–116), and (2) there is "a variable distribution of voters along the scale" (p. 117). Along these lines, various references have observed that the theorem stated above can be generalized to the following result. See, for instance, Davis and Hinich (1966, p. 181), Osborne (1995, Proposition 1; 2004, Section 3.3), Aliprantis and Chakrabarti (2000, the "Generalized Voter Model" on pp. 66–67), or Roemer (2001, Theorem 1.1).

Theorem 4 *Suppose* $\Gamma = (S_1, S_2; \mathrm{EV}^1, \mathrm{EV}^2)$ *satisfies the following assumptions: (i)* X *is a convex subset of* $\mathbb{R}^1$*, (ii)* Γ *is a regular model with a continuous distribution of most-preferred alternatives on* X*, (iii) there is deterministic voting, and (iv) for each* $\omega \in \Omega$*, the preference ordering* $\succeq_\omega$ *satisfies*

$$[[z < y < m(\omega)] \quad or \quad [z > y > m(\omega)]] \Rightarrow [y \succ_\omega z]$$

for each $y, z \in X$*. Then* x *is an equilibrium strategy for a candidate if and only if* x *is the median for the distribution of most-preferred alternatives.*

The first theorem established that, under the assumptions for the Hotelling–Downs model, the candidates' equilibrium strategy is the midpoint of X. Under the assumptions for that model, it is also the median and the mean for the distribution of most-preferred alternatives. So one will conclude that the social choice made through the electoral competition is "centrist" if any of these three measures of center is used. Under the assumptions for the second (more general) theorem, the candidates' equilibrium strategy continues to be the median for the distribution of most-preferred alternatives, but it will not be the midpoint of X unless the midpoint happens to coincide with the median. Similarly, it will not be the mean for the distribution of most-preferred alternatives unless the mean happens to coincide with the median. So, under the assumptions for the more general theorem, *in most cases* the candidates' equilibrium strategy will be neither the midpoint of X nor the mean for the distribution of most-preferred alternatives. Therefore *in most cases* one's conclusion about whether the social choice is "centrist" will depend on the measure of center that is used.

Analogous results have also been obtained for models where the set of voters is finite. For instance, using the connection between Condorcet winners and equilibrium strategies discussed in Section 4.3, the first theorem stated in Section 1 implies the following result.

Theorem 5 *Suppose* $\Gamma = (S_1, S_2; \mathrm{EV}^1, \mathrm{EV}^2)$ *satisfies the following assumptions: (i) the set of voters is finite, (ii)* $(X, (\succeq_1, \ldots, \succeq_{\#\Omega}))$ *is a regular model, (ii) there is an ordering relation* $\leq_o$ *that is such that, for each* $\omega \in \Omega$*, the preference ordering* $\succeq_\omega$ *is single-peaked with respect to* $\leq_o$*, and (iii) there is deterministic voting. Then* $x \in X$ *is an equilibrium strategy for a candidate if and only if* x *is a median for the distribution of most-preferred alternatives* (with respect to $\leq_o$).

This theorem clearly implies (1) if there is an *odd* number of voters, then (s_1^*, s_2^*) is a pure-strategy equilibrium if and only if $s_1^* = s_2^*$ and s_1^* is the unique median for the distribution of most-preferred alternatives; (2) if there is an *even* number of voters, then (s_1^*, s_2^*) is a pure-strategy equilibrium if and only if s_1^* and s_2^* are medians for the distribution of most-preferred alternatives.

These conclusions about electoral competition models are based on Black's analysis of committees. One of the first references to explicitly state *implications* from Black's analysis of committees *for* electoral competition models with a finite number of voters is Barr and Davis (1966, Theorem 1). The implications for electoral competition models with a finite number of voters that follow from Black's analysis of committees have been discussed in Ordeshook (1986, Theorem 4.3 on p. 162; 1992, pp. 103–105), Banks (1991, p. 58), Bierman and Fernandez (1998, Section 5.3), Brams (2003, pp. 598–602), and other references.

These conclusions about electoral competition models with a finite number of voters have some noteworthy features. For instance, in these models, a pure-strategy equilibrium exists. So these theorems imply there are certain policies that each candidate can be expected to embody. In addition, each candidate selects a strategy that is a median for the distribution of most-preferred alternatives.

The specific equilibrium strategies for the candidates establish that the policies a candidate can be expected to embody will be at the median for the distribution of most-preferred alternatives. What's more, when there is an *odd* number of voters, the policies (which the candidates can be expected to embody) are unique and will converge. However, when there is an *even* number of voters, it's possible to have more than one median for the distribution of most-preferred alternatives. So, when there is an *even* number of voters, the policies (which the candidates can be expected to embody) (1) are not unique, and (2) could converge, but will not necessarily converge.

Kramer (1973, 1976) established that when X is a subset of a Euclidean space, assuming single-peakedness is tantamount to requiring X to be one-dimensional. The next section will consider models where X is a subset of a Euclidean space, but is not limited to being one-dimensional.

6. FINITE-DIMENSIONAL MODELS WITH DETERMINISTIC VOTING

Black and Newing (1951) and Black (1958, pp. 131–137) considered a model that is closely related to the committee model discussed in Section 1—with the only significant change being that these references *replaced* the assumption of a unidimensional set of motions *with* the assumption that each motion either has two distinguishable aspects or consists of two separate parts. These references pointed out that, in these circumstances, a motion would be defined by two characteristics—and used a real-valued variable for each characteristic.

Significantly, they showed that, for their two-dimensional model, the assumption that the voters have strictly quasi-concave utility functions on the set of motions is *not* sufficient to assure that a Condorcet winner exists. Using the connection between Condorcet winners and pure-strategy equilibria discussed at the end of Section 4, it follows that, when S is multidimensional and voting is deterministic, assuming that the voters have strictly quasi-concave utility functions on the set of motions is *not* sufficient to assure that a pure-strategy equilibrium exists in an electoral competition.

6.1. Plott's Analysis

As in the earlier work by Black and Newing (1951), research by Plott (1967) analyzed a model of a committee. He assumed that the committee is attempting to decide on the magnitude of several variables (p. 787); more precisely, there is a set of alternatives, which is a subset of $\mathbb{R}^h$, where h is an integer greater than 1. He assumed that each voter has a differentiable utility function, U_ω, on the set of possible alternatives (p. 788).

Plott started with the following "notion of equilibrium":

> *the variables could be changed by any amount. If a change in the variables is proposed and the change does not receive a majority vote, then the "existing state" of the variables remains. If no possible change in the variables could receive a majority vote, then the "existing state" of the variables is an equilibrium. (p. 787)*

Plott noted that an alternative is a "global" equilibrium of this sort, where changes of any amount are considered only if it is also a "local" equilibrium. In his analysis, Plott explicity considered only local equilibria.

When studying local equilibria, Plott specifically considered "motions," $dx = (dx_1, \ldots, dx_h)$ from an "existing situation," x. In the text of his article (see p. 788), Plott suggested that $(dx_1, \ldots, dx_h)$ could be taken to be a "small change" in x. With this interpretation, the inner product $\langle dx, \nabla U_\omega(x)\rangle$ is a total differential. He also suggested (in footnote 4 on p. 788) that $(dx_1, \ldots, dx_h)$ could be taken to be a direction. With this interpretation, $\langle dx, \nabla U_\omega(x)\rangle$ is the directional derivative of U_ω at x (for the direction dx).

Plott considered a committee with an odd number of voters (p. 790). He started with a setting in which there are no constraints on the set of alternatives. He assumed that an individual "votes for" a motion dx *if* $\langle dx, \nabla U_\omega(x)\rangle > 0$ (p. 788). In addition, he considered settings in which an individual also "votes for" a motion *only if* $\langle dx, \nabla U_\omega(x)\rangle > 0$ (see part A of Section II, on p. 790). In these settings, saying that an alternative x is a local equilibrium means that, at x, no motion could receive a majority vote; that is, there is no motion dx where $\langle dx, \nabla U_\omega(x)\rangle > 0$ for more than $(\#\Omega/2)$ voters.

One of the things that Plott proved (see p. 790 and Theorem 1 on p. 797) is the following: for an alternative, x, to be a local equilibrium, there must be at least one voter, ω, with $\nabla U_\omega(x) = 0$. Then Plott considered an alternative, x, which is "a maximum for one and only one individual" (p. 790). And he derived the following necessary condition for such an alternative to be a local equilibrium (see p. 790 and Theorem 2 on p. 799): The remaining individuals can be divided into pairs in such a way that, for each pair $\{\alpha, \beta\}$, there exist positive real numbers $\gamma_\alpha, \gamma_\beta$ such that

$$\gamma_\alpha \cdot \nabla U_\alpha(x) + \gamma_\beta \cdot \nabla U_\beta(x) = 0. \tag{20}$$

Letting $\gamma(\alpha, \beta) = \gamma_\beta / \gamma_\alpha$, (20) implies

$$\nabla U_\alpha(x) = -\gamma(\alpha, \beta) \cdot \nabla U_\beta(x). \tag{21}$$

As Plott points out, this tells us that "all individuals for which the point is not a maximum can be divided into pairs whose interests are diametrically opposed" (p. 790). Plott also obtained analogous results for settings where there is "a single constraint such as a budget constraint" (p. 792).

Plott's results led him to conclude: "The most important point is that there is certainly nothing inherent in utility theory which would assure the existence of an equilibrium. In fact, it would only be an accident (and a highly improbable one) if an equilibrium exists at all" (pp. 790–792).

Plott's results were specifically for local equilibria. However, Sloss (1973) subsequently established that Plott's conditions are necessary and sufficient for the existence of a global equilibrium when Plott's original assumptions are supplemented with the following two assumptions: (1) X is an open set, and (2) each voter's preferences on X can be represented by a pseudo-concave utility function.

When the results discussed in this section are combined with the connection between Condorcet winners and pure-strategy equilibria discussed at the end of Section 4, we get the following analogous conclusion for electoral competition models with finite sets of voters and deterministic voting when S is multidimensional: While pure-strategy equilibria sometimes exist in these electoral competitions, the existence of a pure-strategy equilibrium is something that is relatively rare.

6.2. Sufficient Conditions

In the results discussed in Section 6.1, Plott established important *necessary* conditions for the type of equilibrium that he analyzed. More specifically, those results can be rephrased as follows: (1) under the assumptions stated in Section 6.1, a *necessary* condition for x being the type of equilibrium that Plott analyzed is that, at least one voter has a zero utility gradient at x; and (2) when one *also* assumes there is exactly one voter with a zero utility gradient at x, a *necessary* condition for x being the type of equilibrium that Plott analyzed is that, the other voters can be divided into pairs where the utility gradient (at x) for one of the voters in the pair is a negative scalar multiple of the utility gradient (at x) for the other voter in the pair.

Other authors have identified *sufficient* conditions for equilibria in multidimensional models. Some of the pioneering work on this topic was done by Tullock. In Tullock (1967a) and in Chapter III of Tullock (1967b), he considered the simple majority rule relation in a setting where the set of alternatives has two dimensions—and identified *sufficent* conditions for the existence of a strong Condorcet winner. In Chapter IV of Tullock (1967b), he extended the Hotelling–Downs model to a setting where the strategy set for the candidates is an issue space that has two dimensions. What's more, in Chapter IV, he pointed out that his *sufficent* conditions for the existence of a strong Condorcet winner were *also sufficent* conditions for the existence of a pure-strategy equilibrium in an electoral competition model.

I will first discuss Tullock's conditions in the context of the simple majority rule relation. After stating implications of his conditions for strong Condorcet winners, I will then discuss Tullock's conditions in the context of electoral competitions.

In the context of the simple majority rule relation, there are three key parts for Tullock's conditions: (1) There is a set of social alternatives that is a rectangular region in a plane. (2) Each voter has a most-preferred alternative, and the most-preferred alternatives are uniformly distributed on the rectangular region. (3) For each voter, one alternative (in the rectangular region) is at least as good as another alternative *if and only if* the Euclidean distance from the alternative to his most-preferred alternative is less than or equal to the Euclidean distance from the other alternative to his most-preferred alternative.

The reasoning that Tullock used establishes that, under these conditions, a social alternative is a strong Condorcet winner if and only if it is the the center of the rectangular region. So Tullock's conditions are *sufficent* conditions for the existence of a strong Condorcet winner.

In the extension of the Hotelling–Downs model that is in Chapter IV of Tullock (1967b), he assumed that the set of possible strategies for the candidates is the set of social alternatives considered above. In other words, a candidate's strategy is a choice of a social alternative. This assumption can be interpreted within the framework in Section 3 as $X \subseteq \mathbb{R}^2$ and X is a rectangular region.

Within the framework in Section 3, the second part of Tullock's conditions can be interpreted as Γ is a regular model, with a uniform distribution of most-preferred alternatives.

The assumption about a voter's preferences in the third part of Tullock's conditions is similar to the following assumptions in Hotelling's locational model for duopolists: Each buyer will transport his purchases home at a constant per unit cost, and each buyer's objective is to buy his "unit quantity" at a store that minimizes his transportation cost. In a model of electoral competition, this becomes the assumption that (for any given voter) one location is at least as good as another location *if and only if* the Euclidean distance from the location to the voter's most-preferred alternative is less than or equal to the Euclidean distance from the other location to the voter's most-preferred alternative. The specific assumption that Tullock used is stated precisely in what follows.

As has been noted, Tullock considered a set of alternatives that is in $\mathbb{R}^2$ and is a rectangular region. Take the vectors in $\mathbb{R}^2$ to be column vectors. For any $v \in \mathbb{R}^2$, let v^t denote the transpose of v. Let I_2 denote the (2×2) identity matrix. Euclidean distance for $\mathbb{R}^2$ is (of course) derived from the Euclidean norm—which, for $\mathbb{R}^2$, is $||y||_2 = (y^t I_2 y)^{1/2}$.

The Euclidean norm can be used to precisely state the meaning of the assumption that (for any given voter) one alternative in X is at least as good as another alternative if and only if the Euclidean distance from the alternative to his most-preferred alternative is less than or equal to the Euclidean distance from the other alternative to his most-preferred alternative. In particular, this assumption can be stated precisely as:

$$x \succ_\omega y \quad \text{if and only if} \quad ||x - m(\omega)||_2 < ||y - m(\omega)||_2 \tag{22}$$

and

$$x \sim_\omega y \quad \text{if and only if} \quad ||x - m(\omega)||_2 = ||y - m(\omega)||_2 \tag{23}$$

for each $x, y \in S$.

For each $\omega \in \Omega$, the corresponding preferences can be represented by the following ordinal utility function on X:

$$U_\omega(x) = -[x - m(\omega)]^t I_2 [x - m(\omega)]. \tag{24}$$

The expression on the right-hand side of (24) is (of course) a specific quadratic form. Since this particular quadratic form is being used, if the domain of the function in (24) was all of $\mathbb{R}^2$, then the graph of the function in $x_1 - x_2 - U_\omega$ space would be a circular paraboloid with a global maximum at $m(\omega)$. The graph of the function in (24) is therefore the portion of that paraboloid that is obtained when the domain is restriced to the rectangular region X. The global maximum for the utility function is (of course) 0. Hence, for each $x \in X - \{m(\omega)\}$, we have $U_\omega(x) < 0$. For each possible $k < 0$, (24) implies that the corresponding indifference curve, $\{x \in X : U_\omega(x) = k\}$, is the *intersection of* a circle (where the length of the radius is the positive root of $-k$ and where the center is the voter's most-preferred alternative) *and* the rectangular region X. So these indifference curves are the portions of the concentric circles centered at $m(\omega)$ that are in X. For any two elements in $X - \{m(\omega)\}$ that are on different indifference curves, the voter will prefer the alternative on the indifference curve for which the corresponding circle has the smaller radius.

In Tullock's extension of the Hotelling–Downs model, it is assumed that each voter learns which social alternative is chosen by each candidate. It is also assumed that each voter evaluates the candidates entirely in terms of the social alternatives the candidates have chosen. Within the framework summarized in Section 3, these assumptions can be interpreted as, there is deterministic voting, with each $\omega \in \Omega$ having a preference ordering R_ω on X that satisfies (22) and (23) for each $x, y \in X$.

Within the framework in Section 3, Tullock's result for his extension of the Hotelling–Downs model can be stated as follows.

Theorem 6 *Suppose* $\Gamma = (S_1, S_2; \text{EV}^1, \text{EV}^2)$ *satisfies the following assumptions: (i)* $X \subseteq \mathbb{R}^2$ *and* X *is a rectangular region, (ii)* Γ *is a regular model, with a uniform distribution of most-preferred alternatives, and (iii)* Γ *has deterministic voting, with each* $\omega \in \Omega$ *having a preference ordering,* R_ω*, on* X*, which satisfies (22) and (23) for each* $x, y \in X$*. Then* (s_1^*, s_2^*) *is a pure-strategy equilibrium if and only if* $s_1^* = s_2^*$ *and their common strategy is the center of the rectangular region.*

This tells us that, when a model of electoral competition satisfies Tullock's conditions, some of the important implications that follow are similar to ones that hold for the unidimensional model developed by Hotelling and Downs. For one thing, Tullock's conditions imply the existence of a unique pure-strategy equilibrium. For another, Tullock's conditions imply convergence for the candidates' strategies. In addition, under Tullock's conditions, the common strategy for the candidates is in a "central location."

In some references, (1) the assumption about the set of alternatives has been generalized so that $X \subseteq \mathbb{R}^h$ (where h is a positive integer), *and* (2) the assumptions about voter preferences stated in (22) and (23) have been generalized to let them be based on any metric in a certain class of metrics (which has the Euclidean metric as one of its elements). The second generalization has been accomplished as follows. Take the vectors in $\mathbb{R}^h$ to be column vectors. For any $v \in \mathbb{R}^h$, let v^t denote the transpose of v. Euclidean distance for $\mathbb{R}^h$ (of course) is derived from the Euclidean norm for $\mathbb{R}^h$, which is $||y||_h = [y^t I_h y]^{\frac{1}{2}}$ (where I_h denotes the $(h \times h)$ identity matrix). For a given h, let A denote a symmetric, positive-definite, $(h \times h)$ matrix. The norm $||y||_A = [y^t A_h y]^{\frac{1}{2}}$ is called the "weighted Euclidean norm." For any $x, y \in X$, the number $||x - y||_A$ is called the "weighted Euclidean distance" between x and y. Voter preferences are based on weighted Euclidean distance by assuming that, for any given $\omega \in \Omega$,

$$x \succ_\omega y \quad \text{if and only if} \quad ||x - m(\omega)||_A < ||y - m(\omega)||_A \tag{25}$$

and

$$x \sim_\omega y \quad \text{if and only if} \quad ||x - m(\omega)||_A = ||y - m(\omega)||_A \tag{26}$$

for each $x, y \in X$. That is, for any given voter, one alternative in X is at least as good as another alternative if and only if the weighted Euclidean distance from the alternative to his most-preferred alternative is less than or equal to the weighted Euclidean distance from the other alternative to his most-preferred alternative.

When this assumption is made, for each $\omega \in \Omega$, the corresponding preferences can be represented by the ordinal utility function

$$U_\omega(x) = -[x - m(\omega)]^t A[x - m(\omega)] \tag{27}$$

on X.

As in (24), the expression on the right-hand side of (27) is a quadratic form. This time the form uses the matrix A. Since this particular quadratic form is being used, if $X = \mathbb{R}^2$, then the graph of (27) in $x_1 - x_2 - U_\omega$ space is an elliptical paraboloid with a global maximum at $m(\omega)$. This implies a voter's indifference curves would be ellipses that are concentric (with the common center for the ellipses being his most-preferred alternative). When (as in Tullock's analysis) we have $X \subset \mathbb{R}^2$, a voter's indifference curves would be the portions of these ellipses that are in X. That is, each indifference curve would be the *intersection of* one of the ellipses *and* X. In either case (i.e., if either $X = \mathbb{R}^2$ or $X \subset \mathbb{R}^2$), for any two alternatives that are not on the same indifference curve, the voter prefers the alternative whose indifference curve is closer (in weighted Euclidean distance) to his most-preferred alternative.

Davis and Hinich (1966) specified a model of electoral competition and used assumptions like these as one part of a set of *sufficient* conditions for the existence of a pure-strategy equilibrium. Their conditions correspond to the premise in the following theorem.

Theorem 7 *Suppose* $\Gamma = (S_1, S_2; \text{EV}^1, \text{EV}^2)$ *satisfies the following assumptions: (i)* $X = \mathbb{R}^h$, *(ii)* Γ *is a regular model, with a multivariate normal distribution of most-preferred alternatives, and (iii)* Γ *has deterministic voting where, for each* $\omega \in \Omega$, *(25) and (26) hold for each* $x, y \in X$. *Then* (s_1^*, s_2^*) *is a pure-strategy equilibrium if and only if* $s_1^* = s_2^*$, *and their common strategy is the mean for the distribution of most-preferred alternatives.*

Among other things, this theorem establishes that (like Tullock's conditions) Davis and Hinich's conditions imply (1) there is a unique pure-strategy equilibrium, (2) the candidates' strategies converge, and (3) the candidates' strategies are in a "central location."

There are also other conditions for regular models with infinite sets of voters that have been shown to imply the existence of a Condorcet winner (and, hence, also pure-strategy equilibria in electoral competitions with deterministic voting) when there is a multimensional X. Davis and Hinich (1968, 1971) obtained results for other models with multivariate normal distributions. Davis, Hinich, and Ordeshook (1970), Riker and Ordeshook (1973), and McKelvey (1975) analyzed multivariate distributions that are symmetric. Davis, DeGroot, and Hinich (1972) and Hoyer and Mayer (1975) worked with multivariate distributions that have a total median. McKelvey, Ordeshook, and Ungar (1980) studied multivariate distributions that are weakly symmetric. In addition, extensions of Tullock's model that do not require each voter to have a unique most-preferred alternative were developed by Arrow (1969), Grandmont (1978), and others.

Conditions for models with finite sets of voters that imply the existence of a Condorcet winner (and, hence, also pure-strategy equilibria in electoral competitions with deterministic voting) when there is a multidimensional set of conditions have also been identified. Important results along these lines are in Simpson (1969), Sloss (1973), Wendell and Thorson (1974), McKelvey and Wendell (1976), Matthews (1979, 1980), Enelow and Hinich (1983), Saari (1997), and other sources.

Significantly, in this work, the sufficient conditions either have demanding symmetry requirements for the distribution of most-preferred alternatives or have other demanding requirements—for example, the convexity assumption used by Arrow (1969), the symmetry assumption for sets of intermediate preferences used by Grandmont (1978), or the assumptions about the number of voters whose most-preferred alternative is located at the equilibrium that are in Slutsky (1979) and Enelow and Hinich (1983).

For further discussion about conditions that are sufficient for Condorcet winners when there is a multidimensional alternative set (and pure-strategy equilibria in electoral competition models with deterministic voting and multidimensional strategy sets), see for instance Feld and Grofman (1987), Straffin (1989, 1994), McKelvey (1990, Section 3), Owen (1995, Section XVI.1), Mas-Colell, Whinston, and Green (1995, pp. 805–806), Hinich and Munger (1997, pp. 87–88), or Saari (2004).

6.3. McKelvey's Theorem

McKelvey (1976) discovered an important result about majority rule. He also identified some implications for models of committees.

In his analysis, McKelvey assumed a particular type of majority rule that is different from the "simple majority rule" used in the discussion about Black's analysis of committees in Section 1. The particular type he assumed requires an absolute majority (i.e., more than half of the entire set of voters) for majority preference. More specifically, (i) one alternative beats another one if and only if an absolute majority prefer it, and (ii) otherwise, the two alternatives tie one another.

McKelvey (1976) considered settings where there is a finite set of voters with $\#\Omega \geq 3$. Recall from Section 1.4, for any given $(X, (\succeq_1, \ldots, \succeq_{\#\Omega}))$, the relation "beats or ties" for absolute majority rule is denoted by $\succeq^A$; for any given $(X, (\succeq_1, \ldots, \succeq_{\#\Omega}))$, saying that $x \in X$ is a "(weak) absolute majority Condorcet winner" (or, equivalently, is in the core for a committee that is using absolute majority rule) means $x \succeq^A y, \forall\, y \in X$.

McKelvey (1976) considered settings where (1) X is a multidimensional Euclidean space, and (2) voters have preferences like the ones used in Tullock's conditions. Tullock (1967a, 1967b), of course, only considered a setting where $X \subseteq \mathbb{R}^2$ and X is a rectangular region. For settings where X is any multidimensional Euclidean space and voters have preferences like the ones used in Tullock's conditions, suppose (1) for an integer $h \geq 2$, $X = \mathbb{R}^h$, and (2) for each voter, one element in X is at least as good as another element if and only if the Euclidean distance from the element to his most-preferred element is less than or equal to the Euclidean distance from the other element to his most-preferred element.

The second assumption stated above can be stated precisely by using the Euclidean norm for $\mathbb{R}^h$ to generalize as follows the assumptions about preferences stated in (22) and (23), so that the generalized assumptions apply to $X = \mathbb{R}^h$. For any given $\omega \in \Omega$,

$$x \succ_\omega y \quad \text{if and only if} \quad ||x - m(\omega)||_h < ||y - m(\omega)||_h \tag{28}$$

and

$$x \sim_\omega y \quad \text{if and only if} \quad ||x - m(\omega)||_h < ||y - m(\omega)||_h \tag{29}$$

for each $x, y \in X$. When $X = \mathbb{R}^h$, a voter whose preferences satisfy this assumption is said to have "Euclidean preferences."

McKelvey proved the following theorem.

Theorem 8 *Suppose $(X, (\succeq_1, \ldots, \succeq_{\#\Omega}))$ is a regular model where $\#\Omega \geq 3$, $X = \mathbb{R}^h$ (with $h \geq 2$), and each voter has Euclidean preferences. If there is no (weak) absolute majority Condorcet winner, then for any $x, y \in X$ there exists a finite sequence of alternatives $\{z_1, \ldots, z_N\}$ with $z_1 = x$ and $z_N = y$ such that $z_{j+1} \succ^A z_j, \forall j \in \{1, \ldots, N-1\}$.*

McKelvey's analysis used absolute majority rule. However, when one makes the other assumptions that he used, an alternative is a (weak) absolute majority Condorcet winner if and only if it is a (weak) simple majority Condorcet winner (see, for instance, Theorem 1.1 on p. 146 in McKelvey and Wendell 1976, or Proposition 1 on p. 318 in Kramer 1977b). So his result applies to both types of (weak) Condorcet winner.

The theorem tells us that the following property holds under McKelvey's assumptions when there is no (weak) Condorcet winner: For any given pair of alternatives, there is a sequence (1) that starts at the first alternative in the pair and ends at the second one in the pair, and (2) where each alternative in the sequence is preferred by an absolute majority of voters to the one that immediately precedes it. So when there is no (weak) Condorcet winner, it is possible for such sequences to wander all over the set of alternatives.

6.4. Summing Up

The electoral competition models with deterministic voting and unidimensional strategy sets based on the work of Hotelling and Downs and the work of Black have pure-strategy equilibria, and the candidate strategies in those equilibria are at central locations. In addition, the research discussed in Sections 6.1 and 6.2 identified conditions under which there are pure-strategy equilibria in electoral competition models with deterministic voting and multidimensional strategy sets, and the candidate strategies in those equilibria are at central locations. But, significantly, the sufficient conditions for pure-strategy equilibria in the latter case (i.e., for pure-strategy equilibria in electoral competition models with deterministic voting and multidimensional strategy sets) are severe conditions that are unlikely to be satisfied.

7. PROBABILISTIC VOTING MODELS

7.1. An Overview

The results for electoral competition models discussed in the previous sections were for models with deterministic voting. In other words, they were for models where the alternatives selected by the candidates always fully determined the choice that every nonindifferent voter would make. More specifically, whenever a voter preferred the alternative selected by one candidate to the alternative selected by the other candidate, that voter was certain to vote for the candidate with the preferred alternative.

Section 7.2 and Sections 8 to 10 are about electoral competition models that use a probabilistic model of voter choice—that is, electoral competition models where the voting is not deterministic. More specifically, they will be about models that do *not* assume that the candidates are certain about the choices that will be made by all of the nonindifferent voters. Such models are commonly called "probabilistic voting models," reflecting the fact that the candidates' uncertainty can be modeled by using a probabilistic description of the voters' choice behavior. Section 7.2 will discuss the reasons why people have been interested in probabilistic voting models. Sections 8 to 10 will concentrate on what has been learned about the implications of candidate uncertainty for the existence and location of a pure-strategy equilibrium.

7.2. Reasons for Analyzing Probabilistic Voting Models

Various researchers have become interested in the implications of candidate uncertainty about voters' choices primarily because there are good empirical reasons for believing that actual candidates often *are* uncertain about the choices that voters are going to make on election day. First, candidates tend to rely on polls for information about how voters will vote, but "information from public opinion surveys is not error-free and is best represented as statistical" (Ordeshook 1986, p. 179). Second, even when economists and political scientists have developed sophisticated statistical models of voters' choices and have used appropriate data sets to estimate them, there has consistently been a residual amount of unexplained variation; see, for instance, Fiorina (1981); Enelow and Hinich (1984, Chapter 9); Enelow, Hinich, and Mendell (1986); Merrill and Grofman (1999).

These circumstances have led many empirically-oriented public choice scholars to the following view, expressed in Fiorina's empirical analysis of voting behavior: "In the real world choices are seldom so clean as those suggested by formal decision theory. Thus real decision makers are best analyzed in probabilistic rather than deterministic terms" (1981, p. 155). Some theoretically-oriented public choice scholars have also adopted the same view and have developed and analyzed the theoretical properties of models in which candidates are assumed to have probabilistic (rather than deterministic) expectations about voters' choices. More specifically, these theorists have carried out these studies because, as Ordeshook put it, "if we want to design models that take cognizance of the kind of data that the candidates are likely to possess, probabilistic models seem more reasonable" (1986, p. 179).

In the context of models where X is a set of possible positions on an issue, when the assumption of deterministic voting is used, each nonindifferent voter will definitely vote for the candidate whose position is preferred by that voter. In an analysis of a model of this sort (where they also assumed that, for each voter, there is a utility function on the set of possible positions *and* the magnitudes of utility differences are meaningful), Merrill and Grofman (1999, p. 81) have argued,

> *Yet voters use criteria other than issues to choose candidates. The probability, furthermore, that even an issue-oriented voter will select the candidate of higher utility is certainly less that unity if utilities do not differ greatly.*

Merrill and Grofman (1999, p. 82) have also pointed out that one can "include non-issue effects by adding a probabilistic (or stochastic) component to the issue-oriented utility." This method for including non-issue effects is one (influential) way of specifying what is sometimes called a "probabilistic model of voter choice."

It is reasonable to take the view that deterministic voting models are most appropriate for elections with candidates who are well informed about the voters and their preferences. However, it is also reasonable to think that probabilistic voting models are most appropriate for elections in which candidates have incomplete information about voters' preferences and/or there are random factors that can potentially affect voters' decisions. Because most elections are in this second category, it seems appropriate to agree with Calvert (1986, p. x) that assuming "that candidates cannot perfectly predict the response of the electorate to their platforms is appealing for its realism" (p. 14), a conclusion that, he points out, is in harmony with the "importance attached by traditional political scientists to the role of imperfect information in politics" (p. 54).

8. UNIDIMENSIONAL MODELS WITH PROBABILISTIC VOTING

Comaner (1976) and Hinich (1977) did pioneering research on unidimensional models where candidates are uncertain about whom the individual voters in the electorate will vote for. In their articles, they independently reexamined models with single-peaked preferences and addressed the question, Is choosing a median necessarily an equilibrium strategy?

Comaner (1976) and Hinich (1977) showed that in models with single-peaked preferences, *if* there is indeterminateness in voter choices *then* choosing a median might not be an equilibrium strategy. This result will initially be illustrated with the following example (which is similar to an example used in Hinich 1977, p. 213, to establish the result). The authors were concerned with the consequences of indeterminatess being introduced into the type of electoral competition model that was discussed in the previous sections. As in Hinich's original example, nondeterministic voting will be assumed for the choices of some (but not all) voters in the initial illustration in this section.

Example 1 Let $\Omega = \{1,2,3\}$. Assume $X = [-1,+1]$. Assume the voters' most-preferred alternatives are $m(1) = -1, m(2) = 0$ and $m(3) = +1$. Assume that, for each $\omega \in \Omega$, there is a difference-scale utility function:

$$U_\omega(x) = -|x - m(\omega)|. \tag{30}$$

Also assume that, for each $\omega \in \Omega$, there is a function P_ω (whose domain contains the set $\{z \in \mathbb{R} \mid \exists\ (s_1, s_2) \in X \times X$ such that $U_\omega(s_1) - U_\omega(s_2) = z\}$ and whose range is contained in the set [0,1]) such that, for each $(s_1, s_2), \in X \times X$,

$$\Pr{}^1_\omega(s_1, s_2) = P_\omega(U_\omega(s_1) - U_\omega(s_2)). \tag{31}$$

By (31) and (30),

$$\Pr{}^1_\omega(s_1, s_2) = P_\omega(|s_2 - m(\omega)| - |s_1 - m(\omega)|). \tag{32}$$

Assume that $P_1(y) = P_2(y), \forall y$ and that (for $\omega = 1,2$) (a) P_ω is differentiable, (b) $P'_\omega(y) \geq 0, \forall y$, (c) there exists an $r > 0$ such that $P'_\omega(y) > 0, \forall y \in [0, r)$ and (d) $P_\omega(0) = 1/2$.

For $\omega = 3$, assume deterministic voting. Using (31), it follows that

$$P_3(y) = \begin{cases} 1 & \text{if} \quad y > 0 \\ \dfrac{1}{2} & \text{if} \quad y = 0 \\ 0 & \text{if} \quad y < 0. \end{cases} \tag{33}$$

The following argument shows that, in Example 1, even though the median for the distribution of most-preferred alternatives, $x_{\text{med}} = 0$, is a feasible strategy for each candidate, $(x_{\text{med}}, x_{\text{med}})$ is *not* a pure-strategy equilibrium in the two-candidate game $(S_1, S_2;\ \text{EV}^1,\ \text{EV}^2)$. The assumptions in the example imply there exists some $\rho \in (0, r)$ such that $\text{Pr}_1^1(\rho, x_{\text{med}}) > 1/4$, $\text{Pr}_2^1(\rho, x_{\text{med}}) > 1/4$, and $\text{Pr}_3^1(\rho, x_{\text{med}}) = 1$. This implies $\text{EV}^1(\rho, x_{\text{med}}) > 3/2$. Since $\text{EV}^1(x_{\text{med}}, x_{\text{med}}) = 3/2$, candidate 1 would be better off if he unilaterally changed his strategy from x_{med} to ρ. Therefore this example shows that a median is not necessarily an equilibrium strategy for a candidate when probabilistic voting is introduced.

The reason for including Example 1 was to illustrate the type of example used in Hinich (1977). The preceding analysis of this example also illustrated the type of logical argument that he used.

Hinich's original example assumed deterministic voting for one voter. Since that assumption was in his example, it was also included in Example 1. Because there is a deterministic voter in Hinich's example and Example 1, they clearly establish that having *some* deterministic voting (in a model with single-peaked preferences) is NOT sufficient for a median to be an equilibrium strategy.

At the same time, because there is a discontinuity at $y = 0$ for the P_ω of the deterministic voter in both Example 1 and Hinich's example, those examples do not establish whether (in a model with single-peaked preferences) a median can fail to be an equilibrium strategy IF *each* P_ω is assumed to be continuous. *A fortiori,* they also do not settle this question for the stronger assumption of differentiability for each P_ω.

The following variation on Example 1 will illustrate the fact that the same basic reasoning can be used *without* assuming there is a nondifferentiable (or, alternatively, a discontinuous) P_ω.

Example 2 Everything assumed in Example 1 up through (32) will also be assumed in this example. However, unlike in Example 1, in this example there will be a specific (and differentiable) P_ω function for each voter.

For each $\omega \in \Omega$, we will use the following function (with the domain $S_1 \times S_2$):

$$z_\omega(s_1, s_2) = |s_2 - m(\omega)| - |s_1 - m(\omega)|. \tag{34}$$

For each $\omega \in \Omega$, the domain of P_ω will be an open interval that contains the range of the function z_ω.

For $\omega = 1$ and $\omega = 2$, assume that (at each element in its domain)

$$P_\omega(y) = \begin{cases} 1 \quad \text{if} \quad y \geq 1 \\ \dfrac{1}{2} + \left(\dfrac{3}{4}\right) y - \left(\dfrac{1}{4}\right)(y^3) \quad \text{if} \quad -1 < y < +1 \\ 0 \quad \text{if} \quad y \leq -1. \end{cases} \tag{35}$$

For $\omega = 3$, assume that (at each element in its domain)

$$P_3(y) = \begin{cases} 1 & \text{if } y \geq \frac{1}{6} \\ \frac{1}{2} + \left(\frac{3}{4}\right)y - \left(\frac{1}{4}\right)(y^3) & \text{if } -\frac{1}{6} < y < +\frac{1}{6} \\ 0 & \text{if } y \leq -\frac{1}{6}. \end{cases} \tag{36}$$

Suppose that, in Example 2, $s_1 = 1/3$ and $s_2 = x_{\text{med}}$. Then we have $\text{EV}^1(1/3, x_{\text{med}}) = P_1(z_1(1/3, 0)) + P_2(z_2(1/3, 0)) + P_3(z_3(1/3, 0)) \approx .2595 + .2595 + 1$. Therefore $\text{EV}^1(1/3, x_{\text{med}}) \approx 1.518$. Since $\text{EV}^1(x_{\text{med}}, x_{\text{med}}) = 1.5$, it follows that $(x_{\text{med}}, x_{\text{med}})$ is *not* a pure-strategy equilibrium in the game $(S_1, S_2; \text{EV}^1, \text{EV}^2)$ in Example 2.

Comaner (1976) provided examples with skewed distributions of most-preferred alternatives where there is a pure-strategy equilibrium at an alternative that is not a median. Hinich (1977) provided two examples where there is a pure-strategy equilibrium at an alternative measure of the center for the distribution of most-preferred alternatives. The first example illustrated the fact that, when the candidates are uncertain about the voters' choices, there can be a pure-strategy equilibrium at the mean for the distribution of most-preferred alternatives, rather than at the median. It also showed that the equilibrium can be far from the median. The second of these examples illustrated the fact that, when the candidates are uncertain about voters' choices, there can be a pure-strategy equilibrium at the mode for the distribution of most-preferred alternatives, rather than at either the median or the mean. Related analyses of unidimensional models have been carried out by Kramer (1978a), Ball (1999), Kirchgassner (2000), Laussel and Le Breton (2002), and others.

The most important point made by the material discussed in this section is that there are important conclusions for models of electoral competition with deterministic voting that can change when one introduces candidate uncertainty about voters' choices into the models.

9. FINITE-DIMENSIONAL MODELS WITH PROBABILISTIC VOTING

9.1. Hinich's Model

Hinich (1978) analyzed *both* unidimensional *and* multidimensional models with probabilistic voting. One of the things he did was identify conditions where, if a pure-strategy equilibrium exists, it must be at the mean. Sufficient conditions for the existence of such a pure-strategy equilibrium were also presented.

Hinich assumed that $X = \mathbb{R}^h$ (without restricting h to be 1). He also assumed that the set of voters is finite. In addition, he assumed that, for each $\omega \in \Omega$, there are a most-preferred alternative $m(\omega) \in X$, and an $(h \times h)$, symmetric, positive-definite matrix, $A(\omega)$, which enter into ω's evaluation of each candidate's strategy. More specifically, he assumed that they enter into the determination of a policy-related "loss" (or negative utility) associated with the winning candidate's choice of a particular $x \in X$. In particular, Hinich assumed that this loss is the number assigned by the following function (which depends on the "distance" between s and $m(\omega)$):

$$L_\omega(s) = M(||s - m(\omega)||_{A(\omega)}) \tag{37}$$

where M is a monotonically increasing function and $||y||_A = [y^t Ay]^{\frac{1}{2}}$. He also assumed that, for each $\omega \in \Omega$, there is a nonpolicy loss, $e_1(\omega)$, for ω if candidate 1 is elected and a nonpolicy loss, $e_2(\omega)$, for ω if candidate 2 is the winner.

Hinich assumed that the candidates are uncertain about the choices that the voters are going to make on election day *because* the candidates are uncertain about the following characteristics for any given $\omega \in \Omega$: the most-preferred alternative $m(\omega)$; the matrix $A(\omega)$; and the nonpolicy losses, $e_1(\omega)$ and $e_2(\omega)$. This uncertainty was formulated by assuming that, for any given $\omega \in \Omega$, the candidates' expectations are given by a random variable on a set of possible values for $m(\omega)$, $A(\omega)$, $e_1(\omega)$ and $e_2(\omega)$. So the formulation of a candidate's expectations about a voter's characteristics is like the standard formulation of expectations about a statistical observation *prior* to it being randomly selected from a population with a known distribution.

Hinich assumed that, for any given pair of strategy choices $(s_1, s_2) \in S_1 \times S_2$, the probability that candidate 1 will get the vote of a particular individual ω (conditional on the voter having a particular most-preferred alternative m, matrix A, and nonpolicy values e_1 and e_2) is

$$\begin{aligned} &\mathrm{P}^1_\omega(s_1, s_2 | m(\omega) = m, A(\omega) = A, e_1(\omega) = e_1, e_2(\omega) = e_2) \\ &= \begin{cases} 1 & \text{if } \; M(||s_1 - ||_A) + e_1 < M(||s_2 - m||_A) + e_2 \\ 0 & \text{otherwise.} \end{cases} \end{aligned} \tag{38}$$

That is, ω will vote for candidate 1 if and only if his total loss (his policy-related loss plus nonpolicy loss) from having candidate 1 elected is smaller than his total loss from having candidate 2 elected. An analogous assumption (with 2 replacing 1 and 1 replacing 2, on the right-hand side of (38)) was made about the conditional probability that ω will vote for candidate 2 at any particular strategy $(s_1, s_2) \in S_1 \times S_2$. Equation (38) can, of course, be rewritten as

$$\begin{aligned} &\mathrm{Pr}^1_\omega(s_1, s_2 | m(\omega) = m, A(\omega) = A, \varepsilon(i) = \varepsilon) \\ &= \begin{cases} 1 & \text{if } \; M(||s_2 - m||_A) - M(||s_1 - m||_A) > \varepsilon \\ 0 & \text{otherwise} \end{cases} \end{aligned} \tag{39}$$

where $\varepsilon = e_1 - e_2$. Hinich denoted the conditional distribution function for ε (given m and A) by F_ε. Using this notation, (39) leads to the conclusion that

$$\Pr^1_\omega(s_1, s_2 | m(\omega) = m, A(\omega) = A) = F_\varepsilon[M(||s_2 - m||_A) - M(||s_1 - m||_A)] \tag{40}$$

for each possible s_1, s_2, m and A. He assumed as well that F_ε has a continuous density function f_ε.

These assumptions imply that, at any given $(s_1, s_2) \in S_1 \times S_2$, the expected vote for candidate 1 is

$$\mathrm{EV}^1(s_1, s_2) = (\#\Omega) \cdot (E\{F_\varepsilon[M(||s_2 - m||_A) - M(||s_1 - m||_A)]\}) \tag{41}$$

with the expected value on the right specifically being taken with respect to the joint distribution of m and A. (41) leads to

$$P\ell^1(s_1, s_2) = (\#\Omega) \cdot (2 \cdot E\{F_\varepsilon[M(||s_2 - m||_A) - M(||s_1 - m||_A)]\} - 1) \tag{42}$$

at each $(s_1, s_2) \in S_1 \times S_2$ (as in Hinich's Equation (5), 1978, p. 364).

In his analysis of the resulting game for the candidates, Hinich considered two models that satisfy his assumptions. The first is the "absolute value model," where $M(y) = |y|$. Hinich pointed out that in the absolute value model, when X has one dimension, each candidate choosing a median most-preferred alternative is a pure-strategy equilibrium.

The second model that Hinich considered is the "quadratic model," where $M(y) = y^2$. Hinich (1978, p. 365) established the following result for the quadratic model:

Theorem 9 *Consider the quadratic model and assume that $f_\varepsilon > 0$ with positive probability for all $(s_1, s_2) \in S_1 \times S_2$. If a pure-strategy equilibrium exists, then both candidates choose*

$$\alpha = [E\{f_\varepsilon(0)A\}]^{-1} E\{f_\varepsilon(0)Am\}. \tag{43}$$

Hinich used this result to identify conditions where, if a pure-strategy equilibrium exists, it must be at the mean. In particular, he pointed out that if (a) $f_\varepsilon(0)$ is independent of m and A, and (b) m and A are uncorrelated, then α is the mean ideal point.

Hinich also obtained a stronger result for quadratic models where "f_ε is a normal density whose mean is zero and whose variance σ^2 is small" (Hinich 1978, p. 368). In particular, building on the previous theorem, Hinich (1978, p. 368) established the following result for unidimensional election models.

Theorem 10 *Let $p(m)$ be a density function for the voters' most-preferred alternatives. Assume there is an interval $[a, b]$ such that $p(m) = 0, \forall\, m \notin [a, b]$ and $p(m) > 0, \forall\, m \in [a, b]$. Consider* *the quadratic model where ε has a normal distribution with mean 0 and variance σ^2. There exists $\rho > 0$ such that if $0 < \sigma < \rho$ then*

(i) *a pure-strategy equilibrium exists, and*
(ii) *(s_1^*, s_2^*) is a pure-strategy equilibrium if and only if $s_1^* = s_2^* = \alpha$.*

Hinich pointed out that, "for a one dimensional space, we know that the median ideal point is a global equilibrium when $\sigma = 0$" (p. 367). He then observed that his theorem "shows that there is a discontinuity in the equilibrium of the expected plurality game as $\sigma \to 0$; the equilibrium jumps from α to the median as σ hits zero" (p. 368). This led Hinich to conclude that "a small amount of error in the choice rule is sufficient to destroy the generality and elegance of the Black–Downs unidimensional deterministic result" (p. 370).

In this analysis, Hinich focused on cases where σ is small—since he wanted to *compare* the equilibria in deterministic voting models *with* the equilibria in "nearby" probabilistic voting models (with σ serving as his measure of proximity). Hinich's analysis did not provide results for cases where σ is not small.

At the end of the theoretical analysis in his paper, Hinich concluded: "Unless the reader is willing to accept either the quadratic or the absolute value model, it is difficult to say anything about the outcome of majority rule voting using the spatial model with the uncertainty element in it" (1978, p. 370).

9.2. Expectations Based on a Binary Luce Model

Considering the implications of candidates having uncertainty about voters' choices naturally raises the more general question of how one should model individuals' choices when there is uncertainty about what the individuals will choose. Mathematical psychologists and others have provided useful ways of thinking about this question; see, for instance, Luce and Suppes (1965), Krantz *et al.* (1971), or Roberts (1979). As is well known, the most famous model for such situations is (using the terminology of Becker, DeGroot, and Marschak 1963, p. 43) the "Luce model," which was originally developed by Luce (1959). This model and variations on it have served as the basis for statistical models of paired comparisons (see, for instance, Bradley 1985).

When each voter is assumed to vote (and, hence, is simply deciding whether to vote for candidate 1 or candidate 2), he is making a type of paired comparison. One of the elements (in the pair that is being compared) is candidate 1 and the strategy that candidate 1 has chosen. The other element is candidate 2 and the strategy that candidate 2 has chosen. In this particular setting, the appropriate version of Luce's model is (again using the terminology of Becker, DeGroot, and Marschak 1963, p. 44) the "binary Luce model." Stated in the context of electoral competition models, the binary Luce model for the individuals' selection probabilities assumes: For each $\omega \in \Omega$, there exists a positive, real-valued "scaling function," $f_\omega(x)$, on X such that

$$\mathrm{Pr}^1_\omega(s_1, s_2) = \frac{f_\omega(s_1)}{f_\omega(s_1) + f_\omega(s_2)} \tag{44}$$

and

$$\mathrm{Pr}^2_\omega(s_1, s_2) = \frac{f_\omega(s_2)}{f_\omega(s_1) + f_\omega(s_2)} \tag{45}$$

for each $(s_1, s_2) \in S_1 \times S_2$.

A number of authors who have analyzed Luce models have suggested that the scaling function used for a particular individual could be taken to be a utility function for that individual (see, for instance, Luce and Suppes 1965, p. 335). That is, in the notation used in this chapter, $f_\omega \equiv U_\omega$, $\forall\, \omega \in \Omega$.

Coughlin and Nitzan (1981) proved the following result for electoral competition models with probabilistic voting which satisfy these two assumptions (along with some other assumptions, which are stated in the premise of the theorem).

Theorem 11 *Suppose $(S_1, S_2; P\ell^1, P\ell^2)$ satisfies the following assumptions: (i) Ω is a finite set, (ii) X is a nonempty, compact, convex subset of $\mathbb{R}^h$ (where h is a positive integer), (iii) each $\omega \in \Omega$ has a positive, concave, differentiable, ratio-scale utility function U_ω on X, and (iv) for each $\omega \in \Omega$,*

$$\mathrm{Pr}^1_\omega(s_1, s_2) = \frac{U_\omega(s_1)}{U_\omega(s_1) + U_\omega(s_2)} \tag{46}$$

and

$$\mathrm{Pr}^2_\omega(s_1, s_2) = \frac{U_\omega(s_2)}{U_\omega(s_1) + U_\omega(s_2)} \tag{47}$$

for each $(s_1, s_2) \in S_1 \times S_2$. Then (s_1^*, s_2^*) is a pure-strategy equilibrium if and only if s_1^* and s_2^* maximize

$$W(x) = \sum_{\omega=1}^{n} \ln(U_\omega(x)) \tag{48}$$

on X (where $\ln(v)$ denotes the natural logarithm of v).

What follows is an outline of the proof that is in Coughlin and Nitzan (1981).

1. Since $(S_1, S_2; P\ell^1, P\ell^2)$ is zero-sum and symmetric, (s, t) is a pure-strategy equilibrium if and only if (s, s) and (t, t) are pure-strategy equilibria.
2. Since the game is symmetric, (ψ, ψ) is a pure-strategy equilibrium if and only if $P\ell^1(x, \psi)$ achieves a global maximum at $x = \psi$.
3. The premise for the theorem implies $P\ell^1(x, \psi)$ is concave in x. Hence, since X is convex, $P\ell^1(x, \psi)$ achieves a global maximum at $x = \psi$ if and only if $P\ell^1(x, \psi)$ achieves a local maximum at $x = \psi$.
4. The premise for the theorem implies $W(x)$ is concave in x. Hence, since X is convex, $W(x)$ achieves a global maximum at $x = \psi$ if and only if $W(x)$ achieves a local maximum at $x = \psi$.
5. Evaluating the gradients of $P\ell^1(x, \psi)$ and $W(x)$ at $x = \psi$ establishes that

$$\nabla_x P\ell^1(x, \psi)]_{x=\psi} = (1/2) \cdot \nabla W(x)]_{x=\psi}. \tag{49}$$

6. Using (49), it follows that $P\ell^1(x, \psi)$ achieves a local maximum at $x = \psi$ if and only if $W(x)$ achieves a local maximum at $x = \psi$.
7. By the conclusions in 3, 4, and 6, $P\ell^1(x, \psi)$ achieves a global maximum at $x = \psi$ if and only if $W(x)$ achieves a global maximum at $x = \psi$.
8. By the conclusions in 2 and 7, (ψ, ψ) is a pure-strategy equilibrium if and only if $W(x)$ achieves a global maximum at $x = \psi$.
9. By the conclusions in 8 and 1, (s, t) is a pure-strategy equilibrium if and only if W achieves a global maximum at s and at t.

Coughlin and Nitzan (1981) pointed out that, under the premise for the theorem, the following result holds.

Corollary 1 *There is a pure-strategy equilibrium.*

Under the premise of the theorem, there can be more than one pure-strategy equilibrium. But Coughlin and Nitzan (1981) also pointed out the following implication of the theorem (which identifies sufficient conditions for uniqueness).

Corollary 2 *If at least one voter has a strictly concave utility function, then there is a unique pure-strategy equilibrium.*

The theorem also establishes a connection between pure-strategy equilibria in electoral competitions and a social welfare function that has been analyzed by Sen (1970, Chapter 8), Kaneko and Nakamura (1979), and others. Suppose that (a) there is a distinguished alternative x_0 (which is not in X) that is one of the worst possible alternatives for all individuals, and (b) we set $U_\omega(x_0) = 0, \forall\, \omega \in \Omega$. When this assumption is added to the premise for the theorem, (48) is a "Nash social welfare function" (see Kaneko and Nakamura 1979, p. 432). In addition, the theorem implies that (s_1^*, s_2^*) is a pure-strategy equilibrium if and only if s_1^* and s_2^* maximize this Nash social welfare function.

It will be useful to contrast the implications of these results with the ones obtained when there is deterministic voting under the following assumptions: (i) Ω is a finite set, (ii) X is a nonempty, compact, convex subset of $\mathbb{R}^1$, and (iii) each $\omega \in \Omega$ has a positive, strictly concave, differentiable, ratio-scale utility function U_ω on X. Under these assumptions, for each $\omega \in \Omega$, the preference ordering $\succeq_\omega$ is single-peaked (with respect to the ordering relation "is less than or equal to" for real numbers). So the last theorem in Section 5 (that is the theorem in Section 5 for electoral competitions with a finite set of voters) implies that x is an equilibrium strategy for a candidate if and only if x is a median for the distribution of most-preferred alternatives (with respect to $\leq$).

First consider the cases where $\#\Omega$ is *odd*. When there is deterministic voting:

(a) there is exactly one equilibrium in pure strategies, and
(b) at the equilibrium in pure strategies, each candidate chooses the unique median for the distribution of most-preferred alternatives.

In the probabilistic voting model with (46) and (47) satisfied, (a) there is exactly one equilibrium in pure strategies, and (b) at the equilibrium in pure strategies, each candidate chooses the unique alternative that maximizes the Nash social welfare function. So, both models have a unique prediction for the candidates' equilibrium strategies, *but* the predictions do not match unless the alternative that maximizes the Nash social welfare function happens to coincide with the median for the distribution of most-preferred alternatives. So, when $\#\Omega$ is *odd*, *in most cases* the equilibrium strategy in the probabilistic voting model with (46) and (47) satisfied will **not** be a median.

Now consider the cases where $\#\Omega$ is *even*. When there is deterministic voting:

(1) If there is a unique median for the distribution of most-preferred alternatives, then
  (a) there is exactly one equilibrium in pure strategies, and
  (b) at the equilibrium in pure strategies, each candidate chooses the unique median for the distribution of most-preferred alternatives.
(2) If there is not a unique median for the distribution of most-preferred alternatives, then
  (a) there is more than one equilibrium in pure strategies, and
  (b) at each equilibrium in pure strategies, each candidate chooses a median for the distribution of most-preferred alternatives.

Once again, in the probabilistic voting model with (46) and (47) satisfied, (a) there is exactly one equilibrium in pure strategies, and (b) at the equilibrium in pure strategies, each candidate chooses the unique alternative that maximizes the Nash social welfare function. The comparison with (1) is the same as when $\#\Omega$ is *odd*. For (2), there are two noteworthy comparisons: first, only the probabilistic voting model with (46) and (47) satisfied has a unique prediction for the candidates' equilibrium strategies; second, like when $\#\Omega$ is *odd*, *in most cases* the equilibrium strategy in the probabilistic voting model with (46) and (47) satisfied will **not** be a median.

Samuelson (1984) subsequently studied election models in which the candidates use a binary Luce model, with the added feature that the candidates' strategies are restricted. The restrictions on the candidates' strategies were specifically included by assuming that each candidate has (a) an initial position, $w_c \in X$, and (b) a nonempty, compact, convex set, $S_c(w_c) \subseteq X$, of feasible options open to him. Samuelson also assumed (a) there is a nonempty, compact, Euclidean set of possible voter characteristics, (b) each scaling function is a concave function of the possible candidate strategies, (c) each scaling function is a continuous function of *both* the possible candidate strategies *and* the possible voter characteristics, and (d) the electorate can be summarized by a continuous density function on the set of possible voter characteristics. Samuelson (1984, p. 311) established that the resulting model has the following property: for each $(S_1(w_1), S_2(w_2); P\ell^1, P\ell^2)$ there exists a pure-strategy equilibrium.

Samuelson used his result to analyze (a) a sequence of elections in which a series of opposition candidates challenged incumbents, and (b) the apparent incumbency advantage that has been observed in recent congressional elections.

In light of the discussion in Section 9.1, a natural question is whether there are any noteworthy connections *between* the models discussed in this section *and* models in which voters have additively separable loss functions like the ones studied by Hinich (1978). It is known that results about binary Luce models have direct implications for models in which utility/loss can be written as the sum of a nonrandom utility/loss function and a random "error" term (see, for instance, Luce and Suppes 1965, Section 5.2). The established connection between these alternative models can be used in the context of electoral competition models as follows. Suppose that (a) each voter, ω, has a policy-related loss function, $L_\omega(s) = -\ln(f_\omega(s)) - b_\omega$ (where f_ω is a positive, real-valued function on X and b is a constant), (b) analogous to (39), for each ω and each $(s_1, s_2) \in S_1 \times S_2$,

$$\Pr^1_\omega(s_1, s_2) = \begin{cases} 1 & \text{if} \quad L_\omega(s_2) - L_\omega(s_1) > \varepsilon_\omega \\ 0 & \text{otherwise} \end{cases} \tag{50}$$

and (c) ε_ω has a logistic distribution. Then, using the argument in the proof of Luce and Suppes' Theorem 30 (1965, p. 335) it follows that the candidates are using a binary Luce model. Therefore, when the remaining assumptions for the theorem in this section are also made, the conclusion of that theorem holds for the corresponding model with separable policy-related and nonpolicy voter utilities/losses.

9.3. Lindbeck and Weibull's Model

Lindbeck and Weibull developed a model of "balanced-budget redistribution between socio-economic groups as the outcome of electoral competition between two political parties" (1987, p. 273) in which the parties have "incomplete information as to political preferences . . . related to ideological considerations and politicians personalities" (p. 274). Since they modeled redistribution between groups, in each case where there are three or more groups, the strategy set for the parties is multidimensional. As a consequence, as with the multidimensional election models discussed in Section 9.2, "the presence of uncertainty is crucial for *existence* of equilibrium in [their] model" (p. 280).

Lindbeck and Weibull assumed that the set of voters, Ω, is finite and that each $\omega \in \Omega$ has a fixed gross income, $Y_\omega \in \mathbb{R}^1_{++}$. They also assumed that the candidates have a (common) partition, $\Theta = \{1,\ldots,m\}$, of the electorate (with $m \geq 2$). Note that in what follows, the elements in Θ will be used as indices for the groups as well as to denote the sets of voters that constitute the candidates' partition. For each $\theta \in \Theta$, n_θ will denote the number of voters in θ.

Lindbeck and Weibull assumed that the strategies available to the candidates are vectors, $x = (x_1,\ldots,x_m) \in \mathbb{R}^m$, of possible transfers to the members of the m groups. In addition, they assumed that each candidate must select a balanced-budget redistribution in which each individual's net income must be positive. Hence

$$X = \left\{ x \in \mathbb{R}^m : \sum_{\theta=1}^{m} n_\theta \cdot x_\theta = 0 \quad \text{and} \quad Y_\omega + x_\theta > 0, \forall\, \omega \in \theta, \forall\, \theta \in \Theta \right\}. \tag{51}$$

As in many of the analyses that have already been discussed, Lindbeck and Weibull assumed that any given voter's utility for a particular candidate's election is the *sum of* his utility for the candidate's strategy *and* an additional component that reflects "other factors" that affect his preferences for the candidates. For each $\omega \in \Omega$, his "final" (or "net") income will be $c_\omega = Y_\omega + x_\theta$ where θ is the group that contains ω. They explicitly assumed that each voter has a twice-differentiable utility function, $v_\omega(c_\omega)$. Using this notation, any particular ω's utility function on X can be written as

$$U_\omega(x) = v_\omega(Y_\omega + x_\theta) \tag{52}$$

where θ is the group which contains ω. Lindbeck and Weibull assumed that, for each $\omega \in \Omega$,

$$v'_\omega(z) > 0 \quad \text{and} \quad v''_\omega(z) < 0, \forall\, z > 0 \tag{53}$$

and

$$\lim_{z\to 0} v'_\omega(z) = +\infty \quad \text{and} \quad \lim_{z\to\infty} v''_\omega(z) = 0. \tag{54}$$

Lindbeck and Weibull assumed that, for each $\omega \in \Omega$ and each $(s_1, s_2) \in S_1 \times S_2$,

$$\mathrm{Pr}^1_\omega(s_1, s_2) = \begin{cases} 1 & \text{if } \; U_\omega(s_1) - U_\omega(s_2) > a_\omega - b_\omega \\ 0 & \text{otherwise} \end{cases} \tag{55}$$

where "a_ω is the utility that individual ω derives from other policies in candidate [1's] political program and likewise with b_ω [and candidate 2]" (p. 276). They also made an analogous assumption about $\mathrm{Pr}^2_\omega(s_1, s_2)$ (with *both* 1 and 2 *and* a and b interchanged on the right-hand side of (55) or, equivalently, with the inequality on the right-hand side of (55) reversed).

Lindbeck and Weibull assumed that the two parties treat a_ω and b_ω as random variables. More specifically, they assumed that the parties have a twice continuously differentiable probability distribution, F_ω, for $b_\omega - a_\omega$. Letting $f_\omega(y) = F'_\omega(y)$, Lindbeck and Weibull additionally assumed that $f_\omega(y) > 0$, $\forall\, y \in \mathbb{R}^1$.

One of the things that Lindbeck and Weibull did was identify a necessary condition for a pure-strategy equilibrium in their model (p. 278). Their necessary condition is stated in the following theorem.

Theorem 12 *If* (s_1, s_2) *is a pure-strategy equilibrium, then*

(i) $s_1 = s_2 \equiv s^*$, *and*
(ii) *there exists* $\lambda > 0$ *such that, for each* $\theta \in \Theta$,

$$\sum_{\omega \in \theta} v'_\omega(Y_\omega + s^*_\theta) \cdot f_\omega(0) = n_\theta \cdot \lambda. \tag{56}$$

Equation (56) is of particular significance because it is also a first-order necessary condition for maximizing the weighted Benthamite social welfare function

$$W(x) = \sum_{\omega=1}^{\#\Omega} v_\omega(c_\omega) \cdot f_\omega(0) \tag{57}$$

on the set X. Lindbeck and Weibull pointed out that, if the parties use the same candidate preference distribution for each voter (i.e., $F_\alpha = F_\beta$, $\forall\, \alpha, \beta \in \Omega$), then "in this special case democratic electoral competition for the votes of selfish individuals produces the same income distribution as would an omnipotent Benthamite government" (p. 278).

In addition, Lindbeck and Weibull (1987, p. 280) identified a sufficient condition for the existence of a unique pure-strategy equilibrium in their model. Their condition used a "concavity index" from Debreu and Koopmans (1982, p. 27): $\iota(v_\omega) = \inf_r \{|v''_\omega(r)| / (v'_\omega(r))^2\}$.

Theorem 13 *If*

$$\sup_t \{|f_\omega'(t)|/f_\omega(t)\} \leq \iota(v_\omega), \forall\, \omega \in \Omega, \tag{58}$$

then a unique pure-strategy equilibrium exists.

They also drew attention to the fact that (58) is "more easily satisfied the larger is the degree of uncertainty" (p. 281).

Lindbeck and Weibull also examined what happens to the results stated above when additional (or alternative) features are included in their model. The particular extensions that they considered were (a) administration costs (which could vary from group to group), (b) abstentions, (c) a role for party activists who do more for a candidate than simply vote for him, and (d) each candidate wanting to maximize his probability of winning (rather than his expected plurality). The conclusions that they arrived at were very similar (albeit not identical) to the two theorems stated above. The minor differences that result from using these alternative assumptions were discussed in detail in the corresponding sections in Lindbeck and Weibull's article.

10. PROBABILISTIC VOTING MODELS WITH FIXED CANDIDATE CHARACTERISTICS AND VOTER PREDICTIONS

10.1. Fixed Candidate Characteristics

Enelow and Hinich (1982) analyzed an election model in which fixed candidate characteristics (i.e., characteristics that the candidates cannot alter during the election being considered) are important. The particular model that they analyzed is very similar to the one in Hinich (1978) (which was discussed in Section 9.1). In particular, as the ensuing discussion will make clear, most of their assumptions correspond to ones that were made by Hinich en route to his existence theorem. However, their existence result (the theorem in this section) is *not* a special case for Hinich's earlier existence theorem. Thus their analysis succeeded in identifying a new sufficient condition for the existence of an electoral equilibrium.

Enelow and Hinich (1982) assumed that the (common) strategy set, X, for the candidates is such that $[0, 1] \subset X \subseteq \mathbb{R}^1$—with the positions in X interpreted as expenditure levels on a single public-spending issue. As did Hinich (1978), they assumed that, for each $\omega \in \Omega$, there is an most-preferred alternative, $m(\omega) \in X$, that enters into ω's evaluation of each candidate's strategy. One part of the premise for Hinich's existence theorem is that there is a density function, $p(m)$, for the voters' most-preferred alternatives such that (a) $p(m) = 0$ for m outside an interval $[a, b]$ and (b) $p(m) > 0$ inside. Enelow and Hinich (1982), by contrast, assumed that the electorate can be partitioned into two groups,

$\theta = 1$ and $\theta = 2$ (with n_1 and n_2 voters, respectively), and that (a) each $\omega \in \theta = 1$ has the most-preferred alternative $m(\omega) = 0$ and (b) each $\omega \in \theta = 2$ has the most-preferred alternative $m(\omega) = 1$.

Enelow and Hinich (1982) assumed that each $\omega \in \Omega$ makes a numerical assessment of the nonspatial characteristics of candidate 1 (and also the nonspatial characteristics of candidate 2), denoted by $\chi_{\omega 1}$ (respectively, $\chi_{\omega 2}$). This assessment was supplemented by a positive, numerical measure of the importance that ω attaches to the candidates' strategies (relative to their nonpolicy characteristics), denoted by a_ω. They assumed that, for each $\omega \in \Omega$ and each $(s_1, s_2) \in S_1 \times S_2$,

$$\mathrm{Pr}^1_\omega(s_1, s_2) = \begin{cases} 1 & \text{if } ((s_2 - m(\omega)))^2 - ((s_1 - m(\omega)))^2 > \varepsilon_\omega \\ 0 & \text{otherwise} \end{cases} \tag{59}$$

where $\varepsilon_\omega = (\chi_{\omega 2}/a_\omega) - (\chi_{\omega 1}/a_\omega)$. An analogous assumption (with 2 replacing 1, and 1 replacing 2, on the right-hand side of (59) and in the definition of ε_ω) was made about $\mathrm{Pr}^2_\omega(s_1, s_2)$. Note that in (59) (a) $(s_c - m(\omega))^2$ corresponds to Hinich's loss function (being, in particular, the special case of Hinich's quadratic model that arises when $X \subseteq \mathbb{R}^1$ and $A = [1]$), and (b) $-\chi_{\omega 1}/a_\omega$ and $-\chi_{\omega 2}/a_\omega$ correspond to e_1 and e_2, respectively, in Hinich (1978). Or, equivalently (translating this observation from "loss" terms into "utility" terms), $U_\omega(x) = -(x - m(\omega))^2$ can be thought of as a policy-related utility function for voter ω and $(\chi_{\omega 1}/a_\omega)$ (or $(\chi_{\omega 2}/a_\omega)$) can be thought of as a nonpolicy value for ω if candidate 1 (respectively, candidate 2) wins the election.

In his existence theorem, Hinich (1978) assumed that the variance, σ^2, for the nonpolicy difference, ε_ω, is the same for each voter. Enelow and Hinich (1982), on the other hand, assumed that the candidates believe that (a) the distribution of ε_ω *across the group* $\theta = 1$ is normal with mean 0 and variance σ_1^2, and (b) the distribution of ε_ω *across the group* $\theta = 2$ is normal with mean 0 and variance σ_2^2 (as the notation suggests, σ_2 need not equal σ_1). This distributional assumption is consistent with assuming that the candidates know the nonpolicy difference for each voter and is, alternatively, also consistent with assuming that they are uncertain about the nonpolicy value for any particular voter but (nonetheless) know the distribution of the nonpolicy values across each group.

In order to be able to state their result in a relatively simple way, Enelow and Hinich (1982) used the following notation:

$$\bar{x} \equiv [n_2 \cdot \sigma_1]/[n_1 \cdot \sigma_2 + n_2 \cdot \sigma_1]. \tag{60}$$

The number, $\bar{x}$, for any special case is, as they pointed out, a weighted mean most-preferred alternative (which has the property that, *if* $\sigma_1 = \sigma_2$, *then* $\bar{x}$ is the unweighted mean most-preferred alternative). Using this notation, the existence result in Enelow and Hinich (1982, pp. 123–124) can be stated as follows.

Theorem 14 *If* $\sigma_1^2 > 2 \cdot (1 - \bar{x})^2$ *and* $\sigma_2^2 > 2 \cdot [1 - (1 - \bar{x})^2]$,

(i) *an equilibrium exists, and*
(ii) (s_1^*, s_2^*) *is an equilibrium if and only if* $s_1^* = s_2^* = \bar{x}$.

This result is similar to Hinich's (1978) existence result in that the conclusion is that a unique equilibrium exists and is located at a weighted mean of the voters' most-preferred alternatives. In addition to the differences in the underlying assumptions that were noted above, Enelow and Hinich's (1982) result also differs from Hinich's (1978) existence theorem in that (a) the sufficient condition involves inequalities that require relatively large variances for the nonpolicy values (rather than relatively small variances), and (b) the result provides precise inequalities for the variances (rather than just assuring that an appropriate inequality exists).

Enelow and Hinich (p. 127) argued that σ_1^2 and σ_2^2 "will be of sufficient size in a large society" for their premise to be satisfied. In particular, they suggested that this will be the case "since the size of these parameters is a function of the number of different views concerning relative differences between candidates' nonspatial characteristics and issue salience." They did not identify what happens if the variances are not large enough to satisfy the inequalities in their premise.

Enelow and Hinich argued that it is especially significant that the equilibrium in their election model is at a "compromise" position, rather than at the most-preferred alternative of one of the two groups. They pointed out that this property implies that (in their model) the minority group has some influence over the outcome and, therefore, there is not a "tyranny of the majority." They argued that this implication reflects an important difference between (a) representative democracy (where the citizens vote for candidates who both propose policies and have fixed characteristics that the voters care about), and (b) direct democracy (where the citizens vote solely on policies).

10.2. Predictive Maps

Enelow and Hinich (1984, Sections 5.1, 5.2, and 5.4) extended their earlier analysis of election models with fixed candidate characteristics by considering cases where there are "predictive mappings" for the voters. These mappings, which are discussed in detail in Enelow and Hinich (1984, Chapter 4), allow each voter to map *from* a candidate's strategy *to* the policies he thinks will actually be adopted if the candidate is elected. The predictive mappings, therefore, allow for the possibility that voters will interpret candidates' strategies in their own individual ways, instead of simply believing that each candidate will carry out the policies that he advocates during the election.

Enelow and Hinich assumed that the candidates' strategy set is the closed interval $[-1/2, +1/2]$ (1984, pp. 101–102 in Appendix 5.1). As before, they assumed that there are two groups, $\theta = 1$ and $\theta = 2$ (with n_1 and n_2 voters, respectively). They made two particular assumptions about the groups: (a) they partition the electorate, and (b) for each $\theta \in \Theta = \{1,2\}$, the voters in the group have a common most-preferred alternative, $m_\theta \in \mathbb{R}^2$, and a common predictive map,

$$w(s_c) = b_\theta + s_c \cdot v_\theta \tag{61}$$

(with domain $[-1/2, +1/2]$). Enelow and Hinich specifically assumed that each predictive map goes from the unidimensional strategy adopted by a candidate to a two-component vector of "predicted policies." Thus, for any given $(s_1, s_2) \in S_1 \times S_2$, the corresponding $w_\omega(s_1) \in \mathbb{R}^2$ (and the corresponding $w_\omega(s_2) \in \mathbb{R}^2$) is the two-dimensional vector of policies that each person in θ thinks will actually be adopted if candidate 1 (respectively candidate 2) is elected. Note that, since the candidates' strategies are in $\mathbb{R}^1$ and the predicted policies are in $\mathbb{R}^2$, the b_θ and v_θ parameters in (61) are two-component vectors, which can therefore be written as $b_\theta = (b_{\theta 1}, b_{\theta 2})^t$ and $v_\theta = (v_{\theta 1}, v_{\theta 2})^t$. Similarly, the common most-preferred alternative for the individuals in a given group, θ, can be written as $m_\theta = (m_{\theta 1}, m_{\theta 2})^t$.

This time around, Enelow and Hinich (1984, p. 83) explicitly interpreted the groups in their model as "interest groups," making the following argument for this interpretation:

> *The ... homogeneous groups can be thought of as the politically salient interest groups in the electorate. Each interest group has a common set of policy concerns and looks at the candidates the same way.... This conception of an interest group is particularly appropriate from the point of view of the candidates. It is a common practice in campaigns to view the electorate as being composed of homogeneous issue groups .... This practice is a shorthand device that permits candidates to plan campaign strategies without becoming lost in the complexities of individual voter attitudes.*

As before, they also assumed that each voter places a nonpolicy value on candidate 1's winning the election and a nonpolicy value on candidate 2's winning. Accordingly, analogous to equation (59), Enelow and Hinich assumed that, for each $\omega \in \Omega$ and each $(s_1, s_2) \in S_1 \times S_2$,

$$\Pr{}^1_\omega(s_1, s_2) = \begin{cases} 1 & \text{if} \quad \|w_\omega(s_2) - m_\theta\|_2^2 - \|w_\omega(s_1) - m_\theta\|_2^2 > \varepsilon_\omega \\ 0 & \text{otherwise} \end{cases} \tag{62}$$

where (a) $||y||_2 = (y^t I_2 y)^{1/2}$ and (b) ε_ω is (again) the *difference between* the nonpolicy value for ω if candidate 2 is elected *and* the nonpolicy value for ω if candidate 1 is elected. An analogous assumptions (with the inequality on the right-hand side of (62) reversed) was made about $\Pr^2_\omega(s_1, s_2)$ (with 1 and 2 interchanged). In addition, Enelow and Hinich assumed that the candidates believe that the distribution of ε_ω *across a given interest group* θ is normal with mean zero and variance σ_θ^2.

For each group θ, Enelow and Hinich (p. 102) used B_θ to denote any number that is greater than or equal to both $(v_{\theta 1}^1 + v_{\theta 2}^2)^{1/2}$ and $[(m_{\theta 1} - b_{\theta 1})^2 + (m_{\theta 2} - b_{\theta 2})^2]^{1/2}$ (the elements that appear in these two equations are specifically the corresponding components in the vectors $v_\theta, m_\theta, b_\theta$). For instance, for each θ, B_θ could simply be the larger of the two numbers. Enelow and Hinich (1984, pp. 85–86, pp. 101–102) established:

Theorem 15 *If $\sigma_1 > 3 \cdot (1.5)^{1/2} \cdot (B_1)^2$ and $\sigma_2 > 3 \cdot (1.5)^{1/2} \cdot (B_2)^2$, then (i) an electoral equilibrium exists, and (ii) (s_1^*, s_2^*) is an electoral equilibrium if and only if $s_1^* = s_2^*$*

$$= \frac{\{n_1\sigma_1^{-1}[v_{11}(m_{11} - b_{11}) + v_{12}(m_{12} - b_{12})] + n_2\sigma_2^{-1}[v_{21}(m_{21} - b_{21}) + v_{22}(m_{22} - b_{22})]\}}{[n_1\sigma_1^{-1}(v_{11}^2 + v_{12}^2) + n_2\sigma_2^{-1}(v_{21}^2 + v_{22}^2)]}. \tag{63}$$

Enelow and Hinich (1984, pp. 87–88) supplemented their analysis with an example of an election model with fixed candidate characteristics, predictive maps, and interest groups.

Example 3 Assume that group $\theta = 1$ is twice as large as group $\theta = 2$ (that is, $n_1 = 2 \cdot n_2$). Also assume that each voter in group $\theta = 1$ has the most-preferred alternative $m_1 = (.2, .8)^t$ and the predictive map

$$w_\omega(s) = \begin{bmatrix} +.3 \\ +.7 \end{bmatrix} + s \cdot \begin{bmatrix} +.2 \\ -.2 \end{bmatrix} \tag{64}$$

and that each voter in group $\theta = 2$ has the most-preferred alternative $m_2 = (.35, .65)^t$ and the predictive map

$$w_\omega(s) = \begin{bmatrix} +.2 \\ +.8 \end{bmatrix} + s \cdot \begin{bmatrix} +.3 \\ -.3 \end{bmatrix}. \tag{65}$$

Enelow and Hinich (1984) pointed out that their result directly implies that (in their example) if $\sigma_1 > 3 \cdot (1.5)^{1/2} \cdot B_1^2 = .294$ and $\sigma_2 > 3 \cdot (1.5)^{1/2} \cdot B_2^2 = .661$, then there is a unique equilibrium, $(s_1^*, s_2^*) \in S_1 \times S_2$, with

$$s_1^* = s_2^* = \frac{\{-.08\sigma_1^{-1} + .09\sigma_2^{-1}\}}{[.16\sigma_1^{-1} + .18\sigma_2^{-1}]}. \tag{66}$$

They also pointed out that if one makes the further assumption that $\sigma_1 = \sigma_2$, then their result provides the even more precise conclusion that $s_1^* = s_2^* = .03$.

Enelow and Hinich (1984, Section 5.4) also used this example to illustrate the fact that when their sufficient condition is not satisfied, their model with fixed candidate characteristics, predictive maps, and interest groups need not have an equilibrium. They did so by (more specifically) showing that, when this example is supplemented with the alternative assumption that $\sigma_2 = 0$ and $.06 < \sigma_1 < .12$, there is no electoral equilibrium.

10.3. Summing Up

One reason why results that have been derived for probabilistic voting models are important is that equilibrium existence results have been obtained for distributions of voter preferences that have no Nash equilibrium when voting is deterministic. This is illustrated by the theorems stated in Sections 9.2 and 9.3. More specifically, the theorems apply to multidimensional strategy spaces but do not require any symmetry properties for the distribution of voter preferences.

A second reason why results that have been derived for probabilistic voting models are important is that, when there is a Nash equilibrium in a deterministic voting model, there may be a different Nash equilibrium for a corresponding probabilistic voting model. For example, consider the assumptions in the premise of the theorem stated in Section 9.2. A relevant special case (for the assertion made at the beginning of this paragraph) is the one where $S \subseteq \mathbb{R}^1$. In this special case, a Nash equilibrium exists, with each candidate's strategy being a number that maximizes the Nash social welfare function in (48). If we now replace the assumption of probabilistic voting with the assumption of deterministic voting, then Theorem 5 applies. Therefore a Nash equilibrium exists, with each candidate's strategy being a median for the distribution of most-preferred alternatives. However, the other assumptions that have been made do *not* imply that the median will maximize the Nash social welfare function in (48). There are some circumstances where there are equilibrium strategies for a deterministic voting model that are the same as the equilibrium strategies for a corresponding probabilistic voting model. But that is the exception rather than the rule.

11. ALTERNATIVE SOLUTION CONCEPTS

The *absence* of a pure-strategy equilibrium for a pair of political candidates could be described as follows: The process of trying to second-guess the other candidate is hopeless. For each possible alternative, the other candidate should select a different alternative. But given this alternative, the first candidate should select yet another alternative. This description suggests that, when there is no pure-strategy equilibrium, there is no definite prediction about what will happen. This conclusion has led Ordeshook (1986) to argue that "it is unsatisfactory to conclude that pure-strategy equilibria need not exist in two-candidate elections, since this conclusion leaves us without any hypotheses about eventual strategies and outcomes for a wide class of situations" (p. 180).

Because pure-strategy equilibria are rare in multidimensional election models with deterministic voting, some authors have concluded that only a fundamental reformulation of how the competitive process works will allow for meaningful predictive deductions about candidate decisions in multidimensional election models. Some authors have proposed a solution concept that generalizes the notion of a pure-strategy equilibrium (by including pure-strategy equilibria in the set of solutions when they exist and allowing for a nonempty set of solutions when there is no pure-strategy equilibrium). Others give up on the idea of studying pure-strategy equilibria and use a different type of solution concept.

11.1. A Dynamical Approach

Some authors have concluded that analyses of electoral competition in the substantively important multidimensional case must be based on explicit hypotheses about disequilibrium behavior. For instance, Kramer (1977b) used hypotheses about disequilibrium choices by political candidates in an analysis of sequences of elections.

Kramer assumed that there is a finite set of voters. He assumed that there is a set of alternatives and that this set is a multidimensional Euclidean space. He also assumed that each voter has a most-preferred alternative and Euclidean preferences.

Kramer considered two political candidates that compete in a sequence of elections. In any given election, (1) each candidate competes by advocating a particular alternative, (2) there is deterministic voting, and (3) if one of the candidates gets more votes than the other, he or she wins; otherwise the winner is selected by the toss of a fair coin. The winning candidate then enacts the alternative it advocated. In the next election, the incumbent must defend the alternative, and the challenger chooses an alternative that maximizes its vote. A sequence of successively enacted alternatives that is generated by this process is called a "vote-maximizing sequence (or trajectory)." (x_t) will be used to denote any such sequence.

Kramer also used the following concepts, which had previously been developed by Simpson (1969). For any given $(X, (\succeq_1, \ldots, \succeq_{\#\Omega}))$, he considered the following function on X:

$$v(x) = \max_{y \in X} \#\{\omega_\omega \in \Omega : y \succ_\omega x\}. \tag{67}$$

The number

$$v^* = \min_{x \in X} v(x) \tag{68}$$

is called the minmax number. The set

$$M(v^*) = \{x \in X : v(x) = v^*\} \tag{69}$$

is called the minmax set.

Kramer used the term "(x_t) enters $M(v^*)$" to mean $\exists\ t$ such that $x_t \in M(v^*)$. Saying "(x_t) enters $M(v^*)$ in period t" will mean $x_t \in M(v^*)$ and $x_{t-1} \notin M(v^*)$. Kramer pointed out that, under the assumptions stated above, there exist vote-maximizing sequences of alternatives that do *not* enter the minmax set.

When a (weak) simple majority Condorcet winner exists, the minmax set is the set of (weak) simple majority Condorcet winners. So, when there is a pure-strategy equilibrium in the one-period game $(X, X; \mathrm{VS}^1, \mathrm{VS}^2)$, the minmax set is the set of equilibrium strategies. Hence, in any such situation, if (x_t) enters $M(v^*)$ in period t then $x_r \in M(v^*)$ for each x_r in the sequence with $r > t$.

Kramer argued that, when a (weak) simple majority Condorcet winner does not exist, the elements of the minmax set are the ones that "most resemble" (weak) simple majority Condorcet winners. He also pointed out that, under the assumptions he considered, the minmax set is typically a small proper subset of the society's set of alternatives.

Kramer also used the following definition of the distance from a point $x \in \mathbb{R}^h$ to a set $Z \subset \mathbb{R}^h$:

$$d(x, Z) = \inf_{z \in Z} ||x - z||_h. \tag{70}$$

Kramer described the following theorem as "the main result" (p. 320) in his analysis.

Theorem 16 *Suppose* $(X, (\succeq_1, \ldots, \succeq_{\#\Omega}))$ *is a regular model where* $X = R^h$ *(with* $\#\Omega > h \geq 2$*) and each voter has Euclidean preferences. Consider any vote-maximizing trajectory,* (x_t)*. For any* t *where* $x_t \notin M(v*)$*,*

$$d(x_{t+1}, M(v^*)) < d(x_t, M(v^*)). \tag{71}$$

Kramer pointed out that his theorem implies that, for any vote-maximizing trajectory, the distance to the minmax set must be monotonically decreasing *until* the trajectory reaches the set (p. 320). He described this property of his model by stating that "every vote-maximizing trajectory will tend to approach the minmax set." Kramer also described this property by saying that every vote-maximizing trajectory "necessarily converges on the minmax set" (p. 323). However, the convergence is limited because (1) it is possible for a trajectory to never enter the minmax set, and (2) when there is no pure strategy equilibrium in $(X, X; \mathrm{VS}^1, \mathrm{VS}^2)$ there exist sequences of alternatives that enter the minmax set but have infinite subsequences that are outside the minmax set (e.g., because, whenever the minmax set is reached, the next vote-maximizing proposal selected is outside the minmax set).

11.2. Mixed-Strategy Equilibria

The most prominent research on electoral competition using a solution concept that generalizes the notion of a pure-strategy equilibrium is research that has replaced the concept of a pure-strategy equilibrium for the candidates with the concept of a mixed-strategy equilibrium. The pioneering work on this topic was done by Shubik (1968, 1970, 1982, p. 387; 1984, pp. 625–629).

Shubik derived the mixed-strategy equilibria for some specific electoral competitions. Additionally, he considered the relation *between* mixed-strategy equilibria *and* pairwise comparisons made with simple majority rule. His analysis of this relation included the following important comment: "If there is a set of outcomes which are intransitive among themselves but are preferred to all others, the resulting game of strict opposition between the two candidates will call for a mixed strategy over the set of outcomes which display the intransitivity" (p. 348).

The consequences of assuming that candidates may play mixed-strategies have also been explored by Kramer (1978b), Calvert (1986), Laffond, Laslier, and Le Breton (1993, 1994), Laslier (1997, Section 10.1; 2000), Dutta and Laslier (1999, Sections 3.3 and 4.3), Banks, Duggan, and Le Breton (2002), and others. Some of the authors who have studied mixed-strategy equilibria have suggested that they could be interpreted as situations where, when the voters compare the candidates, the voters are comparing lotteries that correspond to the candidates' mixed strategies (e.g., Shubik 1968, 1970, 1982; Laffond, Laslier, and Le Breton 1994; and Laslier 2000).

Critiques of the idea of using a mixed-strategy equilibrium as the equilibrium concept for election models have been written by Riker and Ordeshook (1973, p. 340), McKelvey and Ordeshook (1976, pp. 1174–1175), Kramer (1977a, pp. 695–696), Ordeshook (1986, pp. 180–182; 1992, pp. 107–108), Artale and Gruner (2000, pp. 20–29), Ansolabehere and Snyder (2000, p. 334), and others.

One line of criticism of mixed-strategy equilibria is based on the empirical observation that political candidates do not use random devices to select strategies. For instance, Ordeshook (1986, p. 181) states: "it seems silly to conceptualize candidates spinning spinners or rolling dice to choose policy platforms."

A second line of criticism is based on the idea that, even if the political candidates did use random devices to select pure strategies, they would have to communicate the pure strategies to the voters before election day. In this context, Ordeshook (1986) has suggested that it is useful to distinguish *between* a candidate using a "mixed strategy" *and* a candidate using a "risky strategy." His rationale is, "In an election context, if a candidate abides by some mixed strategy, then, ultimately, the electorate sees only the pure strategy he chooses by lottery. If a candidate adopts a risky strategy, though, then the electorate sees the lottery as that candidate's platform. Risky strategies are pure strategies" (p. 186). The second line of criticism argues that in cases where there is no pure-strategy equilibrium (1) once the "selected pure strategies" (i.e., the ones that result from the candidates adopting mixed strategies and then using random devices to select pure strategies) are communicated to the voters, at least one of the candidates will be better off changing his pure strategy; (2) at the strategy pair that results from this change, at least one of the candidates will be better off changing his pure strategy; (3) the conclusion in (2) applies over and over again (ad infinitum). As a result there is no definite prediction about what will happen.

Artale and Gruner (2000) presented another argument against viewing a mixed-strategy equilibrium as a reasonable solution for an electoral competition. They first suggested (pp. 20–21) that a reasonable solution will reflect the following "stylized facts of political life in representative democracies": the presence of "political stability" and "the absence of discrimination against single groups." Then they considered the hypothesis that a mixed-strategy equilibrium is a reasonable solution for an electoral competition.

They began by deriving the mixed-strategy equilibrium for an electoral competition (with deterministic voting) where the alternatives are possible income distributions. By analyzing the mixed-strategy equilibrium, they were able to show that it (1) "cannot explain high degrees of political stability (p. 29), and (2) implies that one should "observe frequent cases of discrimination against single groups" (p. 29). Since these properties do not match with their stylized facts, they rejected the hypothesis that a mixed-strategy equilibrium is a reasonable solution for an electoral competition.

The preceding arguments against viewing a mixed-strategy equilibrium as a reasonable solution for an electoral competition interpret a mixed-strategy as a "chance mechanism" for selecting a pure strategy. Calvert (1986, Section 4.6) has suggested that Harsanyi's (1973) alternative interpretation of a mixed-strategy equilibrium may provide a more useful way to think about mixed-strategies in an electoral competition.

In Harsanyi's view, mixed-strategies are not the results of deliberate randomization. Rather, in his view, they result from imperfect knowledge by one player of another. Roemer (2001, p. 145) has provided the following description of what Harsanyi's interpretation means in the specific context of an electoral competition:

> *parties ... can be viewed as playing mixed strategies, as follows. Suppose that each party does not know for certain the type of the other party .... Each party has only a probability distribution over the other party's type. Each party can compute how the other party will respond to its own policy, for every type that it may be, and this induces a "mixed strategy"—that is, party 1 views party 2 as responding with a probability distribution over strategies, induced by the probability distribution that party 1 has over party 2's type. The appropriate concept of equilibrium, in this case, is a mixed-strategy equilibrium.*

Calvert observed that, when Harsanyi's interpretation is used, "an equilibrium in mixed-strategies in a game of full information, such as deterministic electoral competition between candidates, is really just a summary of the distribution of outcomes that would be observed if the candidates were slightly uncertain about one another's perceptions of the plurality function" (p. 41). He added that this using this approach "provides information about a form of candidate uncertainty different from that addressed by the probabilistic voting models" (p. 42).

11.3. Some Other Solutions That Have Been Proposed

Various other solutions have also been proposed for electoral competitions with deterministic voting. This section briefly describes some of them.

One approach has been to view the set of undominated candidate strategies as a solution set. A variation on this approach has been to take the solution set to be the set of strategies that remains after iterated elimination of (weakly or strongly) undominated candidate strategies. References that have used this type of approach include McKelvey and Ordeshook (1976), Cox (1989), and Ordeshook (1992).

Another approach has been based on the so-called "uncovered set." Saying that alternative x "covers" alternative y means that (i) a majority prefers x to y, and (ii) for all $z \in X - \{x, y\}$, if a majority prefers alternative y to z, then there is also a majority that prefers x to z. An alternative is in the "uncovered set" if and only if it is *not* covered by any other alternative. When all majority comparisons are strict (e.g., because there is an odd number of voters and each voter has strict preferences), saying that an alternative y is in the "uncovered set" can (alternatively) be stated as follows: for each other alternative, x, either (a) a majority prefers y to x, or (b) a majority prefers y to a third alternative, z, which a majority prefers to x (i.e., a majority prefers y to z *and* a majority prefers z to x). References that have taken the uncovered set to be a solution set for an electoral competition include Miller (1980, pp. 89–93), McKelvey (1986, Section 6), Ordeshook (1986, pp. 184–187), and Mueller (2003, Chapter 11). A variation on this approach has been developed by Schofield (1999, Section 5; 2002, Sections 2 and 3)—using a *superset* of the uncovered set that he calls the "political heart."

Yet another approach has been to take the solution set to be the support of a mixed-strategy equilibrium. References where this approach has been suggested for an electoral competition with a finite set of alternatives include Laffond, Laslier, and Le Breton (1993, 1994), Laslier (1997), and Dutta and Laslier (1999). With this approach, in a game with a finite set of alternatives, the solution set would consist of all of the alternatives that have a positive probability of being chosen by a candidate. The references listed above established that, in games with a finite sets of alternatives, this solution set is a *subset* of the uncovered set. Subsequently, Banks, Duggan, and Le Breton (2002) proved that (under fairly general assumptions) the same conclusion holds for games with infinite sets of alternatives.

The approaches described in the preceding paragraphs all predict that policies will tend to be in a specific, identifiable subset of the society's set of alternatives. However, as was pointed out in Section 6, the models of electoral competition discussed in that section (which have multidimensional sets of alternatives and deterministic voting) rarely have pure-strategy equilibria, so the solution concepts discussed in this subsection all have the following problem: a candidate who confidently selects a policy position using one of these approaches will (usually) subsequently want to change his position—since his opponent will (usually) be able to respond with a position that is preferred by a majority of voters.

12. CONCLUSION

In this chapter about probabilistic and spatial models of voting, I have viewed the terms "spatial models of voting" and "probabilistic models of voting" as closely related but not interchangeable terms.

I have thought about the term "spatial models of voting" in the way that it is used, for instance, in Enelow and Hinich (1984) book *The Spatial Theory of Voting: An Introduction.* In addition to using a variation of the term in the title of their book, they also use a variation of the term in the title of Chapter 1 ("Spatial Voting Models: The Behavioral Assumptions"). In the first paragraph of that chapter, they state "the spatial theory of voting . . . can be traced back as far as the 1920s in the work of Hotelling (1929). The first major works are those of Downs (1957) and Black (1958)" (p. 1). Then, as they proceed through the book, they describe models that are built on the foundation provided by Hotelling, Downs, and Black.

I have thought about the term "probabilistic models of voting" in the way that it is used, for instance, in my book *Probabilistic Voting Theory* (Coughlin 1992). In addition to using a variation of the term in the title of my book, Chapter 1 described models of electoral competition where "both candidates are . . . uncertain about the voters' decisions," and pointed out that they are commonly "called *probabilistic voting models* (reflecting the fact that the candidates' uncertainty requires a probabilistic description of the voters' choice behavior)" (p. 21).

Since the title for this chapter is "Probabilistic and Spatial Models of Voting," my goal has been to cover *both* probabilistic voting models *and* other spatial voting models that are *closely related to* probabilistic voting models—and to state important results about *both* probabilistic voting models *and* other *closely related* spatial voting models. The other *closely related* spatial voting models have included Black's model, the Hotelling–Downs model, and the subsequent literature on electoral competition where candidates are certain about the decisions that will be made by voters who are not indifferent between the policies embodied by the candidates.

ACKNOWLEDGMENTS

I would like to acknowledge helpful comments and suggestions provided by Kenneth Arrow.

REFERENCES

Aliprantis, C., & Chakrabarti, S. (2000). *Games and decision making.* Oxford: Oxford University Press.

Ansolabehere, S., & Snyder, J. (2000). Valence politics and equilibrium in spatial election models. *Public Choice, 103*, 327–336.

Aranson, P., Hinich, M., & Ordeshook, P. (1973). Campaign strategies for alternative election systems. In H. Alker *et al.* (Eds.), *Mathematical approaches to politics* (pp. 193–229). Amsterdam: Elsevier.

Arrow, K. (1963). *Social choice and individual values* (2nd ed.). New York: Wiley.
Arrow, K. (1969). Tullock and an existence theorem. *Public Choice, 6*, 105–111.
Arrow, K. (1987). Arrow's theorem. In J. Eatwell *et al.* (Eds.), *The New Palgrave: a dictionary of economics* (Vol. 1, pp. 124–126). London: Macmillan.
Artale, A., & Gruner, H. (2000). A model of stability and persistence in a democracy. *Games and Economic Behavior, 33*, 20–40.
Ball, R. (1999). Discontinuity and non-existence of equilibrium in the probabilistic spatial voting model. *Social Choice and Welfare, 16*, 533–555.
Banks, J. (1991). *Signalling games in political science*, Vol. 46 of *Fundamentals of pure and applied economics*. Chur: Harwood Academic Publishers.
Banks, J., Duggan, J., & Le Breton, M. (2002). Bounds for mixed strategy equilibria and the spatial model of elections. *Journal of Economic Theory, 103*, 88–105.
Barr, J., & Davis, O. (1966). An elementary political and economic theory of the expenditures of local governments. *Southern Economic Journal, 33*, 149–165.
Becker, G., DeGroot, M., & Marschak, J. (1963). Stochastic models of choice behavior. *Behavioral Science, 8*, 41–55.
Bierman, S., & Fernandez, L. (1998). *Game theory with economic applications* (2nd ed.). Reading, MA: Addison-Wesley.
Black, D. (1948a). On the rationale for group decision making. *Journal of Political Economy, 56*, 23–34.
Black, D. (1948b). The decisions of a committee using a special majority. *Econometrica, 16*, 245–261.
Black, D. (1949). The theory of elections in single-member constituencies. *The Canadian Journal of Economics and Political Science, 15*, 158–175.
Black, D. (1958). *The theory of committees and elections.* Cambridge: Cambridge University Press.
Black, D., & Newing, R. (1951). *Committee decisions with complementary valuation.* London: William Hodge and Company.
Bowen, H. (1943). The interpretation of voting in the allocation of economic resources. *Quarterly Journal of Economics, 58*, 27–48.
Bradley, R. (1985). Paired comparisons. In S. Kotz *et al.* (Eds.), *Encyclopedia of statistical sciences* (Vol. 6, pp. 204–210). New York: Wiley.
Brams, S. (2003). Chapter 17: Electing the president. In *For all practical purposes* (6th ed.) (pp. 592-632). New York: W. H. Freeman and Company.
Buchanan, J. (1968). Democracy and duopoly. *American Economic Review, Papers and Proceedings, 58*, 322–331.
Calvert, R. (1985). Robustness of the multidimensional voting model: candidate motivations, uncertainity, and convergence. *American Journal of Political Science, 29*, 69–95.
Calvert, R. (1986). *Models of imperfect information in politics*, Vol. 6 of *Fundamentals of pure and applied economics.* Chur: Harwood Academic Publishers.
Comaner, W. (1976). The median voter rule and the theory of political choice. *Journal of Public Economics, 5*, 169–178.
de Condorcet, M. (1785). *Essai sur l'application de l'analyse a la probabilite des decisions rendues a la pluralite de voix.* Paris.
Coughlin, P. (1992). *Probabilistic voting theory.* Cambridge: Cambridge University Press.
Coughlin, P., & Nitzan, S. (1981). Electoral outcomes with probabilistic voting and Nash social welfare maxima. *Journal of Public Economics, 15*, 113–121.
Cox, G. (1989). Undominated candidate strategies under alternative voting rules. *Mathematical and Computer Modelling, 12*, 451–459.
Davis, O., DeGroot, M., & Hinich, M. (1972). Social preference orderings and majority rule. *Econometrica, 40*, 147–157.

Davis, O., & Hinich, M. (1966). A mathematical model of policy formation in a democratic society. In J. Bernd (Ed.), *Mathematical applications in political science II* (pp. 175–208). Dallas: Southern Methodist University Press.

Davis, O., & Hinich, M. (1968). On the power and importance of the mean preference in a mathematical model of democratic choice. *Public Choice, 5*, 59–72.

Davis, O., & Hinich, M. (1971). Some extensions to a mathematical model of democratic choice. In B. Lieberman (Ed.), *Social choice* (pp. 323–347). New York: Gordon and Breach.

Davis, O., Hinich, M., & Ordeshook, P. (1970). An expository development of a mathematical model of policy formation in a democratic society. *American Political Science Review, 64*, 426–448.

Debreu, G., & Koopmans, T. C. (1981). Additively decomposed quasiconvex functions. *Mathematical Programming, 24*, 1–38.

Denzau, A., & Parks, R. (1975). The continuity of majority rule equilibrium. *Econometrica, 43*, 853–866.

Downs, A. (1957). *An economic theory of democracy*. New York: Harper & Row.

Dutta, B., & Laslier, J. (1999). Comparison functions and choice correspondences. *Social Choice and Welfare, 16*, 513–532.

Enelow, J., & Hinich, M. (1982). Non-spatial candidate characteristics and electoral competition. *Journal of Politics, 44*, 115–130.

Enelow, J., & Hinich, M. (1983). On Plott's pairwise symmetry conditions for majority rule equilibrium. *Public Choice, 40*, 317–321.

Enelow, J., & Hinich, M. (1984). *The spatial theory of voting*. Cambridge: Cambridge University Press.

Enelow, J., Hinich, M., & Mendell, N. (1986). An empirical evaluation of alternative spatial models of elections. *Journal of Politics, 48*, 675–693.

Feld, S., & Grofman, B. (1987). Necessary and sufficient conditions for a majority winner in n-dimensional spatial voting games. *American Journal of Political Science, 31*, 709–728.

Fiorina, M. (1981). *Retrospective voting in American national elections*. New Haven: Yale University Press.

Fishburn, P. (1973). *The theory of social choice*. Princeton: Princeton University Press.

Grandmont, J. M. (1978). Intermediate preferences and majority rule. *Econometrica, 46*, 317–330.

Harsanyi, J. (1973). Games with randomly distributed payoffs: a new rationale for mixed strategy equilibrium points. *International Journal of Game Theory, 2*, 1–23.

Hinich, M. (1977). Equilibrium in spatial voting. *Journal of Economic Theory, 16*, 208–219.

Hinich, M. (1978). The mean versus the median in spatial voting games. In P. Ordeshook (Ed.), *Game theory and political science* (pp. 357–374). New York: New York University Press.

Hinich, M., & Munger, M. (1997). *Analytical politics*. Cambridge: Cambridge University Press.

Hotelling, H. (1929). Stability in competition. *Economic Journal, 39*, 41–57.

Hoyer, R., & Mayer, L. (1973). Social preference orderings under majority rule. *Econometrica, 43*, 803–806.

Johnson, N., Kotz, S., & Kemp, A. (1992). *Univariate discrete distrubitions* (2nd ed.). New York: Wiley.

Kaneko, M., & Nakamura, K. (1979). The Nash social welfare function. *Econometrica, 47*, 423–435.

Kirchgassner, G. (2000). Probabilistic voting and equilibrium. *Public Choice, 103*, 35–48.

Kramer, G. (1973). On a class of equilibrium conditions for majority rule. *Econometrica, 41*, 285–297.

Kramer, G. (1976). A note on single-peakedness. *International Economic Review, 17*, 498–502.

Kramer, G. (1977a). Theories of political processes. In M. Intriligator (Ed.), *Frontiers of quantitative economics III* (pp. 685–702). Amsterdam: North-Holland.

Kramer, G. (1977b). A dynamical model of political equilibrium. *Journal of Economic Theory, 16*, 310–334.

Kramer, G. (1978a). Robustness of the median voter result. *Journal of Economic Theory, 19*, 565–567.

Kramer, G. (1978b). Existence of electoral equilibria. In P. Ordeshook (Ed.), *Game theory and political science* (pp. 371–389). New York: New York University Press.

Kramer, G., & Klevorick, A. (1974). Existence of a "local cooperative equilibrium" in a class of voting games. *Review of Economic Studies, 41*, 539–547.

Krantz, D., *et al.* (1971). *Foundations of measurement* (Vol. 2). New York: Academic Press.
Laffond, G., Laslier, J., & Le Breton, M. (1993). The bipartisan set of a tournament game. *Games and Economic Behavior, 5*, 182–201.
Laffond, G., Laslier, J., & Le Breton, M. (1994). Social choice mediators. *American Economic Review, Papers and Proceedings, 84*, 448–453.
Laslier, J. (1997). *Tournament solutions and majority voting.* Berlin: Springer-Verlag.
Laslier, J. (2000). Interpretation of electoral mixed strategies. *Social Choice and Welfare, 17*, 283–292.
Laussel, D., & Le Breton, M. (2002). Unidimensional Dowsian politics. *Economics Letters, 76*, 351–356.
Lindbeck, A., & Weibull, J. (1987). Balanced-budget redistribution as the outcome of political competition. *Public Choice, 52*, 273–297.
Luce, R. D. (1959). *Individual choice behavior.* New York: Wiley.
Luce, R. D., & Suppes, P. (1965). Preference, utility and subjective probability. In R. D. Luce, R. Bush & E. Galanter (Eds.), *Handbook of mathematical psychology* (pp. 249–410). New York: Wiley.
Mas-Colell, A., Whinston, M., & Green, J. (1995). *Microeconomic theory.* Oxford: Oxford University Press.
Matthews, S. (1979). A simple direction model of electoral competition. *Public Choice, 34*, 141–156.
Matthews, S. (1980). Pairwise symmetry conditions for voting equilibria. *International Journal of Game Theory, 9*, 141–156.
McKelvey, R. (1975). Policy related voting and electoral equilibria. *Econometrica, 43*, 815–844.
McKelvey, R. (1976). Intransitivities in multidimensional voting models and some implications for agenda control. *Journal of Economic Theory, 12*, 472–482.
McKelvey, R. (1986). Covering, dominance and institution-free properties of social choice. *American Journal of Political Science, 30*, 283–314.
McKelvey, R. (1990). Game theoretic models of voting in multidimensional issue spaces. In T. Ichiishi, A. Neyman & Y. Tauman (Eds.), *Game theory and applications* (pp. 317–335). New York: Academic Press.
McKelvey, R., & Ordeshook, P. (1976). Symmetric spatial games without majority rule equilibria. *American Political Science Review, 70*, 1172–1184.
McKelvey, R., & Ordeshook, P. (1990). A decade of experimental research on spatial models of elections and committees. In J. Enelow & M. Hinich (Eds.), *Advances in the spatial theory of voting* (pp. 99–144). Cambridge: Cambridge University Press.
McKelvey, R., Ordeshook, P., & Ungar, P. (1980). Conditions for voting equilibria in continuous voter distributions. *SIAM Journal of Applied Mathematics, 39*, 161–168.
McKelvey, R., & Wendell, R. (1976). Voting equilibria in multidimensional choice spaces. *Mathematics of Operations Research, 1*, 144–158.
Merrill, S., & Grofman, B. (1999). *A unified theory of voting.* Cambridge: Cambridge University Press.
Miller, N. (1980). A new solution set for tournaments and majority voting. *American Journal of Political Science, 24*, 68–96.
Mueller, D. (2003). *Public choice III.* Cambridge: Cambridge University Press.
Myerson, R. (1995). Analysis of democratic institutions. *Journal of Economic Perspectives, 9*, 77–89.
Nakamura, K. (1979). The vetoers in a simple game with ordinal preference. *International Journal of Game Theory, 8*, 55–61.
Ordeshook, P. (1986). *Game theory and political theory.* Cambridge: Cambridge University Press.
Ordeshook, P. (1992). *A political theory primer.* New York: Routledge.
Ordeshook, P. (1997). The spatial analysis of elections and committees. In D. Mueller (Ed.), *Perspectives on public choice* (pp. 247–270). Cambridge: Cambridge University Press.
Osborne, M. (1995). Spatial models of political competition under plurality rule. *Canadian Journal of Economics, 28*, 261–301.
Osborne, M. (2004). *An introduction to game theory.* Oxford: Oxford University Press.

Owen, G. (1995). *Game theory* (3rd ed.). New York: Academic Press.

Patty, J. (2002). Equivalence of objectives in two candidate elections. *Public Choice, 112*, 151–166.

Plott, C. (1967). A notion of equilibrium and its possibility under majority rule. *American Economic Review, 57*, 787–806.

Riker, W., & Ordeshook, P. (1973). *An introduction to positive political theory*. Englewood Cliffs, NJ: Prentice Hall.

Roberts, F. (1979). *Measurement theory*, Vol. 7 in *Encyclopedia of mathematics and its applications*. Reading, MA: Addison-Wesley.

Roemer, J. (2001). *Political competition: theory and applications*. Cambridge, MA: Harvard University Press.

Rubin, J. (1967). *Set theory*. San Francisco: Holden-Day.

Samuelson, L. (1984). Electoral equilibria with restricted strategies. *Public Choice, 43*, 307–327.

Saari, D. (1997). The generic existence of a core for q-rules. *Economic Theory, 9*, 219–260.

Saari, D. (2004). Geometry of chaotic and stable discussions. *American Mathematical Monthly, 111*, 377–393.

Schofield, N. (1999). The C^1 topology on the space of smooth preference profiles. *Social Choice and Welfare, 16*, 445–470.

Schofield, N. (2002). Representative democracy as social choice. In K. Arrow, A. Sen & K. Suzumura (Eds.), *Handbook of social choice and welfare* (Vol. 1, pp. 425–455). Amsterdam: Elsevier.

Sen, A. (1970). *Collective choice and social welfare*. San Francisco: Holden-Day.

Shepsle, K., & Bonchek, M. (1997). *Analyzing politics*. New York: W. W. Norton & Company.

Shubik, M. (1968). A two party system, general equilibrium, and the voters' paradox. *Zeitscrift fur National-Okonomie, 28*, 341–354.

Shubik, M. (1970). Voting or a price system in a competitive market structure. *American Political Science Review, 65*, 1141–1145.

Shubik, M. (1982). *Game theory in the social sciences*. Cambridge, MA: MIT Press.

Simpson, P. (1969). On defining areas of voter choice. *Quarterly Journal of Economics, 83*, 478–490.

Sloss, J. (1973). Stable outcomes in majority voting games. *Public Choice, 15*, 19–48.

Slutsky, S. (1979). Equilibrium under α-majority voting. *Econometrica, 47*, 1113–1125.

Stokes, D. (1966). Spatial models of party competition. In A. Campbell *et al.* (Eds.), *Elections and the political order* (pp. 161–179). New York: Wiley.

Straffin, P. (1989). Spatial models of power and voting outcomes. In F. Roberts (Ed.), *Applications of combinatorics and graph theory to the biological and social sciences* (pp. 315–335). Berlin: Springer-Verlag.

Straffin, P. (1994). Power and stability in politics. In R. Aumann & S. Hart (Eds.), *Handbook of game theory* (Vol. 2, pp. 1128–1151). Amsterdam: North-Holland.

Tullock, G. (1967a). The general irrelevance of the general impossibility theorem. *Quarterly Journal of Economics, 81*, 256–270.

Tullock, G. (1967b). *Toward a mathematics of politics*. Ann Arbor: University of Michigan Press.

Vorobev, N. (1977). *Game theory*. Berlin: Springer-Verlag.

Wendell, R., & Thorson, S. (1974). Some generalizations of social decisions under majority rule. *Econometrica, 42*, 893–912.

Wittman, D. (1977). Candidates with policy preferences. *Journal of Economic Theory, 14*, 180–189.

CHAPTER TWENTY-SEVEN

Geometry of Voting

Donald G. Saari
Director, Institute for Mathematical Behavioral Sciences, Distinguished Professor; Economics and Mathematics, University of California, Irvine, CA

Contents

Abstract

It is shown how simple geometry can be used to analyze and discover new properties about pairwise and positional voting rules as well as for those rules (e.g., runoffs and Approval Voting) that rely on these methods. The description starts by providing a geometric way to depict profiles, which simplifies the computation of the election outcomes. This geometry is then used to motivate the development of a "profile coordinate system," which evolves into a tool to analyze voting rules. This tool, for instance, completely explains various longstanding "paradoxes," such as why a Condorcet winner need not be

Handbook of Social Choice and Welfare, Volume II
ISSN: 0169-7218, DOI: 10.1016/S0169-7218(10)00027-4

elected with certain voting rules. A different geometry is developed to indicate whether certain voting "oddities" can be dismissed or must be taken seriously, and to explain why other mysteries, such as strategic voting and the no-show paradox (where a voter is rewarded by not voting), arise. Still another use of geometry extends McGarvey's Theorem about possible pairwise election rankings to identify the actual tallies that can arise (a result that is needed to analyze supermajority voting). Geometry is also developed to identify all possible positional and Approval Voting election outcomes that are admitted by a given profile; the converse becomes a geometric tool that can be used to discover new election relationships. Finally, it is shown how lessons learned in social choice, such as the seminal Arrow's and Sen's Theorems and the expanding literature about the properties of positional rules, provide insights into difficulties that are experienced by other disciplines.

1. INTRODUCTION

A goal of the "geometry of voting" is to capture the sense that "a picture is worth a thousand words." Geometry after all, has long served as a powerful tool to provide a global perspective of whatever we are studying while exposing unexpected relationships. This is why we graph functions, plot data, study the Edgeworth box from economics, and use diagrams to enhance lectures. Similarly, a purpose of the geometry of voting is to create appropriate geometric tools to enable us more easily to capture global aspects of decision and voting rules while exposing new relationships. Since most if not all practical voting rules combine pairwise or positional methods (e.g., runoffs, Approval Voting, cumulative voting, etc.), or use the rule directly, these are the emphasized methods.

A major reason why the area of social choice is so complex is that it is subject to the "curse of dimensionality"; for example, this curse is what prevents us from using standard geometric approaches to address the challenges of this area. Already with the first interesting setting of three alternatives, the $3! = 6$ dimensions of profile space overwhelm any hope to use standard graphs to connect profiles with election outcomes. (Unless stated otherwise, a profile specifies how many voters have each preference ranking.) As standard "graphing" approaches fail, we need to create new geometric tools. This is the purpose of this chapter.

As illustrations, in Section 2 profiles are geometrically depicted in a manner to simplify the tallying process. Lessons learned from this geometric tallying approach are then used to create a "coordinate system" for the six-dimensional profile space; as will be shown, this profile coordinate system allows us to better understand basic mysteries of social choice and voting theory. In Section 3, a geometric approach is created to more easily determine (e.g., rather than computing likelihoods) whether various paradoxical settings must be taken seriously, or can be dismissed as isolated anomalies. The section ends by describing the geometry of the three-candidate profile space in a manner that identifies which profiles give different outcomes for different voting rules.

A different theme, developed in Section 4, is motivated by those "nail-biting" close elections that involve three or more candidates. For many of us, encountering such an election creates an irresistible temptation to explore whether the outcome would have changed had a different election rule been used. (Had a different voting rule been used in the 2000 U.S. presidential election, for instance, could Gore have beaten Bush?) Published results exploring these concerns typically consider only certain better-known methods, which leads us to wonder what could happen had any of the infinite number of other rules been used. The geometric approach in Section 4 resolves this problem by showing how to depict *all possible positional and Approval Voting outcomes* for any specified profile. The provided references show how to discover all possible outcomes for any voting rule that offers a voter more than one way to tally his ballot; for example, cumulative voting. The converse of these approaches creates a tool to identify new election relationships.

The theme of Section 5 is motivated by the wealth of surprising conclusions and information that have been discovered in social choice. What connects this information with concerns coming from other disciplines is that social choice emphasizes aggregation rules—rules of voting and group decision making. But aggregation methods are widely used in almost all disciplines (e.g., statistics creates ways to aggregate data), which makes it reasonable to wonder whether the hard-won results found in social choice might transfer to other disciplines. Can other areas benefit from, say, the insights of Arrow's and Sen's results, or from the substantial amount of new knowledge that has been discovered about voting rules? As will be shown, this is the case.

2. FROM SIMPLE GEOMETRY TO PROFILE COORDINATES

As a way to partly sidestep that dimensionality cure, I show how to list profiles in a manner that roughly mimics the structure of profile space. An advantage of this *geometric profile representation* is that it makes it much easier to tally positional and pairwise ballots. An added benefit of this tallying approach is that it identifies why, with the same profile, different rules can have conflicting election outcomes. This information, which is exploited to create a "coordinate system" for profiles, is used to answer several voting theory concerns.

2.1. Using Geometry to Represent Profiles

A traditional way to describe a profile for the three alternatives A, B, C is to list how many of the voters' preferences are represented by each of the six rankings; e.g.,

Number	Ranking	Number	Ranking
7	$A \succ B \succ C$	12	$C \succ B \succ A$
15	$A \succ C \succ B$	4	$B \succ C \succ A$
2	$C \succ A \succ B$	12	$B \succ A \succ C$

(1)

But, let us be honest, tallying such a ballot can be be tedious; it requires sifting through the data to find how many voters rank each candidate in different ways. To avoid this annoyance, I developed the following geometric approach (Saari 1994, 1995a, 2001a) that significantly simplifies the tallying process. (For applications, see Nurmi 1999, 2000, 2002 and Tabarrok 2001.)

To start, identify each candidate with a vertex of an equilateral triangle (Figure 27.1a). A point in the triangle defines a ranking according to its distances to the three vertices where "closer is better." As the points on the vertical line of Figure 27.1a are an equal distance from the A and B vertices, for instance, they represent the $A \sim B$ tie or indifference. Similar lines define the $A \sim C$ and $B \sim C$ regions. This binary relationship divides the triangle into the thirteen Figure 27.1a regions: the six small open triangles represent strict rankings, and the seven remaining ranking regions, which include tied outcomes, are portions of the lines. In Figure 27.1a, for instance, the number 15 is in the region that is closest to the A vertex, next closest to C, and farthest from B; this region corresponds to an $A \succ C \succ B$ ranking. This geometric positioning of ranking regions is similar to that of profile space in that adjacent "ranking regions" differ only by the ranking of an adjacent pair.

The *geometric profile representation* places the number of voters with a particular ranking in the associated ranking region; for example, Figure 27.1a represents the Equation (1) profile. When representing a profile in a vector form, the convention is to start with the number of voters with the $A \succ B \succ C$ ranking and list the values in a clockwise manner ending with the $B \succ A \succ C$ value. Thus the numbers in Figure 27.1b denote the "ranking types"; for example, a type-two ranking (the Figure 27.1b region with a 2) is $A \succ C \succ B$. With this notation, the Figure 27.1a profile has the vector representation $(7, 15, 2, 12, 4, 12)$.

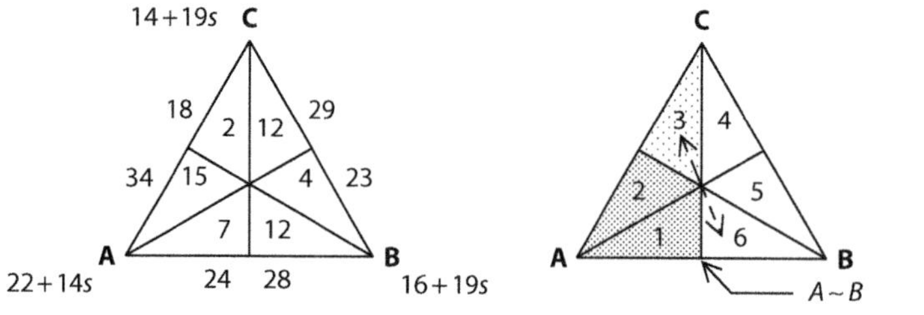

(a) Profile (b) Tallying process and type numbers

Figure 27.1. Profile Representation, Tallies, and Ranking Types.

To find the $\{A,B\}$ majority vote tally, observe that those voters preferring A to B are listed to the left of the vertical $A \sim B$ line. Thus, A's tally in an $\{A,B\}$ election is the sum of values placed in the type $\{1,2,3\}$ regions; these terms would be in the Figure 27.1b three shaded regions; B's tally would be the sum from the three unshaded regions (types $\{4, 5, 6\}$). With the Figure 27.1a profile, the $B \succ A$ tally of 28:24 is listed under the A–B leg. All other pairwise tallies are similarly computed and listed near the appropriate triangle edge. The outcome is the *cycle* $B \succ A, A \succ C, C \succ B$.

Candidate A's plurality tally is the number of voters who have her top-ranked, so this tally would be the Figure 27.1b sum of the numbers in the two heavily shaded regions (types $\{1, 2\}$). Using this approach with Figure 27.1a, the plurality ranking is $A \succ B \succ C$ with a 22:16:14 tally: these are the $s = 0$ values for the expressions located next to the appropriate vertices.

A *positional election* assigns specified points to candidates based on how they are *positioned* on a ballot; for three candidates, such a rule is defined by the *voting vector* (w_1, w_2, w_3), $w_1 \geq w_2 \geq w_3$, $w_1 > w_3$, where w_j points are assigned to the jth positioned candidate, To normalize these rules, let $w_3 = 0$ and divide the weights by w_1 to obtain $\mathbf{w}_s = (\frac{w_1}{w_1}, \frac{w_2}{w_1}, 0) = (1, s, 0)$ for $0 \leq s \leq 1$. For instance, a rule assigning 7, 5, and 0 points, respectively, to a voter's first, second, and third positioned candidate has the voting vector $(7,5,0)$ with the normalized $\mathbf{w}_{\frac{5}{7}} = (\frac{7}{7}, \frac{5}{7}, 0)$ form. (The $(7,5,0)$ tally is seven times the normalized $\mathbf{w}_{\frac{5}{7}}$ tally.) The plurality and antiplurality[1] rules are defined, respectively, by $(1,0,0)$ and $(1,1,0)$, while the Borda Count is defined by $(2,1,0)$ with the normalized $\mathbf{w}_{\frac{1}{2}} = (1, \frac{1}{2}, 0)$. (For n candidates, the Borda Count is defined by $(n-1, n-2, \ldots, 1, 0)$.)

With this normalization, A's $\mathbf{w}_s$-election tally adds s times the number of voters who have her second ranked to her plurality tally. In Figure 27.1b, this is A's plurality vote plus s times the sum of type 3 and 6 voters, or

> [the sum of the numbers in the two heavily shaded regions] plus ***s*** times [the sum of numbers in the two adjacent regions indicated by the arrow].

Using Figure 27.1a, this $[15+7] + s[2+12] = 22 + 14s$ tally is listed by the A vertex. The similarly computed $\mathbf{w}_s$-tallies for the two other candidates are posted by the appropriate vertices.

2.2. Different Information, Different Voting Outcomes

As shown next, these triangles can be used to identify the source of most "voting paradoxes": namely, different rules use different information from a profile. If this comment is true, then we must anticipate different outcomes coming from different rules. Indeed,

[1] It is called "antiplurality" because it is equivalent to voting against one candidate.

as the geometry of voting reveals, *all differences in election outcomes, all conflicts (including Arrow's and Sen's Theorems), reflect differences in how voting rules use, or ignore, information from a profile.*

To develop intuition about this comment, let me suggest that the reader use this profile representation and the tallying approach to solve (before reading ahead) the following three problems:

1. While fixing the plurality tallies, modify the Figure 27.1a profile so that the pairwise votes define the opposite cycle of $A \succ B$, $B \succ C$, $C \succ A$.
2. While fixing the plurality tallies, modify the Figure 27.1a profile so that the paired comparisons define the $B \succ A \succ C$ outcome where B is the Condorcet winner. (A candidate is the Condorcet winner if she beats all other candidates in two-person majority votes.)
3. While fixing the plurality tallies, modify the Figure 27.1a profile so that the antiplurality election ranking now is $C \succ B \succ A$.

To fix the Figure 27.1a plurality tallies, the sum of the two numbers by a vertex must equal the sum of the Figure 27.1a values; for example, the integers adjacent to the A vertex must sum to 22.

The geometric tallying approach simplifies these challenges. To create a profile with the specified cycle, for instance, move voter preferences so that enough of them are in the $A \succ B$ vertical region (the light shaded region of Figure 27.2a), the $B \succ C$ upward sloping shaded region, and the heavier shaded $C \succ A$ region; this defines the Figure 27.2a shaded triangle. Thus, by concentrating the voter preferences (from each vertex's two ranking regions) in the regions with a vertex of the shaded triangle—types $\{1, 3, 5\}$—we can create the desired cycle that has the strongest supporting tallies.

Not only do the Figure 27.2a plurality votes remain the same as in Figure 27.1a, but moving three of the 22 voters from the $A \succ B \succ C$ region to $A \succ C \succ B$ (indicated by the Figure 27.2a arrow) creates the $(19, 3, 14, 0, 16, 0)$ profile where the tallies for *all positional rules* agree with their Figure 27.1a values, but the paired comparisons cycle in the opposite direction. Stated in terms of the consequences for voting rules, this

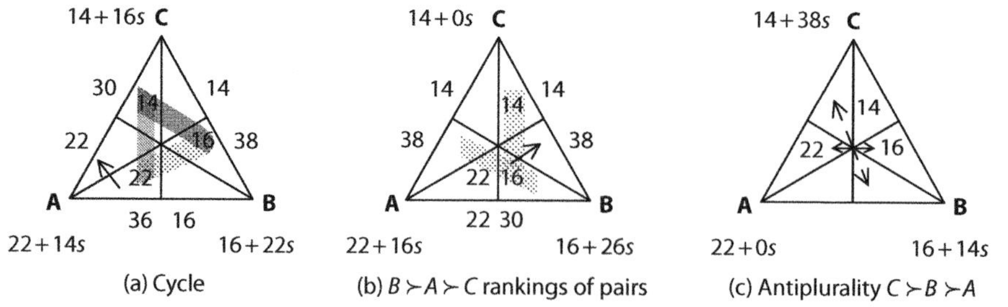

Figure 27.2. Creating "Paradoxes."

construction indicates that there exists a partial disconnect between positional outcomes and the majority votes over pairs. The next exercise provides added support for this comment.

This second question is handled with a similar geometric approach. Namely, move enough voters to the two shaded Figure 27.2b regions (where numbers remain in regions next to the same vertex to fix the Figure 27.1a plurality outcomes) to attain the desired outcome. To create an example where the paired rankings define $B \succ C \succ A$, just slide the slanted shaded region above the $A \sim C$ indifference line; for example, for an extreme choice, move the 16 voters from $B \succ A \succ C$ into the adjacent region, as indicated by the Figure 27.2b arrow, to create the $(22, 0, 0, 14, 16, 0)$ profile.

These exercises capture the essence of my comment that differences in election outcomes reflect how different rules use different aspects of information from a profile. Each shaded region in Figures 27.2a and 27.2b, for instance, describes the information needed to determine a specified paired comparison outcome, but each shaded region also contributes to (i.e., influences) the plurality outcome for *two of the candidates.* As two shaded regions can meet regions defining the plurality outcome for all three candidates (Figure 27.2b), it now becomes easy to adjust a profile so that the plurality tallies remain fixed, but the majority vote outcomes can vary. In other words, anticipate results asserting that *the plurality and paired comparison rankings need not have anything in common.* This is made precise below. (While there are restrictions, the first analysis exploring this concern that I have seen is a 2005 preprint of McDonald and Sieberg 2010.)

The third exercise identifies informational differences that create different positional outcomes. To reduce A's $\mathbf{w}_s$ tally while fixing the plurality outcome, decrease her second-place votes—the values in the two Figure 27.2c regions (types 3 and 6) with dashed arrows. Similarly, to increase C's antiplurality tally, move some of these voters into the regions (with solid arrows—types 2 and 5) providing second-place votes for C. Guided by these arrows, the extreme Figure 27.2c case has the $C \succ B \succ A$ antiplurality tally of 52:30:22; there are many more moderate examples.

The informational difference between plurality and other positional methods, then, is captured by the "second-place" arrows; two of the three choices are indicated in Figure 27.2c. As each arrow meets the plurality regions for two candidates, expect assertions that there need not be any compatibility between the plurality and, say, the antiplurality rankings. This, too, is made precise below.

2.3. Profile Coordinates

The geometric tallying method, then, identifies which portions of a profile are used by different rules. The natural next step is to exploit this information to create a general tool that I call *profile coordinates* (Saari 1999, 2000a, 2000b, 2008), which allows us more easily to analyze voting rules. Before doing so, notice that a coordinate system is of particular value if it simplifies the problem of interest by capturing relevant structures. Rather than helping, the normally useful x-y Cartesian system, for instance, can complicate the analysis of tracking a satellite; polar coordinates which specify the radius and angle defined by the object are more natural and valuable. In the same spirit, a way to significantly simplify the analysis of voting problems is to convert natural configurations of voter preferences into a profile coordinate system.

Start with what I call the "kernel profile"; these are the "neutral" profiles in that they merely yield complete ties for all positional rules and majority votes over pairs. A basis vector for this space is $\mathbf{K}^3 = (1,1,1,1,1,1)$; this is where each ranking is supported by one voter. A general kernel profile, then, is given by $c\mathbf{K}^3$ for scalar $c > 0$. For three candidates, the kernel vectors define a one-dimensional subspace. But for $n > 3$ candidates, the kernel vectors reside in an $[n! - 2^{n-1}(n-2) - 1]$-dimensional space; for example, for six candidates, this expression requires the kernel to consume over 80% of the 720 dimensions (591 of them) of profile space, and for ten candidates the kernel claims over 99.88% of the profile space dimensions! With the kernel voraciously devouring so many dimensions from the $n!$-dimensional profile space (Saari, 2000a, 2000b), we reach the ironic conclusion that a major source of the dimensionality curse plaguing social choice is due to profiles that, alone, do nothing!

The next natural profile direction (motivated by Figure 27.2a) identifies those configurations of preferences that affect pairwise tallies, but nothing else. The extreme setting (Figure 27.2a) assigns a voter to each ranking region with a vertex of the shaded triangle (types {1, 3, 5}); this defines $\mathbf{v} = (1,0,1,0,1,0)$. To create a coordinate system with vectors orthogonal to $\mathbf{K}^3$ (to reduce technical problems), the sum of the coordinates must equal zero; I use $\mathbf{C}^3 = 2\mathbf{v} - \mathbf{K}^3 = (1,-1,1,-1,1,-1)$ (the Figure 27.3a listing). Interpret the -1 terms in $\mathbf{C}^3$ as representing where a voter leaves this preference to adopt a preference with a $+1$; that is, treat $\mathbf{C}^3$ as a vector that changes a given profile without changing the number of voters. The relevant properties of this *Condorcet profile* $\mathbf{C}^3$ are captured by the Figure 27.3a tallies: $\mathbf{C}^3$ does not change any positional tally, but it generates a majority vote cycle. Even stronger, as asserted below, all

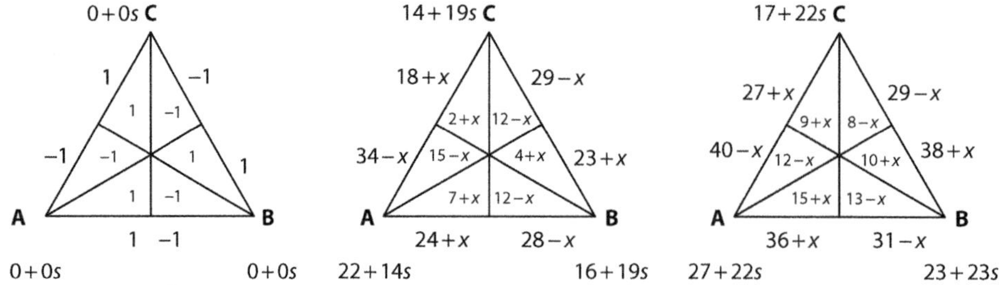

(a) $\mathbf{C}^3$ (b) Changes in pairwise tallies (c) Another example

Figure 27.3. $\mathbf{C}^3$: Condorcet Profile Direction.

possible inconsistencies and problems with three-candidate pairwise rankings and tallies are caused by $\mathbf{C}^3$; *nothing else is involved.*

Figure 27.3b illustrates this $\mathbf{C}^3$ effect; it lists all ways to fix *all of the Figure 27.1a positional tallies* while changing the majority vote tallies. To do so, just add $x\mathbf{C}^3$ to the Figure 27.1a profile where, to ensure non-negative Figure 27.3b profile entries, x is an integer satisfying $-2 \leq x \leq 12$. The pairwise outcomes start with the $B \succ A, A \succ C, C \succ B$ cycle (for $-2 \leq x \leq 1$), progress to where A is the Condorcet (and Borda) winner with $A \succ B \succ C$ $(3 \leq x \leq 7)$, and conclude with the $A \succ B, B \succ C, C \succ A$ cycle $(9 \leq x \leq 12)$; with all 15 profiles, all positional tallies remain fixed. The Figure 27.3c example is described below.

To find the basis for $n \geq 3$ candidates, start with a ranking of n-candidates, say $B \succ A \succ D \succ C \succ \cdots \succ Z$, and construct the "Condorcet n-tuple" by moving the top-ranked candidate to bottom place in the next ranking; for example, the next two rankings are $A \succ D \succ C \succ \cdots \succ Z \succ B$ and $D \succ C \succ \cdots \succ Z \succ B \succ A$. For each ranking in this n-tuple, assign -1 voters to the reversal of the ranking. I call this configuration of $2n$ preference rankings a *Condorcet basis vector.*

An analysis of voting rules often requires determining whether a given profile has some portion in a Condorcet (or other) direction. To show how to do so, recall that if vector $\mathbf{b}$ has Euclidean length $||\mathbf{b}||$, then the amount of vector $\mathbf{a}$ in the direction $\frac{1}{||\mathbf{b}||}\mathbf{b}$ is given by the scalar product $< \mathbf{a}, \frac{1}{||\mathbf{b}||}\mathbf{b} >$. So, because $||\mathbf{C}^3|| = \sqrt{1^2 + (-1)^2 + \cdots + (-1)^2} = \sqrt{6}$, the amount of the Figure 27.1a profile in the $\frac{1}{\sqrt{6}}\mathbf{C}^3$ direction is the fairly large value

$$< (7,15,2,12,4,12), \frac{1}{\sqrt{6}}(1,-1,1,-1,1,-1) >= \frac{1}{\sqrt{6}}[7-15+2-12+4-12]$$
$$= -\frac{26}{\sqrt{6}}.$$

This means that the Figure 27.1a profile has a $-\frac{26}{\sqrt{6}}[\frac{1}{\sqrt{6}}\mathbf{C}^3] = -\frac{13}{3}\mathbf{C}^3$ component; the negative value corresponds to the sign of x in $x\mathbf{C}^3$; it means that the direction of the cyclic effect of the pairs is given by $B \succ A, A \succ C, C \succ B$. In comparison, as

$$< (3,6,2,1,2,0), \frac{1}{\sqrt{6}}\mathbf{C}^3 >= \frac{1}{\sqrt{6}}[3-6+2-1+2-0] = 0, \tag{2}$$

the profile $(3,6,2,1,2,0)$ does not have any Condorcet components; it is orthogonal to this space.

2.3.1. Cycles and "Borda vs. Condorcet"

The Condorcet basis vectors can be used to answer several long-standing concerns from social choice, including the 230-year debate as to whether the Borda or the Condorcet winner more accurately reflects the views of the voters. An often repeated criticism (based on Condorcet's 1784 example) of the Borda Count is that it need not elect the Condorcet winner. The next theorem identifies both why this can happen and what is the source of all the possible differences between the rankings of the two approaches. Another criticism of the Borda Count involves examples that can be created to illustrate inconsistencies in Borda rankings over different subsets of candidates; this theorem identifies the total cause of all possible Borda difficulties.

Theorem 1 (Saari 1999, 2000a, 2000b, 2008) *Assume there are $n \geq 3$ candidates.*

(1) *There are $\frac{(n-1)!}{2}$ linearly independent Condorcet basis vectors; that is, they form an $\frac{(n-1)!}{2}$-dimensional subspace of the $n!$-dimensional profile space. The n-candidate positional tally of a Condorcet basis vector is zero for each candidate, but the pairwise rankings include a cycle where each tally is $(n-2) : -(n-2)$.*

(2) *A profile is orthogonal to all Condorcet basis vectors if and only if the pairwise rankings define a transitive ranking and for each X, Y, Z triplet, the tallies satisfy*

$$\tau(X,Y) + \tau(Y,Z) = \tau(X,Z) \tag{3}$$

where $\tau(X,Y)$ is the difference between X's and Y's majority vote tallies in an $\{X,Y\}$ vote. (Thus, all possible pairwise cycles are completely due to Condorcet terms in a profile.)

(3) *All possible differences between an n-candidate Borda ranking and the majority vote rankings of the pairs are due to Condorcet terms in a profile.*

(4) *The n-candidate Borda tally for candidate X is the sum of the number of points she received over all of her majority vote pairwise comparisons. For any k satisfying $3 \leq k < n$, there is a constant depending on k so that candidate X's n-candidate Borda tally is this multiple times the sum of her Borda tallies over all subsets of k candidates.*

(5) *All possible differences between a Borda ranking of a set of k alternatives, $k \geq 2$, and the Borda ranking of $n > k$ alternatives are caused by Condorcet terms in a profile.*

As profile $(3,6,2,1,2,0)$ is orthogonal to $\mathbf{C}^3$ (Eq. (2)), it illustrates the surprising Equation (3) equality; that is, the outcome $A \succ B$ is by 11:3, $C \succ B$ by 9:5, and $A \succ C$ by 9:5, so $\tau(A,B) = 11 - 3 = 8$, $\tau(B,C) = 5 - 9 = -4$, and $\tau(A,C) = 9 - 5 = 4$, which satisfies $\tau(A,B) + \tau(B,C) = \tau(A,C)$. In contrast, the Figure 27.1a profile (with $\mathbf{C}^3$ components) defines $\tau(A,B) = -4$, $\tau(B,C) = -6$, $\tau(A,C) = 16$, which fails to satisfy Equation (3). By using $\tau(A,C) = -\tau(C,A)$, it is easy to prove for three candidates that the sign of $\tau(A,B) + \tau(B,C) + \tau(C,A)$ is the sign of the profile's multiple of $\mathbf{C}^3$.[2]

[2] With the unanimity profile $(1,0,0,0,0,0)$, $\tau(A,B) = \tau(A,C) = \tau(B,C) = 1$ so $\tau(A,B) + \tau(B,C) + \tau(C,A) = 1$. The guaranteed $\mathbf{C}^3$ component manifests itself in that the pairwise tallies of $\tau(A,B) = \tau(A,C) = 1$ fail to distinguish whether A is "more preferred" over B, or over C.

Parts 3 and 4 of Theorem 1 explain all possible differences between the Borda and majority vote rankings; namely, the Condorcet terms do not affect the Borda Count ranking but they do alter the pairwise tallies and can distort the pairwise rankings. This is nicely illustrated with Figure 27.3c, where $\mathbf{C}^3$ components are added to the base profile of $(15, 12, 9, 8, 10, 13)$. As ensured by part 4, each candidate's Borda tally is the sum of her tallies in her two pairwise votes; as this summation adds a $+x$ to a $-x$, the Borda tally cancels all Condorcet effects. Thus, over all 18 profiles represented in Figure 27.3,[3] the Borda ranking remains $A \succ B \succ C$ with a fixed 76:69:56 tally. In contrast, the pairwise rankings start with the cycle $A \succ C$, $C \succ B$, $B \succ A$ for the $-9 \leq x \leq -5$ values, advance to where the Condorcet winner in $B \succ A \succ C$ differs from the Borda winner for $x = -4, -3$, change the pairwise ranking to $A \succ B \succ C$ to agree with the Borda ranking for the nine $-2 \leq x \leq 6$ values, and conclude with the opposite cycle of $A \succ B$, $B \succ C$, $C \succ A$ for the remaining $x = 7, 8$ values. (It turns out that the Borda and Condorcet winners can differ with three candidates only if the difference between the Borda tallies of the first- and second-place candidates is smaller than the difference between the second- and third-place candidates (Saari 2001c); e.g., here it is $76 - 69 < 69 - 56$. Another result is that for any family, such as Figures 27.3b and 27.3c, there always are more choices where the Borda and transitive Condorcet rankings agree than disagree.)

Parts 4 and 5 explain all possible paradoxical Borda Count outcomes. To expand on the statement, notice that all positional rules have a complete tie for any Condorcet four-tuple such as $\mathbf{C}^4 = \{A \succ B \succ C \succ D, B \succ C \succ D \succ A, C \succ D \succ A \succ B, D \succ A \succ B \succ C\}$. But dropping any one candidate, say D, from $\mathbf{C}^4$ defines the Condorcet triplet $A \succ B \succ C, B \succ C \succ A, C \succ A \succ B$, where all three candidate positional rules have a complete tie, *plus* the extra $A \succ B \succ C$ ranking. This extra ranking affects *all* three-candidate positional outcomes, but, surprisingly, the Condorcet directions are the *only* profile terms that can alter Borda outcomes for subsets of candidates.[4]

Over the four sets of three candidates, the extra rankings define a new kind of cycle,

$$A \succ B \succ C, \quad B \succ C \succ D, \quad C \succ D \succ A, \quad D \succ A \succ B \tag{4}$$

where each candidate is in first, second, and third place in different triplets. This listing makes it clear how to create all possible examples of profiles with, say, the Borda ranking is $A \succ D \succ C \succ B$, but by dropping bottom-ranked B, the new Borda ranking is the reversed $C \succ D \succ A$. Namely, start with a profile that has the desired Borda ranking of

[3] To have non-negative entries in the profile, x must be an integer satisfying $-9 \leq x \leq 8$.

[4] Other positional rules are affected by other terms; e.g., the profile $A \succ B \succ C \succ D, D \succ C \succ B \succ A, B \succ A \succ D \succ C, C \succ D \succ A \succ B$ creates complete ties for all pairs and all four-candidate positional outcomes. When restricted to triplets, however, only the Borda Count has a complete tie.

$A \succ D \succ C \succ B$, and then add a strong enough multiple of a $\mathbf{C}^4$ component to ensure that the extra $C \succ D \succ A$ terms dominate the three-candidate Borda tally. (The $\mathbf{C}^4$ term does not affect the four-candidate Borda tally.) This approach makes it easy to create examples with Borda Count inconsistencies over different sets of candidates, and (Theorem 1) it is the only way.

While Theorem 1 makes it easy to create such examples, it also follows from Equation (4) that if the Borda winner A does poorly in one subset of three candidates, she will do better in the other two subsets. This statement is further supported by part 4, which requires A's low Borda tally in one subset to be offset by higher tallies in other subsets. (Part 4 does not hold for any other positional voting rule; instead, a wide array of outcomes could occur.)

Because *all possible differences* between the two rules are caused by Condorcet terms, it follows that to support the Condorcet approach over Borda, one must justify why a Condorcet n-tuple, such as $A \succ B \succ C$, $B \succ C \succ A$, $C \succ A \succ B$ (where each candidate is once in each position), should not be a complete tie. Until such a justification is developed, Condorcet's criticism is reversed; *a weakness of the Condorcet paired comparison approach is that it need not elect the Borda winner.*

2.3.2. Positional Differences

The next profile directions reflect the Figure 27.2c symmetries. These coordinates have no influence on pairwise or Borda rankings, but they cause all possible differences that could ever occur among positional rules.

Of the several ways to define my *reversal* directions, I prefer to emphasize a particular candidate's plurality region; in Figure 27.2c, both arrows are in the region emphasizing candidate B. The $\mathbf{R}_A$ choice in Figure 27.4a, which I call "A-reversal," highlights candidate A; the negative values (where the coordinates sum to zero) make this choice orthogonal to both $\mathbf{K}^3$ and $\mathbf{C}^3$; they create the sense of voters changing preferences. The directions $\mathbf{R}_B$ and $\mathbf{R}_C$ are similarly defined; that is, place a voter in each region where

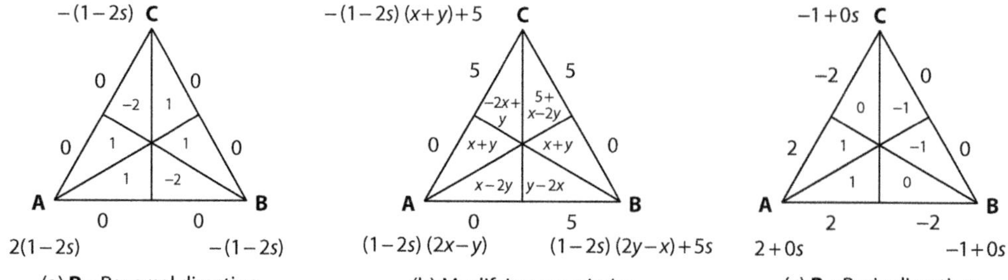

(a) $\mathbf{R}_A$; Reversal direction (b) Modifying unanimity (c) $\mathbf{B}_A$; Basic direction

Figure 27.4. Reversal Profiles.

the indicated candidate is either top-, or bottom-ranked, and -2 voters in each region where the candidate is middle-ranked.

The Figure 27.4a tallies identify the properties of Reversal profile directions; namely, they have no impact whatsoever on pairwise and Borda rankings ($s = \frac{1}{2}$), but they influence all other positional rules. Notice how the outcomes for rules with $s < \frac{1}{2}$ have one kind of outcome, but those with $s > \frac{1}{2}$ have the opposite ranking. The basic properties of Reversal profiles follows:

Theorem 2 (Saari 1999, 2000a, 2000b, 2008) *Assume the three candidates are* $\{A, B, C\}$.

(1) *The reversal profiles satisfy*

$$\mathbf{R}_A + \mathbf{R}_B + \mathbf{R}_C = \mathbf{0}, \tag{5}$$

so they define a two-dimensional subspace of the six-dimensional profile space.

(2) *The* $\mathbf{R}_X$ *tally for candidate* X *is zero for the Borda Count and all majority votes over pairs; the* $\mathbf{w}_s$ *tally is* $2(1-2s)$ *for* X *and* $-(1-2s)$ *for the other two candidates. Thus, the* $\mathbf{w}_s$ *tally of a reversal profile has one ranking for* $s < \frac{1}{2}$ *and the opposite ranking for* $s > \frac{1}{2}$.

(3) *Reversal components of a profile create differences between the tallies of candidates for different positional rules; all possible differences between the tallies of candidates for different rules are due to a profile's Reversal components.*

According to part 1, it suffices to select any two of these three profile directions to serve as a basis (but it is not orthogonal); my choice usually is $\mathbf{R}_A$, $\mathbf{R}_B$. Part 3 has a surprising message; it means that the extensive literature describing differences among positional rules reduces to analyzing how positional rules behave over reversal components of a profile. These differences are specified in part 2.

This reversal effect is illustrated with Figure 27.4b, which starts with a unanimity profile of five voters preferring $C \succ B \succ A$ and then adds $x\mathbf{R}_A + y\mathbf{R}_B$. Different from Figures 27.3b and 27.3c, this time I did not include $\mathbf{K}^3$ components. So, after creating a desired example, add a $k\mathbf{R}^3$ vector where k is large enough to ensure that all components are non-negative.

As guaranteed by Theorem 2, part 2, all choices of x and y have the same pairwise tallies with $\tau(B,A) = \tau(C,B) = \tau(C,A) = 5$ and the same Borda Count ranking of $C \succ B \succ A$. The other positional rankings, however, can be converted into whatever is desired by assigning appropriate choices for the two variables. To have a conflicting Figure 27.4b $A \succ B \succ C$ plurality ranking (i.e., $s = 0$), for instance, just solve the associated inequalities $2x - y > 2y - x > 5 - (x + y)$ (which reduce to $3y > 5, x > y$) with solutions $x = 3, y = 2$. By adding $4\mathbf{K}^3$, the resulting profile $(3, 9, 0, 8, 9, 0)$ has the desired properties.

The two remaining profile directions come from what I call the *Basic profiles*; the one for A is given in Figure 27.4c. More generally, to create the direction for $\mathbf{B}_X$, assign one voter to each ranking where X is top-ranked and -1 to each ranking where X is bottom-ranked. The properties of the Basic profile are reflected by the Figure 27.4c tallies.

Theorem 3 (Saari 1999, 2000a, 2000b, 2008) *Assume the three candidates are* $\{A, B, C\}$.

(1) *The Basic profiles satisfy*

$$\mathbf{B}_A + \mathbf{B}_B + \mathbf{B}_C = \mathbf{0}, \tag{6}$$

so they define a two-dimensional subspace of the six-dimensional profile space.

(2) *For* all *positional rules, the* $\mathbf{B}_X$ *tally assigns two points to candidate X and* -1 *points for each of the other two candidates. In pairwise votes, X receives two points and the other candidate receives zero points. The pairwise vote between the two other candidates is a zero-zero tie.*

(3) *Basic components of a profile have the same ranking for all positional rules and paired comparisons. Indeed, for this Basic component, the difference between tallies for any two candidates is precisely the same for all positional outcomes and* $\frac{3}{4}$ *the difference between majority vote tallies of these two candidates.*

(4) *The common positional tally of a profile's Basic component equals the Borda Count tally of the profile minus the Borda Count's tally of the* $k\mathbf{K}^3$ *component.*

In other words, nothing goes wrong with a Basic profile! Not only do pairwise and *all* positional rules share the same ranking, but, for these rules, even differences in the tallies between any two candidates agree. The reason for this amazing property comes from the Figure 27.2 shading approach, which identifies the different information from a profile used by different rules; the Basic profiles are orthogonal to these configurations of rankings that cause differences in outcomes.

The importance of profile coordinates for three alternatives is that they completely identify a profile's informational content in terms of the behavior of all positional and pairwise rules (along with voting methods that are built using these rules). Namely, everything that can happen with a positional method comes from the Basic and Reversal components of a profile; everything that can happen with the majority vote over pairs comes from the Basic and Condorcet components of a profile. Everything that can happen with the Borda Count, on the other hand, is based strictly on the Basic component of a profile. Because different rules use information from orthogonal subsets of information, different outcomes with different rules must be anticipated.

To provide extra content for this comment about the Borda Count, consider the profile $\mathbf{p} = 3\mathbf{B}_A + 2\mathbf{B}_B + 3\mathbf{R}_A + 9\mathbf{K}^3 = (6, 13, 10, 0, 11, 14)$. For all positional methods, the $3\mathbf{B}_A + 2\mathbf{B}_B$ tally is $(4, 1, -5)$. The normalized Borda outcome of $\mathbf{p}$ is $(31, 28, 22)$ while its tally of $9\mathbf{K}^3$ is $(27, 27, 27)$, and, indeed $(32, 28, 22) - (27, 27, 27) = (4, 1, -5)$. In other words, the Borda Count tally of a profile captures the common positional tally of the profile's Basic components; all possible differences in tallies reflect how different $\mathbf{w}_s$ rules handle reversal components.

2.4. Resolving Classical Problems and "Paradoxes"

As a way to illustrate the power of this profile coordinate system, I now use it to explain what causes some of the better-known classical three-candidate voting paradoxes.[5]

1. *"The Condorcet paradox: Given that the preference ordering of every voter ... is transitive, the (amalgamated) preference ordering of the majority of the voters ... may nevertheless be intransitive."*
   The answer is immediate; a necessary and sufficient condition for this to occur is if the profile has a sufficiently large $\mathbf{C}^3$ component. As will be explained in Section 3.4.1, this $\mathbf{C}^3$ component has the effect of vitiating the crucial assumption that voters have transitive preferences!
2. *"The Condorcet Winner paradox: An alternative x is not elected despite the fact that x is preferred by a majority of the voters over each of the other competing alternatives."*
   Two explanations (with combinations) cover all possibilities. The first is captured by Figures 27.3b and 27.3c and Theorem 1, which show that a profile's $\mathbf{C}^3$ components have absolutely no impact on positional outcomes, but they definitely influence pairwise outcomes. Thus an appropriately large multiple of $\mathbf{C}^3$ can change the Condorcet winner (as true with certain Figure 27.3c values of x) without changing the outcome of any rule that is not affected by $\mathbf{C}^3$ terms (such as positional methods, or any method based on positional rules such as Approval or cumulative voting). The second effect reflects the fact that a profile's Reversal components have no impact on the pairwise rankings, but they can alter a non-Borda positional outcome to anything desired; for example, the winner of such a positional method need not have anything to do with the paired comparison outcomes. (For more details, see Saari 2002.) Thus, if one accepts this paradox as a serious problem, all rules that give nontied outcomes to $\mathbf{C}^3$ and/or to Reversal components should be avoided; this includes all rules based on paired comparisons and non-Borda positional outcomes.
3. *"The Condorcet Loser ... paradox: An alternative x is elected despite the fact that a majority of the voters prefer each of the remaining alternatives to x."*
   The complete answer is the Reversal component of a profile; this profile component, and only this kind of component, can force a non-Borda positional rule's outcome to be completely independent of the pairwise rankings. Rules constructed from non-Borda positional methods are subject to this problem if they do not include a pairwise vote.
4. *"The Absolute Majority paradox: An alternative x may not be elected despite the fact that it is the only alternative ranked first by an absolute majority of the voters."*

[5] I took this list directly from the charge for a August 2010 "Voting Power in Practice" workshop in Normandy, France, where a goal was "to try and formulate necessary and/or sufficient condition(s) for the occurrence of the main paradoxes [that they listed]." As shown here, this objective is readily accomplished with profile coordinates.

Such an alternative must be top-ranked with the plurality rule, but it need not be so ranked with any other positional rule. The explanation is a combination of the Reversal and $\mathbf{C}^3$ components. To see the idea, suppose 1000 voters prefer $A \succ B \succ C$ and 1000 prefer $B \succ C \succ A$; who do they prefer? Both A and B are in first place precisely 1000 times, but B is in second place while A is in last place the other 1000 votes, so it is easy to argue that B is the robust winner. Yet, by adding just one more voter in favor of A, she becomes the absolute majority winner and the plurality winner, but she is not the winner with most other positional rules. Again, it is easy to argue *for this kind of profile* that this behavior indicates a weakness, rather than a strength, of the plurality vote. With a modification of the above profile decomposition (Saari 2002), it has been shown that this "paradox" occurs *only* with profiles of this kind; thus, it is arguable that the intended criticism of the paradox is poorly directed; it should be directed at the failings of the plurality vote. (Computing the scalar product of this profile with $\mathbf{C}^3$ and $\mathbf{R}_A$ shows that it has the strong components in these directions.)

5. *"The Absolute Loser paradox: An alternative x may be elected despite the fact that it is ranked last by a majority of the voters."*
   This property cannot occur with majority votes over pairs, so it is strictly a feature of how the Reversal profiles can force non-Borda positional methods to ignore information about pairs. This is the total explanation; as an illustration, the plurality vote where 202 prefer $A \succ C \succ B$, 201 prefer $B \succ C \succ A$, and 200 prefer $C \succ B \succ A$ has nearly two-thirds of the voters with A bottom-ranked, but she is the plurality winner. The scalar product of this profile $(0, 202, 0, 200, 201, 0)$ with $\mathbf{R}_A$ demonstrates the profile's exceptionally strong Reversal component. Rules constructed from these positional methods, such as Approval and cumulative voting, are subject to this problem.

Other concerns are similarly addressed; for example, there is a literature examining which voting rules will elect a Condorcet winner when one exists. The above profile decomposition provides a partial answer: The Condorcet winner is strictly determined by information from the Basic and Condorcet components, so, for a rule to elect the Condorcet winner, it must *not* be influenced by other types of profile information such as the Reversal components of a profile, but it *must be influenced* by Condorcet components. The statement about Reversal components means that all non-Borda Count positional rules, or methods based on these rules, cannot have this property. The second condition about Condorcet components means that the Borda Count cannot have this property, but methods that are based on the Borda Count over subsets of candidates might have this property. (This is because the Condorcet components affect Borda Count outcomes over subsets of candidates. This comment is reflected with the Nanson method, which is a Borda runoff, where at each stage all candidates not receiving at least the average number of votes are dropped. This leads to a Condorcet winner.)

The description of what happens for $n > 3$ alternatives is, as one must anticipate, more complicated. The intrepid reader is directed to Saari (2000a, 2000b).

3. GEOMETRY OF THE LIKELIHOODS OF VOTING PROBLEMS

While Section 2 explains what goes wrong with standard voting rules, one might wonder whether these problems are isolated anomalies that can be safely ignored, or issues that must be seriously considered. In other words, how likely are the various paradoxes?

The real objective has nothing to do with finding precise likelihood values; after all, it is not clear where, if anywhere, such precise values have ever proved to be of any value. Adding doubt to the validity of these values is that often they are based on questionable probability distributions,[6] which means that the numerical values must not be taken seriously. But, while flawed, what makes these conclusions valued contributions to the social choice literature is that they provide insights about which voting behaviors are essentially isolated phenomena and which ones reflect important, realistic difficulties. Because the real goal is to find this kind of qualitative information, it is natural to wonder whether answers can be found more easily by using the geometry of voting. This is the case; ways to do so are described after outlining a technical approach.

3.1. Central Limit Theorem

A way to appreciate what should be treated as an unexpected outcome (e.g., paradox) and what should not is to notice how easy it is to create Figure 27.2b-type examples with the same plurality tallies but with different pairwise and positional rankings. It is instructive, for instance, to use the Section 2 structures to find all profiles fixing the plurality $A \succ B \succ C$ tally of 17:16:15, but with different pairwise and/or antiplurality rankings.

Now, keeping the same 17:16:15 plurality tally, let me ask the reader to find all examples that exhibit complete agreement; that is, the pairwise, plurality, and antiplurality rankings all share the same $A \succ B \succ C$ outcome. Try it, but you might not like the challenge problem, which is more difficult to solve because there are not many examples! As the numbers of possible examples serve as a surrogate for the likelihoods of various behaviors, this exercise suggests that consistency is more unlikely than inconsistency.

[6] An often used choice, for example, is "the impartial anonymous culture" (IAC) assumption popularized by W. Gehrlein, P. Fishburn, and others. While IAC asserts that all profiles are equally likely, I doubt whether anyone really believes that a profile with one voter preferring $A \succ B \succ C$ and 49 preferring $C \succ B \succ A$ is as likely as where the 50 voters are split, say, 24 preferring one choice and 26 the other.

This counterintuitive observation forces us to wonder whether *the true paradoxical setting is to have complete consistency over all positional and pairwise rules, rather than inconsistencies.*

Such an assertion runs against accepted beliefs, but it is supported by analysis. By using methods of differential geometry and the central limit theorem combined with a geometric voting result described later (the "procedure line" in Section 4.3), Maria Tataru (a former graduate student of mine) and I developed an approach (Saari and Tataru 1999) to determine the likelihood that all positional outcomes agree.

Theorem 4 (Saari and Tataru 1999) *Assume there is a probably distribution for n voters over how they rank the three candidates where, in the limit, the distribution is IID with a mean at complete indifference and with a positive standard distribution. In the limit and with probability 0.69, a profile will have different rankings of the candidates when tallied with certain different positional rules.*

In other words, with only the surprisingly small likelihood of 0.31 can we expect a profile to have common $\mathbf{w}_s$ rankings. Moreover (as suggested by Figures 27.3b and 27.3c), this likelihood decreases once we include pairwise comparisons. (See Saari and Tataru 1999 for more general results.) This Saari–Tataru technique has subsequently been used by Merlin, Tataru, and Valognes (2000, 2001) to determine the likelihood that the *winner* will change with the procedure and the likelihood of Condorcet profiles; other papers include Lepelley and Merlin (2001) and Tataru and Merlin (1997).

3.2. Geometry of Paired Comparisons

It is not uncommon to hear, after an election involving majority votes over pairs, how the outcome reflects the "will of the voters." But this need not be the case; for example, Brams, Kilgour, and Zwicker (1998) describe a California "Yes–No" initiative election where not one of the millions of voters agreed with all of the actual outcomes. Partly motivated by their paper, Katri Sieberg (who did the statistical analysis for their paper) and I developed a geometric approach (Saari and Sieberg 2001a) to explain and provide geometric insights into these kinds of issues.

Start with a pairwise outcome where A beats B by receiving 60% of the vote. Geometrically represent this outcome on a line interval with endpoints A and B by placing a point 60% of the way from B to A. This point represents the profile and the outcome; with 100% certainty, 60% of these voters prefer A to B. Similarly with the two pairs $\{A, B\}$ and $\{C, D\}$, suppose A beats B and C beats D with, respectively, 60% and 55% of the vote. If the horizontal and vertical axes of a square depict, respectively, the A–B (A is on the right) and C–D (C is on the top) outcomes, then point $\mathbf{q}$ in the first quadrant of Figure 27.5a represents this joint outcome.

While with certainty 60% of the voters prefer A to B, and 55% prefer C to D, how should this outcome be interpreted? To capture the potential ambiguity of the interpretation, Sieberg created an example where 100 voters in a school district must decide whether to increase benefits for teachers (B is yes, A is no) and/or their salary (D is yes, C is no). Does this joint outcome, where both propositions are defeated with at least a 55% vote, signal the voters' forceful rejection of the teachers? After all, 55% of voters might embrace both negative conclusions because

- 55 of them vote against both proposals ($A \succ B, C \succ D$),
- 5 vote against benefits ($A \succ B$) but accept a salary increase ($D \succ C$),
- while the remaining 40 voters support both proposals ($B \succ A, D \succ C$).

But this interpretation could be incorrect because the same negative election tallies occur where, rather than rejecting the teachers, 85% of the voters are trying to help them! Because of financial constraints, these voters choose to provide support in one or the other way. Namely,

- only 15 voters vote against the teachers on both issues ($A \succ B$, $C \succ D$),
- 45 of the 100 voters support a salary increase ($D \succ C$) over improving benefits ($A \succ B$),
- and 40 of the voters prefer improving benefits ($B \succ A$) over a salary increase ($C \succ D$).

Both issues lose by sizable margins, but because 85% of these voters wanted to help the teachers in one way or the other, they would be very disappointed with the combined decision.

The social choice issue is to determine whether this disappointment is an anomaly that can be safely ignored, or an issue that must be seriously addressed. To tackle these kinds of concerns we developed a geometric approach (Saari and Sieberg 2001a) to connect profiles with their Figure 27.5a outcome. Let $\nu(A,C)$ be the fraction of all voters preferring $A \succ B$ and $C \succ D$; by using a similar notation with the other three choices, a profile becomes

$$\mathbf{p} = (\nu(A,C), \nu(A,D), \nu(B,C), \nu(B,D)). \tag{7}$$

Divide the voters into the "rightists"—the $A \succ B$ voters with preferences on the right edge, and the "leftists"—the $B \succ A$ voters with preferences on the left edge. (The

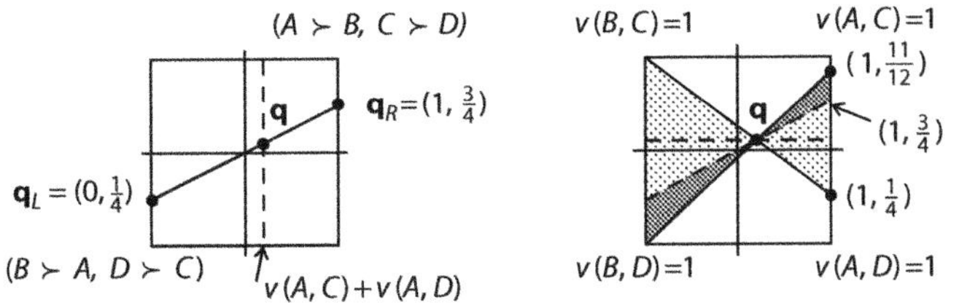

(a) A profile line (b) Finding all supporting profiles

Figure 27.5. Representing Profiles.

horizontal axis is selected so that for $\mathbf{q} = (q_1, q_2)$, we have $q_1 \geq q_2$.) Further divide the rightists according to how they rank C and D; this defines the $\mathbf{q}_R$ point on the Figure 27.5a right edge. A similar division of the leftist party defines $\mathbf{q}_L$ on the left edge. To interpret these points, as $\mathbf{q}_R$ is above the midpoint on the right edge, over half of the rightists support $C \succ D$; the lower position of $\mathbf{q}_L$ proves that most leftists prefer $D \succ C$. The general formulation for these points is

$$\mathbf{q}_L = \left(0, \frac{\nu(B,C)}{\nu(B,C)+\nu(B,D)}\right) = \left(0, \frac{\nu(B,C)}{1-(\nu(A,C)+\nu(A,D))}\right),$$
$$\mathbf{q}_R = \left(1, \frac{\nu(A,C)}{\nu(A,C)+\nu(A,D)}\right). \tag{8}$$

The straight line connecting $\mathbf{q}_L$ and $\mathbf{q}_R$, given by $(1-t)\mathbf{q}_L + t\mathbf{q}_R$, $0 \leq t \leq 1$, passes through $\mathbf{q}$ for $t = \nu(A,C) + \nu(A,D)$ (which is A's vote in the $\{A,B\}$ election); at this point we re-obtain the joint election outcome

$$\mathbf{q} = (\nu(A,C)+\nu(A,D), \nu(B,C)+\nu(A,C)).$$

In geometric terms, $\mathbf{q}$ is at the intersection of the Figure 27.5a solid line connecting the endpoints and the dashed vertical line representing the $\{A,B\}$ pairwise tally. The important observation is that a profile can be equated with a line segment with

1. endpoints on the left and right edges of the square and
2. a distinguished point $\mathbf{q}$ on the line; $\mathbf{q}$ identifies the joint election outcome.

Call the line segment with its distinguished point a *profile line.*

Of particular importance is that the converse is true: a line segment with these properties defines an Equation (7) profile where the segment becomes the profile line. The profile is found by carrying out the reverse computations. To illustrate, use the 60% vote of A over B along with the endpoints $\mathbf{q}_L = (0, \frac{1}{4})$ and $\mathbf{q}_R = (1, \frac{3}{4})$. As $\mathbf{q}_R$ requires $\frac{3}{4}$ of the rightists to prefer $C \succ D$, it follows that $\nu(A,C) = (0.6)(\frac{3}{4}) = 0.45$ while $\nu(A,D) = (0.6)(\frac{1}{4}) = 0.15$. Similarly, $\frac{1}{4}$ of the leftists prefer $C \succ D$, so $\nu(B,C) = (0.4)(\frac{1}{4}) = 0.1$ while $\nu(B,D) = (0.4)(\frac{3}{4}) = 0.3$. This particular *profile line*, then, represents the profile

$$(\nu(A,C), \nu(A,D), \nu(B,C), \nu(B,D)) = (0.45, 0.15, 0.10, 0.30).$$

To review, *all lines with endpoints on the side edges that pass through* $\mathbf{q}$ *represent profiles with outcome* $\mathbf{q}$. The set of all profiles with pairwise outcomes $\mathbf{q}$ are all lines in the shaded wedge of Figure 27.5b; call it the *profile cone.* (To find the cone, set $\mathbf{q}_L$ at its extreme settings at the top and bottom vertices. The line from each of these vertices through $\mathbf{q}$

defines the cone's boundaries.) This profile cone identifies *all possible supporting profiles for the specified pairwise outcomes.*

3.3. Geometric Likelihood Estimates

The ability to geometrically identify all profile lines (i.e., all profiles) supporting a specified $\mathbf{q}$ outcome is what allows us to geometrically represent the likelihoods of different events. Motivated by Sieberg's example demonstrating the ambiguity of interpreting the Figure 27.5a joint outcomes, it is natural to question how likely it is for certain percentages of the voters to accept both outcomes. A geometric answer is found by comparing the relative abundance of profile lines that satisfy a specified property relative to the full cone (Saari and Sieberg 2001a).

To examine the reasonable assumption that at least 55% of the Figure 27.5 voters prefer both $A \succ B$ and $C \succ D$ outcomes, find all of the profiles lines that support this property. As only rightists support the $A \succ B$ conclusion, the analysis reduces to determining what fraction of them, given by y, must also support $C \succ D$. This y value must satisfy $y(0.60) \geq 0.55$, or $y \geq \frac{11}{12}$; according to Figure 27.5b, *precisely one profile satisfies this constraint.* With a smooth probability profile distribution, then, *a 55% level of support has essentially zero likelihood of occurring.*

This geometric approach makes it easy to determine whether 52%, or 50%, or any other percentage of the voters support both outcomes. To illustrate by examining the more modest condition that at least 45% of the voters support both outcomes, we must determine when $\nu(A, C) \geq 0.45$. To do so, find the fraction y of rightists with $C \succ D$ preferences, which is $y(0.60) \geq 0.45$, or $y \geq \frac{3}{4}$. In Figure 27.5b, the relatively small size of this profile subset—the heavier shaded region in the profile cone—geometrically shows how unlikely it is to have even at least 45% of the voters supporting both outcomes![7]

The reader who prefers having actual probability values needs to specify a probability distribution for the profile lines. If one assumes, for instance, that each profile line is equally likely, then the likelihood (see Saari and Sieberg 2001a) is the length of the heavily shaded portion on the right edge divided by the length of the shaded portion on the right edge, or only $[\frac{11}{12} - \frac{3}{4}]/[\frac{11}{12} - \frac{1}{4}] = \frac{1}{4}$. Different distributions yield different outcomes; for example, the more realistic binomial probability distribution drops the likelihood of 0.25 to a smaller value.

The geometry for more pairs is higher-dimensional. With three pairs, for instance, the square describing the outcomes for two pairs is replaced with a cube. But while

[7] To determine what outcome has a 50% likelihood, find the midpoint of the right edge in the cone, or $y = \frac{7}{12}$. As $\frac{7}{12}(0.6) = \frac{7}{20} = 0.35$, for a conclusion to be supported with a 50% likelihood, all we can say is that both outcomes are shared by at least 35% of the voters. Similar to the Theorem 4 conclusion, "consistency" need not be as likely as inconsistency.

the geometry is more complicated, the cone structure extends. For a sample of new results, it follows from the geometry of the square that with any two-pair outcome, there always exist voters who agree with the combined outcome.[8] For three or more pairs, however, it follows from the geometry that it is possible for no voter to completely agree with the final outcome. Notice how this assertion becomes a theoretical explanation for the Brams, Kilgour, and Zwicker (1998) empirical result. For details, more results, and examples, and applications to "bundled voting," see Saari and Sieberg (2001a).

3.4. Explaining and Interpreting Pairwise Voting Outcomes

As demonstrated in Section 3.2, as soon as voters vote over several pairs, it is likely that only a small fraction of the voters, or maybe even none, support all outcomes; that is, any sense that the pairwise votes accurately reflect the views of most voters over all outcomes is doubtful. Why is this so, and how should such conclusions be interpreted? Explanations and interpretations are needed.

3.4.1. An Explanation

Start with the problem of selecting a committee that must have a member from each of three groups. Each group has two candidates; from the *West*: (Deanna, Eric); from the *East*: (Florence, George); and from the *North*: (Helen, Joe). To keep everything simple, suppose there are only three voters, where each is to vote for a candidate from each of the three districts. If Eric, George, and Joe each wins by 2:1, the social choice issue is to determine whether the voters are content with this outcome; does the conclusion reflect their aggregated views?

To analyze this problem, use reverse engineering by analyzing all possible supporting profiles. By ignoring the identity of each voter, there are five such profiles where, in the following list, the first letter of each candidate's name is used:

1. Voter 1: (E, G, J); Voter 2: (D, F, H); Voter 3: (E, G, J).
2. Voter 1: (D, G, J); Voter 2: (E, F, H); Voter 3: (E, G, J).
3. Voter 1: (E, F, J); Voter 2: (D, G, H); Voter 3: (E, G, J).
4. Voter 1: (E, G, H); Voter 2: (D, F, J); Voter 3: (E, G, J).
5. Voter 1: (D, G, J); Voter 2: (E, F, J); Voter 3: (E, G, H).

The (E, G, J) outcome appears to be reasonable for the first four profiles. This is because the directly opposing preferences of the first two voters create a tie that is broken by the remaining voter. But beyond appealing to the 2:1 tallies, justifying

[8] To see why, let $\mathbf{q}$ be any point in the top quadrant of Figure 27.5a satisfying the required $q_1 \geq q_2$. The worse situation is if $\mathbf{q}_L$ is located at the top, left vertex. But as the corresponding profile line passing through $\mathbf{q}$ still hits the right edge above the bottom vertex, there always must be a positive fraction of the rightists that accept both outcomes.

this conclusion for the last profile is problematic. A comforting observation, however, is that the outcome reflects the combined views of the voters for the vast majority of the scenarios—80% of them.

But suppose the outlier, the last profile, is the actual one where each voter is disappointed with the outcome because each wanted to have at least one woman and one man on the committee: this wish reflects how they voted. On the other hand, it is reasonable to question whether this example constitutes a realistic criticism of the voting rule; after all, nothing is built into the rule to reflect this "mixed gender" requirement—or any other newly imposed stipulation. But, as described next, this mixed gender condition identifies the source of all pairwise voting paradoxes.

To illustrate what happens, convert this committee example into an equivalent but more familiar setting just by changing names. Replace D with $B \succ A$ and E with $A \succ B$, F with $C \succ B$ and G with $B \succ C$, H with $A \succ C$ and J with $C \succ A$. With this name change, *the "mixed gender" condition is equivalent to the social choice requirement that voters have transitive preferences;* a voter's "same gender" rankings of all men, or all women, translate, respectively, to the *cyclic* preferences $A \succ B$, $B \succ C$, $C \succ A$ or $B \succ A$, $A \succ C$, $C \succ B$.

The first four committee profiles correspond, then, to where at least one voter has cyclic preferences. Only the last one, the outlier, represents voters with transitive preferences: the preferences of voters 3, 1, and 2 correspond, respectively, to

$$A \succ B \succ C, \quad B \succ C \succ A, \quad C \succ A \succ B. \tag{9}$$

Recall how this Equation (9) "Condorcet triplet" played a central role in Section 2.3.1.

As the only difference between the committee election and pairwise voting is a name-change, the analysis of both examples must be identical. Namely,

1. The majority vote over pairs loses information by severing all information that connects the pairs. Beyond the mixed gender requirement, the vote emasculates the individual rationality assumption by dropping all information about the transitivity of individual rankings.
2. Rather than responding to a specified profile, the majority vote reacts to the set of all profiles that support the specified tallies; it selects an outcome that best reflects "the largest portion" of these profiles.

These comments explain the majority vote cycle associated with the Equation (9) Condorcet triplet; the cycle arises because it best reflects the properties of most (here, 80%) of the supporting profiles, rather than the specified one. The fact that this cycle reflects an appropriate outcome for nonadmissible profiles (as they have cyclic voters) is immaterial—not to us, but to the mechanics of the voting rule. The rule strips away and ignores the connecting information and requirements that we accept as valuable when determining pairwise outcomes. (For more, see Saari 2006, 2008.)

3.4.2. Other Consequences

The above explanation is compatible with earlier interpretations of paired comparison results that were advanced in Saari and Sieberg (2001a) and Saari (2004). A convenient one comes from the geometry of the Figure 27.5b profile cone where $\nu(A, C)$ *has the largest component value* for most of the profile lines supporting $\mathbf{q}$. This suggests that the true role of $\mathbf{q}$ is *not* to identify what outcomes most voters in a specified profile prefer (which is false), but rather to identify which profile entry has the largest value for the largest number of supporting profiles in the profile cone. (For one pair, this statement supports common expectations; for several pairs, it conflicts with popular interpretations.) Thus, consistent with the Section 3.4.1 comments, rather than reflecting a specified profile, the outcome is appropriate for the largest portion of supporting profiles. "Paradoxes," then, are generated by the outliers in the set of supporting profiles.

Theorem 5 (Saari and Sieberg 2001a) *Let the probability distribution over profiles be either the uniform or the binomial distribution with* $p = \frac{1}{2}$. *For two or more pairs, the combined pairwise outcome agrees with the component that has the largest value with the largest number of profiles.*

To convert this theorem into a working tool, notice that two pairs define a profile with *four components,* so, according to Theorem 5, all we can say in general is that the dominating component value for the largest number of profiles is greater than $\frac{1}{4}$, not $\frac{1}{2}$. By using geometry (or the analytic approach as suggested by footnote 8), an even smaller value is needed to assert with 50% likelihood that the fraction of the voters support all outcomes. With N pairs, we only know that the dominating component is larger than $(\frac{1}{2})^N$; so, with $N = 3$ or 4 pairs, we only know, respectively, that the largest number of profile lines are where at least $\frac{1}{8}$ or $\frac{1}{16}$ of the voters approve all outcomes. With $N = 20$ "Yes–No" issues on the ballot, all we can expect is that largest number of profile lines have the combined outcome supported by $\frac{1}{1{,}048{,}576}$ of the voters.

So (without added information), there is no reason to expect the joint outcomes over several pairs to enjoy much support. A lesson of particular importance coming from the profile cone geometry is that pairwise majority vote outcomes need not reflect the properties of an actual profile; they reflect a statistical sense of the set of all possible profiles that yield the same result.

3.5. Geometry of All Three-Candidate Pairwise and Positional Outcomes

A geometric representation of profile space showing all possible interactions among all three-candidate majority vote and positional outcomes would be very useful. If possible, we would like to have this geometry identify all inconsistencies among the outcomes for different rules, specify all supporting profiles, and indicate their likelihoods. A method that does some of this (using profile coordinates) is in Saari (1999). The approach outlined next, which comes from Saari and Valognes (1998, 1999), captures these objectives by describing the geometry of profile space.

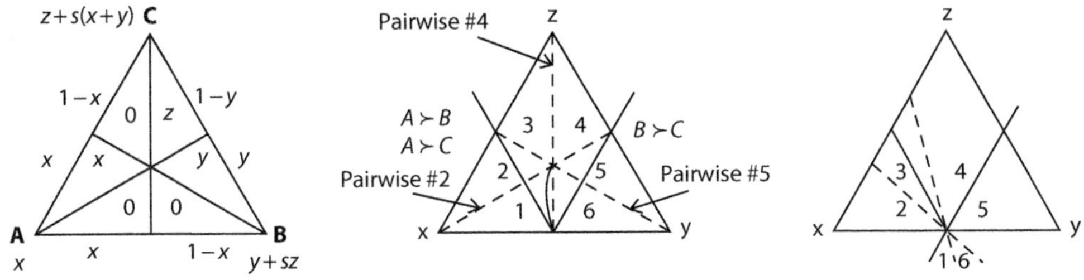

(a) Class of profiles (b) Pairwise and $s=0$ (c) Pairwise and $s=\frac{1}{2}$

Figure 27.6. Three-Candidate Geometry.

For reasons explained later, start with any profile involving only three types; the Figure 27.6a choices are voters of types 2, 4, and 5 (Figure 27.1b). If x, y, z represent the fraction of voters of the indicated types, then the positional and pairwise tallies are as specified in Figure 27.6a.

3.5.1. Geometrically Comparing Positional and Pairwise Outcome

Reflecting my preferred and persistent use of equilateral triangles, notice how this set of points $\{(x, y, z) \in \mathbb{R}^3 \mid 0 \leq x, y, z, x+y+z=1\}$ defines a simplex (equilateral triangle in Figure 27.6b) that passes through the three points $(1,0,0), (0,1,0), (0,0,1)$; these points capture, respectively, where $x=1, y=1$, and $z=1$. To find all profiles supporting specific election outcomes, on this triangle find the boundaries (i.e., ties) of the majority vote outcomes over pairs. According to Figure 27.6a, the $A \sim B$ outcome is given by the line $x=\frac{1}{2}$; this is the solid downward slanting line in Figure 27.6b.

As the notation in Figure 27.6b indicates, all profiles in the triangle to the left of this line represent $A \succ B$; the profiles to the right represent $B \succ A$. The same line captures the $A \sim C$ boundary, so all that remains is to find the $B \sim C$ boundary, which is given by the line $y=\frac{1}{2}$ and the upward slanted line in Figure 27.6b. This profile space, then, is divided into three open regions; the small equilateral triangle on the left corresponds to type 2 profiles defining $A \succ C \succ B$, the small equilateral triangle on the right identifies all profiles defining the opposite type 5 rankings, and the remaining quadrilateral are all profiles defining a type 4 pairwise ranking.

While the same approach identifies which profiles define what positional outcomes, it is easier to handle the rules separately and then describe how they are connected. The $A \sim B$ plurality ($s=0$) boundary of profiles is given (Figure 27.6a tallies) by the line $x=y$—the vertical dashed line in Figure 27.6b. Similarly, the $A \sim C$ and $B \succ C$ boundaries are given, respectively, by the $x=z$ and $y=z$ dashed lines. (The curved line is explained later.)

Results identifying differences in election outcomes are immediate; for example, Figure 27.6b proves for profiles of the Figure 27.6a type that any of the thirteen possible plurality rankings can be accompanied by a type 4 ($C \succ B \succ A$) pairwise ranking. The geometry even shows how to find supporting profiles; for example, to have a type 1 plurality outcome with the reversed type 4 pairwise ranking, just select a point (x, y, z) in the indicated region; in addition, any point satisfying $z < y < x < \frac{1}{2}$ suffices, such as $x = \frac{5}{12}, y = \frac{4}{12}, z = \frac{3}{12}$. The integer form of this profile is $(0, 5, 0, 4, 3, 0)$.

Figure 27.6c compares the pairwise and Borda outcomes. To compute the Borda ($s = \frac{1}{2}$) $A \sim B$, $B \sim C$, $A \sim C$ boundaries, it follows from the Figure 27.6a tallies that we should graph, respectively, the Figure 27.6c lines $x = y + \frac{x}{2}$, $y + \frac{x}{2} = z + \frac{1}{2}(x + y)$, $x = z + \frac{1}{2}(x + y)$. (The graphing is simple; two points determine each line, and they can be found by setting one of the variables equal to zero.) Notice how the figures capture significant differences between the plurality and Borda ranking with respect to the pairwise outcomes: all profiles leading to a type 5 pairwise outcome define the same Borda ranking, but this is not so with the plurality rule. Profiles defining a type 4 pairwise outcome require a type 3 or 4 Borda outcome, but all possible plurality rankings can emerge. Indeed, with Figure 27.6a profiles, it is impossible to have a Borda type 1 or 6 ranking.

The remaining extreme setting is the antiplurality vote ($s = 1$); here the $A \sim B$ boundary coincides with the $A \sim B$ pairwise boundary, the $A \sim C$ boundary is the vertex $(1, 0, 0)$ (or $x = 1$), and the $B \succ C$ boundary is the right triangle edge. In other words, with these profiles, the only strict antiplurality outcomes are of type 3 (the triangle near the x vertex) and type 4. Comparing the dashed lines of Figures 27.6b and 27.6c, it follows that there exist plenty of profiles providing a type 4 Borda ranking, and anything desired (i.e., any of the thirteen possibilities) for the plurality ranking.

To relate the outcomes for the various positional rules, plot how the completely tied $\mathbf{w}_s$ election point moves as s varies. As this point is the intersection of the $A \sim B$ and $B \sim C$ boundary surfaces, it follows from the associated algebraic equations that these tied points satisfy

$$(x, y, z) = \left(\frac{1 + s}{3}, \frac{1 - s + s^2}{3(1 - s)}, \frac{1 - 2s}{3(1 - s)}\right), \quad 0 \leq s \leq 1. \tag{10}$$

The $0 \leq s \leq \frac{1}{2}$ part of this curve is plotted in Figure 27.6b; the rest of the curve is out of the triangle. In other words, as s increases, the $\mathbf{w}_s$ point of complete indifference moves down this curve from the plurality point carrying a modified version of the boundary lines for the $\mathbf{w}_s$ ranking regions.

3.5.2. Surprising Conclusions

This geometry makes it surprisingly easy to pick out fascinating conclusions. For instance, notice how the type 4 region for any $\mathbf{w}_s$, $0 < s \leq \frac{1}{2}$, contains portions of *all plurality regions*. In fact because of the tilting of the $A \sim B$ indifference line, the geometry makes it simple to show that if $0 \le s_1 < s_2 \le \frac{1}{2}$, then *any* $\mathbf{w}_{s_1}$ ranking can be accompanied with a type 4 $\mathbf{w}_{s_2}$ ranking. For another property, select any point $\mathbf{p}$ in the region between the curved line and the $A \sim B$ plurality boundary. The plurality outcome winner is A. But as s increases, regions 6, 5, and 4 pass over $\mathbf{p}$; namely, for any such profile $\mathbf{p}$, *each candidate becomes the winner with some* $\mathbf{w}_s$. The geometry also shows that this is the only region in this setting where, as s changes, all three candidates can win. On the other side of the curved line, however, regions 5 and 6 cannot cross a point, but regions 2 and 3 can. So, in an appropriately selected portion, it follows for any such profile that both A and C can be a $\mathbf{w}_s$ winner, but B never can.

Finding the likelihoods of various events also becomes immediate. For the practical purpose of determining whether various inconsistencies are serious, or can be ignored, the answer is geometrically represented by the size of the appropriate regions relative to the area of the full triangle. Letting n_2, n_5, n_4 represent the number of voters of the various types, where $n = n_2 + n_4 + n_5$, we have that $x = \frac{n_2}{n}$, $y = \frac{n_5}{n}$, and $z = \frac{n_4}{n}$. As the value of n becomes much larger, it is not difficult to prove that the ratio of the areas of various regions tends, in the limit, to agree with the ratio of the number of points of these types in different regions. In other words, the geometry makes it easy to compute likelihoods, such as to find how likely it is for a Figure 27.6a profile to have all candidates as winners by varying $\mathbf{w}_s$, compute the ratio of the region between the Figure 27.6b curved line and vertical axis relative to the area of the triangle. Handling more realistic probability distributions involves integration over regions. Examples for all of this are in Saari and Valognes (1998, 1999).

3.5.3. The Full Profile Space for Three Candidates

The huge obstacle imposed by a three-candidate profile space is its large $3! = 6$ dimension. One dimension can be dropped by replacing the number of voters having each ranking with the fraction of all voters that have this ranking. To drop another dimension, notice that we can assign zero voters to some one ranking. To analyze $(4, 6, 3, 9, 7, 2)$, for instance, subtract $2\mathbf{K}^3$ to obtain $(2, 4, 1, 7, 5, 0)$. (This reduction primarily reduces the number of majority vote cycles.) By changing names, if necessary, the choice of the ranking with zero voters is arbitrary; in Figure 27.7a it is type 6. Thus, relative to the $k\mathbf{K}^3$ reduction and the six possible name changes, Figure 27.7a reflects a general profile. This set

$$\mathcal{P} = \{(x, y, z, u, v) \in \mathbb{R}^5 \,|\, x, y, z, u, v \ge 0, x + y + z + u + v = 1\} \tag{11}$$

defines an equilateral tetrahedron in a four-dimensional space. But it remains challenging to envision four-dimensional objects. Another step is necessary.

The approach is to determine what happens on $\mathcal{P}$'s "faces" where a variable equals zero. If, say, $v = 0$, the remaining variables, $\{(x, y, z, u) \in \mathbb{R}^4 \,|\, x, y, z, u \ge 0,\ x + y + z +$

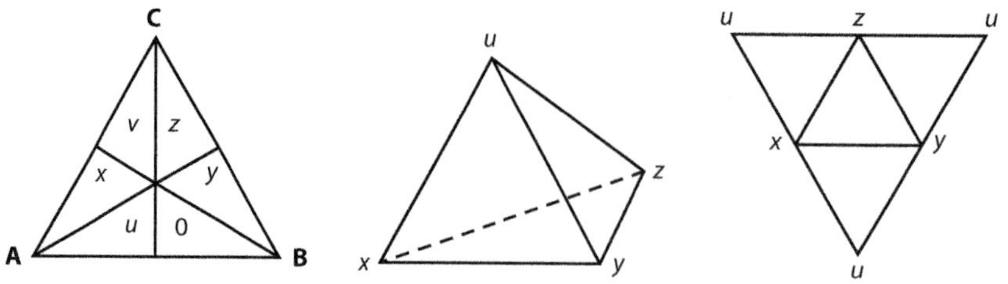

(a) All profiles (b) Tetrahedron for four types (c) Opened tetrahedron

Figure 27.7. Finding the Geometry of Profile Space.

$u = 1\}$, create an equilateral tetrahedron as depicted in Figure 27.7b. To understand the geometry of voting rules on this tetrahedron (i.e., with these four voter types), open it up. That is, select a vertex, say u, and cut down the three connecting edges. Folding the faces out generates a Figure 27.7c-type figure. In each of these four triangles, carry out an analysis similar to that used in Figure 27.6 to determine what profiles cause what kinds of behaviors with different voting rules.[9] (This analysis, but one in which a right triangle is used rather than equilateral triangles, is developed in Saari and Valognes 1998, 1999.) Folding the edges up creates an excellent picture of the relationships among the outcomes for the rules.

Similar to how Figure 27.7b is converted into Figure 27.7c, "open" the Equation (11) four-dimensional equilateral tetrahedron into five three-dimensional tetrahedrons; each is defined by setting one of the five variables equal to zero. Just as the opened three-dimensional tetrahedron attaches three equilateral triangles to edges of a central equilateral triangle, the four-dimensional object attaches four equilateral tetrahedrons each to a face of a central equilateral tetrahedron. The analysis of behavior on each tetrahedron is known, so examining connecting boundaries of tetrahedrons provides a picture of $\mathcal{P}$. This structure allows surprising results to be "seen."

4. OTHER GEOMETRIC VOTING RESULTS

The reasonably sized literatures that discuss either paired comparisons or strategic voting make it worth indicating how geometry allows us to better "see" what is occurring in either case. Some of the geometry is outlined; details are left to references. A third concern reflects what many of us do after a close election; we check to see whether there would have been a different outcome had a different election rule been used. But the

[9] Readers interested in extending to four candidates the Section 2 geometric approach to represent three-candidate profiles and to compute the tallies should use this unfolding of the tetrahedron. Details are in Saari (2000a).

complexity of the analysis often means that we can check only what might have occurred with a couple of standard voting rules. The last part of this section shows how to use geometry to capture what would have happened with a wide selection of rules.

4.1. Paired Comparisons: Extending McGarvey's Theorem

A valued paired comparison result is McGarvey's Theorem (1953) asserting that all possible pairwise rankings are possible. Namely, for each of the $\binom{n}{2}$ pairs of n alternatives, select one of the three possible rankings: there exists a profile yielding all of these majority vote rankings. The next step is to move beyond knowing what combination of rankings can arise to specify all possible tallies. This is of interest, for instance, when analyzing supermajority voting where McGarvey's result does not apply. The approach to do so (Saari 1994, 1995a) mimics aspects of the construction in Sections 3.2 and 3.3[10] where an interval is identified with each pair of alternatives and a point x of the distance from X toward Y represents where Y receives the fraction x of the $\{X, Y\}$ vote. For three alternatives, the three pairs define a cube. (Thus n alternatives define an $\binom{n}{2}$ dimensional cube.) A convenient choice selects the vertices for each line to be at the values of ± 1 so that 0 represents a tie and a negative or positive value represents a victory for the appropriate candidate.

Not all points in the cube represent pairwise tallies; it is impossible to use transitive preferences to attain the point representing unanimous support for $A \succ B$, $B \succ C$, and $C \succ A$, for example. To find which tallies *are* admissible for $n = 3$, notice that only two of the eight vertices represent unanimity cyclic outcomes and they are diametrically located. (For n alternatives, there are $2^{\binom{n}{2}} - n!$ such vertices; e.g., for $n = 5$, the ten-dimensional cube has $2^{10} - 5! = 1024 - 120 = 904$ nontransitive and 120 transitive vertices.) Draw hyperplanes through vertices with transitive rankings where only non-transitive vertices are on one side; throw this side away. With three candidates, then, two oppositely located pyramids, each with a cyclic vertex, are dismissed (Saari 1994, 1995a). All remaining points can be attained with pairwise outcomes; with k voters, for example, these are all points in the truncated cube that have a common denominator k.

By using $-1 \leq x_{X,Y} \leq 1$ for each pair of candidates where, say, $x_{A,B} = x_{B,C} = x_{C,A} = 1$ means that the first listed candidate in each pair wins unanimously, it follows that all rational points in

$$\{(x_{A,B}, x_{B,C}, x_{C,A}) \mid -1 \leq x_{X,Y} \leq 1, \quad -1 \leq x_{A,B} + x_{B,C} + x_{C,A} \leq 1\} \tag{12}$$

are paired comparison election tallies for some profile; no other points have this property. As an illustration, suppose we wish to determine all possible $\{B, C\}$ outcomes that can

[10] The approaches differ in that the Sections 3.2 and 3.3 development identifies all associated profiles.

occur if A wins both of her elections with 90% of the vote (so $x_{A,Y} = -1 + .9(1 - (-1)) = .8$). The answer from Equation (12) is that $-1 \leq 0.8 + x_{B,C} - 0.8 \leq 1$, or $-1 \leq x_{B,C} \leq 1$, which means that there are no restrictions whatsoever on the $x_{B,C}$ tally.

This argument can be used to prove McGarvey's result. With the alternatives $\{A_1, \ldots, A_n\}$, the center point of each face of the $\binom{n}{2}$-dimensional cube is the pairwise tally for some profile; such as a way to realize the center point of the $A_1 \succ A_2$ face, given by point $(1,0,\ldots,0)$ (so, A_1 is the unanimous winner over A_2 and all other paired comparisons end in a tie), is to consider all rankings where A_1 is ranked immediately above A_2; the desired outcome arises by assigning one voter to each of these rankings.[11] As such, the convex hull defined by these midpoints generates a subset of the tallies that are achievable with profiles. This convex set includes a sizable neighborhood about the midpoint of the cube (given by $(0,\ldots,0)$), so it intersects all ranking regions. In turn, this means that any listing of pairwise rankings can be achieved. (But to have ties, the number of voters—which is given by a common denominator of a point—must have an even value.)

To connect this geometry with the profile coordinates, create what I call the *transitivity plane*; it is the set of pairwise tallies in the cube that satisfy Equation (3) for each triplet. (The plane's normal directions are defined by the Condorcet basis directions described in Section 2.3.) This plane provides an interesting, geometric way to represent the tallies for different voting rules (Saari 2000a). As an example, for any pairwise tally $\mathbf{q}$ in the cube, the associated Borda Count outcome (and normalized tally) is the closest point (with the usual Euclidean distance) in the transitivity plane to $\mathbf{q}$. Associated with the Borda rule is the Copeland rule; this is where a winner of a pairwise outcome is assigned one point, the loser zero, and with a tie both receive $\frac{1}{2}$ points. (To use the cube with $[-1,1]$ edges, change the Copeland tallies to 1, -1, and 0.) Find the vertex of the original uncut cube that is closest to $\mathbf{q}$, and then find the point in the transitivity plane that is closest to this vertex; this is the Copeland outcome. The Kemeny outcome (another well-studied voting rule) is the closest region to $\mathbf{q}$ with a transitive ranking (where "closest" now is the l_1 distance, or the sum of the magnitudes of the coordinates), and so forth (Saari 2000a). (For definitions of these voting rules, see the descriptions that Brams and Fishburn (2002) give in Chapter 4 of volume I of this *Handbook*.)

This geometry makes it possible to create a fairly complete description of all Copeland and Kemeny outcomes and paradoxes that can occur by dropping candidates, or comparing them with other procedures (Saari and Merlin 1996, 2000a). Merlin and I proved, for instance, that the Kemeny method always ranks the Borda winner above the Borda loser, and the Borda method always ranks the Kemeny winner above the Kemeny loser. Our

[11] Clearly, A_1 beats A_2 with a unanimous vote. For all other pairs, treat the $A_1 \succ A_2$ ranking as a unit denoted by Z, which reduces the number of variables to $n-1$. Because each ranking of these variables is accompanied by its reversal, the paired comparison ranking for all other pairs is a complete tie.

paper (Saari and Merlin 2000a) extends many of the nice results about Kemeny's method that were discovered by Le Breton and Truchon (1997) and by Young (1978, 1988).

As true throughout social choice, expect to discover delightful surprises. As an illustration, while the Kemeny method handles cyclic rankings by finding the "closest" transitive ranking, the Dodgson method seeks a "winner" rather than a ranking (see Ratliff 2001, 2002, 2003), so it selects the "closest" ranking that has a Condorcet winner. The similarity between these rules makes it is reasonable to expect that the Dodgson winner is Kemeny top-ranked. This, however, need not be the case: by using my geometry of pairwise tallies, Ratliff (2001) proved that the Dodgson winner can be ranked *anywhere within a Kemeny ranking*, even last! He even proved (2002) that no relationship need exist between the Dodgson winner and the Borda ranking. When Ratliff (2003) generalized Dodgson's approach to create a method to select a committee (a committee of size k is found from $\mathbf{q}$ by finding the nearest ranking where each of the k candidates is preferred to all of the remaining $n - k$ candidates), he discovered all sorts of surprising conclusions. The "best" committee of five selected by his method, for instance, need not include anyone from the "best" committee of two, nor even the Dodgson winner. No wonder the area of social choice is so intriguing! (These mysteries, of course, are caused by a profile's Condorcet terms, which mix up behavior among different subsets of candidates. See Section 2.3.)

4.2. Geometry of Strategic Behavior

For other appealing issues, recall the Brams and Fishburn (1983) "no-show" paradox where a voter obtains a personally better outcome by not voting, and the Gibbard (1973)–Satterthwaite (1975) conclusion asserting that with three or more candidates, settings exist where voters can achieve personally better outcomes by voting strategically. These kind of results involve changes in profiles. Namely, if F is the voting rule and $\mathbf{p}$ the original profile, then the goal of these kinds of problems (i.e., strategic voting, voters not voting, voters changing their views, or whatever else a theoretician may wish to examine) is to compare the $F(\mathbf{p}+\mathbf{v})$ outcome with that of $F(\mathbf{p})$, where $\mathbf{v}$ represents the change in the profile. For the outcomes to differ, $F(\mathbf{p}+\mathbf{v})$ and $F(\mathbf{p})$ must be in different ranking regions. If the change involves a limited number of voters (so $||\mathbf{v}||$ is "small"), both outcomes must be near a boundary.[12] A simple, nonmathematical way to address these kinds of issues is to examine outcomes near ties and determine who benefits by breaking them (Saari 2003).

In Figure 27.8a, for instance, the bullet represents a $B \succ C \succ A$ plurality election outcome with a close vote between the top two candidates. Of the three Figure 27.6a

[12] For the more mathematically inclined reader, the comparison of $F(\mathbf{p}+\mathbf{v})$ and $F(\mathbf{p})$ suggests a Taylor series approximation with the directional derivative product $(\nabla F(\mathbf{p}), \mathbf{v})$. This observation motivated the geometric approach in Saari (1995, 2001a) where $\nabla F(\mathbf{p})$ is replaced by the normal to the profile boundary of tied election outcomes.

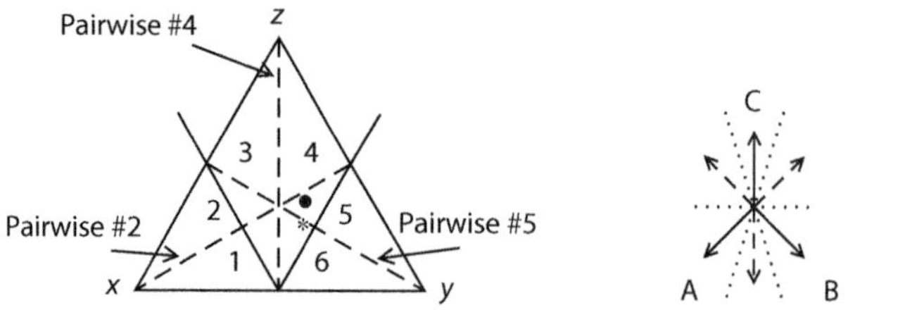

(a) Plurality and runoffs (b) Changing the outcome

Figure 27.8. Strategic Voting and Unexpected Behavior.

voter types, voters of types 2 and 4 may be disappointed in the outcome. Can either of these types be strategic to achieve a personally better conclusion? The geometry of what can occur is in Figure 27.8b.

If a type 4 voter votes sincerely, the outcome helps C; this is the upward arrow pointing toward C in Figure 27.8b. To be strategic, the voter does not vote for C, which is the Figure 27.8b downward dashed arrow, and votes either for A or B, one of the two downward sloping solid arrows pointing toward the appropriate candidate's name. The combination of these actions changes the outcome in one of the two downward directions indicated by the dotted line. As both move the outcome more solidly into the type 5 region, this voter has no strategic opportunities. The type 2 voter, on the other hand, does have a strategic option. To see this, because a sincere vote is represented by the solid arrow pointing to the left, not voting moves the outcome in the opposite direction given by the dashed arrow pointing upward to the right. By voting for C, the solid arrow pointing upward, the combination moves the outcome, the bullet, in the direction of the upward dotted line, which can cross the boundary and change the winner.

Figure 27.8b captures the essence of the seminal Gibbard–Satterthwaite Theorem. Namely, whatever the voting rule, as long as each candidate can win with some profile, there exist boundaries of ties, or transitions, between what profiles elect one or another candidate. For a profile sufficiently near such a boundary, the question is whether there is a tactical way to cross it. To see what happens, first notice that the plurality vote offers only three possible ways to vote, but the combinations of not voting in one way (i.e., sincerely) and voting in another manner creates six directions (the dotted lines). Because the arrows are not all on one side of any line passing through the center point of Figure 27.8b, it follows that at least one of these arrows (i.e., at least one strategy) will cross the boundary no matter how it is positioned. To extend this insight into a general result, conditions are imposed on the voting rule to ensure that at a point, the voters' possible votes are not all on one side of a line. This condition can be accomplished in several ways, such as requiring that votes for a candidate will help her, or even that such votes will hurt her.

To "see" the geometry of the no-show paradox, where the act of not voting creates a personally better outcome, suppose the outcome for a plurality runoff is given by the asterisk in Figure 27.8a. As the plurality outcome is $B \succ A \succ C$, candidates A and B advance to the runoff where, as the figure shows, the pairwise outcome is of type 4, so B wins. As this winner is a type 2 voter's bottom choice, it is easy to imagine scenarios where he refuses to vote. But by not voting, the outcome moves in the direction of the Figure 27.8b dashed arrow pointing upward and to the right. This action, then, could move the asterisk, the plurality outcome, into the type 5 region where B and C are advanced to the runoff. Here C, our negligent voter's second-ranked candidate, wins: by not voting, the voter achieved a personally better outcome. Beyond the geometry, expect the no-show paradox, or violations of monotonicity (so more support can hurt a candidate), and so on, to occur with any rule, such as a runoff, involving two or more votes (Saari 1995a). The problem is that if the first vote determines who gets advanced to the second vote, all sorts of problems can arise.

One might wonder whether it is possible for a voter to elect his top choice by forgetting to vote. This is what Nurmi (2001) calls the *strong no-show paradox*. As it turns out, the geometry of Figure 27.8b prevents this strong no-show paradox from occurring with the plurality vote. Other $\mathbf{w}_s$ methods, however, change the directions represented in Figure 27.8b, so the conclusion changes. The following result, described in terms of "positive involvement," is proved in Saari (1994, 1995a). Extensions to $n > 3$ candidates are immediate.

Theorem 6 *All three-candidate $\mathbf{w}_s$-runoff methods admit the "no-show" paradox. With the exception of the plurality vote ($s = 0$), all other $\mathbf{w}_s$-runoff procedures allow the strong no-show paradox.*

The geometry of strategic behavior leads to other conclusions. For instance, because all procedures can be manipulated, the next question is to determine *which voting rules are least likely to allow a successful manipulation by a small fraction of the voters.* I answered this question for positional methods with any number of candidates in Saari (1990a); the conclusion for three alternatives is reproduced in Saari (1995a). While precise definitions are left to the references, think of the "level of susceptibility" as the number of profiles where a small number of voters can successfully manipulate the outcome; that is, a positional procedure that permits fewer successful strategic opportunities is less susceptible.

Theorem 7 (Saari 1990a, 1995a) *The positional method $\mathbf{w}_s$ that is least susceptible to a small, successful manipulation is the Borda Count. As the value of $|s - \frac{1}{2}|$ increases, so does the level of susceptibility of the positional method.*

The most manipulable methods include the plurality vote, which is manifested by the "Don't waste your vote!" cries heard during three-candidate plurality elections. A reason the Borda Count is least susceptible is that strategic voting involves two components, opportunity and approach. With the assumption of a limited number of strategic voters, "opportunity" requires the sincere tally to be nearly tied for the two top-ranked candidates. Thus, a major part of the analysis involves finding the relative sizes of such boundaries in profile space. The conclusion reflects those problems of finding the rectangle of area one with the minimum perimeter, or the ellipse of area one with the smallest circumference. In both cases, the answer is the most symmetric figure—a square and a circle. Similarly in voting, the answer is the $\mathbf{w}_s$ method exhibiting the most symmetry between assigned w_j points: the Borda Count. A major reason for this conclusion, then, is that the Borda Count minimizes the opportunities for a small number of voters to engage successfully in strategic behavior.

4.3. Could My Candidate Have Won with a Different Voting Rule?

At least for me, a close "nail-biting" election creates an irresistible temptation to explore whether a different voting rule would have changed the outcome—particularly if "my" candidate lost. Could this be done more easily with the geometry of voting? It can, and the converse of the approach becomes a tool that allows us to better understand the theoretical structure of voting rules.

The clue suggesting how to find the outcomes for *all* positional methods is in Figures 27.1a and 27.9a: the tallies define a linear equation. In Figure 27.9a, the plurality votes, or "first-place tallies," are $\mathbf{FPT} = (20, 15, 10)$. The "second-place tallies" specify how often each candidate is ranked in second place; for example, for A it is the sum of voters with types 3 and 6 preferences. With Figure 27.9b, we have $\mathbf{SPT} = (6, 13, 26)$.[13] The general positional outcome has the form of a straight line

$$\mathbf{w}_s \text{ vote tally} = \mathbf{FPT} + s\,\mathbf{SPT}, \quad 0 \le s \le 1. \tag{13}$$

Thus in $\mathbb{R}^3$(where the x, y, and z axes are identified, respectively, with the tallies of A, B, and C), the Figure 27.9a and Equation (13) tallies define a line connecting the the plurality ($s = 0$) and antiplurality ($s = 1$) endpoints. In the space of normalized tallies (i.e., where $x + y + z = 1$, which is, again, an equilateral triangle), just plot the normalized plurality and antiplurality tallies (depicted, respectively, in Figure 27.9b with $\bullet_P$ and $\bullet_A$).[14] The connecting line (which I call a "procedure line") identifies all possible $\mathbf{w}_s$ tallies (see Figure 27.9b). As the line crosses seven regions, the Figure 27.9a profile defines seven different election rankings ranging from $A \succ B \succ C$ to the reversed $C \succ B \succ A$.

Use elementary algebra to determine which rules define which outcomes; in Figure 27.9b, for example, the first tie is $B \sim C$, which means that $15 + 13s = 10 + 26s$,

[13] For more candidates, compute the "third-place tallies," etc.

[14] Namely, there are 45 voters, so plot $(\frac{20}{45}, \frac{15}{45}, \frac{10}{45})$ for the plurality vote and $(\frac{26}{90}, \frac{28}{90}, \frac{37}{90})$ for the normalized antiplurality tally.

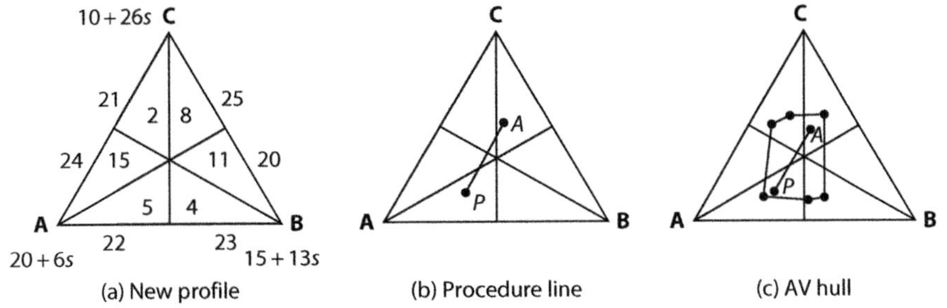

Figure 27.9. Finding all Possible Outcomes.

or $s = \frac{5}{13}$. Thus the $\mathbf{w}_s$ outcome for this profile is $A \succ B \succ C$ for $0 \leq s < \frac{5}{13}$ and $A \succ B \sim C$ for $s = \frac{5}{13}$.

As an application of procedure lines, recall that W. Clinton won the 1992 U.S. Presidential election with less than a majority vote. It is reasonable to wonder whether one of his opponents, Bush or Perot, could have won with a different election method. But by using the procedure line, Tabarrok (2001) showed that Clinton's support was more solid than previously believed: Clinton would have been victorious with *any* positional method. On the other hand, by using the technique from Saari (1995a) that is described in the next subsection, Tabarrok showed with Approval Voting (AV) that any candidate—Bush, Clinton, or Perot—could have won depending on which voters voted for one or two candidates. Tabarrok then showed how to use the procedure line to make it into a useful tool to analyze whether a candidate is the voters' solid choice. Elsewhere, Tabarrok and Spector (1999) used the higher-dimensional version of this approach (Saari 1992, 2001a) to analyze the important 1860 U.S. presidential election that precipitated the Civil War. Also see Nurmi (2002).

The 1992 election provides an interesting setting to discuss AV outcomes. Start with the reality that it is strategically irrational for an AV voter to vote for his second-place candidate if this candidate could beat his top choice. A voter with Clinton $\succ$ Bush $\succ$ Perot preferences, for instance, would *not* vote for Clinton and Bush as it would cancel his impact on the {Clinton, Bush} outcome. Thus it is reasonable to believe that only those AV voters with Perot second-ranked would vote for two candidates; if enough had done so, we would have had President Perot. In other words, Approval Voting has troubling properties.

4.3.1. *AV and Hulls for Multiple Voting Rules*

To find all Approval Voting outcomes (where voters can vote for one or two candidates) for the Figure 27.9a profile, notice that A's tally is 20 should she receive only first-place votes, and 26 should she receive the votes of everyone who ranked her in first or second place. Thus, A has seven possible tallies. In general, the number of different AV tallies for a candidate is one more than her SPT value; the total number of different AV tallies is the product of these values. The Figure 27.9a profile, then, admits $7 \times 14 \times 27 = 2646$ different AV tallies.

Plotting all 2646 values is not realistic. Fortunately, however, they can be found in terms of the eight extreme AV tallies where candidates receive either all possible first- and second-place votes, or only first-place votes. These tallies are $(20,15,10)$, $(26,15,10)$, $(20,28,10)$, $(20,15,36)$, $(26,28,36)$, $(20,28,36)$, $(26,15,36)$, $(26,28,10)$, with the associated normalized tallies $(\frac{20}{45}, \frac{15}{45}, \frac{10}{45})$, $(\frac{26}{51}, \frac{15}{51}, \frac{10}{51})$, $(\frac{20}{58}, \frac{28}{58}, \frac{10}{58})$, $(\frac{20}{71}, \frac{15}{71}, \frac{36}{71})$, $(\frac{26}{90}, \frac{28}{90}, \frac{36}{90})$, $(\frac{20}{84}, \frac{28}{84}, \frac{36}{84})$, $(\frac{26}{77}, \frac{15}{77}, \frac{36}{77})$, $(\frac{26}{64}, \frac{28}{64}, \frac{10}{64})$. To obtain what I call the *AV hull*, plot these eight normalized points, and connect them to find the associated convex hull. (See Figure 27.9c where the lines defining the convex region is the AV hull.) The 2644 AV normalized values are close to being equally spaced within this region.

Notice that the plurality and antiplurality tallies always must be among the eight AV hull vertices. This requires any $\mathbf{w}_s$ outcome for a profile to also be an AV outcome; if a profile has an excellent, or a questionable, $\mathbf{w}_s$ outcome, this same ranking occurs with AV. AV, however, admits many other outcomes; with the Figure 27.9a profile, for example, it follows from Figure 27.9c that *any of the thirteen ways* to rank three candidates is an admissible AV ranking for this profile. The AV hull includes the procedure line and usually much more, so with any natural probability or statistical assumption on voter preferences, it is unlikely for the AV outcome to agree with a positional tally.

The following illustrates another kind of result that follows from the geometry: While the outcome is described for three alternative, it holds for any number of them.

Theorem 8 *If* $\mathbf{p}$ *is a profile where some* $\mathbf{w}_s$ *method allows a voter to be strategic, then* $\mathbf{p}$ *also offers AV strategic opportunities. On the other hand, there are sets of profiles permitting AV strategic settings for some voter, but no strategic opportunities for any positional method.*

The reason AV is more prone to strategic action follows directly from the geometry. The procedure line is a subset of the AV hull, so if a positional outcome is near a tie allowing a strategic opportunity, then so are AV outcomes. The AV hull, however, admits other strategic settings near a tie where no positional method does. (See Saari 1995a, 2001a.)

The properties and outcomes associated with other "multiple voting rules" are found in a similar manner (Saari 2010a). A multiple rule is where a voter ranks the candidates and then selects a voting rule to tally his ballot. The following makes this more precise.

Definition 1 *An n-candidate scoring vector is given by* $\mathbf{s} = (s_1, s_2, \ldots, s_n)$ *where the* $s_j \in \mathbb{R}$ *has a specified value. A multiple rule is defined by a specified set of scoring vectors* $\mathcal{S}_{rule}$*. In voting, a voter ranks the candidates and then selects* $\mathbf{s} \in \mathcal{S}_{rule}$ *to tally the ballot.*

An example of a multiple rule is where a voter strategically truncates his ballot to avoid assigning points to lower-ranked candidates. If the specified positional rule is $(7,4,0)$, for instance, and if the one candidate listed on a truncated ballot is assigned seven points, then $\mathcal{S}_{truncate} = \{(7,4,0),(7,0,0)\}$. A standard strategic plurality vote is to vote for your second-ranked choice, so $\mathcal{S}_{plurality} = \{(1,0,0),\ (0,1,0)\}$. To provide examples of other multiple rules, see the following definitions.

Definition 2 *"Approval Voting" (AV) is where a voter votes "yes" or "no" for each candidate; in tallying the ballot, a candidate receiving a "yes" vote receives one point. For three candidates, then,* $\mathcal{S}_{AV} = \{(1,0,0),(1,1,0),(1,1,1)\}$.

"Cumulative voting" (CV) is where, with n candidates, each voter has $n-1$ points; the voter assigns integer values to the candidates in any desired manner as long as the sum does not exceed the specified value. For three candidates, $\mathcal{S}_{CV} = \{(2,0,0),(1,1,0),(1,0,0)\}$.

"Divide the points voting" (DPV) is where each voter is given a fixed number of points. The voter assigns non-negative values to the candidates, whether integer valued or not, in any desired manner as long as the sum equals the specified value; say 2. For three candidates, $\mathcal{S}_{DPV} = \{(w_1,w_2,0)\,|\,w_1+w_2=2\}$.

"Range Voting" (RV) is where each voter assigns to each candidate a number of points coming from a specified range, say, any integer between 0 and 100. Thus, for three candidates, $\mathcal{S}_{RV} = \{(w_1,w_2,w_3)\,|\,0 \leq w_1 \leq 100,\ 0 \leq w_2 \leq w_1,\ 0 \leq w_3 \leq w_2\}$.

In all cases, each candidate is ranked according to the sum of assigned points.

For each multiple rule, a "tally hull" can be constructed in a manner similar to the approach used to construct the AV hull. Of importance for what is described in the next section, the hulls for multiple rules using positional methods can be constructed just by knowing the FPT and SPT values. See Saari (2010a) for details.

Definition 3 *For a voting rule and a profile* $\mathbf{p}$, *the voting rule's "tally hull" is the convex hull of all outcomes after each tally is normalized to represent the fraction of the total vote assigned to each candidate. It is denoted by* $\mathcal{TH}_{voting\ rule}(\mathbf{p})$.

This tool makes it possible to discover differences among multiple rules; the approach is to compare the structure of their hulls. For instance, is it possible to have a Borda outcome that could never occur with Cumulative voting? Theorem 9, which proves that this is impossible, identifies what can occur with positional and the four defined multiple rules.

Theorem 9 (Saari 2010a) *For any given profile* $\mathbf{p}$ *and* $n \geq 3$ *candidates, the following inequality holds:*

$$\mathcal{TH}_{positional\ rule}(\mathbf{p}) \subset \mathcal{TH}_{AV}(\mathbf{p}) \subset \mathcal{TH}_{CV}(\mathbf{p}) = \mathcal{TH}_{DPV}(\mathbf{p}) \subset \mathcal{TH}_{RV}(\mathbf{p}). \qquad (14)$$

To illustrate Theorem 9, notice how Figure 27.9c displays the ample opportunities for AV strategic opportunities; they are where the AV hull crosses tied vote boundaries. According to Theorem 9 these strategic opportunities only increase with Cumulative and Range voting.

A worrisome property of multiple rules is how they spawn a large set of admissible outcomes rather than one conclusion. To avoid the trouble of having to compute and determine the appropriate tally hull, it would be useful if we had simple "rules of thumb" that would identify all outcomes that can occur with each multiple rules. Such an approach follows from the geometry of the tally hulls; I illustrate the ideas with AV primarily because the arguments are easier.

It is reasonable to expect that the AV bottom-ranked candidates are those who are not highly ranked by most voters. The next definition pushes this notion to an extreme by excluding only those candidates who are bottom-ranked by too many voters.

Definition 4 *Candidate X is said to be "in the mix" with candidate Y if the number of voters who do not have X bottom-ranked is more than the number of voters who have Y top-ranked.*

To illustrate, suppose A and B receive, respectively, 45% and 40% of the first-place rankings, while C is bottom-ranked by 51% of the voters. As 49% of the voters do not have C bottom-ranked, she is in the mix with both A and B. As A is not bottom-ranked by at least 45% of the voters and as C is top-ranked by 15%, A is in the mix with everyone; as B is not bottom-ranked by at least 51% of the voters (who have C bottom-ranked), she too is in the mix. The next theorem provides a quick way to use this tool to find all possible admissible AV rankings.

Theorem 10 (Saari 2010a) *For a given three-candidate profile, if X is in the mix with Y, there exists a sincere AV election outcome where X beats Y. If each candidate is in the mix with any other candidate, then all possible ways to rank the candidates is an admissible AV election outcome. However, if X is not in the mix with Y, then no AV outcome can rank X above Y.*

As the above example has all candidates in the mix with all other candidates, any of the thirteen ways to rank three candidates is an admissible AV outcome. For rules-of-thumb addressing the CV outcomes and so on, see Saari (2010a).

4.3.2. Creating Examples

Rather than using a profile to find the procedure line, the converse approach would be to start with a line segment and then determine whether it is the procedure line for some profile. If it is possible to do this, then properties of voting rules can be found just by considering all admissible ways to position lines in the space of normalized election tallies (Saari 1995). Similarly, rather than searching for a profile to create a desired kind of tally hull for a specified multiple rule, an easier way to find the rule's properties would be if we could start with what appears to be a hull and then determine if it is supported by some profile. All of this can be done for the procedure line and several multiple rules, such as AV, CV, and DPV. Details are in Saari (2010a), but the main steps are outlined next.

The first step is to understand how a change in a profile can change the shape and size of the various hulls. A clue comes from the assertion that the hulls described in Theorem 9 rely on FPT and SPT information; that is, all vertices of a hull are determined from the plurality and antiplurality tallies. This dependency on SPT accurately suggests that a profile's reversal components (Theorem 2) play major roles in changing the size and shape of the hull. An interesting feature is that these hulls are centered about a particular positional voting rule's outcome. The Borda outcome, for example, is always located at the center of the AV tally hull: by connecting the opposite vertices of the AV hull, the four lines cross at the Borda outcome (Saari 2010a). (With the Figure 27.9a profile, the Borda outcome is $A \sim C \succ B$, or where the procedure line crosses the $A \sim C$ line in Figure 27.9b. It is not difficult to see which pairs of vertices of the AV hull connect and pass through the Borda outcome.) Thus, a first step in designing a hypothetical hull is to select appropriate potential choices for the plurality, antiplurality tallies.

The problem reduces to determining which choices of potential plurality and antiplurality tallies can be supported by profiles. When a supporting profile does exist, a candidate's antiplurality tally, A_X, is bounded below by her plurality tally Pl_X, or $Pl_X \leq A_X$. As each voter has twice as many antiplurality votes, when normalizing with n candidates, we have $\frac{1}{2}\frac{Pl_X}{n} \leq \frac{A_X}{2n}$. As a candidate can receive at most half of the antiplurality votes, her normalized $s = 1$ tally is bounded above by $\frac{1}{2}$. That is,

$$\frac{1}{2}\frac{Pl_X}{n} \leq \frac{A_X}{2n} \leq \frac{1}{2}. \tag{15}$$

Surprisingly, Equation (15) suffices to ensure that selecting points are supported by a profile; namely, if any two rational points in the simplex, $\mathbf{p}_j = (p^j_A, p^j_B, p^j_C)$, $j = 1, 2$, satisfy $\frac{1}{2}p^1_X \leq p^2_X \leq \frac{1}{2}$ (i.e., Equation (15)), then $\mathbf{p}_1$ and $\mathbf{p}_2$ serve as the normalized plurality and antiplurality tallies for some profiles! The class of supporting profiles differs in two ways; the first (reflecting the $\mathbf{K}^3$ profile component) is a scaling factor that allows a supporting profile to be multiplied by any positive integer to create another supporting profile. The second way profiles can differ is by adding multiples of $\mathbf{C}^3$.

To illustrate, because $\mathbf{p}_1 = (\frac{4}{13}, \frac{3}{13}, \frac{6}{13})$ and $\mathbf{p}_2 = (\frac{8}{26}, \frac{8}{26}, \frac{5}{13})$ satisfy Equation (15), they are normalized plurality and antiplurality tallies for a class of profiles. To find these profiles, first find integer tallies for these points; to find a plurality tally, multiply $\mathbf{p}_1$ by its common denominator of 13 to have $(4, 3, 6)$. The associated antiplurality tally is found by multiplying $\mathbf{p}_2$ by twice this value, or 26, to obtain the antiplurality tally of $(8, 8, 10)$. This means that $SPT = (8, 8, 10) - (4, 3, 6) = (4, 5, 4)$, while the plurality tallies provide the FPT information.

To find one supporting profile, assign zero voters to some ranking. To do so, notice that the smallest FTP and STP value is where B has only three first-place votes. So, assign zero voters to one ranking where B is top-ranked, say $B \succ C \succ A$, and three to the other ranking $B \succ A \succ C$. This choice of a ranking with zero voters and C's STP value of 4 means that four voters have the $A \succ C \succ B$ ranking. Now that three entries are known, the rest of the profile of $(0, 4, 1, 5, 0, 3)$ is easily found. Thus, for any positive integer t, $(0, 4t, t, 5t, 0, 3t)$ is another supporting profile.

For each t, the class of supporting profiles can be further enlarged by adding appropriate $x\mathbf{C}^3$ terms. To illustrate with $t = 1$, we find the following 13-voter profiles:

Number	Ranking	Number	Ranking
x	$A \succ B \succ C$	$5 - x$	$C \succ B \succ A$
$4 - x$	$A \succ C \succ B$	x	$B \succ C \succ A$
$1 + x$	$C \succ A \succ B$	$3 - x$	$B \succ A \succ C$

where the $0 \leq x \leq 3$ admissible x values define the different $\mathbf{C}^3$ multiples.

For any selected rational points that satisfy Equation (15), the set of supporting profiles can be found in this same simple manner.

5. EXPORTING LESSONS LEARNED FROM SOCIAL CHOICE

Voting rules are aggregation methods: the rule aggregates the voters' preferences into a societal ranking or outcome. But aggregation procedures are central to almost all disciplines; in astronomy, for instance, each particle's angular rotation is aggregated into the system's angular momentum; in statistics, data are aggregated to provide information about the "whole"; in economics, each individual's willingness to buy and sell at a given price is aggregated into a price mechanism that, hopefully, finds the appropriate price where supply equals demand. Indeed, much of what we analyze in the social and behavioral sciences involves aggregation.

The theme to be explored in this section is whether the various insights about aggregation rules that have been developed in social choice can provide guidance about what to expect with the aggregation rules from other disciplines. This can be done; an immediate example is Saari (2005), which shows how to use information about voting rules to significantly extend Luce's (1959) insightful axioms for human discision making. While several other illustrating examples could be provided, the ones used in this section suffice to make my point. (1) I show how the profile decomposition of Section 2 provides insights into the structure of nonparametric statistics; (2) how Arrow's Theorem (1952) speaks to concerns as disperse as alcoholism and nanotechnology; (3) how Sen's Theorem (1970) provides insights into those troubling periods of transition within a society; and (4) how Chichilnisky's topological dictator (1982) can be used to better understand concerns from psychology.

5.1. From Voting to Nonparametric Statistics

When asking about which nonparametric test should be used in a particular setting, a common response is that the choice is subjective. This comment suggests that the structure of the various statistical tests is unknown. Here, social choice has much to offer because of the strong relationship between these tests and positional voting rules.

To explain, suppose the goal is to test the level of some ingredient (where more is better) in three brands of coffee; the data is in the first table of Equation (16). An approach to handle this nonparametric analysis is to replace the actual data values with rankings where more is better; this leads to the second table's ranked data set.

A	B	C
3.2	2.9	3.3
2.7	3.4	3.0

A	B	C
4	2	5
1	6	3

(16)

Next, combine the ranking values in all possible ways, which defines the eight triplets $(1,6,3)$, $(4,6,3)$, $(1,2,3), (1,6,5), (4,2,5), (1,2,5), (4,6,5), (4,2,3)$. One way in which conclusions about this data are obtained is to analyze the triplets; for example, one test counts how often an alternative is top-ranked in a triplet. Notice that the way in which these triplets are used means that they can be converted into a profile; none of these triplets have $A \succ B \succ C$, for example, but one of them has $A \succ C \succ B$. The associated profile, then, is $(0,1,1,2,3,1)$. Thus, the application of this approach to the Equation (16) data set reduces to the social choice problem of computing the plurality outcome for the profile; the outcome is $B \succ C \succ A$.

I asked my former graduate student Deanna Haunsperger to more carefully examine these connections. As part of her Ph.D. thesis (1992), she proved that a large class of nonparametric statistical rules can be analyzed precisely in this manner; that is, first convert the data into profiles, and then use a positional voting rule to rank the alternatives. The ranking associated with the widely used Kruskal–Wallis rule, for instance, is determined in this manner by using the Borda Count. (The Kruskal–Wallis ranking of the Equation (16) data is $B \sim C \succ A$.) Haunsperger then used my results (Saari 1989) about the dictionaries of positional voting rules[15] to characterize all possible paradoxical behavior that could ever occur with any specified nonparametric rules.

Closely related to Haunsperger's article is a paper by Laruelle and Merlin (2002) where they mapped cooperative games into profiles. Laruelle and Merlin then used a different dictionary result of mine (where I found all possible positional outcomes that could be associated with a profile; Saari 1992) to demonstrate the wild behavior of power

[15] These dictionaries list all possible rankings that ever could occur when specified positional rules are used with profiles; i.e., these results extend McGarvey's paired comparison conclusion to all positional rules.

indices. Independently, Sieberg and I (2001b) obtained similar conclusions, but we did so by developing a direct geometric approach.[16]

From Haunsperger's results, we now know that should different nonparametric rules be applied to the same data set, they can define different rankings. The natural next question is to understand what aspects of data affect different methods; for instance, it would useful to have a data decomposition similar to the Section 2 profile decomposition. This was done in Bargagliotti and Saari (2009) where, surprisingly, everything is similar to the Section 2 description. Current projects by Bargagliotti and Orrison and another by Crisman are advancing this approach.

5.2. "Divide and Conquer": A Generalized Arrow's Theorem

A way to appreciate why Arrow's seminal theorem (1952) has implications in a variety of areas that were previously unsuspected is to offer a different interpretation. Recall that his assumptions are:

1. Voters have complete and transitive preferences; there are no restrictions.
2. The societal outcome is complete and transitive.
3. (Pareto) If everyone ranks some pair in the same manner, then that common ranking is the society ranking of the pair.
4. (IIA) The outcome of any pair depends only on the relative rankings of that pair. That is, if $\mathbf{p}_1$ and $\mathbf{p}_2$ are two profiles where each voter has the same relative ranking of a specified pair, then the pair's societal ranking is the same for both profiles.

The conclusion, of course, is that with three or more alternatives, the only rule satisfying these conditions is a dictator; that is, there is a voter so that, for all profiles, the societal outcome always agrees with that voter's ranking.

First, notice how the conditions that are imposed on the rule mandate that the societal ranking is constructed by determining appropriate outcomes for each pair. In a real sense, these conditions require the rule to adopt a "divide-and-conquer" approach where the structure of the whole—the societal outcome—is determined by dividing the problem into its parts—the pairs.

Now, suppose for $n \geq 3$ alternatives that an appropriate societal ranking always exists. After all, I suspect that the supporters of different voting rules might argue that their approach always delivers the "correct" outcome. In this setting, Arrow's result asserts that

if an appropriate complete and transitive societal ranking always exists, there are settings where this ranking cannot be obtained in terms of finding appropriate outcomes for each of the pairs;

[16] Although Saari and Sieberg (2001b) was published first, I expect that Laruelle and Merlin (2002) obtained their main results before we did.

that is, there always exist settings where the divide-and-conquer approach fails. The same statement holds in trying to construct a "whole" from the parts.

This "divide-and-conquer" methodology is commonly used in many disciplines: this is true in engineering, the nano-sciences, medicine, economics, alcoholic addiction, organizational design, and just about everything. With the above interpretation of Arrow's result, one must wonder whether a similar message extends to other disciplines; for instance, are there settings where the whole cannot be obtained from the parts? It does (Saari 2010b); the proof of this assertion is based on replacing a transitivity definition of rankings with conditions that encompass more general settings.

This objective is accomplished by examining the structure of transitivity and extracting appropriate properties. Transitivity, for instance, divides the ranking into pairs, so assume that the divide-and-conquer approach defines disjoint sets of objects $\mathcal{C}_j, j = 1, \ldots, k$. To illustrate, for an industry that is producing a product, divide the process into the components of design $\mathcal{D}$, manufacturing $\mathcal{M}$, and sales $\mathcal{S}$. $\mathcal{D}$, for example, could consist of the infinite number of possible designs that may be based on results coming from partial differential equations, and so forth.

In transitivity, completeness means that any admissible combination of pairs must include a ranking for each pair. For a general setting, assert that a combination $(c_1, \ldots, c_k)$, $c_j \in \mathcal{C}_j$, is complete only if it has an entry from each component part. To illustrate with the industry problem, for completeness we need a triplet (d, m, s) where $d \in \mathcal{D}$ is a suggested design, $m \in \mathcal{M}$ is a proposed manufacturing approach, and $s \in \mathcal{S}$ is the marketing plan.

Transitivity asserts that there is a right way, and a wrong way, to assemble the pairs. But if the pairs define a nontransitive outcome, the set of rankings can be converted into a transitive one with an appropriate change in some entries. (For instance, the pairs $A \succ B$, $B \succ C$, $C \succ A$ can be converted into a transitive ranking by reversing any one of these pairwise rankings.) A similar condition is imposed on divide-and-conquer approaches. For instance, it may be that (d, m, s) is incompatible with a specified feasibility condition because the design, d, cannot be manufactured. But this triplet can be altered by selecting a different design d^* so that (d^*, m, s) is compatible.

The component sets $\mathcal{C}_j$ could be anything; a continuum, solutions of partial differential equations, plans for design and marketing, and so forth. The restrictions arise by how "compatibility" is defined: these conditions are determined by the field of interest; they list when a combination is, or is not, acceptable. After imposing these conditions, the rest of the structure of Arrow's Theorem extends. The conclusion is that there must be settings where the divide-and-conquer approach fails.

As the true goal is to find positive conclusions, a first step requires finding a positive version of Arrow's result (see Chapter 2 in Saari 2008). The approach to do so is based on Section 3.4.1, which essentially shows that the IIA condition nullifies the assumption that voters have transitive preferences. (A geometric proof is in the Appendix of Saari 2001b.) Namely, similar to the way the pairwise vote ignores the "mixed gender" condition of Section 3.4.1, the IIA condition strips away the connecting information that the voters connect the pairs in a transitive manner. Consequently, to achieve a positive condition, IIA needs to be modified to allow using the crucial assumption that voters have transitive preferences.[17] A similar story applies to the generalized version of Arrow's result as applied to divide-and-conquer methods, but general results have yet to be found.

5.3. Dysfunctional Societies: Lessons from Sen's Theorem

The Section 3.4.1 argument also explains the source of Sen's important theorem (1970). It is interesting how, by doing so, Sen's result gains wider interest.

Sen's only requirements for a rule (which leads to the impossibility of a Paretian liberal) are that it satisfies Arrow's Pareto condition and the minimal liberal condition (where at least two agents are assigned at least one pair; each "decisive agent" determines the societal outcome of the assigned pairs). This emphasis on pairs, then, means that the rule must dismiss the information that voters have transitive preferences. So, rather than the usual assertion about a conflict between Pareto and Minimal Liberalism, the result reflects the emphasis on building a result by analyzing pairs. As such, it now becomes easy to create all possible Sen cycles (Saari 2008).

In other words, select a desired societal cyclic ranking, and assign it to all voters; for example, select the "two-cycle" choice of $A \succ B, B \succ C, C \succ A, C \succ D, D \succ B$. Temporarily assign these rankings to all agents. Next, assign at least two decisive agents to each cycle where each is decisive over at least one of the pairs. As an illustration, the $\{B, C\}$ pair is in both cycles, so let Ann be decisive over $\{B, C\}$. Let Barb be decisive over $\{A, B\}$ and $\{D, B\}$—a pair from each of the two cycles.

If an agent is decisive over a pair, the way all other voters rank this pair is immaterial. So, where necessary, reverse a pair's ranking for the nondecisive agent to create a transitive preference; this always can be done! To illustrate, as Anne is decisive over $\{B, C\}$, reversing Barb's ranking of this pair converts her original cyclic rankings into the transitive preferences of $C \succ A \succ D \succ B$. Similarly, Barb is decisive over two pairs; reversing Ann's rankings of each of these pairs converts her originally assigned cyclic rankings into her new transitive preference ranking of $B \succ C \succ D \succ A$. This assignment of decisive voters and transitive preferences generates the desired two cycles.

Notice how Ann's choice of $B \succ C$ over her assigned pair creates a "strong negative externality" for Barb in that not only does Barb disagree with this societal ranking, but she strongly disagrees, as reflected by the fact that another alternative separates her $C \succ B$ ranking. Similarly, Ann suffers a strong negative externality over each of Barb's choices. This is a general conclusion.

[17] For instance, if IIA is modified so that the rule can use each voter's relative ranking of a pair, and the number of alternatives that separate the two alternatives, Arrow's dictator conclusion is replaced by the Borda Count.

Theorem 11 (Saari 2008) *In any Sen cycle, all agents suffer a strong negative externality.*

As developed in Saari (2001b), Saari and Petron (2006), and Li and Saari (2008), and summarized in Saari (2008), this strong negative externality feature can be used to temper the Sen cycles, and it also introduces new issues. The fact that each person suffers a strong negative externality, for instance, introduces opportunities to create a "tit-for-tat" structure from the Prisoners' Dilemma to reduce the effects of the Sen cycles.

The fact that *everyone* must suffer a strong negative externality suggests that a Sen cycle also models dysfunctional societal settings. It can, for instance, capture the occasionally disruptive transition stage that can occur when a previously disenfranchised group finally gains power. As an example, consider smoking in restaurants with the three options of $A =$ "Smoking is acceptable," $B =$ "Smoking is not acceptable," and $C =$ "Complain to the maitre de." Nonsmokers' preferences are $B \succ C \succ A$, while a smoker has the preferences $A \succ B \succ C$. Prior to no-smoking requirements, the smoker was a decisive agent over $\{A, B\}$, so he smoked and created a strong negative externality for the nonsmoker. While the nonsmoker has the right to take action over $\{A, C\}$, the problem is that she is not decisive, so the outcome remains $C \succ A$, which defines the transitive $A \succ B \succ C$. But during the transition stage to nonsmoking, the nonsmoker does become decisive, and a Sen cycle emerges. Once the new social "nonsmoking" social norm becomes solidified, the smoker no longer is decisive, so the transitive societal outcome of $B \succ C \succ A$ now holds. Thus, Sen's cycle in this example captures the transition behavior between the two social norms.

5.4. Applying Chichilnisky's Topological Dictator to Psychology

Another delightful result is Chichilnisky's (1982) topological dictator conclusion. A simple case (that differs from Chichilnisky's intent) is where two agents are trying to decide where to picnic on the beach of an island. In this setting, each person's preferred choice can be described as a point on a circle S^1. As the circle also is the space of outcomes, the decision rule F can be described as

$$F : S^1 \times S^1 \to S^1. \tag{17}$$

Natural properties to impose on F are (1) continuity (we do not want trivial changes in an agent's choice to create a jump in the outcome); (2) unanimity (if both people want to picnic at the same spot, that should be the outcome); and (3) Pareto (if there is an arc of shortest distance between the two agents' preferred location, then the outcome should be on that arc, e.g., if one agent wants to be on the east side while the other on the north, then the outcome should not be in the southwest side). Chichilnisky's surprising conclusion is that any such F must be "homotopic to a dictator." Stating this conclusion in a more reader-friendly manner, it means that one agent makes the decision while the other, up to certain bounds, can modify the outcome.

The connection between this result and problems in psychology is that many psychological processes involve two or more "parts," such as two eyes, or the two sides of a brain. Also, stimuli can be higher-dimensional, such as the color circle, or faces expressing emotions. As such, Equation (17) can model the psychological process using essentially the same requirements on F. In this way the mathematics from social choice can explain why one side of the brain can dominate in some tasks. This direction along with others are being developed with my colleague Louis Narens.

As indicated above (and developed in Saari 2008), what causes Arrow's and Sen's results is their emphasis on constructing the whole from pairs; this means that the intended transitivity information about the domain, the space of individual preferences, is not being used. A similar explanation holds for Chichilnisky's result. As described in Kronewetter and Saari (2007) and developed more extensively in Saari (2008), the culprit is the continuity of F. To explain, continuity is a technical condition ensuring that what occurs at a point is similar to what occurs nearby. As such, continuity alone forces F to treat the domain as a line, or a "contractable space." But if the space does not have this feature (and a circle does not), expect negative results to occur. Thus, to develop a positive result, information about the true structure of the domain must be included.

6. SUMMARY

A goal of this chapter is to make the geometry of voting more intuitive by emphasizing approaches that, after described, should be transparent and applicable elsewhere, and to indicate a variety of new results and techniques. My expectation is that the descriptions will suggest to the reader new ways to analyze other choice rules and problems.

To suggest what else is possible, by combining geometry with other techniques such as concepts from dynamical "chaos" (Saari 1995b), it becomes possible to list all possible paradoxical positional election outcomes that can occur with any number of candidates, any combination of positional procedures (for the different subsets of candidates) and any profile Saari (1989, 1995b). In other words, we now know all possible election paradoxes that could ever occur with any positional and pairwise methods, and, by extension, for all voting rules that use them. These conclusions identify a surprisingly large numbers of paradoxes.

Conversely, suppose that a voting rule never admits certain kinds of election rankings. These missing listings constitute properties of the rule; for example, the Borda Count never ranks a Condorcet loser over a Condorcet winner. It is easy to convert missing listings into an "axiomatic characterization." Because the Borda Count admits, by far, the smallest number and kinds of lists of election rankings over the different subsets of candidates (Saari 1989, 1990b), it enjoys the most "properties," which makes it possible to generate all sorts of new "axiomatic characterizations" for the Borda Count (Saari 1990b, 1995b).

This comment, suggesting how to find new "axiomatic" representations, leads to my concluding point. While the geometry of voting has provided many new and different insights into several choice theory issues, this approach remains at an early stage of development. This approach can and should be extended in other directions.

ACKNOWLEDGMENTS

This research was supported by NSF grants DMI-0233798, DMI-0640817, and DMS-0631362. My thanks to a referee and to K. Arrow, N. Baigent, H. Nurmi, T. Ratliff, M. Salles, and K. Sieberg, among others, for comments on earlier drafts.

REFERENCES

Arrow, K. J. [1952] (1963). *Social choice and individual values* (2nd ed.). New York: Wiley.

Bargagliotti, A., & Saari, D. G. (2009). Symmetry of nonparametric statistical tests on three samples, Working Paper, Institute for Mathematical Behavioral Sciences, University of California, Irvine.

Black, D. (1958). *The theory of committees and elections.* London, New York: Cambridge University Press.

Brams, S., Kilgour, D., & Zwicker, W. (1998). The paradox of multiple elections. *Social Choice & Welfare, 15*, 211–236.

Brams, S., & Fishburn, P. (2002). "Voting Procedures", Chap. 4 in ed. K. J. Arrow, A. K. Sen & Kotaro Suzumura, *Handbook of Social Choice and Welfare, Vol. 1*, Elsevier, Amsterdam.

Condorcet, M. (1785). *Essai sur l'application de l'analyse à la probabilite des decisions rendues à la pluralite des voix.* Paris.

Chichilnisky, G. (1982). The topological equivalence of the Pareto conditions and the existence of a dictator. *Journal of Mathematical Economics, 9*, 223–233.

Fishburn, P., & Brams, S. (1983). Paradoxes of preferential voting. *Mathematics Magazine, 56*, 207–214.

Gibbard, A. (1973). Manipulation of voting schemes: a general result. *Econometrica, 41*, 587–601.

Haunsperger, D. (1992). Dictionaries of paradoxes for statistical tests on k samples. *Journal of the American Statistical Association, 87*, 149–155.

Kalai, E., Muller, E., & Satterthwaite, M. (1979). Social welfare functions when preferences are convex, strictly monotonic, and continuous. *Public Choice, 34*, 87–97.

Kronewetter, J., & Saari, D. G. (2007). From decision problems to dethroned dictators. *Journal of Mathematical Economics, 44*, 745–761.

Laruelle, A., & Merlin, V. (2002). Different least square values, different rankings. *Social Choice Welfare, 19*, 533–550.

Le Breton, M., & Truchon, M. (1997). A Borda measure for social choice functions. *Mathematical Social Sciences, 34*, 249–272.

Lepelley, D., & Merlin, V. (2001). Scoring runoff paradoxes for variable electorates. *Economic Theory, 17*, 53–80.

Linfang, Li, & Saari, D. G. (2008). Sen's theorem: geometric proof and new interpretations. *Social Choice & Welfare, 31*, 393–434.

Luce, R. D. (1959). *Individual choice behavior; a theoretical analysis.* New York: John Wiley and Sons. Dover edition, 2005.

McDonald, M., & Sieberg, K. K. (2010). Probability and plausibility of cycles in three-party systems: a mathematical formulation and application. *British Journal of Political Science.* (2005 preprint.)

McGarvey, D. C. (1953). A theorem on the construction of voting paradoxes. *Econometrica, 21,* 608–610.

Merlin, V., & Saari, D. G. (1997). Copeland method II: manipulation, monotonicity, and paradoxes. *Journal of Economic Theory, 72,* 148–172.

Merlin, V., Tataru, M., & Valognes, F. (2000). On the probability that all decision rules select the same winner. *Journal of Mathematical Economics, 33,* 183–208.

Merlin, V., Tataru, M., & Valognes, F. (2001). The likelihood of Condorcet's profiles. *Social Choice and Welfare.*

Nanson, E. J. (1882). Methods of elections. *Transactions and Proceedings of Royal Society of Victoria, 18,* 197–240.

Nurmi, H. (1999). *Voting paradoxes and how to deal with them.* New York: Springer-Verlag.

Nurmi, H. (2001). *Monotonicity and its cognates in the theory of choice.* Finland: Department of Political Science, University of Turku. mimeo.

Nurmi, H. (2002). *Voting procedures under uncertainty.* New York: Springer-Verlag.

Ratliff, T. (2001). A comparison of Dodgson's method and Kemeny's rule. *Social Choice and Welfare, 18,* 79–89.

Ratliff, T. (2002). A comparison of Dodgson's method and the Borda count. *Economic Theory, 20,* 357–372.

Ratliff, T. (2003). Some startling paradoxes when electing committees. *Social Choice & Welfare, 10,* 433–454.

Saari, D. G. (1989). A dictionary for voting paradoxes. *Journal of Economic Theory, 48,* 443–475.

Saari, D. G. (1990a). Susceptibility to manipulation. *Public Choice, 64,* 21–41.

Saari, D. G. (1990b). The Borda dictionary. *Social Choice and Welfare, 7,* 279–317.

Saari, D. G. (1991). Calculus and extensions of Arrow's theorem. *Journal of Mathematical Economics, 20,* 271–306.

Saari, D. G. (1992). Millions of election outcomes from a single profile. *Social Choice & Welfare, 9,* 277–306.

Saari, D. G. (1994). *Geometry of voting.* Heidelberg: Springer-Verlag.

Saari, D. G. (1995a). *Basic geometry of voting.* Heidelberg: Springer-Verlag.

Saari, D. G. (1995b). A chaotic exploration of aggregation paradoxes. *SIAM Review, 37,* 37–52.

Saari, D. G. (1998). Connecting and resolving Sen's and Arrow's theorems. *Social Choice & Welfare, 15,* 239–261.

Saari, D. G. (1999). Explaining all three-alternative voting outcomes. *Journal of Economic Theory, 87,* 313–335.

Saari, D. G. (2000a). Mathematical structure of voting paradoxes I: pairwise vote. *Economic Theory, 15,* 1–53.

Saari, D. G. (2000b). Mathematical structure of voting paradoxes II: positional voting. *Economic Theory, 15,* 55–101.

Saari, D. G. (2001a). *Chaotic elections! A mathematician looks at voting.* Providence, RI: American Mathematical Society.

Saari, D. G. (2001b). *Decisions and elections; explaining the unexpected.* New York: Cambridge University Press.

Saari, D. G. (2001c). Analyzing a "nail-biting" election. *Social Choice & Welfare, 18,* 415–430.

Saari, D. G. (2002). Adopting a plurality vote perspective. *Mathematics of Operations Research, 27,* 45–64.

Saari, D. G. (2003). Unsettling aspects of voting theory. *Economic Theory, 22,* 529–556.

Saari, D. G. (2004). Analyzing pairwise voting rules. In M. Wiberg (Ed.), *Reasoned choices* (pp. 318–342). Turku, Finland: Finnish Political Science Association.

Saari, D. G. (2005). The profile structure for Luce's choice axiom. *Journal of Mathematical Psychology, 49,* 226–253.

Saari, D. G. (2006). Which is better: the Condorcet or Borda winner? *Social Choice & Welfare, 26*(1), 107–130.

Saari, D. G. (2008). *Disposing dictators, demystifying voting paradoxes.* New York: Cambridge University Press.

Saari, D. G. (2010a). Systematic analysis of multiple voting rules. *Social Choice & Welfare* (Online First, 2009), *34*, 217–247.

Saari, D. G. (2010b). Source of complexity in the social and managerial sciences: an extended Sen's theorem (forthcoming). *Social Choice & Welfare* (In press).

Saari, D. G., & Merlin, V. (1996). Copeland method I: dictionaries and relationships. *Economic Theory, 8*, 51–76.

Saari, D. G., & Merlin, V. (2000a). A geometric examination of Kemeny's rule. *Social Choice & Welfare, 17*, 403–438.

Saari, D. G., & Merlin, V. (2000b). Changes that cause changes. *Social Choice & Welfare, 17*, 691–705.

Saari, D. G., & Petron, A. (2006). Negative externalities and Sen's liberalism theorem. *Economic Theory, 28*, 265–281.

Saari, D. G., & Sieberg, K. (2001a). The sum of the parts can violate the whole. *American Political Science Review*, 415–433.

Saari, D. G., & Sieberg, K. (2001b). Some surprising properties of power indices. *Games and Economic Behavior, 36*, 241–263.

Saari, D. G., & Valognes, F. (1998). Geometry, voting, and paradoxes. *Mathematics Magazine, 4*, 243–259.

Saari, D. G., & Valognes, F. (1999). The geometry of Black's single peakedness and related conditions. *Journal of Mathematical Economics, 32*, 429–456.

Saari, D. G., & Tataru, M. (1999). The likelihood of dubious election outcomes. *Economic Theory, 13*, 345–363.

Saari, D. G., & Van Newenhizen, J. (1988). Is approval voting an "unmitigated evil"? *Public Choice, 59*, 133–147.

Satterthwaite, M. (1975). Strategyproofness and Arrow's conditions. *Journal of Economic Theory, 10*, 187–217.

Sen, A. (1970). The impossibility of a Paretian liberal. *Journal of Political Economy, 78*, 152–157.

Tabarrok, A. (2001). President Perot or fundamentals of voting theory illustrated with the 1992 election, or could Perot have won in 1992? *Public Choice, 106*, 275–297.

Tabarrok, A., & Spector, L. (1999). Would the Borda count have avoided the Civil War? *Journal of Theoretical Politics, 11*, 261–288.

Tataru, M., & Merlin, V. (1997). On the relationships of the Condorcet winner and positional voting rules. *Mathematical Social Sciences, 34*, 81–90.

Young, H. P. (1988). Condorcet's theory of voting. *American Political Science Review, 82*, 1231–1244.

Young, H. P., & Levenglick, A. (1978). A consistent extension of Condorcet's election principle. *SIAM Journal of Applied Mathematics, 35*, 285–300.

INDEX

A

F

G

J

K

L

M

Q

R

W